DONGOLESE NUB.
A LEXICON

DONGOLESE NUBIAN

A LEXICON

BY THE LATE
CHARLES HUBERT ARMBRUSTER

NUBIAN—ENGLISH
ENGLISH—NUBIAN

CAMBRIDGE
AT THE UNIVERSITY PRESS
1965

CAMBRIDGE UNIVERSITY PRESS
Cambridge, New York, Melbourne, Madrid, Cape Town, Singapore,
São Paulo, Delhi, Dubai, Tokyo

Cambridge University Press
The Edinburgh Building, Cambridge CB2 8RU, UK

Published in the United States of America by Cambridge University Press, New York

www.cambridge.org
Information on this title: www.cambridge.org/9780521153140

© Cambridge University Press 1965

This publication is in copyright. Subject to statutory exception
and to the provisions of relevant collective licensing agreements,
no reproduction of any part may take place without the written
permission of Cambridge University Press.

First published 1965
This digitally printed version 2010

A catalogue record for this publication is available from the British Library

ISBN 978-0-521-04051-8 Hardback
ISBN 978-0-521-15314-0 Paperback

Cambridge University Press has no responsibility for the persistence or
accuracy of URLs for external or third-party internet websites referred to in
this publication, and does not guarantee that any content on such websites is,
or will remain, accurate or appropriate.

PUBLISHER'S NOTE

Mr Armbruster died without reading the proofs of this book. The task of seeing the book through the press at all its stages has been most generously undertaken by Professor P. L. Shinnie of the University of Ghana.

TO MY WIFE, STEFANA
WITHOUT WHOSE CONSTANT HELP
THIS BOOK COULD NOT HAVE BEEN
WRITTEN

PREFACE

THE §§ refer to my Dongolese Nubian grammar. The phonetic alphabet, etc., is as there, §§ 268 ff.

As headings, words are given in their liaison form, with the pausal form, if it differs, added in a bracket. The liaison form gives the stem for declension of nouns, adjectives, pronouns and numerals.

Of a verb the conjugation-stem (§§ 2763–70) forms the heading.

For verbs and verb-complexes ending in a hyphen, see §§ 2771–2.

In cases where I have heard more than one form of the same word I have usually given as the main heading the form I have heard most commonly used, e.g. áur‿ *wing*; under áwɪr‿, probably an older form historically, one is referred to áur‿.

Words from Arabic such as hakím‿ and hókum‿, halḗ and hŏwwɪlḗ, that would come under the same heading in an Arabic dictionary, are not so grouped here.

C.H.A.

ABBREVIATIONS, SIGNS AND SYMBOLS

ABBREVIATIONS

abbr. abbreviated, -tion
abs. absolute
acc. accusative
adj. adjective, -tival
adv. adverb, -bial
Ag. Agə̄u
al. aliter
Amh. Amharic
Anm. Anmerkung
ap. apud
API L'Association Phonétique Internationale
apod. apodosis
app., appar. apparently
approx. approximate(ly)
Ar. Arabic
ass. assimilated, -tion
aux. auxiliary
Bar. Barea, Barya
Bd. Band (volume)
Beḍ. Beḍáujɛt, Beḍáwiɛt
Bil. Bilín
c. consonant
⌣c. subsequent consonant (§3ƒ)
card. cardinal
caus. causative
cft. confert
ch. chapter
cogn. cognate (with)
coll. collective
compl. complement(ary)
compos. composition
concr. concretion
cond. conditional
conj. conjunction, -tive
conjug. conjugation
conn. connected
constr. constructed
Copt. Coptic
cp. compare
cpd. compared
cps. compares
cpx. complex
*d hypothetic sound (§269)
D. Duŋgulándi, Duŋguláwi, Dongoláwi, Dongolese, dialect of of Dóngola; all Nubian words given are D. unless marked K., M., MN. or ON.
dat. dative
def. definitive (§3801)
dem. demonstrative
denom. denominal, -ative
deprec. depreciative
det. determinative
Di. Dinka
dic. dicendi
dim. diminutive
distr. distributive
e.g. exempli gratia
ed. edition
Eg. Egyptian
Eg. Ar. Egyptian Arabic
Eng. English

esp. especial(ly)
Eth. Ethiopic
etym. etymological(ly)
euph. euphonic
Eur. European
ext. extension
F. Fijadiččančíndi (subdialect of M.)
fam. family
fem. feminine
ff. (&) following
fin. ad finem
Fr. French
freq. frequentative
fut. future
G. (ap. Reinisch) Ge'ez = Gíɛ̣ız
Gal. Galla
gen. genitive
Ger. German
ger. gerundial
Gk. Greek
Ham.-Sem. Hamito-Semitic
i. intransitive
i.e. id est
ibid. ibidem
id. idem
I.-Eur. Indo-European
imit. imitative, -ting, imitandi
imperat. imperative
imperf. imperfect
ind. indicative
indef. indefinite
inf. infinitive
init. ad initium
int. intensive
interj. interjection
interr. interrogative
IPA International Phonetic Association
iron. ironical(ly)
irreg. irregular
It. Italian
K. Kunūzíndi, Kénzi dialect
Ka. Káfā
Kh. Xamír
Ku. Kunáma
L. Lepsius
Lat. Latin
Lib. Libyan, Libyco-Berber (*MCL*, p. 136)
lit. literal(ly)
loc. locative
M. Máḥasi, Massınčíndi, dialect of Máḥas
masc. masculine
Mer. Meroitic
Mɪd. Mɪdóbi
MN. Mountain Nubian (§90)
MS manuscript
N. northern, pronunciation or form I hear at El-Órdi and northward
N. pronunciation I have heard of northern speakers, but have not ascertained to be universal in N.
n. noun (= nomen substantivum, cp. *TG*, xiii)
n. act. nomen actionis
n.b. nota bene
n. dic. nomen dicendi

n. ess.   nomen essentiae
n. imit.   nomen imitandi
n. instr.   nomen instrumenti
n. un.   nomen unitatis
n. v.   nomen verbi
neg.   negative
no.   number
nom.   nominative
not heard = not heard by me (§66)
Nub.   Nubian
num.   numeral, numéro
obj.   object(ive)
occ.   occasional(ly)
ON.   Old Nubian, Index I in *GNT*
onom.   onomatopœia, -œic
opp.   opposed
or.   origin(al, -ally), i.e. of (at) some earlier date
p.   passive
p. (before number)   page
part.   participle, -cipial
paus.   pausal (ending a breath-group §371)
perf.   perfect
pers.   person(al)
pl.   plural
Port.   Portuguese
pos.   positive
poss.   possessive
postp.   postposition
pp.   pages
pred.   predicate (-ative, -ation, -ating)
pref.   prefix(ed)
prep.   preposition
pres.   present
prob.   probable, -ly
pron.   pronoun, pronominal
prop.   proper(ly)
prot.   protasis
q.s.   quod sciam
q.v.   quod (quae) vide
Qw.   Qwắrắ
R.   Reinisch
recip.   reciprocal
ref.   reference
reg.   regular
rel.   relative
rhyth.   rhythmical(ly)
S.   southern, pronunciation or form I hear south of Hándag⌣
*S   Ursudan (*WS*, p. 107)
s.v(v).   sub voce (vocibus)
sc.   scilicet
sep.   separate
serv.   used by servants of Europeans
sg.   singular
Sōm.   Sōmǎli
Sp.   Spanish
sp.   species
stat.   stative
subj.   subjunctive
subord.   subordinating
subst.   substantival(ly)
Sud.   Sudanian
suff.   suffix(ed, -es)
syll.   syllable(s)
t.   transitive
Tĕ.   Tigrĕ
Tña.   Tigriñña
Turk.   Turkish
uninfl.   uninflected
uss.   usitatissimum
usu.   usual(ly)
v.   verb
v.   vowel

⌣v.   subsequent vowel (§3*f*)
vb.-cpx.   verb-complex
⌣vc.   subsequent vowel or consonant
voc.   vocative
W.   a speaker to *X*.
W. in §§170-95   Westermann
w.   with
w.w.   water-wheel
X.   a speaker
Y.   a listener
Z.   another listener
y   former or adverbial part of verb-complex (§§3743-4)
z   latter or verbal part of verb-complex (§§3743-4)

SIGNS

§   paragraph
=   equals, is equivalent to
˘   short (§59*a*)
¯   long (§59*a*)
˜   long or short. n.b. (§§1468-70) a long syllable may contain a long or a short vowel: tōgırkŏlgǎ? ¯ ¯ ˘ ˘ *one (obj.) that has struck?*
´   over a vowel indicates that the *syllable* is stressed (§59*b*)
`   over a vowel indicates secondary stress (§1410)
⌒   marks a diphthong
⌣   the sign of liaison (§3)
⌢   the pausal stop (§371)
| shows division into syllables (§14)
+   obstruction for consonant (§293)
..   stop of consonant (§293)
...   repeats word(s) (§9) or indicates unknown word(s)
- -   friction of consonant (§293)
!   release of stop or friction (§293)
ɯ   vowel (§284)
√   root (§§2007-9)
†   not in general use, e.g. a neologism or foreign word
*   hypothetic; supposed earlier sound or form, such as those with *d (§879); inferred meaning, e.g. √íšk- **sit*
>   becomes, is developed (reduced, formed) into, as Eng. *shall not* > *shan't*
<   arises from, is developed (etc.) from, as *shan't* < *shall not*; e.g. téddo⌣ < *térdo⌣ = téddo⌣ arises from a theoretical earlier térdo⌣
¶   my remark on quoted matter
I, II, III, etc. of derived forms of Arabic verb as in *WAG*, I, §35 (see *c*, ibid.)

NOTE ON ⌣ THE SIGN OF LIAISON

I have to thank H. Schäfer for the sign ⌣, as its special value was first brought home to me on reading *SNK*.

The sign ⌣ tells the reader when the pronunciation of adjacent words is continuous; e.g. it shows that the two words n⌣ágın? *who is there?* are pronounced nágın?, as if they were one word.

The primary function, then, of ⌣ is to show that a space in writing is to be disregarded in speaking, that no hiatus should occur: thus ténn⌣ur *his head* is pronounced ténnur, in syllables tén|nur, as one might write in English not⌣at⌣all to indicate the pronunciation nɒ|tə|tɔ́l rather than nɒt|ət|ɔ́l.

⌣ is a reminder to the reader (who reads words rather than syllables) to avoid making a hiatus in cases where it is not made by a native speaker (who utters syllables rather than words); such cases are:

(i) when the division into words and that into syllables are not the same (§435): ín⌣εsέn⌢ *this is thin* syll. í|nε|sέn⌢;

(ii) where the sound ending a word assimilates or is assimilated by that beginning the next: káǧ⌣ǧĕr⌣ *one horse* < káǧ⌣wĕr⌣ (§553); íŋ⌣kádε⌣ *this cloth* < ín⌣kádε⌣ (§655).

⌣, if not printed, is implicit under any hyphen (§13): tǎr-an⌢ *tell him to come* = tǎr⌣-an⌢, pronounced tǎran⌢, syll. tǎ|ran⌢; sáb-bĕr⌣ *a cat* = sáb⌣-bĕr⌣ < sáb⌣wĕr⌣ (§517).

⌣, if not printed, is implicit between all contiguous words closely connected by their sense: ín durón⌢ *this is thick*, more fully written ín⌣durón⌢.

⌣ supplies a conveniently abbreviated means of showing whether the next word begins with a vowel or a consonant, a condition on which the shape of many Nubian words depends; thus, with *v.* = vowel, *c.* = consonant, we can show when alternative forms of the genitive are used:

  káǧ⌣ *horse*; gen. káǧn⌣*v.* as in káǧn⌣úr⌣ *the horse's head*; gen. káñ⌣*c.* as in káñ⌣témɛn⌣ *the price of the horse*.
  ínın⌣*v.* as in ínın⌣íllar⌣ *because of this*; ınín⌣*c.* as in ınín⌣témɛn⌣ *the price of this*.

⌣ attached to an isolated word will remind the reader that the isolation is academic or artificial, and does not occur in Nubian speech:
  ⌣ɛ́ *say, be* does not start a breath-group;
  ógıǧ⌣ *man* does not end one.

ENGLISH AMBIGUITIES

In the English translations from Nubian:
The masculine is intended unless the feminine is specified.
The singular of verbs is intended unless the plural is specified.
Ambiguous words such as *you, your*, are singular unless marked plural (*pl.*).
An English verb in the 2nd person is singular unless marked pl.
  Come = *come thou.*   *You come* = *thou comest.*
pl.... after the translation of a phrase = the same phrase with the *subject* in the plural:
  Come at dawn fəǧírro⌣tắrɛ⌢, pl....⌣tắwɛ⌢ = *Come (thou) at dawn* fəǧírro⌣tắrɛ⌢, *come (ye) at dawn* fəǧírro⌣tắwɛ⌢.

USE OF BRACKETS

In English:
  (*a*) Inclusive: (*s*)*he* (*it*) *eats* = *he eats* and *she eats* and *it eats*.
  (*b*) Explanatory: *temple* (*of head*).
  (*c*) Implementary: enclosing addition(s) required or allowed by English idiom: kálan⌢ *tell* (*him, her*) *to eat* (*it, them*).
In Nubian:
  tódk(ı)⌣ = tódk⌣ and tódkı⌣.
  kát(¹)rɛ⌣ = kátrɛ⌣ and kát¹rɛ⌣.
Square brackets [ ] enclose:
  (1) API symbols (§ 268);
  (2) etymological or historical notes (see § 494).

USE OF HYPHEN

(*a*) Analytic hyphen: this shows the component grammatical or etymological parts (not the sounds) of a word or phrase, as if we wrote *al-one* to show that *alone* < *all one*; so when bɛ́lgá? (*do you mean*) *the one that kills?* is written bɛ́-l-g-á? it is to show the analysis: bɛ́- verbal stem, *kill*; -l- participial; -g- objective; -á? interrogative.
  búru⌢ *it is a girl* = búru- a girl + -n⌢ *it is*.

(*b*) A terminal hyphen, as in suwắn-⌣an- (*to*) *go to Aswán* (§ 3910), bɛ́-kattı- (*to*) *be killed* (§ 4093), serves as a reminder that these are only stems, not complete words, and distinguishes them from stems like bɛ́r-an (*to*) *tell to kill* (§ 3890), ǧu⌣nál- (*to*) *see by going, ascertain,* that are also complete words, bɛ́ran⌢ *tell* (*him*) *to kill* (*it*), ǧunál⌢ *ascertain*.
  dogóǧır⌢ *raise it* is a sentence (§ 4664).
  dogōǧır- *upwards* is part of a word (§ 4136).

(*c*) Abbreviatory hyphen: when the latter part of a word varies, the hyphen is a convenient abbreviation of its earlier part: nóǧın⌢ (-gĭ⌢, -gí⌢) = nóǧın⌢ (nóǧĭ⌢, nóǧí⌢).
  The abbreviatory hyphen need only carry enough of the word to show how it varies: gīrắd⌣ ¼, pl. -ắdı⌣ (-dĭ⌢) = pl. gīrắdı⌣ (gīrắdĭ⌢).
  The abbreviatory hyphen takes no account of previous analytic hyphens: e.g. once ǧíñıran⌢ *tell him (her) to go and wait* has been shown to be compounded of ǧ(u) + íñır + an, it is no longer necessary to write ǧ-íñır-an⌢. So ǧ-íñır-an⌢ (-rā⌢, -rá⌢) = ǧ-íñır-an⌢ (ǧíñırā⌢, ǧíñırá⌢).

USE OF SYLLABLE-DIVIDER

The syllable-divider | is a guide to pronunciation (as if we wrote *a|lone*): bú|run⌢ *it is a girl*; su|wắ|nan- (*to*) *go to Aswán*.

While, then, - analyses the sense, | analyses the sound:
  bɛ̄rıréllɛ́? (*one*) *that killed* (more than one object)?
  bɛ̄-r-ır-ɛ́-l-lɛ́? details of sense: the elements are: bɛ̄- verbal stem, *kill*; -r-ır plural-object suffix; -ɛ́ expresses the past; -l participial; -lɛ́? interrogative.
  bɛ̄|rı|rɛ́l|lɛ́? details of sound: the syllables are bɛ̄, rı, rɛ́l, lɛ́?

ABBREVIATIONS OF PROPER NAMES AND OF TITLES OF PUBLICATIONS

Numbers refer primarily to §§ or sections; where these do not exist, to pages. Some extensive titles are here reduced.
  AZN, LN, RN, etc. where no § or page is cited = *s.v.* in the respective vocabularies.
  Botanists' names are cited from *BSP* and have been checked in J. C. Willis, *A Dictionary of Flowering Plants and Ferns* (4th ed. Cambridge, 1919).

AAE *Initia Amharica*, by C. H. Armbruster, Part III, Amharic-English Vocabulary, Vol. I, *ʋ–ñ* (Cambridge, 1920).
AAG *Ibid.* Part I, Grammar (Cambridge, 1908).
AÆSI *Einleitung in ein ägyptisch-semitisch-indoeuropäisches Wurzelwörterbuch*, von Carl Abel (Leipzig, 1886).
AB *Die Bischari-Sprache Tū-Beḏāwie in Nordost-Afrika beschreibend und vergleichend dargestellt*, von Herman Almkvist. I and II (Uppsala 1881); III (Uppsala, 1885).
ABW = Part III of *AB*.
AEA *Initia Amharica*, Part II, English-Amharic Vocabulary (Cambridge, 1910).
AESA *English-Arabic Vocabulary for the use of Officials in the Anglo-Egyptian Sudan*, by Captain H. F. S. Amery (Cairo, Al-Mokattam Printing-Office, 1905).
API L'Association Phonétique Internationale (= IPA). Rédaction: Department of Phonetics, University College, London, W.C.1.
ASIN *Die Verbalformen des abhängigen Satzes (Subjunktiv und Infinitive) im Nubischen*, von Hans Abel (Heidelberg, 1921).
ATM *Extrait du Vocabulaire de la langue Tigre parlée à Muçawwʻa*, compilé par Antoine d'Abbadie (Leipzig, 1865). Printed at end of *MT*.
AZA *Kleine Beiträge zur Lexikographie des Vulgär-arabischen*, II. Aus dem Nachlass Prof. H. Almkvist's herausgegeben von K. V. Zetterstéen. Le Monde Oriental, vol. XIX (Uppsala, 1925).
AZN *Nubische Studien im Sudān*, 1877–78, aus dem Nachlass Prof. Herman Almkvist's herausgegeben von K. V. Zetterstéen (Uppsala, 1911).
BB البستان وهو معجم لغويّ تأليف الشيخ عبد الله البستاني اللبناني عُفِيَ عنهُ (Beyrout, 1927.)
BEH *On English Homophones*, by Robert Bridges. S.P.E. Tract no. 2 (Oxford, Clarendon Press, 1919).
BES *Cook's Handbook for Egypt and the Sûdân*, by E. A. Wallis Budge (2nd ed. London, 1906).
BHS *Gibt es einen hamitischen Sprachstamm?* von C. Brockelmann. *Anthropos*, tome XXVII, 1932, pp. 797–818 (St. Gabriel-Mödling bei Wien, 1932).
BMM كتاب محيط المحيط تاليف المعلم بطرس البستاني عُفِيَ عنهُ (Beyrout, 1286 = 1870.)
BNS *Die Nominalbildung in den semitischen Sprachen*, von J. Barth (zweite Ausgabe, Leipzig, 1894).
BNT *Texts relating to Saint Mêna of Egypt and Canons of Nicaea, in a Nubian dialect*, ed. by E. A. Wallis Budge (London, British Museum, 1909).
BR Vme *Congrès International des Linguistes, Bruxelles 28 août–2 septembre 1939. Deuxième publication. Rapports* (Bruges, 1939).
BRQ Vme *Congrès, etc. Première publication. Réponses au Questionnaire* (Bruges, 1939).
BRQS Vme *Congrès, etc. Première publication. Réponses au Questionnaire (Suite)* (Bruges, 1939).
BSLP *Bulletin de la Société de Linguistique de Paris* (Paris, Édouard Champion, C. Klincksieck).

BSP Catalogue of Sudan Flowering Plants, compiled by A. F. Broun, Director of Woods & Forests, Sudan Government (Khartoum, 1906).

BSWE Spoken and Written English, by Henry Bradley (Oxford, 1919).

BT Vocabolario Tigray-Italiano e Repertorio Italiano-Tigray, di Padre Francesco da Bassano (Roma, 1918).

BVS Grundriss der vergleichenden Grammatik der semitischen Sprachen, von Carl Brockelmann (I. Band. Berlin, 1908; II. Band. Berlin, 1913).

CAN Angels of the Nile, by J. W. Crowfoot (*SNR* II, 183–97, Khartoum, 1919).

CChS Les Résultats acquis de La Grammaire comparée chamito-sémitique, par Marcel Cohen, Directeur d'études à l'École pratique des Hautes Études. *Revue des Cours et Conférences*, 35ᵉ Année (Iʳᵉ Série) no. 3, 15 Janvier 1934 (Paris, Boivin, 1934).

CGA A Practical Introduction to Greek Accentuation, by H. W. Chandler (2nd ed. Oxford, 1881).

CLA A Sketch of the Modern Languages of Africa, by Robert Needham Cust (London, 1883).

COD = FCOD.

CSW Spinning and Weaving in the Sudan, by Grace M. Crowfoot (*SNR* IV, 20–38, Khartoum, 1921).

CVS Du verbe sidama (dans le groupe couchitique), par Marcel Cohen. (*BSLP*, no. 83, pp. 169–200, Paris, 1927).

DAA Über die Anfänge des Axumitischen Reiches, von A. Dillmann (Abhandlungen der Königl. Akademie der Wissenschaften zu Berlin 1878, Berlin, 1879).

DAG Some Arab Games and Puzzles, by R. Davies (*SNR* VIII, 137–52, Khartoum, 1925).

DBGÆ Grammatik der Äthiopischen Sprache, von August Dillmann, zweite verbesserte und vermehrte Auflage, von Carl Bezold (Leipzig, 1899).

DLÆ Lexicon Linguae Aethiopicae, von Chr. Fr. Augusti Dillmann (Lipsiae, 1865).

DNN La Numération chez les Nègres, par Maurice Delafosse (unfinished) (*JIA*, 1, 3, pp. 387–90, Oxford and London, 1928).

DSA Supplément aux Dictionnaires Arabes, par R. Dozy (Leyde, 1881).

DVT Vocabolario della Lingua Tigrigna, di L. De Vito. Introduzione e indice italiano-tigrigna del Dott. Conti Rossini Carlo (Roma, 1896).

EÆGl Aegyptisches Glossar, von Adolf Erman (Berlin, 1904).

EÆGr Ägyptische Grammatik, von Adolf Erman (3. Aufl., Berlin, 1911).

EÆGr⁴ Ägyptische Grammatik, von Adolf Erman (4. Aufl. Berlin, 1928).

EMR E. M. Roper, Sudan Government (personal communication).

FCOD The Concise Oxford Dictionary of Current English, adapted by H. W. Fowler and F. G. Fowler from the Oxford Dictionary. New (2nd) ed. revised by H. W. Fowler (Oxford, 1929).

FG Greek Grammar Rules, by Frederic W. Farrar (London, Longmans, 1866–1920, etc.).

FKE The King's English, by H. W. and F. G. Fowler (2nd ed. Oxford, Clarendon Press, 1918).

FKE³ Ibid. 3rd ed. (Oxford, 1930).

FLA Lexicon Arabico-Latinum, by G. W. Freytag (Halis Saxonum, 1830).

FMEU A Dictionary of Modern English Usage, by H. W. Fowler (Oxford, Clarendon Press, 1926).

FPOD The Pocket Oxford Dictionary of Current English, compiled by F. G. Fowler and H. W. Fowler (Oxford, Clarendon Press, 1924).

GBH Wilhelm Gesenius' *Hebräisches und Aramäisches Handwörterbuch über das Alte Testament*, in Verbindung mit Prof. Dr. H. Zimmern, Prof. Dr. W. Max Müller u. Dr. O. Weber bearbeitet von Frants Buhl, Prof. a.d. Un. Kopenhagen. 15. Auflage (Leipzig, 1910).

GCD Christian Documents from Nubia, by F. Ll. Griffith (*Proceedings of the British Academy*, vol. XIV, London, Milford, 1928).

GEA Egyptian Colloquial Arabic, by W. H. T. Gairdner, assisted by Sheikh Kurayyim Sallām (Cambridge, Heffer, 1917).

GEG Egyptian Grammar, by Alan H. Gardiner (Oxford, 1927).

GHKC Gesenius' Hebrew Grammar, as edited and enlarged by E. Kautzsch. 2nd English (from 28th German) ed. revised by A. E. Cowley (Oxford, 1910).

GNT The Nubian Texts of the Christian Period, ed. by F. Ll. Griffith (Abhandlungen der Königl. Preuss. Akademie der Wissenschaften. Jahrgang 1913. Phil.-Hist. Klasse, Nr. 8, Berlin, 1913).

GPA The Phonetics of Arabic, by W. H. T. Gairdner (Oxford, 1925).

GSL The Theory of Speech and Language, by Alan H. Gardiner (Oxford, 1932).

GVA Vocabolario Amarico-Italiano, compilato da Ignazio Guidi (Roma, 1901).

HESA Sudan Arabic: English-Arabic Vocabulary, by S. Hillelson (published by the Sudan Government, London, 1925).

HESA² Ibid., 2nd ed. (London, 1930.)

HKN Beiträge zur Kenntnis der Kordofan-nubischen Sprache, von J. J. Hess. ZE Band X, Heft 1 (Berlin, 1920).

HKNO K. D. D. Henderson's letter on *KNO* (*SNR* XXI, 1, 222–4, Khartoum, 1938).

HNO Nubian Origins, by S. Hillelson (*SNR* XIII, 1, 137–48, Khartoum, 1930).

HSAT Sudan Arabic Texts, with translation and glossary, by S. Hillelson (Cambridge, 1935).

HWJ Brig.-Gen. Sir Herbert W. Jackson, K.B.E., C.B., Governor of Dóngola 1902–22 (personal communication).

IMM اِنْجِيل يَسُوع اَلْمَسِيحِن لِن مَرْقُسِن فَايسِين نَقتَا اسكندريل ١٨٩٩

IPA International Phonetic Association (= API). University College, London.

JAS Journal of the African Society (London).

JCK Kordofân-Texte im Dialekt von Gebel Dair, von H. Junker und W. Czermak (Wien, 1913).

JEP An English Pronouncing Dictionary (on strictly phonetic principles), by Daniel Jones (London, 1917).

JIA AFRICA, Journal of the International Institute of African Languages and Cultures (University Press, Oxford).

JL Language, its Nature, Development and Origin, by Otto Jespersen (London, George Allen and Unwin Ltd., 1922).

JLP Lehrbuch der Phonetik, von Otto Jespersen, Vierte Auflage (Leipzig, Teubner, 1926).

JPG The Philosophy of Grammar, by Otto Jespersen (London, George Allen and Unwin Ltd., 1924).

JPS Phonetic Spelling, by Sir Harry Johnston (Cambridge, 1913).

JRAS Journal of the Royal Asiatic Society (London).

JSNK Nubische Texte im Kenzi-Dialekt, von H. Junker und H. Schäfer. 1. Band (Wien, A. Hölder, 1921).

KB Die bergnubische Sprache (Dialekt von Gebel Delen), von P. Daniel Kauczor (Wien, A. Hölder, 1920).

KBW Bergnubisches Wörterverzeichnis, von P. Daniel Kauczor F. S. C. Bibliotheca ethnologica-linguistica Africana, herausgegeben... von Albert Drexel, Rektor. Band III, Heft 4, pp. 243–83 (Afrikanisches Institut, Innsbruck, 1920).

KNH Natural History Notes (made in Dongola), by H. H. King (*SNR* IV, 39–43, Khartoum, 1921).

KNO A Survey of Nubian Origins, by L. P. Kirwan (*SNR*, XX, 1, 47–62, Khartoum, 1937).

LA An Arabic-English Lexicon, by Edward William Lane (London, 1863–93).

LN Nubische Grammatik, mit einer Einleitung über die Völker und Sprachen Afrika's, von R. Lepsius (Berlin, 1880).

LNW = LN Wörterbuch.

LSA Standard Alphabet for reducing unwritten languages and foreign graphic systems to a uniform orthography in European letters, by C. R. Lepsius (2nd ed. London and Berlin, 1863).

LSF A Latin Dictionary, founded on Andrews' edition of Freund's..., by Charlton T. Lewis and Charles Short (Oxford, 1890).

LSG Die semitischen Fremdwörter im Griechischen, von Heinrich Lewy (Berlin, 1895).

map AFRICA 1:250,000, sheets 45A 1920, 45E, F 1921 (Survey Office, Khartoum, Survey Dept., Giza, Cairo, and Stanford, London).

MAS *A History of the Arabs in the Sudan*, by H. A. MacMichael (2 vols. Cambridge University Press, 1922).

MCL *Les Langues du Monde*, par un groupe de linguistes sous la direction de A. Meillet et Marcel Cohen (Paris, 1924).

MDL *Darfur Linguistics*, by H. A. MacMichael (*SNR* III, 197–216, Khartoum, 1920).

MEG *English Grammar*, by C. P. Mason (40th ed. London, G. Bell and Sons, 1901).

MGC *Grammaire copte*, par Alexis Mallon, S.J. (deuxième éd. Beyrouth, 1907).

MGG *Grammatica teorico-practica della Lingua Galla*, di Martino Mario Moreno (Casa Editrice A. Mondadori, Roma, 1939).

MH *Die Sprachen der Hamiten*, von Carl Meinhof (Hamburg, 1912).

MK *Eine Studienfahrt nach Kordofan*, von Carl Meinhof (Hamburg, 1916).

MND *Nubian elements in Darfur*, by H. A. MacMichael (*SNR* I, 30–48, Khartoum, 1918).

MNK *Wörterbuch des nubischen Kunûzi-Dialektes mit einer grammatischen Einleitung*, von G. von Massenbach (Mitteilungen des Seminars für Orientalische Sprachen, Jahrgang XXXVI, dritte Abteilung, pp. 99–227, Berlin, 1933).

MOS *Ostafrikanische Studien*, von Werner Munzinger (Schaffhausen, 1864).

MP *Le Maître Phonétique*. Organe de l'Association Phonétique Internationale, 20 Rue de la Madeleine, Bourg-la-Reine (Seine), France. Rédaction: Daniel Jones, University College, London, W.C.1.

MSA *Die moderne Sprachforschung in Afrika*, Hamburgische Vorträge von Carl Meinhof (Berlin, 1910).

MSAW *An Introduction to the Study of African Languages*, by Carl Meinhof, translated by A. Werner (London, 1915). Contains valuable amplifications and adaptations to English of *MSA*.

MSM *Die Sprache von Meroe*, von Carl Meinhof, ZE, Band XII, Heft 1 (Berlin, 1922).

MT *Vocabulaire de la langue Tigré*, par Werner Munzinger (printed with *ATM* at the end of *DLÆ*; also (with *ATM*) separately) (Leipzig, 1865).

MZM *Notes on the Zaghâwa and the People of Gebel Midób, Anglo-Egyptian Sudan*, by H. A. MacMichael (*Journal of the Royal Anthropological Institute of Great Britain and Ireland*, vol. XLII, pp. 288–344, London, 1912).

NB *Beiträge zur semitischen Sprachwissenschaft*, von Theodor Nöldeke (Strassburg, 1904).

NGP *General Phonetics*, by G. Noël-Armfield (3rd ed. Cambridge, Heffer, 1924).

NGP⁴ Ibid. 4th ed., revised and enlarged (Cambridge, Heffer, 1931).

NNB *Neue Beiträge zur semitischen Sprachwissenschaft*, von Theodor Nöldeke (Strassburg, 1910).

NSD *The Sakia in Dongola Province*, by W. Nicholls (*SNR* I, 21–4, Khartoum, 1918).

NSS تاريخ السودان لمؤلفه نعوم بك شقير بمصر ١٩٠٣

NSTD *Sagia Terminology in Dongola*, by H. A. Nicholson (*SNR* XVIII, II, 314–22, Khartoum, 1935).

PA *Die amharische Sprache*, von Franz Praetorius (Halle, 1879).

PBÆ *Beiträge zur äthiopischen Grammatik und Etymologie*, von Franz Praetorius. In *Beiträge zur Assyriologie und vergleichenden semitischen Sprachwissenschaft*, herausgegeben von Friedrich Delitzsch und Paul Haupt. 1. Band, Heft 1, pp. 21–47 (Leipzig, 1889).

PEP *A First Course of English Phonetics*, by Harold E. Palmer (Cambridge, Heffer, 1917).

PF *Seasonal Occurrence and Edibility of Fish at Khartoum*, by Waino Pekkola (*SNR* I, 88–98, Khartoum, 1918).

PG *Zur Grammatik der Gallasprache*, von Franz Praetorius (Berlin, 1893).

PHO *Über die hamitischen Sprachen Ostafrika's*, von Franz Prætorius. Beiträge zur Assyriologie, II. Band, Heft 2, pp. 312–41 (Leipzig, 1892).

PLC *Lexicon Linguæ Copticæ*, studio Amedei Peyron (Taurini, 1835).

PT *Grammatik der Tigriñasprache in Abessinien*, von Franz Praetorius (Halle, 1871).

PVL *The New Latin Primer*, by J. P. Postgate and C. A. Vince (London, Cassell, 1922).

QMA *The Holy Qur-án*, Arabic text with English translation and commentary by Maulvi Muhammad Ali (2nd ed. Lahore, 1920).

RAW *Die 'Afar-Sprache*, von Leo Reinisch. II, 'Afar-deutsches Wörterbuch (Wien, 1887).

RB *Die Beḍauye-Sprache in Nordost-Afrika*, von Leo Reinisch (I and II Wien, 1893; III and IV Wien, 1894).

RBW *Wörterbuch der Beḍauye-Sprache*, von Leo Reinisch (Wien, 1895).

RBi *Die Bilīn-Sprache in Nordost-Afrika*, von Leo Reinisch (Wien, 1882).

RBiW *Die Bilīn-Sprache*, von Leo Reinisch, zweiter Band (*Wörterbuch der Bilīn-Sprache*, Wien, 1887).

RCh *Die Chamirsprache in Abessinien*, von Leo Reinisch, I and II (Wien, 1884).

REM R. E. Massey, Sudan Government Botanist (personal communication).

RK *Die Kafa-Sprache in Nordest-Afrika*, von Leo Reinisch, I (Wien, 1888).

RKW RK II, *Kafa-deutsches Wörterbuch* (Wien, 1888).

RKu *Die Kunama-Sprache in Nordost-Afrika*, von Leo Reinisch. I, Grammatik (Wien, 1881); II, Texte (Wien, 1889).

RKuW RKu III, *Kunama-deutsches Wörterbuch* (Wien, 1890).

RMB *Die Barea-sprache, Grammatik, Text und Wörterbuch*, nach den handschriftlichen Materialen von Werner Munzinger Pascha bearbeitet von Leo Reinisch (Wien, 1874).

RN *Die Nuba-Sprache*, von Leo Reinisch. Erster Theil, *Grammatik und Texte* (Wien, 1879).

RNs.v. = *RNWs.v.*

RNW RN, zweiter Theil, *Nubisch-deutsches und deutsch-nubisches Wörterbuch* (Wien, 1879).

RP *Das persönliche Fürwort und die Verbalflexion in den chamitosemitischen Sprachen*, von Leo Reinisch (Wien, 1909).

RQ *Die Quarasprache in Abessinien*, von Leo Reinisch. I, Grammatik (Wien, 1885).

RQW RQ II, Textproben u. *Quarisch-deutsches Wörterbuch* (Wien, 1885).

RSG *Die Somali-Sprache*, von Leo Reinisch. III, Grammatik (Südarabische Expedition, Band V, Teil 1) (Wien, 1903).

RSN *Die sprachliche Stellung des Nuba*, von Leo Reinisch (Wien, 1911).

RSW *Die Somali-Sprache*, von Leo Reinisch. II, Wörterbuch (Südarabische Expedition, Band II) (Wien, 1902).

RoB *Tu Beḍawie*, by E. M. Roper (Sudan Government; printed by S. Austin and Sons, Ltd., Hertford, 1928).

SAE *An Arabic-English Vocabulary of the Colloquial Arabic of Egypt*, by Socrates Spiro (Cairo and London, 1895).

SAE² *Arabic-English Dictionary of the Modern Arabic of Egypt*, by S. Spiro Bey (2nd ed., revised and considerably enlarged, Cairo, 1923). [Omits imperfect of verb.]

SAP *Abyssinische Pflanzennamen*, von G. Schweinfurth. Aus dem Anhang zu den Abhandlungen der königl. preuss. Akademie der Wissenschaften zu Berlin vom Jahre 1893 (Berlin, 1893).

SE *The Characteristics and Distribution of the Human Race: an Introduction to Ethnology*, by C. G. Seligman. In *An Outline of Modern Knowledge* (London, Gollancz, 1931).

SGB *Greek Lexicon of the Roman and Byzantine periods*, by E. A. Sophocles (New York, Scribner's, 1900).

SKG *Koptische Grammatik...*, von Georg Steindorff. Neudruck der zweiten Auflage mit Nachträgen (Berlin, 1930).

SL *Language, an Introduction to the Study of Speech*, by Edward Sapir (Oxford, 1921).

SMN *A Study in Medieval Nubian*, by B. H. Stricker. *Bulletin of The School of Oriental Studies* (University of London), vol. X, part 2, pp. 439–54 (London, 1940).

SNK *Nubische Texte im Dialekte der Kunûzi (Mundart von Abuhôr)*, von Prof. Dr. Heinrich Schäfer. Abhandlungen der königl. preuss. Akademie der Wissenschaften, Jahrgang 1917 (Berlin, 1917).

SNR *Sudan Notes and Records* (Khartoum; began 1918).

SOED *The Shorter Oxford English Dictionary on Historical*

Principles, prepared by William Little, H. W. Fowler, J. Coulson; revised and edited by C. T. Onions (Oxford, 1933).

SP A Primer of Phonetics, by Henry Sweet (3rd ed. Oxford, 1906).

SSG The Soul of Grammar, by E. A. Sonnenschein (Cambridge, 1927).

SSL Introduction to the Science of Language, by A. H. Sayce, 2 vols. (4th ed. London, 1900).

SW Word-Division, by Kenneth Sisam. SPE. Tract no. XXXIII (Oxford, 1929).

TEG Elementi di Glottologia, di Alfredo Trombetti (Bologna, 1923).

TESS Die Entstehung des semitischen Sprachtypus..., von Harry Torczyner (Erster Band, Wien, 1916).

TG On the Terminology of Grammar, being the Report of the Joint Committee on Grammatical Terminology. Revised 1911 (London, John Murray, 1935).

TGD Dictionary of the Galla Language, by Charles Tutschek (*Lexicon der Galla Sprache*, von Karl Tutschek) (Munich, 1844).

TOB Le Origini della Lingua Basca, di Alfredo Trombetti (Bologna, 1925).

TWEG English Grammar Descriptive and Historical, by T. G. Tucker and R. S. Wallace (Cambridge, 1917).

VAM The Spoken Arabic of Mesopotamia, by the Rev. John Van Ess (Oxford, undated (?1919)).

VBA The Modern Egyptian Dialect of Arabic: a Grammar: from the German of K. Vollers, translated by F. C. Burkitt (Cambridge, 1895).

VH Was sind Hamitensprachen? von Werner Vycichl. *JIA*, vol. VIII, no. 1, pp. 76–89 (Oxford and London, 1935).

VL Le Langage: Introduction Linguistique à l'Histoire, par J. Vendryes (Paris, 1921).

WAE The Spoken Arabic of Egypt, by J. Selden Willmore (3rd ed. London, David Nutt, 1919). [Derived forms of verb renumbered.]

WAG A Grammar of the Arabic Language, translated from the German of Caspari by W. Wright (3rd ed. revised by W. Robertson Smith and M. J. de Goeje, Cambridge University Press, 1896).

WAS The Verb 'to say' as an Auxiliary in Africa and China, by A. Waley and C. H. Armbruster. *Bulletin of the School of Oriental Studies*, vol. VII, part 3, pp. 573–6 (London, 1934).

WCES Charakter und Einteilung der Sudansprachen, von Deidrich Westermann. *JIA* VIII, 2, pp. 129–48 (Oxford and London, 1935).

WCS Lectures on the Comparative Grammar of the Semitic Languages. From the papers of the late William Wright. Ed. by W. Robertson Smith (Cambridge, 1890).

WLA The Language-Families of Africa, by A. Werner (London, 1915).

WS Die Sudansprachen, eine sprachvergleichende Studie, von Deidrich Westermann (Hamburg, 1911).

WSG Sudanese Grammar, by Allan Worsley (London, S.P.C.K., 1925).

WWP Practical Phonetics for Students of African Languages, by D. Westermann and Ida C. Ward (Oxford, 1933).

WZKM Wiener Zeitschrift für die Kunde des Morgenlandes.

ZDMG Zeitschrift der Deutschen Morgenländischen Gesellschaft (Leipzig).

ZDN Zur Stellung des Dārfūr-Nubischen, von Ernst Zyhlarz. *WZKM*, XXXV, pp. 84-123, 188–212 (Wien, 1928).

ZE Zeitschrift für Eingeborenen-Sprachen (Berlin (Reimer) and Hamburg (Boysen)).

ZGFH Das geschichtliche Fundament der hamitischen Sprachen, von Ernst Zyhlarz. *JIA*, vol. IX, no. 4 (Oxford and London, 1936).

ZMS Das meroïtische Sprachtproblem, von Dr. Ernst Zyhlarz. *Anthropos*, Band XXV, pp. 409–63 (St Gabriel-Mödling bei Wien, 1930).

ZNA Neue Sprachdenkmäler des Altnubischen, von Ernst Zyhlarz. In *Studies presented to F. Ll. Griffith* (Egypt Exploration Society, London, 1932).

ZNG Grundzüge der nubischen Grammatik im christlichen Frühmittelalter (Altnubisch), von Ernst Zyhlarz (Leipzig, 1928).

ZS Zeitschrift für Semitistik und verwandte Gebiete (Leipzig, Brockhaus).

ZUSA Ursprung und Sprachcharakter des Altägyptischen, von E. Zyhlarz. *ZE*, Band XXIII, Hefte 1–4 (Berlin, 1932-3).

NUBIAN–ENGLISH

-á⌢ (-ă⌢, a⌢ §939) *say (to), tell* = án⌢ (§§3890–3906).

-á? interrogative particle (§§4260–6, 5838–43) suffixed to: (*a*) verb in indicative (§§3050–6); (*b*) objective case of noun, adjective, pronoun, numeral, participle; (*c*) adverb in -gi⌢ or -ki⌢; (*d*) objective case of verb in subjunctive (§§3063, 3065).
   tăriá? *shall* (§5369*b*) *I come?*
   nálná? *do you (does (s)he, it) see?*
   sándıná? *are you (is (s)he, it) afraid?*
   ɛsmăn⌣óddıná? *is ɣoθmăn ill?*
   wăndıgorandɛ́? ımbéllıá? *have they come in sight? shall I start?*
   asálgı⌣bımbélluá? *shall we (will you pl.) start to-morrow?*
   tărandıá? *am I to tell him (her) to come?*
   másıl⌣ābbélná? *is the sun rising?*
   X. tékkı⌣tír⌢ *give it (them) to him (her).*
   Y. nígi? áligá? *to whom?, to ɣáli?*
   X. nógan⌢ *tell him (her) to go.*
   Y. áhmɛdká? *Áḥmad?*
   X. áli⌣tăran⌢ (-t⌣t- < -g⌣t- §707) *tell ɣáli to come.*
   Y. ál⌣ıdrıská? *ɣáli Idrıs?*
   X. kándıg⌣étta⌢ *bring the knife.*
   Y. dúlgá? *the large one?*
   X. dɛ́n⌢ *give it to me.*
   Y. ıngá? *this?*
   X. tır⌣ówwın⌣nálli⌢ (-n⌣n- < -g⌣n-, §625) *I see the two of them.*
   Y. tır⌣ówwıgá? *the two of them?*
   X. tékk⌣úwɛ⌢ *call him (her).*
   Y. nogílgá? *the one that is going?*
   X. áɣıŋ⌣gúššıgó⌢ *the leather (has) got broken.*
   Y. ékkɛnɛgá? *now?*
   X. kåg̊k⌣étta⌢ *bring the snake.*
   Y. aı⌣bɛ́sıgá? *that I killed?*
    ɛr⌣bɛ́sıngá? *that you killed?*
    tɛr⌣bɛ́sıngá? *that (s)he (it) killed?*
    ar⌣bɛ́sugá? *that we killed?*
    ır⌣bɛ́sugá? *that you (pl.) killed?*
    tır⌣bɛ́sangá? *that they killed?*

— not elided before following vowel (§1134):
   tɛr⌣uñúrná⌣ár⌣ısáır⌣ɛrugi? *does (s)he (it) know where we are?*
   tɛr⌣uñúrná⌣ɛ́r⌣ısáır⌣ɛ́ŋgi? *does (s)he (it) know where you are?*

— second consecutive -á? sometimes dropped (§5841):
   tɛr⌣índo⌣bıkálná?, sahắŋg⌣éttari? *will (s)he eat (it, them) here?, shall (§5369*b*) I bring a plate?*

— in alternative question -á? not repeated (§5842):
   álı⌣tágoná⌣wálla⌣sắlum? *did (has) ɣáli come or Sắlım?*
   ar⌣índo⌣tɛgruá⌣wálla⌣kándu? *are we to (§5468) stay here or go home?*
   bābúr⌣gatírkı⌣bɛrğɛ́ná⌣wálla⌣bímbɛlın? *will the steamer wait for the train or will it start?*
   mugóıá⌣wáll⌣úwɛri? *shall (§5369*b*) I leave him (her) alone or call him (her)?*
   mugóıá? < mugósrıá? (§982).

— in an alternative question -á? may be absent throughout (§5843):
   álı⌣wálla⌣sắlum⌣tắgo? *did (has) ɣáli or Sắlım come?*

-ā⌢ (-á⌢, -a⌢ §939) *say (to), tell* = -an⌢ (§§3890–3906).

á⌣, ⌣ā⌣ (§1066), -ă⌣ (§2374*b*) n. (*a*) *heart*; (*b*, used as reflexive pronoun, §§2688ff., 5170–1) *self* [§4491].
   obj. ág⌣v., -g⌣ assimilated to ⌣c. (§511), ági⌣.
   pl. ánč(ı)⌣.

— note stress (§1671) of:
   ánn-ā⌣ *my heart* (§2374*b*).
   ɛ́nn-ā⌣ *your heart.*
   ténn-ā⌣ *his (her, its) heart.*
   ánn-ā⌣ *our hearts.*
   ínn-ā⌣ *your hearts.*
   tínn-ā⌣ *their hearts.*
   obj. ánn⌣ág⌣ and ánn-āg⌣ (*a*) *my heart, our hearts,* (*b*) *myself, ourselves.*
   ánna⌣áıg⌣óddıgon⌢ *I had a pain in my heart,* lit. *my heart hurt me.*
   tínna⌣tírg⌣óddın⌢ *they have a pain in the heart.*
   aı⌣ánn-áb⌣bıbɛ́rı⌣ɛgó⌢ (-b⌣b- < -g⌣b- §519) *(s)he (you) said 'I shall kill myself'.*
   tɛ́r⌣bı⌣ténn-āb⌣bɛ́⌢ (§§939, 5384) *(s)he will kill himself (herself).*
   tıntımbáb⌣ténn-áb⌣bɛ́gó⌢ *their father (has) killed himself.*
   N. ógıg̊⌣ówwı⌣tínn-āb⌣bɛ́koran⌢ *two men (have) killed themselves.*
   ɛr⌣ɛnnán⌣ádun⌣ *you are your own enemy.*
   ténn⌣ágonom⌣báññın⌢ *he talks to (lit. with) himself (she talks to herself).*
   aı⌣ánnán⌣nálkori⌢ and (§513).
   aı⌣ánnāg⌣nálkori⌢ (*a*) *I saw (have seen) myself,* (*b*) *I myself saw (have seen) him (her, it, them).*
   aı⌣ánn⌣ágɛn⌣nálkori⌢ (-n⌣n- < -d⌣n- §624) *I myself saw (have seen) him (her, it, them).*
   ánnaw⌣wɛ́rı⌢ (-w⌣w- < -g⌣w- §719) (*a*) *I say it to myself,* (*b*) *I myself say it.*
   tɛr⌣ténnas⌣sérēn⌣ɛgó⌢ (-s⌣s- < -g⌣s- §678) *he said to himself (she said to herself) 'Good!'.*
   aı⌣ánnas⌣sérēn⌣ɛwɛ́gori⌢ *I said to myself 'Good!'.*
   ɛ́nnāb⌣bálko! (-b⌣b < -g⌣b- §519) and ɛ́nn-āb-bálko! (*a*) *take care of yourself!;* (*b*) *take care yourself!*
   ɛ́nnāb⌣bálkor⌣ɛgóri⌢ *I said 'take care (of) yourself!'.*

án-d(ı)⌣ (§§2545ff.) adj. *appertaining to the heart, of the heart, cardiac.*
   obj. -dıg⌣.
   pl. -dınč(ı)⌣.

ā-dūl-kṍ- (§4116) v.i. *be proud:* (*a*, in good sense) *have proper pride, be self-respecting;* (*b*, in bad sense) *be conceited, be vain.*
   pres. aı⌣ādūlkóri⌢, ɛr⌣ādūlkón⌢ (-kṍ⌢, -kṍ⌢, -kṍ⌢ §939).
   perf. aı⌣ādūlkṍgori⌢
   part. pres. ādúlkōl⌣ (ādūlkól⌣ §1708) *(one that is) proud (etc.).*

á-sɛrɛ́-kōl⌣ (§2578) adj. *sincere, unassuming.*

áb v.t. *catch* (a thrown or falling body).
   pres. aı⌣áb(ı)rı⌢, ɛr⌣ábın⌢ (⌣ábī⌢, ⌣ábí⌢).
   perf. aı⌣ábkori⌢ (⌣ápk-).
   imperat. áp!, pl. ábwɛ! (ábwé!).
   kúlug⌣ábın⌢ *(s)he catches (you catch) the stone.*
   bıtáŋ⌣kúrag⌣ápkó⌢ *the boy (has) caught the ball.*

— of an object falling from above:
   āddígırın⌣áp! *he's (she's, it's) falling, catch him (her, it)!*

ábar⌣ (ábúr⌣; §§2200ff.) and abíd⌣ (§§2256ff.) n. *catching.*

átt(ı)⌣ n. *wheel catching and raising water, vertical wheel on end of horizontal axle* (tórɛ⌣) *in water-wheel* (kólɛ⌣); *over it pass cables* (álası⌣) *bearing jars* (béšɛnč(ı)⌣) [< *áp-t(ı)⌣ < *ábt(ı)⌣ *catching,* nomen actionis *of* áb v.t *catch,* §2325β].
   obj. -tıg⌣.
   pl. -tınč(ı)⌣.
   áttın⌣sɛ́n⌣ *rope binding together the shoreward ends of all the transverse limbs* (fášɛnč(ı)⌣) *of spokes of* átt(ı)⌣; *it forms a* rim *corresponding to the* g̊ómbo⌣ *at riverward end of* fášɛnč(ı)⌣.

⌣ábtı-r⌣ (⌣áptır⌣, ⌣áttır⌣ §5894) postp. = prep. *at (to) the side (of), alongside, beside, by, near;* follows the genitive (§4375): [áb-tı-r *in catching, in contact with* (in RN, §383 confused with -abd(ı)⌣)].
   tɛr⌣ánn⌣ábtır⌣ágın⌢ *(s)he squats (etc., s.v. ág) beside me (us);* (cp. RN, §383).
   ánn⌣áttır⌣tɛ́p⌢ *stay (stand) by my (our) side.*
   zɛ́rbɛn⌣áttır⌣élkori⌢ *I found him (her, it, them) by the fence.*
   g̊ébɛln⌣áttır⌣bıdágoran⌢ *they came (have come) alongside the mountain.*
   X. kánd⌣ısɛ́? *where's the knife?*
   Y. ɛ́nn⌣áttır⌢ *it's beside you.*

áb-an (§3890) v.t. *tell to catch, let catch.*
abɛd-ǎg- (§3877) v.t. *be in the situation of having caught.*
  kúlug⏜abɛdágın⏝ *(s)he has caught the stone.*
áb-katti- (ápk-; §4093) v.p. *be caught.*
  kúṛ⏜ápkattın⏝ *the ball is caught.*
áb⏜ n. *top of river-bank* (= Sudan Ar. gέf).
  obj. ábk(ı)⏜, ápk(ı)⏜, -ki⏝.
  gen. ábn⏜v., ám⏜c. (§586).
  pl. ábı⏜.
áb v.t. *net, catch with a net.*
  pres. aı⏜áb(¹)ri⏝, ɛr⏜ábın⏝ (⏜ábī⏝, ⏜ábí⏝).
  perf. aı⏜ábkori⏝ (⏜ápk-).
  kǎrɛg⏜ábı⏜ *fisherman.*
  kǎrɛš⏜šébɛkɛgɛd⏜ábın⏝ (-š⏜š- < -g⏜š- §695) *he catches fish with a net.*
ábar⏜ (ábár⏜; §§2200ff.) and
ábíd⏜ (§§2256ff.) n. *netting, catching with a net.*
ábɛ⏜ (§2234δ) n. *small fishing-net.*
  obj. ábɛg⏜.
  pl. ábɛnč(ı)⏜.
áb-an (§3890) v.t. *tell to net, etc., let net, etc.*
áb-bŭ- (§3931β) v.i. stat. *be in a netted (etc.) state or condition.*
  kǎr⏜ábbŭn⏝ *the fish is (has been, are §4696d, have been) netted.*
ābɛd-ǎg- (§3877) v.t. *be in the situation of having netted, etc.*
áb-katti- (ápk-; §4093) v.p. *be netted, etc.*
  kǎr⏜ápkattın⏝ *the fish is (are) netted.*
ábadan⏜ (ébɛdɛn⏜ §956a) and
abadáŋ(ı)⏜ (ɛbɛdéŋ-, -gi⏝; §5998) adv. *(a, with negative) ever, at all; (b, without negative) never, not at all* [< أَبَدً id.].
  abadáŋı⏜dǎmunun⏝ *there isn't any at all.*
  abadáŋı⏜nalkómunan⏝ *they never saw (have never seen) him (her, it, them §5083).*
abǎg n. *(a) buttock; (b) buttocks, posterior (§4696a); (c) hinder part, back part, rear; (d) latter part, end.*
  obj. -ǎgk(ı)⏜, -ǎkk(ı)⏜, -ki⏝.
  gen. -ǎgn⏜v., -ǎŋ⏜c. (§642), -ǎm⏜ before ⏜b- (§591).
  pl. -ǎgı⏜.
  únn⏜abǎm⏜bókkom⏜biñírran⏝ *they will wait till the end of the month.*
abǎgk-ɛd⏜ (-ǎkk-; -ɛt⏝ §469, -έ⏝ §966; §6007) adv. *(a, space) by (etc., s.v. -ɛd⏜) the hinder part, behind, at (to) the back, backwards; (b, time) afterwards.*
  abǎgkɛd⏜dɛfégoran⏝ *afterwards they paid.*
⏜**abǎgkɛd**⏜ (-ǎkk-; -ɛt⏝, -έ⏝; §§4380a, 5860) postp. (= prep. §4287) *(a, space) behind, after; (b, time) after.*
— follows the genitive:
  tínn⏜abǎkkɛn⏜nókkoran⏝ (-n⏜n- < -d⏜n- §624) *they went (have gone) behind (after) them.*
abǎg-ır (§6007) adv. *(a, space) on (in, at, to) the hinder part, behind, on (etc.) the back, backwards; (b, time) afterwards.*
  abǎgır⏜ *(s)he (it) is (they are) at the back (behind).*

⏜**abǎgır**⏜ (§§5860, 5893) postp. (= prep. §4287) *(a) behind, at (on, to) the back of; (b, of place and time) after, following.*
— follows the genitive (§4358):
  ténn⏜abǎgır⏜ǧómkó⏝ *(s)he (it) (has) struck him (her, it) behind.*
  tír⏜kǎn⏜abǎgır⏝ *they are behind the house.*
  urtínčın⏜abǎgır⏜nókkon⏝ *(s)he (it) went (has gone) after the animals.*
  únn⏜abǎgır⏜bıtáran⏝ *they will come at the end of the month.*
abǎn-d(ı)⏜ (§§2545ff.) adj. *appertaining to the buttocks, hinder, back, posterior, latter.*
  obj. -dıg⏜.
abǎg-an- (§3913β) v.i. *move (go, come) to(wards) the hinder part, back(wards), retire, retreat.*
abǎgam-bŭ- (§3950β) v.i. stat. *be in a state of backward motion, be on one's way back(wards), be retiring.*
abǎganɛd-ǎg- (§§3965ff.) v.i. *be in the situation of having gone (come) back(wards), etc.*
abǎgan-nóg (§§3973, 4150) v.i. *go (away) back(wards), retire, retreat.*
  imperat. abǎgannók!
abǎgan-nóg-bŭ- (-nóggŭ- §546; §§3974, 4153) v.i. stat. *be in a state of motion (going) back(wards).*
abǎgan-nog(¹)r-ɛg-ǎg- (§3980) v.i. = abāgannogɛdól-.
abǎgan-nog-ɛ-dól- (-gᵒdól- §1178; §3979) and
abǎgan-nog(¹)r-ɛ-dól- (-rᵒdól-; §3981) v.i. *be about to go (away) back(wards).*
abǎgan-nog-ɛ-mǎ- (§3982) and
abǎgan-nog(¹)r-ɛ-mǎ- (§3983) v.i. *become unable to go (away) back(wards).*
abǎgk-ır (-ǎkk-; §3698) v.t. *(a) cause or allow to be behind; (b) place behind, put back.*
  énn⏜ıbǎrrotŏ⏜kınnέg⏜abǎkkırkŏ⏝ *(s)he (has) put it (them) a little behind your mark (i.e. the mark you made).*
abǎgkır-óčč(ı) (-ǎkk-; §4136) v.t. *drag backwards, drag back.*
abǎgkır-óčči-katti- (-ǎkk-; N. -ıha-; §4144) v.p. *be dragged backwards.*
abǎgkır-tólle (-ǎkk-; §4140) v.t. *pull backwards, pull back.*
abǎgkır-úskur (-ǎkk-; §4141) v.t. *put (etc. s.v. úskur) at the back, put behind.*
abǎgǎǧ (-ǎčّ⏝) n. *Um Agag (on map), a small island near Šābánɛ, about seven miles above El-Xándaq.*
  obj. -ǎgk(ı)⏜, -ǎčk(ı)⏜, -ǧk-, -čk- (§323), -ki⏝.
abáıa (ıb-) n. *cloak* [< عَبَايَة id.].
  obj. -ag⏜.
  pl. -anč(ı)⏜.
ábajó! apocritic sentence-word (§4488) *O yes! (ironically), I dare say, possibly, etc. (implying I don't believe you).*
  X. mudír⏜sándıbŭn⏝ *the governor is frightened.*
  Y. ábajó! *O yes!*
  X. énn⏜íg⏜úndur, ín⏜íg⏜orófélun⏝ *put your hand in, this fire is cold.*
  Y. ábajó! *I dare say it is.*

abaláñ⏜ n. *ape, Cercopithecus sp.* [-ñ⏜ dim. §2304; RSN, §129; cp. Sudan Ar. عبالنج ,ابالنج (ε)abaláng id.].
  obj. -áñg(ı)⏜, -gi⏝.
  pl. -áñi⏜.
abǎr⏜ explanation = ıbǎr⏜.
abátte n. *Abatta (on map), a village and district on the right bank of the Nile near the northern end of Árgo Island; opposite it, on the island, are another village and district of the same name.*
  obj. abáttɛg⏜, abáttég⏝ (§1532).
āb-bǎg- (āg-bǎg- §519; §§3831ff.) v.t. *(a) be engaged in distributing, etc. (s.v. bǎg); (b) continually (habitually) distribute, etc.*
— takes two objectives (§5345):
  tórbarım⏜márɛg⏜ābbagırríddan⏝ (-m⏜m- <-g⏜m- §601) *they are distributing (habitually) distribute) (the) millet to the peasants.*
āb-bǎg- (ág-bǎg- §519; §§3831ff.) v.t. *(a) be engaged in dividing, etc. (s.v. bǎg); (b) continually (habitually) divide, etc.*
āb-bagǎše- (ág-ba- §519; §§3831ff.) v.t. *(a) be engaged in stepping over; (b) continually (habitually) step over.*
āb-bagítte- (ág-ba- §519; §§3831ff.) v.t. = ābbǎg-.
āb-bǎǧ- (ág-bǎǧ- §519; §§3831ff.) v.t. *(a) be engaged in writing, etc. (s.v. bǎǧ); (b) continually (habitually) write, etc.*
  ind. pres. aı⏜ābbǎǧ(¹)ri⏝.
  έn⏜tém⏜míssıg⏜ābbǎǧın⏝ *the woman habitually paints her eyes (§4696a; (the) women (§4647) habitually paint their eyes; sc. with antimony).*
āb-bǎı- (ág-bǎı- §519; §§3831ff.) v.t. *(a) be engaged in procuring on hire; (b) continually (habitually) procure on hire.*
āb-bǎn- (ág-bǎn- §519; §§3831ff.) v.i. *(a) be engaged in dancing; (b) continually (habitually) dance.*
āb-báññi- (ág-báñ- §519; §§3831ff.) v.i. *(a) be engaged in speaking, etc. (s.v. báñ(ı)); (b) continually (habitually) speak, etc.*
āb-bǎr- (ág-bǎr- §519; §§3831ff.) v.t. *(a) be engaged in sorting, etc. (s.v. bǎr); (b) continually (habitually) sort, etc.*
āb-bǎr- (ág-bǎr- §519; §§3831ff.) v.t. *(a) be engaged in scratching; (b) continually (habitually) scratch.*
āb-bǎrıǧ- (āg-bǎ- §519; §§3831ff.) v.t. = ābbǎr-.
āb-bārıkέdɛn (āg-bā- §519; §3839) v.t. *(a) be engaged in congratulating (the speaker); (b) continually (habitually) congratulate (the speaker).*
āb-bārıkέtır (āg-bā- §3839) v.t. *(a) be engaged in congratulating (other than the speaker); (b) continually (habitually) congratulate (other than the speaker).*
āb-baríski- (āg-ba- §519; §§3831ff.) v.t. *(a) be engaged in vomiting; (b) continually (habitually) vomit.*
āb-bέ- (āg-bέ- §519; §§3831ff.) v.t. *(a) be engaged in killing, etc. (s.v. bέ); (b) continually (habitually) kill, etc.*
  íkk⏜ābbέran⏝ *(a) they are putting the fire (light) out; (b) they continually (habitually) put the fire (light) out.*

āb-bɛdɛ́- (āg-bɛ- §519; §§3831ff.) v.t. *be engaged in beginning, etc.* = ābbɛtɛ́-.

āb-bɛ́jjı- (āg-bɛ́- §519; §§3831ff.) v.i. (a) *be engaged in bleating*; (b) *continually (habitually) bleat.*
bɛ́rt⌒abbɛ́jjın⌒ *the goat is (goats are* (§4696d), *keep(s) on) bleating.*

āb-bɛ́l- (āg-bɛ́l- §519; §§3831ff.) v.i. (a) *be engaged in issuing, etc.* (s.v. bɛ́l); (b) *continually (habitually) issue, etc.*
kår⌒abbɛ́lın⌒ *the fish are (keep on) escaping* (§4696d).

āb-béndıg- (āg-bén- §519; §§3831ff.) v.t. and i. (a) *be engaged in begging, etc.* (s.v. béndıg); (b) *continually (habitually) beg, etc.*

āb-bɛ́r- (āg-bɛ́r- §519; §§3831ff.) v.i. and t. (a) *be engaged in becoming sated (with);* (b) *continually (habitually) become sated (with).*

āb-bɛ́r- (āg-bɛ́r- §519; §§3831ff.) v.i. (a) *be sprouting;* (b) *continually sprout.*

āb-bérığ- (āg-bé- §519; §§3831ff.) v.t. (a) *be engaged in massacring, etc.* (s.v. bérığ); (b) *continually (habitually) massacre, etc.*

āb-bɛ́s- (āg-bɛ́s- §519; §§3831ff.) v.t. (a) *be engaged in combing;* (b) *continually (habitually) comb.*

āb-bɛtɛ́- (āg-bɛ- §519; -bɛdɛ́-; §§3831ff.) v.t. (a) *be engaged in beginning;* (b) *continually (habitually) begin.*

āb-bɛ́u- (āg-bɛ́u- §519; §§3831ff.) v.t. (a) *be engaged in unravelling, etc.* (s.v. bɛ́u); (b) *continually (habitually) unravel, etc.*

āb-bír- (āg-bír- §519; §§3831ff.) v.t. (a) *be engaged in transporting;* (b) *continually (habitually) transport.*
ind. pres. āı⌒abbírrı⌒.

āb-bíllı- (āg-bíl- §519; §§3831ff.) v.t. (a) *be engaged in picking, etc.* (s.v. bíll(ı)); (b) *continually (habitually) pick, etc.*

abbıré v.t. *measure, ascertain the length, area or volume of* (=ās) [< imperat. or imperf. stem of Sudan Ar. عبر *id.*+-ɛ́ §3638].
ind. pres. āı⌒abbıréri⌒, ɛr⌒abbırén⌒ (-ré⌒, -rɛ́⌒); perf. āı⌒abbırɛ́gori⌒ (N. -ɛ́ko-, -ɛ́ho-).
imperat. abbıré!
írıg⌒ókked⌒abbıréran⌒ *they measure rope by the fathom.*
kådɛk⌒kɛ́uged⌒abbıréran⌒ *they measure cloth by the cubit.*
arítkı⌒šåged⌒abbıréran⌒ *they measure (the) land with a (the) fathom rod.*
márɛk⌒kɛ́laged⌒abbıréran⌒ *they ascertain the amount of millet with a measure.*
ír⌒óg⌒muhóttırɛ⌒dåbuŋ⌒abbıré⌒ (§6122) and
írıg⌒óg⌒mıŋkóttēr⌒dåbuŋ⌒abbıré⌒ (§6131) *measure how many fathoms of rope there are.*
arítk⌒abbıréróskoran⌒ *they have measured the land.*

abbırérar⌒ (-rår⌒; §§2200ff., 2207) and **abbıréríd⌒** (§§2256ff., 2260) n. *measuring, measurement.*

abbırér-an (§§3890, 3899) v.t. *tell to measure, etc., let measure, etc.*

abbıré-bū- (§3931β) v.i. stat. *be in a measured state or condition.*

abbırēred-åg- (§§3877ff.) v.t. *be in the situation of having measured.*

abbıré-kattı- (N. -ɛ́ha-; §4093) v.p. *be measured.*

āb-bíttı- (āg-bít- §519; §§3831ff.) v.t. (a) *be engaged in picking up, etc.* (s.v. bítt(ı)); (b) *continually (habitually) pick up, etc.*

āb-bóban- (āg-bó- §519; §3839) v.i. *be (in process of) becoming adolescent, etc.* (s.v. bób-an-).

āb-bód- (āg-bód- §519; §§3831ff.) v.i. (a) *be engaged in running, etc.* (s.v. bód), *run about;* (b) *continually (habitually) run, etc.*

āb-bóg- (āg-bóg- §519; §§3831ff.) v.t. and i. (a) *be engaged in pouring, etc.* (s.v. bóg); (b) *continually (habitually) pour, etc.*
éssıg⌒abbókkori⌒ (a) *I was (engaged in) pouring the water out (away);* (b) *I habitually poured the water out (away).*
áru⌒marıssóddēr⌒abbógı⌒ *a very little rain* (a) *is falling,* (b) *continually falls.*
šeríkkɛd⌒abbógın⌒ *in the east it is (keeps on) pouring (with) rain.*
ğåkk⌒abbógın⌒ (a) *the jug is leaking;* (b) *the jug always leaks.*

āb-bógır- (āg-bó- §519; §3838) v.t. and i. (a) *be engaged in causing or allowing (liquid, etc.) to pour or leak, etc.* (s.v. bógır); (b) *continually (habitually) cause or allow to pour, etc.*
íŋ-gırbåd⌒éssıg⌒abbógırın⌒ and
íŋ⌒gırbåd⌒abbógırın⌒ *this water-skin is (keeps on) leaking.*

āb-bókkı- (āg-bók- §519; §§3831ff.) v.i. (a) *be engaged in hiding (oneself) etc.* (s.v. bókk(ı)); (b) *continually (habitually) hide (oneself), etc.*

āb-bókkı- (āg-bók- §519; §§3831ff.) v.t. (a) *be engaged in unloading;* (b) *continually (habitually) unload.*

āb-bókkır- (āg-bók- §519; §3838) v.t. (a) *be engaged in concealing;* (b) *continually (habitually) conceal.*

āb-bór- (āg-bór- §519; §§3831ff.) v.i. (a) *be falling down, etc.* (s.v. bór); (b) *continually fall down, etc.*
múgd°abbórın⌒ *the upright post (of the water-wheel* kólɛ⌒) *is (keeps on) falling down.*

āb-bórkığ- (āg-bór- §519; §3838) v.t. (a) *be engaged in pulling down, etc.* (s.v. bórk-ığ); (b) *continually (habitually) pull down, etc.*
kåg⌒abbórkığ¹ran⌒ *they are pulling the house down.*

āb-bórkır- (āg-bór- §519; §3838) v.t. caus. (a) *be (engaged in) causing or allowing to fall down, etc.* (s.v. bórk-ır); (b) *continually (habitually) cause or allow to fall down, etc.*

āb-bóttı- (āg-bót- §519; §§3831ff.) v.i. (a) *be in process of peeling off, etc.* (s.v. bótt(ı)); (b) *continually (habitually) peel off, etc.*

āb-bóttıgır- (āg-bót- §519; §3838) v.t. caus. (a) *be causing or allowing to peel off, etc.;* (b) *continually (habitually) cause or allow to peel off, etc.*

āb-bóttır- (āg-bót- §519; §3838) v.t. (a) *be engaged in detaching, etc.* (s.v. bóttır); (b) *continually (habitually) detach, etc.*

āb-bówwı- (āg-bów- §519; §§3831ff.) v.i. (a) *be engaged in bathing* (i.), *etc.* (s.v. bów(ı)); (b) *continually (habitually) bathe* (i.), *etc.*

āb-bówwíddı- (āg-bōw- §519; §3838) v.t. (a) *be engaged in bathing* (t.); (b) *continually (habitually) bathe* (t.).

āb-bū- *said not to be in use* (§67).

abdallanårt(ı)⌒ (-ti⌒) n. *Abdullinarti (on map), a small island three miles below Argo [ɣabdálla's Island].*
obj. -tıg⌒.

abdɛ́ v.t. (a) *worship, adore, pray to;* (b) *ask in prayer, implore* [عابد *worshipper*+-ɛ́ §3631].
ind. pres. āı⌒abdɛ́ri⌒; perf. āı⌒abdɛ́gori⌒ (N. -ɛ́ko-).
imperat. abdɛ́!
årtıg⌒abdɛ́ran⌒ *they worship God.*
tɛr⌒åñıŋg⌒abdɛ́n⌒ (§6122) *(s)he prays (that (s)he may be allowed) to live.*
tɛ́r⌒åñıŋg⌒årtıg⌒abdɛ́n⌒ (§6135) *(s)he prays to God to let him (her) live.*
tír⌒åñıraŋg⌒årtıg⌒abdɛ́ran⌒ *they implore God that they may live.*

abdɛ́rar⌒ (-rår⌒; §§2200ff.) and **abdɛ́ríd⌒** (§§2256ff.) n. *worship, adoration.*
årtın⌒abdɛ́ríd⌒ *adoration of God.*

abdɛ́-kattı- (N. -ɛ́ha-; §4093) v.p. *be worshipped, be adored.*

abdɛnnū́r⌒ n. *one of the sorts of date growing in Dóngola, s.v.* bént(ı)⌒; *with coll. sg.* (§4696b), [< عبد النور *id.*].
obj. -núrk(ı)⌒, -kı⌒.
pl. -núru⌒.

ábd(ı) v.t. *meet* [§2868].
ind. pres. āı⌒ábdırı⌒, ɛr⌒ábdın⌒ (-dí⌒, -dí⌒); fut. āı⌒bábdırı⌒; perf. āı⌒ábdıgori⌒ (N. -ıko-).
imperat. ábdi!
ar⌒tékkı⌒ógwwın⌒áttır⌒ábdıgoru⌒ *we met him (her) by the well.*
árg⌒abdıríddan⌒ *they meet us.*
árgı⌒babdıríddan⌒ *they will meet us.*

ábd-an (§3890) v.t. *tell to meet, let meet.*

-abd(ı)⌒ (-add(ı)⌒, -dí⌒) postp. *(to meet, and so* = *prep.* §4287) *in the direction of, towards, to;* suffixed to the objective (§4335); (in *RN*, §383 confused with ⌒ábtı-r⌒).
kågabdı⌒nókkoran⌒ *they went (have gone) towards the house.*
āı⌒sūgkabdı⌒nógbūri⌒ *I am on my way to the market.*
írıg⌒ékkaddı⌒n⌒tólle!* pull the rope to-(wards) you!*
kåg⌒ğebénn⌒togógaddı⌒dıgrín⌒ (-nn t-<-lnt- §814) *snakes (§4647) are plentiful towards the foot of the mountain.*
X. maíngaddı⌒kállí⌒ *push it (them) to-wards the left.*
Y. *pushes in another direction.*
X. íŋgémmunun, maíngaddıgı! (§4336) *not like that, towards the left!*

ábɛ⌒ *small fishing-net s.v.* áb.

abgússı⌒ (-si⌒) n. *Abu Gussi (on map), a small village on the left bank of the Nile, about six miles above Old Dóngola* [<أَبُو قُسِّي].
obj. -sıg⌒.

ábkoñ — ād-déssan-

ábkoñ (ápk-) n. *castor-oil plant, Ricinus communis*, Linn. (BSP, 528) [-ñ dim. §2304].
  obj. abkóñg(ı), -gi.
ábol n. *steep declivity, sudden drop in level of ground.*
  obj. abólg(ı), -gi.
  pl. ábol.
  úrun ábol *steep bank of river.*
  hórn ábol *steep bank of watercourse.*
  abóllo dıgíkori *I fell on (over, down) the declivity.*
  ábon tógor (-n t- < -ln t- §814; §5858) *(s)he (it) is (they are) under the steep bank.*
  ábon kóččır (-ŋ k- < -ln k- §653) *(s)he (it) is (they are) on the steep bank.*
abrahín n. *Abraham* [< اِبْراهيم id. §§1290, 1339].
  obj. -íŋg(ı), -gi.
ábrɛ n. *dry fermented-millet-bread* [Sudan Ar. أُبْرِي id. §2236].
  obj. ábrɛg, -gi.
  ábrᵉíwırtōn áukattın ábrɛ *is made from great millet.*
abríš n. *Abu Rish* (on map), *an island five miles below Débba* [< أَبُو رِيش].
  obj. -íšk(ı), -ki.
absóg n. *hedgehog, porcupine* [< أَبُو شَوْك id. §1297].
  obj. -ógk(ı), -ókk(ı), -ki.
  pl. absóg.
ábir postp. *alongside (of)* sv. áb.
abufátma n. *Abu Fatma* (on map), *a domed tomb* (قُبَّة) *near Aškán on the right bank of the Nile ten miles below Árgo; this is the linguistic frontier between Dóngola and Máḥas.*
  obj. -nag [< أَبُو فاطمة].
ábug n. *wool* [RSN, §200 s.v. *bāg*].
  obj. abúgk(ı), -úkk(ı).
  gen. abúgn v., -úŋ c. (§642).
  ɛgédn ábug *sheep's wool.*
  kámn ábug *camel's wool.*
  ín ábugun *this is wool.*
abún-d(ı) (§§2545 ff.) adj. *appertaining to (the) wool, of (the) wool, woollen.*
  obj. -dıg.
abúrrɛ n. *Tripoli senna, Cassia obovata,* Collad. (BSP, 166).
  obj. -rɛg.
abušébɛd n. *a large spider, of rapid pace and (?) venomous* [أَبُو شَبَت id.].
  obj. -šɛbédk(ı), -étk(ı), -étt(ı) (§2462), -ki, -ti.
  pl. šébɛdı.
áčč(ı) v.t. *bite* [cogn. ág-ıl *mouth* §2864].
  ind. pres. āi áččıri, ɛr áččɛn (-či-, -čí-); fut. āi báččıri, perf. āi áččıgori (N. -ıko-, -ıho-).
  imperat. ácci!
  subj. past āi áččısı (-su).
  wél bıtáŋg áččóskó *the dog has bitten the child.*
áččar (-čár; §§2200 ff.) and
áččíd (§§2256 ff.) n. *biting.*

áčč-an (§3890) v.t. *tell to bite, let bite.*
áčči-bŭ- (§3931β) v.i. stat. *be in a bitten state or condition.*
  wél áččıbūn *the dog is (has been) bitten.*
áččır-ɛg-ág- (§§4071 ff.) v.t. = aččɛdól-.
  wél aččırɛgágın *the dog is just going to bite.*
áčč-ɛ-dól- (-čᵒdól- §1178; §4022) and
áččır-ɛ-dól- (-rᵒdól-; §4027) v.t. *be about to bite.*
áčč-ɛ-má- (§4036) and
áččır-ɛ-má- (§4041) v.t. *become unable to bite.*
áččɛd-ág- (§3877) v.t. *be in the situation of having bitten.*
  wél bıtáŋg aččɛdágın *the dog has bitten the child.*
áčči-kattı- (N. -ıha-; §4093) v.p. *be bitten.*
ád n. *handle, helve, hilt (of wood or substitute fitted to metal); usually distinguished from f,* q.v. [cogn. *ăr seize* §2061].
  obj. ádk(ı), átk(ı), átt(ı) (§2462), -ki, -ti.
  pl. ád.
  fåsn ád *handle of axe.*
  gálamn ád *handle of pen, penholder.*
  kándın ád *handle of knife.*
  siwídn ád *hilt of sword* = siwídn f.
  šākúšn ád *handle of hammer.*
  túbron ád *handle of hoe.*
  túrubn ád *handle of sickle.*
ád-kıññ(ı)- (átk-; §2536) adj. *without a handle.*
áda n. *basket-work plate or tray* [< أَداة *utensil* or (?) < قَدَح *bowl* §1278].
  obj. ádag.
  pl. adánč(ı).
ádam, ádəm *human being* = ádɛm.
ād-dáb- (āg-dáb- §534; §§3831 ff.) v.i. (a) *be (in course of) disappearing, etc.* (s.v. *dáb*) *be coming to an end*; (b) *continually (habitually) disappear, etc.*
  árᵘ āddábın *the rain is coming to an end.*
ād-dábır- (āg-dá- §534; §3838) v.t. (a) *be engaged in causing or allowing to disappear, etc.* (s.v. *dábır*); (b) *continually (habitually) cause or allow to disappear, etc.*
  ind. pres. āi āddabíddi and āi āddabírri.
ād-dáğı- (āg-dá- §534; §3838) v.i. (a) *be engaged in walking about, etc.* (s.v. *dáğı-*); (b) *continually (habitually) walk about, etc.*
ād-dárrı- (āg-dár- §534; §3831 ff.) v.i. (a) *be engaged in ascending, etc.* (s.v. *dárr(ı)*); (b) *continually (habitually) ascend, etc.*
ād-darrı-mér- (āg-dar- §534; §3839) v.t. (a) *be engaged in ascending and cutting*; (b) *continually (habitually) ascend and cut.*
ād-dáttı- (āg-dát- §534; §§3831 ff.) v.i. (a) *be engaged in walking stumblingly, etc.* (s.v. *dátt(ı)*); (b) *continually (habitually) walk stumblingly, etc.*
addɛ́ v.t. *finish, end, complete* (= tɛmmɛ́) [? < a stem of قَضَّى *finish* + -ɛ́ §§1277, 3642].
  ind. pres. āi addɛ́ri (occ. -déri §1073), ɛr addɛ́n (-dɛ́-, -dɛ́- §939); occ. -dén, -dé, -dɛ́); fut. āi baddɛ́ri (occ.

-déri); perf. āi addɛ́gori (N. -ɛ́ko-, -ɛ́ho-).
def. perf. āi addɛróskori.
addɛ́! *finish!, have done!*, pl. addɛ́wɛ! (addɛ́wɛ́!).
  sútte tékk addɛ́ *finish it (that §5103) quickly.*
  ğéllıg addɛgómunan *they did not finish (have not finished) the work.*
  ín ğéllıg addɛróskın ánnár ta *as soon as you finish this matter (work) come to me.*
addɛ́rar (-rár; §§2200 ff.) and
addɛ́ríd (§§2256 ff.) n. *finishing, completion.*
addɛ́r-an (§3890) v.t. *tell to finish, etc., let finish, etc.*
addɛ́-bŭ- (§3931β) v.i. stat. *be in a finished (etc.) state or condition.*
addɛ́r-ɛg-ág- (§§4071 ff.) v.t. = addɛrɛdól-.
addɛ́r-ɛ-dól- (-rᵒdól- §1178; §§4017, 4022, 4027) v.t. *be about to finish, etc.*
addɛ́r-ɛ-má- (§§4036, 4041) v.t. *become unable to finish, etc.*
addɛ́rɛd-ág- (§3877) v.t. *be in the situation of having finished, etc.*
addɛ́-kattı- (N. -ɛ́ha-; §4093) v.p. *be finished, etc.*
  ékkɛnɛ baddɛ́kattı *it will be finished immediately* (lit. . . . . *now*).
ād-dɛfɛ́ (āg-dɛ- §534; §§3831 ff.) v.t. (a) *be engaged in paying*; (b) *continually (habitually) pay.*
ād-dɛfɛ́dɛn- (-ág-dɛ- §534; §3839) v.t. (a) *be engaged in paying* (to the speaker, s.v. dɛfɛ́-dɛn); (b) *continually (habitually) pay (etc.).*
ād-dɛfɛ́tır- (āg-dɛ- §534; §3839) v.t. (a) *be engaged in paying* (to other than the speaker, s.v. dɛfɛ́-tır); (b) *continually (habitually) pay (etc.).*
ād-dég- (āg-dég- §534; §§3831 ff.) v.t. and i. (a) *be engaged in putting on, etc.* (s.v. dég), (b) *continually (habitually) put on, etc.*
ād-dég- (āg-dég- §534; §§3831 ff.) v.t. (a) *be engaged in irrigating*; (b) *continually (habitually) irrigate.*
  désseg āddégın *he (it) is irrigating (habitually irrigates) the vegetables (crops), etc.,* s.v. désse.
ād-dékkı- (āg-dék- §534; §§3831 ff.) v.i. (a) *be engaged in hopping*; (b) *continually (habitually) hop.*
ād-dɛn- (āg-dɛn- §534; §§3831 ff.) v.t. (a) *be engaged in giving* (to the speaker, s.v. dɛ́n); (b) *continually (habitually) give (etc.).*
ād-déñ- (āg-déñ- §534; §§3831 ff.) v.t. s.v. déñ.
ād-déŋgɛlan- (āg-déŋ- §534; §3839) v.i. (a) *be in process of becoming solid, etc.* (s.v. déŋgɛl-an-); (b) *continually become solid, etc.*
ād-dɛréñɛ- (āg-dɛ- §534; §3839) v.i. (a) *be engaged in bending down, etc.* (s.v. dɛréñɛ); (b) *continually (habitually) bend down, etc.*
ād-déssan- (āg-dés- §534; §3839) v.i. (a) *be in process of becoming green, etc.* (s.v. déss-an-); (b) *continually become green, etc.*

ād-détte- (āg-dét- §534; §§3831 ff.) v.i. (*a*) *be dripping, etc.* (s.v. détte); (*b*) *continually drip, etc.*
 éssɪ‿bɛ́šɛrtōn‿āddéttɛn⌒ *the water is dripping* (*continually drips*) *from the jar*(*s* §4647) sc. *of the water-wheel* kólɛ‿.
 áru‿bōgedā́gɪn‿ólgon‿āddéttɛn⌒ *the rain has poured* (*come down*) (*and* §6240) *it is still drizzling.*

ād-dí- (āg-dí- §534; §§3831 ff.) v.i. (*a*) *be dying* (*of flame*), *be going out*; (*b*) *continually be extinguished, keep on going out.*

ād-díŋgɪr- (āg-díŋ- §534; N. -ŋkɪr-; §3838) v.t. (*a*) *be causing or allowing to die, etc.*; (*b*) *continually* (*habitually*) *cause or allow to die, etc.*

-add(ɪ)- postp. *towards, to,* <-abd(ɪ)‿ s.v. ábd(ɪ).

ād-díd- (āg-díd- §534; §§3831 ff.) v.t. (*a*) *be engaged in reviling, etc.* (s.v. díd); (*b*) *continually* (*habitually*) *revile, etc.*

ād-dígɪr- (āg-dí- §534; §3838) v.t. (*a*) *be engaged in tying, etc.* (s.v. dígɪr s.v. díg); (*b*) *continually* (*habitually*) *tie, etc.*

ād-dígɪr (āg-dí- §534; §§3831 ff.) v.i. (*a*) *be falling*; (*b*) *continually* (*habitually*) *fall.*

ād-dɪgɪrtṓ- (āg-dɪ- ; §3839) v.i. (*a*) *be falling in*; (*b*) *continually* (*habitually*) *fall in.*

ād-dɪgrīgɪrbáññɪ- (āg-dɪ- §534; N. -īkɪr-, -īhɪr-; §3839) v.i. (*a*) *be engaged in speaking a great deal, etc.* (s.v. dɪgrīgɪrbáññ(ɪ)); (*b*) *continually* (*habitually*) *speak a great deal, etc.*

ād-dɪgrīgɪrbṓg- (āg-dɪ- §534; N. -īkɪr-, -īhɪr-; §3839) v.t. and i. (*a*) *be engaged in pouring a great deal, etc.* (s.v. dɪgrīgɪrbṓg); (*b*) *continually* (*habitually*) *pour a great deal, etc.*

ād-dɪgrīgɪrgɛrɟɛ́- (āg-dɪ- §534; N. -īkɪr-, -īhɪr-, -gɛrɛ́- ; §3839) v.t. and i. (*a*) *be engaged in reading much, etc.* (s.v. dɪgrīgɪrgɛrɟɛ́); (*b*) *continually* (*habitually*) *read much, etc.*

ād-dɪgrīgɪrkál- (āg-dɪ- §534; N. -īkɪr-, -īhɪr-; §3839) v.t. and i. (*a*) *be engaged in eating a great deal, etc.* (s.v. dɪgrīgɪrkál); (*b*) *continually* (*habitually*) *eat a great deal, etc.*

ād-dɪgrīgɪrkórrɛ- (āg-dɪ- §534; N. -īkɪr-, -īhɪr-; §3839) v.i. (*a*) *be engaged in snoring a great deal, etc.* (s.v. dɪgrīgɪrkórrɛ); (*b*) *continually* (*habitually*) *snore a great deal, etc.*

ād-dɪgrīgɪrnóg- (āg-dɪ- §534; N. -īkɪr-, -īhɪr-; -gɪnnóg- §628; §3839) v.i. (*a*) *be engaged in going a great deal, etc.* (s.v. dɪgrīgɪrnóg); (*b*) *continually* (*habitually*) *go a great deal, etc.*

ād-dɪgrīgɪrsándɪ- (āg-dɪ- §534; N. -īkɪr-, -īhɪr-; §3839) v.i. and t. (*a*) *be much afraid* (*of*), *etc.* (s.v. dɪgrīgɪrsándɪ); (*b*) *continually* (*habitually*) *be much afraid* (*of*), *etc.*

ād-dɪgrīgɪrsándɪgɪr- (āg-dɪ- §534; N. -īkɪr-, -īhɪr-, -dɪkɪr-, -dɪhɪr-; §3839) v.t. (*a*) *be engaged in frightening a great deal, etc.* (s.v. dɪgrīgɪrsándɪgɪr); (*b*) *continually* (*habitually*) *frighten a great deal, etc.*

áddo‿ *on* (*etc.*) *me* (*us*) s.v. -r‿ (§2611).

ād-dóg- (āg-dóg- §534; §§3831 ff.) v.t. (*a*) *be engaged in kissing*; (*b*) *continually* (*habitually*) *kiss.*

ād-dōhɛ́- (āg-dō- §534; -dōxɛ́-; §§3831 ff.) v.i. (*a*) *be* (*in process of*) *becoming giddy*; (*b*) *continually* (*habitually*) *become giddy.*

ād-dól- (āg-dól- §534; §§3831 ff.) v.t. (*a*) *be desiring, etc.* (s.v. dól); (*b*) *continually* (*habitually*) *desire, etc.*
 búru‿diélg‿āddólkó⌒ *he used to be in love with the* (*a*) *girl that died.*

ād-dóñ- (āg-dóñ- §534; §§3831 ff.) v.t. (*a*) *be engaged in rearing, etc.* (s.v. dóñ); (*b*) *continually* (*habitually*) *rear, etc.*

ād-dóš- (āg-dóš- §534; §§3831 ff.) v.t. (*a*) *be engaged in covering, etc.* (s.v. dóš); (*b*) *continually* (*habitually*) *cover, etc.*

ād-dowwɪrɛ́- (āg-dow- §534; -wᵘrɛ́-; §§3831 ff.) v.t. (*a*) *be engaged in causing to revolve, etc.* (s.v. dowwɪrɛ́); (*b*) *continually* (*habitually*) *cause to revolve, etc.*

ād-dúg- (āg-dúg- §534; §§3831 ff.) v.i. (*a*) *be in process of becoming clouded, etc.* (s.v. dúg); (*b*) *continually* (*habitually*) *become clouded, etc.*

ād-dúkkɪ- (āg-dúk- §534; §§3831 ff.) v.t. (*a*) *be engaged in extracting, etc.* (s.v. dúkk(ɪ)); (*b*) *continually* (*habitually*) *extract, etc.*
 árabɪ‿hálar‿ǧáddɪg‿árɪdɪrtōn‿āddúkkɪran⌒ *the Arabs in the desert are engaged in* (*make a practice of*) *extracting natron from the ground.*

ād-dúlan- (āg-dú- §534; §3839) v.i. (*a*) *be* (*in process of*) *becoming great, etc.* (s.v. dúl-an-); (*b*) *continually become great, etc.*
 ǧóww‿āddúlanɪn⌒ (*a*) *the tree is* (*trees are* §4696b) *growing large*; (*b*) *the trees continually grow large.*

ād-dúr- (āg-dúr- §534; §§3831 ff.) v.t. (*a*) *be engaged in reaching, etc.* (s.v. dúr); (*b*) *continually* (*habitually*) *reach, etc.*

ádɛm‿ (ádàm‿, ádam‿) n. *human being, person* [<آدم‎ id. §1391].
 obj. adémg(ɪ)‿, -gi⌒.
 pl. ádɛm‿.
 ádàm‿ɪndonč‿ɛ́goran⌒ (-m‿í- < -mɪ‿í- §1122) *the people* (*persons, homines*) *were here* (§4449).
 ádɛm‿mállɛn‿dógor‿nósōn⌒ (*s*)*he* (*it*) *is taller than anybody, lit. than every person.*
 íw‿wél‿adémg‿áččɪn⌒ (-w‿w- < -n‿w- §720) *this* (*that*) *dog bites.*

ádɛs‿ n. *lentil*; with coll. sg. (§4696b) [<عدس‎ id.].
 obj. adésk(ɪ)‿, -ki⌒.

ádɪr n. *winter* [cp. ⲣⲁⲱⲡ RSN, §129; Eg. ḥt-ḥr *house of Horus,* هاتور Eth. ϩⲁⲧⲱⲣ 'Aθύρ *month* 10 *Nov.-*9 *Dec.*].
 obj. adɪ́rk(ɪ)‿, -ki⌒.
 pl. ádrɪ‿.
 ɪnnóww‿ádɪr‿dɪgrí⌒ *to-day is very wintry* (§4719).
 ɪnnówwɪg‿ádɪr‿dɪgrí⌒ *to-day it's very wintry.*

adírk(ɪ) (§4433) and
adir-ro‿ adv. *in* (*the*) *winter.*

ádɪr-an- (§3913α, ν) v.i. *become winter.*
 ádɪraŋkó⌒ *it has become* (*became*) *winter.*

ádɪram-bŭ- v.i. stat. (*a*, §3949) *be in the state of becoming winter*; (*b*, §3953) *be in the state of having become winter, be winter.*
 ádɪrambūn⌒ (*a*) *winter is coming on*; (*b*) *winter has set in.*

adɪran-ɛ-dól- (-nᵒdól- §1178; §4026) and
adɪrand-ɛ-dól- (-dᵒdól-; §4034) v.i. *be about to become winter.*
 adɪran(d)ɛdólɪn⌒ *winter is just starting.*

ádŭ‿ n. *enemy* [<عدو‎ id.].
 obj. ádŭg‿.
 pl. ádunč(ɪ)‿.
adún-d(ɪ)‿ (§§2545 ff.) adj. *appertaining to the* (*an*) *enemy, of the* (*an*) *enemy, hostile.*

ā-dūl-kó- *be proud* s.v. ắ‿.

āfɛ́- v.t. *pardon, forgive* [<ɛaf- عفو‎ *forgiveness* or of عفاعن‎ *forgive*+-ɛ́ §§1351, 3627].
 ind. pres. āɪ‿āfɛ́rɪ⌒; perf. āɪ‿āfɛ́gorɪ⌒ (N. -ɛ́ko-, -ɛ́ho-).
 imperat. āfɛ́!
 def. imperat. (§3793) āfɛ́ros! (-ɛ́ró! §962); pl. āfɛ́rósswɛ! (-óswé!, -ówwɛ! §724, -wɛ́!, -ósse! §687, -sɛ́).
 sɪǧínd‿undúrkoran, bádkɛd‿āfɛ́goran⌒ *they put him* (*her, them*) *in prison,* (*but*) *afterwards they pardoned him* (*her, them* §5083).
 X. āɪg‿āfɛ́ró! *forgive me!*
 Y. sɛ́rɛn, ɛ́kk‿āfɛ́róskorɪ⌒ *all right, I have forgiven you.*

āfɛ́rar- (-rár‿; §§2200ff.) and
āfɛ́ríd- (§§2256 ff.) n. *pardon, forgiveness.*

āfɛ́r-an (§3890) v.t. *tell to pardon, etc., let pardon, etc.*

āfɛ́-kattɪ- (N. -ɛ́ha-; §4093) v.p. *be pardoned, etc.*
 tímbɛs‿sɪǧíndotōm‿bélkon, āfɛ́kattɪgó⌒ *his brother has come* (*came*) *out of prison, he has been* (*was*) *pardoned.*
 ín‿āfɛ́kattɪmunun⌒ *this* (*one*) *cannot* (§4097) *be pardoned* (*this thing* (*person*) *is unpardonable*).

áfɛš‿ n. *baggage, luggage, stuff, belongings* [<عفش‎ id. §§1258, 1358].
 obj. afɛ́šk(ɪ)‿, -ki⌒.

affád- (-át⌒) n. *Affát* (*Affat on map*), a village on the right bank of the Nile, about 16 miles above Débba.
 obj. -ádk(ɪ)‿, -átk(ɪ)‿, -ki⌒.
 affád-ar (*at*) *to*) *Affát.*
 affádɪr⌒ (*s*)*he* (*it*) *is* (*they are*) *at Affát.*

āf-fadlɛ́- (āk-fad-, āg-fad- §541; §§3831 ff.) v.i. (*a*) *be* (*in process of*) *remaining behind, etc.* (s.v. fadlɛ́); (*b*) *continually* (*habitually*) *remain behind, etc.*

āf-fáttɛ- (āk-fát-, āg-fát- §541; §§3831 ff.) v.i. (*a*) *be having a fit*; (*b*) *continually have fits.*

āf-fattɪrɛ́- (āk-fat-, āg-fat- §541; §§3831 ff.) v.i. (*a*) *be engaged in breakfasting*; (*b*) *habitually breakfast.*

āf-fɛ́kkagɪr- (āk-fɛ́k-, āg-fɛ́k- §541; -fák-, -fák-; §3838) v.t. =affɛkkɛ́-.

āf-fɛkkɛ́- (āk-fɛk-, āg-fɛk- §541; §§3831 ff.) v.t. (*a*) *be engaged in changing* (*into smaller coin*); (*b*) *continually* (*habitually*) *change* (*etc.*).

āf-fɛttɪšɛ́- (āk-fɛt-, āg-fɛt- §541; §§3831 ff.) v.t. (*a*) *be engaged in examining, etc.* (s.v. fɛttɪšɛ́); (*b*) *continually* (*habitually*) *examine, etc.*

āf-fɪlátti- (āk-fɪ-, āg-fɪ- §541; -lítti-; §§3831 ff.) v.i. *be shining, etc.* = āffɪlínči-.

āf-fɪlínči- (āk-fɪ-, āg-fɪ- §541; §§3831 ff.) v.i. (*a*) *be shining, etc.* (s.v. fɪlínč(ɪ)); (*b*) *continually shine, etc.*

āf-fírrɪ- (āk-fír-, āg-fír- §541; §§3831 ff.) v.i. (*a*) *be engaged in flying;* (*b*) *continually (habitually) fly.*

āf-físsɪ- (āk-fís-, āg-fís- §541; §§3831 ff.) v.t. (*a*) *be engaged in splashing;* (*b*) *continually (habitually) splash.*

āf-fórrɛ- (āk-fór-, āg-fór- §541; §§3831 ff.) v.i. (*a*) *be engaged in snorting, etc.* (s.v. fórrɛ); (*b*) *continually (habitually) snort, etc.*

āf-fúčɛ- (āk-fú-, āg-fú- §541; §§3831 ff.) v.i. (*a*) *be engaged in blowing one's nose;* (*b*) *continually (habitually) blow one's nose.*

áfja n. *health, good health* [< عَافِية *id.*].
obj. -ag.

afránğɪ adj. and n. *European* [< أَفْرَنْجِي *id.*].
obj. -ğɪg.
pl. -ğɪnč(ɪ).

ág (§§2806, 3815, 4491) v.i. (*a*) *squat;* (*b*) *sit down, sit;* (*c*) *settle;* (*d*) *reside, live;* (*e*) *remain, stay, wait (not depart);* (*f*) *be in a situation, position or place, be continuously, remain, stay, keep (not change position);* (*g*) *be present, be here, be there;* (*h*) *be* [cp. ON. ⴰⵔ *id.* GNT, s.v.; RSN, §129; contains √á- §4491].
— used of persons, like its synonym tég, while dā- is more commonly used of things, and téb is used of either.
ind. pres. āɪ-ág(¹)ri, ɛr-ágɪn (-ágĩ, -ágɪ); fut. (āɪ-bágri heard but not in general use, replaced by) āɪ-bɪtégri (s.v. tég); perf. āɪ-ágkori (-ákko-).
subj. past āɪ-ágsɪ (áksɪ §679; -su).
ák! *sit down!* (to one seated = *don't get up!*).
pl. ágwɛ! (ágwé!, ággɛ! §547, -gé!).
índ-ág-egó (*s*)*he said 'sit here'.*
part. pres. ágɪl (*one*) *that squats, etc., squatter, etc., squatting, etc.*, obj. āgílg(ɪ).
part. past ágɛl (*one*) *that squatted, etc., squatter, etc., squatting, etc.*, obj. āgélg(ɪ).
neg. pres. āɪ-ágmunun (áŋŋunun §661, -unũ, -unu, -un §947).
kúrsɪr-ágɪn (*s*)*he sits on (in) the (a) chair.*
tɛr-ɪmbélmɛŋgon-ágɪn (§5743) (*a*) (*s*)*he (it) remains squatting instead of getting up;* (*b*) (*s*)*he (it) remains instead of starting.*
šétɪl-ɪmbélmɛŋŋon-ágɪn the young plant remains stunted instead of growing up.
X. álɪ-míŋg-āgáwɪn? *what is ɣáli doing?*
Y. sūdɪr-ágɪn *just sitting, i.e. nothing* (=قَاعِد سَاكِت).
índ-ákkoran *they (have) settled (etc.) here.*
X. sáɪr-ágran? *where do they live?*

Y. mássín-dār-ágran *they live in Máḥas.*
ógɪğ-ídɪw-nogóskoran, tósk-ágran *eight men have gone, three remain.*
murásli-wēr-ágɪn *a messenger is waiting (is in attendance).*
X. íŋg-éttārɛl-ágná? *is the person that brought this waiting?*
Y. éjj-ágɪn *yes (s)he is.*
āɪ-ágríddo-bɪtégri *I shall remain where I am* (§6207).
n-ágɪn? (nágī?, nágí?; < ní-ágɪn? §1125) *who's here?, who's there?*
mán-kúbɪr-n-ágɪn? *who's in that boat (over there)?*
áŋ-gɛr-índ-áŋŋunun *there's no-one here but me (us).*
zāmɛndotōn-ágɪn (*s*)*he has been sitting (here, there) for a long time.*
šáhíd-dēr-ákkon (-d-d- < -d-w- §533) *a witness was present.*
tíŋ-kár-ágran *they are in their house (are at home).*
hémar-ágɪn (*s*)*he is in the tent.*
álɪ-méktɛbɪr-ágɪn *ɣáli is in the office.*
zábɪnn-agárro-n-ágɪn? (-nn- < -dn- §624) *who is (present, acting) in place of the officer?*
kálɪŋŋon-ágran (§5738) *they are (engaged in) eating* = ākkállan.
āɪ-gɛrjéŋgon-ágri (-jéŋŋon) *I am engaged in reading.*
ɛr-gɛrjéŋgon-ágɪn (-jéŋŋon) *you are engaged in reading.*
tɛr-gɛrjéŋgon-ágɪn (-jéŋŋon) (*s*)*he is engaged in reading.*
ar-gɛrjéŋgon-ágru (-jéŋŋon) *we are engaged in reading.*
ɪr-gɛrjéŋgon-ágru (-jéŋŋon) *you are engaged in reading.*
tɪr-gɛrjéŋgon-ágran (-jéŋŋon) *they are engaged in reading.*

ágar (ágar; §§2200 ff.) and
āgíd (§2256 ff.) n. *squatting, etc.*

ágar n. *place, position, space* [< ágar §2215].
obj. agárk(ɪ), -ki.
pl. ágarɪ.
tínn-ɪllár-ágar-dámunun *there's no place (room) for them.*
ínɪn-ɪllár-agárk-áu *make a place (make room) for this (one).*
mohámmɛd-fadílgɪ-wél-tónn-agárkɪ-géndɪgɪran *let Muḥámmad Faḍl mend the place* (sc. *in the fence*) *where the dog comes in;* mohámmɛd-fadílgɪ a noun-complex (§4751), indirect object of -an (§3892); -wél tónn a noun-clause in the genitive (§6156).
sūdn-ágar and sūdnagar n. *time or situation in which one has nothing to do, spare time, leisure.*
obj. sūdn-agárk(ɪ), sūdnagárk(ɪ).
āɪ-sūdnagárkɪ-dólli *I want (like) leisure.*
agár-ro (§6007) adv. *in (to) the place.*
kúšar-ténn-agárró (§1989) *the key is in its place.*
kɪtābɪ-tínn-agárró *the books are in their place.*

X. kúšar-ɪsέ? *where's the key?*
Y. ténn-agárró *it's in its place.*
-agárro (§§5860, 5893 ff.) postp. (= prep. §4287) *in the place (of), instead (of).*
— follows the genitive:
hánuk-kágn-agárr-ɛttágoran *they (have) brought the (a) donkey instead of the (a) horse.*
X. ɛsmán-tɛr-mén-tágomɛnɪn? *why didn't (hasn't) ɣoθmán come?*
Y. álɪ-ténn-agárró *ɣáli is instead of him.*
íŋgu-tínn-agárró *these are (a) in their (own) place;* (*b*) *instead of them.*

ág-an (§3890) v.t. *tell to squat (etc.), all senses, let squat, etc.*
āɪ-tékk-ágandi *I('ll §5369b) tell him (her) to sit down (etc.).*
iškártɪg-áŋgarɛr-ágan (§5392) *let the guest sit on the bedstead.*

*****āgɛd-ág-**, ***āg-ɛ-dól-**, ***āg-ɛ-má-** *not heard; replaced by tég-complexes.*

ágɪl-dā- (ágɪllā- §578; §3985) v.i. *be present squatting, etc., be at hand squatting, etc., be, squatting (etc.) at hand.*
hakím-ágɪllānā? *is the (is there a) doctor present (in residence)?*

ag-ídd(ɪ) (§3722) v.t. caus. *cause or allow to squat or sit, give a seat to, seat* [ág- > ag- §1062].
ind. pres. āɪ-agíddɪri; fut. āɪ-bagíddɪri; perf. āɪ-agíddɪgori (N. -iko-, -iho-).
imperat. agíddi!
pl.-obj. agíddɪr.
def. imperat. agɪddós!
āɪ-tékk-agíddɪri *I'll (§5369b) make (let) him (her) sit down.*
tɛr-āig-agíddɪn (*s*)*he makes (lets) me sit down.*
āɪ-tékkɪ-níbɪdɪr-bagíddɪri *I shall seat him (her) on the (a) mat.*
tɛr-āig-áŋgarɛr-agíddɪgó (*s*)*he seated me on the (a) bedstead.*

agíddar (-dar; §§2200 ff.) and
agɪddíd (§2256 ff.) n. *causing or allowing to squat or sit, giving a seat.*

agídd-an (§3890) v.t. *tell to give a seat to, let give a seat to.*
álɪ-tékk-agíddan (-t-t- < -g-t- §707) *let ɣáli give him (her) a seat (tell ɣáli to make him (her) sit down).*

āg-áb- (§§3831 ff.) v.t. (*a*) *be engaged in catching (a thrown or falling body);* (*b*) *continually (habitually) catch.*

āg-áb- (§§3831 ff.) v.t. (*a*) *be engaged in netting, etc.* (s.v. áb), (*b*) *continually (habitually) net, etc.*
kárɛg-āgáb¹ran (*a*) *they are netting fish;* (*b*) *they habitually net fish.*

ágaba n. *desert* [< عَقَبَة *id.*].
obj. -bag.
pl. -banč(ɪ).

āg-abágan- (§3839) v.i. (*a*) *be engaged in moving backwards, etc.* (s.v. abág-an-); (*b*) *continually (habitually) move backwards, etc.*

āg-abágkɪr- (-ákkɪr-; §3838) v.t. caus. (*a*) *be engaged in causing or allowing to be behind, etc.* (s.v. abágk-ɪr s.v. abág);

(b) continually (habitually) cause or allow to be behind, etc.

āg-abbɪrɛ́- (§3838) v.t. (a) be engaged in measuring, etc. (s.v. abbɪrɛ́); (b) continually (habitually) measure, etc.

āg-abdɛ́- (§3838) v.t. (a) be engaged in worshipping, etc. (s.v. abdɛ́); (b) continually (habitually) worship, etc.

āi-áñ¹rɪŋ‿kɛ́lg‿āi‿ártɪg‿āgabdɛ́ri⌒ (-ŋ‿ k-<-nn‿k- §657; §6156) as long as I live I (shall §5369b) continue praying to God.

āg-ábd(ɪ)- (§§3831ff.) v.t. (a) be engaged in meeting; (b) continually (habitually) meet.

āg-áčči- (§§3831ff.) v.t. (a) be engaged in biting; (b) continually (habitually) bite.

āg-addɛ́- (§3838) v.t. (a) be engaged in finishing, etc. (s.v. addɛ́); (b) habitually finish, etc.

ágadɛ‿ n. Agada (on map), a village on the right bank of the Nile at the southern end of Argo Island. obj. -dɛg‿.

āg-agáu- (§3838) v.t. (a) be engaged in twisting (s.v. agáu); (b) continually (habitually) twist.

āg-ágɪs- (§3838) v.t. (a) be engaged in rousing, etc. (s.v. ágɪs); (b) continually (habitually) rouse, etc.

āg-aǧǧɪrɛ́- (§3838) v.t. (a) be engaged in procuring on hire; (b) continually (habitually) procure on hire.

āg-aǧǧɪrɛ́dɛn- (§3839) v.t. (a) be engaged in letting, etc. (to the speaker; s.v. aǧǧɪrɛ́- dɛn); (b) continually (habitually) let, etc. (to the speaker).

āg-aǧǧɪrɛ́tɪr- (§3839) v.t. (a) be engaged in letting, etc. (to other than the speaker; s.v. aǧǧɪrɛ́-tɪr); (b) continually (habitually) let, etc. (to other than the speaker).

āg-ăhhɛrɛ́- (-ăhhárɛ́-, etc., s.v. ăhhɛrɛ́; §3838) v.i. (a) be (in process of) becoming late, etc. (s.v. ăhhɛrɛ́); (b) continually (habitually) become late, etc.

āg-ăhhɛrɛ́gɪr- (-ăhhár- etc.; §3838) v.t. caus. (a) be engaged in causing or allowing to become late, etc.; (b) continually (habitually) cause or allow to become late, etc.

āg-āmɪnɛ́- (§3838) v.t. (a) be trusting, etc. (s.v. ámɪnɛ́); (b) habitually trust, etc.

āg-amíntɪ- (§3838) v.t. (a) be engaged in showing; (b) continually (habitually) show.

āg-áñgɪr- (§3838) v.t. (a) be engaged in animating, etc. (s.v. áñg-ɪr); (b) continually (habitually) animate, etc.

tɛr‿ígk‿āgáñgɪrɪn⌒ (s)he is (keeps on) stirring the fire.

āg-áŋgɪs- v.t.=āg-ágɪs-.

āg-áŋɪs- v.t.=āg-ágɪs-.

ágar n. place, etc. s.v. āg.

āg-ár- (§3838) v.t. (a) be engaged in seizing, etc. (sv. ár); (b) continually (habitually) seize, etc.

āg-ár-an- (-áróan-, -áróan-; §3839) v.i. (a) be in process of becoming white; (b) continually become white.

ín‿āgaranɪn⌒ this is turning (always turns) white.

āg-árbɪr- (§3838) v.t. (a) be engaged in folding; (b) continually (habitually) fold.

āg-aríkkɪ- (§§3831ff.) v.t. (a) be engaged in throwing, etc. (s.v. aríkk(ɪ)); (b) continually (habitually) throw, etc.

āg-árkɪ- v.t.=āgaríkkɪ-.

āg-árkɪ- (§§3831ff.) v.i. (a) be in process of burning (flagrans); (b) continually burn.

āg-árk-ɪr- (§3838) v.t. (a) be engaged in kindling; (b) continually (habitually) kindle.

āg-ás- (§§3831ff.) v.t. (a) be engaged in measuring; (b) continually (habitually) measure.

āg-as|kkɪ- (§3838) v.t. (a) be engaged in borrowing; (b) continually (habitually) borrow.

āg-asíkkɪdɛn- (§3839) v.t. (a) be engaged in lending (to the speaker, s.v. asíkkɪ-dɛn); (b) continually (habitually) lend (to the speaker).

āg-asíkkɪtɪr- (§3839) v.t. (a) be engaged in lending (not to the speaker, s.v. asíkkɪ- tɪr); (b) continually (habitually) lend (not to the speaker).

āg-ásɪl- (§§3831ff.) v.t. (a) be engaged in frying; (b) continually (habitually) fry.

āg-átɪñ- (§§3831ff.) v.i. (a) be engaged in sneezing; (b) continually (habitually) sneeze.

āg-átɪš- v.i.=āgáttɪñ-.

āg-atšɛ́- (§3838) v.i. (a) be thirsting, be (in process of) becoming thirsty; (b) continually (habitually) be or become thirsty.

āg-atšɛ́gɪr- (§3838) v.t. caus. (a) be engaged in (in process of) causing or allowing to thirst, etc. (s.v. atšɛ́g-ɪr); (b) continually (habitually) cause or allow to thirst, etc.

āg-áttɪ- (§§3831ff.) v.t. (a) be engaged in beating up (liquid dough) with the hand (s.v. áttɪ); (b) continually (habitually) beat up, etc.

ɛŋ‿kaníssɛg‿āgáttɪn⌒ the woman is beating up (habitually beats up) the (liquid) dough with her hand.

āg-attɪlɛ́- (§3838) v.t. (a) be engaged in hindering, etc. (s.v. attɪlɛ́); (b) continually (habitually) hinder, etc.

agáu v.t. form (rope) by twisting, twist [< agáu make while squatting §2861].

ind. pres. āi‿agáurɪ, ɛr‿agáuɪn⌒ (-áuî⌒, -áuî⌒); perf. āi‿agáukori⌒.

imperat. sg. ágáu!

tɛr‿alásk‿agáuɪn⌒ he twists rope.

agáuar (-áudr‿; §§2200ff.) and **agaūíd-** (§§2256ff.) n. twisting.

agáu-an (§3890) v.t. tell to twist, let twist.

agáu-bŭ- (§3931β) v.i. stat. be in a twisted state or condition.

agáu-kattɪ- (§4093) v.p. be twisted.

āg-áu- (§§3831ff.) v.t. (a) be engaged in doing, etc. (s.v. áu); (b) continually (habitually) do, etc.

ɛŋ-kúsug‿āgáwɪn⌒ (a) the woman is cooking the meat; (b) the woman habitually cooks the meat.

āg-awíddɪ- (§3838) v.t. (a) be engaged in spreading, etc. (s.v. awíddɪ-); (b) continually (habitually) spread, etc.

āg-áwɪǧ- (§3838) v.t. (a) be engaged in plaiting, etc. (s.v. áwɪǧ); (b) continually (habitually) plait, etc.

tínnɛssɪn‿díltɪg‿āgáwɪǧɪn⌒ (a) she is plaiting her sister's hair; (b) she habitually plaits her sister's hair.

ɛ́n‿nɪbítk‿āgáwɪǧɪn⌒ (a) the woman is making the (a) mat; (b §4647) women make (the) mats.

āg-awwɪrɛ́- (-áuwɪ-, -wᵘrɛ́-; §3838) v.t. (a) be engaged in wounding, etc. (s.v. awwɪrɛ́); (b) continually wound, etc.

āg-awwugɛ́- (-áuwu-; §3838) v.t.=āgaw- wɪrɛ́-.

āgb- s.v. ābb- (§519).

āg-báǧ- be engaged in writing, etc. s.v. āb- báǧ-.

āgd- s.v. ādd- (§534).

āg-dáb- be disappearing, etc. s.v. ād-dáb-.

āg-ɛ́bɪr- (§§3831ff.) v.t. (a) be engaged in stopping, etc. (s.v. ɛ́bɪr); (b) continually (habitually) stop, etc.

āg-ɛ́d- (§§3831ff.) v.t. (a) be engaged in marrying (s.v. ɛ́d); (b) habitually marry.

āi‿ɛskɪtámunun, āi‿āgɛ́drɪ⌒ I can't come, I'm getting married.

āg-ɛgɛ́čč-ɛ- (§3838) v.i. (a) be lying supine; (b) continually (habitually) lie supine.

āg-ɛgɛ́čč-ɛ- (§3838) v.i. (a) be engaged in ascending; (b) continually (habitually) ascend.

āg-ɛ́gɪr- (§3838) v.t. (a) be engaged in riding (on, s.v. ɛ́gɪr); (b) continually (habitually) ride (on).

āg-ɛǧ-ǧŭ́- (§3839) v.t. (a) be engaged in proceeding after taking, etc. (s.v. ɛǧ-ǧŭ́, s.v. ɛ́d); (b) continually (habitually) proceed after taking, etc.

āg-ɛ́kkɪ- (§§3831ff.) v.i. and t. (a) be engaged in evacuating the bladder, etc. (s.v. ɛ́kk(ɪ)); (b) continually (habitually) evacuate the bladder, etc.

āg-ɛ́l- (§§3831ff.) v.t. (a) be engaged in finding, etc. (s.v. ɛ́l); (b) continually find, etc.

āg-ɛ́lɛw- (§§3831ff.) v.t. (a) be engaged in rinsing, etc. (s.v. ɛ́lɛw); (b) continually (habitually) rinse, etc.

āg-ɛ́r- (§§3831ff.) v.t. (a) be engaged in plundering, etc. (s.v. ɛ́r); (b) continually (habitually) plunder, etc.

āg-ɛ́r- (§§3831ff.) v.t. (a) be engaged in impregnating, fertilizing (palms); (b) continually (habitually) impregnate, etc.

āg-ɛrǧɛ́- (-ɛrɛǧɛ́-, etc.; §3838) v.i. and t. (a) be engaged in waiting (for), etc. (s.v. ɛrǧɛ́); (b) continually (habitually) wait (for), etc.

āg-ɛ́sɛ- (§§3831ff.) v.i. (a) be engaged in belching; (b) continually (habitually) belch.

āg-ɛttá- and **āg-ɛ́ttă-** (§3839) v.t. (a) be engaged in bringing, etc. (s.v. ɛt-tá, s.v. ɛ́d); (b) continually (habitually) bring, etc.

ɛskɛ́tk‿āgɛ́ttăran⌒ they are bringing (habitually bring) soil.

āg-ɛ́u- (§§3831ff.) v.t. (a) be engaged in washing; (b) continually (habitually) wash.

āg-ɛ́u- (§§3831ff.) v.t. (a) be engaged in sending; (b) continually (habitually) send.

āg-ɛ́wɪr- (§3838) v.t. (a) be engaged in exchanging, etc. (s.v. ɛ́wɪr); (b) continually (habitually) exchange, etc.

ind. pres. āi‿āgɛwírrɪ⌒.

āg-ɛ́wɪr- (§3838) v.t. (a) be engaged in cultivating, etc. (s.v. ɛ́wɪr); (b) continually (habitually) cultivate, etc.

āg-ɛwírkıddı- — āg-íu-

X. sálum‿míng‿agáwın? *what is Sálim doing?*
Y. kólɛg‿agéwırın⌒ *he is cultivating an estate (an irrigated area).*
ɛr‿míng‿agéwırın? *and* ɛr‿ámmıŋgéwırın? (§§601, 5601) *what are you growing?*
âı‿íllɛg‿agɛwírrı⌒ (a) *I am growing wheat;* (b) *I habitually grow wheat.*
kól‿agéurın⌒ *the water-wheel is working.*

āg-ɛwírkıddı- (§3838) v.t. caus. (a) *be engaged in causing or allowing to cultivate, etc.* (s.v. ɛwírk-ıdd(ı)); (b) *continually (habitually) cause or allow to cultivate, etc.*
tórbarıg‿agɛwırkıddıríddı⌒ (a) *I am making (letting) the peasants work at cultivation;* (b) *I always make (let) the peasants work at cultivation.*

āgf- s.v. āff- (§541).

āg-fírrı- *be engaged in flying, etc.,* s.v. āf-fírrı-.

āg-gābılɛ́- (§3838) v.t. (a) *be engaged in meeting, etc.* (s.v. gābılɛ́); (b) *continually (habitually) meet, etc.*

āg-gág- (§§3831 ff.) v.t. and i. (a) *be engaged in (in process of) splitting, etc.* (s.v. gág); (b) *continually (habitually) split, etc.*

āg-gajırɛ́- (§3838) v.t. (a) *be engaged in changing, etc.* (s.v. gajırɛ́); (b) *continually (habitually) change, etc.*

āg-galabɛ́- (§3838) v.t. (a) *be engaged in tiring, etc.* (s.v. galabɛ́); (b) *continually (habitually) tire, etc.*

āg-gālıtɛ́- (§3838) v.t. and i. (a) *be engaged in disputing with, etc.* (s.v. gālıtɛ́); (b) *continually (habitually) dispute with, etc.*

āg-gǎn- (§§3831 ff.) v.t. (a) *be engaged in licking;* (b) *continually (habitually) lick.*

āg-gāngiddı- (§3838) v.i. (a) *be engaged in yawning, in gaping;* (b) *continually (habitually) yawn, gape.*

āg-gáññı- (§§3831 ff.) v.t. and i. (a) *be engaged in shaving, etc.* (s.v. gáññ(ı)); (b) *continually (habitually) shave, etc.*

āg-gǎr- (§§3831 ff.) v.t. (a) *be engaged in crushing* (grain); (b) *continually (habitually) crush.*

āg-gárɛ- (§3838) v.t. (a) *be engaged in embracing, etc.* (s.v. gárɛ); (b) *continually (habitually) embrace, etc.*

āg-gásıǧ- (§3838) v.t. (a) *be engaged in splitting up, etc.* (s.v. gásıǧ); (b) *continually (habitually) split up, etc.*

āg-gǎš- (§§3831 ff.) v.i. (a) *be engaged in coquetting, etc.* (s.v. gǎš); (b) *continually (habitually) coquet, etc.*
ém-bur‿aggášın⌒ *your daughter is (always) flirting.*

āg-gáškır- (§3838) v.t. (a) *be engaged in coaxing, etc.* (s.v. gáškır); (b) *continually (habitually) coax, etc.*
tınɛ́n‿tém‿bıtǎng‿aggáškırın⌒ *the mother is (keeps on) petting her child.*

āg-gašɛ́- (§3838) v.t. (a) *be engaged in passing, etc.* (s.v. gašɛ́); (b) *continually (habitually) pass, etc.*

āg-gašɛ́gır- (§3838) v.t. caus. (a) *be engaged in causing or allowing to pass, etc.;* (b) *continually (habitually) cause or allow to pass, etc.*

bōlís‿aıg‿aggašɛ́gırmunun⌒ *the policeman won't let (never lets) me pass.*

āg-gāwılɛ́- (§3838) v.i. (a) *be engaged in contracting, etc.* (s.v. gāwılɛ́); (b) *continually (habitually) contract, etc.*

āg-gáwwı- (-gáuwı-; §§3831 ff.) v.t. (a) *be engaged in hulling, etc.* (s.v. gáww(ı)); (b) *continually (habitually) hull, etc.*

ággɛ! (⸌⸍) < ágwɛ! imperat. pl. of āg *squat, etc.*

āg-gɛddımɛ́- (-dumɛ́-; §3838) v.t. and i. (a) *be engaged in advancing, etc.* (s.v. gɛddımɛ́); (b) *continually (habitually) advance, etc.*

āg-gɛddımɛ́-tá (-dum-; §3839) v.i. (a) *be engaged in coming ahead, etc.* (s.v. gɛddımɛ́-tá); (b) *continually (habitually) come ahead, etc.*
bābŭr‿ín‿nɛhárıg‿aggɛddumɛ́tān⌒ *the steamer (train) these days keeps coming early (before its appointed time);* the stressing emphasizes -gɛddumɛ́- (§1419).

āg-géddımkattı- (-dum-; §3839) v.i. = āggɛddımɛ́- i.

āg-gégɛr- (§§3831 ff.) v.t. (a) *be engaged in rolling into a ball, etc.* (s.v. gégɛr); (b) *continually (habitually) roll into a ball, etc.*
bıtánı‿síbɛg‿aggɛgérran⌒ *the children are (keep on) rolling the mud into balls.*

āg-gɛlan- (§3839) v.i. (a) *be in process of turning red, etc.* (s.v. gɛ́l-an-); (b) *continually turn red, etc.*

āg-gɛ́lɛgır- (N. -ɛkır-, -ɛhır-; §3838) v.t. (a) *be engaged in reddening, etc.* (s.v. gɛ́lɛg-ır); (b) *continually (habitually) redden, etc.*

āg-géndıgır- (N. -ıkır-, -ıhır-; §3838) v.t. (a) *be engaged in rendering good, etc.* (s.v. géndıg-ır s.v. gén‿); (b) *continually (habitually) render good, etc.*

āg-gɛndıgırbíttı- (§3839) v.t. (a) *be engaged in picking up properly, etc.* (s.v. gɛndıgırbítt(ı)); (b) *continually (habitually) pick up properly.*

āg-gɛndıgırkób- (§3839) v.t. (a) *be engaged in shutting properly, etc.* (s.v. gɛndıgırkób); (b) *continually (habitually) shut properly, etc.*

āg-gɛndıgırkús- (§3839) v.t. (a) *be engaged in opening properly, etc.* (s.v. gɛndıgırkús); (b) *continually (habitually) open properly, etc.*

āg-gɛrjɛ́- (-gɛrɛ́-; §3832) v.t. (a) *be engaged in reading, etc.* (s.v. gɛrjɛ́); (b) *continually (habitually) read, etc.*

āg-gíd- (§§3831 ff.) v.t. (a) *be engaged in choking, etc.* (s.v. gíd); (b) *continually (habitually) choke, etc.*
íŋ‿kál‿aıg‿aggídın⌒ *this food is choking me.*

āg-gıdbɛ́- (§3839) v.t. (a) *be engaged in strangling;* (b) *continually strangle.*

āg-gíǧır- (§3831 ff.) v.t. (a) *be engaged in perceiving, etc.* (s.v. gíǧır); (b) *continually (habitually) perceive, etc.*
tɛr‿óddıbūng‿aggíǧırná? *are you hearing (do you from time to time hear) that (s)he is ill?*
âı‿habašíncım‿báññın‿gɛrk‿aggıgırkómunun⌒ (-m‿b-<-n‿b- §592, -ŋ‿g-<-dn‿g- §644) *I never used to hear anything but the language of the Abyssinians.*

āg-gırídɛ- (§3838) v.i. (a) *be engaged in revolving, etc.* (s.v. gırídɛ); (b) *continually (habitually) revolve, etc.*

āg-góbır- (§§3831 ff.) v.t. (a) *be engaged in (in process of) surrounding;* (b) *continually surround.*

āg-góǧ- (§§3831 ff.) v.t. (a) *be engaged in slaughtering;* (b) *continually (habitually) slaughter.*

āg-góllı- (§§3831 ff.) v.t. (a) *be engaged in swallowing;* (b) *continually (habitually) swallow.*

āg-góñ- (§§3831 ff.) v.t. (a) *be engaged in building or weaving* (s.v. góñ); (b) *continually (habitually) build or weave.*
kádɛg‿aggóñın⌒ (a) *he is weaving cloth;* (b) *he (habitually) weaves cloth.*
ógıǧ‿duhángɛg‿góññag‿aggóñın⌒ (-g‿g- <-d‿g- §545) *the man is weaving (habitually weaves) cloth on the loom.*

āg-gŏr- (§§3831 ff.) v.t. (a) *be engaged in gnawing;* (b) *continually (habitually) gnaw.*

āg-goššɛ́- (§3838) v.t. (a) *be engaged in deceiving, etc.* (s.v. goššɛ́); (b) *continually (habitually) deceive, etc.*
âıg‿aggoššɛ́goran⌒ *they were (have been) deceiving me.*
árg‿aggoššɛ́ríkkoran⌒ *they were (have been) deceiving us.*

āg-gúllı- (§§3831 ff.) v.t. (a) *be engaged in scattering, etc.* (s.v. gúll(ı)); (b) *continually (habitually) scatter, etc.*

āg-gŭñčı- (§3838) v.i. and t. (a) *be engaged in looking (at), etc.* (s.v. gŭñč(ı)); (b) *continually (habitually) look (at), etc.*

āg-gūñčıkób- (§3839) v.t. (a) *be engaged in looking at (etc.) and shutting, etc.* (s.v. gūñčı-kób); (b) *continually (habitually) look at (etc.) and shut, etc.*
âı‿kobídk‿aggūñčıkóbrı⌒ (a) *I am shutting the door carefully;* (b) *I habitually shut the door carefully.*
âı‿kobídk‿aggūñčıkópkorı⌒ *I was (have been) shutting (used to shut) the door carefully.*

āg-gúššı- (§§3831 ff.) v.t. and i. (a) *be engaged in (in process of) breaking, etc.* (s.v. gúšš(ı)); (b) *continually (habitually) break, etc.*

āgǧ- s.v. āǧǧ- (§551).

āg-ǧǎl- *be engaged in shouting, etc.,* s.v. āǧ-ǧǎl-.

ággɛ‿ n. *Akja* (on map), a village on the left bank of the Nile just north of Úrdi. obj. ággɛg‿, ággɛ́g‿ (§1532).

ágh- s.v. āhh- (§559).

āg-híkkı- *be engaged in kneeling, etc.* s.v. āhhíkkı-.

āg-íg- (§3838) v.t. (a) *be engaged in telling, etc.* (s.v. íg); (b) *continually (habitually) tell, etc.*

āg-ír- (§3838) v.t. (a) *be engaged in counting, etc.* (s.v. ír); (b) *continually (habitually) count, etc.*

āg-íu- (-íᵘ-, -íw-; §§3831 ff.) v.t. (a) *be engaged in tending at pasture, etc.* (s.v. íu); (b) *continually (habitually) tend at pasture, etc.*

āg-íu- (-íᵘ-, -íw-; §§3831 ff.) v.t. (a) *be forgetting;* (b) *continually (habitually) forget.*

āg-ıbırtıgúndur- (§3839) v.t. (*a*) *be engaged in twisting* (s.v. ıbírt(ı)); (*b*) *continually (habitually) twist.*

agídd(ı) *cause to squat, etc.* s.v. ăg.

āg-íddı- (§§3831ff.) v.t. (*a*) *be engaged in asking, etc.* (s.v. ídd(ı)); (*b*) *continually (habitually) ask, etc.*

āg-ıgíddı- (§3838) v.t. (*a*) *be engaged in watering, etc.* (s.v. ıgídd(ı)); (*b*) *continually (habitually) water, etc.*

ágıl⌣ n. (*a*) *mouth*; (*b*) *aperture*; (*c*, *of knife, etc.*) *blade* [cp. M. ág⌣ *id.*, ON. ᚨᚢᛚ *the* (ZNG, §76) *mouth* (§2277); cogn. áčč(ı) *bite* (§4492); RSN, §§129, 200; TOB, §143, 187].
obj. agílg(ı)⌣, -gi⌢.
pl. áglı⌣.
kån⌣ágıl⌣ *doorway of house.*
zérben⌣ágıl⌣ *opening (gate) of fence.*
kándın⌣ágıl⌣ *blade of knife.*
sıwídn⌣ágıl⌣ *blade of sword.*
énn⌣agílgı⌣kóp! *close your mouth (shut up)!*
ínn⌣áglık⌣kóbwé! (-k⌣k- < -g⌣k- §569) *close (pl.) your mouths (shut up)!*
tér⌣āig⌣agílgeğ⌣gómın⌢ (-ğ⌣ğ- < -d⌣ğ- §550) *(s)he shouts me down, lit. (s)he hits me with his (her) mouth.*

ágıl⌣ adj. *intelligent, wise* [< عاقل *id.*].
obj. āgílg(ı)⌣, -gi⌢.
pl. åg(ı)lı⌣.

ágıldā- (-ıllā-) *be present squatting, etc.* s.v. ăg.

āg-ımbél- (āgímbɛl- §1880; §3838) v.i. (*a*) *be engaged in rising, etc.* (s.v. ım-bél); (*b*) *continually (habitually) rise, etc.*

āg-índı- (§3838) v.t. (*a*) *be engaged in lifting, etc.* (s.v. ınd(ı)); (*b*) *continually (habitually) lift, etc.*

āg-ındɛğğŭ- (§§3839, 5722) v.t. (*a*) *be engaged in proceeding (conveying) after lifting* (*etc.* s.v. ınd-ɛğ-ğŭ); (*b*) *continually (habitually) proceed (convey) after lifting, etc.*

āg-ınd-ɛttā- (-ɛttă-; §3839) v.t. (*a*) *be engaged in bringing after lifting, etc.* (s.v. ınd-ɛt-tå); (*b*) *continually (habitually) bring after lifting, etc.*

āg-iñır- (-iñír-; §§3831ff.) v.i. and t. (*a*) *be engaged in waiting (for), etc.* (s.v. íñır); (*b*) *continually (habitually) wait (for), etc.*

āg-ıriñ- v.i. and t. = āgíñır-.

āg-írrı- (§§3831ff.) v.i. (*a*) *be engaged in roaring*; (*b*) *continually (habitually) roar.*

ágıs v.t. (*a*) *rouse, wake*; (*b*) *sharpen, whet* [< åg⌣ *heart* (obj.) + -ıs caus. (§2894), quasi *hearten*] = ángıs, áñıs.
ind. pres. aĭ⌣ágısrı⌢ (⌐⌐ §1760), ɛr⌣ágısın⌢ (-sí⌢, -sí⌢); fut. aĭ⌣bágısrı⌢; perf. aĭ⌣ágıskori⌢ (⌐⌐).
kándıg⌣ágıskori⌢ *I (have) sharpened the knife.*

āgısar⌣ (-sår⌣; §§2200ff.) and
agısíd⌣ (§§2256ff.) n. *rousing, etc.*

ágıs-an (§3890) v.t. *tell to rouse, etc., let rouse, etc.*

ágıs-kattı- (§4093) v.p. *be roused, etc.*

āg-ıstɛlɛmɛ́- (§3838) v.t. (*a*) *be engaged in taking over, etc.* (s.v. ıstɛlɛmɛ́); (*b*) *continually (habitually) take over, etc.*

āg-ıšın- (-ıšín-; §§3831ff.) v.t. (*a*) *be engaged in sending*; (*b*) *continually (habitually) send.*

āg-íwıs- (āg-íwıs-; §§3831ff.) v.t. (*a*) *be engaged in twisting, etc.* (s.v. íwıs); (*b*) *continually (habitually) twist, etc.*

āgk- s.v. ākk- (§569).

āg-káčči- *be engaged in playing, etc.* s.v. ăkkáčči-.

áglo⌣ n. *wooden rung* between the two cables (álası⌣) that pass over the wheel over the water (áttı⌣) in the water-wheel (kólɛ⌣, q.v.); a belt resembling an endless rope-ladder is formed by the cables and these rungs, to pairs of which, at intervals, are lashed the jars (bɛ́šɛnčı⌣) in their cradles (kórısı⌣) [< عَقْلَة *shackle* §§1271, 1345; the rungs keep the cables in position.]

— with coll. sg. (§4696d):
obj. áglog⌣ [> Sudan Ar. لَغْلُوق laglúg *id.* (AESA, p. 426), of which l- arises from the Ar. article].
pl. áglonč(ı)⌣.

āgm- s.v. āmm- (§601).

āg-mɛr- v.t. *be engaged in cutting, etc.* s.v. ām-mɛr-.

āgn- s.v. ānn- (§625).

āg-ní- v.t. *be engaged in drinking, etc.* s.v. ān-ní-.

āgñ- s.v. āññ- (§638).

āg-ñúrrı- *be engaged in growling, etc.* s.v. āñ-ñúrrı-.

āg-ó- (§§3831ff.) v.t. (*a*) *be engaged in singing*; (*b*) *continually (habitually) sing.*

āg-ób- (§§3831ff.) v.i. (*a*) *be in process of becoming inverted, etc.* (s.v. ób); (*b*) *continually become inverted, etc.*

āg-óbır- (§3838) v.t. (*a*) *be engaged in inverting, etc.* (s.v. ób-ır); (*b*) *continually (habitually) invert, etc.*

āg-óčči- (§§3831ff.) v.t. (*a*) *be engaged in dragging, etc.* (s.v. óčč(ı)); (*b*) *continually (habitually) drag, etc.*

āg-ógolan- (§3839) v.i. (*a*) *be engaged in going ahead, etc.* (s.v. ógol-an-); (*b*) *continually (habitually) go ahead, etc.*

āg-óğı- (§3838) v.t. (*a*) *be engaged in conveying, etc.* (s.v. óğı); (*b*) *continually (habitually) convey, etc.*

āg-óñ- (§3838) v.i. and t. (*a*) *be engaged in (be)wailing, etc.* (s.v. óñ); (*b*) *continually (habitually) (be)wail, etc.*

āg-órığ- (§3838) v.t. and i. (*a*) *be engaged in (in process of) tearing up, etc.* (s.v. órığ); (*b*) *continually (habitually) tear up, etc.*

āg-orófɛgır- (N. -ɛkır-, -ɛhır-; §3838) v.t. (*a*) *be engaged in cooling, etc.* (s.v. orófɛg-ır); (*b*) *continually (habitually) cool, etc.*

āg-orófɛlan- (§3839) v.i. (*a*) *be in process of cooling, etc.* (s.v. orófɛl-an-); (*b*) *continually (habitually) cool, etc.*

āg-órrı- (§§3831ff.) v.t. and i. (*a*) *be engaged in tearing, etc.* (s.v. órr(ı)); (*b*) *continually (habitually) tear, etc.*
kádɛg⌣ágórrın⌢ *(s)he (it) is (keeps on) tearing the cloth.*
kád⌣ágórrın⌢ *the cloth is (keeps on) tearing.*

āg-ós- (§§3831ff.) v.t. *be engaged in causing to issue, etc.* (s.v. ós); (*b*) *continually (habitually) cause to issue, etc.*

āg-óšog- (-ošóg-; §3838) v.t. (*a*) *be engaged in shaking, etc.* (s.v. óšog); (*b*) *continually (habitually) shake, etc.*

āg-óšoŋ- (-ošóŋ-; §3838) v.t. = āg-óšog-.

āg-ošóškı- (§3838) v.t. (*a*) *be engaged in dragging, etc.* (s.v. ošóšk(ı)); (*b*) *continually (habitually) drag, etc.*

āgs- s.v. āss- (§679).

āg-sándı- *be afraid, etc.* s.v. ās-sándı-.

āgš- s.v. ăšš- (§697).

āg-šɛ́g- *be engaged in planting, etc.* s.v. āš-šɛ́g-.

āgt- s.v. ātt- (§708).

āg-tå- *be engaged in coming, etc.* s.v. āt-tå-.

āg-úbbı- (§§3831ff.) v.i. (*a*) *be in process of getting a hole, etc.* (s.v. úbb(ı)); (*b*) *continually (habitually) get holes, etc.*

āg-úbbuğ- (§3838) v.t. (*a*) *be engaged in perforating, etc.* (s.v. úbbuğ); (*b*) *continually (habitually) perforate, etc.*

āg-úbbur- (§3838) v.t. (*a*) *be engaged in tearing a hole in, etc.* (s.v. úbbur); (*b*) *continually (habitually) tear a hole in, etc.*

āg-úffɛ- (§3838) v.i. and t. (*a*) *be in process of (engaged in) blowing, etc.* (s.v. úffɛ); (*b*) *continually (habitually) blow, etc.*
ınnówwıg⌣ɛ́skɛd⌣āgúffɛn⌢ *today the dust is (keeps on) blowing about.*

āg-ŭkkı- (§§3831ff.) v.i. (*a*) *be engaged in barking, etc.* (s.v. ŭkk(ı)); (*b*) *continually (habitually) bark, etc.*

āg-úllı- (§§3831ff.) v.t. (*a*) *be engaged in kindling, etc.* (s.v. úll(ı)); (*b*) *continually (habitually) kindle, etc.*

āg-úndur- (§3838) v.t. (*a*) *be engaged in putting in, etc.* (s.v. úndur); (*b*) *continually (habitually) put in, etc.*

āg-úrrı- (§§3831ff.) v.t. (*a*) *be engaged in pressing, etc.* (s.v. úrr(ı)); (*b*) *continually (habitually) press, etc.*

āg-úskı- (§3838) v.t. (*a*) *be engaged in giving birth to, etc.* (s.v. úsk(ı)); (*b*) *continually (habitually) give birth to, etc.*

āg-úskur- (§3838) v.t. (*a*) *be engaged in setting, etc.* (s.v. úskur); (*b*) *continually (habitually) set, etc.*
šahárro⌣kån⌣úğrɛr⌣rijål⌣díčč⌣āguskúddi⌢ (-r⌣r- < -g⌣r- §669) *I am paying five dollars a month house-rent.*

āg-ússı- (§§3831ff.) v.i. and t. (*a*) *be engaged in defecating, etc.* (s.v. úss(ı)); (*b*) *continually (habitually) defecate, etc.*

āg-úsu (§§3831ff.) v.i. (*a*) *be engaged in laughing*; (*b*) *continually (habitually) laugh.*
aĭ⌣tén⌣kóččır⌣āgúsurı⌢ *I am laughing (always laugh) at him (her, it).*

āg-ŭwɛ- (§3838) v.t. (*a*) *be engaged in calling, etc.* (s.v. ŭwɛ); (*b*) *continually (habitually) call, etc.*

āgw- s.v. āww- (§719).

āg-wákkı- *be engaged in omitting, etc.* s.v. āw-wákkı-.

ağabɛ́ (*a*) v.i. *wonder, marvel, be astonished*; (*b*) v.t. *wonder (etc.) at* [< عجب *astonishment* + -ɛ §3622].
ind. pres. aĭ⌣ağabɛ́rı⌢; perf. aĭ⌣ağabɛ́gori⌢ (N. -ɛ́ko-, -ɛ́ho-).
imperat. ağabɛ́!
aĭ⌣tékk⌣ağabɛ́rı⌢ *I am astonished at him (her, it).*

ağabɛ́rar⌣ (-rár⌣; §§2200ff.) and
ağabɛ́ríd⌣ (§§2256ff.) n. *wondering, etc., astonishment.*

ağabég-ır (N. -ɛ́kır, -ɛ́hır; §3681) (a) v.t. caus. *cause or allow to wonder, etc.*; (b) v.t. *astonish, surprise.*
tɛr‿áıg‿ağabɛ́gırın⌒ *(s)he (it) astonishes me.*

ağabɛ́-kattı- (§4093) v.p. *be wondered at, etc.*

āğ-ğábɛ- (āg-ğá- §551; §3838) v.t. (a) *be engaged in touching, etc.* (s.v. ğábɛ); (b) *continually (habitually) touch, etc.*

āğ-ğág- (āg-ğáğ- §551; §§3831 ff.) v.t. (a) *be engaged in kneading, etc.* (s.v. ğág); (b) *continually (habitually) knead, etc.*

āğ-ğákkı- (āg-ğák- §551; §3838) v.t. (a) *be engaged in pressing, etc.* (s.v. ğákk(ı)); (b) *continually (habitually) press, etc.*

āğ-ğál- (āg-ğál- §551; §§3831 ff.) v.i. (a) *be engaged in shouting, etc.* (s.v. ğál); (b) *continually (habitually) shout, etc.*
ind. pres. áı‿āğğálli⌒, ɛr‿āğğálın⌒ (-lí⌒, -lí⌒).

āğ-ğámmɛ- (āg-ğám- §551; §3838) v.i. (a) *be engaged in (in process of) coming together, etc.* (s.v. ğámmɛ); (b) *continually (habitually) come together, etc.*
ıŋglíz‿āğğámmɛran⌒ (-z‿ā- < -zı‿ā- §1122) *the English (a) are congregating;* (b) *habitually congregate.*

āğ-ğán- (āg-ğán- §551; §§3831 ff.) v.t. (a) *be engaged in trading in, etc.* (s.v. ğán); (b) *continually (habitually) trade in, etc.*
ind. pres. áı‿āğğándi⌒, ɛr‿āğğánın⌒ (-ní⌒, -ní⌒).

āğ-ğáŋgı- (āg-ğáŋ- §551; §§3831 ff.) v.t. (a) *be engaged in filling, etc.* (s.v. ğáŋg(ı)); (b) *continually (habitually) fill, etc.*

āğ-ğáwwı- (āg-ğáw- §551; -ğáuwı-, -wᵘ- §1202; §§3831 ff.) v.i. (a) *be engaged in brawling, etc.* (s.v. ğáww(ı)); (b) *continually (habitually) brawl, etc.*
ind. pres. áı‿āğğáwwırı⌒.

āğ-ğāzɛ́- (āg-ğā- §551; §3838) v.t. (a) *be engaged in requiting, etc.* (s.v. ğāzɛ́); (b) *continually (habitually) requite, etc.*

āğ-ğɛ́d- (āg-ğɛ́d- §551; §§3831 ff.) v.i. and t. (a) *be engaged in swearing, etc.* (s.v. ğɛ́d); (b) *continually (habitually) swear, etc.*

āğ-ğɛ́llıg-áu- (āg-ğɛ́l- §551; §§1879, 3839, 5632) v.i. (a) *be engaged in working, etc.* (s.v. ğɛ́llıg-áu); (b) *continually (habitually) work, etc.*
tɛr‿āğğɛ́llıgāwın⌒ (a) *(s)he is at work;* (b) *(s)he habitually works.*

āğ-ğɛrrıbɛ́- (āg-ğɛr- §551; -rubɛ́-; §3838) v.t. (a) *be engaged in trying, etc.* (s.v. ğɛrrıbɛ́); (b) *continually (habitually) try, etc.*

āğ-ğígıd- (āg-ğí- §551; §§3831 ff.) v.t. (a) *be engaged in rubbing, etc.* (s.v. ğígıd); (b) *continually (habitually) rub, etc.*

āğ-ğíllɛ- (āg-ğíl- §551; §3838) v.t. (a) *be engaged in thinking, etc.* (s.v. ğíllɛ); (b) *continually (habitually) think, etc.*

āğ-ğíllɛgır- (āg-ğíl- §551; §3838) v.t. caus. (a) *be engaged in causing to think, in reminding* (s.v. ğíllɛg-ır); (b) *continually (habitually) cause to think, etc.*

ağğırɛ́ v.t. *hire, procure on hire* [< imperat. or imperf. stem of Sudan Ar. أَجِر *let on hire* §6269 + -ɛ́ §3637].
ind. pres. áı‿ağğırɛ́rı⌒; fut. áı‿bağğırɛ́rı⌒; perf. áı‿ağğırɛ́gorı⌒ (N. -ɛ́ko-, -ɛ́ho-).
imperat. ağğırɛ́!
bélɛnn‿tūr‿kā-wēg‿ağğırɛ́goran⌒ (-nn‿t- < -dn‿t- §630; tūr‿ enclitic and atonic §1671) *they (have) hired a house in the town.*

ağğırɛ́rar‿ (-rár‿; §§2200 ff.) and **ağğırɛrɛ́d‿** (§§2256 ff.) n. *hiring.*

ağğırɛ́r-an (§§3890, 3899) v.t. *tell to hire, let hire.*

ağğırɛ́-dɛn (§§3996–7) v.t. *grant on hire, let (to the speaker).*

ağğırɛ́-tır (§§3998–9) v.t. *grant on hire, let (to other than the speaker).*
kăn‿tírt‿ağğırɛ́tırırın⌒ (§1964) *the owner of the house lets it (to more than one person).*

ağğırɛ́-kattı- (N. -ɛ́ha-; §4093) v.p. *be hired.*

āğ-ğóbbɛ- (āg-ğób- §551; §3838) v.i. (a) *be engaged in waiting, etc.* (s.v. ğóbbɛ); (b) *continually (habitually) wait, etc.*

āğ-ğóg- (āg-ğóg- §551; §§3831 ff.) v.t. (a) *be engaged in grinding, etc.* (s.v. ğóg); (b) *continually (habitually) grind, etc.*
nógo‿ğúğ‿ağğógın⌒ *the female slave (a) is grinding;* (b) *habitually grinds.*
nógo‿nórtıg‿ağğógın⌒ *the female slave (a) is grinding flour;* (b) *habitually grinds flour.*

āğ-ğógor- (āg-ğóg- §551; §3838) v.t. and i. (a) *be engaged in squeezing, etc., be in process of crumpling, etc.* (s.v. ğógor); (b) *continually (habitually) squeeze, etc., crumple, etc.*

āğ-ğókkı- (āg-ğók- §551; §3838) v.t. (a) *be engaged in chewing;* (b) *continually (habitually) chew.*

āğ-ğóm- (āg-ğóm- §551; §§3831 ff.) v.t. (a) *be engaged in striking, etc.* (s.v. ğóm); (b) *continually (habitually) strike, etc.*
ıŋ-gúr‿níššıgɛd‿ağğómın⌒ *this bull (habitually) butts.*
kōrábk‿ağğómran⌒ *they are raising (habitually raise) a great cry.*
tórbar‿ısísk‿ağğómın⌒ and tórbar‿usúsk‿ağğómın⌒ *the peasant is (keeps on) whistling.*

āğ-ğombɛ́- (āg-ğom- §551; §§3770, 3839) v.t. (a) *be engaged in beating to death (etc. s.v. ğom-bɛ́);* (b) *continually (habitually) strike dead (etc.).*

āğ-ğór- (āg-ğór- §551; §3831 ff.) v.t. (a) *be engaged in reaping, etc.* (s.v. ğór); (b) *habitually reap, etc.*
ind. pres. áı‿ağğórrı⌒.
bɛ́rk‿ağğórran⌒ *they are cutting (habitually cut) wood (fuel).*

āğ-ğúde- (āg-ğú- §551; §3838) v.t. and i. (a) *be engaged in (in process of) dissolving, etc.* (s.v. ğúdɛ); (b) *continually (habitually) dissolve, etc.*

āğ-ğúg- (āg-ğúg- §551; §§3831 ff.) v.i. (a) *catching fire, etc.* (s.v. ğúg); (b) *continually catch fire, etc.*
kă‿ağğúgın⌒ *the house is on fire.*
bɛ́r‿ağğúgın⌒ *the wood is (keeps on) catching fire.*

āğ-ğúgran- (āg-ğúg- §551; §3839) v.i. (a) *be in process of becoming hot, etc.* (s.v. ğúgr-an); (b) *continually become hot, etc.*

āğ-ğugrígır- āg-ğug- §551; N. -fkır, -íhır-; §3838) v.t. (a) *be engaged in heating;* (b) *continually (habitually) heat.*
ind. pres. áı‿ağğugrígıddı⌒, ɛr‿ağğugrígırın⌒ (-rí⌒, -rí⌒).

āğ-ğúgur- (āg-ğú- §551; §3838) v.t. (a) *be engaged in burning;* (b) *continually (habitually) burn.*
ind. pres. áı‿āğğugúrrı⌒.

āğ-ğúkkı- (āg-ğúk- §551; §3838) v.t. (a) *be engaged in sucking;* (b) *continually (habitually) suck.*

āğ-ğúrrı- (āg-ğúr- §551; §§3831 ff.) v.t. and i. (a) *be engaged in squeezing, etc.* (s.v. ğúrr(ı)); (b) *continually (habitually) squeeze, etc.*

āğ-ğúrum- (āg-ğú- §551; §§3831 ff.) v.t. (a) *be engaged in crumbling, etc.* (s.v. ğúrum); (b) *continually crumble, etc.*

ág̱ın‿ n. (a) *skin, hide;* (b) *prepared skin, leather* [RSN, §§129, 200].
obj. ağíŋg(ı)‿, -gi⌒.
pl. áğ(ı)nı‿.
áğın‿déss(ı)‿ *raw hide.*
áğıŋ‿kárğɛl‿ (‿káğğɛl‿) and áğıŋ‿kárğıbūl‿ (‿káğğı-) *tanned hide, leather.*
bɛ́rtın‿áğın‿ and búttuln‿áğın‿ *goatskin.*
míssın‿áğın‿ *eyelid(s §4696a).*
kúffın‿úrn‿áğın‿ *prepuce.*

áğız‿ adj. *weak, feeble, powerless, disabled* [< عاجز id. §1258].
obj. ağízk(ı)‿ (ağísk(ı)‿; áğı- §1522), -ki⌒.
pl. áğızı‿.
áğızun⌒ *(s)he is weak (etc.).*

āğızɛ́ v.i. *become weak, etc., weaken* [§3631].
ind. pres. áı‿āğızɛ́rı⌒; perf. áı‿āğızɛ́gorı⌒ (N. -ɛ́ko-, -ɛ́ho-).
def. perf. áı‿āğızɛróskorı⌒.

āğızɛ́rar‿ (-rár‿; §§2200 ff.) and **āğızɛrɛ́d‿** (§§2256 ff.) n. *weakening, feebleness, inability.*

āğızɛ́-bū- (§3935) v.i. stat. *be in a weak (etc.) state or condition.*
āğızɛ́būran‿āšál‿ğúgr‿ɛnn‿íllɛr⌒ *they are in a weak state because the weather is hot.*
— *takes an infinitive in the objective* (§3936):
ımbɛlláŋg‿āğızɛ́būran⌒ *they are too weak to get up.*

áğwa‿ n. *soft dates in mass* (= kúra‿) [< عجوة id. §1258].
obj. -wag‿.

āh-haddırɛ́- (āg-had- §559; §3838) v.t. (a) *be engaged in preparing;* (b) *continually (habitually) prepare.*

āh-haddırɛ́gır- (āg-had-) v.t. = āhhaddırɛ́-.

āh-hadmɛ́r- (āg-had- §559, āx-xad-, āk-xad-, ag-xad- §563; §3838) v.t. and t. (a) *be engaged in serving, etc.* (s.v. hadmɛ́); (b) *continually (habitually) serve, etc.*

āh-hağğırɛ́- (āg-hağ- §559; §3838) v.t. (a) *be engaged in forbidding, etc.* (s.v. hağğırɛ́); (b) *continually (habitually) forbid, etc.*

āh-halbıtɛ́- (āg-hal- §559, āx-xal-, āk-xal-, ag-xal- §563; §3838) v.t. (a) *be engaged in confusing, etc.* (s.v. halbıtɛ́); (b) *continually (habitually) confuse, etc.*

āh-halḗ- (āg-ha- §559; §3838) v.t. (a) *be engaged in scaring, etc.* (s.v. halḗ); (b) *continually (habitually) scare, etc.*

āh-hallısḗ- (āg-hal- §559; āx-xal-, āk-xal-, āg-xal- §563; §3838) v.t. (a) *be engaged in saving, etc.* (s.v. hallısḗ); (b) *continually save, etc.*

āh-hamdḗ- (āg-ham- §559; §3838) v.t. (a) *be engaged in praising*; (b) *continually (habitually) praise.*

āh-harbḗ- (āg-har- §559; āx-xar-, āk-xar-, āg-xar- §563; §3838) v.t. (a) *be engaged in ruining, etc.* (s.v. harbḗ); (b) *continually (habitually) ruin, etc.*

āh-hárrı- (āg-hár- §559; §§3831 ff.) v.i. (of dog) (a) *be engaged in growling*; (b) *continually (habitually) growl.*

āh-hāsıbḗ- (āg-hā- §559; §3838) v.t. (a) *be engaged in calculating, etc.* (s.v. hāsıbḗ); (b) *continually (habitually) calculate, etc.*

āh-has(ı)lḗ- (āg-has- §559; §3838) v.i. (a) *be (in process of) happening, etc.* (s.v. has(ı)lḗ); (b) *continually happen, etc.*

ăhherḗ (-hárḗ, -hırḗ; ăxxerḗ, -xárḗ, -xırḗ §1397) v.i. *get delayed, get late* [ăhhɛr- (etc.) < part of a stem of Sudan Ar. اتأخر = تأخر id. §3652; -ḗ §3603].

ind. pres. âi‿ăhherḗriᴖ; perf. âi‿ăhherḗgoriᴖ (N. -ḗko, -ḗho-).
gátır‿axxerḗgonᴖ *the train (has) got (is) late (delayed).*

ăhherḗrar‿ (-hár-, etc., -rár‿; §§2200ff.) and
ăhherḗríd‿ (-hár-, etc.; §§2256ff.) n. *getting delayed, etc.*

ăhherḗ-bŭ- (-hár-, etc.; §3931 α) v.i. stat. *be in a delayed state or condition.*
gátır‿axxárḗbūnᴖ *the train is late.*
tén‿sắ dagíga dımíŋɡ‿ăhhırḗbūnᴖ *his (her) watch (clock) is ten minutes slow;* ‿dagíga dımíŋɡ‿ a noun-complex (§4783) in the objective showing duration of time (§4666).

ăhherḗgır (-hár-, etc., N. -ḗkır, -ḗhır; §3681) (a) v.t. caus. *cause or allow to get delayed, etc.*; (b) v.t. *delay, retard.*

áhher-kattı- (-hár-, etc.; §4100) v.p. *be delayed.*
âi‿axxırkáttıgoriᴖ (§1938) *I was (have been) delayed.*

āh-híkkı- (āg-hík- §559; §§3831 ff.) v.i. (a) *be engaged in kneeling*; (b) *continually (habitually) kneel.*

āh-híkkıg-ır- (āg-hík- §559; N. -ıkır-, -ıhır-; §3838) v.t. caus. (a) *be engaged in causing or allowing to kneel*; (b) *continually (habitually) cause or allow to kneel.*

āh-híkkı-šŭkkı- (ag-hík- §559; §3839) v.t. (a) *be engaged in washing while kneeling*; (b) *continually (habitually) wash while kneeling.*

āh-hıdmḗ- (āg-hıd-, āx-xıd-, etc.) =āhhadmḗ-.

āh-híŋıŋkı- (āg-hí- §559; §3838) v.i. (a) *be engaged in neighing or whinnying*; (b) *continually (habitually) neigh or whinny.*

āh-hıssḗ- (āg-hıs- §559; §3838) v.t. (a) *be (engaged in) perceiving, etc.* (s.v. hıssḗ); (b) *continually (habitually) perceive, etc.*

X. ɛr‿óddıbūŋ‿ăhhıssḗná? *are you feeling (that you are) ill?*
Y. hıssḗriᴖ *yes,* lit. *I feel (it).*

āh-hıtmḗ- (āg-hıt- §559, āx-xıt-, āk-xıt-, āg-xıt- §563; §3838) v.t. (a) *be engaged in sealing, etc.* (s.v. hıtmḗ); (b) *continually (habitually) seal, etc.*

āh-hızzḗ- (āg-hız- §559; §3838) v.t. (a) *be engaged in shaking, etc.*; (b) *continually (habitually) shake.*

āh-hokmḗ- (āg-hok- §559; -huk-; §3838) v.t. (a) *be engaged in judging, etc.* (s.v. hokmḗ); (b) *continually (habitually) judge, etc.*

āh-hóŋı- (āg-hóŋ- §559; §3838) v.i. (a) *be engaged in braying*; (b) *continually (habitually) bray.*

āh-húŋı- (āg-húŋ- §559; §§3831ff.) v.i. (a) *be kneeling*; (b) *continually (habitually) kneel.*

āh-húŋıg-ır- (āg-húŋ- §559; N. -ıkır-, -ıhır-; §3838) v.t. caus. (a) *be engaged in causing or allowing to kneel*; (b) *continually (habitually) cause or allow to kneel.*

āh-húŋı-ğŏg- (āg-huŋ- §559; §3839) v.t. (a) *be engaged in grinding, etc. while kneeling* (s.v. huŋı-ğŏg); (b) *continually (habitually) grind, etc. while kneeling.*

áhır (áxır §1397) n. *end, extremity* [< آخر id.].

obj. āhírk(ı)‿ (áhrk(ı)‿ §1522), -kiᴖ.
pl. áhırı‿.
ín‿nósōn, ténn‿áhırrotōm‿mḗrᴖ *this is too long, cut some off its end.*

āhír-ro‿ (áxír-; áh-, āx-, §1522; §6007) adv. *at (to) the end.*
āhírroᴖ *(s)he (it) is (they are) at the end.*
‿āhírro‿ (etc. §§5860, 5895) postp. (i = prep. §§4287, 4359) *at (to) the end of.*
— follows the genitive:
úln‿āhírro‿ğákar‿dắbunᴖ *at the end of the line there is a hook.*
úln‿āhírro‿ğákar‿dígbūᴖ *the (a) hook is fastened on to the end of the line.*
ğawắbn‿āhírro‿hítım‿dắbumununᴖ *at the end of the letter there is no seal.*
‿āhírro‿ (etc.) postp. (ii = conj. §§4287, 4360) *at the end of the time during which, after, when once, as soon as,* — follows the subjunctive genitive (§2943):—
âi‿kắlln‿āhírro‿bınógri‿ *I shall go when I have finished eating.*

áhmar adj. *red* [< أحمر].
obj. ahmárk(ı)‿.
gen. áhmarn‿.
pl. áhmarı‿.

áhmɛd (-mắd‿) n. *Aḥmad, a man's name* [< أحمد].
voc. áhmɛt!, -mắt!
obj. ahmɛ́dk(ı)‿, -ɛ́tk(ı)‿, -ɛ́tt(ı)‿, -ɛ́kk(ı)‿ §2462; ‿§1522; -kiᴖ, -tiᴖ.
gen. ahmɛ́dn‿v., -mɛ́nn‿v.c., -mɛ́n‿c.; ‿§§778-88.

ahmɛ́n-d(ı)‿ (§§2545ff.) adj. *appertaining to Aḥmad.*

áhsɛn‿ (§1332) adj. *better, best* [< أحسن id.].
obj. áhsɛŋ(ı)‿, -giᴖ.

X. ɛr‿ɛ́kkɛnɛ‿kınnḗg‿áhsɛnmɛn? (-sɛmmɛn? §604) *aren't you a little better now?* (§4256) i.e. *I hope you are ...*
Y. hámdılıllá!, kınnḗg‿áhsɛn‿ériᴖ *praise be to God!, I am a little better.*
tḗŋ‿kŏ́r‿kınnḗg‿áhsɛnunᴖ (§1966) *his (her, its) wound is a little better.*
X. tɛr‿áhsɛnud? *is (s)he (it) better?*
Y. áhsɛnunᴖ *yes.*
tíddᵒ‿áhsɛŋ‿ɛ́ttagoriᴖ (tídd‿áh- §1122) *I (have) brought the better (best) of them.*

āx- s.v. āh-.
āx-xadmḗ- (āk-xad-, āg-xad- §563; -xıd-) *be engaged in serving, etc.* =āh-hadmḗ-.
āx-xalbıtḗ- (āk-xal-, āg-xal- §563) *be engaged in confusing, etc.* =āh-halbıtḗ-.
āx-xallısḗ- (āk-xal-, āg-xal- §563) *be engaged in saving, etc.* =āh-hallısḗ-.
āx-xarbḗ- (āk-xar-, āg-xar- §563) *be engaged in ruining, etc.* =āh-harbḗ-.
āx-xıtmḗ- (āk-xıt-, āg-xıt- §563) *be engaged in sealing, etc.* =āh-hıtmḗ-.

áxır‿ n. *end, etc.* =áhır‿.

âi‿ (áiᴖ, âiᴖ) and commonly unstressed (§1718).

âi‿ pers. pron. *I* (§§2604 ff., 5076-8) [cp. ON. ʌi id., GNT s.v.].
obj. âig(ı)‿, âigiᴖ.
gen. ánn‿v., án‿c., homophonous with gen. of ár‿ (§6290).
pl. ár‿ *we* q.v.
tír‿ắgran, nogedóll‿âiᴖ (§5101) *they remain; I for my part am going to go.*
âigı‿dɛ́ŋkoran‿ *they gave (have given) it (them) to me.*
ánn‿ɛ́ss(ı)‿ (a) *my water;* (b) *our water.*
ám‿bɛ́lɛd‿ (§592) *my (our) country (village).*
án‿dúŋ(ı)‿ *my (our) money.*
ám‿fɛ́rıš (§597) and áf‿fɛ́rıš (§542) *my (our) bed-clothes.*
áŋ‿gadíjɛ (§646) *my (our) lawsuit.*
áŋ‿ğɛ́b‿ *my pocket.*
án‿hánu‿ and áh‿hánu (§560) *my (our) donkey.*
áŋ‿ků (§655) *my (our) house.*
án‿lámba‿ and ál‿lámba‿ (§582) *my (our) lamp.*
ám‿mắr‿ (§604) *my (our) village.*
án‿níbıd‿ *my (our) mat.*
án‿rádd(ı)‿ and ár‿rádd(ı)‿ (§670) *my (our) answer.*
án‿sáfar‿ and ás‿sáfar‿ (§680) *my (our) journey.*
án‿šábákǎ‿ and áš‿šábákǎ‿ (§698) *my (our) net.*
án‿tí‿ *my (our) cow.*
áw‿wɛ́l‿ (§720) *my (our) dog.*
án‿zắbıd‿ and áz‿zắbıd‿ (§735) *my (our) officer.*
ánn-ă‿ *my heart,* án‿ğɛr‿ *my back, etc.* §1671.
áddo‿, N. áido‿ *on (etc. s.v. -r‿) me.*

âi-kırı‿ (§§2539-40, 2635) pers. pron. adj. *like me.*

án-d(ı)‿ (§2637) abs. poss. pron. *that appertaining to me, mine.*
obj. ándıg‿, -giᴖ.
pl. ándınč(ı)‿.
ándıg‿ğíğır‿ *listen to me,* lit. *listen to mine.*

āila⌣ — āk-kuččég-

ándı-kırı⌣ (§2638) pers. pron. adj. *resembling that appertaining to me (us), like mine (ours).*

andínči-kırı⌣ (§2638) pers. pron. adj. *resembling those appertaining to me (us), like mine (ours).*

āila⌣ n. (*a, prop.*) *family*; (*b*, politely for) *wife* [< عايلة, عَيْلَة > عَيْلَة *id.*].
 obj. -lag⌣.
 pl. -lanč(ı)⌣.
 ténn⌣āila⌣saím⌣búrun⌢ (-m⌣b- < dn⌣b- §594) *his wife is Saɛíd's daughter.*
 tér-ón⌣dámɛŋkın, téŋ⌣kák⌣kókkı⌣ ténn⌣āilát⌣tır⌢ (-t⌣t- < -g⌣t- §707) *if he is not there, knock at his door (lit. house) (and §6239) give it (them) to his wife*; ⌣tır⌢ enclitic (§1555).

ák! imperative of **ág** *squat, etc.*

ákaš n. *ear-ring*; with coll. sg. (§4696d) [cp. عَكَشَ *contorta et convoluta fuit coma*, FLA s.v.].
 obj. akášk(ı)⌣, -ki⌢.
 pl. ákašı⌣.
 dúŋgın⌣akaš⌣ *silver ear-ring*.
 nóbrɛn⌣akaš⌣ *gold ear-ring*.

ákıl⌣ n. *food* [< أَكْل *id.* §1359].
 obj. akílg(ı)⌣, -gi⌢.
 pl. ákli⌣.

ákır⌣ n. *Ákır*, a village on the left bank of the Nile, about 17 miles above Úrdi.
 obj. akírk(ı)⌣.
 akírro⌣ (s.v. -r⌣) *at (to) Ákır.*
 akírro⌢ (§6007) *(s)he (it) is (they are) at Ákır.*

āk-káčči- (āg-káč- §569; §§3831 ff.) v.i. and t. (*a*) *be engaged in playing, etc.* (s.v. káčč(ı)); (*b*) *continually (habitually) play, etc.*
 síğag⌣akkáččıran⌢ *they are playing (habitually play)* síğa⌣ (q.v.).
 kuštínag⌣akkáččıran⌢ *they are playing (habitually play) cards.*
 ākkáččıgoran⌢ *they were (kept on) playing (used to play).*

āk-kádub- (āg-kád- §569; -dıb-; §3838) v.t. (*a*) *be engaged in digging the surface of, etc.* (s.v. kádub); (*b*) *continually (habitually) dig the surface of, etc.*
 gabúrk⌣akkádubran⌢ *they are digging the (a) grave.*

āk-kåg- (āg-kåg- §569; §§3831 ff.) v.t. (*a*) *be engaged in carrying on one, etc.* (s.v. kåg); (*b*) *continually (habitually) carry on one, etc.*
 dértıg⌣akkåg¹ran⌢ *they are keeping the fast.*

āk-kagákkı- (āg-ka- §569; §3838) v.i. (*a*) *be engaged in clucking*; (*b*) *continually (habitually) cluck.*

āk-kåğğı- (āg-kåğ- §569) v.i. *be becoming ripe, etc.* = āk-kárğı-.

āk-kåğğı- (āg-kåğ- §569) v.t. *be engaged in testifying, etc.* = āk-kárğı-.

† **āk-káhkıg-aū-** (āg-káh- §569; §3839) v.i. (*a*) *be engaged in making cakes*; (*b*) *continually (habitually) make cakes.*

āk-kåi- (āg-kåi- §569; §§3831 ff.) v.t. (*a*) *be engaged in fashioning, etc.* (s.v. kåi); (*b*) *continually (habitually) fashion, etc.*

āk-kákkɛ- (āg-kák- §569; §3838) v.t. (*a*) *be engaged in getting warm at (in), etc.* (s.v. kákkɛ); (*b*) *continually (habitually) get warm at (in), etc.*
 aī⌣íkk⌣akkákkɛrı⌣ód⌣āig⌣arıŋ⌣karámır⌢ *I am (keep on) warming myself at the fire because I feel the cold, lit. . . . because the cold grips me* (§6215).
 aī⌣masílg⌣akkákkɛrı⌣ód⌣āig⌣arín-karam⌢ *I am (make a practice of) warming myself in the sun because I feel the cold.*

āk-kákkır- (āg-kák- §569; §3838) v.t. (*a*) *be engaged in hatching*; (*b*) *continually (habitually) hatch.*

āk-kál- (āg-kál- §569; §§3831 ff.) v.i. and t. (*a*) *be engaged in eating, etc.* (s.v. kál); (*b*) *continually (habitually) eat, etc.*

āk-kalgíddı- (āg-kal- §569; §3838) v.t. caus. (*a*) *be engaged in feeding, etc.* (s.v. kalgídd(ı)); (*b*) *continually (habitually) feed, etc.*

āk-kálgır- (āg-kál- §569; §3838) v.i. (*a*) *be engaged in making bread*; (*b*) *continually (habitually) make bread.*

āk-kal-nī- (āg-kal- §569) v.i. (*a*) *be engaged in eating and drinking*; (*b*) *continually (habitually) eat and drink.*

āk-kal-ni-bañ̃ñ̃-ō-bån- (āg-kal- §569; §3840; RN, §423) v.i. (*a*) *be engaged in eating, drinking, talking, singing and dancing*; (*b*) *continually (habitually) eat, drink, talk, sing and dance.*

āk-kállı- (āg-kál- §569; §§3831 ff.) v.t. (*a*) *be engaged in pushing, etc.* (s.v. káll(ı)); (*b*) *continually (habitually) push, etc.*

āk-kallıfɛ́- (āg-kal- §569; -kɛl-; §3838) v.t. (*a*) *be engaged in charging (commanding), etc.* (s.v. kallıfɛ́); (*b*) *continually (habitually) charge (command), etc.*

āk-kanıssɛg-áttı- (āg-ka- §569; §3839) v.i. (*a*) *be engaged in beating up* (s.v. átt(ı)) *dough*; (*b*) *continually (habitually) beat up dough.*
 έnč⌣akkanıssɛgáttıran⌢ *the women are beating (habitually beat) up dough.*

āk-károū- (āg-ká- §569; §3838) v.i. (*a*) *be rattling, etc.* (s.v. károū); (*b*) *continually (habitually) rattle, etc.*
 ğέrdel⌣kám⌣kóččır⌣agkárawın⌢ *the bucket is (keeps on) clattering on the camel's back.*

āk-kárğı- (āg-kár- §569; -káğğı-; §§3831 ff.) v.i. (*a*) *be (in process of) becoming ripe, etc.* (s.v. kárğ(ı)); (*b*) *continually become ripe, etc.*

āk-kárğı- (āg-kár- §569; -káğğı-; §§3831 ff.) v.t. (*a*) *be engaged in testifying, etc.* (s.v. kárğ(ı)); (*b*) *continually (habitually) testify, etc.*
 íŋ⌣akkárğıran⌢,
 íŋged⌣akkárğıran⌢ and
 ıŋ⌣ég⌣akkárğıran⌢ *they are (keep on) attesting this* (§5542).
 ɛsmán⌣ınd⌣agsíŋ⌣akkáğğıran⌢,
 ɛsmán⌣ınd⌣agsíŋed⌣akkáğğıran⌢ and
 ɛsmán⌣ınd⌣agsíŋ⌣ég⌣akkáğğıran⌢ *they are (keep on) testifying that ɛoθmán was there* (§5544).
 ɛsmán⌣āli⌣kår⌣tósıŋ⌣nálkor⌣ég⌣ akkáğğın⌢ ɛoθmán *is (keeps on) attesting that he saw ɛáli enter the house.*

múrsıged⌣akkáğğın⌢ *(s)he is giving (habitually gives) false evidence.*

āk-kárğıgır- (āg-kár- §569; -káğğı-; N. -ıkır-, -ıhır- §3838) v.t. (*a*) *be engaged in ripening, cooking, tanning, etc.* (s.v. kárğıg-ır); (*b*) *continually (habitually) ripen, cook, tan, etc.*

āk-kárğıgır- (āg-kár- §569; -káğğı-; N. -ıkır-, -ıhır- §3838) v.t. (*a*) *be engaged in calling to witness, etc.* (s.v. kárğıg-ır); (*b*) *continually (habitually) call to witness, etc.*

āk-kás- (āg-kás- §569; §§3831 ff.) v.t. and i. (*a*) *be engaged in drawing (water), etc.* (s.v. kás); (*b*) *continually (habitually) draw (water), etc.*
 nóg⌣akkásın⌢ *the female slave (a) is drawing water*; (*b*) *habitually draws water.*

āk-kåšɛ- (āg-kå- §569; §3838) v.t. (*a*) *be engaged in stirring*; (*b*) *continually (habitually) stir.*

āk-káttı- (āg-kát- §569; §§3831 ff.) v.t. (*a*) *be engaged in wrapping, etc.* (s.v. kátt(ı)); (*b*) *continually (habitually) wrap, etc.*

ákkɛd⌣ (-ɛt⌢) n. *Akkad* (on map), a village on the left bank of the Nile west of Bádın Island, three miles below Kérma.
 obj. akkétt(ı)⌣ (§716), -ti⌢.

āk-kɛllıfɛ́- (āg-kɛl- §569) v.t. *be engaged in charging (commanding), etc.* = āk-kallıfɛ́.

āk-kérkɛr- (āg-kér- §569; §3838) v.i. (*a*) *be (in process of) oscillating, etc.* (s.v. kérkɛr); (*b*) *continually (habitually) oscillate, etc.*

āk-kíddı- (āg-kíd- §569; §§3831 ff.) v.i. (*a*) *be (in process of) sinking, engaged in diving, etc.* (s.v. kídd(ı)); (*b*) *continually sink, etc., dive, etc.*

āk-kíttɛ- (āg-kít- §569; §3838) v.i. (*a*) *remain silent*; (*b*) *continually (habitually) remain silent.*

āk-kób- (āg-kób- §569; §§3831 ff.) v.t. and i. (*a*) *be engaged in (in process of) shutting, etc.* (s.v. kób); (*b*) *continually (habitually) shut, etc.*

āk-kŏd- (āg-kŏd- §569; §§3831 ff.) v.t. (*a*) *be engaged in scraping, etc.* (s.v. kŏd); (*b*) *continually (habitually) scrape, etc.*

āk-kóhıl- (āg-kó- §569; -kóıl-; §§3831 ff.) v.i. (*a*) *be (engaged in) limping*; (*b*) *continually (habitually) limp.*

āk-kókkı- (āg-kók- §569; §§3831 ff.) v.t. (*a*) *be engaged in knocking*; (*b*) *continually (habitually) knock.*

āk-kómıs- (āg-kó- §569; §§3831 ff.) v.t. (*a*) *be engaged in effacing, etc.* (s.v. kómıs); (*b*) *continually (habitually) efface, etc.*

āk-kórou- (āg-kó- §569; §3838) v.i. (*a*) *be rattling, etc.* (s.v. kórou); (*b*) *continually (habitually) rattle, etc.*
 tåg⌣akkórowın⌢ *the window is (keeps on) rattling (the windows are (keep on) rattling* §4647).

āk-kórrɛ- (āg-kór- §569; §3838) v.i. (*a*) *be snoring*; (*b*) *continually (habitually) snore.*

āk-kŏs- (āg-kós- §569; §§3831 ff.) v.i. *be in process of fermenting, etc.* (s.v. kŏs); (*b*) *continually ferment, etc.*

āk-kuččég- (āg-kuč- §569; §3838) v.t. (*a*) *be engaged in mounting, etc.* (s.v. kuč-čég, s.v. kúğ); (*b*) *continually (habitually) mount, etc.*

āk-kúddɛgır- (āg-kúd- §569; N. -ɛkır-, -ɛhır-; §3838) v.t. (a) *be engaged in clarifying*, etc. (s.v. kúddɛg-ır); (b) *continually (habitually) clarify*, etc.

āk-kúddɛgır- (āg-kúd- §569; N. -ɛkır-, -ɛhır-; §3838) v.t. (a) *be engaged in burning*, etc. (s.v. kúddɛg-ır); (b) *continually (habitually) burn*, etc.

āk-kúg̣ur- (āg-kú- §569; §3838) v.t. (a) *be engaged in placing on*, etc. (s.v. kúg̣ur); (b) *continually (habitually) place on*, etc.

āk-kúl- (āg-kúl- §569; §§3831 ff.) v.t. (a) *be engaged in causing to issue*, etc. (s.v. kúl); (b) *continually (habitually) cause to issue*, etc.

āk-kúñ- (āg-kúñ- §569; §3838) v.i. (a) *be (in process of) sinking*, etc. (s.v. kúñ); (b) *continually sink*, etc.

āk-kúñur- (āg-kú §569; §3838) v.t. (a) *be engaged in burying*; (b) *continually (habitually) bury*.

āk-kŭr- (āg-kŭr- §569; §§3831 ff.) v.t. (a) *be engaged in learning*; (b) *continually (habitually) learn*.

āk-kŭrkır- (āg-kŭr- §569; §3838) v.t. (a) *be engaged in teaching*, etc. (s.v. kŭrk-ır); (b) *continually (habitually) teach*, etc.

āk-kŭrtı- (āg-kŭr- §569; §§3831 ff.) v.t. (a) *be engaged in tangling*; (b) *continually (habitually) tangle*.

āk-kúrub- (āg-kú- §569; §3838) v.i. (a) *be rattling*, etc. (s.v. kúrub); (b) *continually rattle*, etc.

āk-kúrusan- (āg-kú- §569; §3839) v.i. (a) *be (in process of) becoming old*, etc. (s.v. kúrus-an-); (b) *continually become old*, etc.

lúl‿ākkúrusanın⌒ (a) *the bread (food) is getting stale*; (b) *the bread keeps on getting (always gets) stale*.

āk-kús- (āg-kús- §569; §§3831 ff.) v.t. and i. (a) *be engaged in opening*, etc. (s.v. kús); (b) *continually (habitually) open*, etc.

kåg‿ākkúsran⌒ (a) *they are opening the door*; (b) *they keep on opening (always open) the door*.

āk-kútte- (āg-kút- §569; §3838) v.i. (a) *be engaged in descending*; (b) *continually (habitually) descend*.

āk-kúttɛgır- (āg-kút- §569; N. -ɛkır-, -ɛhır-; §3838) v.t. caus. (a) *be engaged in causing or allowing to descend*, etc. (s.v. kúttɛg-ır); (b) *continually (habitually) cause or allow to descend*, etc.

kámlıg‿ākkuttɛgırıddan⌒ *they are unloading (habitually unload) the camels*.

ákrɛs‿ adj. *unlucky* (a) *having bad luck, unfortunate*; (b) *bringing bad luck* [< ἄχαρις *unpleasant, ingratus*].
obj. akrésk(ı)‿, -ki⌒.
pl. ákrɛsı‿.
ın‿ákrɛsun⌒ (a) *this is unfortunate*; (b) *this brings bad luck*.
ın‿ógıg̣‿ákrɛsun⌒ (a) *this man is unfortunate*; (b) *this man brings bad luck*.

akundéna‿ n. *one of the better sorts of date growing in Dóngola* = gundéla‿; s.v. bént(ı)‿; with coll. sg. (§4696 b).
obj. -nag‿.
pl. -nanč(ı)‿.

-al‿ postp. (= conj.) *at the time (in the past) that, when* (§§4337, 5913, 6202) suffixed to subjunctive present objective (§2943), that receives the force of a past, and has in the pl. 3 -waŋ-g- instead of -*d̦aŋ-g- (§2919):

tékkı‿g̣ómrıgal‿dıgírkó⌒ *when I struck him (her, it) (s)he (it) fell down*.

tékkı‿g̣ómıl‿érıgal‿dıgírkon⌒ (§5410) *when I was going to hit him (her, it) (s)he (it) fell down*.

árgı‿nálwaŋgal‿bōdóskoran⌒ *when they saw us they ran off*.

aláma‿ n. *mark, sign, token, symptom*; with coll. sg. (§4696) [< عَلَامَة id.].
obj. -mag‿.
pl. -manč(ı)‿.
sandúg̣‿alámarton‿uñúrkattın⌒ *the box is known by (lit. from) its mark(s)*.
tédd‿aláma-wēg‿áu‿dábmenınn‿ıllár⌒ *make a mark on it, in order that it may not get lost*.

álas‿ n. *cable, thick rope of belt that, in water-wheel* (kólɛ‿), *dips jars* (béšenč(ı)‿) *in water and brings them up over vertical wheel* (átt(ı)‿); *the belt is formed of two endless cables, kept parallel at a suitable distance by pairs of wooden rungs* (áglonč(ı)‿), *to which jars are lashed*. [? < قَلْس id. (§1277); > Sudan Ar. أَلَس id.].
obj. alásk(ı)‿, -ki⌒.
pl. álasi‿.
aláski‿kólen‿íllɛr‿agagáuın⌒ *he is twisting cable for the water-wheel*.

alɛ‿ (a) n. *truth*; (b) adj. *true, genuine, authentic* [ON. ᎠᎶᎡ id. (a) GNT s.v.; ? < *alɛt! (§§963-7) remnant of ἀληθές, ἀληθεία].
obj. alɛg‿, -gi⌒.
pl. alɛnč(ı)‿.
alɛw‿wētíkkori⌒ (-w‿w- < -g‿w- §719) *I (have) told the truth*.
alɛn⌒ *it's true*.
alɛmunun⌒ *it's not true*.
alɛrɛ? *is it true?*
alɛmen? *isn't it true?*
tém‿báññıd‿alɛmunun⌒ *his (her) story is not true*.
hábar‿alɛ‿dāná? *is there authentic (certain) news?*

áli‿ n. ɛáli, *a man's name* [< عَلِي id. = *High*].
voc. áli!
obj. álıg‿.

alınárt(ı)‿, -ti⌒ n. *Alinarti (on map), an island now attached to the right bank of the Nile, about 22 miles above Débba* [ɛáli's Island].
obj. -tıg‿.

alın-d(ı)‿ (§§2545 ff.) adj. *appertaining to ɛáli*.

áli‿ adj. *high, lofty* [< عَالِي id.].
obj. álıg‿.
pl. álınč(ı)‿.
kå‿álın⌒ *the house is high*.
kå‿álımunun⌒ *the house is not high*.

alımálık‿ n. *one of the sorts of date growing in Dóngola, s.v. bént(ı)‿; with coll. sg. (§4696 b)* [< عَلِي مَالِك id.].
obj. -málıkk(ı)‿, -ki⌒.
pl. -málıkı‿.

allág̣a‿ n. *pad of rope at end of cradle* (kórıs‿) *carrying each jar* (béšɛ‿) *of the water-wheel* (kólɛ‿); *its function is to tilt the jar, as a heel tilts a shoe, at the required angle*; with coll. sg. (§4696 d) [? < عَلَاقَة *suspender*, or more prob. *عَلَاجَة (cp. عَلَاج *manipulation*, etc.) §1279].
obj. -g̣ag‿, -gi⌒.
pl. -g̣anč(ı)‿.

álod‿ n. *goose (wild)*; with coll. sg. (§4696 d).
obj. alódk(ı)‿, -ótk(ı)‿, -ki⌒.
pl. álodı‿.

amandákkɛ‿ n. *freshwater turtle* = dárıg‿ (a); with coll. sg. (§4696 d) [< *amann-dár(ı)gkɛ‿ < áman‿ (M.) *water* + gen. -n‿ + dárıg‿ *turtle* + -k obj. suff. + -ɛ‿ §2235].
obj. -kɛg‿.
pl. -kɛnč(ı)‿.

ambáb‿ *my father* s.v. -báb‿.
ám‿báb‿ (§1719) *my (our) door*.
ambánɛss(ı)‿ *my father's sister* s.v. -báb‿.
ambánna‿ (-bénna‿) *my father's brother* s.v. -báb‿.
ámbɛs‿ *my brother* s.v. -bɛs‿.
ámbu- *be going*, etc. s.v. án- go.

amg̣ulúd‿ n. *boil, tumour, abscess*; with coll. sg. (§4696 c) [< Sudan Ar. أُمّ جُلْرُد *deep-seated ulcer covered with thick skin* (§1345)].
obj. -údk(ı)‿, -útk(ı)‿, -ki⌒.
pl. -údı‿.

amınɛ‿ v.t. *trust, have faith in, believe, believe in, trust in, rely on* [< amın- < أَمِن imperat. or imperf. stem of أَمَن id. + -ɛ §3651].
ind. pres. āı‿āmınɛri; perf. āı‿āmınɛgori⌒ (N. -ɛko-, -ɛho-).
imperat. āmınɛ!
ın‿ogígk‿amınɛri⌒ *I trust this man*.
āı‿ın‿sɛrk‿amınɛmunun⌒ *I don't trust this strap, i.e. I think it likely to break*.
āı‿sandúŋ‿kēlúŋ‿amınɛmunun⌒ *I don't trust the lock of the box*.

amınɛrar‿ (-rár‿; §§2200 ff.) and
amınɛríd‿ (§§2256 ff.) n. *trusting*, etc., *trust, faith, belief, reliance*.
amınɛr-an‿ (§§3890, 3899) v.t. *tell to trust*, etc., *let trust*, etc.
amınɛ-bū- (§3934) v. stat. (a) p. *be in a trusted (etc.) state or condition*; (b) t. *be in a trusting (etc.) state or condition*.
ın‿ogíg̣‿amınɛbūn⌒ (a) *this man is trustworthy*; (b) *this man is a believer (a Muslim)*.
sandúŋ‿kēlún‿amınɛbúmunun⌒ (-ŋk- < -gn‿k- §652) *the lock of the box is not to be relied on*.
amınɛred-āg- (§3877) v.t. *be in the situation of having trusted*, etc.
amınɛ-kattı- (N. -ɛha-, §4093) v.p. *be trusted*, etc.
amınɛ-káttı-bū- (N. -ɛha-; §4105) v.i. *be in a trusted (etc.) state or condition*.
amínt(ı) v.t. *show* (§§4664, 5083 ff., 5339) [< *ammínt(ı) (§996) < án- *say* + mín- *what?* + -t dem. (§4593) *say what it (sc. is)* §2860].

ind. pres. âı‿amíntırı⌒, ɛr‿amíntın⌒ (-tī⌒, -tí⌒); fut. âı‿bamíntırı⌒; perf. âı‿amíntıgori⌒ (N. -ıko-, -ıho-).
imperat. amínti!
subj. past âı‿amíntısı‿ (-su‿).
def. perf. âı‿amıntóskori⌒.
samílgı‿ğawâbk‿amíntıgori⌒ *I showed (have shown) the letter to the sheikh.*
âīg‿amıntıgómunan⌒ *they didn't show (haven't shown) me (him, her, it, them, §§5089–90).*
dúŋgıg‿amíntıgoran⌒ *they showed (have shown) (me, you, him, her, us, you (pl.), them) the money (§5091).*
kâg‿amıntıgómunan⌒ *they didn't show (haven't shown) (me, you, him, her, us, you (pl.), them) the house.*
âı‿bamíntımunun⌒ *I shall not show him (her, it, them, to you, him, her, it, you (pl.), them, §5094).*

amíntar‿ (-tır‿; §§2200ff.) and
amıntíd‿ (§§2256ff.) n. *showing, demonstration.*
amínt-an (§3890) v.t. *tell to show, let show.*
amıntır-ɛg-ág- (§§4071ff.) v.t. = amıntɛdól-.
amınt-ɛ-dól- (-tᵒd- §1178; §4022) and
amıntır-ɛ-dól- (-rᵒd-; §4027) v.t. *be about to show.*
amıntır-ɛ-ğű-bű- (§4069) v.t. stat. *be on one's way (coming) to show.*
amınt-ɛ-má- (§4036) and
amıntır-ɛ-má- (§4041) v.t. *become unable to show.*
amıntır-ɛ-nóg- (§§4048ff.) v.t. *go to show.*
amıntır-ɛ-nóg-bŭ- (-nóggŭ- §546; §4058) v.t. stat. *be on one's way (going) to show.*
amıntır-ɛ-tá- (§§4060ff.) v.t. *come to show.*
amínti-kattı- (N. -ıha-; §4093) v.p. *be shown.*
ām-mág- (āg-mág- §601; §§3831ff.) v.t. (a) *be engaged in stealing (from), etc.* (s.v. mág); (b) *continually (habitually) steal (from), etc.*
ām-mágır- (āg-má- §601; §3838) v.t. caus. (a) *be engaged in causing or allowing to be tired, etc.* (s.v. mág-ır-); (b) *continually (habitually) cause or allow to be tired, etc.*
jóm‿dıgríg‿árg‿ammágırkó⌒ (§§4666, 4760, 4695) *(s)he (it) was (has been) annoying us for many days.*
ām-máltan- (āg-mál- §601; §3838) v.i. (a) *be (in process of) becoming (part of) the right bank* (s.v. málṭ-an-); (b) *continually become (part of) the right bank.*
árṭ‿ammáltanın⌒ *the island is (keeps on) becoming part of the right bank (of the Nile).*
ām-mɛdé- (āg-mɛ- §601; §3838) v.t. (a) *be engaged in signing, etc.* (s.v. mɛdé); (b) *continually (habitually) sign, etc.*
ām-mér- (āg-mér- §601; §§3831ff.) v.t. and i. (a) *be engaged in cutting, etc.* (s.v. mér); (b) *continually (habitually) cut, etc.*
súlu‿mɛrkúpk‿ammérın⌒ *the shoemaker is cutting (habitually cuts) out shoes.*
ām-mérɛlan- (āg-mɛ́- §601; §3839) v.i. (a) *be (in process of) curdling* (s.v. mérɛl-an-); (b) *continually curdle.*
íčč‿ammérɛlanın⌒ *the milk is (keeps on) curdling.*

ām-mír- (āg-mír- §601; §3838) v.t. (a) *be engaged in hindering, etc.* (s.v. mír); (b) *continually (habitually) hinder.*
ām-míllan- (āg-míl- §601; §3839) v.i. (a) *be (in process of) becoming bad, etc.* (s.v. míll-an-); (b) *continually become bad, etc.*
ām-mísır- (āg-mí- §601; §3838) v.t. (a) *be missing, etc.* (s.v. mísır); (b) *continually (habitually) miss, etc.*
ām-míssɛ- (āg-mís- §601; §3838) v.t. (a) *be engaged in sprinkling, etc.* (s.v. míssɛ); (b) *continually (habitually) sprinkle, etc.*
ām-mőn- (āg-mőn- §601; §3838) v.t. and i. (a) *be engaged in hating, refusing, etc.* (s.v. mőn); (b) *continually (habitually) refuse, etc.*
ām-mőr- (āg-mőr- §601; §§3831ff.) v.t. (a) *be engaged in tying, etc.* (s.v. mőr); (b) *continually (habitually) tie, etc.*
ām-múg- (āg-múg- §601; §§3831ff.) v.t. (a) *be engaged in leaving, etc.* (s.v. múg); (b) *continually (habitually) leave, etc.*
ām-múkkı- N. (āg-múk- §601; §3838) v.t. (a) *be engaged in cutting, etc.* (s.v. múkk(ı) N.); (b) *continually (habitually) cut, etc.*
ām-múkkı- (āg-múk- §601; §3838) v.t. (a) *be engaged in crossing, etc.* (s.v. múkk(ı)); (b) *continually (habitually) cross, etc.*
ām-murré- (āg-mur- §601; §3838) v.i. (a) *be engaged in strolling, etc.* (s.v. murré); (b) *continually (habitually) stroll, etc.*
ár‿ammurrégoru⌒ (a) *we were (have been) taking a walk;* (b) *we used to go for walks.*
ām-múruğ- (āg-múr- §601; §3838) v.t. (a) *be engaged in cutting off, etc.* (s.v. múruğ); (b) *continually (habitually) cut off, etc.*
ām-múttı- (āg-mút- §601; §3838) v.t. (a) *be engaged in reaping, etc.* (s.v. mútt(ı)); (b) *continually (habitually) reap, etc.*
tín‿díltik‿kısórkɛd‿ammúttın⌒ (-k‿k- <-g‿k §569) *(s)he is cutting (habitually cuts) their hair with scissors.*
amrós (am°rós‿ §1197; armós‿ §899) n. *rainbow* [< ὄμβρος *rain* §2393].
obj. -ósk(ı)‿, -ki⌒.
amuntógo (amın- §1197) n. *Amentego (on map), a village on the right bank of the Nile, 16 miles above El-Xándaq (Hándaq‿).*
obj. -togóg‿.
amuntógor‿ (s.v. -r‿) *at (to) Amentego.*
amuntógor⌒ (§6007) *(s)he (it) is (they are) at Amentego.*
ámur‿ n. *order, command* [< أَمْر id. §1363].
obj. amúrk(ı)‿, -ki⌒.
pl. awāmır‿ [< أَوَامِر], obj. awāmírk(ı)‿, -ki⌒.
ámur‿bélkon⌒ *the (an) order came (has come) out (was, has been, issued).*
amúrk‿ osóskona? *has (s)he issued the (an) order?*
tér‿amúrkı‿dɛŋkó⌒ *(s)he gave (has given) me the (an) order.*
án‿ *of me, my,* gen. of âı‿ (§2604).
án‿ *of us, our,* gen. of ár‿ (§2604).
án (§§3888-9, 5487-91, 6140) v.t. (a) *say;* (b) *say, tell, bid, so;* (c) *let, allow* [specialized use of ‿án *have a tendency* (§211)].
ind. pres. âı‿...ándı⌒, ɛr‿...ánın‿ (‿ánī⌒, ‿ánī⌒); perf. âı‿...áŋkori⌒.
subj. past âı‿...ánsı‿ (‿ássı §680, -su‿).
álım‿mudfr‿ɛkkı‿dólın‿an⌒ (-m‿m- <-g‿m- §601) *tell ɛáli that the manager wants him,* lit. *say to ɛáli 'the manager wants you'.*
X. tékk‿éssı‿ğúgrı‿dıgrín‿an⌒ *tell him (her) (that) the hot water is (too) much.*
Y. marískır‿ándıá? *shall I tell him (her) to make less?*
X. éjjo⌒ *yes.*
tókkon‿tágomunan‿ámmɛn! *don't say they didn't (haven't) come!*
tókkon‿tágomunan‿ámmɛwwé! *don't (pl.) say they didn't (haven't) come!*

— usually constituting (z) the verbal part of a verb-complex (§§3890ff., 5644ff.).
— commonly in:
imperat. -an! (-ā!, -á!, -a! §939), pl. -áwwɛ! (-áwwɛ́!).
neg. imperat. tókkon‿...-ámmɛn! (-mĕ!, -mé!); pl. tókkon‿...-ámmɛwwé! (...-ámmɛndé!).
def. imperat. -ános! (-anó! §962); pl. -anóswɛ! (-oswé!, -ówwɛ́! §724, -wé!, -óssɛ! §687, -sé!).
X. âı‿tékkı‿bınógandi⌒ *I shall tell him (her) to go.*
Y. ɛr‿bıwémunun⌒ *you will not tell him (her).*
âı‿tírgı‿nógwanıddi⌒,
âı‿tírgı‿nógwanırıddi⌒,
âı‿tírgı‿nóganıddi⌒,
âı‿tírgı‿nóganırıddi⌒,
âı‿tírgı‿nógandi⌒ and
âı‿tírgı‿nógandi⌒ *I tell them to go* (§5659).
X. tâgorandé? *have they come?*
Y. síkkandi⌒ *I'll send to inquire,* lit. *I (will §5369b) tell (someone §4664) to ask.*
— the imperative of this complex provides a jussive mood (§§5649-53):
nógan! *tell him (her) to go!, let him (her) go!*
sālúmgı‿nógan! *tell Sâlım to go!, let Sâlım go!*
álı‿ı‿tân‿tấ‿sālúmg‿âıgı‿wédēnan⌒ *let Sâlım tell me when ɛáli comes.*
tékk‿âıgı‿wédēnanó! *let him (her) tell me!*
âıgı‿nógan! *let me go!*
âıgı‿nógawwé! *let (pl.) me go!*
âıg‿ıŋg‿áwan⌒ *let me do this (see that I do this).*
álıj‿já‿kítterai‿já‿nógan! (-ij‿j- -ıg‿j- §566, -aj‿j- <-an‿j- §567) *let ɛáli either be silent or go away!*
sámıl‿nógan‿é⌒ *the sheikh says (s)he (it) is to go,* lit. *...says 'tell (him, her, it) to go, ...says 'say go'.*
— providing a negative jussive (α, §5654):
tòkkon-nógmɛnan! *tell him (her) not to go!, let him (her) not go!*
tòkkon-nógmɛnawwé! *tell (pl.) him (her) not to go!, let him (her) not go!*

— or (β) -an itself may be placed in the negative:
tókkon‿tékkı‿nogámmɛn! *don't tell him (her) to go!, (s)he is not to go!, let him (her) not go!*
tókkon‿tékkı‿nogámmɛwwɛ́! *don't (pl.) tell him (her) to go!, etc.*
tókkon‿tírgı‿nogwámmɛn! *don't tell them to go!, they are not to go!, let them not go!*
tókkon‿tírgı‿nogwámmɛwwɛ́! *don't (pl.) tell them to go!, etc.*

— or (γ) both verbs may be placed in the negative (the two negatives do not make a positive):
tókkon‿tékkı‿nógmɛnammɛn! *don't tell him (her) to go!, (s)he is not to go!, let him (her) not go!*, lit. *don't tell him (her) not to go!*
tókkon‿tékkı‿nógmɛnammɛwwɛ́! *don't (pl.) tell him (her) to go!, etc.*
tókkon‿tírgı‿nógmɛwwammɛn! *don't tell them to go!, etc.*
ind. pres. âı‿...‿andári⌒, ɛr‿...‿andân⌒ (-dá̃⌒, -dá⌒; ‿ándān⌒ §1933a); perf. âı‿...‿andágori⌒ (N. -áko-, -áho-).
ár‿bıtámunan‿andágoru⌒, ár‿tír‿bıtámunan‿andágoru⌒ and ár‿tírgı‿bıtámunan‿andágoru⌒ *we thought they would not come.*
wɛ́run‿andágori⌒ *I thought that it was (some)one.*
ár‿tír‿íŋgı‿bıdólmunan‿andágoru⌒ *we thought they would not like (want) this.*
tír‿ár‿íŋgı‿bıdólmunun‿andágoran⌒ *they (XX) thought they (XX) should not like (want) this* (§5110).
ɛr‿tır‿uñúddan‿andágoná? (§6142) and ɛr‿tírgı‿uñúddan‿andágoná? (§6147) *did you think they knew?*
tókkon‿tírgı‿nógmɛwwammɛwwɛ́! *don't (pl.) tell them to go!, etc.*
tókkon‿tírgı‿nógmɛnammɛn! (§5657) *don't tell them to go!, etc.*
tókkon‿tírgı‿nógmɛnammɛwwɛ́! *don't (pl.) tell them to go!, etc.*

— the logical subject of the jussive may precede tókkon‿ (§5658):
tírgı‿tòkkon-nógmɛwwan! *tell them not to go!, let them not go!*
tírgı‿tòkkon-nógmɛnwáwwɛ́! *tell (pl.) them not to go!, let them not go!*

— redundantly with wɛ́tır *tell* (§5667):
wɛ́tır‿nógan⌒ *tell him (her) to go.*

‿an-dá- (§§3844, 6140) v.t. *suppose, think, believe* (=‿ɛ-dá-) [*be present saying* sc. *to oneself*].

‿aw-wɛ́ (‿ā-wɛ́, ‿a-wɛ́ §976; §3845) v.t. (a) *say*; (b) *say to, tell, bid* [‿an pleonastic: ‿awwɛ́ri⌒ *I say, saying*].
âı‿nóg‿awwɛ́ri⌒ *I say 'go'.*
âı‿ɛ́kkı‿nóg‿awwɛ́ri⌒ *I tell you to go.*
âı‿nóg‿awwɛ́gori⌒ and âı‿nóg‿áŋgı‿wɛ́gori⌒ (§5582) *I said 'go'.*
âı‿tókkon‿áumɛn‿awwɛ́ri⌒ and âı‿tókkon‿áumɛn‿áŋgı‿wɛ́ri⌒ *I say 'don't do it'.*

‿aw-wɛ́-dĕn (‿ā-wɛ́-, ‿a-wɛ́- §976; §§3845, 3996-7) v.t. *say to* (the speaker), *inform, tell, bid, instruct* (the speaker).
imperat. ‿awwɛ́dĕn! (-dĕ̃!, -dē̃!, -dɛ́!).

‿aw-wɛ́-tır (‿ā-wɛ́-, ‿a-wɛ́-; §§3845, 3998-9) v.t. *say to* (other than the speaker), *inform, tell, bid, instruct* (other than the speaker).
bɛlóskoran‿awwɛ́tır⌒ *say to him (her) 'they have gone (come) out'.*
nógw‿awwɛ́tırır⌒ *tell (each of §5456) them to go.*

‿án- (-an-; §§3888-9, 5492-96) v.i. -(a) *become, grow, turn, get, go*; (b) *go, move along*; (c, of time) *go or come by, pass going or coming, elapse* [specialized use of ‿án *have a tendency* (§211)].

— requires an adverbial complement (§5493), constructed without a postposition, and commonly in composition (§§3910ff.):
ind. pres. âı‿...-andi⌒ (‿ándi⌒, §§1923-26a, 5555ff.), ɛr‿...-anın⌒ (-aní⌒, -aní⌒; ‿ánın⌒, etc.); fut. âı‿bı-...-andi⌒ (...-ándi⌒); perf. âı‿...-aŋkori⌒ (´´⌒).
subj. past âı‿...-ansı‿ (-assı‿ §680, -su‿; ´´).
def. perf. âı‿...-anóskori⌒.
núgud‿áŋkó⌒ *he has become (became) a slave.*
téw‿wézın‿rátul‿ídıw‿áŋkó⌒ (-w‿w- < -n‿w- §722) *its weight was (is, lit. went to, has gone to, became, has become) 8 lb.*
éssı‿gɛzáz‿ówwı‿búgon, gɛzáz‿zɛ́r‿ áŋkon⌒ (-z‿z- < -z‿w- §737) *the water was two bottles (and, but §6239), it became (has become, shrank, has shrunk, to) one bottle.*
ékkɛnɛ‿šăkúškır‿anóskó⌒ *now it has got like a hammer.*
gŭ‿urúmm‿áŋkın‿ (§5557) and gŭ‿urúmmaŋkın‿ *when it gets dark.*
bı-súg-ándi⌒ and bısúgandi⌒ *I shall go to (the) market.*
súg‿áŋkon⌒ and súgaŋkon⌒ (s)he (it) *went (has gone) to (the) market.*
âı‿súg‿andáŋgı‿dólli⌒ *I want to go to (the) market* (§2963).
másur‿áŋkoran⌒ *they went (have gone) to Egypt (Cairo).*
dúŋgul‿anóskoran⌒ *they have gone to Old Dóngola.*
kă‿anóskŏ⌒ (ka‿an- §1135, kanóskŏ⌒, s.v. k-án s.v. kă‿) (s)he (it) *has gone home.*
ɛr‿¹s‿ánın? *where are you going to?*
s‿áŋkon? (-kŏ?, -kó?) (< sɛ‿áŋkon? §1122) (a) *where did you go (have you gone)?*; (b) *where did (s)he (it) go (has (s)he (it) gone)?*; (c) *what became (has become) of him (her, it)?*
s‿áŋkon! (-kŏ!, -kó!) *heaven knows where (s)he (it) went (has gone)!, heaven knows what became (has become) of him (her, it)!*
kınnēr‿áŋkın‿ *when it becomes a little (time),* i.e. *in a little time, soon.*
X. áru‿dabóskŏ⌒ *the rain has disappeared.*

Y. búmɛntān, téw‿wékıd‿anóskó⌒ (-w‿w- < -n‿w- ;722) *oh, it will come, it's due now,* lit. ....*it has become its time.*
šáhar‿ŏww‿anóskon‿ar‿tékkı‿nalsúd-dotōn⌒ *it is now (lit. it has become) two months since we saw him (her, it)* (§§6208, 6177).

‿ám-bŭ- (§3927) v.i. stat. *be in a state or condition of becoming, of motion, of elapsing, be on one's way, be going.*
ind. pres. âı‿...‿ámbūri⌒ (‿ambūri⌒ (§1927); ɛr‿...‿ámbūn⌒ (-bŭ̃⌒, -bŭ⌒, -bŭ⌒).
súg‿ámbūri⌒ and súgambūri⌒ *I am on my way to (the) market.*
ɛr‿¹s‿ámbun? *where are you going to?*

-an-nog-ɛ-dól- (§3979) v.i. *be about to go, be on the point of going, be just going to go.*
ind. pres. âı‿...-annogɛdólli⌒, ɛr‿...-annogɛdólın⌒ (-lĩ⌒, -lí⌒).

-an-nog-ɛ-má- (§3982) v.i. *become unable to go.*

†ánasa‿ n. *rhinoceros* [< Sudan Ar. عَنَ id. AZA s.v., AESA s.v. *rhinoceros*].
obj. -sag‿.
pl. anasánč(ı)‿.

ánda‿ *my home, our home,* s.v. dá‿.
‿andá- *suppose, etc.* v.t. s.v. ‿án *say*.
andándi‿ *I go to my (our) home* s.v. dá‿.
andánd(ı)‿ *Dóngola Nubian* s.v. dá‿.
ánd(ı)‿ *mine* s.v. âı.
ánd(ı)‿ *ours, Dóngola Nubian* s.v. ár‿.
án(n) *of me, my,* gen. of âı (§2604).
án(n) *of us, our,* gen. of ár‿ (§2604).

ān-naddífɛ- (āg-nad- §625; §3838) v.t. (a) *be engaged in cleaning*; (b) *continually (habitually) clean.*

ān-nadífkır- (āg-na- §625; §3838) v.t. caus. =ān-naddífɛ-.

ān-nag(ı)sɛ́gır- (āg-nā- §625; N. -ɛ́kır-, -ɛ́hır-; §3838) v.t. caus. (a) *be engaged in decreasing, etc.*; (b) *continually (habitually) decrease, etc.*

ān-nál- (āg-nál- §625; §§3831ff.) v.t. (a) *be engaged in seeing, etc.* (s.v. nál); (b) *continually (habitually) see, etc.*

ān-nālɛ́- (āg-nā- §625; §3838) v.t. (a) *be engaged in cursing*; (b) *continually (habitually) curse.*

ánnaŭ‿ *my grandmother* s.v. -aŭ‿.

ān-nɛ́ñ- (āg-nɛ́ñ- §625; §§3831ff.) v.i. (a) *be (in process of) soaking, etc.* (s.v. nɛ́ñ); (b) *continually soak, etc.*

ān-nɛ́ñgır- (āg-nɛ́ñ- §625; N. -ñkır-; §3838) v.t. (a) *be engaged in soaking, etc.* (s.v. nɛ́ñg-ır); (b) *continually (habitually) soak, etc.*

ān-nɛ́r- (āg-nɛ́r- §625; §§3831ff.) v.i. (a) *be sleeping, be asleep*; (b) *continually (habitually) sleep.*

ánn-ess(ı)‿ *my sister* s.v. -ess(ı); ánn‿ɛss(ı)‿ *my (our) water.*

ān-nɛššígɛ- (āg-nɛš- §625; §3838) v.t. (a) *be engaged in giving snuff to*; (b) *continually (habitually) give snuff to.*

ān-nɛ́wɛ- (āg-nɛ́- §625; §3838) v.i. (a) *be breathing*; (b) *continually (habitually) breathe.*

ánn-i‿ *my hand(s), our hands,* s.v. í‿.

ān-ní- (āg-ní- §625; §§3831ff.) v.t. (a) *be engaged in drinking, etc.* (s.v. ní); (b) *continually (habitually) drink, etc.*

X. šăıgı‿nígoná? *did (s)he drink (has (s)he drunk) (the) tea?*
Y. ānní‿ *(s)he is drinking it.*
šăıgoŋ‿gáhwagoŋg‿ānníri, nɛbítt‿ānnímunun‿ *I habitually drink tea and coffee, I never drink wine.*

ān-nís- (āg-nís- §625; §§3831ff.) v.t. *(a) be engaged in compressing, etc.* (s.v. nís); *(b) continually (habitually) compress, etc.*

ān-níb- (āg-níb- §625; §§3831ff.) v.t. *(a) be engaged in roasting, etc.* (s.v. níb); *(b) continually (habitually) roast, etc.*

ān-níǧ- (āg-níǧ- §625; §§3831ff.) v.t. *(a) be engaged in sewing, etc.* (s.v. níǧ); *(b) continually (habitually) sew.*
ānníǧmunan‿ and ānníññunan‿ (§629) *(a) they are not sewing; (b) they never sew.*

ān-nımíntı- (āg-nı- §625; -míttı- §710; §3838) v.i. *(a) be blinking; (b) continually (habitually) blink.*

ān-nób- (āg-nób- §625; §§3831ff.) v.t. *(a) be engaged in stewing, etc.* (s.v. nób); *(b) habitually stew, etc.*
ɛn‿ǧakútt‿ānnóbın‿ *the woman is cooking (habitually cooks) the stew.*

***ánn-od‿** my father-in-law* not heard‿; s.v. -od‿.

ān-nóddı- (āg-nód- §625; §§3831ff.) v.t. *(a) be engaged in cutting, etc.* (s.v. nódd(ı)); *(b) continually (habitually) cut, etc.*

ān-nóg- (āg-nóg- §625; §§3831ff.) v.i. *(a) be engaged in (in process of) going, etc.* (s.v. nóg); *(b) continually (habitually) go, etc.*

ánnogo‿ *my mother-in-law* s.v. -ogo‿.

ān-nór- (āg-nór- §625; §§3831ff.) v.t. *(a) be engaged in grinding; (b) continually (habitually) grind.*
nógo‿nórtıg‿ānnórın‿ *the female slave is grinding (habitually grinds) flour.*

ánnu‿ *my grandfather* s.v. -u‿.

ān-nŭr- (āg-nŭr- §625; §§3831ff.) v.t. *(a) be engaged in threshing* (s.v. nŭr); *(b) continually (habitually) thresh.*

ánod‿ *my father-in-law* s.v. -od‿.

ansára‿ *oil-press* = assára‿.

antımbáb‿ *our father* s.v. -báb‿.

antımbáness(ı)‿ *our paternal aunt* s.v. -báb‿.

antımbánna‿ *our paternal uncle* s.v. -báb‿.

antımbénna‿ *our paternal uncle* s.v. -bénna‿.

antımbes‿ *our brother* s.v. -bes‿.

antınén‿ *our mother* s.v. -én‿.

antınéŋkegıd‿ *our maternal aunt* s.v. -én‿.

antınnaū‿ *our grandmother* s.v. -aū‿.

antınness(ı)‿ *our sister* s.v. -ess(ı)‿.

antınnogo‿ *our mother-in-law* s.v. -ogo‿.

antınnu‿ *our grandfather* s.v. -u‿.

antınod‿ *our father-in-law* s.v. -od‿.

antıŋgı‿ *our maternal uncle* s.v. -gı‿.

ántıssód‿ *our sister's child* s.v. -ssód‿.

áñ v.i. *live, be alive* [< √á- dem. (§4491) + -ñ (§2895); RSN, §129 cps. Eg. ꜥnx *id.*; ON. ⲁⲡⲓ *id.* GNT s.v.].
ind. pres. āı‿áñ(¹)rı‿, ɛr‿áñın‿ (‿áññı‿, ‿áñí‿); perf. āı‿áñkori‿.
part. pres. áñıl‿ *(one) that lives, liver, living;* past áñɛl‿ *(one) that lived, liver, living.*
máll‿áñran‿ *they are all alive* (§4950).

tér-on‿áñkın‿sérēn‿ *if (s)he (it) lives, it is well.*

áñıd‿ n. *life.*
obj. áñídk(ı)‿, -ítk(ı)‿, -ítt(ı)‿ §2462; -kı‿, -tı‿.
gen. -ídn‿v., -ín‿c. §§778–88.

áñ-bŭ- (§3931 α) v.i. stat. *be alive.*

áñ-ır (N. áñkır; §3683) *(a)* v.t. caus. *cause or allow to live; (b)* v.t. *animate, rouse.*
ind. pres. āı‿áñgıddi‿, ɛr‿áñgırın‿ (-rí‿, -rí‿).
ígk‿áñgırın‿ *stir the fire.*

áñgır-an (§§3890, 3904) v.t. *tell to animate, etc., let animate, etc.*
ɛn‿hɛ́lg‿áñgıran‿ *tell him (her) to be energetic* (etc. s.v. hɛ́l‿).

āñ-nál (§3747 ε') v.t. *see by living, live to see.*
imperat. áñnal! (§1871).
— Bairam greeting:
kórɛg‿áñnal! *live to see the feast!* (sc. again) = *many happy returns!*

āñ-ñárrı- (āg-ñár- §638; §§3831ff.) v.i. *(of dog) (a) be engaged in growling; (b) continually (habitually) growl.*

āñ-ñúrrı- (āg-ñúr- §638; §§3831ff.) v.i. *(a) be engaged in growling (purring* s.v. ñúrr(ı)*); (b) continually (habitually) growl (purr).*

aŋgálle‿ n. *lupine*, Lupinus termis, Forsk. (BSP, 117); with coll. sg. (§4696b).
obj. -lɛg‿.
pl. -lɛnč(ı)‿.
tíštı‿dúl-lēg‿éttaran, aŋgállɛt‿téddo‿ bógran‿kurúpkon‿ɛ́ssıgoŋg‿undúddan, jóm‿tóskım‿múgran, aŋgálle‿ bássaranın‿ (-l-l- < -l-w- §580, -t‿t- < -g‿t- §707, -m‿m- < -g‿m- §601) *they get a large pan, pour the lupines into it, put in earth and water, leave it for three days, (and) the lupines lose their bitter taste.*

áŋgarɛ‿ (-gárɛ‿) n. *(a) bedstead; (b) the Great Bear (constellation;* as in Sudan Ar. العنقريب *id. a* and *b*) [< Beḍ. aŋgárɛ *id.* 'aus amgarē für magarē = مَقْرَى *lectus*' RB, §72].
obj. -rɛg‿.
pl. aŋgarénč(ı)‿.
(s.v. ǧígıd‿, mírıg‿)—the two side-pieces (mírıgı‿) and two end-pieces (ǧígıdı‿) form a frame, that rests on four legs (óssınč(ı)‿).
aŋgarɛn‿óssınč(ı)‿ *(a) legs of bedstead; (b) the Great Bear.*

áŋgı‿ *my maternal uncle* s.v. -gı‿.

áŋgıs v.t. *(a) rouse, wake; (b) sharpen, whet* [< *áŋgıs < áñ *live* +-g- obj. suff. (§3683) +-ıs caus. (§2894), quasi *enliven*] = ágıs.
ind. pres. āı‿áŋgısri‿, ɛr‿áŋgısın‿ (-sí‿, -sí‿); perf. āı‿áŋgıskori‿.
kándıb‿báŋgısri‿ (-b‿b- < -g‿b- §519) *I'll* (§5383) *sharpen the knife.*

áŋgısar‿ (-sárɛ‿) (§§2200ff.) and

áŋgısíd‿ (§§2256ff.) n. *rousing, etc.*

áŋgıs-an (§§3890, 3904) v.t. *tell to rouse, etc., let rouse, etc.*

áŋgıs-kattı- (§4093) v.p. *be roused, etc.*

áŋıs v.t. *rouse, etc.* = áŋgıs.

‿áŋkın‿ *if (when) (s)he (it) becomes, etc.* s.v. ‿áñ- *become.*

áŋŋunan‿ (§661) *they do not squat* (etc.) < ágmunan‿ s.v. ág.

ápkoñ‿ *castor-oil plant* = ábkoñ‿.

‿áptır‿ postp. *beside, etc.* = ‿ábtır‿ s.v. áb.

ár‿ and commonly unstressed (§1718)

ar‿ pers. pron. *we* (§§2604ff., 5076ff.).
obj. árg(ı)‿, -gi‿.
gen. ánn‿v. (< árn‿ §628), án‿c., homophonous with gen. of áı‿ (§6290).
árgonon‿tágoran‿ *they came (have come) with us.*
áddo‿ *on* (etc. s.v. -r‿) *us.*
ánn‿éged‿ *(a) our sheep; (b) my sheep.*
ám‿bér‿ (§595) *our (my) wood.*
án‿dégır‿ *our (my) saddle.*
án‿fáıda‿, ám‿fáıda‿ (§597) and áf‿fáıda‿ (§543) *our (my) advantage.*
áŋ‿gámbu‿ (§648) *our (my) axe.*
áŋ‿ǧákud‿ *our (my) stew.*
án‿hág‿ *our (my) right.*
áŋ‿kárɛ‿ (§659) *our (my) fish.*
án‿lıǧám‿ and ál‿lıǧám‿ (§583) *our (my) bridle.*
ám‿méksɛb‿ (§608) *our (my) profit.*
án‿nógo‿ *our (my) female slave.*
án‿rıjál‿ and ár‿rıjál‿ (§671) *our (my) dollar.*
án‿súkkar‿ and ás‿súkkar‿ (§681) *our (my) sugar.*
án‿šákúš‿ and áš‿šákúš‿ (§699) *our (my) hammer.*
án‿tábla‿ *our (my) padlock.*
áw‿wésıl‿ (§722) *our (my) receipt.*
án‿zál‿ and áz‿zál‿ (§736) *our (my) anger.*
ánn-i‿ *our hands* (§4696a), ánn-urı‿ *our heads, etc.* §1671.

án-d(ı)‿ (§2637) *(a)* abs. poss. pron. *that appertaining to us, ours; (b)* n. *our language, Dóngola Nubian, Dongolese.*
obj. -dıg‿, -gi‿.
pl. ándınč(ı)‿.
X. ándıg‿uñúrná? *does (s)he know Dóngola Nubian?*
Y. marıssoddég‿uñurın‿ *(s)he knows a very little.*
ándıb‿báññi‿ (-b‿b- < -g‿b- §519) and
ándıgeb‿báññi‿ (-b‿b- < -d‿b- §518) *speak Dóngola Nubian.*
ándıged‿dámunun‿ = ám‿baññítked‿dámunun‿ *there isn't any (there is no such expression) in our language.*

ár-kırı‿ (árkírı §1701; §§2539–40, 2635) pers. pron. adj. *like us.*

ándı-kırı‿ (§2638) pers. pron. adj. *resembling that appertaining to us (me), like ours (mine).*

andınčı-kırı‿ (§2638) pers. pron. adj. *resembling those appertaining to us (me), like ours (mine).*

ár‿ n. *shore, river-bank, waterside* (= gár‿, nár‿) [specialization of nominal presentation §2049 of the thing-meant whose verbal presentation is ár *hold* (§2858, so or. *holding, *holder, sc. of river; §2141].
obj. árk(ı)‿, -ki‿.
pl. árı‿.

ắrro‿tếpꜛ *stand (wait) on (stop at) the bank.*
kúb‿ắrro‿tébıŋꜛ *the boat stops at (waits by) the bank.*
éssıŋ‿ắrro‿tébranꜛ *they stand (wait) at the waterside.*
úrun‿ắrróꜛ *(s)he (it) is (they are) on the river-bank (§5858).*

ắr v.t. *(a) seize, grip, grasp, catch, capture, take, so (b) obtain, get, and (c) grasp, comprehend, understand* [< ă‿ *heart* +-ɾ‿ *to, in, at,* so *(sc. take) to heart, *(sc. have) at heart (§2858);* ON. ᚱp *id.* GNT, s.v.; cogn. ắd‿ *handle (§2061)*].
ind. pres. aı̄‿ắrrıꜛ, ɛɾ‿ắrıŋꜛ (árīꜛ, áríꜛ); fut. aı̄‿bắrrı; perf. aı̄‿ắrkorıꜛ.
imperat. ắr!, pl. ắrwɛ! (ắrrɛ! §672, ``).
pl.-obj. ind. pres. aı̄‿ăríddıꜛ, ɛɾ‿ắrırıŋꜛ (-ırí‿ꜛ, -ırí‿ꜛ).
pl.-obj. imperat. ắrır!
def. perf. aı̄‿ăróskorıꜛ and aı̄‿ăredkorıꜛ (-étk-).
def. imperat. ắros!
sắb‿kắuırtɛg‿ắrkōꜛ *the cat (has) caught the (a) bird.*
wél-gěl-lēg‿ắrkonꜛ (-l-l- < -l-w- §580) *the dog (has) caught a gazelle.*
kobíttı‿šɛŋkélgɛd‿ắrꜛ *catch the door with the hook.*
káb‿bájıl‿dúŋgıt‿tírıŋ, bǎıtırıl‿dúŋgıg‿ắrıŋꜛ (-b‿b- < -g‿b- §519, -t‿t- < -g‿t- §707) *the tenant of the house gives (the) money, the landlord takes it.*
ód‿ắrg‿ắrıŋꜛ and (§4623) ắrg‿ód‿ắrıŋꜛ *we are cold,* lit. *the cold seizes us.*
tékkı‿mínč‿ắrkonꜛ *(s)he (it) (has) got hungry.*
tírgı‿mínč‿ắríkkonꜛ *they (have) got hungry.*
ízıŋ‿ắrkonꜛ *(s)he (has) obtained permission.*
éssıg‿ắrkonꜛ *(s)he (has) got (the) water.*
aı̄‿tím‿bǎññıdk‿ắrkómununꜛ *I didn't catch (hear, understand) what they said.*
X. míŋg‿énꜛ *what does (s)he say?*
Y. ărkómununꜛ *I didn't catch (hear, understand).*
kóleŋ‿gíråd‿děg‿ắrkorıꜛ (-d‿d- < -d‿w- §533) *I took (have taken, i.e. have) bought) one twenty-fourth share of the (an) irrigable estate; here* ắr = ğan-ắr (s.v. ğăn).

ắrar‿ (ắrăr‿; §§2200 ff.) and
ắrıd‿ (§§2256 ff.) n. *seizure, etc.*

ắr-an (§3890) v.t. *tell to seize, etc., let seize, etc.*

ắr-bǔ- (§3931β) v.i. stat. *be in a seized (etc.) state or condition.*
éddı‿bígıdır‿ắrbūnꜛ *the (a) hyaena is (has been) caught in the trap.*

ắr-ɛ-dól- (ắrᵒd- §1178; §4022) and
ắrr-ɛ-dól- (rᵒd-; §4027) v.t. *be about to seize, etc.*

ắrr-ɛg-ắg- (§§4071 ff.) v.t. = ăɾɛdól-.

ắrr-ɛ-ğǔ-bǔ- (§4069) v.t. stat. *be on one's way (coming) to seize, etc.*

ắr-ɛ-mā- (§4036) and
ắrr-ɛ-mắ- (§4041) v.t. *become unable to seize, etc.*

ắrr-ɛ-nóg- (§§4048 ff.) v.t. *go to seize, etc.*

ắrr-ɛ-nóg-bǔ- (-nóggǔ- §546; §4058) v.t. stat. *be on one's way (going) to seize, etc.*

ắrr-ɛ-tắ- (§§4060 ff.) v.t. *come to seize, etc.*

ắrɛb-bítt(ı) (§§4169 ff.; ărɛggıbítt(ı) §§4176-8) v.t. *pick up (etc.* s.v. *bítt(ı)) after, seizing, etc.*
wasáha‿málleš‿šıbírk‿ărɛbbıttóskoranꜛ (-š‿š- < -g‿š- §695) *they have taken baskets (§4647) and picked up all the dirt;* §5599.

ārɛd-ắg- (§3877) v.t. *be in the situation of having seized, etc.*
sắb‿ğıgír-rēg‿ărɛdắgınꜛ (-r-r- < -r-w- §672) *the cat has caught a mouse.*
ğakútk‿ắwıl‿dúmmadé‿wēg‿ărɛdắgınꜛ *the cook has got (i.e. bought) a fowl.*
ískıd‿ăıg‿ărɛdắgınꜛ *I have a cold in the head.*
ǎıgı‿mínč‿ărɛdắgınꜛ *I have got hungry.*
tírgı‿mínč‿ărɛdắgırırınꜛ *they have got hungry.*

ārɛd-dā- (§3990; ărɛggıdā- §§3993-4) v.t. *be going along having seized, etc., be going along gripping.*

ārɛd-ɛğ-ğǔ (§4200) v.t. *after seixing (etc.) move (i.) along with (etc.* ɛğğǔ s.v. *éd).*
ǎlı‿tén‿dúŋg‿ărɛdtɛŋkārɛğğǔgóꜛ (§5606) *ɛáli on getting his money took it along to his house.*

ārɛğ-ğǔ-bǔ- (§4220; -ɛd-gı-ğǔ-bǔ-, -ɛg-gı- §4221) v.t. stat. *be on one's way (coming) after seizing, etc.*

ārɛn-nóg (§§4169 ff.; ărɛdgınóg, -ɛggı- §§4176-8) v.t. *go (etc.* s.v. *nóg) after seizing, etc., take away, carry off.*
ind. fut. aı̄‿bārɛnnógrıꜛ.
imperat. ărɛnnók! (" " §1954).
ır‿mén‿ǎıg‿írgonon‿ărɛnnókkomendu? *why didn't you (pl.) take me with you?*

ārɛn-nóg-bǔ- (§4220; ărɛdgı-nóg-bǔ-, -ɛggı- §4221; -nóggǔ- §546) v.t. stat. *be on one's way (going) after seizing, etc., be carrying off.*

ārɛt-tắ (occ. ărɛd-tắ §§4169 ff.; ărɛggıtắ, occ. -ɛdgı- §§4176-8) v.t. *come after seizing, etc.*
ind. pres. aı̄‿ărɛttắrıꜛ, ɛɾ‿ărɛttắnꜛ (-tắꜛ, -tắꜛ); perf. aı̄‿ărɛttắgorıꜛ (N. -tắko-, -tắho-).
imperat. ărétta!, ăréggıta!
íŋgı‿wakílnartōn‿ărɛttắgoꜛ *(a) (s)he came (has come) after getting this from the station-master (etc.* s.v. *wakíl‿); (b §5723) after getting this from the station-master (etc.) (s)he has brought it (ărɛttắgoꜛ from* ăr-ɛttā *infra).*

ār-ɛttắ and
ār-ɛttắ (§3855) v.t. *bring (ɛttắ s.v. éd) after seizing, etc.*
ind. pres. aı̄‿ărɛttắrıꜛ and ărɛttắrıꜛ; ɛɾ‿ărɛttắnꜛ (-tắꜛ, -tắꜛ), ‿ărɛttắnꜛ (-tắꜛ, -tắꜛ, -ɛttắꜛ); perf. aı̄‿ărɛttắgorıꜛ (N. -ắko-, -ắho-), and ‿ărɛttắgorıꜛ (N. -ắko-, -ắho-).
ráddıg‿ărɛttắgoꜛ *(s)he (has) got and brought back the (an) answer.*

ār-étta-děn (" " §1532; §4000) v.t. *after seizing (etc.) and bringing give (to the speaker), seize (etc.) and bring to or for (the speaker).*
súgırtōn‿ǎıgı‿tumbắkk‿ărɛttắdéꜛ *get me some tobacco from the market.*

ār-étta-tır (" " §4000) v.t. *after seizing (etc.) and bringing give (to other than the speaker), seize (etc.) and bring to or for (other than the speaker).*

āríŋg-ır (" " ; §3688) v.t. caus. *cause or allow to seize, etc.*

ắr-kattı- (§4093) v.p. *be seized, etc.*
údlañ‿ărkắttımununꜛ *the hare is not (cannot be §5379) caught.*

ắr-kúttɛgır (§4132) v.t. *after seizing (etc.) lower.*
aı̄‿nórɛn‿ărkuttɛgírkorıꜛ *taking hold of him (her, it) I lowered him (her, it) gently.*

ārós-děn (§§4180 ff.; -óddɛn §538; -ósgı-děn, -ózgı-, -óggı- §4185) v.t. *after seizing (etc.) give (to the speaker), seize (etc.) for (the speaker).*
gắtırtōn‿ăróddɛnꜛ *get it for me from the train.*

ārós-tır (§§4180 ff.; -óttır §714; -ósgıtır, -ózgı-, -óggı- §4185) v.t. *after seizing (etc.) give (to other than the speaker), seize (etc.) for (other than the speaker).*

ắt-tă (§3856) v.t. *bring (an animate object)* [< *ắr-tă (§713) *come having seized, seize and come*].
ind. pres. aı̄‿ắttărıꜛ; fut. aı̄‿bắttărıꜛ; perf. aı̄‿ắttăgorıꜛ (N. -ắko-, -ắho-).
ogíčči‿mufɛttíšnar‿ắttagoranꜛ *they (have) brought the man to the inspector.*

ắrab‿ n. *Arab;* sg. not coll. (§4708) [< عَرَب *Arabs* (§2403)].
obj. arắbk(ı)‿, -ắpk(ı)‿, -kıꜛ.
gen. arắbn‿*n.*, -ắmn‿*n.c.*, -ắm‿*c.* (§586).
pl. ắrab‿.
ărắb-bēɾ‿tắgóꜛ (-b-b- < -b-w- §517) *an Arab came (has come).*
arắbn‿ɛgétk‿éttăꜛ and arắmn‿ɛgetk‿éttăꜛ *bring the Arab's sheep.*
arắm‿hắnug‿éttăꜛ *bring the Arab's donkey.*

ắrabı‿ n. *Arabic (the language)* [< عَرَبِي *id.*].
obj. ắrabıg‿.
ărabıgɛb‿bắññıranꜛ (-b‿b- < -d‿b- §518) *they talk Arabic.*
marísseɾ‿nūbab‿bắññın, dıgrínč‿ărabıb‿bắññıranꜛ (-b‿b- < -g‿b- §519) *a few speak Nubian, many speak Arabic.*

arabín-d(ı)‿ (§§2545 ff.) adj. *appertaining to (the) Arabs, (the) Arabs', Arab.*

arabnắrt(ı)‿, -tıꜛ n. *Arabnarti (on map), a village on the left bank of the Nile, about three miles above Old Dóngola* [Arab's Island; *but now joined to the left bank*].
obj. -tıg‿.

arắm-d(ı)‿ (§§2545 ff.) adj. *appertaining to the (an) Arab, of the (an) Arab, the (an) Arab's.*

arabíjɛ‿ (-jă‿, -ja‿) n. *vehicle, cart, carriage* [< عَرَبِيَّة *id.*].
obj. -jɛg‿.
pl. -bíjɛnč(ı)‿.

aradéb‿ n. *tamarind, Tamarindus indica,* Linn. (BSP, 171); *with coll.* sg. (§4696b); [< Beḍ. aradéb, obj. of aradé *id.* RB, §74].

arág⌣ — **aríkk(ı)**

obj. -έbk(ı)⌣, -έpk(ı)⌣, -kı⌢.
gen. -έbn⌣v., -έm⌣c.
pl. -έbı⌣.

arág⌣ n. *mustard-tree*, Salvadora persica, Garcin (BSP, 334); with coll. sg. (§4696b); [< أَرَاك *id*.].
obj. -ágk(ı)⌣, -ákk(ı)⌣, -kı⌢.
gen. -ágn⌣v., -áŋ⌣c.
pl. -ágı⌣.
kág⌣araŋ⌣túr⌣bókkın⌢ *the snake hides in the (bush of the) mustard-tree (...among the mustard-trees)*.

ár-an- *become white* s.v. áro⌣.

árbaha⌣ n. *Wednesday* [< الأَرْبِعَاء *id*. §§1264, 1389].
obj. árbahag⌣, arbáhag⌣ (§1532).
pl. arbahánč(ı)⌣.
árbaha⌣jóm⌣ (§4750),
árbahan⌣jóm⌣ (§4810),
árbaha⌣nahár⌣ (⌣náh-, ⌣nεh-) and árbahan⌣nahár⌣ *Wednesday*.
arbáhag⌣, arbáhag⌣, -gı⌢ (§4665),
árbahar⌣,
árbaha⌣nahárk(ı)⌣, -kı⌢ and
árbaha⌣nahárro⌣ *on Wednesday*.
árbahartŏn⌣ and
árbaha⌣nahárrotŏn⌣ *since Wednesday*.
árbaham⌣móŋkon⌣ and
árbaham⌣bókkon⌣ *till Wednesday*.
ásal⌣árbahan⌢ (-há⌣, ⌣árbahá⌢ §939) *tomorrow is Wednesday*.

arbahán-d(ı)⌣ (§§2545ff.) adj. *appertaining to Wednesday, Wednesday's*.

arbaín (§956a) card. num. *forty* [< أَرْبَعِين *id*. §1258].
obj. -íng⌣.

arbaín-d(ı)⌣ (§§2545ff., 2738) adj. *appertaining to 40, of 40, 40's*.

arbaín-int(ı)⌣ (-ínint(ı)⌣; §2742) ord. num. *fortieth*.

arbaín-kırı⌣ (-íŋkırı⌣ §1701; §2736) num. adj. *about forty*.

arbátašar⌣ *fourteen* [< أَرْبَعَتَاشَر *id*.].
arbátašarn⌣unátt(ı)⌣ (-šann⌣un- §628) = dımındokémısn⌣unátt(ı)⌣ *full moon* [< اِبْن أَرْبَعَتَاشَر *id*.].

√**árb(ı)** *be compact* (§4495).

árbı-bŭ- (§3940) v.i. stat. *be in a folded state or condition*.
kád⌣árbıbūn⌢ *the cloth is (has been) folded*.

árb-ır (§3674) v.t. *fold*.
ind. pres. aī⌣arbíddı⌢, εr⌣árbırın⌢ (-rī⌢, -rí⌢); perf. aī⌣arbírkorı⌢.
kádεg⌣arbíddan⌢ *they fold the cloth*.

árbırar⌣ (-rár⌣; §§2200ff.) and

arbıríd⌣ (§§2256ff.) n. *folding*.
ténn⌣arbırídırtóm⌣mεr⌢ (-m⌣m- < -n⌣m- §604) *cut it along the fold*, lit. *cut (it) from its folding*; ⌣mεr⌣ enclitic (§1742).

árbır-an (§§3890, 3904) v.t. *tell to fold, let fold*.

árbı-kattı- (N. -ıha-; §4102) v.p. *be folded*.

ardahál⌣ n. *petition, formal petition to Government* [< عرضحال *id*.].
obj. -álg(ı)⌣, -gı⌢.
pl. -álı⌣.

ardahálg⌣geddımégorı⌢ *I (have) submitted a petition*.
ardahálg⌣ánn⌣ıllar⌣báčkó⌢ *he wrote (has written) the (a) petition for (on behalf of) me (us)*.
ardahálg⌣ádd⌣undúkkó⌢ *(s)he (has) put in a petition against me (us)*; ⌣ádd⌣ ⌣áddo⌣ s.v. -r⌣.
ardahálg⌣bágıl⌣ (§5407) *petition-writer*.

árd(ı)⌣ n. *warp (in weaving*, applied to طول) (< عرض *width*, misapplied §2408].
obj. -dıg⌣.
pl. -dınč(ı)⌣.

arduán⌣, **-án**⌢ *Arduan (on map)*, a large island in Máhas, near the head of the third cataract.
obj. -áŋg(ı)⌣, -gi⌢.
arduánn⌣árt(ı)⌣ *the island of Arduan*.
arduándo⌣ (s.v. -r⌣) *on (to) Arduan*.
arduándo⌢ (§6007) *(s)he (it) is (they are) on Arduan*.

árε⌣ n. *interior, inner part, inside* [<á⌣ *heart* + -r⌣ *in* + -ε⌣ of n. ess., so ⁎*what is in the heart* §2316].
obj. árεg⌣.
pl. árεnč(ı)⌣.
árεg⌣aī⌣nalkómunun⌢ (§4623) *I didn't see (haven't seen) the inside*.
árεr⌣ (s.v. -r⌣) adv. *in (to) the interior, inside, within, indoors*.
árεnčır⌣ adv. *in (to) the interiors, inside, within*.

árén-d(ı)⌣ (§§2545ff.) adj. *appertaining to the interior, etc., inner, interior*.
obj. -dıg⌣.
pl. -dınč(ı)⌣.
— in the water-wheel (kólε⌣) árεn⌣, árεnd(ı)⌣ = *towards the river, nearer to the river*.

ár-an- (§3910β) v.i. *go to the interior, etc*.

árám-bŭ- (áramb ŭ-; §3950β) v.i. stat. *be in a state of motion towards the interior, etc., be on one's way (going) in, be going in*.

áranεd-ág- (§3966β) v.i. *be in the situation of having gone to the interior, etc*.

árgadε⌣ n. *cog-wheel* [<⁎árgedε⌣ (§§1048, 1175) < ár *seize* + gédε⌣ *circle*, so ⁎*circle of seizure, that seizes*, i.e. *wheel that engages, gears* §2246].
obj. -dεg⌣.
pl. -dεnč(ı)⌣.
árgadεŋ⌣gédε⌣ *(a) horizontal cog-wheel turning counter-clockwise on vertical axle* (míšš(ı)⌣) *in water-wheel* (kólε⌣); *its cogs engage with those of the* árgadεn⌣tód⌣; *(b) rim of (a)*.
árgadεŋ⌣gédεn⌣túndınč(ı)⌣ *spokes of horizontal cog-wheel*.
árgadεn⌣tód⌣ *vertical cog-wheel* on the same axle (tórε⌣) as the wheel over the water (átt(ı)⌣); its cogs (súl-gadεnč(ı)⌣) engage with those of the árgadεŋ⌣gédε⌣; it rotates between two beams (kág⌣ and kómε⌣); called ⌣tód⌣ *small* as contrasted with the horizontal cog-wheel.
árgadεn⌣tóŋ⌣gédε⌣ (-ŋ-g- < -dn⌣g- §644) *rim of vertical cog-wheel*.
árgadεn⌣tón⌣túndınč(ı)⌣ (-n⌣t- < -dn⌣t- §630) *spokes of vertical cog-wheel*.

árgı⌣, **-gi**⌢ n. *Argi (on map)*, name of an island two miles and of another (*Old Argi*) three miles below Débba.
obj. árgıg⌣, árgíg⌣ (§1532).
árgı⌣gedíd⌣ *New Argi*.
árgı⌣kúrus⌣ *Old Argi*.

árgo⌣ n. *Argo (on map)*, an island 18 miles long, beginning 8 miles north of El-Órdi.
obj. -gog⌣, -gogi⌢.
árgor⌣ágın⌢ and árgor⌣sákınun⌢ *(s)he lives in Árgo*.
árgoŋ⌣kóñ⌣ *(a) head (up-stream extremity*, lit. *face) of Árgo*; *(b) El Koin (on map)*, a village in the south-eastern end of Árgo.

argon-sáb⌣ (-ossáb⌣ §680) and **argo-sáb**⌣ (§2361) n. *Argosab (on map)*, name of the northern end of Árgo Island.
obj. -sábk(ı)⌣, -sápk(ı)⌣, -kı⌢.
argosénε⌣ *Argo colossus (-si)* s.v. sénε⌣.

árı⌣ (§§2714, 5227ff.) card. num. *twenty* [§2254, RSN, §125].
obj. árıg⌣, -gi⌢ (§6290).
gen. árın⌣.
jóm⌣árım⌣bádır⌣bıtáran⌢ *they will come after 20 days*.
— in compounds arrε-, arr°- [<⁎ar-ro-, s.v. -r⌣]:
arrε-wέr⌣ (-r°w-) 21.
arr-óww(ı)⌣ 22.
arrε-tósk(ı)⌣ (-r°t-) 23, etc.

árı-kırı⌣ (§2539) num. adj. *about 20*.

arín-d(ı)⌣ (§§2545ff.) adj. *appertaining to 20, of 20, 20's*.

arínt(ı)⌣ (árınt(ı)⌣, §2742) ord. num. *twentieth*.

arıntínd(ı)⌣ (§2743) adj. *appertaining to the twentieth*.

arıŋgár⌣ (§2758) n. *the whole 20, all (the) 20*.
obj. -gárk(ı)⌣.

árıd⌣ n. *earth, soil, ground, land* [<أَرْض *id*.].
obj. arídk(ı)⌣, -ítk(ı)⌣, -ítt(ı)⌣, -íkk(ı)⌣, -kı⌢, -ti⌢ (§§2462, 6290).
gen. árıdn⌣, -ın⌣c. (§2472).
pl. ár(ı)dı⌣.
árıd⌣bŭr⌣ (§4750) *fallow, land left uncultivated*.
árın⌣harág⌣ and árın⌣túlba⌣ *land-tax*.
árın⌣tírt(ı)⌣ *the owner of the land*.
árıdır⌣ adv. *on (in, to) the ground*.
árıdır⌣ (§5858) *(s)he (it) is (they are) on the ground, it is (they are) in the ground*.

árıg⌣ n. *side* [RSN, §129].
obj. arígk(ı)⌣, -íkk(ı)⌣, -kı⌢ (§6290).
pl. ár(ı)gı⌣ (§6290).
mán⌣aríkkεb⌣bŭn⌢ (-b⌣b- < -d⌣b- §518) *(s)he (it) lies on that (other) side*.
ín⌣aríkkεn⌣nókkoran⌢ (-n⌣n- < -d⌣n- §624) *they went (have gone) in this direction*.

aríkk(ı) (árk(ı)⌣, q.v.) v.t. *(a) cast, throw aside, off, down, away*; *(b) drop, let fall*; *(c) throw [objective (i.e. adverbial) case of árıg⌣ side stereotyped as verbal stem, or. (sc. put) aside §2852]*.
ind. pres. aī⌣aríkkırı⌢, εr⌣aríkkın⌢ (-kı⌢, -kí⌢); fut. aī⌣baríkkırı⌢; perf. aī⌣arík-kıgorı⌢ (N. -iko-, -iho-).

18

imperat. aríkki!
subj. past aî‿aríkkısı‿ (-su‿).
  X. fúlla‿sέ? *where's the cork?*
  Y. arıkkóskori⁀ *I've thrown it away.*
  S.X. (being carried) dókkon‿âig‿
    aríkkımεwwέ! and
  S.Y. (being carried) dókkon‿âig‿aríkkımεndέ! *don't (pl.) drop me!*
  Z. έkkı‿barıkkımunun⁀.
  W. békk‿aríkkımunun⁀.
  V. έkkı‿bar‿aríkkımunun⁀ *we shan't drop you.*
aríkkar‿ (-kdr‿, §§2200ff.) and
arıkkíd‿ (§§2256ff.) n. *casting, etc.*
aríkk-an (§3890) v.t. *tell to cast, etc., let cast, etc.*
aríkkı-bŭ- (§3931β) v.i. stat. *be in a cast (etc.) state or condition.*
  arίkkıbūn, nefέmunun⁀ *it's (it has been) thrown away, it's useless.*
arıkkεd-ág- (§3877) v.t. *be in the situation of having cast, etc.*
arıkkır-εg-ắg- (§4071ff.) v.t. = arıkkεdól-.
arıkk-ε-dól- (-kᵒd- §1178; §4022) and
arıkk-ε-dól- (-rᵒd-; §4027) v.t. *be about to cast, etc.*
arıkk-ε-mắ- (§4036) and
arıkkır-ε-mắ- (§4041) v.t. *become unable to cast, etc.*
arıkkır-ε-nóg-(§§4048ff.) v.t. *go to cast, etc.*
arıkkır-ε-nóg-bŭ- (-nόggŭ- §546; §4058) v.t. stat. *be going to cast, etc., be on one's way to cast, etc.*
arıkkı-ǧóm (§3747ε') v.t. *hit by throwing at, throw at and hit.*
arıkk-úndur (§§3769, 3782) v.t. *cast (etc.) in(to).*
  kawíšk‿ígır‿arıkkundúkkó⁀ *(s)he threw (has thrown) the rubbish into the fire.*
arıkk-undos-tá (-ottá §714; §4189; -osgıtắ, -ozgı-, -oggı- §4190) v.t. *come after casting (etc.) in(to), just (s.v. -tá) cast (etc.) in(to), go and (§5713) cast (etc.) in(to).*
  imperat. arıkkundósta! (-ótta!, -ósgıta!, -ozgı-, -óggı-).
  bústar‿ǧawâb-bēg‿arıkkundoggıtári⁀ (-b-b- < -b-w- §517) *I'm just going to drop a letter into the post.*
aríñčε‿ n. *small bead* esp. *for necklaces and bracelets*; *with coll. sg.* (§4696c)
  [< *ár(ı)ñtε‿ (§1062) < ár *clasp*+-ı- euph. +-ñ dim. (§4572)+-t dem. or dim. +-ε‿ of n. ess., so **the little thing(s) for a clasp* §2229].
  obj. -čεg‿.
  pl. -čεnč(ı)‿.
árk(ı) v.t. (a) *cast, throw aside, off, down, away*; (b) *drop, let fall*; (c) *throw* [worn-down form of arίkk(ı) id.].
  ind. pres. aî‿árkırı⁀, εr‿árkın⁀ (-kῖ⁀, -kí⁀); fut. aî‿bárkırı⁀; perf. aî‿árkıgori⁀ (N. -ıko-, -ıho-).
  imperat. árki!, pl. árkıwε! (-wέ!).
  subj. past aî‿árkısı‿ (-su‿).
  neg. imperat. tókkon‿árkımεn! (-mε̃!, -mέ!); pl. tókkon‿árkımεwwε! (-wέ!) and tókkon‿árkımεndέ!
  X. fúlla‿sέ? *where's the cork?*
  Z. arkóskori⁀ *I've thrown it away.*
  túrug‿bárkın⁀ *the wind will throw it down.*
  X. (being carried) tókkon‿âig‿árkımεwwέ! and
  Y. (being carried) tókkon‿âig‿árkımεndέ! *don't (pl.) drop me!*
  Z. ar‿έkkı‿bárkımunun⁀.
  W. ar‿békk‿árkımunun⁀.
  V. έkkı‿bar‿árkımunun⁀ *we shan't drop you.*
  kúlug‿úrur‿árki⁀ *throw a (the) stone into the river.*
árkar‿ (-kdr‿; §§2200ff.) and
arkíd‿ (§§2256ff.) n. *casting, etc.*
árk-an (§3890) v.t. *tell to cast, etc., let cast, etc.*
árkı-bŭ- (§3931β) v.i. stat. *be in a cast (etc.) state or condition.*
arkεd-ág- (§3877) v.t. *be in the situation of having cast, etc.*
arkır-εg-ág- (§4071ff.) v.t. = arkεdól-.
ark-ε-dól- (-kᵒd- §1178; §4022) and
arkır-ε-dól- (-rᵒd-; §4027) v.t. *be about to cast, etc.*
ark-ε-mắ- (§4036) and
arkır-ε-mắ- (§4041) v.t. *become unable to cast, etc.*
arkır-ε-nóg- (§§4048ff.) v.t. *go to cast, etc.*
arkır-ε-nóg-bŭ- (-nόggŭ- §546; §4058) v.t. stat. *be going to cast, etc., be on one's way to cast, etc.*
arkı-ǧóm (§3747ε') v.t. *hit by throwing at, throw at and hit.*
  kåkkı‿kúlug‿arkıǧómkó⁀ *(s)he threw a stone at the snake and hit it,* lit. *(s)he hit the snake with a stone by throwing.*
ark-úndur (§§3769, 3782) v.t. *cast (etc.) in(to).*
ark-undos-tá (-ottá §714; §4189; -osgıtắ, -ozgı-, -oggı- §4190) v.t. *come after casting (etc.) in(to), just (s.v. -tá) cast (etc.) in(to), go and (§5713) cast (etc.) in(to).*
  imperat. arkundósta! (-ótta!, -ósgıta!, -ózgı-, -óggı-).
árk(ı) v.i. *burn (flagrare), catch fire, light.*
  ind. pres. tεr‿árkırı⁀ (-kí⁀, -kí⁀); perf. tεr‿árkıgon⁀ (N. -ıkon⁀, -ıhon⁀; -gõ⁀, -gó⁀).
  íg‿árkın⁀ *the fire burns (lights).*
árkı-bŭ- (§3931α) v.i. stat. *be in a burning state, be on fire, be alight.*
  íg‿arkıbūn⁀ *the fire is alight.*
  lámb‿árkıbūn⁀ *the lamp is alight.*
árk-ır (§3672a) (a) v.t. caus. *cause or allow to burn, etc.;* (b) v.t. *kindle, set on fire, light.*
  ind. pres. aî‿arkíddi⁀ (árkıddi⁀ §1806), εr‿árkırın⁀ (-rí⁀, -rí⁀); perf. aî‿ār-kírkori⁀.
  ígk‿árkıddan⁀ *they light the (a) fire (light).*
  lámbag‿arkírkori⁀ *I (have) lit the lamp.*
árkır-an (§§3890, 3904) v.t. *tell to kindle, etc., let kindle, etc.*
armós (§899) n. = am(ᵒ)rós *rainbow.*
áro‿ adj. *white, light in colour, pale* [contains √ár- **sky* (§4493); §2562; RSN, §§129, 200].
  obj. arógı‿, -gı⁀.
  pl. arónč(ı)‿.
— *used as noun* (§§4964–5):
  béntın‿áro‿ *pale one(s) of the dates* (§4696b), i.e. *dates that begin to ripen, turning from green to light yellow.*
  kúmbun‿áro‿ *white of egg.*
  míssın‿áro‿ *white of eye.*
ár-an- (áróan-, árᵒan- §1114; §3910α) v.i. *become (grow, turn) white, etc.*
  ind. pres. aî‿árandi⁀, εr‿áranın⁀ (-nῖ⁀, -ní⁀); fut. aî‿bárandi⁀; perf. aî‿árankori⁀.
  subj. past aî‿áransı‿ (-assı‿ §680, -su‿).
áram-bŭ- (árᵒam-, árᵒam-; §§3949ff.) v.i. stat. *be in a state of becoming or having become (etc.) white (etc.).*
aróg-ır (N. -ókır, -óhır; §3701) (a) v.t. caus. *cause or allow to become white, etc.;* (b) v.t. *whiten.*
  ind. pres. aî‿arógıddi⁀.
arogíttεl‿ adj. *whitish, pale* [< *arogírtεl‿ (§713) < *aróǧırtεl‿ (§1068) < aróg‿+-ır caus. (§3665)+-t dem. (§4593)+-έ *say* (§213)+-l‿ part. -ing (§2958), so **that saying 'make white'* §2526].
  obj. -gıttέlg(ı)‿, -gı⁀.
  pl. -gíttεl‿.
aró‿ (§§2539–40) adj. *whitish, whity.*
aró? *we?* s.v. -ó?
arrágı‿ n. *shirt* [< *Sudan Ar.* عَرَّاقِي *undervest (to absorb perspiration);* cp. our *sweater*].
  obj. -rágıg‿.
  pl. -rágınč(ı)‿.
arrahâu‿ (⁻, ⸌⸍ §1524) n. *crane, stork* (= ráhau‿); *with coll. sg.* (§4696d) [< الرَّهْو *id.* §§1388, 1357].
  obj. -háug‿.
  pl. -háwı‿ (arráhawı‿, ⸌⸍).
árrε‿ n. *wave* [< *ánrε‿ (§670) < ‿án- *go*+intensive -r (§4586)+-ε‿ of n. act. (§2234γ), so **much going, vehement motion* §2317].
  obj. árrεg‿.
  pl. árrεnč(ı)‿.
arrε- *in compounds* = árı‿ *twenty-* (§2715).
  arrε-wέr‿ 21.
-árrε‿ *in* kån-árrε‿ *neighbour* s.v. kắ‿.
ár-rεjjıhέ- (āg-rεj- §669; §3838) v.t. (a) *be engaged in quieting, etc.* (s.v. rεjjıhέ); (b) *habitually quiet, etc.*
árt(ı)‿ n. *God* [< √ár **sky* (§4493)+-t (§2326); RN, §292 al.].
  obj. -tıg‿, -gı⁀.
  árt‿úñurın⁀ *God knows* (sc. *I don't*); = اللّٰه أَعْلَم.
  árt‿ár‿mállεn‿tımbábun⁀ (§5118) and árt‿ár‿mállεn‿tımbáb-taran⁀ (§5791) *God is the father of us all;* ár‿mállεn‿ *a pronoun-complex* (§5196).
árt(ı)‿ n. *island* [< å-r‿ *in the heart* i.e. *centre* (sc. *of the river*)+-t(ı)‿ §2331; cp. TOB, §143, 34].
  obj. -tınč(ı)‿.
  pl. -tınč(ı)‿.
  ártın‿kón‿ *head or nose (up-stream extremity) of island.*
  ártın‿sâb‿ *tail (down-stream extremity) of island.*

artıgáša⌣ — áss(ı)⌣

— several places whose names end in -árt(ı)⌣ are now no longer islands or only become islands at high Nile (s.v. mált-an-, tıŋgắr-an-).

ārtín-d(ı)⌣ (§§2545ff.) adj. *appertaining to the (an) island, of the (an) island, insular.*

artıgáša⌣ n. *Artigashi* (on map), an island just north of Argo.
  obj. -šag⌣.

artımóga⌣ n. *Artimoga* (on map), a village on the left bank of the Nile, about 24 miles above Débba.
  obj. -gag⌣.

áru⌣ n. *rain* [< √ár- §4493; ON. ⲁⲣⲟⲩ *GNT*, s.v.].
  obj. árug⌣, -gi⌢.
  pl. arúnč(ı)⌣.
    ár⌣abbógın⌢ (§1122) *the rain is (keeps on) coming down.*
    ár-ón⌣tăgın⌢ *if (when) (the) rain comes.*
  arún-d(ı)⌣ (§§2545ff.) adj. *appertaining to (the) rain, of (the) rain.*

ắs v.t. *measure, ascertain the length, area or volume of* (= abbıré).
  ind. pres. āi⌣ắs(ı)ri⌢, ɛr⌣ắsın⌢ (⌣ắsi⌢, ⌣ắsí⌢); perf. āi⌣ắskori⌢.
  imperat. ắs!, pl. ắswɛ! (-wé!, ắssɛ! §687, -sé!).
    írıg⌣ókkɛd⌣ắsran⌢ *they measure rope by the fathom* (óg⌣).
    kádɛk⌣kéugɛd⌣ắsran⌢ *they measure cloth by the cubit.*
    arítkı⌣šăgɛd⌣ắsran⌢ *they measure (the) land with a (the) fathom rod.*
    arítk⌣āsóskoran⌢ *they have measured the land.*
    íuk⌣kéłagɛd⌣ắsran⌢ *they measure grain (a) with a measure; (b) by the kéła⌣ (q.v.).*
    íug⌣ắskorandé? *did they measure (have they measured) the grain?*

ásar (ásar⌣; §§2200ff.) and
ásíd (§§2256ff.) n. *measuring.*

asıdd(ı)⌣ n. *measured amount, measure* [ás- > as- §1062; §§2271-2].
  obj. -dıg⌣.
  pl. -dınč(ı)⌣.
    kéła⌣gắŋgıbūgoná? tɛr⌣asíddıg⌣ošóŋkoná? *was the measure (vessel) full?, did (s)he shake the measure (amount) down?*

ás-an (§3890) v.t. *tell to measure, let measure.*

áz-bū- (§§727, 3931β) v.i. stat. *be in a measured state or condition.*
    íu⌣ăzbūn⌢ *the grain is (has been) measured.*

ās-ɛ-má- (§4036) and
ās(ı)r-ɛ-má- (§4041) v.t. *become unable to measure.*

āsɛd-ág- (§3877) v.t. *be in the situation of having measured.*

ás-kattı- (§4093) v.p. *be measured.*

ásab n. *(a) sinew, (b) muscle* [< عَصَب id.], with coll. sg. (§4696a).
  obj. asábk⌣, -ápk(ı)⌣, -ki⌢.
  gen. ásabn⌣v, -am⌣c.
  pl. asábk⌣.

asám-d(ı)⌣ (§§2545ff.) adj. *appertaining to the (a) sinew (muscle), of the (a) sinew (muscle).*
    ódd⌣asámd(ı)⌣ *muscular pain.*

ásal⌣ n. *morrow, to-morrow (dies crastinus), next day* [<*ásıl⌣ (§1175) < ás- *morrow* (cp. Eth. ጌሰ: *mane agere RSN*, §34) + -ıl⌣ determinative (§2277) §2193].
  obj. asálg(ı)⌣, -gi⌢.
    ásal⌣bušnóñ-taran⌢,
    ásal⌣bušnóñun⌣ (-ñū⌢, -ñú⌢) *to-morrow is Tuesday.*
    asáln⌣íčč(ı) *to-morrow's milk (milk for to-morrow).*
    asálg(ı)⌣, -gi⌢ (§4431) adv. *to-morrow (cras).*
    asálgı⌣bıtáran⌢ *they will come to-morrow.*
    asál⌣šărɛg(ı)⌣ adv. *to-morrow evening.*
    asál⌣šărɛb⌣bıtáran⌢ (-b⌣b- < -g⌣b- §519) *they will come to-morrow evening.*
    asál⌣wáhákk(ı)⌣ (s.v. wahag-) adv. *the day after to-morrow.*

asáln-d(ı)⌣ (asánd(ı)⌣ §807; §§2545ff.) adj. *of to-morrow, to-morrow's.*
  obj. -dıg⌣, -dıgi⌢.

ásal n. *honey* [< عَسَل id.].
  obj. asálg(ı)⌣, -gi⌢.
    asáln⌣kúlt(ı)⌣ (asán⌣k-, asáŋ⌣k- §810) *bee(s §4696c).*

asánd(ı)⌣ *to-morrow's* s.v. ásal *morrow.*

asıdd(ı)⌣ *measured amount* s.v. ắs.

asíkk(ı) v.t. *borrow* [<*an-síkk(ı) *ask saying* §2861].
  ind. pres. āi⌣asíkkıri⌢; perf. āi⌣asíkkıgori⌢ (N. -ıko-, -ıho-).
  imperat. asíkki⌢.

asíkk-an (§§3890ff.) v.t. *tell to borrow, let borrow.*

asíkkı-dĕn (§§3996-7) v.t. *lend (to the speaker).*
  ind. pres. ɛr⌣asíkkıdɛnın⌢ (-ní⌢, -ní⌢).
  imperat. asíkkıdɛn! (-dḗ!, -dḗ!, -dé!, -dɛ!).
    ɛsmán⌣āigı⌣rıjál⌣árıg⌣asıkkıdéŋkó⌢ ɛθmán (has) *lent me twenty dollars.*

asíkkı-tır (§§3998-9) v.t. *lend (to other than the speaker).*
  ind. pres. āi⌣asíkkıtıddi⌢.
  imperat. asíkkıtır!
    āi⌣tékkı⌣rıjál⌣kɛmísk⌣asıkkıtíkkori⌢ *I (have) lent him (her) four dollars.*

ásıl v.t. *fry* [identified in *AZN*, s.v. with أَصْلَى *roast;* §2844].
  ind. pres. āi⌣asíllı⌢, ɛr⌣ásılın⌢ (-lí⌢, -lí⌢); fut. āi⌣basíllı⌢; perf. āi⌣asílkori⌢.
    kărɛd⌣déskɛb⌣básılın⌢ (-d⌣d- < -g⌣d- §534, -b⌣b- < -d⌣b- §518) *(s)he will fry the fish in (lit. with) butter.*

ásılar (-lăr⌣; §§2200ff.) and
asılíd⌣ (§§2256ff.) n. *frying.*

ásıl-an (§§3890ff.) v.t. *tell to fry, let fry.*

asíl-bū- (§3931β) v.i. stat. *be in a fried state or condition.*
    kăr⌣asílbūn⌣ *the fish is (has been) fried.*

asíl-kattı- (§4093) v.p. *be fried.*

áskar n. *soldier, policeman* [< عَسْكَر *troops* §2403].
  obj. askárk(ı)⌣, -ki⌢.
  pl. áskarı⌣.

ās-sabré- (āk-sab-, āg-sab- §679; §3838) v.i. and t. *(a) be engaged in having patience (with),* etc. (s.v. sabré); *(b) continually (habitually) have patience (with),* etc.

ās-sădé- (āk-sā-, āg-sā- §679; §3838) v.t. *(a) be engaged in helping; (b) continually (habitually) help.*

ās-saffıré- (āk-saf-, āg-saf- §679; §3838) v.i. *(a) be engaged in whistling (with instrument); (b) continually (habitually) whistle.*

ās-saggıré- (āk-sag-, āg-sag- §679; §3838) v.i. *(a) be in process of rusting; (b) continually rust.*

ās-sallé- (āk-sal-, āg-sal- §679; §3838) v.i. *(a) be engaged in praying,* etc. (s.v. sallé); *(b) continually (habitually) pray,* etc.
    tíŋ⌣kúpkı⌣tolléŋgon⌣āssalléran⌢ *they are chanting (habitually chant) while towing their boat;* ⌣tolléŋgon §§5726ff., 1965a.

ās-săm- (āk-săm-, āg-săm §679; §§3831ff.) v.i. *(a) be engaged in becoming intoxicated; (b) continually (habitually) become intoxicated.*

ās-sándı- (āk-sán-, āg-sán- §679; §3838) v.i. and t. *(a) be afraid (of), be frightened (of); (b) continually (habitually) be afraid (of),* etc.

ās-sándıgır- (āk-sán-, āg-sán- §679; N. -ıkır-, -ıhır-; §3838) v.t. caus. *(a) be engaged in frightening,* etc. (s.v. sándıgır-); *(b) continually (habitually) frighten,* etc.

assára⌣ (ansă-) n. *oil-press* [< عَصَّارَة id.].
  obj. -rag⌣.
  pl. -ranč(ı)⌣.

ās-său- (āk-săŭ-, āg-săŭ- §679; §§3831ff.) v.i. *(a) be (in process of) mingling,* etc. (s.v. săŭ); *(b) continually (habitually) mingle,* etc.

ās-săwır- (āk-să-, āg-să- §679; -săwᵘr-, etc.; §3838) v.t. *(a) be engaged in mingling; (b) continually (habitually) mingle.*

ās-sɛjjıdé- (āk-sɛj-, āg-sɛj- §679; -sējıdé-; §3838) v.t. *(a) be engaged in hunting; (b) continually (habitually) hunt.*

ās-sɛlgé- (āk-sɛl-, āg-sɛl- §679; §3838) v.t. *(a) be engaged in boiling (in a liquid); (b) continually (habitually) boil (etc.).*

ās-sɛllımé- (āk-sɛl-, āg-sɛl- §679; -lumé-; §3838) v.t. *(a) be engaged in greeting,* etc. (s.v. sɛllımé); *(b) continually (habitually) greet,* etc.

ās-sɛndé- (āk-sɛn-, āg-sɛn- §679; §3838) v.t. *(a) be engaged in supporting,* etc. (s.v. sɛndé); *(b) continually (habitually) support,* etc.

ās-sɛ́r- (āk-sɛ́r-, āg-sɛ́r- §679; §§3831ff.) v.t. *(a) be engaged in chopping,* etc. (s.v. sɛ́r); *(b) continually (habitually) chop,* etc.

ās-sɛrɛgırmér- (āk-sɛ-, āg-sɛ- §679; N. -ēkır-, -ēhır-; §3839) v.t. *(a) be engaged in cutting well,* etc. (s.v. sɛrɛgır-mér-); *(b) continually (habitually) cut well,* etc.
    ɛŋ⌣kánd⌣ékkɛn⌣ āssɛrɛgımérın⌢ *now your knife is cutting well;* ɛŋ⌣kánd⌣ékkɛnɛ⌣sɛrɛgırámmérın⌢ (§5634).

áss(ı)⌣ n. *small branch, twig, shoot;* with coll. sg. (§4696c) [<*áns(ı)⌣ (§680) < ⌣án- *become, grow* + -s dim., so *little growth* §2319].

obj. -sɪgᴗ.
pl. -sɪnč(ɪ)ᴗ.
béntɪnᴗáss(ɪ)ᴗ *shoot(s) of date-palm.*

ās-sɪgíddɪ- (āk-sɪ-, āg-sɪ- §679; §§3831ff.) v.i. (*a*) *be engaged in praying, in saying one's prayers*; (*b*) *continually* (*habitually*) *pray, etc.*

ās-síkkɪ- (āk-sík-, āg-sík- §679; §3838) v.t. (*a*) *be engaged in asking, etc.* (s.v. síkk(ɪ)); (*b*) *continually* (*habitually*) *ask, etc.*

ās-síllɪ- (āk-síl-, āg-síl- §679; §§3831ff.) v.t. (*a*) *be engaged in winnowing, etc.* (s.v. síll(ɪ)); (*b*) *continually* (*habitually*) *winnow, etc.*

ās-sínnɛgɪr- (āk-sín-, āg-sín- §679; N. -ɛkɪr-, -ɛhɪr; §3838) v.t. (*a*) *be engaged in vexing, etc.* (s.v. sínnɛg-ɪr); (*b*) *continually* (*habitually*) *vex, etc.*

ássŏdᴗ *my sister's child* s.v. -ssŏdᴗ.

ās-sóg- (āk-sóg-, āg-sóg- §679; §§3831ff.) v.t. (*a*) *be engaged in accompanying, etc.* (s.v. sóg); (*b*) *continually* (*habitually*) *accompany, etc.*

ās-sōkɛrɛ́- (āk-sō-, āg-sō- §679; §3838) v.t. (*a*) *be engaged in registering* (*at post-office*); (*b*) *continually* (*habitually*) *register.*

ās-sókkɛ- (āk-sók-, āg-sók- §679; §3838) v.t. (*a*) *be engaged in taking up, etc.* (s.v. sókkɛ); (*b*) *continually* (*habitually*) *take up, etc.*

X. mohámmɛ́tᴗtaᴗíndo!, mohámmɛsᴗsɛ́? (-tᴗt- < -dᴗt- §706, -sᴗs- < -dᴗs- §677) *Muḥámmad, come here!—where is Muḥámmad?,* ᴗtaᴗ *enclitic* (§§1557, 1742).

Y. ğŭbū̄: téŋᴗkádɛgᴗassókkɛ̀̃ *he's coming: he's getting* (lit. *picking up*) *his clothes* (§4696d).

ās-sóllɪgɪr- (āk-sól-, āg-sól- §679; N. -ɪkɪr-, -ɪhɪr-; §3838) v.t. (*a*) *be engaged in suspending, etc.* (s.v. sóllɪg-ɪr); (*b*) *continually* (*habitually*) *suspend, etc.*

ās-sŏ́wwɪ- (āk-sŏw-, āg-sŏw- §679; §§3831ff.) v.i. (*a*) *be* (*in process of*) *getting dry, etc.* (s.v. sŏ́ww(ɪ)); (*b*) *continually* (*habitually*) *get dry, etc.*

ɛ́ssᴗassŏ́wwɪnˆ *the water is* (*keeps on*) *drying up.*

ās-sŏwwíddɪ- (āk-sŏw-, āg-sŏw-§679; -wúd- §1201; §3838) v.t.(*a*) *be engaged in drying, etc.* (s.v. sŏww-ídd(ɪ)); (*b*) *continually* (*habitually*) *dry, etc.*

ās-súd- (āk-súd-, āg-súd- §679; §§3831ff.) v.t. (*a*) *be engaged in missing, etc.* (s.v. súd); (*b*) *continually* (*habitually*) *miss, etc.*

ās-súg- (āk-súg-, āg-súg- §679; §§3831ff.) v.t. (*a*) *be engaged in baking, etc.* (s.v. súg); (*b*) *continually* (*habitually*) *bake, etc.*

ɛ́nᴗsúkkɪᴗdɛ́wɪrᴗassúgɪnˆ *the woman is baking* (*habitually bakes*) *the cake* (s.v. súgᴗ) *on the bake-stone.*

ās-súkkɪ- (āk-súk-, āg-súk- §679; §3838) v.t. (*a*) *be engaged in chewing* (*tobacco*); (*b*) *continually* (*habitually*) *chew.*

tumbákᴗassúkkɪnˆ (*a*) *he is chewing tobacco*; (*b*) *he chews tobacco.*

ās-súndɛ- (āk-sún-, āg-sún- §679; -súnnɛ-; §3838) v.t. (*a*) *be engaged in sniffing, etc.* (s.v. súndɛ); (*b*) *continually* (*habitually*) *sniff, etc.*

ğŏ́wwɪnᴗígkᴗassúndɛranˆ *they are* (*keep on*) *sniffing the blossoms* (§4696c) *of the tree*(*s* §4696b).

ās-sunúkkɪ- (āk-su-, āg-su- §679; §3838) v.t. (*a*) *be engaged in pinching*; (*b*) *continually* (*habitually*) *pinch.*

ās-sursúkkɪ- (āk-sur-, āg-sur- §679; §3838) v.i. (*a*) *be* (*in process of*) *stumbling, etc.* (s.v. sursúkk(ɪ)); (*b*) *continually* (*habitually*) *stumble, etc.*

ās-sursúkkɪgɪr- (N. āk-sur-; āg-sur- §679; N. -ɪkɪr-, -ɪhɪr- §3838) v.t. caus. (*a*) *be causing or allowing to stumble, etc.*; (*b*) *continually cause or allow to stumble, etc.*

ās-sursurúkkɪ- (N. āk-sur-; āg-sur-) v.i.= ās-sursúkkɪ-.

ās-sursurúkkɪgɪr- (N. āk-sur-; āg-sur-; N. -ɪkɪr-, -ɪhɪr-) v.t. caus.=ās-sursúkkɪgɪr-.

ásur n. *(late) afternoon* (*about 3 p.m. to 5 p.m.*) [< عَصْر *id.* §1363].

obj. asúrk(ɪ)ᴗ.

asúrro (ásurroᴗ §1562; s.v. -rᴗ) *in the* (*late*) *afternoon.*

asúrroᴗnókkoranˆ *they went in the* (*late*) *afternoon.*

asúrrᴗíndᴗɛgóˆ (*s*)*he* (*it*) *was here late in the afternoon.*

asúrróˆ (§§1989, 5858) *it is in the* (*late*) *afternoon.*

áša n. *dinner* [< عَشَاء *id.*].

obj. ášagᴗ, -giˆ.

pl. ašánč(ɪ)ᴗ.

ášarᴗágranˆ *they are at dinner.*

ášāı n. *place, region* [cp. Sudan Ar. أَشْوْ].

ašŭu *country* (*as opposed to town*); see K. *éšei Land* in *SNK*, 2, 1008[5]; *RSN*, §129 s.v. *Išey*; cp. Kh. *šéwa Ebene* RCh. §74, Ka. *šǎwō Erde, Land RK*, s.v., Qw. *sawā Feld, Landschaft, Bezirk RQ*, s.v.; §2191].

obj. ašāıgᴗ, -giˆ.

pl. ášāıᴗ, ášajıᴗ.

āıᴗínᴗašāıgᴗuñúmmununˆ *I don't know this place.*

— used like gúᴗ (q.v.), دُنْيَه and Sudan Ar.

وَطَاء:

ášāıᴗgúgrɪnˆ *the weather is hot* حَمَّى, Sudan Ar. حَارَّة (وَطَاء).

ášāıᴗdúgbūnˆ *it* (*the weather*) *is misty.*

ášāıᴗorōfóskóˆ *it* (*the weather*) *has turned cold.*

ášāıᴗurúmmᴗáŋkonˆ and ášāıᴗurúmmaŋkonˆ (§5564) *it* (i.e. *the day*) (*has*) *got dark* (Sudan Ar. بَقَتِ الْوَطَاء ظُلْمَة).

ášāıᴗúgᴗɛ́ŋgedᴗárgɪᴗbusursukkígɪrɪnˆ *because it's dark it'll make us stumble* (cp. HESA s.v. *when*).

mánᴗugrɛ́skᴗášāıᴗníččᴗɛgónˆ *on that day it was cloudy*; mánᴗugrɛ́skᴗ an adv.-cpx. (§6050).

ášāıᴗsɛ́lunˆ *there is a stink.*

aškǎnᴗ (-ǎnᴗ) n. *a village on the right bank of the Nile opposite Kabrɪnárti, near Abufátna, about ten miles below Argo.*

obj. -áŋg(ɪ)ᴗ, -giˆ.

ašk(ɪ)ᴗ (N. ášš(ɪ)ᴗ) n. *large lizard, monitor*, Varanus niloticus.

obj. -kɪgᴗ.

pl. -kɪnč(ɪ)ᴗ.

ášma (uncommon §986) n. *fibre* (*from bark*) *of date-palm*=hášmaᴗ.

ašrāfnárt(ɪ)ᴗ (-tiˆ) n. *Lebab* (on map), *an island about 12 miles south of Urdi* [*Island of the* أَشْرَاف].

obj. -tɪgᴗ.

ašraŋkǎñ n. *bean*=ašráŋkɛᴗ; with coll. sg. (§4696b) [-ñᴗ *dim.* §2304].

obj. -káñgᴗ, -giˆ.

pl. -káñɪᴗ.

ašráŋkɛᴗ (ášraŋkɛᴗ §1573) *bean*, Phaseolus mungo, Linn. (*BSP*, 149); with coll. sg. (§4696b) [? cp. Copt. ⲁⲣϣⲓⲛ *Linse* (*SKG*, p. 65*), ⲁⲛϣⲓⲣⲓ *species phaseoli viridis* (*PLC*); §2389].

obj. -kɛgᴗ, -giˆ.

āš-šākɪlɛ́- (āk-šā-, āg-šā- §697; §3838) v.i. and t. (*a*) *be engaged in quarrelling* (*with*); (*b*) *continually* (*habitually*) *quarrel* (*with*).

āš-šákkɪ- (āk-šák-, āg-šák- §697; §§3831ff.) v.t. (*a*) *be engaged in shaking* (*milk*) *in a skin, etc.* (s.v. šákk(ɪ)); (*b*) *continually* (*habitually*) *shake in a skin, etc.*

áššāu n. *Ashau* (on map), *a village on the left bank of the Nile about six miles below Kérma, just in Máḥas.*

obj. aššáugᴗ.

áššaunᴗárt(ɪ)ᴗ *the island of Ashau.*

āš-šɛ́g- (āk-šɛ́g-, āg-šɛ́g- §697; §§3831ff.) v.t. (*a*) *be engaged in implanting, etc.* (s.v. šɛ́g); (*b*) *continually* (*habitually*) *implant, etc.*

béntɪnᴗšɛ́tlɪgᴗaššɛ́g'ranˆ *they are planting* (*habitually plant*) *out the palm-shoots.*

āš-šɛ́gɪg- (āk-šɛ́-, āg-šɛ́- §697; §3838) v.t. (*a*) *be engaged in implanting* (*etc.*) *in several places, etc.* (s.v. šɛ́gɪg); (*b*) *continually* (*habitually*) *implant in several places, etc.*

āš-šɛkkɛ́- (āk-šɛk-, āg-šɛk- §697; §§3831ff.) v.i. and t. (*a*) *be engaged in complaining* (*of*), *etc.* (s.v. šɛkkɛ́); (*b*) *continually* (*habitually*) *complain* (*of*), *etc.*

ɛrᴗmíŋᴗaššɛkkɛ́ñ? (§5601) and ɛr-ām-míŋɪ-šɛkkɛ́n? *what are you* (*always*) *complaining of?*

írᴗnígᴗaššɛkkɛ́ru?, írᴗāg-nɪš-šɛkkɛ́ru? and írᴗännɪššɛkkɛ́ru? *whom are you* (*pl.*) (*always*) *complaining about?*

tírᴗmɛ́nᴗaššɛkkɛ́ran?, tírᴗāg-mɛn-šɛkkɛ́ran? and tírᴗämmɛššɛkkɛ́ran? (§5605) *why are they* (*continually*) *complaining?*

āš-šɛklɛ́- (āk-šɛk-, āg-šɛk- §697; §3838) v.i. and t.=āš-šākɪlɛ́-.

āš-šɛ́log- (N.; āk-šɛ́-, āg-šɛ́- §697; §§3831ff.) v.t. and i.=āš-šúlug-.

āš-šɛŋkɪlɛ́- (āk-šɛŋ-, āg-šɛŋ- §697; -šǎŋ-; §3838) v.t. (*a*) *be engaged in hooking, etc.* (s.v. šɛŋkɪlɛ́); (*b*) *continually* (*habitually*) *hook, etc.*

āš-šɛrkɛ́- (āk-šɛr-, āg-šɛr- §697; §3838) v.t. (*a*) *be engaged in sharing, etc.* (s.v. šɛrkɛ́); (*b*) *continually* (*habitually*) *share, etc.*

ášš(ɪ)ᴗ (N.)=ášk(ɪ)ᴗ Varanus niloticus.

āš-šír- (āk-šír-, āg-šír- §697; §§3831ff.) v.t. (*a*) *be engaged in plaiting, etc.* (s.v. šír); (*b*) *continually* (*habitually*) *plait, etc.*

āš-šog(o)lɛ́- — āt-tó-

hawwǎd‿ğakárk‿āššíriŋ⌢ *the fisherman is hauling the hook in.*
āš-šog(o)lɛ́- (āk-šo-, āg-šo-) v.i. = āš-šuglɛ́-.
āš-šókkɪ- (āk-šók-, āg-šók- §697; §§3831ff.) v.t. (*a*) *be engaged in pounding, etc.* (s.v. šókk(ɪ)); (*b*) *continually* (*habitually*) *pound, etc.*
āš-sólog- (āk-šó-, āg-šó-) v.t. and i. *be engaged in* (*in process of*) *shaking, etc.* = āš-šúlug-.
āš-šóndɪ- (āk-šón-, āg-šón- §697; §§3831ff.) v.t. (*a*) *be engaged in shaking*; (*b*) *continually* (*habitually*) *shake.*
āš-šórogɪr- (āk-šó-, āg-šó- §697; N. -okɪr-, -ohɪr-; §3838) v.t. (*a*) *be engaged in lightening, etc.* (s.v. šórog-ɪr); (*b*) *continually* (*habitually*) *lighten, etc.*
āš-šúg- (āk-šúg-, āg-súg- §697; §§3831ff.) v.t. (*a*) *be engaged in driving, etc.* (s.v. šúg); (*b*) *continually* (*habitually*) *drive, etc.*
āš-šuglɛ́- (āk-šúg-, āg-šug- §697; -šoglɛ́-, -šogolɛ́-; §3838) v.i. (*a*) *be engaged in working, etc.* (s.v. šuglɛ́, *be at work*); (*b*) *continually* (*habitually*) *work, etc.*
āš-šúgum- (āk-šú-, āg-šú- §697; §§3831ff.) v.t. (*a*) *be engaged in shaking, etc.* (s.v. šúgum); (*b*) *continually* (*habitually*) *shake, etc.*
āš-šúgur- (āk-šú-, āg-šú- §697; §§3831ff.) v.i. (*a*) *be engaged in* (*in process of*) *descending*; (*b*) *continually* (*habitually*) *descend.*
āš-šugúddɪ- (āk-šu-, āg-šu- §697; §3838) caus. (*a*) *be engaged in causing or allowing to descend, etc.* (s.v. šugúdd(ɪ)); (*b*) *continually* (*habitually*) *cause or allow to descend, etc.*
āš-šúkɪ- (N.; āk-šú-, āg-šú-) v.t. = āššúkkɪ-.
āš-šúkkɪ- (āk-šúk-, āg-šúk- §697; §3838) v.t. (*a*) *be engaged in washing*; (*b*) *continually* (*habitually*) *wash.*
āš-šúlug- (āk-šú-, āg-šú- §697; -šólog-; N. -šélog-; §§3831ff.) v.t. and i. (*a*) *be engaged in* (*in process of*) *shaking, etc.* (s.v. šúlug); (*b*) *continually* (*habitually*) *shake, etc.*
átar n. *track, footprint, spoor*; with coll. sg. (§4696d) [< أَثَر id.].
obj. atárk(ɪ)‿, -kɪ⌢.
pl. átarɪ‿.
íŋ‿átar‿tɪnčíndɪkɪrɪŋ⌢ *this track is* (*these tracks are*) *like those of cattle.*
átbara‿ (átbára‿ §1532) n. *the Atbara,* Ἀσταβόρας, *the northernmost tributary of the Nile* [át-<*átt(a)-<*ást(a)-*water* (=*ést(ɪ)‿ s.v. éss(ɪ)‿), as in Ἀτάπους *White Nile,* Ἀστασόβας *Blue Nile* RNW, s.v. éssi, RSN, §129].
obj. -rag‿.
átɪñ v.i. *sneeze* (= átɪš) [onom.].
ind. pres. âɪ‿atíñrɪ⌢, ɛr‿átɪñrɪ⌢ (-ñí⌢, -ñí⌢); fut. âɪ‿batíñrɪ⌢; perf. âɪ‿atíñkorɪ⌢.
def. perf. âɪ‿atɪñóskorɪ⌢.
atɪñíŋ-ɪr (N. -ŋkɪr; §3688) v.t. caus. *cause or allow to sneeze.*
íñ‿âɪg‿atɪñíŋgɪrɪrɪŋ⌢ *this makes me sneeze.*
átɪš v.i. *sneeze* (= átɪñ) [onom., cp. عَطس id.].
ind. pres. âɪ‿atíšrɪ⌢, ɛr‿átɪšrɪ⌢ (-ší⌢, -ší⌢); fut. âɪ‿batíšrɪ⌢; perf. âɪ‿atíškorɪ⌢.

atɪšíŋ-ɪr (N. -ŋkɪr; §3688) v.t. caus. *cause or allow to sneeze.*
íŋ‿árg‿atɪšíŋgɪrɪrɪŋ⌢ *this makes* (*each of*) *us sneeze.*
atšɛ́ v.i. *get thirsty* [< Sudan Ar. عَطش n. *thirst* (§1258)+-ɛ́ §3618].
ind. pres. âɪ‿atšɛ́rɪ⌢; perf. âɪ‿atšɛ́gorɪ⌢ (N. -ɛ́ko-, -ɛ́ho-).
atšɛ́rar‿ (-rár‿; §§2200ff.) and
atšɛ́ríd‿ (§§2256ff.) n. *getting thirsty.*
atšɛ́-bŭ- (§3931α) v.i. stat. *be in a thirsty state or condition.*
ind. pres. âɪ‿atšɛ́bŭrɪ⌢.
atšɛ́g-ɪr (N. -ɛ́kɪr, -ɛ́hɪr; §3681) (*a*) v.t. caus. *cause or allow to get thirsty*; (*b*) v.t. *render thirsty.*
íñ‿âɪg‿atšɛ́gɪrɪrɪŋ⌢ *this makes me thirsty.*
áttä *bring* s.v. ár *seize.*
āt-tá- (āk-tá-, āg-tá- §708; §§3831ff.) v.i. (*a*) *be engaged in coming*; (*b*) *continually* (*habitually*) *come.*
āt-tábbɛ- (āk-táb-, āg-táb- §708; §3838) v.t. (*a*) *be engaged in moistening, etc.* (s.v. tábbɛ); (*b*) *continually* (*habitually*) *moisten, etc.*
āt-tabhɛ́- (āk-tab-, āg-tab- §708; -bɛ́-; §3838) v.t. (*a*) *be engaged in cooking*; (*b*) *continually* (*habitually*) *cook.*
āt-tágɪr- (āk-tá-, āg-tá- §708; §3838) v.t. (*a*) *be engaged in covering, etc.* (s.v. tág-ɪr); (*b*) *continually* (*habitually*) *cover, etc.*
āt-taggɪsɛ́- (āk-tag-, āg-tag- §708; §3838) v.t. (*a*) *be engaged in depreciating*; (*b*) *continually* (*habitually*) *depreciate.*
attál‿ n. *porter, carrier* [< عَتّال id.].
obj. -álg(ɪ)‿, -gɪ⌢.
pl. -álɪ‿.
āt-talabɛ́- (āk-ta-, āg-ta- §708; -tálabɛ́- §3838) v.t. (*a*) *be engaged in demanding*; (*b*) *continually* (*habitually*) *demand.*
āt-támug‿ (āk-tá-, āg-tá- §708; §§3831ff.) v.i. (*a*) *be engaged in fighting, etc.* (s.v. támug); (*b*) *continually* (*habitually*) *fight, etc.*
āt-táncɛ- (āk-tán-, āg-tán- §708; §3838) v.t. (*a*) *be engaged in tasting*; (*b*) *continually* (*habitually*) *taste.*
āt-táŋgɪr- (āk-táŋ-, āg-táŋ- §708; §3838) v.t. caus. (*a*) *be engaged in causing or allowing to come, in sending* (s.v. táŋg-ɪr s.v. tá); (*b*) *continually* (*habitually*) *cause or allow to come, continually* (*habitually*) *send.*
ár‿íŋkɪrɪg‿āttáŋgɪrmun⌢ (§947) *we are not letting* (*never let*) *this kind come;* ‿íŋkɪrɪg‿ §1532.
āt-tɛbɛ́- (āk-tɛ-, āg-tɛ- §708; §3838) v.t. (*a*) *be engaged in seeking, etc.* (s.v. tɛbɛ́); (*b*) *continually* (*habitually*) *seek, etc.*
āt-tɛlɛ́wɛ- (āk-tɛ-, āg-tɛ- §708; §3838) v.i. (*a*) *be in process of melting, etc.* (s.v. tɛlɛ́wɛ); (*b*) *continually* (*habitually*) *melt, etc.*
āt-tɛlɛ́wɛgɪr- (āk-tɛ-, āg-tɛ- §708; N. -ɛkɪr; -ɛhɪr-; §3838) v.t. (*a*) *be engaged in melting, etc.* (s.v. tɛlɛ́wɛ-ɪr); (*b*) *continually* (*habitually*) *melt, etc.*
āt-tɛmmɛ́- (āk-tɛm-, āg-tɛm- §708; §3838) v.t. (*a*) *be engaged in completing, etc.* (s.v. tɛmmɛ́); (*b*) *continually* (*habitually*) *complete, etc.*

āt-tɛ́r- (āk-tɛ́r-, āg-tɛ́r- §708; §§3831ff.) v.t. (*a*) *be engaged in sowing, etc.* (s.v. tɛ́r); (*b*) *continually* (*habitually*) *sow, etc.*
átt(ɪ)‿ *wheel raising water* s.v. áb.
átt(ɪ) v.t. *beat up* (*liquid dough*) *with the hand* (*preparatory to kneading* (*ğág*) *that is done when it becomes viscous*).
ind. pres. âɪ‿áttɪrɪ⌢; fut. âɪ‿báttɪrɪ⌢; perf. âɪ‿áttɪgorɪ⌢ (N. -ɪko-, -ɪho-).
ɛ̂ŋ‿kanísseg‿áttɪŋ⌢ *the woman beats up the* (*liquid*) *dough with her hand.*
áttar‿ (-tár‿; §§2200ff.) and
áttíd‿ (§§2256ff.) n. *beating up with the hand.*
átt-an (§§3890ff.) v.t. *tell to beat up, etc., let beat up, etc.*
áttɪ-bŭ- (§3931β) v.i. stat. *be in a beaten up state or condition.*
áttɪ-katt(ɪ)- (N. -ɪha-; §4093) v.p. *be beaten up, etc.*
kaníss‿áttɪkattɪŋ⌢ *the dough is beaten up.*
attɪlɛ́ v.t. *hinder, impede, detain, delay* [< imperat. or imperf. stem of عَطّل id. + -ɛ́ §3638].
ind. pres. âɪ‿attɪlɛ́rɪ⌢; fut. âɪ‿battɪlɛ́rɪ⌢; perf. attɪlɛ́gorɪ⌢ (N. -ɛ́ko-, -ɛ́ho-).
imperat. attɪlɛ́!
N. âɪg‿attɪlɛ́horan⌢ *they* (*have*) *hindered* (*delayed*) *me.*
attɪlɛ́rar‿ (-rár‿; §§2200ff.) and
attɪlɛ́ríd‿ (§§2256ff.) n. *hindering, etc.*
attɪlɛ́r-an (§§3890, 3899) v.t. *tell to hinder, etc., let hinder, etc.*
attɪlɛ́-bŭ- (§3931β) v.i. stat. *be in a hindered* (*etc.*) *state or condition.*
gátɪr‿attɪlɛ́bŭn⌢ *the train is delayed* (*late*).
áttɪl-katt(ɪ)- (§4100) v.p. *be hindered, etc.*
N. attɪlkáttɪkorɪ⌢ *I was* (*have been*) *hindered* (*delayed*).
ɛr‿mɛ́n‿attɪlkáttɪgō? *why were you* (*have you been*) *delayed* (*why were* (*are*) *you late*)?
gátɪr‿attɪlkáttɪgō⌢ *the train was* (*has been*) *delayed.*
ğéllɪ‿báttɪlkattɪŋ⌢ *the work will be hindered.*
attɪl-káttɪ-bŭ- (§4105) v.i. stat. *be in a hindered* (*etc.*) *state or condition.*
gátɪr‿attɪlkáttɪbūn⌢ *the train is late.*
āt-tíllɛ- (āk-tíl-, āg-tíl- §708; §3838) v.i. (*a*) *be* (*in process of*) *sweating*; (*b*) *continually* (*habitually*) *sweat.*
āt-tínan- (āk-tí-, āg-tí- §708; §3839) v.i. (*a*) *be* (*in process of*) *becoming* (*part of*) *the left bank* (s.v. tín-an-); (*b*) *continually become* (*part of*) *the left bank.*
 árt‿āttínanɪn⌢ *the island is* (*keeps on*) *becoming part of the left bank* (*of the Nile*).
āt-tɪŋgáran- (āk-tɪŋ-, āg-tɪŋ-) v.i. = āttínan-.
‿**áttɪr**‿ postp. *beside, etc.* <‿ábtɪr‿ s.v. áb.
āt-tír- (āk-tír-, āg-tír- §708; §3838) v.t. (*a*) *be engaged in giving* (*not to the speaker*); (*b*) *continually* (*habitually*) *give* (*etc.*).
āt-tɪššɛ́- (āk-tɪš-, āg-tɪš- §708) v.i. *be straying, etc.* = āt-tuššɛ́-.
āt-tó- (āk-tó-, āg-tó- §708; §§3831ff.) v.i. (*a*) *be engaged in entering*; (*b*) *continually* (*habitually*) *enter.*

āt-tóbbɛ- (āk-tób-, āg-tób- §708; §3838) v.t. (a) be engaged in patting, etc. (s.v. tóbbɛ); (b) continually (habitually) pat, etc.

āt-tóččɛ- (āk-tóč-, āg-tóč- §708; §3838) v.i. (a) be in process of cracking (making sudden sharp noises); (b) continually crack.

āt-tóg- (āk-tóg-, āg-tóg- §708; §§3831 ff.) v.t. (a) be engaged in heating, etc. (s.v. tóg); (b) continually (habitually) heat, etc.
 álɪ‿téŋ‿kórk‿ígɪr‿āttógɪn⁀ ɛáli is warming (continually warms) his wound at the fire.

āt-tóg- (āk-tóg-, āg-tóg- §708; §§3831 ff.) v.t. (a) be engaged in striking, etc. (s.v. tóg); (b) continually (habitually) strike, etc.
 ɛm‿bɪtāŋg‿āttógɪn⁀ (§5601) and ɛn‿abbɪtāŋgɪtógɪn⁀ the woman is (keeps on) beating the child.

āt-tókkɪ- (āk-tók-, āg-tók- §708; §§3831 ff.) v.i. (a) be (in process of) limping; (b) continually (habitually) limp.

āt-tókkɪgɪr- (āk-tók-, āg-tók- §708; N. -ɪkɪr-, -ɪhɪr-; §3838) v.t. (a) be (engaged in) laming, etc. (s.v. tókkɪg-ɪr); (b) continually (habitually) lame, etc.

āt-tóllɛ- (āk-tól-, āg-tól- §708; §3838) v.t. (a) be engaged in pulling, etc. (s.v. tóllɛ); (b) continually (habitually) pull, etc.

āt-tómbɪ- (āk-tóm-, āg-tóm- §708; §§3831 ff.) v.t. and i. (a) be engaged in (in process of) breaking, etc. (s.v. tómb(ɪ)); (b) continually (habitually) break, etc.

āt-tóskɪ- (āk-tós-, āg-tós- §708; §§3831 ff.) v.i. (a) be (engaged in) coughing; (b) continually (habitually) cough.

āt-túb- (āk-túb, āg-túb- §708; §§3831 ff.) v.t. (a) be engaged in sweeping, etc. (s.v. túb); (b) continually (habitually) sweep, etc.

āt-túbbɪ- (āk-túb-, āg-túb-) v.i. be (in process of) lying down, etc. = āt-túrbɪ-.

āt-túffɪ- (āk-túf-, āg-túf- §708; §§3831 ff.) v.t. (a) be engaged in spitting, etc. (s.v. túff(ɪ)); (b) continually (habitually) spit, etc.

āt-túkkɪ- (āk-túk-, āg-túk- §708; §§3831 ff.) v.t. (a) be engaged in pounding, etc. (s.v. túkk(ɪ)); (b) continually (habitually) pound, etc.

āt-túlɛ- (āk-tú-, āg-tú- §708; §3838) v.i. (a) be engaged in (in process of) stooping, etc. (s.v. túlɛ); (b) continually (habitually) stoop, etc.

āt-tulúnčɪ- (āk-tu-, āg-tu- §708; §3838) v.i. (a) be shining, etc. (s.v. tulúnč(ɪ)); (b) continually shine, etc.

āt-túŋgɪ- (āk-túŋ-, āg-túŋ- §708; §§3831 ff.) v.t. (a) be engaged in carding, etc. (s.v. túŋg(ɪ)); (b) continually (habitually) card, etc.

āt-túr- (āk-túr-, āg-túr- §708; §§3831 ff.) v.t. (a) be engaged in driving away, etc. (s.v. túr); (b) continually (habitually) drive away, etc.

āt-túrbɪ- (āk-túr-, āg-túr- §708; -túbbɪ-; §3838) v.i. (a) be in process of lying down, engaged in resting, etc. (s.v. túrb(ɪ)); (b) continually (habitually) lie down, etc.

āt-tús- (āk-tús-, āg-tús- §708; §§3831 ff.) v.t. (a) be engaged in cursing; (b) continually (habitually) curse.

āt-tuššɛ́- (āk-tuš-, āg-tuš- §708; -tɪššɛ́-; §3838) v.i. (a) be (in process of) straying, etc. (s.v. tuššɛ́); (b) continually (habitually) stray, etc.

-áū‿ n. grandmother [RSN, §129; cp. GBH, s.v. אָב, LSF, s.v. āvus].
 obj. -áūg‿, -áūgɪ⁀.
 pl. -awɪ‿, -áwɪ‿.
 Always with a form of the possessive personal pronoun (§2622) prefixed, thus:
 ánnaū‿ my grandmother.
 ínnaū‿ your grandmother.
 tínnaū‿ his (her) grandmother.
 antínnaū‿ our grandmother.
 ɪntínnaū‿ your (pl.) grandmother.
 tɪntínnaū‿ their grandmother.
 tínnáūn‿nálkori⁀ (-n‿n- < -g‿n- §625) I saw (have seen) his (her) grandmother.
 tɪnnáwɪn‿nálkori⁀ I saw (have seen) his (her) grandmothers.

áu, áw, áu (a) v.t. do, perform; (b) v.t. make, construct, form; (c) v.i. work, act, behave; (d) v.t. cook [cp. ON. ᚨᛦ, ᚨᛦᛟᛦ id. GNT, s.v.; RSN, §129].
 ind. pres. āɪ‿áuri⁀ (áwʲri⁀), ɛr‿áwin⁀ (áuɪn‿; áwí⁀, áwí⁀ §939); fut. āɪ‿bāuri⁀; perf. āɪ‿áukori⁀ (N. áuho-).
 imperat. áu!, pl. áuwɛ! (áuwɛ́!).
 sub. past āɪ‿áusɪ‿ (-su‿).
 cond. pres. āɪ-on‿áukɪrɪ‿.
 part. pres. áwɪl‿ (ául‿) (one) that does, etc., doer, etc., doing, etc.; obj. āwílg(ɪ)‿ (áwɪlg(ɪ)‿ §1522).
 part. past. áwɛl‿ (one) that did, etc., doer, etc., doing, etc.; obj. āwélg(ɪ)‿ (áwelg(ɪ)‿).
 interr. ind. pres. āɪ‿áuriá⁀, ɛr‿áuná?
 def. pres. āɪ‿āwósri⁀ (áuós-); perf. āɪ‿āwóskori⁀ (áuós-); imperat. sg. áuó!
 tókkon‿ɪŋk‿áumɛn⁀ (a) don't do (make, etc.) it like that; (b) don't behave like that.
 míŋg‿áuri? what do I (shall I, am I to §5469) do? (asking for instructions).
 mín‿áuri! what am I to do! (expressing perplexity), lit. how (mínɛ‿ §1122) shall I act?
 bɪ-míŋg‿áuru? what shall we do? (asking for information or instructions).
 bɪ-mín‿áuru! what shall we do! (expressing perplexity).
 súlɛgɛm‿míŋg‿áuran? (-m‿m- < -d‿m- §600) what do they do with the pot?
 ɛr‿dúŋgɪm‿mín‿áukon⁀ (-m‿m- < -g‿m- §601) what have you done with (about) the money?
 tókkon‿tékkɛg‿áumɛn! (a) don't do it in that way!; (b) don't behave like that!
 tókkon‿tékkɛg‿áumɛwwɛ́! (a) don't (pl.) do it in that way!; (b) don't (pl.) behave like that!
 súttɛ‿áukan‿sérɛn⁀ (§5449) it's (a) good (thing) to do it quickly.
 naūútkɛd‿áuran⁀ they do it (make it, work) with an adze.
 sandúg-gɛg‿áukon⁀ (-g-g- < -g-w- §547) he (has) made a chest.
 tɛr‿áukon⁀ (s)he (has) made (the) rope = írɪg‿írkon⁀.
 ɛnčɪ‿kálg‿áw'ran⁀ the women make bread (prepare food).
 ɛŋ‿kúsug‿āwóskon⁀ the woman has cooked the meat.

áwar‿ (áwar‿; §§2200 ff.) and

áwíd‿ (§§2256 ff.) n. doing, deed, performance, action; making, construction, formation; working, behaviour; cooking.

áw-an (§§3890 ff.) v.t. tell to do, etc., let do, etc.
 álɪg‿áwan⁀ tell ɛáli to do (etc.) it (let ɛáli do it).
 gáhwa‿toddɛ́g‿áwan⁀ tell him (her) to make a little coffee.
 ɛ́ssɪ‿ugrís‿sútt‿áwan⁀ (-s‿s- < -g‿s- §678) tell him (her) to make the (some) hot water quickly.

áu-bǔ- (§3931 β) v.i. stat. be in a done (etc.) state or condition.
 kús‿áubúná? is the meat done (fully cooked)?

áu-děn (§§3996–7) v.t. do (etc.) to (the speaker), do (etc.) for (the speaker).
 ind. pres. ɛr‿áudɛnɪn⁀ (áudɛnɪn‿; -ní⁀, -ní⁀); perf. ɛr‿áudɛŋkon⁀ (áudɛŋkon‿; -kǒ⁀, -kó⁀).
 imperat. áudɛn! (-děʼ!, -děʼ!, -děʼ!, -děʼ! §945).
 subj. past ɛr‿áudɛnsɪn‿ (áudɛnsɪn‿; -sun‿).
 ɪŋg‿áug‿áuděʼ⁀ do (etc.) this for me.
 tɛr‿áik‿kɪlkílg‿áuděŋkon⁀ (s)he (it) (has) tickled me.

áur-ɛg-ág- (§§4071 ff.) v.t. = āwedól-.

áw-ɛ-dól- (áwᵒdól- §1178; §4022) and

áur-ɛ-dól- (-ᵒdól-; §4027) v.t. be about to do, etc.

áur-ɛ-ğǔ-bǔ- (§4069) v.t. stat. be on one's way (coming) to do, etc.

áw-ɛ-má- (§4036) and

áur-ɛ-má- (§4041) v.t. become unable to do, etc.

áur-ɛ-nóg- (§§4048 ff.) v.t. go to do, etc.

áur-ɛ-nóg-bǔ- (-nóggū- §546; §4058) v.t. stat. be on one's way (going) to do, etc.

áur-ɛ-tá- (§§4060 ff.) v.t. come to do, etc.

áwɛd-ág- (§3877) v.t. be in the situation of having done, etc.

áu-ɛttä (áwɛttä §3855) v.t. bring after making, etc.
 ind. pres. āɪ‿áuɛttāri⁀ (-éttāri⁀); fut. āɪ‿bāuɛttāri⁀ (-éttāri⁀); perf. āɪ‿áuɛttāgori⁀ (-éttāgori⁀).
 bárrād‿kɪññār‿ɛkkɪ‿šāig‿āwéttār‿ɛn⁀ (s)he says you are to make tea in the small tea-pot and bring it, lit. (s)he says to you (‿ɛ́kkɪ‿) 'make tea etc.' s.v. ‿ɛ- say.

áu-kárğɪgɪr (-káğğɪ-; N. -ɪkɪr, -ɪhɪr; §4132) v.t. cook fully, finish cooking.
 ɛŋ‿kúsug‿áukağğɪgɪróskó⁀ the woman has done cooking the meat.

áu-kattɪ- (N. áuha-; §4093) v.p. be done, etc.
 áukattɪgon⁀ it was (has been) done, etc.
 áukattɪgómunun⁀ it was not (has not been) done, etc.
 míndotōn‿áukattɪran? what are they made of?
 ábrɛ‿marɛ́rtōn‿áukattɪn⁀ ábrɛ‿ is made from great millet.

áuos-ɛtta (āwos-; §4203) v.t. bring after making.
 áuosɛttāgori⁀ I (have) made and brought it.

áuos-tá (ăwos-, -ottá §714; §§4180-4; -osgitá, -ozgı-, oggı- §4185) v.t. *come after doing, etc.*
  imperat. áuósta! (-ótta!, -ósgıta!, -ózgı-, -óggı-).
  awottắrı⌢ *I'll* (§5369b) *come as soon as I've done (etc.) it.*
  áuottắgorı⌢ *I came as soon as I had done (etc.) it.*
  ɛr⌣dúŋgım⌣mín⌣awottắgon? (-m⌣m- <-g⌣m- §601) *here you are* (-tắgon⌢), *what have you done about (with) the money?* ⌣mín <⌣mínɛ⌣ (§1122); lit. *having done how about (with) the money have you come?*

áu-tır (§§3997-8) v.t. *do (etc.) to* (other than the speaker), *do (etc.) for* (other than the speaker).
  ind. pres. ăı⌣áutıddı⌢, ɛr⌣áutırın⌢ (-rı⌢, -rí⌢); perf. ăı⌣áutırkorı⌢ (-tıkko- §571; áutír-, -tík-).
  subj. past ăı⌣áutırsı⌣ (-tıssı⌣ §683; -su⌣).
  íŋgı⌣tékk⌣áutır⌢ *do (etc.) this for him (her).*
  íŋgı⌣tírg⌣áutır⌢ *do (etc.) this for them.*
  íŋgı⌣tírg⌣áutırır⌢ *do (etc.) this for (each of) them.*
  ékkı⌣kılkílg⌣áutıkkoná? *did (s)he (it) tickle you?*

áur⌣ (áuᵘr⌣, áuır⌣, áwır⌣ q.v.) n. (a) *wing,* then *of tree;* (b) *branch, twig.*
  With coll. sg. (§4696) [<*áu-ır allow or enable to act (not in use as verb) caus. stem (§3671) of áu act stereotyped as noun what enables one to act, instrument §2148].
  obj. áurk(ı)⌣ (áuᵘrk(ı)⌣, etc.), -ki⌢.
  pl. áurı⌣ (áuᵘrı⌣, etc.).

áuun-togo⌣ n. *armpit;* with coll. sg. (§4696a) [<áuurn-togo *wing's underpart* §2150].
  obj. áuuntogóg⌣, -gi⌢.
  pl. -togónč(ı)⌣.

áurı⌣ *friend* s.v. áwrı⌣.

awadán-da⌣ n. *Dar el Awada* (on map), a district on the eastern side of Argo Island; on the right bank of the Nile, a little to the north, is another district of the same name.
  obj. -dandág⌣.
  awadandắr⌣ (s.v. -r⌣) *at (to) Dar el Awada.*
  awadandắr⌢ (§6007) *(s)he (it) is (they are) in Dar el Awada.*

awắmır⌣ *orders* s.v. ámur⌣.

áw-an *tell to do, etc.* s.v. áu.

ăwéttắ *bring after making, etc.* s.v. áu.

awíččɛ⌣ *palm-leaf fibre* s.v. áwığ.

ăwídd(ı) v.t. *spread, spread out* [extension in -d(ı) of áwır⌣ wing, quasi *make a wing of §2866].
  ind. pres. ăı⌣ăwíddırı⌢; perf. ăı⌣ăwíddıgorı⌢ (N. -iko-, -ıho-).
  imperat. ăwíddı!
  kádɛg⌣awíddıran⌢ *they spread out the (a) cloth.*
  súfran⌣fútag⌣awíddıri⌢ *I('ll* §5369b) *lay the table-cloth.*
  fɛrísk⌣awíddı⌢ *make the (a) bed.*
  N. ar⌣síum⌣mısídır⌣awíddıkoru⌣

(-m⌣m <-g⌣m- §601) *we (have) laid down sand in (i.e. on the floor of) the mosque.*

ăwíddar⌣ (-dắr⌣; §§2200ff.) and

ăwıddíd⌣ (§§2256ff.) n. *spreading, etc.*

ăwídd-an (§§3890ff.) v.t. *tell to spread, etc., let spread, etc.*
  nıbítt⌣awíddan⌢ *let him (her) spread out the (a) mat.*

ăwíddı-bŭ- (§3931β) v.i. stat. *be in a spread (etc.) state or condition.*
  níbıd⌣awíddıbūn⌢ *the (a) mat is (has been) spread.*

ăwíddɛd-ắg- (§3877) v.t. *be in the situation of having spread, etc.*

ăwíddı-kattı- (N. -ıha-; §4093) v.p. *be spread, etc.*

áwığ v.t. (a) *plait;* (b) *form by plaiting* [extension in -ğ (§2884) of áu *do, make*].
  ind. pres. ăı⌣áwığ(¹)rı⌢, ɛr⌣áwığın⌢ (-ğı⌢, -ğí⌢); perf. ăı⌣awíğkorı⌢ (-íčk-; -ğk-, -čk- §323).
  imperat. áwıč!
  ɛnčı⌣wɛrwɛn⌣díltıg⌣áwığran⌢ *(the) women plait one another's hair.*
  ɛnčı⌣níbdıg⌣áwığran⌢ *(the) women make mats.*

awíččɛ n. *palm-leaf fibre* (>Sudan Ar. عويش id. AESA, s.v. palm) [<*awíğtɛ⌣ (§526) <áwığ+-t of n. act.+-ɛ⌣ of n. ess., so *plaiting-material §2229].
  obj. -čɛg⌣.

áwığ-an (§§3890ff.) v.t. *tell to plait, etc., let plait, etc.*

áwığ-kattı- (-íčk-, -ığk-, -íčk- §323; §4093) v.p. *be plaited, etc.*
  X. níbıd⌣míndotōn⌣awíčkattın? *what is the mat (are mats §4647) made of?*
  Y. béntın⌣háurtertōn⌢ *of the leaf of the date-palm.*

áwır⌣ *wing, branch* = áur⌣ q.v.
  obj. awírk(ı)⌣ (áwırk(ı)⌣ §1522), -ki⌢.
  pl. áw(ı)rı⌣.

áwrı⌣ (áurı⌣; §2377) n. *friend* (=tíwrı⌣) [<*án-wrı⌣ §§2349, 2634].
  obj. -rıg⌣.
  pl. áwrınč(ı)⌣ (awrínč(ı)⌣).

āw-wád- (āg-wád- §719; §§3831ff.) v.t. and i. (a) *be engaged in bleeding, etc.* (s.v. wád); (b) *continually (habitually) bleed, etc.*

āw-waddé- (āg-wad- §719; §3838) v.i. (a) *be engaged in performing ablutions (before prayer);* (b) *continually (habitually) perform ablutions (etc.).*

āw-wáddı- (āg-wád- §719; §§3831ff.) v.t. (a) *be engaged in digging, etc.* (s.v. wádd(ı)); (b) *continually (habitually) dig, etc.*
  gabúrk⌣āwwaddıran⌢ *they are digging the (a) grave.*

āw-wádıñ- (āg-wá- §719; §3838) v.t. (a) *be engaged in kicking;* (b) *continually (habitually) kick.*

āw-waffıré- (āg-waf- §719; §3838) v.t. (a) *be engaged in saving, etc.* (s.v. waffıré); (b) *continually (habitually) save, etc.*

āw-wajjé- (āg-waj- §719; §3838) v.i. (a) *be (in process of) recovering, etc.* (s.v. wajjé); (b) *continually (habitually) recover, etc.*

āw-wajjégır- (āg-waj- §719; N. -ékır; -éhır; §3838) v.t. caus. (a) *be engaged in curing, etc.* (s.v. wajjég-ır); (b) *continually (habitually) cure, etc.*

āw-wákkı- (āg-wák- §719; §3838) v.t. (a) *be engaged in omitting, etc.* (s.v. wákk(ı)); (b) *continually (habitually) omit, etc.*

āw-wálag- (āg-wá- §719; §§3831ff.) v.t. (a) *be engaged in waving (about), etc.* (s.v. wálag); (b) *continually (habitually) wave (about), etc.*

āw-wắndı- (āg-wắn- §719; §§3831ff.) v.i. (a) *be (in process of) appearing, etc.* (s.v. wắnd(ı)); (b) *continually (habitually) appear, etc.*

āw-wár- (āg-wár- §719; §§3831ff.) v.i. (a) *be engaged in jumping, etc.* (s.v. wár); (b) *continually (habitually) jump, etc.*

āw-wárığ- (āg-wá- §719; §3838) v.i. (a) *be engaged in jumping about, etc.* (s.v. wárığ); (b) *continually (habitually) jump about, etc.*

āw-wárıs- (āg-wá- §719; §3838) v.t. (a) *be engaged in stretching, etc.* (s.v. wárıs); (b) *continually (habitually) stretch, etc.*

āw-wắs- (āg-wắs- §719; §§3831ff.) v.i. (a) *be in process of boiling, etc.* (s.v. wắs); (b) *continually boil, etc.*
  éss⌣āwwắsın⌢ *the water is (keeps on) boiling.*

āw-wắskıddı- (āg-wắs- §719; §3838) v.t. caus. (a) *be engaged in boiling, etc.* (s.v. wắsk-ıdd(ı)); (b) *continually (habitually) boil, etc.*
  ăı⌣éssıg⌣āwwắskıddırı⌢ *I am (keep on) boiling (the) water.*

āw-wắu- (āg-wắu- §719; §3838) v.t. (a) *be engaged in rowing, etc.* (s.v. wắu); (b) *continually (habitually) row, etc.*

āw-wazné- (āg-waz- §719; §3838) v.t. (a) *be engaged in weighing;* (b) *continually (habitually) weigh.*

⌣**aw-wé** *say, say to, tell* s.v. án say.

āw-wé- (āg-wé- §719; §§3831ff.) v.t. (a) *be engaged in saying, etc.* (s.v. wé); (b) *continually (habitually) say, etc.*
  ăı⌣tókkon⌣nógmɛn⌣ég⌣awwérı⌢ *I keep on saying 'don't go'.*
  ăı⌣tírgı⌣tókkon⌣áumɛnd⌣ég⌣awwéri⌢ *I keep on telling them not to do it* (§6229).
  ăı⌣tírgı⌣tókkon⌣áumɛnw⌣áŋg⌣awwéridd-i⌢ *I keep on telling (each of §5456) them not to do it* (§6229a).
  múrsıg⌣āwwéran⌢ (a) *they are telling a lie (lies* §4696d); (b) *they habitually tell lies.*

āw-wédɛn- (āg-wé- §719; §§3839, 3996-7) v.t. (a) *be engaged in telling, etc.* (the speaker, s.v. wé-dɛn); (b) *continually (habitually) tell, etc.*
  tɛr⌣ăıg⌣awwédɛnın⌢ *(s)he is (keeps on) telling me.*

āw-wétir- (āg-wé- §719; §§3839, 3998-9) v.t. (a) *be engaged in telling, etc.* (other than the speaker, s.v. wé-tır); (b) *continually (habitually) tell, etc.*
  ăı⌣tékk⌣awwétıddı⌢ *I am (keep on) telling him (her).*

āw-wéd- (āg-wéd- §719; §§3831ff.) v.i. (a) *be (in process of) floating;* (b) *continually (habitually) float.*

āw-wéd- (āg-wéd- §719; §§3831ff.) v.t. (a) be engaged in spinning; (b) continually (habitually) spin.
āw-wélɛg- (āg-wé-) = āwwálag-.
āw-wɛllɛ́- (āg-wɛl- §719; §3838) v.t. (a) be engaged in kindling, etc. (s.v. wɛllɛ́); (b) continually (habitually) kindle, etc.
āw-wɛ́rsı- (āg-wɛ́r- §719; -wéssı-; §§3831ff.) v.t. (a) be (engaged in) wanting, etc. (s.v. wɛ́rs(ı)); (b) continually (habitually) want, etc.
āw-wíd- (āg-wíd- §719; §§3831ff.) v.i. (a) be engaged in wandering, etc. (s.v. wíd); (b) continually (habitually) wander, etc.
āw-wíg- (āg-wíg- §719; §§3831ff.) v.i. (a) be engaged in crying, etc. (s.v. wíg); (b) continually (habitually) cry, etc.
āw-wídɛ- (āg-wí- §719; -wıdɛ́-, -wᵘdɛ́-; §3838) v.i. (a) be (in process of) turning, etc. (s.v. wídɛ); (b) continually (habitually) turn, etc.
āw-wídɛgır- (āg-wí-; -wıdɛ́-; -wᵘdɛ́-; N. -ɛkır-, -ɛhır-, -ékır-, -éhır-; §3838) v.t. caus. (a) be engaged in causing or allowing to turn, etc. (s.v. wídɛg-ır); (b) continually (habitually) cause or allow to turn, etc.
āw-wıdɛnóg- (āg-wı-, -wᵘd-; §3839) v.i. (a) be (in process of) going back, etc. (s.v. wıdɛ-nóg); (b) continually (habitually) go back, etc.
āw-wıdɛtā́- (āg-wı-, -wᵘd-; §3839) v.i. (a) be (in process of) coming back, etc. (s.v. wıdɛ-tā́); (b) continually (habitually) come back, etc.
āw-wıllı- (āg-wíl- §719; §§3831ff.) v.t. (a) be engaged in demolishing, etc. (s.v. wíll(ı)); (b) continually demolish, etc.
kā́g⌣awwıllıran⌒ they are taking down the house.
awwırɛ́ (aúwı-, -wᵘrɛ́-) v.t. wound, lacerate, injure [< imperat. or imperf. stem of Eg. and Sudan Ar. عَوَّر id. +-ɛ́ §3639].
ind. pres. aī⌣awwırɛ́rı⌒; perf. aī⌣awwırɛ́-gorı⌒ (N. -ɛ́ko-, -ɛ́ho-).
imperat. awwırɛ́!
awwırɛ́rar (aúwı-, -wᵘrɛ́-, -rár⌣; §§2200ff.)
awwırɛ̆ríd⌣ (aúwı-, -wᵘrɛ-; §§2256ff.) n. wounding, laceration.
awwırɛ̆r-an (aúwı-, -wᵘrɛ́-; §§3890, 3899) v.t. tell to wound, etc., let wound, etc.
awwırɛ́-bŭ- (aúwı-, -wᵘrɛ́-; §3931β) v.i. stat. be in a wounded (etc.) state or condition.
ógıǧ⌣awwᵘrēbúmunun⌒ the man is unwounded.
awwırɛ̆r-ɛg-ág- (aúwı-, -wᵘrɛ̄-; §§4071ff.) v.t. = awwırɛ́rɛdól-.
awwırɛ̆r-ɛ-dól- (aúwı-, -wᵘrɛ̄-; -rᵒd- §1178; §4022) v.t. be about to wound, etc.
awwırɛ́-kattı- (aúwı-, -wᵘrɛ́-; N. -ɛ́ha-; §4093) v.p. be wounded, etc.
āw-wᵘdɛ́- (āg-wᵘ-) be turning, etc. = āw-wídɛ-.
awwᵘgɛ́ (aúw⌣-) v.t. hurt, injure [< imperat. or imperf. stem of Sudan Ar. عَوَّق id. +-ɛ́ §3639].
ind. pres. aī⌣awwᵘgɛ́rı⌒; perf. aī⌣awwᵘgɛ́-gorı⌒ (N. -ɛ́ko-, -ɛ́ho-).
imperat. awwᵘgɛ́!

gátar-ón⌣sıddageddágogın⌣dıgrí-wēb⌣ bawwᵘgɛgó⌒ (-b⌣- < -g⌣b- §519) if the train had been running fast it would have injured many persons.
awwᵘgɛ́-kattı- (aúwᵘ-; N. -ɛ́ha-; §4093) v.p. be hurt, injured.
āw-wúkkı- (N.; āg-wúk- §719; §3838) v.i. (a) be engaged in barking, etc. (s.v. wúkk(ı)); (b) continually (habitually) bark, etc. = āgúkkı-.
ázɛb (ázıb⌣) n. widow [< عازبة husbandless woman (§1393) or عزب id. (§1351)].
obj. āzɛbk(ı)⌣, -ɛ́pk(ı)⌣, -kı⌒.
pl. ázɛbı⌣.
ambā́b⌣dígon, índı⌣ázɛbun⌒ my father is dead, my mother is a widow.
ázɛba⌣ n. widow [< عازبة husbandless woman].
obj. -bag⌣, -gı⌒.
pl. -banč(ı)⌣.
ázɛb-an- (§§3910ff.) v.i. become a widow.
āzɛbanóskó⌒ she has become a widow.
āzɛban-ág- (§3926) v.i. live in widowhood.
āz-zālɛ́- (āg-zā- §734; §3838) v.i. (a) be getting angry, etc. (s.v. zālɛ́); (b) continually (habitually) get angry, etc.
āz-zıdɛ́- (āg-zī- §734; §3838) v.t. (a) be engaged in increasing; (b) continually (habitually) increase.

b- before a vowel < bı-, bu- (§2968).
bá! (bá!) let him (her, it) lie, etc. < bu-án! s.v. bú.
bā́⌣ n. plot of irrigable ground with edges raised to hold water (= hód⌣ b); with coll. sg. (§4696c) [cp. Bar. ba field RMB, s.v.].
obj. bág⌣.
pl. bánč(ı)⌣.
bā́⌣ǧáŋgıbūn⌒ the plot is (plots are) full (sc. of water).
bā́⌣mállɛ⌣ǧáŋgıbūn⌒ all the plots are full.
bā́⌣súdun⌒ the plot is (plots are) empty.
ím⌣bā́⌣sówwédun⌒ this plot is dry.
X. ɛ́n⌣túbro⌣sɛ́? where's your hoe?
Y. bā́r⌒ in the plot(s).
bā́n-d(ı)⌣ (§§2545ff.) adj. appertaining to a plot, etc.
-báb⌣ (§2375) n. father [cp. ON. пап id. GNT, s.v.; RSN, §§129, 200].
voc. -báp!
obj. -bábk(ı)⌣, -bápk(ı)⌣, -kı⌒.
gen. -bábn⌣v., -bám⌣c.
pl. -bábı⌣.
Always with a form of the possessive personal pronoun (§2629) prefixed, thus:
ambā́b⌣ my father.
ımbā́b⌣ your father.
tımbā́b⌣ his (her, its) father.
antımbā́b⌣ our father.
ıntımbā́b⌣ your (pl.) father.
tıntımbā́b⌣ their father.
ımbā́p⌣kóbbun⌒ your father is shut up (in prison; §6292).
ánn-ogíñ⌣tımbā́b⌣ my husband's father = ánod⌣ (s.v. -od⌣).
ánn-ēn⌣tımbā́b⌣ my wife's father = ánod⌣ (s.v. -od⌣).

ɛsmā́n⌣antımbā́bun⌒ ʕoθmā́n is our father.
ɛsmā́n⌣ár⌣mā́llɛn⌣tımbā́bun⌒ ʕoθmā́n is the father of us all; ⌣ár⌣mā́llɛn⌣ a pronoun-complex (§5196); ⌣tımbā́b-generalized (§5118).
ambā́bnarton⌣kā́n⌣néukori⌒ I (have) inherited the house from my father; -n⌣n- < -g⌣n- (§625).
-bā́m-d(ı)⌣ (§§2545ff.) adj. appertaining to the (a) father, (the) father's.
dúng⌣ambā́md(ı)⌣ my father's money.
-bā́bna⌣ = -bā́nna⌣ paternal uncle, father's brother.
tımbā́bna⌣ his (her) father's brother.
-bā́n-ɛss(ı)⌣ (§2378) n. paternal aunt, father's sister [< -bā́bn-ɛss(ı)⌣].
obj. -bā́nɛssıg⌣.
pl. -bā́nɛssınč(ı)⌣.
Always with a form of the possessive personal pronoun (§2629) prefixed:
ambā́nɛss(ı)⌣ my father's sister.
ımbā́nɛss(ı)⌣ your father's sister.
tımbā́nɛss(ı)⌣ his (her) father's sister.
antımbā́nɛss(ı)⌣ our father's sister.
ıntımbā́nɛss(ı)⌣ your (pl.) father's sister.
tıntımbā́nɛss(ı)⌣ their father's sister.
-bā́nɛssím-buru⌣ (-bā́nɛssímbúru⌣ §1532) n. and as noun-complex (§4812).
-bā́nɛssım⌣búru⌣ father's sister's daughter, cousin.
obj. -búrug⌣.
pl. -búruı⌣, -búrwı⌣.
Always with a form of the possessive personal pronoun (§2629) prefixed:
ambā́nɛssímburu⌣ my father's sister's daughter.
ımbā́nɛssímburu⌣ your father's sister's daughter, etc.
-bā́nɛssın-tód⌣ n. and as noun-complex (§4812).
-bā́nɛssın⌣tód⌣ father's sister's son, cousin.
voc. -tót!, -tó!
obj. -tódk(ı)⌣, -tótk(ı)⌣, -tókk(ı)⌣, -tótt(ı)⌣ (§2462); -kı⌒, -tı⌒.
gen. -tódn⌣v., -tónn⌣v.c., -tón⌣c. (§§778–88).
pl. -bā́nɛssíntonı⌣.
Always with a form of the possessive personal pronoun (§2629) prefixed:
ambā́nɛssıntód⌣ my father's sister's son.
ımbā́nɛssıntód⌣ your father's sister's son, etc.
-bā́nna⌣ (bábna⌣, -bɛ́nna⌣; §2378) n. paternal uncle, father's brother [< *-bā́b-ɛnna §2300].
obj. -nag⌣.
pl. -nanč(ı)⌣.
Always with a form of the possessive personal pronoun (§2629) prefixed:
ambā́nna⌣ my father's brother.
ımbā́nna⌣ your father's brother.
tımbā́nna⌣ his (her) father's brother.
antımbā́nna⌣ our father's brother.
ıntımbā́nna⌣ your (pl.) father's brother.
tıntımbā́nna⌣ their father's brother.
-bā́nnám-buru⌣ (-bā́nnámbúru §1532) n. and as noun-complex (§4812).
-bā́nnam⌣búru⌣ father's brother's daughter, cousin.
obj. -búrug⌣.
pl. -búruı⌣, -búrwı⌣.

báb⌣ — bág

Always with a form of the possessive personal pronoun (§ 2629) prefixed:
ambānnámburu *my father's brother's daughter.*
ımbānnámburu *your father's brother's daughter, etc.*
-bānnan-tŏd⌣ n. and as noun-complex (§ 4812).
-bānnan⌣tŏd⌣ *father's brother's son, cousin.*
voc. -tŏt!, -tó!
obj. -tŏdk(ı)⌣, -tŏtk(ı)⌣, -tŏkk(ı)⌣, -tŏtt(ı)⌣ (§ 2462); -ki⌢, -ti⌢.
gen. -tŏdn⌣v., -tŏnn⌣v.c., -tŏn⌣c. (§§ 778–88).
pl. -bānnántonı⌣.
Always with a form of the possessive personal pronoun (§ 2629) prefixed:
ambānnantŏd⌣ *my father's brother's son.*
ımbānnantŏd⌣ *your father's brother's son, etc.*
báb⌣ n. *door* [< باب *id.*].
obj. bábk(ı)⌣, bápk(ı)⌣, -ki⌢.
gen. bábn⌣v., bám⌣c.
pl. bábı⌣.
bábn⌣í *handle of door.*
bám⌣kúšar *key of door.*
ím⌣báb⌣kóbbūn⌢ *this door is shut* (§ 6292).
ím⌣bám⌣tŏrtık⌣kóp⌢ *shut half of this door (close this door half-way).*
bám-d(ı)⌣ (§§ 2545 ff.) adj. *appertaining to a (the) door, (the) door's.*
bābúr⌣ n. (a) *steamer* [< بابور < It. *vapore id.*]; (b) *railway train*; (c) *engine, machine*; (d) *stove.*
obj. -úrk(ı)⌣, -ki⌢.
pl. -úrı⌣.
gátır⌣bābúrk⌣ɛrğɛn⌢ *the train waits for the steamer.*
bābúrn⌣kábagı⌣fadlɛ́goran⌢ (bābúŋ⌣ká- § 659) *the steamer's barges (have) remained behind.*
báč! imperat. of **bág** *write, divorce.*
***bád-** [< بَعْد *after* § 1350].
bádk(ı)⌣ (bátk(ı)⌣, bátt(ı)⌣ § 716; -ki⌢, -ti⌢; § 4476) adv. *afterwards, subsequently, later.*
bádkı⌣tăgoran⌢ *they came afterwards.*
⌣**bádk(ı)⌣** (etc.) postp. (i, = prep. §§ 4288, 4356) *after (in point of time)*—follows the genitive, of which -n⌣ usually > -m⌣ (§ 592).
ášam⌣bádkı⌣tăgoran⌢ *they came after (the) dinner.*
⌣**bádk(ı)⌣** (etc.) postp. (ii, = conj. §§ 4288, 4386) *after*—follows the subjunctive bare form or genitive (§§ 2943, 2953):
aı⌣nógrı⌣bádk(ı)⌣ and
aı⌣nógrım⌣bádk(ı)⌣ *after I go.*
aı⌣nógsı⌣bádk(ı)⌣ and
aı⌣nógsım⌣bádk(ı)⌣ *after I went.*
ar⌣nógrum⌣báttı⌣tír⌢ *after we go give it (them) to him (her, it).*
tɛr⌣nógsım⌣ıng⌣ɛ́lkori⌢ *after (s)he (it) had gone I found this.*
bád-ır (§ 6007) adv. *afterwards.*
⌣**bád-ır⌣** postp. (i, = prep. §§ 4288, 4376) *after (in point of time)*—follows the genitive, of which -n⌣ usually > -m⌣ (§ 592); -r⌢ implies predication (§§ 5858–60):
ár⌣sǎ⌣wɛ́m⌣bádır⌣bımbɛ́llu⌢ (m⌣ < *-m⌣b- § 595) *we shall start after one hour (in an hour's time, or ... after one o'clock).*
jŏm⌣díñ⌣bádır⌣bımbɛ́llan⌢ (-ñ⌣b- < -ğn⌣b- § 632) *they will start in five days.*
gátır⌣sǎ⌣wɛ́m⌣bádır⌢ *the train is in an hour's time (or ... after one o'clock).*
⌣**bádır⌣** postp. (ii, = conj. §§ 4288, 4387) *after*—follows the subjunctive bare form or genitive (§§ 2943, 2953, 5910):
aı⌣nógrı⌣bádır⌣ *after I go.*
ɛr⌣nógım⌣bádır⌣ *after you go.*
tɛr⌣nógım⌣bádır⌣ *after (s)he (it) goes.*
ar⌣nógru⌣bádır⌣ *after we go.*
ır⌣nógru⌣bádır⌣ *after you go.*
tır⌣nógram⌣bádır⌣ *after they go.*
aı⌣nógsı(-su⌣)⌣bádır⌣ *after I went.*
ɛr⌣nógsım⌣bádır⌣ (-sum⌣bǎ-) *after you went.*
tɛr⌣nógsım⌣bádır⌣ (-sum⌣bǎ-) *after (s)he (it) went.*
ar⌣nógsu⌣bádır⌣ *after we went.*
ır⌣nógsu⌣bádır⌣ *after you went.*
tır⌣nógsam⌣bádır⌣ *after they went.*
aı⌣nógrım⌣bádır⌣ *after I go.*
ɛr⌣nógım⌣bádır⌣ *after you go.*
tɛr⌣nógım⌣bádır⌣ *after (s)he (it) goes.*
ar⌣nógrum⌣bádır⌣ *after we go.*
ır⌣nógrum⌣bádır⌣ *after you go.*
tır⌣nógram⌣bádır⌣ *after they go.*
aı⌣nógsım⌣bádır⌣ (-sum⌣bǎ-) *after I went.*
ɛr⌣nógsım⌣bádır⌣ (-sum⌣bǎ-) *after you went.*
tɛr⌣nógsım⌣bádır⌣ (-sum⌣bǎ-) *after (s)he (it) went.*
ar⌣nógsım⌣bádır⌣ *after we went.*
ır⌣nógsım⌣bádır⌣ *after you went.*
tır⌣nógsım⌣bádır⌣ *after they went.*
aı⌣nógrım⌣bádır⌣áu⌢ *do (make) it after I go.*
ar⌣nógsum⌣bádır⌣ *it was after we went.*
bádk-ɛd⌣ (bátk-, bátt-; -ɛt⌢, -ɛ́⌢; § 4478a) adv. *afterwards, subsequently, later*; -ɛt⌢, -ɛ́⌢ imply predication (§§ 5858–60, 6007).
ıng⌣bádkɛb⌣báurı⌢ (-b⌣b- < -d⌣b- § 518) *I shall do this afterwards.*
bádkɛn⌣nókkoran⌢ (-n⌣n- < -d⌣n- § 624) *afterwards they went (away).*
X. ékkɛn⌣ɛ́ttāriá? *shall (§ 5369b) I bring him (her, it, them § 5083) now?*
Y. wáram⌣bádké⌢ *no, later on.*
badín⌣ (-ín⌢) n. *Badin (on map), a large island opposite Kérma,* = **bádın⌣**;
—**badín⌣** is said to be an Arabizing (§ 1396) pronunciation of **bádın⌣**.
obj. -díng(ı)⌣, -gi⌢.
bádın⌣ (bádın⌢, bádí⌢, bádí⌢ § 939; badín⌣) n. *Badin (on map), a large island opposite Kérma.*
obj. bádıng(ı)⌣, -gi⌢.
bádınn⌣árt(ı)⌣ *the island of Bádin.*
badíndo⌣ (s.v. -r⌣) *to (in) Bádin.*
badíndo⌢ (§ 6007) *(s)he (it) is (they are) in Bádin.*
bág v.t. *distribute, deal out in shares* [cogn. bág *divide* § 2776; RSN, §§ 129, 200, TOB, § 143, 271].
Constructed with two objectives (§ 5345):
ind. pres. aı⌣bágri⌢; perf. aı⌣bágkori⌢ (bákkori⌢).
ıng⌣bák⌢ *distribute this.*
dúŋgıb⌣bák⌢ (-b⌣b- < -g⌣b- § 519) *distribute the money.*
ɛn⌣mállɛd⌣dúŋgıb⌣bágran⌢ (§ 605; -d⌣d- < -g⌣d- § 534) *they give a share of the money to each woman.*
— this verb is naturally heard commonly in the plural-object conjugation **bágırır** (§ 3033):
ind. pres. aı⌣bagıríddi⌢, ɛr⌣bágırırı⌢ (-rí⌢, -rí⌢); perf. aı⌣bagırírkori⌢ (-íkkori⌢).
aı⌣dúŋgıb⌣bıbagıríddi⌢ (-b⌣b- < -g⌣b- § 519) *I shall distribute the money.*
dúŋgıb⌣bagırírkoran⌢ *they (have) distributed the money.*
tírgı⌣dúŋgıb⌣bágırır⌢ *distribute the money to them.*
ɛnčıd⌣dúŋgıb⌣bagıríddan⌢ (-d⌣d- < -g⌣d- § 534) *they distribute the money to the women.*
bágar (-gár⌣; §§ 2200 ff.) and
bagíd (§§ 2256 ff.) n. *distribution.*
bágıd (§ 2268) n. *share*; with collective sg. (§ 4696d).
obj. bagídk(ı)⌣, -ítk(ı)⌣, -ítt(ı)⌣ (§§ 716, 2462); -ki⌢, -ti⌢.
pl. bág(ı)dı⌣.
bág-an (§§ 3890 ff.) v.t. *tell to distribute, etc., let distribute, etc.*
álıd⌣dúŋgıb⌣bágan⌢ (-d⌣d- < -g⌣d- § 534, -b⌣b- < -g⌣b- § 519) *let ɛáli distribute the money.*
bág-bū- (bággū- § 546; § 3931β) v.i. stat. *be in a distributed (etc.) state or condition.*
dúŋgı⌣bággūn⌢ *the money is (has been) distributed.*
bagr-ɛg-ág- (§§ 4071 ff.) v.t. = bagɛdól-.
bag-ɛ-dól- (-gºdól- § 1178; § 4022) and
bagr-ɛ-dól- (-rºdól-; § 4027) v.t. *be about to distribute, etc.*
bagr-ɛ-ğŭ-bū- (§ 4069) v.t. stat. *be on one's way (coming) to distribute, etc.*
bag-ɛ-má- (§ 4036) and
bagr-ɛ-má- (§ 4041) v.t. *become unable to distribute, etc.*
bagr-ɛ-nóg- (§§ 4048 ff.) v.t. *go to distribute, etc.*
bagr-ɛ-nóg-bū- (-nóggū- § 546; § 4058) v.t. stat. *be on one's way (going) to distribute, etc.*
bagr-ɛ-tă- (§§ 4060 ff.) v.t. *come to distribute, etc.*
bagɛd-ág- (§ 3877) v.t. *be in the situation of having distributed, etc.*
dúŋgıb⌣bagɛdágran⌢ (-b⌣b- < -g⌣b- § 519) *they have distributed the money.*
bagíŋ-ır (⌣ § 1799; N. -ŋkır; § 3688) v.t. caus. *cause or allow to distribute, etc.*
aı⌣tékkın⌣ıŋgı⌣bıbágıŋıddi⌢ *I shall make (let) him (her) distribute this.*
bág-kattı- (bákkat- 569; § 4093) v.p. *be distributed, etc.*
bagırıdd-ɛg-ág- (§ 4077) v.t. = bagırıddɛdól-.

26

bagırıdd-ɛ-dól- (-d°dol- §1178; §4031) v.t. *be about to distribute, etc. (more than one object).*

bagırıdd-ɛ-mǎ- (§4045) v.t. *become unable to distribute, etc. (more than one object).*

bǎg v.t. *divide, divide into shares* (=bagíttɛ) [cogn. bág *distribute* §2776; RSN, §129; WS, p. 108, 6].
 ind. pres. aı⌣bǎgri⌢; perf. aı⌣bǎgkori⌢ (bǎkkori⌢).
 dúŋgıb⌣bǎkkoran⌢ (-b⌣b- < -g⌣b §519) *they (have) divided the money into shares.*
 márɛb⌣bǎkkoran⌢ *they (have) divided the millet into shares.*
 nórtıb⌣bǎkkoran⌢ *they (have) divided the flour into shares.*
 (S.) márog⌣gǔ⌣tóskır⌣bǎk⌢ and
 (S.) márot⌣tóskır⌣bǎk⌢ (-t⌣t- < -g⌣t- §707) *divide the millet into three shares.*
 béntıg⌣gǔ⌣kémsır⌣bǎggɛ⌢ and béntık⌣kémsır⌣bǎgwɛ⌢ *divide (pl.) the dates into four shares.*
 dımındídíwgı⌣tóskı⌣tóskıgɛb⌣bǎkkıŋ⌣ goríččé⌢ (§5327 bıɣ; -b⌣b- < -d⌣b- §518) 18÷3=6.

bǎgar (-gár⌣; §§2200ff.) and
bǎgíd⌣ (§§2256ff.) n. *division into shares.*

bǎg-an (§§3890ff.) v.t. *tell to divide, etc., let divide, etc.*
 íŋgı⌣tékkı⌣(⌣gǔ⌣)⌣kémsır⌣bǎgan⌢ *let him (her) divide this into four shares.*

bǎg-bŭ- (bǎggǔ- §546; §3931β) v.i. stat. *be in a divided (etc.) state or condition.*
 dúŋgı⌣bǎggǔn⌢ *the money is (has been) divided into shares.*

bagr-ɛg-ǎg- (§§4071ff.) v.t. = bǎgɛdól-.

bǎg-ɛ-dól- (-g°dól- §1178; §4022) and
bǎgr-ɛ-dól- (-r°dól-; §4027) v.t. *be about to divide, etc.*

bǎgr-ɛ-gǔ-bŭ- (§4069) v.t. stat. *be on one's way (coming) to divide, etc.*

bǎg-ɛ-mǎ- (§4036) and
bǎgr-ɛ-mǎ- (§4041) v.t. *become unable to divide, etc.*

bǎgr-ɛ-nóg- (§§4048ff.) v.t. *go to divide, etc.*

bǎgr-ɛ-nóg-bŭ- (-nóggǔ- §546; §4058) v.t. stat. *be on one's way (going) to divide, etc.*

bǎgr-ɛ-tǎ- (§§4060ff.) v.t. *come to divide, etc.*

bǎgɛd-ǎg- (§3877) v.t. *be in the situation of having divided, etc.*

bǎgíŋg-ır (⌢ §1799; N. -ŋkır; §3688) v.t. caus. *cause or allow to divide, etc.*
 aı⌣tékk⌣íŋg⌣bǎgıŋgıddı⌢ *I make (let) him (her) divide this into shares.*

bǎg-kattı- (bǎkkat-; §4093) v.p. *be divided, etc.*

bágala n. *mule* [< Sudan Ar. بَغَلَة = بَغْلَة id.; cp. WSG, p. 9, §5 (3)].
 obj. -lag⌣.
 pl. bagalánč(ı)⌣.

bagǎšɛ v.t. *step over* [with -gáš- cp. gaš- of gašɛ́ *pass*; -ɛ §2870].
 ind. pres. aı⌣bagǎšɛri⌢; perf. aı⌣bagǎšɛ-gori⌢ (N. -ɛko-, -ɛho).
 bérkı⌣bagǎšɛ⌢ *step over the (piece of) wood.*
 (N.) máltıb⌣bagǎšɛkori⌢(-b⌣b- < -g⌣b- §519) *I stepped over the runnel.*

bagašándı⌣ n. *step, stride*; with collective sg. (§4696c) [< *bagášandı⌣ (§1068) < *bagáš- *stride*+-andı⌣ (*the fact that*) *I go*, so *(the fact that) I take a stride* §2149].
 obj. -dıg⌣.
 pl. -dınč(ı)⌣.

bagǎšɛrar⌣ (-rár⌣; §§2200ff., 2210) and
bagǎšɛríd⌣ (§§2256ff., 2263) n. *stepping over.*

bagǎšɛr-an (§§3890, 3899) v.t. *tell to step over, let step over.*

bagǎšɛ-bagǎšɛ⌣ (§4438b) adv. *with very rapid strides, with very quick steps, striding or stepping very rapidly.*

bagǎšɛ-bagǎšɛ-nóg- (§3745) v.i. *walk with very rapid strides or very quick steps, walk very fast.*
 hánu⌣bagǎšɛbagǎšɛnógın⌢ *the donkey walks with very quick steps.*

baggáníjɛ⌣ n. *beer (made from dates and millet together)* [< Sudan Ar. بَقَّانِيَّة (HSAT, 63)].
 obj. -jɛg⌣.
 pl. -jɛnč(ı)⌣.

bágg(ı)⌣ n. (a) *bug*, Cimex sp. [< بَقّ id., collective §2403]; (b) *tick*, acaridan with collective sg. (§4696c).
 obj. -gıg⌣.
 pl. -gınč(ı)⌣.

bagíttɛ v.t. *divide, divide into shares* (=bǎg) [< bagídk⌣ɛ́- lit. *say* (i.e. *perform*) *shares* §4001].
 ind. pres. aı⌣bagíttɛri⌢; perf. aı⌣bagítt-ɛgori⌢ (N. -ɛko-, -ɛho-).
 dúŋgıb⌣bagíttɛ⌢ (-b⌣b- < -g⌣b- §519) *divide the money into shares.*
 dúŋgıg⌣gǔ⌣tóskır⌣bagíttɛ⌢ and
 dúŋgıt⌣tóskır⌣bagíttɛ⌢ (-t⌣t- < -g⌣t- §707) *divide the money into three shares.*
 márɛg⌣gǔ⌣díğır⌣bagíttɛ⌢ and
 márɛd⌣díğır⌣bagíttɛ⌢ (-d⌣d- < -g⌣d- §534) *divide the millet into five shares.*
 arrɛwɛ́k⌣kólot⌣kolóttɛb⌣bagíttɛgın⌣tós-kıgɛ́⌢ (-b⌣b- < -d⌣b- §518; §5327b vii) 21÷7=3.
 def. imperat. bagíttos! (-ittó! §962).
 íŋgı⌣bagíttó⌢ *divide this into shares.*
 aı⌣tékkı⌣bagíttóskori⌢ *I have divided it into shares.*

bagíttɛrar⌣ (-rár⌣; §2210) and
bagíttɛríd⌣ (§2263) n. *division into shares.*

bagíttɛr-an (§§3890, 3899) v.t. *tell to divide, let divide, etc.*
 íŋgı⌣tékkı⌣(⌣gǔ⌣)⌣kólodır⌣bagíttɛr-an⌢ *let him (her) divide this into seven shares.*

bagíttɛ-bŭ- (§3931β) v.i. stat. *be in a divided state or condition.*
 dúŋgı⌣bagíttɛbūn⌢ *the money is (has been) divided into shares.*

bagıttɛr-ɛg-ǎg- (§§4071ff.) v.t. = bagıt-tɛrɛdól-.

bagıttɛr-ɛ-dól- (-r°dól- §1178; §4027) v.t. *be about to divide, etc.*

bagıttɛr-ɛ-gǔ-bŭ- (§4069) v.t. stat. *be on one's way (coming) to divide, etc.*

bagıttɛr-ɛ-mǎ- (§4041) v.t. *become unable to divide, etc.*

bagıttɛr-ɛ-nóg- (§§4048ff.) v.t. *go to divide, etc.*

bagıttɛr-ɛ-nóg-bŭ- (-nóggǔ- §546; §4058) v.t. stat. *be on one's way (going) to divide, etc.*

bagıttɛr-ɛ-tǎ- (§§4060ff.) v.t. *come to divide, etc.*

bagıttɛd-ǎg- (§3877) v.t. *be in the situation of having divided, etc.*
 aı⌣dúŋgıb⌣bagıttɛdǎgri⌢ (-b⌣b- < -g⌣b- §519) *I have divided the money into shares.*

bagıttéŋg-ır (bagíttɛŋgır §1799; §3688) v.t. caus. *cause or allow to divide, etc.*

bagíttɛ-kattı- (N. -ɛha-; §4093) v.p. *be divided, etc.*

bágōn⌣ (and ⌣̆; -gō̃⌢, -gó⌢ §956c) n. *summer* [< ⲡⲁϫⲱⲛ (RSN, §129) بؤونة *June* §2389].
 obj. bagōŋ(ı)⌣, -gi⌢.
 pl. bagón⌣.
 bagōndo⌣táran⌢ *they come in summer.*

bagōn-d(ı)⌣ (§§2545ff.) adj. *appertaining to summer, of summer.*

bagōn-an- (§§3910ff.) v.i. *become summer.*

bagōnam-bŭ- (§§3949ff.) v.i. stat. *be in a state of becoming or having become summer, be summer.*

bagōnan-ɛ-dól- (-n°dól- §1178; §4026) and
bagōnand-ɛ-dól- (-d°dól-; §4034) v.i. *be about to become summer.*
 bagōnanɛdólın⌢ *summer is just coming on.*

bǎǧ⌣ (bǎč⌢) n. *El Baja* (on map), *a village on the left bank of the Nile, just below Old Dóngola.*
 obj. bǎǧk(ı)⌣, bǎčk(ı)⌣, -ǧk-, -čk- (§323), -ki⌢.

bǎǧ v.t. (a) *write*; (b) *write on, inscribe* [< *bárǧ (§980) < bár *scratch* (cp. ON. ⲛⲁⲡ *write* GNT, s.v.)+-ǧ iterative (§2890)].
 ind. pres. aı⌣bǎǧ(!)ri⌢; perf. aı⌣bǎǧkori⌢ (bǎčk-, bǎččo- §523; -ǧk-, -čk- §323).
 imperat. bǎč!, pl. bǎǧwɛ! (bǎǧwé!; bǎǧǧɛ! §553, -ǧé!).
 subj. past aı⌣bǎǧsı⌣ (⌣bǎčsı⌣ §529, -su⌣).
 tókkom⌣bǎǧmɛn⌢ (-mē⌢, -mé⌢),
 tókkom⌣bǎǧñɛn⌢ (-ñē⌢, -ñé⌢) and
 (S.) dókkom⌣bǎññɛn⌢ (§639, -ñē⌢, -ñé⌢) *don't write.*
 def. perf. aı⌣bǎǧóskori⌢.
 def. imperat. bǎǧos! (bǎǧó! §962).
 ténn⌣érrıd⌣daftárro⌣bǎǧkoran⌢ (-d⌣d- < -g⌣d- §534; s.v. dáftar⌣) *they wrote (have written) his (her, its) name in the book.*
 ɛ́n⌣nímnɛgɛt⌣tém⌣míssıb⌣bǎǧın⌣tón-ǧıland⌣égi⌢ (-b⌣b- < -g⌣b- §519; §6223) *the woman paints (lit. inscribes) her eyes* (§4696a, *women paint their eyes* §4647) *with antimony in order to become beautiful* (cp. RN, s.v. baj).
 X. bǎǧó! *write it down!*
 Y. bǎǧóskó⌢ *he has.*
 part. pres. bǎǧıl⌣ (*one*) *that writes, etc., writer, clerk; writing, etc.; obj. bǎǧılg(ı)⌣ (bǎǧılg(ı)⌣ §1522).
 part. past bǎǧɛl⌣ (*one*) *that wrote, etc., writer; writing, etc.; obj. bǎǧɛlg(ı)⌣ (bǎǧɛlg(ı)⌣).
 ardahǎlg⌣bǎǧıl⌣ (§5407) *petition-writer.*

bǎǧıl-an- (§3910α) v.i. *become a writer.*

bǎǧar⌣ (-ğár⌣, -ğɛr⌣; §§2200ff.) n. (*action of*) *writing, etc.*

băǧ — bán

băǧíd⌣ (§§ 2256 ff.) and
báǧǐd⌣ (-ǧɪd⌣; § 2268) n. (a) = báǧar⌣; (b, resultant) writing, inscription; with collective sg. (§ 4696 d).
 kúlu⌣bāǧíttɪ⌣kốmunun⌢ the stone has (stones have) no inscription(s).
báčč(ɪ)⌣ n. (action of) writing, etc. [< *bắǧ-t(ɪ)⌣ §§ 526, 2228].
 obj. -čɪg⌣.
 ɪnnówwɪm⌣mɛktébɪr⌣bắččɪ⌣dígr⌣ɛgó⌢ (-m⌣m- < -g⌣m- § 601) today in the office there was (has been) much writing (done).
 bắččɪr⌣tɛ́gɪn⌢ he is sitting and (lit. at) writing (he is busy writing).
băǧ-an (§§ 3890 ff.) v.t. tell to write, etc., let write, etc.
băǧ-bŭ- (bắǧǧŭ- § 552; § 3931 β) v.i. stat. be in a written or inscribed state, be in writing, be written, be written on.
 wāɪkɪŋ⌣kúluncɪ⌣bắǧǧūlɪ⌣dáran⌢ (-ŋk- < -dnk- § 658) there are ancient stones with inscriptions.
băǧ(ˡ)r-ɛg-ǎ́g- (§§ 4071 ff.) v.t. = băǧɛdól-.
băǧ-ɛ-dól- (-ǧᵒdól- § 1178; § 4022) and
băǧ(ˡ)r-ɛ-dól (-rᵒdól- § 4027) v.t. be about to write, etc.
băǧ(ˡ)r-ɛ-ǧ́ŭ-bŭ- (§ 4069) v.t. stat. be on one's way (coming) to write, etc.
băǧ-ɛ-mắ- (§ 4036) and
băǧ(ˡ)r-ɛ-mắ- (§ 4041) v.t. become unable to write, etc.
băǧ(ˡ)r-ɛ-nóg- (§§ 4048 ff.) v.t. go to write, etc.
băǧ(ˡ)r-ɛ-nóg-bŭ- (-nóggŭ- §§ 546, 4058) v.t. stat. be on one's way (going) to write, etc.
băǧ(ˡ)r-ɛ-tắ- (§§ 4060 ff.) v.t. come to write, etc.
băǧɛd-ǎ́g- (§ 3877) v.t. be in the situation of having written, etc.
băǧ-kattɪ- (bắck-, -ǧk, -čk- § 323; § 4093) v.p. be written, etc.
băǧ v.t. divorce [< *băǧǧ < bắɪ be distant + -ǧ causative (§ 2892), so *cause to be distant; popularly regarded as a special use of băǧ write, like كتب عليها].
 ind. pres. āɪ⌣băǧ(ˡ)rɪ⌢; perf. āɪ⌣bắǧkorɪ⌢ (bắck-, bắčo- § 523; -ǧk-, -čk- § 323).
 subj. past āɪ⌣băǧsɪ⌣ (⌣bắčsɪ⌣ § 529; -su⌣).
 def. perf. āɪ⌣băǧóskorɪ⌢.
 ténn⌣ɛ́ŋɪ⌣bắčkó⌢ he (has) divorced his wife.
 tɛr⌣bắǧˡr⌣ɛ́gɪn⌣ténn⌣ɛ́n⌣ắmmónɪn⌢ when he says 'I'll (§ 5369 b) divorce (you)' his wife keeps on (ǎ́g-) refusing, i.e. he is always wanting to divorce his wife, but she prevents him (sc. by refusing to agree about the proposed amount of the نَفَقَة).
băǧar⌣ (-ǧɑr⌣; §§ 2200 ff.) and
băǧíd⌣ (§§ 2256 ff.) n. divorcing.
băǧ-bŭ- (bắǧǧŭ- § 552; § 3931 β) v.i. stat. be in a divorced state or condition.
băǧ(ˡ)r-ɛg-ǎ́g- (§§ 4071 ff.) v.t. = băǧɛdól-.
băǧ-ɛ-dól- (-ǧᵒd- § 1178; § 4022) and
băǧ(ˡ)r-ɛ-dól- (-rᵒd-; § 4027) v.t. be about to divorce.
băǧɛd-ǎ́g- (§ 3877) v.t. be in the situation of having divorced.
băǧ-kattɪ- (bắck-, -ǧk, -čk- § 323; § 4093) v.p. be divorced.

bắɪ- (bắɪ-) I shall < bɪ- (§ 2967) + ắɪ⌣ (ắɪ⌣, § 2604; § 2974).
bắɪ, băj, bắɪ v.i. (a) be distant, be far (away); (b) remain distant, keep away, be averse [WS, p. 108, 6].
 ind. pres. ắɪ⌣bắɪrɪ⌢ (⌣bắj(ˡ)rɪ⌢), ɛr⌣băjɪn⌢ (-jí⌢, -jí⌢); perf. ắɪ⌣bắɪkorɪ⌢ (N. ⌣bắɪho-).
 imperat. bắɪ!, pl. bắɪwɛ! (bắɪwɛ́!).
 índotōm⌣bắɪ⌢ keep away from here (from this, from there, from that, s.v. ín⌣).
 sắb⌣ɛ́ssɪrtōm⌣băjɪn⌢ the (a) cat keeps away from (the) water.
 ɛn⌣safárrotōm⌣băjɪn⌢ the (a) woman is averse from travelling.
băjɛl⌣ adj. distant (§ 2523 a).
 obj. băjɛ́lg(ɪ)⌣.
 tíŋ⌣kắ⌣áŋ⌣kắrtōm⌣băjɛlun⌢ their house is far from my (our) house.
băj-an- (§§ 3890 ff.) v.t. tell to be distant, etc., let be distant, etc.
băjɪŋ-ɪr (bajíŋgɪr § 1799; N. -ŋkɪr; § 3688) (a) v.t. caus. cause or allow to be distant, etc.; (b) v.t. render distant, keep away.
 ind. pres. ắɪ⌣băjɪŋgɪddɪ⌢.
 ắɪ⌣tékk⌣índotōm⌣băjɪŋgɪddɪ⌢ I keep him (her, it) away from here (from this, etc.).
 wɛ́lgɪ⌣kúsurtōm⌣bajíŋgɪr⌣ keep the dog away from the meat.
bắɪ, băj, bắɪ v.t. procure on hire.
 ind. pres. ắɪ⌣bắɪrɪ⌢ (băj(ˡ)rɪ⌢), ɛr⌣băjɪn⌢ (-jí⌢, -jí⌢); perf. ắɪ⌣bắɪkorɪ⌢ (N. ⌣bắɪho-).
 imperat. bắɪ!
 part. pres. băjɪl⌣ procuring on hire, (one) that procures on hire, lessee, tenant; obj. băjɪ́lg(ɪ)⌣.
 káb⌣băjɪl⌣ (-b⌣b- < -g⌣b- § 519) tenant of house.
 káb⌣bắɪkorɪ⌢ I took (have taken) the (a) house on hire.
băj-an (§§ 3890 ff.) v.t. tell to procure on hire, let procure on hire.
bắɪ-bŭ- (§ 3931 β) v.i. stat. be in a hired state or condition.
bắɪ-dɛ̆n (§§ 3996-7) v.t. grant on hire, let (to the speaker).
băjɛd-ǎ́g- (§ 3877) v.t. be in a position of having procured on hire, hold on hire, be the tenant of.
 íŋ⌣káb⌣băjɛdǎ́gran⌣ they are the tenants of this house.
 ín⌣hánub⌣băjɛdǎ́grɪ⌢ I have (taken) this donkey on hire.
bắɪ-kattɪ- (N. bắɪha-; § 4093) v.p. be procured on hire.
bắɪ-tɪr (§§ 3998-9) v.t. grant on hire, let (to other than the speaker).
 part. pres. bắɪtɪrɪl⌣ that grants on hire.
 káb⌣bắɪtɪrɪl⌣ landlord of house.
 káb⌣băjɪl⌣úǧrɛd⌣dɛfɛ́n, bắɪtɪrɪl⌣ɪstɛlɛmɛ́n⌢ (-d⌣d- < -g⌣d- § 534) the tenant of the house pays the rent, the landlord receives it.
bákɪr n. El-Bakri (on map), name of a village on the left bank of the Nile about 19 miles above Hándag [< بكر § 1359].
 obj. bakírk(ɪ)⌣, -kɪ⌢.

bakírro⌣ (s.v. -r⌣) at (to) El-Bakri.
bakírro⌢ (§ 6007) (s)he (it) is (they are) at El-Bakri.
bakɪrnắrt(ɪ)⌣ (-tɪ⌢) Bukri Id. (on map) a small island north of El-Bakri [Bakr's Island].
 obj. -tɪg⌣.
bắl⌣ n. attention, mind [< بال id.].
 obj. bắlg(ɪ)⌣, -gɪ⌢.
 ɛ́m⌣bắlgɪ⌣dắran⌣ (s.v. dắ) pay attention (to him, her, it, them, take care, خَلّي بالَك).
 kắr⌣ɛ́m⌣bắlgɪ⌣dắran⌢ take care of the house.
bắl-ko (§ 4122) (a) v.i. pay attention, attend, take care, mind; (b) v.t. pay attention to, attend to, heed, notice, take care of or about, mind.
 ind. pres. ắɪ⌣bắlkorɪ⌢, ɛr⌣bắlkon⌢ (-kõ⌢, -kó⌢); perf. ắɪ⌣bālkógorɪ⌢ (⌣ⁿ⌣; N. -óko-, -óho-, -oko-, -oho-).
 imperat. bắlko!, bắlkor⌣v. (§ 3533), pl. bắlkowɛ! (⌣ⁿ⌣).
 subj. past ắɪ⌣bắlkosɪ⌣ (-su⌣).
 part. pres. bắlkōl⌣ (one) that pays attention, etc.
 neg. part. pres. bālkŏmɛnɪl⌣ (one) that does not pay attention, etc.
 bắlkoran⌢ they pay attention, etc.
 bālkŏmunan⌢ they do not pay attention, etc.
 ắɪ⌣bắlkogómunun⌢ I didn't notice (didn't pay attention).
 tókkom⌣bắlkomɛn⌣ don't pay attention.
 íŋgɪ⌣bắlko⌢ mind this.
 bắlkor⌣ɛgórɪ⌢ I said 'take care'.
 ténn⌣íb⌣bắlko! (-b⌣b- < -g⌣b- § 519) mind (watch, don't injure) his (her) hand(s § 4696 a)!
 sílkɪb⌣bắlko⌢ mind (beware) of the wire!
 ɛ́ŋ⌣kadénčɪb⌣bắlko: kóbdɪr⌣búja⌣ dắbūn⌢ mind your clothes: there is paint on the doors.
 ɛ́nn⌣ắb⌣bắlko! (§ 1671) and ɛ́nn-āb⌣bắlko! take care! (lit. mind yourself!)
 šắrtɪrtōn⌣ɛ́nn-āb⌣bắlko! mind the iron!, lit. mind yourself from the iron!
 šắrtɪrtōn⌣ɛ́nn-āb⌣bắlkor⌣ɛgórɪ⌢ I said 'mind the iron!'.
bắlkor-an (§§ 3890, 3899) v.t. tell to pay attention, etc., let pay attention, etc.
 kắ⌣sŭdun, álɪb⌣bắlkoran⌢ the house is empty; tell ɛáli to take care of it.
bámbar⌣ n. stool [< Sudan Ar. مِنبر id. < منبر HESA, s.v. stool].
 obj. bambắrk(ɪ)⌣, -kɪ⌢.
 pl. bámbarɪ⌣.
bán⌢ let him (her, it) lie, etc. < bu-án⌢ s.v. bŭ.
bán v.i. dance [WS, p. 108, 5].
 ind. pres. ắɪ⌣bắndɪ, ɛr⌣bắnɪn⌢ (⌣bắnī⌢), bắnɪ⌢ § 939); perf. ắɪ⌣bắŋkorɪ⌢.
 imperat. bán! (bắ!).
 subj. past ắɪ⌣bắnsɪ⌣ (⌣bắsɪ⌣ § 974; -su⌣).
 cond. pres. ắɪ⌣bắŋkɪrɪ⌣.
bánar (-nɑ́r⌣; §§ 2200 ff.) and
bāníd⌣ (§§ 2256 ff.) n. dancing.
bánt(ɪ)⌣ n. dance, dancing [§ 2325 α].
 obj. -tɪg⌣.

bāntín-d(ɪ)◡ (§§ 2545 ff.) adj. *appertaining to the dance.*
bǎn-an (§§ 3890 ff.) v.t. *tell to dance, let dance.*
bǎnɪŋg-ɪr (⁻́◡; N. -ŋkɪr; § 3688) v.t. caus. *cause or allow to dance.*
bándar◡ *town* = **bándɑ́r**◡.
bánd(ɪ)◡ n. *span, i.e. maximum distance between tips of thumb and little finger, approx. 9 inches.*
  obj. -dɪg◡, -gɪ⌒.
  pl. -dɪnč(ɪ)◡.
-bǎnɛss(ɪ)◡ *paternal aunt, father's sister* s.v. **-bǎb**◡.
-bǎnna◡ *paternal uncle, father's brother* s.v. **-bǎb**◡.
bǎññɛn⌒ < bǎǧñɛn⌒ < bǎǧmɛn⌒ (§ 639) s.v. **bǎǧ** *write.*
bǎññi(ɪ) v.i. *speak, talk*; §§ 5532-3 [RSN, § 129 s.v. **bain**].
  ind. pres. aɪ◡bánniri⌒ (bánniri⌒ § 1532), ɛr◡bánnin (-ñi⌒, -ñí⌒); perf. aɪ◡báññŋgori⌒ (báññígori⌒; N. -iko-, -iho-, -íko-, -ího-).
  imperat. báññi!
  subj. past aɪ◡báññɪsɪ⌒ (◡báññɪsɪ◡; -su◡).
  tírgonom◡báññimunan⌒ *they don't speak to* (lit. *with*) *them.*
  tɛr◡ám◡baññítkɪ◡báññimunun⌒ *(s)he doesn't speak my (our) language;* ◡baññítkɪ◡ *adverbial of manner* (§ 4667).
  ándɪb◡báññimɛn? (-b◡b- < -g◡b- § 519) and
  ándɪgɛb◡báññimɛn? (-b◡b- < -d◡b- § 518) *don't you speak Nubian?* i.e. *do* (§ 5485) *speak Nubian.*
  múrsɪb◡báññin⌒ *(s)he tells lies* (§ 4696 d).
báññar◡ (-ñar◡, -ñɛr◡; §§ 2200 ff.) and **baññíd**◡ (§§ 2256 ff.) n. *speaking, talking.*
baññid◡ n. *(a) speaking, speech, talking, talk; (b) word; (c) language, dialect; (d) tale, story.*
  obj. baññídk(ɪ)◡, -ítk(ɪ)◡, -ítt(ɪ)◡ (§ 2462), -kɪ◡, -tɪ◡, gen. báññidn◡v., -ɪn◡c.
  pl. báññɪdɪ◡.
  aɪ◡ém◡baññítt◡uñúrmunun⌒ *I don't understand what you say.*
  ám◡baññítkɪ◡báññiran⌒ and
  ám◡baññítkɛb◡báññiran⌒ (-b◡b- < -d◡b- § 518) *they speak our (my) language.*
  mássɪnčɪm◡baññítkɛb◡báññin⌒ *(s)he talks the Máhasi dialect.*
  ógɪg◡bɛlém◡baññítt◡uñúrmɛnɪl◡nɛfé-munun⌒ (-m◡b- < -dn◡b- § 594) *a man that does not know the language of the country is useless.*
  báññɪd◡ɪsáɪ◡ (-ñɪs◡sáɪ◡ § 677) ◡bɪnɛ-fɛ́n? *what will it be useful to say?*
báññ-an (§§ 3890 ff.) v.t. *tell to speak, etc., let speak, etc.*
báññɪŋg-ɪr (⁻́◡ § 1799; N. -ŋkɪr; § 3688) v.t. caus. *cause or allow to speak, etc.*
bánga◡ n. *(a) locust; (b) cricket,* Acheta sp. with collective sg. (§ 4696 c) [perhaps contains **bǎn** *dance* § 2179].
  obj. -gag◡.
  pl. -ganč(ɪ)◡.
  bángan◡dódɛ◡ *grasshopper.*
  hábɪn◡bánga◡ (-ɪm◡b-) *Poeciloocerus hieroglyphicus, Klug.*

banganárt(ɪ)◡ (-ti⌒) n. *Banganarti (on map), an island now joined to the right bank at low Nile, about five miles above Old Dóngola* [*Locust's Island*].
  obj. -tɪg◡.
bangɪ-báng(ɪ)◡ (§ 4438) adv. *each apart from another, each separately* [báng(ɪ)◡ < bán! *let (him, her, it) be!* (< buán! § 1110) + -g(ɪ)◡ *adverbial* § 4430].
  bangɪbáng◡ággɛ⌒ *sit (pl.) each separately, each by himself (herself).*
  bangɪbáng◡tébbɛ⌒ *stand (pl.) each separately, each by himself (herself).*
  bangɪbáng◡étta⌒ *bring each separately.*
bár v.t. *(a) place in order of excellence or desirability, sort, separate, classify; (b) sort out, select, choose* [cogn. **bǎr** *scratch* § 2776].
  ind. pres. aɪ◡bárrɪ⌒, ɛr◡bárɪn⌒ (-rī⌒, -rí⌒); perf. aɪ◡bárkori⌒.
  subj. past aɪ◡bársɪ◡ (-su◡).
  wíččɪr◡sɛ́rɛ́-wēb◡bárkori⌒ (-b◡b- < -g◡b- § 519) *I (have) selected a good stick.*
  sɛrɛb◡bárɪddan⌒ and
  sɛrɛb◡barɪríddan⌒ *they select every good one* (§§ 4957, 5466).
  sɛ́rɛ-sɛrɛb◡baríkkori⌒ (§ 4955) and
  sɛ́rɛ-sɛrɛb◡barɪríkkori⌒ *I (have) sorted out all the good ones.*
  béntɪb◡barédkori⌒ and
  béntɪb◡baróskori⌒ *I have sorted the dates.*
  ám◡béntɪb◡barédkori⌒ *I have sorted out my (our) dates.*
báred◡ adj. *selected for inferiority, inferior, bad, worse, worst* [§ 2522].
  obj. barédk(ɪ)◡, -étk(ɪ)◡, -étt(ɪ)◡ (§ 2462), -kɪ◡, -tɪ⌒.
  pl. bárɛdɪ◡.
  aɪgɪ◡barédkɪ◡déŋko⌒ *(s)he gave (has given) me the worse (worst)* (§ 4964).
  ím◡béntɪ◡báredun, sókke⌒ *these dates are bad (inferior), take them away;* ◡béntɪ◡ *collective sg.* (§ 4696 b).
bár-an (§§ 3890 ff.) v.t. *tell to sort, etc., let sort, etc.*
bār-bū- (§ 3931 β) v.i. stat. *be in a sorted (etc.) state or condition.*
  béntɪ◡bárbūn⌒ *the dates are (have been) sorted, etc.*
bár-dĕn (§§ 3996-7) v.t. *give (to the speaker) after sorting, etc., sort (etc.) for (the speaker).*
  aɪgɪ◡sɛrɛb◡bardéŋko⌒ (-b◡b- < -g◡b- § 519) *(s)he (has) sorted me out the good ones.*
barr-ɛg-ǎg- (§§ 4071 ff.) v.t. = baredól-.
bar-ɛ-dól- (-rºdól- § 1178; § 4022) and
barr-ɛ-dól- (-rºdól- § 4027) v.t. *be about to sort, etc.*
barr-ɛ-gǔ-bū- (§ 4069) v.t. stat. *be on one's way (coming) to sort, etc.*
barr-ɛ-mǎ- (§ 4036) and
barr-ɛ-mǎ- (§ 4041) v.t. *become unable to sort, etc.*
barr-ɛ-nóg- (§§ 4048 ff.) v.t. *go to sort, etc.*
barr-ɛ-nóg-bū- (-nóggū- § 546; § 4058) v.t. stat. *be on one's way (going) to sort, etc.*
barr-ɛ-tǎ- (§§ 4060 ff.) v.t. *come to sort, etc.*
bared-ǎg- (§ 3877) v.t. *be in the situation of having sorted, etc.*

bared-dĕn (§§ 5690-1) v.t. *after selecting for inferiority give (to the speaker), sort out the worst for (the speaker).*
  tɛr-aɪgɪ◡béntɪb◡bareddéŋko⌒ (-b◡b- < -g◡b- § 519) *(s)he (has) sorted me out the worst of the dates.*
bared-tɪr (-éttɪr; §§ 5690-1) v.t. *after selecting for inferiority give (to other than the speaker), sort out the worst for (other than the speaker).*
  aɪ◡tékkɪ◡béntɪb◡barettíkkori⌒ *I (have) sorted him (her, it) out the worst of the dates.*
bared-ɪšín (-rɛggɪš- § 4176; -íšɪn §§ 4160-73) v.t. *send after sorting out, etc.*
  aɪ◡tékkɪ◡feǧírro◡wéb◡barebbíšindi⌒ *I shall select and send you one tomorrow morning.*
  aɪgɪ◡sɛrɛ́-wéb◡baredíšɪŋkó⌒ (◡baregɪšɪŋkó⌒) *(s)he sent me a good one (s)he had chosen.*
bared-ɪšín-dĕn (§ 5692) v.t. *after sorting out (etc.) send to (the speaker).*
bared-ɪšín-tɪr (§ 5692) v.t. *after sorting out (etc.) send to (other than the speaker).*
  aɪ◡tékkɪ◡wéb◡barebbíšɪntɪddi⌒ (-b◡b- < -g◡b- § 519) *I shall choose and send you one.*
bark-idd(ɪ) (§ 3725) v.t. caus. *cause or allow to sort, etc.*
  imperat. bárkɪddi! (§ 1858).
  aɪ◡tékkɪ◡sɛrɛb◡barkíddiri⌒ *I make (let) him (her) sort out the good ones.*
bár-kattɪ- (§ 4093) v.p. *be sorted, etc.*
bar-sókke (§ 3747 ɛ') v.t. *after sorting out (etc.) take away.*
  ám◡béntɪb◡barsókkegori⌒ (-b◡b- < -g◡b- § 519) *I selected and took (have selected and taken) away my (our) dates.*
bár-tɪr (§§ 3998-9) v.t. *give (to other than the speaker) after sorting, etc., sort (etc.) for (other than the speaker).*
  aɪ◡tékkɪ◡sɛrɛb◡bartíkkori⌒ *I (have) sorted him (her) out the good ones.*
bár- (bar-) *we shall* < bɪ- (§ 2967) + ár◡ (ar◡, § 2604).
bǎr v.t. *scratch* [cogn. **bár** *sort* § 2776; cp. ON. пар *write* GNT, s.v.].
  ind. pres. aɪ◡bárrɪ⌒, ɛr◡bárɪn⌒ (-rī⌒, -rí⌒); perf. aɪ◡bárkori⌒.
  sáb◡aɪgɪ◡bárkó⌒ *the cat (has) scratched me.*
bǎrar◡ (-rɑ́r◡; §§ 2200 ff.) and
bǎríd◡ (§§ 2256 ff.) n. *scratching.*
bǎr-an (§§ 3890 ff.) v.t. *tell to scratch, let scratch.*
bǎr-bū- (§ 3931 β) v.i. stat. *be in a scratched state or condition.*
  ánnɪ◡bárbūn⌒ *my hand (arm) is (hands are* § 4696 a) *scratched.*
bǎrr-ɛg-ǎg- (§§ 4071 ff.) v.t. = bāredól-.
bǎr-ɛ-dól- (-rºd- § 1178; § 4022) and
bǎrr-ɛ-dól- (-rºd-; § 4027) v.t. *be about to scratch.*
bǎred-ǎg- (§ 3877) v.t. *be in the situation of having scratched.*
bǎr-kattɪ- (§ 4093) v.p. *be scratched.*
barakǎwɪ◡ n. *one of the better sorts of date growing in Dóngola* = ɛbéttɛ◡; s.v. bént(ɪ)◡; *with collective sg.* (§ 4696 b) [< Sudan Ar. بَرَكاوي *id.*].

báram — básɛ

obj. -wıg.
pl. -wınč(ı).

báram n. *acacia blossom*; with collective sg. (§4696b) [< بَرَم *fruit of the* عِضَاه *LA*, s.v. برم].
obj. barámg(ı), -gi.
pl. bárami.
báram mórɛn sállɛn gándɛn ğówwın ígun báram *is the blossom of Acacia ehrenbergiana, A. seyal, A. spirocarpa and A. arabica.*

bárandi *I shall become white*, s.v. áro.

bárbarı (bárbári §1532) n. *Nubian* = bérbɛrı.

bargúd n. *flea*; with collective sg. (§4696c) [< بَرْغُوث *id.*].
obj. -údk(ı), -útk(ı), -ki.
pl. -údı.

bárığ v.t. *scratch* [< bár *id.* + -ı- euphonic (§483β) + -ğ or. intensive §2884].
ind. pres. aī bárığ(¹)ri, ɛr bárığın (-ği, -ği); perf. aī barığkori (-íčk-; -ığko-, -íčko- §323).
imperat. bárič!
sáb aīgı baríčkó *the cat (has) scratched me.*
ín sáb barığmunun, ím bárığın *this cat doesn't scratch, that one does.*

bárığar (-ğár; §§2200ff.) and
baríğíd (§§2256ff.) n. *scratching.*

bárığ-an (§§3890ff.) v.t. *tell to scratch, let scratch.*

baríğ-bū- (-ığğū- §552; §3931β) v.i. stat. *be in a scratched state or condition.*

barığ(¹)r-ɛg-ág- (§§4071ff.) v.t. = barığɛ-dól-.

barığ-ɛ-dól- (-ğºd- §1178; §4022) and
barığ(¹)r-ɛ-dól- (-rºd-; §4027) v.t. *be about to scratch.*

barığed-ág- (§3877) v.t. *be in the situation of having scratched.*

baríğ-kattı- (báríğ- §1522; -íčk-; -ígka-, -íčka- §323; §4093) v.p. *be scratched.*
ér kıníssɛgɛb bıbáríčkattın (-b- < -d-b- §518) *you will be scratched by the thorns* (§4696c).

bárığ adj. (a, *of particle or small object*) *above average size, larger* (than the average); (b, *of mass of particles, etc.*) *with particles above average size, coarse*; (c, *of rope*) *coarse, thick* [adjectival presentation of the stem bárığ §2493].
obj. baríğk(ı), -íčk(ı), -íčč(ı) §523; -íğk(ı), -íčk(ı) §323; -ki, -či.
gen. barığn v., -iñ c. 632.
pl. bárığı.
ím béntırtóm bárığ baríčči bítti *pick out each larger one from these dates (pick out all the larger ones...)*; bénti- collective sg. (§4696b); bárığ baríčči §4955.
ín nórtı bárığun *this flour is coarse.*
írı baríğ-ğég éttágoran (-ğ-ğ- < -ğ-w- §553) *they (have) brought a thick rope*; baríğ- §1561.

bārıkɛ́ v.i. *bestow a blessing* [< imperat. or imperf. stem of بَارَك *id.* + -ɛ §3647]. Constructed with -r (-do, etc.) as بارك with في in the formulae used for thanking (§§6264–6):
artón ɛddo bārıkɛr ɛn and (commonly abbreviated to) ɛddo bārıkɛr ɛn (-kɛ́r ɛ́, -kɛr ɛ́) *God bless you, lit. if God say 'I bless you', sc. I am content* (a version of بارك الله فيك *id.*).
íddo bārıkɛr ɛn *God bless you (pl.).*
ártón ɛddo bārıkɛ́r ɛl *God bless you, lit. if God (is) saying 'I bless you', sc. I am content.*

bārıkɛ́-dɛn (§§3996–7) v.t. *congratulate (the speaker).*
ind. pres. ɛr bārıkɛdɛ́nın (-ní, -ní; §1935); perf. ɛr bārıkɛdɛ́ŋkon (-kõ, -kó).
imperat. bārıkɛ́dɛn! (-dɛ̃!, -dɛ̃!, -dɛ̃!).
tɛr aīgı bārıkɛdɛ́nın *(s)he congratulates me.*

bārıkɛ́-tır v.t. *congratulate (other than the speaker).*
ind. pres. aī bārıkɛ́tıddi; perf. aī bārıkɛtírkori (-tíkkori).
imperat. bārıkɛ́tır!

barísk(ı) v.t. *vomit* [§2853].
ind. pres. aī barískıri (barískíri §1532), ɛr barískın (-kī, -kí); perf. aī barískıgori (-ískíg-; N. -ıko-, -ıho-, -íko-, -ího-).
tɛr kalíngı barískın *(s)he (it) vomits what (s)he (it) eats* (§6122).

barískar (-kár; §§2200ff.) and
barískíd (§§2256ff.) n. *vomiting.*

barískır-ɛg-ág- (§§4071ff.) v.t. = barískɛ-dól-.

barísk-ɛ-dól- (-kºdól- §1178; §4022) and
barískır-ɛ-dól- (-rºdól-; §4027) v.t. *be about to vomit.*

barískɛd-ág- (§3877) v.t. *be in the condition of having vomited.*

barískíŋ-ır (⁻ˊ⁻; N. -ŋkır; §3688) v.t. caus. *cause or allow to vomit.*

bárra- بَرَّا *outside*].

bárrar (-rár; §6007) adv. *(at, on, to) outside.*
bárrar ágran *they sit (etc. s.v. ág) outside.*
bárrar *(s)he (it) is (they are) outside.*
X. tír kárɛ́ wálla bárrarɛ́? *are they in the house or outside?*
Y. bárrarɛ *outside.*

barrád *pot, etc.* = bɛrrád.

bárrɛ n. *intervening space, interstice, room between or among*; with collective sg. (§4696c) [< *bágrɛ (§669) < bág *distribute* + intensive -r + -ɛ of n. ess., so *numerous distribution*, concrete *what is numerously distributed* §2317].
obj. -rɛg.
pl. -rɛnč(ı).
bárrɛk kón (-k-k- < -g-k- §569) *it has (they have) an intervening space (intervening spaces).*
bárrɛnčık kón *it has (they have) intervening spaces.*

bárrɛ-r (§6007) adv. *in (to) the intervening space, etc., between.*
bárrɛr *(s)he (it) is (they are) between.*

bárrɛr (§§4361, 5897) postp. (= prep. §4287) *between, among*; follows the genitive, of which -n > -m (§592).
kág kúlum bárrɛr bokkıtúbbın *the snake lies (snakes lie) hid among the stones* (§4696d).
kóbıd ówwım bárrɛr *(s)he (it) is (they are) between (the) two doors.*
kágon ğówwᵘgom bárrɛr *(s)he (it) is (they are) between the house and the tree*; ğówwᵘgom < ğówwıgom (§1192).
kágon úrugom bárrɛr *(s)he (it) is (they are) between the house and the river.*
ɛ́kkon ogíččom bárrɛr *(s)he (it) is (they are) between you and the man*; ogíččom < ogíğkom (§523).
ánda árgogon úrdıgom bárrɛr *my (our) home is between Árgo and El-Órdi.*

barrɛ́n-d(ı) (§§2545ff.) adj. *intervening, middle, central.*

bárr-an (§3913β) v.i. *go to the intervening space, etc.*
tím bárraŋkó *(s)he (it) went (has gone) between (among) them.*

bárram-bŭ- (§3952) v.i. stat. *be in a state of motion towards the intervening space, etc., be going between or among.*

bárr(ı) n. *land as opposed to water, bank, shore* [< بَرّ *id.*].
obj. -rıg.
bárrır (§6007) adv. *on (to, the) land, ashore.*
bárrır ágran *they are (etc. s.v. ág) ashore.*
bárrır *(s)he (it) is (they are) ashore* (§§5858–60).

barrín-d(ı) (§§2545ff.) adj. *appertaining to the land, etc.*

bárr-an (§3913β) v.i. *go ashore, land.*

bárram-bŭ- (§3952) v.i. stat. *be in a state of motion towards the land, be on one's way ashore.*

bárs(ı) n. *twin* [(?) < bár *separate, choose* + -s of n. act. (§2319), so *separation, choice*, cp. the name مُخْتَار; al. WS, p. 114, 29].
obj. -sıg.
pl. -sınč(ı).

bārúd n. (a) *gunpowder* [< بَارُود *id.*]; (b) *cartridge*; with collective sg. (§4696d).
obj. -údk(ı), -útk(ı), -útt(ı), -úkk(ı) (§2462), -ki, -ti.
gen. -údn v., -ún c.
pl. -údı.
bārúd-dɛd-dɛ́n (-d-d- < -d-w- §533, -d-d- < -g-d- §534) *give me a cartridge.*

básɛ n. *pool, esp. long winding pool left by falling river, standing water*; with collective sg. (§4696d) [< *bássɛ (§1011) < *bágsɛ (§678) < bág *distribute* + -s dem. + -ɛ of n. ess., so *that (those) distribution(s)* sc. in river-bed §2320].
obj. -sɛg.
pl. básɛnč(ı).
ín ɛssı básɛn *this water does not flow.*
úr ım básɛm múkko (-m-m- < -g-m- §601) *the river (has) left this pool*; úr ım < úru ím (§1122).

basír‿ n. (a) *craftsman, artisan*, esp. (b) *carpenter that sets up and repairs the water-wheel* (kólɛ‿) [< Sudan Ar. بَصِير *id.* (prop. *discerning, intelligent*)].
  obj. -írk(ı)‿, -ki⌒.
  pl. -írı‿.
  basír-nār‿ (-sínnār‿ §628) ‿išıŋkori⌒ *I (have) sent him (her, it, them* §5083) *to the carpenter.*

báskal‿ n. *small forceps, small pincers, tweezers* (commonly used to remove hair) [? <*mísgal‿ (§1287, cp. §1182) < مِصْقَل *instrument for smoothing;* Griffith cft. with (?) ON. пасκ *punish GNT,* s.v.; *RSN,* §34].
  obj. baskálg(ı)‿.
  pl. báskalı‿.
  díltıb‿baskálgɛd‿dúkkıran⌒ (-b‿b- < -g‿b- §519) *they take out hair(s) with tweezers.*

basláñ‿ n. *Baslan* (on map) *a village on the left bank of the Nile, about* 14 *miles above Hándag.*
  obj. -áñg(ı)‿, -gi⌒.

bássarı‿ adj. *devoid of strong flavour, insipid, tasteless.*
  obj. -rıg‿.
  pl. -rınč(ı)‿.
  ín‿ákıl‿bássarın⌒ *this food is insipid.*

bássar-an- (§§3910 ff.) v.i. *become insipid, etc.*
  tíštı‿dúl‿lēg‿éttaran, aŋgállɛgoŋ‿kurúpkon‿éssıgoŋı‿téddo‿bógran, jóm‿tóskım‿múgran, aŋgállɛ‿bássaranın⌒ (‿dúl-lēg‿ < ‿dúl-wēg‿ §580, -m‿m- < -g‿m- §601) *they fetch a large pan, pour (this) lupines and earth and water into (it), leave it for three days, (and) the lupines lose their bitter taste.*

bássaram-bū- (§§3949ff.) v.i. stat. *be in the state or condition of becoming or having become insipid, etc.*

bastέ v.i. *be pleased, rejoice* [< بَسَط of imperf. stem of اَنْبَسَط *id.* or بَسَط *enjoyment* + -έ §3658].
  ind. pres. āı‿bastέri⌒; perf. āı‿bastέgori⌒ (N. -έko-; -έho-).
  imperat. bastέ!
  āı‿έddotōm‿bastέgori⌒ *I am pleased with you* (أَنَا مَبْسُوط مِنَّك).

bastέrar- (-rár‿; §§2200ff., 2207) and
bastέríd‿ (§§2256ff., 2260) n. *rejoicing.*

bastέ-bū- (§3931 α) v.i. stat. *be in a pleased state.*
  āı‿bastέbūr‿ɛr‿árbaha‿nehárkı‿wıdɛbúŋgi⌒ (§6190b) *I am glad that you are returning on Wednesday.*

bastέg-ır (N. -έkır, -έhır; §3681) (a) v.t. caus. *cause or allow to be pleased, etc.;* (b) v.t. *please, delight.*

báša‿ (-šá‿) n. *pasha* [< بَاشَا *id.*].
  obj. -šag‿, -šág‿).
  pl. -šanč(ı)‿ (-šan-).

†batátıs‿ n. *potato;* with collective sg. (§4696b) [< بَطَاطِس *id.* collective < Eur.].

  obj. batátísk(ı)‿.
  pl. batátısı‿.

battāníjɛ‿ (-já‿, -ja‿) n. *blanket* [< بَطَّانِيَّة *id.*].
  obj. -jɛg‿, -jág‿, -jag‿.
  pl. -jɛnč(ı)‿, -jánč(ı)‿, -janč(ı)‿.

bátt(ı)‿ < bádk(ı)‿ (§716) *afterwards.*

bándar‿ (bénder‿, bándar‿) n. *town* [< بَنْدَر *id.*].
  obj. bándark(ı)‿, -ki⌒.
  pl. bándárı‿.

bárrád‿ *pot, etc.* = bɛrrád‿.

bε̄ (§§3132ff.) v.t. (a) *kill;* (b) *extinguish, put out;* (c) *numb.*
  ind. pres. āı‿bε̄ri, ɛr‿bε̄n‿ (bε̄⌒, bε̄⌒, bε̄⌒); perf. āı‿bε̄gori⌒ (N. bε̄ko-, bε̄ho-).
  imperat. bε̄!, pl. bε̄wɛ! (bε̄wέ!).
  subj. past āı‿bε̄sı‿ (-su‿).
  part. pres. bε̄l‿ *(one) that kills, etc., killer, etc., killing, etc.;* obj. bε̄lg(ı)‿.
  part. past bε̄rɛl‿ *(one) that killed, etc., killer, etc., killing, etc.;* obj. bε̄rélg(ı)‿ (bε̄rélg(ı)‿ §1522).
  ǧúgrıgıd‿āıgı‿bε̄gó⌒ *the heat (has) exhausted* (lit. *killed) me.*
  íkkı‿bε̄rıá? *shall* (§5369b) *I put the fire (light) out?*
  X. ígkı‿bε̄⌒ *put the fire (light) out.*
  Y. āı‿bε̄róskori⌒ *I have* (§§3789ff.).
  káǧıb‿bε̄l‿ (-b‿b- < -g‿b- §519) *rainbow,* lit. *killer of horses.*
  kúltıgɛb‿bε̄ran‿ (§§5452-3) n. *instrument for killing flies, fly-killer.*
  kúltıgɛb‿bε̄ráŋ‿éttari‿ *I'll* (§5369b) *bring the (a) fly-killer.*
  āı‿έddınčıb‿bε̄rıddi⌒ *I kill (the various* §5456*) hyaenas.*

bε̄rar- (-rár‿; §§2200ff., 2207) and
bε̄ríd‿ (§§2256ff., 2260) n. *killing; homicide, murder; extinction, putting out.*

bε̄r-an (§§3890, 3899) v.t. *tell to kill, etc., let kill, etc.*

bε̄r-ɛg-ág- (§§4071ff.) v.t. = bε̄rɛdól-.

bε̄r-ɛ-dól- (-rᵒd- §1178; §§4016-17, 4022, 4027) v.t. *be about to kill, etc.*

bε̄r-ɛ-ǧŭ-bū- (§4069) v.t. stat. *be on one's way (coming) to kill, etc.*

bε̄r-ɛ-má- (§§4016-17, 4036, 4041) v.t. *become unable to kill, etc.*

bε̄r-ɛ-nóg- (§§4048ff.) v.t. *go to kill, etc.*
  gέlıb‿bε̄rɛnókkoran⌒ (-b‿b- < -g‿b- §519) *they went (have gone) gazelle-hunting.*

bε̄r-ɛ-nóg-bū- (-nóggū- §546; §4058) v.t. stat. *be on one's way (going) to kill, etc.*

bε̄r-ɛ-tá- (§§4060ff.) v.t. *come to kill, etc.*

bε̄rɛd-ág- (§§3877ff.) v.t. *be in the situation of having killed, etc.*
  ód‿ánn-íb‿bε̄rɛdágın⌒ (-b‿b- < -g‿b- §519) *the cold has numbed my hands;* ‿ánn-íb‿ §1671; collective sg. (§4696a).

bε̄ŋ-ır (N. bέŋkır; §3688) v.t. caus. *cause or allow to kill, etc.*
  ind. pres. āı‿bε̄ŋgıddi⌒.

bε̄-kattı- (N. bε̄ha-; §4093) v.p. *be killed, etc.*
  íg‿bε̄kattımunun⌒ *the fire is not (cannot be* §5379) *put out.*

bε̄kattar‿ (N. bε̄ha-; -tár‿ §2213) and
bε̄kattíd‿ (N. bε̄ha-; §2266) n. *being killed, etc.*

bε̄kattı-bū- (N. bε̄há-; §4105) v.i. stat. *be in a killed (etc.) or killable (etc.) state or condition.*
  íg‿bε̄kattıbúmunun⌒ *the fire (is in such a state that it) can't be put out.*

béddı (a) v.t. *pray, pray to, beg, entreat, implore, invoke;* (b) v.i. *pray, recite prayer* [< *bénd(ı) cp. béndıg *beg* §2868].
  ind. pres. āı‿béddıri‿, ɛr‿béddın‿ (-dí⌒, -dí⌒); perf. āı‿béddıgori⌒ (N. -ıko-, -ıho-).
  imperat. béddı!
  āı‿ártıb‿béddıri⌒ (-b‿b- < -g‿b- §519) *I pray to God.*
  tέkkonom‿béddı(ı) *pray with him (her),* i.e. *pray (recite the* فَاتِحَة) *over the corpse of a deceased person, attend his (her) funeral service.*
  tɛr‿díŋgal‿āı‿tέkkonom‿béddıgori⌒ *when (s)he died I attended his (her) funeral service.*

béddar‿ (-dár‿; §§2200ff.) and
béddíd‿ (§§2256ff.) n. *prayer, supplication, entreaty.*

béddı-dĕn (§§3996-7) v.t. *invoke God on behalf of (the speaker), bless.*
  imperat. béddıdĕn! (-dε̄!, -dε̄!, -dέ!).
  āıgı‿béddıdεn⌒ *give me a blessing.*

béddı-tır (§§3998-9) v.t. *invoke God on behalf of (other than the speaker), bless.*
  āı‿έkkı‿béddıtıddi⌒ *I bless you.*

bɛddır-ɛ-ǧŭ-bū- (§4069) v.i. and t. stat. *be on one's way (coming) to pray, etc.*

bɛddır-ɛ-nóg- (§§4048ff.) v.i. and t. *go to pray, etc.*
  ártıb‿bɛddırɛnógran⌒ (-b‿b- < -g‿b- §519) *they go to pray to God.*

bɛddır-ɛ-nóg-bū- (-nóggū- §546; §4058) v.i. and t. stat. *be on one's way (going) to pray, etc.*
  aŋgíntonn‿έn‿dıóskó, āı‿bɛddırɛnógbūri⌒ (s.v. -g(ı)‿) *my cousin's (mother's brother's son's) wife has died, I am on my way to pray (to the funeral service).*

bɛddır-ɛ-tá- (§§4060ff.) v.i. and t. *come to pray, etc.*

bɛddırέ v.i. *be early, act early* [< imperat. or imperf. stem of Sudan Ar. بَدَّر *id.* + -έ §3636].
  ind. pres. āı‿bɛddırέri⌒; fut. āı‿bıbɛddırέri⌒ (bub-); perf. āı‿bɛddırέgori⌒ (N. -έko-, -έho-).
  imperat. bɛddırέ!
  máŋgu‿ǧéllık‿kólı‿bɛddırέgoran⌒ *those labourers over there began (have begun) work early.*

bɛddırέrar- (-rár‿; §§2200ff.) and
bɛddırέríd‿ (§§2256ff.) n. *being early, early action.*

bɛddırέ-ágıs (-áŋgıs, -áŋıs; §3747ε') v.t. *rouse (etc. s.v. ágıs) early.*

bɛddırέr-an (§§3890, 3899) v.t. *tell to be early, let be early, etc.*

bɛddırέ-bıčč(ı) (§3747ε') v.i. *wake early.*

bɛddır-ɛt-tá (-ét-tá §3855; §3770) v.t. *bring (ɛt-tá s.v. ɛd) early.*
  imperat. bɛddırétta!

bɛdɛ́ — bɛ́lɛd‿

bɛddɪr-ímbɛl (§ 3767) v.i. (a) rise early; (b) start early.
bɛddɪrē-nóg (§ 3747 ɛ′) v.i. go early.
 imperat. bɛddɪrēnók!, ⁻́.
bɛddɪrē-sókkɛ (§ 3747 ɛ′) v.t. take up (etc. s.v. sókkɛ) early.
bɛddɪrē-tá (§ 3747 ɛ′) v.i. come early.
 ind. pres. āɪ‿bɛddɪrētāri⌒.
 imperat. bɛddɪrēta!
bɛddɪrē-wídɛ (-wɪdɛ́, -wᵘdɛ́; § 3767) v.i. turn (etc. s.v. wídɛ) early.
bɛddɪrē-wídɛ-tá (-wᵘdɛ-; § 3770) v.i. come back early.
 ind. pres. āɪ‿bɛddɪrēwɪdetāri⌒ (-wᵘd-).
 imperat. bɛddɪrēwídeta! (-wɪdéta!, -wᵘdéta!).
bɛdɛ́ begin, etc. = bɛtɛ́.
 ind. pres. āɪ‿bɛdɛ́ri⌒; perf. āɪ‿bɛdɛ́gori⌒ (N. -ɛ́ko-, -ɛ́ho-).
 imperat. bɛdɛ́!, pl. bɛdɛ́wɛ!, ⁻̈.
bédrɪ I shall marry s.v. éd.
***béd(¹)rɪ-** [< بَدْرِي early].
 bédrɪn⌒ (-rī⌒, -rí⌒) it's early.
 bédrɪmunun⌒ it's not early.
béd(¹)rɪ-r‿ (§ 6007) adv. early.
 béd(¹)rɪr⌒ (s)he (it) is (they are) early.
 bédrɪr‿tȧgon⌒ (s)he (it) came (has come) early.
 ɪŋɛ́ŋgɪ‿hartúm‿béd¹rɪr‿bunógru⌒ this year we shall go to Khartoum early.
bɛdrɪg-ɪr- (N. -ɪkɪr-, -ɪhɪr-; § 4139) in composition = bɛddɪrē-.
bɛdrɪgɪr-ágɪs (-áŋgɪs, -áɲɪs) v.t. = bɛddɪrágɪs.
bɛdrɪgɪr-bíčč(ɪ) v.i. = bɛddɪrēbíčč(ɪ).
bɛdrɪgɪr-ɛttá (-ɛ́ttä) v.t. = bɛddɪrɛttá.
 imperat. bɛdrɪgɪrɛ́tta!
bɛdrɪgɪr-ímbɛl v.i. = bɛddɪrímbɛl.
bɛdrɪgɪr-nóg (-ɪnnóg § 628) v.i. = bɛddɪrēnóg.
 imperat. bɛdrɪgɪrnók!, ⁻̈.
bɛdrɪgɪr-sókkɛ v.t. = bɛddɪrēsókkɛ.
bɛdrɪgɪr-tá v.i. = bɛddɪrētá.
 ind. pres. āɪ‿bɛdrɪgɪrtāri⌒; fut. āɪ‿bɛdrɪgɪrbɪtāri⌒ (-but-).
 imperat. bɛdrɪgɪ́rta!
bɛdrɪgɪr-wídɛ (-wɪdɛ́, -wᵘdɛ́) v.i. = bɛdrɪēwídɛ.
bɛdrɪgɪr-wídɛ-tá (-wᵘdɛ-) v.i. = bɛddɪrēwɪdɛtá.
 ind. pres. āɪ‿bɛdrɪgɪrwɪdetāri⌒ (-wᵘd-).
 imperat. bɛdrɪgɪrwídeta! (-wɪdéta!, -wᵘdéta!).
bɛjád n. white (of egg) [< بَيَاض id.].
 obj. -ǎdk(ɪ)‿, -ǎtk(ɪ)‿; -ki⌒.
 kúmbum‿bɛjád‿ (the) white of (the, an) egg.
béjjɛ‿ (§ 2235) n. waist-fringe (رَهَط) of leather, worn by girls under the age of puberty [cp. Tē. ባላት id. RSN, § 80, Beḍ. bálʼa, bála, Bil. balä́t id. RBW, s.v.].
 obj. -jɛg‿.
 pl. -jɛnč(ɪ)‿.
béjji v.i. start the morning, wake in the morning, enter on the morning, be in the morning (= أَصْبَحَ; s.v. sérɛ‿) [< بِيح (§ 1234) imperf. stem of Sudan Ar. باح باح (of dawn) appear (cogn. apparuit), § 2844].
 ind. pres. āɪ‿béjjɪri⌒; perf. āɪ‿béjjɪgori⌒ (N. -ɪko-, -ɪho-).
 imperat. béjji!
 gū‿béjjɪn⌒ the morning begins (it is morning); s.v. gū‿).
 gū‿béjjɪgó⌒ the morning began (has begun, it was (is) morning).
 gū‿bɛjjjóskó⌒ the morning has begun (it is (already) morning).
 ɛr‿bɛjjɪgɪn‿ɪŋɡáu⌒ when you wake in the morning do this.
bɛ́jj(ɪ) v.i. bleat [onom.].
 ind. pres. tɛr‿bɛ́jjɪn⌒ (-jī⌒, -jí⌒); perf. tɛr‿bɛ́jjɪgon⌒ (N. -ɪko-, -ɪho-; -gō⌒, -gó⌒).
 ɛ́ged‿bɛ́jjɪn⌒ the sheep bleats (bleat § 4696 d).
 bɛ́rtɪ‿bɛ́jjɪn⌒ the goat bleats (goats bleat § 4696 d).
bɛ́jjar (-jár‿; §§ 2200 ff.) n. bleating.
 bɛ́rtɪm‿bɛ́jjar‿ (the) bleating of (the) goat(s).
bɛjjíd (§§ 2256 ff.) n. = bɛ́jjar‿.
 ɛ́gem‿bɛjjíd‿ (-m‿b- < -dn‿b- § 594) (the) bleating of (the) sheep.
bɛjjúd (-út‿) n. Bayud (on map), a village on the east bank of the Nile, opposite Argo Island.
 obj. -útt(ɪ)‿ (§ 716), -ti⌒.
 bɛjjúdɪr‿ at (to) Bayud.
 bɛjjúdɪr⌒ (§ 6007) (s)he (it) is (they are) at Bayud.
bɛ́l‿ (one) that lay, etc. s.v. bū.
bɛ́l v.i. (a) issue, emerge, pass out, Fr. sortir, and so (b) come out; (c) go out; (d, of heavenly bodies, like יָצָא, Eth. ወፅአ፡, طَلَعَ) come out sc. of the eastern horizon, rise [cp. ON. ᚾᛖᛚ id. GNT, s.v.; RSN, §§ 129, 200, TOB, § 143, 65; ?cogn. Copt. ⲃⲟⲗ Äusseres SKG, § 393].
 ind. pres. āɪ‿béllin⌒, ɛr‿bélin⌒ (-lī⌒, -lí⌒); fut. āɪ‿bɪbélli⌒ (bub-); perf. āɪ‿bélkori⌒.
 imperat. bél!, pl. bélwɛ! (bélwɛ́!).
 subj. past āɪ‿bélsu⌒ (-su‿).
 kártóm‿bɛl! (§ 1742) come (go) out of the house!
 awámɪr‿bɛlóskoran⌒ orders have been issued.
 unáttɪ‿bɛlóskó⌒ the moon has risen.
 másɪl‿bɛ́lsɪw‿wɛkɪtkɪ‿tȧgoran⌒ (-w‿w- < -n‿w- § 720) they came when the sun rose.
bélar‿ (-lár‿; §§ 2200 ff.) and
bɛlíd (§§ 2256 ff.) n. issuing, emergence, etc.
bɛ́lt(ɪ)‿ (§ 2325 α) n. (a) eruption, outbreak; (b) boil, tumour, abscess, pimple, with collective sg. (§ 4696 c), rash.
 obj. -tɪg‿.
 pl. -tɪnč(ɪ)‿.
bɛ́l-an (§§ 3890 ff.) v.t. tell to issue, etc., let issue, etc.
bɛl-bítt(ɪ) (§ 3747 ɛ′) v.t. pick up after issuing.
bɛl-bɪtti-kál (§ 3765) v.t. eat after issuing and picking up.
bɛl-boččɪr-bɪtti-kál (§ 5605) v.t. eat after issuing and picking up outside.

bɛl-bód (§ 3747 ɛ′) v.i. run while (after) issuing, run out, escape.
bɛ́l-bū- (§ 3931 α) v.i. stat. be in a state of motion outwards, be on one's way out.
 ámbɛs‿tén‿ɡ̌éllɪrtōm‿bɛ́lbūn⌒ my brother is leaving his job.
bɛll-ɛg-ág- (§§ 4071 ff.) v.i. = bɛlɛdól-.
bɛl-ɛ-dól- (-ldól § 1178; § 4022) and
bɛll-ɛ-dól- (-ldól-; § 4027) v.i. be about to issue, etc.
 āɪ‿bɛlɛdóllɪ‿ɡ̌unállɪ‿ɛ́gi⌒ (§ 6222) I'm just going (coming) out to go and see.
bɛl-ɛ-má- (§ 4036) and
bɛll-ɛ-má- (§ 4041) v.i. become unable to issue, etc.
(*bɛlɛd-ág- said not to be used.)
bɛl-ɡ̌ú (§ 3747 ɛ′) v.i. move while (after) issuing, pass along out.
bɛl-ɡ̌ú-bū- (§§ 4198, 3931 α) v.i. stat. be in a state of motion out towards the speaker, be issuing in this direction, be coming out and approaching.
 wél‿kártōm‿bɛlɡ̌úbūn⌒ the dog is coming out of the house towards us.
bɛl-ɡ̌u-nóg- (§ 4146) v.i. go (off) after going along out, pass along out and away.
 imperat. bɛlɡ̌unók!, ⁻̈́, ⁻̈́ (§ 1953).
bɛl-ɡ̌u-tá (§ 4146) v.i. come (back) after going along out, go along out and return.
 imperat. bɛlɡ̌uta! ⁻̈́ (§ 1953).
bɛlk-ídd(ɪ) (§ 3725) (a) v.t. caus. cause or allow to issue, etc.; (b) v.t. send out, out.
 ind. pres. āɪ‿bɛlkíddɪri⌒.
 imperat. bélkɪddi!
 āɪ‿tɛ́kkɪ‿bɛlkíddiri⌒ I'll (§ 5369 b) send (let) him (her, it) out.
bélk-ɪr (§ 3683) v.t. caus. and v.t. = bɛlkídd(ɪ).
 ind. pres. āɪ‿bélkɪddi⌒.
bɛlíŋ-ɪr (bélɪŋgɪr § 1799; N. -ŋkɪr; § 3688) v.t. caus. and v.t. = bɛlkídd(ɪ).
 āɪ‿tɛ́kkɪ‿bélɪŋgíddiri⌒ (⁻̈́, ⁻̈́ § 1812) I'll (§ 5369 b) send (let) him (her, it) out.
bɛl-nóg (§ 3747 ɛ′) v.i. go (away after) issuing, go (away) out.
 ind. pres. āɪ‿bɛlnógri⌒.
 imperat. bɛlnók! (bélnok! § 1871).
 kártōm‿bélnok! go away out of the house!
bɛl-tá (§ 3747 ɛ′) v.i. come (after) issuing, come out.
 ind. pres. āɪ‿bɛltāri⌒.
 imperat. bɛltá!, bélta! (§ 1944).
 kártōm‿bélta! come out of the house (to me, with me)!
bɛl-ta-kál (§ 4146) v.t. eat after coming out.
bɛl-ta-ɡ̌ɛrɪfkɪ-kál (-ruf-; § 5601) v.i. (after) coming out eat (what is growing on) the foreshore.
 ɛ́rɪd‿úrurtōm‿bɛltaɡ̌ɛrɪ́fkɪkálɪn⌒ the hippopotamus coming out of the river eats what is growing on the foreshore.
bélɛd‿ n. (a) district, country; (b) village, town [< بَلَد id.].
 obj. bɛlédk(ɪ)‿, -étk(ɪ)‿, -étt(ɪ)‿ (§ 2462); -ki⌒, -ti⌒.
 gen. béledn‿v., -ɛnn‿v.c., -ɛn‿c. and bélɛdn‿v., -ɛnn‿v.c., -ɛn‿c. (§ 1523).
 pl. bélɛd‿.

pl. gen. bélɛdın⌣.
béledn⌣ábtır⌣ and
bélenn⌣áttır⌣ by the village.
bélenn⌣áttır⌢ (-ɛnn⌣át-) (s)he (it) is (they are) by the village.
bɛlén⌣kɛ́l⌣ the boundary of the district.
bélenn⌣tū́r⌣ and
bélen⌣tū́r⌣ in the district (etc.).
bélenn⌣tū́r⌢ (-ɛn⌣t-) (s)he (it is) (they are) in the district (etc.).
ám⌣bélɛdırtōn⌣tím⌣bélɛn⌣bókkos⌣ sāŋ⌣kémsırén⌢ (s⌣s- < -n⌣s- §680) from my (our) village to their village is a quarter of an hour.
belén-d(ı)⌣ (§§2545ff.) adj. appertaining to the district, etc.
tékkon⌣ám⌣beléndín⌢ (s)he too is of my (our) country (village).
belɛdíje⌣ n. one belonging to the district, etc., native of the district, etc., countryman, compatriot [< بَلَدِّي my countryman].
obj. -jɛg⌣.
pl. -jɛnč(ı)⌣.
tén⌣haddām⌣ám⌣bɛlɛdíjen⌢ his (her) servant is from my (our) country.
bélɛdn⌣íd⌣ (§2363) and
bɛlɛ́dnıd⌣ n. (a) person of the country, inhabitant, native; (b) countryman, rustic.
obj. bélɛdn⌣ídk(ı)⌣, ⌣ítk(ı)⌣, ⌣ítt(ı)⌣ and bɛlɛdnídk(ı)⌣, etc., -kı⌢, -tı⌢.
gen. bélɛdn⌣ídn⌣v., ⌣ín⌣c. and bɛlɛ́d-nıdn⌣v., -ın⌣c.
pl. bélɛdn⌣íri⌣ and bɛlɛdnıri⌣.
beledn̨ırín-d(ı)⌣ (§§2545ff.) adj. (a) appertaining to the inhabitants, native; (b) countrified, rustic.
bélli⌢ I shall find, s.v. él.
bénder⌣ town = bándar⌣.
béndıg (a) v.t. beg, ask as alms; (b) v.i. beg, be a mendicant [with bénd- cp. bédd(ı) entreat; -ıg frequentative §2893].
ind. pres. āı⌣béndıg(ı)rı⌢, ɛr⌣béndıgın⌢ (-gı⌢, -gí⌢); perf. āı⌣bɛndígkorı⌢ (-díkkorı⌢).
imperat. béndık!
part. pres. (§2278) béndıgıl⌣ (one) that begs, etc., beggar, begging; obj. bɛndı-gílg(ı)⌣; pl. bɛndıgılı⌣.
ar⌣íŋg⌣ɛnnartōm⌣béndıgᴵru⌢ we beg this of you.
tén⌣kálgı⌣béndıgí⌢ (s)he begs his (her) bread.
āı⌣bendígmunun⌢ (-munū⌢, munu⌢, -mun⌢ §947; -díŋŋunun⌢ §661) I do not beg (I am not a beggar).
béndıgar⌣ (-gar; §§2200ff.) and
bɛndıgíd⌣ (§§2256ff.) n. begging, mendicancy.
béndıg-an⌣ (§§3890ff.) v.t. tell to beg, etc., let beg, etc.
-bénna⌣ n. paternal uncle, father's brother = -bánna⌣ s.v. -báb⌣ [<-*bāb-énna⌣ §2300].
obj. -bénnag⌣.
pl. -bénnanč(ı)⌣.
Always with a form of the possessive personal pronoun (§2629) prefixed:
ambénna⌣ my father's brother.
ımbénna⌣ your father's brother.
tımbénna⌣ his (her) father's brother.
antımbénna⌣ our father's brother.
ıntımbénna⌣ your (pl.) father's brother.
tıntımbénna⌣ their father's brother.
-bēnnám-buru⌣ (-ámbúru⌣ §1532) father's brother's daughter, cousin.
obj. -búrug⌣.
pl. -búruı⌣.
Always with a form of the possessive personal pronoun (§2629) prefixed:
ambēnnámburu⌣ my father's brother's daughter.
ımbēnnámburu⌣ your father's brother's daughter, etc.
-bēnnan-tŏd⌣ n. father's brother's son, cousin.
voc. -tŏt!, -tó!
obj. -tŏdk(ı)⌣, -tŏtk(ı)⌣, -tŏkk(ı)⌣, -tŏtt(ı)⌣ (§2462); -kı⌢, -tı⌢.
gen. -tŏdn⌣v., -tŏnn⌣v.c., -tŏn⌣c. (§§778–88).
pl. -bēnnán-tonı⌣.
Always with a form of the possessive personal pronoun (§2629) prefixed:
ambēnnantŏd⌣ my father's brother's son.
ımbēnnantŏd⌣ your father's brother's son, etc.
bɛnnág⌣ and (less commonly)
bɛnnáug⌣ n. cotton (-plant, -wool, thread and cloth) [like Ger. Baumwolle < bɛrn-ábug⌣ tree's wool (RN, §47); -nn- < -rn- §628].
obj. -ágk(ı)⌣, -áŋk(ı)⌣, -áugk(ı)⌣, -áuk̆k(ı)⌣, -kı⌢.
pl. -ágı⌣, -áugı⌣.
ím⌣bɛnnágun⌢ this (one) is cotton.
ím⌣bɛnnágırtónun⌢ this is made of cotton.
bɛnnág⌣úl⌣ cotton thread.
bɛnnán-d(ı)⌣ (-ágnd(ı)⌣, -áŋnd(ı)⌣, -áŋŋd(ı)⌣, §643; §§2545ff.) adj. appertaining to cotton, of cotton.
úl⌣bɛnnáŋd(ı)⌣ cotton thread.
bɛnnáŋ-kolɛ⌣ n. gin, wooden machine resembling a mangle, for removing the seeds from cotton.
obj. -lɛg⌣.
pl. -lénč(ı)⌣.
bɛnnáŋkolɛ⌣bɛnnákk⌣éwırıŋ⌣kuk-kósk⌣ósᴵr⌣égı⌢ (§6222) the gin gins the cotton to take out the seeds.
bént(ı)⌣ n. date (palm and fruit), Phoenix dactylifera, Linn. (BSP, 595); with coll. sg. (§4696b) [< Eg. bnj, Copt. ⲃⲛⲛⲉ id. (RSN, §129)+-t (§2323); cp. ON. ⲁⲡⲉⲛⲧⲓ id. GNT, s.v.].
obj. -tıg⌣.
pl. -tınč(ı)⌣.
bénti⌣dígirın⌢ and
bénti⌣bŏgin⌢ the dates fall down (sc. from the tree).
bénti⌣bŏrin⌢ the date-palm falls (-palms fall) down.
béntınči⌣turúŋkaram⌣bórran⌢ the palms fall because of the wind, i.e. …are thrown down by the wind.
bénti⌣béntırtōn⌣āddígirın⌢ the dates are (keep on) dropping from the palm(s).
bénti⌣kúrusaŋkó⌢ the dates (have) got stale.
bénti⌣duráŋkó⌢ (§1924) the date-palm(s) (has, have) got old.
béntın⌣áro⌣ (§§4964–5) pale one(s) of the dates, i.e. dates beginning to ripen, s.v. áro⌣.
bént⌣aroanóskó⌢ the dates have turned yellow (lit. white), i.e. …have begun to ripen.
béntın⌣áss(ı)⌣ shoot(s) of date-palm.
béntın⌣ért(ı)⌣ date-bearing stem(s) of palm.
béntın⌣fás⌣ (-tım⌣fás⌣) date-stone(s).
béntıŋ⌣gól⌣ (cluster of leaves at) top of date-palm.
béntın⌣hášma⌣ and occasionally
béntın⌣ášma⌣ fibre (from bark) of date-palm.
béntın⌣hău(ı)rtɛ⌣ branch(es) or frond(s) of date-palm.
béntın⌣kárr(ı)⌣ female date-palm.
béntın⌣kárro⌣ midrib(s) of date-palm-branch(es).
béntın⌣ónd(ı)⌣ male date-palm.
béntın⌣šége⌣ young date-palm plant(s).
béntın⌣úmbu⌣ trunk(s) of date-palm.
béntın⌣úrsɛ⌣ root(s) of date-palm.
The kinds of date growing in Dóngola are, in approximate order of excellence in native estimation: 1, gundɛ́la⌣=akun-dɛ́na⌣; 2, ɛbɛttamóda⌣; 3, kúrša⌣; 4, ɛbɛ́ttɛ⌣=barakáwi⌣; 5, ğáu⌣; 6, ab-dɛnnū́r⌣; 7, sabbāríjɛ⌣; 8, alımálık⌣; 9, dɛssıkárga⌣; 10, dókna⌣; 11, gélad⌣; 12, kúlma⌣ (kúrma⌣). ğáu⌣ is said to include nos. 6 to 10.
bentín-d(ı)⌣ (§§2545ff.) adj. appertaining to the date (etc.), of the date (etc.).
bénti-kŏ- (§4118) v.i. have date-palms.
árıd⌣béntıkon⌢ (-kò⌢, -kó⌢) the land has date-palms (on it).
árıd⌣bentıkŏmunun⌢ the land has no date-palms (on it).
(part.) béntıkŏl⌣ (§2576) adj. having date-palms; obj. bɛntıkŏlg(ı)⌣, pl. béntıkonı⌣.
ógığ⌣béntıkŏl⌣dámunun⌢ (a) the man that owns date-palms is absent; (b) there is no man present that owns date-palms.
árıd⌣bentıkŏlgı⌣kó⌢ (s)he has land with date-palms.
béñ⌣ n. small skin bag, esp. to hold milk, s.v. masád⌣ [-ñ⌣ dim. §2304].
obj. béŋg(ı)⌣ (occ. approaches *béŋg(ı)⌣ §647), -gı⌢.
pl. béñı⌣.
íččım⌣béñı⌣ (§4685) (a) the (a) skin for milk; (b) the (a) skin (full) of milk.
íččım⌣béñ-wēg⌣éttagon⌢ (s)he (has) brought a skin (full) of milk.
béñ-d(ı)⌣ (§§2545ff.) adj. appertaining to the (a) small skin bag.
bér⌣ n. (a) wood, timber; (b, of tree) trunk; (c) wooden object, pole, beam.
obj. bérk(ı)⌣, -kı⌢.
pl. bérı⌣.
ğówwım⌣bér⌣ (a) wood of tree; (b) trunk of tree.
núbrom⌣bér⌣ pillar of spindle (CSW, p. 21).
núrem⌣bér⌣ post (in centre) of threshing-floor (s.v. núrɛ⌣).
telegrám⌣bér⌣ (-m⌣b- < -fn⌣b- §588) telegraph-pole(s §4696d).

bém-d(ı)⌣ — bért(ı)⌣

bérn⌣gábad⌣ (-rŋ⌣g-) and
bérn⌣kǎčč(ı)⌣ (-rŋ⌣k-) (a) *bark of tree*;
(b) *shaving(s* §4696d).
bérn⌣kǎšš(ı)⌣ (-rŋ⌣k-) *fragment(s) of wood, shaving(s), sawdust.*
bérkı⌣kǎıl⌣ (§2278) *carpenter.*
— also used in sense of *fuel* = ugúllan⌣:
bérkon⌣éssıgoŋgı⌣ğéttaran⌣ (s.v. ğú) *tell him (her) to go and fetch wood and water.*
bēm-d(ı)⌣ (§§2545ff.) adj. *appertaining to (the) wood, etc., of (the) wood, etc., wooden.*
ğérdɛl⌣bérnd(ı)⌣ *the (a) wooden bucket.*
bér-kırı⌣ (bérkírı⌣ §1532; §2539) adj. *resembling wood, like wood.*
bér- (bɛr-) *you will* < bı- (§2967)+ ér⌣ (ɛr⌣, §2604; §2974).
bēr (a) v.i. *get sated, have enough;* (b) v.t. *get sated with, have enough of* [RSN, §129].
ind. pres. aı⌣bérrı⌣, ɛr⌣bérın⌣ (bérı͡⌣, bérí͡⌣); perf. aı⌣bérkorı͡⌣.
imperat. bér!, pl. bérwɛ! (bérwé!).
part. pres. bérıl⌣ (*one) that gets sated, having enough, replete;* obj. bērílg(ı)⌣ (bérílg(ı)⌣ §1526).
part. past bérɛl⌣ (*one) that got sated, having enough, replete;* obj. bērélg(ı)⌣ (bérélg(ı)⌣).
X. ıŋgʼríg⌣éttarıá? *shall* (§5369b) *I bring the sweet?*
Y. wǎram⌣bēróskorı͡⌣ *no, I have had enough* (sc. *to eat;* §6240).
aı⌣íŋgı⌣bēróskorı͡⌣ *I have had enough of this.*
tɛr⌣éssıb⌣bérın͡⌣ (-b⌣b- < -g⌣b- §519) (s)*he (it) has enough water to drink* (...*drinks as much water as (s)he (it) wants*).
bērar⌣ (-rár⌣; §§2200ff.) and
bēríd⌣ (§§2256ff.) n. *satiety, satiation.*
bér-an (§§3890ff.) v.t. *tell to get sated, etc., let get sated, etc.*
bér-bǔ- (§3931α) v.i. stat. *be in a sated state or condition.*
káml⌣éssıgɛb⌣bérbūran͡⌣ (-b⌣b- < -d⌣b- §518) *the camels have had enough water to drink.*
bērr-ɛg-ǎg- (§§4071ff.) v.i. and t. = bērɛdól-.
bēr-ɛ-dól- (-rᵒdól- §1178; §4022) and
bērr-ɛ-dól- (-rᵒdól-; §4027) v.i. and t. *be about to get sated, etc.*
éssıb⌣bērredóllan͡⌣ (-b⌣b- < -g⌣b- §519) *they have nearly had enough water.*
bēr-ɛ-mǎ- (§4036) and
bērr-ɛ-mǎ- (§4041) v.i. and t. *become unable to get sated, etc.*
éssıb⌣bērremǎgoran͡⌣ *they couldn't drink enough water.*
bēred-ǎg- (§3877) v.i. and t. *be in the condition of having got sated, etc.*
bérk-ır (§3683) v.t. caus. and v.t. = bēríŋgır.
ind. pres. aı⌣bérkıddı͡⌣.
íŋ-kál⌣aıgı⌣bérkırın͡⌣ *this food satiates me.*
bēríŋg-ır (⌣ §1799; N. -ŋkır; §3688) (a) v.t. caus. *cause or allow to get sated, etc.;* (b) v.t. *sate, satiate.*

bēr v.i. *sprout, begin to grow, come up, come out.*
ind. pres. tɛr⌣bérın⌣ (-rí͡⌣, -rí͡⌣), pl. tır⌣bérran⌣ (-rä͡⌣, -rá͡⌣); perf. tɛr⌣bérkon⌣ (-kō͡⌣, -kó͡⌣).
part. pres. bérıl⌣ (*one) that sprouts, etc., sprouting;* obj. bērílg(ı)⌣ (bérílg(ı)⌣ §1526).
part. past bérɛl⌣ (*one) that sprouted, etc., sprouting;* obj. bērélg(ı)⌣ (bérélg(ı)⌣).
márɛ⌣bēróskó͡⌣ *the millet has sprouted.*
bérar (-rár⌣ §2200ff.) and
bēríd (§§2256ff.) n. *sprouting.*
X. mám⌣mınéllé? *what's that over there?*
Y. mahádam⌣bērídun͡⌣ *it's the sprouting of the maize.*
bér-bǔ- (§3931α) v.i. stat. *be in a sprouting state or condition.*
márɛ⌣bérbūn͡⌣ *the millet is sprouting.*
bērr-ɛg-ǎg- (§§4071ff.) v.i. = bēredól-.
bēr-ɛ-dól- (-rᵒdól- §1178; §4022) and
bērr-ɛ-dól- (-rᵒdól-; §4027) v.i. *be about to sprout, etc.*
márɛ⌣bērredólın͡⌣ *the millet is about to come up.*
bēr-ɛ-mǎ- (§4036) and
bērr-ɛ-mǎ- (§4041) v.i. *become unable to sprout, etc.*
bēred-ǎg- (§3877) v.i. *be in the condition of having sprouted, etc.*
márɛ⌣bēredǎgın͡⌣ *the millet has started coming up.*
bérk-ıdd(ı) (§3725) v.t. caus. *cause or allow to sprout, etc.*
éssıgom⌣másılgon⌣déssɛb⌣bérkıddın͡⌣ (-b⌣b- < -g⌣b- §519) *water and sun make the vegetation come up.*
bēríŋg-ır (bérıŋgır §1799; N. -ŋkır; §3688) v.t. caus. = bérkıdd(ı).

bérag n. *flag* [< بَيْرَق *id.*].
obj. bēragk(ı)⌣, -ákk(ı)⌣, -kı͡⌣.
pl. béragı⌣.
béram n. *Bairam, festival after Ramaḍán* [< بيرم].
obj. bérámg(ı)⌣, -gı͡⌣.
bérámır⌣ *at Bairam.*
bérber⌣ (bárbár⌣, bárbar⌣ §1327) n. *Berber, a town on the right bank of the Nile about 23 miles below the entry of the Atbara.*
obj. bɛrbérk(ı)⌣, -kı͡⌣.
bɛrbérro⌣ *at (to) Berber.*
bérberı⌣ (bárbárı⌣, bárbarı⌣ §1327; bérbérı⌣, etc. §1532) n. *Nubian* [< بَرْبَرِيّ *id.* (onom., cp. βάρβαροι); LA, s.v., LN, p. II note].
obj. -rıg⌣.
pl. bɛrbɛrınč(ı)⌣.
bérgo⌣ n. *infertile land (high or low; NSD, 24)* [?< bérıǧ *slaughter* +-o⌣ dem. §4573].
obj. -ǧog⌣ [> Sudan Ar. برجوق *id.*].
pl. -ǧonč(ı)⌣.
bérı⌣ n. *side (of animate or inanimate object); with coll. sg.* (§4696a) [§§2251-5; RSN, §129; TEG, §608].
obj. -rıg⌣.
pl. bēríč(ı)⌣.
ém⌣bérı⌣ *your side(s).*
ódam⌣bérı⌣ *the side(s) of the room.*

bérıŋ⌣kíhıd⌣ (etc. s.v. kíhıd⌣) *rib(s).*
tém⌣bérıgɛt⌣túbbın͡⌣ (s)*he (it) lies on his (her, its) side.*
berıgeb-bǔ (§3947) v.i. *lie (be lying) on one's side.*
tém⌣bérıgeb⌣bǔ͡⌣ (-b⌣b- < -d⌣b- §518) and (§§5572, 1931).
tém⌣bērıgébbū͡⌣ (s)*he (it) is lying on his (her, its) side.*
bérıǧ n. *lightning* [< بَرْق *id.* §§1332, 1359].
obj. berígk(ı)⌣, -íkk(ı)⌣, -kı͡⌣.
pl. bérıǧı⌣.
bérıǧ v.t. *massacre, slaughter, kill in numbers* [< bē *kill* +-r app. gerundial (§3556) but perhaps intensive (§4586)+-ǧ intensive §2886].
ind. pres. aı⌣bérıǧ(ʼ)rı⌣, ɛr⌣bérıǧın⌣ (-ǧí͡⌣, -ǧí͡⌣); perf. aı⌣berígkorı͡⌣ (-íčk-; -ǧk-, -čk- §323).
imperat. béríč!
part. pres. bérıǧıl⌣ (*one) that massacres, etc., wholesale killer, massacring, etc.*
part. past bérıǧel⌣ (*one) that massacred, etc., wholesale killer, massacring, etc.*
def. perf. aı⌣berıǧóskorı͡⌣.
ím⌣báŋgab⌣bérıǧrı͡⌣ (-b⌣b- < -g⌣b- §519) *I'll* (§5369) *kill these locusts.*
dɛrewíšı⌣berıčkoran͡⌣ *the Dervishes killed many people.*
bérıǧar⌣ (-ǧár⌣; §2200ff.) and
berıǧíd⌣ (§§2256ff.) n. *massacre, slaughter, carnage.*
bérıǧ-an (§§3890ff.) v.t. *tell to massacre, etc., let massacre, etc.*
bérıǧ-bǔ- (§3931β) v.i. stat. *be in a massacred (etc.) state or condition.*
kúltı⌣bérıǧbūn͡⌣ *the flies* (§4696c) *lie killed in numbers.*
berıǧed-ǎg- (§3877) v.t. *be in the situation of having massacred, etc.*
bérıǧ-kattı- (-íčk-, ⌣, -ǧk-, -čk-; §4093) v.p. *be massacred, etc.*
berrád⌣ (bár-, bar-) n. *pot, kettle, tea-pot* [< Sudan Ar. بَرَّاد *id.*].
obj. -ádk(ı)⌣, -átk(ı)⌣, -átt(ı)⌣ (§2462), -kı͡⌣, -tı͡⌣.
gen. -ádn⌣v., -án⌣c.
pl. -ád⌣.
berrád⌣šáınd(ı)⌣ *tea-pot.*
berránčı⌣ *handle of tea-pot.*
bért(ı)⌣ n. (a, prop.) *she-goat;* (b) *goat (she- and he-). With coll. sg.* (§4696d) [< *bǎjjárt(ı)⌣ < bǎjjár⌣ n. act. of bǎjj(ı)⌣ *bleat* (RN, §294)+-t dem. (§2325β), so *that bleating*].
obj. -tıg⌣.
pl. -tınč(ı)⌣.
bertınčıg⌣íwıl⌣ *goatherd.*
bertın-tód⌣ (§2366) n. *young of goat, kid;* with coll. sg. (§4696d).
voc. -tót!, -tó!
obj. -tódk(ı)⌣, -tótk(ı)⌣, -tókk(ı)⌣, -tótt(ı)⌣ (§2462), -kı͡⌣, -tı͡⌣.
gen. -tódn⌣v., -tónn⌣v.c., -tón⌣c. (§§778-88).
pl. bértıntonı⌣, ⌣⌣ (§1689).
bertıntódun⌣ *it's a kid.*
bértı-tod⌣ (§2369) n. (a) *unsatisfactory, poor or indifferent specimen of goat;* (b) *goat.*

voc. bértıtŏt!, bértıtó!
obj. bértıtŏdk(ı)⌣, -tŏtk(ı)⌣, -tŏkk(ı)⌣, -tŏtt(ı)⌣, -ki⌒, -ti⌒.
gen. bértıtŏdn⌣v., -tŏnn⌣v.c., -tŏn⌣c.
pl. bértıton⌣.
bértıtodun⌒ *it's a (rather poor) goat.*
bɛrtín-d(ı)⌣ (§§ 2545 ff.) adj. *appertaining to the (a) goat, of the (a) goat, (the, a) goat's.*
bɛrtınčín-d(ı)⌣ (§§ 2545 ff.) adj. *appertaining to (the) goats, of (the) goats, (the) goats'.*
bɛrtíndı-kırı⌣ (§ 2541) adj. *like the (a) goat's.*
bɛrtınčíndı-kırı⌣ (§ 2541) adj. *like (the) goats'.*
-bɛs⌣ n. *brother.*
obj. -bésk(ı)⌣, -ki⌒.
gen. -bɛsn⌣, -bɛzn⌣.
pl. -bɛsı⌣.
— always with a form of the possessive personal pronoun (§ 2629) prefixed:
ámbɛs⌣ *my brother.*
ímbɛs⌣ *your brother.*
tímbɛs⌣ *his (her, its) brother.*
antímbɛs⌣ *our brother.*
ıntímbɛs⌣ *your (pl.) brother.*
tıntímbɛs⌣ *their brother.*
aı⌣tímbɛs⌣ɛri⌒ *I am his (her) brother.*
tɛr⌣ámbɛsun⌒ (§ 1966) *he is my brother.*
ámbɛs-sɛ́run⌒ (-s-s- < -s-w- § 687; §§ 1561, 1565) *he is one of my brothers, lit. he is a my brother.*
ámbɛsn⌣ɛn⌣ *my brother's wife.*
ánnɛn⌣tímbɛs⌣ *my wife's brother.*
ánnogıň⌣tímbɛsun⌒ (-ň⌣t- < -ǧn⌣t- § 632) *he is my husband's brother.*
búru⌣tımbɛ́skı⌣dólın⌒ *the girl loves (wants) her brother.*
-bésnd(ı)⌣ (-béznd(ı)⌣, §§ 2545 ff.) adj. *appertaining to a brother, brother's.*
ambésnd(ı)⌣ (-ézn-) *my brother's.*
ımbésnd(ı)⌣ (-ézn-) *your brother's, etc.*
dúŋgı⌣tımbézndı⌣dabóskŏ⌒ *his (her) brother's money has disappeared.*
-bɛstŏd⌣ (§ 2368) n. *brother's child, nephew, niece* [< -*bɛsn-tŏd⌣ § 2474].
voc. -tŏt!, -tó!
obj. -tŏdk(ı)⌣, -tŏtk(ı)⌣, -tŏkk(ı)⌣, -tŏtt(ı)⌣ (§ 2462); -ki⌒, -ti⌒.
gen. -tŏdn⌣v., -tŏnn⌣v.c., -tŏn⌣c. (§§ 778-88).
pl. -tonı⌣.
— always with a form of the possessive personal pronoun (§ 2629) prefixed:
ámbɛstŏd⌣ *my brother's child.*
ímbɛstŏd⌣ *your brother's child.*
tímbɛstŏd⌣ *his (her) brother's child.*
antímbɛstŏd⌣ *our brother's child.*
ıntímbɛstŏd⌣ *your (pl.) brother's child.*
tıntímbɛstŏd⌣ *their brother's child.*
ámbɛstonı⌣ *my brother's children.*
ímbɛstonı⌣ *your brother's children.*
tıntímbɛstonı⌣ *their brother's children.*

bés⌣ adv. *only, just* [بَس id.].
wɛg⌣éttagom⌣bés⌣ *(a) you (have) brought one only; (b) (s)he has brought one only.*
bés⌣íŋk⌣úskur⌒ (⌣iŋk < ⌣iŋkɛ⌣) *put it just like this (that).*
íŋgɛb⌣bés⌒ (-b⌣b- < -d⌣b- § 518) *(put it) just like this (that).*

bés v.t. comb.
ind. pres. aı⌣bésri⌒, ɛr⌣bésın⌒ (bésī⌒, bésí⌒); perf. aı⌣béskori⌒.
ánn-urkı⌣béskori⌒ *I (have) combed my head.*
bés-an v.t. (§§ 3890 ff.) *tell to comb, let comb.*
béz-bū- (§ 3931 β) v.i. stat. *be in a combed state or condition.*
téṇ⌣díltı⌣bézbūn⌒ *his (her) hair is combed.*
bɛsír⌣ and **bésır**⌣ (§§ 1068, 1154) n. *(a) comb; (b) heddle* (CSW, p. 33) [§§ 2283-4].
bɛsír⌣ usually = (b), bésır⌣ usually = (a).
obj. bɛsírk(ı)⌣, bɛsírk(ı)⌣, bésırk(ı)⌣; -ki⌒.
pl. bɛsírı⌣, bésırı⌣.
béssandı⌒ *I shall go to the water,* s.v. éss(ı)⌣.
béšɛ⌣ n. *jar in a water-wheel* (kólɛ⌣); *the jars, each in its cradle* (kórıs⌣), *are lashed to pairs of rungs* (áglonč(ı)⌣) *that are between two endless cables* (álası⌣) *passing over the vertical wheel* (átt(ı)⌣) [< *béššɛ⌣ < *béňšɛ⌣ < *béňsɛ⌣ < béň⌣ *small skin bag* + -s dem. or dim. + -ɛ⌣ of n. ess., from its baglike shape § 2322 β].
obj. -šɛg⌣, -gi⌒.
pl. -šɛnč(ı)⌣.
béšɛŋ⌣kórıs⌣ *cradle of jar.*

bɛté (bɛdé) v.t. *begin, start, commence* [< بَدَأ *beginning* + -ɛ́ §§ 1218, 3626].
ind. pres. aı⌣bɛtéri⌒; perf. aı⌣bɛtégori⌒ (N. -éko-, -ého-).
imperat. bɛté!, pl. bɛtɛ́wɛ!.
aı⌣íŋg⌣ınnówwıb⌣bıbɛtéri⌒ (-b⌣b- < -g⌣b- § 519) *I shall begin this today.*
ár⌣ólgom⌣bɛtɛ́gómunun⌒ *we haven't begun yet.*
ólgoŋ⌣gullíttı⌣bɛdɛgómunan⌒ *they haven't started sowing yet.*
bɛtérar (bɛdé-; -rar⌣; §§ 2200 ff.) and
bɛtɛríd (bɛdé-; §§ 2256 ff.) n. *beginning, start, commencement.*
bɛtɛ́r-an (bɛdɛ́r-; §§ 3890, 3899) v.t. *tell to begin, let begin, etc.*
bɛtɛ́-bū- (bɛdɛ́-; § 3931 β) v.i. stat. *be in a begun (etc.) state or condition.*
ǧɛllı⌣bɛdɛ́būn⌒ *the work is (has been) begun.*
bɛtɛ́r-ɛg-ág- (bɛdɛ́r-; §§ 4071 ff.) v.t. = bɛtɛ́rɛdól-.
bɛtɛ́r-ɛ-dól- (bɛdɛ́r-; -ʳdól-; § 1178; §§ 4016-7, 4022, 4027) v.t. *be about to begin, etc.*
aı⌣níčč⌣ıb⌣bɛtɛ́rɛdólli⌒ (-b⌣b- < -g⌣b- § 519) *I am just going to start sewing.*
bɛtɛ́r-ɛ-ǧú-bū- (bɛdɛ́r-; § 4069) v.t. stat. *be on one's way (coming) to begin, etc.*
bɛtɛ́r-ɛ-má- (bɛdɛ́r-; §§ 4016-17, 4036, 4041) v.t. *become unable to begin, etc.*
bɛtɛ́r-ɛ-nóg- (bɛdɛ́r-; §§ 4048 ff.) v.t. *go to begin, etc.*
bɛtɛ́r-ɛ-nŏg-bū- (bɛdɛ́r-; -nŏggŭ- § 546; § 4058) v.t. stat. *be on one's way (going) to begin, etc.*
bɛtɛ́r-ɛ-tá- (bɛdɛ́r-; §§ 4060 ff.) v.t. *come to begin, etc.*
bɛtɛ́rɛd-ág- (bɛdɛ́r-; § 3877) v.t. *be in the situation of having begun, etc.*
bɛtɛ́ŋ-ır (bɛdɛ́-; N. -ŋkır; § 3688) v.t. caus. *cause or allow to begin, etc.*

ǧɛllıb⌣bɛtɛ́ŋgıddi⌒ (-b⌣b- < -g⌣b- § 519) *I make (let) the work begin (I set the work going).*
aı⌣tékkı⌣ǧɛllıb⌣bɛtɛ́ŋgıddi⌒ and aı⌣ǧɛllıt⌣tékkı⌣bɛtɛ́ŋgıddi⌒ (-t⌣t- < -g⌣t- §§ 707-8) *I make (let) him (her) begin (the) work.*
bɛtɛ́-kattı- (bɛdɛ́-; N. -éha-; § 4093) v.p. *be begun, etc.*

bɛ́u, bɛ́w, bɛ́u v.t. *(a) unravel, untwist, separate the strands of; (b) unwind; (c) disentangle; (d, confused matter) clear up, straighten out; (e) make peace between, reconcile.*
ind. pres. aı⌣bɛ́uri⌒ (⌣bɛ́wʳri⌒), ɛr⌣bɛ́wın⌒ (-wī⌒, -wí⌒); perf. aı⌣bɛ́ukori⌒ (N. -uho-).
írıb⌣bɛwóskon⌒ (-b⌣b- < -g⌣b- § 519) *(s)he has untwisted (etc.) the rope.*
úl⌣káttıbúlgı⌣bɛ́ukó⌒ *(s)he (has) unwound the wound thread.*
ánn⌣ímmab⌣bɛ́ukori⌒ (-b⌣b- < -g⌣b- § 519) *I (have) unwound my turban.*
úl⌣kúrtıbúlgı⌣bɛ́ukó⌒ *(s)he (has) disentangled the tangled thread.*
ɛǧǧwádı⌣šɛklɛ́bulıb⌣bɛwırıddán⌒ (-b⌣b- < -g⌣b- § 519) *peacemakers make peace between the quarrellers.*
šākılēbúgoram⌣bɛwırıkkori⌒ *they were quarrelling (but § 6240) I (have) reconciled them.*
bɛ́war (-wár⌣; §§ 2200 ff.) and
bɛwíd (§§ 2256 ff.) n. *unravelling, etc.; peacemaking, reconciliation.*
bɛ́w-an (§§ 3890 ff.) v.t. *tell to unravel, etc., let unravel, etc.*
bɛ́u-bū- (§ 3931 β) v.i. stat. *be in an unravelled (etc.) state or condition.*
írı⌣bɛ́ubūn⌒ *the rope (a) is (has come) untwisted (has its strands separated = fírtıbūn⌒); (b) is unwound; (c) is disentangled.*
šākılēbúgoran⌣ɛ́kkɛnɛ⌣bɛ́uburan⌒ *they were quarrelling, now they are reconciled.*
bɛ́ur-ɛg-ág- (bɛ́wʳr-; §§ 4071 ff.) v.t. = bɛ́wɛdól-.
bɛ́w-ɛ-dól- (-wᵒdól- § 1178; § 4022) and
bɛ́ur-ɛ-dól- (bɛ́wʳr-; -ʳdol-; § 4027) v.t. *be about to unravel, etc.*
bɛ́ur-ɛ-ǧú-bū- (bɛ́wʳr-; § 4069) v.t. stat. *be on one's way (coming) to unravel, etc.*
bɛ́w-ɛ-má- (§ 4036) and
bɛ́ur-ɛ-má- (bɛ́wʳr-; § 4041) v.t. *become unable to unravel, etc.*
bɛ́ur-ɛ-nóg- (bɛ́wʳr-; §§ 4048 ff.) v.t. *go to unravel, etc.*
bɛ́ur-ɛ-nógbū- (bɛ́wʳr-; -nóggŭ- § 546; § 4058) v.t. stat. *be on one's way (going) to unravel, etc.*
bɛ́ur-ɛ-tá- (bɛ́wʳr-; §§ 4060 ff.) v.t. *come to unravel, etc.*
bɛ́wɛd-ág- (§ 3877) v.t. *be in the situation of having unravelled, etc.*
bɛ́u-kattı- (N. -uha-; § 4093) v.p. *be unravelled, etc.*
šɛklɛbúgoram⌣bɛ́ukattóskoran⌒ *they were quarrelling, they have been reconciled.*

†bíba n. *tobacco-pipe* [< بيبة < It. *pipa* id.].
obj. bíbag⌣, -gi⌒; pl. bíbanč(ı)⌣.

bír⌣ — bíll(1)

bír⌣ n. *bracelet*, worn by women and girls, and by boys at circumcision [*RSN*, §129; ?contains í-r⌣ *on the hand(s)* §4497].
  obj. bírk(ı)⌣, -ki⌢.
  pl. bíri⌣.

bír⌣ v.t. *transport, carry, move* [?contains í-r⌣ *on the hand(s)* §4497].
  ind. pres. aī⌣bírri⌣, ɛr⌣bíri⌢ (-rí⌢, -rí⌢); fut. aī⌣bıbírri⌢ (bub-); perf. aī⌣bírkori⌢.
  part. pres. bírıl⌣ (*one*) *that transports, etc., transporter, etc., transporting, etc.*
  part. past bírɛl⌣ (*on*) *that transported, etc., transporter, etc., transporting, etc.*
  afɛ́sk⌣attáli⌣bıbírran⌢ (*the*) *porters will transport the baggage.*
  kúlu⌣dıgríğ⌣ğɛbéllotōn⌣úrum⌣món⌣kom⌣bírkoran⌢ (-ğ⌣ğ- < -g⌣ğ- §551) *they (have) transported much stone from the mountain(s, desert) to the river.*

bírar⌣ (-rár⌣; §§2200ff.) and
biríd⌣ (§§2256ff.) n. *transport, carriage.*

bir-ăg-óğı- (§§4198, 5634–5) v.t. (a) *be engaged in conveying (etc. s.v. óğı) by transporting, etc., be engaged in carrying along*; (b) *continually (habitually) convey (etc.) by transporting, etc.*
  attál⌣gatírroton⌣afɛ́ski⌣băbúrro⌣bīrăgóğiran⌢ *the porters are conveying (habitually convey) the baggage from the train to the steamer by carrying it.*

bír-an (§§3890ff.) v.t. *tell to transport, etc., let transport, etc.*

bír-bŭ- (§3931β) v.i. stat. *be in a transported (etc.) state or condition.*
  úmbu⌣bírbūn⌢ *the palm-trunk is (has been) transported (...palm-trunks are, etc.* §4647).

birr-ɛg-ág- (§§4071ff.) v.t. = bīrɛdól-.
bir-ɛ-dól- (-rᵒd- §1178; §4022) and
birr-ɛ-dól- (-rᵒd-; §4027) v.t. *be about to transport, etc.*

birr-ɛ-ğŭ-bŭ- (§4069) v.t. stat. *be on one's way (coming) to transport, etc.*

bir-ɛ-má- (§4036) and
birr-ɛ-má- (§4041) v.t. *become unable to transport, etc.*

birr-ɛ-nóg- (§§4048ff.) v.t. *go to transport, etc.*

birr-ɛ-nóg-bŭ- (-nóggŭ- §546; §4058) v.t. stat. *be on one's way (going) to transport, etc.*

birr-ɛ-tá- (§§4060ff.) v.t. *come to transport, etc.*

birɛd-ăg- (§3877) v.t. *be in the situation of having transported, etc.*
  úmbub⌣bīrɛdágran⌢ (-b⌣b- < -g⌣b- §519) *they have transported the palm-trunk(s* §4647).

bír-kattı- (§4093) v.p. *be transported, etc.*
  ín⌣dúllon, bírkattımunun⌢ *this (that) is (too) heavy, it can't (§5379) be moved.*

†**bíra⌣** n. *(European) beer* [< بيرة < It. *birra* id.].
  obj. -rag⌣, -gi⌣.

bitán⌣ (bıt-, but-; §956d) n. (a) *child (of any age), offspring*; like tód⌣, ولد, commonly; (b) *male child, son*; so (c) *boy*; (d, *of animals*) *young*; (e, *of plants*) *fruit, seed*; with collective sg. (§4696b), but- is said to be an Arab mispronunciation [< bıtán⌣ (*that*) *(s)he will come* (§2145); > Sudan Ar. بطان id. plural (*AESA*, s.v. *children*) from confusion with بطون, cp. جابت لي ثلثة بطون *she bore me three children* (Id. ib. s.v. *bear*)].
  obj. -áng(ı)⌣, -gi⌣.
  gen. -ánn⌣v., -án⌣c.
  pl. -áni⌣.
  tím⌣bıtám⌣búrun⌢ *their child is a girl.*
  tɛr⌣ám⌣bitánun⌢ *he is my (our) son.*
  búruı⌣táwaŋgal⌣bıtáni⌣nogóskoran⌢ *when the girls came the boys went away*; ⌣táwaŋgal s.v. al⌣.
  káñ⌣bitán⌣ *colt, foal*; káñ⌣ gen. of káğ⌣.
  ğówwım⌣bıtán⌣ *fruit (seed) of tree.*
  káuırtɛ⌣arán⌣bitáŋgı⌣kálın⌢ *the bird eats (birds eat §4647) the seeds of the mustard-tree.*
  koín⌣bitáŋgı⌣kállan⌢ (-n⌣b- < -dn⌣b- §594) *they eat the fruit of Zizyphus spina-christi.*

bitám-buru⌣ (bıt-, but-; ⌢ §1532; §2363) *son's daughter, grand-daughter.*
  obj. -burug⌣.
  pl. -buru⌣, -burwi⌣.
  tím⌣bıtámburun⌢ *she is their grand-daughter.*

bitán-tód⌣ (bıt-, but-; §2366) *son's son, grandson.*
  voc. -tót!, -tó!
  obj. -tódk(ı)⌣, -tótk(ı)⌣, -tótt(ı)⌣ (§2462); -ki⌢, -ti⌢.
  gen. -tódn⌣v., -tónn⌣v.c., -tón⌣c. (§§778–88).
  pl. bitántonı⌣, bıt-, but-.
  ín⌣ám⌣bitántódun⌢ *this is my (our) son's son.*

bitán-tod⌣ (bıt-, but-; §2369d) *male child up to four or five years of age* (not depreciative).
  voc. bitántot!, bitántó!
  obj. bitántódk(ı)⌣, -tótk(ı)⌣, -tótk(ı)⌣, -tótt(ı)⌣; -ki⌢, -ti⌢.
  gen. bitántódn⌣v., -tónn⌣v.c., -tón⌣c.
  pl. bitántonı⌣.
  ín⌣ám⌣bitántodun⌢ *this is my (our) little boy.*

bitáŋ-kō- (§4115) v.i. *bear fruit, be fructiferous.*
  ín⌣ğówwı⌣bitáŋgı⌣kōn⌢ *this tree has fruit (on it).*
  ín⌣ğówwı⌣bıtáŋkōn⌢ *this tree has fruit (is fructiferous; §5710).*

bı- prefix forming future tense (§§2966ff.).

bíblığ⌣ n. *thick ear-ring of solid gold or silver*; with collective sg. (§4696d) [§2275].
  obj. bıblíğk(ı)⌣; -íčk(ı)⌣, -íč(ı)⌣ (§523); -ğk-, -čk- (§323); -ki⌢, -či⌢.
  pl. bíblığı⌣.

bíčč(1) v.i. (a) *wake, wake up*; (b) *be awake* [cp. ON. пικκ id. *GNT*, s.v.; *RSN*, §200].
  ind. pres. aī⌣bíčči⌣, ɛr⌣bíččın⌢ (-čí⌢, -čí⌢).
  fut. aī⌣bıbíčči⌣ (bub-).
  perf. aī⌣bíčıgori⌢ (N. -ıko-, -ıho-).
  imperat. bíčči!
  bıččóskoran⌢ *they have woken up.*
  X. ɛsmán⌣nɛ́rbūná? *is ɛoθmán asleep?*
  Y. wáram⌣bíčči⌢ *no, he's awake.*

bíččar⌣ (-čár⌣; §§2200ff.) and
bíččíd⌣ (§§2256ff.) n. *waking, awakening.*

bıčč-ăg- (§§3747ɛ', 3875) v.i. *be awake.*
bıčč-bŭ- (§3931α) v.i. stat. *be awake.*
bíčč-ıg-ır (N. -ıkır, -ıhır; §3682) (a) v.t. caus. *cause or allow to wake;* (b) v.t. *wake, rouse.*
bíčči-nál (§3747ɛ') v.t. *see on waking.*

bıdá⌣ v.i. *come* [with -dá cp. dá- *be going along*].
  ind. pres. aī⌣bıdári⌣, ɛr⌣bıdán⌢ (-dá⌢, -dá⌢); fut. aī⌣bıbıdári⌣ (bub-); perf. aī⌣bıdágori⌢ (N. -áko-, -áho-).
  imperat. bída!, pl. bıdáwɛ! (bıdáwɛ!).
  subj. past aī⌣bıdásı⌣ (-su⌣).
  áıgonó⌣bída⌣ *come with me.*
  áru⌣bıdágó⌢ *the rain came (has come).*
  ıškártınčı⌣bıdágoran⌢ *the guests came (have come).*

bígıd⌣ n. *trap, snare, noose.*
  obj. bıgídk(ı)⌣, -ítk(ı)⌣, -ítt(ı)⌣; -ki⌢, -ti⌢.
  gen. bıgídn⌣v., bıgín⌣c.
  pl. bíg(ı)dı⌣.

bílañ⌣ n. *rag* [? < بلى *attrition, wear and tear* + -ñ dim. §2304].
  obj. bıláñg(ı)⌣, -gi⌣.
  pl. bílañ⌣.

bılínč(1) v.i. *flash continually* or *continuously, glitter, sparkle, gleam, shine, be bright, be brilliant* (= fılínč(1), tulúnč(1) [< √bılínč- *flash* (§4499) + -č intensive (§4502) much §2864]).
  ind. pres. tɛr⌣bılínčı⌢ (-čí⌢, -čí⌢), tır⌣bılínčıran⌣ (-rá⌢, -rá⌢); perf. tɛr⌣bılínčıgon⌢ (N. -ıko-, -ıho-; -gō⌢, -gó⌢).
  nóbrɛ⌣masíllo⌣bılínčın⌢ *the gold glitters in the sun.*
  wıssı⌣bılínčın⌢ *the star glitters (...stars glitter §4696d).*
  másıl⌣bılínčın⌢ *the sun shines.*
  unáttı⌣bılínčın⌢ *the moon shines.*
  íg⌣bılínčın⌢ *the fire (light) shines (flashes).*
  búru⌣tónğılun, bılínčın⌢ *the girl is beautiful, she is brilliant.*
  ɛ́lım⌣míssı⌣bılínčıgó⌢ *the crocodile's eye (eyes §4696a) glittered.*

bíllɛ⌣ n. *onion*; with collective sg. (§4696b).
  obj. -lɛg⌣.
  pl. bıllénč(ı)⌣.
  bíllɛg⌣ɛwírran⌣ *they grow onions.*
  bíllɛn⌣írıs⌣ *the smell of the onion(s).*

bíllɛ-kıñ́ñ(ı)⌣ (§§2536–7) adj. *devoid of onions.*

bıllɛn-írís-kıñ́ñ(ı)⌣ (§2538) adj. *devoid of the smell of the onion.*
  kándı⌣bıllɛnírıskıñ́ñı⌣wɛd⌣dólli⌢ (-d⌣d- < -g⌣d- §534) *I want a knife that does not smell of onions.*

bíllɛ-kırı⌣ (§2539) adj. *resembling the onion.*

bíll(1) v.t. *pick, pick apart, pick to pieces, tease, tease out.*
  ind. pres. aī⌣bíllıri⌣, ɛr⌣bíllın⌢ (-lí⌢, -lí⌢); perf. aī⌣bíllıgori⌢ (N. -ıko-, -ıho-).

imperat. bílli!
hášmab‿bílliranᐞ (-b‿b- < -g‿b- §519) *they pick the fibre apart.*
abúkkı‿bílligoranᐞ *they (have) teased out the wool.*
bíllar‿ (-lár‿; §§2200ff.) and
bıllíd‿ (§§2256ff.) n. *picking, etc.*
bíll-an (§§3890ff.) v.t. *tell to pick, etc., let pick, etc.*
bílli-bŭ- (§3931β) v.i. stat. *be in a picked (etc.) state or condition.*
ábug‿bíllıbūnᐞ *the wool is (has been) teased out.*
bıllɛd-ág- (§3877) v.t. *be in the situation of having picked, etc.*
ɛ́n‿abúkkı‿bıllɛdágınᐞ *the woman has teased out the wool.*
bílli-kattı- (N. -ıha-; §4093) v.p. *be picked, etc.*
bínnɛ‿ n. *Gharb Binna (on map), a village on the left bank of the Nile, west of the centre of Árgo Island.*
obj. bínnɛg‿, bínnɛgᐞ (§1532).
bınnɛn-árt(ı)‿ (-tiᐞ) n. *Island of Bínnɛ, an island west of the centre of Árgo Island.*
obj. -tıg‿.
bınníjɛ‿ n. *a large Nile fish of light colour, Barbus bynni, Foskal (PF, p. 94); with collective sg. (§4696 d)* [< بُنِّيّة n. un. of بُنِّي id.].
obj. -jɛg‿.
pl. -jɛnč(ı)‿.
bírbɛ‿ n. *ancient temple* [< بِرْبَة id. < Copt. ⲡⲉⲣⲡⲉ *der Tempel, SKG, §150*].
obj. -bɛg‿.
pl. -bɛnč(ı)‿.
bírd(ı)‿ n. *broom.*
obj. -dıg‿.
pl. -dınč(ı)‿.
bırkíjɛ-már‿ n. *Berkia (on map), a village on the left bank of the Nile, at the northern end of Árgo Island [Bırkíjɛ village].*
obj. -márk(ı)‿, -kiᐞ.
bırkíjɛmárro‿ (s.v. -r‿) *at (to) B.*
bırkíjɛmárroᐞ (§6007) *(s)he (it) is (they are) at B.*
bís!, bíss! and with -s- prolonged indefinitely (§307).
bísss! interj. *to drive away a cat* (= fís!) [onom.].
bıšıráď‿ (-šɛr-) n. *good news* [? < بشارات id. (§1313); cp. Eth. ብሥራት: id.].
obj. -ádk(ı)‿, -átk(ı)‿, -átt(ı)‿; -kiᐞ, -tiᐞ.
gen. -ádn‿v., -án‿c.
pl. -ádı‿.
bıtán‿ child, etc. s.v. bıtán‿.
bıtánᐞ *you ((s)he (it)) will come* s.v. tá.
bítt(ı) v.t. *pick up, gather, gather up.*
ind. pres. aï‿bíttırıᐞ, ɛr‿bíttınᐞ (-tíᐞ, -tíᐞ); perf. aï‿bíttıgoriᐞ (N. -ıko-, -ıho-).
imperat. bítti!
part. pres. bíttıl‿ *(one) that picks up, etc., gatherer, picking up, etc.*
part. past bíttɛl‿ *(one) that picked up, etc., gatherer, picking up, etc.*
háb‿mállɛb‿bıbíttıran‿ (-b‿b- < -g‿b- 519) *they will pick up every grain.*

bıttóskoriᐞ *I have picked it (them) up.*
bíttar‿ (-tár‿; §§2200ff.) and
bıttíd‿ (§§2256ff.) n. *picking up, etc.*
bítt-an (§§3890ff.) v.t. *tell to pick up, etc., let pick up, etc.*
bíttı-bŭ- (§3931β) v.i. stat. *be in a picked up (etc.) state or condition.*
bíttır-ɛg-ág- (§§4071ff.) v.t. = bıttɛdól-.
bıtt-ɛ-dól- (-tᵒd- §1178; §4022) and
bíttır-ɛ-dól- (-rᵒd; §4027) v.t. *be about to pick up, etc.*
bíttır-ɛ-ğŭ-bŭ- (§4069) v.t. stat. *be on one's way (coming) to pick up, etc.*
bítt-ɛ-má- (§4036) and
bíttır-ɛ-má- (§4041) v.t. *become unable to pick up, etc.*
bíttır-ɛ-nóg- (§§4048ff.) v.t. *go to pick up, etc.*
bíttır-ɛ-nóg-bŭ- (-nóggŭ- §546; §4058) v.t. stat. *be on one's way (going) to pick up, etc.*
bíttır-ɛ-tá- (§§4060ff.) v.t. *come to pick up, etc.*
bıttɛd-ág- (§3877) v.t. *be in the situation of having picked up, etc.*
bíttıg-ır (N. -ıkır-, -ıhır; §3682) v.t. *cause or allow to pick up, etc.*
bıttı-kál (§3747ε′) v.t. *eat after picking up, etc.*
bíttı-kattı- (N. -ıha-; §4093) v.p. *be picked up, etc.*
bıtt-ós (§3747ε′) v.t. *take out after picking up, etc.*
iw‿wárag‿mállɛb‿bıttóswɛᐞ (-w‿w- < -n‿w- §720, -b‿b- < -g‿b- §519) *pick (pl.) up all this (that) paper and take it out.*
bıttı-sókkɛ (§3747ε′) v.t. *take away after picking up, etc.*
íŋ‿káššı‿mállɛb‿bıttısókkɛᐞ *pick up all this (that) rubbish and take it away.*
bób‿ n. *adolescent, youth, young man or woman of (more or less) 15 to 25; also, like iuvenis, applied to persons up to 40.*
voc. bóp!
obj. bóbk(ı)‿, bópk(ı)‿; -kiᐞ.
gen. bóbn‿v., bóm‿c.
pl. bóbı‿.
ım‿bób‿ım‿búrug‿áwwérsınᐞ *this (that) young man is wooing this (that) girl.*
bób-an- (§3910α) v.i. *become adolescent, grow into a youth, etc.*
ind. pres. aï‿bóbandiᐞ, ɛr‿bóbanınᐞ (-níᐞ, -níᐞ); fut. aï‿bıbóbandiᐞ (‿bub-); perf. aï‿bóbaŋkoriᐞ.
subj. past aï‿bóbansı‿ (-assı‿ §680, -su‿).
bóbam-bŭ- (§§3949ff.) v.i. stat. *be in a state of becoming or having become adolescent, etc.*
bóbanɛd-ág- (§3966α) v.i. *be in a condition of having become adolescent, etc.*
bócč(ı)‿ n. *exterior, outer part, outside* [< *bóct(ı)‿ < *bókt(ı)‿ < *bógt(ı)‿ < √bóg- *out (§4500) + -t dem. §2228].
obj. -čıg‿.
pl. -čınč(ı)‿.
bóččıg-ɛd (-ɛtᐞ, -ɛ́ᐞ §966; §6007) adv. *by (etc. s.v. -ɛd‿) the exterior, etc., externally, outside, out of doors.*
bóččıgɛdágınᐞ *(s)he (it) is (sits, lives, s.v. ág) outside (out of doors).*

‿bóččıgɛd‿ (-ɛtᐞ, -ɛ́ᐞ §966; §5860) postp. *outside of*—follows the genitive.
bóčč-ı-r‿ (§6007) adv. *on (at, to) the exterior, etc., externally, outside, out of doors* (s.v. -r‿).
tɛr‿éssıb‿bóččır‿arkóskonᐞ (-b‿b- < -g‿b- §519) *(s)he has thrown the water outside.*
‿bóččır‿ (§5860) postp. *outside of*—follows the genitive.
tır‿kám‿bóččırᐞ *they are outside the house.*
bóččín-d(ı)‿ (§§2545ff.) adj. *appertaining to the exterior, etc., outer, outside.*
— in the water-wheel (kólɛ‿) bóččın‿, bóččínd(ı)‿ = *shoreward, away from the river.*
bócč-an- (§3910β) v.i. *go outside, go out.*
ind. pres. aï‿bóččandiᐞ; perf. aï‿bóččaŋkoriᐞ.
ɛr‿bıbóččanná? *shall you go out?*
bóččanóskoranᐞ *they have gone out.*
bóččam-bŭ- (§3950β) v.i. stat. *be in a state of motion towards the exterior, be on one's way (going) out, be going out.*
bóččanɛd-ág- (§3966β) v.i. *be in the situation of having gone outside, etc.*
bóččanɛdágranᐞ *they have gone out.*
bóččan-nogr-ɛg-ág- (§3980) v.i. = bóččan-nogɛdól-.
bóččan-nog-ɛ-dól- (-gᵒd- §1178; §3979) and
bóččan-nog(¹)r-ɛ-dól- (-rᵒd-; §3981) v.i. *be about to go outside.*
bód v.i. (a) *run*; (b) *run off, run away, escape* [cp. Eg. pd, Copt. ⲡⲱⲧ id. RSN, §129].
ind. pres. aï‿bód(¹)riᐞ, ɛr‿bódınᐞ (-diᐞ, -díᐞ); perf. aï‿bódkoriᐞ (bótk-).
imperat. bót!, pl. bódwɛ! (bódwɛ́!; bóddɛ! §583, -dé!).
subj. past aï‿bódsı‿ (bótsı‿, bóssı‿ §688, -su‿).
part. pres. bódıl‿ *(one) that runs, etc., runner, running, etc.*, obj. bódílg(ı)‿, -giᐞ.
part. past bódɛl‿ *(one) that ran, etc., runner, running, etc.*, obj. bōdélg(ı)‿, -giᐞ.
def. perf. aï‿bōdóskoriᐞ.
aï‿tékkı‿ğómrıgal‿bótkóᐞ *when I struck him (her, it) (s)he (it) ran (away).*
bódar‿ (-dár‿; §§2200ff.) and
bōdíd‿ (§§2256ff.) n. *running, etc.*
bōdíd-am-bód (§§4161-3) v.i. *run very fast, run right off, run away.*
imperat. bōdídambót!
bōdídambód-bŭ- (-bóddŭ- §532; §4166) v.i. stat. *be running very fast, etc.*
bōdídk-ır-bód (-ítkır-, -íttır- §716; §4159) v.i. = bōdídambód.
bōdídkırbód-bŭ- (-ítkır-, -íttır-; -bóddŭ- §532; §4165) v.i. stat. = bōdídambódbŭ-.
bódt(ı)‿ (bótt(ı)‿) n. *running* [§2325α].
obj. -tıg‿.
bód-kátt(ı)‿ (bōtkát-) adj. *given to running, etc., fleet, swift-footed, nimble* [§§2534, 2535b].
obj. -tıg‿.
pl. -tınč(ı)‿.
bód-an (§§3890ff.) v.t. *tell to run, etc., let run, etc.*
bōd-ár (§3747ε′) v.t. *seize (etc. s.v. ár) after running.*

bōddŭ- — bókk(ɪ)

wɛ́l‿gɛ́ln‿abágɪr‿bōdárkon⁀ *the dog, running after the gazelle, caught it.*

bōd-bŭ- (bṓddŭ- §532; §3931α) *v.i. stat. be in a running (etc.) state or condition, be a fugitive.*
   aī‿bṓdbūri⁀ (‿bṓddūri⁀) *I am running away (I am a fugitive).*
   bābūr‿bṓdbūn⁀ *the train is going at a good rate.*
   nīgu-tɛ‿mám‿bṓdbuli? *who are those (over there) running (away)?*

bōd-dáb (§3747ᵋ') *v.i. disappear by running, run out of sight.*
   imperat. bṓddáp!
   ǧōmkɪru‿bɪbṓddábɪn⁀ *if you (pl.) beat him (her, it) (s)he (it) will run out of sight;* (ǧōmkɪru‿ *also* = *if we beat* §5079).

bōd(ᴵ)r-ɛg-ág- (§§4071 ff.) *v.i.* = bōdɛdól-.
   gɛ́lɪ‿bōdᴵrɛgágran⁀ *the gazelles are on the point of running away.*

bōd-ɛ-dól- (-dᵒd- §1178; §4022) and
bōd(ᴵ)r-ɛ-dól- (-rᵒd-; §4027) *v.i. be about to run, etc.*

bōd-ɛ-mǎ- (§4036) and
bōd(ᴵ)r-ɛ-mǎ- (§4041) *v.i. become unable to run, etc.*

bōdɛd-ág- (§3877) *v.i. be in the situation or condition of having run, etc.*

bōd-ǧu-tǎ- (bōǧǧu- §550; §4147) *v.i. come after going running, run there and back.*
   sūgɪrtōm‿bōǧǧutári⁀ *I'll* (§5369b) *run to the market and back (I'll just run to the market, s.v. tǎ, §5713).*
   sūgɪrtōm‿bōǧǧuta! and
   suŋ‿móŋkom‿bōǧǧuta! *run to the market and back.*

bōd-tǎ (bōttǎ §706; §3747ᵋ') *v.i. come running.*
   imperat. bōtta!, pl. bōttǎwɛ! (-tǎwɛ́!).
   bōttǎgoran⁀ *they came (have come) running.*

bōd-tō (bōttō §706; §3747ᵋ') *v.i. enter running, run in.*
   imperat. bōtto!
   sǎp‿kǎr‿bōttōgó⁀ *the cat ran (has run) into the house.*

bṓddŭ- (§532) < bṓdbŭ- *be running s.v.* bōd.

bōg (a) *v.t. pour, pour out, pour down, pour away;* (b, *of liquid, grain, etc.*) *v.i. pour, descend in a stream or considerable quantity;* (c, *of vessel, skin, etc.*) *v.t. and i. leak;* (d, *of its contents*) *v.i. leak* [< √bōg- *out* §4500; cp. ON. пок *id. GNT, s.v.; RSN,* §§ 129, 200].
   ind. pres. aī‿bōg(ᴵ)ri⁀, ɛr‿bōgɪn⁀ (-gī⁀, -gí⁀); perf. aī‿bōgkori⁀ (bōkkori⁀).
   imperat. bōk!, pl. bōgwɛ! (bōgwɛ́!; bōggɛ! §547, -gɛ́!).
   subj. past aī‿bōgsɪ‿ (bōksɪ‿ §576; -su‿).
   part. pres. bōgɪl‿ (*one*) *that pours, etc., pourer, etc., pouring, etc.*
   part. past bōgɛl‿ (*one*) *that poured, etc., pourer, etc., pouring, etc.*
   def. imperat. bōgos! (bōgó! §962); pl. bōgōswɛ! (-góswɛ́!, -gówwɛ! §724, -wɛ-, -góssɛ! §687, -sɛ́!).
   ɛ́ssɪb‿bōkkori⁀ (-b‿b- < -g‿b- §519) *I (have) poured the water out (away).*
   ɛ́ssɪb‿bōgɪn⁀ (a) (s)he *pours (out) (the) water;* (b) *it (the vessel) leaks (water).*
   ɛ́ssɪb‿bōgɪn⁀ *(the) water (a) pours down;* (b) *leaks.*
   áru‿bōgkon⁀ *(the) rain fell (has fallen).*
   áru‿bōgóskon⁀ *(the) rain has fallen.*
   gɪrbád‿bōgɪn⁀ *the water-skin leaks.*
   ɛ́ssɪ‿bābūrrotōm‿bōgɪn⁀ (the) water pours down (leaks) from the engine (etc. s.v. bābūr‿).
   bɛ́ntɪ‿bōkkó⁀ *the dates fell (have fallen) down in quantities, sc. from the palm(s).*
   íllɛ‿sílkattɪgɪn‿tabágɪrtōn‿árɪdɪr‿ bōgɪn⁀ *when wheat is winnowed it descends in a stream from the tray to the ground.*

bōgar‿ (-gǎr‿; §§2200 ff.) and
bōgíd‿ (§§2256 ff.) *n. pouring, etc.*

bōg-an (§§3890 ff.) *v.t. tell to pour, etc., let pour, etc.*

bōg-bŭ- (bōggŭ- §546; §3931β) *v.i. stat. be in a poured out (etc.) state or condition.*
   ɛ́ssɪ‿bōgbūn⁀ *the water is (has been) poured out (away).*

bōg-dɛ̄n (§§3996-7) *v.t. give (to the speaker) by pouring out, pour out for (the speaker).*
   imperat. bōgdɛ̄n! (-dɛ̄!, -dɛ̃!, -dɛ̌!, -dɛ̃!, §945).
   šaī‿tōddɛb‿bōgdɛ̄⁀ (-b‿b- < -g‿b- §519) *pour me out a little tea.*

bōg(ᴵ)r-ɛg-ág- (§§4071 ff.) *v.i.* = bōgɛdól-.
   áru‿bōgᴵrɛgágɪn⁀ *the rain's just going to come down.*

bōg-ɛ-dól- (-gᵒd- §1178; §4022) and
bōg(ᴵ)r-ɛ-dól- (-rᵒd-; §4027) *v.t. and i. be about to pour, etc.*
— *of rain:* ɛ́kkɛnɛ‿bōgɛdólɪn⁀ *now it's just going to pour.*

bōg-ɛ-mǎ- (§4036) and
bōg(ᴵ)r-ɛ-mǎ- (§4041) *v.t. and i. become unable to pour, etc.*

bōg-ɪr (§3671) (a) *v.t. caus. of* bōg (b, d) *cause or allow (liquid, etc.) to pour or leak, so* (b) *v.t.* = bōg (a); (c) *v.t. and i.* = bōg (c).
   ind. pres. aī‿bōgɪddi⁀.
   ɛ́ssɪb‿bōgírkori⁀ (-b‿b- < -g‿b- §519) *I (have) poured the water away.*
   gɪrbád‿ɛ́ssɪb‿bōgɪrɪn⁀ *the water-skin lets the water leak.*
   íŋ-gɪrbád‿bōgɪrɪn⁀ *this water-skin leaks.*

bōgɪrar‿ (-rǎr‿ §§2200 ff.) and
bōgɪríd‿ (§§2256 ff.) *n. pouring, leaking.*

bōgk-ɪdd(ɪ) (bōkk-; §3725) *v.t. caus.* = bōgkɪr.
   imperat. bōgkɪddi!
   aī‿tékk‿ɛ́ssɪb‿bōgkɪddɪri⁀ (-b‿b- < -g‿b- §519) *I (I'll* §5369b) *make (let) him (her, it) pour the water out.*

bōgk-ɪr (bōkkɪr; §3683) *v.t. caus. cause or allow to pour, etc.*
   ind. pres. aī‿bōgkɪddi⁀, ɛr‿bōgkɪrɪn⁀ (-rí⁀, -rí⁀).

bōg-kattɪ- (bōkkat-; §4093) *v.p. be poured, etc.*

bōg-tɪr (bōktɪr; §§3998-9) *v.t. give (to other than the speaker) by pouring out, pour out for (other than the speaker).*
   gáhwab‿bōgtɪr⁀ (-b‿b- < -g‿b- §519) *pour him (her) out some coffee.*

bōg-tō (bōktō; §3747ᵋ') *v.i. enter pouring, pour in.*
   ɛ́ssɪ‿wázbūl‿bōgtōgon⁀ *the boiling water (has) poured in.*

bōg-úndur (§4132) *v.t. put in by pouring, pour in.*
   ɛ́ssɪb‿bōgundúrkori⁀ *I (have) poured (the) water in.*

bōgɪǧandi⁀ *I shall become a man, s.v.* ógɪǧ.

bōǧǧuta! *run there and back!, s.v.* bōd.

bōǧō‿ *adj. broad, wide* [< √bōǧ- *out* (§4501) +-ō‿ §2562].
   obj. boǧōg‿.
   pl. boǧōrɪ‿ and boǧōnč(ɪ)‿.
   úru‿bōǧōn⁀ *the river is broad.*
   káde‿bōǧon⁀ *the cloth is broad.*
   sɛ́r‿boǧō-wēd‿dólɪn⁀ (-d‿d- < -g‿d- §534) *(s)he (it) wants a broad strap.*
   ógɪǧ‿boǧōmunun⁀ *the man is not broad in build.*

bóǧogɪd‿ (§2247) *n. breadth, width.*
   obj. boǧogídk(ɪ)‿, -ítk(ɪ)‿, -ítt(ɪ)‿; -kī⁀, -tɪ⁀.

boǧōkanɛ‿ (§2295) *n. breadth, width.*

bóǧ-an- (§3910α) *v.i. become broad, etc., broaden, widen.*

bóǧam-bŭ- (§§3949 ff.) *v.i. stat. be in a broadening (etc.) or broadened (etc.) state or condition.*

boǧōg-ɪr (N. -ókɪr, -óhɪr; §3701) (a) *v.t. caus. cause or allow to be broad, etc.;* (b) *v.t. broaden, widen.*
   ind. pres. aī‿boǧōǧɪddi⁀, ɛr‿boǧōǧɪrɪn⁀ (-rí⁀, -rí⁀).

bók! imperat. *of* bōg *pour.*

bókk(ɪ)‿ *n. thigh; with collective sg.* (§4696a) [§2053; *RSN,* §129].
   obj. -kɪg‿.
   pl. -kɪnč(ɪ)‿.

bókk(ɪ) *v.i. hide (oneself), go into hiding* [§2053].
   ind. pres. aī‿bókkɪri⁀, ɛr‿bókkɪn⁀ (-kī⁀, -kí⁀); perf. aī‿bókkɪgori⁀ (N. -ɪko-, -ɪho-).
   imperat. bókki!
   subj. past aī‿bókkɪsɪ‿ (-su‿).
   def. perf. aī‿bokkóskori⁀.
   márɛn‿tūr‿bókkɪn⁀ *(s)he (it) hides in the (field of) millet.*

bókkar‿ (-kǎr‿; §§2200 ff.) and
bokkíd‿ (§§2256 ff.) *n. hiding.*

bókk-an (§§3890 ff.) *v.t. tell to hide, let hide.*

bókkɪ-bŭ- (§3931α) *v.i. stat. be in a hidden state or condition.*
   ǧawáb‿kɪtám‿tūr‿bokkɪbúgon⁀ (-m‿t- < -bn‿t- §586) *the letter was hidden in the book.*

bókkɪbūl‿ *n. Bakabul (on map) a village on the right bank of the Nile, just above Old Dóngola* [*Hidden*].
   obj. bokkɪbúlg(ɪ)‿, -gi⁀.
   bokkɪbúllo (s.v. -r‿) *at (to) B.*
   bokkɪbúllo⁀ (§6007) *(s)he (it) is (they are) at B.*

bokkɪ-túrb(ɪ) (-túbb(ɪ) §520; §3747ᵋ') *v.i. lie hid.*
   imperat. bokkɪtúrbi!

bokkɪr-ɛg-ág- (§§4071 ff.) *v.i.* = bokkɛdól-.

bokk-ɛ-dól- (-kᵒd- §1178; §4022) and
bokkɪr-ɛ-dól- (-rᵒd-; §4027) *v.i. be about to hide (oneself).*

bokkɪr-ɛ-ǧu-bŭ- (§4069) *v.i. stat. be on one's way (coming) to hide (oneself).*

bokk-ɛ-mǎ- (§4036) and
bokkɪr-ɛ-mǎ- (§4041) *v.i. become unable to hide (oneself).*

bokkır-ɛ-nóg- (§§ 4048 ff.) v.i. *go to hide (oneself).*
bokkır-ɛ-nóg-bŭ- (-nóggŭ § 546; § 4058) v.i. stat. *be on one's way (going) to hide (oneself).*
bokkır-ɛ-tá- (§§ 4060 ff.) v.i. *come to hide (oneself).*
bokkɛd-ág- (§ 3877) v.i. *be in the situation of having hidden (oneself).*
bókk-ır (§ 3672) (*a*) v.t. caus. *cause or allow to become hidden, render hidden*; (*b*) v.t. *hide, conceal.*
   ind. pres. aĭ⌣bókkıddi⌢, ɛr⌣bókkırın⌢ (-rĭ⌢, -rí⌢); perf. aĭ⌣bokkírkori⌢.
   tókkon⌣tékkı⌣bókkırmɛn⌢ *don't hide him (her, it).*
bókkırar⌣ (-rár⌣; §§ 2200 ff.) and
bokkıríd⌣ (§§ 2256 ff.) n. *concealment.*
bokkır-an (§§ 3890, 3904) v.t. *tell to conceal, let conceal.*
bokkıdd-ɛg-ág- (§§ 4071, 4078) v.t. = bokkır-ɛ-dól-.
bokkır-ɛ-dól- (-r⁰d- § 1178; § 4025) and
bokkıdd-ɛ-dól- (-d⁰d-; § 4033) v.t. *be about to conceal.*
bokkıdd-ɛ-ğŭ-bŭ- (§ 4069) v.t. stat. *be on one's way (coming) to conceal.*
bokkır-ɛ-má- (§ 4039) and
bokkıdd-ɛ-má- (§ 4046) v.t. *become unable to conceal.*
bokkıdd-ɛ-nóg- (§§ 4048, 4057) v.t. *go to conceal.*
bokkıdd-ɛ-nóg-bŭ- (-nóggŭ- § 546; § 4058) v.t. stat. *be on one's way (going) to conceal.*
bokkıdd-ɛ-tá- (§§ 4060, 4068) v.t. *come to conceal.*
bokkıred-ág- (§§ 3877, 3883) v.t. *be in the situation of having concealed.*
bokkíng-ır (ˊ˜; N. -ŋkır; § 3688) (*a*) v.t. caus. *cause or allow to hide (oneself)*; (*b*) v.t. *hide, conceal.*
   tókkon⌣tékkı⌣bókkıŋgırmɛn⌢ *don't make (let) him (her, it) hide himself (herself, itself).*
bókk(ı) (*a*) v.t. *unload, remove load from*; (*b*, specialized, of woman) v.i. *miscarry* [< √bóg- *out* (§ 4500) + -k(ı) factitive § 2853].
   ind. pres. aĭ⌣bókkıri⌢, ɛr⌣bókkın⌢ (-kĭ⌢, -kí⌢); perf. aĭ⌣bókkıgori⌢ (N. -ıko-, -ıho-).
   imperat. bókkı!
   subj. past aĭ⌣bókkısı⌣ (-su⌣).
   kámgı⌣bókkıgoran⌢ *they (have) unloaded the camel.*
   kámlıb⌣bokkóskoran⌢ (-b⌣b < -g⌣b- § 519) *they have unloaded the camels.*
   ténnēm⌣bókkıgó⌢ (-m⌣b- < -n⌣b- § 592; -ēn⌣ § 1663) *his wife (has) had a miscarriage.*
bókkar⌣ (-kár⌣; §§ 2200 ff.) and
bokkíd⌣ (§§ 2256 ff.) n. *unloading, miscarriage.*
bókk-an (§§ 3890 ff.) v.t. *tell to unload, etc., let unload, etc.*
   kámgı⌣bókkıwan⌢ *let them unload the camel.*
bókkı-bŭ- (§ 3931 β) v.i. stat. *be in an unloaded state or condition.*
   kám⌣bókkıbūn⌢ *the camel is (has been) unloaded.*

bokkır-ɛg-ág- (§§ 4071 ff.) v.t. and i. = bokkɛdól-.
bokk-ɛ-dól- (-k⁰d- § 1178; § 4022) and
bokkır-ɛ-dól- (-r⁰d-; § 4027) v.t. and i. *be about to unload, etc.*
bokkır-ɛ-ğŭ-bŭ- (§ 4069) v.t. stat. *be on one's way (coming) to unload.*
bokk-ɛ-má- (§ 4036) and
bokkır-ɛ-má- (§ 4041) v.t. *become unable to unload.*
bokkır-ɛ-nóg- (§§ 4048 ff.) v.t. *go to unload.*
bokkır-ɛ-nóg-bŭ- (-nóggŭ- § 546; § 4058) v.t. stat. *be on one's way (going) to unload.*
bokkır-ɛ-tá- (§§ 4060 ff.) v.t. *come to unload.*
bokkɛd-ág- (§ 3877) (*a*) v.t. *be in the situation of having unloaded;* (*b*) v.i. *be in the condition of having miscarried.*
   hánub⌣bokkɛdágran⌢ (-b⌣b- < -g⌣b- § 519) *they have unloaded the donkey.*
bókkı-katti- (N. -ıha-; § 4093) v.p. *be unloaded, have its load removed.*
⌣**bókkon**⌣ (-kõ⌢, -kó⌢, -ko ⌢ § 939) postp. (i = prep. § 4287; § 4381) (*a*, in space) *as far as, out to, up to, down to, to;* (*b*, in time) *till, until* [stereotyped noun-concretion (§ 4898) < *bógkon⌣ < √bóg- *out* (§ 4500) + -k adv. suff. + -on *wish*, so *(if you) wish out (to);* GNT, s.v. πλοῦ cft. -π⌣πλτοτκλ = ἕως οὗ].
   — follows the genitive, of which -n⌣ > -m⌣ (§ 592) or disappears (§§ 2473–4); = ⌣móŋkon⌣.
   úrum⌣bókkon⌣ *as far as the Nile.*
   bɛlén⌣bókkon⌣ (bélɛn⌣bókkon⌣ § 1523; -n⌣b- < -dn⌣b- § 594) *as far as the village.*
   mándotōn⌣débbam⌣bókkon⌣ *from there to Ed-Débba*ʰ.
   ékkɛnɛm⌣sǎ⌣ídıwm⌣bókkon⌣ *from now till 8 o'clock.*
   sǎ⌣kémız⌣bókkon⌣ (-z⌣b- < -sn⌣b- § 855) *till 4 o'clock.*
   ékkɛnɛm⌣bókkon⌣nɛ́rbūgō⌢ *(s)he (it) has been asleep up till now.*
⌣**bókkon**⌣ (etc.) postp. (ii = conj. § 4287; § 4316) (*a*) *till, until;* (*b*) *as long as.*
   — follows the subjunctive bare form (§§ 2943, 2951), that may be introduced by ⌣náman⌣ (§ 4483):
   ar⌣nógru⌣bókkõ⌣tép⌢ (-kõ⌣t- § 979) *wait until we go.*
   aĭ⌣tárı⌣bókkon⌣índo⌣ték⌢ and
   aĭ⌣náman⌣tárı⌣bókkon⌣índo⌣tέk⌢ *wait (sit) here till I come.*
   ɛr⌣tám⌣bókkon⌣índo⌣bıtέgri⌢ and
   ɛr⌣náman⌣tám⌣bókkon⌣índo⌣bıtέgri⌢ *I shall wait here till you come.*
   ar⌣tásu⌣bókkon⌣tέkkoran⌢ *they waited till we came.*
   — of animate objects going away:
   tır⌣nálkattıram⌣bókkon⌣gúñči⌢ *watch them as long as they can* (§ 5379) *be seen.*
   ar⌣náman⌣nέrru⌣bókkon⌣kíttɛwan⌢ *tell them to be quiet while we are asleep.*
   — may be used where we use *before* or *by:*
   másıl⌣tóm⌣bókkon⌣aĭ⌣támɛŋkıri, fān-úsk⌣ıšín⌢ *if I don't come (back) before sunset, send the lantern.*
bōlís⌣ n. *policeman* [< بوليس id. < Fr. *police*].

obj. -lísk(ı)⌣, -ki⌢.
pl. -lísı⌣.
bór v.i. *fall down, fall in, fall in ruin, collapse.*
   ind. pres. tɛr⌣bórın⌢ (-rĭ⌢, -rí⌢), pl. tır⌣bórran⌣ (-rǎ⌢, -rá⌢); perf. tɛr⌣bórkon⌢ (-kõ⌢, -kó⌢).
   béntı⌣bórkó⌢ *the palm(s* § 4696 *b) fell (has, have fallen) down.*
   béntı⌣bōróskon⌢ *the palm has (palms have) fallen down.*
   téŋ⌣kólɛ⌣bōróskó⌢ *his (her) water-wheel has collapsed.*
bórar⌣ (-rár⌣; §§ 2200 ff.) and
bōríd⌣ (§§ 2256 ff.) n. *falling down, etc., collapse.*
bór-an (§§ 3890 ff.) v.t. *let fall down, etc.*
   téŋ⌣kólɛ⌣bóran!* (-b⌣b- < -g⌣b- § 519) *let his (her) water-wheel collapse!,* i.e. *may it collapse!* (§ 5649).
bór-bŭ- (§ 3931 α) v.i. stat. *be in a fallen down (etc.) state or condition.*
   kǎ⌣bórbūn⌢ *the house lies in ruins.*
   tíŋ⌣kólɛ⌣bórbūn⌢ *their water-wheel lies collapsed.*
bórr-ɛg-ág- (§§ 4071 ff.) v.i. = bórɛdól-.
bórr-ɛ-dól- (-r⁰d- § 1178; § 4022) and
bórr-ɛ-dól- (-r⁰d-; § 4027) v.i. *be about to fall down, etc.*
   kǎ⌣bórɛdólkon⌢ *the house was going to fall down.*
bōred-ág- (§ 3877) v.i. *be in the situation (condition) of having fallen down, etc.*
bórk-ığ (§ 2892) v.t. *forcibly cause to fall down, etc., throw down, demolish.*
   ind. pres. aĭ⌣bórkığ(¹)ri⌢, ɛr⌣bórkığın⌢ (-ğĭ⌢, -ğí⌢); perf. aĭ⌣bōrkíğkori⌢ (-íčk-; -ğk-, -čk- § 323).
   imperat. bórkıč!
   kâb⌣bórkığran⌢ (-b⌣b- < -g⌣b- § 519) *they demolish the house.*
   túrug⌣béntınčıb⌣bórkığın⌢ *the wind tears the palms down.*
   — Some speakers do not differentiate bórkığ from bórkır.
   béntıb⌣bórkığran⌢ *they fell the palm(s)* = béntıb⌣bórkıddan⌢.
bórkığar⌣ (-ğár⌣; §§ 2200 ff.) and
bórkığíd⌣ (§§ 2256 ff.) n. *demolition.*
bórkığ-an (§§ 3890 ff.) v.t. *tell to demolish, etc., let demolish, etc.*
bórkığ(¹)r-ɛg-ág- (§§ 4071 ff.) = bōrkığɛdól-.
bórkığ-ɛ-dól- (-ğ⁰d- § 1178; § 4022) and
bórkığ(¹)r-ɛ-dól- (-r⁰d-; § 4027) v.t. *be about to demolish, etc.*
bórkığ(¹)r-ɛ-ğŭ-bŭ- (§ 4069) v.t. stat. *be on one's way (coming) to demolish, etc.*
bórkığ-ɛ-má- (§ 4036) and
bórkığ(¹)r-ɛ-má- (§ 4041) v.t. *become unable to demolish, etc.*
bórkığ(¹)r-ɛ-nóg- (§§ 4048 ff.) v.t. *go to demolish, etc.*
bórkığ(¹)r-ɛ-nóg-bŭ- (-nóggŭ- § 546; § 4058) v.t. stat. *be on one's way (going) to demolish, etc.*
bórkığ(¹)r-ɛ-tá- (§§ 4060 ff.) v.t. *come to demolish, etc.*
bórkığed-ág- (§ 3877) v.t. *be in the situation of having demolished, etc.*
bórk-ır (§ 3683) (*a*) v.t. caus. *cause or allow to fall down, etc.;* (*b*) v.t. *fell, pull down.*

borós — bú

ind. pres. aī‿bórkɪddɪ⁀.
ká̆b‿bórkɪddan⁀ (-b‿b- < -g‿b- §519) (a) *they allow the house to fall down;* (b) *they pull the house down.*
bɛ́ntɪb‿bŏrkɪrɪn⁀ *he fells the palm(s).*
bŏrkɪrar‿ (-rár‿; §§2200ff.) and
bŏrkɪríd‿ (§§2256ff.) n. *causing or allowing to fall down, etc., felling, etc.*
bŏrkɪr-an (§§3890, 3904) v.t. *tell to fell, etc., let fell, etc.*
bŏrkɪdd-ɛg-ắg- (§§4071, 4078) v.t. = bŏrkɪrɛdól-.
bŏrkɪr-ɛ-dól- (-rᵒd- §1178; §4025) and
bŏrkɪdd-ɛ-dól- (-dᵒd-; §4033) v.t. *be about to fell, etc.*
bŏrkɪdd-ɛ-ğŭ-bŭ- (§4069) v.t. stat. *be on one's way (coming) to fell, etc.*
bŏrkɪd-ɛ-mắ- (§4039) and
bŏrkɪdd-ɛ-mắ- (§4046) v.t. *become unable to fell, etc.*
bŏrkɪdd-ɛ-nóg- (§§4048, 4057) v.t. *go to fell, etc.*
bŏrkɪdd-ɛ-nóg-bŭ- (-nóggŭ- §546; §4058) v.t. stat. *be on one's way (going) to fell, etc.*
bŏrkɪdd-ɛ-tắ- (§§4060, 4068) v.t. *come to fell, etc.*
bŏrkɪrɛd-ắg- (§§3877, 3883) v.t. *be in the situation of having felled, etc.*
bŏr-šúgur (§3747ᵉ) v.i. *come down in collapse, come falling down.*
ind. pres. tɛr‿bŏršúgurɪn⁀ (-rī⁀, -rí⁀), tɪr‿bŏršugúrran⁀ (-rā⁀, -rá⁀, -úddan⁀, -dā⁀, -dá⁀).
ká̆‿bŏršugurósko⁀ *the house has come tumbling down.*
borós n. *Buros (on map), an island south of Tángas Island, about 11 miles below Ed-Débbáʰ.*
obj. -ósk(ɪ)‿, -kɪ⁀.
bórra‿ n. *a Nile fish of light colour,* Tilapia nilotica L. (*PF*, p. 96).
obj. -rag‿.
pl. -ranč(ɪ)‿.
bŏ̆t! imperat. of *bŏd run.*
bótt(ɪ) v.i. (a, of superficial layer) *get detached, peel off;* (b) *lose its superficial layer, peel;* (c, of colour) *fade;* (d) *lose its colour, fade* [< *bókt(ɪ) (§707) < *bógt(ɪ) < √bóg- *out* (§4500) + -t (§2900)].
ind. pres. tɛr‿bóttɪn⁀ (-tī⁀, -tí⁀); perf. tɛr‿bóttɪgon⁀ (-gō⁀, -gó⁀; N. -ɪko-, -ɪho-).
— of an enamelled iron plate: sáham‿ bóttɪgon⁀ (-m‿b < n‿b- §592) *the plate (has) lost its enamel.*
ğŏ́wwɪŋ‿kắčč‿bóttɪgó⁀ *the bark of the tree came (has come) off.*
kádɛ‿bóttɪgó⁀ *the cloth (has) faded.*
tɛ́l‿lŏ́m‿bóttɪgo⁀ (-l‿l- < -n‿l- §583) *its colour (is) faded.*
bóttar‿ (-tár‿; §§2200ff.) and
bottíd‿ (§§2256ff.) n. *peeling, etc.*
bóttɪ-bŭ- (§3931 α) v.i. stat. *be in a peeling or peeled (etc.) state or condition.*
sáham‿bóttɪbūn⁀ *the plate has lost its enamel.*
ğŏ́wwɪŋ‿kắčč‿bóttɪbūn⁀ *the bark of the tree is peeling off.*
búja‿bóttɪbūn⁀ (a) *the paint has peeled off;* (b) *the paint has faded.*
bottɪr-ɛg-ắg- (§§4071ff.) v.i. = bottɛdól-.

bott-ɛ-dól- (-tᵒd- §1178; §4022) and
bottɪr-ɛ-dól- (-rᵒd-; §4027) v.i. *be about to peel, etc.*
bottɛd-ắg- (§3877) v.i. *be in the condition of having peeled, etc.*
bóttɪg-ɪr (N. -ɪkɪr, -ɪhɪr; §3682) v.t. caus. *cause or allow to peel off, etc.*
ind. pres. aī‿bóttɪgɪddɪ⁀, ɛr‿bóttɪgɪrɪn⁀ (-rī⁀, -rí⁀).
mắsɪ‿tél‿lŏ́ŋgɪ‿bóttɪgɪrɪn⁀ (-l‿l- < -n‿l- §583) *the sun makes its colour fade.*
bótt-ɪr (§3672) (a) v.t. caus. = bóttɪgɪr; (b) v.t. *detach (superficial layer), peel off.*
ind. pres. aī‿bóttɪrrɪ⁀; perf. aī‿bóttɪrkori⁀.
aī‿ám‿mɛrkúbkɪ‿bóttɪrrɪ⁀ *I ('ll §5369) take off my slippers.*
tén‿komáŋgɪ‿bóttɪrkon⁀ *he took (has taken) his shirt off.*
mắsɪ‿tél‿lŏ́ŋgɪ‿bóttɪrɪn⁀ (-l‿l- < -n‿l- §583) *the sun makes its colour fade.*
bóttɪrar‿ (-rár‿; §§2200ff.) and
bottɪríd‿ (§§2256ff.) n. *causing to peel, etc., detachment.*
bóttɪr-an (§§3890, 3904) v.t. *tell to detach, etc., let detach, etc.*
ím‿mɛrkúbɪb‿bóttɪrwan⁀ (-b‿b- < -g‿b- §519) *let them take their (own §5112) slippers off.*
bottɪr-ɛg-ắg- (§§4071, 4078) v.t. = bottɪrɛdól-.
bottɪr-ɛ-dól- (-rᵒd- §1178; §4025) and
bottɪrr-ɛ-dól- (-rᵒd-; §4033) v.t. *be about to detach, etc.*
bottɪr-ɛ-mắ- (§4039) and
bottɪrr-ɛ-mắ- (§4046) v.t. *become unable to detach, etc.*
bottɪrɛd-ắg- (§§3877, 3883) v.t. *be in the situation (condition) of having detached, etc.*
bottɪríng-ɪr (´⁀‿; N. -ŋkɪr; §3691) v.t. caus. *cause or allow to detach, etc.*
ind. pres. aī‿bottɪríŋgɪddɪ⁀, (§1826).
bŏ̆ww(ɪ) v.i. (a) *bathe, take a bath;* (b) *swim* [*RSN*, §129 s.v. *bǎw*].
ind. pres. aī‿bŏ̆wwɪrɪ⁀ (bŏ̆ww°rɪ⁀ §1202); perf. aī‿bŏ̆wwɪgori⁀ (N. -ɪko-, -ɪho-).
imperat. bŏ̆wwi!
part. pres. bŏ̆wwɪl‿ *(one) that bathes, etc., bather, etc., bathing, etc.*
part. past bŏ̆wwɛl‿ *(one) that bathed, bather, etc., bathing, etc.*
def. perf. aī‿bŏ̆wwóskori⁀ (§3789) and
def. perf. aī‿bŏ̆wwédkori⁀ (-étk-).
bɪbŏ́wwɪná? (bubŏ́wwŭná?) *shall you (plain-future FKE, p. 143) have a bath?*
úrugɛb‿bŏ́wwɪran‿ (-b‿b- < -d‿b- §518; §§5452-3) n. *instrument for swimming in the river, i.e. inflated skin(s).*
bŏ̆wwɪ-kátt(ɪ)‿ (N. -ɪhá-; §2535b) adj. *good at swimming.*
bŏ̆wwar‿ (-wár‿; §§2200ff.) and
bŏ̆wwíd‿ (§§2256ff.) n. *bathing, swimming.*
bŏ̆ww-an (§§3890ff.) v.t. *tell to bathe (i.), etc., let bathe (i.), etc.*
bŏ̆wwɪr-ɛg-ắg- (§§4071ff.) v.i. = bŏ̆wwɛdól-.

bŏ̆ww-ɛ-dól- (-wᵒd- §1178; §4022) and
bŏ̆wwɪr-ɛ-dól- (-wᵘrᵒd-; §4027) v.i. *be about to bathe (i.), etc.*
bŏ̆wwɪr-ɛ-ğŭ́-bŭ- (§4069) v.i. stat. *be on one's way (coming) to bathe (i.), etc.*
bŏ̆wwɪr-ɛ-mắ- (§4036) and
bŏ̆wwɪr-ɛ-mắ- (§4041) v.i. *become unable to bathe (i.), etc.*
bŏ̆wwɪr-ɛ-nóg- (§§4048ff.) v.i. *go to bathe (i.), etc.*
bŏ̆wwɪr-ɛ-nóg-bŭ- (-nóggŭ- §546; §4058) v.i. stat. *be on one's way (going) to bathe (i.), etc.*
bowwɪrɛnógbūran⁀ *they are on their way to bathe.*
bŏ̆wwɪr-ɛ-tắ- (§§4060ff.) v.i. *come to bathe (i.), etc.*
bŏ̆wwɛd-ắg- (§3877) v.i. *be in the condition of having bathed (i.), etc.*
bowwɛdágran⁀ *they have had a bath.*
bŏ̆wwɛt-tắ (§4169ff., 5723a) v.i. *come (back) after bathing (i.), go (§5713; s.v. tắ) and bathe (i.).*
ind. pres. aī‿bŏ̆wwɛttắrɪ⁀.
imperat. bŏ̆wwétta!
bŏ̆ww-ídd(ɪ) (§3721) (a) v.t. caus. *cause or allow to bathe (i.);* (b) v.t. *bathe, give a bath to.*
ind. pres. aī‿bŏ̆wwíddɪrɪ⁀; perf. aī‿bŏ̆wwíddɪgorɪ⁀ (N. -ɪko-, -ɪho-).
imperat. bŏ̆wwíddi!
bŏ̆wwíddar‿ (-dár‿; §§2200ff.) and
bŏ̆wwíddíd‿ (§§2256ff.) n. *bathing, giving a bath.*
bŏ̆wwídd-an (§§3890, 3904) v.t. *tell to bathe (t.), etc., let bathe (t.), etc.*
bŏ̆wwíddɪr-ɛg-ắg- (§§4071, 4078) v.t. = bŏ̆wwɪddɛdól-.
bŏ̆wwɪddɪr-ɛ-dól- (-dᵒd- §1178; §4025) and
bŏ̆wwɪddɪr-ɛ-dól- (-rᵒd-; §4033) v.t. *be about to bathe (t.), etc.*
bŏ̆wwɪddɪr-ɛ-ğŭ́-bŭ- (§4069) v.t. stat. *be on one's way (coming) to bathe (t.), etc.*
bŏ̆wwɪdd-ɛ-mắ- (§4039) and
bŏ̆wwɪddɪr-ɛ-mắ- (§4046) v.t. *become unable to bathe (t.), etc.*
bŏ̆wwɪddɪr-ɛ-nóg- (§§4048, 4057) v.t. *go to bathe (t.), etc.*
bŏ̆wwɪddɪr-ɛ-nóg-bŭ- (-nóggŭ- §546; §4058) v.t. stat. *be on one's way (going) to bathe (t.), etc.*
bŏ̆wwɪddɪr-ɛ-tắ- (§§4060, 4068) v.t. *come to bathe (t.), etc.*
bŏ̆wwɪddɛd-ắg- (§§3877, 3883) v.t. *be in the situation of having bathed (t.), etc.*
bu- (common in S.) = bɪ- prefix forming future tense (§§2966ff.).
bú (§§3567, 5517) v.i. (a) *lie, be lying, be lying down;* (b) *lie, occupy a position, be situated, be* [= *se trouver, trovarsi, hallarse, sich befinden*]; (c) *be, exist;* (d, in composition §§3927ff.) -bŭ- *be in a state or condition.*
— *used of animate and inanimate objects.*
ind. pres. aī‿búrɪ⁀, ɛr‿bún⁀ (‿bŭ‿, ‿bú̆‿ §337, ‿bú̆⁀); perf. aī‿búgori⁀ (N. ‿búko-, ‿búho-).
imperat. bú!, pl. bú̆we! (bú̆wé!).
part. pres. búl‿ *(one) that lies, etc., lying, etc.;* obj. búlg(ɪ)‿, -gi⁀.
part. past bú̆ɛl‿ (bᵘɛ́l‿, bʷɛ́l‿, bɛ́l‿ §1114) *(one) that lay, etc., lying, etc.;* obj. buélg(ɪ)‿ (bᵘélg(ɪ)‿, etc.), -gi⁀.

part. past búrɛl‿ (one) that lay, etc., lying, etc.; obj. búrɛlg(ı)‿ (búrɛlg(ı)‿ §1522), -gı⌒.
aı‿búri⌒ (a) I'll §5369) lie down; (b) I'm lying down) (*ăbbúri⌒ said to be not used).
óggı‿mándo‿búran⌒ the men lie over there.
ógıɛ‿tém‿bérıgɛb‿bŭ⌒(-b‿b- < -d‿b- §518) and (§§5572, 3947-8)
ógıɛ‿tém‿bɛrıgɛbbŭ⌒ the man is lying on his side.
kúb‿sí̵wır‿búgon⌒ the boat lay on the sand.
sámtɛr‿íŋkɛ‿búgon⌒ on Saturday it was (lay) like that (this).
wɛr‿índo‿bŭn⌒ there is one (someone, lying) here.
X. šɛ́ma‿dáná? are there any candles? (§4647).
Y. éjjo, dăn; dōlábır‿bŭn⌒ yes, there are; they are in the cupboard.
X. kúrsı‿dáná? is there a chair?
Y. éjjo, mándo‿bŭ⌒ yes, it's (it stands, lit. it lies) over there (§5531).
ıŋ‿éssı‿zɛmándoton‿índo‿bŭn⌒ this water has been (lying §5372) here for a long time.
mındíl‿índo‿búl‿ándín⌒ the handkerchief lying here is mine.
ɛr‿kıtáb‿mándo‿búlgı‿nálná? do you see the book (that is) lying over there?
ɛr‿kıtáb‿mándo‿bélgı‿nálkoná? did you see (have you seen) the book that was (lying) over there?
kúšar‿índo‿bélgı‿ténn‿agárro‿wᵘdégır⌒ put the key that was (lay) here back into its place.
kánd‿índo‿bél‿sɛ́? where is the knife that was (lay) here?
mındíl‿índo‿bél‿sɛ́? and
mındíl‿índo‿búrɛl‿sɛ́? where is the handkerchief that lay here?
mán‿índo‿búgolgı‿ (N. ‿búkolgı‿) ‿ténn‿agárro‿wᵘdégır (N. ‿wᵘdékır⌒) put that (other) one that was (lay) here back into its place.
búrar (-rɑr‿; §§2200ff., 2207) and
búríd‿ (§§2256ff., 2260) n. lying, being, existence.
bu-án (bᵘán, bwán, bán §§3890ff., 3898, 5661) v.t. tell you to lie, let lie, etc.
imperat. buán!, b(w)án!, b(w)ắ!, b(w)á! (§939).
tékk‿índo‿buán⌒ and
índo‿bán⌒ let him (her, it) be here ((s)he (it) is to lie here).
ǧarásk‿índo‿bwá⌒ (‿bá⌒) the bell is to be here.
lámbag‿índo‿bá⌒ the lamp is to be (set) here.
X. kúrsıs‿sɑ̆ır‿uskúddi? (-s‿s- < -g‿s- §678) where shall (§5369b) I put the chair?
Y. índo‿bá⌒ put (leave) it here (there).
tókkon‿índo‿bámmɛn⌒ don't set it here.
tírg‿índo‿búwan⌒ and
tírg‿índo‿buwánır⌒ let them lie (be) here; tírg‿ may be omitted.
bán-an (§5663) v.t. tell to let lie, tell to set, let put.

ind. pres. aı‿bánandı⌒, ɛr‿bánanın⌒ (-nĭ⌒, -ní⌒).
imperat. bánan! (báná!, bání!).
ár‿tékk‿índo‿bánaŋkoru⌒ we (have) told him (her) to leave (put) it here.
kăn‿tŭr‿báná⌒ let him (her) put (leave) it inside the house.
bu-ɛ-dól- (bᵘódól- §1178; §4022) and
bŭr-ɛ-dól- (-rᵒd-; §4027) v.i. be about to lie, etc.
bu-ɛ-mắ- (§4036) and
bŭr-ɛ-mắ- (§4041) v.i. become unable to lie, etc.
N. aı‿buɛmăkori⌒ I became (have become, am) unable to lie down.
bŭl-dā- (búllā- §578; §3985) v.i. be lying present, be lying at hand, be existing, be (situated) here or there.
búllāgın‿ɛ́tta⌒ if there is any (some) lying (there), bring it.
búd v.i. (of limb) get dislocated [or. *come out, cp. Eth. ⲱⲃⲏ exiit §2056].
ind. pres. tɛr‿búdın⌒ (-dĭ⌒, -dí⌒); perf. tɛr‿búdkon⌒ (bútk-, -kŏ⌒, -kó⌒).
énn‿ı‿bıbúdın⌒ your arm (shoulder, elbow, wrist, finger, thumb) will get dislocated.
énn-ın‿sárbɛ‿bıbúdın⌒ your finger will get dislocated.
— in the water-wheel (kólɛ‿).
súlgad‿árgadɛrtóm‿budóskon⌒ the cogs (§4696d, i.e. of the vertical cogwheel árgadɛn‿tód) have become disengaged from the (horizontal) cogwheel (ár-gadɛŋ‿gédɛ‿) (or vice versa).
búdar (-dɑr‿; §§2200ff.) and
búdíd‿ (§§2256ff.) n. dislocation.
ím‿búdar‿ dislocation of the arm (etc.).
budúrt(ı)‿ n. joint; with collective sg. (§4696a). [< *búdɑrt(ı)‿ (§1175) < búdɑr‿ dislocation + -t dem., or. that dislocation, then that (place of) articulation §2325β].
obj. -tıg‿.
pl. -tınč(ı)‿.
ín‿sárbɛm‿budúrt(ı)‿ finger-joint(s).
búd-bŭ- (búddŭ- §532; §3931α) v.i. stat. be in a dislocated state or condition.
ténn‿ósmar‿búddŭn⌒ his (her, its) shoulder is dislocated.
búd‿ n. bare ground esp. round house(s) [or. *the coming out (búd), i.e. *what one comes out on to §2056].
obj. búdk(ı)‿, bútk(ı)‿, búttı‿, búkk(ı)‿ (§2462), -ki⌒, -tı⌒.
gen. búdn‿v., bŭn‿c.
pl. búdı‿.
kăm‿búd‿ bare ground round a house.
ím‿mahálli‿búdun⌒ this place is bare.
budáɛ‿ (-dăɑ‿, -dáɑ‿ §1352a) n. article for sale, merchandise; with collective sg. (§4696d) [< بِضَاعَة id. = بِضَاعَة].
obj. -áɛg‿, -áăg‿, -áəg‿.
pl. -áɛnč(ı)‿, -áănč(ı)‿, -áənč(ı)‿.
búddŭ- (§532) < búdbŭ- be in a dislocated state s.v. búd.
búga‿ n. (a) Omdurmán [< البُقْعَة id. (§1389) the (sc. holy) spot, i.e. the Mahdi's tomb there]; (b, subsequently applied to) Khartoum.

obj. -gag‿.
búgar‿ at (to) Omdurmán.
búgar‿ (§5858) (s)he (it) is (they are) at Omdurmán.
bugán-d(ı)‿ (§§2545ff.) adj. appertaining to Omdurmán.
búg-an- (§3910β) v.i. go to Omdurmán.
ind. pres. aı‿búgandi⌒; fut. aı‿bıbúgandi⌒ (‿bub-); perf. aı‿búgaŋkori⌒.
sub. past aı‿búgansı‿ (-assı‿ §680, -su‿).
búgam-bŭ- (§3950β) v.i. stat. be in a state of motion towards Omdurmán, be on one's way to Omdurmán, be going to Omdurmán.
bugɛnɛd-ág- (§3966β) v.i. be in the situation of having gone to Omdurmán.
bugan-nog(ı́)r-ɛg-ág- (§3980) v.i. = bugannogɛdól-.
bugan-nog-ɛ-dól- (-gᵒd- §1178; §3979) and
bugan-nog(ı́)r-ɛ-dól- (-rᵒd-; §3981) v.i. be about to go (off) to Omdurmán.
bugan-nog-ɛ-mắ- (§3982) and
bugan-nog(ı́)r-ɛ-mắ- (§3983) v.i. become unable to go (off) to Omdurmán.
bugbúga‿ n. sand-grouse, Pterocles arenarius; with collective sg. (§4696c) [< bugbúg- onom. (§2153) + -a‿ *utterance (§2050) < -án say (§919), so *(what) says 'bugbúk!' (§468); cp. بَقْبَق to gurgle, بَقْباق chatterer].
obj. -gag‿.
pl. -ganč(ı)‿.
búgdo‿ n. potter [cp. Sudan Ar. بَقْداوي id.; §2309].
obj. -dog‿.
pl. búgdŏnč(ı)‿, bugdónč(ı)‿, búgdorı‿.
bugdombúš‿ n. Bugdumbush (on map), ruins on the right bank of the Nile eight miles above Hándag‿ [Potter's Monday].
bugdŏn-d(ı)‿ (§§2545ff.) adj. appertaining to the potter, potter's.
búgdo‿ n. large upright post supporting cross-beam (dfu‿) of water-wheel (kólɛ‿); with collective sg. (§4696d); = múgdo‿ (§1014) q.v. [§§2306-8].
obj. -dog‿ [> Sudan Ar. بِدْقوق id.].
pl. -donč(ı)‿.
†**búja**‿ n. paint [< بويا id.].
obj. -jag‿.
pl. -janč(ı)‿.
búllā- < bŭl-dā- be lying present, etc. s.v. bú.
búll(ı)‿ n. small boat [§2298; RSN, §129].
obj. -lıg‿.
pl. -lınč(ı)‿.
búllı‿wawíddıgɛw‿wăwᵘran⌒ (-ıw‿w- < -ıg‿w- §719, -ɛw‿w- < -ɛd‿w- §718) they row the boat with oars (§4696d).
bullın-árt(ı)‿, -tı⌒ n. Bullinarti (on map), an island to the west of the northern end of Argo Island; official name of Bunnárti⌒ [Small Boat Island].
obj. -tıg‿.
bullín-d(ı)‿ (§§2545ff.) adj. appertaining to a small boat.

búma — čúppp...!

búma⌣ n. *owl*; with collective sg. (§4696d) [< بُومَة *id*.].
　obj. -mag⌣.
　pl. -manč(ı)⌣.
bún⌣ (§956d) n. *bottom, underside, undersurface* [*RSN*, §200].
　obj. búŋg(ı)⌣, -gi⌢.
　pl. búnı⌣.
　sandúŋ⌣búndo⌣báǧǧun⌢ (-ŋ⌣b- < -gn⌣b- §642a) *it is written on the bottom of the box.*
　búndotōm⌣bélkon⌢ *it came (has come) out from the bottom.*
bún-d(ı)⌣ (§2545 ff.) adj. *appertaining to the bottom, etc.*
bún⌣ (§956a) n. *coffee (bean and drink)* = búnn(ı)⌣ (§1370).
　obj. búŋg(ı)⌣, -gi⌢.
　búm⌣marıssōddɛ́d⌣dólli⌢ (-m⌣m- < -n⌣m- §604, -d⌣d- < -g⌣d- §534) *I want a very little coffee.*
bún-d(ı)⌣ (§§2545 ff.) adj. *appertaining to coffee.*
　X. fıŋ⌣ǧáŋgı⌣ǧétta⌢ *go and fetch a cup.*
　Y. búndıgá? *a coffee-cup?*
búndug⌣ n. *gun, rifle* [< بُنْدُق *gun*].
　obj. bundúgk(ı)⌣, -dúkk(ı)⌣; búndu- §1522; -ki⌢.
　pl. búndugı⌣.
　bundúkkɛǧ⌣ǧóm (-ǧ⌣ǧ- < -d⌣ǧ- §550; §5572) *fire at, shoot*, lit. *hit with the gun.*
　bundúkkɛǧ⌣ǧómkori, súdkori⌢ (§6241) *I fired and missed.*
　bundúkkɛǧ⌣ǧómkori, ǧómkō⌢ *I fired and it (sc. the bullet) hit.*
　ɛlúmgı⌣bundúkkɛǧ⌣ǧómkō⌢ *he (has) shot the crocodile.*
bundukk-ɛǧ-ǧóm (§4167) v.t. *fire at, shoot.*
　ɛlúmgı⌣bundukkɛǧǧómkō⌢ *he (has) shot the crocodile.*
búnn(ı) n. *coffee (bean and drink)* = bún⌣ (§1370) [< بُنّ Amh. ቡን *id*.].
　obj. -nıg⌣.
bunnárt(ı)⌣ (-ti⌢) n. *an island to the west of the northern end of Argo Island; popular name of Bullınárti⌢.*
　obj. -tıg⌣.
búr n. *fallow, land left uncultivated* [< Sudan Ar. بُور *id*. = بُور; (appar. not < Beḍ. būr *earth, land*)].
　obj. búrk(ı)⌣.
　pl. búrı⌣.
　ténn⌣árıd⌣málle⌣búrun⌢ *all his (her, its) land is uncultivated.*
　árıd⌣búr⌣mándo⌣dıgrí⌣dán⌣ *over there there is much uncultivated land* (§4750).
búr-an- (§3910α) v.i. *become uncultivated, go out of cultivation.*
búram-bŭ- (§3949 ff.) v.i. stat. *be advanced in the process of going out of cultivation, be getting quite uncultivated.*
búranɛd-ág- (§3966α) v.i. *be in the condition of having become uncultivated.*
　árıd⌣búranɛdágın⌢ *the land has gone out of cultivation.*
búrdanın⌢ *(s)he (it) will go to El-Órdi.* s.v. úrdı⌣.

búrgɛ⌣ *Bergeig (on map), a village on the right bank of the Nile at the northern end of Argo Island.*
　obj. búrgɛg, búrgég⌣ (§1532).
burnɛ́ta⌣ n. *hat, helmet* [< بَرْنِيطَة *id*.].
　obj. -tag⌣.
　pl. -tanč(ı)⌣.
bursūdán⌣ n. *Port Sudan* [? bur- on analogy of بور in بور سعيد < Fr. *Port Saïd*].
　obj. -dáŋ(ı)⌣, -gi⌢.
búru⌣ n. (a) *girl*; (b, esp. enclitic ⌣buru⌣, -buru⌣ §§1663-6, 2374a) *daughter* [2337; *RSN*, §129].
　obj. búrug⌣.
　pl. búruı⌣, búrwı⌣.
　ám-buru⌣ *my (our) daughter.*
　ém-buru⌣ *your daughter.*
　tém-buru⌣ *his (her) daughter.*
　ím-buru⌣ *your (pl.) daughter.*
　tím⌣buru⌣ *their daughter*; ám⌣búru⌣, ɛ́m⌣búru⌣, etc. and am⌣buru⌣, ɛm⌣buru⌣, etc. (§1665) are also heard.
　tínnɛssım⌣buru⌣ and tınnɛssím⌣buru⌣ *his(her) sister's daughter.*
　síttın⌣tınnɛssím-buru⌣ *the lady's sister's daughter* (§4830).
burún-d(ı)⌣ (§§2545 ff.) adj. *appertaining to a girl, etc., girl's, daughter's.*
búr-tod⌣ (§2369d) n. *female child up to about four or five years of age.*
　voc. búrtod!, búrtó!
　obj. búrtodk(ı)⌣, -totk(ı)⌣, -tŏkk(ı)⌣, -tŏtt(ı)⌣ (§2462); -tŏdk(ı)⌣, etc.; -ki⌢, -ti⌢.
　gen. -tŏdn⌣v., tŏnn⌣v.c., -tŏn⌣c. (§§778-88).
　pl. búrtonı⌣.
　ın⌣tím⌣búrtódū⌢ *this is their little girl.*
　ın⌣ám⌣burtódun⌢ *this is my (our) little girl.*
　ın⌣ámburum⌣búrtodun⌢ *this is my (our) daughter's little girl.*
burúm-buru (̋̋ §1532) n. *daughter's daughter, grand-daughter.*
　obj. burumbúrug⌣.
burun-tód (§2366) n. *daughter's son, grandson.*
　voc. -tót!, -tó!
　obj. -tŏdk(ı)⌣, -tŏtk(ı)⌣, etc.
　gen. -tŏdn⌣v., etc.
　pl. burúntonı⌣.
burúkk(ı)⌣ n. *jerboa, Dipus ægyptius*; with collective sg. (§4696d) [§2293; *RSN*, §129].
　obj. -kıg⌣.
　pl. -kınč(ı)⌣.
bústa⌣ n. *post, postal service, post-office* [< Eg. Ar. بُوسْطَة *id*. < It. *posta*].
　obj. -tag⌣.
　bústan⌣ıllar⌣ǧawábık⌣kóná? *have you any letters for the post?*
búsug⌣ n. *leathern sack* [*RSN*, §129].
　obj. busúgk(ı)⌣, -úkk(ı)⌣, -ki⌢.
　pl. búsugı⌣.
búš⌣ n. *Monday* [cp. ON ⲡⲟⲧϣ *id*., *ZNA*, p. 194(?) *week*, *GCD*, p. 11].
　obj. búšk(ı)⌣, -ki⌢.
　gen. búšn⌣v., búš⌣c. (§§861-4).
　pl. búšı⌣.
　búš⌣jóm (§4813) and

　búš⌣nahár⌣ (náh-, nɛh-; §4813) *Monday.*
　búšk(ı)⌣ (§4665),
　búšır⌣,
　búš⌣nahárk(ı)⌣ and
　búš⌣naharro⌣ *on Monday.*
　búšırtōn⌣ and
　búš⌣naharrotōn⌣ *since Monday.*
　búš⌣móŋkon⌣ and
　búš⌣bókkon⌣ *till Monday.*
　ásal⌣búšun⌣ (-šū⌢, búšú⌢ §939) *tomorrow is Monday.*
bŭšn-d(ı)⌣ (§§2545 ff.) adj. *appertaining to Monday, Monday's.*
bŭšn-óñ⌣ (bıšn-) n. *Tuesday* [§2150].
　obj. bušnóñg(ı)⌣, -gi⌢.
　gen. bušnóñn⌣v., -óñ⌣c. (§§838-43).
　pl. bušnóñı⌣.
　bušnóñ⌣jóm⌣ (§4813) and
　bušnóñ⌣nahár⌣ (§4813) *Tuesday.*
　bušnóñg(ı)⌣ (§4665),
　bušnóñır⌣,
　bušnóñ⌣nahárk(ı)⌣ and
　bušnóñ⌣naharro⌣ *on Tuesday.*
　bušnóñırtōn⌣ and
　bušnóñ⌣naharrotōn⌣ *since Tuesday.*
　bušnóñ⌣móŋkon⌣ and
　bušnóñ⌣bókkon⌣ *till Tuesday.*
　ásal⌣bušnóñun⌣ (-óñū⌢, -óñú⌢ *tomorrow is Tuesday.*
bušnóñ-d(ı)⌣ (§§2545 ff.) adj. *appertaining to Tuesday, Tuesday's.*
bután⌣ *child, etc.* s.v. bitán⌣.
bután⌣ *(s)he (it) will come* s.v. tá.
bútte⌣ n. *aftermath, what grows after a plant has been cut down*; with collective sg. (§4696b) [< *búdtɛ⌣ (§706) < búd *come out* + -t dim. + -ɛ⌣ of n. act., so *little coming(s) out, sprout(s)* §2335].
　obj. -tɛg⌣.
　pl. -tenč⌣.
　gín⌣bútte⌣ (-n⌣b- < -dn⌣b- §594, gím⌣b- §595) *after-grass.*
　márɛm⌣bútte⌣ *fresh shoots that grow after millet has been cut.*
bútt(ı)⌣ n. *person of the same age, contemporary* [< *búrt(ı)⌣ (§713) < bú *be* + gerundial -r (§4585) + -t dem. so *that (sc. fellow-)being*; cp. ON ⲛⲓⲁⲧ, ⲛⲓⲧⲧ *friend* (*GNT*, s.v.) < ⲛⲓ *be* + ⲁ + ⲧ §2328β].
　obj. -tıg⌣.
　pl. -tınč(ı)⌣.
　tɛr⌣ám⌣búttín⌣án⌣tíwrímunun⌣ám⌣bɛléndimunun⌢ (§6238) *he is my equal in age (but) not my friend (and) not of my country.*
búttul n. (a) *he-goat*; (b) *buck.*
— with collective sg. (§4696d) [§2343]:
　obj. buttúlg(ı)⌣.
　pl. búttulı⌣.
　gɛ́ln⌣búttul⌣ and
　gɛ́lm⌣búttul⌣ *buck.*
b(w)án! b(w)ǎ!, b(w)á!) *let him (her, it) lie!, etc.* < buán! s.v. bú.

čúp!, čúpp! and with stop prolonged indefinitely (§306).
čúppp...!, interj. *damn!, curse!*
　áıgı⌣čúppp⌣ɛgó⌢ *(s)he (has) cursed at me.*
čubbɛ́ v.t. and i. *curse (at), swear (at)* (= tubbɛ́) [say čúpp! (to) §4080].

ind. pres. āi⌣čubbέri⌢; perf. āi⌣čubbέgori⌢ (N. -έko-, -έho-).
āıgı⌣čubbέgoran⌢ *they swore (have sworn) at me.*
tókkon⌣čubbέmεn! *don't swear (at me, him, her, it, us, them, §5083).*

dá⌣ (-da⌣ §1675; §2376) n. *home, place (house, district or part) where one lives* [§2049].
obj. dág⌣.
pl. dánč(ı)⌣.
nóbrεn-da⌣ *Home of Gold*, name of a village near Sόr⌣ (Suri on map) about six miles below Hándag⌣.
— with sg. of family poss. pron. and (homophonous) pl. of normal pers. pron. (§2632):
ánda⌣ *my home.*
índa⌣ *your home.*
tínda⌣ *his (her) home.*
ánda⌣ *our home.*
índa⌣ *your (pl.) home.*
tínda⌣ *their home.*
án⌣dār⌢, ándār⌣ *in (to) my (our) home.*
ín⌣dār⌣, índār⌣ *in (to) your (sg. and pl.) home.*
tín⌣dār⌣, tíndār⌣ *in (to) his (her, their) home.*
— with predicative -r⌢ (§5858):
án⌣dār⌢ *(s)he (it) is (they are) in my (our) home.*
ín⌣dār⌢ *(s)he (it) is (they are) in your (sg. and pl.) home.*
tín⌣dār⌢ *(s)he (it) is (they are) in his (her, their) home.*
ánda-dān⌣índa-dām⌣bárrεr⌢ *(s)he (it) is (they are) between my (our) home and yours (sg. and pl.).*
ǧızúlın⌣dār⌣ášab⌣bukállan⌢ (-b⌣b- <-g⌣b- §519) *they will dine at Ǧuzúli's.*

dăn-d(ı)⌣ (§§2545 ff.) adj. *appertaining to the home, of the home, domestic.*
andánd(ı)⌣ *appertaining to my (our) home.*
ındánd(ı)⌣ *appertaining to your (sg. and pl.) home.*
tındánd(ı)⌣ *appertaining to his (her, their) home.*
andánd(ı)⌣ n. *Dóngola Nubian* [(sc. the language) *of our home* §4964].
andándıb⌣báññıran⌢ (-b⌣b- <-g⌣b- §519) and
andándıgεb⌣báññıran⌢ (-b⌣b- <-d⌣b- §518) *they speak Dóngola Nubian.*
mássín-da⌣ *Máḥas⌣* =mássínda⌣ s.v. mássı⌣.
mássın⌣dār⌣ *in Máḥas⌣.*
mássın⌣dănd(ı)⌣ adj. *appertaining to Máḥas⌣, Máḥasi.*

-dán (<-dá-an §1111; §§3921-3) v.i. *go to the home;* suffixed to the genitive of the possessor of the home, that must be expressed.
ind. pres. āi⌣ ...-dándi⌢, εr⌣ ...-dánın⌢ (-ní⌢, -ní⌢); fut. āi⌣b(ı)- ...-dándi⌢; perf. āi⌣...-dánkori⌢.
subj. past āi⌣ ...-dánsı⌣ (-dássı⌣ §680, -su⌣).
āi⌣andándi⌢ *I go home.*
εr⌣indánın⌢ *you go home.*
tεr⌣tındánın⌢ *(s)he (it) goes home.*
ar⌣andándu⌢ *we go home.*
ır⌣indándu⌢ *you go home.*
tır⌣tındándan⌢ *they go home.*
āi⌣bandandi⌢ *I shall go home,* εr⌣bandánın⌢ *you will go home.*
āi⌣andánkori⌢ *I went home.*
āi⌣andánsı⌣wεkídkı⌣ *when I went home.*
āi⌣andándi⌢ *I go to my (our) home.*
āi⌣ındándi⌢ *I go to your (sg. and pl.) home.*
āi⌣tındándi⌢ *I go to his (her, their) home.*
ar⌣ındándu⌢ *we go to your (sg. and pl.) home.*
ar⌣tındándu⌢ *we go to his (her, their) home.*
ır⌣tındándu⌢ *you (pl.) go to his (her, their) home.*
tır⌣andándan⌢ *they go to my (our) home.*
tır⌣tındándan⌢ *they go to his (her, their) home.*
tεr⌣bıtındánın⌢ *(s)he will go to his (her, their) home.*
ındán! *go home!* (*-dá!, *-dá! *not heard* §952).
ındáwwε! (-wέ!) *go (pl.) home!*
ındámmεn! (-mε̃!, -mέ! §939) *don't go home!*
ındámmεwwε! (-wέ!) *don't (pl.) go home!*
tókkon⌣ındámmεn! (-mε̃!, -mέ!) *and* ındámmεn⌣tókkó! *don't go home!*
tókkon⌣ındámmεwwε! (-wέ!) *don't (pl.) go home!*
mássın-dándi⌢ *I go to Máḥas.*
bı-mássın⌣dándan⌢ *they will go to Máḥas.*
mássın⌣dáŋkoran⌢ *they went (have gone) to Máḥas.*
mássın-dánsaw⌣wεkítt(ı)⌣ (-w⌣w- <-n⌣w §720) *when they went to Máḥas⌣.*

-dám-bŭ- (§3961) v.i. stat. *be in a state of motion towards the home, be on one's way to the home, be going to the home;* suffixed to gen. of possessor of home:
āi⌣andámbŭri⌢ *I am on my way home.*
εr⌣indámbŭn⌢ *you are on your way home.*
tεr⌣tındámbŭn⌢ *(s)he is on his (her) way home.*
ar⌣andámbŭru⌢ *we are on our way home.*
ır⌣indámbŭru⌢ *you are on your way home.*
tır⌣tındámbŭran⌢ *they are on their way home.*
āi⌣bandámbŭri⌢ *I shall be on my way home.*
āi⌣andámbŭgori⌢ *I was on my way home.*
āi⌣andámbŭsı⌣wεkídk(ı)⌣ *when I was on my way home.*
āi⌣ındámbŭri⌢ *I am on my way to your (sg. and pl.) home.*
āi⌣tındámbŭri⌢ *I am on my way to his (her, their) home.*
ar⌣andámbŭru⌢ *we are on our way to your (sg. and pl.) home.*
ar⌣tındámbŭru⌢ *we are on our way to his (her, their) home.*
ır⌣tındámbŭru⌢ *you (pl.) are on your way to his (her, their) home.*
tır⌣andámbŭran⌢ *they are on their way to my (our) home.*
tır⌣tındámbŭran⌢ *they are on their way to his (her, their) home.*
āi⌣mássındámbŭri⌢ *I am on my way to Máḥas.*

-danεd-ắg- (§3966β) v.i. *be in the situation of having gone to the home;* suffixed to the gen. of the possessor of the home:
tındanεdágın⌢ (a) *(s)he has gone home;* (b) *(s)he has gone to their home.*
tındanεdágran⌢ (a) *they have gone home;* (b) *they have gone to his (her) home.*
mássındanεdágran⌢ *they have gone to Máḥas.*

dá- (§§3818-20) v.i. *be going (along), be proceeding;* common as -dā- (infra) in complex; the simple verb is usually replaced by nógbŭ- [cp. dăǧı *walk about,* dátt(ı) *walk stumblingly,* bıdá *come*].
X. εr⌣ısắır⌣nókkó? *where did you go (have you been) to?*
Y. āi⌣súgır⌣dágori *I was (have been) walking in the market.*
tέkk⌣āi⌣ḥartúmır⌣dásıddo⌣nálkori⌢ *I saw him (her, it) when I was going about Khartoum.*

-dā- (in verb-complexes §3987) *be moving* (i.) *along, be proceeding, be travelling, be going.*

dá- (§§3533, 3558) v.i. (a) *be present, be at hand;* (b) *exist, be* [§2049; cp. ON. ᴀᴀ *be* GNT, s.v.; prob. a specialization of dá- *be going* (§3819), cp. (a) *going* and *current=existing, to be had*].
— usually of things or unknown persons, as ắg of known persons:
ind. pres. āi⌣dári⌢, εr⌣dán⌢ (⌣dắ⌢, ⌣dắ⌢ §337, ⌣dắ⌢ §942; ⌣dān⌢ §1786); perf. āi⌣dắgori (N. ⌣dắko-, ⌣dắho-).
subj. past āi⌣dắsı⌣ (-su⌣).
part. pres. dắl⌣ (one) *that exists,* etc., *existing,* etc.; obj. dắlg(ı)⌣, -gi⌢.
part. past dārεl⌣ (one) *that existed,* etc., *existing,* etc.; obj. dārεlg(ı)⌣ (dắrεlg(ı)⌣), -gi⌢.
tεr⌣ímmam⌣mássır⌣dăn⌢ *he is present without a turban.*
ógıǧ⌣díǧ⌣dăn⌢ *there are five men.*
ám⌣bέlεdır⌣dắmunun⌢ *in my (our) country there isn't any.*
wǐlgı⌣dắgomunun⌢ *yesterday (a) there wasn't one (any); (b) (s)he (it) was not present.*
wǐlgı⌣dắgomunan⌢ *yesterday (a) there weren't any; (b) they were not present.*
X. bún⌣dắmεní? *isn't there any coffee?*
Y. súgır⌣dắ⌢ *there is some in the market.*
wǐldotōn⌣dắmunun⌢ (a) *there has been (§5372) none since yesterday;* (b) *(s)he (it) has been absent since yesterday.*
X. εr⌣ısắır⌣εgó? *where were you? (where have you been?).*
Y. āi⌣súgır⌣dắgori *I was (have been) in the market* (s.v. dá- *be going*).
tέkk⌣ár⌣ḥartúmır⌣dásuddo⌣nálkori⌢ *I saw him (her, it) when we were at Khartoum.*

dá- — dabbúra⌣

X. éssɪg⌣étta⌢ *bring water.*
Y. marɪssóddɛ́r⌣dān⌢ (§1786) *there is very little.*
X. dálg⌣étta⌢ *bring what there is.*
dárɛlg⌣étta⌢ *bring what (the one that) there was.*
nɪ́g⌣índo⌣dárɛlgɪ⌣nálkoná? *did you see the one that was here last year?*
ğawǎbɪ⌣bústan⌣ıllǎr⌣dǎrandɛ́? *are there (any) letters for the post?*
såkɪnɪ⌣dǎmunan⌢ *(a) the residents are absent;* (b) *there are no residents.*
X. súğɪrtōm⌣mǐŋg⌣éttagon? *what did you bring (have you brought) from the market?*
Y. éttagorɪ⌣dǎmunun⌢ (§6118) *I (have) brought nothing,* lit. '*I (have) brought' doesn't exist.*
X. mǐŋg⌣ǎuın? *what are you doing?*
Y. åurɪ⌣dǎmunun⌢ *I'm not doing anything.*
bukálɪn⌣dǎná? *will (§5383) you eat something?*
dǎŋkɪrɪn⌢ (§5057) *there seems to be some.*

— with ⌣d- assimilated to preceding -l⌣ (§578):
X. nɪ́⌣tagon? *who came (has come)?*
Y. tågol⌣dǎmunun⌢ and
Z. tågol⌣lǎmunun⌢ *there's nobody that came (has come).*
dǎgol⌣dǎná? and
dǎgol⌣lǎná? *is there anyone (present) that was present? (is there anyone here that was there?).*

-dān⌣ (-dǎ⌣, -dā⌣)...-dān⌣ (etc.) *both ...and* s.v. -dān⌣.

dǎr-an (§§3890, 3899) v.t. *tell to be present, etc., let be present, etc.*
imperat. dǎran! (-rǎ!, -rá!).
ém⌣bálg⌣ǎddo⌣dǎrǎ! *attend to me (us)!,* lit. *tell your attention to be (directed) to me (us)!*

dá-bŭ- (§§3927ff.) v.i. stat. *be in a state of existence, exist, be present, be situated, be (se trouver, hallarse, trovarsi, sich befinden).*
ind. pres. āɪ⌣dǎburi⌢; perf. āɪ⌣dǎbŭgori⌢ (N. -ŭko-, -ŭho-).
part. pres. dǎbūl⌣ *(one) that exists, etc., existing, etc.;* obj. dǎbūlg(ɪ)⌣.
part. past dǎbŭɛl⌣ (-bwɛl⌣, -bɛl⌣) *(one) that existed, etc., existing, etc.;* obj. dǎbŭɛlg(ɪ)⌣ (-bwɛlg(ɪ)-, -bɛlg(ɪ)-).
X. kɪbrɪ́dkɪ⌣dólná? *do you want matches?* (§4696c).
Y. dǎn, án⌣ğɛ̌bɪr⌣dǎbūn⌢ *there are (i.e. I have) some, they are in my pocket.*
sɪğɪndo⌣dǎbun⌢ *(s)he is (spending his (her) time) in prison.*
bánga⌣korráñn⌣agíllo⌣dǎbūgó⌢ *the cricket was (actually) in the gecko's mouth.*
ígɪr⌣dǎbugo⌢ *it was (has been) in the fire.*
ámbestonɪ⌣dǎbugoran⌢ *my brother's children were present.*
hán⌣ugúgoŋgɪ⌣dǎbugo⌢ *the donkey was present during (§4666) the night also.*
índo⌣dǎbɛlgɪ⌣dólli⌢ *I want (like) the one that was here.*
índo⌣dǎbugómunan⌢ *they were not (have not been) here.*

X. såɪr⌣nókkó? *where did (s)he (it) go (has (s)he (it) gone) to?*
Y. āɪ⌣uñúmmunun, āɪ⌣ǎrɛr⌣dǎburi⌢ *I don't know, I have been (lit. am) inside (indoors)?*
índ⌣úmbud⌣dǎbumunun⌢ *there is no salt here (in this).*

dǎl-dā- (dállā- §578; §§3985-6) v.i. (a) *be present existing, be existing at hand;* (b) *be existing, be in existence.*
X. dállāná? (dáldāná?) *is there any (some, anything)?*
Y. dállāmunun⌢ *there is none (nothing).*
Z. dallāmunun⌢ *there is none (nothing).*
X. ténnɛ⌣dállāná? *is (are) there any more?*
Y. dállān⌢ *there is (are).*
sɛ́riñ⌣dallǎgɪn⌣ğɪsíkkɪ⌢ (§6152ii) *go and ask whether there is any barley.*
(N.) ğawǎb⌣dallǎkɪn⌣ɪsíkkɪrɪ⌢ *I'll §5369b) ask whether there's a letter (there are letters §4647).*

dǎŋ-ɪr (N. -ŋkɪr; §3688) v.t. caus. *cause or allow to exist, etc.*

dáb v.i. (a) *disappear, vanish;* (b) *become lost, get lost* [cp. ON. ⲧⲁⲛⲡⲓ *be lost* GNT, s.v. Bed. *ḍāb, ḍāb entflichen* RBW, s.v.].
ind. pres. āɪ⌣dáb(ɪ)ri⌢, ɛr⌣dǎbɪn⌢ (-bí⌢, -bí⌢); perf. āɪ⌣dábkori⌢ (dápk-).
imperat. dáp! *be off!,* pl. dábwɛ! (dábwɛ́!).
subj. past āɪ⌣dábsɪ⌣ (⌣dápsɪ⌣, -su⌣).
def. imperat. dábos! (dabós!, dabó! §962); pl. dabóswɛ! (-bóswɛ́!, -bówwɛ́!, -wɛ́!, -bóssɛ́! §687, -sɛ́!).
tén⌣dúŋgɪ⌣dabóskó⌢ *his (her) money has disappeared.*
āɪ⌣kuljómgɪ⌣dówwab⌣bɪnír⌣ín⌣amğulúd⌣dǎbɪm⌣bókkö⌢ (-b⌣b- < -g⌣b- §519) *I shall drink the medicine every day until this boil (these boils §4696c) disappear(s).*

— of a small (slippery, etc.) object:
bálko!, bɪdábɪn⌢ *mind!, it will get lost.*

dábar⌣ (-bǎr⌣; §§2200ff.) and
dabíd⌣ (§§2256ff.) n. *disappearance.*
dabíd-an-dáb (§4161) v.i. *disappear (etc.) utterly, get quite lost, disappear (etc.) for good.*
imperat. dabídandáp!

dáb-an (§§3890ff.) v.t. *tell to disappear, etc., let disappear, etc.*

dáb-bŭ- (§3931α) v.i. stat. *be in a vanished or lost state or condition.*
míndo⌣dǎbbūn? *what has disappeared? (what is lost?).*

dab(ɪ)r-ɛg-ǎg- (§§4071ff.) v.i. =dabɛdól-.
élum⌣dabrɛgǎgɪn⌢ *the crocodile is just going to disappear.*

dab-ɛ-dól- (-b°d- §1178; §4022) and
dab(ɪ)r-ɛ-dól- (-r°d-; §4027) v.i. *be about to disappear, etc.*
wɪ́lgɪ⌣dabɛdólkori, ígkɪ⌣nálmensugɛ́⌢ (§6203) *yesterday I nearly got lost because I did not see the fire (light).*

dab-ɛ-mǎ- (§4036) and
dab(ɪ)r-ɛ-mǎ- (§4041) v.i. *become unable to disappear, etc.*

dabɛd-ǎg- (§3877) v.i. *be in the situation of having disappeared, etc.*

dab-ğŭ (§3747ɛ') v.i. *go out of sight, go off.*
ind. pres. āɪ⌣dabğŭri⌢.
imperat. dabğŭ!

X. míndo⌣dabğŭgó? *where has (s)he (it) disappeared (did (s)he (it) disappear) to?*
Y. āɪ⌣tɛr⌣dabğŭsɪn⌣agárk⌣uñúrmunun⌢ *I don't know the place (s)he (it) went off to.*
Z. dabɪdandabóskó⌢ *(s)he (it) has disappeared for good.*

dáb-ɪr (§3671) (a) v.t. caus. *cause or allow to disappear, etc.;* (b) v.t. *get rid of, get through, waste, squander;* (c) v.t. *lose.*
ind. pres. āɪ⌣dabíddi⌢ and ⌣dabírri⌢ (⌣ᵃ⌣), ɛr⌣dábɪrɪn⌢ (-rí⌢, -rí⌢); fut. āɪ⌣bɪdabíddi⌢ (⌣bud-, -írri⌢); perf. āɪ⌣dabírkori⌢.
subj. past āɪ⌣dabírsɪ⌣ (-íssɪ⌣ §683, -su⌣).
tókkon⌣såbid⌣dábɪrmɛn⌢ (-d⌣d- < -g⌣d- §534; §5457) *don't let the cats run away.*
ténnɛ́n⌣tén⌣dúŋgɪ⌣málɛd⌣dábɪrɪn⌢ *his wife squanders all his (her) money.*
tókkon⌣dúŋgɪd⌣dábɪrmɛn⌢ *don't lose (etc.) the money.*
án⌣zummǎrad⌣dabróskori⌢ (-d⌣d- < -g⌣d- §534; §1080) *I have lost my pipe (flute).*

dabɪrɛd-ǎg- (§§3877, 3883) v.t. *be in the situation of having caused or allowed to disappear, etc.*
tín⌣dúŋgɪd⌣dabɪrɛdǎgran⌢ *they have lost (etc.) their money.*

dabíŋ-ɪr (dǎbɪŋgɪr §1799; N. -ŋkɪr; §3688) v.t. caus. and v.t. =dábɪr.
ind. pres. āɪ⌣dabɪŋgíddi⌢ (⌣dábɪŋgíddi⌢), ɛr⌣dabíŋgɪrɪn⌢ (-rí⌢, -rí⌢).
tókkon⌣dúŋgɪd⌣dábɪŋgɪrmɛn⌢ *don't lose (etc.) the money.*
såbkɪ⌣tókkon⌣dabɪŋgírmɛn⌢ *don't let the cat(s) run away.*

dabɪ́ríŋ-ɪr (dǎbɪrɪŋgɪr §1799; N. -ŋkɪr; §3691) v.t. caus. *cause or allow to get rid of, etc.*
ind. pres. āɪ⌣dabɪríŋgíddi⌢ (⌣dábɪrɪŋgíddi⌢, ⌣ⁿⁿⁿⁿ⌣ §1820), ɛr⌣dabɪ́rɪŋgɪrɪn⌢ (-rí⌢, -rí⌢).
tókkon⌣tékkɪ⌣dúŋgɪd⌣dábɪrɪŋgɪrmɛn⌢ *don't let him (her) waste (etc.) the money.*

dabos-tǎ- (-ottá §714; §§4180-4; -osgɪtǎ-, -ozgɪ-, -oggɪ- §4185) v.i. *come (back) after disappearance, etc.*
ír⌣nógsun⌣ɛgéttɪr⌣jóm⌣mɛ́d⌣dabottǎgó⌢ (-m⌣m- < -m⌣w- §603, -d⌣d- < -g⌣d- §534) *soon after you (pl.) went away (s)he disappeared for one day and then returned.*

dábba⌣ (déb-) n. *Debba (on map), Ed-Débbà*, a station on the left bank of the Nile about 46 miles south-east of Hándag⌣ [< الدَّبَّة *the sandy hill*; §1389].
obj. -bag⌣.

dabbúra⌣ n. *star (badge of rank);* with collective sg. (§4696d) [< Sudan Ar. دبورة id.].
obj. -rag⌣.
pl. -ranč(ɪ)⌣.
dabbúra⌣tóskɪk⌣kó⌢ *he (it) has three stars.*

†**dabbûs**‿ n. *pin*; with collective sg. (§4696c) [< دبوس *id*.].
  obj. -úsk(ı)‿, -kiᴑ.
  pl. -úsı‿.
-**dabíss(ı)**‿ n. *cousin* (a) *father's brother's son*; (b) *father's brother's daughter*.
  voc. -si!
  obj. -sıg‿.
  pl. -sınč(ı)‿.
— always with a form of the possessive personal pronoun (§§2622, 2629a) prefixed:
  andabíss(ı)‿ *my father's brother's child*.
  ındabíss(ı)‿ *your father's brother's child*.
  tındabíss(ı)‿ *his (her) father's brother's child*.
  antındabíss(ı)‿ *our father's brother's child*.
  ıntındabíss(ı)‿ *your (pl.) father's brother's child*.
  tıntındabíss(ı)‿ *their father's brother's child*.
dábja n. *leathern bag* (esp. to carry grain) [< Sudan Ar. ضَبِيَّة *id*.].
  obj. -jag‿.
  pl. -janč(ı)‿.
  máron‿dábja‿ *the bag of (for) sorghum* (§4685).
  íllɛn‿dábja‿ *the bag of (for) wheat*.
  símsım‿dábja‿ (-m‿d- < -mn‿d- §817) *the bag of (for) sesame*.
dádd(ı)‿ and **dád(ı)**‿ n. *pan, dish, bowl or similar vessel*; with collective sg. (§4696c) [RSN, §129, SMN, p. 451].
  obj. -dıg‿.
  pl. -dınč(ı)‿.
  úmbun‿dád(ı)‿ *salt-bowl*, of pottery, about a foot in diameter, stands on a stool in the kitchen.
  †tubúrtın‿dád(ı)‿ *ash-tray* (not native).
dáftar‿ *note-book* = dáftɐr‿.
dagíga‿ n. *minute*; with collective sg. (§4696c) [< دَقِيقَة *id*.].
  obj. -gag‿.
  pl. -ganč(ı)‿.
dắgı v.i. *walk about, walk to and fro, ramble, roam, wander* [< -dá- *be going along* + -ğ iterative §2887].
  ind. pres. aı‿dắğırı‿; perf. aı‿dắğıgorıᴑ (N. -ıko-, -ıho-).
  imperat. dắğı!
  tókkon‿dắğımɛn, índ‿ák‿ *don't wander about, sit down here*.
dắğɛt-tá (§§4169ff.) v.i. *come (back) after walking about, etc*.
  aı‿dắğettagorıᴑ *I (have) arrived after wandering about*.
dắğı- v.i. (a) *be present, be at hand*; (b) *exist, be* [< dá- *be present* + -ğ §2887].
  ind. pres. aı‿dắğırı‿; perf. aı‿dắğıgorıᴑ (N. -ıko-, -ıho-).
  X. ɛ́ssı‿dắná? *is there (any) water?*
  Y. ɛ́ssı‿dắğınᴑ *yes, there is*, lit. *water is present*.
  kál‿dắğımununᴑ *there's no food (bread)*.
  íŋon‿dắğınᴑ *that, too, exists*.
dáhal‿ (§4717) (a) n. *evil spirit possessing a person or object, madness*; (b) n. *mad person or animal*; (c) adj. *mad* [< διάβολ- of διάβολος, ON. ᛞᛁᚨᛒᚬᛚᚨᛋ, §2393].
  obj. dahálg(ı)‿, -giᴑ.
  pl. dahalı‿.

tɛr‿dahálgı‿kónᴑ (‿kóᴑ, ‿kóᴑ) and (§4672)
tɛr‿dahál‿kónᴑ (‿kóᴑ, ‿kóᴑ) (s)he (it) is mad (δαιμόνιον ἔχει Luke vii. 33).
dahálgı‿kóranᴑ and
dahál‿kóranᴑ *they are mad*.
ín‿dáhalunᴑ *this (that) is a mad person (animal) (this one is mad)*.
ɛ́n‿dáhál-lɛn‿nálkoriᴑ (-l-l- < -l-w- §580, -n‿n- < -g‿n- §625) *I saw (have seen) a madwoman*.
wɛ́l‿dahál-lɛb‿bɛ́goranᴑ (-b‿b- < -g‿b- §519) *they (have) killed a mad dog*.
dáhal-an- (§3910α) v.i. *go mad*.
  dáhalaŋkóᴑ *(s)he (it) went (has gone) mad*.
dahalan-ɛ-dól- (n°d- §1178; §4026) and
dahaland-ɛ-dól- (-d°d-; §4034) v.i. *be about to go mad*.
  dahalanɛdólınᴑ *(s)he (it) will very soon go mad*.
dahál-kŏ- (§4118) v.i. *be mad*.
  dahálkon‿ (-kŏᴑ, -álkóᴑ, -koᴑ) *you are ((s)he (it) is) mad*.
  dahálkoranᴑ *they are mad*.
  part. pres. dahálkōl‿ (dahalkól‿) *(one that is) mad*.
  ín‿dahalkólunᴑ *this (that) is a mad person (animal) (this (that) one is mad)*.
  ɛ́n‿dahálkól-lɛn‿nálkoriᴑ (-l-l- < -l-w- §580, -n‿n- < -g‿n- §625) *I saw (have seen) a madwoman*.
dalál‿ (dàl-) n. *wattle (of cock)*; with collective sg. (§4696a) [cp. دَلَال *chevelure, celle du front DS*, دَلْدَال *motion* of a thing suspended *LA*; in Sudan Ar. دَلْدَال = Amh. እንጥጣቲ *lobe or wattle on goat's neck*].
  obj. -álg(ı)‿, -giᴑ.
  pl. -álı‿.
  kuglúŋ‿dalál‿ *cock's wattle(s)*.
dállā- (§578) < dáldā- *be present existing, etc*. s.v. dá- *be present*.
dálu n. (a) *bucket of skin*, esp. for use at well [< دَلْو *id*.]; (b, in water-wheel, kólɛ‿) *final channel receiving water from smaller trough (ğaráttarɛ‿) and leading to runnel (mált(ı)‿)*.
  obj. dálug‿.
  pl. dalúnč(ı)‿.
  ɛ́ssıg‿gŏ́wwırtōn‿dálugɛs‿sókkeranᴑ (-s‿s- < -d‿s- §677) *they lift water from the well by means of a bucket*.
dámbo‿ n. *Dambo (on map)*, a village on the left bank of the Nile, about three miles above Hándag‿.
  obj. -bog‿.
-**dān**‿ (-dā̆-, -dā §979)...-dān‿ (etc.) *concretion-forming postposition both... and* (§4402) *suffixed to nom*. [<‿dān‿ *there is* §4390].
  áli-dān‿ɛsmán-dān‿nókkoranᴑ *ɛáli and ɛoθmán went (have gone)*.
  ánda‿árgo‿dān‿úrdi‿dām‿bárrerᴑ *my (our) home is between Argo and El-Ordi*.
  kám-dān‿hánu-daw‿wɛl-dān‿dabóskoranᴑ (-w‿w- < -n‿w- §720) *the camel, donkey and dog have disappeared*.

ugúllan-dān‿ɛ́ssı-dāŋ‿ɛ́ttagoranᴑ *they (have) brought (the) fuel and water* (§4901).
ɛsmán-dā‿mohámmɛd-dāŋ‿ín‿fıríččıb‿bɛ́wáᴑ (-b‿b- < -g‿b- §519) *let ɛoθmán and Muhámmad kill these wasps* (§4696c).
dáp! imperat. of dáb *disappear*.
dắr‿ n. *(inhabited) district, (inhabited) country* [<‿دَار *dwelling-place*].
  obj. dắrk(ı)‿, -kiᴑ.
  pl. dắrı‿.
  árabın‿dắrrṓᴑ (§§5858-60) *(s)he (it) is (they are) in the Arabs' country*.
dára‿ n. *screen, shelter*, esp. that erected, against the wind, round the trough (sáblo‿) of the water-wheel (kólɛ‿) [cp. دَرْوَة *id*. (§1339), دَرْو *projecting part* §2411].
  obj. dárag‿.
  pl. daránč(ı)‿.
dárıb‿ (-rub‿) *path, road* = dárıb‿.
dárıg‿ n. (a) *freshwater turtle* (= amandákkɛ‿); (b) *terrestrial turtle, tortoise*.
— with collective sg. (§4696d) [cp. Sudan Ar. دريقة *id*.; دريقة dim. of دَرَقَة *shield*]:
  obj. darígk(ı)‿, -íkk(ı)‿, -kiᴑ.
  pl. dárıgı‿.
  dárıg‿úrun‿túgon‿hálagond‿ɛ́lkattınᴑ (-d‿ɛ́- < -do‿ɛ́- §1122; §§6085) *the turtle is found both in the river and in the desert*.
  ám‿bélɛdır‿dárıŋ‿kúsu‿kálkattınᴑ (-ıŋ‿k- < -gıı‿k- §652) *in my (our) country the flesh of the turtle is eaten*.
  tússı‿dárıg‿ *a shrub*, Bergia suffruticosa, Fenzl. (BSP, 48).
darín-d(ı)‿ (§§2545 ff.) adj. *appertaining to the turtle*.
darímd(ı)‿ (-rúm-) adj. *appertaining to the (a) path, etc*. = dárımd(ı)‿.
dárr(ı)‿ v.i. *ascend, go or come up, climb*.
  ind. pres. aı‿dárrırı‿, ɛr‿dárrın‿ (-ríᴑ, -ríᴑ); perf. aı‿dárrıgoriᴑ (N. -ıko-, -ıho-).
  imperat. dárri!
  sáp‿tarabɛ́zar‿dárrın‿ *the cat gets up on to the table*.
  mán‿ğébɛln‿dógor‿dárrıgoru‿ *we (you pl.) (have) climbed on to the top of that mountain*.
dárrar (-rắr‿; §§2200 ff.) and
darríd‿ (§§2256 ff.) n. *ascent*.
darr-ám-mér- (-ág-mér- §601; §4198) v.t. (a) *be engaged in cutting after ascending (etc*.); (b) *continually (habitually) cut after ascending (etc*.).
  gŏ́wwır‿darrámmérkoranᴑ and (§5582)
  gŏ́wwır‿dárrıg‿ámmérkoranᴑ *they used after climbing the trees to cut them*.
dárr-an‿ (§§3890 ff.) v.t. *tell to ascend, etc*., *let ascend, etc*.
dárrı-bū- (§3931 α) v.i. stat. *be in an ascending (etc.) state or condition, be on the way up*.
  béntır‿dárrıbūnᴑ *he is on his way up the date-palm*.
dárrır-ɛg-ág- (§§4071 ff.) v.i. = darrɛdól-.

darr-ɛ-dól- (-r⁰d- § 1178; § 4022) and
darrɪr-ɛ-dól- (-r⁰d-; § 4027) v.i. *be about to ascend, etc.*
darrɪr-ɛ-ğŭ-bŭ- (§ 4069) v.i. stat. *be on one's way (coming) to ascend, etc.*
darr-ɛ-mǎ- (§ 4036) and
darrɪr-ɛ-mǎ- (§ 4041) v.i. *become unable to ascend, etc.*
darrɪr-ɛ-nóg- (§§ 4048 ff.) *go to ascend, etc.*
darrɪr-ɛ-nóg-bŭ- (-nóggŭ- § 546; § 4058), v.i. stat. *be on one's way (going) to ascend, etc.*
darrɪr-ɛ-tǎ- (§§ 4060 ff.) v.i. *come to ascend, etc.*
darred-ág- (§ 3877) v.i. *be in the situation of having ascended, etc.*
dárrɪg-ɪr (N. -ɪkɪr, -ɪhɪr; § 3682) (a) v.t. caus. *cause or allow to ascend, etc.*; (b) v.t. *send up.*
(N.) aı⌣bɪtáŋɪ⌣béntɪr⌣dárrɪkɪddɪ⌢ *I'll § 5369 b) send the boy up the date-palm.*
darrɪ-mér (§ 3747 ɛ́) v.t. *cut after ascending, etc.*
darrɪ-túrb(ɪ) (-túbb(ɪ) § 520; § 3747 ɛ́) v.i. *lie down (etc. s.v. túrb(ɪ)) after ascending, etc.*
sáb⌣ğówwɪr⌣darrɪtúbbɪn⌢ *the cat rests up in the tree.*
dárub⌣ n. *path, road = dárɪb*⌣.
obj. darúbk(ɪ)⌣, -úpk(ɪ)⌣, -kɪ⌢; gen. darúbn⌣v., -rúm⌣c.; pl. dár(u)bɪ⌣.
darúm⌣tŭr⌢ *in (on, to) the path.*
darúm-d(ɪ)⌣ (§§ 2545 ff.) adj. *appertaining to the (a) path, etc.*
darŭrɪ⌣ adj. *necessary* [<ضَرُورِيّ id.].
obj. -rɪg⌣.
pl. -rɪnč(ɪ)⌣.
dáško⌣ n. *a large Nile catfish, of light colour, Bagrus bayad Forskal (PF, p. 90); with collective sg. (§ 4696d).*
obj. -kog⌣.
pl. -konč(ɪ)⌣.
dátt(ɪ) v.i. *walk stumblingly, walk a few steps and stumble, totter* [<*dárt(ɪ) (§§ 1048, 713) < dǎ- *be going* +gerundial -r (§ 4585) +-t § 2901].
ind. pres. aı⌣dáttɪrɪ⌢; perf. aı⌣dáttɪgorɪ⌢ (N. -ɪko-, -ɪho-).
báŋga⌣dáttɪn⌢ *the grasshopper (locust) walks a few steps and stumbles.*
bɪtantód⌣dattosko⌢ *the infant has begun to walk a few steps and stumble.*
dáttar (-tǎr⌣; §§ 2200 ff.) and
dattíd⌣ (§§ 2256 ff.) n. *stumbling walk.*
datted-ág- (§ 3877) v.i. *be in the situation of having walked stumblingly, etc.*
dáw(w)a⌣ (dów-; § 1386) n. *medicine* [<دَوَاء id.].
obj. -ag⌣.
pl. -anč(ɪ)⌣.
dáwan⌣hábba⌣ *pill.*
dáftar⌣ (dáftar⌣, déftar⌣) n. *book, esp. for writing in, note-book, register* [<دَفْتَر id.].
obj. dáftark(ɪ)⌣, -kɪ⌢.
pl. dáftarɪ⌣.
dárɪb⌣ (dár-, dér-, -rub⌣) n. *path, road* [<دَرْب id. § 1361].
obj. dárɪbk(ɪ)⌣, -ɪpk(ɪ)⌣, -kɪ⌢; gen. dárɪbn⌣v., -rím⌣c.; pl. dár(ɪ)bɪ⌣.

dárɪm⌣tǔr⌢ (§§ 5858–60) *(s)he (it) is (they are) in (on) the path.*
dárɪm-d(ɪ)⌣ (dar-, der-, -rúm-; §§ 2545 ff.) adj. *appertaining to the (a) path, etc.*
-dɛ!, -dɛ́! alternative ending of negative imperative plural (§ 3092).
tókkon⌣úskurmɛndɛ́! = tókkon⌣úskur-mɛwwɛ́! *don't (pl.) put it!*
-dɛ́? (after -n) = -rɛ́?, interrogative (a) sign of predication (§ 4240); (b) particle (§ 4273).
ólgon⌣ *still, yet;* ólgondɛ́? *is (s)he (it, are they) still?*
nógran⌢ *they go;* nógrandɛ́? *do they go?*
dɛ́!, dɛ̌!, dɛ̂! imperat. of dɛ́n *give (to the speaker).*
débba⌣ Ed-Débbaʰ s.v. dábba⌣.
dɛfɛ́ v.t. *pay, give in payment, give to in payment* [<دَفْع payment + -ɛ́ § 3620].
ind. pres. aı⌣dɛfɛ́rɪ⌢, ɛr⌣dɛfɛ́n⌢ (-fɛ́⌢, -fɛ̂⌢); perf. aı⌣dɛfɛ́gorɪ⌢ (N. -ɛ́ko-, -ɛ́ho-).
imperat. dɛfɛ́!, pl. dɛfɛ́wɛ! (ⁿ⁻ɛ́).
subj. past aı⌣dɛfɛ́sɪ⌣ (-su⌣).
part. pres. dɛfɛ́l⌣ (one) *that pays, payer, paying,* obj. dɛfɛ́lg(ɪ)⌣, -gɪ⌢ and occ. (§ 3535) dɛfɛ́rɪl⌣, = dɛfɛ́l⌣, obj. dɛfɛ-rílg(ɪ)⌣.
part. past dɛfɛ́rɛl⌣ (one) *that paid, payer, paying,* obj. dɛfɛ́rɛlg(ɪ)⌣, -gɪ⌢.
dúŋgɪ⌣budɛfɛ́ran⌢ (-b⌣b- § 519) *they will pay (the) money.*
tórbarɪd⌣dɛfɛ́gorɪ⌢ (-d⌣d- < -g⌣d- § 534) and (§ 5456).
tórbarɪd⌣dɛfɛ́rɪkkorɪ⌢ *I (have) paid the (agricultural) labourers.*
dɛfɛ́rar (-rǎr⌣; §§ 2200 ff., 2207) and
dɛfɛ́ríd⌣ (§§ 2256 ff., 2260) n. *payment.*
dɛfɛ́r-an (§§ 3890 ff., 3899) v.t. *tell to pay, let pay.*
dɛfɛ́-dɛn, dɛfɛ́-tɪr, infra.
dɛfɛ́r-ɛg-ág- (§§ 4071 ff.) v.t. = dɛfɛ́rɛdól-.
dɛfɛ́r-ɛ-dól- (-r⁰d- § 1178; §§ 4017-17, 4022, 4027) v.t. *be about to pay.*
dɛfɛr-ɛ-ğŭ-bŭ- (§ 4069) v.t. stat. *be on one's way (coming) to pay.*
dɛfɛr-ɛ-mǎ- (§§ 4016-17, 4036, 4041) v.t. *become unable to pay.*
tɛššáš⌣dúŋgɪd⌣dɛfɛ́mágon⌢ (-d⌣d- < -g⌣d- § 534) *the pedlar couldn't (was unable to) pay the money.*
dɛfɛ̄r-ɛ-nóg- (§§ 4048 ff.) v.t. *go to pay.*
dɛfɛ̄r-ɛ-nóg-bŭ- (-nóggŭ- § 546; § 4058) v.t. stat. *be on one's way (going) to pay.*
dɛfɛ̄r-ɛ-tǎ- (§§ 4060 ff.) v.t. *come to pay.*
dɛfɛ́-kattɪ- (N. -ɛ́ha-; § 4093) v.p. *be paid.*
dúŋgɪ⌣dɛfɛ́kattɪgon⌢ *the money was (has been) paid.*
tórbarɪ⌣dɛfɛ́kattɪgómunan⌢ *the labourers were not (have not been) paid.*
dɛfɛ́-dɛn (§§ 3996-7) v.t. *give (to the speaker) in payment, pay (the speaker).*
imperat. dɛfɛ́dɛn! (-dɛ̂!, -dɛ̌!, -dɛ́!, -dɛ̂!, § 945).
aıgı⌣dúŋgɪd⌣dɛfɛ́dɛ́ŋkoran⌢ *they (have) paid me the money.*
dɛfɛ̄dɛ̄nd-ɛ-ğŭ-bŭ- (§ 4069) v.t. stat. *be on the way (coming) to pay (the speaker).*
aıgı⌣dɛfɛ̄dɛndɛğúburan⌢ *they are coming to pay me.*
dɛfɛ̄dɛ̄nd-ɛ-tǎ- (§§ 4060 ff.) v.t. *come to pay (the speaker).*

tɛr⌣aıgı⌣dɛfɛ̄dɛndɛtágó⌢ *(s)he came (has come) to pay me.*
dɛfɛ̄dɛ̄nd-ág- (§ 3877 ff.) v.t. *be in the situation of having paid (to the speaker).*
dɛfɛ́-tɪr (§§ 3997-8) v.t. *give (to other than the speaker) in payment, pay (other than the speaker).*
tórbarɪd⌣dɛfɛ́tíkkorɪ⌢ (-d⌣d- < -g⌣d- § 534) and
tórbarɪd⌣dɛfɛ́tɪríkkorɪ⌢ *I (have) paid the labourers.*
tɪ́rgɪ⌣dúŋgɪd⌣dɛfɛ́tɪríkkoran⌢ *they (have) paid (each of) them the money.*
dɛfɛ́tɪdd-ɛ-ğŭ-bŭ- (§ 4069) v.t. stat. *be on one's way (coming) to pay (other than the speaker).*
dɛfɛ́tɪdd-ɛ-nóg- (§§ 4048 ff.) v.t. *go to pay (other than the speaker).*
tɪr⌣tékkɪ⌣dɛfɛ́tɪdɛnókkoran⌢ *they went (have gone) to pay him (her).*
dɛfɛ́tɪdd-ɛ-nóg-bŭ- (-nóggŭ- § 546; § 4058) v.t. stat. *be on one's way (going) to pay (other than the speaker).*
dɛfɛ́tɪdd-ɛ-tǎ- (§§ 4060 ff.) v.t. *come to pay (other than the speaker).*
dɛfɛ́tɪred-ág- (§§ 3877 ff.) v.t. *be in the situation of having paid (other than the speaker).*
défter⌣ *note-book* = dáftar⌣.
dég (a) v.i. *cover one's loins by putting a garment round them* [cogn. with díg *get bound,* dúg *become clouded,* tág *get covered* (§ 2781), dɛ́g *irrigate* (§ 2776); cp. ON. ᴀᴋ- bedecken ZNG, s.v., ᴀᴋᴋɪ hide GNT, s.v.]; (b) v.t. *put a garment) round one's loins;* (c) v.i. *put on clothes, dress oneself, dress;* (d) v.t. *put a garment) on, wear;* (e) v.t. *put a saddle on, saddle* (this seems to be the commonest sense now in regard to an animal unless the situation shows that f or g is meant); (f) v.t. *place a burden on, load;* (g) v.t. *place (a burden) on, load.*
ind. pres. aı⌣dég(¹)rɪ⌢, ɛr⌣dégɪn⌢ (-gɪ̂⌢, ⌣dégí⌢); perf. aı⌣dégkorɪ⌢ (dékko-).
imperat. dék!, pl. dégwɛ! (dégwɛ́!; déggɛ! § 547, -gɛ́!).
part. pres. dégɪl⌣ (one) *that covers the loins, etc.*
part. past dégɛl⌣ (one) *that covered the loins, etc.*
tén⌣káded⌣dékkô⌢ (-d⌣d- < -g⌣d- § 534) *(s)he (has) put on his (her) clothes (4696d); ...dressed himself, herself).*
aı⌣ín⌣tagíab⌣budéŋŋunun⌢ (-b⌣b- < -g⌣b- § 519, -ŋŋ- < -gm- § 661) *I shall not wear this cap.*
búr⌣akášk⌣úlugɪr⌣dékkan⌢ *the girl wears the ear-rings in her ears (§ 4696c, a).*
kámgɪ⌣dék⌢ (a) *saddle the camel;* (b) *load the camel.*
hánud⌣dékkorɪ⌢ (-d⌣d- < -g⌣d- § 534) (a) *I (have) saddled the donkey;* (b) *I (have) loaded the donkey.*
afɛ́škɪ⌣dékkorɪ⌢ *I (have) put the baggage on (the animal's back), I (have) loaded the baggage.*
umbúdkɪ⌣dék⌢ *load the salt (sc. on to the animal).*
éssɪd⌣dék⌢ *load the water.*

dégar͜ (-gár͜-; §§2200ff.) and
dɛgíd͜ (§§2256ff.) n. (a) covering one's loins (etc.), dressing, wearing, saddling, loading; (b) burden, load.
dégır͜ n. saddle [§2286α].
 obj. dɛgírk(ı)͜, -ki͡.
 pl. dég(ı)rı͜.
 dégırn͜hızám͜ and
 dégın͜hızám͜ (-n͜h- < -rn͜h- §614) girth.
dég-an (§§3890ff.) v.t. tell to cover, etc., let cover, etc.
 álıh͜hánud͜dégan͡ (-h͜h- < -g͜h- §559, -d͜d- < -g͜d- §534) let ẓáli saddle (load) the donkey.
dég-bŭ- (déggŭ- §546; §3931) v.i. stat. be in a state or condition of having one's loins covered, etc.
 aı͜dɛgbúri͡ I am dressed (I have my clothes on).
 aı͜dɛgbúmunun͡ I am not dressed.
 tɛr͜káded͜dɛgbún͡ (a) (s)he is covered with the (a) cloth; (b) (s)he is wearing clothes (§4696d).
 hánu͜déggūn͡ (a) the donkey is saddled; (b) the donkey is laden.
 hán͜aféšked͜dɛgbūn͡ the donkey is laden with (the) baggage.
 áfeš͜dɛgbūn͡ the baggage is loaded.
 áfeš͜hánun͜kóččır͜dɛgbūn͡ the baggage is loaded on the donkey.
— on a journey, when a start is being attempted:
 ádámı͜dɛgbūran͡ the men have (got) the (their) baggage loaded.
dɛg(ı)r-ɛg-ág- (§§4071ff.) v.i. and t. = dɛgɛdól-.
 hánud͜dɛgɪrɛgágrı͡ I am just going to saddle (load) the donkey.
dɛg-ɛ-dól- (-gᵒd- §1178; §4022) and
dɛg(ı)r-ɛ-dól- (-rᵒd-; §4027) v.i. and t. be about to cover one's loins, etc.
dɛg(ı)r-ɛ-gŭ-bŭ- (§4069) v.t. stat. be on one's way (coming) to saddle or load.
 hánud͜dɛgɪrɛgúbūn͡ he is coming to saddle (load) the donkey.
 aféški͜dɛgrɛgúbūran͡ they are coming to load the baggage.
dɛg-ɛ-má- (§4036) and
dɛg(ı)r-ɛ-má- (§4041) v.i. and t. become unable to cover one's loins, etc.
 kámgı͜dɛgɪrɛmágoran͡ they couldn't saddle (load) the camel.
dɛg(ı)r-ɛ-nóg- (§§4048ff.) v.t. go to saddle or load.
dɛg(ı)r-ɛ-nóg-bŭ- (-nóggŭ- §546; §4058) v.t. stat. be on one's way (going) to saddle or load.
dɛg(ı)r-ɛ-tá- (§§4060ff.) v.t. come to saddle or load.
 hánud͜dɛgɪrɛtágoran͡ (-d͜d- < -g͜d- §534) they came (have come) to saddle (load) the donkey.
dɛgɛd-ág- (§3877) v.i. and t. be in the condition or situation of having covered one's loins, etc.
 án͜káded͜dɛgɛdágrı͡ I have got my clothes on.
 aı͜dɛgɛdágrı͡ I am dressed.
 ár͜dɛgɛdágmɛndu͜tókkon͜támɛn͡ don't come when (if, while) we are not dressed (don't come before we are dressed §6188).
dɛgɛd-ággɛllıgáu- (-ággél- §551; §5637) v.t. after putting (a garment) on be engaged in working, etc. (s.v. ággɛ́llıgáu-), be at work (etc.) wearing.
 tórbar͜tés͜sagírtıd͜dɛgɛdággɛllıgáu-kon͡ (-s͜s- < -n͜s- §680, -d͜d- < -g͜d- §534) the peasant was at work (habitually worked) in his shorts.
dɛgɛd-áššuglé- (-ākšug-, -āgšug-; -šog(o)lé-; §5636) v.t. after putting (a garment) on be engaged in working, etc. (s.v. áššuglé-), be at work wearing.
 tórbar͜sagírtıd͜dɛgɛdáššogolén͡ the peasant is at work (habitually works) in shorts.
dɛgéb-bŭ- (§§3947-8) v.i. stat. lie with loins covered, etc., lie down in one's clothes.
 imperat. dɛgébbu!
 aı͜dɛgɛbbúri͡ I lie with my loins covered (etc.).
dɛgéd-dā- (§3992; -éggı-dā-, occ. -édgı- §§3993-4) v.i. and t. be going along covering one's loins, etc., be going along with one's loins covered, etc.
 ɛn͜tén͜kadɛ́nčıd͜dɛgɛ́ddān͡ (-d͜d- < -g͜d- §534) the woman is walking along wearing her (various) clothes.
 kám͜umbúdkı͜dɛgɛ́ddān͡ the camel is proceeding with a (the) load of salt.
 ógıǧ͜hánur͜káded͜dɛgɛ́ddān͡ the man is going along with a donkey laden with (the) cloth (... is proceeding with a (the) load of cloth on a donkey).
dɛgɛǧ-ǧɛllıgágau- (§5638) v.t. after putting (a garment) on be engaged in working, etc. (s.v. ǧɛllıgágau-), be at work (etc.) wearing.
 tórbarı͜tés͜sagírtıd͜dɛgɛǧǧɛllıgágau-ran͡ (-s͜s- < -n͜s- §680, -d͜d- < -g͜d- §534) the peasants are working (habitually work) in their shorts.
dɛ́g-kattı- (dékka-; §4093) v.p. be put round one's loins, be worn, be saddled, be laden, be loaded.
dég v.t. irrigate, water [phonetic variant of dég cover specialized to mean cover with water §2776].
 ind. pres. aı͜dég͜ri͡, ɛr͜dégın͡ (-gí͡), dégí͡); perf. aı͜dégkori͡ (dékko-).
 imperat. dék!, pl. dégwɛ! (dégwé!; dégge! §547, -gé!).
 part. pres. dégıl͜ (one) that irrigates, etc., irrigator, etc., irrigating, etc.
 obj. dégılg(ı)͜, -gi͡.
 part. past dégɛl͜ (one) that irrigated, etc., irrigator, etc., irrigating, etc.
 obj. dégɪlg(ı)͜, -gi͡.
 márɛj͜jóm͜kémızm͜bádır͜dégran͡ (-j͜j- < -g͜j- §566, -zm͜b- < -sn͜b- §731) they water the millet every (lit. after) four days.
dégar͜ (-gár͜-; §§2200ff.) and
dɛgíd͜ (§§2256ff.) n. irrigation.
dég-an (§§3890ff.) v.t. tell to irrigate, etc., let irrigate, etc.
dég-bŭ- (déggŭ- §546; §3931β) v.i. stat. be in an irrigated (etc.) state or condition.
 árıd͜dégbūn͡ the land has been watered.
dɛg(ı)r-ɛg-ág- (§§4071ff.) v.t. = dɛgɛdól-.

dɛg-ɛ-dól- (-gᵒd- §1178; §4022) and
dɛg(ı)r-ɛ-dól- (-rᵒd-; §4027) v.t. be about to irrigate, etc.
dɛg(ı)r-ɛ-gŭ-bŭ- (§4069) v.t. stat. be on one's way (coming) to irrigate, etc.
dɛg-ɛ-má- (§4036) and
dɛg(ı)r-ɛ-má- (§4041) v.t. become unable to irrigate, etc.
dɛg(ı)r-ɛ-nóg- (§§4048ff.) v.t. go to irrigate, etc.
dɛg(ı)r-ɛ-nóg-bŭ- (-nóggŭ- §546; §4058) v.t. stat. be on one's way (going) to irrigate, etc.
dɛg(ı)r-ɛ-tá- (§§4060ff.) v.t. come to irrigate, etc.
dɛgɛd-ág- (§3877) v.t. be in the situation of having irrigated, etc.
 (S.) márod͜dɛgɛdágran͡ (-d͜d- < -g͜d- §534) they have watered the millet.
dég-kattı- (dékka-; §4093) v.p. be irrigated, etc.
 ín͜árıd͜dékkattın, mán͜dékkáttımunun͡ this island is irrigated, that yonder is not (this land can be irrigated, that can't §5704).
déggɛ! (``) < dégwɛ! imperat. pl. of dég cover one's loins, etc.
déggɛ! (``) < dégwɛ! imperat. pl. of dég irrigate.
déggŭ- < dégbŭ- s.v. dég.
déggŭ- < dégbŭ- s.v. dég.
dék! imperat. of dég.
dék! imperat. of dég.
dékk(ı) v.i. hop.
 ind. pres. aı͜dékkırı͡; perf. aı͜dékkıgorı͡ (N. -ıko-, -ıho-).
demír͜ɛ (-rá͜, -ra͜) n. high Nile, inundation, time of the inundation = mısór͜.
 [< Eg. Ar. دمير < Copt. ⲦⲈⲘⲎⲢⲈ id. W. Spiegelberg ZS, 4, 1, p. 61; AZN, s.v.].
 obj. -rɛg͜.
 pl. -rɛnč(ı)͜.
dén (§§3584-92, 5534) v.t. give (to the speaker) [cp. ON. ⲀⲈⲚ, ⲀⲒⲚ id. GNT, s.v.; RSN, §§129, 200].
 ind. pres. (t)ɛr͜dénın͡ (͜dḗ́ni͡, ͜déní͡);
 fut. (t)ɛr͜bıdénın͡ (͜bud-, etc.); perf. (t)ɛr͜dénkon͡ (͜dḗ́k-, dḗ́k-, dék-, -kṍ͡, -kó͡).
 imperat. dén! (dḗ́!, dé!, dḗ́!), sometimes enclitic (§§1742-3) ͜dén! (͜dḗ́!, ͜dḗ́!, ͜dḗ́!).
 imperat. pl. dénwɛ! (dḗ́wɛ!, dḗ́ᵋwɛ!; déwwɛ! (§720); ``).
 subj. past (t)ɛr͜dénsın͡ (͜dḗ́s-, ͜dḗ́ᵋs-, ͜dés-; -sun͡).
 neg. ind. pres. (t)ɛr͜dénmunun͡ (͜dḗ́m-mu-, -munū͡, -munu͡, -mun͡ §947).
 neg. imperat. tókkon͜dénmɛn! (͜démm-, -mḗ!, -mé!, -mɛ!); pl. tókkon͜dén-mewwɛ! (͜démm-, -wé!).
 pl.-obj. stems dénčır and dénčırır (dḗ́č-, dḗ́ᵋč-, déč-).
 ind. pres. (t)ɛr͜dénčırın͡ (-rí͡, -rí͡, -rı͡); perf. (t)ɛr͜dénčırkon͡ (`--`; -číkkon͡, -kõ͡, -kó͡, -ko͡), (t)ɛr͜dénčırírkon͡ (`---`; -íkkon͡, -kõ͡, -kó͡, -ko͡).

dḗn — **dért(ɪ)**

dḗn and âɪgɪ-dḗn *give it (them* §5457) *to me.*
íŋg‿âɪgɪ‿dḗ *give me this (that).*
íŋgug‿âɪgɪ‿dḗ (§5457) *give me these (those).*
éssíd‿dɛn (§1742; -d‿d- < -g‿d- §534) *give me the (some) water.*
árgɪ‿dḗnčɪrɪr *give them to us.*
íŋg‿árgɪ‿dḗnčɪrɪr *give this to us.*
árg‿íŋgud‿dḗnčɪr (-d‿d- < -g‿d- §534) *give us these (those).*
árgɪ‿dúŋgɪd‿dḗnčɪrɪr *give (each of) us money.*
âɪgɪ‿dúŋgɪb‿bɪdḗmmunan (-b‿b- < -g‿b- §519) *they will not give me the money.*
tɛr‿árgɪ‿dúŋgɪb‿bɪdḗnčɪnná? *will (s)he give us (the) money?*
ɛr‿árgɪ‿dúŋgɪb‿bɪdḗnčɪrínná? *will you give us (the) money?*
tɪr‿árgɪ‿dúŋgɪb‿bɪdḗnčɪríddandḗ? *will they give us (the) money?*
érōn‿árgɪ‿dúŋgɪd‿dḗnčɪkkɪm‿bɪnógru *if (when) you give us (the) money we shall go.*

dḗn-an (§§3890 ff.) v.t. *tell to give (to the speaker), let give (to the speaker).*
tékk‿âɪgɪ‿dḗnan *let him (her) give it (them) to me.*

dḗn-ɛ-dól- (-nᵒd- §1178; §4022) v.t. *be about to give (to the speaker).*

dēnd-ɛ-ǧú-bŭ- (§4069) v.t. stat. *be on the way (coming) to give (to the speaker).*

dḗn-ɛ-má- (§4036) v.t. *become unable to give (to the speaker).*
ér‿âɪgɪ‿dúŋgɪd‿dḗnɛmaná? (-d‿d- < -g‿d- §534) *can't you give me the money?*

dēnd-ɛ-tá- (§4060 ff.) v.t. *come to give (to the speaker).*

dēnɛd-ág- (§3877) v.t. *be in the situation of having given (to the speaker).*
íŋg‿âɪgɪ‿dēnɛdágran *they have given me this (that).*

dḗnos (§3789) v.t. *give (to the speaker).*
imperat. dḗnos! (dḗnó!, dḗno! §962), N. occ. dḗnōs!; pl. dḗnoswɛ! (-oswḗ!, -ówwɛ! §724, -wɛ́!, -ósse! §687, -sḗ!)
âɪgɪ‿dḗnó! *give it (them) to me!*

dḗnos-an (§§3890, 3905) v.t. *tell to give (to the speaker).*
dēnóswan! (-swã̄!, -swá!, -ówwan!, -wwã̄!, -wwá!, -óssan!, -ssã̄!, -ssá!) *tell them to give it (them) to me!*

dḗn (§956a) n. *debt* [< دين *id.*].
obj. dḗŋg(ɪ)‿, -gɪ.
pl. dḗnɪ.
álɪr‿dḗn‿tḗbɪn *áli owes the (a) debt.*
dḗn-wēr‿áddo‿tḗbɪn (déw-wēr‿§720, dḗn-nēr §627) *I (we) have (owe) a debt.*
dḗn‿áddo‿tḗb¹ran (-n‿á- < -nɪ‿á- §1122) *I (we) have got debts.*
t‿én‿dḗŋgɪ‿kóbɪn *he discharges his (she discharges her) debt.*
dḗn‿éddo‿kúgɪn *you ought to pay the debt,* lit. *the debt is incumbent on you.*

dḗñ v.t. *inire* (Latin) [RSN, §129 s.v. danj].
ind. pres. âɪ‿dḗñɪrɪ, ɛr‿dḗñɪn (-ñɪ, -ñí); perf. âɪ‿dḗñkorɪ.
ógɪg‿ḗŋgɪ‿dḗñɪn.

gúr‿tíd‿dḗñɪn (-d‿d- < -g‿d- §534).
gúr‿tíd‿dḗñkó.

dḗñar (-ñár; §§2200 ff.) and
dēñíd (§§2256 ff.) nomen verbi.

dēññára n. *harlot* [< dḗñ- + -ár- nominal -ing (§§2200-2) + -a *utterance (§2178), so *that says 'copulation'*].
obj. -rag.
pl. -ranč(ɪ).

dḗñ-bŭ- (§3931 β) v.i. stat.
ɛ́n‿dḗñbūn.
tí‿dḗñbūn.

dḗñɪŋ-ɪr (N. -ŋkɪr; §3688) v.t. caus.
ind. pres. âɪ‿dḗñɪŋgɪddɪ.
ɛ́n‿ogíčč‿dḗñɪŋgɪrɪn.
tí‿gúrkɪ‿dḗñɪŋgɪrɪn.

dḗñ-kattɪ- (§4093) v.p. iniri.
ɛ́n‿dḗñkattɪn.
tí‿dḗñkattɪn.

déŋge v.i. *become solid, rigid, firm, hard, tough, strong* (opp. to ǧagádɛ) [§§2870 ff.].
ind. pres. âɪ‿déŋgɪrɪ; perf. âɪ‿déŋgegorɪ (N. -ɛko-, -ɛho-).
dés‿ódɪr‿déŋgen *(the) butter gets hard in (the) cold weather.*
šéma‿bɪdéŋgé (§1793) *this skin does (will §5369) not get hard.*
áǧɪn‿deŋgóskó *the hide has got hard.*

déŋgerar (-rár; §§2200 ff., 2210) and
deŋgeríd (§§2256 ff., 2263) n. *becoming solid, etc., solidification, etc., solidity, etc.*

déŋgel (part. pres. §2523) adj. *solid, rigid, firm, hard, tough, strong.*
obj. déŋgélg(ɪ)‿, -gɪ.
pl. déŋgelɪ.
íŋ‿kúmbu‿déŋgélun (§1966) *this egg is (these eggs are §4696c) hard(-boiled).*
ín‿áǧɪn‿déŋgélun *this leather is tough.*
šártɪ‿bérn‿dógor‿déŋgélun *iron is stronger than wood.*

déŋgel-an (§3910α) v.i. *become solid, etc., solidify (i.), etc.*

déŋgelam-bŭ- (deŋgelámbŭ- §1932a; §§3949 ff.) v.t. stat. *be in a solidifying (etc.) state or condition, be advanced in the process of solidification, etc.*
dés‿deŋgelámbūn *the butter has begun to get hard.*

deŋgelám-bᵘ-an (-b(w)an; §3964) v.t. *let be in a solidifying (etc.) state or condition.*
imperat. deŋgelámbᵘan! (-b(w)an!, -b(w)ã̄!, -b(w)á!).

deŋgelanɛd-ág- (§3966α) v.i. *be in a condition of having become solid, etc.*
dés‿deŋgelanɛdágɪn *the butter has got (quite) hard.*

déŋgɛ-bŭ- (§3931 α) v.i. stat. *be in a solid (etc.) state or condition.*

déŋgɛ-bᵘ-an (-b(w)an; §3962) v.t. *let be in a solid (etc.) state or condition.*
imperat. déŋgebᵘan! (-b(w)an!, -b(w)ã̄!, -b(w)á!).
kúmbud‿déŋgebá (-d‿d- < -g‿d- §534) *let the egg(s) be hard(-boiled).*

deŋger-eg-ág- (§§4071 ff.) v.i. = deŋgeredól-.

deŋger-ɛ-dól- (-rᵒd- §1178; §§4016-7, 4022, 4027) v.i. *be about to become solid, etc.*

deŋgeg-ɪr (N. -ɛkɪr, -ɛhɪr; §3679) (a) v.t. caus. *cause or allow to become solid, etc.; (b) v.t. render solid, etc., solidify, harden, toughen.*

deŋgegɪr-selgé (§§4140, 3783) v.t. *render solid (etc.) by boiling, boil hard.*
imperat. deŋgegɪrselgé!
kúmbud‿âɪgɪ‿deŋgegɪrselgégorɪ *I (have) boiled the egg(s) hard.*

deŋgegɪr-selgé-dɛn (§4000) v.t. *after boiling hard give (to the speaker), boil hard for (the speaker).*
imperat. deŋgegɪrselgédɛn! (-dḗ!, -dɛ!, -dḗ!, -dɛ̄! §945).
kúmbud‿âɪgɪ‿deŋgegɪrselgédɛn *boil me the egg(s) hard.*

deŋgegɪr-selgé-tɪr (§4000) v.t. *after boiling hard give (to other than the speaker), boil hard for (other than the speaker).*

deŋge-selgé-bŭ- (§5683; cp. §3943) v.i. stat. *be in a hard-boiled state or condition.*
kúmbu‿deŋgeselgébūn *the egg is (eggs are) hard-boiled.*

déŋnunun (§661) < dégmunun *I (etc.) do not cover my loins (etc.)* s.v. dég.

dɛrḗñɛ v.i. *(a) stoop, bend down; (b) bow oneself, bow; (c) slant downward, slope* (= túlɛ) [§§2870 ff., 2509].
ind. pres. âɪ‿dɛrḗñɪrɪ, ɛr‿dɛrḗñɪn (-ḗñɪ, -ḗñí); perf. âɪ‿dɛrḗñegorɪ (N. -ɛko-, -ɛho-).
def. perf. âɪ‿dɛrḗñeróskorɪ and dɛrḗñóskorɪ (§3540).

dɛrḗñerar (-rár; §§2200 ff., 2210) and
dɛrḗñeríd (§§2256 ff., 2263) n. *stooping, bending down; bowing, bow; downward slant, slope.*

dɛrḗñ-áb-bíttɪ- (-ágbít- §519; §4198) v.t. *be stooping (etc.) engaged in picking up, etc.* (s.v. ábbíttɪ-).
tɛ́rid‿dɛrḗñábbíttɪgoran (-d‿d- < -g‿d- §534) *they were stooping (used to stoop) gathering up (the) seed.*

dɛrḗñ-ās-sɪgíddɪ- (-ākṣɪ, -āgsɪ- §679; §4198) v.i. *be bowing engaged in prayer.*
dɛrḗñassɪgíddɪran *they are bowing in prayer.*

dɛrḗñ-bŭ- (§3931α) v.i. stat. *be in a stooping (etc.) state or condition.*

dɛrḗñeg-ɪr (N. -ɛkɪr, -ɛhɪr; §3679) v.t. caus. *cause or allow to stoop, etc.*
ind. pres. âɪ‿dɛrḗñegɪddɪ.

dɛrḗñe-ǧáŋ(ɪ) (§3747ʹ) v.t. *fill while (after) stooping, etc.*
kúbed‿dɛrḗñeǧáŋɪgó (-d‿d- < -g‿d- §534) *bending down (s)he filled the jar.*

dɛrḗñe-tēb-sɪgíddɪ- (§4198) v.i. *be bowing engaged in prayer.*
dɛrḗñetēbsɪgíddɪran *they are bowing in prayer.*

dɛrewíš n. *dervish* [< درويش pl. of درويش *id.* §2405].
obj. -wíšk(ɪ), -kɪ.
pl. -wíšɪ.

dérɪb (-rub) *path, road* = dárɪb.

derímd(ɪ) (-rúm-) *appertaining to the (a) path, etc.* = dárɪmd(ɪ).

dért(ɪ) n. *fast* [§§2323 ff.; cp. ON. ᛅᛁᛔᛏ *id.* GNT, s.v.].
obj. -tɪg.
pl. -tɪnč(ɪ).
dértɪk‿kágran *they keep the fast.*

48

dertín-d(ı) (§§2545ff.) adj. *appertaining to the (a) fast.*

derwíš n. *dervish* (=dɛrɛwíš) [< درويش *id.*].
obj. -wíšk(ı), -ki.
pl. -wíšı.

dés n. *(a) fatty part of milk, butter; (b) vegetable oil* [RSN §129].
obj. désk(ı), -ki.
pl. désı.
símsım dés *sesame oil.*

désn-d(ı) (§§2545ff.) adj. *appertaining to butter, etc., of butter, etc.*

dɛsɛgíttɛl *greenish* s.v. **désse**.

désen v.c. (dɛsén c.; -sɛn, -sẽ, -sé) adv. *very, exceedingly, very much* [§4425].
ín désen sérēn,
ín dɛsén sérɛn and
ín dɛsés sérɛn (-s- <-n s- §680) *this (that) is very good.*
ín désem míllın *this (that) is very bad.*
X. ğúgrɪré? *is it hot?*
Y. éjjo, dɛsé yes, *very.*
ténn-ur dɛsén dúlun *his (her, its) head is very large.*
désen sútte tágoran (ɛs sút-) *they came (have come) very quickly.*
désen dóllan *they like (want) him (her, it, them §5083) very much.*
désem móndan *they dislike him (etc.) very much.*
désem bódran *they run very hard.*

désse (α) adj. (a) *green;* (b) *light blue* [déss-é *saying 'unripe'* §§2517-18]; (β, used as) n. *green vegetable, growing crop, plant, vegetation;* with coll. sg. (§4696 b).
obj. -sɛg.
pl. -sɛnč(ı).
gíd désseⁿ (désse, déssé §939) *the grass is green.*
séma déssen *the sky is light blue.*
déssed dɛkkómunan (-d d- <-g d- §534) *they did not water (have not watered) the vegetables (etc.).*

déss-an- (§3910α) v.i. *become green, etc.*

déssam-bŭ- (§§3949ff.) v.i. stat. *be in a state of becoming or having become green, etc.*

dɛssanɛd-ág- (§3966α) v.i. *be in the condition of having become green, etc.*

désseg-ır (N. -ɛkır, -ɛhır; §3701) v.t. caus. *cause or allow to become green, etc.*

dɛsɛgíttɛl adj. *greenish, light-bluish* [<*dɛsɛgírtɛl (§713) <*désseg ırtɛl (§1010) <désseg +-ır caus. (§3665) +-t dem. (§4593) +-ɛ say (§213) +-l part. -*ing* (§2958), so *that saying 'make green'* §2526].
obj. -gíttɛlg(ı), -gi.
pl. -gíttɛlı.

désse-kırı (§§2539-40) adj. *greenish, light-bluish.*

déss(ı) adj. (a) *unripe;* (b) *uncooked, raw* [cp. ON. ⲁⲉϭϭⲓ *green* GNT, s.v.; RSN, §§129, 200].
obj. -sıg.
pl. -sınč(ı).
bénti déss(ı) *unripe date(s* §4696b*) =* gállo díffe.

ím bɛnti déssın (déssı, déssí §939) *this date is (these dates are) unripe.*
X. móz dámɛn? *aren't there any bananas?*
Y. wǎran, déssın *no, they're not ripe.*
kúsu déss(ı) *raw meat.*
kúsu déssın (déssí, déssí) *the meat is raw.*
kúmbu déssın (-sí, -sí) *the egg is (eggs are §4696c) raw.*
áğın déss(ı) *raw hide.*

dɛssıkárğa n. *one of the sorts of date growing in Dóngola* (s.v. bɛnt(ı)), *that when ripe looks unripe;* with collective sg. (§4696b) [<dɛssı- +-kárğ(ı)- *get ripe* +-a(n) *say,* so **that ripening says 'unripe'* §2178].
obj. -ğag.
pl. -ğanč(ı).

dɛstúr n. *leave to go off duty, dismiss* [Sudan Ar. دستور *id.*].
obj. -úrk(ı), -ki.
dɛstúrk áu *go off duty, knock off.*
mıráslıd dɛstúrk áuan (-d d- <-g d- §534) *tell the messenger to knock off.*
dɛstúrk áuwan *tell them to knock off.*

détte v.i. *drip, fall in drops* [lit. *say 'détt!'* §§2870ff.].
ind. pres. tɛr détten (-tẽ, détté);
perf. tɛr déttegon (N. -ɛkon, -ɛhon; -gõ, déttegó).
gálon tógor éssı détten *under the water-jar the water drips.*
gɛu kórroton détten *the blood drips from the wound.*
áru détten (a) *the rain comes down in drops (at starting);* (b) *the rain drizzles.*

détterar (-rár), **déttar** (-tár; §§2200ff., 2211) and **detteríd**, dettídu (§§2256ff., 2264) n. *dripping, falling in drops.*
éssın détt(ɛr)ar and
éssın dett(ɛr)íd *the dripping of (the) water.*

detténg-ır (dettɛŋgır §1801; N. -ŋkır; §3688) v.t. caus. *cause or allow to drip, etc.*
ášai ğúgr án tıláttid detténgırın (-d d- <-g d- §534) *the hot weather makes me drip with perspiration,* lit.... *makes my sweat drip.*

dɛu, dɛ́u n. *bake-stone, plate of stone or metal on which bread is baked.*
obj. dɛ́ug(ı), -gi.
pl. dɛ́uı, dɛ́wı.
ɛ́nčı kálgı dɛ́uged áuran *the women make bread by means of the bake-stone.*
ɛ́nčı kálgı dɛ́ur undúddan *the women bake bread on the bake-stone,* lit. *the women put bread in (sc. the fire) on the bake-stone.*
dɛ́uŋ ká *bake-house, kitchen.*

dɛ́wwɛ! (§720) <dɛ́nwwɛ! *give (pl.) me!* s.v. dɛn.

di v.i. (a) *die;* (b) *be extinguished, go out* [cp. ON. ⲁⲓ, ⲁⲉⲓ *id.* GNT, s.v.; RSN, §§129, 200].
ind. pres. aí dírın, ɛr dín (dí); perf. tɛr dígon (-gõ, -gó,

N. díkon, -kõ, -kó, díhon, -hõ, -hó).
subj. past tɛr dísın (-sun).
part. pres. díl (one) *that dies, etc., dying, going out;* obj. dílg(ı), -gi.
part. past díɛl (one) *that died, etc., dead, extinguished;* obj. díɛlg(ı), -gi.
def. perf. tɛr díóskon (díós-, -kõ, -kó).
ádun íged dígon *he was killed by the enemy,* lit. *he died by the enemy's hand* (Amh. በጠላኝ እጅ ሞተ).
íg díóskó *the fire (light) has gone out.*
díɛl gabúrro túbbın *the dead (person) lies in the grave.*
wɛ́li díɛlí (§939) *the dogs are dead.*
tɛr díɛlmunun, áñılun (s)he (it) *is not dead,* (s)he (it) *is alive.*
kándın ágı díɛlun *the knife's blade is blunt.*
kándı díɛlun *the knife is blunt.*

díar (díár, díɛr; §§2200ff.) n. *death, extinction.*
obj. díárk(ı) (díárk(ı), díárk(ı), díɛrk(ı)), -ki.

dí-an (§§3890ff.) v.t. *tell to die, let die, etc.*

dí-bŭ- (§3931α) v.i. stat. *be in a dead (etc.) state or condition, lie dead.*
part. pres. díbūl *dead, extinguished.*
ánn-i ótked díbun *my hands (§4696a) are numbed with (the) cold.*

dír-ɛg-ág- (§§4071ff.) v.i. =díɛdól-.
íg díɛgágın *the fire (light) is just going out.*

dĭ-ɛ-dól- (§4022) and **dír-ɛ-dól-** (-rᵒd- §1178; §4027) v.i. *be about to die, etc.*
ánnɛssı díɛdólın *my sister is at the point of death.*
íg díɛdólkó *the fire (light) nearly went out.*

díŋ-ır (N. -ŋkır; §3688) v.t. caus. *cause or allow to die, etc.*
ín tékki díŋırkó *this (has) led to his (her, its) death.*
íkki díŋırkó *let the fire (light) go out.*

diráŋ-ır (—; N. -ŋkır; §3689) v.t. caus. *cause or allow (more than one object) to die, etc.*
ín tírgı díraŋırkó *this (has) led to their death.*

díos-áñ (§4180) v.i. *having died come to life again, come to life after dying.*
díosáñkó *after dying (s)he (it) came (has come) to life again.*

díje n. *blood-money, compensation paid to relatives for manslaughter* [<دية *id.*].
obj. -jɛg.
díjed dɛfégoran (-d d- <-g d- §534) *they (have) paid the blood-money.*

dímɛ and **dímɛg** (-gi; §4477) adv. *constantly, continually, always* [< Sudan Ar. ديما *id.*].
dábın, dímɛ wᵘdɛtán (s)he (it) *disappears, but (§6239) (s)he (it) always comes back.*
dímɛ dídın (s)he *always abuses one.*
X. tíŋkár nógın (s)he (it) *goes to their house.*

dímɛn⌣ — dígır

Y. sınták? *when?*
X. dímɛgi⌢ *always.*

dímɛn⌣ (-mɛ̃⌢, dímɛ́⌢ §939) and
dímɛŋ(ı)⌣ (-gi⌢; §4477) *adv. constantly, continually, always* [< دايماً *id.* §1325].

dís *n. reed,* Cyperus *sp.* (*BSP*, 628); with collective sg. (§4696b) *sedge;* = góu⌣ [< ديس *id.*].

obj. dísk(ı)⌣, -ki⌢.
pl. dísı⌣.

díséssın⌣tūr⌣ımbélın, téddotōm⌣ báččıŋ⌣galámgı⌣mérran⌢ *the reed grows in the water; from it they cut the pen for writing.*

dísırtōŋ⌣gálamım⌣mérran⌢ (-m⌣m- < -g⌣m- §601) and
gálamıd⌣dísırtōm⌣mérran⌢ (-d⌣d- < -g⌣d- §534, -m⌣m- < -n⌣m- §604) *they cut pens from the reeds.*

díu⌣, díw⌣ *n. horizontal beam,* so (*a*) *lintel;* (*b,* in water-wheel, kólɛ⌣) *cross-beam,* usually a palm-trunk (úmbu⌣), supported at each end by posts (múgdonč(ı)⌣); in its centre, underneath, is a socket (dfun⌣úbbur⌣) in which the apex of the vertical axle (míššın⌣úr⌣) revolves; Sudan Ar. ديو *id.;* (*c,* in loom, duhán⌣) *bar* or *rod* from which heddles (bɛsfrı⌣) *swing;* (Sudan Ar. مِعْلَاق *id. CSW,* p. 37) [? cogn. M. *diyi gross, stark, vil RNW,* s.v., ON. ⲁⲓⲉ, ⲁⲉⲓⲉ *GNT,* s.v.; or from material used Beḍ. *diwa* Mimosa nilotica *RBW* s.v., cp. Tña. ድዋ Grewia venusta, Fres. *BT,* s.v., Tɛ. ድወት eine akazienorte *RBiW,* s.v. *duwá*].

obj. díug⌣, díwg(ı)⌣.
pl. díunč(ı)⌣, díwınč(ı)⌣.

-d(ı)⌣, adj. *in,* §§2545ff.

dib⌣ *n. castle, fortress* (now ruined) [cp. ON. ⲁⲓⲡⲡⲓ *town, village GNT,* s.v.].

obj. díbk(ı)⌣ (dípk(ı)⌣), -ki⌢.
pl. díbı⌣.

wad-nımérın⌣díbır⌣ *at the castle of Wad Nıméri* (*ruins about ten miles above Urdi*).

dím-d(ı)⌣ (§§2545ff.) *adj. appertaining to the (a) castle, etc.*

dič⌢ pausal form (§469) of díg⌣ *five.*

díd *v.t. revile, abuse, scold.*
ind. pres. āı⌣díd(ı)ri⌢; perf. āı⌣dídkori⌢ (⌣dítk-).
imperat. dít!

dıdar⌣ (-dɑ́r⌣; §§2200ff.) and
dıdíd (§§2256ff.) *n. reviling, etc.*
dıdt(ı)⌣ (dítt(ı)⌣) *n.* = dídar [§2325α].
obj. -tıg⌣.
pl. -tınč(ı)⌣.

díd-an (§§3890ff.) *v.t. tell to revile, etc., let revile, etc.*
díd-bū- (§3931β) *v.i. stat. be in a reviled (etc.) state or condition.*
díd(¹)r-ɛg-ág- (§§4071ff.) *v.t.* = dıdɛdól-.
dıd-ɛ-dól- (-dᵒd- §1178; §4022) and
díd(¹)r-ɛ-dól- (-rᵒd- §4027) *v.t. be about to revile, etc.*
dıdɛd-ág- (§3877) *v.t. be in the situation of having reviled, etc.*
āıgı⌣dıdɛdágın⌢ *(s)he has reviled me.*
díd-kattı- (dítk-; §4093) *v.p. be reviled, etc.*

diffɛ⌣ *n. unripe date(s) at summit of palm;* with collective sg. (§4696b) [< diff-*summit + -ɛ⌣* of n. ess., so *what is the summit §2234β*].

obj. -fɛg⌣ [> Sudan Ar. دقيك dıffɛ́k *id.*

coll., with nomen unitatis دَقِيقَة dıfféga §§469², 2412].
pl. -fɛnč(ı)⌣.

díg *v.i.* (*a*) *get bound, get tied, get tied up;* (*b*) *get bound by a bet, bind oneself by a bet, bet, wager, have a bet or wager.* -ɛd⌣ (§4341) shows the amount or subject of the bet (§6204); -onon⌣ (§4347) shows the person to whom the bet is offered (§5538) [cogn. dég *cover one's loins,* dúg *become clouded,* tág *get covered* §2781].

ind. pres. āı⌣dígri; perf. āı⌣dígkori⌢ (⌣díkkori⌢).
imperat. dík!

ógıǧ⌣dígın⌢ *the man gets bound.*
ógıǧ⌣díkkó⌢ *the man got (has been) bound.*
tárıd⌣dıgóskon⌢ *the parcel has been tied up.*
gíd⌣dıgóskó⌢ *the grass has been tied up (...tied into a bundle).*
ter⌣gírıš⌣dımíŋgɛd⌣díkkon⌢ *(s)he (has) bet ten piastres, lit. (s)he (has) got bound by (s.v. -ɛd⌣) ten piastres.*
āı⌣ékkonon⌣ter⌣bıtáŋgɛb⌣bıdígri⌢ (-b⌣b- < -d⌣b- §518) and
āı⌣ékkonom⌣budígri⌣ter⌣butáŋgé⌢ *I'll bet you (s)he (it) will come.*
āı⌣ékkonon⌣ter⌣támɛnıŋgɛb⌣bıdígri⌢ and
āı⌣ékkonom⌣bıdígri⌣ter⌣támɛnıŋgé⌢ *I'll bet you (s)he (it) doesn't (i.e. won't §5369a) come.*
ter⌣āıgonon⌣tır⌣támɛndaŋgɛg⌣gírıš⌣díččɛd⌣díkkó⌢ (-g⌣g- < -d⌣g- §545) *(s)he (has) bet me five piastres that they do (i.e. will) not come.*
āı⌣ékkonom⌣bıdígri⌣ter⌣támɛnıŋgɛg⌣ǧínɛ⌣wɛ́gé⌢ (-ǧ⌣ǧ- < -d⌣ǧ- §550) *I'll bet you a pound (s)he (it) doesn't (i.e. won't) come.*
āı⌣nálsıgɛd⌣ékkonom⌣bıdígri⌢ *I'll bet you I saw him (her, it, them).*
āı⌣ékkonon⌣āı⌣uñúddıgɛǧ⌣ǧínɛ⌣wɛ́gɛd⌣dígri⌢ *I bet you a pound that I know.*
X. ér⌣tékkı⌣nálmɛnsıŋgɛb⌣bıdígri⌢ (-b⌣b- < -d⌣b- §518) *I'll bet you didn't see him (her, it).*
Y. āı⌣nálsıgɛg⌣gírıš⌣dímın⌣dımíŋgɛd⌣dígru⌣ (-g⌣g- < -d⌣g- §545; §§5250, 5376) *let's have a bet of ten piastres each on whether I saw him (her, it), sc. I betting ten that I did, you betting ten that I didn't.*

dıgar⌣ (-gɑ́r⌣; §§2200ff.) and
dıgíd (§§2256ff.) *n. getting bound, etc.; betting.*
díg-an (§§3890ff.) *v.t. tell to bet, let bet.*
díg-bū- (díggū- §546; §3931β) *v.i. stat. be in a bound (etc.) state or condition, be the subject of a bet.*
ind. pres. āı⌣dígburi⌢ (⌣díggurı⌢).
fānús⌣díggun⌢ *the lantern is (has been) tied on (up).*

bértı⌣wígın⌣díggüŋgé⌢ (s.v. -ɛd⌣) *the goat bleats because it is tied up.*
úln⌣áxırro⌣ǧákar⌣dígbun⌢ *the hook is fastened to the end of the line.*
íŋ⌣gírıš⌣dımíŋgɛd⌣díggun⌢ *ten piastres have been wagered about this.*

dig-ır (§§3671, 3710) *v.t. tie, tie up, tie on, bind, fasten, tether.*
ind. pres. āı⌣dıgírri (⌣dígırri⌢, §1803), ɛr⌣díg(ı)rın⌢ (-rí⌢, -rí⌢); perf. āı⌣dıgırkori⌢.
imperat. dígır!, pl. dıgırwɛ! (⌣⌣, ⌣⌣,).
part. pres. díg(ı)rıl⌣ *(one) that ties, etc., tier, etc., tying, etc.;* obj. dıg(ı)rílg(ı)⌣, -gi⌢.
part. past díg(ı)rɛl⌣ *(one) that tied, etc., tier, etc., tying, etc.;* obj. dıg(ı)rélg(ı)⌣, -gi⌢.
def. imperat. dıgrós! (-ró! §962) *tie it (etc.) up!;* pl. dıgrósweɛ! (-róswé!, -rówwe! §724, -wé!, -rósse! §687, -sé!).
írıd⌣dígrı⌢ (-d⌣d- < -g⌣d- §534) *tie the rope.*
írıgɛd⌣dígrı⌢ *tie it (him, her, them) with (the) rope.*
úlgɛd⌣dígrı⌢ *tie it (them) with thread.*
káčkı⌣dıgírkori⌢ *I (have) tethered the horse.*

dígırar⌣ (-rɑ́r⌣; §§2200ff., 2212) and
dıgırfd (§§2256ff., 2265) *n. tying, etc.*
dıgır-an (§§3890ff., 3904) *v.t. tell to tie, etc., let tie, etc.*
dıgırr-ɛg-ág- (§§4071ff.) *v.t.* = díg(ı)rɛdól-.
díg(ı)r-ɛ-dól- (-rᵒd- §1178; §4025) and
dıgırr-ɛ-dól- (-rᵒd- §4033) *v.t. be about to tie, etc.*
dıgırr-ɛ-ǧŭ-bū- (§4069) *v.t. stat. be on one's way (coming) to tie, etc.*
díg(ı)r-ɛ-mǎ- (§4039) and
dıgırr-ɛ-mǎ- (§4046) *v.t. become unable to tie, etc.*
dıgırr-ɛ-nóg- (§§4048, 4057) *v.t. go to tie, etc.*
dıgırr-ɛ-nóg-bū- (-nóggū- §546; §4058) *v.t. stat. be on one's way (going) to tie, etc.*
dıgırr-ɛ-tǎ- (§§4060, 4068) *v.t. come to tie, etc.*
dıgırɛd-ág- (§§3877, 3883) *v.t. be in the situation of having tied, etc.*
dıgır-kattı- (§4093) *v.p. be tied, etc.*
díggū- (§546) < díg-bū- *be in a bound (etc.) state s.v.* díg.

dígır (§§2836, 3575) *v.i. fall, fall down, drop* [cp. šúgur *descend*].
ind. pres. āı⌣dıgırri (⌣dígırri⌢), ɛr⌣díg(ı)rın⌢ (-rí⌢, -rí⌢); perf. āı⌣dıgırkori⌢.
part. pres. díg(ı)rıl⌣ *(one) that falls, etc., falling, etc.;* obj. dıg(ı)rílg(ı)⌣, -gi⌢.
part. past díg(ı)rɛl⌣ *(one) that fell, etc., falling, etc.;* obj. dıg(ı)rélg(ı)⌣, -gi⌢.
def. perf. āı⌣díg(ı)róskori⌢.

béntı⌣dıgírkó⌢ *the dates (§4696b) fell (have fallen), sc. from the palm(s)* = béntı⌣bógkó⌢.
árıdır⌣dıgírkoran⌢ *they fell (have fallen) to (on) the ground.*

dígırar⌣ (-rɑ́r⌣; §§2200ff.) and

dıgıríd͡ (§§ 2256 ff.) n. *falling.*
dígır-an (§§ 3890 ff.) v.t. *let fall, etc.*
dígır-bŭ- (dıgírbŭ- § 1522; § 3931α) v.i. stat. *be in a fallen state or condition, be prostrate, lie fallen.*
 ǵówwı͡dígırbŭn⌒ *the tree lies fallen.*
 sɛmafór͡dıgırbŭgon, ımbɛlóskon⌒ *the signal was down and has gone up.*
dıgırr-ɛg-ág- (§§ 4071 ff.) v.i. = dıg(ı)rɛ-dól-.
 kắrı͡dıgırrɛgákkoran⌒ *the houses were very nearly falling down.*
dıg(ı)r-ɛ-dól- (-rᵒd- § 1178; § 4022) and
dıgırr-ɛ-dól- (-rᵒd-; § 4027) v.i. *be about to fall, etc.*
dıgır-fáttɛ (§ 3783) v.i. *fall in a fit.*
dıgır-fatfád-ko- (-átko-; § 3783) v.i. *fall in a fit.*
dıgır-gúšš(ı) (§ 3747ᵉ´) v.t. and i. *break* (t. and i. s.v. gúšš(ı)) *by falling, etc.*
 tɛr͡sahángı͡dıgırgúššıgó⌒ and (§ 5601) tɛr͡dıgır͡sahangı͡gúššıgó⌒ *(s)he fell and broke (has fallen and broken) the (a) plate.*
 dógortōn͡dıgırgúššıgon⌒ *it fell from above and broke (it has fallen from above and broken).*
dıgırk-idd(ı) (§ 3725) v.t. caus. and v.t. = dıgírkır.
 ind. pres. aı͡dıgırkíddırı⌒; perf. aı͡dıgırkíddıgorı⌒ (N. -ıko-, -ıho-).
 imperat. dıgírkıddı!
 tɛr͡aıg͡árıdır͡dıgırkíddıgó⌒ *(s)he (it) made (let) me fall to the ground.*
dıgírk-ır (§ 3683) (a) v.t. caus. *cause or allow to fall, etc.*; (b) v.t. *drop, throw down.*
 ind. pres. aı͡dıgırkíddı⌒, ɛr͡dıgírkırın⌒ (-rí⌒, -rí⌒); perf. aı͡dıgırkírkorı⌒.
 aı͡tɛ́kk͡árıdır͡dıgırkírkorı⌒ *I (have) made (let) him (her, it) fall to the ground.*
 X. tókkon͡dıgırkírmɛn⌒ *don't drop it (him, her, them, § 5083).*
 Y. bıdıgırkírmunun⌒ *I shan't (§ 5364).*
díg(ı)rıŋ-ır (⏑̆, ⏑̆; N. -ŋkır; § 3688) v.t. caus. and v.t. = dıgírkır.
 tókkon͡dígırıŋgırmɛn⌒ (͡dıgırıŋgírmɛn⌒, ⏑̆ § 1846) *don't drop it (etc.).*
dıgır-tó (§ 3747ᵉ´) v.i. *enter by falling (etc.), fall (etc.) in.*
 bɛ́rtı͡ǵówwır͡dıgırtógon⌒ *the she-goat fell (has fallen) into the well.*
 úrur͡dıgırtōróskoran⌒ *they have fallen into the river.*
dıgır-tō-dí (§ 3766) v.i. *die after falling in, fall in and die.*
 bɛ́rtı͡ǵówwır͡dıgırtōdígon⌒ *the she-goat was (has been) killed by falling into the well.*
dıgır-tómb(ı) (§ 3747ᵉ´) v.t. and i. *break* (t. and i. s.v. tómb(ı)) *by falling, etc.*
dígrı͡ (dıgrí͡) adj. *great in quantity or number, abundant, plentiful, numerous* [perhaps contains díg *get bound*; -rī § 2564; cp. ON. *ᕒᑌ- *viel sein* ZNG, s.v.].
 obj. dıgrí͡.
 pl. dıgrínč(ı)͡.
 tín͡dúŋgı͡dıgrín⌒ (-grí͡, -grí⌒ § 942) *their money is plentiful.*

 tín͡dúŋgı͡dígr͡ɛgón⌒ (͡ɛgó⌒, ͡ɛgó⌒) and
 N. tín͡dúŋgı͡dígrı͡ɛkó⌒ *their money was plentiful.*
 árıd͡dıgrí͡dắn⌒ *there is much land.*
 dárbı͡dıgrínčí⌒ (§ 1161) *the paths are many.*
 kúltı͡dıgrín⌒ *the flies (§ 4696c) are numerous.*
dıgríg- (-gi⌒; § 4667) adv. *much, exceedingly, very.*
 márra͡dıgríg͡ (-gi⌒) *many times, often.*
dıgrí-an-,
dígri-an- (-rıan-) and
dígr-an- (§ 3910α) v.i. *become much, increase.*
 áru͡bókkıŋ͡kág͡dıgránın⌒ *when the rain pours (the) snakes (§ 4696d) become numerous.*
dıgríam-bŭ-,
dıgriámbŭ- (-rıám-) and
dıgrámbŭ- (§§ 3949 ff.) v.i. stat. *be in an increasing or increased state or condition.*
dıgranɛd-ág- (§ 3966α) v.i. *be in the condition of having become abundant, etc.*
dıgran-ímbɛl- (§ 4152) v.i. *rise (etc. s.v. ímbɛl), having become abundant, etc., rise in a great quantity.*
 gutắr͡dıgranımbɛ́lkó⌒ *the dust rose (has risen) in a great quantity.*
dıgran-ímbɛl-bŭ- (-ımbɛ́lbŭ-; § 4153) v.i. stat. *be in a state or condition of rising (having risen) in a great quantity.*
 gutắr͡dıgranımbɛ́lbŭn⌒ *the dust is rising (has risen) in a great quantity.*
dıgríg-ır (N. -íkır, -íhır; § 3701) (a) v.t. caus. *cause or allow to be or become abundant, etc.*; (b) v.t. *make much, increase.*
 ind. pres. aı͡dıgrígıddı⌒, ɛr͡dıgrígırın⌒ (-rí⌒, -rí⌒).
dıgrígır (N. -íkır, -íhır; § 4466) and
dıgrígrg(ı)͡ (N. -íkır-, -íhır-; -gi⌒; §§ 4467, 5981) adv. *much, increasingly, exceedingly, very, (of occasions) often.*
 X. hándaŋ͡háwa͡sérén⌒ *the climate of Hándag is good.*
 Y. éjjo, dıgrígırn⌒ *yes, very.*
 tıntımbáb͡dıgrígır͡dúlun⌒ *their father is very old.*
 aı͡téddotōn͡dıgrígırgı͡mabsúd͡érı⌒ (-sút͡érı⌒ § 1399) *I am exceedingly pleased with him (her, it).*
dıgrígır- (N. -íkır-, -íhır-) in composition (§ 4989) *a great deal, much, exceedingly, very.*
 kắ͡dıgrígır͡dúlun⌒ *the house is very large.*
 éssı͡dıgrígır͡orófélun⌒ *the water is very cold.*
 dıgrıgırsɛrɛ́-wɛd͡dólli⌒ (-d͡-<-gud-§ 534) *I want a very good one.*
dıgrıgır-ábbáññı- (N. -íkır-, -íhır-; -ágbáñ- § 519; § 4142) v.i. *be engaged in speaking (etc. s.v. ábbáññı-) a great deal, in talking excessively.*
 ɛsmắn͡dıgrīgırābbáññın⌒ ɛθmắn (a) *is speaking at great length*; (b) *always talks so much.*
dıgrıgır-ábbóg- (N. -íkır-, -íhır-; -ágbóg- § 519; § 4142) v.t. and i. *be engaged in pouring (etc. s.v. ábbóg-) a great deal, etc.*

dıgrıgır-ággɛrɉɛ́- (N. -íkır-, -íhır-; -gɛrɛ́-; § 4142) v.t. *be engaged in reading (etc. s.v. ággɛrɉɛ́-) a great deal, etc.*
dıgrıgır-ákkál- (N. -íkır-, -íhır-; -ágkál- § 569; § 4142) v.t. *be engaged in eating (etc. s.v. ákkál-) a great deal, etc.*
dıgrıgır-ákkórrɛ- (N. -íkır-, -íhır-; -ágkór- § 569; § 4142) v.i. *be snoring (etc. s.v. ákkórrɛ-) a great deal, etc.*
dıgrıgır-ánnóg- (N. -íkır-, -íhır-; -ágnóg- § 625; § 4142) v.i. *be engaged in going (etc. s.v. ánnóg-) often.*
dıgrıgır-ássándı- (N. -íkır-, -íhır-; -áksán-, -ágsan- § 679; § 4142) v.i. and t. *be much afraid (of, etc. s.v. ássándı-).*
dıgrıgır-ássándıgır- (N. -íkır-, -íhır-, -dıkır-; -áksán-, -ágsán- § 679; § 4142) v.t. *be engaged in frightening (etc. s.v. ássándıgır-) a great deal, etc.*
dıgrıgır-báññ(ı) (N. -íkır-, -íhır-; § 4137) v.i. *speak a great deal, talk much, talk excessively.*
dıgrıgır-bárıkɛ́ (N. -íkır-, -íhır-; § 4140) v.i. *bestow many blessings; for construction s.v. bárıkɛ́.*
— in the expressions:
 éddo͡dıgrīgırbārıkɛ̄r͡ɛn⌒ *I thank you very much.*
 íddo͡dıgrīgırbārıkɛ̄r͡ɛn⌒ *I thank you (pl.) very much.*
dıgrıgır-bóg (N. -íkır-, -íhır-; § 4137) v.t. and i. *pour (etc. s.v. bóg) a great deal, pour (etc.) very heavily.*
 wílg͡áru͡áddo͡dıgrīgırbókko⌒ *yesterday the rain came down very heavily on me (us).*
dıgrıgır-dól- (N. -íkır-, -íhır-; § 4137) v.t. *love (etc. s.v. dól) much.*
 ind. pres. aı͡dıgrīgırdólli⌒, ɛr͡dıgrīgırdólin⌒ (-lí⌒, -lí⌒).
 subj. past aı͡dıgrīgırdólsı͡ (-su⌒).
dıgrıgırɛd-ág- (N. -íkır-, -íhır-; §§ 3877, 3883) v.t. *be in the situation of having caused or allowed to be much, etc.*
dıgrıgır-él (N. -íkır-, -íhır-; § 4137) v.t. *find in a large quantity.*
dıgrıgır-él-kattı- (N. -íkır-, -íhır-; § 4144) v.p. *be found in a large quantity.*
dıgrıgır-ɛskı-nóg- (N. -íkır-, -íhır-; § 4142) v.i. *be able to go (etc. s.v. nóg) much (far, often).*
 X. dárıg͡dıgrīgırɛskınógmunun⌒ *the tortoise can't walk much.*
 Y. ɛskınógın, bōdkáttın⌒ *it can walk, it goes at a good pace, lit. . . . it is apt to run.*
dıgrıgır-ɛttá and
dıgrıgır-ɛ́ttä (N. -íkır-, -íhır-; § 4142) v.t. *bring much, many, often.*
dıgrıgır-gɛrɉɛ́ (N. -íkır-, -íhır-; -gɛrɛ́; § 4140) v.t. *read much, recite much.*
 goráŋgı͡dıgrīgırgɛrɉɛran⌒ *they read (recite) the Coran a great deal.*
dıgrıgır-gɛrɉɛred-ág- (N. -íkır-, -íhır-; -gɛrɛ́-; § 3884) v.t. *be in the situation of having read (recited) much.*
dıgrıgır-gɛrɉɛ́-kattı- (N. -íkır-, -íhır-; -gɛrɛ́-; § 4144) v.p. *be much read, be much recited.*
dıgrıgır-hóŋ(ı) (N. -íkır-, -íhır-; § 4137) v.i. *bray much.*

dɪgrīgɪr-kál (N. -īkɪr-, -īhɪr-; §4137) v.t. eat (etc. s.v. kál) a great deal, eat much.

dɪgrīgɪr-kalĕğ-ğu-bókk(ɪ) (N. -īkɪr-, -īhɪr-; §4179a) v.i. and t. (-kal- can have an object) after eating much go and hide (oneself).
   ín⌣sáb⌣dɪgrīgɪrkalĕğğubókkɪn⌢ this cat after eating much goes and hides.
   élum⌣kárɛd⌣dɪgrīgɪrkalĕğğubókkɪn⌢ (-d⌣d- < -g⌣d- §534) the crocodile after eating a large quantity of fish goes and hides.

dɪgrīgɪr-kál-kattɪ- (N. -īkɪr-, -īhɪr-; §4144) v.p. be eaten much.

dɪgrīgɪr-kórrɛ (N. -īkɪr-, -īhɪr-; §4140) v.i. snore much, snore heavily.

dɪgrīgɪr-nóg (N. -īkɪr-, -īhɪr; -gɪnnóg §628; §4137) v.i. go (etc. s.v. nóg) much, go far, walk much, walk far.

dɪgrīgɪr-sándɪ (N. -īkɪr-, -īhɪr-; §4140) (a) v.i. be much afraid; (b) v.t. be much afraid of, fear much.
   éddotōn⌣dɪgrīgɪrsándɪran⌢ and ékkɪ⌣dɪgrīgɪrsándɪran⌢ they are much afraid of you.

dɪgrīgɪr-sándɪgɪr (N. -īkɪr-, -ɪkɪr-, -īhɪr-, -ɪhɪr; §4141) v.t. frighten (etc. s.v. sándɪgɪr) a great deal, etc.

dɪgrīgɪr-sɛllɪmɛ́ (N. -īkɪr-, -īhɪr-; -lum-; §4140) v.t. greet many times, i.e. heartily.
   tɛr⌣ékkɪ⌣dɪgrīgɪrsɛllɪmɛ́gon⌢ (s)he sent you many greetings.

dɪgrīgɪr-sɛllɪmɛ́-dɛn (N. -īkɪr-, -īhɪr-; -lum-; §4142) v.t. give many greetings to (the speaker).

dɪgrīgɪr-sɛllɪmɛ́-tɪr (N. -īkɪr-, -īhɪr-; -lum-; §4142) v.t. give many greetings to (other than the speaker).

dɪgrīgɪr-sínnɛ (N. -īkɪr-, -īhɪr-; §4140) v.i. become very angry.

dɪgrīgɪr-sínnɛ-bŭ- (N. -īkɪr-, -īhɪr-; §4142) v.i. stat. be in a very angry state.

dɪgrīgɪr-tíllɛ (N. -īkɪr-, -īhɪr-; §4140) v.i. perspire profusely.

díğ (díč⌢; §§2699, 2707) card. num. five [RSN, §§120, 200].
   obj. díğk(ɪ)⌣, -díčk(ɪ)⌣, díčč(ɪ)⌣ §523; -ğk-, -čk §323; -kɪ⌢, -čɪ⌢.
   gen. díğn⌣, díñ⌣c. §632.
   pl. díğɪ⌣, -ğɪ⌢.
   díğun⌢ (-ğŭ⌢, -ğú⌢ §§939, 5232) and tɛr⌣díğun⌢ (tɛr⌣ §5233) it's (they're) five.
   díğin⌢ (-ğí⌢, -ğí⌢ §5235) and tír⌣díğín⌢ (tɪr⌣ §5236) they're five.
   díč tágon⌢ and díč tágoran⌢ five came (have come; §5229).
   tír⌣díğ nókkon⌢ and tír⌣díğ nókkoran⌢ the five of them went (have gone; §5245).
   wɛl⌣díğ bɛlbótkon⌢ and wɛl⌣díğ bɛlbótkoran⌢ five dogs ran (have run) out (§5239).
   sắ⌣díğɪ díğun⌢ and (more commonly in N. than in S.) sắ⌣díğğɪ díğun⌢ it's 5·5 (s.v. sắ⌣).

dɪğín-d(ɪ)⌣ (§2737b) adj. = díñd(ɪ)⌣.

dɪğ-int(ɪ)⌣ (díğɪnt(ɪ)⌣; §2740) ord. num. fifth.
   obj. -tɪg⌣.

dɪğɪntínd(ɪ)⌣ (§2743) adj. appertaining to the fifth.

dɪğɪrɛ⌣ (§2745) n. ⅕, fifth part [< díğ- 5 + -ɪr *(action of) making + -ɛ⌣ of n. ess., so *one of what makes into 5 §2287].
   obj. -rɛg⌣.
   pl. -rɛnč(ɪ)⌣.

díñ-d(ɪ)⌣ (§2737a) adj. appertaining to five, of five, five's.

dɪŋgár⌣ (§§2758, 5261-7) num. the whole five, all five [<*dɪñgár (§645) < díñ⌣ of 5 + -g- obj. suff. + -ár⌣ *seizure, so *comprehension of the 5 §2218].
   obj. -árk(ɪ)⌣, -kɪ⌢.
   tɛr⌣dɪŋgárk⌣étta⌢ bring them all five; tɛr⌣dɪŋgárk⌣ a pronoun-complex (§5199).

díğ-kɪrɪ⌣ (díčkɪrɪ⌣; -ğk-, -čk- §323; §1532; §2736) num. adj. about five.

díğ-an- (§2760) v.i. become five.

díğam-bŭ- (§2761) v.i. stat. be in a state or condition of becoming five.

díğk-ɪr (díčkɪr-, -ğk-, -čk-; díčč̄ɪr §523; §2759) v.t. caus. make into five.

díğkɪr-bág (díčkɪr- etc.; §4138) v.t. divide into five.
   imperat. díğkɪrbák!
   dúngɪd⌣díčkɪrbákkori⌢ and dúngɪd⌣díččɪrbákkori⌢ (-d⌣d- < -g⌣d- §534) I (have) divided the money into five shares.

díkkɛ⌣ n. string or band (passing round waist) suspending drawers [< دكّة id.].
   obj. -kɛg⌣.
   pl. -kɛnč(ɪ)⌣.

dílt(ɪ)⌣ n. (a) hair (anywhere on body); (b, of animal) fur, coat; (c, of bird) feathers, plumage with collective sg. (§4696a) [cp. MN. tɛl id. coll. KB, §126, tɛlŭ id. HKN 9; -t(ɪ)⌣ §§2323, 2326; RSN, §§129, 200].
   obj. -tɪg⌣.
   pl. -tɪnč(ɪ)⌣.
   kámn⌣dílt(ɪ)⌣ and (§817).
   kám⌣dílt(ɪ)⌣ the camel's coat.
   wɛln⌣dílt(ɪ)⌣ and (§806).
   wɛl⌣dílt(ɪ)⌣ the dog's coat (fur).
   ɛgɛn⌣dílt(ɪ)⌣ (-n⌣d- < -dn⌣d- §612) the sheep's fleece.
   sắm⌣dílt(ɪ)⌣ (-m⌣d- < -bn⌣d- §586) the cat's fur.
   kắuɪrten⌣dílt(ɪ)⌣ the bird's feathers.

dɪltín-d(ɪ)⌣ (§§2545 ff.) adj. appertaining to hair, etc., of hair, etc., hair's.

díltɪ-kɪñ̄(ɪ)⌣ (§§2536-7) adj. devoid of hair, etc., hairless.

dímɪn⌣ (§§956d, 2699, 2707) card. num. ten [cp. Beḍ. támɪn id., etc. RSN, §§123-4; ON. тимін id. ZNG, s.v.: 'hamitisches Lehnwort' MSM, p. 15¹; DNN, p. 389].
   obj. dɪmíŋ(ɪ)⌣, -gɪ⌢.
   pl. dím(ɪ)nɪ⌣.
   dím(ɪ)nun⌢ (-nŭ⌢, -nú⌢ §§939, 5232) and tɛr⌣dím(ɪ)nun⌢ (tɛr⌣ §5233) it's (they're) ten.
   dím(ɪ)nín⌢ (-ní⌢, -ní⌢ §5235) and tír⌣dím(ɪ)nín⌢ (tɪr⌣ §5236) they're ten.
   X. dúngɪ⌣mɪŋkóttɛrré⌢ how much is the money?
   Y. gɪríš⌣dímnun⌢ it's ten piastres.
   gɪríš⌣dímɪn⌣fadlɛ́n⌢ ten piastres remain (§5239).

dɪmɪn-d(ɪ)⌣ (§2737a) adj. appertaining to ten, of ten, ten's.

dɪm(ɪ)nín-d(ɪ)⌣ (§2737b) adj. = dɪmínd(ɪ)⌣.

dɪmɪn-d-ídɪw⌣ (§2712) card. num. eighteen.
   obj. -ɪdíwg(ɪ)⌣, -ídɪwg(ɪ)⌣.

dɪmɪn-d-ískŏd⌣ (-ɪskŏ́d⌣; §2712) card. num. nineteen.
   obj. -ɪskŏ́dk(ɪ)⌣, etc. s.v. ískŏd⌣.

dɪmɪn-d-ŏ́wwɛl⌣ (-ŏ́uwɛl, -ŏ́wɛl⌣ §§1041, 989, -wắl⌣, -wɛl⌣ §1332a; §2741) ord. num. eleventh (= dɪmɪndowɛ́rínt(ɪ)⌣).
   dɪmɪndŏwwɛ́lg⌣étta⌢ and dɪmɪndowɛ́rintɪg⌣étta⌢ bring the eleventh.

dɪmɪn-d-ŏ́ww(ɪ)⌣ (-ŏ́uw(ɪ)⌣, -w⌣ §§1041, 1202; -ŏ́wᵘ⌣ §1012; §2712) card. num. twelve.
   obj. -wɪg⌣, -wᵘg⌣.
   dɪmɪndŏwwín⌢ (-wí⌢, -wí⌢ §§939, 1970, 5232) and tɛr⌣dɪmɪndŏwwín⌢ (tɛr⌣, -wí⌢, -wí⌢ §5233) it's (they're) twelve.
   tír⌣dɪmɪndŏwwín⌢ (tɪr⌣, -wí⌢, -wí⌢ §5237) they're twelve.

dɪmɪn-d-ŏ́ww-int(ɪ)⌣ (-ŏ́wwɪnt(ɪ)⌣; §2742) ord. num. twelfth.

dɪmɪn-díğ⌣ (-díč⌣; §2716) card. num. fifty.

dɪmɪn-do-díğ⌣ (-díč⌢; §2712) card. num. fifteen.
   obj. -díğk(ɪ)⌣, etc. s.v. díğ⌣.

dɪmɪn-do-górɪğ⌣ (-ɪč⌢; §2712) card. num. sixteen.
   obj. -gorɪ́ğk(ɪ)⌣, etc. s.v. górɪğ⌣.

dɪmɪn-do-kémɪs⌣ (§2712) card. num. fourteen.
   obj. -kɛmísk(ɪ)⌣, -kém(ɪ)sk(ɪ)⌣, -kɪ⌢.
   dɪmɪndokémɪsn⌣unátt(ɪ)⌣ full moon [cp. اِبْن أَرْبَعْتَاشَر id.].

dɪmɪn-do-kólod⌣ (-ot⌢; §2712) card. num. seventeen.
   obj. -kolódk(ɪ)⌣ etc. s.v. kólod⌣.

dɪmɪn-do-tósk⌣ (§2712) card. num. thirteen.
   obj. -kɪg⌣.

dɪmɪn-do-tosk-int(ɪ)⌣ (-tóskɪnt(ɪ)⌣; §2742) ord. num. thirteenth.

dɪmɪn-do-wɛ̄r⌣ (§2712) card. num. eleven.
   obj. -wɛ́g⌣.
   dɪmɪndowɛ́run⌢ (-rŭ⌢, -rú⌢ §§939, 5232) and tɛr⌣dɪmɪndowɛ́run⌢ (tɛr⌣ §5233) it's (they're) eleven.
   dɪmɪndowɛ́rín⌢ (-rí⌢, -rí⌢ §5235) and tír⌣dɪmɪndowɛ́rín⌢ (tɪr⌣ §5236) they're eleven.

dɪmɪn-do-wɛ̄r-int(ɪ)⌣ (-wɛ̄rint(ɪ)⌣; §2741) ord. num. eleventh (= dɪmɪn-dŏ́wwɛl⌣).

dɪmɪn-ídɪw⌣ (§2716) card. num. eighty.

dɪm(ɪ)n-int(ɪ)⌣ (dím(ɪ)nɪnt(ɪ)⌣; §2740) ord. num. tenth.

dɪm(ɪ)nɪntínd(ɪ)⌣ (§2743) adj. appertaining to the tenth.

dɪm(ɪ)nɪrɛ⌣ (§2745) n. ¹⁄₁₀, tenth part [< dímɪn- 10 + -ɪr *(action of) making +

dırārnárt(ı) — dól

-ɛ of n. ess., so *one of what makes into 10 §2287].
  obj. -rɛg.
  pl. -rɛnč(ı).
dımın-ískŏd (-ıskód; §2716) card. num. *ninety*.
dımın-tósk(ı) (§2716) card. num. *thirty*.
dımıŋgắr (§§2758, 5261-7) n. *the whole ten, all ten*.
  obj. -árk(ı), -ki.
  ır-ter-dımıŋgárk-ettágoruá? *did you (pl.) bring (have you (pl.) brought) the whole ten?* (§5199).
dımıŋ-górığ (-ič; §2716) card. num. *sixty*.
dımıŋ-kémıs (§2716) card. num. *forty*.
dımíŋ-kırı (-kírı §1532; §2736) num. adj. *about ten*.
dımıŋ-kólod (-ot; §2716) card. num. *seventy*.
dím(ı)n-an- (§2760) v.i. *become ten*.
dím(ı)nam-bŭ- (§2761) v.i. stat. *be in a state or condition of becoming ten*.
dımíŋ-ır (N. -ŋkır; §2759) v.t. caus. *make into ten*.
dımıŋgır-bág (N. -ŋkır-; §4138) v.t. *divide into ten*.
  imperat. dımıŋgırbák!
dımıŋgır-gásığ (-ič; N. -ŋkır-; §4138) v.t. *split into ten*.
  imperat. dımıŋgırgásıč!
dımıŋgır-órığ (-ič; N. -ŋkır-; §4138) v.t. *tear into ten*.
dırārnárt(ı) (-rānnā- §628; -ti) n. *Derar (on map), two islands about 14 miles above Urdi*.
  obj. -tıg.
dírr(ı) n. *(bird's) crest, comb* = kúğ (a).
  obj. -rıg.
  pl. -rınč(ı).
  dúrmadɛn-dírr(ı) *fowl's comb*.
  kugulún-dírr(ı) *cock's comb*.
dírr(ı) n. *notch near top of spindle* (CSW, p. 21) [either (§2408) < Sudan Ar. درّ *whorl* (HESA, s.v. spindle), or specialization of dírr(ı) *crest*].
  obj. -rıg.
  pl. -rınč(ı).
  núbron-dírr(ı) *notch of spindle*.
dít! imperat. of díd *revile*.
-do postp. *on, in, at, to* s.v. -r.
dódɛ n. *grasshopper*; with collective sg. (§4696c).
  obj. dódɛg.
  pl. dódɛnč(ı).
  báŋgan-dódɛ *grasshopper*.
dŏg v.t. *kiss* [RSN, §129].
  ind. pres. āı-dŏg(¹)rı; perf. āı-dógkori (dókkori).
  imperat. dók!, pl. dógwɛ! (dógwé!; dógɛ! §547, -gé!).
  ánnɛssıd-dókko (-d-d- < -g-d- §534) *(s)he (has) kissed my sister*.
dógar (-går; §§2200ff.) and
dōgíd (§§2256ff.) n. *kissing*.
dŏg-an (§§3890ff.) v.t. *tell to kiss, let kiss*.
dŏg-bŭ- (dóggŭ- §546; §3931β) v.i. stat. *be in a kissed condition*.
dŏg-katti- (dókkat-; §4093) v.p. *be kissed*.
dóggɛ! < dógwɛ! *kiss! (pl.)* s.v. dŏg.

dŏggŭ- < dógbŭ- *be in a kissed condition* s.v. dŏg.
dŏgır n. (a) *magician, sorcerer*; (b) *sorceress, witch* [§2286β; cp. ON. ᛬ᚩᚱ 'wise man; cf. Lat. doctus' GNT, s.v.; SNK, 866].
  obj. dōgírk(ı), -ki.
  pl. dŏg(ı)rı.
  dógırn-ónd(ı) (§4687) = dógır (a).
  dógır-kárr(ı) = dógır (b).
  dógır-ádamık-kálın (-k-k- < -g-k- §569) *the magician (witch) eats human beings*.
dógo n. *upper part, top, summit* [§2310; cp. ON. ᛬ᚩᚱ ride (GNT, s.v.) i.e. *be on*, M. dōg *sich auf etwas setzen, reiten* AZN, s.v., -o directional §4574; §4577; RSN, §129].
  obj. dogógı-c., -óg-v.c. (§512), -ógi.
  pl. dogónč.
  dogós-sókkɛgoran (§678) and
  dogógı-sókkɛgoran *they took (have taken) off (away) the top*.
  kán-dógo and (§2363)
  kándógo *top of house, roof*.
dogóg-ed (-ɛt-, -é §966; §6007) adv. *by* (etc. s.v. -ɛd) *the upper part, etc.*
dógōr (§6007) adv. *on (in, at, to) the upper part, etc., above, aloft, up, upwards*.
  dógōr (s)he (it) is (they are) on (in, at) the upper part, etc.
  X. tɛr-ólgon-dógōré? *is (s)he (it) still above?*
  Y. éjjo, dógōr *yes, (s)he (it) is*.
-dógōr (§§5860, 5898) postp. (= prep. §4287), (a, of position and motion) *above, over, on top of*; (b, in comparison §§4966ff.) *more*.
— follows the genitive (§§4362-3):
  kídi-wɛrwɛ́n-dógor-búran *the bones lie one on top of the other*.
  tógo-dógon-dógor-sérɛn *the lower part is better than the upper part*.
  béled-mállɛn-dógor-ín-sérɛn *this is the best of all countries* (§4968).
  mán-ínın-dógor-ɛ́ččɛlun *that (other, yonder) is different from this*.
— sometimes atonic:
  wíl-dogor-oróffélun (-l-d- < -ln-d- §806) *it's colder than yesterday*.
dogŏn-d(ı) (§§2545ff.) adj. *appertaining to the upper part, etc., upper*.
  obj. -dıg.
  pl. -dınč(ı).
dogŏndı-kırı (§2541) adj. *resembling the upper*.
dóg-an- (§3913β) v.i. *move (go, come) to(wards) the upper part, etc., move up(wards), ascend*.
  doganóskoran *they have gone (come) up*.
dogám-bŭ- (§3952) v.i. stat. *be in a state of upward motion, be on one's way up, be ascending*.
doganɛd-ág- (§§3965ff.) v.i. *be in the situation of having ascended*.
dogan-ɛgéččɛ (§4150) v.i. *ascend to the upper part, etc.*
  doganɛgɛččóskoran *they have gone up aloft*.
dogan-ɛgéčče-bŭ- (§4153) v.i. stat. *be in a state of motion ascending to the upper part, etc.*

doganɛgéččɛr-an (§3905) v.t. *tell to ascend to the upper part, etc., let ascend to the upper part, etc.*
dogan-nóg (§4150) v.i. *go upwards, ascend*.
dogan-nóg-bŭ- (-nóggŭ- §546; §4153) v.i. stat. *be in a state of motion (going) upwards*.
dogóg-ır (N. -ókır, -óhır; §3697) (a) v.t. caus. *cause or allow to be or become the upper part, etc.*; (b) v.t. *raise, elevate*.
  ind. pres. āı-dogógıddi, ɛr-dogógırın (-rí, -rí).
dogōgır- (N. -ókır-, -óhır-) in composition *aloft, up, upwards*.
dogōgır-sókkɛ (N. -ókır-, -óhır-; §4140) v.t. *raise aloft, hoist*.
dogōgır-tóllɛ (N. -ókır-, -óhır-; §4140) v.t. *pull upwards, pull up*.
dogōgır-úskur (N. -ókır-, -óhır-; §4141) v.t. *set (etc. s.v. úskur) in the upper part, etc. (s.v. dógor), put (etc.) up*.
dogōgır-wár (N. -ókır-, -óhır-; §4136) v.i. *jump upwards, jump up*.
  ind. pres. āı-dogōgırwárri, ɛr-dogōgırwárın (-rí, -rí); perf. āı-dogōgırwárkori.

dōhɛ́ (dōxɛ §1397) v.i. *get giddy* [< دوخ *giddiness* or دوخ imperf. stem of داخ *get giddy* + -ɛ §3624].
  ind. pres. āı-dōhɛ́ri; perf. āı-dōhɛ́gori (N. -ɛ́ko-, -ɛ́ho-).
dōhɛ̆rar (-rår; §§2200ff.) and
dōhɛ̆ríd (§§2256ff.) n. *becoming giddy, giddiness*.
dōhɛ́-bŭ- (§3931α) v.i. stat. *be in a giddy state or condition, be giddy*.
dōhɛ̆r-ɛg-ág- (§§4071ff.) v.i. = dōhɛrɛ-dól-.
dōhɛ̆r-ɛ-dól- (-r°d- §1178; §§4016-17, 4022, 4027) v.i. *be about to become giddy*.
dōhɛ́g-ır (N. -ɛ́kır, -ɛ́hır; §3681) v.t. caus. *cause or allow to become giddy*.
  ɛn-tumbág-āıgı-dōhɛ́gırın *your tobacco makes me giddy*.
dŏk! imperat. of dŏg *kiss*.
S. dókkon (-kŏ, -kó) neg. adv. = tókkon.
dókna n. *one of the sorts of date growing in Dóngola*; s.v. bént(ı); with collective sg. (§4696b).
  obj. -nag.
  pl. -nanč(ı).
dól v.t. (a) *desire, wish, wish for, want*; (b) *like, love*; (c) *want, require* [cp. ON. ᛬ᚩᛚ wish GNT, s.v.; RSN, §129].
  ind. pres. āı-dólli, ɛr-dólın (-lí, -lí); perf. āı-dólkori.
  subj. past āı-dólsı (-su).
  míŋgı-dólın? *what do you (does (s)he (it)) want?*
  āı-nográŋgı-dólli (§5443) *I wish to go*.
  āı-tır-nográŋgı-dólli (§5443) *I wish them to go*.
  X. (to Y., thinking that Y. has called him)
  āıgı-dólmɛn? *don't you want me?*
  āıgı-dólmɛn? also = *doesn't (s)he like (want) me?* (§3119).
  n-āıgı-dólın? *who wants me?*
  ugúg-udúdɛd-dólmunun (-d-d- -g-d- §534) *I (etc. §3077) don't like thunder at night* (§4665).

dōláb⌣ — dúg

kúmbud⌣dólná⌢ *do you (does (s)he (it)) like (want) eggs (§4696d)?*
désɛn⌣dóllan⌢ *they like him (her, it) very much.*
šăɪgɪ⌣ğúgr⌣ɛn⌣dólli⌢ (§6187) *I like tea hot.*
íŋgud⌣dolíddi⌢ (-d⌣d- < -g⌣d- §534) *and*
íŋgud⌣dolıríddi⌢ *I like (want) these.*
ín⌣néfıs⌣ówwıd⌣dóln⌣sókkɛrann⌣íllɛr⌢ (-d⌣d- < -g⌣d- §534) *this (one) requires two persons to lift it (him).*

-dól- (at the end of a complex in -ɛ- §§4021ff.) *be about to, be on the point of, be just going to.*

dólar⌣ (-làr⌣; §§2200ff.) and
dolíd⌣ (§§2256ff.) *n. desire, wish, wanting; liking; love, affection.*

dolidk-ır-dól (-ıtkır-, -ıttır- §716; §4156) *v.t. desire (etc.) intensely.*
íŋi⌣dolídkırdóllan⌢ *they desire (etc.) this (one) very much indeed.*

dólt(ı)⌣ *n.* = dólar [§2325α].

dól-bŭ- (§3931β) *v.i. stat. be in a desired (etc.) state or condition.*

dolɛd-ág- (§3877) *v.t. be in the situation of having desired, etc.*

dolíŋ-ır (dólıŋgır §1799; N. -ŋkır; §3688) *v.t. caus. cause or allow to desire, etc.*
tɛr⌣ăıg⌣íŋi⌣dólıŋgırın⌢ *(s)he (it) makes me want (etc.) this.*

dōláb⌣ *n. (a) water-wheel, wheel to raise water for irrigation; (b) cupboard* [< دُولاب *id.*].
obj. -ábk(ı)⌣, -ápk(ı)⌣, -ki⌢.
gen. -ábn⌣v., -ám⌣c.
pl. -ábi⌣.

dōlám-d(ı)⌣ (§§2545ff.) *adj. appertaining to the (a) water-wheel, etc.*

dóll(ı)⌣ *adj. deep* [cp. MN. twale *id.* KB, §115].
obj. -lıg⌣.
pl. -lınč(ı)⌣.
éssı⌣dóllın⌢ *the water is deep.*

dóllıgıd⌣ *n. depth* [§§2247–8].
obj. dollıgídk(ı)⌣, -ıtk(ı)⌣, -ítt(ı)⌣ §2462; -ki⌢, -ti⌢.
tén⌣dóllıgıd⌣mıŋkóttɛrré⌢ *what is its depth?*
tén⌣dollıgíttı⌣nál⌢ *see what its depth is.*

dóll-an- (§3910α) *v.i. become deep, deepen.*

dóllam-bŭ- (§§3949ff.) *v.i. stat. be in a deepening or deepened state or condition.*

dollanɛd-ág- (§3966α) *v.i. be in the condition of having become deep.*

dóllıg-ır (N. -ıkır, -ıhır; §3701) *(a) v.t. caus. cause or allow to become deep; (b) v.t. make deep, deepen.*

dollıgır-kúñur (N. -ıkır-, -ıhır-; §4141) *v.t. bury deep.*
ar⌣dollıgırkuñúrkoru⌢ *we (have) buried him (her, it, them) deep.*
ar⌣bıdollıgırkuñúrru⌢ *we shall bury him (her, it, them) deep.*

dóñ *v.t. rear, bring up* [§§2056, 2895a].
ind. pres. ăı⌣dóñ(ı)ri⌢, ɛr⌣dóñın⌢ (-ñi⌣, -ñí⌢); perf. ăı⌣dóñkori⌢.

dóñar⌣ (-ñár⌣, -ñɛr⌣; §§2200ff.) and
dōñíd⌣ (§§2256ff.) *n. rearing, bringing up.*

dóñɛd⌣ *n. (a) rearing, bringing up; (b) child or animal reared, etc., nursling* [§2242].

obj. dōñɛ́dk(ı)⌣, -ɛ́tk(ı)⌣, -ɛ́tt(ı)⌣ §2462; -ki⌢, -ti⌢.
gen. dóñɛdn⌣v., -ɛn⌣c.
pl. dóñɛdi⌣.
ím⌣búr⌣án⌣dóñɛdun⌢ *I (we) brought this girl up.*

dóñır⌣ *n. ram* [< *dōñír⌣ §1154; §2286α].
obj. doñírk(ı)⌣, -ki⌢.
pl. dóñırı⌣.

dóñ-kattı- (§4093) *v.p. be reared, etc.*
X. ɛr⌣sáır⌣dóñkattıgō? *where were you brought up?*
Y. (N.) árgor⌣dóñkattıkori⌢ *I was brought up in Argo.*

dōr⌣ *n. turn (successive occasion)* [< Eg. Ar. دَوْر *id.*].
obj. dórk(ı)⌣, -ki⌢.
pl. dórı⌣.
X. án⌣dórré? *is it my turn?*
Y. éndín⌢ *yes,* lit. *it is yours.*
X. álı⌣mén⌣tăgogo? (§939) *why had ξáli come?*
Y. dōr⌣ténd⌣ɛgo⌢ *it was his turn,* lit. *the turn was his (tén-d(ı)⌣ s.v. tér⌣).*

dōr⌣ *n. week* [< Sudan Ar. دَوْر *id.*].
obj. dórk(ı)⌣, -ki⌢.
pl. dórı⌣.
dōr⌣wɛr⌣jóm⌣kólodun⌢ (and dōr⌣ rɛr⌣...§672) *one week is seven days.*
dórro⌣jóm⌣kólod⌣dábun⌢ *there are seven days in the week.*
šahárro⌣dōr⌣kɛmıs⌣dábun⌢ (and -ız⌣ dá- §729) *there are four weeks in the month.*
hamís⌣tálɪn⌣dórkı⌣bıtáran⌢ *they will come on Thursday week;* §4665 (يجو دور الخميس الجاي)
X. bıtáran⌢ *they will come.*
Y. sıntá? *when?*
X. hamís⌣tálɪn⌣dórro⌢ *on Thursday week.*

dōš *v.t. provide with a fixed or permanent cover (as distinguished from tágır), cover, cover over, cover up, plaster the roof of.*
ind. pres. ăı⌣dōš(¹)ri⌢; perf. ăı⌣dōškori⌢.
subj. past ăı⌣dōšsı⌣ (-su⌣).
gabúrkı⌣kúluged⌣dōšran⌢ *they cover the grave with stones* (§4696d).
kán⌣dogós⌣síbeged⌣dōšran⌢ (-s⌣s- < -g⌣d- §678) *they cover over (plaster) the roof of the house with mud.*
nuggáran⌣agílg⌣ağíŋed⌣dōšran⌢ *they cover over the opening of the (e.g. jar forming the) drum with skin.*
kád⌣dōššan⌣wekíttı⌣íŋ⌣áukoran⌢ (-d⌣d- < -g⌣d- §534) *they did this when they plastered the roof of the house.*

dōšar⌣ (-šár⌣; §§2200ff.) and
dōšíd⌣ (§§2256ff.) *n. covering.*
dérıb⌣dōšín⌣kóčči̥geg⌣gašɛbún⌢ (-n⌣k- < -dn⌣k- §612, -g⌣g- < -d⌣g- §545) *the path crosses over on* (lit. *by means of (-ɛd⌣) the top of) the covering.*

dōš-an (§§3890ff.) *v.t. tell to cover, etc., let cover, etc.*

dōž-bŭ- (§§738, 3931β) *v.i. stat. be in a covered (etc.) state or condition.*
túrbɛ⌣kúluged⌣dōžbún⌢ *the grave is covered with stones.*

máltı⌣dárum⌣tógor⌣dōžbun⌢ *the runnel is roofed over under the path.*
éssı⌣máltı⌣dōžbúln⌣tǔgen⌣nógın⌢ (-n⌣n- < -d⌣n- §624) *the water passes through the covered runnel.*

dōš(¹)r-ɛg-ág- (§4071ff.) v.t. = dōšɛdól-.

dōš-ɛ-dól- (-š°d- §1178; §4022) and
dōš(¹)r-ɛ-dól- (-r°d-; §4027) *v.t. be about to cover, etc.*

dōš-ɛ-má- (§4036) and
dōš(¹)r-ɛ-má- (§4041) *v.t. become unable to cover, etc.*

dōšɛd-ág- (§3877) *v.t. be in the situation of having covered, etc.*

dōšíŋ-ır (dōšıŋgır §1799; N. -ŋkır; §3688) *v.t. caus. cause or allow to cover, etc.*

dōš-kattı- (§4093) *v.p. be covered, etc.*
máltı⌣béntın⌣úmbuged⌣dōškattın⌢ *the runnel is (runnels are §4647) covered over with palm-trunks* (§4696b).
moís⌣úmbuged⌣dōškattın⌢ *the cattle-track (of the water-wheel s.v. kólɛ⌣) is covered over with (i.e. is made of) palm-trunks.*

-do-tŏn⌣ *postp. from, of* s.v. -r-tŏn⌣.

dów(w)a⌣ *medicine* = dáw(w)a⌣.

dowwır (-wᵘr-) *v.t. cause to revolve, (a) turn round* = gırídegır; *(b) stir* = kăše [< imperat. or imperf. stem of دَوْر *id.* + -ɛ §3639].
ind. pres. ăı⌣dowwıréri⌢; perf. ăı⌣dowwırégori⌢ (N. -ɛ́ko-, -ɛ́ho-).
imperat. dowwıré!

dowwırérar⌣ (-wᵘr-; -rár⌣; §§2200ff., 2207) and
dowwırérid⌣ (-wᵘr-; §§2256ff., 2260) *n. turning round, etc.*

dowwırɛ́r-an⌣ (-wᵘr-; §§3890, 3899) *v.t. tell to turn round, etc., let turn round, etc.*

dowwırɛ́-kattı- (-wᵘr-; N. -ɛ́ha-; §4093) *v.p. be turned round, etc.*

dubára⌣ *n. string* [< دُبَارة *id.*].
obj. -rag⌣.
pl. -ranč(ı)⌣.

dúffa⌣ *n. (a) rudder; (b, in weaving) upper part of batten (CSW, pp. 30, 31)* [< دَفَّة *id.* §1336].
obj. -fag⌣.
pl. -fančı⌣.

dúg *v.i. become clouded, become overcast, become misty* [cogn. dég *cover one's loins*, díg *get bound*, tág *get covered* §2781].
ind. pres. tɛr⌣dúgın⌢ (-gí⌣, ⌣dúgí⌢); perf. tɛr⌣dúgkon⌢ (⌣dúkkon⌢, -kŏ⌢, -kó⌢).
séma⌣dúgın⌢ *the sky gets cloudy.*

dúgar⌣ (-gár⌣; §§2200ff.) and
dugíd⌣ (§§2256ff.) *n. becoming clouded, etc., cloudiness, mistiness.*

dúg-bŭ- (dúggŭ- §546; §3931α) *v.i. stat. be in a clouded (etc.) state or condition.*
séma⌣dúgbūn⌢ *the sky is cloudy (overcast)* = séma⌣níččın⌢.
áša⌣dúggūn⌢ *it (the weather) is misty.*

dug-ɛ-dól- (-g°d- §1178; §4022) and
dug(¹)r-ɛ-dól- (-r°d-; §4027) *v.i. be about to become clouded, etc.*
séma⌣dugɛdólın⌢ *the sky is about to get overcast.*

dúgal‿ (-gál‿, -gɛl‿) n. *lock* [? cogn. díg *get bound* or ? < دَغَل *thicket*].
  obj. dugálg(ı)‿, -gálg(ı)‿, -gélg(ı)‿; -gi⌒.
  pl. dúgalı‿, -gálı‿, -gɛlı‿.
  kúšar‿dugállo‿tón⌒ *the key enters the lock.*
  kúšer‿dúgello‿tōráŋŋı‿móní⌒ *the key won't go into the lock.*
dúgus‿ and **dúŋus‿** (§ 1018) n. *intestine, gut, entrails*; with collective sg. (§ 4696a).
  obj. dugúsk(ı)‿, -ki⌒.
  pl. dúgusı‿.
duhắn‿ (§ 956a) n. *loom* [< N. dukắn‿ *id.* § 1027].
  obj. -áŋg(ı)‿, -gi⌒.
  pl. -áŋı‿.
  duhắŋ‿kórıs‿ *treadle(s* § 4696d) *of loom.*
duhắn-d(ı)‿ (§§ 2545 ff.) adj. *appertaining to the (a) loom, of the (a) loom.*
duhānín-d(ı)‿ (§§ 2545 ff.) adj. *appertaining to (the) looms, of (the) looms.*
duhắn-goñ‿ (-áŋg-) n. *(a) loom-maker* [s.v. góñ‿] = (b) *weaver.*
  obj. duhāngóñg(ı)‿, -gi⌒.
  pl. duhắŋgoñı‿.
  duhắŋgoñ‿tén‿duhắŋg‿áwın⌒ *the weaver sets up his loom.*
duhắŋgoñı‿ n. = duhắŋgoñ‿ [of which it is pl. used as sg. § 2143].
  obj. -ñıg‿, -gi⌒.
  pl. -ñınčı‿.
  duhắŋgoñıt‿tārá⌒ (-t‿t- < -g‿t- § 707) *tell the weaver to come.*
duhāníjɛ‿ n. (a) *loom-maker*; (b) *weaver* [< a pl. *دُكَّانِيَّة *loom-men* § 2405] *(a)* = *(b),* the weaver sets up his loom.
  obj. -íjɛg‿.
  pl. -íjɛnč(ı)‿.
  duhāníjɛ‿duhắŋg‿áwın, bắdkı‿góñ-ñag‿góñın⌒ *the duhāníjɛ makes the loom and (§ 6239) afterwards weaves the cloth.*
duhhắn‿ (duxxắn; § 956a) n. *tobacco* [< دُخَّان *id.*].
  obj. -áŋg(ı)‿, -gi⌒.
dúhur‿ n. *noon* [< ظُهْر *id.* § 1363].
  obj. duhúrk(ı)‿, -ki⌒.
  duhúrro‿ *at noon.*
  duhúrn‿owwéllo‿ *before noon.*
  duhúrm‿bắdk(ı)‿ and
  duhúrm‿bắdır‿ *after noon.*
  duhúr‿áŋkım‿bıtắran⌒ *they will come at noon,* lit. .... *when it becomes noon.*
dúhur-an- (§ 3910α) v.i. *become noon.*
  bıdúhuranın⌒ *it will become noon.*
  ékkɛnɛ‿dúhuraŋkó⌒ *it's now noon,* lit. *now it has become noon.*
  dúhuraŋkın‿ *at (by) noon.*
dúhuram-bŭ- (§§ 3949 ff.) v.i. stat. *be becoming noon.*
duhuran-ɛ-dól- (-nᵒd- § 1178; § 4026) and
duhurand-ɛ-dól- (-dᵒd-; § 4034) v.i. *be about to become noon.*
  duhuranɛdólın‿ *it's nearly noon.*
dukắn‿ (N.; § 956a) n. *loom* (= duhắn‿) [< دُكَّان *id.,* bench].
  obj. -áŋg(ı)‿, -gi⌒.
  pl. -áŋı‿.

dukắn-d(ı)‿ (N.; §§ 2545 ff.) adj. *appertaining to the (a) loom, of the (a) loom.*
dukānín-d(ı)‿ (N.; §§ 2545 ff.) adj. *appertaining to (the) looms, of (the) looms.*
dukắn-goñ‿ (N.) n. *(a) loom-maker* = (b) *weaver.*
  obj. dukāngóñg(ı)‿, -gi⌒.
  pl. dukắŋgoñı‿.
dukkắn‿ (§ 956a) n. *shop* [< دُكَّان *id.*].
  obj. -káŋg(ı)‿, -gi⌒.
  pl. -káŋı‿.
  dukkáŋgı‿kúskó⌒ *he (has) opened the (a) shop.*
  álı‿dukkándó⌒ *ɛáli is at (in) the shop.*
dukkắn-d(ı)‿ (§§ 2545 ff.) adj. *appertaining to the (a) shop.*
dúkk(ı) v.t. (a) *extract, pull out, uproot;* (b, *apparel*) *take off.*
  ind. pres. aı‿dúkkırı⌒; perf. aı‿dúkkıgori⌒ (N. -ıko-, -ıho-).
  imperat. dúkki!
  def. imperat. dúkkos! (dukkós!, -kó! § 962); pl. dukkóswɛ! (-kóswɛ!, -kówwɛ! § 724, -wɛ́!, -kóssɛ! § 687, -sɛ́!).
  hakím‿tén‿nél‿ówwıd‿dúkkıgó⌒ (-d‿d- < -g‿d- § 534; § 4859) *the doctor took (has taken) out two of his (her) teeth.*
  íŋ‿kınıssɛg‿ánn‿óssırtōn‿dúkkıgon⌒ *(s)he (has) extracted this thorn from my foot.*
  túrug‿ın‿ǵówwıd‿dukkóskó⌒ *the wind has uprooted this tree.*
  ın‿ǵówwıg‿árdırtōn‿dukkóskó⌒ *(s)he (it) has pulled this tree out of the ground.*
  ɛŋ‿kádɛd‿dúkki⌒ *take your clothes* (§ 4696d) *off (undress).*
  ɛn‿hızámgı‿dúkki⌒ *take your belt off.*
  nɛwértıd‿dúkkıgó⌒ *(s)he breathed deeply (sighed).*
— used intransitively in:
  ɛn‿nɛwértı‿dúkkın‿ *you are out of breath,* lit. *your breath pulls (itself) out.*
dúkkar‿ (-kár‿; §§ 2200 ff.) and
dukkíd‿ (§§ 2256 ff.) n. *extraction, etc.*
dúkk-an‿ (§§ 3890 ff.) v.t. *tell to extract, etc., let extract, etc.*
dúkkı-bŭ- (§ 3931β) v.i. stat. *be in an extracted (etc.) state or condition.*
  nél‿dúkkıbūn‿ *the tooth is out (has been extracted).*
dúkkı-děn‿ (§§ 3996-7) v.t. *extract (etc.) for (the speaker).*
  hakím‿nél‿áıg‿oddélgı‿bıdukkıdénın⌒ (§ 4805) *the doctor will take out for me the tooth that hurts me.*
dúkkı-tır (§§ 3998-9) v.t. *extract (etc.) for (other than the speaker).*
  hakím‿nél‿ékk‿oddélgı‿bıdúkkıtırın⌒ *the doctor will take out for you the tooth that hurts you.*
dukkır-ɛg-ág- (§§ 4071 ff.) v.t. = dukkɛdól-.
dukk-ɛ-dól- (-kᵒd- § 1178; § 4022) and
dukkı-ɛ-dól- (-rᵒd-; § 4027) v.t. *be about to extract, etc.*
dukk-ɛ-má- (§ 4036) and
dukkı-ɛ-má- (§ 4041) v.t. *become unable to extract, etc.*
dukkɛd-ág- (§ 3877) v.t. *be in the situation of having extracted, etc.*
  hakím‿nélgı‿dukkɛdágın⌒ *the doctor has taken the tooth out.*

dúkkı-kattı- (N. -ıha-; § 4093) v.p. *be extracted, etc.*
dukkós-děn‿ (-óddɛn § 538; §§ 4180-4, 3995 ff.) v.t. *extract (etc.) for (the speaker).*
  hakím‿nél‿áıg‿oddélgı‿dukkoddɛ́ŋ-kó⌒ *the doctor took (has taken) out for me the tooth that hurt me.*
dukkós-tır (-óttır § 714; §§ 4180-4, 3995 ff.) v.t. *extract (etc.) for (other than the speaker).*
  hakím‿nél‿ékk‿oddélgı‿dukkottíkkoná? *did the doctor take (has the doctor taken) out for you the tooth that hurt you?*
dukkos-tő (-ottő § 714; §§ 4180-4; -osgıtő, -ozgı-, -oggı- § 4185) v.t. *enter after extracting, etc.*
  ind. pres. aı‿dukkostóri⌒ (-ottóri⌒, etc.).
  imperat. dukkósto! (-ótto!, -ósgıto!, -ózgı-, -óggı-).
  téŋ‿kádɛd‿dukkottōróskon⌒ (-d‿d- < -g‿d- § 534) *having taken off his clothes* (§ 4696d) *he (her clothes she) has gone in.*
dukkos-urur-tő (-osgur-, -ozgur-, -oggur- §§ 4185, 5605) v.t. *enter the river after extracting, etc.*
  áŋ‿kádɛd‿dukkosururtōróskori⌒ *having undressed I went into the river.*
dúl‿ adj. (a) *great, large, big;* then, like كبير, *maior;* (b) *aged, old* [§ 2543; either < *dúrl < dúr *attain* + -l‿ part., so *attaining,* or dú- is cogn. with ON. ᚦᛅᚢ-, ᚦᛅᚢᛅ- *gross sein* ZNG, s.v.; RSN, §§ 129, 200].
  obj. dúlg(ı)‿, -gi⌒.
  gen. dúln‿v., dún‿c. (§§ 807, 810, 814).
  pl. dúlı‿ and dúlınč(ı)‿.
  kā‿dúln‿tírtın⌒ and
  kā‿dún‿tírtın⌒ *he is master (owner) of the (a) large house.*
  tím‿báññıd‿dúlun⌒ *their talk is loud.*
  téh‿híssı‿dúlun‿ (-h‿h- < -n‿h- § 561) *his (her) voice (its sound) is very loud.*
  tımbáb‿dúlun‿ *his (her) father is old.*
dúlkanɛ‿ (§ 2295) n. (a) *greatness, largeness, size;* (b) *being aged, old age, age.*
dúl-an- (§ 3910α) v.i. *become great, etc., grow, increase.*
  ind. pres. aı‿dúlandi, ɛr‿dúlanın‿ (-ni⌒, -ní⌒); fut. aı‿bıdúlandi (bud-); perf. aı‿dúlaŋkori⌒.
  subj. past aı‿dúlansı‿ (-assı‿ § 680, -su‿).
  úru‿dúlaŋkın‿ *when the river rises.*
  dégır‿dúlaŋkó⌒ *the saddle (has) turned out (to be) too large.*
  ambáb‿dúlaŋkó⌒ *my father has grown old.*
dúlam-bŭ- (§§ 3949 ff.) v.i. stat. *be in an increasing (etc.) or increased (etc.) state or condition.*
  ambáb‿dúlambūn⌒ *my father is getting to be an aged man (...is well on in years).*
dūland-ɛg-ág- (§ 3977) v.i. = dūlanɛdól-.
dūlan-ɛ-dól- (-nᵒd- § 1178; § 3975) and

dūland-ɛ-dól- (-dᵒd-; §3978) v.i. *be about to become great, etc.*
  úru͜dūlanɛdólın⌒ *the river is about to rise.*
dūland-ág- (§3966α) v.i. *be in a condition of having become great, etc., be in an increased condition.*
  ambáb͜dūlanɛdágın⌒ *my father is an aged man.*
dúlg-ır (N. dúlkır; §3702) (a) v.t. caus. *cause or allow to be or become great, etc.*; (b) v.t. *render great, etc., enlarge, increase.*
  ind. pres. aı͜dúlgıddi⌒, ɛr͜dúlgırın⌒ (-rī⌒, -rí⌒); perf. aı͜dúlgırkori⌒.
  tén͜nɛfískı͜dúlgırın⌒ *(s)he is conceited.*
  N. tókkon͜ɛn͜nɛfískı͜dúlkırmɛn⌒ *don't be conceited.*
dúlgır-an (N. -lkı-; §§3890, 3904) v.t. *tell to enlarge, etc., let enlarge, etc.*
dūlgır-bañ́ñ(ı) (N. dūlkır-; §4137) and emphasizing dūlgır-.
dúlgır-bañ́ñ(ı) (N. dúlkır-; §1964) v.i. *speak loud.*
  imperat. dúlgırbañ́ñı!
dúlgır-ó (N. -lkı-; §4137) v.i. *sing loud.*
dúllo͜ adj. (a) *heavy, weighing much*; (b) *ponderous, dull, slow*; (c) *oppressive, tyrannical, unjust*; (d) *difficult, hard*; (e, of drink) *strong* [§2561β; ?cogn. dúl͜ *great*].
  obj. -log͜.
  pl. -lorı͜ and -lonč(ı)͜.
  áfɛš͜dúllòn⌒ *the baggage is heavy.*
  tín͜hāsıbērid͜dúllòn⌒ (§4713) (a) *their calculation is heavy, i.e. they are slow in calculating*; (b) *their calculation is difficult, i.e. they are difficult to be calculated.*
  tín͜nálar͜dúllòn⌒ (a) *their sight is dull, i.e. they do not see well*; (b) *they are hard to see, i.e. to be seen.*
  dɛrɛwíšın͜hókum͜dúll͜ɛgó⌒ *the rule of the dervishes was oppressive.*
  nóbım͜báñ́ñıd͜ówwalɛn͜dúllon⌒ *the Nubians' language* (i.e. Máhasi, s.v. nób͜) *is difficult at first.*
  dértıŋ͜kāgíd͜dúllon͜tumbágın͜ıllár⌒ *keeping the fast is hard because of tobacco (sc. its being forbidden).*
  bún͜dúllo͜ *strong coffee.*
  šāı͜dúllod͜dóllan⌒ (-d͜d- < -g͜d- §534) *they like strong tea.*
  mérsɛ͜dúllomunun⌒ *the beer is not strong.*
dúllogıd͜ n. *heaviness, dullness, etc.* [§§2247–8].
  obj. dullogídk(ı)͜, -ítk(ı)͜, -ítt(ı)͜ (§2462), -tı⌒.
dúllokanɛ͜ (§2295) n. *heaviness, dullness, etc.*
dúll-an- (§3910α) v.i. *become heavy, etc.*
  šāı͜dúllaŋkŏ⌒ *the tea (has) got strong.*
dúllam-bŭ- (§§3949ff.) v.i. stat. *be in a state or condition of becoming or having become heavy, etc.*
dullanɛd-ág- (§3966α) v.i. *be in the condition of having become heavy, etc.*
  šāı͜dullanɛdágın⌒ *the tea has got strong.*
dúllog-ır (N. -okır, -ohır; §3701) (a) v.t. caus. *cause or allow to be or become heavy, etc.*; (b) v.t. *render heavy, etc.*
  ind. pres. aı͜dúllogıddi⌒, ɛr͜dúllogırın⌒ (-rī⌒, -rí⌒).
  šāıgı͜dúllogırkon⌒ and (§514a)
  šāıd͜dúllogırkŏ⌒ *(s)he has (you have) made the tea strong.*
dúllogır-an (N. -okır-, -ohır-; §§3890, 3904) v.t. *tell to render heavy, etc., let render heavy, etc.*
  gáhwak͜kınnéd͜dúllogıran⌒ (-k͜k- < -g͜k- §569, -d͜d- < -g͜d- §534) *tell him (her) to make the coffee rather strong.*
dullogır-áu (N. -okır-, -ohır-; §4137) v.t. *make (a drink) strong.*
  mérsɛd͜dullogıráuran⌒ *they make the beer strong.*
dullogıráw-an (N. -okır-, -ohır-; §§3890, 3905) v.t. *tell to make (a drink) strong, let make strong.*
  šāıgı͜dullogıráwan⌒ *tell him (her) to make the tea strong.*
dúmmadɛ͜ (§607) < dúrmadɛ͜ *hen, etc.*
dúŋ(ı)͜ n. (a) *silver*; (b) *money*; (c) *coin* [§2032].
  obj. dúŋıg͜.
  pl. dúŋınč(ı)͜.
  dúŋın͜ákaš͜ *silver ear-ring.*
  dúŋın͜tábıd͜ *silversmith.*
  dúŋ͜ándın⌒ *the money is mine (ours).*
  dúŋık͜kóran⌒ *they have (the, some) money.*
  X. ıŋgı͜fɛkké⌒ *change this.*
  Y. dúŋıgá͜wála͜warákk͜éttari? (§4647) *shall (§5369b) I bring coin or notes?*
  X. dúŋıd͜dén, aı͜warákkı͜dólmunun⌒ (-d͜d- < -g͜d- §534) *give me coin: I don't want notes.*
duŋgín-d(ı)͜ (§§2545ff.) adj. *appertaining to (the) silver, etc., of (the) silver, etc.*
dúŋı͜kıñ́ñ(ı)͜ (§§2536-7) adj. *without money, penniless.*
dúŋıkıñ́ñıg-ır (ᵇ⌣ᵘ⌣; N. -ıkır, -ıhır; §§3703, 5708) v.t. *cause or allow to become without money, render or leave penniless.*
dúŋı-kŏ (§§4109, 4115) v.i. *have money, be well off.*
  part. pres. dúŋıkŏl͜ *(one) that has money, well off;* obj. duŋıkŏlg(ı)͜, -gi⌒.
  neg. part. pres. duŋıkómɛnıl͜ *(one) that has no money, penniless;* obj. duŋıkómɛnílg(ı)͜, -gi⌒.
  dúŋıkŏran⌒ *they have money (are well off).*
dúŋula͜ n. (a, *the village now called*) *Old Dóngola* (on map), دَنْقَلَا الْعَجُوز, = túŋgul͜ (a); (b, *the country*) *Dóngola* (on map) ['may be for Do-oŋgo-la "Do in the south"' GCD, p. 28; 'An older form of 'Donkola' was 'Domkola' (e.g. see Yákūt, Geogr. مدينة النوبه اسمها دمقلة).' MAS, II, p. 329].
  obj. -lag͜, -gi͜.
  dúŋgular͜nókkoran⌒ and
  dúŋgul͜áŋkoran⌒ *they went (have gone) to (Old) Dóngola.*
duŋulán-d(ı)͜ (§§2545ff.) (a) adj. *appertaining to Old Dóngola, etc., of Dóngola, Dongolese;* (b) n. *the language of Dóngola, Dongolese Nubian.*
  duŋulándıb͜báñ́ñıran⌒ (-b͜b- < -g͜b- §519) and
  duŋulándıgɛb͜báñ́ñıran⌒ (-b͜b- < -d͜b- §518) *they talk Dongolese Nubian.*
duŋuláwı͜ (-lāuı͜) n. *Nubian (native) of Dóngola, Dongolese* [< دَنْقَلَاوِي id.].
  obj. -wıg͜.
  pl. -áwınč(ı)͜.
duŋuláwın-d(ı)͜ (-lāuín-; §§2545ff.) adj. *appertaining to the (a) Nubian of Dóngola.*
duŋuláwınčín-d(ı)͜ (-lāuın-; §§2545ff.) (a) adj. *appertaining to (the) Nubians of Dóngola, of the Dongolese, Dongolese;* (b) n. *the language of the Nubians of Dóngola, Dongolese Nubian.*
  duŋulawınčíndıb͜báñ́ñıran⌒ and duŋulawınčíndıgɛb͜báñ́ñıran⌒ *they speak Dongolese Nubian.*
dúŋul-an- (§3910β) v.i. *go to Old Dóngola, etc.*
  dúŋulaŋkoran⌒ *they went (have gone) to Old Dóngola (etc.).*
dúŋgur͜ adj. *blind* [§§2033-4, 2569; <*dúŋır͜ < dúg *become clouded* + -ır͜ *making or made* §2496].
  obj. duŋgurk(ı)͜, -ki⌒.
  pl. dúŋgurı͜.
dúŋgúrkanɛ͜ (§2295) n. *blindness.*
dúŋgur-an- (§3910α) v.i. *become blind, go blind.*
  ind. pres. aı͜dúŋgurandi⌒; perf. aı͜dúŋguraŋkori⌒.
dúŋguram-bŭ- (§§3949ff.) v.i. stat. *be in a state of going blind, be advanced in the process of going blind.*
duŋguranɛd-ág- (§3966α) v.i. *be in the condition of having gone blind, be quite blind.*
duŋgútt(ı)͜ n. *thick spoke of wheel raising water* (átt(ı)͜) *in water-wheel* (kólɛ͜); *there are four, alternating with four thin spokes* (tarantarénč(ı)͜) [§2347; <*duŋgúnt(ı)͜ (§710), cp. F. dununti id. SNK, 377A, 10; ?cogn. with dúŋus-gut (s.v. dúgus͜); for -t(ı)͜ see §2323].
  obj. -tıg͜.
  pl. -tınč(ı)͜.
dúŋus͜ *intestine, etc.* = dúgus͜.
dúr v.t. (a) *reach, attain*; (b) *overtake*; (c) *obtain, get* [§4505].
  ind. pres. aı͜dúrın⌒, ɛr͜dúrın⌒ (-rī⌒, -rí⌒); perf. aı͜dúrkori⌒.
  béntır͜dárrıgori, béntid͜dúrkómunun⌒ (-d͜d- < -g͜d- §534) *I climbed up the palm but couldn't reach the dates* (§4696b).
  gátır͜urúm͜bāburkı͜dúrkómunun⌒ *the train didn't catch the steamer.*
  ǧawáb͜bústab͜bıdúrmunun⌒ (-b͜b- < -g͜b- §519) *the letter will not catch the post.*
  aı͜tékkı͜bundúkkɛǧ͜ǧómkori, dúrkori⌒ (-ǧ͜ǧ- < -d͜ǧ- §550) *I fired at and* (§6239) *hit him (her)*.
  tén͜abágır͜bódkori, dúrkómunun⌒ *I ran after him (her, it) but couldn't* (§5475) *catch him (her, it) up.*
  tén͜hánu͜dúŋı͜dıgríd͜dúrkŏ⌒ (-d͜d- < -g͜d- §534) *his (her) donkey*

(has) fetched a good price, lit. ...*obtained much money*.
án⌣táttı⌣dūróskó⌢ *my time on duty (in cultivation by water-wheel) is ended*, lit. ...*has reached sc. its end*.
dūrar⌣ (-rár⌣; §§2200ff.) and
dūríd⌣ (§§2256ff.) n. *reaching, attainment, etc.*
dúr-an (§§3890ff.) v.t. *tell to reach, etc., let reach, etc.*
dúr-bŭ- (§3934) v. stat. (a) i. *be in an attained (attainable, etc.) state or condition*; (b) t. *be in a state or condition to attain, etc.*
bénti⌣dúrbūmunun⌢ *the dates are out of reach*, lit....*are not in an attainable state*.
akundéna⌣dúŋgı⌣dıgrĭd⌣dúrbūn⌢ akundéna⌣ (*dates*) *are fetching a lot of money*, lit....*are in a state to obtain much money*.
dur-bundukk-eğ-ğóm (§5605) v.t. *hit by attaining with a gun, fire at and hit*.
aı⌣tékkı⌣dūrbundukkeğğómkori⌢ *I fired at and hit him (her, it)*.
dūrr-ɛg-åg- (§§4071ff.) v.t. = dūrɛdól-.
dūr-ɛ-dól- (-rᵒd- §1178; §4022) and
dūrr-ɛ-dól- (-rᵒd-; §4027) v.t. *be about to reach, etc.*
dūr-ɛ-må- (§4036) and
dūrr-ɛ-må- (§4041) v.t. *become unable to reach, etc.*
dūrr-ɛ-nóg- (§§4048ff.) v.t. *go to reach, etc.*
dūrr-ɛ-nóg-bŭ- (-nóggŭ- §546; §4058) v.t. stat. *be going to reach, etc., be on one's way to reach, etc.*
dūrɛd-åg- (§3877) v.t. *be in the situation of having reached, etc.*
dúr-katti- (§4093) v.p. *be reached, etc.*
dūr-kátti-bŭ- (§4105) v.i. stat. *be in an attained (attainable, etc.) state or condition*.
dúra⌣ n. (a) *forearm* (=ğɛríd⌣); (b) *cubit of 21 or 22 inches* (=kɛ́u⌣) *with collective sg.* (§4696a) [<Sudan Ar. durá⌣ =
ذِرَاع id.].
obj. dúrag⌣.
pl. duránč(ı)⌣.
dúrmadɛ⌣ (dúmmadɛ⌣ §607) n. (a) *hen*; (b) *fowl* [§2187; with dúr- cp. Eth. ዶርሆ *fowl*].
obj. -dɛg⌣.
pl. durmadénč(ı)⌣.
dúrmadɛ⌣kárr(ı)⌣ *hen*.
dúrmadɛŋ⌣dírr(ı)⌣ and
dúrmadɛŋ⌣kúğ⌣ *fowl's comb*.
dúrmadɛŋ⌣tód⌣ *young of fowl, chicken(s §4696d)*.
durmadɛn-tŏd⌣ (dumma-; §2366) n. *chicken; with collective sg.* (§4696d).
obj. -tŏdk(ı)⌣, -tŏtk(ı)⌣, -tŏkk(ı)⌣, -tŏtt(ı)⌣ (§2462), -ki⌢, -ti⌢.
gen. -tŏdn⌣v., -tŏnn⌣v.c., -tŏn⌣c. (§§778–88).
pl. durmadéntonı⌣.
durmadé-tod⌣ (dumma-; §2369) n. (a) *rather poor fowl, indifferent specimen of fowl*; (b) =dúrmadɛ⌣.
obj. -détŏdk(ı)⌣, -tŏtk(ı)⌣, -tŏkk(ı)⌣, -tŏtt(ı)⌣; -dɛtŏdk(ı)⌣, etc., -ki⌢, ti⌢.
gen. -détŏdn⌣v., -tŏnn⌣v.c., -tŏn⌣c.
pl. -détonı⌣.
dummadétodun⌢ *it's a (rather poor) fowl*.

durmadén-d(ı)⌣ (dumma-; §§2545ff.) adj. *appertaining to the (a) fowl, of the (a) fowl, (the, a) fowl's*.
dúrŏ⌣ adj. (a) *thick (ample in one or two dimensions)*; (b, of animate objects) *stout, broad in figure* [< √dúr- *attain* (§4505) +-ŏ⌣ (§2562)].
obj. duróg⌣.
pl. durŏ́rı⌣.
íŋ⌣dúrŏ́n⌢ *this (that) is (too) thick*.
kádɛ⌣dúrŏ́n⌢ *the cloth is (too) thick*.
wíččır⌣dúrŏ́n⌢ *the stick is (too) thick*.
dúrŏ́-wɛd⌣dóllan⌢ (-d⌣-<-g⌣d- §534) *they want a thick one*.
ógığ⌣dúrŏ́n⌢ *the man is broad in figure*.
durókanɛ⌣ (§2295) n. *thickness, stoutness*.
dúr-an- (duróan-, -rᵒan-; §3910α) v.i. *become thick, etc.*
habɛšínčın⌣ór⌣duráŋkó⌢ *the king of the Abyssinians grew (has grown) stout* (§6290).
durám-bŭ- (duroám-, -rᵒam-; §§3949ff.) v.i. stat. *be in a state or condition of becoming or having become thick, etc.*
duranɛd-åg- (duróan-, -rᵒan-; §3966α) v.i. *be in the condition of having become thick, etc.*
dúru⌣ adj. *aged, old, of animate objects* [< √dúr- *attain* (§4505) +-u⌣ dem. (§4596)].
obj. dúrug⌣.
pl. dúruı⌣ (dúrwı⌣).
ambåb⌣dúrun⌢ *my father is old*.
índı⌣dúrun⌢ *my mother is old*.
ógıŋ⌣dúru⌣ (§4687) *old man*.
tíŋ⌣dúru⌣ *old cow* (etc. s.v. tí⌣).
dúrukanɛ⌣ (§2295) n. *being aged, old age*.
dúr-an- (dúruan-, -rwan-; §3910α) v.i. *become aged, grow old*.
habɛšínčın⌣ór⌣duráŋkó⌢ (§6290) *the king of the Abyssinians grew (has grown) old*.
šídar⌣duráŋkó⌢ *the tree(s §4696b, has, have) got old*.
durám-bŭ- (-ruám-, -rwám-; §§3949ff.) v.i. stat. *be in an aging or aged state or condition*.
duran-ɛ-dól- (-nᵒd- §1178; §4026) and
durand-ɛ-dól- (-dᵒd-; §4034) v.i. *be about to become aged, grow old*.
ambåb⌣durandɛdólın⌢ *my father is beginning to grow old*.
duranɛd-åg- (duruán-, -rwan-; §3966α) v.i. *be in the condition of having become aged, etc.*

*d §269.

-é⌢ *because* s.v. -ɛd⌣.
⌣é- (⌣ɛ- §§1789ff.; §§3500ff.) v.t. (a) *say*; (b, with question as object) *ask*; (c) *say to, tell*; (d) *say of (to), call, name*. =wɛ́ [*intend §213].
ind. pres. aı⌣éri⌢, ɛr⌣én⌢ (⌣é⌢, -é⌢, ⌣en⌢, ⌣é⌢, ⌣eɛ⌢); perf. aı⌣égori⌢ (N. ⌣éko-, ⌣ého-; ~⌢).
subj. past aı⌣ésı⌣ (⌣ésu⌣).
— often unstressed and enclitic (§1791).
— before ⌣é- most verbal stems ending in a vowel receive gerundial -r⌣ (§§3531ff.).

— if ⌣é- *has a sentence as its object, or as one of its objects, the sentence is in oratio recta without -g⌣* (§6140).
— for usage see §§5500ff., 6140ff.).
íŋ⌣éri⌢ *I say this*.
míŋ⌣én? *what do you (does (s)he) say?*
fɛğırr⌣éri⌢ *I say 'at dawn' (...'early tomorrow')*.
fɛğırr⌣egó⌢ *you ((s)he) said 'at dawn'*.
aı⌣båğ¹r⌣émunun⌢ *I do not say 'I('ll* §5369b) *write (it'; 'I'll divorce you'*, s.v. båğ), i.e. *I'm not going to write (etc.)* = aı⌣båğɛdólmunun⌢.
tåɡomunun, óddın⌣erán⌢ *(s)he didn't (hasn't) come, they say (s)he's ill*.
nóg⌣ɛgóri⌢ (§5078) and
aı⌣ɛkki⌣nóg⌣ɛgóri⌢ *I said 'go'*.
aı⌣ékkı⌣nóg⌣ɛgóri⌢ *I told you to go (I bade you go)*.
ékkı⌣nóg⌣ɛn⌢ *(s)he says you are to go*.
írgı⌣nógw⌣én⌢ *(s)he says you (pl.) are to go*.
síttı⌣åıgı⌣kår⌣nóg⌣ɛgó⌢ *the lady told me to go to the house*.
tår⌣ɛgóri⌢ *I said 'come'*.
ékkı⌣tår⌣én⌢ and
ékkı⌣tår⌣én⌢ *(s)he says you are to come (is calling you, has sent for you)*.
írgı⌣tåw⌣én⌢ (⌣en⌢) *(s)he says you (pl.) are to come*.
ékkı⌣såmıl⌣sútte⌣tår⌣ɛn⌢ *the sheikh wants you at once* (lit....*says to you 'come quickly'*).
ğóbber⌣ɛgóri⌢ *I said 'have patience' ('wait')*.
ter⌣åıgı⌣ğóbber⌣ɛgó⌢ *(s)he told me to have patience (wait)*.
tır⌣åıgı⌣ğóbber⌣ɛgoran⌢ (⌣ɛgóran⌢) *they told me to wait*.
ɛr⌣tékkı⌣ğóbber⌣ɛgoná? *did you tell him (her) to wait?*
ğúwer⌣ɛgóri⌢ *I said 'go and call (him, her, it, them)'*.
ékkı⌣kítter⌣ɛn⌢ *(s)he says you are to be silent*.
írgı⌣kíttew⌣én⌢ *(s)he says you (pl.) are to be silent*.
aı⌣ékkı⌣sókker⌣ɛgóri⌢ *I told you to take it up* (...*to carry it*, ...*to remove it*, s.v. sókkɛ).
ékkı⌣tóller⌣ɛn⌢ *(s)he says you are to pull (it, them §5083)*.
írgı⌣tóllew⌣én⌢ *(s)he says you (pl.) are to pull (it, them)*.
aı⌣ékkı⌣håsıber⌣ɛgóri⌢ *I told you to reckon*.
aı⌣ékkı⌣fɛttıšér⌣ɛgóri⌢ *I told you to investigate*.
aı⌣ékkı⌣bɛter⌣ɛgóri⌢ *I told you to begin*.
aı⌣ékkı⌣addér⌣ɛgóri⌢ *I told you to finish (it)*.
aı⌣ékkı⌣sabrer⌣ɛri⌢ *I tell you to be patient*.
ékkı⌣fadlér⌣ɛgóri⌢ *I told you to remain behind*.
ékkı⌣nf⌣én⌢ *(s)he says you are to drink (it)*.
írgı⌣nfw⌣én⌢ *(s)he says you (pl.) are to drink (it)*.
aı⌣ékkı⌣nf⌣ɛgóri⌢ *I told you to drink (it)*.

‿ɛ-

ékkı‿gābılēráŋgı‿dóllˏɛ́⌢ (s)he says that (s)he wishes to meet you, lit. (s)he says to you 'I wish to meet'.
aĭ‿nŏrtı‿marıssoddɛ́d‿dóll‿egóri⌢ (-d‿d- < -g‿d- §534) I said I wanted (lit. want) just a little flour.
wɛ́b‿bıšínd͡iegó⌢ (-b‿b- < -g‿b- §519) he said he (she said she) would send one (…someone).
N. ogíčči‿bıšínd‿ekorā⌢ they promised to send the man, lit. …said 'we shall send (‿bıšíndu‿)…'.
ár‿bıtámunun‿eráŋ⌢ they say 'we shall not come', i.e. they say they will not come.
míŋg‿āurı‿ɛ́⌢ (s)he asks what (s)he is to do, lit. (s)he says 'what am I to do?' ((s)he asks for instructions).
mín‿āur‿egó⌢ (s)he asked what (s)he was to do, lit. (s)he said 'how do I act? ((s)he expressed perplexity); mín‿ < míne‿…?
er‿míŋg‿āgáwın‿ɛ̃⌢ (s)he asks what you are doing.
ékkı‿santăg‿gádak‿kállu‿ɛ́⌢ (s)he asks you when we shall (you (pl.)) have lunch, lit. (s)he says to you 'when do we (you, pl.) eat lunch?'.
šerǐf‿ékk‿ɛ́t‿kómbomen‿egó⌢ the Šerǐf (a §1122) asked whether you were well, lit. …said to you 'are you not well?'
ıblískı‿dămunun‿égın, tér‿tắŋ⌢ if you say of the devil that he doesn't exist, he comes.
ter‿éddo‿dıgrīgırbărıkér‿en‿egó⌢ (s)he said 'thank you very much' (s.v. bărıkɛ̆́).
aĭ‿wắran‿éri⌢ and
aĭ‿wăraŋg‿éri⌢ I say no.
íŋgı‿míŋg‿erán? what do they call this (that)?
ékkı‿níg‿eran? what is your name? lit. whom do they call you?
X. tékkı‿níg‿eran? what is his name?
Y. ahmétk‿erán⌢ his name is Aḥmad.
aĭ‿íŋg‿erıá? do I say this?
er‿íŋg‿ená? do you say this?
ter‿íŋg‿ená? does (s)he say this?
ar‿íŋg‿eruá? do we say this?
ır‿íŋg‿eruá? do you (pl.) say this?
tır‿íŋg‿erandé? do they say this?
tır‿íŋg‿erandé? do they say this.
-ɛ- in verb-complexes (§§4009ff.) indicates the intention or attitude of the subject.
-ɛ*g‿ (§4340) postp. = prep. intending; suffixed to obj. case of noun in the infinitive-complex that is the formula for nomina instrumenti (§§5452-5):
kúltıgeb‿bɛ̆ran‿ (-b‿b- < -g‿b- §519) fly-killer.
tíŋcıgeš‿šúgran‿ (-š‿š- < -g‿š- §695) switch for driving cattle.
‿ég‿ (‿égı‿ §5919, ‿égi⌢; ‿eg‿, ‿egı‿, ‿egi⌢; §§4333, 5920-3, 6219ff.) postp. = conj. (a) saying, that, to the effect that; (b) intending, in order that.
aĭgı‿mírkoran, tókkon‿nógmen‿égi⌢ they forbade me to go, lit. they stopped me, saying 'don't go'.
dắgın‿ékkı‿bıtíddi; dăme̦ŋkın‿dámunun‿ébıwĕri⌢ (-b‿b- < -g‿b- §519) if there is one (some) I shall give you it; if there isn't I shall say there isn't.
ar‿sándıru‿gălo‿bıgússın‿égi⌢ (بزج) we are afraid that the water-jar (بزج) will break.
éssı‿ğúgrıd‿dóll‿ánn‿óssıg‿ĕwⁱr‿égi⌢ (-d‿d- < -g‿d- §534) I want some hot water to wash my feet (§4696a).
ár‿maŋ-kámbūr‿éssın‿nír‿égi⌢ (-n‿n- < -g‿n- §625) we are on our way to that house to drink water.
úlud‿dŭlgı‿sókkeruá‿mufettísk‿amíntır‿égi? shall we take the large (piece of) coal to show it to the inspector?
ıškártıg‿geddımér‿én‿nókkori⌢ (-n‿n- < -g‿n- §625) I went (have been) to see the guests off.
— pleonastically with -an say (§5669):
ğawáb‿oŋgárk‿eğğusandūgırúnduran‿ég‿āıgı‿déŋkon⌢ (s)he gave (has given) me both the letters telling me to take them along and put them into the box.
‿ɛ-dǎ- (§§3846, 6140) v.t. suppose, think, believe (= ‿an-dǎ-) [be present saying sc. to oneself].
ind. pres. aĭ‿edárı⌢, er‿edán⌢ (‿edắ⌢, ‿edă⌢; ‿edán⌢, ‿edá⌢, ‿edā⌢ §1933a); fut. aĭ‿ebıdắri⌢ (§§3777, 5610); perf. aĭ‿edágori⌢ (N. -áko-, -áho-).
imperat. ‿éda.
ár‿bıtámunan‿edáru⌢,
ár‿tír‿bıtámunan‿edáru⌢ and
ár‿tírgı‿bıtámunan‿edáru⌢ we think they will not come.
aĭ‿wĕrun‿edágori⌢ I thought that it was (some)one.
ar‿wĕrun‿edágoru⌢ we thought that it was (some)one.
ín‿āıgı‿sándıgırkon: kắgun‿edágori⌢ this (that) frightened me: I thought it was a snake.
kắuırtén‿edáran, lákıŋ‿kắuırte‿dắmunun⌢ (-tén‿ §§1532, 1970) they think it is a (the) bird, but there is no bird.
aĭ‿ambéskı‿kăn-tu-wĕrro‿bŭn‿edári⌢ I think my brother is inside some house (or other).
aĭ‿ambéskı‿kăn-tu-wĕrro‿bŭgon‿edágori⌢ I thought my brother was inside some house.
tér‿íčči‿dăn‿edăn⌢ (s)he (it) thinks there is some milk.
aĭ‿dắn‿ebıdắri⌢ and (§5611)
aĭ‿bı-dắn‿edắri⌢ I shall think that (s)he (it) is present (that there is some).
ég-ır (§3710) v.t. ride, ride on [lit. cause (horse, etc.) to act §3687].
ind. pres. aĭ‿egírri⌢, er‿egırın⌢ (-rí⌢, -rí⌢); fut. aĭ‿begírri⌢; perf. aĭ‿egírkori⌢ (occ. ᵋᵉⁿⁿ, ᵋᵉⁿⁿ).
subj. past aĭ‿egírsı⌢ (-su‿).
def. imperat. eg(ı)rét! (-ré! §965); pl. eg(ı)rédwe! (-édwé!).
hánug‿egírkori⌢ I rode the (a) donkey.
íŋg‿egré! ride this!
égırar‿ (-răr‿; §2200ff.) and
egırǐd‿ (§§2256ff.) n. riding.

égır-an (§§3890, 3904) v.t. tell to ride (on), let ride (on).
álıh‿hánug‿égıran⌢ (-h‿h- < -g‿h- §559) let ɛáli ride the donkey.
ɛg(ı)rɛn-nóg (§4169; -rɛggınóg §4176) v.t. go mounted on, ride off on.
ind. perf. aĭ‿ɛg(ı)rɛnnókkori⌢.
hánu-wĕg‿ɛgrɛnnókkŏ⌢ (s)he rode (has ridden) off on a donkey.
ɛg(ı)rɛt-tǎ́ (§4169; -rɛggıtǎ́ §4176) v.t. come mounted on, ride up on.
ind. perf. aĭ‿ɛg(ı)rɛttágori⌢ (N. -áko-, -áho-).
ɛgír-kattı- (§4093) v.p. be ridden.
ıŋ‿kắğ‿ɛgırkáttımunun⌢ this horse is not (cannot be §5704) ridden.
‿ɛ-wɛ́ (§§3847, 6140) v.t. (a) say; (b) say to, tell, inform; (c) tell, bid, order [‿ɛ-pleonastic; ‿ewéri⌢ I say, saying].
ind. pres. aĭ‿ewɛ́ri⌢; fut. aĭ‿bewɛ́ri⌢ and aĭ‿ebıwĕri⌢ (§§3777, 5609); perf. aĭ‿ewĕgori⌢ (N. -ĕko-, -ĕho-).
imperat. ‿ewĕ!
aĭ‿nóg‿ewĕri⌢ I say 'go!'.
aĭ‿tókkon‿nógmen‿ewĕgori⌢ I said 'don't go!'.
aĭ‿dắn‿ebıwĕri⌢ and (§5611)
aĭ‿bı-dắn‿ewĕri⌢ I shall say that (s)he (it) is present (that there is some).
aĭ‿dắmunun‿ebıwĕri⌢ and
aĭ‿bı-dắmunun‿ewĕri⌢ I shall say that (s)he (it) is absent (that there is none).
éssı‿dămeŋkın‿dắmunun‿ebıwĕri⌢ if there isn't any water I shall say there isn't.
aĭ‿ɛr‿nókkon‿ebıwĕri⌢ and
aĭ‿bɛr-nókkon‿ewĕri⌢ I shall say that you went (have gone).
aĭ‿tır‿nókkoran‿ewĕri⌢ and
aĭ‿bı-tır‿nókkoran‿ewĕri⌢ I shall say that they went (have gone).
er‿aĭ‿nókkori‿bewĕn⌢ and
er‿baĭ-nókkori‿ewĕn⌢ you will say that I went (have gone).
ténnās‿sérēn‿ewĕgó⌢ (-s‿s- < -g‿s- §678) he said to himself (she said to herself) 'good!'; s.v. ắ‿.
aĭ‿ékk‿índo‿tắr‿ewĕgori⌢ I told you to come here.
‿ewĕr-ɛ-dól- (-rᵒd- §1178; §§4016-17, 4022, 4027) v.t. be about to say, etc.
‿ɛ- (‿ɛ- §§1790-1; §§2803, 3500ff., 5509ff.) v.i. be [*exhibit a tendency §213].
aĭ‿erı⌢.
ar‿ırğĕn‿éru⌢ we are rich.
ır‿ırğĕn‿éru⌢ you (pl.) are rich.
tır‿ırğĕn‿éran (‿erā⌢, ‿erá⌢, ‿erán⌢, ‿erắ⌢, ‿erá⌢) they are rich.
aĭ‿índ‿egóri⌢ I was (have been) here.
er‿índ‿egón⌢ (‿egó⌢, ‿egó⌢) you were (have been) here.
ter‿índ‿egón⌢ (‿egó⌢, ‿egó⌢) (s)he (it) was (has been) here.
ar‿índ‿egóru⌢ we were (have been) here.
ır‿índ‿egóru⌢ you (pl.) were (have been) here.
tır‿índ‿egóran⌢ (-rā⌢, ‿egórá⌢) they were (have been) here.
In subordinate clauses the present tense, now subjunctive, is complete.
aĭ‿ırğĕn‿érın‿ıllar‿ because I am rich.

ɛr‿ırğɛn‿ɛnn‿ıllar‿ because you are rich.
tɛr‿ırğɛn‿ɛnn‿ıllar‿ because (s)he is rich.
ar‿ırğɛn‿ɛrun‿ıllar‿ because we are rich.
ır‿ırğɛn‿ɛrun‿ıllar‿ because you (pl.) are rich.
tır‿ırğɛn‿ɛrann‿ıllar‿ because they are rich.
āı‿índ‿ɛ́sı‿wɛkítt(ı)‿ when I was here.
ɛr‿índ‿ɛ́sıw‿wɛkítt(ı)‿ (-w‿w-<-n‿w- §720) when you were here.
tɛr‿índ‿ɛ́sıw‿wɛkítt(ı)‿ when (s)he (it) was here.
ar‿índ‿ɛ́su‿wɛkítt(ı)‿ when we were here.
ır‿índ‿ɛ́su‿wɛkítt(ı)‿ when you (pl.) were here.
tır‿índ‿ɛ́saw‿wɛkítt(ı)‿ when they were here.
ɛ́ss‿oróf ɛl‿ɛ́n‿nírɑn͡ and (§6187)
ɛ́ssıg‿oróf ɛl‿ɛ́n‿nírɑn͡ they drink the water cold (‿ɛ́n‿ provided it be, when it is).
kårɛ‿sıɛ́l‿ɛn‿ɛ́ttagó͡ (s)he (has) brought the fish stinking.
g̊úgr‿ɛ́n‿dóllan͡ they like it hot.
íŋgı‿dóllan‿dúl‿ɛnn‿íllar͡ they want (like) this because it is large.
X. tá! come (here)!
Y. āı‿índ‿ɛ́rı͡ here I am! (me voici!, eccomi!)
ɛ́kkɛn‿índ‿ɛ́gő͡ just now (s)he (it) was here.
fɛğírr‿índo‿gón͡ (§1142) (s)he (it) was here in the morning.
bůšk‿ód‿ɛgón͡ on Monday it (the weather) was cold.
X. álı‿mɛ́n‿tågogon? why had ɣáli come?
Y. tɛ́n‿dőr‿ɛŋgɛ́͡ because it was his turn; ‿ɛ́ŋgɛ́͡ lit. because (-ɛ́͡ s.v. -ɛd‿) it is.
márɛ‿sówwɛd‿ɛ́ŋgɛs‿ɛ́rɛ̄n͡ (-s‿s-<-d‿s- §677) the millet's good because it's dry.
nádd‿ɛ́ŋŋɛm‿móndan͡ (-ŋŋ-<-ŋg-<-ng- §662, -m‿m-<-d‿m- §600) because it is bitter they dislike it.
kúl‿ɛ́ŋŋon‿ulúdkı‿gálıgın͡ (kúl‿<kúlu‿§1122; ‿ɛ́ŋŋon‿<‿ɛ́ŋgon‿ s.v. -on‿) though it is stone it resembles coal.
kåg‿íŋkır‿ɛ́ŋŋon‿dúlú͡ (§939) the snake is like this but larger (§4969).
tɛrōm‿mánd‿ɛ́gım‿mugótta͡ if (s)he (it) is (over) there leave him (her, it) and come.

‿ɛ́- (§§3524-9) v.t. say [app. a variant pronunciation of ‿ɛ́- say; <wɛ́ say RN, §42³].

ɛbbıdá bring, fetch s.v. ɛ́d.

ɛ́bɛdɛn‿ (ɛbɛdɛ́ŋ(ı)‿) ever, never=ábadan‿.

ɛbɛ́tta‿ n. a sort of date=ɛbɛ́ttɛ‿.
 obj. -tag‿.
 pl. -tanč(ı)‿.

ɛbɛttamóda‿ (ıbɛ-, -tɛm-) n. one of the better sorts of date growing in Dóngola, s.v. bɛ́nt(ı)‿; with collective sg. (§4696b).

obj. -dag‿.
pl. -danč(ı)‿.

ɛbɛ́ttɛ‿ (-ta‿) n. one of the better sorts of date growing in Dóngola=barakåwı‿; s.v. bɛ́nt(ı)‿; with collective sg. (§4696b) [cp. K. ɛbɛ́ttɛ‿ clitoris].
 obj. -tɛg‿.
 pl. -tɛnč(ı)‿.

ɛ́bır v.t. stop (check the motion of) [§2837].
 ind. pres. āı‿ɛbírrı͡, ɛr‿ɛ́bırın͡ (-rī͡, -rí͡); perf. āı‿ɛbírkorı͡.
 imperat. ɛ́bır!, pl. ɛbírwɛ! (ɛbírwɛ́!).
hánug‿ɛ́bır͡ stop the donkey.
bābúrk‿ɛbírkoran͡ they (have) stopped the steamer (train).

ɛ́bir-an (§§3890ff.) v.t. tell to stop, let stop.
hánug‿ɛ́bıran͡ let him (her) stop the donkey.

ɛbír-kattı- (§4093) v.p. be stopped.
gátır‿índ‿ɛbırkáttımunun͡ the train is not (to be §5704) stopped here.

√ ɛ́čč- apart, separate [§4513].

ɛ́ččɛ- [a verbal stem in -ɛ (§§2870ff.)=be apart, be alone, be separate, differ; the subj. pres. sg. 3 is stereotyped as an adverb, and the pres. participle is used as an adjective].

ɛ́ččɛn‿ (§§4422, 5961) adv. separately, alone, by oneself, by itself.
ın‿ɛ́ččɛn‿dåbugó͡ (a) this person was (present) by himself (herself); (b) this was (present) by itself (separately).
tɛ́kk‿íŋgı‿tír, íŋgoŋg‿ɛ́ččɛn‿tír͡ (§§1561, 1797) give him (her) this, and give him (her) this (that) separately.
ɛ́ndıg‿ɛ́ččɛn‿ɛ́n‿ıšíŋkorı͡ (§6187) I (have) sent yours separately.

ɛ́ččɛn-ɛ́ččɛn‿ (§4438a) adv. each apart from other, each separately.
ɛ́ččɛnɛ́ččɛn‿tågoran͡ they came each by himself (herself, itself).
kullwahídk‿ɛ́ččɛnɛ́ččɛn‿tɛ́r͡ plant each one by itself.

ɛ́ččɛl‿ adj. different, other; used as indefinite pronoun (§§2680, 5165-6).
 obj. ɛččɛ́lg(ı)‿, -gı͡.
 pl. ɛ́ččɛlı‿.
ın‿ɛ́ččɛlun‿ and (§1967)
ın‿ɛ́ččɛlun͡ this is different (another).
ɛ́ččɛ́l‿lɛ̄d‿dóllan͡ (-l-l-<-l-w- §580, -d-d-<-g‿d- §534) they want a different one.
índo‿dúŋgulam‿bañ ñidk‿uñúrmunan, tím‿báññid‿ɛ́ččɛlun͡ here they do not know the language of Dóngola, their language is different.
— constructed with ‿dógor‿:
ím‿bélɛd‿mánın‿dógor‿ɛ́ččɛlun͡ this country is different from that one.
ɛ́ndın‿dógor‿ɛ́ččɛl-lɛ̄d‿dóllu͡ we want a different one from yours.

ɛ́ččɛln-d(ı)‿ (§§2545ff.) adj. appertaining to (a) different, etc.

ɛ́ččɛl-an- (§3910α) v.i. become different, change, alter.

ɛ́ččɛlg-ır (N. -lkır; §3702) (a) v.t. caus. cause or allow to be or become different, etc.; (b) v.t. render different, change, alter.

ɛ́d v.t. (a) take in marriage, marry; (b, in complex and composition in earlier unspecialized sense) take [verbal specialization of *ɛ*d (§2062); cogn. ɛ́r carry off as plunder (§2775); cp. ON. ɛιτ (ɛτ, ɛττ) take, receive GNT, s.v.; RSN, §129].
 ind. pres. āı‿ɛ́drı͡, ɛr‿ɛ́dın͡ (‿ɛ́dī͡, ‿ɛdí͡); fut. āı‿bɛ́drı͡; perf. āı‿ɛ́dkorı͡ (‿ɛ́tk-).
 imperat. ɛ́t!, pl. ɛ́dwɛ! (ɛ́dwɛ́!).
 subj. past āı‿ɛ́dsı‿ (‿ɛ́tsı‿, ‿ɛ́ssı‿ §688; -su‿).
búrug‿ɛ́tkő͡ he (has) married the (a) girl.
ogíčk‿ɛ́tkő͡ she (has) married the (a) man.
tɛr‿ɛ́tkő͡ (s)he (has) married.
ɛ́m‿búrug‿ɛdílgı‿tír͡ give it to the man that is marrying your daughter.
ɛ́m‿búrug‿ɛdɛ́lgı‿tír͡ give it to the man that married your daughter.

ɛ́dar‿ (ɛ́dår‿; §§2200ff.) and
ɛdíd‿ (§§2256ff.) n. marrying, marriage.

ɛ́rkanɛ‿ (§2296) n. marriage [<*ɛ́*d-kanɛ‿ (§873); ɛ́r- *taking, nominal specialization of *ɛ́*d (§§2062, 873)].
 obj. -nɛg‿.
 pl. -nɛnč(ı)‿.

ɛ́rkanɛ-kől‿ (§§2382, 2486) n. party to a marriage, bridegroom, bride.
 obj. ɛ́rkanɛkólg(ı)‿, -gı͡.
 pl. ɛrkánɛkonı‿.

ɛ́rt(ı)‿ n. mamma, teat, nipple, dug, udder, breast; with collective sg. (§4696a) [<*ɛ́d-t(ı)‿ (§874)<ɛ́d- take+-t dim., or. the little thing that is taken §2325γ].
 obj. ɛ́rtıg‿.
 pl. ɛ́rtınč(ı)‿.
bɛ́ntın‿ɛ́rt(ı)‿ date-bearing stem(s) of palm.

ɛrtín-d(ı)‿ (§§2545ff.) adj. appertaining to the mamma, etc.

ɛ́rt(ı)‿ (a) n. dirt, filth; (b §4719, used as) adj. dirty, filthy, foul, soiled [<*ɛ́d-t(ı)‿ (§874)<ɛ́d- take+-t of n. act., or. taking(s), what is taken, what one gathers, e.g. while working §2325β].
 obj. ɛ́rtıg‿.
 pl. ɛ́rtınč(ı)‿.
án‿ǧísım‿ɛ́rtın͡ I am dirty, lit. my body is dirt.
bıtåw-wɛ̄r‿ɛ́rtın‿nálkorı͡ (-w-w-<-n‿w- §720, -n‿n-<-g‿n- §625) I saw a dirty child.

ɛ́rt-an- (§3910α) v.i. become dirty, etc.

ɛ́rtam-bů- (§§3949ff.) v.i. stat. be in the state or condition of becoming or having become dirty, etc.

ɛrtanɛd-åg- (§3966α) v.i. be in the condition of having become dirty, etc.

ɛ́rtıg-ır (N. -lkır, -ıhır; §3701) (a) v.t. caus. cause or allow to be dirty, etc.; (b) v.t. render dirty, etc., foul, soil.

ɛ́tt(ı)‿ n. bile, gall [<*ɛ́d-t(ı)‿ (§706)<ɛ́d take+t of n. act., or. taking, secretion, then what is secreted §2325β].
 obj. -tıg‿.

ɛttín-d(ı)‿ (§§2545ff.) adj. appertaining to the bile or gall.

ɛ́d-an (§§3890ff.) v.t. tell to marry, let marry.

ɛb-bıdá (§3851) v.t. (a distant object) bring, fetch, (a near object) hand, pass, give [<*ɛd-bıdå (§518) come after taking].

ɛd

ind. pres. āɪ‿ɛbbɪdári⌒; fut. āɪ‿bɛb-bɪdári⌒; perf. āɪ‿ɛbbɪdágori⌒ (N. -áko-, -áho-).
imperat. ɛ́bbɪda! (ˊˊˊ, ˉˊˊ), pl. ɛbbɪ-dáwɛ! (ˉˊˊˊ).
ɛ́ssɪɡ‿ɛbbɪdágoran⌒ *they (have) brought (the) water.*

ɛ́d-bŭ- (ɛ́ddū- §532; §3931β) v.i. stat. *be in a married state or condition, be a married woman.*
āɪ‿ɛ́dbūri⌒ (‿ɛ́ddūri⌒) *I am a married woman.*
ám-bur‿ɛ́ddun⌒ *my daughter is (has been) married.*
ím‿bur‿ɛddúmunun⌒ *(a) this (that) girl is unmarried; (b) your (pl.) daughter is unmarried.*

ɛdɛd-ág- (§3877) v.t. *be in the condition of having married, be a married person,* esp. *a married man.*
āɪ‿ɛdɛdágri⌒ *I am in the condition of having married,* esp. *I am a married man.*
tím‿búrug‿ɛdɛdágɪn⌒ *he has married their daughter.*
ɛr‿ɛdɛdágmɛn⌒? *aren't you married?*
ín‿tód‿ɛdɛdágɪn⌒ *(a) this (that) young man is married; (b) your (pl.) son is married.*
ín‿tód‿ɛdɛdágmunun⌒ (-áŋŋu- §661) *(a) this (that) young man is unmarried; (b) your (pl.) son is unmarried.*
āɪɡon‿ámbɛ́skon‿óɡɪɡ̑‿ɡ̑ɛ́m‿búr‿ówwɪɡ‿ɛdɛdágru; ántɪnod‿áñɪn⌒(-ɡ̑‿ɡ̑-<-ɡ̑‿w- §553, -m‿b- <-n‿b- §592) *I and my brother (are in the position of having) married the two daughters of one man; our father-in-law is alive.*
āɪ‿ɛdɛdāɡríddotōn‿sɛ́na‿tóskɪ-tánnan⌒ (-ríndo- §535) *I have been married for three years,* lit. *it is three years since I am married.*

ɛdk-íddɪ (ɛtk- §3725) v.t. *(a, first object) cause or allow to marry; (b, second object) give in marriage.*
ind. pres. āɪ‿ɛdkíddɪri⌒.
imperat. ɛ́dkɪddɪ!
āɪ‿tékk‿ám‿búruɡ‿ɛdkíddɪɡori⌒ *I gave (have given) him my daughter in marriage,* lit. *I (have) allowed him to marry my daughter.*
āɪ‿ɛ́kk‿ám‿búrub‿bɛdkíddɪri⌒ (-b‿b- <-ɡ‿b- §519) and ám‿búruɡ‿ɛ́kkɪ‿bɛdkíddɪri⌒ *I shall give you my daughter in marriage.*

ɛdos-tɛ́ɡ (ɛdottɛ́ɡ §714; §§4180-4; -osɡɪ-tɛ́ɡ, -ozɡɪ-, -oɡɡɪ- §4185) v.t. *reside after marrying.*
imperat. ɛdóstēk! (-óttēk!, -ósɡɪtēk!, -ózɡɪ-, -óɡɡɪ-).
índ‿ám-buruɡ‿ɛdóttēk⌒ and N. (§1103)
ám-buruɡ‿ɛdōsíndotēk⌒ (§5605) *marry my (our) daughter and live here.*
téddo‿tím‿búruɡ‿ɛdottɛ́kkō⌒ (N. ‿ɛdōttɛ́kkó⌒) *he has settled there after marrying their daughter.*

ɛɡ̑-ɡ̑ŭ (§3853) v.t. *(a) proceed after taking, move (i.) along with, take along, transport, carry, convey, transfer,* and so *(b, a near object) take away, remove* [< *ɛd-ɡ̑ŭ §550].
ind. pres. āɪ‿ɛɡ̑ɡ̑úri⌒, ɛr‿ɛɡ̑ɡ̑ún⌒ (-ɡ̑ú⌒, -ɡ̑ú⌒); fut. āɪ‿bɛɡ̑ɡ̑úri⌒; perf. āɪ‿ɛɡ̑ɡ̑úgori⌒ (N. -úko-, -úho-).
imperat. ɛ́ɡ̑ɡ̑u!, pl. ɛɡ̑ɡ̑úwɛ! (-ɡ̑ŭwɛ́!).
subj. past āɪ‿ɛɡ̑ɡ̑úsɪ‿ (-su‿).
íŋɡ‿ɛɡ̑ɡ̑úriá⌒? *shall I take this (that) along? (...away from here?).*
íŋɡɪ‿méktɛbɪr‿ɛɡ̑ɡ̑úriá⌒? *shall I take this (that) to the office?*
kúrsɪnčɪm‿mákt ābɪrtōm‿bābúrr‿ɛɡ̑ɡ̑úgoran⌒ (-m‿m- <-g‿m- §601,-r‿ɛɡ̑- <-ro‿ɛɡ̑- §1122) *they took (have taken) (the) chairs from the office to the train (steamer).*

ɛ́ɡ̑ɡ̑u-an (-ɡ̑ᵘan, -ɡ̑wan, -ɡ̑an §§3890, 3898, 3905) v.t. *tell to proceed after taking, etc., let proceed after taking, etc.*
hánuɡɛd‿ɛ́ɡ̑ɡ̑wá⌒ *tell him (her) to transport him (her, it) on the (a) donkey.*
álɪm‿márɛh‿hánuɡɛd‿índotōn‿ɛɡ̑-ɡ̑wan⌒ (-m‿m- <-ɡ‿m- §601, -h‿h- <-ɡ‿h- §559) *tell ɣáli to take the millet away from here on the (a) donkey.*
kámɡɛd‿ɛɡ̑ɡ̑úwan⌒ *let them transport him (her, it) on the (by) camel.*

ɛɡ̑-ɡ̑-árk(ɪ) (ɛɡ̑ɡ̑aríkk(ɪ); §4147) v.t. *throw (etc., s.v. árk(ɪ), aríkk(ɪ)) after moving (i.) along with, etc.*
íŋɡ‿ɛɡ̑ɡ̑árki⌒ *take this (that) and throw it away.*

ɛɡ̑ɡ̑árk-an (-aríkk-; §§3890, 3905) v.t. *tell to throw (etc.) after removing, let throw (etc.) after removing.*
íŋɡ‿ɛɡ̑ɡ̑árká⌒ *tell him (her) to take this (that) and throw it away.*

ɛɡ̑ɡ̑ⁿ-awídd(ɪ) (-ɡ̑wawí-, -ɡ̑awí-; §4147) v.t. *spread (etc., s.v. awídd(ɪ)) after moving (i.) along with, etc.*
nɪbítt‿ɛɡ̑ɡ̑awíddi⌒ *take along the (a) mat and spread it out.*

ɛɡ̑-ɡ̑u-bóɡ (§4147) v.t. *pour (etc., s.v. bóɡ) after moving (i.) along with.*
kášš ɪɡ‿ɡumámar‿ɛɡ̑ɡ̑ubóɡran⌒ *they take the rubbish along and pour it into the rubbish-hole.*

ɛɡ̑ɡ̑ubóɡ-an (§§3890, 3905) v.t. *tell to pour (etc.) after moving (i.) along with, let pour (etc.) after moving (i.) along with.*

ɛɡ̑-ɡ̑ŭ-bŭ- (§3854) v.t. stat. *be in a state or condition of motion towards the speaker (-ɡ̑ŭbū-) with (ɛɡ̑- < ɛd-), be on one's way (coming) with, be bringing.*
fānusk‿ɛɡ̑ɡ̑úbun⌒ *(s)he is coming with the (a) lantern.*
X. álɪ‿kándɪɡ‿ɛɡ̑ɡ̑úbuná⌒? *is ɣáli bringing the knife?*
Y. wăran, āssókkɛn⌒ *no, he is taking it away.*

ɛɡ̑ɡ̑ⁿ-ɛ-dól- (-ɡ̑ɛd-, -ɡ̑ᵒd-, -ɡ̑ud-, §§1178, 4022, 4026) and
ɛɡ̑ɡ̑úr-ɛ-dól- (-rᵒd-; §§4027, 4034) v.t. *be about to proceed taking, etc.*

ɛɡ̑ɡ̑ⁿ-ɛ-má- (-ɡ̑ɛmá- §§4036, 4040) and
ɛɡ̑ɡ̑úr-ɛ-má- (§§4041, 4047) v.t. *become unable to proceed after taking, etc.*

ɛɡ̑ɡ̑u-ɡ̑án (-ɡ̑ᵘɡ̑-, -ɡ̑¹ɡ̑- §1199, 4147) v.t. *sell after taking along, etc.*
ind. pres. āɪ‿ɛɡ̑ɡ̑uɡ̑ándi⌒.
íŋɡ‿ɛɡ̑ɡ̑uɡ̑án⌒ *take this (that) (away) and sell it.*

ɛɡ̑ɡ̑u-ɡ̑óm (-ɡ̑ᵘɡ̑-, -ɡ̑¹ɡ̑- §§1199, 4147) v.t. *strike, etc. (s.v. ɡ̑óm) after taking along, etc.*
wílɡɪ‿tɛllɛɡráfk‿ɛɡ̑ɡ̑¹ɡomóskó⌒ *yesterday (s)he (you) took the telegram and went and sent it off.*

ɛɡ̑ɡ̑u-ɡ̑úɡur (§§4147, 3769) v.t. *burn after taking along, etc.*

ɛɡ̑ɡ̑u-kárɡ̑ɪɡɪr (-káɡ̑ɡ̑ɪ-; §4147, 3769) v.t. *after taking along (sc. to court) cause to testify, etc. (s.v. kárɡ̑ɪɡɪr).*
āɪ‿ɛ́kk‿ɛɡ̑ɡ̑ukáɡ̑ɡ̑ɪɡɪddi⌒ *I shall (§5369a) take you along and call you as a witness.*

ɛɡ̑ɡ̑-úndur (-ɡ̑wún-; §§4147, 3769) v.t. *put in after taking along (away).*

ɛɡ̑ɡ̑úndur-an (-ɡ̑wún-; §§3890, 3905) v.t. *tell to put in after taking along (away), let put in after taking along (away).*

ɛɡ̑ɡ̑u-sandūɡɪr-úndur (§5605) v.t. *after taking along (away) put into the (a) box.*
ɡawábk‿ɛɡ̑ɡ̑usandūɡɪrundúrkon⌒ *(s)he took the letter along and put it into the box.*

ɛɡ̑ɡ̑-úskur (-ɡ̑wús-; §§4147, 3769) v.t. *set (down, etc. úskur) after taking along (away).*

ɛɡ̑ɡ̑úskur-an (-ɡwús-; §§3890, 3905) v.t. *tell to set (down, etc.) after taking along (away), let set (down, etc.) after taking along (away).*

ɛɡ̑ɡ̑-uskuros-tá (-ɡ̑wus-; -ottá §714; §§4180-4; -osɡɪtá, -ozɡɪ-, -oɡɡɪ- §4185) v.t. *after taking along (away) and setting (down, etc.) come (back), just (-tá s.v. tá) take away and set (down), etc.*
ɛɡ̑ɡ̑uskurottári⌒ *I'll just take it away and put it down.*
íŋɡ‿ɛɡ̑ɡ̑uskurottá⌒ *take this (that) away, put it down and come back (just take and set this down away from me).*

ɛt-tá *and*

ɛ́t-tă (§3855) v.t. *(a) bring, fetch; (b) bring back, fetch back; (c, a near object) hand, pass, give* [< *ɛd-tá (§706) come after taking].
ind. pres. āɪ‿ɛttári⌒ and ‿ɛttári⌒, ɛr‿ɛttán⌒ (-tă⌒, -tă⌒) and ‿ɛttán⌒ (-tă⌒, -tă⌒, -tă⌒); fut. āɪ‿bɛttári⌒ and ‿béttári⌒; perf. āɪ‿ɛttágori⌒ (N. -áko-, -áho-) and ‿ɛttágori⌒ (N. -ăko-, -ăho-).
imperat. ɛ́tta!, pl. ɛttáwɛ! (ˉˊˊ) and ɛ́ttawɛ! (ˊˊˊ).
subj. past āɪ‿ɛttásɪ‿(-su‿) and ‿ɛttásɪ‿(-su‿).
part. pres. ɛ́ttāl‿ *(one) that brings, etc., bringer, bringing;* obj. ɛttálɡ(ɪ)‿, -ɡi⌒.
part. fut. béttāl‿ *(one) that will bring, etc., bringer, bringing.*
part. past ɛ́ttārɛl‿ *(one) that brought, etc., bringer, bringing;* obj. ɛttārélɡ(ɪ)‿, -ɡi⌒.
pl.-obj. imperat. ɛttárɪr! and ɛ́ttārɪr!; pl. ɛttárɪrwɛ!, -ɪwwɛ!, ˉˊˊˊ and ɛttárírwɛ!, -íwwɛ!, ˊˊˊ.
neg. ind. perf. āɪ‿ɛttáɡomunun⌒ (N. -áko-, -áho-).
neg. imperat. tókkon‿ɛttámɛn! and ...‿ɛttámɛn!; pl. tókkon‿ɛttámɛwwɛ!, ˉˊˊ and ...‿ɛttámɛwwɛ!, ˊˊˊ.

def. perf. aī‿ɛttāróskori⌒.
sáig‿éttari? *which am I to (...shall I §5369b) bring?*
ékkɛnɛ‿béttari⌒ *I shall bring him (her, it, them, some, §5083) now.*
X. (N.) saítti‿nírɛ‿béttā? *who will fetch Sa̧ɣíd?*
Y. kól‿bitån⌒ *he'll come by himself.*
X. íŋgi‿n‿ɛttāgó? (§1125) *who brought this (person, thing)?*
Y. aī‿ɛttāgori⌒ *I did (cp. §5364).*
íŋgi‿ténnartōn‿étta⌒ *bring this (pointing to a receipt-form) back from him (her).*
íŋg‿étta⌒ *hand me that.*
aī‿bústar‿nóggūri, ǧawåbig‿étta⌒ *I am going to the post, (so §6239) give (me) the letters (for it).*
íŋg‿éttāl‿såiré? *where is the bringer of ((s)he that brings) this?*
íŋg‿éttarél‿sé? *where is (s)he that brought this?*
íŋg‿éttarɛl‿nókkoná? *has (s)he that brought this gone?*
ɛttarélgi‿tébaⁿ⌒ *let the one that brought it (them) wait.*
sámil‿ékki‿dúŋg‿énnar‿dålg‿éttar‿ɛ⌒ (‿ɛ̌⌒ < ‿ɛn⌒) *that you are to bring what money you have, lit. ...the money that is (‿dålg‿) with you (‿én-nar‿).*
X. ɛr‿ánn‿illår‿míŋg‿ɛttågon‿ɛ́⌒ *(s)he asks 'what have you brought for me?' (i.e. for him (her) §5107).*
Y. aī‿ɛttågori‿dåmun⌒ (§947) *I haven't brought anything, lit. there is no 'I (have) brought' (§6118).*
ɛttárar‿ (-rår‿; §§2200ff., 2207) and
ɛttāríd‿ (§§2256ff., 2260) *n. bringing, fetching, etc.*
ɛttār-an (§§3890, 3899, 3905) *v.t. tell to bring, etc., let bring, etc.*
éttar-an (§§3890ff.) *v.t. = ɛttār-an.*
ahmétk‿ɛttarándia? *shall I (§5369b) tell Ahmad to bring him (her, it, them)?*
dúŋgig‿éttawan⌒ *let them bring the money.*
ɛtta-båǧ (§4146a) *v.t. write (etc. s.v. båǧ) after bringing.*
índ‿årōr‿ɛttabåč⌒ *bring (it) here and write (it) in (-r‿) the light.*
étta-dɛn (¨¨¨ §§1532, 1557; §4000) *v.t. after bringing (etc.) give (to the speaker), bring to or for (the speaker).*
imperat. **éttadɛn!** (-dɛ̌!, -dɛ̄!, -dɛ́!, -dɛ̌! §945), ¨¨¨.
éssi‿toddɛ̌g‿éttádɛn⌒ *bring me a little water.*
ɛttār-ɛg-åg- (§§4071ff.) *v.t. = ɛttārɛdól-.*
ɛttār-ɛ-dól- (-rᵒd- §1178; §§4016-17, 4022, 4027) *v.t. be about to bring, etc.*
ɛttār-ɛ-må- (§§4016-17, 4036, 4041) *v.t. become unable to bring, etc.*
ɛttār-ɛ-nóg- (§§4048ff.) *v.t. go to fetch.*
ɛttār-ɛ-nóg-bŭ- (-nóggŭ- §546; §4058) *v.t. stat. be going to fetch, be on one's way to fetch.*
ɛttārɛd-åg- (§§3877, 3884) *v.t. be in the position of having brought, etc.*
ar‿íŋgi‿búgartōn‿ɛttaredågru‿ *we have brought this from Omdurmån (we have this that we brought from Omdurmån §3880).*

ɛttāros-tá (-ottā §714; §§4180-4; -osgitå, -ozgi-, -oggi- §4185) *v.t. come after fetching, come bringing.*
ɛttārostår-an (-ottår-, etc., §§3890, 3899, 3905) *v.t. tell to come after fetching, etc., let come after fetching, etc.*
ɛttāros-widɛ (-owwí- §724; §§4180-4; -osgiwí-, -ozgi-, -oggi- §4185; -widé, -wᵘdé) *v.t. go back again after bringing.*
aī‿ɛttarowwidéri⌒ *I'll (§5369b) bring him (her, it, them, §5083) and go back.*
ǧawåbk‿ɛttarowwᵘdégō⌒ *after bringing the letter (s)he went back.*
étta-tɪr (¨¨ §§1532, 1557; §4000) *v.t. after bringing (etc.) give (to other than the speaker), bring (etc.) to or for (other than the speaker).*
éssi‿toddɛ̌g‿éttátɪr⌒ *bring him (her, it) a little water.*
ɛttāgoŋg-ɪr (¨¨¨; N. -ŋkɪr; §3695) *v.t. caus. cause or allow to have brought.*
ind. pres. sg. 1 ‿ɛttāgoŋgiddi⌒ (¨¨¨¨) —only in Bairam formulae, s.v. kórɛ‿.

-ɛd (§§3789ff.) *forms a definitive conjugation.*
In the body of a complex -ɛd- in some instances contributes its primary sense take (§4193):
wɛ́lgi‿šūgonnókkoran⌒ *after driving off the dog they went (away).*
wɛ́lgi‿šūgennókkoran⌒ (-nn- < -dn- §624) *they went (away) driving the dog off with them.*

-ɛd- (-ɛt- §469, -ɛ́⌒ §966; §§4341-4) postp. suffixed to objective case:
(i = prep. §4287) (a, taking as instrument, means) *with, by,* and so (b, method, manner) *by, according to;* (c, price, rate) *for, at;* (d, accompaniment) *together with, cum;* (e, cause or origin) *because of, on account of, out of;* (f, cause or manner, ablative) *by, of, from;* (g, position, locative) *at, on, in;* (h, direction) *to, towards.*
— not used to express the agent (§5706) [stereotyped form of éd *take,* so originally *taking* (λαβών, ἔχων) *as means or instrument, as method, as price or rate, as cause, as companion or accompaniment, as position or direction.*]
— -ɛt⌒, -ɛ́⌒ *may imply predication* (§§5858-60).
(a) kušárkɛk‿kóbbūn⌒ (-k‿k- < -d‿k- §568) *it is locked, lit. it is (has been) shut with (by means of) a key.*
X. íŋgi‿míŋgɛm‿mérri? (-m‿m- < -d‿m- §600) *what shall (§5369b) I cut this with?*
Y. jå‿kándigɛj‿jå‿kɪsŏrkɛ⌒ (-j‿j- < -d‿j- §565) *either with a knife or with scissors.*
márɛk‿kɛ́lagɛd‿åskoran⌒ *they (have) ascertained the amount of millet with a measure.*
ulúkkɛg‿gi̧gɪrkáttimunan, soríŋgɛg‿gi̧gɪr-káttiran⌒ (-g‿g- < -d‿g- §545) *they are not perceived by the ear, they are perceived by the nose.*
(a, b) élim‿ténn‿ɛugɛt‿tógɪn⌒ *the crocodile lashes with its tail.*
túpkɛd‿åggóñrandɛ́? *are they building in brick?*

éssigɛm‿míssɛgō⌒ (-m‿m- < -d‿m- §600) *(s)he (has) sprinkled it with water.*
tɛlɛgráfkɛw‿wɛ́tɪr⌒ (-w‿w- < -d‿w- §718) *inform him (her) by telegram.*
siwíttɛb‿bɛ́kattɪgoran⌒ (-b‿b- < -d‿b- §518) *they fell (lit. were killed) by the sword.*
diárkɛh‿hukmɛ́gon⌒ (-h‿h- < -d‿h- §558) *he (has) sentenced him to (lit. with) death* (حَكَمَ عَلَيْهِ بِالْمَوْتِ).
gɛzázɪk‿kúlugɛš‿šúkkosɪr⌒ (-š‿š- < -d‿š- §694) *wash the bottles out with stones (§4696d), sc. shaking stones and water in them.*
máror‿rahåiɛgɛn‿nórran⌒ (-r‿r- < -g‿r- §669, -n‿n- < -d‿n- §624) *they grind (the) millet in a (the) hand-mill.*
X. sígam‿míŋgɛk‿káččiran? (-m‿m- < -g‿m- §601, -k‿k- < -d‿k- §568) *what do they play sìǧa with?*
Y. jå‿korótkɛd‿jå‿kámlɪn‿túrkɛt⌒ *either with pebbles or with camels' dung.*
sígaw‿wɛ́l‿arrɛkɛmískɛk‿káččiran⌒ (-w‿w- < -g‿w- §719, -k‿k- < -d‿k- §568) *they play sìǧa with 24 pieces.*
X. (N.) úrub‿bumúkkɪran⌒ (-b‿b- < -g‿b- §519) *they will cross the river.*
Y. (N.) níŋ‿kúpkɛt? *in whose boat?*
aī‿káčkɛb‿bi̧gúri⌒ (-b‿b- < -d‿b- §518) *(a) I shall travel on horseback; (b) I shall go for a ride.*
tɛr‿kámgɛt‿tågon⌒ *(s)he (it) came (has come) by camel.*
W. bidågoran⌒ *they have come.*
X. hánugɛ? *(is it) by donkey?*
Y. hánugɛdɪré? *(is it) by donkey?*
Z. hánugɛdó? *(is it) by donkey?*
hánuigɛn‿nogóskoran⌒ (-n‿n- < -d‿n- §624) *they have gone on donkeys.*
ténn‿óssigɛn‿nógɪn⌒ (-n‿n- < -d‿n- §624) *(s)he goes on foot.*
ǧawåpk‿åligɛd‿išíŋkori⌒ *I (have) sent the letter by ɣáli.*
(a, b, c) gíriš‿dimíŋgɛd‿dígbūn⌒ *there is a bet of ten piastres about it; s.v. díg.*
(a, b, f) íččɪk‿kébɛgɛn‿nírran⌒ (-n‿n- < -d‿n- §624) *they drink (the) milk from (lit. taking) the (a) gourd.*
(a, b, g) gɛzázkɪ‿kádɛgɛk‿kattɛddågori⌒ (-k‿k- < -d‿k- §568) *I (have) carried the (a) glass (bottle) wrapped in a cloth.*
(a) íŋgɛm‿mér⌒ (-m‿m- < -d‿m- §600) *(i) cut it (them) with this.*
(f, g) (ii) *cut it (off, out, some) here (there).*
(a, g) íŋgɛk‿kɪnnɛm‿mér⌒ (-k‿k- < -d‿k- §568, -m‿m- < -g‿m- §601) *(i) cut off (out) a little with this; (ii) cut off (out) a little here.*
(b) mám‿båpkɛb‿bélkó⌒ (-b‿b- < -d‿b- §518) *(s)he (it) came (has come, went, has gone) out by that (other) door.*
íŋgɛt‿tómunan⌒ *they do not enter this way (by this entrance).*
ín‿darúpkɛd‿ɛgɛ́ttirɛ́? *is this the nearest way?, lit. by this path is it near?*
án‿dárub‿íŋgɛt⌒,

éd

án⌣dárub⌣íŋgé⌒ and án⌣dárub⌣íŋgedun⌒ *my (our) way is in this direction (by this route), i.e. I (we) go this way.*
X. án⌣dárub⌣íŋgedó? *do I (we) go this way?*
Y. éjj°⌣íŋgé⌒ *yes, this way.*
tín⌣dárub⌣ŋgémmunun⌒ *their way is not this,* lit. ....*not by this.*
W. bɪdágoran⌒ *they have come.*
X. máŋgé? *(by) that way?*
Y. máŋged¹ré? *(by) that way?*
Z. máŋgedó? *(by) that way?*
sâɪget⌣tâgoran? *which way (by what route) did (have) they come?*
âɪ⌣úrdɪget⌣tâgori⌒ *I came (have come) via El-Ordi.*
togógen⌣nók⌒ (-n⌣n- < -d⌣n- §624) *go by the lower path.*
hákkeh⌣hokmégo⌒ (-h⌣h- < -d⌣h- §558) *he (has) decided according to law.*
arabíndɪgeb⌣báññɪran⌒ (-b⌣b- < -d⌣b- §518) *they talk Arabic.*
tím⌣baññídkeb⌣báññɪran⌒ *they speak in their language.*
ter⌣nahâr⌣kolódkeb⌣bunógin⌒ *(s)he (it) will go in (taking) seven days* (...*be seven days on the road*).
éssɪ⌣mâsúrageb⌣bélin⌒ (-b⌣b- < -d⌣b- §518) *the water goes (comes) out by the pipe.*
mâsúran⌣tûgen⌣nókkó⌒ (-ɛn⌣n- < -ed⌣n- §624) *it (has) passed through the pipe.*
álɪǧ⌣ǧawápked⌣ɪšíŋkori⌒ (-ǧ⌣ǧ- < -g⌣ǧ- §551) *I (have) sent ɛáli with the (a) letter.*
híttaged⌣áššugléran⌒ *they are working (habitually work) by the piece.*
táttɪ́ɪ́lliged⌣uñúrkattɪn⌒ *the watch (time on duty) is known by the shadow* (e.g. *the position of the shadow at noon marks the end of the watch*).
wɛrwéged⌣dábran⌒ *one by one they disappear.*
márra⌣wéget⌣tâgoran⌒ *(a) they came all at once (on the same occasion); (b) they came suddenly.*
ambâb⌣tínn⌣ɪged⌣dígon⌒ *my father was killed by them,* lit. ....*died by their hand.*
ánn⌣i⌣kɪníssegeb⌣báričkattɪgó⌒ (-b⌣b- < -d⌣b- §518) *my hand was (has been) scratched by a thorn (my hands were scratched by (the) thorns §4696a, c).*
ɛŋ⌣kéfké⌒ *as you like,* lit. *according to your liking* (كيفك).
(b, f) tâgaged⌣úwe⌒ *call (him, her, them) from (through) the window.*
(b, f, g) ín⌣ǧámbɪgét⌣ta⌒ *come on (by, along) this side.*
(c) íŋgɪ⌣gírɪš⌣tɔ́rtɪgeǧ⌣ǧâŋkori⌒ (-ǧ⌣ǧ- < -d⌣ǧ- §550) *I (have) bought (sold, s.v. ǧán) this (that) for (at) half a piastre.*
X. ínɪn⌣témem⌣mukóttéré? (-m⌣m- < -n⌣m- §604) *what's the price of this?*
Y. gírɪš⌣šéget⌣ta⌒ (-š⌣š- < -š⌣w- §704) *a piastre,* lit. *(it's) at one piastre.*
gírɪš⌣tɔ́rtɪged⌣ (⌣tɔ́rtɪget⌒, ⌣tɔ́rtɪgé⌒) *for (at) half a piastre.*

gírɪš⌣wéged⌣ (N. ⌣wék(k)ed⌣; ⌣wégɛt⌒, ⌣wégé⌒, N. ⌣wék(k)ɛt⌒, ⌣wék(k)é⌒) *for (at) one piastre.*
gírɪš⌣šéged⌣ (-š⌣š-<-š⌣w- §704) (N. ⌣šék(k)ed, šék(k)ɛt⌒, ⌣šék(k)é⌒) *for (at) one piastre.*
gírɪš⌣wɛrɪ⌣tɔ́rtɪged⌣ (etc.) *for (at) a piastre and a half.*
gírɪš⌣ówwɪged⌣ (⌣ówwɪgɛt⌒, ⌣ówwɪgé⌒) *for (at) two piastres.*
gírɪš⌣owwɪ-tɔ́rtɪged⌣ (etc.) *for (at) two piastres and a half.*
gírɪš⌣tɔ́skɪged⌣ (etc.) *for (at) three piastres.*
gírɪš⌣kém(ɪ)sked⌣ (⌣kemísked⌣, kém(ɪ)skɛt⌒, ⌣kém(ɪ)ské⌒, kemískɛt⌒, kemísṕé⌒) *for (at) four piastres.*
gírɪš⌣díǧked⌣ (⌣díǧked⌣, ⌣díčked⌣, ⌣díčked⌣, ⌣díčced⌣, -kɛt⌒, -čet⌒, -ké⌒, -čé⌒) *for (at) five piastres.*
gírɪš⌣goríǧked⌣ (-íǧked⌣, -íčked⌣, etc. like ⌣díǧked⌣) *for (at) six piastres.*
gírɪš⌣kolódked⌣ (⌣kolótked⌣, -ótted⌣, ⌣kolódkɛt⌒, -ótkɛt⌒, -óttɛt⌒, ⌣kolódké⌒, -ótké⌒, -ótté⌒) *for (at) seven piastres.*
gírɪš⌣ɪdíwged⌣ (⌣ɪdíwgɛt⌒, ⌣ɪdíwgé⌒) *for (at) eight piastres.*
gírɪš⌣ɪskódked⌣ (⌣ɪskótked⌣, etc. like ⌣kolódked⌣) *for (at) nine piastres.*
gírɪš⌣dɪmíŋged⌣ (⌣dɪmíŋgɛt⌒, ⌣dɪmíŋgé⌒) *for (at) ten piastres.*
rɪjâl⌣léǧeǧ⌣ǧâŋkori⌒ (-l⌣l- < -l⌣w- §580, -ǧ⌣ǧ- < -d⌣ǧ- §550) *I (have) bought (sold, s.v. ǧán) it for one dollar.*
X. rɪjâl⌣mɪŋkottégeǧ⌣ǧânárkon? *for how many dollars did you ((s)he) buy?*
Y. díččé⌒ *(for) five.*
rɪjâl⌣díčkeǧ⌣ǧântíkkori⌒ *I (have) sold it for five dollars.*
âɪ-on⌣ékk⌣íŋged⌣ám⌣budáet⌣tíkkɪri, âɪ⌣hasrébúri⌒ (-t⌣t- < -g⌣t- §707) *if I give you my goods at that price I shall be (§5369a) a loser.*
(d) mándo⌣ténn⌣éŋged⌣ágɪn⌒ *he lives over there with his wife.*
ténn⌣éssɪ⌣tékkek⌣kaǧǧélgɪ⌣dólin⌒ (-k⌣k- < -d⌣k- §568) *(s)he wants the water it was boiled in,* lit. *(s)he wants its water that got boiled with it;* ténn...kaǧǧélgɪ *a noun-complex* (§4864).
(e) sahâpken⌣nálkattɪmunun⌒ (-n⌣n- < -d⌣n- §624) *it is not (cannot be §5379) seen because of the cloud(s §4696d).*
turúkkeg⌣gɪǧɪrmunun⌒ (-g⌣g- < -d⌣g- §545) *(s)he (it) doesn't (can't §5377) hear on account of (is prevented from hearing by) the wind.*
X. gɪǧɪ́rmunan⌒ *they don't hear.*
Y. turúkké⌒ *it's on account of the wind,* < turúkkɛt⌒.
kúltɪged⌣ɛskɪšuglémunan⌒ *they can't work for (because of) the flies* (§4696c).
mínčɪged⌣dígoran⌒ *they (have) died of hunger.*
ɛssɪnɛ́rked⌣dígoran⌒ *they (have) died of thirst.*
(e, f) ɛskédkɪ⌣ténn-urro⌣weǧádkeb⌣bógɪn⌒ (-b⌣b- < -d⌣b- §518) *(s)he pours

earth on his (her) head for (as a sign of) mourning.*
bérked⌣âuran⌒ *they make it (them) of wood.*
tékked⌣álɪǧ⌣úwe⌒ and álɪǧ⌣úwe⌣tékké⌒ *from there (where you are) call ɛáli.*
(g) wél⌣tén⌣ǧérket⌣túbbɪn⌒ *the dog lies on its back.*
bóččɪged⌣ágran⌒ *they are (sit, live, s.v. ág) outside (out of doors).*
šartɪndɪt⌣togóged⌣úskur, mušemmándɪd⌣dogógek⌣kúǧur⌒ (-t⌣t- < -g⌣t- §707, -d⌣d- < -g⌣d- §534, -k⌣k- < -d⌣k- §568) *put the iron one underneath, put the canvas one on top.*
ar⌣nógrun⌣ogóllo⌣jóm⌣ówwɪget⌣tékkɪ⌣bɪkóbru⌒ *we shall close it (shut him, her, it, up) two days before we go.*
(h) áŋ⌣kóle⌣mârroton⌣íŋgedun⌒ *my (our) water-wheel (irrigable estate) is on this side of the village,* lit. ....*is in this direction from the village.*
kârtōm⌣máŋgen⌣nókkoran⌒ (-n⌣n- < -d⌣n- §624) *they went (have gone) to (by) that (the other) side of the house (beyond) the house.*
— *expressing the sum* (§§5309, 5312):
kɛmískoŋ⌣goríčkon⌣dɪmíŋgé⌒ *4+6=10.*
— *expressing the product* (§5316):
kólod⌣ówwɪ⌣dɪmɪndokemíské⌒ *7 × 2 = 14.*
ówwɪ⌣díǧɪr⌣dɪmíŋgé⌒ *2 × 5 = 10.*
kémɪz⌣górɪǧɪr⌣arrekemíské⌒ *4 × 6 = 24.*
tóskɪ⌣gūtóskɪrbûl⌣ɪskótké⌒ *3 × 3 = 9.*
kémɪz⌣gūkémsɪrbûl⌣dɪmɪndogoríčcé⌒ *4 × 4 = 16.*
tóskɪ⌣gūkólodɪrbûl⌣arrewégé⌒ *3 × 7 = 21.*
— *expressing the divisor* (§5322):
dɪmíŋg⌣ówwɪgeb⌣bagíttegɪrɪ⌣díǧ⌣díčké⌒ (-b⌣b- < -d⌣b- §518) *10 ÷ 2 = 5.*
— *expressing the quotient* (§5326γ):
ɪdíwg⌣ówwɪr⌣bagíttegɪŋ⌣kɛmɪské⌒ *8 ÷ 2 = 4.*

-ɛd (-ɛt, -é⌒) *postp.* (ii, =*conj.* §§4287, 4344) *because.*
— *suffixed to objective form of subjunctive* (§§2943, 2953, 6203-5):
sándɪŋged⌣íǧn⌣áttɪr⌣tégɪn⌒ *because (s)he is afraid (s)he sits by the fire (light).*
íŋgɪ⌣kállɪ⌣tékkɪ⌣dóllɪgɛt⌒ *I eat this because I like it.*
âɪ⌣tékkɪ⌣dólsɪgek⌣kálkori⌒ (-k⌣k- < -d⌣k- §568) *I ate (have eaten) it because I liked (wanted) it.*
wílgɪ⌣dabɛdólkoru⌣ɪ́gkɪ⌣nálmɛnsugé⌒ *yesterday we were nearly lost because we didn't see the light (fire).*
X. álɪ⌣fâtnad⌣dólná? (-d⌣d- < -g⌣d- §534) *does ɛáli like Fâtima?*
Y. wâram⌣mɪšíndɪl⌣éŋged⌣dólmunun⌒ *no, he doesn't like her because she is ugly.*
X. ín⌣séren; mán⌣súgɪrtom⌣míll⌣egó⌒ *this is good; that (other) from the market was bad.*
Y. gedím⌣éŋgé⌒ *because it was* (lit. *is*) *stale.*

orófɛl⌣éŋgem⌣múgran⌢ (-m⌣m- < -d⌣m- §600) *they leave it because it is cold.*
ám⌣béledır⌣ténn⌣íg⌣dúlanın⌣árıs⌣ séréŋgɛt⌢ (-s⌣s- < -d⌣s- §677) *in my (our) country its blossom gets large because the soil is good.*
[-ɛ⌢ is the last element in íŋké⌢, máŋké⌢, tékké⌢ (s.v. tér⌣) *thus*.]

⌣ɛ-dắ- v.t. *suppose (that)*, etc., s.v. ⌣é- *say*.
édd(ı)⌣ n. *hyaena*, H. striata; with collective sg. (§4696d) [§2232; *RSN*, §129 s.v. *adi* cps. Eg. ḫt-t, Copt. ϩⲟⲉⲓⲧⲉ id.].
 obj. -dıg⌣.
 pl. -dınč(ı)⌣.
éddo⌣ *on* (etc.) *you*, s.v. -r⌣.
ɛddór adv. (a) *perhaps, possibly*; (b) *probably, I think* [< Sudan Ar. أَنْدُور id. *HSA* s.v. *think*].
 ɛddór⌣bélli, ɛddór⌣bımısírri⌢ *perhaps I shall find him (her, it, some), perhaps I shan't.*
 X. éssı⌣dăná? *is there water?*
 Y. uñúrmunun, ɛddór⌣dắ, ɛddór⌣dắmunun⌢ *I don't know: perhaps there is, perhaps there isn't.*
 ɛddór⌣wăran⌣dógor⌣éjjon⌣ɛgéttín⌢ *ɛddór is nearer to yes than to no.*
 X. gíríš⌣mukottɛ́r⌣ɛgón? *how many piastres (§4696d) were they?*
 Y. ɛddór⌣kéms⌣ɛgón⌢ *I think they were four.*
 X. ɛsmăn⌣ısáır⌣dắ? *where is ϩⲟθⲙắⲛ?*
 Y. ɛddór⌣máktáb⌣áŋkŏ⌢ *I believe he's gone to the office.*
éddŭ- < édhŭ- *he married*, s.v. éd.
ɛféndı⌣ n. *gentleman, official, officer (not said of Europeans)* [< أَفَنْدِي < αὐθέντης = δεσπότης].
 obj. ɛféndıg⌣.
 pl. ɛfendínč(ı)⌣.
ɛgéčče (§3849) v.i. *lie supine, lie on the back* [< ɛǧékke id. §901b].
 ind. pres. âı⌣ɛgéččɛri⌢; perf. âı⌣ɛgéččɛgori⌢ (N. -ɛko-, -ɛho-).
 árıdır⌣ɛgéčče⌢ *lie on your back on the ground.* (árıdır⌣ defines the homophone.)
ɛgéččɛrar (-rár⌣; §§2200ff., 2210) and
ɛgéččɛríd (§§2256ff., 2263) n. *lying supine.*
ɛgéččɛg-ır (N. -ɛkır, -ɛhır; §3679) (a) v.t. caus. *cause or allow to lie supine*, etc.; (b) v.t. *lay supine.*
 âı⌣tékk⌣árıdır⌣ɛgéččɛgıddi⌢ *I lay him (her, it) on his (her, its) back on the ground.*
ɛgéččɛgır-úskur (§4135) v.t. *lay supine*—serves to define the homophone ɛgéččɛgır.
 âı⌣tékk⌣ɛgéččɛgıruskúddi⌢ *I lay him (her, it) on his (her, its) back.*
ɛgéčče-túrb(ı) (-túbb(ı); §3747ɛ′) v.i. *lie supine,* etc.; defines the homophone ɛgéčče.
 árıdır⌣ɛgéččɛtúbbi⌢ *lie on your back on the ground.*
ɛgéčče-turbır-ɛg-ǎg- (-tubbır-; §§4071ff.) v.i. *be about to lie supine,* etc.
ɛgéččɛr-an (§§3890ff., 3899) v.t. *tell to lie supine, let lie supine,* etc.

ɛgéčče-bŭ- (§3931α) v.i. stat. *be in a supine condition.*
 tɛr⌣ǧérkɛd⌣ɛgéččɛbŭn⌢ *(s)he (it) is lying supine.* (⌣ǧérkɛd⌣ *on his (her, its) back* defines the homophone.)
ɛgéčče v.i. *ascend, come up, go up* [a specialized use of ɛgéčče *lie supine* §3850].
 ind. pres. âı⌣ɛgéččɛri⌢, ɛr⌣ɛgéččɛn⌢ (čě⌢, -čé⌢); fut. âı⌣bɛgéččɛri⌢; perf. âı⌣ɛgéččɛgori⌢ (N. -ɛko-, -ɛho-).
 def. perf. âı⌣ɛgɛččóskori⌢.
 tɛr⌣béntır⌣bɛgéččɛn⌢ *he (it) will climb up the date-palm.*
ɛgéččɛrar (-rár⌣; §§2200ff., 2210) and
ɛgéččɛríd (§§2256ff., 2263) n. *ascent.*
ɛgéčče-kátt(ı) (N. -ɛhá-; §§2534-5) adj. *given to ascending,* etc.
 obj. -tıg⌣.
 pl. -tınč(ı)⌣.
 sáb⌣ɛgéččɛkáttın⌢ *the cat is a climber.*
 kág⌣ɛgéččɛkáttın⌢ *the snake is (snakes are) given to climbing.*
 kág⌣ɛgéččɛkáttınčí⌢ (§§1122, 939) *(the) snakes are given to climbing.*
ɛgéččɛr-an (§§3890ff., 3899) v.t. *tell to ascend, etc., let ascend,* etc.
ɛgéčče-bŭ- (§3931α) v.i. stat. *be in an ascending state or condition.*
 bıtám⌣béntır⌣ɛgéččɛbŭn⌢ *the boy is on his way up the date-palm.*
ɛgéčče-dárr(ı) (§3747ɛ′) v.i. *ascend,* etc. defines the homophone ɛgéčče.
ɛgéččɛr-ɛg-ǎg- (§§4071ff.) v.i. = ɛgéččɛrɛdól-.
ɛgéččɛr-ɛ-dól- (-rᵒd- §1178; §§4016-17, 4022, 4027) v.i. *be about to ascend,* etc.
ɛgéččɛr-ɛ-má- (§§4016-17, 4036, 4041) v.i. *become unable to ascend,* etc.
ɛgéččɛd-ǎg- (§3877ff.) v.i. *be in the situation of having ascended,* etc.
ɛgéččɛg-ır (N. -ɛkır, -ɛhır; §3679) (a) v.t. caus. *cause or allow to ascend,* etc.; (b) v.t. *send up.*
 âı⌣tékkı⌣béntır⌣ɛgéččɛgıddi⌢ *I send him up the date-palm.*
ɛ́gɛd n. *sheep*; with collective sg. (§4696d) [*RSN*, §129].
 obj. ɛgédk(ı)⌣, -étk(ı)⌣, -étt(ı)⌣ (§2462), -kı⌣, -tı⌢.
 gen. ɛgédn⌣v., ɛgénn⌣v.c., ɛgén⌣c. (§2472).
 pl. ɛgɛdu⌣.
 ɛ́gɛd⌣kárr(ı)⌣ (§1691) *ewe.*
 ɛgén⌣dílt(ı)⌣ *sheep's fleece.*
 ɛgén⌣hóss(ı)⌣ and
 ɛgén⌣kálle⌣ *sheep's droppings.*
 ɛgén⌣kúsu⌣ *mutton.*
 ɛgén⌣témɛn⌣ *the price of a (the) sheep.*
ɛgen-tŏd (§2366) n. *lamb*; with collective sg. (§4696d).
 obj. -tŏdk(ı)⌣, -tŏtk(ı)⌣, -tŏkk(ı)⌣, -tŏtt(ı)⌣ (§2462), -kı⌣, -tı⌢.
 gen. -tŏdn⌣v., -tŏnn⌣v.c., -tŏn⌣c. (§§778-88).
 pl. ɛgéntonı⌣.
 ɛgentŏdun⌢ *it's a (the) lamb.*
ɛgét-tod (§2369) n. (a) *rather poor sheep*; (b) = ɛ́gɛd.
 voc. ɛgéttot!, ɛgéttŏ!
 obj. ɛgéttŏdk(ı)⌣, -tŏtk(ı)⌣, -tŏkk(ı)⌣, -tŏtt(ı)⌣, -kı⌣, -tı⌢.
 gen. ɛgéttŏdn⌣v., -tŏnn⌣v.c., -tŏn⌣c.

 pl. ɛgéttonı⌣.
 ɛgéttŏdun⌢ *it's a (rather poor) sheep.*
ɛgédn-d(ı)⌣ and
ɛgén-d(ı)⌣ (§§2545ff.) adj. *appertaining to the (a) sheep, of the (a) sheep, (the, a) sheep's.*
 kús⌣ɛgénd(ı)⌣ *mutton.*
ɛgedín-d(ı)⌣ (§§2545ff.) adj. *appertaining to (the) sheep, of (the) sheep, (the) sheep's.*
ɛgédndı-kırı⌣ (ɛgén-; §2541) adj. *like the (a) sheep's.*
 tén⌣dílt⌣ɛgéndıkırın⌢ *its coat is like a sheep's.*
ɛgedíndı-kırı⌣ (§2541) adj. *like (the) sheep's.*
 tín⌣dílt⌣ɛgedíndıkırın⌢ *their coats are like sheep's.*
ɛgétt(ı)⌣ (a) n. *nearness (in space or time), propinquity, vicinity*; (b, §4720, used as predicative) adj. *near* [< *ɛgédt(ı)⌣ < √ɛ́gɛd *near (§4515) + -t §2326].
 obj. -tıg⌣.
 pl. -tınč(ı)⌣.
 âı⌣ɛgéttɛri⌢ *I am (too) near, propinquus sum.*
 tɛr⌣ɛgéttın⌢ (-tí⌢, -tí⌢) *(s)he (it) is (too) near.*
 tır⌣ɛgéttınčín⌢ (-čí⌢, -čí⌢) *they are (too) near.*
 ín⌣ɛgéttımunun⌢ *this (that) is not near (enough).*
ɛgétti-r (§6007) adv. *near, (of time) soon.*
 ɛgéttın⌢ *(s)he (it) is (they are) near.*
 âı⌣ɛgéttın⌢ *I am near, prope sum.*
 ambáb⌣ɛgéttır⌣ágın⌢ *my father sits (lives) near.*
 tɛr⌣ɛgéttır⌣bŭn⌢ *(s)he (it) lies near.*
⌣ɛgéttır (§§5860, 5899) postp. (= prep. §4287) *near*—follows the genitive (§4364).
 kán⌣ɛgéttır⌣ *near the (a) house.*
 énn⌣ɛgéttır⌢ *(s)he (it) is (they are) near you.*
ɛgettín-d(ı)⌣ (§§2545ff.) adj. *near, nearer.*
ɛgétt-an- (§3910α) v.i. *become near(er), get near(er), approach.*
 índotŏn⌣ɛgettanóskó⌢ *(s)he (it) has got near here (has come close to this place).*
 árun⌣tăríd⌣ɛgettanóskó⌢ *the advent of the rain(s) has approached.*
ɛgéttam-bŭ- (§§3949ff.) v.i. stat. *be in an approaching state or condition.*
ɛgettanɛd-ǎg- (§3965ff.) v.i. *be in the situation of having become near(er),* etc.
ɛgettan-nóg (§§3973, 4150) v.i. *go near(er).*
 imperat. ɛgettannók!
ɛgettan-tắ (§4150) v.i. *come near(er).*
ɛgettır-bŭ (§§3947-8, 1931) v.i. *lie near, be near.*
 ind. pres. âı⌣ɛgettırbúri⌢.
 imperat. ɛgettırbu!, ɛgéttırbu!
ɛgéttıg-ır (N. -ıkır, -ıhır; §3697) (a) v.t. caus. *cause or allow to be near or soon*; (b) v.t. *take near, bring near.*
 ind. pres. âı⌣ɛgéttıgıddi⌢, ɛr⌣ɛgéttıgırın⌢ (-rí⌢, -rí⌢).
ɛgettıgır-áu (N. -ıkır, -ıhır-; §4136) v.t. *do (etc. s.v. áu) near or soon.*
 ar⌣ɛgettıgırbáuru⌢ and (§5570)
 ar⌣ɛgettıgırgı⌣báuru⌢ *we shall (a) make it near*; *(b) do it soon.*

εgettıgır-úskur (N. -ıkır-, -ıhır-; §4141) v.t. set (etc. s.v. úskur) near.
  ind. pres. āɩ‿εgettıgıruskúddıⁿ, εr‿εgettεgıruskurınⁿ (-rīⁿ, -ríⁿ).
εgétt(ɩ)‿ sheep (obj.), s.v. εgεd‿.
εgiⁿ that, in order that, s.v. ‿έ- say.
égır v.t. ride, ride on, s.v. ‿έ- say.
εğέkkε v.i. lie supine, lie on the back [<*ε-ğέrk-έ (§§571b, 2039) be on the back §3848] (understood, but apparently being superseded by εgέččε id.).
  ind. pres. āɩ‿εğέkkεrıⁿ; perf. āɩ‿εğέkkεgorıⁿ (N. -εko-, -εho-).
εğέkkε v.i. ascend, come up, go up [a specialized use of εğέkkε lie supine §3850] (understood, but apparently being superseded by εgέččε id.).
  ind. pres. āɩ‿εğέkkεrıⁿ; perf. āɩ‿εğέkkεgorıⁿ (N. -εko-, -εho-).
εğğú proceed after taking, s.v. έd.
εğğwåd‿ n. umpire, peacemaker, reconciler [<√εğğ- different (§4516) + √wá*d separation (§4604); -á- > -å- through stress (§1069); -d‿ nominal specialization of -*d (§2061); so *separator of disputants].
  obj. -ådk(ɩ)‿, -åtk(ɩ)‿, -ått(ɩ)‿ §2462, -kiⁿ, -tiⁿ.
  pl. -ådɩ‿.
  εğğwåd-dēg‿έttaⁿ (-d-d- < -d-w- §533) bring an umpire.
  εğğwådɩ‿tågoram‿bēwırídd‿έgiⁿ peacemakers came (have come) to reconcile them (§6222).
έjjε‿ n. neck, = gúmur [RBW, s.v. ê].
  obj. -jεg‿.
  pl. -jεnč(ɩ)‿.
έjjoⁿ (έjjo‿, -jº‿v., -j‿v.; §4488) apocritic sentence-word yes [?contains ‿έ- be].
  έjjo‿εnⁿ (έjjo‿εⁿ, έjjo‿έⁿ §939) (s)he says 'yes'.
  X. uñúmmεnⁿ (§3119) don't you know? Y. έjjoⁿ yes, I do (= uñúddiⁿ). (Not used like Amh. አዎን yes. X. አታውቅም፧ don't you know? Y. አዎን no (= አላውቅም።).)
έkkεd‿ excreta, s.v. έkk(ɩ) urinate, etc.
έkkεnε‿ now, s.v. έr‿.
έkk(ɩ)‿ you (obj.), s.v. έr‿.
έkk(ɩ) (a) v.i. evacuate the bladder, urinate; (b) v.t. evacuate from the bladder; (c) v.i. and t. defecate = úss(ɩ).
  ind. pres. āɩ‿έkkɩrıⁿ; perf. āɩ‿έkkɩgorıⁿ (N. -ɩko-, -ɩho-).
  āɩ‿gεug‿εkkóskorıⁿ I have passed blood from my bladder.
έkkεd‿ n. excreta (human and animal) (a) urine; (b) faeces, dung. With collective sg. (§4696d) [§2242β].
  obj. εkkέdk(ɩ)‿, -έtk(ɩ)‿, -έtt(ɩ)‿ (§2462), -kiⁿ, -tiⁿ.
  gen. έkkεdn‿v., -εnn‿v.c., -εn‿c. (§2472).
  pl. έkkεdɩ‿.
  έkkεdn‿έss(ɩ)‿ urine.
  ádεmn‿έkkεd‿ human excreta (of one person).
  ádεmın‿έkkεd‿ human excreta (of more than one person).
  bέrtın‿έkkεd‿ goat's excreta.
  hánun‿έkkεd‿ donkey's excreta.

έkkar‿ (-kår‿; §§2200ff.) and
έkkíd‿ (§§2256ff.) n. urination, defecation.
εkkır-ε-nóg (§4048) v.i. go to evacuate the bladder, etc.
  ind. pres. āɩ‿εkkɩrεnógrıⁿ.
εkkır-ε-nóg-bŭ- (-nóggŭ- §546; §4058) v.i. stat. be on one's way (going) to evacuate the bladder, etc.
εkkεd-ág- (§§3877ff.) v.i. and t. be in the condition of having evacuated the bladder, etc.
εkkíŋg-ır (´⁔; N. -ŋkɩr; §3688) v.t. caus. cause or allow to evacuate the bladder, etc.
έl v.t. (a) find; (b) obtain, get [cp. ON. ελ id. GNT, s.v.].
  ind. pres. āɩ‿έllıⁿ, εr‿έlıⁿ (έlīⁿ, έliⁿ); fut. āɩ‿bέllıⁿ (‿bᵘέllıⁿ); perf. āɩ‿έlkoriⁿ.
  subj. past āɩ‿έlsɩⁿ (-su‿).
  def. perf. āɩ‿έlóskoriⁿ.
  εr‿dúŋgıg‿έlkoná? did you find (etc., have you found, etc.) the money?
έlar‿ (έlår‿; §§2200ff.) and
έlid‿ (§§2256ff.) n. finding, etc.
  tέnn‿εlar‿dúllonⁿ (s)he (it) is difficult to find.
εl-ε-må- (§4036) and
εll-ε-må- (§4041) v.t. become unable to find, etc.
έl-kattɩ- (§4093) v.p. be found, etc.
  tεr‿εlkáttɩmununⁿ (s)he (it) cannot (§5704) be found.
έlos-bέ (-obbέ §521; §§4180-4; -osgɩbέ, -ozgɩ-, -oggɩ- §4185) v.t. kill on finding.
  āɩ‿ánn‿ádug‿εlobbērόskoriⁿ (RN, §167) as soon as I found my enemy I killed him.
έlbå‿ (-bε‿) small receptacle = ílbε‿.
  obj. έlbåg‿, -bεg‿.
  pl. έlbånč(ɩ)‿, -bεn-.
έlbɩl‿ n. toothless rake, leveller (for levelling and smoothing plots for irrigation; smaller than wåsu; SNK, 376⁶⁷; > Sudan Ar. البل id.) [§2279; cp. erbi D. ebnen AZN, s.v.].
  obj. εlbílg(ɩ)‿.
  pl. έlbɩlɩ‿.
έlεw (έlεu) v.t. rinse, wash out.
  ind. pres. āɩ‿εlέw(ˡ)riⁿ (εlέuriⁿ), εr‿έlεwınⁿ (-wīⁿ, -wíⁿ); perf. āɩ‿εlέwkoriⁿ.
  imperat. έlεw!, έlεu!
  tíštɩb‿bεlέuriⁿ (-b‿b- < -g‿b- §519) I'll rinse the basin.
  sahåŋgon‿εlέuriá? shall (§5369b) I rinse the plate?
  ğεrdέlg‿εlέwosⁿ rinse out the bucket.
έlgon‿ (όlgon‿ q.v.; -gonⁿ, -gõⁿ, -góⁿ §939) adv. (a) yet, still; (b) not yet (so سَّ, Amh. ገና ነው።) [stereotype of έl-gon‿ (§5730) lit. and one finds (§4473); so ON. ελ-on καὶ νῦν GNT, s.v. ελ].
  nokkómunan, έlgon‿índ‿ågranⁿ they didn't go (haven't gone), they are still here [lit. they didn't go, and one finds they are here].
  έlgow‿wárrınčınⁿ (-w‿w- < -n‿w- §720) they are still far off.

  έlgon‿bεlkómunanⁿ they haven't gone (come) out yet.
  X. bústa‿tågona? has the post come?
  Y. έlgónunⁿ (§1966) not yet.
— **έlgon‿** preceding the negative subjunctive (§6198), that may be followed by ‿kóttıg‿= before (antequam, priusquam) with positive verb:
  εr‿έlgon‿nálmεnın, tír‿nálkoranⁿ they saw (him, her, it, them) before you did, lit. before you see they saw.
  εr‿έlgon‿nálkomεnın, tír‿nálkógoranⁿ before you saw (him, her, it, them) they had seen (him, her, it, them).
  āɩ‿έlgon‿ğúmεndɩ‿tέr‿dɩgírkóⁿ and āɩ‿έlgon‿ğúmεndɩ‿kόttɩt‿tέr‿dɩgírkóⁿ (-t‿t- < -g‿t- §707) (s)he (it) fell down before I went.
  āɩ‿έlgon‿nálmεndɩ‿dabóskoranⁿ and āɩ‿έlgon‿nálmεndɩ‿kόttɩd‿dabóskoranⁿ (-d‿d- < -g‿d- §534) before I saw (could see them) they had (§3806) disappeared.
— **έlgon‿** preceding the negative subjunctive verb-concretion (§5744) = before with positive verb:
  āɩ‿έlgon‿árkımεŋgon‿έkkɩ‿bamíntırıⁿ before I throw it (them) away I shall show it (them) to you.
έlıf‿ card. num. thousand [< ألف id. §1359].
  obj. εlífk(ɩ)‿, έlıfk(ɩ)‿ (§1522), -kiⁿ.
  pl. έl(ɩ)fɩ‿.
εlif-kırɩ (-kírɩ‿; §§2539-40, 2736) num. adj. about a thousand.
έlım‿ (έlum‿) n. crocodile [RSN, §129].
  obj. εlímg(ɩ)‿ (εlúmg(ɩ)‿, -giⁿ.
  pl. έl(ɩ)mɩ‿ (έlumɩ‿).
εlım-d(ɩ)‿ (εlúmd(ɩ)‿; §§2545ff.) adj. appertaining to the (a) crocodile, (the, a) crocodile's.
εlwíl‿ n. stay, thin rope, in water-wheel (kóle‿); εlwílɩ‿ extend from horizontal axle (tόrε‿) to shoreward ends of transverse limbs (fåšεnč(ɩ)‿) of spokes of wheel raising water (átt(ɩ)‿).
  obj. -flg(ɩ)‿, -giⁿ.
  pl. -flɩ‿.
έmkın‿ adv. perhaps [app. < يُمْكِن = يَمْكِن id.].
έn‿ of you, your gen. of εr‿.
-έn‿ (§2375) n. mother [RSN, §129].
  obj. -έŋg(ɩ)‿, -giⁿ.
  gen. -έnn‿v., -έn‿c.
  pl. -έnɩ‿.
  pl. obj. -έnɩg‿.
  Always with a form of the possessive personal pronoun (§2626) prefixed, thus: (anέn‿ my mother is M. = D. índ(ɩ)‿, q.v.).
  ɩnέn‿ your mother.
  tınέn‿ his (her, its) mother.
  antınέn‿ our mother.
  ɩntɩnέn‿ your (pl.) mother.
  tıntınέn‿ their mother.
  tınέn‿såɩrέ? where is his (her, its) mother?
-έn-d(ɩ)‿ (§§2545ff.) adj. appertaining to the mother, mother's.
  dúŋg‿ɩnέnd(ɩ)‿ your mother's money.
  dúŋgɩ‿tınέnd(ɩ)‿ his (her) mother's money.
  bɩtán‿tɩnέndɩk‿kalεdólɩnⁿ the child's just going to eat its mother's (food).

-ếŋ-kɛgɩd‿ (-ɛ́nk- §2378) n. *maternal aunt, mother's sister* [< -ɛ́ŋ-k- app. older adverbial case of -ɛ́n‿ + √ɛgɩd *near (§4515)].
  obj. -ēŋkɛgídk(ɩ)‿, -ítk(ɩ)‿, -ítt(ɩ)‿ (§2462), -kiꓥ, -tiꓥ.
  pl. -ếŋkɛgɪdɩ‿.
Always with a form of the possessive personal pronoun (§2626) prefixed:
  ɩnḗŋkɛgɪd‿ *your maternal aunt.*
  tɩnḗŋkɛgɪd‿ *his (her) maternal aunt.*
  antɩnḗŋkɛgɪd‿ *our maternal aunt.*
  ɩntɩnḗŋkɛgɪd‿ *your (pl.) maternal aunt.*
  tɩntɩnḗŋkɛgɪd‿ *their maternal aunt.*
-ếŋkɛgím-buru‿ (-ếŋkɛgímbúru‿ §1532) n. and as noun-complex (§4812)
-ếŋkɛgɪm‿búru‿ *mother's sister's daughter, cousin.*
  obj. -burug‿.
  pl. -buru‿.
Always with a form of the possessive personal pronoun (§2626) prefixed:
  ɩnēŋkɛgímburu‿ (‿ ‿ ‿́ ‿̀) and ɩnḗŋkɛgɪm‿búru‿ *your mother's sister's daughter.*
  tɩnēŋkɛgímburu‿ (‿ ‿ ‿́ ‿̀) and tɩnḗŋkɛgɪm‿búru‿ *his (her) mother's sister's daughter,* etc.
-ếŋkɛgɪn-tŏ́d‿ n. and as noun-complex (§4812)
-ếŋkɛgɪn‿tŏ́d‿ *mother's sister's son, cousin.*
  voc. -tŏ́t!, -tó!
  obj. -tŏ́dk(ɩ)‿, -tŏ́tk(ɩ)‿, -tŏ́kk(ɩ)‿, -tŏ́tt(ɩ)‿ (§2462); -kiꓥ, -tiꓥ.
  gen. -tŏ́dn‿v., -tŏ́nn‿v.c., -tŏ́n‿c. (§§778–88).
  pl. -ếŋkɛgíntonɩ‿.
Always with a form of the possessive personal pronoun (§2626) prefixed:
  ɩnḗŋkɛgɪntŏd‿ and ɩnḗŋkɛgɪn‿tŏ́d‿ *your mother's sister's son.*
  tɩnḗŋkɛgɪntŏd‿ and tɩnḗŋkɛgɪn‿tŏ́d‿ *his (her) mother's sister's son,* etc.
ɛ́n‿ (§956d) n. (a) *woman*; (b) *wife*; in this sense often atonic (§§1663–6).
  obj. ɛ́ŋg(ɩ)‿, -giꓥ.
  gen. ɛ́nn‿v., ɛ́n‿c.
  pl. ɛnč(ɩ)‿ (§2432).
  ɛ́n‿kémɩz‿dăn‿ꓥ and ɛ́ŋ‿kémɩz‿dăn‿ꓥ *there are four women.*
  ɛ́nč‿índončɩn‿ꓥ *the women are here.*
  ɛ́nč‿índončɛ́goran‿ꓥ *the women were here.*
  ín‿ɛ́n‿ (ɩn‿ɛ́n‿ §1721) *this (that near) woman.*
  ánn‿ɛ́n‿ (§§1664, 4844) and ann‿ɛ́n‿ (§1665), but usually án-ɛ́n‿ (§2374) *my wife.*
  ɛ́nnēn‿ *your wife.*
  ténnēn‿sɛ́? and ténnēn‿sáirɛ́? *where is his wife?*
  ánn-ɛ́n‿tɩmbésun‿ (ánn‿ɛ́n‿, ann‿ɛ́n‿) *he's my wife's brother.*
  ánn-ɛ̄n‿tɩnɛ́n‿ *my wife's mother* (= án-nogo‿, s.v. -ogo‿).
  ánn-ɛ̄n‿tínnɛs(ɩ)‿ *my wife's sister.*
  ánn-ɛ̄n‿ír‿tír‿ꓥ *give it into my wife's hand(s §4696a).*
ɛ́n-d(ɩ)‿ (§§2545ff.) adj. *appertaining to the (a) woman, etc., (the, a) woman's, etc.*
  íŋ‿kád‿ɛndɩn‿ꓥ *this garment is a woman's.*

ɛ́ndɪ-kɪrɪ‿ (§2541) adj. *resembling that appertaining to a (the) woman, etc., like a woman's.*
ɛ̄nčín-d(ɩ)‿ (§§2545ff.) adj. *appertaining to (the) women, of (the) women, women's.*
  ím‿báññɩd‿ɛnčíndɪn‿ꓥ *this is how women talk,* lit. *this language is of the women.*
ɛ̄nčíndɪ-kɪrɪ‿ (§2541) adj. *resembling that appertaining to (the) women, etc., like (the) women's.*
ɛ́n-an- (§3910α) v.i. *become a woman.*
  ám-bur‿ɛnaŋkó‿ꓥ *my (our) daughter became (has become) a woman.*
ɛ̄nam-bŭ- (§§3949ff.) v.i. stat. *be in the state of becoming a woman.*
ɛ̄nan-ɛ-dól- (-nᵒd- §1178; §4026) and **ɛ̄nand-ɛ-dól-** (-dᵒd-; §4034) v.i. *be about to become a woman.*
ɛ̄nanɛd-ág- (§3966α) v.i. *be in the condition of having become a woman.*
ɛ́ŋ-kiññ(ɩ)‿ (§§2536–7) adj. *without a woman, without a wife.*
  ín‿ógɩǧ‿ɛŋkiññɩn‿ꓥ *this man has no wife* (said of bachelor or widower or one that has divorced his wife).
ɛ́ŋ-kɪrɪ‿ (ɛ́ŋkírɪ; §§2539–40) adj. *resembling a woman, like a woman.*
ɛ́ndɛ‿ n. *(a) pillar, vertical beam, supporting post, support, prop*; (b) *of ship) mast*; (c) *bulrush millet,* Pennisetum typhoideum, Rich. (BSP, 647) [< *ɛ́rndɛ‿ (§621) < *ɛr- *taking (§2062) + -nd- appertaining to* (§§2545ff.) + -ɛ *of* n. ess. (§2234β), so *thing of taking, i.e. holding, supporting; cp. ɛ́r(i)ndɛ id. AZN s.v., erndē stüze, stamm RNW, s.v.].
  obj. -dɛg‿.
  pl. -denč(ɩ)‿.
  soríñn‿ɛ́ndɛ‿ *bridge of the nose.*
  kúbn‿ɛ́ndɛ‿ *mast.*
ɛ́nd(ɩ)‿ *yours,* s.v. ɛ́r‿.
ɛ́n(n)‿ *of you, your,* gen. of ɛ́r‿.
ɛnnébɪ‿ n. *the Prophet* [< النَّبِيّ id. §1388].
  ɛnnébɪ‿íŋkɛ‿wɛ́gon‿ꓥ *the Prophet said so (...spoke thus).*
  ɛnném‿mohámmɛd‿íŋkɛ‿wɛ́gon‿ꓥ (§1322) *the Prophet Muḥámmad said so.*
ɛ́nn-i‿ *your hand(s),* s.v. í‿.
ɛnnū́r‿ n. *En-Nū́r,* a man's name [< النُّور *the light*].
  obj. -úrk(ɩ)‿, -kiꓥ.
ɛ́r‿ (ɛr‿ §1718; §§2604ff., 5076–8) pers. pron. 2nd sg. *you, thou* [cp. ON. eɪp id. GNT, s.v.].
  obj. ɛ́kk(ɩ)‿ (< *ɛ́rk(ɩ)‿ §571b), -kiꓥ.
  gen. ɛ́nn‿v. (< *ɛ́rn‿ §628b), ɛ́n‿c.
  pl. ír‿ q.v.
  ɛ́kk‿āgúwen‿ꓥ *(s)he is calling you.*
  ɛ́nn‿ágɪ‿ *your mouth.*
  ɛm‿bɛ́lɛd‿ (§595) *your country (village).*
  ɛn‿dúŋ(ɩ)‿ *your money.*
  ɛn‿fádɪl‿, ɛm‿fádɪl‿ and ɛf‿fádɪl‿ (§543) *your kindness.*
  ɛŋ‿gadíǧɛ‿ (§648) *your lawsuit.*
  ɛn‿ǧɛb‿ *your pocket.*
  ɛn‿hánu‿ and ɛh‿hánu‿ (§561) *your donkey.*
  ɛn‿kắ‿ (§659) *your house.*
  ɛn‿lámba‿ and ɛl‿lámba‿ (§583) *your lamp.*

  ɛm‿míss(ɩ)‿ (§608) *your eye(s §4696a).*
  ɛn‿néd‿ *your tongue.*
  ɛn‿rádd(ɩ)‿ and ɛr‿rádd(ɩ)‿ (§671) *your answer.*
  ɛn‿sáfar‿ and ɛs‿sáfar‿ (§681) *your journey.*
  ɛn‿šáwál‿ and ɛš‿šáwál‿ (§699) *your sack.*
  ɛn‿tí‿ *your cow.*
  ɛ́w‿wɛ́l‿ (§722) *your dog.*
  ɛn‿zắbɪd‿ and ɛz‿zắbɪd‿ (§736) *your officer.*
  ɛ́nn-ắ‿ *your heart,* ɛ́n-ǧɛr‿ *your back,* etc. §1671.
  ɛ́ddo‿ *on* (etc. s.v. -r‿) *you.*
  ɛ́kkon‿ (s.v. -on‿) *you also.*
  ɛ́kkoŋ‿āgúwen‿ꓥ *(s)he is calling you too.*
  ɛ́kkonom‿binógri‿ꓥ *I shall go with you.*
ɛ́k-kɪrɪ‿ (ɛ́kkírɪ‿ §1532; §§2539–40, 2635) pers. pron. adj. *like you.*
ɛ́n-d(ɩ)‿ (§2637) abs. poss. pron. *yours.*
  dúŋg‿ɛndɩn‿ꓥ *the money is yours.*
  ɛ́ndɩg‿gɪǧírkori‿ꓥ *I (have) heard what you said (...your story).*
ɛ́ndɪ-kɪrɪ‿ (§2638) pers. pron. adj. *resembling that appertaining to you, like yours.*
ɛ́ndɪ́nčɪ-kɪrɪ‿ (§2638) pers. pron. adj. *resembling those appertaining to you, like yours.*
ɛ́kkɛnɛ‿ (ɛ́kkénɛ‿ §1532; §§4426, 5966–7) adv. *now, just now* (of the present or immediate past or future) = íŋkɛnɛ‿ s.v. ín‿ [< *ɛ́r-k-ɛn-ɛn‿ (§939) *it is (that) it says 'you'*; -ɛn- 213; cp. *there you are!* = *there now!*].
  ɛ́kkɛn‿índ‿ɛgó‿ꓥ *(s)he (it) was here just now.*
  ɛ́kkɛnɛ‿tómb‿gó‿ꓥ (a) *(s)he (it) has just broken it;* (b) *it has just (got) broken.*
  ɛ́kkɛnɛ‿baddɛ́ri‿ꓥ *I shall (I'll §5383) finish it immediately.*
— declined and with postposition (§4479):
  ɛ́kkɛnɛ‿íllár‿kɛfɛ́n‿ꓥ *it's enough for now (...for the present).*
  ɛ́kkɛnɛrtōm‿bŭ́š‿móŋkon‿ *from till Monday.*
ɛ́kkɛnɛg‿ (ɛ́kkénɛg‿ §1532; -gi‿ §5981; §5987) adv. = ɛ́kkɛnɛ‿.
  X. tírgɩ‿tír‿ꓥ *give it to them.*
  Y. ɛ́kkɛnɛgá‿? *now?*
-**ɛ́r**‿ (§2244) *intention, *wish* s.vv. ɛ́ssɪ‿ *water,* nálu‿ *sleep.*
ɛ́r‿ adj. *new, fresh* (= ǧɛdíd‿) [< *taken, *acquired §§2493, 2499].
  obj. ɛ́rk(ɩ)‿.
  pl. ɛ́rɪ‿.
  ɛ́r‿ɛ́nn‿íllár‿ *the new one is (§5858) for you.*
  íŋ‿kád‿ɛ́rkɪ‿ǧắŋkori‿ꓥ *I have bought this new cloth.*
  ún‿ɛ́r‿ *new moon.*
ɛ́rk-ɪr (§3702) (a) v.t. caus. *cause or allow to be or become new;* (b) v.t. *render new, renew, renovate.*
  ind. pres. āɪ‿ɛ́rkɪddi‿ꓥ, ɛr‿ɛ́rkɪrɪn‿ (-rí‿ꓥ, -rí‿ꓥ).
ɛ́r v.t. (a) *carry off as plunder, loot;* (b) *plunder, loot* [cogn. ɛ́d *take* (in marriage) §2775; §2493].
  ind. pres. āɪ‿ɛ́rri‿ꓥ, ɛr‿ɛ́rɪn‿ (‿ɛ́rí‿ꓥ, ‿ɛ́rí‿ꓥ); perf. āɪ‿ɛ́rkori‿ꓥ.

tíncıg‿érkoranͻ *they (have) looted (the) cattle.*
belédk‿érkoranͻ *they (have) looted the country.*
érar‿ (érȧr‿; §§ 2200 ff.) and
ēríd‿ (§§ 2256 ff.) n. *looting, pillage.*
ér v.t. *fertilize, impregnate (palm-tree)* [< √ έ*d take §2775].
ind. pres. aī‿érrinͻ, er‿érinͻ (‿érīͻ, ‿érīͻ); perf. aī‿érkoriͻ.
béntıncıg‿érkoranͻ *they (have) fertilized the palms.*
érar‿ (érȧr‿; §§ 2200 ff.) and
ēríd‿ (§§ 2256 ff.) n. *fertilization.*
ére‿ n. *pollen* [< ér- + -ε‿ of n. act., or. *fertilization §2234δ].
obj. έrεg‿.
pl. έrεnč(ı)‿.
ér-an (§§ 3890 ff.) v.t. *tell to fertilize, etc., let fertilize, etc.*
εrdέ v.i. *be willing, agree, consent* [< أرْضَ of أرْضَى *I consent* + -ε §3630].
ind. pres. aī‿εrdέriͻ; fut. aī‿bεrdέriͻ; perf. aī‿εrdέgoriͻ (N. -έko-, -έho-).
imperat. εrdέ!
def. perf. aī‿εrdērόskoriͻ.
έrdεb‿ n. *ardébb, a measure of capacity of 198 litres, about 5½ bushels* [< أَرْدَبّ id. < ἀρτάβη, Copt. ⲉⲣⲧⲱⲃ, ⲉⲣⲧⲟⲃ].
obj. -εbk(ı)‿, -έpk(ı)‿, -kiͻ.
pl. -εbı‿.
έrdεb‿bέr‿kέla‿dımındόwwınͻ (-b‿b- < -b‿w- §517) *one ardébb is twelve kέla‿.*
εrğέ (εrεğέ, εrεğğέ, εrığέ and N. εrığğέ) (a) v.i. *wait, remain, stay;* (b) v.t. *wait for, await;* (c) v.t. *expect* [< أَرْجَ of أَرْجُو *I await* + -έ §3630 (*pace* Schäfer *SNK*, 676)].
ind. pres. aī‿εrğέriͻ, εr‿εrğέnͻ (-ğέͻ, -ğέͻ, -ğέͻ); fut. aī‿bεrğέriͻ; perf. aī‿εrğέgoriͻ (N. -έko-, -έho-).
imperat. εrğέ!
índ‿aig‿εrεğğέͻ *wait for me here.*
εr‿tέkkı‿bεrğέná? *will you wait for him (her, it)?*
gátır‿urúm‿bābúrk‿εrğέná? *does the train wait for the steamer?*
εrğέrar‿ (εrεğέ-, etc.; -rȧr‿; §§ 2200ff., 2207) and
εrğέrīd‿ (εrεğέ-, etc.; §§ 2256 ff., 2260) n. *(a)waiting, etc.*
εrğέr-an (εrεğέr-, etc.; §§ 3890, 3899) v.t. *tell to (a)wait, etc., let (a)wait, etc.*
εrğέ-bū- (εrεğέ-, etc.; §3931β) v.i. stat. *be in an awaited (etc.) state or condition.*
babūr‿arbāhag‿εrεğğέbūnͻ *the steamer (train) is expected on Wednesday.*
εrğέr-ε-ğú-bū- (εrεğέr-, etc.; §4069) v.i. and t. stat. *be on one's way (coming to) (a)wait, etc.*
εrğέr-ε-mȧ- (εrεğέr-, etc.; §§ 4016–17, 4036, 4041) v.i. and t. *become unable to (a)wait, etc.*
εrğέr-ε-nόg (εrεğέr-, etc.; §§ 4048 ff.) v.i. and t. *go to (a)wait, etc.*
εrğέr-ε-nόg-bū- (εrεğέr-, etc.; -nόggū- §546; 4058) v.i. and t. stat. *be on one's way (going) to (a)wait, etc.*

εrğέr-ε-tȧ (εrεğέr-, etc.; §§ 4060ff.) v.i. and t. *come to (a)wait, etc.*
εrğέred-ȧg- (εrεğέred-, etc.; §§ 3877 ff.) v.i. and t. *be in the situation of having (a)waited, etc.*
εrğέg-ır (εrεğέg-, etc.; §3681) v.t. caus. *cause or allow to (a)wait, etc.*
εrğέ-kattı- (εrεğέ-, etc.; N. -έha-; §4093) v.p. *be awaited, etc.*
érıd‿ n. *hippopotamus* (= έssın‿tíͻ).
obj. erídk(ı)‿, -ítk(ı)‿, -ítt(ı)‿ (§2462), -kiͻ, -tiͻ.
pl. erídı‿.
erίd-dēn‿nálkoranͻ (-d-d- < -d-w- §533) *they saw (have seen) a hippopotamus.*
erίd‿šεllállo‿nálkattınͻ *the hippopotamus is seen in the cataract(s)* (§4696d).
erín-d‿ (§§ 2545 ff.) adj. *appertaining to the hippopotamus.*
έrıg n. (a) *intelligence, understanding, sense, reason;* (b) *thought, idea, opinion* [contains εr- *taking, *grasp §2062].
obj. erίgk(ı)‿, -ίkk(ı)‿, -kiͻ.
pl. erίkkı‿kό (§5709) v.i. *have intelligence, etc.* = erίkkό-.
neg. part. pres. erίkkı‿kόmεnı‿ *having no intelligence, etc.* = εrıkkόmεnı‿.
εrίkkı‿kόmununͻ *(s)he has (you have) no sense.*
erık-kátt(ı)‿ (§§ 2534–5) adj. *intelligent, wise, reasonable.*
obj. -tıg‿.
pl. -tınč(ı)‿.
erıkkáttı-bū- (§3945) v.i. stat. *be intelligent, etc.*
neg. part. pres. erıkkattıbūmεnı‿ (one) *devoid of intelligence, fool.*
erík-kō- (§4118) v.i. *have intelligence, have sense, be intelligent, be sensible.*
ind. pres. aī‿erıkkόriͻ, εr‿erίkkōnͻ (kōͻ, -kōͻ, -kόͻ); perf. aī‿erık-kόgoriͻ (N. -όko-, -όho-).
εrίkkόmεnunͻ = εrίkkı‿kόmununͻ.
ind. part. pres. erίkkōl‿ (§2579α) (a) adj. *intelligent, sensible;* (b) n. *intelligent person.*
neg. part. pres. εrıkkόmεnı‿ (§2581) (a) adj. *unintelligent, stupid, foolish;* (b) n. *unintelligent person, fool.*
erığğέ (N.) v.i. and t. *wait, await, wait for* = εrğέ, q.v.
ind. pres. aī‿εrığğέriͻ; perf. aī‿εrığğέkoriͻ (-έho-).
imperat. εrığğέ!
(N.) kεrίmȧr‿urúm‿bābū́r‿gatίrk‿εrığğέhόmununͻ *at Kεrίma the steamer didn't wait for the train.*
erığğέk-ır (N.; -έhır; §3681) v.t. *cause or allow to (a)wait, etc.*
érkanε‿ *marriage*, s.v. éd.
érr(ı)‿ n. *name* [< *έrεr‿ *saying of, calling, naming*, n. act. in -εr‿ (§§ 2200, 2203) of ‿έ- *say of, call, name* (§3508)].
obj. -rıg‿.
pl. -rınč(ı)‿.
ínın‿έrrım‿mίng‿εrán? (-m‿m- < -g‿m- §601) *what's the name of this?*, lit. *what do they call the name of this?*

énn‿έrrın‿nίg‿εrán? (-n‿n- < -g‿n- §625) *what's your name?*, lit. *whom do they call your name?*
nobίndıgεd‿έrrık‿kόmununū͂ *(s)he (it) has no name in Nubian.*
errı-kátt(ı)‿ (N. -ıhá-; §§2534, 2535a) adj. *having the same name, homonymous.*
obj. -tıg‿.
pl. -tınč(ı)‿.
ánn‿errıkáttınͻ *(s)he has the same name as I.*
έrt(ı)‿ *dirt, dirty,* s.v. éd.
έrt(ı)‿ *mamma, teat,* s.v. éd.
έs‿ n. *early afternoon* (about 1 p.m. to 3 p.m.) [K. id. *die Mittagshitze SNK*, 292, 142].
obj. έsk(ı)‿, -kiͻ.
έkkεn‿έsunͻ *it is now early afternoon.*
έsk(ı)‿ (-kiͻ; §§ 4431–3) adv. *in the early afternoon.*
έskı‿tȧgoranͻ *they came in the early afternoon.*
έs-an- (§3910α) v.i. *become early afternoon.*
έsaŋkόͻ *it became (has become, is) early afternoon.*
έsε‿ (§§ 2520–1) adj. *deficient in two dimensions, thin* (= Amh. ቀጭን).
obj. εsέg‿.
pl. εsέrı‿.
wίččır‿εsέnͻ *the stick is (too) thin.*
έsέ-wēg‿έttaͻ *bring a thin one.*
εsέ-tod‿ (§§2484, 2582) adj. *unsatisfactorily (miserably, wretchedly) thin.*
voc. -tot!, -tό!
obj. -tόdk(ı)‿, -tόtk(ı)‿, -tόtt(ı)‿, -tόkk(ı)‿, -kiͻ, -tiͻ.
gen. -tόdn‿v., -tόnn‿v.c., -tόn‿c.
pl. -toni‿.
όgığ‿εsέtodunͻ *the man is miserably thin.*
ír‿εsέtodunͻ *the rope is wretchedly thin.*
ír‿εsέtόd-dēg‿έttagonͻ (-d-d- < -d-w- §533) *(s)he (has) brought a miserably thin rope.*
wίččır‿εsέtodunͻ *the stick is miserably thin.*
wίččır‿εsέtόd-dēd-dέŋkoͻ (-tόd- §1565; -d-d- < -d-w- §533, -d‿d- < -g‿d- §534) *(s)he gave (has given; you gave; have given) me a miserably thin stick.*
έs-an- (§3910α) v.i. *become thin.*
tεr‿εsaŋkόͻ *(s)he (it) became (has become) thin.*
εsέg-ır (N. -έkır, -έhır; §3701) (a) v.t. caus. *cause or allow to be or become thin;* (b) v.t. *render thin.*
ίn‿ákıl‿aig‿εsέgırınͻ *this food makes (leaves) me thin.*
έsed‿ n. *lion* [< أَسَد id.].
obj. εsέdk(ı)‿, -έtk(ı)‿, -έtt(ı)‿ (§2462); -kiͻ, -tiͻ.
pl. έsεdı‿.
έsked‿ n. (a) *loose earth, crumbled soil;* (b) *dust* [cp. ON. ⲉⲓⲥⲕⲓⲧ ἡ γῆ *GNT,* s.v.].
obj. εskέdk(ı)‿, -έtk(ı)‿, -έtt(ı)‿ (§2462); -kiͻ, -tiͻ.
ar‿εskέdkεn‿naddufέgoru‿ (-n‿n- < -d‿n- §624) *we (have) cleaned it (them) with earth.*

ɛskédn-d(ı)‿ and
ɛskén-d(ı)‿ (§§ 2545 ff.) adj. appertaining to loose earth, etc., of loose earth, etc.
ésk(ı) and ísk(ı) v.t. be able to [cp. ON. ⲉⲕⲣⲓ ⲛⲓⲕⲁⲛ GNT, s.v.].
　ind. pres. aī‿éskırī⌒ I can, ɛr‿éskın⌒ (-kī⌒, -kí⌒); fut. aī‿béskırī⌒; perf. aī‿éskıgorī⌒ (N. -ıko-, -ıho-).
　aī‿tékkı‿nallánɡ‿éskımunun⌒ and (§ 3857)
　aī‿tékk‿eskınálmunun⌒ I can't see him (her, it).
ɛskı-báññ(ı)- (ıskı-; § 3857) v.i. be able to speak.
ɛskı-bɛ́- (ıskı-; § 3857) v.t. be able to kill, etc. (s.v. bɛ́).
　káɡk‿eskıbɛ́munan⌒ they can't kill the snake.
ɛskı-bél- (ıskı-; § 3857) v.i. be able to issue, etc. (s.v. bél).
　eskıbélmunan⌒ they can't get out.
ɛskı-dúkkı- (etc.) v.t. be able to extract, etc. (s.v. dúkk(ı)).
　ar‿musmárk‿eskıdúkkımunun⌒ and (§ 5601)
　ar‿èskı-musmárkı-dúkkımunun⌒ we can't get the nail(s § 4696c) out.
　aī‿musmárk‿eskıdúkkımunun⌒ and aī‿èskımusmárkıdúkkımunun⌒ I can't pull the nail(s) out.
ɛskı-ɡíɡır- (etc.) v.t. be able to perceive, etc. (s.v. ɡíɡır).
　ɛr‿ɡ̌ɛrésk‿eskıɡíɡırmen? can't you hear the bell?
ɛskı-ɡ̌ábɛ- (etc.) v.t. be able to touch, etc. (s.v. ɡ̌ábɛ).
ɛskı-kál- (etc.) v.i. and t. be able to eat, etc. (s.v. kál).
ɛskı-mér- (etc.) v.t. be able to cut, etc. (s.v. mér).
ɛskı-nál- (etc.) v.t. be able to see, etc. (s.v. nál).
ɛskı-nɛ́wɛ- (etc.) v.i. be able to breathe.
ɛskı-níɡ̌- (etc.) v.t. be able to sew.
ɛskı-nóɡ- (etc.) v.t. be able to go, etc. (s.v. nóɡ).
ɛskı-sabrɛ́- (etc.) v.i. and t. be able to have patience, be able to endure, etc. (s.v. sabrɛ́).
ɛskı-sókkɛ- (etc.) v.t. be able to take up, etc. (s.v. sókkɛ).
ɛskı-šuɡlɛ́- (etc.; -šoɡlɛ́-, -šoɡolɛ́-) v.i. be able to work.
ɛskı-tǎ- (etc.) v.i. be able to come.
　ɛskıtǎmunan⌒ they can't come.
ɛskı-tabhɛ́- (etc.; -bxɛ́-) v.t. be able to cook.
ɛskı-tɔ́- (etc.) v.i. be able to enter, etc. (s.v. tɔ́).
ɛskı-tɔ́ɡ- (etc.) v.t. be able to strike.
ɛskı-tóllɛ- (etc.) v.t. be able to pull.
ɛskı-wár- (etc.) v.i. be able to jump.
ɛsmán‿ (§ 956a) n. ɛuθmán, ɛoθmán, Osmán, a man's name [< عثمان id.].
　obj. -áŋ(ı)‿, -ɡı⌒.
　ɛsmán‿úr‿ ɛoθmán's head.
　ɛsmán‿dúŋ(ı)‿ ɛoθmán's money.
　ɛsmáŋɡoŋɡı‿tóran⌒ (-máŋŋoŋɡı‿, -máŋŋoŋɡı‿ §§ 502, 662) tell ɛoθmán to come (go) in too.
ɛsmán-d(ı)‿ (§§ 2545 ff.) adj. appertaining to ɛoθmán, of ɛoθmán, ɛoθmán's.

-ɛss(ı)‿ n. sister [< *-ɛns(ı)‿ (§ 680) < ɛn‿ woman (§§ 1048, 1062) + -s dim. or dem. (§ 2319); RN, § 150 et al.; cp. ON. ⲉⲥⲥⲓ id. GNT, s.v.].
　obj. -ɛssıɡ‿.
　pl. -ɛssınč(ı)‿.
Always with a form of the possessive personal pronoun (§ 2625) prefixed:
　ánnɛss(ı)‿ my sister.
　ínnɛss(ı)‿ your sister.
　tínnɛss(ı)‿ his (her) sister.
　antínnɛss(ı)‿ our sister.
　ıntínnɛss(ı)‿ your (pl.) sister.
　tıntínnɛss(ı)‿ their sister.
　antínnɛssınč(ı)‿ and antínnɛssínč(ı)‿ (§ 1526) our sisters.
　ánnɛssın‿tód‿ my sister's child = ássöd‿ (s.v. -ssöd‿).
　ánnɛssın‿óɡıɡ̌‿ my sister's husband.
　ánn‿óɡıñ‿tínnɛss(ı)‿ (-ñ‿t- < -ɡn‿t- § 632) my husband's sister.
　tér‿tínnɛssıŋ‿káŋkó⌒ (s)he went (has gone) to his (her) sister's house.
-ɛssín-d(ı)‿ (§§ 2545 ff.) adj. appertaining to a sister, sister's.
　dúŋ‿annɛssínd(ı)‿ my sister's money.
éss(ı)‿ n. water [< *ést(ı)‿ (§ 2319); older *ást(a) in Ἀσταβόρας, etc. (s.v. átbara‿); cp. ON. ⲉⲧⲧⲱ (GNT, s.v.) MN. ọti (KB, §§ 100e, 133) id.; ZNG, p. 187; ZMS, p. 430³³].
　obj. -ɛssıɡ‿.
　tɛr‿éss‿áŋkō⌒ (§§ 5555 ff.) (s)he (it) went (has gone) to the water.
ɛssın-ɛ́r- n. thirst [< éssın‿ *ɛ́r‿ intention (desire) of water § 2244; cp. MN. ẹr (1) Schlauheit, (2) Durst KB, § 97c].
　obj. -ɛ́rk(ı)‿, -kı⌒.
　ɛssınɛ́r‿áiɡ̌‿árın⌒ and (§ 4623)
　áiɡ‿ɛssınɛ́r‿árın⌒ I am thirsty, lit. thirst seizes me.
　ɛssınɛ́rkɛt‿tēbdín⌒ and
　ɛssınɛ́rkɛd‿addín⌒ (s)he (it) is dying of thirst.
　ɛssınɛ́rkɛd‿diɛdóllan⌒ they are nearly dead of thirst.
　ɛssınɛ́rkı‿sándırı⌒ I am afraid of thirst.
ɛssı-káɡ‿ n. (in water-wheel, kólɛ‿) beam supporting trough (sáblo‿) and horizontal axle (tórɛ‿) towards its river end [lit. carry-water § 2381].
　obj. -káɡk(ı)‿, -kákk(ı)‿, -kı⌒.
　gen. -káɡn‿v., -káŋ‿c.
　pl. -káɡŋ‿.
ɛssıkáɡır‿ n. (in water-wheel, kólɛ‿) block(s, there are two) resting on the ɛssıkáɡ‿ and immediately supporting the trough [lit. on-the-carry-water § 2381a].
　obj. -káɡírk(ı)‿, -kı⌒.
　pl. -káɡırı‿.
éssın‿káɡ‿ and
éssın-tūŋ‿káɡ‿ a Nile fish, of a dark colour, resembling an eel, Polypterus sp. (PF, p. 97) [water-snake].
　obj. ‿káɡk(ı)‿, ‿kákk(ı)‿, -kı⌒.
　pl. ‿káɡıı‿.
éssın-ti‿ (éssín-ti‿, ‿‿, § 2355) hippopotamus, lit. water-cow (= érıd‿) [> Sudan Ar. عيسنتي, ɛésítt id.].
　obj. éssın‿tíɡ‿.

ɛssín-d(ı)‿ (§§ 2545 ff.) adj. appertaining to (the) water, of (the) water.
éssı-kıññ(ı)‿ (§§ 2536-7) adj. waterless.
　ín‿áɡar‿éssıkıññın⌒ this place is waterless.
éssı-kırı‿ (§§ 2539-40) adj. like water, watery.
éss-an- (§ 3910β) v.i. go to (the) water.
　ind. pres. aī‿éssandı⌒, ɛr‿éssanın⌒ (-nī⌒, -ní⌒); fut. aī‿béssandı⌒; perf. aī‿éssaŋkorı⌒.
　subj. past aī‿éssansı‿ (-assı‿ § 680, -su‿).
éssam-bŭ- (§ 3950β) v.i. stat. be in a state of motion towards (the) water, be on one's way to (the) water, be going to (the) water.
éssan-ɛ-dól- (-nᵒd- § 1178; § 4026) and
éssand-ɛ-dól- (-dᵒd-; § 4034) v.i. be about to go to (the) water.
éssanɛd-áɡ- (§ 3966β) v.i. be in the situation of having gone to (the) water.
éssı‿ (§ 688) < édsı‿ (the fact, the one) that I married, s.v. éd.
éssır‿ n. bottle [< éss(ı)‿ water + -ır‿ *(action of) making, then concrete *water-maker § 2286β].
　obj. ɛssírk(ı)‿, -kı⌒.
　pl. éssırı‿.
　dés‿n‿éssır‿ the (a) bottle for (§ 4683, of § 4685) butter.
　íčč‿éssırró⌒ (§ 5858) the milk is in the bottle.
éše v.i. belch [lit. say 'éš!' §§ 2870 ff.].
　ind. pres. aī‿éšerı⌒, ɛr‿éšen⌒ (‿éšɛ⌒, ‿éšé⌒); perf. aī‿éšeɡorı⌒ (N. -ɛko-, -ɛho-).
éšerar‿ (-rár‿; §§ 2200 ff., 2210) and
éšeríd‿ (§§ 2256 ff., 2263) n. belching.
éšátt(ı)‿ n. belch, belching (concrete); with collective sg. (§ 4696d) [§§ 2222-3].
　obj. -tıɡ‿.
　tɛr‿bérsıŋ‿éšáttırtön‿uñúrkorı⌒ I knew by his (her, its) belching that (s)he (it) had had enough.
éš-an (§§ 3890 ff.) v.t. let belch, i.e. give much food and drink to, ply with food and drink.
　aī‿tékk‿éšandı⌒ I('ll § 5369b) feed him (her, it) well.
éšer-eɡ-áɡ- (§§ 4071 ff.) v.i. = éšeredól-.
éšer-ɛ-dól- (-rᵒd- § 1178; §§ 4016-17, 4022, 4027) v.i. be about to belch, have eaten and drunk to repletion.
éšeɡ-ır (N. -ɛkır, -ɛhır; § 3679) (a) v.t. caus. cause or allow to belch; (b) v.t. ply with food and drink.
　ín‿áiɡ‿éšeɡırın⌒ (a) this makes me belch; (b) this person plies me with food and drink.
éšeŋ-ır (N. -éŋkır, ‿‿; § 3688) v.t. caus. and v.t. = éšeɡır.
　aī‿tékk‿éšeɡıddı⌒ (N. ‿éšekıddı⌒) and
　aī‿tékk‿éšeŋɡıddı⌒ (N. ‿éšeŋkıddı⌒) I('ll § 5369b) feed him (her, it) well.
éttā bring, s.v. éd.
étt(ı)‿ bile, gall, s.v. éd.
éu‿ (éw‿, éu) n. tail [§ 2052].
　obj. éuɡ(ı)‿, éuɡ(ı)‿, -ɡı⌒.
　pl. éwı‿.
　káɡn‿éu‿ (a) horse's tail; (b) comet.

ɛ́u — ɛ́wɪr

ɛ̃́u-kŏ́l⌣ (§2579α) (a) adj. *possessing a tail, caudate*; (b) n. *creature* (e.g. monkey) or *thing* (e.g. comet) *with a tail*.
  obj. -kŏ́lg(ɪ)⌣, -giᴖ.
  pl. -kŏ́lɪ⌣.
  wíss⌣ɛukŏ́l⌣ *comet*.
  gírɪd⌣ɛukŏ́lɪ⌣ *monkeys with tails*.
ɛ̃́u-kol⌣ (ɛúkkŏl⌣ §2382) n. *fox, Vulpes vulpes, subsp. aegyptiaca*, Sonn. (*KNH*, 40).
  obj. ɛukólg(ɪ)⌣, ɛukkŏ́lg(ɪ)⌣, -giᴖ.
  pl. ɛ̃́ukolɪ⌣, ɛ́ukkolɪ⌣.
ɛ́u (ɛ́w, ɛ̃́u) v.t. *wash* [§2774].
  ind. pres. ãɪ̃⌣ɛ̃́uriᴖ (⌣ɛ́w¹riᴖ), ɛr⌣ɛ́wɪnᴖ (⌣ɛ̃́wɪ̃ᴖ, ⌣ɛ́wíᴖ); fut. ãɪ̃⌣bɛ́uriᴖ (⌣bɛ́w¹riᴖ); perf. ãɪ̃⌣ɛ̃́ukoriᴖ.
  imperat. ɛ́u!, pl. ɛ̃́uwɛ! (-wɛ́!).
  part. pres. ɛ́wɪl⌣ (*one*) *that washes, washer, washing*; obj. ɛ̃́wɪ́lg(ɪ)⌣.
  part. fut. bɛ́wɪl⌣ (*one*) *that will wash, washer, washing*.
  part. past ɛ́wɛl⌣ (*one*) *that washed, washer, washing*; obj. ɛ̃́wɛ́lg(ɪ)⌣.
  def. imperat. ɛ́wos! (ɛ̃́wó!, ɛ̃́wó!); pl. ɛ̃́wóswɛ! (ɛ̃́wóswɛ́!, -ówwɛ́! §724, -wɛ́!, -ósɛ! §687, -sɛ́!).
  ánn-ib⌣bɛ́uriᴖ (-b⌣b- <-g⌣b- §519) *I shall wash my hand(s* §4696a).
  ánn-ig⌣ɛ̃́ukoriᴖ *I (have) washed my hand(s)*.
  áɲ⌣kádeg⌣ɛ̃́ukoriᴖ *I (have) washed my clothes* (§4696d).
  ɛwɪrɪrᴖ *wash (each of) them* (§5456).
ɛ́war (ɛ́wắr⌣; §§2200ff.) and
ɛ̌wíd (§2256ff.) n. *washing*.
ɛ̃́w-an (§§3890ff.) v.t. *tell to wash, let wash*.
ɛ̃́u-bŭ- (§3931β) v.i. stat. *be in a washed state or condition*.
ɛ̃́ur-ɛg-ắg- (ɛ̃́w¹r-; §§4071ff.) v.t. = ɛ̃́wɛ-dól-.
ɛ̃́w-ɛ-dól- (-wᵒd- §1178; §4022) and
ɛ̃́ur-ɛ-dól- (ɛ̃́w¹r-, -rᵒd-; §4027) v.t. *be about to wash*.
ɛ̃́ur-ɛ-ğŭ-bŭ- (ɛ̃́w¹r-; §4069) v.t. stat. *be on one's way (coming) to wash*.
ɛ̃́w-ɛ-má- (§4036) and
ɛ̃́ur-ɛ-má- (ɛ̃́w¹r-; §4041) v.t. *become unable to wash*.
ɛ̃́ur-ɛ-nóg- (ɛ̃́w¹r-; §§4048ff.) v.t. *go to wash*.
ɛ̃́ur-ɛ-nóg-bŭ- (ɛ̃́w¹r-; -nóggŭ- §546; §4058) v.t. stat. *be on one's way (going) to wash*.
ɛ̃́ur-ɛ-tá- (ɛ̃́w¹r-; §§4060ff.) v.t. *come to wash*.
ɛ̌wɛd-ắg- (§§3877ff.) v.t. *be in the situation of having washed*.
ɛ̌wíng-ɪr (᷄¯; N. -ŋkɪr; §3688) v.t. caus. *cause or allow to wash*.
ɛ̃́u-kattɪ- (§4093) v.p. *be washed*.
ɛ́u (ɛ́w, ɛ̃́u) v.t. *send* [§§2774, 2052].
  ind. pres. ãɪ̃⌣ɛ̃́uriᴖ (⌣ɛ́w¹riᴖ), ɛr⌣ɛ́wɪnᴖ (⌣ɛ̃́wɪ̃ᴖ, ⌣ɛ́wíᴖ); fut. ãɪ̃⌣bɛ́uriᴖ (⌣bɛ́w¹riᴖ); perf. ãɪ̃⌣ɛ̃́ukoriᴖ.
  imperat. ɛ́u!, pl. ɛ̃́uwɛ! (-wɛ́!).
  part. pres. ɛ́wɪl⌣ (*one*) *that sends, sender, sending*; obj. ɛ̃́wɪ́lg(ɪ)⌣.
  part. fut. bɛ́wɪl⌣ (*one*) *that will send, sender, sending*.
  part. past ɛ́wɛl⌣ (*one*) *that sent, sender, sending*; obj. ɛ̃́wɛ́lg(ɪ)⌣, -giᴖ.
  def. imperat. ɛ́wos! (ɛ̃́wó!, ɛ̃́wó!); pl. ɛ̃́wóswɛ! (ɛ̃́wóswɛ́!, -ówwɛ́! §724, -wɛ́!, -ósɛ! §687, -sɛ́!).
  ãɪ̃⌣tɛ́kk⌣úrdɪr⌣bɛ́w¹riᴖ *I shall send him (her, it) to El-Ordi*.
  ogíčkɪ⌣ğawábkɛd⌣ɛ̃́ukoriᴖ *I (have) sent the (a) man with the (a) letter*.
  dúŋɪged⌣ɛ̃́ukoriᴖ *I (have) sent him (her) with the money*.
  ɛ́wɪrɪrᴖ *send (each of) them* (§5456).
ɛ́war (ɛ́wắr⌣; §§2200ff.) and
ɛ̌wíd (§§2256ff.) n. *sending, dispatch*.
ɛ̃́w-an (§§3890ff.) v.t. *tell to send, let send*.
ɛ̃́u-bŭ- (§3931β) v.i. stat. *be in a sent state or condition*.
  ógɪğ⌣ɛ̃́ubūnᴖ *the man is (has been) sent*.
ɛ̃́u-dɛ̄n (§§3996-7) v.t. *send to (the speaker)*.
ɛ̌ur-ɛg-ắg- (ɛ̃́w¹r-; §§4071ff.) v.t. = ɛ̃́wɛ-dól-.
ɛ̃́w-ɛ-dól- (-wᵒd- §1178; §4022) and
ɛ̃́ur-ɛ-dól- (ɛ̃́w¹r-, -rᵒd-; §4027) v.t. *be about to send*.
ɛ̃́w-ɛ-má- (§4036) and
ɛ̃́ur-ɛ-má- (ɛ̃́w¹r-; §4041) v.t. *become unable to send*.
ɛ̌wɛd-ắg- (§§3877ff.) v.t. *be in the situation of having sent*.
ɛ̌wíng-ɪr (᷄¯; N. -ŋkɪr; §3688) v.t. caus. *cause or allow to send*.
ɛ̃́u-kattɪ- (§4093) v.p. *be sent*.
ɛ̃́u-tɪr (§§3998-9) v.t. *send to (other than the speaker)*.
⌣ɛwɛ́ *say*, etc., s.v. ⌣ɛ́- *say*.
ɛ́wɪr v.t. (a) *exchange, alter the ownership of by exchanging*, so (cp. senses of ğán, ğá, óğɪ §§5330-4); (b, when object now owned by subject of past verb) *acquire in exchange*; (c, when object now owned by subject of present or future verb) *give in exchange*; (d, when object not now owned by subject of past verb) *give in exchange*; (e, when object not now owned by subject of present or future verb) *acquire in exchange*; (f) *change (into smaller coin)* = fɛkkɛ́; (g, cotton) *gin, remove the seeds from* [<ɛ̃́u⌣ *tail* + -ɪr *make* (§3665), so *make (sc. *the face into the*) *tail*, *turn round (sc. *the ownership of*), **turn (cotton) round* §3676].
  ind. pres. ãɪ̃⌣ɛwírriᴖ, ɛr⌣ɛ́wɪrnᴖ (-riᴖ, -ríᴖ); fut. ãɪ̃⌣bɛwírriᴖ; perf. ãɪ̃⌣ɛwírkoriᴖ.
  subj. past ãɪ̃⌣ɛwírsɪ⌣ (-íssɪ⌣ §683, -su⌣).
  ár⌣ím⌣bɛ́rtɪg⌣ɛgɛ́d-dɛ́ged⌣ɛwírkoruᴖ (-d-d- <-d-w- §533) (b, *speakers own, or speak for owner(s) of, the goat*) *we (have) got this goat in exchange for a sheep*; (d, *speakers do not own, or speak for owner(s) of the goat*) *we gave (have given) this goat in exchange for a sheep*.
  ím⌣bɛ́rtɪg⌣ɛgɛ́d⌣dᵈged⌣ɛ́wɪrᴖ *exchange this goat for a sheep*, i.e. (c) *give this goat in exchange...*; or (e) *take this goat in exchange...*.
  ár⌣ín⌣hánut⌣tínnārtóɲ⌣kắğ-ğɛ̌ged⌣ ɛwírkoruᴖ (-t⌣t- <-g⌣t- §707, -ğ-ğ- <-ğ-w- §553) *we (have) got this donkey from them in exchange for a horse*.
  íɲ⌣kắğ⌣ãɪ̃⌣ɛwírsu-tànnanᴖ (§6164ii) (b, *speaker owns, or speaks for owner(s) of, horse*) *this horse is the one I (have) got in exchange*; (d, *speaker does not own, or speak for owner(s) of, horse*) *that horse is the one I gave (have given) in exchange*.
  ãɪ̃⌣ğínɛb⌣bɛwírrɪᴖ (-b⌣b- <-g⌣b- §519) *I shall change the (a) pound*.
  bɛnnákkɪ⌣bɛnnāŋkóleged⌣ɛwírranᴖ *they gin cotton with a ginning-machine*.
ɛ́wɪrar (-rắr⌣; §§2200ff.) and
ɛwɪríd (§§2256ff.) n. *exchange, changing, ginning*.
ɛwɪrt(ɪ)⌣ n. *exchange*; obj. -tɪg⌣.
ɛwɪrtɪr (§6007) adv. *in exchange*.
  ɛwírtɪrᴖ *it is (they are) in exchange*.
ɛ́wɪr-an (§§3890, 3904) v.t. *tell to exchange, etc., let exchange, etc.*
ɛwír-bŭ- (§3931β) v.i. stat. *be in an exchanged (etc.) state or condition*.
  íɲ⌣kắğ⌣ɛwírbunᴖ *this horse is one got by exchange*.
  ín⌣ãɪ̃⌣índ⌣uskúrsɪmununᴖ, ɛwírbūnᴖ *this is not what I put here, it is (has been) changed*.
ɛwír-dɛ̄n (§§3996-7) v.t. *give (to the speaker) in exchange*.
  ãɪ̃g⌣íŋg⌣ɛwírdɛ̄nᴖ *give me this in exchange*.
ɛwɪred-ắg- (§§3877ff.) v.t. *be in the situation of having exchanged*, etc.
ɛwɪret-tá (§§4169ff.) v.t. *come after exchanging, etc., just go* (-tá s.v. tá) *and exchange, etc.*
  imperat. ɛwɪrɛtta!
  rijắlg⌣ɛwɪrettắriá? *shall I go and change the dollar?*
ɛ́wɪr-kattɪ- (§4093) v.p. *be exchanged, etc.*
ɛwɪrós-dɛ̄n (-óddɛ̄n §538; §§4180-4; -ósgɪdɛ̄n, -ózgɪ-, -óggɪ- §§4185-6; §§3995-7) v.t. *give (to the speaker) in exchange*.
  X. ãɪ̃g⌣íŋg⌣ɛwɪróddɛ̄nᴖ *give me this in exchange*.
  Y. sɛ́rɛ̄n, ɛwɪrobbɪtíddiᴖ *very well, I will* (§5383).
ɛwɪrós-tɪr (-óttɪr §714; §§4180-4; -ósgɪtɪr, -ózgɪ-, -óggɪ- §§4185-6; §§3998-9) v.t. *give (to other than the speaker) in exchange*.
  ãɪ̃⌣tɛ́kkɪ⌣tĭ-wɛ̃g⌣ɛwɪroggɪtíkkoriᴖ *I gave (have given) him (her) a cow in exchange*.
ɛ́wɪr-tɪr (§§3998-9) v.t. *give (to other than the speaker) in exchange*.
  ãɪ̃⌣tɛ́kkɪ⌣íŋgɪ⌣bɛwírtɪddiᴖ *I shall give him (her) this in exchange*.
  tɛ́kkɪ⌣íŋg⌣ɛwírtɪrᴖ *give him (her) this in exchange*.
  máɲ⌣kắğ⌣ãɪ̃⌣ɛwɪrtɪssu-tànnanᴖ *that horse is the one I gave in exchange*.
ɛwɪrtɪr-ắr (§4127) v.t. *take (obtain, get) in exchange* [ɛwírt-ɪr⌣ supra].
  ãɪ̃⌣íŋgɪ⌣tínnārtóɲ⌣ɛwɪrtɪrắrkoriᴖ *I (have) got this from them in exchange*.

ɛwɪrtɪr-bɛ́lbŭ- (ɛwírtɪrbɛlbŭ- §1964; §§3927 ff.) v.i. stat. *be in a state of motion outwards in exchange, be for exchange.*
   íŋ-káǧ⏜ɛwírtɪrbɛlbūn⏝ *this horse is for exchange.*
ɛ́wɪr v.t. *cultivate (a) use* (land) *for agriculture; (b) raise as a crop, grow* [or. *turn round* (sc. *the water-wheel for*) §3676 = Sudan Ar. دَوَّر *cultivate by water-wheel*].
   ind. pres. aī⏜ɛwírrɪ⏝, ɛr⏜ɛ́wɪrɪn⏝ (⏜ɛ́ú-rɪn⏝, -rí⏝, -rí⏝); fut. aī⏜bɛwírrɪ⏝; perf. aī⏜ɛwírkorɪ⏝.
   subj. past aī⏜ɛwírsɪ⏝ (-íssɪ⏝ §683, -su⏝).
   aī⏜kólɛb⏜bɛwírrɪ⏝ (-b⏜b- < -g⏜b- §519) *I shall cultivate an (irrigated) estate.*
   aī⏜ín⏜arɪ́ttɪ⏜bɛwírmunun⏝ *I shall not cultivate this land.*
   íllɛg⏜ɛwírkorɪ⏝ *I grew (have grown) wheat.*
   márɛg⏜ɛwɪróskoran⏝ *they have grown great millet.*
ɛwɪrar⏝ (-ràr⏝; §§2200 ff.) and ɛwɪríd⏝ (§§2256 ff.) n. *cultivation.*
ɛwɪrátt(ɪ)⏝ n. *driver of water-wheel* (kólɛ⏝) = šúgɪl⏝ [< *ɛwɪrárt(ɪ)⏝ < ɛ́wɪr *turn* (t.) *round* + -ar⏝ ger. *-ing* (§2200) + -t dem. (§2323), so *that turning* (t.) *round*; or -t dim. (§2325 γ), as the driver is usually a small boy; > Sudan Ar. اُورَتِّي *aūrátti*, ōr-, -rétti > اَرْوَتِّي *arwétti id.*].
   obj. -tɪg⏝.
   pl. -tɪnč(ɪ)⏝.
ɛwɪr-kátt(ɪ)⏝ (§§2534, 2535 b) adj. *good at cultivating.*
   íŋ⏜gúr⏜ɛwɪrkáttɪn⏝ *this (that) bull is good at cultivating, i.e. works well at the water-wheel.*
ɛ́wɪr-an (§§3890, 3904) v.t. *tell to cultivate, etc., let cultivate, etc.*
ɛwír-bŭ- (§3931 β) v.i. stat. *be in a state or condition of being cultivated.*
   íŋ⏜kólɛwírbūn⏝ *this estate* (s.v. kólɛ⏝) *is being cultivated.*
   ín⏜árɪd⏜ɛwírbúmunun⏝ *this land is not under cultivation.*
ɛwɪrɛd-ág- (§§3877 ff.) v.t. *be in the situation of having cultivated, etc.*
   tír⏜márog⏜ɛwɪrɛdágran⏝ *they have grown great millet.*
ɛwɪrk-ɪ́dd(ɪ) (§3727) v.t. caus. *cause or allow to cultivate, etc.*
   imperat. ɛwírkɪddi!
   kólɛb⏜bɛwírkɪddɪrɪ⏝ (-b⏜b- < -g⏜b- §519) *I shall set the water-wheel working.*
   tórbarɪg⏜ɛwɪrkɪddɪríddan⏝ *they make (let) the peasants work at cultivation.*
ɛ́wɪr-kattɪ- (§4093) v.p. *be cultivated, etc.*
   ín⏜árɪd⏜bɛwírkattɪn⏝ *this land will be cultivated.*
   rúzzɪ⏜dúŋgular⏜ɛwɪrkáttɪmunun⏝ *rice is not grown in Dóngola.*

fadabál⏝ n. *freedom from care, peace of mind* [< فَضَاء بَال *id.*].
   obj. -álg(ɪ)⏝, -gɪ⏝.
   fadabáll⏜ágɪn⏝ (-ll⏜á- < -llo⏜á-) *(s)he is free from care.*

fádda⏝ n. *para*, ¼ *of piastre; with collective sg.* (§4696 d) [< فَضَّة *id.*].
   obj. -dag⏝.
   pl. -danč(ɪ)⏝.
faddɪlɛ́ v.i. *do the favour* (of coming in, sitting down, helping oneself, etc.) [< a stem of Sudan Ar. تَفَضَّل = اِتْفَضَّل *id.* + -ɛ §3652].
   faddɪlɛ́r⏝ *please come in (etc.).*
   faddɪlɛ́wɛ⏝ *please come* (pl.) *in (etc.).*
At an entrance:
   X. ágná? *is (s)he at home?*
   Y. (a) ágɪn, ɛ́kkɪ⏜faddɪlɛ́r⏜ɛ́n⏝ *yes please come in*, lit. *(s)he is, (s)he says to you 'please come in'*;
   (b) ágɪn, ɪ́rgɪ⏜faddɪlɛ́w⏜ɛ́n⏝ *yes, please come* (pl.) *in.*
fádɪ⏝ adj. *empty, vacant* [< فَاضِي *id.*].
   obj. -dɪg⏝.
   pl. -dɪnč(ɪ)⏝.
fádɪl (fád-) n. (a) *favour, kindness* [< فَضْل *id.*]; (b, *the name*) *Faḍl*.
   obj. fadílg(ɪ)⏝, -gɪ⏝.
   pl. fád(ɪ)lɪ⏝.
   ɛ́m⏜fadíllotōn⏝ (s.v. -rtōn⏝) *if you please* (مِن فَضْلَك).
fadlɛ́ v.i. *remain over, remain, be left, remain behind* [< فَضْل *excess* + -ɛ́ §3615].
   ind. pres. aī⏜fadlɛ́rɪ⏝ (occ. -lérɪ⏝ §1073), ɛr⏜fadlɛ́n⏝ (-lɛ́⏝, -lé §939); occ. -lén⏝, -lɛ́⏝, -éko-, -ého⏝); perf. aī⏜fadlɛ́gorɪ⏝ (N. -éko-, -ého⏝).
   imperat. fadlɛ́!, pl. fadlɛ́wɛ! (-lɛ́wé!).
   part. pres. fadlɛ́l⏝ *(one) that remains over, etc., remainder, etc., remaining over, etc.*; perf. fadlɛ́gol⏝ *(one) that (has) remained over, etc., remainder, etc., having remained over, etc.*; past fadlɛ́rɛl⏝ *(one) that remained over, etc., remainder, etc., remaining over, etc.*
   índo⏜fadlɛ́wé⏝ *remain* (pl.) *here.*
   míndo⏜fadlɛ́n? *what is left?*
   X. míndo⏜fadlɛ́gon? *what was (is) left?*
   Y. dállāmun⏝ *nothing* (s.v. dá- *be present*).
   míndo⏜fadlɛ́róskó? *what's remained over (...been left behind)?*
   téddotōn⏜fadlɛ́goná? (a) *did it remain* (has it remained) *over from it?*; (b) *did some remain* (has some remained) *over from it?*
   téddotōf⏜fadlɛ́gol⏜dáná? (-f⏜f- < -n⏜f- §542) *is there any of it (that has been) left?*
   téddotōf⏜fadlɛ́gol⏜dámɛn? *isn't there any of it left?*
   dɪmɪndówwɪrtōŋ⏜goríčk⏜óskɪŋ⏜góríč⏝ fadlɛ́⏝ *12 - 6 = 6.*
fadlɛ́rar⏝ (ràr⏝; §§2200 ff., 2207) and fadlɛ́ríd⏝ (§§2256 ff., 2260) n. *remaining over, etc.*
fadlɛ́r-an (§§3890, 3899) v.t. *tell to remain behind, let remain over, etc.*
fadlɛ́-bŭ- (§3931 β) v.i. stat. *be in the state or condition of remaining over, etc.*
   gírɪš⏜tóskɪ⏜fadlɛ́būn⏝ *three piastres are left.*

fadlɛ́gol-dā- (-ollā- §578; §§3985-6, 5566) v.i. *be present* (etc. s.v. dá-) *having remained over, etc.*
   téddotōf⏜fadlɛ́gollāná? (-f⏜f- < -n⏜f- §542) *is there any of it left?*
   téddotōf⏜fadlɛ́gollāmɛn? *isn't there any of it left?*
fadlɛrɛd-ág- (§§3877 ff.) v.i. *be in the situation of having remained over, etc.*
fadlɛ́g-ɪr (N. -ékɪr, -éhɪr; §3681) v.t. caus. *cause or allow to remain over, etc.*
fadíčča⏝ (-díč-) = fijadíčča⏝.
fagír (fàg-, fɛg-) n. *Coran-reader or -reciter, schoolmaster; learned man, holy man* [< فَقِير (*poor*) as used in Sudan Ar. §2409].
   obj. -gírk(ɪ)⏝, -kɪ⏝.
   pl. -gírɪ⏝.
   fɛgír⏜hīránɪg⏜gɛrjɛ́gɪrɪrɪn⏝ *the fɛgír teaches* (lit. *causes*) *the pupils to read.*
   fàgírro⏜ǧétkoran⏝ *they swore (have sworn) by the holy man* (i.e. *on his tomb*).
fagír-an- (fàg-, fɛg-; §3910α) v.i. *become a Coran-reader, etc.*
fagíram-bŭ- (fàg-, fɛg-; §§3949 ff.) v.i. stat. *be in the state of becoming a Coran reader, etc.*
fagíranɛd-ág- (fàg-, fɛg-; §3966α) v.i. *be in the condition of having become a Coran-reader, etc.*
fagírɪŋkútt(ɪ)⏝ (fàg-, fɛg-, -tɪ⏝) n. *Fakrinkotti* (on map) *a village on the left bank of the Nile, about 26 miles above Débba* [*Knoll of the Coran-readers*].
   obj. -tɪg⏝.
fáida⏝ (fâida⏝) n. *benefit, advantage, profit, use* [< فَائِدَة *id.*].
   obj. -dag⏝.
   pl. -danč(ɪ)⏝.
   tér⏜fáidak⏜kón⏝ *(s)he (it) has an advantage, etc.*
   ín⏜fáidak⏜kómunun⏝ *this has no advantage, etc.*
fáida-kɪ́ññ(ɪ)⏝ (§§2536-7) adj. *without benefit, etc., unprofitable, useless.*
fáidakɪ́ññɪg-ɪr ("⏝, N. -ɪkɪr, -ɪhɪr; §3703) (a) v.t. caus. *cause or allow to be without benefit, etc.*; (b) v.t. *render unprofitable, etc., sterilize.*
   ǧɛlli⏜mállɛf⏜fáidakɪ́ññɪgírkoran⏝ (-f⏜f- < -g⏜f- §540) *they (have) rendered the whole affair unprofitable* (...made all *the work useless*).
fáida-kō- (§4118) v.i. *have an advantage, be advantageous, be profitable, be useful.*
   part. pres. fáidakōl⏝ (fáidakól⏝ §1708) *(one) that is advantageous, profitable, useful*; obj. fáidakólg(ɪ)⏝, -gɪ⏝.
   ím⏜fáidakon, ím⏜fáidakómunun⏝ *this is advantageous, that isn't.*
fáidád⏝ (§2397) n. = fáida⏝ [< Sudan Ar. فَائِدَات pl. of فَائِدَة *id.*].
   obj. -ádk(ɪ)⏝, -átk(ɪ)⏝, -átt(ɪ)⏝ §2462, -kɪ⏝, -tɪ⏝.
   gen. -ádn⏝v., -án⏝c.
   pl. -ádɪ⏝.
fáidád-kɪ́ññ(ɪ)⏝ (-átk-; §§2536-7) adj. = fáidakɪ́ññ(ɪ)⏝.

fáɩz — fɛhmɛ́

faîdãdkíññıg-ır (-ātk-; N. -ıkır, -ıhır; §3703) v.t. caus. and v.t. = faîdakıññıgır.
fáɩz (fáíz) n. *interest (on money due)* [< قايظ *id.*].
  obj. fáízk(ı)⏜, -ízk(ı)⏜, -ísk(ı)⏜, -ísk(ı)⏜, -ki⏝.
  faízk⏜áwın⏝ and
  faízkɛd⏜áwın⏝ *(s)he lends at interest*.
  faískɛd⏜árın⏝ *(s)he borrows at interest*.
  âı⏜dúŋgıx⏜xawáğanartöf⏜faískɛd⏜árkori⏝ (-x⏜x- <-g⏜x- §562, -f⏜f- <-n⏜f- §542) *I (have) got (the) money from the merchant at interest.*
  hawáğ⏜áıgı⏜dúŋgıf⏜faískɛd⏜dɛŋkó⏝ (-f⏜f- <-g⏜f- §540) *the merchant gave (has given) me the (some) money at interest*.
fákka⏜ n. *change, small coin*, s.v. fɛkka⏜.
fakkɛ́ v.t. *change (money)*, s.v. fɛkkɛ́.
fála⏜ adj. *skilful, adroit, clever* [< فالح *id.* SNK, 798; §§1234, 1340].
  obj. fálag⏜.
  pl. fáları⏜.
  ústa⏜fálan⏝ *the craftsman is skilful*.
  X. tér⏜fálare̊? *is (s)he skilful?*
  Y. fálamunun, kússan⏝ *(s)he's not skilful, (s)he's stupid*.
fál-an- (§3910α) v.i. *become skilful*, etc.
  fálam-bū- (§§3949 ff.) v.i. stat. *be in the state of becoming skilful*, etc.
  fálanɛd⏜ág- (§3966α) v.i. *be in the condition of having become skilful*, etc.
fānū́s⏜ n. *lantern* [< فانوس < φανός *id.*].
  obj. -úsk(ı)⏜.
  pl. -úsı⏜.
  fānúsn⏜ı́⏜ *handle of lantern*.
fárğɛ⏜ n. *Fergi (on map), a village on the left bank of the Nile, about 13 miles above Handag* [< فرجة *relief*].
  obj. fárğɛg⏜, fárğɛ́g §1532.
fás⏜ n. *date-stone; with collective sg.* (§4696b) [< فصى *id.* or < فصّ *stone (of ring), lump* §1372].
  obj. fásk(ı)⏜, -ki⏝.
  pl. fásı⏜.
  béntın⏜fás⏜ (-tım⏜fás⏜) *date-stone(s)*.
fás⏜ n. *axe, hatchet* (= gámbu⏜) [< فاس *id.*].
  obj. fásk(ı)⏜, -ki⏝.
  pl. fásı⏜.
  ín⏜tém⏜fásun⏝ *this is his axe*.
  fásn⏜ád⏜ *handle of axe*.
fássa⏜ n. *labium pudendi muliebris; with collective sg.* (§4696a) [? < فصعة *dilatatum praeputium*].
  obj. -sag⏜.
  pl. -sanč(ı)⏜.
fášɛ⏜ n. *transverse limb at the end of each spoke* (duŋgútt(ı)⏜, tárántarɛ) *of wheel raising water* (átt(ı)⏜) *in water-wheel* (kólɛ⏜); *over these limbs pass cables* (álası⏜) *bearing jars* (bɛ́ššɛnč(ı)⏜) [§2234δ; cp. K. *fašše id.* SNK, 377A10, K. *fašɛ́ sich ausstrecken* AZN].
  obj. -šɛg⏜.
  pl. -šɛnč(ı)⏜.
fašfás⏜ n. *lung* (= ufúff(ı)⏜); *with collective sg.* (§4696a) [< Sudan Ar. فَشْفَاش *id.*].

obj. -ášk(ı)⏜, -ki⏝.
pl. -áši⏜.
fátah⏜ n. *opening chapter of the Coran*, fátıha [< فاتحة *id., the opener* §§1340, 1394].
  obj. fātahk(ı)⏜, -ki⏝.
  fátahkı⏜sókkɛgori⏝ *I (have) recited the fátıha* (شلت الفاتحة).
fātáhkı-tır (§§3998, 5568) v.t. *recite the fátıha over (other than the speaker, s.v. tír)*.
  âı⏜diélgı⏜fātáhkıtıddi⏝ *I (shall §5369a) recite the fátıha over one (the person) that is dead*.
fatfád⏜ n. *fit, epilepsy, apoplexy* [§§2151, 2153; cp. fátte *have a fit*].
  obj. -ádk(ı)⏜, -átk(ı)⏜, -átt(ı)⏜ §2462, -ki⏝, -ti⏝.
  ím⏜fatfádun⏝ *this is a fit*.
  fatfátkı⏜kön⏝ (⏜kón⏝, ⏜kő⏝, ⏜kó⏝ §3566) *(s)he has a fit*.
fatfád-ko- (-átko-; §4118) v.i. *have a fit*.
  part. pres. fatfátköl⏜.
  fatfátkon⏝ (-kő⏝, -kó⏝) *(s)he has a fit*.
fatís⏜ n. *carrion, dead animal* [< فطيس *id.*].
  obj. -ísk(ı)⏜, -ki⏝.
  pl. -ísı⏜.
fatís-kal⏜ (§2381) n. *carrion-eater, vulture; with collective sg.* (§4696d).
  obj. fatīskálg(ı)⏜, -gi⏝.
  pl. fatīskalı⏜.
fátna⏜ n. *Fátıma, a woman's name* [< فاطمة *id.* §1290].
  obj. -nag⏜.
fátte v.i. *have a fit, have a stroke* [< فطّ (§1216) *prostration* + -ɛ (§3613)].
  ind. pres. âı⏜fátteri⏝; perf. âı⏜fáttɛgori⏝ (N. -ɛko-, -ɛho-).
  fattóskó⏝ *(s)he has had a fit*.
fátterar (-rár⏜; §§2200 ff., 2210) and
fatterí́d⏜ (-rár⏜; §§2256 ff., 2263) n. *having a fit (fits), epilepsy, apoplexy*.
fattɛr-ɛ-dól (-r°d- §1178; §§4016–17, 4022, 4027) v.i. *be about to have a fit*.
  fattɛrɛdólın⏝ *(s)he is going to have a fit*.
fattırɛ́ v.i. *breakfast* [< fattır- based on فطر *id.* + -ɛ́ §3644].
  ind. pres. âı⏜fattırɛ́ri⏝; perf. âı⏜fattırɛ́gori⏝ (N. -ɛ́ko-, -ɛ́ho-).
  imperat. fattırɛ́!
  def. perf. âı⏜fattırɛrɛ́dkori⏝.
fattırɛ́rar (-rár⏜; §§2200 ff., 2207) and
fattırɛ́rí́d⏜ (§§2256 ff., 2260) n. *breakfasting*.
fağír⏜ *Coran-reader*, etc. = fagír⏜.
fáğır⏜ n. *dawn* = fɛğır⏜.
fákka⏜ n. *change, small coin* = fɛkka⏜.
fakkɛ́ v.t. *change (money)* = fɛkkɛ́.
†farā́ıd⏜ (serv.) *fried* = fɛrā́ıd⏜.
fɛddán⏜ (§956a) n. *acre* (1·038 acre); *with collective sg.* (§4696d) [< فدّان *id.*].
  obj. -áŋg(ı)⏜, -gi⏝.
  pl. -ánı⏜.
  árıt⏜fɛddán⏜wɛğ⏜ğanárkori⏝ (-t⏜f- <-d⏜f-§705, -ğ⏜ğ- <-g⏜ğ-§551) and
  árın⏜fɛddáw⏜wɛğ⏜ğanárkori⏝ (-w⏜w- <-n⏜w- §720) *I (have) bought one acre of land*.

fɛgír⏜ *Coran-reader*, etc. = fagír⏜.
fɛğıntū́g⏜ *at dawn*, etc., s.v. fɛğır⏜.
fɛğır⏜ (fáğ-) n. (a) *dawn, day-break* [< فجر *id.* §1359]; (b, loosely) *early morning*.
  obj. fɛğírk(ı)⏜, -ki⏝.
  gen. fɛğíri⏜, -ğínn⏜v-, -ğın⏜c.
  féğın⏜mónkon⏜iñírkoran⏝ (-m⏜m- <-rn⏜m- §608) *they waited till dawn*.
fɛğírk(ı)⏜, -ki⏝ (§§4431–3) adv. (a, prop.) *at dawn*; (b, loosely) *early in the morning*; (c) *tomorrow morning, tomorrow*.
  (N.) kám⏜ınnówwı⏜fɛğírkı⏜dábukó⏝ (§6041) *the camel was present today at dawn*.
fɛğırro⏜ (s.v. -r⏜; §6007) adv. = fɛğírk(ı)⏜.
  fɛğírro⏝ *it is at dawn* (etc.).
  fɛğírro⏜så⏜kólodır⏜táwɛ⏜ *come (pl.) in the morning* (sc. *tomorrow*) *at seven o'clock*.
  X. ín⏜tɛ́rıt⏜tɛ́r⏝ (-t⏜t- <-g⏜t- §707) *sow this seed (these seeds §4696c)*.
  Y. ɛ́kkɛnɛgá? *now?*
  X. wǎran, fɛğírro⏝ *no, in the morning* (sc. *tomorrow*).
  kám⏜fɛğírrotów⏜wāhdıgómunun⏝ (-w⏜w- <-n⏜w- §720) *the camel has not appeared since dawn (i.e. ... has not been seen today)*.
fɛğırn⏜ogóllo⏜ and
fɛğınn⏜ogóllo⏜ (§6007) adv. *before dawn, before day-break*.
  fɛğírn⏜ogóllo⏝ (-ínn⏜) *it is before dawn* (etc.).
  főğa⏜fɛğínn⏜ogóll⏜ısfski⏜ğómın⏝ *the little birds* (§4696c) *twitter before day-break*.
fɛğın-tū́g⏜ (§1997) adv. (a, prop.) *at* (lit. *in*, s.v. tū́⏜) *dawn*; (b, loosely, like fɛğírk(ı)⏜) *early in the morning*.
  désse⏜fɛğıntū́b⏜bıččınálkan⏜sɛ́rɛ́n⏝ (-f⏜f- <-g⏜f- §540, -b⏜b- <-g⏜b- §519) *it's good (i.e. lucky) to see* (§5449) *vegetation on waking early in the morning, proverb*.
fɛğırí́jɛ⏜ n. *time from midnight till daybreak, one of the four watches in water-wheel cultivation duty, s.v. tátt(ı)⏜* (SNK, 291, 6) [< Sudan Ar. فجرية *id.*].
  obj. -jɛg⏜.
fɛhmɛ́ v.t. *understand* [< فهم *intelligence or* فاهم *intelligent* + -ɛ́ §3616].
  ind. pres. âı⏜fɛhmɛ́ri⏝; perf. âı⏜fɛhmɛ́gori⏝ (N. -ɛ́ko-, -ɛ́ho-).
  âı⏜ín⏜ogíčkı⏜fɛhmɛ́munun⏝ *I don't understand this man*.
  âı⏜ín⏜báññıdkı⏜fɛhmɛ́munun⏝ *I don't understand what they say*.
fɛhmɛ́rar (-rár⏜; §§2200 ff., 2207) and
fɛhmɛ́rí́d⏜ (§§2256 ff., 2260) n. *understanding, comprehension*.
fɛhmɛ́-bū- (§3934) v. stat. (a) i. *be in an understood state or condition, be intelligible*; (b) t. *be in an understanding state or condition, be intelligent*.
  tím⏜báññıd⏜fɛhmɛbūná? *is their language intelligible?*
  tím⏜báññıd⏜fɛhmɛbúmunun⏝ *their speech is not intelligible*.
  ín⏜ogíğ⏜fɛhmɛbūná? *is this man intelligent?*

fɛhmēr-ɛ-má- (§§ 4016–17, 4036, 4041) v.t. *become unable to understand.*

fɛhmɛ̄red-ág- (§§ 3877 ff.) v.t. *be in the condition of having understood.*

fɛhmḗg-ɪr (N. -ḗkɪr, -ḗhɪr; § 3681) v.t. caus. *cause or allow to understand, explain, explain to.*
  tém⌣baññídk⌣áɪgɪ⌣fɛhmḗgɪr⌢ *explain to me what (s)he says,* lit. *cause me to understand his (her) speech.*

fɛhmḗ-kattɪ- (N. -ḗha-; §§ 4093, 4099) (a) v.p. *be understood;* (b) v.i. *be intelligible.*

fɛhmḗ-káttɪ-bŭ- (N. -ḗha-; § 4108) v.i. stat. *be in an understood or intelligible state or condition.*

fékka (fák-, fák-, -kà⌣, -kɛ⌣) n. *change, small coin* [< فَكَّة *id.*].
  obj. -kag⌣.

fékkag-ɪr (fák-, fák-; N. -akɪr, -ahɪr; § 3697) v.t. *change (into smaller coin).*
  ind. pres. āɪ⌣fékkagɪddɪ⌢ and (§ 1814)
  āɪ⌣warákkɪ⌣bufékkagíddɪ⌢ (-w⌣w- < -n⌣w- § 720) *I shall change this note.*

fɛkkagɪr-ɛt-tá (fɛkkagɪr-ét-tä § 3855; N. -akɪr-, -ahɪr-; § 4142) v.t. *bring after changing (etc.).*
  íw⌣warákkɪ⌣fɛkkagɪrétta⌢ *change this note and bring (it,* sc. *the change).*

fɛkkḗ (fák-, fak-) v.t. *change (into smaller coin;* = ɛwɪr *f*) [< فَكّ *changing (etc.)* + -ɛ́ § 3623].
  ind. pres. āɪ⌣fɛkkḗrɪ⌢; perf. āɪ⌣fɛkkḗgorɪ⌢ (N. -ḗko-, -ḗho-).
  imperat. fɛkkḗ!
  def. imperat. fɛkkḗros! (fɛkkḗró! § 962).
  ín⌣ğínɛf⌣fɛkkḗró⌢ (-f⌣f- < -g⌣f- § 540) *change this pound.*

fɛkkḗrar (fák-, fak-; -rár⌣; §§ 2200 ff., 2207) and

fɛkkḗríd (etc.; §§ 2256 ff., 2260) n. *changing (etc.).*

fɛkkḗr-an (etc.; §§ 3890 ff., 3899) v.t. *tell to change (etc.), let change (etc.).*

fɛkkḗ-dɛn (etc.; §§ 3996–7) v.t. *change (etc.) for (the speaker).*

fɛkkḗ-tɪr (etc.; §§ 3998–9) v.t. *change (etc.) for (other than the speaker).*

fɛkkḗred-ág- (etc.; §§ 3877 ff.) v.t. *be in the situation of having changed (etc.).*

fɛkkḗr-ɛt-tá (etc.; fɛkkḗr-ét-tä § 1074 b; § 4142) v.t. *bring after changing (etc.).*
  ğínɛf⌣fɛkkɛrétta⌢ (-f⌣f- < -g⌣f- § 540) *change and bring the pound.*

fɛkkɛrós-dɛn (etc.; -óddɛn § 538; §§ 4180–4; -ósgɪdɛn, -ózgɪ-, -óggɪ- § 4185) v.t. = fɛkkḗdɛn.
  āɪg⌣íŋgɪ⌣fɛkkɛróddɛ⌢ *change this for me.*

fɛkkɛrós-tɪr (etc.; -óttɪr § 714; -óssɪr § 686; §§ 4180–4; -ósgɪdɪr, -ózgɪ-, -óggɪ- § 4185) v.t. = fɛkkḗtɪr.
  íŋgɪ⌣tékkɪ⌣fɛkkɛróssɪr⌢ *change this for him (her).*
  ğínɛf⌣fɛkkɛrók-kulwāhítkɪ-gírɪš-arrɛdíčkɪ-tɪr⌢ (§ 5604) *when you have changed the pound give each one 25 piastres.*

fɛ́lɛg n. *beam, esp. beam(s) under roof, resting on the cross-beam* (mírɪg⌣) *that lies on the vertical beam* (ɛ́ndɛ⌣); *with collective sg.* (§ 4696 d) [< فَلَق (§ 1358) *id.,* usually *a split palm-trunk*].
  obj. fɛlɛ́gk(ɪ)⌣, -ɛ́kk(ɪ)⌣, -kɪ⌢.
  pl. fɛ́lɛgɪ⌣.
  ğíbɪd⌣fɛ́lɛgɪrtōn⌢ *the platform is made of beams.*

fɛ́rɪš n. *bed, bed-clothes, bedding* [< فَرْش (§ 1359) *id.*].
  obj. fɛrɪ́šk(ɪ)⌣, -kɪ⌢.
  pl. fɛ́r(ɪ)šɪ⌣.
  fɛ́rɪš⌣tagídd(ɪ)⌣ (-š⌣t- < -šn⌣t- § 865) *bedspread.*
  fɛ́ršɪn⌣tagíddɪnč(ɪ)⌣ *bedspreads* (lit. *covers of beds*).

†**fɛrtíd** (§ 2408) = †hartíd⌣ *rhinoceros.*

fɛrtɪgḗ v.i. *burst* [< a stem of اتفرتك *id.* + -ɛ́ § 3655].
  ind. pres. tɛr⌣fɛrtɪgḗn⌢ (-gɛ̄⌢, -gɛ̄́⌢, -gɛ̄⌢); perf. tɛr⌣fɛrtɪgḗgon⌢ (-gō⌢, -gó⌢); N. -ḗkon⌢, -kō⌢, -kó⌢, -ḗhon⌢, -hō⌢, -hó⌢).

fɛttɪšḗ v.t. *examine, inspect, investigate, scrutinize* [< imperat. or imperf. stem of فتّش *id.* + -ɛ́ § 3636].
  ind. pres. āɪ⌣fɛttɪšḗrɪ⌢; perf. āɪ⌣fɛttɪšḗgorɪ⌢ (N. -ḗko-, -ḗho-).
  imperat. fɛttɪšḗ!
  ím⌣mállɛf⌣fɛttɪšḗran⌢ (-f⌣f- < -g⌣f- § 540) (a) *they examine all this;* (b, § 3899) *let him (her) examine all this.*

fɛttɪšḗrar (-rár⌣; §§ 2200, 2207) and

fɛttɪšḗríd (§§ 2256 ff., 2260) n. *examination, etc.*

fɛttɪšḗr-an (§§ 3890 ff., 3899) v.t. *tell to examine, etc., let examine, etc.*

fɛttɪšḗ-bŭ- (§ 3931 β) v.i. stat. *be in an examined (etc.) state or condition.*

fɛttɪšḗr-ɛg-ág- (§§ 4071 ff.) v.t. = fɛttɪšēredól-.

fɛttɪšḗr-ɛ-dól- (-rᵒd- § 1178; §§ 4016–17, 4022, 4027) v.t. *be about to examine, etc.*

fɛttɪšḗred-ág- (§§ 3877 ff.) v.t. *be in the situation of having examined, etc.*

fɛttɪšḗ-kattɪ- (N. -ḗha-; § 4093) v.p. *be examined, etc.*

fɛttɪšḗ-nál (§ 3747 ɛ) v.t. *see by examining, etc., look at carefully.*
  imperat. fɛttɪšḗnal! (§ 1871).
  ím⌣mállɛf⌣fɛttɪšḗnállan⌢ (-f⌣f- < -g⌣f- § 540) *they look carefully at all this.*

fɛttɪšḗnál-an (§§ 3890 ff., 3905) v.t. *tell to see by examining, etc., let see by examining, etc.*
  ím⌣mállɛf⌣fɛttɪšḗnálan⌢ *tell him (her) to look carefully at all this.*

fḗza n. *emergency working-party of voluntary helpers in irrigation by water-wheel* (kólɛ⌣; NSD, 22, 23) [< Sudan Ar. فَزَع *id.* HSA, s.v. *water-wheel*].
  obj. -zag⌣.
  pl. fɛzánč(ɪ)⌣.

†**fəráid** (fár-; serv.) adj. *fried* [< Eng. *fried* regarded as فَرَائِد § 2588].
  obj. -áidk(ɪ)⌣, -âitk(ɪ)⌣, -kɪ⌢.

†**fəráidk-ɪr** (fár-, -âitk-; § 3702) (a) v.t. caus. *cause or allow to be fried;* (b) v.t. *fry.*

†**fəráidkɪr-ɛt-tá** (fár-, -âitk-; -ét-tä § 3855; § 4142) v.t. *bring after frying.*
  kúmb⌣ówwɪf⌣fəráidkɪrétta⌢ (-f⌣f- < -g⌣f- § 540) *fry and bring two eggs.*

fíčč n. *bat (animal);* with collective sg. (§ 4696 d) [< *fíčt(ɪ)⌣ (§ 526) < fíč- onom. + -t dim. or dem. § 2228].
  obj. -čɪg⌣.
  pl. -čɪnč(ɪ)⌣.

fijadíčča (fíja-, fja-, fa-, -díč-) n. *Fadíčča,* name applied to the Nubians and to their language from Sukkót to Koróskó (Reinisch's *Fadīja,* Fadidscha RN, p. vi) [popular etymology RN, 1, p. 180].
  obj. -čag⌣.
  pl. -čanč(ɪ)⌣.

fijadíččančín-d(ɪ) (fíja-, etc.; §§ 2545 ff.) (a) adj. *appertaining to the Fijadíččanči;* (b) n. *the language of the F.,* a subdialect included here in M. (§ 85).

fíl n. *elephant* [< فِيل *id.*].
  obj. fílg(ɪ)⌣, -gɪ⌢.
  pl. fílɪ⌣.

fíl-nél (§ 2358; fílnɛl⌣) *ivory.*
  obj. fílnɛ́lg(ɪ)⌣.
  tɛr⌣fílnɛ́llotōnun⌣ɛríndín⌢ *it is (made) of ivory.*

fíln-d(ɪ) (§§ 2545 ff.) adj. *appertaining to the (an) elephant, of the (an) elephant, the (an) elephant's.*
  ín⌣⌣fílndɪmunun⌣ɛríndín⌢ *this tusk is not an elephant's, it's a hippopotamus's.*

†**fís** (serv.) n. *pantry* [< Sudan Ar. فيس *id.* < Fr. *office* § 2395].
  obj. físk(ɪ)⌣, -kɪ⌢.
  pl. físɪ⌣.
  X. álɪ⌣sɛ́? *where is* ɛáli?
  Y. físɪr⌢ *in the pantry.*

fɪlátt(ɪ) v.i. *flash, glitter, sparkle, gleam, shine* (= fɪlátt(ɪ), q.v.) [imit. < *fɪlátk(ɪ) (§ 716) < √fɪlát- *flash* (§ 4520) + -k (§ 2899)].
  ind. pres. tɛr⌣fɪláttɪn⌢ (-tī⌢, -tí⌢); perf. tɛr⌣fɪláttɪgon⌢ (-gō⌢, -gó⌢; N. -ɪkon⌢, -kō⌢, -kó⌢, -ɪhon⌢, -hō⌢, -hó⌢).
  unátt⌣úrun⌣tūr⌣fɪláttɪn⌢ and
  unátt⌣úrur⌣fɪláttɪn⌢ *the moon sparkles on* (lit. *in*) *the river.*

fɪlatfɪlád (fɪlɛt- § 1176) n. *repeated lightning, flashes of lightning;* with collective sg. (§ 4696 d) [repetition of √fɪlát- *flash* (§ 4520) § 2158].
  obj. -ádk(ɪ)⌣, -átk(ɪ)⌣, -átt(ɪ)⌣ § 2462; -kɪ⌢, -tɪ⌢.
  pl. -ádɪ⌣.
  fɪlɛtfɪlád⌣ğómkó⌢ *repeated lightning (has) flashed.*

fílfɪl n. *pepper* [< فُلْفُل *id.*].
  obj. fɪlfɪ́lg(ɪ)⌣, -gɪ⌢.
  fɪlfɪl⌣hábba (§ 808) *peppercorn.*

fɪlínč(ɪ) v.i. *flash continually or continuously, glitter, sparkle, shine* (= bɪlínč(ɪ), tulúnč(ɪ)) [< √fɪlín- *flash* (§ 4521) + -č intensive (§ 4502) *much* § 2864].
  ind. pres. tɛr⌣fɪlínčɪn⌢ (-čī⌢, -čí⌢), tɪr⌣fɪlínčɪran⌢ (-rā⌢, -rá⌢); perf. tɛr⌣fɪlínčɪgon⌢ (-gō⌢, -gó⌢; N. -ɪkon⌢, -kō⌢, -kó⌢, -ɪhon⌢, -hō⌢, -hó⌢).
  gɛzáz⌣fɪlínčɪn⌢ *(the) glass glitters.*
  ɛ́lum⌣míssɪ⌣fɪlínčɪn⌢ *the crocodile's eye glitters* (... *eyes glitter* § 4696 a).

fılınfıldádɛ — gābılɛ́

nóbrɛ⁀fılínčın⁀ (the) gold is bright.
íg⁀wárrırtōn⁀fılínčın⁀ the fire (light) shines from afar.

fılınfıldádɛ (N.) n. repeated lightning, flashes of lightning (=fılatfıládɛ); with collective sg. (§4696d) [< √fılín- flash (§4521) modified in repetition (§2157) +-ɛ of n. act. (§2234γ); §2188].
  obj. -dɛg.
  pl. -dɛnč(ı).

fılítt(ı) v.i. flash, glitter, sparkle, gleam, shine (=fılátt(ı)) [< *fılínt(ı) (§711) < √fılín- flash (§4521)+-t (§2900); RSN, §129].
  ind. pres. tɛr⁀fılíttın⁀ (-tī⁀, -tí⁀); perf. tɛr⁀fılíttıgon⁀ (-gō⁀, -gó⁀; N. -ıkon⁀, -kō⁀, -kó⁀, -ıhon⁀, -hō⁀, -hó⁀).
  gɛzáz⁀fılíttın⁀ (the) glass glitters.
  élum⁀míssı⁀fılíttın⁀ the crocodile's eye glitters (...eyes glitter) §4696a.
  nóbrɛ⁀fılíttın⁀ (the) gold is bright.
  másıl⁀fılíttın⁀ the sun shines.
  unáttı⁀fılíttın⁀ the moon shines.
  wíssı⁀fılíttın⁀ the star glitters (stars glitter §4696d).
  íg⁀wárrırtōn⁀fılíttın⁀ the fire (light) shines from afar.

fınğán (§956a) n. small cup [< فِنْجان id.].
  obj. -ğáŋg(ı), -gi⁀.
  pl. -ğánı.
  fınğánn⁀í⁀ the handle of the small cup.
  fınğán⁀tɛ́mɛn⁀ (-nt- < -nn⁀t- §613) the price of the small cup.

fırıčč(ı) n. mason wasp, solitary wasp; with collective sg. (§4696c) [< *fırígt(ı) (§525) < fır- of fírr(ı) to fly + íg⁀ fire +-t dim. so *little thing that flies and burns §2228].
  obj. -čıg.
  pl. -čınč(ı).

fírr(ı) v.i. fly [imit.; RSN, §§129, 200, TOB, §143, 276].
  ind. pres. tɛr⁀fírrın⁀ (-rī⁀, -rí⁀); perf. tɛr⁀fírrıgon⁀ (-gō⁀, -gó⁀, N. -ıkon⁀, -kō⁀, -kó⁀, -ıhon⁀, -hō⁀, -hó⁀).
  part. pres. fírrıl⁀ (one) that flies, flier, flying; obj. fırrílg(ı), -gi⁀.

fírrıl (-rıl) n. moth, butterfly, larger winged insect (smaller ones are called kúlt(ı)); with collective sg. (§4696c) [§2281].
  obj. fırrílg(ı), -rílg(ı), -gi⁀.
  pl. fírrılı, fırrílı.
  ár⁀fırrílg⁀ɛru, érrı⁀ɛččɛ́lgı⁀kómunun⁀ we call it fırrfl, it has no other name (said of a dragon-fly).

fırrır-ɛg-ág- (§§4071ff.) v.i. = fırrɛdól-.
fırr-ɛ-dól- (-rᵒd- §1178; §4022) and
fırr-ɛ-dól- (-rᵒd-; §4027) v.i. be about to fly.
fırr-ɛ-má- (§4036) and
fırrır-ɛ-má- (§4041) v.i. become unable to fly.

fırt(ı) v.i. untwist, come untwisted, get its strands separated.
  ind. pres. tɛr⁀fírtın⁀ (-tī⁀, -tí⁀); perf. tɛr⁀fírtıgon⁀ (-gō⁀, -gó⁀; N. -ıkon⁀, -kō⁀, -kó⁀, -ıhon⁀, -hō⁀, -hó⁀).
  írı⁀fírtın⁀ the rope comes (will come §5369a) untwisted.
  írı⁀fırtóskon⁀ the rope has come untwisted.

fírtı-bŭ- (§3931α) v.i. stat. be in an untwisted state or condition, have its strands separated.
  írı⁀fırtıbūn⁀ the rope is (has come) untwisted.

fís! and (§307)
físss! interj. to drive away a cat (=bís!) [onom.].

físs(ı) v.t. and i. splash [imit.].
  ind. pres. aī⁀físsırı⁀; perf. aī⁀físsıgori⁀ (N. -ıko-, -ıho-).
  aī⁀ɛ́dd⁀ɛssıf⁀físsırı⁀ (-dᴗɛ- < -doᴗɛ- §1122, -fᴗf- < -gᴗf- §540) I splash water on to you.
  aī⁀tɛ́kk⁀ɛssıgɛf⁀físsıgorı⁀ (-fᴗf- < -dᴗf- §539) I (have) splashed him (her, it) with water.
  éssı⁀físsın⁀ the water splashes.

físsar (-sárᴗ; §§2200ff.) and
físsíd (§§2256ff.) n. splashing.

físs-an (§§3890ff.) v.t. tell to splash, let splash.

físsı-tó (§§3747ᴱ′, 3783) v.i. and t. enter splashing, splash in.
  éssı⁀áddo⁀fıssıtón⁀ the water splashes in on to me (us).

fítnɛ n. intrigue, plot, conspiracy, treachery, sedition, rebellion [< فِتْنَة id.].
  obj. -nɛg.
  pl. -nɛnč(ı).
  fítnɛg⁀áw¹ran⁀ they make a conspiracy.

fógır adj. poor [appar. < فَقْر poverty §2586].
  obj. fogírk(ı), -ki⁀.
  pl. fóg(¹)rı.

fóğ adj. bald [RSN, §129].
  obj. fóğk(ı), fóčk(ı), fóčč(ı) §523; -ki⁀, -či⁀.
  pl. fóğı.
  úrn⁀fóğ = fóğ.
  ógığ⁀fóğun⁀ the man is bald.

fóğ-an- (§3910α) v.i. get bald.
fóğam-bŭ- (§§3949ff.) v.i. stat. be in the state of getting bald.
fóğanɛd-ág- (§3966α) v.i. be in the condition of having got bald.

fóğa n. small bird; with collective sg. (§4696c) [< *fóğan (§939) < fóğ- onom. +-an *utterance (§2050), so *what says fóč! (§§468-9), chirper, twitterer; cp. Amh. √ፎጨ in ፎጨሎ whistle].
  obj. -ğag.
  pl. fóğanč(ı).

fórrɛ v.i. (a) snort; (b, of cat) spit; (c, of cat) purr (=ñúrr(ı)); (d) snore [lit. say 'fórr!' §§2870ff.].
  ind. pres. aī⁀fórrırı⁀; perf. aī⁀fórrɛgori⁀ (N. -ɛko-, -ɛho-).
  káğ⁀fórrɛgon⁀ the horse snorted.
  sáb⁀fórrɛgon⁀ the cat (a) spat, (b) purred.

fúčɛ v.i. blow one's nose [lit. say 'fúč!' §§2870ff.].
  ind. pres. aī⁀fúčɛrı⁀; perf. aī⁀fúčɛgori⁀ (N. -ɛko-, -ɛho-).

fúčɛrar (-rárᴗ), fúčar (-čárᴗ, -čɛr); §§2200ff., 2211) and
fŭčɛríd, fŭčíd (§§2256ff., 2264) n. nose-blowing.

fúč-an and
fúč-an (§§3890ff., 3540) v.t. tell to blow the nose, let blow the nose.

fúl n. bean, Vicia faba L. (BSP, 141): with collective sg. (§4696b) [< فُول id.].
  obj. fúlg(ı), -gi⁀.
  gen. fúln⁀v.c., fún⁀c. (§612a).
  pl. fúlı.
fúln-d(ı) and
fŭn-d(ı) (§§2545ff.) adj. appertaining to the (a) bean (beans).
  ğakud⁀fúnd(ı) a stew of beans.

fulán (§956a) indef. pron. so-and-so, a certain person [< فُلان id.].
  obj. -áŋg(ı), -gi⁀.
  gen. -ánn⁀v., -ánᴗc.

†**fúlla** n. cork (stopper) [< فِلَّة id.].
  obj. -lag.
  pl. -lanč(ı).

fúndug n. mortar (vessel for pounding) [app. < Sudan Ar. فُنْدُق pestle §2408].
  obj. fundúgk(ı), -úkk(ı), -ki⁀.
  gen. -úgn⁀v., -úŋc., -
  pl. fúndugı.

fúrsa (-sàᴗ) n. fatty part of milk, butter [< فُرْصَة id.].
  obj. -sag.

†**fúrša** n. brush [< فُرْشَة id.].
  obj. -šag.
  pl. -šanč(ı).

fúrun (§956a) n. oven [< فُرْن id. §1363].
  obj. furúŋg(ı), -gi⁀.
  pl. fúrunı.
  furundó and furun⁀tūr in the oven.
  furundó and furun⁀tūr (§6007) it is in the oven.
  kál⁀furúndojó? is the bread in the oven?
  fúrun⁀ğugrírɛ? is the oven hot?

fúta n. cloth, esp. for wiping, towel, napkin [< فُوطَة id.].
  obj. -tag.
  pl. -tanč(ı).
  súfran⁀fúta (Eur.) tablecloth.

futúr n. breakfast [< فُطُور id.].
  obj. -úrk(ı), -ki⁀.

gáb n. Wādi⁀l-Gáɛb, an oasis in the desert about 20 miles north-west of El-Ordi [< القَعْب id., The Bowl, §1389].
  obj. gábk(ı), gápk(ı), -ki⁀.

gába n. wood, forest [< غابَة id.].
  obj. gábag.

gábad n. bark (of tree) (=kắčč(ı)) [RSN, §§129, 200].
  obj. gabádk(ı), -átk(ı), -átt(ı) §2462; -ki⁀, -ti⁀.
  pl. gábadı.
  ğówwıŋ⁀gábad and šídarn⁀gábad bark of tree.
  bérn⁀gábad and bérŋ⁀gábad (a) bark of trunk; (b) shaving(s §4696d).
  hášam⁀gábad (-mᴗg- < -bnᴗg- §586) shaving(s).

gābılɛ́ v.t. meet, come face to face with [< imperf. or imperat. stem of قَابَل id.+-ɛ́ §3647].
  ind. pres. aī⁀gābılɛ́rı⁀; perf. aī⁀gābılɛ́gori⁀ (N. -ɛ́ko-, -ɛ́ho-).

imperat. gābılɛ́!
part. pres. gābılɛ́rıl⌣ (one) that meets, meeter, meeting; past gābılɛ́rel⌣ (one) that met, meeter, meeting.
sámıl⌣ɛkkı⌣gābılɛ́rán̄gı⌣dólın⌢ the chief wants to meet you.
gābılɛ́rar⌣ (-rɑ̀r⌣; §§2200ff., 2207) and
gābılɛ́rıd⌣ (§§2256ff., 2260) n. meeting.
gābılɛ́r-an (§§3890, 3899) v.t. tell to meet, etc., let meet, etc.
gābılɛ́-bŭ- (§3933) v.t. stat. be in the state or condition of meeting or having met, be with on meeting.
ɛsmán⌣tımbéskı⌣gābılɛ́būn⌢ ɟoθmán has met (and is with) his brother.
gābılɛ̄red-ág- (§§3877ff.) v.t. be in the situation of having met, etc.
gābılɛ́-kattı- (N. -ɛ́ha-; §4093) v.p. be met.
tɛ́r⌣gābılɛ́kattın⌢ (s)he is met, can be (§5704) met, is sociable.
ın̄⌣ógıg̈⌣gābılɛkáttımunun⌢ this man is not sociable.
part. gābılɛkattıl⌣ (one) that is (can be) met, sociable.
ádɛm⌣gābılɛkattílgı⌣dóllan⌢ they like a sociable person.
gabul- [< Sudan Ar. قَبْل before, previously (to) = قَبْل §1355].
gabúl-lo⌣ (s.v. -r⌣; §6007) adv. beforehand, previously, formerly.
⌣gabúllo (§5860) postp. (= prep. §4287) before, previously to—follows the genitive.
āı⌣sıgíddaŋ⌣gabúllo⌣waddɛ́gorı⌢ (-ŋ⌣g- < -rn⌣g- §648) I performed the ritual ablutions before saying my prayers.
gábur n. grave, tomb [< قَبْر id. §1363].
obj. gabúrk(ı)⌣, -kı⌢.
pl. gáburı⌣.
gáda⌣ n. lunch [< غَدَاء id.].
obj. -dag⌣.
gádı⌣ n. judge [< قَاضِي id. §1389].
obj. -dıg⌣.
pl. -dınč(ı)⌣.
gadíjɛ⌣ (-jɑ̀⌣, -ja⌣) n. lawsuit, case [< قَضِيَّة id.].
obj. -jɛg⌣.
pl. -jɛnč(ı)⌣.
gádın⌣ogóllo⌣gadíjɛk⌣kórı⌢ (-k⌣k- < -g⌣k- §569) I have a case before the judge.
ɛ́r⌣gadíjɛr⌣gálıb'rɛ́⌣wála⌣mɛglúb'rɛ́? did you win the case or lose it?
gadíb⌣ n. rail (of railway); with collective sg. (§4696d) [< قَضِيب id.].
obj. -díbk(ı)⌣, -dípk(ı)⌣, -kı⌢.
gen. -díbn⌣ɔ, -dím⌣c. (§586).
pl. -díbı⌣.
gáfa⌣ n. nape of neck [< قَفَاء id.].
obj. gáfag⌣.
pl. gafánč(ı).
gág (a) v.t. split, crack, slit, burst; (b) v.i. get split, get cracked, get slit, burst.
ind. pres. āı⌣gág(ı)rı⌢, perf. āı⌣gágkorı⌢ (gákko-).
imperat. gák!

tókkom⌣bérkı⌣gágmɛn⌢ and dókkom⌣bérkı⌣gáŋŋɛn⌢ (§661) don't split the wood.
bér⌣bugágın⌢ the wood will split.
tɛ́ŋ⌣kádɛg⌣gákkō⌢ (s)he (has) slit his (her) cloth (garment).
tɛ́ŋ⌣kádɛ⌣gákkō⌢ his (her) cloth (has) slit.
áw⌣wıččírkı⌣gagóskorı⌢ (-w⌣w- < -n⌣w- §720) I have split my stick.
áw⌣wıččir⌣gagóskō⌢ my stick has split.
búndug⌣gagóskō⌢ the gun has exploded.
gágar⌣ (-gɑ̀r⌣; §§2200ff.) and
gagíd⌣ (§§2256ff.) n. splitting, etc.
gág-an (§§3890ff.) v.t. tell to split, etc., let split, etc.
gág-bŭ- (gággu- §546; §3931 β) v.i. stat. be in a split (etc.) state or condition, be split, etc.
ıŋ⌣gággūn, ıŋ⌣gaggúmunun⌢ this is split (diffissum est) that isn't.
wıččir⌣gággūl⌣ the (a) split stick.
gág-kattı- (gákka-; §4093) v.p. be split, etc.
ıŋ⌣gákkattın, ıŋ⌣gakkáttımunun⌢ this is (can be §5704) split (diffinditur) that isn't (can't).
gággu- < **gág-bŭ-** be split, etc. s.v. gág.
gáhwa⌣ n. coffee (the drink) [< قَهْوَة id.].
obj. -wag⌣.
gáhwad⌣dólná? (-d⌣d- < -g⌣d- §534) do you (does (s)he) want (like) coffee?
gajásk(ı)⌣ (gıjás-, gıas-) n. large sailing-boat [< gaj(j)ás- of قَيَّاسَة id. (§1393) + -k(ı)⌣ §2139].
obj. -kıg⌣.
pl. -kınč(ı)⌣.
gajaskın-d(ı)⌣ (gıjas-, gıas-; §§2545ff.) adj. appertaining to the (a) large sailing-boat.
gajırɛ́ v.t. change, alter [< imperat. or imperf. stem of غَيَّر id. (§1381) + -ɛ́ §3640].
ind. pres. āı⌣gajırɛ́rı⌢; perf. āı⌣gajırɛ́gorı⌢ (N. -ɛ́ko-, -ɛ́ho-).
ɛ́ŋ⌣kádɛg⌣gajırɛ́⌢ change your clothes (§4696d).
gajırɛ́rar⌣ (-rɑ̀r⌣; §§2200ff., 2207) and
gajırɛ́rıd⌣ (§§2256ff., 2260) n. change, alteration.
gajırɛ́r-an (§§3890, 3899) v.t. tell to change, etc., let change, etc.
gajırɛ́-bŭ- (§3931 β) v.i. stat. be in a changed (etc.) state or condition.
gajırɛ̄red-ág- (§§3877ff.) v.t. be in the situation of having changed, etc.
ıŋı⌣gajırɛ̄redágın⌢ you have ((s)he has) changed this.
gajırɛ́-kattı- (N. -ɛ́ha-; §4093) v.p. be changed, etc.
ıŋ⌣gajırɛkattóskon⌢ this has (already §3802) been changed.
-g-al s.v. -al⌣.
galabán (§956a) adj. tired, tired out, worn out, exhausted [< غَلْبَان id.].
obj. -áŋg(ı)⌣, -gı⌢.
pl. -ánı⌣.
tır⌣g̈élligeg⌣galabánın⌢ (-g⌣g- < -d⌣g- §545) they are exhausted by (the) work.
galabɛ́ v.t. tire, tire out, wear out, exhaust [< غَلَب overcoming + -ɛ́ §3621].

ind. pres. āı⌣galabɛ́rı⌢; perf. āı⌣galabɛ́gorı⌢ (N. -ɛ́ko-, -ɛ́ho-).
g̈éll⌣āıgı⌣galabɛ́gō⌢ the work (has) tired me out.
galabɛ́rar⌣ (-rɑ̀r⌣; §§2200ff., 2207) and
galabɛ́rıd⌣ (§§2256ff., 2260) n. tiring, etc., exhaustion.
galabɛ́-bŭ- (§3931 β) v.i. stat. be in a tired (etc.) state or condition.
galabɛ̄red-ág- (§§3877ff.) v.t. be in the situation of having tired, etc.
tɛr⌣āıgı⌣galabɛ̄redágın⌢ (s)he (it) has worn me out.
galabɛ́-kattı- (N. -ɛ́ha-; §4093) v.p. be tired, etc.
gálam n. pen [< قَلَم < κάλαμος id. (reed)].
obj. galámg(ı)⌣, -gı⌢.
pl. gálamı⌣.
gálamn⌣ád⌣ handle of pen, penholder.
galam-rasás n. pencil [< قَلَم رَصَاص id.].
obj. -ásk(ı)⌣, -kı⌢.
pl. -ásı⌣.
gálı⌣ adj. dear, costly [< غَالِي id.].
obj. -lıg⌣.
pl. -lınč(ı)⌣.
gálıg v.t. resemble.
ind. pres. āı⌣gálıg(¹)rı⌢, ɛr⌣gálıgın⌢ (-gī⌢, -gí⌢); perf. āı⌣galígkorı⌢ (-íkko-).
tımbéskı⌣gálıgın⌢ he resembles his (she resembles her) brother.
ulúdkı⌣gálıgın⌢ it's like charcoal.
— also constructed, and forming complex, with object without objective suffix (§§5701-2):
tɛr⌣nórtıg⌣gálıgın⌢,
tɛr⌣nórtı⌣gálıgın⌢ and
tɛr⌣nórtı⌣galıgın⌢ it's like flour; ⌣nórtı⌣galıgın⌢ emphasizes flour.
tımbés⌣gálıgın⌢ he resembles his (she resembles her) brother.
ulúd⌣gálıgí⌢ it's like charcoal.
mín-gálıgın? what's it like?
tɛr⌣tımbáb⌣gálıgın⌢ he resembles his (she resembles her) father.
búru⌣tınɛ́ŋ⌣gálıgın⌢ the girl resembles her mother.
tıntımbáb⌣gálıgran⌢ and timbáb⌣gálıgran⌢ (§§5116-17) they resemble their father.
tód⌣ɛ́ŋgom⌣búrugálıgın⌢ and tód⌣ɛ́ŋgom⌣búrugálıgılun⌢ though he's a boy (s.v. -ón⌣ b) he looks like a girl (§§5731-3).
gālıtɛ́ (a) v.t. dispute with, contradict; (b) v.t. dispute; (c) v.i. dispute, argue [< imperf. or imperat. stem of غَالَط id. + -ɛ́ §3647].
ind. pres. āı⌣gālıtɛ́rı⌢; perf. āı⌣gālıtɛ́gorı⌢ (N. -ɛ́ko-, -ɛ́ho-).
imperat. gālıtɛ́!
āı⌣ɛkkı⌣gālıtɛ́gorı⌢ I (have) contradicted you.
tɛr⌣āıgı⌣gālıtɛ́gō⌢ (s)he (has) contradicted me.
tékkon⌣āıgoŋ⌣gālıtɛ́goru⌣ (s)he and I (have) had a dispute.
gālıtɛ́rar⌣ (-rɑ̀r⌣; §§2200ff., 2207) and
gālıtɛ́rıd⌣ (§§2256ff., 2260) n. disputing, contradiction.

gālıtɛ́-bŭ- (§ 3934) v.i. stat. *be in a disputed (etc.) state or condition, be the subject of or a party in a dispute.*
ín⌣hǎğɛ⌣gālıtɛ́būn⌢ *this matter is the subject of dispute.*
ín⌣hǎğɛr⌣ar⌣gālıtɛ́būru⌢ *in this matter we are in dispute.*

gālıtɛ́rɛd-ǎg- (§§ 3877ff.) v.t. *be in the situation of having disputed with, etc.*
tɛr⌣ǎıgı⌣gālıtɛ́rɛdǎgın⌢ *(s)he has contradicted me.*

gālıtɛ́-kattı- (N. -ɛ́ha-; § 4093) v.p. *be disputed with, etc.*
ín⌣hǎğɛ⌣gālıtɛ́kattın⌢ *this matter is disputed.*

gállo⌣ n. *unripe date*; with collective sg. (§ 4696b) [§ 2306].
obj. -log⌣.
pl. -lonč(ı)⌣.

gálo⌣ n. *large earthenware jar, esp. for storing and cooling water, water-jar* (= Eg. زير) [§ 2308].
obj. -log⌣.
pl. -lonč(ı)⌣.

gālón-d(ı)⌣ (§§ 2545ff.) adj. *appertaining to the (a) water-jar.*

gálo-kırı⌣ (§§ 2539-40) adj. *like the (a) water-jar.*

gámbu⌣ n. *axe, hatchet* [§ 2299; RSN, §§ 129, 200].
obj. -bug⌣.
pl. -bunč(ı)⌣.
gámbun⌣ǎd⌣ *handle of axe or hatchet.*

gámrɛ⌣ n. *Capparis aphylla, Roth.* (BSP, 28); with collective sg. (§ 4696b) [?cp. Amh. ጎምርʼ *Capparis tomentosa, Lam.*].
obj. -rɛg⌣.

gándar⌣ (-dȧr⌣) n. *yolk* [§ 2199].
obj. gandárk(ı)⌣, -kı⌢.
pl. gándarı⌣.
kúmbuŋ⌣gándar⌣ *(the) yolk of (the, an) egg.*

gándɛ⌣ n. *Acacia spirocarpa, Hochst.* (BSP, 181); with collective sg. (§ 4696b) [§ 2303; RSN, § 129].
obj. -dɛg⌣.
pl. -dɛnč(ı)⌣.

gandɛ́n-d(ı)⌣ (§§ 2545ff.) adj. *appertaining to A. spirocarpa.*

ganétt(ı)⌣, -tı⌣ n. *Ganétti (on map), an island about 20 miles above Débba.*
obj. -tıg⌣.
ganéttır⌣ *at (on, to) Ganétti.*
ganéttır⌣ *(s)he (it) is (they are) at (on) Ganétti.*

gānū́n (§ 956a) n. *rule, regulation, law* [< قانون id. < κανών id. LSG, p. 133].
obj. -ū́ŋ(ı)⌣, -gı⌢.
pl. -únı⌣.

gǎñ v.t. *lick* [cogn. gáññ(ı) *shave* (§ 2777)].
ind. pres. aı⌣gǎñrı, ɛr⌣gǎñın (-ñí⌢, -ñí⌢); perf. aı⌣gǎñkorı.
sǎb⌣sahǎŋgı⌣gǎñkon⌢ *the cat (has) licked the plate.*

gǎñar⌣ (-ñȧr⌣; §§ 2200ff.) and **gǎñíd**⌣ (§§ 2256ff.) n. *licking.*

gǎñ-an (§§ 3890ff.) v.t. *tell to lick, let lick.*

gǎñ-bŭ- (gǎñǔ- § 635; § 3931β) v.i. stat. *be in a licked state or condition.*
sáhaŋ⌣gǎñbūn⌢ *the plate is (has been) licked.*

gāñɛd-ǎg- (§§ 3877ff.) v.t. *be in the situation of having licked.*

gǎñ-kattı- (§ 4093) v.p. *be licked.*

√**gǎñ**

gāng-ídd(ı) (§ 3724) v.i. *yawn, gape.*
ind. pres. aı⌣gāngíddırı, ɛr⌣gāngíddın (-dí⌢, -dí⌢); perf. aı⌣gāngíddıgorı (N. -ıko-, -ıho-).

gáññ(ı) (a) v.t. *shave*; (b) v.i. *shave, shave oneself* [cogn. gǎñ *lick* § 2777].
ind. pres. aı⌣gáññırı; perf. aı⌣gáññıgorı (N. -ıko-, -ıho-).
part. pres. gáññıl⌣ *(one) that shaves, shaver, barber, shaving*; obj. gáññılg(ı)⌣, -gı⌢.
úrkı⌣gáññıl⌣ *head-shaver, (said of) hairdresser.*
aı⌣ás⌣sǎmɛ⌣gáññırı⌢ (-s⌣s- < -n⌣s- § 681) *I shave my beard (whiskers).*
ánn-urkı⌣gáññıgon⌢ *he (has) shaved my head.*
súgaŋkoran⌣tínn-urkı⌣gáññırann⌣ íllar⌢ and
súgaŋkoran⌣tínn-urkı⌣gáññır⌣ɛgı⌢ *they went (have gone) to the market to shave their heads, i.e. to get them shaved.*

gáññır n. *razor* [§ 2286α].
obj. gáññírk(ı)⌣, -kı⌢.
pl. gáññırı⌣.

gáññar⌣ (-ñȧr⌣; §§ 2200ff.) and **gáññíd**⌣ (§§ 2256ff.) n. *shaving.*

gáññ-an (§§ 3890ff.) v.t. *tell to shave, etc., let shave, etc.*

gáññ-bŭ- (§ 3931β) v.i. stat. *be in a shaved state or condition, be shaven.*
ténn-ur⌣gáññbūn⌢ *his head is shaven.*

gāññɛd-ǎg- (§§ 3877ff.) v.t. and i. *be in the situation (condition) of having shaved, etc.*
tɛr⌣ánn-urkı⌣gāññɛdǎgın⌢ *he has shaved my head.*
aı⌣gāññɛdǎgrı *I have shaved.*

gáññı-kattı- (N. -ıha-; § 4093) v.p. *be shaved.*

gañños-bǎğ (-obbǎğ § 521; §§ 4180-4) v.t. *write after shaving (oneself).*
kadénčıg⌣gaññobbǎč⌢ *when you have shaved, write (the list of) the clothes.*

gáŋgarɛ⌣ n. = gáŋgarı⌣.
obj. -rɛg⌣.
pl. gaŋgarénč(ı)⌣.

gáŋgarı⌣ n. *ear of wheat, barley, maize or millet when nearly ripe*; with collective sg. (§ 4696b) [RSN, § 129; Sudan Ar. قَنْقَرَة id.].
obj. -rıg⌣.
pl. gaŋgarínč(ı)⌣.
íllɛŋ⌣gáŋgarı⌣ *fresh (nearly ripe) ear(s) of wheat.*
makádaŋ⌣gáŋgarın⌣níbran⌢ (-n⌣- < -g⌣n- § 625) *they roast fresh ears of maize.*

gǎr⌣ n. *shore, bank, waterside* (= ǎr⌣, nǎr⌣) [app. < ON. ᚱᛅᚴ *side* GNT, s.v.; cp. ON. ᚱᛅᚴ id.; RSN, § 129].
obj. gǎrk(ı)⌣, -kı⌢.
pl. gǎrı⌣.
ɛ́ssıŋ⌣gǎrro⌢ *(s)he (it) is (they are § 5858) at the waterside.*
úruŋ⌣gǎrro⌣tɛ́bın⌢ *(s)he stands (waits s.v. tɛ́b) on the riverside.*

gǎr n. *cave* [< غار id.].
obj. gǎrk(ı)⌣, -kı⌢.
pl. gǎrı⌣.
fɛgír⌣gǎrn⌣túr⌣ǎgın⌢ *the holy man lives in the (a) cave.*
gǎrro⌣tógoran⌢ *they went (have gone) into the (a) cave.*

gǎr v.t. *crush (grain).*
ind. pres. aı⌣gǎrrı, ɛr⌣gǎrın (⌣gǎrí⌢, ⌣gǎrí⌢); perf. aı⌣gǎrkorı.
íllɛg⌣gǎrkorı⌢ *I (have) crushed the wheat.*
márɛg⌣gǎrran⌢ *they crush (the) sorghum.*
makádag⌣gǎrran⌢ *they crush (the) maize.*

gǎrar⌣ (-rȧr⌣; §§ 2200ff.) n. *crushing.*

gǎríd⌣ (§§ 2256ff.) n. (a) = gǎrar⌣; (b, § 2268) *crushed grain.*

gǎr-an (§§ 3890ff.) v.t. *tell to crush, let crush.*

gǎr-bŭ- (§ 3931β) v.i. stat. *be in a crushed state or condition.*
íllɛ⌣gǎrbūn⌢ *the wheat is (has been) crushed.*

gǎrk-ıdd(ı) (§ 3725) v.t. caus. *cause or allow to crush.*
aı⌣tɛ́kk⌣íllɛg⌣gǎrkıddırı⌢ *I make (let) him (her) crush (the) wheat.*

gǎr-kattı- (§ 4093) v.p. *be crushed.*

garáma⌣ n. *fine, monetary penalty* [< غرامة id.].
obj. -ag⌣.
pl. -anč(ı)⌣.

gǎrar n. *bag, sack* [cp. غرارة id. §§ 1307, 1394].
obj. garárk(ı)⌣, -kı⌢.
pl. gǎrarı⌣.

gardón⌣ (§ 956a) n. *Gordon* [< Sudan Ar. غَرْدُون ɛardón].
obj. -dóŋ(ı)⌣, -gı⌢.
gardóm⌣bǎša *Gordon Pasha.*

gǎrɛ v.t. *embrace, clasp, put one's arms round, take into one's arms* [§ 2870].
ind. pres. aı⌣gǎrɛrı, ɛr⌣gǎrɛn (-rɛ̃⌢, -rɛ̃⌢); perf. aı⌣gǎrɛgorı (N. -ɛko-, -ɛho-).
ɛsmǎn⌣tɛ́n⌣tíwrıg⌣garóskó⌢ ɛoθmǎn *has embraced his friend.*

gǎrɛrar⌣ (-rȧr⌣; §§ 2200ff., 2210) and **gǎrɛríd**⌣ (§§ 2256ff., 2263) n. *embracing, etc.*

gǎrɛ-bŭ- (§ 3931β) v.i. stat. *be in an embraced (etc.) state or condition.*
bıtǎn⌣gǎrɛbūn⌢ *the child is in his (her, cuiusvis) arms.*

gǎrɛr-ɛg-ǎg- (§§ 4071ff.) v.t. = gǎrɛrɛdól-.

gǎrɛr-ɛ-dól- (-rᵒd-§ 1178; §§ 4016-17, 4022, 4027) v.t. *be about to embrace, etc.*

gǎrɛd-ǎg- (§§ 3877ff., 3540) v.t. *be in the situation of having embraced, etc.*
hásɛm⌣búrug⌣gǎrɛdǎgın⌢ *Hásan has taken the girl into his arms* (RN, s.v. gar).

gǎrɛ-kattı- (N. -ɛha-; § 4093) v.p. *be embraced, etc.*

gǎrɛ-nál (§ 3747ᵉ) v.t. *see with an embrace, etc., embrace (etc.) on seeing* (§ 3783).
aı⌣tɛ́kkı⌣gǎrɛnálkorı⌢ *when I saw him (her) I embraced him (her).*

gārɛ-sókkɛ (§3747ε') v.t. *take up in an embrace.*
   tımbánna⏝bıtáŋgı⏝gārɛsókkɛgó⏜ *its uncle picked up and embraced the child.*
gárıb⏝ n. (a) *west;* (b) *left bank of the Nile* (=tín⏝, tıŋgár⏝) [< غرب *id.* §1359].
   obj. garíbk(ı)⏝, -ípk(ı)⏝, -ki⏜.
   gen. gárıbn⏝v., -rım⏝c.
   gár(ı)bır⏝ (s.v. -r⏝) adv. *in (to) the west, on (to) the left bank.*
   gár(ı)bır⏜ (§6007) *(s)he (it) is (they are) in the west (on the left bank).*
   gárıbır⏝ágran⏜ *they live (etc. s.v. ág) in the west (...on the left bank).*
   tín⏝ká⏝gárıbır⏜ *their house is on the left bank.*
   gárıbırtōn⏝tágoran⏜ *they came (have come) from the west (...left bank).*
   garíb-ɛd⏝ (-ípk-; -kɛt⏝, -ké⏜ §966; §6007) adv. *on the west, by the western route, on (by) the left bank.*
   garípkɛt⏝tágoran⏜ *they came (have come) by the western route (...by the left bank).*
   garíbkɛn⏝nókkoran⏜ (-n⏝n- < -d⏝n- §624) *they went (have gone) by the western route (etc.).*
garím-d(ı)⏝ (§§2545 ff.) adj. *western, of the left bank.*
gárıb-an- (§§3910 ff.) v.i. (a) *go to the west, go to the left bank;* (b) *become (part of) the left bank.*
   ártı⏝gárıbaŋkó⏜ *the island became (has become) part of the left bank.*
garıbkɛb-bél (-ıpk-; §4127) v.i. *issue (sc. from river, boat) on the left bank.*
   imperat. garıbkébbɛl! (§1871).
garıbkɛbbél-an (-ıpk-; §§3890 ff., 3905) v.t. *tell to issue on the left bank, let issue on the left bank.*
garıbkɛn-nóg (-ıpk-; §4127) v.i. *go by the western route, on (by) the left bank.*
   garıbkɛnnókkoran⏜ = garíbkɛn⏝nókkoran⏜.
garıbkɛnnóg-an (-ıpk-; §§3890 ff., 3905) v.t. *tell to go by the western route, etc., let go by the western route, etc.*
garıbkır-nóg (-ıpk-; §4136) v.i. *go westwards, go to the left bank.*
   garıpkırnókkoran⏜ *they went (have gone) westwards (...to the left bank).*
garıbkırnóg-an (-ıpk-; §§3890 ff., 3905) v.t. *tell to go westwards, etc., let go westwards, etc.*
gárja n. *yard* (slung on mast) [< قرية *id.*].
   obj. -jag⏝.
   pl. -janč(ı)⏝.
   gárja⏝kádɛs⏝sókkɛn⏜ (-s⏝s- < -g⏝s- §678) *the yard carries the sail.*
gásıb *violence* = gásub⏝.
gásığ v.t. *split up, split in two, split in pieces, split a quantity of, split in numbers* [intensive extension of gág *split* §2883].
   ind. pres. āī⏝gásıǧ(¹)rı⏜, ɛr⏝gásıǧın⏜ (-ǧı-, -ǧí⏜); perf. āī⏝gásıǧkori⏜ (-íčk-; -ǧk-, -čk- §323).
   imperat. gásıč!
   úmbug⏝gásıǧran⏜ *they split the palm-trunk (-trunks §4696b) in two.*
   bér⏝mállɛg⏝gasíčkoran⏜ *they (have) split up all the wood.*

gásıǧar⏝ (-ǧár⏝; §§2200 ff.) and
gasıǧíd⏝ (§§2256 ff.) n. *splitting up, etc.*
gásıǧ-an (§§3890 ff.) v.t. *tell to split up, etc., let split up, etc.*
gásıǧ-bū- (§3931 β) v.i. stat. *be in a split up (etc.) state or condition.*
   úmbu⏝gásıǧbūn⏜ *the palm-trunk is (-trunks are, has been, have been) split in two.*
gasıǧɛd-ág- (§§3877 ff.) v.t. *be in the situation of having split up, etc.*
gásıǧ-kattı- (-ıčk-; -ǧk-, -čk- §323; §4093) v.p. *be split up, etc.*
gásım n. *a man's hand* [< قاسم abbr. of ابو القاسم].
   obj. gāsímg(ı)⏝, -gi⏜.
gásub⏝ (-sıb⏝) n. *violence* [< غَضَب *id.* §1361].
   obj. gasúbk(ı)⏝, -síbk(ı)⏝, -úpk(ı)⏝, -ípk(ı)⏝, -ki⏜.
   tén⏝gásıbır⏝ (§5858) *in spite of him (her, it)* = غَصْبًا عَنه.
   gasúpkɛk⏝kálli⏜ (-k⏝k- < -d⏝k- §568) *I am forced to eat (I eat in spite of myself)* = اكُل غَصْبًا عَنِّي.
gáš⏝ n. *belt* [§2052].
   obj. gášk(ı)⏝, -ki⏜.
   pl. gáši⏝.
gáš v.i. *coquet, flirt; mince, simper; be spoilt* [§2052].
   ind. pres. āī⏝gášri⏜; perf. āī⏝gáškori⏜.
gášar⏝ (-šár⏝; §§2200 ff.) and
gašíd⏝ (§§2256 ff.) n. *coquetry.*
gášk-ır (§3683) (a) v.t. caus. *cause or allow to coquet, etc.;* (b) v.t. *coax, pamper, pet, spoil, caress, fondle.*
   ind. pres. āī⏝gáškıddi⏜, ɛr⏝gáškırın⏜ (-rí⏝, -rí⏜).
gašé v.t. *pass, go past, come past, cross* [< غش of غشو *coming to* or of غشا *come to* + -é §3627].
   ind. pres. āī⏝gašéri⏜; perf. āī⏝gašégori⏜ (N. -éko-, -ého-).
   imperat. gašé!
   part. pres. gašél⏝ *(one) that passes, etc., passer, etc., passing, etc.;* past gašɛ́rɛl⏝ *(one) that passed, etc., passer, etc., (then) passing, etc., (now) past, etc.*
   hórkı⏝gašégoran⏜ *they (have) passed the (a) watercourse.*
   dérıb⏝máltıg⏝gašén⏜ *the path crosses the runnel(s §4696d).*
   gadíbkı⏝gašégoran⏜ *they (have) crossed the rails.*
   šáhar⏝gašérɛl⏝mahíja-taran⏜ (-l⏝m- < -ln⏝m- §811) *it's the salary of the past month (it's last month's salary).*
   mahíja⏝šahar⏝gašégōldı-taran⏜ *the salary is that of the month that (has) passed.*
gašérar⏝ (-rár⏝; §§2200 ff., 2207) and
gašɛríd⏝ (§§2256 ff., 2260) n. *passing, etc.*
gašér-an (§§3890 ff., 3899) v.t. *tell to pass, etc., let pass, etc.*
gašé-bū- (§3933) v.t. stat. *be in the condition of passing, etc.*
   dérıb⏝máltın⏝kóččır⏝gašébūn⏜ *the path crosses over the runnel(s).*

gašég-ır (N. -ékır, -éhır; §3681) v.t. caus. *cause or allow to pass, etc.*
   āī⏝tékkı⏝gašégıddi⏜ *I('ll §5369b) let him (her, it) pass.*
   N. bōlís⏝áīgı⏝gašékırmunun⏜ *the policeman does (will §5369a) not let me pass.*
gašéŋg-ır (N. -ŋkır; §3688) v.t. caus. *cause or allow to pass, etc.*
   bōlís⏝áīgı⏝gašéŋgırmunun⏜ *the policeman does (will) not let me pass.*
gaším adj. *inexperienced, unsophisticated, simple, credulous, gullible, easily duped* [< غَشِيم *id.*].
   obj. -ímg(ı)⏝, -gi⏜.
   pl. -ími⏝.
gáta n. *cover* = gúta⏝.
gátır (-tar⏝) n. *railway train* [< Sudan Ar. قطر gátar *id.* = قِطار].
   obj. gatírk(ı)⏝, -tárk(ı)⏝, -ki⏜.
   gen. gatírn⏝v.c., gátırn⏝v.c. §1522; -tín⏝c., -tın⏝c., -tárn⏝v.c., etc.
   pl. gát(¹)rı⏝, gátarı⏝.
   gen. pl. gátrın⏝, gátarın⏝.
   gátım⏝harákkı⏝gıǧírri⏜ and gátın⏝harákkı⏝gıǧírri⏜ *I hear the sound of the (a) train.*
   gátrın⏝harákkı⏝gıǧírri⏜ *I hear the sound of (the) trains.*
gáuūn⏝ *sweet melon* s.v. gāwūn⏝.
gawátt(ı)⏝ n. *well under water-wheel* (kólɛ⏝) *into which jars* (béšɛnč(ı)⏝) *dip and fill* (NSD, p. 22) [< غوط *deepen* +-t, so *deepening* §2333].
   obj. -tıg⏝.
   pl. -tınč(ı)⏝.
gāwılé v.i. *make a contract or bargain, contract, bargain* [< imperf. stem of قاول *id.* +-é §3647].
   ind. pres. āī⏝gāwıléri⏜; perf. āī⏝gāwılégori⏜ (N. -éko-, -ého-).
   imperat. gāwılé!
   tékkono⏝gāwılégori⏜ *I (have) made a contract with him (her).*
gāwılérar⏝ (-rár⏝; §§2200 ff., 2207) and
gāwılɛríd⏝ (§§2256 ff., 2260) n. *contracting, etc.*
gāwılérɛd-ág- (§§3877 ff.) v.i. *be in the situation of having made a contract, etc., be on piece-work.*
   gāwılérɛdágran, jōmíjagɛd⏝áumunan⏜ *they are under contract (are on piece-work), they do not work for a daily wage.*
gāwūn⏝ (gáuūn⏝; §956a) n. *sweet melon Cucumis melo, Linn.* (BSP, 206); with collective sg. (§4696b) [< قاوون *id.*].
   obj. -ūŋ(ı)⏝, -gi⏜.
   pl. -ūni⏝.
gáww(ı) (gáuw(ı)⏝) v.t. *take out of its pod (hull, sheath), hull, shell.*
   ind. pres. āī⏝gáwwıri⏜; perf. āī⏝gáwwıgori⏜ (N. -iko-, -iho-).
   imperat. gáwwi!
   ugúdkı⏝tén⏝káččırtōn⏝gáwwıgoran⏜ *they have hulled the beans* (§4696b).
   mahádag⏝gáwwıgoran⏜ *they took (have taken) the maize out of its sheaths.*

gáta — √gēl-

gáwwar‿ (gáūw-, -wάr‿; §§2200ff.) and
gawwíd‿ (gáūw-; §§2256ff.) n. *hulling, etc.*

gáwwı-an (gáūw-; §§3890ff.) v.t. *tell to hull, etc., let hull, etc.*

gáwwı-bŭ- (gáūwı-; §3931β) v.i. stat. *be in a hulled (etc.) state or condition.*
 úgud‿gáwwıbūn⌒ *the beans are (have been) hulled.*

gawwed-ág- (gáūw-; §§3877ff.) v.t. *be in the situation of having hulled, etc.*

gáwwı-kattı- (gáūw-; N. -ıha-; §4093) v.p. *he hulled, etc.*

gáta n. *cover* = gúta.

gázáz‿ (gaz-, gɛz-, gɪz-) n. (a) *glass (substance)* [< Sudan Ar. قزاز *id.* §1329]; (b) *vessel of glass, bottle.*
 obj. -ázk(ı)‿, -ásk(ı)‿, -ki⌒.
 pl. -ázı‿.

-g-έ‿ s.v. -ɛd‿.

N. ‿**gébbel**‿ postp. *opposite* = ‿gébɛl‿.
 N. ám‿béled‿mérkɛzŋ‿gébbélun⌒ (-lū⌒),
 N. ám‿béled‿mérkɛzŋ‿gébbélló⌒ (s.v. -r‿) and
 N. ám‿béled‿mérkɛzŋ‿gébbélgέ⌒ (s.v. -ɛd‿) *my (our) village is opposite the government district office.*

‿**gébel**‿ (N. also ‿gébbel‿; §1386) postp. (= prep. §4287) *opposite, facing, in front of* [< Sudan Ar. قَبَل gábal *id.* = قَبْل §1358]—follows the genitive (§4385).
 tén‿dukkám‿máháttan‿gébelun⌒ *his shop is opposite the station.*
 tíŋ‿kά‿zάptıjɛŋ‿gebél-taran⌒ *their house is that opposite the police-station.*
 sōgdánn‿άrtı‿kérman‿gebél-tánnan⌒ *the island of Sōgdán is that opposite Kérma.*

‿**gebél-lo**‿. (s.v. -r‿; §§5860, 5900) postp. (= prep.) *opposite, facing, in front of;* follows the genitive (§4365).
 bάm‿gebéllo⌒ (-m‿g- < -bn‿g- §586) *(s)he's (it's, they're) opposite the door.*
 mulwάd‿sállıŋ‿gebélló⌒ (§1989) *Mulwάd is opposite Sάllı⌒.*
 άrtı‿kérman‿gebélló⌒ *the island is opposite Kérma.*

-gɛd‿ (RN, §359; -gɛt⌒, -gέ⌒) = -g- objective suffix +-ɛd‿ s.v. éd.

geddımέ (-dum-) (α) v.t. *advance, send forward; put forward, present, submit* [< imperf. or imperat. stem of قَدَّم *id.* +-έ §3636]; (β) v.i. (a, in space) *advance, go or come forward, get ahead* (b, in time) *be ahead, be early* [< a stem of Sudan Ar. تَقَدَّم = اِتْقَدَّم *id.* +-έ §3652].
 ind. pres. aī‿geddımέrı⌒; perf. aī‿geddımέgorı⌒ (N. -έko-, -έho-).
 imperat. geddımέ!
 ıškάrtıg‿geddımέgoran⌒ *they saw (have seen) the guest off (. . . set him on his way).*
 ardahάlg‿άddo‿geddımέgó⌒ and
 N. ardahάlg‿áīdo‿geddımέkó⌒ *(s)he (has) put in a petition against me.*
 X. ɛsmάn‿sέ? *where's ϱoθmάn?*
 Y. geddumέróskó⌒ *he's gone on ahead.*
 sắ‿geddımέn⌒ *the watch (clock) gains.*

geddımέrar‿ (-dum-, -rάr‿; §§2200ff., 2207) and
geddımέríd‿ (-dum-; §§2256ff., 2260) n. *advancing, etc.*

geddımέr-an (-dum-; §§3890ff., 3899) v.t. *tell to advance, etc., let advance, etc.*

geddımέ-bŭ- (-dum-; §§3927ff.) v.i. stat. *be in an advanced (etc.) state or condition.*
 ardahάl‿έddo‿geddımέbūn⌒ *a (the) petition is (has been) submitted against you.*
 X. ɛsmάn‿sέ? *where's ϱoθmάn?*
 Y. geddımέbūn⌒ *he's on ahead.*
 sắ‿geddımέbūná? *is the watch (clock) fast?*

géddım-katt(ı) (-dum-; §4101) v.i. = geddımέ (β).
 imperat. géddımkatti!

geddımέ-kattı- (-dum-; N. -έha-; §4093) v.p. *be put forward, etc.*
 ardahάl‿bıgeddımέkattın⌒ *the petition will be submitted.*

geddımέ-nóg (-dum-; §3747ε´) v.i. *go (on) ahead, go early.*

geddımέ-tá (-dum-; -έ-tá §1419; §3747ε´) v.i. *come (on) ahead, come early.*
 imperat. geddımέta!

geddımέr-ɛ-ğŭ́-bŭ- (-dum-; §4069) v.t. and i. stat. *be on one's way (coming) to put forward, get ahead, etc.*

geddımέr-ɛ-nóg (-dum-; §§4048ff.) v.t. and i. *go to put forward, get ahead, etc.*
 X. ɛsmάn‿sέ? *where's ϱoθmάn?*
 Y. geddımέrenókkó⌒ *he went (has gone) to get ahead.*
 X. tír‿sέ? *where are they?*
 Y. geddımέrenókkoran⌒ *they went (have gone) on to get ahead.*

geddımέr-ɛ-nóg-bŭ- (-dum-; -nóggŭ- §546; §4058) v.t. and i. stat. *be on one's way (going) to put forward, get ahead, etc.*

geddımέr-ɛ-tá (-dum-; §§4060ff.) v.t. and i. *come to put forward, etc., come to get ahead, etc.*

geddımέred-ág- (-dum-; §§3877ff.) v.i. and t. *be in the situation (condition) of having advanced, etc.*
 sắ‿geddımέredágın⌒ *the watch (clock) has gained.*

geddımέrɛn-nóg (-dum-; occ. -ednóg, §4169ff.; -έreggınóg, -ɛdgı- §§4176ff.) v.t. *go (etc. s.v. nóg) after putting forward, etc.*

geddımέros-nóg (-dum-; -onnóg §629; §§4180-4; -osgınóg, -ozgı-, -oggı- §4185) v.t. *go after putting forward, etc.*
 ardahάlg‿geddımέronnókkoran⌒ *they went away after submitting a petition.*

gédɛ n. (a) *circle;* (b) *rim.*
 obj. gédɛg‿.
 pl. gedénč(ı)‿.
 míssın‿gédɛ *pupil of eye.*
 árgadɛŋ‿gédɛ (a) *horizontal cog-wheel of water-wheel (kólɛ‿);* (b) *rim of (a).* (One would expect árgadɛŋ gédɛŋ‿gédɛ, but I do not find this expression in use.)
 árgadɛŋ‿tóŋ‿gédɛ *rim of vertical cog-wheel of water-wheel.*
 núbroŋ‿gédɛ *whorl of spindle (CWS, p. 21).*

gedén-d(ı)‿ (§§2545ff.) adj. *appertaining to a circle, etc.*

gédem n. *foot (lineal or square measure);* with collective sg. (§4696d) [< قَدَم *id.*]
 obj. gedémg(ı)‿, -gi⌒.
 pl. gédemı‿.
 gedémged‿ásran⌒ *they measure by the foot.*
 gédem‿wέr‿ and gédem‿mέr‿ (§603) *one foot.*
 aī‿έkk‿άrıŋ‿gédem‿mέb‿bıtím-munun⌒ (-ŋ‿g- < -dn‿g- §644, -b‿b- < -g‿b- §519) *I shall not give you one (square) foot of land.*

gedím adj. *ancient, old, not new, stale; former* [< قَدِيم *id.*].
 obj. -ímg(ı)‿, -gi⌒.
 pl. -fmı‿.

gédır‿ n. *amount, quantity* (= kótt(ı)‿) [< قَدْر *id.* §1359].
 obj. gedírk(ı)‿, -ki⌒.
 tén‿gedírk‿uñúddan⌒ *they know the amount of it.*
 gédır-taran⌒ (gedír-taran⌒ §1522) and
 gédır-tánnan⌒ (gedír-) *that's the lot, that's all, it's finished, it's ended.*
 ıŋ‿gédır‿taran⌒ *that's the lot, this is all, that's all.*
 gédır‿tέ? *is that the lot?, is that all?, is it finished (ended)?*
 hammάmırtōn‿έr‿gédır‿tέ? *have you done with the bath?*

géger v.t. *roll (yielding substance) into a ball (balls)* [RSN, §129].
 ind. pres. aī‿gegérrı⌒, ɛr‿gégerın⌒ (-rí⌒, -rí⌒); perf. aī‿gegérkorı⌒.
 síbɛg‿gegérran⌒ *they roll the mud into a ball (balls).*

gégerar‿ (-rάr‿; §§2200ff.) and
gegeríd‿ (§§2256ff.) n. *rolling into a ball (balls).*

gegér-bŭ- (§3931β) v.i. stat. *be in a rolled (etc.) state or condition.*
 síbɛ‿gegérbūn⌒ *the mud is (has been) rolled into a ball (balls).*

gegered-ág- (§§3877ff.) v.t. *be in the situation of having rolled, etc.*

gegér-kattı- (§4093) v.p. *be rolled, etc.*

√gēl- *red* [< √gĕ- (be) red (§4523) +-l determinative or participial (§§4558-9); cp. ON. гел red GNT, s.v.].

gέl n. *gazelle, buck* [the red one §2297].
 obj. gέlg(ı)‿, -gi⌒.
 pl. gέlı‿.
 gέln‿búttul‿ and gέlm‿búttul‿ *buck.*

gέl-kırı‿ (gέlkírı‿; §§2539-40) adj. *like a gazelle.*

gɛlad (-lɛd‿ infra) n. *one of the sorts of date growing in Dóngola, s.v. bént(ı)‿;* with collective sg. (§4696b).
 obj. gelάdk(ı)‿, -άtk(ı)‿, -άtt(ı)‿, -άkk(ı)‿ §2462, -ki⌒, -ti⌒.
 gen. -ádn‿v., -ánn‿v.c., -án‿c.
 pl. gelάdnı‿.

gέle adj. *red, reddish, reddish brown* [§§2517-18].
 obj. gέleg‿, -gi⌒.
 pl. gέlenč(ı)‿.
 šάrtı‿gέle‿ *copper, brass.*
 wíssı‿gέle‿ *the red star, Mars.*

gélɛ-kırı (§§ 2539-40) adj. *reddish*.
gél-an- (§ 3910α) v.i. *become red*, etc.
gélam-bŭ- (§§ 3949 ff.) v.i. stat. *be in a reddening (etc.) state or condition, be advanced in the process of becoming red, etc.*
  bíllɛ gélambūn the onions are getting browned (fried brown).
gēlan-ɛ-dól- (-nºd- § 1178; § 4026) and
gēland-ɛ-dól- (-dºd-; § 4034) v.i. *be about to become red*, etc.
gēlanɛd-åg- (§ 3966α) v.i. *be in the condition of having become red*, etc.
gélɛg-ır (N. -ɛkır, -ɛhır; § 3701) (a) v.t. caus. *cause or allow to be red*, etc.; (b) v.t. *render red*, etc., *redden, brown*; (c) v.t. *redden or brown by frying or roasting, fry, roast* (= ḥmr).
  bíllɛd déskɛg gélɛgıddan (-d d- < -g d- § 534, -g g- < -d g- § 545) *and emphasizing* déskɛd (§ 4626).
  déskɛb bíllɛg gélɛgıddan (-b b- < -d b- § 518) *they fry the onions in butter*.
géled n. *sort of date* = gélad *supra*; with collective sg.
  obj. gɛlédk(ı), -étk(ı), -étt(ı), -ékk(ı) § 2462, -ki, -ti.
  gen. -édn v., -énn v.c., -én c.
  pl. géledı.
gelíndɛl adj. *yellow* [< √gél- red + -ı- euphonic + -n genitival + -d (§ 2546) + -ɛ of n. ess. (§ 2234β) + -l participial (§ 2958), so *that is appertaining to red* § 2531].
  obj. gelindélg(ı), -gi.
  pl. gelíndɛlı.
  sållen íg gelíndélun the blossom of Acacia Seyal (طَلْح) is yellow.
  íŋ gelíndélmunun (§ 1978) this (that) is not yellow.
-gɛn (§§ 3596-7, 5520-7) v.i. *be* [§ 2493; RSN, §§ 45, 129, 200]—only used after adjective-concretions and verb-concretions.
  ind. pres. âı-gendi; perf. âı-gɛŋkori.
  imperat. -gɛn!, -gē!, -gé!, pl. -gɛwwɛ! (´̆).
  ar sɛrɛ́rıgoŋ ŋendu mabsúdıgoŋ ŋendu *we are well and we are content*.
  tɛr tɛrígkoŋ geni mummúdkoŋ geni (s)he's deaf and dumb.
  tɛr washåŋgoŋ genim bɛndıgílgoŋ genin and
  tɛr washåŋ ŋoŋ ŋenim bɛndıgílgoŋ ŋenin (s)he's dirty and a beggar.
  kǎ kuróskoŋ ŋeŋkom mílligoŋ ŋeŋkó the house was old and bad.
  dídgoŋ ŋenin tůzgoŋ ŋenin (s)he both scolds and curses; cp. dídıŋgon tůsıŋgon ǎgın (s)he is engaged in scolding and cursing.
  kálgoŋgen nígoŋgen *eat and drink too*.
  kálgoŋgɛwwé nígoŋgɛwwé *eat (pl.) and drink (pl.) too*.
  kíttɛgoŋgɛn ándıgoŋgı gíğır *be silent and listen to me*, lit. ... *and listen to mine*; ándıg-on *a pronominal adjective-concretion* (§ 5226).
gɛn (§ 956d) adj. (a) *good, satisfactory*;
(b) *in good order or condition, sound*;
(c) *in good health, well* (cp. طيب id.)
  [§ 2493; cp. ON. ᚴᛁᚾ -gut sein ZNG, s.v.].
  obj. gɛŋg(ı), -gi.
  pl. gɛ́nı.
  X. ısåı-tɛ gén? (§ 5854) *which is the better?*
  Y. oŋgår wɛrun *they're both the same*.
  íŋ génun, íŋ gémmunun *this (one) is good (etc.), that isn't*.
  tíddo géŋg étta *bring the better (best §4969, one) of* (lit. *in* s.v. -r) them.
  tíddo géŋg étta *bring the better (best, ones) of them*.
  X. ínnówwit tér míne bún? (-t t- < -g t- § 707) *how is (s)he (it) to-day?*
  Y. kınnéw wíl dogor génun (-w w- < -g w- § 719, -l d- < -ln d- § 806) (s)he (it) is a little better than yesterday.
  X. énn óssı géndé? (s.v. -ré?) *is your foot (leg) better?*
  Y. kınnɛ́g åhsénun *it's a little better*.
gén-an- (§ 3910α) v.i. *become good*, etc.
  X. énn-í gɛnáŋkomɛn? *has (lit. hasn't) your hand got better?*
  Y. ólgónun *not yet*, lit. *it's still* (sc. bad).
  X. énn-ur kınnɛ́s sɛráŋkoná? (-s s- < -g s- § 678) *is your head a little better?*
  Y. éjjo, kínnɛg gɛnanóskó *yes, it has got a little better*.
géŋ-ır (N. géŋkır; § 3702) (a) v.t. caus. *cause or allow to be good*, etc.; (b) v.t. *render good*, etc., *set right*.
  ind. pres. âı géŋgıddi.
génd(ı) v.i. *become good*, etc., *get into good order*, etc., *become clean, get cleaned* [§ 2868].
  ind. pres. âı géndırı, ɛr géndın (-di, -dí); perf. âı géndıgori (N. -ıko-, -ıho-).
  ınnówwıg ódå géndın *today the room is (to be) cleaned*.
  ódå géndıgon *the room got (has become, is) clean*.
  âı ért ɛgóri, ékkɛnɛ géndıgori *I was dirty, now I have got clean*.
  áŋ kór gendóskó *my wound has healed*.
  hısáb gendóskó *the account has come right*.
gɛ́ndar (-dår; §§ 2200 ff.) and
gɛndíd (§§ 2256 ff.) n. *becoming good*, etc.
gɛndíd-aŋ-génd(ı) (§§ 4161-3) v.i. *become very good (etc.) indeed*.
  áŋ kór gendídaŋgéndıgó *my wound became (has become) completely healed*.
géndı-bŭ- (§ 3931α) v.i. stat. *be in a good, sound or clean state or condition, be in order, be all right*.
  íŋ géndıbún *this (one) is in a good (etc.) state*.
géndıg-ır (N. -ıkır, -ıhır; § 3682) (a) v.t. caus. *cause or allow to become good*, etc.
(b) v.t. *render good, etc., set right, mend, clean*.
  ind. pres. âı géndıgıddi (´̆), ɛr géndıgırın (-rí, -rí); perf. âı gɛndıgírkori (N. -ıkír-, -ıhír-).
  såg géndıgır *put the clock (watch) right*, i.e. (a) *set it correctly*, or (b) *mend it*.
  kåg géndıgır *put the house (room) in order* (e.g. *clean it*).
  âı washån ɛgóri, ékkɛn án-nɛfísku gɛndıgírkori *I was dirty, now I have cleaned myself*.
  ɛr mén gɛndıgırkómɛnın? *why didn't (haven't) you set it right?*
  náúúdkɛg gɛndıgíddan (-g g- < -d g- § 545) *they set it right with an adze*.
  hakím áŋ kórkı gɛndıgírkó the doctor (has) dressed my wound.
  íŋgug gɛndıgırríkkori (§ 5456) *I (have) set right (each of) these*.
géndıgır-an (§§ 3890 ff., 3904) v.t. *tell to set right*, etc., *let set right*, etc.
gɛndıgır-åbbítti- (-agbí-; § 4142) v.t. *be engaged in picking up (etc.* s.v. åbbítti-*) properly, thoroughly, exhaustively*.
gɛndıgır-åkkób- (-ågkób-; § 4142) v.t. *be engaged in shutting (etc.* s.v. åkkób-*) properly*, etc.
gɛndıgır-åkkús- (-ågkús-; § 4142) v.t. *be engaged in opening (etc.* s.v. åkkús-*) properly*, etc.
gɛndıgır-bítt(ı) (§ 4135) v.t. *pick up (etc.* s.v. bítt(ı)*) properly, thoroughly, exhaustively, gather completely*.
  éš šíkkɛg gɛndıgırbıttıgómunun (-š š- < -n š § 699, -g g- < -d g- § 545) *you did not pick (it, them) up (have not picked (it, them) up) properly on* (-ed) *your side* (šíg).
gɛndıgırbıtt-an (§§ 3890 ff., 3905) v.t. *tell to pick up (etc.) properly*, etc. *(etc.) properly*, etc.
gɛndıgırbítti-bŭ- (§ 4145) v.i. stat. *be in a properly (etc.) picked up (etc.) state or condition*.
gɛndıgırbıttɛd-ǎg- (§ 3883) v.t. *be in the situation of having picked up (etc.) properly*, etc.
gɛndıgıdd-ɛg-ǎg- (§§ 4071 ff.) v.t. = gɛndıgırɛdól-.
gɛndıgıdd-ɛ-dól- (-rºd- § 1178; § 4022) and
gɛndıdd-ɛ-dól- (-dºd-; § 4027) v.t. *be about to set right*, etc.
  íŋı gɛndıgıredólli *I am just going to set this (one) right (... mend, clean this)*.
gɛndıgıdd-ɛ-gŭ-bŭ- (§ 4069) v.t. stat. *be on one's way (coming) to set right*, etc.
gɛndıgır-ɛ-må- (§ 4036) and
gɛndıgıdd-ɛ-må- (§ 4041) v.t. *become unable to set right*, etc.
gɛndıgıdd-ɛ-nóg (§ 4048 ff) v.t. *go to set right*, etc.
gɛndıgıdd-ɛ-nóg-bŭ- (-nóggŭ- § 546; § 4058) v.t. stat. *be on one's way (going) to set right*, etc.
gɛndıgıdd-ɛ-tǎ (§§ 4060 ff.) v.t. *come to set right*, etc.
gɛndıgıred-ǎg- (§ 3883) v.t. *be in the situation of having set right*, etc.
gɛndıgır-ɛttǎ (-éttå § 3855; § 4142) v.t. *bring after setting right*, etc.
  gɛndıgıretta *bring it (them* § 5083) *when you have set it (them) right*.

‿gɛr‿ — -g(ı)‿

ıŋ‿kubbăiag‿gɛndıgıréttagori⌒ *I (have) cleaned and brought this glass.*

gendıgır-kób (§4135) v.t. *shut (etc. s.v. kób) properly, thoroughly.*
  kobídkı‿gɛndıgırkóp⌒ *shut the door properly.*

gendıgırkób-an (§§3890ff., 3905) v.t. *tell to shut (etc.) properly, etc., let shut (etc.) properly, etc.*

gendıgırkób-bŭ- (§4145) v.i. stat. *be in a properly (etc.) shut (etc.) state or condition.*

gendıgırkobɛd-ág- (§§3877ff.) v.t. *be in the situation of having shut properly, etc.*

gendıgır-kús (§4135) v.t. *open (etc. s.v. kús) properly, thoroughly.*

gendıgırkús-an (§§3890ff., 3905) v.t. *tell to open (etc.) properly, etc., let open (etc.) properly, etc.*

gendıgırkúz-bŭ- (§4145) v.i. stat. *be in a properly (etc.) opened (etc.) state or condition.*

gendıgırkusɛd-ág- (§§3877ff.) v.t. *be in the situation of having opened (etc.) properly, etc.*

gendıgıros-kób (-okkób §573; §§4180-4; -osgıkób, -ozgı-, -oggı- §4185) v.t. *shut (etc. s.v. kób) after setting right, etc.*

gendıgıros-sokk-úndur (§4203; -osgı-sokk-, -ozgı-, -oggı- §4205) v.t. *after setting right (etc.) take up and put in(to).*
  íŋgı‿gɛndıgırokkārsokkúndur⌒ (§5605) *when you have set this right take it up and put it in the house.*

gendıgıros-úndur (§§4180-4; -osgún-, -ozgún-, -oggún- §4185) v.t. *put in(to) after setting right, etc.*
  íŋgug‿gɛndıgıroggıkārúndur⌒ (§5605) *when you have set these right put them into the house.*

gendıgıros-úskur (§§4180-4; -osgús-, -ozgús-, -oggús- §4185) v.t. *set (place, put) after setting right, etc.*
  íŋgı‿gɛndıgıroggındúskur⌒ (§5605) *when you have set this (that) right put it here.*

géndı-kattı- (N. -ıha-; §4098) v.p. *be rendered good, etc., be set right, mended, etc.*
  ɛmkıŋ‿gɛndıkattın‿ɛmkıŋ‿gɛndıkáttı-munun⌒ *perhaps it can (§5704) be set right (etc.), perhaps it can't.*

gendı-nóg (§3747ɛ') v.i. *go (etc. s.v. nóg) well, go (etc.) straight.*
  wɛrwégonon‿gɛndınókkoran⌒ *they walked in step.*

‿gɛ́r‿ indef. pron. *other* (=prep. §§5167-8) *besides, except, but* [< غَيْر id.].
  obj. ‿gɛ́rk(ı)‿.
— only after the genitive:
  áŋ‿gɛ́r‿dămunun⌒ *there is nobody (present) but me (us).*
  aî‿ɛŋ‿gɛ́rkı‿bıtírmunun⌒ *I shall not give (it to anyone) but you.*
  hánuŋ‿gɛ́rkı‿nalkómunun⌒ *they saw (have seen) nothing but the donkey.*

gerɛ́ *read, etc. = gerjɛ́.*
  ind. pres. aî‿gɛrɛ́ri⌒; perf. aî‿gɛrɛ́gori⌒ (N. -ɛ́ko-, -ɛ́ho-).
  imperat. gerɛ́!

geredún‿ (§956b) n. *swallow, bird resembling swallow;* with collective sg. (§4696d); = ıŋgɛlɛdúna‿ [< χελιδών RN, s.v. engeledúna].
  obj. -dúŋg(ı)‿, -gi⌒.
  pl. -dún‿.
  gerɛdúŋ-kırı‿ (-kíri‿; §§2539-40) adj. *resembling a swallow.*

geríf n. *small fishing-net* = ábɛ‿ [?cp. غَرَفَ *scoop up* (water with one's hand)].
  obj. -ífk(ı)‿, -ki⌒.
  pl. -ífı‿.

gerjɛ́ (gɛrɛ́) v.t. *(a) read, (b) recite* [< قَرَأَ *reading, recitation* +-ɛ́ §3626].
  ind. pres. aî‿gɛrjɛ́ri⌒ (occ. -jɛ́ri §1073), ɛr‿gɛrjɛ́n⌒ (-jɛ́‿, -jɛ́⌒ §939; occ. -jɛ́n⌒, -jɛ́⌒, -jé⌒; perf. aî‿gɛrjɛ́gori⌒ (N. -ɛ́ko-, -ɛ́ho-; occ. -jégo-, N. -jéko-, -jého-).
  imperat. gerjɛ́!
  goráŋgı‿gɛrjɛ́ran⌒ *(a) they read (recite) the Coran; (b) let (-an⌒) him read (recite) the Coran.*

gerjɛ́rar‿ (gɛrɛ́-; -rár‿; §§2200ff., 2207) and
gerjɛ́ríd‿ (gɛrɛ́-; §§2256ff., 2260) n. *reading, recitation.*

ger(j)ɛ́r-an (§§3890ff., 3899) v.t. *tell to read, etc., let read, etc.*

ger(j)ɛ́-bŭ- (§3931β) v.i. stat. *be in a read (etc.) state or condition.*
  mám‿béledır‿goráŋ‿gɛrjɛbúmunun⌒ *in that country the Coran is not read.*

ger(j)ɛ̄r-eg-ág- (§§4071ff.) v.t. = gɛr(j)ɛ̄redól-.

ger(j)ɛ̄r-ɛ-dól- (-rᵒd-§ 1178; §§4016-17, 4022, 4027) v.t. *be about to read, etc.*

ger(j)ɛ̄r-ɛ-má- (§§4016-17, 4036, 4041) v.t. *become unable to read, etc.*

ger(j)ɛ̄red-ág- (§§3877ff.) v.t. *be in the situation (condition) of having read, etc.*

ger(j)ɛ́g-ır (N. -ɛ́kır, -ɛ́hır; §3681) *(a)* v.t. caus. *cause or allow to read or recite; (b)* v.t. *teach to read, etc.*
  ind. pres. aî‿gɛrjɛ́gıddi⌒.
  pl.-obj. ind. pres. aî‿gɛrjɛ́gıríddi⌒.

ger(j)ɛ́-kattı- (N. -ɛ́ha-; §4093) v.p. *be read, etc.*

-g-ɛt⌒ s.v. -ɛd.

gɛ́u (gɛ̆ᵘ, gɛ́w‿, gɛ̆u‿) n. *(a) blood; (b) menses* (= hɛ́d‿) [< √gɛ̆- (*be*) *red* (§4523) +-u‿ dem. (§2337); RSN, §115].
  obj. gɛ̆ug(ı)‿, -gi⌒ (§514).
  ɛ́n‿gɛ̆u‿ (< ɛ́nn‿g- §613) = gɛ̆u *(b).*
  tɛ́n‿gɛ̆un⌒ *(a,* of a man*) it's his blood; (b,* of a woman*) she has her menses.*
  ɛ́n‿gɛ̆un⌒ (§4719) *the woman has her menses.*

geún-d(ı)‿ (§§2545ff.) adj. *appertaining to (the) blood, of (the) blood, menstrual.*
  ɛ́n‿gɛund(ı)‿ *menstrual.*

gɛ́w-an- (§3910α) v.i. *bleed.*

gɛ́wam-bŭ- (§3949ff.) v.i. stat. *be in a bleeding state or condition.*

gezáz‿ n. *glass, bottle* = gəzáz‿.

-gi⌒, -gu‿, -gı‿ *adverbial* (including objective) *suffix* (§§2036-42).

-gı‿ *maternal uncle* s.v. -g(ı)‿.

gíd n. *grass* [RSN, §129].
  obj. gídk(ı)‿, gítk(ı)‿, gítt(ı)‿, gíkk(ı)‿ §2462; -ki⌒, -ti⌒.
  gen. gídn‿v., gín‿c.
  pl. gídı‿.
  gídn‿ágar‿ *the (a) grassy place.*
  gín‿šəwál‿ *(a) the (a) sack of grass; (b) the (a) sack for grass* = šəwál‿ gínd(ı)‿.
  ágar‿gítti‿kól‿ *the (a) place that has grass, the (a) grassy place.*

gín-d(ı)‿ (§§2545ff.) adj. *appertaining to (the) grass, of (the) grass.*
  šəwál‿gínd(ı)‿ *the (a) sack for grass.*

gĭd-kıññ(ı)‿ (gítk-; §§2536-7) adj. *devoid of grass.*
  ágar‿gítkıññın⌒ and gítkıññın‿ágar⌒ (§4627) *the place is devoid of grass.*

gídkı-ko- (gítkı-, gítti-; §4121) v.i. *have grass, be grassy.*
  (part. pres.) gídkıkól‿ (gítkı-, gítti-; §2575) adj. *grassy.*
  ágar‿gíttıkó⌒ *the place is grassy.*

gírád‿ n. $\frac{1}{24}$, *twenty-fourth part;* with collective sg. (§4696d) [< قِيراط id. < κεράτιον].
  obj. -ádk(ı)‿, -átk(ı)‿, -átt(ı)‿, -ákk(ı)‿ §2462; -ki⌒, -ti⌒.
  gen. -ádn‿v., -án‿c.
  pl. -ádı‿.
  kólɛ‿gīrád‿arrekémısun⌒ *an irrigable estate is (in) twenty-four parts.*
  árıd‿gīrád‿dɛ̆ğ‿ğăntírkori⌒ (-d‿ < -d‿w- §533, -ğ̆-ğ- < -g‿ğ- §551) and
  árıŋ‿gīrád‿dɛ̆ğ‿ğăntíkkori⌒ (-ŋ‿g- < -dn‿g- §644) *I (have) sold $\frac{1}{24}$ of the land.*

gíttıko- *be grassy* s.v. gíd‿.

-g(ı)‿ n. *maternal uncle, mother's brother* [cp. RSN, §129; WS, p. 174, no. 243].
  voc. ⌒.
  obj. -gıg‿.
  pl. -gınč(ı)‿.
  Always with a form of the possessive personal pronoun (§2630) prefixed:
  áŋg(ı)‿ *my maternal uncle,* obj. áŋgıg‿.
  íŋg(ı)‿ *your maternal uncle.*
  tíŋg(ı)‿ *his (her) maternal uncle.*
  antíŋg(ı)‿ *our maternal uncle.*
  ıntíŋg(ı)‿ *your (pl.) maternal uncle.*
  tıntíŋg(ı)‿ *their maternal uncle.*

-gím-buru‿ (-gímbúru‿ §1532) n. *mother's brother's daughter, cousin.*
  obj. -búrug‿.
  pl. -búruı‿.
  Always with a form of the possessive personal pronoun (§2630) prefixed:
  aŋgímburu‿ *my mother's brother's daughter.*
  ıŋgímburu‿ *your mother's brother's daughter, etc.*

-gın-tód‿ (-gíntód‿ §1667) n. *mother's brother's son, cousin.*
  voc. -tót!, -tót!, -tó!
  obj. -gıntódk(ı)‿, -tótk(ı)‿, -tókk(ı)‿, -tótt(ı)‿ §2462; -ki⌒, -ti⌒.
  gen. -gıntódn‿v., -tónn‿v.c., -tón‿c.;
  -gıntódn‿v., -tónn‿v.c., -tón‿c.
  pl. -gıntonı‿.
  Always with a form of the possessive personal pronoun (§2630) prefixed:
  aŋgıntód‿ (aŋgíntód‿) *my mother's brother's son.*

ɪŋgɪntŏd⏜ (ɪŋgíntŏd⏜) *your mother's brother's son, etc.*

-gɪ⏜ (-g⏜, -gi⏜) *adverbial (including objective) suffix* (§§ 2036–42).

giásk(ɪ)⏜ *large sailing-boat* = gajásk(ɪ)⏜.

gíd *v.t. choke, throttle, suffocate.*
ind. pres. aī⏜gíd(¹)ri⏜, ɛr⏜gídɪn⏜ (-dī⏜, -dí⏜); perf. aī⏜gídkori⏜ (gítk-).
imperat. gít!
ín⏜túll⏜áɪgɪ⏜gídɪn⏜ *this smoke suffocates me.*

gídar⏜ (-dar⏜; §§ 2200 ff.) *and*
gidíd⏜ (§§ 2256 ff.) *n. choking, suffocation.*

gɪd-bέ (§ 3747 ε') *v.t. kill by choking, etc., strangle.*

gíd-bŭ- (§ 3931 β) *v.i. stat. be in a choked (etc.) state or condition.*

gɪdɛd-ág- (§§ 3877 ff.) *v.t. be in the situation of having choked, etc.*
kíd⏜tékkɪ⏜gɪdɛdágɪn⏜ *the (a) bone has choked him (her, it).*

gíd-katti- (gítk-; § 4093) *v.p. be choked, etc.*

gífɪl⏜ (gúful⏜ § 1342) *n. lock, esp. padlock* [< قُفْل *id.* § 1361].
obj. gɪfílg(ɪ)⏜, gufúlg(ɪ)⏜, -gi⏜.
pl. gífl⏜, gúf(u)l⏜.

gíğɪr (§ 2837) *v.t. perceive with ear or nose, so (a) v.t. hear; (b) v.t. listen to; (c) v.i. listen; (d) v.t. smell (gíğɪr does not = understand).*
ind. pres. aī⏜gɪğírri⏜ *and* aī⏜gɪğíddi⏜, ɛr⏜gíğɪrɪn⏜ (-rí⏜, -rí); perf. aī⏜gɪğírkori⏜.
subj. past aī⏜gɪğírsu⏜ (-íssi⏜ § 683, -su⏜).
wέlɪ⏜ūkkídkɪ⏜gɪğírkori⏜ *I (have) heard the barking of the (a) dog(s* § 4696 *d).*
mohámmɛs⏜sέ?, gɪğírkomέ? (-s⏜s- <-d⏜s- § 677) *where's Muhámmad?, didn't he hear?*
gɪğírkorandέ?, uñúddandέ? *did they hear? (have they heard?), do they understand?*
aī⏜tém⏜bannídkɪ⏜gɪğɪrkómunun⏜ *I did not hear (have not heard) what (s)he said.*
ándɪg⏜gíğɪr⏜ *listen to me (us),* lit. *listen to mine (ours).*
írís-sēg⏜gɪğírri⏜ (-s-s- <-s-w- § 687) *I smell an odour.*
ğugfdn⏜wírɪskɪ⏜gɪğírri⏜ *I notice a smell of burning.*

gíğɪrar⏜ (-rar⏜; §§ 2200 ff.) *and*
gɪğɪríd⏜ (§§ 2256 ff.) *n. perception by ear or nose.*

gíğɪr-ɛ-má- (§ 4036),
gíğɪrr-ɛ-má- (§ 4041) *and*
gɪğɪdd-ɛ-má- (§ 4041) *v.t. become unable to perceive, etc.*

gɪğɪrɛd-ág- (§§ 3877 ff.) *v.t. be in the condition of having perceived, etc.*

gɪğɪrk-ídd(ɪ) (§ 3725) *v.t. caus. cause or allow to perceive, etc.*
ind. pres. aī⏜gɪğɪrkíddɪri⏜.
imperat. gɪğɪrkíddi! *and* ◌.

gɪğɪr-katti- (gɪğírk- § 1522; § 4093) *v.p. be perceived, etc.*
ín⏜ulúkkɛg⏜gɪğɪrkáttimunun, soríñgɛg⏜gɪğɪrkáttɪn⏜ (-g⏜g- <-d⏜g- § 545) *this is not perceived by the ear, it is perceived by the nose.*

gɪğírkattar⏜ (-tar⏜; §§ 2200 ff., 2213) *and*
gɪğírkattíd⏜ (§§ 2256 ff., 2266) *n. being perceived, etc.*

gɪğɪros-tá (-ottá § 714; §§ 4180–4; -osgɪtá, -ozgɪ-, -oggɪ- § 4185) *v.t. come on perceiving, etc.*
imperat. gɪğɪrósta! (-ótta!, -ósgɪta!, -ózgɪ-, -óggɪ-).
tínn⏜ūwɛrítkɪ⏜gɪğɪrottágó⏜ *(s)he (it) came on hearing their call.*

gɪğɪroz-bŏd-tá (§ 727; -obbŏd- § 521; § 4205; -osgɪbŏd-, -ozgɪ-, -oggɪ- § 4205; -bŏttá § 706) *v.t. come running on perceiving, etc.*
imperat. gɪğɪrozbódta! (-obbód-, etc.).
έnn⏜ūwɛrárkɪ⏜gɪğɪrobbóttágori⏜ *and* N. έnn⏜ūwɛríttɪ⏜gɪğɪroggɪbóttákori⏜ *I came (have come) running on hearing your call.*
aī⏜mánd⏜óŋgor⏜ğŭsɪm⏜bádk⏜ím⏜bannídkɪ⏜gɪğɪrobbŏdtágori⏜ *after I had gone over there to the south I came running back on hearing your (pl.) talking.*

gijásk(ɪ)⏜ *large sailing-boat* = gajásk(ɪ)⏜.

-g-ɪr = -g- *objective suffix* (§ 909) + -ɪr *causative suffix* (§ 3665; *RN*, §§ 181, 380).

gɪr- *n. time, occasion* (Fr. *fois*, Ger. *-mal*, It. *volta*, Sp. *vez*): with collective sg. (§ 4696 *d*) [cp. K. gír *id.*, *path*; -gɪr⏜ in tɪŋgɪr⏜ s.v. tí⏜; § 2101].
— *used to form numeral adverbs* (§ 2762) = márra⏜:
gɪrrέt⏜tágoran⏜ (-rr- <-rw- § 672, -t⏜t- <-g⏜t- § 707) *they came (have come) once.*
gɪrówwɪn⏜nókkoran⏜ (-n⏜n- <-g⏜n- § 625) *they went (have gone) twice.*
gɪrárɪn⏜nálkori⏜ *I saw (have seen) him (her, it,* them) *twenty times.*

gírba⏜ *n. water-skin* [< قِرْبَة *id.*].
obj. -bag⏜.
pl. -bančʿ(ɪ)⏜.

gɪrbád⏜ *n. water-skin* [apparently < a pl. *قِرْبَات of قِرْبَة *id.* § 2397].
obj. -bádk(ɪ)⏜, -bátk(ɪ)⏜, -bátt(ɪ)⏜ § 2462; -ki⏜, -ti⏜.
pl. -bádɪ⏜.
έssɪ⏜gɪrbád-dēg⏜étta⏜ (-d-d- <-d-w- § 533) *bring a skin (full) of water.*

gírgɪd⏜ *n. gum (gingiva); with collective sg.* (§ 4696 *a*) [§ 2270].
obj. gɪrgɪdk(ɪ)⏜, -gítk(ɪ)⏜, -gítt(ɪ)⏜ § 2462; -ki⏜, -ti⏜.
gen. -gídn⏜v., -gín⏜c.
pl. -gɪdɪ⏜.

gɪrgíttɛ⏜ *n. cricket (Gryllus sp.); with collective sg.* (§ 4696 *c*) [< *gɪdgídtɛ⏜ (§§ 872, 706) < gɪd-gíd- onom. +t dim. +-ɛ⏜ of n. dic., so *little thing that says 'gɪd-gíd-' § 2335].
obj. -tɛg⏜.
pl. -tɛnč(ɪ)⏜.

gɪríde *v.i. (a) revolve, turn oneself round; (b) take a turn, walk round, walk about, stroll* [§§ 2870 ff.].
ind. pres. aī⏜gɪrídɛri⏜; perf. aī⏜gɪrídɛgori⏜ (N. -ɛko-, -ɛho-).

gɪríderar⏜ (-rar⏜; §§ 2200 ff., 2210) *and*
gɪrídɛríd⏜ (§§ 2256 ff., 2263) *n. revolving, etc.*

gɪrídɛ-bŭ- (§ 3931 α) *v.i. stat. be in a rounded state or condition, be round, be circular.*
(part. pres.) gɪrídɛbūl⏜ adj. *round, circular*; obj. gɪrídɛbúlg(ɪ)⏜.
ín⏜tábag⏜gɪrídɛbún⏜, mán⏜gɪrídɛbúmunun⏜ *this basket-work tray is circular, that other isn't.*

gɪrídɛg-ɪr (N. -ɛkɪr, -ɛhɪr; § 3679) (*a*) *v.t. caus. cause or allow to revolve, etc.; (b) v.t. turn round.*

gɪrídɛgɪr-mér (N. -ɛkɪr, -ɛhɪr-; § 4135) *v.t. cut while turning (t.) round.*

gírid⏜ *n. ape, baboon, monkey* [< قِرْد *id.* § 1359].
obj. gɪrídk(ɪ)⏜, -ítk(ɪ)⏜, -ítt(ɪ)⏜ § 2462; -ki⏜, -ti⏜.
pl. gír(ɪ)dɪ⏜.

gɪríš⏜ *n. piastre; with collective sg.* (§ 4696 *d*)
[< قِرْش *id.* < *Groschen*; § 1359].
obj. gɪríšk(ɪ)⏜, -ki⏜.
pl. gír(ɪ)šɪ⏜.

gísma⏜ *n. nose-ring* [?cp. خِزَام *id.*]
obj. -mag⏜.
pl. -manč(ɪ)⏜.
έn⏜gísma⏜ (-n⏜g- <-nn⏜g- § 613) *woman's nose-ring.*
kám⏜gísma⏜ (-m⏜g- <-mn⏜g- § 819) *camel's nose-ring.*

gɪzáz⏜ *n. glass, bottle* = gazáz.

góbɪr (§ 2837) *v.t. surround* [*RSN*, § 129].
ind. pres. aī⏜gobírri⏜, ɛr⏜góbɪrɪn⏜ (-rī⏜, -rí⏜); perf. aī⏜gobírkori⏜.
ğɪnέnaz⏜zέrbɛgɛg⏜gobírkoran⏜ (-z-z- <-g⏜z- § 734, -g⏜g- <-d⏜g- § 545) *they (have) surrounded the garden with a fence.*

gób(ɪ)rar⏜ (-rar⏜; §§ 2200 ff.) *and*
gob(ɪ)ríd⏜ (§§ 2256 ff.) *n. (action of) surrounding.*

góbɪr-an (§§ 3890 ff.) *v.t. tell to surround, let surround.*

gobɪr-ár (§ 3747 ε') *v.t. seize (etc.) s.v. ár after surrounding.*
ár⏜tékkɪ⏜gobɪrárkoru⏜ *we (have) surrounded and caught him (her, it).*

góbɪr-bŭ- (§ 3931 β) *v.i. stat. be in a surrounded state or condition.*
kā⏜šídan⏜séllɛr⏜góbɪrbūn⏜ (-n⏜s- <-rn⏜s- § 614) *the house is surrounded in the middle of (the) trees,* i.e. *the house is surrounded by (the) trees, of which it is in the middle.*
írɪ⏜wɛrwέgɛg⏜góbɪrbūn⏜ (-g⏜g- <-d⏜g- § 545) *and*
írɪ⏜góbɪrbūn⏜ *the ropes* (§ 4649) *are intertwined,* lit. *are surrounded (each by the other).*

gobɪrɛd-ág- (§§ 3877 ff.) *v.t. be in the situation of having surrounded.*

góbɪr-kattɪ- (§ 4093) *v.p. be surrounded.*

góg⏜ *n. raven-vulture* [onom. § 4526].
obj. gógk(ɪ)⏜, -gókk(ɪ)⏜, -ki⏜.
pl. gógk⏜.
góg⏜gurám⏜dógor⏜dúlun, fatískɪ⏜kálin⏜ (-m⏜d- <-bn⏜d- § 586) *the raven-vulture is larger than the crow, (and) eats carrion.*

gogládɛ n. *a weed that grows among cultivation*, Amaranthus blitum, Linn. (REM; BSP, 488) [§2188].
obj. -dɛg.

gŏglatt(ı) n. *frog, toad*; with collective sg. (§4696c) [<*gŏglart(ı)<gŏgl- onom. (√gŏg- §4526; cp. M. *gogele* quaken LN)+-ar gerundial -*ing* (§2200)+-t dem. or dim. (§§2324, 2325γ), so *that (little) croaking*; §§2221, 2225].
obj. gōglátttɪg.
pl. gōgláttɪnč(ı).

góǧ v.t. *slaughter, kill for food* [perhaps extension in -ǧ of √gó- *cut*; cogn. Sōm. *gŏy, gō* schneiden RSW, s.v.; cp. ON. δοδ *sacrifice* GNT, s.v.; §2891].
ind. pres. aī góǧ(ˡ)ri, ɛr góǧın (-ǧiˆ, -ǧíˆ); perf. aī góǧkori (gŏćk-; -ǧk-, -čk- §323; gŏćčo- §523).
imperat. góć!, pl. góǧwɛ! (góǧwé!; góǧǧɛ! §553, -ǧé!).
subj. past aī góǧsɪ (gŏćsɪ §529, -su).
ámbɛs ɛgɛd-dɛg goǧósko (-d-d- <-d-w- §533) *my brother has slaughtered a sheep*.

gŏǧar (-ǧár; §§2200ff.) and
gŏǧíd (§§2256ff.) n. *slaughtering*.

góǧ-an (§§3890ff.) v.t. *tell to slaughter, let slaughter*.

góǧ-bŭ- (góǧǧŭ- §552; §3931β) v.i. stat. *be in a slaughtered state or condition*.
ɛgɛd góǧǧūn *the sheep is (has been) slaughtered*.

goǧɛd-ág- (§§3877ff.) v.t. *be in the situation of having slaughtered*.
ámbɛs ınnówwıg ɛgɛ́tkı goǧɛdágın *my brother has slaughtered the (a) sheep today*.

góǧ-kattı- (góćk-; -ǧk-, -čk- §323; §4093) v.p. *be slaughtered*.

gŏkka n. *pigeon, dove*; with collective sg. (§4696d) [<*gŏkkar (§959) <*gŏg-kar (§569) <√gŏg- onom. of *cooing* (§4526)+-k intensive (§2853)+-ar ger. -*ing* (§2200), so *much cooing*, specialized in concrete sense; §2176].
obj. -kag.
pl. -karı.
gŏkkan hánu (-kah há- §560) and hánuŋ gŏkka *large pigeon*.

gól n. *upper or foremost part* [a remnant of ógol front, q.v.].
obj. gólg(ı), -gi.
pl. gólı.
béntıŋ gól *(cluster of leaves at) top of date-palm*.
gázázıŋ gól *neck of bottle*.
ſuŋ gól *head (ear; heads, ears §4696b) of corn*.
kúm gól (-m g- <-bn g- §586) *bow (prow) of boat*.
núbroŋ gól *top (notched end) of spindle* (CSW, p. 21).

gōlíd (ıt) n. *El-Goled (on map), name of two villages on the left bank of the Nile, about ten miles above Hándag*.
obj. gōlídk(ı), -lítk(ı), -ki.
gōlıd kánnɛ *Gōlid North*.
gōlıd óngo *Gōlid South*.
índotŋ gōlın móŋkon *from here to Gōlid*

góll(ı) v.t. *swallow*.
ind. pres. aī gólllıri.
perf. aī gólllıgori (N. -ıko-, -ıho-).
imperat. gólli!
dáwag gólllıgori *I (have) swallowed the medicine*.

góllar (-lár; §§2200ff.) and
gollíd (§§2256ff.) n. *swallowing*.

góll-an (§§3890ff.) v.t. *tell to swallow, let swallow*.

goll-ɛ-má- (§4036) and
gollır-ɛ-má- (§4041) v.t. *become unable to swallow*.

gollɛd-ág- (§§3877ff.) v.t. *be in the condition of having swallowed*.

góllı-kattı- (N. -ıha-; §4093) v.p. *be swallowed*.

golmódd(ı) n. *side-piece of yoke* (íslam) borne by cattle working water-wheel (kólɛ) [<*golmŏrd(ı) (§537) <gŏl- *foremost part*+√mŏr- *bind* (§4564)+-d of n. instr. (§2231), so *what binds the foremost part*].
obj. -dıg.
pl. -dınč(ı).

-g-on s.v. -on.

gonıssɛ n. *gum* [§§2291-2; RN, s.v. gonıssɛ].
obj. -sɛg.

gonıssɛ-kırı- (§§2539-40) adj. *resembling gum*.

gonıssɛ-kŏ- (§4118) v.i. *have gum, be gummiferous*.
(part. pres.) gonıssɛkōl (gonıssɛkŏl §1708) adj. *that has gum, gummiferous*.
ɪŋ gŏwwı gonıssɛkóm *this tree has gum*.
ín gŏwwı gonıssɛkómunun *this tree has no gum*.

-g-on-on with, *as soon as* s.v. -on-on.

góñ v.t. (a) *build*; (b) *weave* [cp. MN. kwań id. (a) KB, §496; RSN, §129].
ind. pres. aī góñ(ˡ)ri, ɛr góñın (-ñi, -ñíˆ); perf. aī góñkori.
part. pres. góñɪl *(one) that builds (weaves), builder, weaver, building, weaving*; past góñɛl *(one) that built (wove), builder, weaver, building, weaving*.
kág góñɪl *builder*.
kádɛg góñɪl *weaver*.
ká dɪgríg góñkoran *they (have) built many houses* (§4647).
góññab bɛnnágírton góñran (-b b- <-g-b- §519) *they weave (the) cloth out of cotton*.

góñar (-ñár, -ñɛr; §§2200ff.) and
goñíd (góñıd; §§2256ff.) n. *building, weaving*.
goñídk ágawın *he is working as a builder (weaver), lit....working at building (weaving)*.

góñña n. *cloth* (=Ar. دَمُور) [<*gŏñ-ñar (§979) *what is woven*=gónar §2177].
obj. -ñag.
pl. -ñanč(ı).
kúm góñña (-m g- <-bn g- §586) *sail*.

góñt(ı) n. *building, weaving* (=gónar) [§2325α].
obj. -tıg.
ɛr káŋ góñtıg uñúrná? *do you know how to build a house?*

góñ-an (§§3890ff.) v.t. *tell to build, etc., let build, etc.*

góñ-bŭ- (góñǧŭ- §635; §3931β) v.i. stat. *be in a built or woven state or condition*.
wáırtŏŋ góñbūgon *it was built in ancient times*, lit. *it has been in a built state since ancient times*.

goñ(ˡ)r-ɛg-ág- (§§4071ff.) v.t. =goñɛdól-.

goñ-ɛ-dól- (-ñod- §1178; §4022) and
goñ(ˡ)r-ɛ-dól- (-rod-; §4027) v.t. *be about to build, etc.*

goñ-ɛ-má- (§4036) and
goñ(ˡ)r-ɛ-má- (§4041) v.t. *become unable to build, etc.*

góñ-kattı- (§4093) v.p. *be built, etc.*

gŏr n. *ant*; with collective sg. (§4696c) [§2053; RSN, §129 s.v. guar; TOB, §143, 80; WS, p. 140, no. 138].
obj. gŏrk(ı), -ki.
pl. gŏrı.
gŏrn kám and occasionally gŏrŋ kám *large ant*; with collective sg.
gŏrn kám fırrıl *large winged ant*; with collective sg.

gŏr v.t. *gnaw* [§2053].
ind. pres. aī gŏrri; perf. aī gŏrkori.
wɛl kítkı gŏrın *the dog gnaws the bone*.

gŏrar (-rár; §§2200ff.) and
gōríd (§§2056ff.) n. *gnawing*.

gŏrɛ n. *couch-grass*, Cynodon dactylon, Pers. (BSP, 666) [<gŏr-+-ɛ of n. act. *what gnaws (from its manner of growth)* §2234δ].
obj. -rɛg.
pl. -rɛnč(ı).

gŏr-bŭ- (§3931β) v.i. stat. *be in a gnawed state or condition*.
kíd gŏrbūn *the bone is (has been) gnawed*.

gŏr-kattı- (§4093) v.p. *be gnawed*.

gorán (gur-; §956a) n. *Coran* [< اَلْقُرْآن id. §1389].
obj. -áŋg(ı), -gi.
gorándo *it is* (§5858) *in the Coran*.
gorándotónun *it is from the Coran*.

gorán-d(ı) (§§2545ff.) adj. *Coranic*.

gordád n. *tassel*; with collective sg. (§4696c) [app. < قُرْطَات a pl. of قُرْط *pendant, cluster* §2397].
obj. -ádk(ı), -átk(ı), -átt(ı) §2462; -ki, -ti.
gen. -ádn v., -ánn v.c., -án c.
pl. -ádı.
díkkɛn gordád *tassel(s on ends) of band suspending drawers*.
béjjɛŋ gordád *tassel(s) of (girl's) waist-fringe*.

górıǧ (-ıčˆ; §§2699, 2707) card. num. *six* [<*górdıǧ 1(+)5 RSN, §114].
obj. gorıǧk(ı), -íčk(ı), -íčč(ı) (§523); gór(ı)ǧk(ı), gór(ı)čk(ı) (§1522); -ǧk-, -čk (§323); -ki, -či.
gen. gorıǧn v., gór(ı)ǧn v., goríñ c. (§632), gór(ı)ñ c. (§1522).
pl. gór(ı)ǧı.
gór(ı)ǧun (-ǧū, -ǧúˆ §§939, 5232) and
tɛr gór(ı)ǧun (tɛr §5233) *it's (they're) six*.

gór(ı)ğín⌒ (-ğí⌒, -ğí⌒ §5235) and tír‿gór(ı)ğín⌒ (tır‿ §5236) *they're six.*
górıč‿tágon⌒ and górıč‿tágoran⌒ *six came (have come;* §5229).
tír‿górığ‿nókkon⌒ and tír‿górığ‿nókkoran⌒ *the six of them went (have gone;* §5245).
ógığ‿górığ‿nógın⌒ and ógığ‿górığ‿nógran⌒ *six men go* (§5239).
så‿gór(ı)ğı‿díğır⌒ *it's at 6·5* (s.v. så‿).

gor(ı)ğín-d(ı) (§2737b) adj. = goríñd(ı)‿.
gor(ı)ğ-ínt(ı)‿ (gór(ı)ğınt(ı)‿; §2740) *ord. num. sixth.*
gor(ı)ğıntín-d(ı)‿ (§2743) adj. *appertaining to the sixth.*
gór(ı)ğırε‿ (§2745) n. ⅙, *sixth part* [< gór(ı)ğ- 6 + -ır *(action of) making* + -ε‿ of n. ess., so *one of what makes into 6 §2287].
obj. -rεg‿.
pl. -rεnč(ı)‿.

gorín-d(ı)‿ (§2737a) adj. *appertaining to six, of six, six's.*
goriŋgår‿ (§§2758, 5261-7) num. *the whole six, all six* [< *gorıñgår‿ (§645) < góríñ of 6 + -g- obj. suff. + -år *seizure, so *comprehension of the 6 §2218].
obj. -árk(ı)‿, -ki⌒.
tεr‿goriŋgårk‿étta⌒ *bring the six of them;* tεr‿goriŋgårk‿ *a pronoun-complex* (§5199).

gorığ-kırı‿ (-íčkı-; -ğk-, -čk- §323; -kírı‿ §1532; §2736) num. adj. *about six.*
gór(ı)ğ-an- (§2760) v.i. *become six.*
gór(ı)ğam-bŭ- (§2761) v.i. stat. *be in a state or condition of becoming six.*
gorígk-ır (-íčk-, -ğk-, -čk-; N. -íččır §523; §2759) v.t. caus. *make into six.*
gorığkır-båg (-íčk-, etc.; §4138) v.t. *divide into six.*
imperat. gorığkırbåk!

gós‿ *Adam's apple* = góz‿.
góška adj. *one-eyed* = góško‿.
obj. -kag‿.
pl. -kanč(ı)‿.
ín‿ógığ‿góškan⌒ (‿góškå⌒, ‿góšká⌒ §939) *this man is one-eyed.*
góško adj. *one-eyed* = góško‿.
obj. -kog‿.
pl. -korı‿, -konč(ı)‿.
ín‿ógığ‿góškon⌒ (‿góškõ⌒, góškó⌒ §939) *this man is one-eyed.*

goššé v.t. *deceive, trick, dupe, cheat* [< Sudan Ar. ġúšš (=غشّ) *deceit* + -έ §3623].
ind. pres. åı‿goššérı⌒, εr‿goššén⌒ (-šέ⌒, -šέ §939); occ. -šén⌒, -šέ⌒, -šέ⌒ §1073); perf. åı‿goššégori⌒ (N. -έko-, -έho-).
imperat. goššé!
part. pres. goššέl‿ *(one) that deceives, etc., cheat, cheating, dishonest.*
έkkı‿goššéróskoran⌒ *they have deceived you.*
goššérar‿ (-rår‿; §§2200ff., 2207) and **goššέrid**‿ (§§2256ff., 2260) n. *deceiving, etc.*

goššέridk-ır-goššέ (-ítkır-, -íttır- §716; §4156) v.t. *deceive completely, utterly.*
åıgı‿goššέrídkırgoššέgoran⌒ and N. åıgı‿goššέrīttırgoššέkoran⌒ *they (have) completely deceived me.*
goššέ-bŭ- (§3931β) v.i. stat. *be in a deceived (etc.) state or condition.*
goššέrεd-ág- (§§3877ff.) v.t. *be in the situation of having deceived, etc.*
goššέ-kattı- (N. -έha-; §4093) v.p. *be deceived, etc.*
åı‿goššέkattóskori⌒ *I have been deceived.*

góu‿ (ɡów‿) n. *reed, Cyperus sp.* (BSP, 628); *with collective sg.* (§4696b); = dís‿ [< *gόww‿ §486β].
obj. góug‿, gówg‿.
pl. gówı‿.
gów‿έssın‿túr‿ımbélın⌒ *the reeds grow in the water.*
góu‿kúluŋ‿kóččır‿έssın‿túr‿ımbélın⌒ *the reeds grow on stones in the water.*
gówırtóŋ‿galámgı‿mérran⌒ *they cut pens* (§4647) *from (the) reeds.*

góuwε‿ (gówwε‿) n. *bed or growth of reeds, sedge* [< *gόww- *reed* + -ε‿ *existence, so *reed-existence* §2234β].
obj. -wεg‿.
pl. -wεnč(ı)‿.

góww(ı)‿ (góuw(ı)‿, -w(u)‿ §1202) n. *well* [cp. ON. ϙⲟⲣεıλ *id.* GNT, s.v. (-ⲁ predicative ZNG, §70)].
obj. -wıg‿.
pl. -wınč(ı)‿.

góz‿ n. *dune* [< Sudan Ar. قُوْز gōz *id.*].
obj. gózk(ı)‿, gósk(ı)‿, -ki⌒.
pl. gózı‿.
sfuŋ‿góz‿ *elevated part of sand-bank, sand banked up by wind, dune.*

góz‿ (gós‿ §1300) n. *(a) Adam's apple* [cp. Eg. Ar. جوزة الزور *id.* SAE², s.v. جوز; RSN, §129 s.v. *gōs*]; *(b), applied to) larynx, interior of throat.*
obj. gózk(ı)‿, gósk(ı)‿, -ki⌒.
X. εŋ‿góz‿έkk‿óddıná? *does your throat (lit. Adam's apple) hurt you?*
Y. έjjo, zíkm‿εŋέ⌒ (§6203) *yes, because I have a cold, lit.... because it is catarrh.*

-gu forms pl. of ín‿ *this,* mán‿ *that,* ní? *who?* and of subjunctive (§§2070d, 6169, 6171).

gú‿ (occ. g‿v. §1128) n. *(a) earth; (b) ground, floor; (c) place* [cp. M. gúr *id.*; WS, p. 137, no. 120].
obj. gúg‿.
gå‿máll‿fεttıšgori⌒ (-f‿f- < -g‿f- §540) *I (have) examined all the ground.*
gúr‿ágın⌒ (s)he (it) *squats (etc. s.v. ág) on the ground.*
gúr‿búran⌒ *they lie on the ground.*

— like åšåı‿ (q.v.) and Ar. دنيا (SNK, 641), Sudan Ar. وطاء *earth, ground, used vaguely of the place, time or weather:*
gú‿urúmmén⌒ (§1532; -mέ⌒, -mέ⌒) *it's (the time or place is) dark* (الوطاء بقت ظلمة).

gú‿ğugrín⌒ *it's (the weather's) hot* (الوطاء حارّة).
gú‿ğugr‿εgó⌒ *it (the weather) was (has been) hot* (كانت الوطاء حارّة).
ınnówwıg‿g‿orófélun⌒ *today it's (the weather's) cold.*
gú‿béjjın⌒ *it is morning (the morning is starting, s.v. béjj(ı)).*

gú‿ and **gŭ-c.**, **g-v.**—*in division* (§5324d, f): *share, lit. place.*
márεg‿gú‿tóskır‿båk⌒ *divide the millet into three shares.*
béntıg‿gú‿kémsır‿bagíttε⌒ *divide the dates into four shares.*
dúŋgıg‿gú‿ídıwır‿båk⌒ *divide the money into eight shares.*
hamsínıgoríčkı‿gú‿kólodır‿båkkın‿ ídıw‿ıdíwgέ⌒ 56 ÷ 7 = 8.
ımílgıg-árır‿bagíttεgın‿díğ‿díčké⌒ 100 ÷ 20 = 5.

— *in multiplication* (§§5319-21) gŭ-, g-v. *is used as we use* times *in expressing the multiplier:*
ídıw‿gówwırbūl‿dımındogoríčče⌒ 8 × 2 = 16.
kémız‿gútóskırbūl‿dımdówwıgέ⌒ 4 × 3 = 12.
kólot‿kolótkεg‿guídıwırbūl‿hamsínıgoríčké⌒ 7 × 8 = 56.
ídıw‿ıdíwgεg‿guıskódırbūl‿sabaınówwıgέ⌒ 8 × 9 = 72.
ıskód‿ıskóttεg‿gūdımíndobūl‿tısaíŋgέ⌒ 9 × 10 = 90.
dımındo‿årır‿gūdımındówwırbūl‿míllέr‿arbaínıkemíské⌒ 12 × 12 = 144.

— *this participle also expresses fractions* (§2747):
gūtóskırbūlg‿εttágoran⌒ *they (have) brought three-quarters.*

gŭn-d(ı)‿ (§§2545ff.) adj. *appertaining to the earth, etc.*
gubår n. *travelling or suspended dust, dustiness, dusty day, dusty weather* [< غبار *id.*].
obj. -árk(ı)‿, -ki⌒.
pl. -årı‿.

gúbba n. *dome, esp. dome over tomb of saint* [< قبّة *id.*].
obj. gúbbag‿, gúbbåg‿ (§1532), -gi⌒.
pl. -banč(ı)‿.
abufåtnaŋ‿gúbba-tånnan⌒ *it's the dome (over the tomb) of Abu Fåtima.*

gúful‿ n. *lock, esp. padlock* = gífıl‿.
obj. gufúlg(ı)‿, -gi⌒.
pl. gúf(u)lı‿.

gúl n. (a) *sorcerer, wizard;* (b) *sorceress, witch* [< غول *demon*].
obj. gúlg(ı)‿, -gi⌒.
pl. gúlı‿.
gúln‿ónd(ı)‿ = gúl‿ (a).
gúl‿kårr(ı)‿ = gúl‿ (b).

gúlgul n. *cotton-seed; with collective sg.* (§4696b); = kukkós‿ [< Sudan Ar. غَلْغُل *id.*].
obj. gulgúlg(ı)‿, -gi⌒.
pl. gúlgulı‿.

gúlla‿ n. (a) *earthenware water-bottle* [< قُلَّة *id.*]; (b) *(whole) gourd in which hole has*

gúll(ı)⌣ — gússa⌣

been made so that it can be used as a receptacle.
obj. -lag⌣.
pl. -lanč(ı)⌣.

gúll(ı)⌣ n. *seed (nut) of dōm-palm*; with collective sg. (§ 4696b) [§ 2053].
obj. -lıg⌣.
pl. -lınč(ı)⌣.
hámbuŋ⌣gúll(ı)⌣ = gúll(ı)⌣.

gúll(ı) v.t. (a) *scatter, throw here and there*; (b) *sow (by scattering)*; (c) *throw about, dissipate, squander* [§ 2053].
ind. pres. aî⌣gúlliri↷; perf. aî⌣gúlligori↷ (N. -ıko-, -ıho-).
imperat. gúlli!
ar⌣sfum⌣mısídır⌣gúllıgoru↷ (-m⌣m- < -g⌣m- § 601) *we (have) scattered (the) sand in (i.e. on the floor of) the mosque.*
tɛ́rıg⌣gúllıran↷ *they sow the seed(s).*
ɛsmán⌣tén⌣dúŋgıg⌣gullóskon↷ ɛoθ-mán *has squandered his money.*

gúllar⌣ (-lár⌣; §§ 2200 ff.) and
gullíd⌣ (§§ 2256 ff.) n. *scattering, etc.*

gúll-an (§§ 3890 ff.) v.t. *tell to scatter, etc., let scatter, etc.*

gúllı-bŭ- (§ 3931 β) v.i. stat. *be in a scattered (etc.) state or condition.*
tɛ́rı⌣gúllıbūn↷ *the seed is (has been) sown.*

gullır-ɛg-ág- (§§ 4071 ff.) v.t. = gulledól-.

gull-ɛ-dól- (-lᵒd- § 1178; § 4022) and
gullır-ɛ-dól- (-rᵒd-; § 4027) v.t. *be about to scatter, etc.*

gulled-ág- (§§ 3877 ff.) v.t. *be in the situation of having scattered, etc.*

gúllı-kattı- (N. -ıha-; § 4093) v.p. *be scattered, etc.*

gullıkáttı-bŭ- (N. -ıha-; § 4105) v.i. stat. = gúllıbŭ-.
tɛ́rı⌣gullıkáttıbūn↷ = tɛ́rı⌣gúllıbūn↷

gumáma⌣ n. *place where rubbish is thrown, rubbish-hole* [< قُمَامَة *sweepings*].
obj. -mag⌣.
pl. -manč(ı)⌣.
kǎrıg⌣góñkaŋ⌣kúl-lēw⌣wáddıran, wa-sáhab⌣bógran⌣téddó, gumámag⌣ɛrán↷ (-l-l- < -l-w- § 580, -w⌣w- < -g⌣w- § 719, -b⌣b- < -g⌣b- § 519) *when they build houses they dig a hole (sc. in taking earth for mud for building), they throw refuse into it, they call it the* gumáma; ⌣téddó, § 1532, cp. § 4630.

gumár⌣ n. *gambling* [< Sudan Ar. قُمَار *id.*].
obj. -árk(ı)⌣.
gumárkı⌣káččıran↷ *they gamble.*
tén⌣dúŋgıg⌣gumárro⌣dábırın↷ *he loses (wastes) his money in gambling.*

gúmɛ⌣ n. *time before dawn, about 4 a.m.* (SNK, 291, 5) [قُمْ *rise!* + -ɛ⌣ *utterance* § 2236].
obj. -mɛg⌣.
pl. guménč(ı)⌣.
gúmɛr⌣ımbɛlóskoran↷ *they have started before dawn.*

gúmmud⌣ n. *foam.*
obj. gummúdk(ı)⌣, -útk(ı)⌣, -útt(ı)⌣ § 2462; -ki↷, -ti↷.

gúmur n. *neck* = ɛ́jjɛ⌣ [RSN, § 129].
obj. gumúrk(ı)⌣, -ki↷.
pl. gúmuru⌣.

gŭ́nč(ı) v.i. and t. *look, etc.* occasional pronunciation of gúñč(ı).

gundéla⌣ n. *one of the better sorts of date growing in Dóngola* = akundɛ́na⌣; s.v. bɛ́nt(ı)⌣; with collective sg. (§ 4696b).
obj. -lag⌣.
pl. -lanč(ı)⌣.

guntár⌣ n. *weight of 100 pounds* (rátul⌣) = 45 *kilograms, hundredweight*; with collective sg. (§ 4696d) [< Sudan Ar. قِنْطَار < قَنْطَار *id.*].
obj. -árk(ı)⌣, -ki↷.
pl. -árı⌣.

gúñč(ı) (gŭ́nč(ı) § 1210) (a) v.i. *look, look out, watch*; (b) v.t. *look at, watch, keep an eye on*; (c) v.t. *look out for, watch for* [cp. M. gúñ *id.*; -č *intensive* § 2864].
ind. pres. aî⌣gúñčiri↷; perf. aî⌣gúñčigori↷ (N. -ıko-, -ıho-).
imperat. gŭ́nči!
bābúrkı⌣bıgúñčıru↷ *we shall (you pl. will) look out for the steamer (train).*

gúñčar⌣ (-čár⌣; §§ 2200 ff.) and
gūñčíd⌣ (§§ 2256 ff.) n. *looking, etc.*
tén⌣gūñčíd⌣sérēn↷ (§ 4682) (a) *(s)he (it) keeps a good look-out*; (b) *it is good to look out for him (her, it).*

gúñč-an (§§ 3890 ff.) v.t. *tell to look (at), etc., let look (at), etc.*

gúñčı-bŭ- (§ 3931 β) v.i. stat. *be in a watched (etc.) state or condition.*

gūñčɛd-ág- (§§ 3877 ff.) v.i. and t. *be in the situation of having looked (at), etc., be still looking (at), etc.*
ɛ́kkı⌣gūñčɛdágın↷ *(s)he has been (sc. and still is) looking out for you.*

gúñčı-kób (§ 3747ᵉ′) v.t. *shut (etc. s.v. kób) after looking (at), etc.*
imperat. gūñčıkóp!
kobídkı⌣gūñčıkópkó↷ *(s)he (has) closed the door carefully.*

gūñčıkobɛd-ág- (§§ 3877 ff.) v.t. *be in the situation of having shut (etc.) after looking (at), etc.*
kobídk⌣úgu⌣mállɛg⌣gūñčıkobɛdák-koran↷ *they were (have been) shutting the door carefully every night.*

gūñčı-nál (§ 3747ᵉ′) v.t. *look at carefully, examine well.*
imperat. gūñčınál! (⌣ᵕ).

gūñčı-nóg (§ 3747ᵉ′) v.i. and t. *go (etc. s.v. nóg) while looking (at), etc., watch as one goes.*
imperat. gūñčınók!
ar⌣án⌣togóg⌣gūñčınógru↷ *we watch (the ground) under us as we go.*

gúr⌣ n. *bull.*
obj. gúrk(ı)⌣, -ki↷.
pl. gúrı⌣.

gúrn-d(ı)⌣ (§§ 2545 ff.) adj. *appertaining to the (a) bull, of the (a) bull, bull's.*
kúsu⌣gúrnd(ı)⌣ *beef.*

gur-tŏd⌣ (§ 2370) n. *calf.*
obj. -tŏdk(ı)⌣, -tŏtk(ı)⌣, -tŏkk(ı)⌣, -tŏtt(ı)⌣ (§ 2462); -ki↷, -ti↷.
gen. -tŏdn⌣v., -tŏnn⌣v.c., -tŏn⌣c. (§§ 778–88).
pl. gúrtonı⌣.
gurtódun↷ *it's the (a) calf.*

gúr-tod⌣ (§ 2370) n. (a) *rather poor bull, bull of poor quality*; (b) = gúr⌣.
obj. gúrtŏdk(ı)⌣, -tŏtk(ı)⌣, -tŏkk(ı)⌣, -tŏtt(ı)⌣; -tŏdk(ı)⌣, etc.; -ki↷, -ti↷.
gen. -tŏdn⌣v., -tŏnn⌣v.c., -tŏn⌣c.
pl. gúrtonı⌣.
gúrtodun⌣ (gúrtódun↷ § 1966) *it's the (a) (rather poor) bull.*

guráb⌣ n. *crow, raven* [< غُرَاب *id.*].
obj. -ábk(ı)⌣, -ápk(ı)⌣, -ki↷.
gen. -ábn⌣v., -ám⌣c.
pl. -ábı⌣.

gurán⌣ *Coran* = gorán⌣.

gúrgud⌣ adj. *frizzly* [< *gúdgud⌣ § 2507].
obj. gurgúdk(ı)⌣, -útk(ı)⌣, -útt(ı)⌣ § 2462; -ki↷, -ti↷.
pl. gúrgudı⌣.
díltı⌣gurgúdkı⌣kól⌣ *with frizzly hair.*
núgun⌣díltı⌣gurgúdun↷ (-n⌣d- < -dn⌣d- § 612) *the slave's hair is frizzly.*

gúrrɛ v.i. *become glad, become happy, get pleased, rejoice* [< gúrr- either cogn. with ON. коур *be glad* (GNT, s.v.) or < فَرِح *rejoicing after grief* (§ 1393) + -ɛ § 2874].
ind. pres. aî⌣gúrrɛri↷, ɛr⌣gúrrɛn↷ (-ré↷); perf. aî⌣gúrrɛgori↷ (N. -ɛko-, -ɛho-).

gúrrɛrar⌣ (-rár⌣; §§ 2200 ff., 2210) and
gurrɛríd⌣ (§§ 2256 ff., 2263) n. *becoming glad, etc.*

gurrɛríd-an-gúrrɛ (§ 4161) v.i. *become exceedingly glad, etc.*

gúrrɛ-bŭ- (§ 3931 α) v.i. stat. *be in a state of gladness.*
part. pres. gúrrɛbūl⌣ *(one) that is in a glad state, glad, happy, joyful.*
dárıg⌣gúrrɛbū, mabsúdū, ággırídē↷ *the tortoise is happy, it's content, it's walking about.*

gúrrɛbūrar⌣ (-rár⌣; §§ 2200 ff., 2207) n. *joy, happiness.*
obj. gurrɛbūrárk(ı)⌣ (-búrárk(ı)⌣).

gúrrɛ-dɛ́n (§§ 3996–7) v.t. *congratulate (the speaker).*
aîgı⌣gúrrɛdɛ́ŋkoran↷ *they (have) congratulated me.*

gúrrɛ-tır (§§ 3998–9) v.t. *congratulate (other than the speaker).*
aî⌣tékk⌣ínın⌣íllar⌣gurrɛtíkkori↷ *(have) congratulated him (her) on this.*

gurúnt(ı)⌣ n. *alluvial soil, newly-formed alluvial land* (included in kúrub⌣); = Sudan Ar. قَرِير gurɛr (AESA; HESA, s.v. soil; NSD, p. 24) [? < *ku-rúbn-t(ı)⌣ § 2329].
obj. -tıg⌣.
pl. -tınč(ı)⌣.

gurúnt(ı)⌣ (-ti↷) *Gronti* (on map), *a village on the western side of Argo Island about 5 miles from its northern end.*
obj. -tıg⌣.

gússa⌣ n. *large receptacle for storing grain, bin*; with collective sg. (§ 4696d): (SNK, 509) [< قَصْعَة *large trough* (AZA, p. 59)].
obj. -sag⌣.
pl. -sanč(ı)⌣.

gússa⌣síbɛrtónū, íwın⌣íllár; dıgrígır⌣ dúlū, ogíččı⌣sókkē; gırídébū, gátawēk⌣kŏ; togógɛd⌣úbbúr-rēk⌣kŏ; íud⌣dogógɛb⌣bōgundúddā, togógɛd⌣ubbúrkɛd⌣ós'rā⁀ (-r-r- < -r-w- §672, -d⌣d- < -g⌣d- §534, -b⌣b- < -d⌣b- §518) *the gússa is (made) of clay, it is for grain; it is very large, it holds a man; it is circular, it has a cover; below it has a hole; they pour the grain in at the top, they take it out below by the hole.*
gúss⌣ɛ́rdɛb⌣tóskıkırım⌣bókkos⌣sókkɛn⁀ (-m⌣b- < -n⌣b- §592, -s⌣s- < -n⌣s- §680) *a gússa holds up to about three arắdıb.*
gušábı⌣ (-bı⁀) n. *Goshabi (on map), a village on the left bank of the Nile, about eleven miles above Ed-Débbaᵇ.*
obj. -bıg⌣.
gúšš(ı) (a) v.t. *break*; (b) v.i. *get broken, break* (= tómb(ı), but commoner).
ind. pres. aī⌣gúššırı⁀, ɛr⌣gúššın⁀ (-ší⁀, -ší⁀); perf. aī⌣gúššıgori⁀ (N. -ıko-, -ıho-).
imperat. gúšši!
sáb⌣saháŋgı⌣gúššıgó⁀ *the cat broke (has broken) the plate.*
sáhaŋ⌣gúššıgó⁀ *the plate broke (has got broken).*
fıŋǧaw-wēg⌣gúššıgori⁀ (-w-w- < -n-w- §720) *I broke (have broken) a cup.*
fıŋǧaw-wēr⌣gúššıgó⁀ *a cup (has) got broken.*
súlɛ⌣gŏwwıgaddı⌣tɛméllın⌣nókkıŋ⌣ gúššın⁀ (-n⌣n- < -g⌣n- §625) *if the pot goes continually to the well it gets broken.*
tém⌣maínn⌣óssı⌣gúššıgó⁀ *his (her) left leg was (has got) broken.*
gúššar⌣ (-šár⌣; §§2200 ff.) and
gúššíd (§§2256 ff.) n. *breaking, fracture.*
guššid-aŋ-gúšš(ı) (§4162) v.i. *get completely broken, get smashed to pieces.*
guššid-aŋ-gúššı-bū- (§4166) v.i. stat. *be in a completely broken (etc.) state or condition.*
gálo⌣guššídaŋgúššíbūn⁀ *the water-jar is (has been) broken to pieces.*
guššídk-ır-gúšš(ı) (-ītkır-, -īttır- §716; §§4156-8) v.t. *break completely, smash to pieces.*
gúššɛd adj. *broken* [§2522].
obj. guššédk(ı)⌣, -étk(ı)⌣, -ki⁀.
pl. gúššɛdı⌣.
íŋgu⌣guššédí⁀ (§1161) *these are broken.*
gúšš-an (§§3890 ff.) v.t. *tell to break, let break.*
gúšši-bū- (§3931 β) v.i. stat. *be in a broken state or condition.*
éssır⌣gúššıbūn⁀ *the bottle is (lies) broken.*
guššır-ɛg-ág- (§§4071 ff.) v.t. and i. = guššɛdól-.
sandúkkı⌣gúššıɛgákkon⁀ *(s)he was (you were) just going to break the box.*
sandúg⌣guššıɛgákkon⁀ *the box was just going to break.*
guš-ɛ-dól- (-šᵒd- §1178; §4022) and
guššır-ɛ-dól- (-rᵒd- §4027) v.t. and i. *be about to break.*
ɛr⌣ɛssírkı⌣guššɛdólın⁀ *you are about to break the bottle.*

éssır⌣guššɛdólın⁀ *the bottle is about to break.*
sandúkkı⌣guššɛdólkó⁀ *(s)he was (you were) just going to break the box.*
guš-ɛ-má- (§4036) and
guššır-ɛ-má- (§4041) v.t. and i. *become unable to break.*
aī⌣ǧɛrrıbɛ́gori, aī⌣tékkı⌣guššɛmágori⁀ *I (have) tried, I couldn't break it.*
guššɛd-ág- (§§3877 ff.) v.t. and i. *be in the situation of having broken.*
ɛssírkı⌣guššɛdágın⁀ *(s)he (it) has (you have) broken the bottle.*
gúšši-kattı- (N. -ıha-; §4093) v.p. *be broken.*
gúta⌣ (gáta⌣, gáta⌣) n. *cover, lid* [< غطاء, Sudan Ar. غطا *id.*].
obj. -tag⌣.
pl. -tančı⌣.
gutár⌣ (-tár⌣) n. *dust in commotion, dust-storm, sand-storm.*
obj. -ark(ı)⌣, -ki⁀.
ǧ- (§1111) < ǧú *proceed.*
ǧabád⌣ n. *haunch-bone, haunch, buttock*; with collective sg. (§4696a) [< Sudan Ar. جعمات pl. of جَعْمَة *id.* §2397].
obj. -ádk(ı)⌣, -átk(ı)⌣, -átt(ı)⌣ §2462; -ki⁀, -ti⁀.
gen. -ádn⌣v., -án⌣c.
pl. -ádı⌣.
ǧabárkal⌣ (-bákkal⌣ §571a) n. *purslane, Portulaca oleracea,* Linn. (BSP, 45) [< *ǧabr- (جبر) *slave* + kál⌣ *food*, so *slave-food §2294].
obj. ǧabarkálg(ı)⌣, -gi⁀.
ǧábbɛd⌣ n. *woman's waist-cloth.*
obj. ǧabbédk(ı)⌣, -étk(ı)⌣, -étt(ı)⌣ §2462; -ki⁀, -ti⁀.
gen. ǧábbɛdn⌣v., -bɛn⌣c.
pl. ǧábbɛdı⌣.
ǧábɛ v.t. *touch, feel, handle* [< جَعَل inversion, *turning over, inside out* (§1350) + -ɛ §3610].
ind. pres. aī⌣ǧábɛrı, ɛr⌣ǧábɛn⁀ (-bē⁀, -bé⁀); perf. aī⌣ǧábɛgori⁀ (N. -ɛko-, -ɛho-).
part. pres. ǧábɛl⌣ (one) *that touches, etc., toucher, etc., touching, etc.*; obj. ǧabél(ı)⌣, -gi⁀.
part. fut. bíǧábɛl⌣ (one) *that will touch, etc., toucher, etc., touching, etc.*
part. past ǧábɛrɛl⌣ (one) *that touched, etc., toucher, etc., touching, etc.*; obj. ǧabɛrélg(ı)⌣, -gi⁀.
tókkon⌣íŋı⌣ǧábɛmɛn⁀ *don't touch this.*
ǧábɛrar⌣ (-rár⌣; §§2200 ff., 2210) and
ǧábɛríd⌣ (§§2256 ff., 2263) n. *touching, etc.*
ǧábɛr-an (§§3890 ff., 3899) v.t. *tell to touch, etc., let touch, etc.*
ǧábɛ-dég (§3747ɛ') v.t. *by handling cover one's loins (etc. s.v. dég), take and put round one's loins* (§3783).
imperat. ǧábɛdɛk! [> Sudan Ar. جبديق ǧabadég⌣, -ék⌣ *waist-cloth*].
aī⌣ǧabɛdékkori *I took (have taken) and put it round my waist.*
íŋı⌣ǧábɛdék⁀ *put this round your waist.*

íŋ⌣kádɛǧ⌣ǧábɛdék⁀ *put this cloth round your waist.*
ǧábɛr-ɛg-ág- (§§4071 ff.) v.t. = ǧábɛrɛdól-.
ǧábɛr-ɛ-dól- (-rᵒd- §1178; §§4016-17, 4022, 4027) v.t. *be about to touch, etc.*
ǧábɛr-ɛ-má- (§§4016-17, 4036, 4041) v.t. *become unable to touch, etc.*
ǧábéŋ-ır (´˜; N. -ŋkır; §3688) v.t. caus. *cause or allow to touch, etc.*
ind. pres. aī⌣ǧábéŋıddi⁀ (´˜˜).
ar⌣íŋı⌣wēb⌣bíǧábɛŋírmunun⁀ (-b⌣b- < -g⌣b- §519) *we shall not let anyone touch this.*
ǧábɛ-kattı- (N. -ɛha-; §4093) v.p. *be touched, etc.*
ǧábríjɛ⌣ n. *Gabria (on map), a village on the left bank of the Nile, about 7 miles below Ed-Débbaʰ* [< خابرية].
obj. -jɛg⌣.
ǧádd(ı)⌣ n. *natron* [< *ǧárd(ı)⌣ §537].
obj. -dıg⌣ [> Sudan Ar. جردقة *id.* AESA, s.v.].
ǧáfar⌣ (-fár⌣) n. *Gáɛfar, a man's name* [< جعفر *id.*].
obj. ǧafárk(ı)⌣, ǧáfárk(ı)⌣, -ki⁀.
ǧáfárn-d(ı)⌣ (ǧáfárnd(ı)⌣; §§2545 ff.) adj. *appertaining to Gáɛfar.*
ǧág v.t. *knead (i.e. mix by kneading)* [cogn. ǧákk(ı) *compress* §2777].
ind. pres. aī⌣ǧágri, ɛr⌣ǧágın⁀ (-gī⁀, -gí⁀); perf. aī⌣ǧágkori⁀ (⌣ǧákkori⁀).
imperat. ǧák!
ɛŋ⌣kaníssɛǧ⌣ǧágın⁀ (-ǧ⌣ǧ- < -g⌣ǧ- §551) *the woman kneads the dough.*
ǧágar⌣ (-gár⌣; §§2200 ff.) and
ǧágíd (§§2256 ff.) n. *kneading.*
ǧág-an (§§3890 ff.) v.t. *tell to knead, let knead.*
ǧág-bū- (-ǧággū- §546; §3931 β) v.i. stat. *be in a kneaded state or condition.*
kaníssɛ⌣ǧágbūn⁀ *the dough is (has been) kneaded.*
ǧágɛd-ág- (§§3877 ff.) v.t. *be in the situation of having kneaded.*
ǧág-kattı- (ǧákka-; §4093) v.p. *be kneaded.*
kaníssɛ⌣ǧákkattóskó⁀ *the dough has been kneaded.*
ǧágad⌣ adj. *weak* [cogn. ǧágadɛ (´˜˜) v.i. *melt* §2495].
obj. ǧagádk(ı)⌣, -átk(ı)⌣, -átt(ı)⌣ §2462; -ki⁀, -ti⁀.
pl. ǧágadı⌣.
ǧágad-an- (§3910α) v.i. *become weak, weaken.*
ǧágadam-bū- (§§3949 ff.) v.i. stat. *be in a weakening (i.) state or condition.*
ógıǧ⌣ǧágadambūn, dígırbūn⁀ *the man is growing weak, he has fallen down, lit. lies fallen.*
ǧágadanɛ-ág- (§3966α) v.i. *be in the condition of having become weak.*
ǧágádɛ (´˜, ´˜ §§1794, 2878) v.i. (a) *pass from solid towards liquid state, melt;* (b) *become pliant, relax, soften;* (c) *become effeminate (molliri).*
opp. to déŋɛ; [< ǧágád- cogn. ǧágad *weak* §2495) + -ɛ (-ɛ́) §2870].
ind. pres. aī⌣ǧágádɛrı (˜˜, ˜˜˜);
perf. aī⌣ǧágádɛgori⁀ (˜˜˜, ˜˜˜);
N. -ɛko-, -éko-, -ɛho-, -ého-).

ğăggŭ- — ğámmɛ

def. perf. aı̂‿ğagadóskori⁀ (⌣́⌣́⌣⌣).
šéma‿masíllo‿bığagádé⁀ the candle(s §4647, wax) will melt in the sun.
áğın‿ğagádegó⁀ the skin (leather) became (has become) pliant.
(part. pres.) ğagádɛl⁀ (⌣́⌣́, ⌣́⌣́⌣́⌣́; §2524) adj. melting, pliant, relaxed, soft, effeminate.
kúsu‿ğagadélun⁀ the meat is tender.
ín‿ógığ‿ğagádɛlun⁀ this man is effeminate.

ğagádɛrar (⌣⌣́⌣́, ⌣́⌣́⌣́⌣́; -rɑ̆r; §§2200ff., 2210) and
ğagādɛríd (§§2256ff., 2263) n. melting, relaxation, softening, etc.

ğagádɛl-an- (⌣⌣́⌣, ⌣́⌣́⌣; §3910α) v.i. = ğagádɛ.

ğagādɛlam-bŭ- (⌣⌣́⌣⌣, ⌣́⌣́⌣⌣; ⌣⌣́⌣⌣; §1932a; §§3949ff.) v.i. stat. be in a melting (etc.) state or condition, be advanced in the process of melting, etc.
dés‿ğagādɛlámbun⁀ the butter has begun to melt.

ğagādɛlámbᵘ-an (-b(w)an; §3962) v.t. let be in a melting (etc.) state or condition, etc.
ağíngı‿ğagādɛlámbá⁀ let the hide (leather) be in a pliant condition.

ğagādɛlanɛd-ăg- (§3966α) v.i. be in a condition of having melted, etc.

ğagádɛ-bŭ- (⌣⌣́⌣, ⌣́⌣́⌣; §3931α) v.i. stat. be in a melted (etc.) state or condition.

ğagádɛbᵘ-an (-gādébᵘan, -gādɛ́-; -b(w)an; §3962) v.t. let be in a melted (etc.) state or condition.
šémağ‿ğagādɛbá⁀ (-ğ‿ğ- <-g‿ğ-§551) let the wax be in a melted state.

ğagādɛr-ɛg-ăg- (§4071ff.) v.i. = ğagādɛrɛdól-.

ğagādɛr-ɛ-dól- (-rᵒd- §1178; §§4016-17, 4022, 4027) v.i. be about to melt, etc.

ğagádɛg-ır (⌣⌣́⌣, ⌣́⌣́⌣; N. -ɛkır, ⌣́⌣, -ɛhır, ⌣́⌣; §3680) (a) v.t. caus. cause or allow to melt, etc.; (b) v.t. melt, relax, soften.

ğagādɛgır-sɛlgɛ́ (N. -ɛkır-, -ɛhır-; §4135) v.t. boil rendering soft, render soft by boiling, boil (leaving) soft.
N. kúmb‿ówwığ‿ğagādɛkırsɛlgɛ́⁀ (-ğ‿ğ- <-g‿ğ- §551) boil two eggs soft.

ğagādɛgır-sɛlgér-an (N. -ɛkır-, -ɛhır-; §4142) v.t. tell to boil soft, let boil soft.

ğagādɛ-sɛlgɛ́-bŭ- (§5683; cp. §3943) v.i. stat. be in a soft-boiled state or condition.
kúmbu‿ğagādɛsɛlgɛ́būgó⁀ the egg was (eggs were §4647, has (have) been) soft-boiled.

ğagādɛgır-sɛlgɛ́-dĕn (N. -ɛkır-, -ɛhır-; §§4142, 3995ff.) v.t. after boiling soft give (to the speaker), boil soft for (the speaker).
kúmb‿ówwığ‿ğagādɛgırsɛlgɛ́dĕn⁀ boil me two eggs soft.

ğagādɛgır-sɛlgɛ́-tır (N. -ɛkır-, -ɛhır-; §§4142, 3995ff.) v.t. after boiling soft give (to other than the speaker), boil soft for (other than the speaker).

ğăggŭ- (§546) < ğăg-bŭ- be in a kneaded state s.v. ğăg.

ğăham (ğăh-, ğĕh- §1150a) = ğákam cheek.

ğăhar = ğákar n. hook.

ğáhud = ğákud n. stew.

ğákam (ğáham §1027, ğắh-, ğɛ́h-) n. cheek (=tíbıl); with collective sg. (§4696a) [RSN, §129; §2137].
obj. ğákamg(ı) (ğáham-, ğắh-, ğɛ́h-), -gi⁀.
pl. ğákamı (ğáhamı, ğắh-, ğɛ́h-).

ğákar (ğáhar §1027; N. ğákkar) n. hook, fish-hook.
obj. ğákark(ı), -ki⁀.
pl. ğákarı.

†**ğakɛ́ta** (ğakkɛ́- §1380) n. jacket, coat [< جاكيتة < giacchetta].
obj. -tag.
pl. -tanč(ı).

N. **ğákkar** n. hook = ğákar.
obj. ğákkark(ı) (ğákkark(ı) §1522), -ki⁀.
pl. ğákkarı.

ğákk(ı) v.t. (a) press, press down, compress, squeeze (= úrr(ı)); (b) massage [cogn. ğăg knead §§2777, 2853].
ind. pres. aı̂‿ğákkıri⁀; perf. aı̂‿ğákkıgori⁀ (N. -ıko-, -ıho-).
imperat. ğákki!
def. perf. aı̂‿ğakkóskori⁀.
tɛr‿ánn‿íğ‿ğákkıgó⁀ (-ğ‿ğ- <-g‿ğ- §551) (s)he squeezed my hand(s §4696a).
antımbésk‿ğákkıgori⁀ I (have) massaged our brother.

ğákkar (-kɑ̆r; §§2200ff.) and
ğakkíd (§§2256ff.) n. pressure, etc.

ğákk-an (§§3890ff.) v.t. tell to press, etc., let press, etc.

ğákkı-bŭ- (§3931β) v.i. stat. be in a pressed (etc.) state or condition.
wíččır‿kúlu‿dŭl‿tógor‿ğákkıbūn⁀ (-l‿t- <-ln‿t- §813) the stick is (being) pressed under the (a) large stone (sc. to straighten it).
áğıŋ‿kúlu‿dŭlğɛ‿ğákkıbūn⁀ (-ğ‿ğ- <-d‿ğ- §550) the hide is (being) pressed out (i.e. flattened) with the (a) large stone.

ğákkı-kattı- (N. -ıha-; §4093) v.p. be pressed, etc.

ğákud (ğáhud §1027) n. stew (of meat or vegetables or both), cookery.
obj. ğakúdk(ı), -útk(ı), -útt(ı) §2462; -ki⁀, -ti⁀.

ğakúdk‿ău v.i. cook (in general).
aı̂‿ğakúdk‿ɑ̆uri⁀ I cook.
part. pres. ğakúdk‿ắwıl (‿ắul) (one) that cooks, cook, cooking.
ğakútk‿uñurắwin⁀ (s)he knows (you know) how to cook.

ğál v.i. shout, talk in loud tones [RSN, §§129, 200].
ind. pres. aı̂‿ğálli⁀, ɛr‿ğálin⁀ (-li⁀, -lí⁀); perf. aı̂‿ğálkori⁀.

ğálɛ n. shouting, noisy talk [§2234γ].
obj. -lɛg.
pl. -lɛnč(ı).
mán‿ádɛmığ‿ğálɛm‿mugówwan⁀ (-ğ‿ğ- <-g‿ğ- §551, -m‿m- <-g‿m- §601) tell those people to stop shouting.

ğál-kátt(ı) (§§2534-5) adj. given to shouting, etc., clamorous.

ğáll-ɛg-ăg- (§§4071ff.) v.i. = ğálɛdól-.

ğál-ɛ-dól- (-lᵒd- §1178; §4022) and
ğáll-ɛ-dól- (-lᵒd-; §4027) v.i. be about to shout, etc.

ğálús n. cob, clay, mud layer (style of building of native houses and walls in Dóngola); with collective sg. (§4696d) [< جالوص id.].
obj. -úsk(ı), -ki⁀.
X. kăg‿ăggóñran⁀ they are building a house.
Y. túbkɛw‿wála‿ğalúskɛ́? (-w‿w- <-d‿w- §718) in (lit. with) brick or in mud layers?
X. síbɛgedun⁀ it's in mud.
Z. ğalúskedun⁀ it's in mud layers.

ğáma n. mosque [< جامع id.].
obj. -mag.
pl. -manč(ı).

ğamánč(ı) n. pl. company, group, set of persons [pl. of *ğáma (sg. not heard) < جمع crowd, gathering].
obj. -čıg.
án‿ğamánčı‿sɛ́? where are our people?
án‿ğamánčı‿hádırıré? are our fellows ready?
ínn-ugúg‿án‿ğamánčırtom‿bunógıl‿dámɛn? isn't there one of our people that will go tonight?

ğámbo n. side = ğémbo.

ğámmɛ v.i. come together (one to another), assemble, collect, gather [< جمع assembly (§1262) + -ɛ §3611].
ind. pres. ar‿ğámmɛru⁀; perf. ar‿ğámmɛgoru⁀ (N. -ɛko-, -ɛho-).
úrtu‿ğámmɛn⁀ the goats (sheep §4696d) gather together.

ğámmɛrar (-rɑ̆r; §§2200ff., 2210) and
ğámmɛríd (§§2256ff., 2263) n. coming together, assembly, etc.

ğámmɛr-an (§§3890ff., 3899) v.t. tell to come together, etc., let come together, etc.
úrtığ‿ğámmɛran⁀ (-ğ‿ğ- <-g‿ğ- §551) let the flock assemble.

ğámmɛ-bŭ- (§3931α) v.i. stat. be in an assembled (etc.) state or condition.
ind. pres. ar‿ğámmɛbūru⁀.

ğámmɛrɛd-ăg- (§§3877ff.) v.i. be in the situation of having come together (one to another), etc.

ğámmɛg-ır (N. -ɛkır, -ɛhır; §3679) (a) v.t. caus. cause or allow to come together, etc.; (b) v.t. bring together, assemble, collect, gather.
ind. pres. aı̂‿ğámmɛgıddi⁀.
úrtınčığ‿ğámmɛgır⁀ (-ğ‿ğ- <-g‿ğ- §551) gather the goats (sheep) together.

ğámmɛgırar (N. -ɛkır, -ɛhır; -rɑ̆r; §§2200ff., 2212) and
ğámmɛgıríd (N. -ɛkır-, -ɛhır-; §§2256ff., 2265) n. bringing together, assembly, etc.

ğámmɛ-nóg (§3747ε') v.i. go after assembling, go one with another, go together.
ind. pres. ar‿ğámmɛnógru⁀.

ğámmɛ-nog (§1964) v.i. go together (not each separately).
ind. pres. ar‿ğámmɛnogru⁀.

ğámmɛnogge! (§547) go together!

ğámmɛ-tá (§3747ε') v.i. come one with another, come together.
ind. pres. ar‿ğámmɛtăru⁀.

ğámmɛ-tā (§ 1964) v.i. *come together* (*not each separately*).
ind. pres. ar‿ğámmɛtaru⌢.

ğammɛ-tég (§ 3747ɛ') v.i. *squat* (*etc. s.v.* tég) *one with another, sit together*.

ğắn v.t. (*a*) *alter the ownership of by a commercial transaction, trade in, deal in,* and so (cp. senses of éwɪr *exchange*); (*b*, when object now owned by subject of past verb) *buy*; (*c*, when object now owned by subject of present or future verb) *sell*; (*d*, when object not now owned by subject of past verb) *sell*; (*e*, when object not now owned by subject of present or future verb) *buy*. See §5330 [cp. ON. δaп *id.* GNT, s.v.; RSN, §129, TEG, §614, 1].
ind. pres. aı‿ğắndi⌢, ɛr‿ğánın⌢ (-nī⌢, -ní⌢); perf. aı‿ğáŋkori⌢.
def. pres. aı‿ğánosri⌢; perf. aı‿ğanóskori⌢.
kálgı‿ğánıl‿ *bread-dealer*.
tɛr‿íččığ‿ğánın⌢ (-ğ‿ğ- < -g‿ğ- § 551) (*s)he deals in milk*.
tɛr‿íččığ‿ğánın, ğānármunun⌢ (*s)he sells milk, she doesn't buy it*.
X. ín‿hánun‿n‿ɛkkı‿tıkkó? (-n‿n‿ < -g‿n‿ § 625, ‿nɛ́-<‿nɪ́ɛ- § 1125) *who gave* (*has given*) *you that* (*this*) *donkey?*
Y. ğáŋkori⌢ *I* (*have*) *bought it*.
X. ɛ́n‿hánu‿sáŋkon? *what has become of your donkey?*
Y. ğáŋkori⌢ *I* (*have*) *sold it*.
X. ɛ́n‿hánub‿bı-mín-áwın? (§ 5384, -b‿b- < -g‿b- § 519, -n-ǎ- < -nɛ-ǎ § 1111) *what will you do with your donkey?*
Y. bığánosri⌢ *I shall sell it*.
X. hánu-wɛs‿sáir‿bélın? (-s‿s- < -g‿s- § 678) *where will you find a donkey?*
Y. wɛb‿bığándi⌢ (-b‿b- < -g‿b- § 519) *I shall buy one*.
X. (pointing to something of Y.'s) ɛr‿íŋgı‿mıŋkottégɛğ‿ğáŋkó? *what did you pay for that?*, lit. *at* (-ɛğ‿ < -ɛd‿ § 550) *how much did you buy that?*
Y. arrɛdíččɛ⌢ 25 (sc. *piastres*), lit. *at 25*.
X. ɛ́n‿sántəm‿muhottégɛğ‿ğáŋkó? (-m‿m- < -g‿m- § 601, -ğ‿ğ- < -d‿ğ- § 550) (*a*, when Y. owns it) *what did you pay for your valise?*, (*b*, when Y. does not own it) *for how much did you sell your valise?*
Y. rıjál‿díččɛt⌢ (*for*) *5 dollars*.
íŋgı‿ğínɛ‿wɛ́gɛğ‿ğáŋkori⌢ (-ğ‿ğ- < -d‿ğ- § 550) (*a*, if I own it) *I bought this for a pound*; (*b*, if I do not own it) *I sold that for a pound*.

ğánar‿ (-nár; §§ 2200 ff.) and
ğāníd⌢ (§§ 2256 ff.) n. *trading in, etc., purchase, sale*.

ğán-an (§§ 3890 ff.) v.t. *tell to trade in, etc., let trade in, etc*.

ğán-ár (§ 3747ɛ') v.t. *obtain by a commercial transaction, buy*.
ind. pres. aı‿ğānárri⌢.
máller‿rıjál‿lɛ́gɛğ‿ğānárkori⌢ (-r‿r- < -g‿r- § 669, -l‿l- < -l‿w- § 580, -ğ‿ğ- < -d‿ğ- § 550) *I* (*have*) *bought it all for one dollar*.

ğānárran, ğāntímmunan⌢ *they buy, they don't sell* (*it*).
gírıš‿šégɛğ‿ğānāróskori⌢ (-š‿š- < -š‿w- § 704) *I have* (*just* § 3804) *bought it for one piastre*.

ğán-bū- (§ 3931 β) v.i. stat. *be in a bought or sold state or condition*.

ğán-dáb-ır (§ 4132) v.t. *get rid of by a commercial transaction, dispose of by sale, sell off, sell*.
ind. pres. aı‿ğāndabíddi⌢ (-bírri⌢ § 3712), ɛr‿ğāndábırın⌢ (-rī⌢, -rí⌢).
ğāndabírkó⌢ (*s)he* (*has*) *sold* (*etc.*) *it*.
X. ɛ́n‿hánu‿sɛ́? *where's your donkey?*
Y. aı‿ğāndabírkori⌢ *I've sold it*.

ğán-dɛn (§§ 3996-7) v.t. *sell* (to the speaker).
ind. pres. ɛr‿ğāndénın⌢ (-nī⌢, -ní⌢).
íŋgı‿ğāndɛn⌢ *sell this to me*.

ğānd-ɛg-ág- (§§ 4071 ff.) v.t. = ğānɛdól-.

ğān-ɛ-dól- (-nᵒd- § 1178; § 4022) and
ğānd-ɛ-dól- (-dᵒd-; § 4027) v.t. *be about to buy, be about to sell*.

ğānd-ɛ-ğŭ-bū- (§ 4069) v.t. stat. *be on one's way* (*coming*) *to trade in, etc*.

ğānd-ɛ-má- (§ 4036) and
ğānd-ɛ-má- (§ 4041) v.t. *become unable to buy, become unable to sell*.

ğānd-ɛ-nóg (§§ 4048 ff.) v.t. *go to trade in, etc*.

ğāndɛnóg-bū- (-nóggu- § 546; § 4058) v.t. stat. *be on one's way* (*going*) *to trade in, etc*.

ğānd-ɛ-sùğır-ɛğğŭ- (§ 6295) v.t. *proceed with to the market* (*intending*) *to sell*.
imperat. ğāndɛsùğɛ́ğğu!

ğānd-ɛ-tá (§ 4060 ff.) v.t. *come to trade in, etc*.

ğānɛd-ág- (§§ 3877 ff.) v.t. *be in the situation of having traded in, etc*.
X. ín‿ɛ́ndımunun⌢ *this isn't yours*.
Y. ándín, aı‿ğānɛdágri⌢ *it's mine, I've bought it*.

ğānɛt-tá (§ 5723) v.t. *come after buying, go* (§ 5713) *and buy*.
imperat. ğānétta!
aı‿b-íčči-toddég‿gānɛttāriá? (§ 5384) *shall* (§ 5383) *I go and buy a little milk?* lit. *shall I come after buying a little milk?*

ğānɛttár-an (§§ 3890 ff., 3905) v.t. *tell or allow to come after buying, tell or allow to go and buy*.

ğān-ɛttá (-ɛ́ttā; § 5723) v.t. *bring after buying*.
imperat. ğānétta!
íčči‌d‿dólná? toddég‿gānɛttāriá? (-d‿d- < -g‿d- § 534, -ğ‿ğ- < -g‿ğ- § 551) *do you want* (*some*) *milk?, shall* (§ 5369 *b*) *I buy and bring a little?*
gírıš‿šégɛğ‿ğānettagori⌢ (-š‿š- < -š‿w- § 704, -ğ‿ğ- < -d‿ğ- § 550) *I* (*have*) *bought* (*it*) *for one piastre and brought it*.

ğānéttar-an (§§ 3890 ff., 3905) v.t. *tell or allow to bring after buying*.

ğáŋ-kattı (§ 4093) v.p. *be traded in, etc*.

ğān-sókkɛ (§ 3747ɛ') v.t. *take up* (*away*) *after buying*.

ğán-tır (§§ 3998-9) v.t. *sell* (to other than the speaker).
ind. pres. aı‿ğāntıddi⌢, ɛr‿ğāntırın⌢ (-rī⌢, -rí⌢).

tɛr‿íččığ‿ğāntırın⌢ (-ğ‿ğ- < -g‿ğ- § 551) (*s)he sells milk*.
ğāntıddan, ğānármunan⌢ *they sell, they don't buy* (*it*).
káñ‿kárrığ‿ğāntıkkori, hánu‿kárrığ‿ğānárkori⌢ (-ñ‿k- < -ğn‿k- § 632) *I* (*have*) *sold the mare and bought a she-ass*.

ğánı‿ n. *evil spirit, devil, fiend, demon* [<*ğánnı‿ (§§ 997-9) < جانّ *spirits* + euphonic -ı‿ (§ 486) § 2403].
obj. -nıg‿.
pl. -nınč(ı)‿.
mán‿ɛ́n‿ğánık‿kó⌢ *that woman has an evil spirit*.

ğánín-d(ı)‿ (§§ 2545 ff.) adj. *appertaining to an evil spirit, fiendish, devilish*.

ğánı-ko- (§ 4119) v.i. *have* (*be possessed by*) *an evil spirit, etc*.
mán‿ɛ́n‿ğánıkó⌢ *that woman has an evil spirit*.
— of a vexing inanimate object:
íŋ‿kóbıd‿ğánık‿kó⌢ and
íŋ‿kóbıd‿ğánıkó⌢ *the devil is in this door*.
ín‿tága‿ğánık‿kó⌢ and
ín‿tága‿ğánıkó⌢ *the devil is in this window*.

ğáŋg(ı) (*a*) v.i. *get full, fill* [cp. ON. δ̄ῡr-р *cause to be full* GNT, s.v. δıпʀ]; (*b*, more commonly) v.t. *make full, fill*; (*c*) v.t. *make full of, fill with*.
ind. pres. aı‿ğáŋg(ı)ri⌢, ɛr‿ğáŋgın⌢ (-gī⌢, -gí⌢).
ğɛrdíčığı‿ğáŋgıgori⌢ *I* (*have*) *filled the bucket*.
íŋ‿ɛ́ssıgɛb‿bığáŋgri⌢ (-b‿b- < -d‿b- § 518) and
íŋ‿ɛ́ssıb‿buğáŋg'ri⌢ (-b‿b- < -g‿b- § 519) *I shall fill this* (*that*) *with water*.
sǎ́ğ‿ğáŋgı⌢ (-ğ‿ğ- < -g‿ğ- § 551) *wind up the watch* (*clock*).

ğáŋgar‿ (-gár‿; §§ 2200 ff.) and
ğaŋgíd⌢ (§§ 2256 ff.) n. *filling*.

ğáŋg-an (§ 3890 ff.) v.t. *tell to fill, etc., let fill, etc*.

ğáŋgı-bū- (§§ 3934, 5682) v. stat. (*a*) i. *be in a filled state or condition, be full*; (*b*) t. *be in a filling* (t.) *state or condition, be numerous* (i.), *be plentiful* (in).
part. pres. ğáŋgıbūl‿ adj. *full*; obj. ğaŋgıbúlg(ı)‿, -gi⌢.
gırbád‿ɛ́ssı‿ğáŋgıbun⌢ (§ 4656) *the skin is full of water*.
gırbád‿ɛ́ssı‿ğáŋgıbūran⌢ (-d‿ɛ́s- < -dı‿és- § 1122) *the skins are full of water*.
gırbátt‿éssı‿ğáŋgıbūn⌢ (§ 4622) *the water fills the skin*.
káml‿éssıgɛğ‿ğáŋgıbūran⌢ (-ğ‿ğ- < -d‿ğ- § 550) *the camels are full up* (i.e. *fully laden*) *with water;* (*the camels are full of water, i.e. have had enough to drink* = káml‿éssıgɛb‿bérbūran⌢ -b‿b- < -d‿b- § 518).
mán‿ártın‿núgdı‿ğáŋgıbūrá, ténn‿ɛ́rrı‿sōgdánu⌢ *slaves are numerous in* (lit. *are in a state of filling*) *that island,* (*so*) *its name is Sōgdán* (q.v.). (*a*) -n‿n- < -g‿n- (§ 625); ‿ğáŋgıbūrá, t.; (*b*) ‿ártın‿ genitive; ‿ğáŋgıburá, i.

ǧaráđɛ — ǧéd

ǧaŋgɛd-ág- (§§ 3877ff.) v.t. *be in the situation of having made full, etc.*
gırbắtk͟ɛssıǧ͟ǧaŋgɛdágran⌒ (-ǧ͟ǧ <-g͟ǧ- §551) *they have filled the skin with water.*

ǧaŋgéd-dā- (§3990; -éggı-dā-, occ. -édgıdā- §§3993-4) v.i. and t. *be going along after getting full, making full, etc.*
hán͟ɛssıǧ͟ǧaŋgéddan⌒ *the donkey is carrying along a full load of water.*
káml͟ɛssıǧ͟ǧaŋgeddáran⌒ *the camels are going along fully laden with water.*

ǧaŋgɛt-tá (§§4169ff., 5723; ǧaŋgeggı-tá §4176) v.t. *come after filling, go* (§5713) *and fill.*
imperat. ǧaŋgétta!, ǧaŋgéggıta!
ǧɛrdélg͟ɛssıǧ͟ǧaŋgettágori⌒ (-ǧ͟ǧ- <-g͟ǧ- §551) *after filling the bucket with water I came (have come) = I went (have been) and filled the bucket with water.*

ǧaŋ-ɛttá (-éttā; §5723) v.t. *bring after filling, bring full.*
imperat. ǧaŋgétta!
ǧɛrdélg͟ɛssıǧ͟ǧaŋgéttagori⌒ *I (have) brought the bucket full of water.*

ǧáŋgı-kattı- (N. -ıha-; §4093) v.p. *be filled.*
gırbád͟ɛssıgeǧ͟ǧáŋgıkattın⌒ (-ǧ͟ǧ- <-d͟ǧ- §550) *the skin is filled with water.*

ǧaŋgı-sókkɛ (§3747ɛ') v.t. *take up after filling, carry full, take away full.*
ǧɛrdélgı͟ǧaŋgısókkegó⌒ *after filling the bucket (s)he took it away.*

ǧaŋgós-dɛ̌n (-óddɛn §538; §§4180-4, 3995ff.; -ósgıdɛn, -ózgı-, -óggı- §4185) v.t. *give (to the speaker) after filling, fill for (the speaker).*
šaı͟fıŋǧán-nɛ̌ǧ͟ǧaŋgóddɛn⌒ (-n-n- <-n-w- §627, -ǧ͟ǧ- <-g͟ǧ- §551) *fill me a cup of tea;* šaı͟fıŋǧán-nɛ̌ǧ- a noun-complex (§4755).

ǧaŋgós-tır (-óssır §686, -óttır §714; §§4180-4, 3995ff.; -ósgıtır, -ózgı-, -óggı- §4185) v.t. *give (to other than the speaker) after filling, fill for (other than the speaker).*
búŋgı͟fıŋǧán-nɛ̌ǧ͟ǧaŋgóttır⌒ (§5343) and
bún͟fıŋǧán-nɛ̌ǧ͟ǧaŋgóttır⌒ *fill him (her) a cup of coffee.*

ǧaráđɛ n. *Garada (on map), a village on the left bank of the Nile, at the southern end of Argo Island* [< جرادة *locust*].
obj. ǧaráđɛg, ǧarádɛg (§1538), -gi⌒.

ǧáras (ǧárǎs, ǧérɛs) n. *bell* [جرس *id.*].
obj. ǧarásk(ı), -ki⌒.
pl. ǧárası.

ǧaráttarɛ n. *smaller trough through which water raised by water-wheel* (kólɛ) *flows from the channel* (urówwa) *leading from the larger trough* (sáblo) *to the final channel* (dálu).
obj. -rɛg.
pl. -rɛnč(ı).

ǧárk(ı) (ǧaríkk(ı)) *go and throw, etc.* s.v. ǧú.

ǧáu n. *name of several sorts of date growing in Dóngola,* s.v. bént(ı); *with collective sg.* (§4696b).
obj. ǧáug.
pl. ǧáunč(ı).

ǧáu *go and do, etc.* s.v. ǧú.

ǧawáb n. *letter (written message)* [< جواب *reply, letter*].
obj. -ábk(ı), -ápk(ı), -ki⌒.
gen. -ábn v., -ám c.
pl. -ábı.
én͟ǧawám͟ráddı͟tánnan⌒ *it's the answer to your letter.*

ǧáww(ı) (ǧáuw(ı); -wᵘ §1202) v.i. *brawl, quarrel noisily, dispute noisily* [onom., cp. ON. δαʀ *proclaim, crow* GNT, s.v.].
ind. pres. aı͟ǧáwwıri⌒; perf. aı͟ǧáwwıgori⌒ (N. -iko-, -iho-).
tér͟aıgonon͟ǧáwwın⌒ (a) *(s)he disputes noisily with me;* (b) *(s)he scolds me.*
ɛrom͟bértın͟tírtın͟nálkın, tékkonon͟ǧáwwı (-n͟n- <-g͟n- §625) *if (when) you see the owner of the goat(s* §4696d), *give him a talking-to.*

ǧáwwɛ (ǧáuwɛ) n. *brawl, noisy quarrel, noisy dispute.*
obj. -wɛg.
pl. -wɛnč(ı).

ǧáwwı-kátt(ı) (ǧáuwı, -wᵘk-; N. -ihá-) adj. *given to brawling, etc.* [§§2534-5 b].
obj. -tıg.
pl. -tınč(ı).
mán͟ǧáuwᵘkáttıd͟dólmunū̌ (-d͟d- <-g͟d- §534) *I* (§5079) *don't like (want) that brawler.*

ǧáwwur (ǧáuwur) adj. *moist, damp.*
obj. ǧawwúrk(ı), -ki⌒.
pl. ǧáwwurı.
áǧın͟ǧáwwur͟én͟šártıg͟úndur⌒ *when the leather is damp put the iron in.*

ǧáwwur-an- (ǧáuwur-; §3910α) v.i. *become moist, etc.*

ǧáwwuram-bǔ- (ǧáuwur-; ˜˜ §1932a; §3949ff.) v.i. stat. *be in a state or condition of becoming moist, etc.*

ǧáwwuranɛd-ág- (ǧáuwur-; §3966α) v.i. *be in the condition of having become moist, etc.*

ǧáwwúrk-ır (ǧáuwúrk-; §3702) (a) v.t. caus. *cause or allow to be moist, etc.;* (b) v.t. *moisten, damp.*
aı͟tékkı͟ǧawwúrkıddi⌒ (a) *I let it get moist;* (b) *I moisten it.*

†**ǧáz** n. *petroleum, kerosene* [<جاز *id.*].
obj. ǧázk(ı), ǧásk(ı), -ki⌒.

ǧāzɛ́ v.t. (a) *requite;* (b) *punish* [< a stem of جازى *id.* +-ɛ́ §3650].
ind. pres. aı͟ǧāzɛ́ri⌒; perf. aı͟ǧāzɛ́gori⌒ (N. -ɛ́ko-, -ɛ́ho-).
imperat. ǧāzɛ́!
tén͟hɛ́rkı͟hɛ́rkɛǧ͟ǧāzɛ́goran⌒ (-ǧ͟ǧ- <-d͟ǧ- §550) *they (have) requited his (her) kindness with kindness.*
gádı͟tékkı͟ǧarámageǧ͟ǧāzɛ́gó⌒ *the judge (has) punished him (her) with a fine.*

ǧāzɛ́rar (-rár-; §§2200ff., 2207) and
ǧāzɛ́ríd (§§2256ff., 2260) n. *requiting, etc., requital, punishment.*

ǧāzɛ́r-ɛ-má- (§§4016-17, 4036, 4041) v.t. *become unable to requite, etc.*

ǧāzɛ́rɛd-ág- (§§3877ff.) v.t. *be in the situation of having requited, etc.*

ǧāzɛ́-kattı- (N. -ɛ́ha-; §4093) v.p. *be requited, etc.*

mágas͟ǧāzɛ́kattıgon⌒ *the thief was (has been) punished.*
ǧınáʒe͟ǧāzɛ́kattıgon⌒ *the crime was (has been) punished.*

ǧāzɛ́kattar (N. -ɛ́ha-; -tár; §§2200ff., 2213) and
ǧāzɛ́kattíd (§§2256ff., 2266) n. *being requited, etc., requital, punishment.*

ǧázma (ǧáz-, ǧéz-, -má) n. *boot, shoe;* with collective sg. (§4696d) [< جزمة *id.*].
obj. -mag.
pl. ǧazmanč(ı), -mán-, -mɛn-.
†kán-ǧazma *European slippers.*

†**ǧág** (ǧég; serv.) n. *jug* [<*jug*].
obj. ǧágk(ı), ǧákk(ı), ǧégk(ı), ǧékk(ı), -ki⌒.
gen. ǧágn v., ǧégn v., ǧáŋ c., ǧéŋ c.
pl. ǧágı, ǧégı.
ǧágn͟í *handle of jug.*

ǧáham = ǧáham *cheek.*

*****ǧákk(ı)** (ǧék-; serv.) n. *jug* [<*jug*].
obj. -kıg.
pl. -kınč(ı).
ǧákkın͟í *handle of jug.*

ǧáras = ǧáras *bell.*

ǧázma = ǧázma *boot, shoe.*

ǧéb n. *pocket;* with collective sg. (§4696d) [<جيب *id.*].
obj. ǧébk(ı), ǧépk(ı), -ki⌒.
gen. ǧébn v., ǧém c.
pl. ǧébı.

ǧébɛl n. (a) *mountain, hill;* with collective sg. (§4696d); (b) *desert* (= hála) [< جبل *id.* (a), and in Sudan Ar. also (b)].
obj. ǧebɛ́lg(ı), -gi⌒.
pl. ǧébɛlı and ǧıbál [< جبال *id.* §2444].
ǧɛbéllo (s.v. -r; §6007) adv. *on (in, to) the mountain(s, desert).*
ǧɛbéllo⌒ *(s)he (it) is (they are) on (in) the mountain(s, desert).*

ǧébɛl-an- (§3910β) v.i. *go to the mountain(s, desert).*

ǧébɛlam-bód (§4150) v.i. *run off to the mountain(s, desert).*

ǧébɛlam-bǔ- (§3949) v.i. *be on one's way to the mountain(s, desert).*

ǧébɛna n. *coffee-pot of earthenware* [< جبنة *id.*].
obj. -nag.
pl. ǧɛbɛnánč(ı).

ǧɛbɛnán-d(ı) (§§2545ff.) adj. *appertaining to an earthenware coffee-pot.*
bún͟ǧɛbɛnándıd͟dólli⌒ (-d͟d- <-g͟d- §534) *I want (like) coffee made in an earthenware pot.*

ǧéd (a) v.i. *take oath, swear;* (b) v.t. *affirm on oath, swear.* See §§5540, 5922, 6123, 6125.
ind. pres. aı͟ǧédri⌒; perf. aı͟ǧédkori⌒ (ǧétk-).
imperat. ǧét!
subj. past aı͟ǧédsı (ǧétsı, ǧéssı §688, -su).
ıŋkɛ͟ǧétkō⌒ *(s)he (you) swore (has, have sworn) thus (to this effect).*
ǧú͟fɛgırro͟ǧét *go (and* §6239) *swear on (sc. the tomb of) the holy man;* also as complex: ǧufɛgırroǧét⌒ *id.* (§5605).

kıtăpkı‿ğédran⌒ *they swear on the Book*, sc. *the Coran.*
tɛr‿âı‿uñúmmunun‿έğ‿ğédın⌒ *(s)he (X.) swears that (s)he (X.) does not know,* lit. *(s)he swears saying* (‿έğ‿ < ‿έg‿ §§ 551, 5922) '*I do not know*'.
âı‿nalménsığ‿ğédrı⌒ and âı‿ğédrı‿âı‿nalménsıgı⌒ *I swear that I did not see.*
álı‿âı‿nalménsığ‿ğédın⌒ and álı‿ğédın‿âı‿nalménsıgı⌒ *ɛáli swears that he (ɛáli) did not see.*
álı‿tɛr‿nalménsıŋgı‿ğédın⌒ and álı‿ğédın‿tɛr‿nalménsıŋgı⌒ *ɛáli swears that he (another, she, it) did not see.*
tɛr‿âı‿sokkeménsığ‿ğédın⌒ and tɛr‿ğédın‿âı‿sokkeménsıgı⌒ *(s)he (X.) swears that (s)he (X.) did not take it,* lit. *(s)he swears 'I did not take'.*
tɛr‿sokkeménsıŋgı‿ğédın⌒ and tɛr‿ğédın‿tɛr‿sokkeménsıŋgı⌒ *(s)he (X.) swears that (s)he (Y.) did not take it.*

ğédar‿ (-dảr‿, -dɛr‿; §§ 2200ff.) and
ğedíd‿ (§§ 2256ff.) n. *swearing, affirmation on oath, oath.*

ğédtı‿ (ğéttı‿ § 706) n. *swearing, oath* [§ 2325 α].
   obj. -tıg‿.
   pl. -tınč(ı)‿.

ğéd-an (§§ 3890ff.) v.t. *tell to swear, etc., let swear, etc.*
   fɛgírro‿ğétkırkoran⌒ *let him (her) swear on* (sc. *the tomb of*) *the holy man.*

ğed-bŭ- (§ 3927ff., 3938) v.i. stat. *be in a sworn state or condition.*
   έn‿ğédbūn, tékkı‿ğétkırkoran⌒ *the woman is sworn, they have sworn her.*

ğedr-ɛ-nóg (§§ 4048ff.) v.i. and t. *go to swear, etc.*

ğedr-ɛ-nóg-bŭ- (-nóggŭ- § 546; 4058) v.i. and v. stat. *be on one's way (going) to swear, etc.*
   fɛgírro‿ğedrenógbūran⌒ *they are on their way to swear on* (sc. *the tomb of*) *the holy man.*

ğedɛd-ág- (§§ 3877ff.) v.i. and t. *be in the situation of having sworn, etc.*

ğedk-ır (ğétkır; § 3683) (*a*) v.t. caus. *cause or allow to swear, etc.*; (*b*) v.t. *administer oath to swear.*

ğedíd adj. *new, fresh* (= ɛr‿) [< جديد id.].
   obj. ğedídk(ı)‿, -ítk(ı)‿, -ítt(ı)‿ § 2462; -kı⌒, -tı⌒.
   pl. ğedídı‿.
   ısảı-tɛ‿ğedít? (§ 469) *which is the newer (newest)?*

ğedíd-an- (§ 3910α) v.i. *become new, grow afresh.*
   έssıg‿élkın‿ğedídanın⌒ *if it gets water it grows (will grow § 5369α) afresh.*

ğéham‿ = **ğáham‿** *cheek.*

ğehénnɛb‿ n. *hell* [< جهنّم id. § 1288].
   obj. ğehennébk(ı)‿, -épk(ı)‿, -kı⌒.
   gen. -hénnɛbn‿v., -hénnɛm‿c.
   tír‿ğehénnébır⌒ *they are in hell.*
   έn‿ğehénnɛbır‿nók! *go to hell!,* lit. *go to your hell!*

ğehɛnném-d(ı)‿ (§§ 2545ff.) adj. *appertaining to hell, hellish, infernal.*

ğehɛnnéb-kırı‿ (-épk-; -kírı‿; §§ 2539-40) adj. *resembling hell.*
   tím‿bélɛd‿ğehennébkırın⌒ *their country is like hell.*

†**ğékk(ı)‿** = **ğákk(ı)‿** *jug.*

ğékk(ı) (§ 1111) *go and relieve nature,* s.v. ğŭ.

ğél (§ 1111) *go and find,* s.v. ğŭ.

ğéllı‿ n. (*a*) *affair, matter;* with collective sg. (§ 4696d); (*b*) *occupation, business, work, task, job* [stereotyped form of ğ-éllı‿ (the fact that) *I go and find,* s.v. ğŭ, § 2385; cpd. with ON. δαλλ λατρεία GNT, s.v., δaλλι ZNG, s.v.].
   obj. -lıg‿.
   pl. -lınč(ı)‿.
   ğéllı‿ténnǎr‿dān⌒ (§ 1786) *(s)he (it) is occupied (engaged, busy).*
   ɛr‿mınín‿ğéllıg‿ảgảwın? *what work* (lit. *the work of what*) *are you doing?*
   ğéllık‿kŏ v.i. *have work, be employed.*
   ğéllık‿kóran⌒ *they have work.*
   ğéllık‿kómunan⌒ *they have not got work.*
   ɛr‿ğéllık‿kóná? *have you got work?* (... *a job?*).
   part. pres. ğéllık‿kól‿ *worker, labourer;* obj. ğéllık‿kólg(ı)‿, -gı⌒; pl. ğéllık‿kólı‿.

ğéllı-kŏ- (§ 4118) v.i. *be occupied, engaged, busy.*
   ind. pres. âı‿ğéllıkórı⌒; perf. âı‿ğéllı‿kŏgorı⌒ (N. -ıkŏ-, -ıhŏ-).
   ɛr‿ğéllıkóná? *are you engaged (... busy)?*
   part. pres. ğéllıkól‿ (*one*) *that is occupied, etc.*; obj. ğéllıkólg(ı)‿, -gı⌒.

ğéllıg-ág-aŭ (§ 5632) v.i. (*a*) *be engaged in working, in labouring, be at work;* (*b*) *habitually work, labour habitually* = ảğğéllıgaŭ-.
   tέr‿dúngık‿kómeŋŋon‿ğéllıgágaŭmunun⌒ (§ 5743) *though he has no money he is not working.*

ğéllıg-áŭ (-âw; § 1879; § 3747α′, b, 2; § 5578) v.i. *work, labour.*
   ind. pres. âı‿ğéllıgaŭrı⌒ (‾‾′), ɛr‿ğéllıgawın⌒ (‾‾′, -wí‿, -wí⌒).
   imperat. ğéllıgaŭ!

ğéllıg-aŭ-kátt(ı)‿ (N. -aŭhá-) adj. *hard-working, industrious, diligent* [§§ 2534-5 c].
   obj. -tıg‿.
   pl. -tınč(ı)‿.
   ín‿ógıg‿ğéllıgaŭkáttın⌒ *this man is industrious.*

ğɛm‿ c. gen. of **ğέb‿** *pocket.*

ğɛmb(ı)‿ (ğám-) n. *side;* with collective sg. (§ 4696a) [< جنب id.].
   obj. -bıg‿.
   pl. -bınč(ı)‿.
   tέr‿kản‿ğɛmbır⌒ *it is at (on) the side of the house.*
   kúm‿ğɛmb(ı)‿ (-m‿ğ- < -bn‿ğ- § 586) *boat's side.*
   kumáttɛn‿ğɛmb(ı)‿ *labium* (*labia* § 4696a) *pudendi muliebris.*

ğέn‿ (§ 956d) n. *year;* with collective sg. (§ 4696d) [cp. ON. δεμ, ᴦεм id. GNT, s.v.; TEG, § 614, 1].
   obj. ğέŋ(ı)‿, -gı⌒.
   gen. ğέnn‿v., ğɛn‿c.
   pl. ğέnı‿.
   tɛr‿ğέn‿dıgríg‿índ‿egó⌒ (§ 4666) *(s)he (it) was (has been) here many years.*
   ğέn‿έr‿ *the new year.*
   ğέn‿έrro‿ *in the new year.*
   ín‿ğέn‿ and íŋgέn‿ (§ 4867) n. *this year.*
   obj. ín‿ğέŋ(ı)‿, ıŋğέŋ(ı)‿, -gı⌒.
   ín‿ğɛn‿ódun‿ and íŋgɛn‿ódun⌒ *this year is cold.*
   ıŋğέŋ(ı)‿ (-gı⌒) adv. *this year.*
   ıŋğέŋ‿ódun⌒ *this year it's cold.*
   ıŋğέn-d(ı)‿ (§§ 2545ff.) adj. *appertaining to this year, of this year, this year's.*
   béntı‿nínd‿ıd‿dólmunun, ıŋğέnd‿ıd‿dóllı⌒ (-d‿d- < -g‿d- § 534) *I don't want last year's dates, I want this year's.*
   ğέn‿nógɛl (§ 4794) noun-complex *last year;* obj. ğέn‿nogέlg(ı)‿, -gı⌒.
   ğέn‿nogέllo‿, -gı⌒ (§ 4735) and ğέn‿nogέllo‿ (s.v. -r‿; § 4739) adverb-complex (*during*) *last year.*
   ğέn‿nogέn-d(ı)‿, -dı⌒ (§§ 807, 5014) complex adj. *appertaining to last year, of last year, last year's.*
   ğέn‿tǎl‿ (§ 4794) noun-complex *next year;* obj. ğέn‿tǎlg(ı)‿, -gı⌒.
   ğέn‿tǎlg(ı)‿, -gı⌒ (§ 4735) and ğέn‿tǎllo‿ (s.v. -r‿; § 4739) adverb-complex (*during*) *next year.*
   ğέn‿tǎln-d(ı)‿, -dı⌒ (‿tǎnd(ı)‿ § 807; § 5014) complex adj. *appertaining to next year, of next year, next year's.*

ğeŋɛnísse‿ n. *lizard;* with collective sg. (§ 4696c) [< ğen-ğen- imit. of repeated rapid movement (§ 2151) + -ísse‿ dim. § 2291].
   obj. -sɛg‿.
   pl. -sɛnč(ı)‿.

ğenzír‿ n. *chain* [< زَنْجِير = جَنْزِير id.].
   obj. -írk(ı)‿, -kı⌒.
   pl. -írı‿.

ğér‿ n. *back* [cp. Amh. ጀርባ id.; RSN, § 129].
   obj. ğérk(ı)‿, -kı⌒.
   pl. ğérı‿.
   — often atonic (§§ 1671-3):
   án‿ğɛr‿âıg‿óddın⌒ *my back hurts me.*
   ín‿ğɛr‿ *back of hand*(s § 4696a).

ğér-ro‿ (s.v. -r‿; § 6007) adv. *on (in, at, to, into) the back, behind.*
   ğérro‿ (ğérró⌒ § 1989) *(s)he (it) is (they are) on (in, at) the back.*
   ‿ğérro‿ (§§ 5860, 5901) postp. (= prep. § 4287) *at the back of, behind;* follows the genitive (§ 4366).
   kản‿ğérro‿dảmunun⌒ *behind the house there is none.*
   tɛr‿kóbın‿ğérró⌒ (-n‿ğ- < -dn‿ğ- § 612) *(s)he (it) is behind the door.*
   ğɛbéln‿ğérró⌒ *(s)he (it) is (they are) behind the mountain.*

ğérk-ɛd‿ (-ɛt⌒, -έ⌒ § 966; § 6007) adv. = ğérro‿.

ğérkɛd‿ (-ɛt⌒, -έ⌒; § 5860) postp. (= prep. § 4287) = ‿ğérro‿; follows the genitive.
   ğówwı‿kản‿ğérké⌒ *the tree is (trees are* § 4696b) *behind the house.*
   kản‿ğérkɛt‿tέbın⌒ *(s)he (it) stands behind the house.*

ğérdɛl — ğillɛ

ógığ⌣kǎn⌣ğérkɛ́⌢ the man is behind the house.
ógığ⌣kǎn⌣ğérkɛb⌣bún⌢ (-b⌣b- < -d⌣b- §518) the man is (lying) behind the house.

ğérdɛl⌣ n. bucket, pail [< جَرْدَل id.].
  obj. ğɛrdɛ́lg(ı)⌣, -gi⌢.
  pl. ğɛrdɛlı⌣.
  ğérdɛln⌣í⌣ handle of bucket.
  ğérdéllo⌣bókkori⌢ I (have) poured it into the bucket.

ğérɛs⌣ = ğáras⌣ bell.

ğɛrğɛ́ (ğɛrɛğ(ğ)ɛ́, ğɛrığ(ğ)ɛ́) go and wait, etc. s.v. ğŭ.

ğɛríd n. forearm (= dúra⌣); with collective sg. (§4696a) [Sudan Ar. خَرِيدَة id.].
  obj. -ídk(ı)⌣, -ítk(ı)⌣, -ítt(ı)⌣ §2462; -ki⌢, -ti⌢.
  gen. -ídn⌣v., -ín⌣c.
  pl. -ídı⌣.

ğɛríf (-ruf⌣) n. land along water's edge, esp. that left bare by falling river, foreshore [< جَرْف id. §1361].
  obj. ğɛrífk(ı)⌣, -ki⌢.
  pl. ğɛr(ı)fı⌣.

ğɛrrıbɛ́ (-rubɛ́) v.t. try, attempt, test [< imperf. or imperat. stem of جَرَّب id. + -ɛ́ §3636].
  ind. pres. aî⌣ğɛrrıbɛ́ri⌢; perf. aî⌣ğɛrrıbɛ́gori⌢ (N. -éko-, -ého-).
  imperat. ğɛrrıbɛ́!
  aî⌣ğɛrrubɛ́gori, aî⌣ɛ́skimunun⌢ I (have) tried (and) I can't (do it).
  kobídkı⌣bığɛrrıbɛ́rı⌣tɛ́r⌣óŋ⌣kuskattın⌢ I shall try the door, whether it can (§5704) be opened.
  ɛr⌣ğɛrrıbɛ́gın⌣élın⌢ if you try you (will) find him (her, it, them).

ğɛrrıbɛ́rar⌣ (-rub-, -rár⌣; §§2200ff., 2207) and
ğɛrrıbɛ́ríd⌣ (-rub-; §§2256ff., 2260) n. trying, etc.

ğɛrrıbɛ́r-an (-rub-; §§3890ff., 3899) v.t. tell to try, etc., let try, etc.

ğɛrrıbɛ́-kattı- (-rub-; N. -ɛ́ha-; §4093) v.p. be tried, etc.

ğɛrrıbɛ́-nál (-rub-; §3747ɛ́) v.t. see (etc.) s.v. nál) by trying, etc.
  imperat. ğɛrrıbɛnál! and ğɛrrıbɛ́nal! (§1871).

ğɛrrıbɛ́-nal (-rub-; §1964) v.t. see (etc.) by trying, etc., try so as to see, etc., try in order to see, etc. (§3783).
  gurɑ́b⌣ırıb⌣bukálkattıgın⌣ğɛrrubɛ́nalın⌢ (-b⌣b- < -g⌣b- §519) the crow tries the rope to see whether it can (§5705, lit. will) be eaten.

ğɛrt(ı)⌣ n. ornament (bracelet, necklace) worn by either sex at circumcision and marriage (CAN, pp. 185ff.); with collective sg. (§4696d) [§§2323ff.]
  obj. -tıg⌣ [> جِرْتك HSA, s.v. bridegroom].
  pl. -tınč(ı)⌣

ğɛruf (-rıf⌣) n. land along water's edge, esp. that left bare by falling river, foreshore [< جَرْف id. §1361].
  obj. ğɛrúfk(ı)⌣, -ki⌢.
  pl. ğɛrufı⌣.

ɛrıd⌣ğɛrúfkı⌣kálın⌢ the hippopotamus eats (what is growing on) the foreshore.

ğét! imperat. of ğɛd swear.
ğɛ́tta go and fetch s.v. ğŭ.
ğɛ́zma⌣ = ğázma⌣ boot, shoe.
ğɛzzár n. butcher [< جَزَّار id.].
  obj. -árk(ı)⌣, -ki⌢.
  pl. -árı⌣.

ğír⌣ n. lime, calcium oxide [< جِير id.].
  obj. ğírk(ı)⌣, -ki⌢.

ğír (i.e. ğ-ír < ğᵘ-ír §1114) go and count, etc. s.v. ğŭ.

ğıbál pl. of ğébɛl⌣ mountain.

ğıbéd (§3598) v.i. defective proceed, come, go [app. < *ğu-b-éd (§1195) < ğu-bu-éd (§1114), a def. imperat. of ğŭ-bŭ-, s.v. ğŭ].
— only heard in:
  aîgonon⌣ğıbét! (⌣ğıbé! §965) come (go) with me.
  aîgonon⌣ğıbéd⌣ɛn⌣ you say (he, she says) 'come (go) with me'.
  aîgonon⌣ğıbédwɛ! (-béwwɛ! §718, §2915) come (pl., go pl.) with me.

ğıbél (§1195) < ğubél go (come) along out s.v. ğŭ.
  aîgonon⌣ğıbél! come along out with me = aîgonon⌣ğubél!

ğíbıd n. platform of water-wheel (kólɛ⌣) bearing track (moís⌣) round which cattle walk (SNK, 377A9) [< *ğı-b-íd⌣ (§1154) < *ğu-b-íd⌣ (§1196) < *ğŭ-bŭ-íd⌣ (§1111), so *making (sc. the cattle) be coming (ğŭ-bŭ- s.v. ğŭ) §2268].
  obj. ğıbıdk(ı)⌣, -ítk(ı)⌣, ğıbıtt(ı)⌣ §2462 [> Sudan Ar. جبت id.], -ki⌢, -ti⌢.
  gen. ğıbıdn⌣v., -bınn⌣v.c., -bın⌣c.
  pl. ğıbıdı⌣.
  ğıbıd⌣félɛgırton, tén⌣kóččır⌣ɛ́skedun⌢ the platform is (made) of beams, (and) on top of it is earth.
  moís⌣ğıbın⌣kóččır⌢ the cattle-track is on the platform.

ğíbın (§956a) n. cheese (= ğíbna⌣) [< جِبْن id. §1359].
  obj. ğıbíng(ı)⌣, -gi⌢.

ğíbna (-na⌣) n. cheese [< جِبْنَة id.].
  obj. -nag⌣, -nág⌣.
  pl. -nanč(ı)⌣, -nánč(ı)⌣, -nɛnč(ı)⌣.

ğídda⌣ (ğítta⌣) n. body [< Sudan Ar. جَّة id., corpse = جَّة §1228].
  obj. -dag⌣.
  pl. -danč(ı)⌣.

ğıgıd n. head-piece or foot-piece of frame of bedstead (ángarɛ⌣); with collective sg. (§4696d) [RSN, §129].
  obj. ğıgıdk(ı)⌣, -ítk(ı)⌣, -ítt(ı)⌣ §2462; -ki⌢, -ti⌢.
  gen. ğıgıdn⌣v., -ín⌣c.
  pl. ğíg(ı)dı⌣.

ğıgıd v.t. (a) rub; (b) polish; (c) wipe.
  ind. pres. aî⌣ğıgídri⌢ (⌣ğıgídri §1760), ɛr⌣ğıgıdın⌢ (-dí⌢, -dí⌢); perf. aî⌣ğıgídkori⌢ (-ítk-).
  imperat. ğígıt!, pl. ğıgídwɛ! (-gídwɛ́!, -gídde! §533, -dɛ́!).
  ím⌣bérkı⌣kınnɛ́ğ⌣ğıgıt⌢ (-ğ⌣ğ- < -g⌣ğ- §551) polish this wood a little.
  tém⌣míssır⌣ğıgídın⌢ (a) (s)he rubs his (her) eye(s §4696a), lit. (s)he rubs in his (her) eye; (b) (s)he wipes his (her) eye(s).

ğıgıdar⌣ (-dár⌣; §§2200ff.) and
ğıgıdíd⌣ (§§2256ff.) n. rubbing, etc.

ğıgıd-an (§§3890ff.) v.t. tell to rub, etc., let rub, etc.

ğıgıd-bŭ- (ğıgídbŭ-; §3931β) v.i. stat. be in a rubbed (etc.) state or condition.

ğıgıdr-ɛg-ág- (§§4071ff.) v.t. = ğıgıdɛdól-.

ğıgıd-ɛ-dól- (-dᵒd- §1178; §4022) and
ğıgıd-ɛ-dól- (-rᵒd-; §4027) v.t. be about to rub, etc.
  íŋguk⌣kınnɛ́ğ⌣ğıgıdɛdólli⌢ (-k⌣k- < -g⌣k- §569, -ğ⌣ğ- < -g⌣ğ- §551) I am just going to polish these a little.
  íŋguk⌣kınnɛ́ğ⌣ğıgıdɛdolíddi⌢ (§5615) and
  íŋguk⌣kınnɛ́ğ⌣ğıgıddɛdólli⌢ (§5616) I am just going to polish (each of §5456) these a little.

ğıgıdɛd-ág- (§§3877ff.) v.t. be in the situation of having rubbed, etc.

ğıgıd-kattı- (-ıtk-; §4093) v.p. be rubbed, etc.

ğıgılt(ı)⌣ (ğıgílt(ı)⌣ §1522) n. kidney; with collective sg. (§4696a) [2324, TOB, §143, 115, TEG, §614, 1].
  obj. ğıgíltıg⌣.
  pl. ğıgıltınč(ı)⌣.
  án⌣ğígılt⌣aîg⌣óddın⌢ I have a pain in the kidneys.

ğıgır n. (a) mouse, (b) rat; with collective sg. (§4696c) [< ğıg- (ğík⌣ §469) onom. + -ır⌣ *(action of) making, then concrete squeaker §2386β; > Sudan Ar. جُقَّر id. (a)].
  obj. ğıgırk(ı)⌣, -ki⌢.
  pl. ğíg(¹)rı⌣.

ğıgırnárt(ı)⌣, -ti⌢ Gigernarti (on map), an island between about 26 miles above Ed-Débbaʰ [Mouse Island].
  obj. -tıg⌣.

ğıgír-kıri⌣ (-kíri⌣; §§2539-40) adj. resembling the mouse or rat, mouselike, ratlike

ğíllɛ v.t. (a) think; (b) think of, think about; (c) remember [cp. ON. δıλ id. GNT, s.v. §§2870ff.].
  ind. pres. aî⌣ğılleri⌢, ɛr⌣ğíllɛn⌢ (-lɛ̃⌢, -lé⌢); perf. aî⌣ğıllɛgori⌢ (N. -ɛko-, -ɛho-).
  subj. past aî⌣ğılléssı⌣ (-su⌣).
  def. perf. aî⌣ğılóskori⌢
  ɛr⌣míŋgı⌣ğíllɛn? (a) what are you thinking about?; (b) what do you remember?
  ar⌣nálmɛŋkıru⌣ğíllemunun⌢ unless we see him (her, it, them) we don't think of (can't remember §5377) him (her, it, them), lit. if we don't see him....

ğíllɛrar⌣ (-rár⌣; §§2200ff., 2210) and
ğíllɛríd⌣ (§§2256ff., 2263) n. thinking, etc.

ğíllɛr-an- (§§3890ff., 3899) v.t. tell to think, etc., let think, etc.

ğíllɛ-bŭ- (§3931β) v.i. stat. be in a thought-of (etc.) state or condition.

dɛnˬáddoˬtɛ́bılˬǧíllɛbūn͡ the debt against me (us) is remembered (constantly borne in mind).
ǧíllɛd-åg (§§ 3877 ff.) v.t. be in the condition of having thought, etc.
ǧíllɛg-ır (N. -ɛkır, -ɛhır, § 3679) (a) v.t. caus. cause or allow to think, etc.; (b) v.t. remind.
  ind. pres. aiˬǧíllɛgıddi͡, ɛrˬǧíllɛgırın͡ (-rī͡, -rí͡).
  aigˬasálgıˬǧíllɛgırˬaiˬtɛ́kkiˬwɛ́tıddi͡ remind me tomorrow to tell him (her), lit. remind me tomorrow (and § 6239) I (shall § 5369 a) tell him (her).
  aigıˬǧíllɛgırˬaiˬtírgıˬdúŋgıtˬtıríddi͡ (-tˬt- < -gˬt- § 707) remind me to give them the money.
  aiˬtírgıˬdúŋgıtˬtıríddıgˬaigıˬǧíllɛgır͡ and (§ 6126)
  aigıˬǧíllɛgırˬaiˬtírgıˬdúŋgıtˬtıríddıgi͡ remind me that I gave (lit. give) them the money.
ǧíllɛgır-an (N. -ɛkır-, -ɛhır-; §§ 3890 ff., 3904) v.t. tell to remind, let remind.
  mohammɛ́ttˬaigıˬǧíllɛgıran͡ tell Muḥammat to remind me.
ǧíllɛ-kattı- (§ 4093) v.p. be thought of, etc.
ǧima n. Friday (= móšono) [< آلْجُمْعَة id. § 1390].
  obj. -mag.
  pl. ǧımánč(ı).
  ǧimaˬjóm (§ 4750),
  ǧimanˬjóm (§ 4810),
  ǧimaˬnahǻr (ˬnåh-, ˬnɛh-; § 4750) and
  ǧimanˬnahår (§ 4810) Friday.
  ǧimag, -gi (§ 4665),
  ǧimar,
  ǧimaˬjómg(ı), -gi,
  ǧimaˬjómır,
  ǧimaˬnahårk(ı), -ki and
  ǧimaˬnahårro on Friday.
  ǧimartōn,
  ǧimaˬjómırtōn and
  ǧimaˬnahårrotōn since Friday.
  ǧimamˬmóŋkon and
  ǧimamˬbókkon till Friday.
  ásalˬǧiman (ˬǧimå, ˬǧimá § 939) tomorrow is Friday.
  ǧimán-d(ı) (§§ 2545 ff.) adj. appertaining to Friday, Friday's.
ǧımbɛ́z n. sycamore fig-tree, Ficus sycomorus, Linn. (BSP, 533); with collective sg. (§ 4696 b) [< جُمَّيْز id.].
  obj. -ɛ́zk(ı), -ɛ́sk(ı), -ki.
  pl. -ɛ́zı.
ǧınáje (-jå, -ja) n. crime, offence [< جناية id.].
  obj. -jɛg.
  pl. -jɛnč(ı).
ǧınd(ı) go and lift, etc. s.v. ǧú.
ǧınɛ n. pound (of 100 piastres) [< جُنَيْه id.].
  < guinea.
  obj. ǧınɛg.
  pl. ǧınɛnč(ı).
ǧınɛ́na (-nå) n. garden [< جَنَّة id.].
  obj. -nag.
  pl. -nanč(ı).

ǧınıs (ǧíns(ı) q.v.; § 483β) n. species, sort, kind, class, tribe, race [< جنس id. § 1368].
  obj. ǧınísk(ı), -ki.
  pl. ǧín(ı)sı.
  X. esmánˬɛnˬǧınısré? is ʕoθmán (of) your tribe?, lit. is ʕoθmán the tribe of you?
  Y. éjjoˬánˬǧınısū? yes, he is (of) my tribe.
  ímˬmínınˬǧınısre? (ˬǧınısré?) (a) of what kind is this?, lit. is this the kind of what? (s.v. -ré?); (b) of what tribe is this person?
ǧíns(ı) (ǧınıs q.v.; § 483α) n. species, sort, kind, class, tribe, race [< جنس id. § 1368].
  obj. ǧínsıg.
  pl. ǧínsınč(ı).
  terˬmínınˬǧínsıré? (a) of what sort is it?; (b) of what tribe is (s)he?
  ínˬógıgˬmínınˬǧínsıré? of what tribe is this man?
  ténˬǧínsıˬmín¹rɛ? and ténˬǧínsıˬminéllɛ? (a) what kind is it?; (b) what is his (her) tribe?
  mínınˬǧínsıˬdån? what sort is there (present)?, lit. of what is the sort present?
  ɛrˬmínınˬǧínsısˬsíkkın? (-sˬs- < -gˬs- § 678) what (the) kind do you mean?, lit. of what (the) kind do you ask?
  ínınˬǧínsırtōn and (§ 5119)
  ínınˬǧínsırtōnˬdóllan and
  ínınˬǧínsırtōnˬdóllan they want (one, some) of this kind.
ǧíŋır go and wait, etc. s.v. ǧú.
ǧírɛ n. Girra (on map), a village on the left bank of the Nile, about six miles above Ed-Débbåh.
  obj. ǧírɛg.
ǧırɛnárt(ı) (-ti) Island of Ǧírɛ, Girra Id. (on map).
ǧırɛ́ v.i. happen [< a مصدر or stem of جَرَى id. + -ɛ § 3628].
  ind. pres. sg. 3 ǧırɛ́n (-rɛ́, -rɛ́); fut. sg. 3 bıǧırɛ́n (buǧ-, -rɛ́, -rɛ́, -rɛ́); perf. sg. 3 ǧırɛ́gon (-gō, -gó, N. -ɛ́kon, -kō, -kó, -ɛ́hon, -hō, -hó).
  míndoˬtɛ́ddoˬǧırɛ́gó? what (has) happened to him (her, it)?
ǧırɛ́f n. Gireif (on map), a village on the left bank of the Nile, about 11 miles below Ed-Débbåh [< جُرَيْف dim. of جرف river's edge].
  obj. -ɛ́fk(ı), -ki.
ǧırıŋ go and wait, etc. s.v. ǧú.
ǧısıkk(ı) go and ask, etc. s.v. ǧú.
ǧísım n. body [< جسم id. § 1359].
  obj. ǧısímg(ı), -gi.
  pl. ǧís(¹)mı.
ǧíšın go and send s.v. ǧú.
gitta n. body = ǧídda, q.v.

ǧíza n. (a) requital; (b) retribution, punishment, penalty [< جَزَاء id.].
  obj. -zag.
  pl. ǧızánč(ı).
  gådıˬtínˬǧízašˬšórogırkon (-šˬš- < -gˬš- § 695) the judge (has) reduced their punishment.
ǧızúli n. Ǧuzúli, a man's name [< الجُزُولى § 1389].
  obj. -lıg.
ǧızúlín-d(ı) (§§ 2545 ff.) adj. appertaining to Ǧuzúli.
ǧóbbɛ v.i. (a) have patience; (b) wait, stay [§§ 2870 ff.].
  ind. pres. aiˬǧóbbɛri; perf. aiˬǧóbbɛgori (N. -ɛko-, -ɛho-).
  part. pres. ǧóbbɛl (one) that has patience, etc., patient, etc.
  ínˬógıǧˬǧóbbɛlun this man is patient.
  part. past ǧóbbɛl (one) that had patience, etc., patient, etc.
  terˬtåmˬbókkonˬǧóbbɛ (-mˬb- < -nˬb- § 592) and terˬtåmˬmóŋkonˬǧóbbɛ wait till (s)he (it) comes (back).
ǧóbbɛrar (-rår, §§ 2200 ff., 2210) and
ǧóbbɛríd (§§ 2256 ff., 2263) n. patience, waiting, etc.
ǧóbbɛr-an (§§ 3890 ff., 3899) v.t. tell to have patience, etc., let have patience, etc.
  íŋˬɛttarélgıˬǧóbbɛran tell the bringer of this to wait.
ǧóbbɛ-bū- (§ 3931 α) v.i. stat. be in a patient state or condition.
  ínˬógıǧˬǧóbbɛbun this man is patient.
ǧóbbɛl-an- (§ 3910 α) v.i. grow patient.
ǧóbbɛlam-bū- (§ 3949 ff.) v.i. stat. be in a state or condition of growing or having grown patient.
ǧobbɛlanɛd-åg- (§ 3966 α) v.i. be in the condition of having grown patient.
ǧóbbɛr-ɛ-må- (§§ 4016-17, 4036, 4041) v.i. become unable to have patience, etc.
  árˬǧóbbɛrɛmågoru we couldn't (were unable to) wait.
ǧóbbɛ-nóg (§ 3747 ɛ') v.i. go (etc. s.v. nóg) slowly.
ǧóbbɛ-nog (§ 1964) v.i. go (etc.) slowly.
ǧóbbɛ-nóg-bū- (-nóggū- § 546; § 4058) v.i. stat. be going (etc.) slowly.
  båbúrˬǧóbbɛnógbun the steamer (train) is travelling slowly.
ǧóčč(ı) go and drag s.v. ǧú.
ǧóg v.t. (a) grind; (b) work, work on (stone for grinding); (c) turn (hand-mill) [cogn. ǧókk(ı) chew § 2777; ?cogn. ǧú nether stone for grinding; RSN, § 129].
  ind. pres. aiˬǧóg(¹)ri; perf. aiˬǧókkori (ˬǧókkori).
  imperat. ǧók!
  subj. past aiˬǧógsı (ˬǧóksı, -su).
  part. pres. ǧógı (one) that grinds, grinder, grinding.
  åmˬbéledırˬǧógıˬɛ́n-tánnan in my (our) country the one that grinds is the (a) woman.
  nógoˬmárɛˬǧógın (-ǧˬǧ- < -gˬǧ- § 551) the female slave grinds the millet.
  nógoˬǧuntókkɛǧˬǧógın (-ǧˬǧ- < -dˬǧ- § 550) the female slave grinds

gogor — gom

with the upper stone (i.e. has it in her hands).
nógo⌣ğŭğ⌣ğógın⌢ (-ğ⌣ğ- < -g⌣ğ- §551) *the female slave works (on) the stone for grinding*, i.e. *the female slave grinds*.
rahā́ıɛğ⌣ğógran⌢ (-ğ⌣ğ- < -g⌣ğ- §551) *they turn the hand-mill*.

ğógar (-gàr⌣; §§ 2200 ff.) *and*
ğōgíd (§§ 2256 ff.) *n. grinding, etc.*

ğóg-an (§§ 3890 ff.) *v.t. tell to grind, etc., let grind, etc.*

ğóg-bŭ- (ğóggŭ- §546; §3931 β) *v.i. stat. be in a ground state or condition*.
íu⌣ğóggŭn⌢ *the corn is (has been) ground*.

ğōgɛd-ág- (§§ 3877 ff.) *v.t. be in the situation of having ground, etc.*
nógo⌣márɛğ⌣ğōgɛdágın⌢ (-ğ⌣ğ- < -g⌣ğ- §551) *the female slave has ground the millet*.

ğógk-ıdd(ı) (ğókk-; §3725) *v.t. caus. cause or allow to grind, etc.*
imperat. ğógkıddi!
āī⌣nógoğ⌣ğókkıddırı⌢ (-ğ⌣ğ- < -g⌣ğ- §551) *I make the female slave grind*.
nógog⌣íllɛğ⌣ğókkıddóskoran⌢ (§5343) *they have made the female slave grind the wheat*.

ğóg-kattı- (ğókkat-; §4093) *v.p. be ground, etc.*
íllɛ⌣ğókkattın⌢ *the wheat is ground*.

ğógor (a) *v.t. squeeze, compress in the hand, crumple*; (b) *v.i. get squeezed, etc., crumple, shrivel* [< *ğógır (§1175) < √ğóg- *squeeze* (§4529) + -ı- euphonic + -r intensive §4586].
ind. pres. āī⌣gogórrı⌢, ɛr⌣ğógorın⌢ (-rī⌢, -rí⌢); perf. āī⌣gogórkori⌢.
tɛr⌣ánn-īt⌣ténn⌣ígɛğ⌣ğogórkon⌢ (-t⌣t- < -g⌣t- §707, -ğ⌣ğ- < -d⌣ğ- §550) *(s)he squeezed my hand with his (hers)*; ⌣ánn-īt⌣ §1671; ⌣ténn⌣ígɛğ⌣ §1673.
nóbrɛn⌣ákaš⌣ğogoróskó⌢ *the gold earring has (ear-rings have §4696d) got crumpled*.
tímɛ⌣ğógorın⌢ *the water-melon shrivels*.

ğógorar (-ràr⌣; §§ 2200 ff.) *and*
ğogoríd (§§ 2256 ff.) *n. squeezing, crumpling, etc.*

ğógor-an (§§ 3890 ff.) *v.t. tell to squeeze, etc., let squeeze, etc.*

ğógor-bŭ- (§3931 β) *v.i. stat. be in a squeezed (etc.) state or condition*.
ín⌣tímɛ⌣ğógorbūn⌢ *this water-melon is (these water-melons are §4696b) shrivelled*.

ğogoríŋg-ır (N. -ŋkır; §3688) (a) *v.t. caus. cause or allow to squeeze, etc.*; (b) *v.i. crumple, shrivel*.
másıl⌣tímɛğ⌣ğogoríŋgırın⌢ (-ğ⌣ğ- < -g⌣ğ- §551) *the sun shrivels the water-melon(s)*.

ğógor-tómb(ı) (§3747 ε′) *v.t. break by squeezing, etc.*

ğógı *go and carry, etc. s.v. ğŭ.*
ğók! imperat. of *ğóg grind.*

ğókk(ı) *v.t. chew, masticate* (food; distinguish from súkk(ı) *chew tobacco*) [cogn. ğóg *grind* §2777; §2853].
ind. pres. āī⌣ğókkırı⌢; perf. āī⌣ğókkıgori⌢ (N. -ıko-, -ıho-).
imperat. ğókki!
kúsuğ⌣ğókkıran⌢ (-ğ⌣ğ- < -g⌣ğ- §551) *they chew the meat*.

ğókkar (-kàr⌣; §§ 2200 ff.) *and*
ğokkíd (§§ 2256 ff.) *n. mastication.*

ğókk-an (§§ 3890 ff.) *v.t. tell to chew, etc., let chew, etc.*

ğókkı-bŭ- (§3931 β) *v.i. stat. be in a chewed (etc.) state or condition*.
kúsu⌣ğókkıbūn⌢ *the meat is in a masticated condition*.

ğókkı-kattı- (N. -ıha-; §4093) *v.p. be chewed, etc.*
íŋ⌣kúsu⌣dɛŋgélun, ğokkıkáttımunun⌢ *this meat is tough, it cannot (§5704) be chewed*.

ğóm (a) *v.t. strike, hit, beat, play* (an instrument); (b) *v.i. strike, beat, sound* [RSN, §129].
ind. pres. āī⌣ğómrı⌢; perf. āī⌣ğómkori⌢.
imperat. ğóm!, pl. ğómwɛ! (ğómwɛ́!, ğómmɛ! §603, -mɛ́!).
subj. past āī⌣ğómsı⌢ (-su⌣).
tókkon⌣ğómmɛn! (-ko⌣ğóm- §554, -mɛ̃!, -mɛ́!) *don't strike (etc.), him, her, it, them)*.
kák⌣kúsmɛŋŋon⌣ğóm⌢ (§§ 5747 ff.) *knock at the door (lit. house) before you open it*.
bértı⌣níššıgɛğ⌣ğómın⌢ (-ğ⌣ğ- < -d⌣ğ- §550) *the goat butts, lit....strikes with (his) horn.*
ɛlúmgı⌣búndúkkɛğ⌣ğómkori⌢ *I (have) shot the crocodile*.
óddī, kıníssɛ⌣ğómkō⌢ *it hurts, a thorn (has) pierced it*.
fıríčč⌣āīgı⌣ğómkō⌢ *the (a) mason wasp (has) stung me*.
asáln⌣kúlt⌣adémgı⌣ğómın⌢ (§4696c) *bees sting (§5340)*.
íŋ⌣kúltı⌣adémgı⌣ğómın⌢ *these flies sting (bite)*.
tér⌣āīg⌣agílgɛğ⌣ğómkó⌢ (-ğ⌣ğ- < -d⌣ğ- §550) *(s)he shouted me down*, lit. *(s)he struck me with his (her) mouth*.
kúltıgɛğ⌣ğómran⌢ (§§ 5452-3) *n. instrument for hitting flies, fly-switch*.
kúragɛğ⌣ğómran⌢ *instrument for hitting a ball, polo-stick, etc.*
kúblır⌣bújağ⌣ğóm⌢ (-ğ⌣ğ- < -g⌣ğ- §551) *and* (§5344)
kúblıb⌣bújağ⌣ğóm⌢ (-b⌣b- < -g⌣b- §519) *paint the boats*.
kúblıb⌣bújağ⌣ğómır⌢ (§3033) *paint (each of §5456) the boats*.
ɛŋ⌣kádɛf⌣fúrsagɛğ⌣ğóm⌢ (-f⌣f- < -g⌣f- §540, -ğ⌣ğ- < -d⌣ğ- §550) *brush your clothes (§4696d)*.
ğaráskı⌣ğóm⌢ *ring the bell*.
kórabkı⌣ğómkoran⌢ *and*
kórağkı⌣ğómkoran⌢ *they (have) uttered a shout*.
tórbar⌣ısískı⌣ğómın⌢ *the peasant whistles*.
bābŭr⌣suffarağ⌣ğómın⌢ (-ğ⌣ğ- < -g⌣ğ- §551) *the steamer (engine of the train) whistles*.
réıs⌣suffarağ⌣ğómóskó⌢ *the steersman has sounded the whistle*.
nuggárağ⌣ğómın⌢ *he beats (plays) the drum*.
kısírkı⌣ğómın⌢ *he plays the guitar*.
zummárağ⌣ğómın⌢ *he plays on the (a) pipe*.
tābağ⌣ğóm⌢ *put the (a) stamp on* (sc. the letter).
tɛlɛgráfkı⌣ğómkon⌢ *(s)he (has) sent the (a) telegram* (cp. ضرب تلغراف).

— used intransitively (cp. §5341):
ğárǎs⌣ğomóskó⌢ *the bell has (just) rung*.
suffára⌣ğomóskó⌢ *the whistle has (just) sounded*.
fılɛtúfılád⌣ğóm⌢ *the lightning flashes*.
ududɛ⌣ğómın⌢ *the thunder sounds (it thunders)*.

ğómar⌣ (-màr⌣; §§ 2200 ff.) *and*
ğomíd (§§ 2256 ff.) *n. striking, etc.*

ğomıdk-ır-ğóm (-ītkır-, -īttır- §716; §4156) *v.t. strike (etc.) much, strike (etc.) heavily, give a sound beating to*.
magáskı⌣ğomītkırğómkori⌢ *I gave (have given) the thief a good thrashing*.

ğomıdkırğóm-bŭ- (-ītkır-, -īttır-; §4164) *v.i. stat. be in a thoroughly well beaten state or condition*.

ğóm-an (§§ 3890 ff.) *v.t. tell to strike, etc., let strike, etc.*

ğom-bɛ́ (§3747 ε′) *v.t. kill by striking, etc., strike dead, beat to death*.
ím⌣báŋgağ⌣ğombɛ́⌢ (-ğ⌣ğ- < -g⌣ğ- §551) *kill this locust (these locusts §4696c) by hitting it (them)*.
fılɛtufılád⌣tékkı⌣ğombɛ́gó⌢ *the lightning (has) struck him (her, it) dead*.
nugúttı⌣ğombɛ́goran⌢ *they beat (have beaten) the slave to death*.

ğom-bɛ́rığ (§3747 ε′) *v.t. massacre (etc. s.v. bérığ) by striking (etc.), beat to death in numbers*.
ím⌣báŋgağ⌣ğombɛ́rıč⌢ *hit and kill (all) these locusts (§4696c)*; -bérıč⌢ implies that they are numerous.

ğóm-bŭ- (§3931 β) *v.i. stat.* (a) *be in a struck (etc.) state or condition*; (b) *be the victim of a stroke (e.g. of epilepsy), be in a fit*; (c) *be insane*.
ín⌣ógığ⌣ğómbūn⌢ *this man (a) has been struck (etc., has had a beating)*; (b) *has had a stroke (is in a fit)*; (c) *is insane*.
unáttıgɛğ⌣ğómbŭ- (-ğ⌣ğ- < -d⌣ğ- §550) *be epileptic*, lit. *be moonstruck*.

ğóm-dɛ̄n (§§ 3996-7) *v.t. give (to the speaker) by striking, etc., strike (etc.) for (the speaker)*.
tɛlɛgráfk⌣āīgı⌣ğómdɛ̄ŋkó⌢ *(s)he (has) sent me a telegram*.

ğómdɛ̄n-an (and ⌣; §§ 3890 ff., 3905) *v.t. tell to give (to the speaker) by striking, etc., let give (to the speaker) by striking, etc.*
tɛlɛgráfk⌣āīgı⌣ğómdɛ̄nan⌢ *tell him (her) to send me a telegram*.

ğóm-tır (§§ 3998-9) *v.t. give (to other than the speaker) by striking, etc., strike (etc.) for (other than the speaker)*.
tɛlɛgráfkı⌣ğómtır⌢ *send him (her, them) a telegram*.

ğómtır-an (§§ 3890 ff., 3905) *v.t. tell to give (to other than the speaker) by striking, etc., let give (to other than the speaker) by striking, etc.*
tɛlɛgráfkı⌣ğómtıran⌢ *tell him (her) to send him (her, them) a telegram*.

ğomr-ɛg-ág- (§§ 4071 ff.) *v.t. = ğomɛdól-.*

ğom-ɛ-dól- (-mᵒd- §1178; §4022) and
ğomr-ɛ-dól- (-rᵒd-; §4027) v.t. *be about to strike, etc.*
ğomr-ɛ-ğǔ-bū- (§4069) v.t. stat. *be on one's way (coming) to strike, etc.*
ğom-ɛ-mǎ- (§4036) and
ğomr-ɛ-mǎ- (§4041) v.t. *become unable to strike, etc.*
ğomr-ɛ-nóg (§§4048ff.) v.t. *go to strike, etc.*
ğomr-ɛ-nóg-bū- (-nóggū- §546; §4058) v.t. stat. *be on one's way (going) to strike, etc.*
āī⌣tɛlɛgrǎfkī⌣ğomrɛnógbūrī⌢ *I am on my way to send the (a) telegram.*
ğomr-ɛ-tǎ (§§4060ff.) v.t. *come to strike, etc.*
ğomɛd-ǎg- (§§3877ff.) v.t. *be in the situation of having struck, etc.*
fīríčč̄-ēr⌣āīgī⌣ğomɛdǎgīn⌢ (-čč-ēr⌣ < -čč-wēr⌣ §522) *a mason wasp has stung me.*
ğom-ğɛrrıbɛ́ (-rubɛ́; §3747ɛ′) v.t. *try to strike, etc.*
āīgī⌣ğomğɛrrıbɛ́gon⌢ *(s)he (it) tried to hit me.*
ğomíng-ır (and ̓⌣, N. -ŋkır; §3688) v.t. caus. *cause or allow to strike, etc.*
ğóm-kattı- (§4093) v.p. *be struck, etc.*
ğomkattos-kōrābk-āğ-ğóm- (§5601; §4207; -okkō- §573; -osgıkō-, -ozgı-, -oggı- §4208; -āpk-, -āğğóm-) v.i. *having been struck, etc., be engaged in raising (etc. s.v. āğğóm-) a loud cry, be engaged in raising (etc.) a loud cry on being struck, etc.*
wɛ́l⌣ğomkattokkorapkağğómın⌢ *the dog is howling (always howls) on being beaten.*
ğomos-tǎ (-ottā §714; §§4180-4; -osgıtǎ, -ozgı-, -oggı- §4185) v.t. *come after striking, etc., just (s.v. tǎ) strike, etc., go and (§5713) strike, etc.*
imperat. ğomósta! (-ótta!, -ósgıta!, -ózgı-, -óggı-).
ğomos-tǒ (-ottō §714; §§4180-4; -osgıtō, -ozgı-, -oggı- §4185) v.t. *enter (i.) after striking, etc., knock before entering (§3783).*
imperat. ğomostó! (-ottó!, -ozgı-, -oggı-) and ğomósto! (-ótto!, -ósgıto!, -ózgı-, -óggı-).
ğom-tómb(ı) (§3747ɛ′) v.t. *break by striking, etc.*
tókkon⌣ğomtómbımɛn⌢ *don't break it when you hit it.*
ğómbo⌣ n. *(in water-wheel, kólɛ⌣) rope binding together ends nearer river of all transverse limbs (fǎšɛnč(ı)⌣) of spokes of wheel over water (átt(ı)⌣); it forms a* rim *corresponding to the* átt(ı)⌣sɛ́n⌣ *binding shoreward ends of* fǎšɛnč(ı)⌣.
obj. -bog⌣.
pl. -bonč(ı)⌣.
ğómmɛ́! (§603) < ğómwɛ́! *strike (pl.)!* s.v. ğóm.
ğómmɛ́ (§939) < ğómmɛn! *don't strike!* (§§3093, 5477-8).
ğóndo⌣ adj. *sticky, adhesive, glutinous, viscous.*
obj. -dog⌣.
pl. -dorı⌣, -donč(ı)⌣.

gonı́ssɛ⌣ğóndón⌢ *(the) gum is sticky.*
dı⌣ğóndó⌢ (§939) *(the) edible hibiscus is sticky.*
kúmbum⌣bɛjād⌣ğóndón⌢ (-m⌣b- < -n⌣b- §592) *white of egg is sticky.*
ğónd-an- (§3910α) v.i. *become sticky, etc.*
ğóndam-bū- (̀́~ §1932a; §§3949ff.) v.i. stat. *be in a state or condition of becoming sticky, etc., be getting sticky, etc.*
ğondanɛd-ǎg- (§3966α) v.i. *be in the condition of having become sticky, etc.*
ğóndog-ır (N. -okır, -ohır; §3701) v.t. caus. *cause or allow to be or become sticky, etc., render sticky, etc.*
kúmbum⌣bɛjād⌣ánn-ığ⌣ğóndogırkó⌢ (-ğ⌣ğ- < -g⌣ğ- §551) *the white of egg (has) made my hand(s §4696a) sticky;* ⌣ánn-ığ⌣ §1671.
ğōr v.t. *reap, cut (crop, fodder, fuel, building-material) [RSN, §§129, 200; TEG, §614, 1].*
ind. pres. āī⌣ğórrı⌢, ɛr⌣ğórın⌢ (-rī⌢, -rí⌢); perf. āī⌣ğórkorī⌢.
imperat. ğōr!, pl. ğórwɛ! (ğórwɛ́!, ğórrɛ! §672, -rɛ́!).
part. pres. ğórıl⌣ (*one) that reaps, etc., reaper, etc., reaping, etc.*; obj. ğōrılg(ı)⌣, -gı⌢.
part. past ğórɛl⌣ (*one) that reaped, etc., reaper, etc., reaping, etc.*; obj. ğōrɛ́lg(ı)⌣, -gı⌢.
íllɛğ⌣ğórran⌢ (-ğ⌣ğ- < -g⌣ğ- §551) *they reap the wheat.*
márob⌣bīğórran⌢ (-b⌣b- < -g⌣b- §519) *they will cut the sorghum.*
béntığ⌣ğōr *cut down the dates (§4696b from the palm)* = N. béntım⌣múkki⌢.
nógo⌣gídkı⌣ğōrın⌢ *the female slave cuts grass (for fodder).*
gídkı⌣ğōrkoru⌢ (gítti⌣) *we (you pl., have) cut (the) grass.*
bérkı⌣ğórran⌢ *they cut (down) wood (fuel).*
ğōrar- (-rār⌣; §§2200ff.) and
ğōríd (§§2256ff.) n. *reaping, etc.*
ğōr-an (§§3890ff.) v.t. *tell to reap, etc., let reap, etc.*
ğōr-bū- (§3931β) v.i. stat. *be in a reaped (etc.) state or condition.*
márɛ⌣ğōrbūn⌢ *the sorghum is (has been) cut.*
ğōrr-ɛg-ǎg- (§§4071ff.) v.t. = ğōrɛdól-.
ğōrr-ɛ-dól- (-rᵒd- §1178; §4022) and
ğōrr-ɛ-dól- (-rᵒd-; §4027) v.t. *be about to reap, etc.*
ğōrr-ɛ-ğǔ-bū- (§4069) v.t. stat. *be on one's way (coming) to reap, etc.*
ğōr-ɛ-mǎ- (§4036) and
ğōrr-ɛ-mǎ- (§4041) v.t. *become unable to reap, etc.*
ğōrr-ɛ-nóg (§§4048ff.) v.t. *go to reap, etc.*
ğōrr-ɛ-nóg-bū- (-nóggū- §546; §4058) v.t. stat. *be on one's way (going) to reap, etc.*
ğōrr-ɛ-tǎ (§§4060ff.) v.t. *come to reap, etc.*
ğōrɛd-ǎg- (§§3877ff.) v.t. *be in the situation of having reaped, etc.*
ğōrɛt-tǎ (§5723; ğōrɛggı-tǎ §4176) v.t. *come after reaping, etc., go (§5713) and reap, etc.*
imperat. ğōrétta!
ğōr-ɛttǎ (-ɛ́ttā; §5723) v.t. *bring after reaping, etc.*
imperat. ğōrétta!

ğōr-kattı- (§4093) v.p. *be reaped, etc.*
ğōś *go and cause to issue, etc.* s.v. ğǔ.
ğów(ı)⌣ (ğóuw(ı)⌣, -w(ᵘ) §1202) n. *(a) tree (excluding bént(ı)⌣, hámbu⌣); (b) =* ğówwᴗurúmmɛ⌣.
With collective sg. (§4696b):
obj. -wıg⌣.
pl. -wınč(ı)⌣.
wāla⌣béntıw⌣wāla⌣hámbuğ⌣ğówwıg⌣ émunan⌢ (-w⌣w- < -g⌣w- §719, -ğ⌣ğ- < -g⌣ğ- §551) *they do not call either the date-palm or the dōm-palm* ğówwı⌢.
ğówwᴗurúmmɛ⌣ *the black tree, Acacia arabica, Willd. (BSP, 181).*
ğówwım⌣bɛ́r⌣ (-m⌣b- < -n⌣b- §592) *(a) wood of tree; (b) trunk of tree.*
ğówwım⌣bıtǎn⌣ (bıt-) *fruit (seed) of tree.*
ğówwın⌣úlug⌣ *leaf (leaves §4696c) of tree.*
ğǔ n. *nether stone for grinding [?cogn. ğóg grind; RSN, §129].*
obj. ğǔg⌣.
pl. ğǔnč(ı)⌣.
nógo⌣ğǔg⌣āğğógın⌢ *the female slave (a) is grinding, lit.... is working the stone for grinding; (b) habitually grinds (etc.).*
ğūn-tǒd⌣ (§2366) *smaller i.e. upper stone for grinding.*
obj. -tǒdk(ı)⌣, -tǒtk(ı)⌣, -tǒkk(ı)⌣, -tǒtt(ı)⌣ (§2462), -kı⌢, -tı⌢.
gen. -tǒdn⌣., -tǒnn⌣v.c., -tǒn⌣c.
pl. ğǔntonı⌣.
ğǔn-tod (§2371) = ğūntǒd⌣.
obj. ğǔntǒdk(ı)⌣, -tǒtk(ı)⌣, -tǒkk(ı)⌣, -tǒtt(ı)⌣, -kı⌢, -tı⌢.
gen. -tǒdn⌣v., -tǒnn⌣v.c., -tǒn⌣c.
pl. ğǔntonı⌣.
ğǔntodun⌢ and
ğǔntodun⌢ *it's an upper stone for grinding.*
ğǔ v.i. *(a) move along, pass along, proceed, travel, and so (b, when the motion begins or occurs in the presence or vicinity of the speaker, his audience or his agent)* go, *and (c, when it does not) go, come, according to situation. See §5332;—in composition -ǔ- is often elided before a vowel (§1111) [cp. ON. δo-, δω-, δοσ- id. GNT, s.v.].*
ind. pres. āī⌣ğúrı⌢, ɛr⌣ğǔn⌢ (⌣ğǔ⌢, ⌣ğǔ⌢, ⌣ğǔ⌢); perf. āī⌣ğúgorı⌢ (N. -úko-, -úho-).
imperat. ğu⌣, ğú! *go!,* pl. ğǔwɛ! (ğǔwɛ́!).
subj. past āī⌣ğǔsı⌣ (-su⌣).
def. perf. sg. 3 ğúoskon⌢ (ğᵘós-, ğwós-, -kō⌢, -kó⌢).
X. tı́rsɛ́? *where are they?*
Y. kār⌣ğúgoran⌢ *they went (have gone) to the house.*
X. tókkon⌣súgır⌣nógmɛn⌢ *don't go to the market.*
Y. wǎran, súgır⌣bığúmun⌣ *no, I won't (cp. §5365).*
kār⌣ğúrı⌣tǎd⌣íngı⌣dɛ́n⌢ *when I get to the house (sc. to which I am going) give me this.*
úrdır⌣ğúgogan⌣síkkan⌢ *tell him (her) to ask whether they went (have gone) to El-Ordi (§6152, ii).*
kār⌣ğwóskoran⌢ *they have gone to the house.*

ǧú

ǧúrar⌣ (-rár⌣; §§2200ff., 2207) and
ǧurĭd⌣ (§§2256ff., 2260) n. *linear motion, passage, going, coming.*

— In view of their number and the frequent reduction of ǧu- to ǧ-, the following complexes are placed in their actual (instead of their etymological) alphabetical order. For the ǧu- complex, see §§3859–64; for the ǧŭ- complex §3858.

ǧ-amínt(ɪ) v.t. *go and show.*
   káčči⌣ǧamínti⌢ *go and show him (them) the horse.*

ǧamínt-an v.t. *tell to go and show, let go and show.*
   álɪk⌣káčči⌣ǧamíntā⌢ *let ɛáli go and show him (them) the horse.*

ǧán *tell to go* s.v. *ǧŭ-an.*

ǧ-ár v.t. *go and seize, etc.* (s.v. ár).

ǧár-an v.t. *tell to go and seize, etc., let go and seize, etc.*

ǧ-árk(ɪ) (ǧaríkk(ɪ)) v.t. *go and throw, etc.* (s.v. árk(ɪ), aríkk(ɪ)).
   íŋgɪ⌣ǧárki⌢ *go and throw this away.*

ǧárk-an (ǧaríkkan) v.t. *tell to go and throw, etc., let go and throw, etc.*

ǧ-áu v.t. *go and do, etc.* (s.v. áu).
   kúsuǧ⌣ǧáu⌢ (-ǧ⌣ǧ- < -g⌣ǧ- §551) *go and cook the meat.*

ǧáw-an v.t. *tell to go and do, etc., let go and do, etc.*

ǧ-ékk(ɪ) v.i. *go and relieve nature* (s.v. ékk(ɪ)).

ǧ-él v.t. *go and find.*

ǧél-an v.t. *tell to go and find, let go and find.*

ǧ-erǧɛ́ (ǧerɛǧɛ́, ǧerɛǧǧɛ́, ǧerɪǧɛ́, ǧerɪǧǧɛ́) v.i. and t. *go and wait (for).*

ǧerǧɛ́r-an (ǧerɛǧɛ́r-, etc.) v.t. *tell to go and wait (for), let go and wait (for).*

ǧ-étta v.t. *go and fetch.*
   šáɪg⌣áukogɪn, ǧétta⌢ *if he has (you have) made tea, go and fetch it.*

ǧéttar-an v.t. *tell to go and fetch, let go and fetch.*
   ugulláŋgɪ⌣ǧéttawan⌢ *let them go and fetch fuel.*

ǧettár-an v.t. = ǧéttar-an.

ǧ-ír *go and count, etc.* = ǧu-ír.

ǧ-ídd(ɪ) *go and ask, etc.* = ǧu-ídd(ɪ).

ǧ-ɪgídd(ɪ) *go and water, etc.* = ǧu-ɪgídd(ɪ).

ǧ-índ(ɪ) v.t. *go and lift, etc.* (s.v. índ(ɪ)).

ǧínd-an v.t. *tell to go and lift, let go and lift, etc.*

ǧ-íñɪr v.i. and t. *go and (a)wait, etc.* (s.v. íñɪr).

ǧíñɪr-an v.t. *tell to go and (a)wait, etc., let go and (a)wait, etc.*

ǧ-íriñ v.i. *go and (a)wait, etc.* (s.v. íriñ).

ǧíriñ-an v.t. *tell to go and (a)wait, etc., let go and (a)wait, etc.*

ǧ-ɪsíkk(ɪ) v.t. *go and ask, etc.* = ǧusíkk(ɪ).
   imperat. ǧɪsíkki!
   aɪ⌣ǧɪsíkkɪrɪ⌢ *I('ll §5369b) go and ask.*

ǧɪsíkk-an v.t. *tell to go and ask, let go and ask, etc.*

ǧ-íšɪn (ǧɪšín) v.t. *go and send.*

ǧíšɪn-an v.t. *tell to go and send, let go and send.*

ǧ-óbɪr v.t. *go and invert, etc.* (s.v. óbɪr).

ǧóbɪr-an v.t. *tell to go and invert, etc., let go and invert, etc.*

ǧ-óčč(ɪ) v.t. *go and drag, etc.* (s.v. óčč(ɪ)).
   kúbkɪ⌣ǧóččɪwé⌢ *go (pl.) and tow the boat.*

ǧóčč-an v.t. *tell to go and drag, etc., let go and drag, etc.*

ǧ-óǧɪ v.t. *go and carry, etc.* (s.v. óǧɪ).

ǧóǧ-an v.t. *tell to go and carry, etc., let go and carry, etc.*

ǧ-ós v.t. *go and cause to issue, etc.* (s.v. ós) = ǧu-ós.

ǧós-an v.t. *tell to go and cause to issue, etc., let go and cause to issue, etc.*

ǧ-ošóšk(ɪ) v.t. *go and drag, etc.* (s.v. ošóšk(ɪ)).

ǧošóšk-an v.t. *tell to go and drag, etc., let go and drag, etc.*

ǧŭ- (ǧúan, ǧuán, ǧᵘán, ǧwán, ǧán; §3858) v.t. *tell to go, let go.*

ǧu-bág (§§3859–64) v.t. *go and distribute, etc.* (s.v. bág).
   imperat. ǧúbak!, ǧubák! (§1900).

ǧúbag-an (⌣́⌣ §1907; §5645) v.t. *tell to go and distribute, etc., let go and distribute, etc.*

ǧubagíŋg-ɪr (⌣́⌣ §1799; N. -ŋkɪr; §§4212, 5621) v.t. caus. *cause or allow to go and distribute, etc.*
   aɪ⌣tékkɪ⌣dúŋgɪǧ⌣ǧubágɪŋgɪddi⌢ (-ǧ⌣ǧ- < -g⌣ǧ- §551) *I('ll §5369b) make (let) him (her) go and distribute the money.*

ǧubagíŋgɪr-an (N. -ŋkɪr; §5645) v.t. *tell to cause or allow to go and distribute, etc., let cause or allow to go and distribute, etc.*

ǧu-bág v.t. *go and divide into shares.*
   imperat. ǧúbāk!, ǧubák! (§1900).
   dúŋgɪǧ⌣ǧúbāk⌣ *go and divide the money into shares.*

ǧubág-an v.t. *tell to go and divide into shares, let go and divide into shares.*
   álɪd⌣dúŋgɪǧ⌣ǧubágā⌢ (-d⌣d- < -g⌣d- §534) *let ɛáli go and divide the money into shares.*

ǧu-bagíttɛ v.t. *go and divide into shares.*

ǧubagíttɛ-an v.t. *tell to go and divide into shares, let go and divide into shares.*

ǧu-bǎǧ v.t. *go and write, etc.* (s.v. bǎǧ).
   imperat. ǧúbač!, ǧubáč! (§1900).

ǧubǎǧ-an v.t. *tell to go and write, etc., let go and write, etc.*

ǧu-bár v.t. *go and sort, etc.* (s.v. bár).
   imperat. ǧúbar!, ǧubár!

ǧúbar-an (ǧubáran) v.t. *tell to go and sort, etc., let go and sort, etc.*

ǧu-bɛ́ v.t. *go and kill, etc.* (s.v. bɛ́).
   pl.-obj. ǧu-bɛ́rɪr.
   íkkɪ⌣ǧúbɛ⌢ *go and put the fire (light) out.*

ǧubɛ́r-an v.t. *tell to go and kill, etc., let go and kill, etc.*
   álɪg⌣íkkɪ⌣ǧubɛ́ran⌢ *let ɛáli go and put the fire (light) out.*

ǧu-bél v.i. *go and issue* (s.v. bél), *go along out.*
   imperat. ǧúbel!, ǧubél! (§1900), ǧɪbél! (§1195).
   tɛr⌣áɪgonon⌣gububélɪn⌢ (§3777) *(s)he (it) will go along out with me.*
   árgonon⌣ǧúbel⌢ and árgonon⌣ǧɪbél⌢ *come along out with us.*

ǧúbɛl-an (⌣́⌣) v.t. *tell to go along out, let go along out.*

ǧu-bɛtɛ́ (-bɛdɛ́) v.t. *go and begin.*

ǧubɛtɛ́r-an (-ɛdɛ́-) v.t. *tell to go and begin, let go and begin.*

ǧu-bɛu (-bɛ́u) v.t. *go and unravel, etc.* (s.v. bɛu).

ǧubɛ́w-an v.t. *tell to go and unravel, etc., let go and unravel, etc.*

ǧu-bír v.t. *go and transport, etc.* (s.v. bír).
   imperat. ǧúbɪr!, ǧubír!

ǧubír-an v.t. *tell to go and transport, etc., let go and transport, etc.*

ǧu-bítt(ɪ) v.t. *go and pick up, etc.* (s.v. bítt(ɪ)).
   imperat. ǧubítti!

ǧubítt-an v.t. *tell to go and pick up, etc., let go and pick up, etc.*

ǧu-bókk(ɪ) v.i. *go and hide (oneself).*
   imperat. ǧubókki!

ǧubókk-an v.t. *tell to go and hide (i.), let go and hide (i.).*

ǧu-bŏkk(ɪ) (a) v.t. *go and unload;* (b) v.i. *go and miscarry.*
   imperat. ǧubókki!

ǧubŏkk-an v.t. *tell to go and unload, let go and unload.*

ǧu-bókkɪr v.t. *go and conceal.*

ǧubókkɪr-an v.t. *tell to go and conceal, let go and conceal.*

ǧu-bŏrkɪǧ v.t. *go and demolish, etc.* (s.v. bŏr).

ǧubŏrkɪǧ-an v.t. *tell to go and demolish, etc., let go and demolish, etc.*

ǧu-bŏrkɪr v.t. *go and fell, etc.* (s.v. bŏr).

ǧubŏrkɪr-an v.t. *tell to go and fell, etc., let go and fell, etc.*

ǧu-bŏww(ɪ) v.i. *go and bathe (i.), go and swim.*
   imperat. ǧubŏwwi!

ǧubŏww-an v.t. *tell to go and bathe (i.), etc., let go and bathe (i.), etc.*

ǧu-bŏwwídd(ɪ) v.t. *go and bathe (t.).*
   imperat. ǧubŏwwíddi!

ǧubŏwwídd-an v.t. *tell to go and bathe (t.), let go and bathe (t.).*

ǧŭ-bu- (§3858) v.i. stat. *be in a state of motion towards the speaker, be engaged in travelling hither, be on the (subject's) way (coming), be approaching.*
   X. wo⌣saít, tá! *O Saɛíd, come (here)!*
   Y. aɪ⌣ǧúbūri *I'm coming.*
   ǧúbun⌢ *(s)he (it) is on his (her, its) way hither (is coming).*
   X. ɛsmán⌣ǧúbuna? *is ɛoɵmán coming?*
   Y. (N.) ólgō⌣wándɪkómunū⌢ *he has not yet come in sight.*
   X. sámɪl⌣sé? *where is the headman?*
   Y. índo⌣ǧúbū⌢ *he is on his way hither.*
   áru⌣ékkenɛ⌣ǧúbuná⌢ *is (the) rain coming now?*
   ɛn-nār⌣ǧúburu⌢ *we are on our way to (chez) you (your house).*
   ɛnnār⌣ǧúbugoru⌢ *we were on our way to you.*
   búš⌣ǧúbūlg(ɪ)⌣, -gi⌢ (§4665) *on Monday next.*

ǧu-dárr(ɪ) v.i. *go and ascend, etc.* (s.v. dárr(ɪ)).

ǧudárr-an v.t. *tell to go and ascend, etc., let go and ascend, etc.*

ǧu-dɛfɛ́ v.t. *go and pay.*

ǧudɛfɛ́r-an v.t. *tell to go and pay, let go and pay.*

ǧu-dɛfɛ́tır v.t. *go and pay (other than the speaker).*
ǧudɛfɛ́tır-an v.t. *tell to go and pay (other than the speaker), let go and pay (etc.).*
ǧu-dɛ́g v.i. and t. *go and cover one's loins, etc.* (s.v. dɛ́g).
 imperat. ǧúdɛk!, ǧudɛ́k! (§ 1900).
 hánuǧ‿ǧúdɛk⌒ (-ǧ‿ǧ- < -g‿ǧ- § 551) *go and saddle (load) the donkey.*
 afɛ́ški‿ǧudɛ́gwɛ⌒ *go (pl.) and load the baggage.*
ǧúdɛg-an (˘´˘ § 1907) v.t. *tell to go and cover his (her) loins, etc., let go and cover his (her) loins, etc.*
 álıh‿hánuǧ‿ǧúdɛgá⌒ (-h‿h- < -g‿h- § 559) *let ɛáli go and saddle (load) the donkey.*
ǧu-dɛ́g v.t. *go and irrigate, etc.* (s.v. dɛ́g).
 imperat. ǧúdɛk!, ǧudɛ́k! (§ 1900).
ǧudɛ́g-an v.t. *tell to go and irrigate, etc., let go and irrigate, etc.*
ǧu-dígır v.t. *go and tie, etc.* (s.v. díg-ır).
 imperat. ǧúdıgır!, ǧudígır! (§ 1905).
ǧúdıgır-an (˘´˘˘ § 1909) v.t. *tell to go and tie, etc., let go and tie, etc.*
ǧu-dŭr v.t. *go and get, etc.* (s.v. dŭr).
 imperat. ǧúdŭr!, ǧudŭ́r! (§ 1900).
ǧudŭ́r-an v.t. *tell to go and get, etc., let go and get, etc.*
ǧu-gɛ́ddımɛ́ (-dumɛ́) v.t. and i. *go and put forward, go and get ahead, etc.* (s.v. gɛddımɛ́).
ǧugɛddımɛ̄r-an (-dum-) v.t. *tell to go and put forward, etc., let go and put forward, etc.*
ǧu-gɛ́ddımkatt(ı) (-dum-) v.i. *go and get ahead, etc.* (s.v. gɛddımɛ́).
 imperat. ǧugɛ́ddımkatti!
ǧugɛ́ddımkatt-an (-dum-) v.t. *tell to go and get ahead, etc., let go and get ahead, etc.*
ǧu-géndıgır (N. -ıkır, -ıhır) v.t. *go and set right, etc.* (s.v. géndıgır).
ǧugéndıgır-an (N. -ıkır-, -ıhır-) v.t. *tell to go and set right, etc., let go and set right, etc.*
ǧu-gídd(ı) (§ 1140) v.t. *go and water, etc.* (s.v. ıgídd(ı)).
 imperat. ǧugíddi!
 kámlıǧ‿ǧugíddırır⌒ (-ǧ‿ǧ- < -g‿ǧ- § 551) *go and water (each of § 5456) the camels.*
ǧugídd-an v.t. *tell to go and water, etc., let go and water, etc.*
ǧu-ǧɛ́d v.i. and t. *go and swear, etc.* (s.v. ǧɛ́d).
 imperat. ǧúǧɛt!, ǧuǧɛ́t!
 ǧufɛgı̄rroǧɛ́t! *go and swear on (sc. the tomb of) the holy man* (§ 5605), pl. -ǧédwɛ!, -ǧédwɛ́!
ǧúǧɛd-an (˘´˘) v.t. *tell to go and swear, etc., let go and swear, etc.*
ǧu-ǧóm v.t. *go and strike, etc.* (s.v. ǧóm).
 imperat. ǧúǧom!, ǧuǧóm!
ǧúǧom-an (˘´˘) v.t. *tell to go and strike, etc., let go and strike, etc.*
ǧuǧomos-tá (-ottá § 714; §§ 4180-4; -osgıtá, -ozgı-, -oggı- § 4185) v.t. *come after going and striking, etc., just* (s.v. tá) *go and strike, etc.*
 imperat. ǧuǧomósta! (-ótta!, -ósgıta!, -ózgı-, -óggı-).

ǧaráskı‿ǧuǧomótta⌒ *just go and ring the bell.*
ǧu-ǧŏr v.t. *go and reap, etc.* (s.v. ǧŏr).
 imperat. ǧúǧōr!, ǧuǧŏr!
ǧúǧōr-an v.t. *tell to go and reap, etc., let go and reap, etc.*
ǧu-ǧúgur v.t. *go and burn, etc.* (s.v. ǧúgur).
 ind. pres. āi‿ǧuǧugúrri⌒, ɛr‿ǧuǧúgurın⌒ (-rī⌒, -rí⌒).
 imperat. ǧúǧugur!, ǧuǧúgur! (§ 1905).
ǧúǧugur-an (˘´˘˘ § 1909) v.t. *tell to go and burn, etc., let go and burn, etc.*
ǧu-haddırɛ́ v.t. *go and make ready, go and prepare.*
ǧuhaddırɛ̄r-an v.t. *tell to go and make ready, etc., let go and make ready, etc.*
ǧu-haddırɛ́gır (N. -ɛ́kır, -ɛ́hır) v.t. = ǧuhaddırɛ́.
ǧuhaddırɛ́gır-an (N. -ɛ́kır-, -ɛ́hır-) v.t. = ǧuhaddırɛ̄ran.
ǧu-hallısɛ́ (ǧuxal-) v.t. *go and save, go and finish.*
ǧuhallısɛ̄r-an (ǧuxal-) v.t. *tell to go and save, etc., let go and save, etc.*
 ǧéllıǧ‿ǧuhallısɛ́ran⌒ (-ǧ‿ǧ- < -g‿ǧ- § 551) *let him (her) go and finish the work.*
ǧu-hāsıbɛ́ v.t. *go and count.*
ǧuhāsıbɛ̄r-an v.t. *tell to go and count, let go and count.*
ǧuhāsıbɛ̄r-éttă v.t. *bring after going and counting.*
 ind. pres. āi‿ǧuhāsıbɛ̄réttări⌒; perf. āi‿ǧuhāsıbēréttăgori⌒ (N. -ăko-, -ăho-).
ǧu-húŋ(ı) v.i. *go and kneel.*
 imperat. ǧuhúŋi!
ǧu-ír (ǧwír, ǧír § 1114) v.t. *go and count, etc.* (sv. ír).
ǧuír-an (ǧwír-, ǧír-) v.t. *tell to go and count, etc., let go and count, etc.*
ǧu-ídd(ı) (ǧwíd-, ǧíd-) v.t. *go and ask, etc.* (s.v. ídd(ı)).
 imperat. ǧuíddi! (ǧwíd-, ǧíd-).
ǧuídd-an (ǧwíd-, ǧíd-) v.t. *tell to go and ask, etc., let go and ask, etc.*
ǧu-ıgídd(ı) (ǧwıg-, ǧıg- § 1114) v.t. *go and water, etc.* (s.v. ıgídd(ı)) = ǧugídd(ı).
 imperat. ǧuıgíddi! (ǧwıg-, ǧıg-).
ǧuıgídd-an (ǧwıg-, ǧıg-) v.t. *tell to go and water, etc., let go and water, etc.*
ǧu-índ(ı) (ǧwín-, ǧín-) v.t. *go and lift, etc.* (s.v. índ(ı)).
 imperat. ǧuíndi! (ǧwín-, ǧín-).
ǧuínd-an (ǧwín-, ǧín-) v.t. *tell to go and lift, etc., let go and lift, etc.*
ǧu-íñır (ǧwíñ-, ǧíñ-; ǧuıñír, ǧwíñ-, ǧíñ-) v.i. and t. *go and (a)wait, etc.* (s.v. íñır).
ǧuíñır-an (ǧwíñ-, ǧíñ-; ǧuıñıran, ǧwíñ-, ǧıñ-) v.t. *tell to go and (a)wait, etc., let go and (a)wait, etc.*
ǧu-íšın (ǧwíš-, ǧíš-; ǧuıšín, ǧwíš-, ǧíš-) v.t. *go and send.*
 ǧu-wɛ̄g-ınd-isín⌒ (§ 5607) *go and send (some)one here.*
ǧuíšın-an (ǧwíš-, ǧíš-; ǧuıšínan, ǧwíš-, ǧíš-) v.t. *tell to go and send, let go and send.*
ǧu-káčč(ı) v.i. and t. *go and play, etc.* (s.v. káčč(ı)).
 imperat. ǧukáčči!

ǧukáčč-an v.t. *tell to go and play, etc., let go and play, etc.*
ǧu-kál v.i. and t. *go and eat.*
 imperat. ǧúkal!, ǧukál!
ǧúkal-an (ǧukálan) v.t. *tell to go and eat, let go and eat.*
ǧu-kalbɛ́r v.i. and t. *go and eat one's fill (of).*
ǧukalbɛ́r-an v.t. *tell to go and eat to repletion, let go and eat to repletion.*
ǧu-kalgídd(ı) (N. -lkí-) v.t. *go and feed (t.).*
 imperat. ǧukalgíddi!
ǧukalgídd-an (N. -lkí-) v.t. *tell to go and feed (t.), let go and feed (t.).*
ǧu-kálgır v.i. *go and make bread.*
ǧukálgır-an v.t. *tell to go and make bread, let go and make bread.*
ǧu-kárǧ(ı) (-káǧǧ(ı)) v.t. *go and testify, etc.* (s.v. kárǧ(ı)).
 imperat. ǧukárǧi!, ǧukáǧǧi!
ǧukárǧ-an (-káǧǧan) v.t. *tell to go and testify, etc., let go and testify, etc.*
ǧu-kás v.t. and i. *go and draw, go and draw water.*
 imperat. ǧúkas!, ǧukás!
ǧúkas-an (ǧukásan) v.t. *tell to go and draw, etc., let go and draw, etc.*
ǧu-kób v.t. *go and shut, etc.* (s.v. kób).
 ind. pres. āi‿ǧukóbri⌒.
 imperat. ǧúkop!, ǧukóp!
ǧúkob-an (ǧukóban) v.t. *tell to go and shut, etc., let go and shut, etc.*
ǧu-kókk(ı) v.i. and t. *go and knock.*
 imperat. ǧukókki!
ǧukókk-an v.t. *tell to go and knock, let go and knock.*
ǧu-kúddɛgır v.t. *go and burn.*
ǧukúddɛgır-an v.t. *tell to go and burn, let go and burn.*
ǧu-kúǧur v.t. *go and place on, etc.* (s.v. kúǧur).
 éssıǧ‿ǧukúǧur⌒ (-ǧ‿ǧ- < -g‿ǧ- § 551) *go and put the water on* (sc. *the fire*).
 bǎrrǎtkı‿ǧukúǧur⌒ *go and put the kettle on.*
ǧukúǧur-an v.t. *tell to go and place on, etc., let go and place on, etc.*
ǧu-kúñ (ǧúkuñ) v.i. *go and sink.*
 imperat. ǧúkuñ!, ǧukúñ!
— the imperative ˘´ (§ 1903) is a common curse:
 ǧúkuñ! *go to the devil!*
ǧúkuñ-an (˘´˘) v.t. *tell to go and sink, let go and sink.*
 álıǧ‿ǧúkuña! (-ǧ‿ǧ- < -g‿ǧ- § 551) *let ɛáli go to the devil!*
ǧu-kús v.t. *go and open, etc.* (s.v. kús).
 imperat. ǧúkus!, ǧukús!
 X. kobbúlıǧ‿ǧukúsırır⌒ *go and release (each of* § 5456) *the prisoners.*
 Y. kusırıddɛnóggūri⌒ *I am on my way to let them out.*
ǧúkus-an (˘´˘) v.t. *tell to go and open, etc., let go and open, etc.*
ǧ-úll(ı) v.t. *go and kindle.*
 íkki‿ǧúlli⌒ *go and light the (a) fire (light).*
ǧúll-an (v.t. *tell to go and kindle, let go and kindle.*
ǧu-mág v.t. *go and steal, etc.* (s.v. mág).
 imperat. ǧúmǎk!, ǧumǎ́k!
ǧumág-an v.t. *tell to go and steal, etc., let go and steal, etc.*

ǧu-mɛ́r v.t. *go and cut, etc.* (s.v. mɛ́r).
imperat. ǧúmɛr!, ǧumɛ́r!
ǧúmɛr-an (˘ˊ˘) v.t. *tell to go and cut, etc., let go and cut, etc.*
ǧu-mǒr v.t. *go and bind, etc.* (s.v. mǒr).
imperat. ǧúmōr!, ǧumǒr!
ǧumǒr-an v.t. *tell to go and bind, etc., let go and bind, etc.*
ǧu-nál v.t. and i. *go and see, go and look, etc.* (s.v. nál).
imperat. ǧúnal!, ǧunál!
âɩ‿ǧunálliá? *shall* (§ 5369 b) *I go and see?*
mufɛ́ttɩš‿ɛ́r-on‿ágkɩn‿ǧunál *go and see whether the new inspector is there.*
ǧúnal-an (˘ˊ˘) v.t. *tell to go and see, etc., let go and see, etc.*
tírgɩ‿tíŋ‿kǎr‿ákkan‿wɛ́ǧ‿ǧunálan (-ǧ‿ǧ- <-g‿ǧ- § 551) *let someone go and see whether they are at home.*
ǧunalɛt-tá v.t. *just go and see*, lit. *come after going and seeing* (§ 5713).
ind. pres. âɩ‿ǧunalɛttárɩ.
imperat. ǧunalétta!
ǧ-úndur (ǧwúndur) v.t. *go and insert, etc.* (s.v. úndur).
kálgɩ‿ǧúndur *go and bake (the) bread.*
ǧúndur-an (ǧwún-) v.t. *tell to go and insert, etc., let go and insert, etc.*
ǧu-nɛ́r v.i. *go and sleep.*
imperat. ǧúnēr!, ǧunɛ́r!
ǧunɛ́r-an v.t. *tell to go and sleep, let go and sleep.*
ǧu-ní v.i. and t. *go and drink.*
imperat. ǧúni! (occ. ǧúnī!), ǧuní! (occ. ǧunī́!).
ǧuní-an v.t. *tell to go and drink, let go and drink.*
ǧu-ós (ǧwós) v.i. *go* (def. §§ 3789 ff.).
ǧu-ós (ǧwós, ǧʷós, ǧós) v.t. *go and cause to issue, etc.* (s.v. ós).
ǧuós-an (ǧwós-, ǧʷós-, ǧós-) v.t. *tell to go and cause to issue, etc., let go and cause to issue, etc.*
ǧu-sɩgídd(ɩ) v.i. *go and pray, go and say one's prayers.*
imperat. ǧusɩgíddi!
ǧusɩgídd-an v.t. *tell to go and pray, etc., let go and pray, etc.*
ǧu-síkk(ɩ) v.t. *go and ask, etc.* (s.v. síkk(ɩ)) = ǧɩsíkk(ɩ) supra, q.v.
imperat. ǧusíkkɩ!
ǧusíkk-an v.t. *tell to go and ask, etc., let go and ask, etc.*
ǧu-sɩkkɩnál v.t. *go and see by asking, go and ascertain.*
ind. pres. âɩ‿ǧusɩkkɩnálli.
imperat. ǧusɩkkɩnál!, ǧusíkkɩnal! (§ 1871).
gátɩr‿tɛ́m‿mawaɩ́dɩré? moháttaǧ‿ǧusíkkɩnal (-m‿m- <-n‿m- § 608, -ǧ‿ǧ- <-r‿ǧ- § 555) *is the train on time? go and find out at the station;* or (-ǧ‿ǧ- <-g‿ǧ § 551) moháttaǧ obj. of -síkkɩ- (cp. § 5592).
ǧusíkkɩnal-an (˘˘˘ˊ˘ § 1872) v.t. *tell to see by going and asking, let see by going and asking.*
ǧ-úskur (ǧwúskur) v.t. *go and set, etc.* (s.v. úskur).
ind. pres. âɩ‿ǧuskúddi.
ǧúskur-an (ǧwús-) v.t. *tell to go and set, etc., let go and set, etc.*

ǧu-sóg v.t. *go and accompany, etc.* (s.v. sóg).
imperat. ǧúsok!, ǧusók!
ǧúsog-an (˘ˊ˘) v.t. *tell to go and accompany, etc., let go and accompany, etc.*
ǧu-sókkɛ v.t. *go and take up, etc.* (s.v. sókkɛ).
ǧusókkɛr-an v.t. *tell to go and take up, etc., let go and take up, etc.*
ǧu-suttɛ-tá (§ 5605) v.i. *go and quickly return.*
ind. pres. âɩ‿ǧusuttɛtárɩ; perf. âɩ‿ǧusuttɛtágorɩ (N. -áko-, -áho-).
imperat. ǧusútteta!, pl. ǧusuttɛtáwɛ! (-tāwé!).
ǧusuttɛtár-an v.t. *tell to go and quickly return, let go and quickly return.*
ǧu-šúg v.t. *go and drive, etc.* (s.v. šúg).
imperat. ǧúšūk!, ǧušúk!
ǧušúg-an v.t. *tell to go and drive, etc., let go and drive, etc.*
ǧu-šuglɛ́ (-šoglɛ́, -šogolɛ́) v.i. *go and work.*
imperat. ǧušuglɛ́!
ǧušuglɛ́r-an (-šogl-, -šogol-) v.t. *tell to go and work, let go and work.*
ǧu-šúkk(ɩ) (N. -šúk(ɩ)) v.t. *go and wash.*
ɛ́ŋ‿kádeǧ‿ǧušúkki (-ǧ‿ǧ- <-g‿ǧ- § 551) *go and wash your clothes* (§ 4696 d).
ǧušúkk-an v.t. *tell to go and wash, let go and wash.*
álɩg‿ɛ̀ŋ-kàdeǧ-ǧušúkkan *let ɣáli go and wash his (own* § 5670*) clothes.*
ǧu-tá v.i. *go and come back*, just (s.v. tá) *go.*
imperat. ǧúta!, ǧutá!
X. súgɩrtōn‿ǧutárɩ *I'm going (I'll go* § 5369 b*) to the market and back (I'm just going to the market).*
Y. ǧúta! *very well!*, lit. *after going come!*
ǧutár-an v.t. *tell to go and come back, etc., let go and come back, etc.*
ǧu-tɛbɛ́ v.t. *go and seek, etc.* (s.v. tɛbɛ́).
imperat. ǧutɛbɛ́!
ǧutɛbɛ́r-an v.t. *tell to go and seek, etc., let go and seek, etc.*
ǧu-tɛ́g v.i. *go and squat, go and sit.*
imperat. ǧutɛ́k!, ǧutɛ́k!
def. imperat. ǧutɛgó! *go and sit down!*, pl. ǧutɛgówwɛ! (-ówwé!).
ǧutɛ́g-an v.t. *tell to go and squat, etc., let go and squat, etc.*
ǧu-tír v.t. *go and give* (to other than the speaker).
imperat. ǧútir! (§ 1900), ǧutír! (§ 1948).
mákt
àbɩr‿dámɛŋkɩn, tɛ́ŋ‿kǎr‿ǧútɩr *if he is not at the office, go to his house and give it to him.*
ǧútɩr-an v.t. *tell to go and give* (to other than the speaker), *let go and give* (to other than the speaker).
ǧu-tó v.i. *go and enter, go along in.*
imperat. ǧúto!, ǧutó!
ǧutór-an v.t. *tell to go and enter, etc., let go and enter, etc.*
ǧu-tóg v.t. *go and strike, go and beat.*
imperat. ǧútōk!, ǧutók!
ǧutóg-an v.t. *tell to go and strike, etc., let go and strike, etc.*
ǧu-tóllɛ v.t. *go and pull.*
ǧutóllɛr-an v.t. *tell to go and pull, let go and pull.*
ǧu-tómb(ɩ) v.t. *go and break.*
imperat. ǧutómbi!

ǧutómb-an v.t. *tell to go and break, let go and break.*
ǧu-túrb(ɩ) (-túbb(ɩ)) v.i. *go and lie down, etc.* (s.v. túrb(ɩ)).
imperat. ǧutúrbi!
âɩ‿ǧutubbóskori *I have gone to bed.*
ǧutúrb-an (-túbban) v.t. *tell to go and lie down, etc., let go and lie down, etc.*
ǧ-úwɛ v.t. *go and call.*
imperat. ǧúwɛ!, pl. ǧúwɛwɛ! (ǧúwɛwɛ́!).
ǧúwɛr‿ɛgó (s)*he said 'go and call him (her, it)'.*
ǧúwɛr-an v.t. *tell to go and call, let go and call.*
ǧu-wɛ́ v.t. *go and say, etc.* (s.v. wɛ́).
ǧuwɛ́r-an v.t. *tell to go and say, etc., let go and say, etc.*
ǧu-wɛllɛ́ v.t. *go and kindle, etc.* (s.v. wɛllɛ́).
ǧuwɛllɛ́r-an v.t. *tell to go and kindle, etc., let go and kindle, etc.*
ǧu-wɛ́tɩr v.t. *go and tell, etc.* (other than the speaker, s.v. wɛ́-tɩr).
ind. pres. âɩ‿ǧuwɛ́tɩddi, ɛr‿ǧuwɛ́tɩrɩn (-rī, -rí).
ǧuwɛ́tɩr-an v.t. *tell to go and tell* (other than the speaker), *let go and tell* (other than the speaker).
tékk‿íŋgɩ‿ǧuwɛ́tɩran *let him (her) go and tell him (her) this.*
ǧu-wídɛgɩr (-wɩdɛ́g-, -wᵘdɛ́g-, N. -ɛkɩr, -ɛhɩr-, -ɛ́kɩr-, -ɛ́hɩr-) v.t. *go and cause or allow to turn* (i.), *etc.* (s.v. wídɛgɩr).
ǧu-bùruw-wídɛgɩr (§ 5601, -w-w- <-g-w- § 719) *go and make the girl turn back.*
ǧuwídɛgɩr-an (-wɩdɛ́g-, -wᵘdɛ́g-, N. -ɛkɩr-, -ɛhɩr-, -ɛ́kɩr-, -ɛ́hɩr-) v.t. *tell to go and cause or allow to turn* (i.), *etc., let go and cause or allow to turn* (i.), *etc.*
ǧúdɛ (a) v.t. *dissolve, melt*; (b) v.i. *get dissolved, get melted.*
ind. pres. âɩ‿ǧúdɛrɩ, ɛr‿ǧúdɛn (-dɛ̄, ‿ǧúdɛ́); perf. âɩ‿ǧúdɛgorɩ (N. -eko-, -ɛho-).
sukkárk‿ɛ́ssɩr‿ǧúdɛri *I dissolve (the) sugar in (the) water.*
éssi-sukkárkɩ‿ǧúdɛn (*the) water dissolves (the) sugar.*
súkkar‿ɛ́ssɩr‿ǧúdɛn (*the) sugar dissolves in (the) water.*
ɛn‿ágwaǧ‿ǧúrumɩn‿íččɩr‿ǧúdɛŋ-karámɩr (§ 6214, -ǧ‿ǧ- <-g‿ǧ- § 551) *the woman kneads (a lump of) soft dates that they may melt in the milk.*
ǧúdɛrar (-ràr; §§ 2200 ff., 2210) and
ǧúdɛríd (§§ 2256 ff., 2263) n. *dissolving, dissolution.*
ǧúdɛr-an (§§ 3890 ff., 3899) v.t. *tell to dissolve, etc., let dissolve, etc.*
sukkárkɩ‿ǧúdɛran (a) *tell him (her* § 5083*) to dissolve the sugar;* (b) *let the sugar dissolve.*
ǧúdɛ-bū- (§ 3931) v.i. stat. *be in a dissolved (etc.) state or condition.*
súkkar‿ɛ́ssɩr‿ǧúdɛbūn *the sugar is (has been) dissolved in the water.*
ǧúdɛd-áǧ- (§§ 3877 ff.) v.t. and i. *be in the situation of having dissolved, etc.*
sukkárkɩ‿ǧúdɛdáǧrɩ *I have dissolved the sugar.*
ǧúdɛrɛd-áǧ- v.t. and i. = ǧúdɛdáǧ- (§ 3540).

ğúdɛ-kattı- (N. -ɛha-; §4093) v.p. *be dissolved*, etc.
  tarkíñ‿éssır‿ğúdɛkattıŋ⌒ *fish-paste is dissolved in water.*
ğúg v.i. (a) *catch fire, take fire, ignite, burn;* (b) *flare up, have an outburst of anger* [RSN, §129; TOB, §143, 306].
  ind. pres. aı‿ğúgri⌒, ɛr‿ğúgıŋ⌒ (-gī⌒, -gí⌒); perf. aı‿ğúgkori⌒ (‿ğúkkori⌒).
  imperat. ğúk!
  subj. past aı‿ğúgsı‿ (‿ğúksı‿, -su‿).
  part. pres. ğúgıl‿ *(that) that catches fire,* etc., *burning,* etc., obj. ğugílg(ı)‿, -gi⌒; past ğúgɛl‿ *(that) that caught fire,* etc., *burning,* etc., obj. ğugélg(ı)‿, -gi⌒.
  íg‿ğúgıŋ⌒ (and íǵ‿ğúgıŋ⌒ §551) *the fire lights.*
  bér‿ğúgıŋ⌒ *the wood burns.*
  ím‿bér‿ğúgmunuŋ⌒ *this (that) wood does (will §5369a) not burn.*
  ğáku‿ğúkkoŋ⌒ (-ğ‿ğ-<-d‿ğ- §550) *the stew (has) got burnt.*
  tɛr‿aıgı‿báññıd‿míllıw‿wɛŋgal‿ğúkkori⌒ (-w‿w-<-g‿w- §719) *when (s)he used evil language to me I flared up.*
ğúgar (-gàr‿; §§2200 ff.) n. = ğugíd‿.
ğúgɛd adj. *burnt* [§2522].
  obj. ğŭğédk(ı)‿, -étk(ı)‿, -étt(ı)‿ §2462, -ki⌒, -ti⌒.
  pl. ğŭgɛdı‿.
  kúsu‿ğŭğeduŋ⌒ *the meat is burnt (is in a burnt state).*
  kúsu‿ğŭğédmunuŋ⌒ *the meat is not burnt.*
  kúsu‿ğŭğɛd‿ɛgó⌒ *the meat was burnt.*
  aı‿kúsu‿gugédkı‿bıkálmunuŋ⌒ *I shall not eat burnt meat.*
ğúgɛd-an- (§3910α) v.i. *become burnt, get burnt.*
ğugíd (§§2256 ff.) n. *catching fire, ignition,* etc.
  íŋ‿gugíd‿ (-ŋ‿ğ-<-gn‿ğ- §650) *the ignition of (the) fire.*
  bér‿gugíd‿ *the burning of (the) wood.*
  ğákun‿ğugíd‿ (-n‿ğ-<-dn‿ğ- §612) *the burning of the (a) stew.*
ğúg-bŭ- (ğúggŭ- §546; §3931α) v.i. stat. *be in a burnt state or condition* = ğúgur-bŭ-.
  bér‿ğúgbūŋ⌒ *the wood is (has been) burnt.*
  kå‿ğúgbūŋ⌒ *the house is (has been) burnt.*
ğúg-ur (§3673) v.t. caus. *cause to burn (i.), burn, set fire to* [< *ğúg-ır §1189].
  ind. pres. aı‿gugúrri⌒, ɛr‿gúgurıŋ⌒ (-rī⌒, -rí⌒); fut. aı‿bı̆gugúrri⌒ (buğ-); perf. aı‿gugúrkori⌒.
  imperat. ğúgur!, pl. ğugúrwɛ! (-úrwɛ́!).
  íg‿bérkı‿ğúgurıŋ⌒ *the fire burns the wood.*
  X. ér‿warákkı‿mín‿àukon? *what (lit. how) did you do (have you done) with the paper?*
  Y. ğugúrkori⌒ *I (have) burnt it.*
ğúg (§§2200 ff., 2212) and **ğug(ⁿ)ríd** (§§2256 ff., 2265) n. *burning.*
ğúgur-an (§§3890 ff., 3904) v.t. *tell to burn, let burn.*
ğugur-bɛ́ (§3747ᵉ') v.t. *burn and kill, kill by burning, burn to death.*

ğúgur-bŭ- (§3937) v.i. stat. *be in a burnt state or condition* = ğúgbŭ-.
  bér‿ğúgurbūŋ⌒ *the wood is (has been) burnt.*
  kå‿ğúgurbūŋ⌒ *the house is (has been) burnt.*
ğugurr-ɛg-ág- (§§4071 ff.) v.t. = ğugurɛdól-.
ğugur-ɛ-dól- (-rᵒd- §1178; §4025) and **ğugurr-ɛ-dól-** (-rᵒd-; §4033) v.t. *be about to burn.*
ğugurr-ɛ-ğŭ-bŭ- (§4069) v.t. stat. *be on one's way (coming) to burn.*
ğugurr-ɛ-nóg (§§4048 ff.) v.t. *go to burn.*
ğugurr-ɛ-nóg-bŭ- (-nóggŭ- §546; §4058) v.t. stat. *be on one's way (going) to burn.*
ğugurr-ɛ-tá (§§4060 ff.) v.t. *come to burn.*
ğugurɛd-ág- (§§3877 ff.) v.t. *be in the situation of having burnt.*
ğuguríŋ-ır ("---, N. -ŋkır; §3691) v.t. caus. *cause or allow to burn.*
  N. íkkı‿tókkon‿ğúguriŋkırmɛn⌒ *don't let the fire burn it.*
ğúgur-kattı- ("--- §1940; §4093) v.p. *be burnt.*
ğúgri adj. *hot* [2564].
  obj. ğugríg‿, ğúgrig‿.
  pl. ğugríńč(ı)‿.
  éssı‿ğugríg‿ɛbbıdágori⌒ and éssı‿ğúgríg‿ɛbbıdágori⌒ *I (have) brought (the) hot water.*
  búški‿ğúgr‿ɛgóŋ⌒ *it (the weather) was hot on Monday* (§4665).
  éssıt‿tɛron‿ğúgr‿ɛgıŋ‿nálli⌒ (-t‿t-<-g‿t- §707) *I('ll §5369b) see whether the water is hot.*
  éssı‿ğugríŋ⌒ (-rī⌒, -rí⌒ §942; ‿ğúgrīŋ⌒ §1974) *the water is hot.*
  éssı‿ğugrímunuŋ⌒ *the water is not hot.*
  ğúgr‿én‿dólli⌒ (§6186) *I like it hot.*
ğúgrıgıd n. *heat* [§§2247-8].
  obj. ğugrıgídk(ı)‿, -ítk(ı)‿, -ítt(ı)‿ §2462, -ki⌒, -ti⌒.
ğúgr-an- (§3910α) v.i. *become hot, get hot.*
ğúgram-bŭ- (§§3949 ff.) v.i. stat. *be in a state or condition of becoming hot,* etc.
  ášaı‿duhúrro‿ğugrambúgoŋ⌒ *at noon the weather had turned hot.*
ğugríg-ır (N. -íkır, -íhır; §3701) (a) v.t. caus. *cause or allow to be hot;* (b) v.t. *render hot, heat.*
  ind. pres. aı‿gugrígıddi⌒, ɛr‿gugrígırıŋ⌒ (-rī⌒, -rí⌒).
ğuhúdı‿ *Jew* = juhúdı‿.
ğúkk(ı) v.t. *suck* [imit. §2853].
  ind. pres. aı‿ğúkkırı⌒; perf. aı‿ğúkkıgori⌒ (N. -ıko-, -ıho-).
  imperat. ğúkki!
  bıtán‿tɛron‿ín‿sárbɛğ‿ğúkkıŋ⌒ (-ğ‿ğ- <-g‿ğ- §551) *the child sucks its finger(s §4696a).*
ğúkkar (-kàr‿; §§2200 ff.) and **ğúkkíd** (§§2256 ff.) n. *sucking.*
ğúkk-an (§§3890 ff.) v.t. *tell to suck, let suck.*
ğúkkı-bŭ- (§§3931β) v.i. stat. *be in a sucked state or condition.*
  értı‿ğúkkıbuŋ⌒ *the teat is (has been) sucked.*
ğúkkı-kattı- (N. -ıha-; §4093) v.p. *be sucked.*
  értı‿ğúkkıkattıŋ⌒ *the teat is sucked.*

ğúma n. *week* [< جُمْعَة id.].
  obj. -mag‿.
  pl. ğúmanč(ı)‿.
ğumán-d(ı) (§§2545 ff.) adj. *appertaining to the (a) week, of the (a) week, weekly.*
ğŭntŏd‿, ğŭntod‿ *upper stone for grinding,* s.v. ğŭ‿.
†**ğurnál‿** n. *newspaper* [< جُرْنَال id. < It. *giornale* or Fr. *journal*].
  obj. -nálg(ı)‿, -gi⌒.
  pl. -nálı‿.
ğúrr(ı) (α) v.t. (a) *squeeze (to extract liquid);* (b) *squeeze out (liquid);* (β) v.i. *flow with strong current* [possibly < جَرَّ imperf. stem of جَرَّ *draw* §2844a].
  ind. pres. aı‿ğúrrırı⌒, ɛr‿ğúrrıŋ⌒ (-rī⌒ -rí⌒); perf. aı‿ğúrrıgori⌒ (N .-ıko- -ıho-).
  lēmŭŋgı‿ğúrri⌒ *squeeze the lime(s §4696b).*
  tíğ‿ğúrrıgoŋ⌒ (-ğ‿ğ- <-g‿ğ- §551) *he (has) milked the cow.*
  núgud‿íččığ‿ğúrrıŋ⌒ *the (male) slave draws the milk.*
  mán‿agárr‿úru‿ğúrrıŋ⌒ *at* (-ro‿ §1122) *that point the river has a strong current.*
ğúrrar (-ràr‿; §§2200 ff.) and **ğurríd** (§§2256 ff.) n. *squeezing,* etc.
ğúrr-an (§§3890 ff.) v.t. *tell to squeeze,* etc., *let squeeze,* etc.
  bértı‿ğúrran⌒ (-ğ‿ğ- <-g‿ğ- §551) *let him milk the goat(s §4696d).*
ğúrrı-bŭ- (§3931β) v.i. stat. *be in a squeezed (etc.) state or condition.*
  tí‿ğúrrıbūŋ⌒ *the cow has been milked.*
ğúrrı-dɛn (§§3996-7) v.t. *give (to the speaker) after squeezing,* etc., *squeeze,* etc., *for (the speaker).*
  lēmŭŋgı‿ğúrrıdɛŋ⌒ *squeeze me a lime.*
ğurrɛd-ág- (§§3877 ff.) v.t. *be in the situation of having squeezed,* etc.
  tíğ‿ğúrrɛdágri⌒ (-ğ‿ğ- <-g‿ğ- §551) *I have milked the cow.*
ğurret-tá (§5723; -rɛggıtá §4176) v.t. *come after squeezing,* etc., *go* (§5713) *and squeeze,* etc.
  imperat. ğurrétta!, ğurréggıta!
  bértı‿ğurrétta⌒ *go and milk the goat(s).*
ğurr-ɛttá (-éttă; §5723) v.t. *bring after squeezing,* etc.
  íččığ‿ğurrétta⌒ (-ğ‿ğ- <-g‿ğ- §551) *draw and bring the (some) milk.*
  ğurrétta-kàddır‿úndur‿ (§5605) *after drawing and bringing it put it into the (a) jar.*
ğúrrı-kattı- (N. -ıha-; §4093) v.p. *be squeezed,* etc.
  tí‿ğúrrıkattıgoŋ⌒ *the cow was (has been) milked.*
ğúrrı-tır (§§3998-9) v.t. *give (to other than the speaker) after squeezing,* etc., *squeeze (etc.) for (other than the speaker).*
ğúrtɛ n. *pod of Acacia arabica* (ğówwurúmmɛ‿), Sudan Ar. كَرْط; with collective sg. (§4696b) [< ğur- (*Acacia gummifera* AZN) + -t dim. + -ɛ‿ of n. ess. §2335].

ğurud — hadíje

obj. -tɛg.
pl. -tɛnč(ı).
ğurud n. *saliva*.
obj. ğurúdk(ı), -útk(ı), -útt(ı) §2462, -ki, -ti.
gen. ğurúdn v., -un c.
ğúrum v.t. *knead (i.e. disintegrate by kneading), work with the hand, squeeze, crumble or crush in the hand.*
ind. pres. aĭ ğurúm(ı)ri, ɛr ğurumın (-mĭ, -mí); perf. aĭ ğurúmkori.
— not used of kneading dough:
kaníssɛ ğurumkáttımunun, áttıkattın, ğăkkattın dough is not disintegrated by kneading, it is mixed by beating up, mixed by kneading.
ɛ́nč ágwağ ğurúmran íččır noptónkaram (6214, -ğ ğ- < -g ğ- §551) *(the) women knead (a mass of) soft dates that they may melt (s.v. nob-tó) into the milk.*
ɛ́n umbúdk éssın tŭr ténn ígɛğ ğurumın (-ğ ğ- < -d ğ- §550) *the woman crushes the salt in the water with her hand(s §4696a).*
ğúrumar (-măr; §§2200ff.) and
ğurumíd (§§2256ff.) n. *kneading, etc.*
ğúrum-an (§§3890ff.) v.t. *tell to knead, etc., let knead, etc.*
ğúrum-bŭ- (§3931β) v.i. stat. *be in a kneaded (etc.) state or condition.*
ágwa ğurúmbūn *the lump of soft dates is (i.e. has been) kneaded.*
ğurumɛd-ág- (§§3877ff.) v.t. *be in the situation of having kneaded, etc.*
ğurúm-kattı- (§4093) v.p. *be kneaded, etc.*
ğwír *go and count, etc.* = ğu-ír s.v. ğú.
ğwúndur *go and insert, etc.* = ğúndur s.v. ğú.

háb n. *(a) grain, corn; (b) bead* (=hábba §1393); with collective sg. (§4696b) [< حَبّ *id.*].
obj. hábk(ı), hápk(ı), -ki.
p!. háb.
ín símsım hábun *this is (a) grain of sesame.*
símsım háb bɛ́g élkori (-m h- < -mn h- §821, -b b- < -b w- §517) *I (have) found a grain of sesame.*
fílfıl hápk úndur (-l h- < -ln h- §808) *put a peppercorn (some peppercorns) in.*
hábar (xáb- §1397; -băr) n. *news, information* [< خبر *id.*].
obj. habárk(ı), hábárk(ı), -ki.
pl. hábarı.
aĭgı habárkı dɛ́ndan *they inform me.*
aĭgı habárkı bıdɛ́ndan *they will inform me.*
ɛ́kkı habárkı tíddı *I'll* (§5369b) *let you know.*
ɛ́kkı habárkı bıtíddı *I shall let you know.*
hábarkı-dĕn (§5568) v.t. *give news to, inform, let know, tell (the speaker).*
aĭgı habárkıdɛndan *they inform me.*
aĭgı bıhabárkıdɛ́nın *(s)he will inform me.*
hábarkı-tır (§5569) v.t. *give news to, inform, let know, tell (other than the speaker).*

ɛ́kkı habárkıtíddı *I'll* (§5369b) *let you know.*
ɛ́kkı bıhabárkıtıddı *I shall let you know.*
hábăšı (-bašı, -bɛšı) n. *Abyssinian* [< حَبَشِيّ *id.*].
obj. -šıg.
pl. habăšínč(ı).
hábba n. *(a) grain, corn; (b) bead* (=háb); with collective sg. (§4696b) [< حَبَّة *id.*].
obj. -bag.
pl. -bănč(ı).
márɛn hábba *grain(s) of millet.*
símsım hábba (-m h- < -mn h- §821) *grain(s) of sesame.*
fílfıl hábba (-l h- < -ln h- §808) *peppercorn(s).*
dáwan hábba *pill(s).*
hábbu n. *syphilis, syphilitic sore;* with collective sg. (§4696d) [< حَبّ *pimple*].
obj. -bug.
pl. hábbunč(ı) *syphilitic sores.*
hábbă ádd ımbɛlóskon and
N. hább aĭd ımbɛlóskó *I have contracted syphilis,* lit. *syphilis has risen on me.*
habír n. *guide* [< خبير *id.*].
obj. -írk(ı), -ki.
pl. -írı.
hábıd n. Calotropis procera, *a shrub,* عُشَر (BSP, 347); with collective sg. (§4696b).
obj. habídk(ı), -ítk(ı), -ítt(ı) §2462, -ki, -ti.
gen. hábıdn v., ınn v.c., -ın c.
hábın óllı bún *(s)he (it) is (lies) in the shade of the* C. procera.
hábın bánga and
hábım bánga *Poecilocerus hieroglyphicus, Klug.*
haddám n. *servant* [< خَدَّام *id.*].
obj. -ámg(ı), -gi.
pl. -ámı.
haddám-an- (§3910α) v.i. *become a servant.*
haddáman-ág- (§3926) v.i. *having become a servant, reside; live as a servant.*
hakímgonon haddămanágın *he's the doctor's servant,* lit. *having become a servant he lives with the doctor.*
haddıré v.t. *make ready, prepare* [< imperat. or imperf. stem of خَضَّر *id.* +-ɛ §3635].
ind. pres. aĭ haddıréri; perf. aĭ haddırégori (N. -éko-, -ého-).
imperat. haddıré!
def. imperat. haddıréros!
hammámgı haddırégó *he (has) got the (a) bath ready.*
aĭ ınguh haddıréddı (-h h- < -g h- §559) *I prepare (each of §5456) these.*
tɛr ınguh haddıréırın *(s)he prepares (each of) these.*
haddırérar (-răr; §§2200ff., 2207) and
haddırérıd (§§2256ff., 2260) n. *preparation.*
haddırér-an (§§3890ff., 3899) v.t. *tell to make ready, etc., let make ready, etc.*

hammámgı haddıréran *(a) let him prepare the (a) bath; (b,* §6281) *they prepare the (a) bath.*
haddırḗr-ɛg-ág- (§§4071ff.) v.t. = haddırérɛdól-.
haddırḗr-ɛ-dól- (-rᵒd- §1178; §§4016-17, 4022, 4027) v.t. *be about to make ready, etc.*
haddırḗr-ɛ-ğŭ-bŭ- (§4069) v.t. stat. *be on one's way (coming) to make ready, etc.*
haddırḗr-ɛ-mă- (§§4016-17, 4036, 4041) v.t. *become unable to make ready, etc.*
haddırḗr-ɛ-nóg (§§4048ff.) v.t. *go to make ready, etc.*
haddırḗr-ɛ-nóg-bŭ- (-nóggŭ- §546; §4058) v.t. stat. *be on one's way (going) to make ready, etc.*
haddırḗr-ɛ-tá (§§4060ff.) v.t. *come to make ready, etc.*
haddırḗrɛd-ág- (§§3877ff.) v.t. *be in the situation of having made ready, etc.*
kálgı haddıréredágran *they have prepared (the) food.*
haddıréğ-ır (N. -ékır, -éhır; §3693) *(a)* v.t. caus. *cause or allow to be ready; (b)* v.t. *make ready, prepare.*
ind. pres. aĭ haddırégıddı, ᴸᴵᴸᴬ.
X. hammámgı haddırégır *get the bath ready.*
Y. haddırɛróskori *I have got it ready.*
haddıréğır-an (N. -ékır-, -éhır-; §§3890ff., 3904) v.t. *tell to make ready, etc., let make ready, etc.*
haddıréğıdd-ɛg-ág- (§§4071ff.) v.t. = haddıréregág-.
haddıréğır-ɛ-dól- (N. -ékır-, -éhır-; -rᵒd- §1178; §4022) and
haddıréğıdd-ɛ-dól- (-dᵒd-; §4027) v.t. = haddıréredól-.
haddıréğıdd-ɛ-ğŭ-bŭ- (§4069) v.t. stat. = haddıréreğŭbŭ-.
haddıréğır-ɛ-mă- (N. -ékır-, -éhır-; §4036) and
haddıréğıdd-ɛ-mă- (§4041) v.t. = haddırérema-.
haddıréğıdd-ɛ-nóg (§§4048ff.) v.t. = haddırérenóg.
haddıréğıdd-ɛ-nóg-bŭ- (-nóggŭ- §546; §4058) v.t. stat. = haddırérenógbŭ-.
haddıréğıdd-ɛ-tá (§§4060ff.) v.t. = haddıréretá.
haddıréğırɛd-ág- (N. -ékır-, -éhır-; §§3877ff.) v.t. = haddıréredág-.
kúbkı sáfarn íllăr haddıréğıredágkoran *they had got the boat ready for the journey.*
haddıré-kattı- (§4093) v.p. *be made ready, etc.*
hadíje (-jă, -ja) n. *present, gift* [< هَدِيَّة *id.*].
obj. -jeg.
plur. -jenč(ı).
hadíjeg-ır (N. -ékır, -éhır; §3697) v.t. caus. *cause or allow to be a present, make a present of.*
hadíjegır (N. -ékır, -éhır) and
hadíjegırg(ı) (N. -ékır-, -éhır-; §5587) adv. *as a present, gratis.*
íngı tékkı hadíjegır bıtíddı and
íngı tékkı hadíjegırgı bıtíddı *this I shall give him (her) as a present.*

hadíjɛgır-dĕn (N. -ɛkır-, -ɛhır-; §§3995, 4136) v.t. *give as a present* (to the speaker).
 íŋg⌣äıgı⌣hadíjɛgırdɛŋkoran⌢ *this they gave (have given) me as a present*.
hadíjɛgır-tır (N. -ɛkır-, -ɛhır-; §§3995, 4136) v.t. *give as a present* (to other than the speaker).
 íŋgı⌣tékkı⌣bıhadíjɛgırtıddi⌢ *this I shall give him (her) as a present*.
hǎdır adj. *ready* [< حاضر *id*.].
 obj. hǎdırk(ı)⌣ (§1521), -ki⌢.
 pl. hǎdırı⌣.
hǎdır-an (-dər-; §3910α) v.i. *get (become) ready*.
 hǎdıraŋkogın⌣ɛtta⌢ *when (s)he (it) is (lit. has got) ready, bring him (her, it)*.
hǎdıram-bŭ- (-dər-; §§3949ff.) v.i. stat. *be in a state or condition of getting or having got ready*.
hādırámbⁿ-an (-dər-; -b(w)an; §3964) v.t. *tell to be (let be) in a state of getting or having got ready*.
 imperat. hādırámbⁿan! (-b(w)an!, -b(w)ǎ!, -b(w)á!).
 ɛsmǎŋgı⌣hadərámban⌢ *tell ɛoθmán to get ready and wait (in readiness)*.
hādıran-ɛ-dól- (-dər-; -nᵒd- §1178; §4026) and
hādırand-ɛ-dól- (-dər-; -dᵒd-; §4034) v.i. *be about to get ready, be almost ready*.
hādıraned-ǎg- (-dər-; §3966α) v.i. *be in the condition of having got ready*.
hadmɛ́ v.i. and t. *serve, esp. be a domestic servant* (= hıdmɛ́) [< hadm- < خادم *servant* or خدمة *service* + -ɛ́ §3615].
 ind. pres. āı⌣hadmɛ́ri⌢.
 imperat. hadmɛ́!
 āı⌣hartúmır⌣hadmɛ́gori⌢ *I was a servant at Khartoum*.
 āı⌣tékkı⌣hadmɛ́gori⌢ *I served him (her)*.
 āı⌣ténnar⌣hadmɛ́gori⌢ *I (have) served in his (her) house* (s.v. -när⌣).
hadmɛ́rar⌣ (-rǎr-; §§2200f., 2207) and **hadmɛ́ríd**⌣ (§§2256ff., 2260) n. *service*.
hafír⌣ n. *Hafir* (on map), a village on the left bank of the Nile about 4 miles below Argo Island [< حفير *pit*].
 obj. -írk(ı)⌣, -ki⌢.
hág⌣ n. (a) *right, justice*; (b) *lawful right, rights, due*; (c) *truth* [حق *id*. §1370]; (d) *law* (= hágg(ı)⌣).
 obj. hágk(ı)⌣, hákk(ı)⌣, -ki⌢.
 gen. hágn⌣v., hán⌣c.
 pl. hágı⌣.
 gádı⌣hákkɛd⌣āhhokmɛ́n⌢ *the judge habitually decides according to justice*.
 āı⌣án⌣hákkı⌣dólli⌢ *I want my rights*.
 álı⌣tén⌣hákk⌣ɛlkoná⌢ *did ɛáli get (has ɛáli got) his rights?*
 hákkı⌣báñi⌢ *tell the truth*.
 gádı⌣hákkı⌣wɛn⌢ *the judge states the law*.
 hán⌣kıtáb⌣ *book of the law, legal book*.
hágɛ⌣ n. *stalk, esp. of millet*; with collective sg. (§4696b) [RSN, §129 s.v. *agɛ́*].
 obj. -gɛg⌣.
 pl. hagɛnč(ı)⌣.

márɛn⌣hágɛ⌣ *millet-stalk(s)*.
makádan⌣hágɛ⌣ *maize-stalk(s)*.
hágg(ı)⌣ n. *right, justice, etc*. = hág⌣ [< حقّ *id*. §1370].
 obj. hággıg⌣.
 pl. hággınč(ı)⌣.
 āı⌣án⌣hággıd⌣dólli⌢ (-d⌣d- <-g⌣d- §534) *I want my right(s)*.
 hággıb⌣báñi⌢ (-b⌣b- < -g⌣b- §519) *tell the truth*.
haggán⌣ adj. (a) *right, just, equitable, fair*; (b) *lawful, legally due*; (c) *truthful*; (d) *legal* [< حقّاني *id*.].
 obj. -nıg⌣.
 pl. -nınč(ı)⌣.
 ín⌣ógığ⌣haggánın⌢ *this man is just*.
hág⌣ (hɛ́g⌣, híg⌣) n. *pilgrimage* (= hágg(ı)⌣) [< حجّ *id*. §§1328, 1373].
 obj. hágk(ı)⌣, háck(ı)⌣, hácč(ı)⌣ §523, -ki⌢, -či⌢.
hǎg⌣ n. *pilgrim* [< حاج *id*. §1372].
 obj. hágk(ı)⌣, háck(ı)⌣, hácč(ı)⌣ §523, -ki⌢, -či⌢.
 pl. hǎgı⌣.
 tɛr⌣hágun⌢ *(s)he is a pilgrim*.
hǎgɑ⌣ (-gɑ⌣, -gɛ⌣) n. (a) *object, thing, something*; (b) *subject, matter* [< حاجة *id*.].
 obj. -gɑ̆g⌣, -gag⌣, -gɛg⌣.
 pl. -gǎnč(ı)⌣, -ganč(ı)⌣, -gɛnč(ı)⌣.
hǎgɑ-kıñ(ı)⌣ (-gak-, -gɛk-; §§2536-7) adj. (a) *devoid of anything, without anything, bare*; (b) *destitute, without resources*.
hǎgɑkıññır⌣ (-gak-, -gɛk-; §6007) adv. *in destitution*.
 X. saɛ́d⌣mabsúdrɛ́? *is Saɛid content?*
 Y. wǎran, tɛr⌣hǎgakıññır⌢ *no, he is in destitution*.
 Z. hǎgakıññır-ágın⌢ *he is (lives) in destitution*.
hǎgɑkıññıg-ır (⌣, -gak-, -gɛk-, N. -ıkır, -ıhır; §§3703, 5708) v.t. caus. *cause or allow to be destitute, etc., render or leave destitute*.
 sǎmɑr⌣tékkı⌣hǎgakıññıgírko⌢ *drinking (has) brought him to beggary*.
hǎgɑ-kō- (-gakō-, -gɛkō-; §§4109, 4115) v.i. *have property, have money, be well-to-do*.
 part. pres. hǎgɑkōl⌣ (-gak-, -gɛk-) (*one) that has property, well-to-do*; obj. hɑğɑkólg(ı)⌣ (-gak-, -gɛk-).
 tɛr⌣hǎgɑkólun⌢ (-gak-, -gɛk-) *(s)he's well-to-do*.
 neg. part. pres. hǎgɑkómɛnıl⌣ (-gak-, -gɛk-) *(one) that has no property, destitute*.
hágğ(ı)⌣ (hǎgı⌣, hɛ́gğ⌣, hígğ(ı)⌣) n. *pilgrimage* (= hág⌣) [< حجّ *id*. §§1328, 1373].
 obj. hág(ğ)ıg⌣.
 hággır⌣nókkoran⌢ *they went (have gone) on the pilgrimage*.
 hággır⌣ágın⌢ *(s)he is on pilgrimage*.
hağğırɛ́ v.t. *forbid, prohibit* [< a stem of حجر or تحجّر *id*. + -ɛ́ §3645].

ind. pres. āı⌣hağğırɛ́ri⌢ (occ. -rɛ́ri⌢ §1073); perf. āı⌣hağğırɛ́gori⌢ (N. -ɛ́ko-, -ɛ́ho-).
imperat. hağğırɛ́!
subj. past āı⌣hağğırɛ́sı⌣ (-su⌣).
def. imperat. hağğırɛ́rɛt!
hağğırɛ́rar⌣ (-rǎr-; §§2200ff., 2207) and **hağğırɛ́ríd**⌣ (§§2256ff., 2260) n. *prohibition*.
hağğırɛ́r-an (§§3890ff., 3899) v.t. *tell to forbid, etc., let forbid, etc*.
hağğırɛ́-bŭ- (§3931β) v.i. stat. *be (in a state of being) forbidden, be prohibited*.
hağğırɛ́red-ǎg- (§§3877ff.) v.t. *be in the situation or attitude of having forbidden, etc*.
 íŋgı⌣gǎdı⌣hağğırɛ́redágın⌢ *the judge has prohibited this*.
 hukúma⌣núgudığ⌣ğandáŋgı⌣hağğırɛ́redágın⌢ (-ğ⌣ğ- < -g⌣ğ- §551) *the government has prohibited trading in slaves*.
hağğırɛ́-kattı- (N. -ɛ́ha-; §4093) v.p. *be forbidden, etc*.
hǎgib⌣ n. *eyebrow*; with collective sg. (§4696a) [< حاجب *id*.].
 obj. hǎgíbk(ı)⌣, -ípk(ı)⌣, -ki⌢.
 gen. hǎgın⌣v., -ım⌣c.
 pl. hǎg(ı)bı⌣.
 míssın⌣hǎgıb⌣ *eyebrow(s)*.
hǎgım-d(ı)⌣ (§§2545ff.) adj. *appertaining to the eyebrow, of the eyebrow, eyebrow's*.
hakím⌣ n. *doctor* [< حكيم *id*.].
 obj. -ímg(ı)⌣, -gi⌢.
 pl. -ímı⌣.
hǎkum⌣ n. *ruler, governor* [< حاكم *id*.].
 obj. hākúmg(ı)⌣, -gi⌢.
 pl. hākumı⌣.
hál⌣ (xál⌣) n. *vinegar* [< خلّ *id*.].
 obj. hálg(ı)⌣, -gi⌢.
 ín⌣hálun⌢ *this is vinegar*.
hǎl n. *state, condition* [< حال *id*.].
 obj. hálg(ı)⌣, -gi⌢.
 ɛn⌣hǎl⌣mínɛ⌣bún? (ɛh⌣hǎl⌣ §561) *how are you?* (كيف حالك).
 tɛn⌣hǎl⌣mínkírırɛ́? (tɛh⌣hǎl⌣) *how is (s)he (it)?*
 X. sɛraŋágmɛn? *how are you?* (s.v. sɛ́rɛ⌣).
 Y. árton⌣ɛh⌣hálgı⌣sɛrɛ́gırın⌢ *God bless you!* (§6252)
 X. sɛrambɛ́jjıgomɛn? *good morning* (s.v. sɛ́rɛ⌣).
 Y. árton⌣ɛh⌣hálgı⌣sɛrɛ́gırın⌢ = *good morning*.
 X. (N.) sɛrambɛ́jjıkomɛn? *good morning* (s.v. sɛ́rɛ⌣).
 Y. (N.) árton⌣ɛh⌣hálgı⌣sɛrɛ́kırın⌢ = *good morning*.
hála⌣ n. *desert, uninhabited country, bush, veldt* [< خلا *id*.].
 obj. hálag⌣.
 hálar⌣nókkó⌣ and
 hál⌣áŋkó⌣ *(s)he (it) went (has gone) into the desert (etc.)*.
 X. íččın⌣noğğɛtta⌣ (-nun-<-gun- §625) *go along (-gu-) and fetch (the, some) milk*.

halás⌣ — hāmεdn-ā́rt(ı)⌣

Y. úrtıncı⌣hálar⌢ *the goats are out at pasture*, lit. *...in the country* (§6007).
halán-d(ı)⌣ (§§2545 ff.) adj. *appertaining to the desert, etc., wild*.
hál-an- (§3910 β) v.i. *go to the desert, etc.*
ind. pres. āı⌣hálandi⌢, εr-hálanın⌢ (-nı⌢, -ní⌢); fut. āı⌣bıhálandi⌢ (⌣buh-); perf. āı⌣hálaŋkori⌢.
hálam-bŭ- (§3950 β) v.i. stat. *be in a state of motion towards the desert, etc., be on one's way to the desert, etc., be going to the desert, etc.*
halanεd-ā́g- (§3966 β) v.i. *be in the situation of having gone to the desert, etc.*
halás⌣ adv. *at an end, finished, done with* [< خَلَاص id.].
halásun⌢ and
halás-taran⌢ *it's an end, etc.*
halás-an- (§3910 α) v.i. *come to an end, get finished, etc.*
sεrĩ⌣halásaŋkım⌣márεt⌣tír⌢ (-t⌣t- <-g⌣t- §707) *when the barley comes to an end give him (her, it) millet.*
šāı⌣halásáŋkıs⌣sıǧarat⌣tír⌢ (-s⌣s- <-n⌣s- §680) *when tea is over give them cigarettes.*
halásam-bŭ- (§§3949 ff.) v.i. stat. *be in a state or condition of coming to an end, etc.*
halāsan-ε-dól- (-nᵒd- §1178; §3975) and
halāsand-ε-dól- (-dᵒd-; §3978) v.i. *be about to come to an end, etc.*
ǧεllı⌣halásanεdóln⌢ (-andεdóln⌢) *the work is nearly done.*
bún⌣halásandεdóln⌢ *the coffee is almost finished.*
*halásanεd-ā́g- not heard.
halbıtέ (xal-; §1397) v.t. *confuse, mix, mix up, muddle* [< imperf. or imperat. stem of Sudan Ar. خَلْبَط id. (=لْجَبَط)+-έ §3634].
ind. pres. āı⌣halbıtέri⌢; perf. āı⌣halbıtέgori⌢ (N. -έko-, -έho-).
imperat. halbıtέ!
εr⌣hısábkı⌣halbıtέgon⌢ and (N.) εr⌣hısápkı⌣xalbıtέkõ⌢ *you (have) muddled the account.*
halbıtέrar⌣ (xal-; -rár⌣; §§2200 ff., 2207) and
halbıtεríd⌣ (xal-; §§2256 ff., 2260) n. *confusion, etc.*
halbıtεrídk-ır-halbıtέ (xal-, -ītkır-, -ıttır-, -xal-; §4156) v.t. *confuse (etc.) utterly, thoroughly.*
tέr⌣hısábkı⌣halbıtεrídkırhalbıtέgon⌢ *(s)he (has) got the account into a thorough muddle.*
halbıtέ-bŭ- (xal-; §3931 β) v.i. stat. *be in a confused (etc.) state or condition.*
hısáb⌣tεmámmunun, halbıtέbūn⌢ *the account isn't right, it's muddled.*
halbıtέrεd-ā́g- (xal-; §§3877 ff.) v.t. *be in the situation of having confused, etc.*
halbıtέg-ır (xal-; N. -έkır, -έhır; §3681) v.t. caus. *cause or allow to confuse, etc.*
ind. pres. āı⌣halbıtέgıddi⌢,
halbıtέ-katti- (xal-; N. -έha-; §4093) v.p. *be confused, etc.*
halέ v.t. *scare, startle* [prob. < حَلّ *striking* + -έ §3626].

ind. pres. āı⌣halέri⌢; perf. āı⌣halέgori⌢ (N. -έko-, -έho-).
imperat. halέ!
halέrar⌣ (-rár⌣; §§2200 ff., 2207) and
halεríd⌣ (§§2256 ff., 2260) n. *scaring, etc.*
hálε-hatti- (hálaha-, hálha- §1031; §4101) v.p. *be scared, etc.*
halífa⌣ (xa-, -fa⌣, -fε⌣) n. (a) *caliph, vicar*; (b) *the Khalifa* عبد الله التعايشي [< خَلِيفَة id.].
obj. -fág⌣, -fag⌣, -fεg⌣.
pl. -fánč(ı)⌣, -fanč(ı)⌣, -fεnč(ı)⌣.
hálıs (xǎ-) adv. *quite, very* [< خَالِص id.].
— *follows an adjective, with which it can form an adjective-complex* (§4988):
sέrεn⌣xálıs⌢ *(s)he (it) is very good.*
ís⌣sέrε⌣hálısun⌢ (-s⌣s- <-n⌣s- §680) *this (that) is very good.*
hallıs-**έ** (xal-) v.t. (a) *save, deliver, rescue*; (b) *finish, complete* [< imperf. or imperat. stem of خَلَّص id. + -έ §3635].
ind. pres. āı⌣hallısέri⌢; perf. āı⌣hallısέgori⌢ (N. -έko-, -έho-).
imperat. hallısέ!
ǧεllıh⌣hallısέgó⌢ (-h⌣h- <-g⌣h- §559) *(s)he (has) finished the work.*
hallısέrar⌣ (xal-, -rár⌣; §§2200 ff., 2207) and
hallısεríd⌣ (xal-; §§2256 ff., 2260) n. *saving, etc.*
hallısέr-an (xal-; §§3890 ff., 3899) v.t. *tell to save, etc., let save, etc.*
εsmáŋgı⌣ǧεllıh⌣hallısέran⌣ (h⌣h- <-g⌣h- §559) *tell εoθmán to finish the work.*
hallısέ-bŭ- (xal-; §3931 β) v.i. stat. *be in a saved (etc.) state or condition.*
ǧεllı⌣hallısέbun⌢ *the work is (i.e. has been) finished.*
hallısέr-εg-ā́g- (xal-; §§4071 ff.) v.t. = hallısεrεdól-.
hallısέr-ε-dól- (xal-; -rᵒd- §1178; §§4016-17, 4022, 4027) v.t. *be about to save, etc.*
hallısέr-ε-ǧŭ-bŭ- (xal-; §4069) v.i. stat. *be on one's way (coming) to save, etc.*
hallısέr-ε-mā́- (xal-; §§4016-17, 4036, 4041) v.t. *become unable to save, etc.*
wīlgı⌣ǧεllı⌣hallısέrεmágoran⌢ (-h⌣h- <-g⌣h- §559) *they couldn't finish the work yesterday.*
hallısέr-ε-nóg- (xal-; §§4048 ff.) v.t. *go to save, etc.*
hallısέr-ε-nóg-bŭ- (xal-; -nóggŭ- §546; §4058) v.t. stat. *be on one's way (going) to save, etc.*
ǧεllıh⌣hallısεrεnóggúran⌢ *they are on their way to finish the work.*
hallısέr-ε-tā́- (xal-; §§4060 ff.) v.t. *come to save, etc.*
hallısέrεd-ā́g- (xal-; §§3877 ff.) v.t. *be in the situation of having saved, etc.*
hallısέ-katti- (xal-; N. -έha-; §4093) v.p. *be saved, etc.*
hallısέros-tā́ (xal-; -ottá §714; §§4180-4; -osgıtá, -ozgı-, -oggı- §4185) v.t. *come after saving, etc., just* (s.v. -tā́) *save, etc., go and* (§5713) *save, etc.*
imperat. hallısεrósta! (-ótta!, -ósgıta!, -ózgı-, -óggı-).
tέkki⌣hallısεrótta⌢ *just finish it (go and finish it).*

hallúf⌣ n. *boar, pig* [< خَلُّوف *boar*].
obj. -úfk(ı)⌣, -ki⌢.
pl. -úfı⌣.
hálwa (xál-) n. (a) *room or shed (usually near mosque) for accommodation of strangers*; (b) *village school, primary school* [< خَلْوَة id.].
obj. -wag⌣.
pl. -wanč(ı)⌣.
hamártε n. *a deeply-rooted grass, Desmostachya cynosuroides, Stapf.* (BSP, 674), خَلْفَاء
obj. -tεg⌣, -ártεg⌣ §1532.
hamartέn-d(ı)⌣ (§§2545 ff.) adj. *appertaining to D. cynosuroides.*
hámbu⌣ n. *dōm-palm, Hyphaene thebaica, Mart.* (BSP, 600); *with collective sg.* (§4696b) [§2299; RSN, §129].
obj. -bug⌣.
pl. -bunč(ı)⌣.
hámbun⌣úmbu *trunk(s) of dōm-palm.*
hambún-d(ı)⌣ (§§2545 ff.) adj. *appertaining to the dōm-palm, of the dōm-palm.*
obj. -dıg⌣.
pl. -dınč(ı)⌣.
hambundíb⌣ (-díp⌢) n. *Hambundíb Id.* (on map) *an island now attached to the left bank of the Nile about twelve miles above Ed-Débba*ʰ [*Dōm-palm Castle*].
obj. -díbk(ı)⌣, -dípk(ı)⌣, -ki⌢.
hambundıbnā́rt(ı)⌣, -ti⌢ *the island of Hambundíb.*
hambu-kól⌣ (§§2572 ff.) adj. *having dōm-palms.*
obj. -kólg(ı)⌣, -gi⌢.
mán⌣ágar⌣hambukólun⌢ *that place has dōm-palms.*
hambu-kól n. *Abu-Dóm, a village on the left bank of the Nile about fifteen miles above Ed-Débba*ʰ *and twenty-five below Umbukól.*
hambukóllo⌣ (s.v. -r⌣) *at (to) Abu-Dóm.*
hambukólló⌢ (§6007) *(s)he (it) is (they are) at Abu-Dóm.*
hamdέ v.t. *praise* [< حَمْد *praise* + -έ §3615].
ind. pres. āı⌣hamdέri⌢, εr-hamdέn⌢ (-dέ⌢, -dέ⌢; occ. -dέn⌢, -dέ⌢, -dέ⌢ §1073); perf. āı⌣hamdέgori⌢ (N. -έko-, -έho-).
imperat. hamdέ!
X. εr⌣sεranágmεn? *are you (not) well?*
Y. ā́rtıh⌣hamdέri⌢ (-h⌣h- <-g⌣h- §559) *I praise God, i.e.* الْحَمْدُ لِلَّه i.e. *yes, thanks.*
hamdέrar⌣ (-rár⌣; §§2200 ff., 2207) and
hamdεríd⌣ (§§2256, 2260) n. *praising.*
hamdέ-katti- (N. -έha-; §4093) v.p. *be praised.*
hámdılıllá! and
hámdıllá! interj. *praise be to God!* [< الْحَمْدُ لِلَّه (§1389), abbr. ḥamdıllá*ʰ id.].
X. εr⌣sεranágmεn? *are you (not) well?*
Y. hámdıllá! (yes), *praise be to God!*
hāmεdn-ā́rt(ı)⌣ (-εnnā́- §624; -ti⌢; §4810) n. *Hamed Narti* (on map), *a village (district) to the south-east of*

hamís — harbån

Argo Island, now part of right bank [Ḥámɪd's Island].
  obj. -tɪg⌣.
  hāmɛdnårtɪ⌣maltanóskó⌢ Ḥámɪd's Island has become part of the east bank.

hamís (xa-) n. *Thursday* [< خَمِيس in اَلْخَمِيس *id.* §1389].
  obj. -ísk(ɪ)⌣, -ki⌢.
  gen. -ísn⌣v., -ís⌣c. §§855, 857–9.
  pl. -ísu⌣.
  hamís⌣jóm⌣ (§4813) and hamís⌣nahår⌣ (nȧh-, nɛh-; §4813) *Thursday.*
  hamísk(ɪ)⌣ (-ki⌢; §4665), hamísɪr⌣, hamís⌣nahårk(ɪ)⌣, -ki⌢ and hamís⌣nahårro⌣ *on Thursday.*
  hamísɪrtōn⌣ and hamís⌣nahårrotōn⌣ *since Thursday.*
  hamís⌣móŋkon⌣, hamís⌣bókkon⌣ and hamíz⌣bókkon⌣ (-z⌣b- < -sn⌣b- §728) *till Thursday.*
  ásal⌣xamísun⌣ (-ísū⌣, -ísú⌣ §939) *tomorrow is Thursday.*
  hamísn-d(ɪ)⌣ (xa-; §§2545 ff.) adj. *appertaining to Thursday, Thursday's.*

hammám⌣ n. *bath* [< حَمَّام *id.*].
  obj. -åmg(ɪ)⌣, -gi⌢.
  pl. -åmɪ⌣.

hammúr⌣ n. *Hamur (on map), an island about 3 miles above Old Dóngola.*
  obj. -úrk(ɪ)⌣, -ki⌢.
  hammúrnårt(ɪ)⌣ and **hammúnnårt(ɪ)⌣** (§628; -ti⌢) *the island of H.*

hamsín (xa-; §956a) card. num. *fifty* [< خَمْسِين *id.*].
  obj. -íŋ(ɪ)⌣, -gi⌢.
  hamsín-d(ɪ)⌣ (xa-; §§2545 ff., 2738) adj. *appertaining to 50, of 50, 50's.*
  hamsın-ínt(ɪ)⌣ (-sínınt(ɪ)⌣; §2742) ord. num. *fiftieth.*
  hamsíŋ-kırı⌣ (-kírı⌣ §1701; §2736) num. adj. *about fifty.*

hánag⌣ n. (a) *palate*, (b) *lower jaw* [< حَنَك *id.*].
  obj. hanágk(ɪ)⌣, -ákk(ɪ)⌣, -ki⌢.
  gen. hánagn⌣v., -naŋ⌣c.
  pl. hánagɪ⌣.

hánag⌣, -ak⌣ n. *Hannek (on map), a village on the left bank of the Nile about 7 miles below Kɛ́rma, just in Máḥas.*
  obj. hanákk(ɪ)⌣, -ki⌢.
  hánagɪr⌣ (s.v. -r⌣) *at (to) H.*
  hánagɪr⌣ (§6007) *(s)he (it) is (they are) at H.*

hándag⌣ n. *El-Xándaq, a small town (and district) on the left bank of the Nile, forty-four miles south of El-Ordi (§1389).*
  obj. handágk(ɪ)⌣, -ákk(ɪ)⌣, -ki⌢.
  gen. hándagn⌣v., -aŋ⌣c.
  [Called by the Arabs الخندق *the trench, moat,* of which I see no traces at Hándag; possibly Κανδάκη (Strabo, Bk. xvii, chap. 1, §54, Acts viii. 27) = handákkɪ⌣; see Budge in *Cook's Handbook for Egypt and the Sudan* (1906), p. 737].

ám⌣bélɛd⌣hándak-tànnan⌢ *my country is El-Xándaq.*
  hándagɪr⌣ (hándágɪr⌣ §1532; §6007) *at (to) El-Xándaq.*
  hándagɪr⌣ (⌢) *(s)he (it) is (they are) at El-Xándaq.*
hándag-an- (§3910β) v.i. *go to El-Xándaq.*
  hándagaŋkoran⌢ *they went (have gone) to El-Xándaq.*
  bɪhándagandan⌢ *they will go to El-Xándaq.*
  handaganóskorandɛ́? *have they gone to El-Xándaq?*
hándagam-bŭ- (§3950β) v.i. stat. *be in a state of motion towards El-Xándaq, be on one's way to El-Xándaq.*
  bɪhándagambūran⌢ *they will be on their way to El-Xándaq.*
handaganɛd-åg- (§3966β) v.i. *be in the situation of having gone to El-Xándaq.*
  handaganɛdågran⌢ *they have gone to El-Xándaq.*
handagan-nog(ʰ)r-ɛg-åg- (§3980) v.i. = handagannogɛdól-.
handagan-nog-ɛ-dól- (-gᵒd- §1178; §3979) and
handagan-nog(ʰ)r-ɛ-dól- (-rᵒd-; §3981) v.i. *be about to go off to El-Xándaq.*
  handagannogrɛdóllan⌢ *they are just going to go off to El-Xándaq.*
handagan-nog-ɛ-må- (§3982) and
handagan-nog(ʰ)r-ɛ-må- (§3983) v.i. *become unable to go off to El-Xándaq.*
  handagannogɛmågoran⌢ *they couldn't (have become unable to) go off to El-Xándaq.*

hannág⌣, -åk⌣ n. *Khanag (on map), a village on the left bank of the Nile about 2 miles above El-Ordi.*
  obj. -ågk(ɪ)⌣, -åkk(ɪ)⌣, -ki⌢.

hánu⌣ *ass, donkey* [< hán- onom. (cp. hóŋ(ɪ) *bray* حَنّ (of camel) *whinny* LA, s.v., SNR, x, p. 212, 40) + -u⌣ §2337; RSN, §129].
  obj. hánug⌣.
  pl. hánuɪ⌣, -nwɪ⌣.
  hánu⌣kárrɪ⌣ *she-ass.*
  gókkan⌣hánu⌣ (-kah⌣há- §560) and hánuŋ⌣gókka⌣ *large pigeon.*
  †šártɪn⌣hánu⌣ *bicycle.*
  hánun⌣tŭnd(ɪ)⌣ *donkey-girth.*
  — indicating stupidity:
  aı⌣tén⌣dógor⌣hánun⌣nalkómunun⌢ (-n⌣n- < -g⌣n- §625) *I never saw (have never seen) a greater donkey than him.*
  hanún-d(ɪ)⌣ (§§2545 ff.) adj. *appertaining to (an) ass, asinine.*
  hánu-kırı⌣ (§2539–40) adj. *like an ass, resembling an ass.*
  hánuɪkırínčın⌢ (§§1702, 1970) *they are like asses.*
  hánu-kōl⌣ (§2576) adj. *possessing a donkey or donkeys.*
  obj. hanukólg(ɪ)⌣, -gi⌢ (§1706).
  ógɪg⌣hánukól-lɛn⌣nálkori⌢ (-l-l- < -l-w- §580, -n⌣n- < -g-n- §625) *I saw a man with a donkey.*
  hánuɪ-kōl⌣ (-nwɪ-; §2577) adj. *possessing donkeys.*

hanun-tŏd⌣ (§2366) n. *ass's colt or foal.*
  voc. -tŏt!, -tó!
  obj. -tŏdk(ɪ)⌣, -tŏtk(ɪ)⌣, -tŏkk(ɪ)⌣, -tŏtt(ɪ)⌣ (§2462), -ki⌣, -ti⌢.
  gen. -tŏdn⌣v., -tŏnn⌣v.c., -tŏn⌣c. (§§778–88).
  pl. hánuntonɪ⌣, ⌣ (§1689).
  hanuntódun⌢ *it's an (the) ass's colt (foal).*
hánu-tod⌣ (§2369) (a) *poor donkey, indifferent donkey;* (b) = hánu⌣.
  voc. hánutŏt!, hánutó!
  obj. -tŏdk(ɪ)⌣, -tŏtk(ɪ)⌣, -tŏkk(ɪ)⌣, -tŏtt(ɪ)⌣, -ki⌣, -ti⌢.
  gen. -tŏdn⌣v., -tŏnn⌣v.c., -tŏn⌣c.
  pl. hánutonɪ⌣.
  hánutodun⌢ *it's a (poor) donkey.*
  hánutokk⌣ɛ́tta⌢ *bring the donkey.*

*hárab- [< خَرَب v.t. *ruin*].
  hárab-kattı- (-apka-, ⌣; §§4093, 4101) v.p. *be ruined, be destroyed, be spoilt* (= harbɛ́kattı-).

hárag⌣ n. *sound of moving object(s), noise made by movement* (= háraka⌣) [< حَرَك *motion, stirring* §1357].
  obj. harágk(ɪ)⌣, -ákk(ɪ)⌣, -ki⌢.
  gen. háragn⌣v., -raŋ⌣c.
  pl. háragɪ⌣.
  hárag⌣nalkáttımunun, ulúkkɛg⌣gíğɪrkattın⌢ (-g⌣g- < -d⌣g- §545) *hárag cannot (§5704) be seen, it is perceived by the ear.*
  tén⌣hárag⌣dúlun⌢ *the noise (s)he (it) makes (in moving) is great, lit. his (her, its) noise is great.*
  tūruŋ⌣hárag⌣dúlun⌢ (-ŋ⌣h- < -gn⌣h- §650a) *the wind makes a great noise.*
  gátɪrn⌣hárag⌣v. (and ⌣, ⌣v. §1690) *the sound of the train.*
  gátɪrn⌣harákk(ɪ)⌣ (>⌣ §1692) *the sound (obj.) of the train.*
  gátɪn⌣harákkɪ⌣gɪğírran⌢ (gátɪnn⌣ha-, -tɪrn-ha- §622) *they hear the sound of the train.*
  turumbíl⌣nokkáttɪn, harákk⌣åumunun⌢ *the car goes well and (§6239) makes no noise.*
  harákkɪ⌣kŏmunan⌢ *they make (lit. have) no noise (in moving).*

haråğ⌣ (xar-) n. *tax* [< خَرَاج *id.*].
  obj. -åğk(ɪ)⌣, -åčk(ɪ)⌣, -åčč(ɪ)⌣ §523, -ki⌣, -či⌢.
  pl. -åğɪ⌣.
  árɪn⌣haråğ⌣ *land-tax.*
  haråñ-d(ɪ)⌣ (xar-; §§2545 ff.) adj. *appertaining to a (the) tax.*

háraka⌣ n. *sound of moving object(s), noise made by movement* (= hárag⌣) [< حَرَكَة (a) *motion, stirring,* (b) *sound or noise of* (a)].
  obj. -kag⌣.
  pl. harakánč(ɪ)⌣.

háram⌣ n. *pyramid* [< هَرَم *id.*].
  obj. harámg(ɪ)⌣, -gi⌢.
  pl. háramɪ⌣.

harbån⌣ (xar-) adj. *ruined, destroyed, spoilt* [< خَرْبَان *id.*].
  obj. -åŋ(ɪ)⌣, -gi⌢.
  pl. -ånɪ⌣.

99

harbḗ — hḗǧ⏑

aı⏑tén⏑táblag⏑ámın ḗmunū̆, xarbắnū⌒ *I don't trust his (her, its) padlock, it's spoilt.*

harbḗ (xar-; §1397) v.t. *ruin, destroy, spoil* [< خرب *devastation* + -ḗ §3615].
  ind. pres. aı⏑harbḗri⌒; perf. aı⏑harbḗgori⌒ (N. -ḗko-, -ḗho-).
  imperat. harbḗ!
  part. pres. harbḗl⏑ *(one) that ruins, etc.*
  part. past harbḗrɛl⏑ *(one) that ruined, etc.*
  kıtábıh⏑harbḗgoran⌒ (-h⏑h- < -g⏑h- §559) *they (have) destroyed the books.*
  híbır⏑kádeh⏑harbḗgon⌒ *the ink (has) spoiled the cloth.*
  ém⏑mɛrkúbkı⏑dúkkı⏑sıǧǧắǧah⏑harbḗmɛnınn⏑íllár⌒ *take off your slippers in order not to spoil the carpet.*

harbḗrar⏑ (xar-, -rár⏑; §§2200ff., 2207) and
harbḗrid⏑ (xar-; §§2256ff., 2260) n. *ruining, destruction.*

harbēr-ɛ-dól- (xar-; -rᵒd- §1178; §§4016-17, 4022, 4027) v.t. *be about to ruin, etc.*

harbēr-ɛ-mǎ- (xar-; §§4016-17, 4036, 4041) v.t. *become unable to ruin, etc.*

harbḗ-kattı- (xar; N. -ḗha-; §4093) v.p. *be ruined, etc.*
  N. **hárbɛ-kattı-** (xar-; §4101) v.p. = harbḗkattı-.

hárr(ı) v.i. *(of dog) growl* [onom.].
  wɛ́l⏑hárrın⌒ *the dog growls.*
  wɛ́l⏑hárrıgó⌒ *the dog growled.*

†**hartíd⏑** (xar-; §2408) n. *rhinoceros* [< خرتيت *id.*].
  obj. -ídk(ı)⏑, -ítk(ı)⏑, -ki⌒.
  pl. -ídı⏑.

hartū́m⏑ (xar-) n. *Khartoum, capital of the Sudan* [< خرطوم in ٱلخرطوم §1389].
  obj. -ū́mg(ı)⏑, -gi⌒.
  gen. -ū́mn⏑v., -ū́m⏑c.
  hartū́mır⏑ắgran⌒ *they live in Khartoum.*
  hartū́m⏑háwa⏑ *the climate of Khartoum.*

hartū́m-d(ı)⏑ (xar-; §§2545ff.) adj. *appertaining to Khartoum, of Khartoum.*

hartū́m-an- (xar-; §3910β) v.i. *go to Khartoum.*

hartū́mam-bŭ- (xar-; §3950β) v.i. stat. *be in a state of motion towards Khartoum, be on one's way to Khartoum (etc. as s.v. hándag).*

hásab (-sáb⏑, -sɛb⏑) n. *care, attention* [< حسب *consideration, esteem*].
  obj. hasábk(ı)⏑, -ápk(ı)⏑, -ki⌒.
  ín⏑án⏑hásabır⌒ (§5858) *this (one) is in my (our) care.*
  ártın⏑hásabır! *good-bye!*, lit. *(may you be) in God's care!*, reply to hɛ́rro! s.v. hɛ́r⏑.

hásɛd⏑ n. *stumps of crop remaining after harvest, stubble* [< حصد *reaping* §1358].
  obj. hasédk(ı)⏑, -étk(ı)⏑, -étt(ı)⏑ §2462, -ki⌒, -ti⌒.
  gen. hasédn⏑v., -énn⏑v.c., -én⏑c.; hásɛdn⏑v., -enn⏑v.c., -ɛn⏑c. §1522.
  hasénn⏑káčč(ı)⏑ and hasén⏑káčč(ı)⏑ (-éŋk- §658) *refuse of reaped crop, straw.*

hásɛn⏑ (-san; §956a) n. *Ḥásan, a man's name* [< حسن *id.*].
  obj. haséŋgı⏑, -sáŋ-, -gi⌒.

hāsıbḗ v.t. *calculate, reckon, count* [< imperat. or imperf. stem of حاسب *settle accounts with* + -ḗ §3647].
  ind. pres. aı⏑hāsıbḗri⌒; perf. aı⏑hāsıbḗgori⌒ (N. -ḗko-, -ḗho-).
  imperat. hāsıbḗ!
  dúŋgıh⏑hāsıbḗgoran⌒ (-h⏑h- < -g⏑h- §559) *they (have) counted the money.*
  kumbúnčıh⏑hāsıbḗgori⌒ *I (have) counted the eggs.*

hāsıbḗrar⏑ (-rár⏑; §§2200ff., 2207) and
hāsıbḗrid⏑ (§§2256ff., 2260) n. *calculation.*

hāsıbḗr-an (§§3890ff., 3899) v.t. *tell to calculate, etc., let calculate, etc.*

hāsıbḗrɛt-tǎ (§5723) v.t. *come after counting, go (§5713) and count.*
  imperat. hāsıbḗrɛtta!

hāsıbḗr-ɛttǎ (-éttä; §5723) v.t. *bring after counting.*
  imperat. hāsıbḗrɛtta!

hāsıbḗ-kattı- (N. -ḗha-; §4093) v.p. *be calculated, etc.*

hāsıbḗ-nál (§3747ᵉ) v.t. *see by counting, see the number or amount of.*
  imperat. hāsıbḗnál! and hāsıbḗnal! (§1871).

hāsıbḗ-nal (§1964) v.t. *see by calculating, etc., calculate (etc.) by looking at* (§3783).

has(ı)lḗ v.i. *happen, occur* [< حاصل *result* + -ḗ §3631].
  ind. pres. sg. 3 has(ı)lḗn⌒ (-lḗ⌒, -lḗ⌒ §942, occ. -lén⌒, -lḗ⌒, -lḗ⌒ §1073);
  perf. sg. 3 has(ı)lḗgon⌒ (-gō⌒, -gó⌒, N. -ḗkon⌒, -ḗkõ⌒, -ḗkó⌒, -ḗhon⌒, -ḗhū⌒, -ḗhó⌒).
  míndo⏑haslḗgó? *what (has) happened?*

*****hasrḗ-** (xas-) [< خسر *loss (in transaction)* + -ḗ §3615].

hasrḗ-bŭ- (xas-; §3931α) v.i. stat. *be in the state or condition of losing (in a transaction), be* خسران *, be a loser, suffer a loss.*
  ín⏑tɛm ḗŋgɛǧ⏑ǧắntıkkan, hasrḗbūran⌒ (-ǧ⏑ǧ- < -d⏑ǧ- §550) *if they sell (it) at that price they are out of pocket.*

hášab (xá-) n. *wood, timber* [< خشب *id.*].
  obj. hašábk(ı)⏑, -ápk(ı)⏑, -ki⌒.
  gen. hášabn⏑v., -šam⏑c.
  pl. hášabı⏑.
  hášam⏑gábad⏑ and
  hášam⏑káčč(ı)⏑ *shaving(s* §4696d).
  hášam⏑kášš(ı)⏑ (§4696d) *fragment(s) of wood, shaving(s), sawdust.*

hášma⏑ (occ. ášma⏑ §986) n. *fibre (from bark) of date-palm* (= ليف) [app. < هشمة a n.un. of هشم *crushing, bruising* §2411].
  obj. -mag⏑ [> Sudan Ar. عشميق ɛašmḗg⏑ *id.*].
  pl. -manč(ı)⏑.

hatíb⏑ (xa-) n. *betrothed, accepted suitor, bridegroom elect, bride elect* [< خطيب *bridegroom*].
  obj. -tíbk(ı)⏑, -típk(ı)⏑, -ki⌒.
  gen. -tíbn⏑v., -tím⏑c.
  pl. -tíbı⏑.

esmán⏑ám⏑búrun⏑hatíbun⌒ ɛoθmán *is my (our) daughter's betrothed.*
fátna⏑tín⏑tón⏑hatíbū⌒ *Fátima is their son's betrothed.*

hắtım⏑ (xá-) n. *seal, signet-ring* [< خاتم *id.*].
  obj. hātímg(ı)⏑, -gi⌒.
  pl. hát(ı)mı⏑.

hattắna⏑ n. *Hetani (on map), a village on the left bank of the Nile about thirty-two miles above Ed-Débba*ʰ.
  obj. -nag⏑.
  hattắnan⏑ágaba *the desert (east) of H.*

háu(ı)rtɛ⏑ *palm-frond, etc.* = háwırtɛ⏑.

háwa⏑ n. (a) *air, atmosphere;* (b) *weather, climate;* (c) *air in motion, wind* [< هواء *id.*].
  obj. háwag⏑.

hawán-d(ı)⏑ (§§2545ff.) adj. *appertaining to the air, etc., of the air, etc.*

háwa-kıññ(ı)⏑ (§§2536-7) adj. *devoid of air, etc.*
  kắ⏑háwakıññıŋ⏑kóbbūn⌒ (§6240) *the house is stuffy, it's shut up.*

hawáǧɛ⏑ (xa-, -ǧắ⏑, -ǧa⏑) n. (a) *(non-Moslem) gentleman, esp.;* (b) *commercial gentleman, (Greek, Syrian, etc.) shopkeeper or merchant* [< خواجة *id.*].
  obj. -ǧɛg⏑.
  pl. -ǧenč(ı)⏑.

háwırtɛ⏑ (háu(ı)rtɛ⏑) n. *palm-frond, palm-branch (of date-palm) frond, (of dōm-palm) fan-shaped leaf; with collective sg.* (§4696b) [< h- prob. dem. (§2165) + áwır *branch* + -tɛ⏑ (§2335); doublet of káwırtɛ⏑ *bird*].
  obj. -tɛg⏑.
  pl. -tenč(ı)⏑.
  béntın⏑háurtɛ⏑ *frond(s) of date-palm, branch(es) of date-palm.*
  hámbun⏑háurtɛ⏑ *leaf (leaves) of dōm-palm.*
  háurtɛ⏑béntıgon⏑hámbugonn⏑úlugun⌒ *háurtɛ is the leaf of the date-palm and of the dōm-palm.*

hawwád⏑ n. *fisherman* [< حوات *id.*].
  obj. -ádk(ı)⏑, -átk(ı)⏑, -átt(ı)⏑ §2462, -ki⌒, -ti⌒.
  gen. -ádn⏑v., -án⏑c.
  pl. -ádı⏑.
  ámbɛs⏑hawwádun⌒ *my brother is a fisherman.*

hḗ! interj. *calling attention hey!, hi!, hullo!*
  hḗ! índo⏑tá! *hi! come here!*
  hḗ⏑nógil! *hullo (you) walking (there)!*
  hḗ⏑hánu! *hi! (you) donkey!*

hébır n. *ink* s.v. híbır⏑.

hḗd⏑ n. *menses* [< حيض *id.*].
  obj. hḗdk(ı)⏑, hḗtk(ı)⏑, hḗtt(ı)⏑ §2462, -ki⌒, -ti⌒.
  pl. hḗdı⏑.
  tén⏑hḗdun⌒ *she has* (lit. *she is* §4719) *her menses.*
  ín⏑én⏑hḗdun⌒ *this woman has her menses.*

hḗǧ⏑ n. *pilgrimage* (= háǧ §1328).
  obj. hḗǧk(ı)⏑, hḗčk(ı)⏑, hḗčč(ı)⏑ §523, -ki⌒, -či⌒.

héǧǧ(ı)⏜ (héǧı⏜) n. *pilgrimage* (= háǧǧ(ı)⏜).
obj. héǧ(ǧ)ıg⏜.
héǧǧır⏜nókkó⏝ *(s)he has gone (went) on the pilgrimage.*
héǧǧır⏜ágran⏝ *they are on pilgrimage.*

héhúp! interj. *used (sung) by sailors in pushing or lifting.*

héjjın⏜ adj. *easy* [< هَيِّن *id.*].
obj. hejjíŋ(ı)⏜, -gi⏝.
pl. héjjını⏜.

hél⏜ n. *vigour, energy* [< حَيْل *id.*].
obj. hélg(ı)⏜, -gi⏝.
ter⏜hélgı⏜kómunun⏝ and (§ 4672)
ter⏜hél⏜kómunun⏝ *(s)he (it) has no energy.*
én⏜hélg⏜áŋgır! *be energetic! (rouse yourself!, 'buck up!',* شدّ حَيْلَك).

hélě! interj. *used (sung) by sailors in hauling, yoho!*
X. (hauling) hélɛ! *yoho!*
YY., ZZ. (hauling with X.) jálla!
X. hélɛ!
YY., ZZ. jálla!
da capo, ad lib. (and s.v. sálé!).

hélésa! and
hé-élésa! interj. *used (sung) by sailors in hauling, yoho!*

hɛlǽwa⏜ (xɛ-) n. *Kheleiwa (on map), a village on the left bank of the Nile, about 9 miles below Old Dóngola* [< خلوة dim. of خَلْوة s.v. hálwa⏜].
obj. hɛlɛ́wag⏜, hɛlɛ́wág⏝ (§ 1538).

hɛ́ma⏜ (xɛ-, -ma⏜) n. *tent* [< خَيْمَة *id.*].
obj. hɛ́mag⏜ (-mɑ̀g-).
pl. hɛ́manč(ı)⏜ (-mɑ̀n-, -mɛn-).
hɛ́maŋ⏜kóǧır *tent-peg(s* § 4696c).

hɛmmé v.i. *be anxious, concerned, troubled* [< هَمّ *anxiety* + -é § 3623].
ind. pres. aī⏜hɛmmɛ́ri⏝; perf. aī⏜hɛmmɛ́gori⏝ (N. -éko-, -éhο-).
imperat. hɛmmé!
tín⏜tódn⏜ıllár⏜hɛmmɛ́ran⏝ *they are anxious about their son.*

hɛmmɛ́rar⏜ (-rɑ̀r⏜; §§ 2200 ff., 2207) and
hɛmmɛ́ríd⏜ (§§ 2256 ff., 2260) n. *anxiety.*

hɛnné (hınnɛ́) v.i. *yearn, long, be fond, be affectionate* [< *imperf. stem of* حَنّ يَحِنّ *id.* + -é § 3623].
— constr. with -r⏜ (q.v.).
ind. pres. aī⏜hɛnnɛ́ri⏝, ɛr⏜hɛnnɛ́ni⏝ (-nɛ́⏝, -né⏝); perf. aī⏜hɛnnégori⏝ (N. -éko-, -ého-).
imperat. hɛnné!
én⏜uw⏜bitándo⏜hɛnnén⏝ *the woman longs for her child.*
aī⏜tíddo⏜hınnɛ́ri⏝ *I am fond of them.*
tín⏜tódır⏜hɛnnɛ́ran⏝ *they are fond of their son.*
wél⏜áddo⏜hınnɛ́gon, ténn⏜ɛuw⏜wɛlékkon⏝ (-w⏜w- < -g⏜w- § 719) *the dog was pleased to see me (us), it wagged its tail.*

hɛnnɛ́rar⏜ (hın-, -rɑ̀r⏜; §§ 2200 ff., 2207) and
hɛnnɛ́ríd⏜ (hın-; §§ 2256 ff., 2260) n. *yearning, etc.*

hɛr⏜ (xɛr⏜) n. (*a*) *well-being, welfare, prosperity*; (*b*) *well-doing, kindness, generosity* [< خَيْر *id.*].
obj. hɛrk(ı)⏜, -ki⏝.
X. hɛ́rró! (§ 1989) *good-bye!*, lit. *(may you be) in (a state of) well-being!*
Y. ártın⏜hásabır! *good-bye!*, lit. *(may you be) in God's care!*
X. to Y. hɛ́rro⏜túbbi! and
hɛ́rró! *good-night!*, lit. *(sleep) well (in well-being)!*
Y. ékkon⏜hɛ́rro⏜túbbi! *good-night!*, lit. *you too (s.v. ɛr⏜) sleep well!*
X. to Y. and Z. hɛ́rro⏜túbbıwɛ! (túbbᵘwɛ́!) *good-night!*
X. and Y. hɛ́rro⏜túbbi! *good-night!*
Z. írgon⏜hɛ́rro⏜túbbıwɛ́! *good-night!*, lit. *you (pl.) too sleep well!*
X. hɛ́rro⏜túbbi! *good-night!*
Y. ártın⏜hásɛbır! *good-night!*
ár⏜ékkı⏜hɛ́rkɛb⏜biǧázɛru⏝ (-b⏜b- < -d⏜b- § 518) *we shall requite you with kindness.*
X. on receiving a gift:
én⏜hɛ́ron⏜dígranıl! (§ 6266) *thank you,* lit. *may your prosperity increase!* = كَثَّر خَيرَك.

hɛ́r-an- (xɛ́r-; § 3910α) v.i. *become prosperous, prosper.*
tén⏜ǧélli⏜hɛranóskó⏝ *his (her) affair has (affairs have* § 4647) *gone well.*

hɛ́ram-bū- (xɛ́r-; §§ 3949 ff.) v.i. stat. *be in a prospering state or condition.*

hɛ́ranɛd-ág- (xɛ́r-; § 3966α) v.i. *be in the condition of having become prosperous.*

hɛ́raníŋ-ır (¯´¯, xɛ̄r-, N. -ŋkır; § 4213) (*a*) v.t. caus. *cause or allow to become prosperous;* (*b*) v.t. *render prosperous, prosper.*
ind. pres. aī⏜hɛraníŋıddi⏝.
árt⏜ékki⏜bihɛraníŋırın⏝ *God will prosper you.*
árt⏜én⏜ǧéllı⏜b⏜bihɛraníŋırın⏝ (-b⏜b- < -g⏜b- § 519) *God will prosper your affair(s).*

hɛ́rk-ır (xɛ́rk-; § 3698) (*a*) v.t. caus. *cause or allow to be prosperous;* (*b*) v.t. *render prosperous, prosper.*
ind. pres. aī⏜hɛ́rkıddi⏝.
árt⏜ékki⏜bihɛ́rkırın⏝ *God will prosper you.*
ártı⏜tín⏜ǧéllı⏜b⏜bihɛ́rkırın⏝ *God will prosper their affair(s).*

híkk(ı) v.i. *kneel (see húŋ(ı))* [? onom., cp. خخخ *xxx!* interj. *to urge camel to kneel.*]
ind. pres. aī⏜híkkıri⏝, ɛr⏜híkkın⏝ (-kí⏝, -kí⏝); perf. aī⏜híkkıgori⏝ (N. -ıko-, -ıho-).
imperat. híkki!
ǧógıl⏜tén⏜ǧéllın⏜ıllɛr⏜híkkın⏝ *the grinder (sc. of corn) kneels for (to do) her work.*
— some distinguish: húŋ(ı) *kneel erect,* as the grinder or washer does; híkk(ı) *kneel recumbently, on all fours,* as the camel does.
ádɛm⏜húŋgın, kám⏜híkkın⏝.

híkkar⏜ (-kɑ̀r⏜; §§ 2200 ff.) and
híkkíd⏜ (§§ 2256 ff.) n. *kneeling.*

híkk-ǎǧ-ǧóg- (-áǧǧóg-; § 4198) v.t. *be engaged in grinding, etc.* (s.v. ǎǧǧóg-) *while kneeling.*
nógo⏜ǧúh⏜híkkǎǧǧóg̣ın⏝ (-h⏜h- < -ǧ⏜h- § 559) *the female slave is kneeling and working (habitually kneels and works) (on) the stone for grinding.*

híkk-an (§§ 3890 ff.) v.t. *tell to kneel, let kneel.*

híkk-ǎš-šúkkı- (-āk-šúk-, -āǧ-šúk-; § 4198) v.t. *be engaged in washing, etc.* (s.v. áššúkkı-) *while kneeling.*
nógo⏜kadénčıh⏜híkkāššúkkın⏝ *the female slave has knelt down and is engaged in washing (habitually kneels and washes) the clothes.*

híkkı-ǧóg (§ 3747ᵋ) v.t. *grind, etc.* (s.v. ǧóg) *while kneeling.*
nógo⏜mároh⏜híkkıǧógın⏝ *the female slave kneels and grinds the millet.*
nógo⏜ǧúh⏜híkkıǧógın⏝ *the female slave works the grinding-stone kneeling.*

híkkıg-ır (N. -ıkır, -ıhır; § 3682) v.t. caus. *cause or allow to kneel.*
árab⏜tén⏜kámlıh⏜híkkıgırırın⏝ *the Arab makes (each of* § 5456) *his camels kneel.*

híkkı-šúkk(ı) (§ 3747ᵋ) v.t. *wash while kneeling.*
nógo⏜kadénčıh⏜híkkıšúkkıgó⏝ (-h⏜h- < -g⏜h- § 559) *the female slave (has) knelt and washed the clothes.*

hīrán⏜ (§ 956a) n. *pupil, student* [< *Sudan Ar.* حيران, pl. of حُوَّار *id.* § 2405].
obj. -áŋ(ı)⏜, -gi⏝.
pl. -ání⏜.

híbır⏜ (héb-) n. *ink* [< حِبْر *id.*].
obj. hıbírk(ı)⏜, híbırk(ı)⏜, -ki⏝.
pl. híbrı⏜.

hıdmé (xıd-) v.i. and t. *serve* (= hadmé) [< hıdm- < خِدْمَة (§ 1393) *service* + -é § 3617].
ind. pres. aī⏜hıdmɛ́ri⏝; perf. aī⏜hıdmɛ́gori⏝ (N. -éko-, -ého-).
imperat. hıdmé!

híǧ⏜ n. *pilgrimage* (= háǧ⏜ § 1328) [< حَجّ *id.* § 1370].
obj. híǧk(ı)⏜, híčk(ı)⏜, híčč(ı)⏜ § 523, -ki⏝, -či⏝.
tɛr⏜híǧır⏜nókkó⏝ *(s)he went (has gone) on pilgrimage.*

hıǧáz⏜ (heǧ-) n. (*a*) *the Ḥıǧáz,* الحِجَاز (§ 1389); (*b*) *pilgrimage, the Ḥıǧáz being popularly supposed in Dóngola to be so named after the pilgrimage* (حَجّ, s.v. híǧǧ(ı)⏜).
obj. -ázk(ı)⏜, -ásk(ı)⏜, -ki⏝.

hıǧáz-an- (heǧ-; § 3910β) v.i. *go to the Ḥıǧáz, go on pilgrimage.*

hıǧázam-bū- (heǧ-; § 3950β) v.i. stat. *be in a state of motion towards the Ḥıǧáz, be on one's way to the Ḥıǧáz, be on pilgrimage.*
hıǧázambūran⏝ *they are on their way to the Ḥıǧáz (they are on pilgrimage).*

híǧǧ(ı)⌣ — hókum⌣

híǧǧ(ı)⌣ (híǧı⌣) n. *pilgrimage* (= háǧǧ(ı)⌣)
[< حِجّ *id.*].
obj. híǧ(ǧ)ıg⌣.

híǧıl⌣ n. *anklet*; with collective sg. (§ 4696 d)
[< حِجْل *id.* § 1359].
obj. hıǧílg(ı)⌣, -gi⌢.
pl. híǧ(ı)lı⌣.

hıǧlíd⌣ n. *Balanites ægyptiaca, Del.* (BSP, 88); with collective sg. (§ 4696 b)
[< هجليج < هجليد *id.* § 867].
obj. -ídk(ı)⌣, -ítk(ı)⌣, -ítt(ı)⌣ § 2462, -ki⌢, -ti⌢.
gen. -ídn⌣v., -ín⌣c.
pl. -ídı⌣.

hílıb⌣ n. *anchor* [< هُلْب *id.* § 1359].
obj. hılíbk(ı)⌣, -ípk(ı)⌣, -ki⌢.
pl. híl(ı)bı⌣.

híllɛ⌣ (lú⌣, -la⌣) n. *village* [< حِلّة *id.*].
obj. -lɛg⌣.
pl. -lɛnč(ı)⌣.

hılwád⌣ (xıl-) n. *closet, store*, for books, etc., adjoining mosque, used as *Coran school*, *guest-room* [< Sudan Ar. خَلْوَات *id.* pl. § 2397].
obj. -ádk(ı)⌣, -átk(ı)⌣, -átt(ı)⌣ § 2462, -ki⌢, -ti⌢.
gen. -ádn⌣v., -án⌣c.
pl. -ádı⌣.

hınáī⌣ n. *what's-its-name, thingamy* [< Sudan Ar. هناي, هِنَاية (§ 1393) *id.*].
obj. -náīg(ı)⌣, -gi⌢.
pl. -najínč(ı)⌣.

hınné⌣ v. *yearn*, refl. = hɛnné.

híŋıŋk(ı)⌣ v.i. *neigh, whinny* [onom., as our words are; § 2855].
ind. pres. tɛr⌣híŋıŋkın⌣ (-kī⌢, -kí⌢);
perf. tɛr⌣hıŋíŋkıgon⌣ (-gō⌢, -gó⌢, N. ıkon⌢, -kō⌢, -kó⌢, -ıhon⌢, -hō⌢, -hó⌢).

hısáb⌣ n. *calculation, reckoning, account* [< حِساب *id.*].
obj. -ábk(ı)⌣, -ápk(ı)⌣, -ki⌢.
pl. -ábı⌣.

hısɛ́n⌣ (§ 956 a) n. *Ḥusáin*, a man's name [< حُسَين].
obj. -ɛ́ŋg(ı)⌣, -gi⌢.

hısɛnnárt(ı)⌣, -ti⌢. n. *Husseinárti* (on map), an island about thirty-two miles above Ed-Débbaʰ [*Ḥusáin's Island*].
obj. -tıg⌣.

hıssɛ́⌣ v.t. *perceive (by sense), feel, notice* [< حِسّ *perception* + -ɛ́ § 3623].
ind. pres. aī⌣hıssɛ́ri⌢; perf. aī⌣hıssɛ́gori⌢ (N. -ɛ́ko-, -ɛ́ho-).
imperat. hıssɛ́!

hıssɛ́rar⌣ (-rár⌣; §§ 2200, 2207) and
hıssɛríd⌣ (§§ 2256 ff., 2260) n. *perception*.

hıssɛ́-kattı- (N. -ɛ́ha-; § 4093) v.p. *be perceived*, etc.

híss(ı)⌣, -si⌢ n. *sound, noise, voice* = híz⌣ [< حِسّ *id.* § 1370].
obj. -sıg⌣.
pl. -sınč(ı)⌣.

tɛn⌣híssı⌣dúlun⌢ *his (her) voice (its sound) is loud*.
búnduŋ⌣híssıg⌣gıǧírkori⌢ (-ŋ⌣h- < -gn⌣h- § 650 a) *I heard the report of the (a) gun*.

hítım⌣ (xí- § 1397) n. *seal, signet*; *impression of seal* [Sudan Ar. خَتْم = خِتْم *id.* § 1359].
obj. hıtímg(ı)⌣, -gi⌢.
pl. hít(ı)mı⌣.

hıtmɛ́⌣ (xı-) v.t. *seal, affix one's seal to* [< Sudan Ar. خَتْم *seal* + -ɛ́ § 3617].
ind. pres. aī⌣hıtmɛ́ri⌢; perf. aī⌣hıtmɛ́gori⌢ (N. -ɛ́ko-, -ɛ́ho-).
imperat. hıtmɛ́!

hıtmɛ́rar⌣ (xı-, -rár⌣; §§ 2200 ff., 2207) and
hıtmɛríd⌣ (xı-; §§ 2256 ff., 2260) n. *sealing*.

hıtmɛ́r-an⌣ (xı-; §§ 3890 ff., 3899) v.t. *tell to seal, let seal*.

hıtmɛ́-bū- (xı-; § 3931 β) v.i. stat. *be in a sealed state or condition*.
ǧawáb⌣mɛdɛ́bun⌣, hıtmɛ́būmunun⌢ *the letter is signed, not sealed*.

hıtmɛ́-kattı- (xı-; N. -ɛ́ha-; § 4093) v.p. *be sealed*.

hítta⌣ (hɛ́t-) n. *bit, morsel*; with collective sg. (§ 4696 d) [< حِتّة *id.*].
obj. -tag⌣.
pl. -tanč(ı)⌣.

híz⌣ n. *sound, noise, voice* (= híss(ı)⌣) [< حِسّ *id.* § 1370].
obj. hízk(ı)⌣, hísk(ı)⌣, -ki⌢.
pl. -hízı⌣.
tín⌣híz-taran⌣ *it's their voices*.
tɛn⌣hízı⌣dúlun⌢ *his (her) voice (its sound) is loud*.
búnduŋ⌣hískıg⌣gıǧírkori⌢ (-ŋ⌣h- < -gn⌣h- § 650 a) *I heard the report of the (a) gun*.
ín⌣hískıg⌣gıǧırráŋı⌣dólmunun⌢ *I don't want to hear (a) your (pl.) voices; (b) this sound*.

hızám⌣ n. *belt, girth* [< حِزام *id.*].
obj. -ámg(ı)⌣, -gi⌢.
pl. -ámı⌣.
dɛ́gırn⌣hızám⌣ and
dɛ́gın⌣hızám⌣ (§ 622) *girth*.
kán⌣hızám⌣ (-ñ⌣h- < -ǧn⌣h- § 632) *horse-girth*.
hánun⌣hızám⌣ *donkey-girth*.

hızzɛ́ v.t. *shake* (= óšog, óšoŋ) [< imperf. stem of هَزَّ يَهِزّ *id.* + -ɛ́ § 3623].
ind. pres. aī⌣hızzɛ́ri⌢; perf. aī⌣hızzɛ́gori⌢ (N. -ɛ́ko-, -ɛ́ho-).
imperat. hızzɛ́!
tɛr⌣aīgı⌣hızzɛ́gó⌢ *(s)he (it) shook (has shaken) me*.
ɛ́n⌣tɛm⌣bıtáŋgı⌣hızzɛ́gon⌢ *the woman shook her child*.
tɛr⌣tarabɛ́zah⌣hızzɛ́⌣ (-h⌣h- < -g⌣h- § 559) *(s)he (it) shakes the table*.

hızzɛ́rar⌣ (-rár⌣; §§ 2200 ff., 2207) and
hızzɛríd⌣ (§§ 2256 ff., 2260) n. *shaking*.

hızzɛ́r-an⌣ (§§ 3890 ff., 3899) v.t. *tell to shake, let shake*.

hızzɛ́-bū- (§ 3931 β) v.i. stat. *be in a shaken state or condition*.

áfɛš⌣sandúgır⌣dábul⌣hızzɛ́būn⌢ *the stuff that is in the box is in a shaken condition*.

hızzɛ́rɛd-áǧ- (§§ 3877 ff.) v.t. *be in the situation of having shaken*.
sandúgır⌣dábulgı⌣hızzɛ́rɛdáǧran⌢ *they have shaken the contents of the box*.

hızzɛ́ŋ-ır (N. -ŋkır; § 3688) v.t. caus. *cause or allow to shake*.
tókkon⌣hızzɛ́ŋgırmɛn⌢ *don't make (let) him (her) shake him (her, it, them* § 5083).

hızzɛ́-kattı- (N. -ɛ́ha-; § 4093) v.p. *be shaken*.

hód⌣ n. (a) *depression made in the ground to hold water, pan or trough made in the ground for watering animals*; (b) *plot, with edges raised to hold water, of irrigable ground* (= bá⌣); with collective sg. (§ 4696 d) [< حَوْض *id.*].
obj. hódk(ı)⌣, -hótk(ı)⌣, hótt(ı)⌣ § 2462, -ki⌢, -ti⌢.
gen. hódn⌣v., hónn⌣v.c., hón⌣c.
pl. hódı⌣.

hodár⌣ (xo-) n. *green vegetables, greens*; with collective sg. (§ 4696 b) [< خُضار *id.*].
obj. -árk(ı)⌣, -ki⌢.
pl. -árı⌣.

hóhép! interj. used (sung) by sailors in hauling, *yoho!*

hóī! (hóī!) and repeated

hóī⌣hóī! interj. (a) *hullo!, hi!*; (b, answering to one's name) *yes!*
X. wó⌣mohámmɛt! and
Y. mohámmɛt! *Muḥammad!*
Z. (answering to his name) hóī! *yes!*

hokmɛ́⌣ (huk-) v.t. (a) *decide judicially, judge, try*; (b) *pass judgment on, sentence, condemn*; (c) *rule, govern* [< حُكم *judgment* + -ɛ́ § 3617].
ind. pres. aī⌣hokmɛ́ri⌢; perf. aī⌣hokmɛ́gori⌢ (N. -ɛ́ko-, -ɛ́ho-).
imperat. hokmɛ́!
X. írgı⌣mínɛ⌣hukmɛríkkó? *how did he decide your (pl.) case?*, lit. ...*decide you (pl.)?*
Y. aī⌣mɛnsúr⌣ɛ́ri⌢ *I've won*.
Z. aī⌣mɛglúb⌣ɛ́ri⌢ *I've lost*.
gádı⌣tɛ́kkı⌣diárkɛh⌣hukmɛ́gó⌢ (-h⌣h- < -d⌣h- § 558) *the judge (has) condemned him (her) to death*.
mahkáma⌣tírgı⌣sıǧíŋgɛd⌣hokmɛ́rıkkon⌢ *the court (has) sentenced them to imprisonment*.

hokúm-kattı- (-kóm-, -mha-; § 4100) v.p. *be decided judicially*, etc.
X. diárkɛh⌣hokómkattıgoná? *was (s)he (has (s)he been) condemned to death?*
Y. wáran, sıǧíŋgɛ́⌢ *no, to imprisonment*.

hókum⌣ (húk-, hókom⌣) n. (a) *judicial decision, judgment* [< حُكم *id.* § 1364]; (b) *sentence, condemnation*; (c) *rule, government*.
obj. hokúmg(ı)⌣, hukúmg(ı)⌣, hokómg(ı)⌣, -gi⌢.
pl. hók(u)mı⌣, húk(u)mı⌣, hókomı⌣.
sıǧın⌣hókum⌣ (-n⌣h- < -nn⌣h- § 613) *sentence of imprisonment*.
díar⌣hókum⌣ (-r⌣h- < -rn⌣h- § 848 a) *sentence of death*.

dɛrɛwíšın‿hókum‿ *the rule of the dervishes.*
hóŋg(1) v.i. *bray* [onom., cp. hánu‿ *donkey*; §2856].
ind. pres. tɛr‿hóŋgın‿ (-gĭ‿, -gí‿); perf. tɛr‿hóŋgıgon‿ (-gŏ‿, -gó‿, N. -ıkon‿, -kŏ‿, -kó‿, -ıhon‿, -hŏ‿, -hó‿).
hánu‿hóŋgın‿ *the donkey brays.*
hóŋgar‿ (-gȧr‿; §§2200ff.) and
hōŋgíd‿ (§§2256ff.) n. *braying.*
hór‿ (xór‿) n. *watercourse, valley* [< خَوْر *id.*].
obj. hórk(1)‿, -ki‿.
pl. hórı‿.
hórro‿síwır‿búgoran‿ *they were (lay) in the watercourse in the sand.*
hóss(1)‿ n. *(a) animal's dung, droppings,* esp. *(b) dung of horse, donkey or cattle.*
— with collective sg. (§4696d) [< *hóst(1)‿ (§686) < h- prob. dem. +ós *put out* + -t dem. or dim. (§2324), so *what is put out, discharged §2165].
obj. -sıg‿.
pl. -sınč(1)‿.
hánun‿hóss(1)‿ *donkey's dung.*
hánuın‿hóss(1)‿ *donkeys' dung.*
káñ‿hóss(1)‿ (-ñ‿h- < -ǧn‿h- §632) *horse's dung.*
káğlın‿hóss(1)‿ *horses' dung.*
tín‿hóss(1)‿ *cow's dung.*
tínčın‿hóss(1)‿ *cows' dung.*
kám‿hóss(1)‿ (-m‿h- < -mn‿h- §821) *camel's dung* = kám‿tŭr‿.
kámlın‿hóss(1)‿ *camels' dung* = kámlın‿tŭr‿.
úrtın‿hóss(1)‿ *goat's (sheep's) droppings* = úrtıŋ‿kállɛ‿.
hóš‿ n. *enclosure, courtyard* [< حَوْش *id.*].
obj. hóšk(1)‿, -ki‿.
pl. hóšı‿.
hóšn-d(1)‿ (§§2545ff.) adj. *appertaining to the (an) enclosure, etc., of the (an) enclosure, etc.*
X. kobídkı‿kúswé‿ *shut (pl.) the door.*
Y. hóšndıgá? *of the courtyard?*
hŏwwılɛ́‿ *(a)* v.i. *be astonished, amazed, surprised,* constr. with -rton‿ (q.v.).; *(b)* v.t. *be astonished, etc. at* [< hŏwwıl- < هَوَّلَ عَلَيْهِ *be terrified,* or < part of a stem of تَهَوَّلَ *terribilis fuit* understood as اِهْتَالَ *territus fuit* + -ɛ́ §3646].
ind. pres. aı‿hŏwwılɛ́rı‿; perf. aı‿hŏwwılɛ́gorı‿ (N. -ɛ́ko-, -ɛ́ho-).
aı‿téddoton‿howwılɛ́rı‿ and aı‿tékkı‿howwılɛ́rı‿ *I am astonished at him (her, it).*
ógğ‿índo‿míne‿fırrıráŋgı‿howwılɛ́rı‿ *I am amazed at how men fly in this (that);* —ógğ‿ is obj. of ‿howwılɛ́rı‿ (§6122).
hŏwwılɛ́rar‿ (-rȧr‿; §§2200ff., 2207) and
hŏwwılɛ́ríd‿ (§§2256ff., 2260) n. *astonishment.*
hukmɛ́ *decide judicially, etc.* = hokmɛ́.
húkum‿ *judicial decision, etc.* = hókum‿.
hukŭma‿ (-mȧ‿) n. *government* [< حُكُومَة *id.*].
obj. -mag‿.

húmma‿ (-mȧ‿) n. *fever* [< حُمَّى *id.*].
obj. -mag‿.
húŋ(1)‿ v.i. *kneel* (see híkk(1)).
ind. pres. aı‿húŋgırı‿; perf. aı‿húŋgıgorı‿ (N. -ıko-, -ıho-).
imperat. húŋgi!
X. kám‿húŋgın‿ *the camel kneels.*
Y. kám‿húŋgımunun, híkkın‿.
húŋar‿ (-gȧr‿; §§2200ff.) and
huŋgíd‿ (§§2256ff.) n. *kneeling.*
huŋ-ȧǧ-ǧóg- (-ȧǧǧóg-; §4198) v.t. *be engaged in grinding, etc.* (s.v. ȧǧǧóg-) *while kneeling.*
nógo‿huŋgȧǧǧógın‿ *the female slave (a) is on her knees grinding; (b) habitually kneels and grinds.*
nógo‿mároh‿huŋgȧǧǧógın‿ (-h‿h- < -g‿h- §559) *the female slave (a) is kneeling and grinding (the) millet; (b) habitually kneels and grinds (the) millet.*
húŋ-an (§§3890ff.) v.t. *tell to kneel, let kneel.*
huŋ-ān-nór- (-āŋnór-; §4198) v.t. *be engaged in grinding, etc.* (s.v. ānnór-) *while kneeling.*
nógıllɛh‿huŋānnórın‿ *the female slave (a) is kneeling and grinding (the) wheat; (b) habitually kneels and grinds (the) wheat.*
huŋır-ɛ-nóg (§§4048ff.) v.i. *go to kneel* (esp. in order to grind).
huŋır-ɛ-nóg-bŭ- (-nóggŭ- §546; §4058) v.i. stat. *be on one's way (going) to kneel.*
aı‿ğŭr‿huŋırɛnógbūrı‿ *I am on my way to kneel at the stone for grinding.*
huŋı-ǧóg (§3747ᵉ) v.t. *grind, etc.* (s.v. ǧóg) *while kneeling.*
nógo‿ğŭh‿huŋıǧógın‿ *the female slave works the grinding-stone kneeling.*
húŋıg-ır (N. -ıkır, -ıhır; §3682) v.t. caus. *cause or allow to kneel.*
ind. pres. aı‿húŋgıddı‿.
X. kámlıh‿huŋgırkó‿ (-h‿h- < -g‿h- §559) *he (has) made the camels kneel.*
Y. kámlıh‿huŋgırkómunun, híkkıgírkó‿ (§1964).
húrr(1)‿ adj. *free* [< حُرّ *id.*].
obj. -rıg‿.
pl. -rınč(1)‿.
húruǧ (xú-) n. *saddle-bag* [< خُرْج *id.* §1363].
obj. huruǧk(1)‿, -účk(1)‿, -účč(1)‿ §523, -ki‿, -či‿.
pl. húr(u)ği‿.
húruǧ‿ (úr- §986) n. *Acacia albida,* Del. (BSP, 181); with collective sg. (§4696b) [cp. حَرَاز *id.*].
obj. huruǧk(1)‿, -účk(1)‿, -účč(1)‿ §523, -ki‿, -či‿.
pl. húr(u)ği‿.
husūsan (xu- §956a) adv. *especially, particularly* [< خُصُوصًا *id.*].
dıgrıgırɛ́lkattın, husūsam‿moḥámmem‿bɛ́ledır‿ (m‿b- < -dn‿b- §594) *it is found in great quantities, especially in Muḥammad's country.*

xábar‿ *news* = hábar‿.
xál‿ *vinegar* = hál‿.

xalbıtɛ́ *confuse* = halbıtɛ́.
xális‿ *quite, very* = hális‿.
xálwa‿ *room for strangers, village school* = hálwa‿.
xamís‿ *Thursday* = hamís‿.
xamsín‿ *fifty* = hamsín‿.
xarȧǧ‿ n. *tax* = harȧǧ‿.
xarbɛ́ v.t. *ruin, etc.* = harbɛ́.
xášab‿ *wood, timber* = hášab‿.
xátım‿ n. *seal, etc.* = hátım‿.
xawȧǧɛ‿ (-gȧ‿, -ǧa‿) *shopkeeper, etc.* = hawȧǧɛ‿.
xítım‿ n. *seal, etc.* = hítım‿.
xıtmɛ́ v.t. *seal* = hıtmɛ́.
xodȧr‿ *vegetables* = hodȧr‿.
xusūsan‿ *especially* = husūsan‿.

í‿, -í‿ (§2374b) n. *(a) hand; (b) arm; (c) handle;* usually distinguished from ȧd‿, q.v.
— with collective sg. (§4696a) [prob. < *íjı‿, see fjı-n §2140; cp. ON. ei *id.* GNT, s.v.; RSN, §129].
obj. íg‿.
pl. ínč(1)‿.
Enclitic (§1671) in:
ánn-í‿ *my hand(s).*
ɛ́nn-í‿ *your hand(s).*
ténn-í‿ *his (her) hand(s).*
ánn-í‿ *our hands.*
ínn-í‿ *your (pl.) hands.*
tínn-í‿ *their hands.*
obj. ánn-ıg‿ and ánn-íg‿; ɛ́nn-ıg‿ and ɛ́nn-íg‿, etc.
ánni‿óddın‿ *my hand hurts (hands hurt).*
ánni‿nadífun‿ *my hand is (hands are) clean.*
ténni‿búdbūn‿ *his (her) arm (at shoulder, elbow, wrist or finger) is dislocated.*
ténn‿ír‿tíkkorı‿ and more commonly ténnır‿tíkkorı‿ *I gave (have given) it into his (her) hand(s).*
ɛnnıg‿ɛ́wó‿ (§962) and ɛ́nnıš‿šúkki‿ (-š‿š- < -g‿š- §695) *wash your hand(s).*
núgud‿árabın‿íged‿dígó‿ *the slave was (has been) killed by the Arabs,* lit. *...died by the hand of the Arabs.*
tínn‿íged‿dígó‿ *(s)he (it) was (has been) killed by them.*
bȧbn‿í‿ *handle of door.*
bɛrrȧdn‿í‿ *handle of tea-pot, etc.*
fȧnŭsn‿í‿ *handle of lantern.*
fıŋǧȧnn‿í‿ *handle of small cup.*
†ǧȧgn‿í‿ and
†ǧȧkkın‿í‿ *handle of jug.*
ǧérden‿í‿ *handle of bucket.*
kub(b)ȧian‿í‿ *handle of cup.*
kúsn‿í‿ and kúzn‿í‿ *handle of mug.*
lámban‿í‿ *handle of lamp.*
mȧlagan‿í‿ *handle of spoon.*
sandúgn‿í‿ *handle(s) of box, etc.*
sıwídn‿í‿ *hilt of sword* = sıwídn‿ȧd‿.
šȧntan‿í‿ *handle of valise, etc.*
šókan‿í‿ *handle of fork.*
bȧbn‿í‿gúššıgon‿ *the door-handle broke (has broken).*
sandúkkı‿ténn‿íges‿sókke‿ (-s‿s- < -d‿s- §677) *take the box up by its handle(s).*

sandúkkɩ⌣ténn⌣íɡɛt⌣tókkon⌣sókkɛ-mɛn⌢ *don't pick the box up by its handle(s)*.
ím⌣budúrt(ɩ)⌣ *joint(s) of arm (at shoulder, elbow, wrist or of finger)*.
ín-ğɛr⌣ (§1672) n. *back of hand(s)*.
ánn-ɩn⌣ğɛ́rro⌣ (§1565) *on the back of my hand(s)*.
ín⌣kuɡúnd(ɩ)⌣ (íŋ⌣k-) *elbow(s)*.
ín⌣sárbɛ⌣ and ís⌣sárbɛ⌣ (§680) *finger(s)*.
ánn-ɩn⌣sárbɛ⌣ *my finger(s)*.
ɛ́nn-ɩn⌣sárbɛ⌣ *your finger(s)*.
ín-tu⌣ (§2363) n. *palm (of hand)*; with collective sg. (§4696 a).
obj. íntūɡ⌣, ín⌣tūɡ⌣.
gen. ín⌣tūn⌣.
ín-tún-d(ɩ)⌣ (§§2545 ff.) adj. *appertaining to the palm of the hand*.
í-kɩñ́ñ(ɩ)⌣ (§§2536–7) adj. *without hands, etc.*
fɩnğǎn⌣íkɩñ́ñ(ɩ)⌣ *small cup without a handle*.
ín-d(ɩ)⌣ (§§2545 ff.) adj. *appertaining to the hand, etc., of the hand, etc., the hand's etc.*
id⌣ n. *man, etc.* = íd⌣.
íɡ⌣ n. (a) *fire, flame*; (b) *light (e.g. candle, match)*; (c) *blossom, flower*; with collective sg. (§4696 b) [cp. نَارٌ ذَنُ *flame*, نُورٌ ذَنُ *blossom*; RSN, §129].
obj. íɡk(ɩ)⌣, íkk(ɩ)⌣, -kɩ⌢.
gen. íɡn⌣v., íŋ⌣c.
pl. íɡɩ⌣.
íkk⌣úllɩ⌢ *light the fire (light)*.
íkkɩ⌣bé⌢ *put the fire (light) out*.
íɡɩr⌣ (a = íɡ-ɩr §484β) *on (in, to) the fire*; (b = íɡɩ-r⌣ §6288) *on (in, to) the fires*.
íɡɩr⌢ (§5858) *it is (they are) on (in) the fire(s)*.
íŋ⌣kóččɩr⌣būn⌢ *it is on the fire*.
mán⌣íɡ⌣áŋ⌣kǎndɩré? *is that light (yonder) the one of our house?*
ğówwɩn⌣íɡ⌣ and
šídɑ̌rn⌣íɡ⌣ *tree's blossom(s)*.
íɡ-kɩñ́ñ(ɩ)⌣ (íkk-; §§2536–7) adj. *devoid of fire, etc.*
ğóww⌣íkkɩñ́ñ(ɩ)⌣ *the (a) tree without blossoms*.
íŋ-d(ɩ)⌣ (íɡnd(ɩ)⌣, íɡɩ̌nd(ɩ)⌣, íŋ̌ṇd(ɩ)⌣ §792; §§2545 ff.) adj. *appertaining to (the) fire, etc., of (the) fire, etc.*
íɡ v.t. (a) *tell, narrate*; (b) *propound (riddle)* [< í-ɡ⌣ *in (on) the hand(s)*, adverbial case of í⌣ *hand* §2857].
ind. pres. aĩ⌣íɡ(¹)rɩ⌢, ɛr⌣íɡɩn⌢ (⌣íɡī⌢, íɡí⌢); perf. aĩ⌣íɡkorɩ⌢ (⌣íkko-).
imperat. ík!
subj. past aĩ⌣íɡsɩ⌣ (⌣íksɩ⌣, -su⌣).
ɩɡíd-děɡ⌣íɡkó⌢ (-d-d-⌣-d-w- §533) *(s)he (has) told a tale (propounded a riddle)*.
íɡar⌣ (íɡɑ̌r⌣; §§2200 ff.) n. *telling, narration, propounding*.
ɩɡídn⌣íɡar⌣ *the telling of a tale (propounding of a riddle)*.
íɡɩd n. (a) *tale, story*; (b) *tale of which the meaning is to be guessed, riddle* [< *íɡɩd⌣ §§2268, 1154].
obj. ɩɡídk(ɩ)⌣, -ítk(ɩ)⌣, -ítt(ɩ)⌣ §2462, -kɩ⌢, -tɩ⌢.
pl. íɡɩdɩ⌣.

íɡ-an (§§3890 ff.) v.t. *tell to tell, etc., let tell, etc.*
ɩɡítk⌣íɡan⌢ *let him (her) tell the tale (propound the riddle)*.
íɡ-bŭ- (íɡɡū- §546; §3931β) v.i. stat. *be in a told (etc.) state or condition*.
íɡɩd⌣íɡbūn⌢ (a) *the tale is (has been) told*; (b) *the riddle is (has been) propounded*.
íɡɛd-áɡ- (§3877 ff.) v.t. *be in the situation of having told, etc.*
íɡídk⌣íɡɛdáɡɩn⌢ (a) *(s)he has (you have) told the (a) tale*; (b) *(s)he has (you have) propounded the (a) riddle*.
íɡ-kattɩ- (íkkat-; §4093) v.p. *be told, etc.*
íjɩn⌣ (§956 d) n. *right hand*, usually in contracted form ín⌣, q.v. [stereotyped gen. of *íjɩ⌣ *hand* §2140].
ík! imperat. of íɡ *tell, etc.*
íkk(ɩ)⌣ obj. of íɡ⌣ *fire, etc.*
ín⌣ (§956 d) this s.v. ín⌣.
obj. íŋɡ(ɩ)⌣, -gɩ⌢.
gen. ínɩn⌣.
pl. ínɡu⌣.
pl. obj. íŋɡuɡ⌣.
ín⌣ gen. of í⌣ *hand, etc.*
ín⌣ n. *right hand* [< íjɩn⌣ id.].
obj. íŋɡ(ɩ)⌣, -gɩ⌢.
ɛ́nn⌣íŋɡɛd⌣áu⌢ *do it with your right hand*.
ánn⌣íŋɡɛd⌣árkorɩ⌢ *I (have) seized him (her, it) with my right hand*.
X. tír⌣sé? *where are they?*
Y. ɛ́nn⌣íŋɡé⌢ (§966) *on your right.*
íŋɡɛn⌣nókkoran⌢ (-n⌣n- < -d⌣n- §624) *they went (have gone) to the right*.
íŋɡaddɩ⌣kállɩ⌢ *push it (them) towards the right*.
ɛ́nn⌣ínn⌣óssɩs⌣sókkɛ⌢ (-s⌣s- < -ɡ⌣s- §678) *raise your right leg*.
ín-d(ɩ)⌣ (§§2545 ff.) adj. *appertaining to the right hand, right-hand*.
íntu⌣ *palm of hand* s.v. í⌣.
íŋ⌣c. gen. of íɡ⌣ *fire, etc.*
ír⌣ n. (a) *number* [< í-r⌣ *on the hand(s)*, where the decimal (< quinary RSN, §113) system arose §2141]; (b) *mark, sign, written symbol*.
— with collective sg. (§4696 d):
obj. írk(ɩ)⌣, -kɩ⌢.
pl. írɩ⌣.
X. ténn⌣ír⌣mukóttɛ́rré? *how many are they?*, lit. *how much is his (her, its) number?*
Y. aĩ⌣ténn⌣írk⌣uñúmmunun⌢ *I don't know how many they are*.
téddʊ̌⌣írk⌣au⌣dábmenɩnn⌣íllɑ̌r⌢ *make a mark on it so that it should not get lost*.
sandúɡ⌣ténn⌣írrotōn⌣uñúrkattɩn⌢ *the box is known by (lit. from) its mark(s)*.
ír v.t. (a) *make (rope) by rolling between the hands*; (b) *count* [< í-r⌣ *on the hand(s)*, sc. (a) *between the palms*, (b) *on the fingers* §2858].
ind. pres. aĩ⌣írrɩ⌢, ɛr⌣írɩn⌢ (⌣írī⌢, ⌣írí⌢); perf. aĩ⌣írkorɩ⌢.
írɩ-wěɡ⌣ír⌢ *make a rope*.
kúmbuɡ⌣ír⌢ *count the eggs* (§4696 d).
kámlɩɡ⌣írwé⌢ *count (pl.) the camels*.
dúŋɡɩɡ⌣írkoran⌢ *they (have) counted the money*.

írar⌣ (írɑ̌r⌣; §§2200 ff.) and
iríd⌣ (§§2256 ff.) n. *counting, etc.*
írɩ⌣ n. *rope* [< *írɩ⌣ (§1154) < ír *make by rolling between the hands* + -ɩ⌣ (§§2252–5)].
obj. írɩɡ⌣.
pl. ɩrínč(ɩ)⌣.
ɑ̌rɛn⌣ɛ́ssɩn⌣írɩ⌣ *inner water rope, stay securing end of cross-beam (díu⌣) of water-wheel (kólɛ⌣) near weaker post (múɡdo⌣kárrɩ⌣) to beam (ɛssɩkáɡ⌣) under trough*.
bóččɩn⌣ɛ́ssɩn⌣írɩ⌣ *outer water rope, stay securing same end of cross-beam as ɑ̌rɛn⌣ɛ́ssɩn⌣írɩ⌣ in the opposite (shoreward) direction to a peg (kóɡɩr⌣) driven into the ground*.
ír-an (§§3890 ff.) v.t. *tell to count, etc., let count, etc.*
ír-bŭ- (§3931β) v.i. stat. *be in a counted (etc.) state or condition*.
úrt⌣írbūn⌢ *the goats (sheep) are (have been) counted*.
irr-ɛɡ-áɡ- (§§4071 ff.) v.t. = íredol-.
ir-ɛ-dól- (īrᵒd- §1178; §4022) and
irr-ɛ-dól- (-rᵒd-; §4027) v.t. *be about to count, etc.*
irr-ɛ-ğŭ-bŭ- (§4069) v.t. stat. *be on one's way (coming) to count, etc.*
ir-ɛ-mǎ- (§4036) and
irr-ɛ-mǎ- (§4041) v.t. *become unable to count, etc.*
irr-ɛ-nóɡ (§§4048 ff.) v.t. *go to count, etc.*
irr-ɛ-nóɡ-bŭ- (-nóɡɡu- §546; §4058) v.t. stat. *be on one's way (going) to count, etc.*
irr-ɛ-tǎ- (§4060 ff.) v.t. *come to count, etc.*
irɛd-áɡ- (§§3877 ff.) v.t. *be in the situation of having counted, etc.*
úrtɩɡ⌣íredáɡran⌢ *they have counted the flock*.
ír-kattɩ- (§4093) v.p. *be counted, etc.*
ir-nál (§3747ᵋ) v.t. *see by counting, see the number of*.
ind. pres. aĩ⌣írnállɩ⌢.
imperat. ɩrnál! and írnal! (§1871).
kúmbuɡ⌣írnal⌢ *count the eggs and see (how many they are)*.
ɛɡɛdɩɡ⌣írnálkorandé? *did they see (have they seen) the number of the sheep?*
íu⌣, íⁿ⌣, íw⌣ n. (a) *grain, corn*, esp.; (b) *great millet, Sorghum vulgare* (= márɛ⌣); (c) *bread*.
— with collective s.g.(§4696 b) [§2052; RSN, §129]
obj. fuɡ⌣, íuɡ⌣, íwɡ(ɩ)⌣, -gɩ⌢.
gen. íun⌣, íⁿn⌣.
pl. íwɩ⌣.
obj. pl. íwɩɡ⌣.
gen. pl. íwɩn⌣.
fuɡɩ⌣ğōɡedáɡran⌢ *they have ground the corn*.
íu⌣ğedídun⌢ *the bread is new*.
íuŋ⌣ɡól⌣ and
íun⌣núd⌣ *ear(s) of corn, head(s) of millet*.
íu-kɩñ́ñ(ɩ)⌣ (§§2536–7) adj. *devoid of grain, etc.*
iún-d(ɩ)⌣ (§§2545 ff.) adj. *appertaining to grain, etc., cereal*.
iwín-d(ɩ)⌣ (§§2545 ff.) adj. *appertaining to grains, etc., cereal*.

íu, í︎ⁿ, íw v.t. *tend at pasture, lead to pasture, graze, pasture* [cp. ON. ᚺᛏ *id. GNT*, s.v.; §2052].
ind. pres. aı‿íuri⌢ (‿í︎ᵘri⌢, ‿íw(ᵎ)ri⌢), ɛr‿íwın⌢ (‿íwı⌢, ‿íwí⌢); fut. aı‿bíuri⌢ (‿bí︎ᵘri⌢, ‿bíw(ᵎ)ri⌢); perf. aı‿íukori⌢ (‿í︎ᵘk-, ‿íw(ᵎ)k-, N. -uho-).
subj. past aı‿íusı‿ (‿í︎ᵘsı‿, ‿íw(ᵎ)sı‿, -su‿).
part. pres. íwıl‿ *herdsman*.
úrtıg‿íwıl‿ (-tug‿í-) *goatherd.*
tíncıg‿íwıl‿ *neat-herd, cowherd.*
X. ní‿bɛrtíncıg‿íwırırın? *who pastures the goats?*
Y. bıtáw-wɛr⌢ (-w-w- < -n-w- §720) *a boy.*
kámg‿íwri⌢ *I graze the camel.*
kámlıg‿íwıríddi⌢ (§3038) *I graze the camels.*
bıtán‿úrtıg‿íwın⌢, bıtán‿urtíncıg‿íwın⌢ and bıtán‿urtíncıg‿íwırırın⌢ *the boy pastures the goats (sheep).*
árab‿égedıg‿íwırırın⌢ *the Arab grazes the sheep (pl.).*
íwar‿ (íwar‿; §§2200 ff.) and **iwíd‿** (§§2256 ff.) n. *tending at pasture, etc.*
íwıd‿ (§2268) n. (a) *pasture, place for grazing;* (b) = íwíd‿.
úrt‿íwıdır⌢ (§5858) (a) *the goat (sheep) is at pasture;* (b §4696d) *the goats (sheep) are at pasture.*
aı‿tékk‿úrtun‿íwıdır‿ıšíndi⌢ *I send him (her) to pasture the goats (sheep).*
íw-an (§§3890 ff.) v.t. *tell to tend at pasture, etc., let tend at pasture, etc.*
[***íu-bŭ-** reported not used; perhaps because animals do not *lie* at pasture.]
iwɛd-ág- (§§3877 ff.) v.t. *be in the situation of having tended at pasture, etc.*
úrt‿íwɛdágın⌢ *(s)he has led the goats (sheep) to pasture.*
[***íuk-ır** reported not used.]
iwíŋ-ır (íwıŋgır; N. -ŋkır; §3688) v.t. caus. *cause or allow to tend at pasture, etc.*
aı‿tékk‿úrtıg‿íwıŋgıddi⌢ and N. aı‿tékk‿úrtıncıg‿íwıŋkıddi⌢ *I make (let) him (her) graze the goats (sheep).*
íu-kattı- (í︎ᵘka-; N. fuha-, í︎ᵘha-; §4093) v.p. *be tended at pasture, etc.*
úrt‿í︎ᵘkattın⌢ *the goats (sheep) are led to (etc.) pasture.*

íu, í︎ⁿ, íw v.t. *forget* [cp. ON. ᚺᛏ *hide GNT*, s.v.; §2052].
ind. pres. aı‿íuri⌢ (‿í︎ᵘri⌢, ‿íw(ᵎ)ri⌢), ɛr‿íwın⌢ (‿íwı⌢, ‿íwí⌢); fut. aı‿bíuri⌢ (‿bí︎ᵘri⌢, ‿bíw(ᵎ)ri⌢); perf. aı‿íukori⌢ (‿í︎ᵘk-, ‿íw(ᵎ)k-, N. -uho-, -ᵘho-).
subj. past aı‿íusı‿ (‿í︎ᵘsı‿, ‿íw(ᵎ)sı‿, -su‿).
neg. fut. aı‿bíumunun⌢ (‿bí︎ᵘm-, ‿bíwm-, -munú‿, -munu⌢, -mun⌢).
éwu‿wıččírk‿íᵘkon⌢ (-w-w- < -n-w- §722) *you have forgotten your stick.*
ténn‿írk‿í︎ᵘkori⌢ *I forgot (have forgotten) their* (lit. *its* §4647) *number, i.e. how many they were.*
íwar‿ (íwar‿; §§2200 ff.) and **iwíd‿** (§§2256 ff.) n. *forgetting.*

íu-bŭ- (í︎ᵘbŭ-; §3931β) v.i. stat. *be in a forgotten state or condition.*
támugıd‿í︎ᵘbūn⌢ *the war is (has been) forgotten.*
iwɛd-ág- (§§3877 ff.) v.t. *be in the condition of having forgotten.*
íwk-ır (í︎ᵘk-, íuk-; §3683) v.t. caus. *cause or allow to forget.*
iwíŋ-ır (‵̄-, N. -ŋkır; §3688) v.t. caus. = íwkır.
íu-kattı- (í︎ᵘk-, íwk-; N. -uha-, -ᵘha-; §4093) v.p. *be forgotten.*
íwıs v.t. *wring, twist* = íwıs.
ıbáıa n. *cloak* = abáıa‿.
ıbár (ab- §1339) n. (a) *explanation;* (b) *explanatory mark, sign;* with collective sg. (§4696d) [< عِبَارَة *id.* §1393].
obj. -árk(ı)‿, -ki⌢.
pl. -árı‿.
árıdır‿ıbárk‿áukō⌢ *(s)he (has) made explanatory marking(s) on the ground.*
ıbɛttamóda‿ *sort of date* = ɛbɛttamóda‿.
ıbırt(ı)‿ n. *twist;* with collective sg. (§4696d) [§§2323 ff.].
obj. -tıg‿.
pl. -tınč(ı)‿.
úl‿ıbírtık‿kón⌢ *the thread (line, etc. s.v. úl‿) has a twist (has twists, is twisted).*
ıbırtı-dá-bŭ- (§3943) v.i. stat. *be in a twisted state or condition.*
úl‿ıbırtıdábūn, géndıgır⌢ *the thread (etc.) is twisted, put it right.*
ıbırtıg-úndur (§4130) v.t. *twist.*
ind. pres. aı‿ıbırtıgundúddi⌢, ɛr‿ıbırtıgúndurın⌢ (-rí⌢, -rí⌢); perf. aı‿ıbırtıgundúrkori⌢.
káǧ‿ténn‿írıg‿ıbırtıgundúrkon⌢ *the horse (has) twisted its rope (tether, etc.).*
ıbırtıgúndur-an (§§3890 ff., 3905) v.t. *tell to twist, let twist.*
ıbırtıgundurıŋ-ır (N. -ŋkır; §4211) v.t. caus. *cause or allow to twist.*
tókkoh‿hánut‿ténn‿írıg‿ıbırtıgundurıŋgırmen‿ (-h- < -n-h- §560, -t-t- < -g-t- §707) *don't let the donkey twist its rope.*
ıblís n. *devil, demon* [< اِبْلِيس *id.*].
obj. -ísk(ı)‿, -ki⌢.
pl. -ísı‿.
ıblís-d(ı)‿ (§§2545 ff.) adj. *appertaining to the (a) devil, devilish, diabolical.*
ıblísín-d(ı)‿ (§§2545 ff.) adj. *appertaining to devils, devilish, diabolical.*
ıbríg n. *pot* [< إِبْرِيق *id.*].
obj. -ígk(ı)‿, -íkk(ı)‿, -ki⌢.
gen. -ígnᵛ‿, -íŋ‿c.
pl. -ígı‿.
ıčč(ı)‿ n. *milk* [< *ígt(ı)‿ (§525) < √íg- *drink (§4532) + -t of n. act. (§2325), so *drinking §2228; cp. MN. ej pl. Milch KBW, s.v.].
obj. -číg‿.
íččıǧ‿ǧúrrıgon⌢ (-ǧ-ǧ- < -g-ǧ- §551) *(s)he drew (has drawn) the milk (from the cow, etc.).*
íččım‿mɛrɛl‿ (-m-m- < -n-m- §604) *curdled milk.*
íččın‿nébɛd‿ and íččın‿némɛd‿ *cream of milk.*

ıččín-d(ı)‿ (§§2545 ff.) adj. *appertaining to (the) milk, of (the) milk, (the) milk's.*
ıččı-kátt(ı)‿ (N. -ıhá-; §§2534-5) adj. *possessing much milk, rich in milk.*
ín‿tí‿ıččıkáttın⌢ *this cow yields much milk.*
ıččı-kıñň(ı)‿ (§§2536-7) adj. *devoid of milk.*
tí‿ıččıkıñň(ı)‿ *the (a) cow without milk.*
ıččı-kırı‿ (§§2539-40) adj. *like milk, resembling milk.*
ıččı-ko (§§4109, 4119) v.i. *have milk, be in milk (lactare).*
(part. pres.) íččıkōl‿ (‵̄-́, ‵̄-́ §1708) adj. *in milk (lactans);* obj. ıččıkólg(ı)‿, pl. ıččıkonı‿.
(neg. part. pres.) íččıkōmɛnıl‿ adj. *not in milk, without milk.*
tí‿íččıkō⌢ *the cow is in milk.*
bért‿íččıkōl‿dıgó⌢ *the milch-goat (has) died.*
bért‿íččıkōmenílgı‿déŋkó⌢ *(s)he gave (has given) me a goat that has no milk.*
ıččín (čí- §939) n. *scorpion* [< *ígtírñ‿ (§§1154, 525, 615) < íg- *fire* + -t (§2326) + -ír *causation* (§2283) + -ñ‿ dim. (§4572), particularized in concrete sense *little causer of fieriness §2282].
obj. -číŋg(ı)‿, -gi⌢.
pl. -čínı‿.
tɛr‿ıččınú⌢ *(s)he's a scorpion, i.e. a person that makes spiteful (stinging) remarks.*
ıččín-bɛr‿ (-ím-bɛr‿ §§593, 2363) n. *a prostrate herb, Aristolochia bracteata, Retz* (R. E. Massey; *BSP*, 502).
ıččíŋ-kırı‿ (-kírı‿; §§2539-40) adj. *resembling a scorpion.*
tém‿báññıg‿ıččíŋkırın⌢ *(s)he has a stinging tongue,* lit. *his (her) speech is like a scorpion.*
íd‿ (íd‿) n. (a) *man (vir);* (b) *husband;* (c) *person* [nominal specialization of *í*d *doer, 'hand'* §§2061, 2141; cp. ON. ⲉⲓⲧ *person GNT*, s.v.].
obj. ídk(ı)‿, ítk(ı)‿, ítt(ı)‿ §2462, -ki⌢, -ti⌢.
gen. ídnᵛ‿, íŋ‿c.
pl. írı‿.
íd‿ is Massınčíndi, and not universal in Duŋgulándi except in compounds.
ténn‿íd‿ısáıré? *where is her husband?* = ténn‿ógıǧ‿ısáıré?
ín‿íd‿béndıgın⌢ *this person begs (is a beggar).*
kán‿íd‿ (§4811) and kánıd‿ (§§2354, 2363) *inmate of house, householder;* obj. kán‿ídk(ı)‿ (etc.) and kánídk(ı)‿; gen. kán‿ídnᵛ‿ (etc.) and kán‿íŋ‿c; pl. kán‿írı‿ and kánırı‿.
kánır‿ágmunan⌢ *the inmates are not at home.*
bélɛdn‿íd‿ and bélɛdnıd‿ (§2363) (a) *person of the country, inhabitant, native;* (b) *countryman, rustic* (declension s.v. bélɛd‿).
ídd(ı)‿ v.t. (a) *ask, inquire, question, ask of, inquire of;* (b) *ask for, request* (= síkk(ı)‿) [< *ígd(ı)‿ (§§534, 1048) *cause to tell* < íg *tell* + -d caus. §2865; cp. ON. ⲉⲣⲓⲁ, ⲉⲕⲓⲁ πυνθάνομαι *GNT*, s.v.].

ind. pres. aī‿íddırı⌢, ɛr‿íddın⌢ (-dī⌢, -dí⌢); fut. aī‿bíddırı⌢; perf. aī‿íddıgori⌢ (N. -iko-, -iho-).
imperat. íddı⌢.
subj. past aī‿íddısı⌣ (su‿).
aī‿tírg‿ıddıríddı⌢ I('ll §5369) ask (each of §5458) them.
aī‿ólgon‿nónŋɛŋŋon‿ɛkkı‿bíddırı⌢ before I go I shall ask you sc. whether I may; ‿nónŋɛŋŋon‿ < ‿nógmɛŋon‿ §§661–2; §5744.
aī‿bı‿maŋ-kánd‿ɛssıg‿íddır‿ɛgi⌢ I shall go to that house to ask for water; maŋ-kán s.v. kå‿; ‿ɛgi⌢ §6223.
íddar‿ (-dår‿; §2200ff.) and
ıddíd‿ (§§2256ff.) n. *asking, inquiry, question, request.*
ídd-an (§§3890ff.) v.t. *tell to ask, etc., let ask, etc.*
tɛ́kkı‿íddan⌢ *let him (her) ask him (her).*
ıddır-ɛ-ğŭ-bŭ- (§4069) v.t. stat. *be on one's way (coming) to ask, etc.*
ıddır-ɛ-nóg (§§4048ff.) v.t. *go to ask, etc.*
ıddır-ɛ-nóg-bŭ- (-nóggŭ- §546; §4058) v.t. stat. *be on one's way (going) to ask, etc.*
ıddır-ɛ-tå- (§§4060ff.) v.t. *come to ask, etc.*
íddı-kattı- (N. -ıha-; §4093) v.p. *be asked, etc.*
íddo‿ *on (etc.) you (pl.) s.v. -r‿.*
ídıw‿ (§§2699, 2707) card. num. *eight* [RSN, §§116–18].
obj. ídıwg(ı)‿, ídıwg(ı)‿ §1522, -gi⌢.
pl. íd(ı)wı‿.
íd(ı)wun⌢ (-wũ⌢, -wú⌢ §§939, 5232) and
tɛr‿íd(ı)wun⌢ (tɛr‿ §5233) *it's (they're) eight.*
íd(ı)wín⌢ (-wí⌢, -wí⌢ §5235) and
tír‿íd(ı)wín⌢ (tır‿ §5236) *they're eight.*
gírıš‿ídıw‿dabóskó⌢ *eight piastres have disappeared* (§5239).
så‿íd(ı)wun⌢ *it's eight o'clock.*
ıdíwn-d(ı)‿ (§2737a) adj. *appertaining to eight, of eight, eight's.*
ín‿súfr‿ıdíwndın⌢ *this table is for (a party of) eight.*
ıd(ı)wín-d(ı)‿ (§2737b) adj. = ıdíwnd(ı)‿.
ıd(ı)w-ínt(ı)‿ (íd(ı)wınt(ı)‿; §2740) ord. num. *eighth.*
ıd(ı)wıntínd(ı)‿ (§2743) adj. *appertaining to the eighth.*
íd(ı)wırɛ‿ (§2745) n. ⅛, *eighth part* [< ídıw 8 + -ır *action of making + -ɛ‿ of n. ess., so *one of what makes into 8 §2287].
obj. -rɛg‿.
pl. -rɛnč(ı)‿.
ıdíw-kırı‿ (-kírı‿ §1532; §2736) num. adj. *about eight.*
ıdıwngår‿ (-wŋg-; §§2758, 5261–7) num. *the whole eight, all eight.*
obj. -årk(ı)‿, -ki⌢.
tɛr‿ıdıwngårk‿ɛttågoran⌢ *they (have) brought the whole eight* (§5199).
kám‿ıdıwngårkı‿ğånårkoran⌢ *they (have) bought all eight camels.*
ídıw-an- (§2760) v.i. *become eight.*
ídıwam-bŭ- (§2761) v.i. stat. *be in a state or condition of becoming eight.*
ıdíwg-ır (N. -ıwkır; §2759) v.t. caus. *make into eight.*
ıdıwgır-båg (N. -ıwkır-; §4138) v.t. *divide into eight.*
imperat. ıdıwgırbåk!
ıdrís n. *Idrís, a man's name* [< إِدْرِيس].
obj. -ísk(ı)‿, -ki⌢.
ígıd‿ *tale, etc. s.v. íg tell, etc.*
ıgídd(ı) (§3723) v.t. *water, give drink to.*
ind. pres. aī‿ıgíddırı⌢; perf. aī‿ıgíddıgori⌢ (N. -iko-, -iho-).
wɛ́lg‿ɛ́ssıg‿ıgíddı⌢ *give the dog some water to drink.*
kámlıg‿ıgıddıríddan⌢ *they water (each of §5458) the camels.*
ıgíddar‿ (-dår‿; §§2200ff.) and
ıgıddíd‿ (§§2256ff.) n. *watering, etc.*
ıgídd-an (§§3890ff.) v.t. *tell to water, etc., let water, etc.*
ıgíddı-bŭ- (§3931β) v.i. stat. *be in a watered (etc.) state or condition.*
tínč‿ıgíddıbūran⌢ *the cows (cattle, s.v. tí‿) are (have been) watered.*
ıgıddır-ɛg-ǻg- (§§4071ff.) = ıgıddɛdól-.
ıgıddır-ɛ-dól- (-dᵒd- §1178; §4022) and
ıgıddır-ɛ-dól- (-rᵒd-; §4027) v.t. *be about to water, etc.*
ıgıddır-ɛ-ğŭ-bŭ- (§4069) v.t. stat. *be on one's way (coming) to water, etc.*
ıgıdd-ɛ-må- (§4036) and
ıgıddır-ɛ-må- (§4041) v.t. *become unable to water, etc.*
ıgıddır-ɛ-nóg (§§4048ff.) v.t. *go to water, etc.*
ıgıddır-ɛ-nóg-bŭ- (-nóggŭ- §546; §4058) v.t. stat. *be on one's way (going) to water, etc.*
tíg‿ıgıddırɛnóggūn⌢ *(s)he is on his (her) way to water the cow.*
kámlıg‿ıgıddıríddɛnóggūran⌢ *they are on their way to water (each of §5458) the camels.*
ıgıddır-ɛ-tå- (§§4060ff.) v.t. *come to water, etc.*
ıgıddɛd-ǻg- (§§3877ff.) v.t. *be in the situation of having watered, etc.*
ıgıddíŋ-ır ("̄-, N. -ŋkır; §3688) v.t. caus. *cause or allow to water, etc.*
tíg‿ıgıddıŋgíddı⌢ I('ll §5369) *have the cow watered.*
tɛ́kkı‿káčč‿ıgıddıŋgíddan⌢ *they make (let) him water the horse.*
ıgrígı‿ adj. and n. *Greek* [< Sudan Ar. اَفْرِيقِي ıgrígi id. < Greek].
obj. ıgrígıg‿.
pl. ıgrígınč(ı)‿ (-īgınč(ı)‿ §1636).
ıgrígıgɛb‿bánnıran⌢ (-b‿b- < -d‿b- §518) *they talk Greek.*
ıgrígıt‿tír‿ (-t‿t- < -g‿t- §707) *give it (them) to the Greek.*
ığåza n. *leave of absence* [< إِجَازَة id.].
obj. -zag‿.
ığåzag‿årkon⌢ *he (has) got leave of absence.*
ığåzar‿åŋkó⌢ and
ığåz‿åŋkó⌢ (§5493) *he went (has gone) on leave.*
ıláttɛ‿ n. *Letti (on map), a district on the right bank of the Nile, from Amuntógo to opposite Båg, below Old Dóngola.*
obj. ıláttɛg‿, ıláttɛg‿ (§1532).
ílbɛ‿ (ɛ́l-, -bå‿, -ba‿) n. *small receptacle, small box, tin* [< عُلْبَة id.].
obj. -bɛg‿.
pl. -bɛnč(ı)‿.
ílla‿ (i) prep. (§4282) *less, minus, except* [< إِلَّا id.].
ídıw‿ílla‿rúbu‿ (§5297) and
ídıwır‿ílla‿rúbu‿ (§5301) (a) 7¾; (b, of the time) *a quarter to eight* (s.v. så‿).
(ii) conj. (§4483) *except that.*
aī‿dúŋgı‿mállɛg‿ɛ́lkor‿ílla‿rıjål‿ tóskıg‿ɛlkómunun⌢ I *(have) found all the money except three dollars (that) I did not find.*
‿ıllår‿ (-lar‿, -lɛr‿ §1327) postp. (i = prep. §4287; §4377) *(a) for, intended for, for the purpose of; (b) for, for the sake of, on account of, because of* [< ﷲ *relationship* + -r‿ *in*]—follows the genitive (§5902); in pause also predicative (§§5858–60).
ğawåb‿dåná‿bústan‿ıllar? *is there a letter for the post?*
ín‿hébırn‿ıllår, ín‿hébırn‿ıllårmunun⌢ *this (that) is for ink, this (that) is not for ink.*
mállɛ́nn‿ıllår⌢ *it is all for you.*
ín‿ɛ́nn‿ıllaró? *is this for you?*
ín‿ánn‿ıllårmunun⌢ *this is not for me (us).*
tím‿báññɛ́g‿ánn‿ıllår‿dúllon⌢ *their language is difficult for me (us).*
aī‿ɛ́nn‿íllɛr‿nógburi⌢ I *am going on your account (...for your sake).*
‿ıllår‿ (-lar‿, -lɛr‿ §1327) postp. (ii = conj. §4287; §§4378, 6210–13) *(a) in order that; (b) because.*
— follows subjunctive genitive (§§2943, 2953):
aī‿gɛddımɛ́rın‿ıllar‿bódri⌢ I('ll §5369) *run that I may get ahead.*
aī‿gɛddımɛ́sın‿ıllår‿bótkori⌢ I *ran (have run) in order that I might get ahead.*
wīlg‿kobíttı‿kópkoran‿aī‿tírgı‿nálmɛndın‿ıllår⌢ *yesterday they closed the door in order that I should not see them.*
súttɛ‿nóg‿ɛ́r‿ğómkattımɛnınn‿ıllår⌢ *go quickly that you may not be beaten (propera ne vapules).*
sɛrɛ́gırúskur, túrug‿årkɛmɛnın‿ıllar⌢ *set it well, so that the wind should not throw it down.*
bålkoran‿dígırmɛndann‿ıllår⌢ *they take care lest they fall.*
aī‿bóssun‿ıllar‿gɛddımɛ́gori⌢ (‿bóssun‿ < ‿bódsun‿ §688) *because I ran I (have) got ahead.*
ɛr‿ɛskığåbɛmunun‿ğúgr‿ɛ́nn‿ıllår⌢ *you can't touch it because it is (too) hot.*
íččıg‿ɛr‿ıšínsınn‿ıllår‿ɛ́kkı‿šɛkkırɛ́n⌢ *(s)he thanks you for sending the milk, lit. ...thanks you because you sent....*
sándıgoran‿ar‿tuššɛ́ssun‿ıllɛr⌢ *they were alarmed at our getting lost, lit. ...because we got lost.*
íllɛ‿ n. *wheat* [RSN, §80; cp. ON. ⲉⲓⲗⲗⲉ id. GNT, s.v.].
obj. -lɛg‿.

pl. -lɛnč(ı)⌣.
illɛ⌣kárǧın⌣tå⌣turúpkɛm⌣múttıran, ǧámmɛgıddan, nŭrɛm⌣bérro⌣šóndıran⌢ (-m⌣m- < -d⌣m- §600) *when the wheat gets ripe they reap it with sickles, gather it together, and strew it round the post in the threshing-floor.*
íllɛr⌣ *in the wheat.*
íllɛr⌢ (§§5858–60) *(s)he (it) is (they are) in the wheat.*
ıllɛ́n-d(ı)⌣ (§§2545 ff.) adj. *appertaining to wheat, of wheat.*
⌣íllɛr⌣ *for, etc.* = ⌣ıllår⌣.
ím⌣ < ín⌣ *this, your (pl.) before b, f, m* (§§592, 595–7, 604, 608).
ımắnı⌣, -ni⌢ n. *Eimani (on map), a village on the right bank of the Nile, near the southern end of Argo Island* [< إيماني].
obj. -nıg⌣.
ımắnır⌣ (s.v. -r⌣) *at (to) Imáni.*
ımắnır⌢ (§6007) *(s)he (it) is (they are) at Imáni.*
ımắnın-árt(ı)⌣, -ti⌢ n. *a village and district now part of the south-eastern end of Argo Island* [*Imáni's Island*].
obj. -tıg⌣.
ımbáb⌣ *your father* s.v. -båb⌣.
ím⌣båb⌣ *this door.*
ımbábn⌣úsut! *a vulgar curse* s.v. usud⌣.
ımbánɛss(ı)⌣ *your paternal aunt* s.v. -båb⌣.
ımbánna⌣ *your paternal uncle* s.v. -båb⌣.
ım-bél (ímbɛl §1880) v.i. (a) *rise, get up, come up, go up;* (b) *start* [< *ınbél < √ín- (on, after) rising (§4533) + bél issue* §2861; *RN*, §164].
ind. pres. âı⌣ımbélli⌢, ɛr⌣ımbélın⌢ (⌣ímbɛlın⌢; -li⌢, -lí⌢); fut. âı⌣bımbélli⌢; perf. âı⌣ımbélkori⌢.
imperat. ímbɛl!, pl. ımbélwɛ! (ímbɛl-, -wɛ́!).
subj. past âı⌣ımbélsı⌣ (-su⌣).
neg. imperat. tókkon⌣ımbélmɛn! (⌣ímbɛl-), pl. tókkon⌣ımbélmɛwwɛ! (⌣ímbɛl-, -wɛ́!).
âı⌣tɛ́g⌣ɛwɛ̆ri, tókkon⌣ímbɛlmɛn! *I say 'sit down', don't get up.*
šɛ́tıl⌣ågın, ımbélmunun⌢ *the young plant remains (stunted), it does not come up.*
gŭ⌣dámunun⌣tɛr⌣ímbɛlnn⌣íllår⌢ *there is no soil for (to enable) it to come up (in).*
X. sáırtōn⌣tågoru? *where have you come from?*
Y. wılgı⌣hándagırtōn⌣ımbélkoru⌢ *we left (lit. started from) El-Xándaq yesterday.*
X. båbŭr⌣sıntåb⌣bımbélın? (-b⌣b- < -d⌣b- §518 or -g⌣b- §519) *when will the steamer (train) start?*
Y. ımbɛlóskó⌢ *it has started.*
ar⌣índotōn⌣ımbélkıru⌣tɛ́kk⌣âıgı⌣ǧíllɛgır⌢ *when we leave here remind me of it (him, her).*
ímbɛlar⌣ (-lår⌣; §§2200 ff.) and
ımbɛlíd⌣ (§§2256 ff.) n. *rising, starting.*
ímbɛl-an (§§3890 ff.) v.t. *tell to rise, etc., let rise, etc.*
ımbɛl-bél (§4133) v.i. *issue after rising, etc., start out.*
imperat. ímbɛlbɛl!

ımbɛlbɛlíŋg-ır ($\overline{--}$, N. -ŋkır; §4214) v.t. caus. *cause or allow to start out.*
âı⌣tékk⌣ımbɛlbɛlıŋgírkori⌢ *I (have) made (let) him (her) start out.*
ımbɛlbɛlk-ídd(ı) (§4215) v.t. caus. *cause or allow to start out.*
ind. pres. âı⌣ımbɛlbɛlkíddıri⌢.
imperat. ımbɛlbélkıddı!
âı⌣tékk⌣ımbɛlbɛlkíddıgori⌢ *I (have) made (let) him (her) start out.*
ımbél-bŭ- ($\acute{-}\tilde{\;}$; §3931 α) v.i. stat. *be in a rising (etc.) state or condition.*
ind. pres. âı⌣ımbɛ́lbŭri⌢, $\acute{-}\tilde{\;}$.
gámrɛ⌣máktåbn⌣áttır⌣ímbɛlbūn⌢ *Capparis aphylla is coming up by the office.*
ımbɛll-ɛg-ắg- (§§4071 ff.) v.i. = ımbɛlɛdól-.
ımbɛll-ɛ-dól- (-lᵒd- §1178; §4022) and
ımbɛll-ɛ-dól- (-lᵒd; §4027) v.i. *be about to rise, etc.*
ımbɛl-ɛ-má- (§4036) and
ımbɛll-ɛ-má- (§4041) v.i. *become unable to rise, etc.*
ımbɛlɛd-ắg- (§§3877 ff.) v.i. *be in the situation of having risen, etc.*
ımbɛlk-ídd(ı) (§3726) v.t. caus. and v.t. = ımbɛlíŋgır.
imperat. ímbɛlkıddı!
âı⌣tékk⌣ımbɛlkíddıri⌢ *I make (left) him (her, it) rise, etc. (I start him (her, it)).*
båbŭrkı⌣så⌣ídıwır⌣ımbɛlkíddıran⌢ *they start the steamer (train) at 8 o'clock.*
ımbɛlíŋg-ır ($\acute{-}\tilde{\;}$, N. -ŋkır; §3688) (a) v.t. caus. *cause or allow to rise, etc.;* (b) v.t. *raise, start.*
gatírkɛ⌣så⌣kólodır⌣ımbɛlıŋgíddan⌢ *they start the train at 7 o'clock.*
ımbɛlos-wídɛ (-owwídɛ §724; §§4180–4; -osgıwídɛ, -ozgı-, -oggı- §4185; -wídɛ́, -wᵘdɛ́) v.i. *turn (etc. s.v. wídɛ) after rising, etc., start back.*
ımbɛlowwıdɛrósru, másıl⌣så⌣tóskın owéllo⌣butōrosíŋgɛt⌢ (*RN*, §167) *let us start back, because* (-ɛt⌢ s.v. -ɛd⌣ (ii) s.v. éd) *before three hours the sun will (certainly) set.*
ımbɛl-sumắrkı-nóg (§4198) v.i. *(after) rising (etc.) go (away) in haste.*
imperat. ımbɛlsumărkınók!
ımbɛlsumărkınókkoran⌢ *they got up and hurried off.*
ımbɛl-sumắrkı-tá (§4198) v.i. *(after) rising (etc.) come in haste.*
imperat. ımbɛlsumărkıtá! and $\overline{---\cup\underline{\;}\;\;}$ (§1871)
ımbɛlsumarkıtågoran⌢ *they got up and came in haste.*
ımbɛl-wídɛ (-wıdɛ́, -wᵘdɛ́; §3747 ɛ′) v.i. *(after) rising (etc.) turn (etc. s.v. wídɛ), start back.*
ımbɛlwídɛru! (§5376) *let us start back!*
ımbénna⌣ *your paternal uncle* s.v. -bénna⌣.
ímbɛs⌣ *your brother* s.v. -bɛs⌣.
ımdɛ⌣ n. *signature* [< مْضَى *id.*].
obj. -dɛg⌣.
pl. -dɛnč(ı)⌣.
ímıl⌣ (§2730) card num. *hundred.*
obj. ımílg(ı)⌣, -gı⌢.

ógıǧ⌣ímıl⌣tågon⌢ and less commonly ógǧı⌣ímıl⌣tågoran⌢ *a hundred men came (have come).*
ímıl⌣wɛr⌣ and ímıl⌣lɛr⌣ (§580) *one hundred.*
ımíl-wɛr⌣ and ımíl-lɛr⌣ (§2731) *a hundred.*
ımíln-d(ı)⌣ (ımínd(ı)⌣ §807, ımíld(ı)⌣ §806; §2738) adj. *appertaining to 100, of 100, 100's.*
ımılínt(ı)⌣ (ímılınt(ı)⌣; §2742) ord. num. *hundredth.*
ımíl-kırı⌣ (-kírı⌣ §1701; §2736) num. adj. *about 100.*
ımíl-an- (§2760) v.i. *become 100.*
ımílam-bŭ- (§2761) v.i. stat. *be in a state or condition of becoming 100.*
ímmå⌣ (-ma⌣) n. *turban* [< عِمَّة *id.*].
obj. -måg⌣, -mag⌣.
pl. -månč(ı)⌣, -manč(ı)⌣, -mɛnč(ı)⌣.
ímmam⌣másır⌣ *without a turban.*
ımmam⌣másır⌢ (§§5858–60) *he is without a turban.*
in⌣ *of you (pl.), your (pl.)* gen. of ír⌣.
ín⌣ (ín⌣ §1155; ın⌣ §§1721–2; §956 d; §§2639–41) dem. pron. *this, that (near)* [< ín⌣ *of the hand;* cp. ON. ειη *id.* *GNT*, s.v.; cp. *JL*, pp. 402–3; *RSN*, §72].
obj. íŋg(ı)⌣, íŋ-, -gi⌢.
gen. íŋın⌣v.c., ınín⌣c. (ínn-, ınn- §2640).
pl. íŋgu⌣.
pl. obj. íŋgug⌣.
— used substantively and adjectively (§§5120–1):
ín-taran⌢ (a) *this is (s)he (it);* (b) *it's this (one).*
ímmunun⌢ *it's not this (one).*
íŋguŋ⌣kóččır⌣úskur⌢ *put it (them) on top of these.*
ínım⌣bıtắn⌣sɛ́? *where is this one's child?*
ínn⌣ugŭ́g⌣, -gi⌢ adv. *tonight.*
ínn⌣ugŭ́b⌣bıtåran⌢ (-b⌣b- < -g⌣b- §519) *they will come tonight.*
ín⌣ádåm⌣ *this person* (§4866).
ín⌣ádåmı⌣ *these persons.*
ín⌣dúŋ(ı)⌣ (a) *this money;* (b) *your (pl.) money* (s.v. ír⌣).
ím⌣bélɛd⌣ (-m⌣b- < -n⌣b- §592) *this (your, pl.) country (village).*
ín⌣fádıl⌣, ím⌣fádıl⌣ and íf⌣fádıl⌣ (§542) *this (your, pl.) kindness.*
íŋ⌣gadíjɛ⌣ (§646) *this (your, pl.) lawsuit.*
ín⌣ǧéll(ı)⌣ *this (your, pl.) work.*
ín⌣hám⌣ *this (your, pl.) donkey.*
íŋ⌣kám⌣ (§655) *this (your, pl.) camel.*
íŋ⌣kámlı⌣ *these (your, pl.) camels.*
ín⌣lámbå⌣ and íl⌣lámbå⌣ (§581) *this (your, pl.) lamp.*
ím⌣mår⌣ (§604) *this (your, pl.) village.*
ín⌣nórt(ı)⌣ *this (your, pl.) flour.*
ín⌣rádd(ı)⌣ and ír⌣rádd(ı)⌣ (§670) *this (your, pl.) answer.*
ín⌣såfar⌣ and ís⌣såfar⌣ (§680) *this (your, pl.) journey.*
ín⌣šåbåkå⌣ and íš⌣šåbåkå⌣ (§698) *this (your, pl.) net.*
ın⌣tí⌣ *this (your, pl.) cow.*

nd⌣ — índ(ı)

íw⌣wél⌣ (§720) *this (your, pl.) dog.*
íw⌣wélı⌣ *these (your, pl.) dogs.*
ín⌣zábıd⌣ and íz⌣zábıd⌣ (§735) *this (your, pl.) officer.*
ín-do⌣ (s.v. -r⌣) *(a) on (in) this (that); (b) to this (that).*
ín-do⌣ (§§4448–9, 6007) *adv. (a) here, there (near); (b) hither.*
  índ⌣ágın⌣ *(s)he (it) sits (lives, etc. s.v. ág) here.*
  ékkεn⌣índ⌣εgó⌢ *(s)he (it) was here (just) now.*
  índo⌣tá⌢ *come here.*
  índ⌣étta⌢ *bring him (her, it, them) here.*
  tεr⌣índon⌢ (⌣índõ⌢, ⌣índó⌢ §§5770–1, ⌣índo⌣ §6007) *(s)he (it) is here.*
  kám⌣índón⌢ (§1970; ⌣índon⌢, ⌣índõ⌢, índó⌢, ⌣índo⌢) *the camel is here.*
  tır⌣índončín⌢ *they are here.*
  X. wó⌣saıt! Sɑɣíd!
  Y. áı⌣índó! *here I am!* and índo⌣áı! *I'm here!* (§4626).
  áı⌣índo-taran⌢ and áı⌣índo-tànnan⌢ *it is I here.*
  X. tér⌣índorέ? *is (s)he (it) here?*
  Y. índómunun⌢ *(s)he (it) isn't here.*
  X. tır⌣índoré? *are they here?*
  Y. índómunan⌢ *they are not here.*
  kál⌣índoré? and kál⌣índojó? (-doʲó?) *is the food here?*
índo⌣ *may form a genitive (§4479):*
  índon⌣ádır⌣ *the winter here, lit.…of here.*
ındón-d(ı)⌣ (§§2545ff., §2553) *adj. appertaining to here, of this place (Ger. hiesig).*
ín-do-tŏn⌣ (s.v. -r-tŏn⌣; §§5858–60) *from this.*
ín-do-tŏn⌣ (§§4453, 6007) *adv. from here, hence.*
íŋg-εd⌣ (-εt⌣ §469, ⌢⌣ §1532, -έ⌢ §966; §§5858–60) *(a) by (with, at, to, from, etc. s.v. -εd⌣) this (that); (b) adv. (§§4461, 6007) in this (that) way, thus, so.*
  X. sεrēgıruskur, íŋgé! *put it properly, like that.*
  Y. *misplaces it.*
  X. ıŋgémmunun, tékké! (-mm- < -dm- §600) *not like that, like that! (showing).*
  án⌣dárub⌣íŋgέ⌢ *my (our) road is in this direction.*
  kóle⌣mám⌣mármárrotón⌣íŋgέ⌢ (§6031) *the water-wheel (irrigable estate) is on this side of (s.v. -rtŏn⌣) that village.*
nín-d(ı)⌣ (§§2545ff.) *adj. appertaining to this (that), of this (that).*
ŋgún-d(ı)⌣ (§§2545ff.) *adj. appertaining to these (those), of these (those).*
íŋk-ε⌣ (íŋkέ⌢ §1532; §§4411, 5940, 5956) *adv. in this (that) manner, like this (that), in this (that) position, posture or direction, so, thus [*having a tendency to this < íŋk- obj. (§4410)+-έ *have a tendency to §213].*
  tεr⌣íŋkε⌣wέgó⌢ *(s)he said so (tεr⌣ unless emphatic tέr⌣ commonly absent §§5078–9).*
  íŋg⌣íŋk⌣uskúrkori⌢ *I (have) put this like this (…like this, like that).*
  íŋkε⌣bán⌢ (s.v. bú) *let him (her, it) be so (…like this, like that).*

íŋk⌣áukattıgõ⌢ *it was (has been) done in this (that) way.*
íŋkε⌣kannέn⌣íŋk⌣óŋgon⌢ *in this direction is north (and §6239) in that is south.*
tεr⌣íŋkémunun⌢ *it's not so ((s)he's not like that; tεr⌣ commonly absent).*
íŋkémunan⌢ *they're not like that (…in that position, etc.).*
íŋk-εg⌣, -gi⌢ (§§4412–13, 5983) *adv. = íŋkε⌣.*
tókkon⌣íŋk⌣áumεwwέ⌢ and íŋkεt⌣tókkon⌣áumεwwέ⌢ (-t⌣t- < -g⌣t- §707) *don't (pl.) behave (do it, etc. s.v. áu) like that.*
íŋkεk⌣kınnέgi! *(come, move it, etc.) a little this way! (…in this direction!).*
X. sεrēgıráu, íŋkέ⌣ (§1964) *do it properly, like this.*
Y. *does it wrong.*
X. ıŋkémmunun, tékké! (-mm- < -gm- §601) *not like that, like that! (showing).*
íŋkεnε⌣ (⌢⌣⌣ §1532; §§4428, 5968) *adv. now, just now (of the present or immediate past or future) = ékkεnε⌣. s.v. έr⌣ [< *íŋ-k-εn-εn (§939) it is (that) it says 'this'; -εn- §213].*
íŋkεnεg⌣ (⌢⌣⌣ §1532; -gi⌢ §5981; §5988) *adv. = íŋkεnε⌣.*
íŋ-kırı⌣ (⌢⌣⌣, ⌢⌣⌣; §§2539–40) *adj. resembling this (that), like this (that), of this (that) kind.*
íŋgu-kırı⌣ (§§2539–40) *adj. resembling these (those), like these (those).*
ınındí-kırı⌣ (§2651) *adj. like that appertaining to this (that), like this (that) one's.*
ınıŋgúndı-kırı⌣ (§2651) *adj. like that appertaining to these (those).*
ınındínčı-kırı⌣ (§2651) *adj. like those appertaining to this (that).*
ıŋgundínčı-kırı⌣ (§2651) *adj. like those appertaining to these (those).*
ıŋ-kótt(ı)⌣ (§2648) *dem. pron. as much (many) as this (that), so much (many) [< ín⌣ this (that)+kótt(ı)⌣ amount, quantity, size].*
  obj. -tıg⌣, -gi⌢.
  ıŋkóttıg⌣étta⌢ *bring as much as this.*
ıŋkótt-ēr⌣ (§2683) *indef. dem. pron. (about) as much (many) as this (that), (about) so much (many) [< *ıŋkótt-wēr⌣ §717 as much?].*
  obj. ıŋkóttēg⌣, ⌢⌣ , ⌢⌣ (§1728), -gi⌢.
  gen. ıŋkóttērn⌣v., -tēnn⌣v., -tēn⌣c.
  ıŋkóttēg⌣étta⌢ *bring (about) as much as this.*
  tεr⌣mén⌣ıŋkottēg⌣εttágō? *why did (s)he bring (has (s)he brought) so much?*
  ıŋkóttεrré? and ıŋkóttēré? (§1004) *is it so much?*
  tεr⌣mén⌣ıŋkóttεrré? (-tēré?) *why is it so much?*
  tεr⌣ıŋkóttεrun⌢ (§1728) *it's as much as this (that).*
  tεr⌣ıŋkóttεrmunun⌢ *it's not so much.*
índ (before a vowel §1122) < índo⌣ *here s.v. ín⌣.*
índa⌣ *your home,*
  ındán! *go home!,*

ındándi⌢ *I go to your (sg. and pl.) home* and
ındáwwε! *go (pl.) home! s.v. dá⌣ home.*
ındεǧǧú *carry along s.v. índ(ı).*
ındεnnóg *carry off s.v. índ(ı).*
ındétta⌢ *go and fetch it s.v. índ(ı).*
índ⌣étta⌢ (< índo⌣étta⌢) *bring it here.*
índ(ı)⌣ (§2302) *my mother (s.v. -ɛ́n⌣) [RSN, §129].*
voc. wºíndi! (wín-, s.v. wó⌣!).
obj. índıg⌣, -dıgi⌢.
gen. índın⌣.
tínness⌣índí⌢ (§939) *his (her) sister is my mother.*
índınarton⌣néukori⌢ *I (have) inherited it from my mother.*
índıkεgíd⌣ *my mother's sister, my maternal aunt [s.v. -έn⌣].*
obj. índıkεgídk(ı)⌣, -ítk(ı)⌣, -ítt(ı)⌣ §2462, -kı⌢, -ti⌢.
pl. índıkεgıdı⌣.
índıkεgímburu⌣ (⌢⌣⌣⌢ §1532) *and as noun-complex.*
índıkεgım⌣búru⌣ (§4812) *my mother's sister's daughter.*
índıkεgıntŏ́d⌣ and **índıkεgın⌣tŏ́d⌣** *my mother's sister's son.*
ındín-d(ı)⌣ (§§2545ff.) *adj. appertaining to my mother, my mother's.*
  dúŋg⌣ındínd(ı)⌣ *my mother's money.*
índ(ı)⌣ *yours (pl.) s.v. ír⌣.*
índ(ı)⌣ v.t. (a) *lift, take up, pick up; (b) take away, remove* [< √ín- rise (§4533)+-d caus., so cause to rise §2865; RSN, §129].
  ind. pres. áı⌣índırı⌢, εr⌣índın⌢ (-dí⌢, -dí⌢); fut. áı⌣bíndırı⌢; perf. áı⌣índıgorı⌢ (N. -ıko-, -ıho-).
  imperat. índi!, pl. índıwε! (-wέ!).
  subj. past áı⌣índısı⌢ (-su⌢).
  tέr⌣dúlg⌣índıgó, áı⌣kíññarıs⌣sandúgır⌣undúkkori⌢ (-s⌣s- < -g⌣s- §678) *(s)he took (has taken) away the big one(s §4647) and (but §6239) I (have) put the small ones into the box.*
índar⌣ (-dár⌣; §§2200ff.) *and.*
índíd⌣ (§§2256ff.) *n. lifting, etc.*
índ-an (§§3890ff.) *v.t. tell to lift, etc., let lift, etc.*
índı-bŭ- (§3931β) *v.i. stat. be in a lifted (etc.) state or condition.*
índır-εg-ág- (§§4071ff.) *v.t. = ındεdól.*
ınd-ε-dól- (-dºd- §1178; §4022) *and*
ındır-ε-dól- (-rºd-; §4027) *v.t. be about to lift, etc.*
ındır-ε-ǧŭ-bŭ- (§4069) *v.t. stat. be on one's way (coming) to lift, etc.*
ınd-ε-má- (§4036) *and*
ındır-ε-má- (§4041) *v.t. become unable to lift, etc.*
ındır-ε-nóg- (§§4048ff.) *v.t. go to lift, etc.*
ındır-ε-nóg-bŭ- (-nóggŭ- §546; §4058) *v.t. stat. be on one's way (going) to lift, etc.*
ındır-ε-tá- (§§4060ff.) *v.t. come to lift, etc.*
ındεd-ág- (§§3877ff.) *v.t. be in the situation of having lifted, etc.*
ındεb-bítt(ı) (§§4169ff.; -dεggıbít- §§4176–8) *v.t. pick up (etc. s.v. bítt(ı)) after lifting, etc.*
  ím⌣mállεš⌣ıbírk⌣ındεbbíttırı⌢ (-š⌣š- < -g⌣š- §695) *I (shall, will §5369)*

take a basket and pick all this up; § 5599; ímᴗmállɛᴗ *a pronoun-complex* (§ 5210).

ındéd-dā- (§ 3990; -déggıdā- §§ 3993-4) v.t. *be going along having lifted, etc., be going along bearing.*

ındeğ̌-ğ̌ú (§§ 4169ff., 5722; ındɛggığ̌ú §§ 4176-8) v.t. *proceed (etc. s.v. ğ̌ú) after lifting, etc., carry along, carry away.*
imperat. ındéğ̌ğ̌u!, ındéggığ̌u!

ınd-ɛğ̌ğ̌ú (§§ 4169ff., 5722) v.t. *convey (etc. s.v. ɛğ̌ğ̌ú s.v. éd) after lifting, etc., carry along, carry away.*
imperat. ındéğ̌ğ̌u!

ındéğ̌ğ̌u-an (-ğ̌ᵘan, -ğ̌wan, -ğ̌an § 3898; § 3905) v.t. *tell to carry along (away), let carry along (away).*

ındɛğ̌ğ̌-ārk(ı) (-aríkk(ı); § 3766) v.t. *throw (away) after carrying along (away).*

ındɛğ̌ğ̌ārk-an (-aríkkan; §§ 3890ff., 3905) v.t. *tell to throw (away) after carrying along (away), let throw (away) after carrying along (away).*

ındɛğ̌ğ̌-éwır (§ 3765) v.t. *exchange after carrying along (away).*
árᴗíŋgıᴗdólmunun, ındɛğ̌ğ̌éwırᴖ *we don't like this, take it away and exchange it.*

ındɛğ̌ğ̌éwır-an (§§ 3890ff., 3905) v.t. *tell to exchange after carrying along (away), let exchange after carrying along (away).*

ındɛğ̌ğ̌u-bőg (§ 3765) v.t. *pour (away) after carrying along (away).*
imperat. ındɛğ̌ğ̌ubők!

ındɛğ̌ğ̌ubőg-an (§§ 3890ff., 3905) v.t. *tell to pour (away) after carrying along (away), let pour (away) after carrying along (away).*

ındɛğ̌-ğ̌u-bŭ- (§§ 4220, 5724; -dɛggığ̌ú- § 4221) v.t. stat. *be on one's way (coming) after lifting, etc., be coming laden with.*

ınd-ɛğ̌ğ̌ubŭ- (§§ 4220, 5724) v.t. stat. *be on one's way (coming) with after lifting, etc., be bringing after lifting, etc.*
X. marákkᴗéttagoná? *has he brought (did he bring) the soup?*
Y. ındɛğ̌ğ̌úbūnᴖ *he (has) picked it up and is bringing it.*
X. ɛsmánó? (*who is?*—) ɣoθmán?
éndısᴗsaɣídᴗındɛğ̌ğ̌úbūnᴖ (-sᴗs- < -gᴗs- § 678) *Saɣíd is getting and bringing yours.*

ınden-nóg (§§ 4169ff., 4193; -dɛggınóg §§ 4176-8) v.t. *go (etc. s.v. nóg) after lifting, etc., bear away, carry off.*
ind. fut. aîᴗbındɛnnógríᴖ.
imperat. ındɛnnók! (́ ̀ § 1954), pl. -nógwɛ!, -nógwé!
fānúskᴗındɛnnókᴖ *take the lantern and go.*
sāḃᴗındɛnnogóskó̂ᴖ *and*
sāḃᴗındɛggınogóskó̂ᴖ *the cat has carried it off.*
sāmtőḋkᴗındɛnnógruá? *are we to (shall we § 5369b) take the kitten away?*

ınden-nóg-bŭ- (§ 4220; ındɛggı-nóg-bŭ- § 4221; -nóggŭ- § 546) v.t. stat. *be on one's way (going) after lifting, etc., be bearing away, be carrying off.*

ındet-tấ (§§ 4169ff., 5723; -dɛggıtấ §§ 4176-8) v.t. *come after lifting, etc., lift (etc.) and come, just go (§ 5713) and get, fetch, bring.*
imperat. ındétta!, ındéggıta!, pl. ındɛttấwɛ!, ⁻ ́ ⁻ ̌, ındɛggıtấwɛ!, ⁻ ́ ⁻ ̌.
sultāníjᴗıččíndıgᴗındéttaᴖ *go and get the milk-bowl.*
kúmḃᴗówwıgᴗındéttaᴖ *bring two eggs with you.*

ınd-ɛttấ (-éttä § 3855, § 5723) v.t. *bring (ɛttā s.v. éd) after lifting, etc.*
imperat. ındétta!, pl. ındéttấwɛ!, ⁻ ́ ⁻ ̌.
warákkᴗaîgononᴗasálgıᴗbındéttariᴖ *I shall (take up and) bring the paper with me tomorrow.*

ındett-áu (-åw, -áu; § 3765) v.t. *make (etc. s.v. áu) after bringing, etc.*
írıgᴗíndᴗındéttáuᴖ (ᴗíndᴗ < ᴗíndo) *pick up the rope, bring and make (construct) it here.*

ındett-úskur (§ 3765) v.t. *set (etc. s.v. úskur) after bringing, etc.*
sandúgᴗéččél-lēgᴗındettuskúddiᴖ (-l-l- < -l-w- § 580) *I('ll § 5369b) fetch another box and set it down.*

índıg-ır (N. -ıkır, -ıhır; § 3682) v.t. caus. *cause or allow to lift, etc.*

índı-kattı- (N. -ıha-; § 4093) v.p. *be lifted, etc.*

ındos-nóg (-onnóg § 629; §§ 4180-4; -osgınóg, -ozgı-, -oggı § 4185) v.t. *go (away) after lifting, etc.*
tóḋᴗdıgírkó, ámbɛsᴗındonnókkóᴖ *the child fell down; my brother after picking it up went away (sc. leaving the child).*

índıkɛgıd *my mother's sister* s.v. índ(ı).
índo *in this, here, etc.* s.v. ín.
ınɛ́n *your mother* s.v. -ɛ́n.
ınɛ́ɲᴗkumáttɛ! *a vulgar curse* s.v. kumáttɛ.
ınɛ́ŋkɛgıd *your mother's sister* s.v. -ɛ́n.
ıněén *this year* = ínᴗɣɛ́n (§ 1694) s.v. ɣɛ́n.
ínın *of this* gen. of ín.
ınn *of you (pl.), your (pl.)* gen. of ír.
ınn *of this* in ínnᴗuğúğ *tonight.*
ınnáū *your grandmother* s.v. -áū.
ınn-i *your (pl.) hands* s.v. í.
ínnɛss(ı) *your sister* s.v. -ɛss(ı).
ínnogo *your mother-in-law* s.v. -ogo.

N. **ınnóŋg(ı)** and
N. **ınóŋg(ı)** n. *today (hodiernus dies) = ınnóww(ı) [< ínın of this + -ón (§ 646) + -g(ı) § 2139; RSN, § 129].*
obj. -óŋgıg.

N. **ınnóŋgıg, -gi** and
N. **ınóŋgıg, -gi** (§ 4665) adv. *today (hodie).*
N. gutārᴗınóŋgıdᴗdıgranımbélbūn (-dᴗd- < -gᴗd- § 534) *the dust has blown up today in a great quantity.*

ınnőww(ı) (ınnów(ı)) n. *today (hodiernus dies) [contains ínın of this].*
obj. -wıg.
ınnőwwᴗádırun *today is wintry* (§ 4719).
ınnőwwᴗtúrugun, aîᴗbsafarémunun *today is (too) windy, I shall not travel,* lit. *today is wind...* (§ 4719).
ınnőwwᴗnɛhấr (§ 4750),
ınnőwwᴗnɛhấr (§ 4810),
ınnőwwᴗugrɛ́s (§ 4750) and
ınnőwwınᴗugrɛ́s (§ 4810) = ınnőw-w(ı).

hánᴗınnőwwıᴗfɛğ̌írkıᴗdåbugóᴖ *the donkey was present today at dawn (early this morning;* § 4750).

ınnőwwıg (ınnőwıg, -gi § 4665) adv. *today (hodie).*
ınnőwwıgᴗádırun *today it's wintry.*
ınnőwwıtᴗtålūgráfkıᴗgómkó (-tᴗt- < -gᴗt- § 707) *today (s)he (has) sent a telegram.*
hánᴗınnőwwıdᴗdabóskó (-dᴗd- < -gᴗd- § 534) *the donkey has disappeared today.*
X. aîᴗtékkıᴗbığāzɛ́ri *I shall punish him (her, it).*
Y. ınnőwwımᴗmugó (-mᴗm- < -gᴗm- § 601) *let him (her, it) off this time.*
ınnőwwᴗugrɛ́sk(ı),
ınnőwwᴗugrɛ́sır,
ınnőwwᴗugrɛ́sk(ı) and
ınnőwwınᴗugrɛ́sır *adverb-complex today.*

ınnőwwín-d(ı) (-nōwín-; §§ 2545ff.) adj. *appertaining to today, of today, today's.*
ınnőwwíndın *it is today's.*

ınnőwwíndı-kırı (-nōwín-; § 2541) adj. *resembling that of today, like today's.*
ınnowwíndıkırıdᴗdóllan (-dᴗd- < -gᴗd- § 534) *they like it (want some) like today's.*

ínnu *your grandfather* s.v. -u.
ínod *your father-in-law* s.v. -od.
ıntấ? adv. *when?* [remains of ısantắt. § 4439].
X. álıᴗtågon ɣáli *came (has come).*
Y. ıntấ? *when?*

ıntágk(ı)...? (-ákk-, -ki?) adv. *when...?* [remains of ısantágk(ı)...? § 4441].

ıntíllɛ n. *needle;* with collective sg. (§ 4696c) [RSN, § 80].
obj. -lɛg.
pl. -lɛnč(ı).

ıntımbáb *your (pl.) father* s.v. -báb.
ıntımbánɛss(ı) *your (pl.) paternal aunt* s.v. -báb.
ıntımbánna *your (pl.) paternal uncle* s.v. -báb.
ıntımbánna *your (pl.) paternal uncle* s.v. -bénna.
ıntımbɛs *your (pl.) brother* s.v. -bɛs.
ıntınɛ́n *your (pl.) mother* s.v. -ɛ́n.
ıntınɛ́ŋkɛgıd *your (pl.) maternal aunt* s.v. -ɛ́n.
ıntınnáū *your (pl.) grandmother* s.v. -áū.
ıntınnɛss(ı) *your (pl.) sister* s.v. -ɛss(ı).
ıntınnogo *your (pl.) mother-in-law* s.v. -ogo.
ıntınnu *your (pl.) grandfather* s.v. -u.
íntınod *your (pl.) father-in-law* s.v. -od.
ıntíŋg(ı) *your (pl.) maternal uncle* s.v. -g(ı).
íntıssőd *your (pl.) sister's child* s.v. -ssőd.

íñır (ıñír § 1752) (a) v.i. *wait, remain, stay;* (b) v.t. *wait for, await;* (c) v.t. *expect* [< ıríñ id. § 899].
ind. pres. aîᴗíñırri, ɛrᴗíñırın (́ ̌, -ri, -ri); fut. aîᴗbıñírri; perf. aîᴗíñírkori.
índoᴗbıñírran *they will wait (etc.) here.*
ɛrᴗnígᴗíñırın? *whom are you waiting for (...do you expect)?*

√iŋ-, √íŋg- — ırğέn⌣

jŏm⌣árıkırıg⌣íñırkoran⌢ they (have) waited (etc.) for about (-kırıg⌣) twenty days (§4666).
iñırar⌣ (-rár⌣; §§2200ff.) and
iñıríd⌣ (§§2256ff.) n. waiting, etc.
íñır-an (íñíran; §§3890ff.) v.t. tell to wait (for), etc., let wait (for), etc.
íñır-bŭ- (íñírbŭ-; §3931β) v.i. stat. be in an awaited (etc.) state or condition.
 bústa⌣kırăgεg⌣íñírbŭn⌢ the mail is expected on Sunday.
íñırr-ε-ğŭ́-bŭ- (§4069) v.i. and t. stat. be on one's way (coming) to wait (for), etc.
iñır-ε-mǎ- (§4036) and
iñırr-ε-mǎ- (§4041) v.i. and t. become unable to wait (for), etc.
iñırr-ε-nóg (§§4048ff.) v.i. and t. go to wait (for), etc.
iñırr-ε-nóg-bŭ- (-nóggŭ- §546; §4058) v.i. and t. stat. be on one's way (going) to wait (for), etc.
iñırr-ε-tǎ́ (§§4060ff.) v.i. and t. come to wait (for), etc.
iñıred-ăg- (§§3877ff.) v.i. and t. be in the situation of waiting (for), etc., be engaged in waiting (for), etc.
 íŋgu⌣gatírk⌣íñıredágran⌢ these are waiting for the train.
 âı⌣tåsı⌣wekídkı⌣tén⌣haddámı⌣tέkk⌣ iñıredágkoran⌢ when I arrived his servants were waiting for (expecting) him.
iñıreb-bŭ́ (§§3947-8, 4169ff.; -εggı-bŭ́ §§4176-8, §1931) (a) v.i. lie (etc. s.v. bŭ́) waiting, remain lying; (b) v.t. wait by, remain with, stay and mind.
 imperat. iñırέbbu!, iñıréggıbu!
 tεr⌣afésk⌣iñırέbbun⌣ (⌣iñıréggıbun⌢) (s)he stays and minds the baggage.
iñıréb-bŭ- (§3931β) v.i. stat. = iñırbŭ-.
 bābŭ́r⌣ınnŏwwıg⌣iñırέbbun⌢ the steamer (train) is expected today.
iñır-έtta (§4198) v.t. bring after awaiting, await and bring.
iñıréttar-an (§§3890ff., 3905) v.t. tell to bring after awaiting, etc., let bring after awaiting, etc.
iñıred-έtta (§4200; -rεggıtta §4201) v.t. bring after awaiting.
iñıredέttar-an (§§3890ff., 3905) v.t. = iñıréttaran.
 réddıg⌣iñıredέttaran⌢ let him (her) await and bring the answer.
iñırεt-tέb (§§4169ff.; -εggı-tέb §4176-8) v.i. and t. stand (stop, etc. s.v. tέb) waiting (for).
 imperat. iñıréttεp!, iñıréggıtεp! (§§1954-5).
 gatírk⌣iñırεttέbran⌢ they are waiting for the train.
 âıg⌣iñıréttεp⌢ stop and wait for me.
iñırεttέb-an (§§3890ff., 3905) v.t. tell to stand (etc.) waiting (for), let stand (etc.) waiting (for).
 X. tεbíñırın⌣ (s)he is waiting.
 Y. iñırεttέban⌢ let him (her) go on waiting.
iñırεt-tέg (§§4169ff.; -εggı-tέg §4176-8) v.i. and t. squat (sit, etc. s.v. tέg) waiting (for).
 imperat. iñıréttεk!, -έggıtεk!

 gatírk⌣iñırεttέgran⌢ they are waiting for the train.
 âı⌣bı-gatírk-iñırεttέgrı⌢ (§5384) I shall sit and wait for the train.
iñırεt-túrb(ı) (§§4169ff.; -εggı-túrb(ı) §§4176-8; -túbb(ı) §520) v.i. and t. (a) lie down (etc. s.v. túrb(ı)) waiting (for); (b) lie down keeping a watch on, lie down minding.
 afésk⌣índ⌣iñırεttúbbi⌢ lie here and mind the luggage.
íñır-kattı- (íñír-; §4093) v.p. be waited for, etc.
iñıros-έtta (§4203; -rosgέtta, -rozg-, -rogg- §4205) v.t. bring after awaiting.
 tírg⌣iñırosέtta⌢,
 tírg⌣iñırosέttarır⌢,
 tírg⌣iñırosırέtta⌢ and
 tírg⌣iñırosırέttarır⌢ (§5616) wait for them and bring them.
√íŋ-, √íŋg- (§4534) sweet.
iŋgíttεl adj. (a) rather sweet, a little sweet, sweetish; (b) sweet (=íŋg(ı)rĭ⌣) [<*iŋgírtεl⌣ (§713) <√íŋ-+-g obj. suff.+-ır causative suff. (§3665)+-t dem. (§4593) +-έ say (§213)+-l part. -ıŋg (§2958), so *that saying 'make sweet' §2526].
 obj. -gıttέlg(ı)⌣, -gi⌢.
 pl. -gíttεlı⌣.
 tímε⌣kınnέg⌣iŋgíttεlun⌢ (§1966) the water-melon is a little sweet.
 súkkar⌣ıŋgíttεlun⌢ (the) sugar is sweet.
íŋg(¹)rĭ⌣ adj. sweet [< √íŋg-+-r intensive (§4586)+-ĭ adjectival §2564].
 obj. ıŋg(¹)ríg⌣.
 pl. ıŋg(¹)ríŋč(ı)⌣, -rín-.
 súkkar⌣íŋgrín⌣ (the) sugar is sweet.
 íŋgrírέ? is it sweet?
íŋg(¹)r-an- (§3910α) v.i. become sweet.
íŋg(¹)ram-bŭ- (ıŋg(¹)rámbŭ §1932a; §§3949ff.) v.i. stat. be in a sweetened state or condition.
 gáhw⌣ıŋgrámbun⌢ the coffee is (has become) sweetened.
ıŋg(¹)ríg-ır (N. -íkır, -íhır; §3701) (a) v.t. caus. cause or allow to be sweet; (b) v.t. render sweet, sweeten.
ıŋgεlεdū́na n. swallow, bird resembling swallow = gεrεdū́n⌣ [<(τ)ήν χελιδόνα id. (χελιδών RN s.v. engeledūna)].
 obj. -nag⌣, -gi⌢.
 pl. -nanč(ı)⌣.
íŋg(ı)⌣ obj. of ín⌣ this.
íŋg(ı)⌣ your maternal uncle s.v. -g(ı)⌣.
ıŋglíz⌣ n. Englishman, English person [<اِنْكْلِيز id. collective §2403].
 obj. -ízk(ı)⌣, -ísk(ı)⌣, -ki⌢.
 pl. -ízı⌣.
 ıŋglíz-zēr⌣âıg⌣dέŋkon⌣ (-z-z- <-z-w- §737) an Englishman gave it to me.
ıŋglízn-d(ı)⌣ (§§2545ff.) adj. appertaining to (an) Englishman.
ıŋglızín-d(ı)⌣ (§§2545ff.) adj. appertaining to the English, English.
 ín⌣tumbág⌣ıŋglızíndıré? is this tobacco English?
ıŋglízı⌣ adj. English [<اِنْكْلِيزيّ id.].
 obj. -zıg⌣.
 pl. -zınč(ı)⌣.

ıŋglízı⌣ n. English (the language) [<اِنْكْلِيزيّ id.].
 obj. -zıg⌣.
 ıŋglízıg⌣uñúrmunan⌢ they don't know English.
 ıŋglízıb⌣bάññıran⌢ (-b⌣b- < -g⌣b- §519) and
 ıŋglízıgεb⌣bάññıran⌢ (-b⌣b- < -d⌣b- §518) they speak English.
íŋgrı⌣ sweet s.v. √íŋ-.
íŋgu⌣ these s.v. ín⌣.
íŋnon⌣ and this < íŋgon⌣ s.v. -on⌣.
íŋkε⌣, íŋkεg⌣ thus s.v. ín⌣.
íŋkεnε⌣, íŋkεnεg⌣ now s.v. ín⌣.
ıŋkótt(ı)⌣ as much as this s.v. ín⌣.
-ır⌣ postp. on, in, at, to s.v. -r⌣.
ír⌣ (ır⌣ §1718; §§2604ff., 5076ff.) pers. pron. 2nd pl. you [cp. ON. oʻp rarely εıp id. GNT s.v.].
 obj. írg(ı)⌣, -gi⌣.
 gen. ínn⌣v. (< *írn⌣ §628b), ín⌣c.
 írgonom⌣bınógru⌢ we shall go with you (pl.).
 íddo⌣ on (etc. s.v. -r⌣) you (pl.).
 ínn⌣έss(ı)⌣ your (pl.) water.
 ím⌣bélεd⌣ (§595) (a) your (pl.) country (village); (b) this country (village) s.v. ín⌣.
 ín⌣dúŋ(ı)⌣ your (pl.) (this) money.
 ín⌣fádıl⌣, ím⌣fádıl⌣ and íf⌣fádıl⌣ (§543) your (pl.) (this) kindness.
 íŋ⌣gámbu⌣ (§648) your (pl.) (this) axe.
 íŋ⌣géll(ı)⌣ your (pl.) (this) work.
 ín⌣hánu⌣ your (pl.) (this) donkey.
 íŋ⌣kắrε⌣ (§659) your (pl.) (this) fish.
 ín⌣lığám⌣ and íl⌣lığám⌣ (§583) your (pl.) (this) bridle.
 ím⌣mékseb⌣ (§608) your (pl.) (this) profit.
 ín⌣nógo⌣ your (pl.) (this) female slave.
 ín⌣rıjăl⌣ and ír⌣rıjăl⌣ (§671) your (pl.) (this) dollar.
 ín⌣sámıl⌣ and ís⌣sámıl⌣ (§681) your (pl.) (this) chief.
 ín⌣šăwăl⌣ and íš⌣šăwăl⌣ (§699) your (pl.) (this) sack.
 ín⌣tórt(ı)⌣ your (pl.) (this) half.
 íw⌣wésıl⌣ (§722) your (pl.) (this) receipt.
 ín⌣zέd⌣ and íz⌣zέd⌣ (§736) your (pl.) (this) oil.
 ínn-i⌣ your (pl.) hands (§4696a), ínn-urı⌣ your (pl.) heads, etc. (§1671).
ín-d(ı)⌣ (§2637) (a) abs. poss. pron. yours (pl.), of you (pl.); (b) n. your (pl.) language.
 obj. -dıg⌣.
 pl. índınč(ı)⌣.
ír-kırı⌣ (írkírı⌣ §1701; §§2539-40, 2635) pers. pron. adj. like you (pl.).
índı-kırı⌣ (§2638) pers. pron. adj. resembling that appertaining to you (pl.), like yours (pl.).
índínči-kırı⌣ (§2638) pers. pron. adj. resembling those appertaining to you (pl.), like yours (pl.).
-ı-ré⌣ s.v. -ré⌣.
ırğέn⌣ (-ğέn⌣; -ğέj §942) adj. rich.
 obj. -ğέŋg(ı)⌣, -gi⌣.
 pl. -ğέnı⌣.
 ırğέnkanε⌣ (-έŋk-; §2295) n. wealth, opulence.

rı‿ men, etc. s.v. íd‿.
rı‿ rope s.v. ír.
riñ (a) v.i. wait, remain, stay; (b) v.t. wait for, await; (c) v.t. expect (= íñır §899) [§2895; cp. ON. ⲉⲓⲣ̄ⲯ guard, preserve GNT s.v.].
 ind. pres. aî‿ıríñ(ˡ)ri⌒, ɛr‿íriñin⌒ (-ñí⌒, -ñí⌒); fut. aî‿bıríñ(ˡ)ri⌒; perf. aî‿ıríñ-kori⌒.
 índo‿bıríñran⌒ they will wait (etc.) here.
 bābúrk‿ıríñkoran⌒ they waited for the steamer (train).
 sắg‿ıríñkoran⌒ they (have) waited for an hour (§4666).
 tır‿nɪ́g‿ıríñˡran? whom are they waiting for (do they expect)?
íriñar‿ (-ñắr‿; §§2200ff.) and
ıriñíd‿ (§§2256ff.) n. waiting, etc.
íriñ-an (§§3890ff.) v.t. tell to wait (for), etc., let wait (for), etc.
iríñ-bŭ- (§3931β) v.i. stat. be in an awaited (etc.) state or condition.
 bābúr‿ıríñbūn⌒ the steamer (train) is expected.
ıriñ(ˡ)r-ɛ-g̊ŭ-bŭ- (§4069) v.i. and t. stat. be on one's way (coming) to wait (for), etc.
ıriñ-ɛ-mắ- (§4036) and
ıriñ(ˡ)r-ɛ-mắ- (§4041) v.i. and t. become unable to wait (for), etc.
ıriñ(ˡ)r-ɛ-nóg (§§4048ff.) v.i. and t. go to wait (for), etc.
ıriñ(ˡ)r-ɛ-nóg-bŭ- (-nóggŭ- §546; §4058) v.i. and t. stat. be on one's way (going) to wait (for), etc.
ıriñ(ˡ)r-ɛ-tắ (§§4060ff.) v.i. and t. come to wait (for), etc.
ıriñɛd-ắg- (§§3877ff.) v.i. and t. be in the situation of waiting (for), etc., be engaged in waiting (for), etc.
 bābúrk‿ıriñɛdágran⌒ they are waiting for the steamer (train).
ıriñɛb-bŭ (§§3947-8, 4169ff.; -ɛggı-bú §§4176-8; §1931) (a) v.i. lie (etc. s.v. bú) waiting, remain lying; (b) v.t. wait by, remain with, stay and mind.
 imperat. ıriñébbu!, ıriñéggıbu!
 tɛr‿afɛ́šk‿ıriñébbūn⌒ (‿ıriñéggıbūn⌒) (s)he stays and minds the baggage.
ıriñéb-bŭ- (§3931β) v.i. stat. = ıríñbu-.
 būst‿ınnówwıg‿ıriñébbūn⌒ the mail is expected today.
ıriñ-étta (§4198) v.t. bring after awaiting, await and bring.
 tírg‿ıriñétta⌒ and
 tírg‿ıriñéttarır⌒ (§5458) wait for them and bring them.
ıriñéttar-an (§§3890ff., 3905) v.t. tell to bring after awaiting, etc., let bring after awaiting, etc.
ıriñɛd-étta (§4200; -ñɛggɛtta §4201) v.t. bring after awaiting.
 tírg‿ıriñɛdırétta⌒ (§5616) wait for and bring (each of §5458) them.
ıriñɛdéttar-an (§§3890ff., 3905) v.t. = ıriñéttaran.
ıriñet-tɛ́b (§§4169ff.; -ɛggı-tɛ́b §§4176-8) v.i. and t. stand (stop, etc. s.v. tɛ́b) waiting (for).
 imperat. ıriñéttēp!, ıriñéggıtēp! (§§1954-5).

bābúrk‿ıriñɛttɛ́bran⌒ they are waiting for the steamer (train).
árg‿ıriñéttēp! stay and wait for us!
ıriñétteb-an (§§3890ff., 3905) v.t. tell to stand (etc.) waiting (for), let stand (etc.) waiting (for).
ıriñet-tɛ́g (§§4169ff.; -ɛggı-tɛ́g §§4176-8) v.i. and t. squat (sit, etc. s.v. tɛ́g) waiting (for).
 imperat. ıriñéttēk!, -ɛ́ggıtēk!
 bābúrk‿ıriñɛttɛ́gran⌒ they are waiting for the steamer (train).
 aîg‿ıriñéttēk⌒ sit and wait for me.
ıriñet-túrb(ˡ) (§§4169ff.; -ɛggı-túrb(ˡ) §§4176-8; -túbb(ˡ) §520) v.i. and t. (a) lie down (etc. s.v. túrb(ˡ)) waiting (for); (b) lie down keeping a watch on, lie down minding.
 tínn‿afɛ́šk‿ıriñɛggıtúbbıran⌒ they lie by their baggage and mind it.
ıríñ-katti (§4093) v.p. be waited for, etc.
ıriños-étta (§4203; -ñosgétta, -ñozg-, -ñogg- §4205) v.t. bring after awaiting.
íris n. odour, smell.
 obj. ırísk(ˡ)‿, -ki⌒.
 pl. ír(ˡ)sı‿.
 ıríski‿kố⌒ and
 íris-sēk‿kố⌒ (-s-s- < -s-w- §687, -k‿k- < -g-k- §569) (s)he (it) emits (lit. has) a smell.
 ıríski‿kốmunun⌒ (s)he (it) has no smell.
ıris-kíñ(ˡ) (§§2536-7) adj. devoid of odour, without smell.
írís-ko (§§4109ff., 4118) v.i. have a smell, be odoriferous.
 (part. pres.) ırískōl‿ (¯¯, ¯¯ˡ §1708) adj. odoriferous, smelling, scented.
 g̊óww‿ırískól-lēr‿dắn⌒ (-l-l- < -l-w- §580) there is a scented tree.
 (neg. part. pres.) ırıskốmɛnıl‿ adj. devoid of smell, odourless.
 ırıskố⌒ (s)he (it) is scented.
 ırıskốmunun⌒ (s)he (it) is not scented.
ırısn-árt(ˡ)‿, -tı‿ n. Irs I. (on map), an island west of Argo Island towards its southern end [?Isle of the Inheritance (ارث)].
 obj. -tıg‿.
írr(ˡ) v.i. roar [onom.].
 ind. perf. tɛr‿írrıgon⌒ (-gō⌒, -gó⌒, N. -ıkon⌒, -kō⌒, -kó⌒, -ıhon⌒, -hō⌒, -hó⌒).
 kố‿írrın⌒ the lion roars.
írtıd‿, -ıtı‿ n. Ertidi ('n map), a village on the left bank of the Nile just above Urdi.
 obj. ırtídk(ˡ)‿, -ítk(ˡ)‿, -ki⌒.
ir-tōn‿ postp. from, of, since, s.v. -r-tōn‿.
ıs‿ v. where…? s.v. *ısɛ‿…?
ísa! (§3600) v.t. take!, pl. ísawɛ! (-wɛ́!).
 íng‿ísa⌒ take this (near one).
 máng‿ísa⌒ take that (other, distant one).
ısắı‿…? (ˡs-, sắı- §1075; -ắı‿, -ắı?) interr. pron. (§§2656, 5133, 5136) (a, of a definite number) which?; (b, of an indefinite number) who?, what? [RSN, §129 s.v. ızáy].
 obj. -ắıg(ˡ)‿…?, -ắıg(ˡ)‿…?, -gi?; pl. nom. -ắıgu‿…?, -ắıgu…?; obj. -ắıgug‿…?, -ắıg-.
 tíddo‿sắıg‿kúsri which of them shall (§5369b) I open?

ógıg̊‿ısắı‿tắgon? which man came (has come)?
ógg̊‿ısắıgu‿nókkoran? which men went (have gone)?
ɛr‿kánd‿ısắıg‿ɛ́lkó? which knife did you find (have you found)?
tɛr‿sắı‿tɛ́? which is (s)he (it)?
tɛ́m‿bɛ́lɛd‿ˡsắı‿tɛ́? what (which) is his (her) village?
ısắı-tɛ‿nokkốmɛnıl? (§§5139, 5854) which (who) is (s)he that did not go (has not gone)?
ısắı-tɛ‿dúro? (of two) which is the thicker?; (of more than two) which is the thickest?
ˡsắıgu‿tɛ́ddɛ́‿tír? which are they? (§5101).
ısắın-d(ˡ)‿…? (ˡs-, sắı-, -ắın-; §§2545ff.) interr. pron. adj. appertaining to which?, of which?
ısắıgún-d(ˡ)‿…? (ˡs-, sắı-, -ắıg-; §§2545ff.) interr. pron. adj. appertaining to which (pl.), of which (pl.)?
ısắıg-ɛd…? (ˡs-, sắ-, -ắıg-; -ɛt; §469, -ɛ́? §966; §§4464, 5858-60) adv. by (with, etc. s.v. -ɛd‿) which?, by what?, which way?, how?
ısắıgɛb‿bıbéllan? (-b‿b- < -d‿b- §518) how will they get out?
sắıgɛt‿tắran? which way (how) do (will §5369a) they come?
ısắıgɛn‿nókkoran? (-n‿n- < -d‿n- §624) which way did they go (have they gone)?
X. nog̊óskoran⌒ they have gone.
Y. ˡsắıgɛ́? which way?
ısắık-ɛ‿…? (ˡs-, sắı-, -ắı-; -k-ɛ́?; §§4419, 5959) adv. in which (what) manner (position, direction)?, how? [*having a tendency to what? < sắık- obj. (§4419) +-ɛ́ *have a tendency to §213].
sắık‿ắukattıgon? how was it (has it been) done (made)?
ısắıkɛ‿nókkoran? which way (in which direction, by which route) did they go (have they gone)?
X. belóskoran⌒ they have got out.
Y. ısắıké? how?
ısắık-ɛg…? (ˡs-, sắık-, -ắık-; -ɛgi?; §§4420, 5986) adv. = ısắıkɛ‿…?
sắıkɛb‿béllan? (-b‿b- < -g‿b- §519) how do they get out?
ısắı-kırı…? (ˡs-, sắı-, -ắık-, -ri?; §§2539-40) interr. pron. adj. resembling which (what)?, like which (what)?
ısắı-kott(ˡ)‿…? (ˡs-, sắı-, -ắık-, -ti?; §§2663, 5141, 5147-8, 5355) interr. pron. how much?, how many? [< ısắı- what + kótt(ˡ)‿ amount, quantity].
 obj. -tıg‿…?, -gi?
 ısắıkottı‿dắbūn? how much is there?
 tɛr‿sắıkottır ɛ́? how much is (there of) it?
 ógıg̊‿sắıkottı‿tắgon? and
 ógıg̊‿sắıkottı‿tắgoran? how many men came (have come)?
ısắıkottırɛ…? (ˡs-, sắı-, -ắık-; §2664)= ısắıkott(ˡ)‿…?
ısắıkott-ɛr…? (ˡs-, sắı-, -ắık-; §§2684, 5141, 5147-8, 5355) interr. pron. adj. (about) how much?, (about) how many? [< sắı-kott-wɛr‿…? (§717) a how much?].

sándi? — íss(ı)

obj. ısáıkottēgꞈ...?, ısäıkottég ꞈ...?
(§1728), -gi?
ógığꞈısáıkottērꞈtágon? and
ógığꞈısáıkottērꞈtágoran? *how many men came (have come)?*
tɛrꞈdúngꞈısáıkottēdꞈdólın? (-dꞈd-
< -gꞈd- §534) *how much money does (s)he want?*
dúngꞈısáıkottērꞈdān? (§1786) and
dúngꞈısáıkottērꞈdábun? *how much money is there?*
— with -rɛꞈ (§§2685, 5144):
ısáıkottērrɛꞈdán?,
ısáıkottērɛꞈdán? and
ısáıkottēr(r)ɛꞈdábun? *how much is there?*
ısáı-r...? (ˈs-, sǎı-, -ǎı-; §§4450, 6018) adv. *(a, on (in, at) which?, on (in, at) what?) where?; (b, to (into) which?, to (into) what?) where to?, whither?*
kıtābꞈısáırꞈbún? *where is the book?*
sálumꞈˈsáırꞈnókkó? *where did Sálım go (has Sálım gone) to?*
tɛrꞈdúngıgꞈısáırꞈuskursíŋgıꞈnál꞊ and
tɛrꞈdúngısꞈsáırꞈuskursíŋgıꞈnál꞊
(§6152, i; -sꞈs- < -gꞈs- §678) *see where (s)he put the money.*
ısáıré? (ˈs-, sǎı-, -ǎır-; §§4251, 5820-3) locative interrogative sign of predication *where are (sg. and pl.)?, where is?* [< ısáır + -ré? (*-dé?) §1007].
X. ˈsáıré? *where is (s)he (it)?*
Y. ındó꞊ (§5771) *(s)he (it) is here.*
ırꞈısáıré? *where are you (pl.)?*
ɛsmǎnꞈısáıré? *where's ɛoθmǎn?*
ısáı-r-tōnꞈ...? (ˈs-, sǎı-, -ǎır-; -tõ?, -tõ?, -tõ? §939; §4454) adv. *from where?, whence?*
sǎırtōnꞈtágoran? *where did (have) they come from?*
ínꞈısáırtōndé? *where is this from?*
sándi? *where shall I go?* s.v. *ısɛꞈ...?*
sándi *be afraid, fear* s.v. sándı.
santádꞈ...? (ˈs-, san-, -sın-, sın- (q.v.) §1075; -tát? §469; -tǎ? §967; ıntá?) adv. *when?* [< *ısáın-tádꞈ...? *(at the) coming of what?*; s.v.v. ısáıꞈ...?, -tádꞈ §4439].
kágꞈɛkkꞈısıntádꞈáččıgó? (ꞈékkıꞈsın-tádꞈ) *when did the snake bite you?*
santágꞈ...? (ˈs-, san-, -sın-, sın-; -tǎk? §469) adv. *when?* [< *ısáın-tǎ-gꞈ...? *at the coming of what?* (§§4658, 4665); or perhaps a back formation (cp. JL, p. 173) from sántákk(ı)ꞈ...?].
santánꞈnállan? (-nꞈn- < -dꞈn- §624 or §625) *when do they see him (her, them §5083)?*
ɛsmǎnꞈálıgꞈısantánꞈnálkon? *when did ɛoθmǎn see ɛáli?*
santábꞈbunálli? (-bꞈb- < -dꞈb- §518 or < -gꞈb- §519) *when shall I see him (her, it, them)?*
sıntábꞈbıtáran? *when will they come?*
N. santátꞈtáhorǎ? (§1021; -tꞈt- < -dꞈt- §706 or < -gꞈt- §707) *when did they come?*
ɛrꞈsıntámꞈbókkonꞈíndꞈǎgın? (-mꞈb- < -dnꞈb- §594 or < -gnꞈb- §591) and ɛrꞈsantámꞈmóŋkonꞈíndꞈǎgın? (-mꞈm- < -dnꞈm- §606 or < -gnꞈm- §602) *for how long will you be here?, lit. till when are you here?*

ısantág-k(ı)ꞈ...? (ˈs-, san-, -sın-, sın-, -tǎkk(ı)ꞈ...?, -ki?) adv. *when?* [ısantǎk-k(ı)ꞈ...? prob. or. < *ısantádk(ı)ꞈ...? §574; §§4658, 4665].
ɛsmǎnꞈálıgꞈısantákkıꞈnálkon? *when did ɛoθmǎn see ɛáli?*
santákkıꞈnállan? *when do they see him (her, it, them)?*
santákkıꞈbunálli? *when shall I see him (her, it, them)?*
***ısɛ**ꞈ...? [unstressed proclitic form of ısé? (infra); cp. ON. ειc, ċ *what?* GNT s.v.].
ısꞈv.? (ˈsꞈv.?, sꞈv.?, ꞈsɛꞈc.? §4418) adv. *where...?, whither...?* (= ısáırꞈ...?).
ɛrꞈısánın? *where are you going to?,* lit. *where do you go?* = ɛrꞈısánın?
ısꞈánkon? (sꞈánkon?) *where did you (he, she, it) go to?*
ıs-án? (ˈsán-?, sán-?; §3915) v.i. *go where to?*
ind. pres. aıꞈısándı?, ɛrꞈısánın? (-nī?, -ní?); perf. aıꞈısánkori?
ɛrꞈısánın? *where are you going to?*
tırꞈısansáŋgꞈǎıꞈuñúmmununꞈ (§6122) *I don't know where they went (have gone) to.*
— used exclamatorily to express dismay, horror or despair (§5471):
ısándı! *(heaven knows) what is to become of (will happen to) me!*
ısánın! (-nī!, -ní!) *(heaven knows) what is to become of (will happen to) you (him, her, it)!*
ısáŋkon! (-kõ!, -kó!) *(goodness knows) what has become of him (her, it)!*
ısé? (ˈsé?, sé? §1075; §4249) locative interr. sign of predication *where are?, where is?, where are (pl.)?* (= ısáıré?).
ɛrꞈısé? *where are you?*
ɛsmǎnꞈısé? *where is ɛoθmǎn?*
tírꞈˈsé? *where are they?*
ısís n. (a) *whistle, whistling*; (b) of bird *piping, song* = usús [onom. §2153].
obj. -ísk(ı)ꞈ, -kiꞈ.
pl. -ísıꞈ.
káwırte꞊ısísky ꞈgómınꞈ *the birds sing (the birds sing §4647).*
ısíkk(ı) v.t. *ask, ask of, ask for,* more commonly sík(ı) (§1075), q.v. [< *(ı)síg꞊(ı) < (ı)sꞈ *where?* + ıg *tell* + -k caus., so **cause to tell where* §2854].
ind. pres. aıꞈısíkkırıꞈ; fut. aıꞈbısíkkırıꞈ; perf. aıꞈısíkkıgorıꞈ (N. -iko-, -ıho-).
imperat. ısíkki!
ısın (§956d) n. *clarified butter.*
obj. ısíŋ(ı)ꞈ, -gıꞈ.
pl. ísınıꞈ.
déskꞈígırꞈkaǧǧıgíddamꞈbádırꞈısíŋ ɛránꞈ *after they have cooked (lit. cook) butter on the fire they call it ísın.*
ısk(ı) v.t. *be able to* = ésk(ı).
ind. fut. aıꞈbískırıꞈ (ꞈbísk-).
ıskı-kál- *be able to eat* = eskı-kál-.
ıskıdɛ (úskadɛ; "" §1532) n. *catarrh in nose or throat, cold in the head* [< ısk-imit. sound of snivelling + -ıd gerundial

-ing (§§2256-7) + -ɛꞈ of n. ess. (§2234β); §2273].
obj. -dɛgꞈ.
ínꞈískídɛ-tànnan꞊ *this is catarrh (etc.).*
ǎıgꞈıskıdꞈǎrɛdǎgın꞊ *I have a cold in the head.*
ıskŏdꞈ (ıskŏdꞈ; §§2699, 2707) card. num. *nine* [RSN, §122].
obj. ıskŏdk(ı)ꞈ, -ótk(ı)ꞈ, -ótt(ı)ꞈ (§716), -ki꞊, -ti꞊.
gen. -ódnꞈv., -ónnꞈv.c., -ónꞈc.
pl. -ódıꞈ.
ıskódunꞈ (-düꞈ, -dúꞈ §§939, 5232) and tɛrꞈıskódunꞈ (tɛrꞈ §5233) *it's (they're) nine.*
ıskódínꞈ (-dīꞈ, -díꞈ §5235) and tírꞈıskódínꞈ (tırꞈ §5236) *they're nine.*
rıjálꞈıskódꞈfadlénꞈ (§5239) *nine dollars remain.*
sǎꞈıskódunꞈ *it's nine o'clock.*
ıskŏn-d(ı)ꞈ (§2737a) adj. *appertaining to nine, of nine, nine's.*
ıskŏdín-d(ı)ꞈ (§2737b) adj. = ıskónd(ı)ꞈ.
ıskŏd-ínt(ı)ꞈ (ískódınt(ı)ꞈ, ıskódınt(ı)ꞈ; §2740) ord. num. *ninth.*
ıskŏdıntínd(ı)ꞈ (§2743) adj. *appertaining to the ninth.*
ıskŏdırɛꞈ (§2745) n. ⅑, *ninth part* [< ıskód-9 + -ır *(action of) making + -ɛꞈ of n. ess., so *one of what makes into 9* §2287].
obj. -rɛgꞈ.
pl. -renčıꞈ.
ıskŏd-kırıꞈ (-ótkı-; -kírıꞈ §1532; §2736) num. adj. *about nine.*
ıskŏŋgărꞈ (§§2758, 5261-7) num. *the whole nine, all nine.*
obj. -árk(ı)ꞈ, -ki꞊.
tɛrꞈıskŏŋgárkꞈɛttágorandé? (§5199) *have they brought the whole nine?*
ıskŏd-an- (§2760) v.i. *become nine.*
ıskŏdam-bŭ- (§2761) v.i. stat. *be in a state or condition of becoming nine.*
ıskŏdk-ır (-ótkır, -óttır §716; §2759) v.t. caus. *make into nine.*
ıskŏdkır-bág (-ótkır-, -óttır-; §4138) v.t. *divide into nine.*
imperat. ıskŏdkırbák!
íslam n. *yoke borne by cattle working water-wheel* (kólɛꞈ) [< Sudan Ar. اسلام id. AESA, p. 424; an intentional mispronunciation §1307].
obj. ıslámg(ı)ꞈ, -giꞈ.
pl. íslamıꞈ.
ısmaílꞈ n. *Ismāɛıl,* a man's name [< اسمعيل].
obj. -ílg(ı)ꞈ, -giꞈ.
íssǎ adv. *now* [< الساعة *the present time*].
ısságꞈ, -giꞈ (§4477) adv. = íssǎꞈ.
ıssábꞈbıdágoranꞈ (-bꞈb- < -gꞈb- §519) *they have just come.*
íss(ı) n. *louse*; with collective sg. (§4696c) [< *íts(ı)ꞈ; with ít- cp. MN. itid *Laus* KBW s.v.], -s(ı)ꞈ §2319; RSN, §129].
obj. -sıgꞈ.
pl. -sınč(ı)ꞈ.
íssıꞈkídırtōmꞈbélinꞈ *lice come out of the bone(s §4647).*
íssıŋꞈkúmbuꞈ *nit(s §4696c).*

ssŏd⌣ *your sister's child* s.v. -ssŏd⌣.
stɛlɛmɛ́ v.t. *take over, take charge of, receive*
  [< a stem of اِسْتَلَمَ *id.* + -ɛ́ §3659].
  ind. pres. aĭ⌣ɪstɛlɛmɛ́rɪ⌢, ɛr⌣ɪstɛlɛmɛ́n⌢
    (-mɛ́⌣, -mɛ́⌢).
  imperat. ɪstɛlɛmɛ́!
  dúŋgɪg⌣ɪstɛlɛmɛ́goran⌢ *they took (have taken) over the money*.
ɪstɛlɛmɛ́rar⌣ (-rár⌣; §§2200ff., 2207) and
ɪstɛlɛmɛ́ríd⌣ (§§2256ff., 2260) n. *taking over, reception*.
ɪstɛlɛmɛ́r-an (§§3890ff., 3899) v.t. *tell to take over, etc., let take over, etc.*
ɪstɛlɛmɛ́rɛd-ág- (§§3877ff.) v.t. *be in the situation of having taken over, etc.*
  dúŋgɪg⌣ɪstɛlɛmɛ́rɛdágran⌢ *they have taken over the money*.
ɪstɛlɛmɛ́-kattɪ- (N. -ɛ́ha-; §4093) v.p. *be taken over, etc.*
šɪn (ɪšín §1752) v.t. *send*.
  ind. pres. aĭ⌣ɪšíndɪ⌢, ɛr⌣íšɪnɪn⌢ (⌣íšínɪn⌢ -nɪ⌢, -ní⌢); fut. aĭ⌣bɪšíndɪ⌢; perf. aĭ⌣ɪšíŋkorɪ⌢.
  imperat. ɪšín!, ɪšín! (§952).
  subj. past aĭ⌣ɪšínsɪ⌣ (-íssi §680; -ínsu⌣, -íssu⌣).
  part. pres. ɪšɪnɪl⌣ (ɪšínɪl⌣) (*one*) *that sends, sender, sending*; obj. ɪšɪníɪg(ɪ)⌣; past íšɪnɛl⌣ (ɪšínɛl⌣) (*one*) *that sent, sender, sending*; obj. ɪšɪnɛ́lg(ɪ)⌣.
  wɛ́g⌣ɛ́tt⌣ɪšíndɪ⌢ (§6181) (*a*) *bring me one to send* (sc. *it*); (*b*) *bring someone for me to send (a messenger)*.
  aĭ⌣tɛ́kk⌣ɪšɪssúddoton⌣jóm⌣tóskɪtaran⌢ *it is three days since I sent him (her, it)*.
íšɪnar⌣ (ɪšín-; -nár⌣; §§2200ff.) and
ɪšíníd⌣ (§§2256ff.) n. *sending, despatch*.
íšɪn-an (ɪšín-; §3890ff.) v.t. *tell to send, let send*.
  wɛ́g⌣íšɪnan⌢ *let him (her) send one (someone)*.
ɪšɪn-dɛ́n (§§3996-7) v.t. *send as a gift to (the speaker), send to or for (the speaker)*.
  máŋg⌣aĭg⌣ɪšíndɛn⌢ *send me that (other) one (...that one over there)*.
ɪšɪn-tɪr (§§3998-9) v.t. *send as a gift to (other than the speaker), send to or for (other than the speaker)*.
  ind. pres. aĭ⌣ɪšíntɪddɪ⌢.
  ğawábkɪ⌣samɪlg⌣ɪšɪntíkkorɪ⌢ *I (have) sent the (a) letter to the sheikh*.
ɪšɪnd-ɛg-ág- (§§4071ff.) v.t. = ɪšɪnɛdól-.
ɪšɪn-ɛ-dól- (-nᵒd- §1178; §4022) and
ɪšɪnd-ɛ-dól- (-dᵒd-; §4027) v.t. *be about to send*.
ɪšɪn-ɛ-má- (§4036) and
ɪšɪnd-ɛ-má- (§4041) v.t. *become unable to send*.
ɪšɪnɛd-ág- (§§3877ff.) v.t. *be in the situation of having sent*.
  ɪšɪnɛdágrɪ⌢ *I have sent him (her, it, them §5083)*.
  aĭ⌣tɛ́kk⌣ɪšɪnɛdágrɪ⌢ *I have sent him (her, it)*.
  aĭ⌣tírg⌣ɪšɪnɛd(ɪr)ágɪríddɪ⌢ (*a*) *I have sent (each of §5456) them*; (*b*) *I have sent him (her, it, them) to (each of) them*.
  X. ɛr⌣nĭ⌣tɛ? *who are you?*
  Y. aĭgɪ⌣sámɪl⌣ɪšɪnɛdágɪn⌢ *the sheikh has sent me*.

ɪšɪn-ɛttá (ɪšɪn-ɛ́ttá §3855; §4198) v.t. *fetch by sending, send and fetch, send for*.
  hánug⌣ɪšɪnɛ́ttarɪá? *shall I send for the (a) donkey?*
ɪšɪnɛt-tɛ́g (§§4169 ff.; ɪšɪnɛggɪtɛ́g §§4176-8) v.t. *wait after sending*.
ɪšɪnos-tɛ́g (-ottɛ́g §714; §§4180-4; -osgɪtɛ́g, -ozgɪ-, -oggɪ- §4185) v.t. = ɪšɪnɛttɛ́g.
√**išk-** *sit [§4536].
íškarɪ n.pl. *guests* [< √išk- + -ar⌣ -ing of n.v. (§2200) + -ɪ of pl., so *sittings sc. at a meal §2215].
  obj. -rɪg⌣.
  íškarín-ká⌣ (§1676) *guests' quarters, guest-room*; obj. íškarín-kág⌣, íškarɪŋ⌣kág⌣.
ɪškarín-d(ɪ)⌣ (§§2545ff.) adj. *appertaining to (the) guests, of (the) guests, guests'*.
ɪškárt(ɪ)⌣ n. *guest* [-t(ɪ)⌣ of n. un. §2327].
  obj. -tɪg⌣.
  pl. -tɪnč(ɪ)⌣.
ɪškartín-d(ɪ)⌣ (§§2545ff.) adj. *appertaining to (the) guest, of (the) guest, guest's*.
íttɛ n. *clothes-moth, tinea*; with collective sg. (§4696c) [< Sudan Ar. عِتَّة ɛittá *id.*].
  obj. -tɛg⌣.
  pl. -tɛnč(ɪ)⌣.
íwɪs (occ. íwɪs) v.t. (*a*) *wring, wring out*; (*b*) *twist* [< *íwɪs (§1154) < íw⌣ *disappearance* underlying notion of íw *forget* (§2052) + -ɪs caus., so *cause disappearance (sc. of water) from §2894; cp. K. íwɪs *wenden, drehen* MNK s.v.].
  ind. pres. aĭ⌣íwɪs(¹)rɪ⌢, ɛr⌣íwɪsɪn⌢ (-sí⌢, -sí⌢); perf. aĭ⌣íwɪskorɪ⌢.
  kádɛ⌣tábbɛbúlg⌣íwɪs⌢ *wring out the wet cloth (garment)*.
  tɛ́r⌣ánn⌣íg⌣íwɪskó⌢ (*s)he (it) (has) twisted my arm (hand)*.
íwɪsar⌣ (íw-, -sár⌣; §§2200ff.) and
íwɪsíd⌣ (iw-; §§2256ff.) n. *wringing, etc.*
íwɪs-an (íw-; §§3890ff.) v.t. *tell to wring, etc., let wring, etc.*
íwɪz-bŭ- (íw-; §727; §3931β) v.i. stat. *be in a wrung (etc.) state or condition*.
  hɪzám⌣íwɪzbúgon, gɛndɪgɪróskorɪ⌢ *the girth (belt) was twisted, I have put it right*.
íwɪsɛd-ág- (iw-; §3877ff.) v.t. *be in the situation of having wrung, etc.*
íwɪs-kattɪ- (íw-; §4093) v.p. *be wrung, etc.*
ɪzn⌣ n. *permission* [< إِذْن *id.*].
  obj. ízng(ɪ)⌣, ízng(ɪ)⌣, -gɪ⌢.

já⌣...já⌣... conj. *either...or* [< Eg. and Sudan Ar. يا...يا *id.*].
  íŋgɪ⌣já⌣sókkɛ⌣já⌣mugó; ɛŋ⌣kɛ́fun⌣ *either take this or leave it: it's as you like*.
  X. káčč⌣ɛ́ttaríá⌣wálla⌣hánugɪ? *shall I bring the (a) horse or the (a) donkey?*
  Y. mállɛ⌣wɛ́run, já⌣káčč⌣ɪ⌣já⌣hánugɪ *it's all the same, (bring) either the (a) horse or the (a) donkey*.
jálla! interj. (*urging, inciting or encouraging*) *come!* [< يا اللّٰه jálla! *id.*].
jálla! sɪ́gak⌣káččɪru⌣ (§5376) *come, let's play sɪ́ga*.

jálla! nogó! *come, be off!*
jálla! dárri! *come, climb up!* and s.v. hɛ́lɛ!, sálɛ́!
jɛmín⌣ (§956a) n. *right hand, right* [< يَمِين *id.*].
  obj. -íng(ɪ)⌣, -gɪ⌢.
  gadíbkɪ⌣gašɛ́m⌣bádɪr⌣ɛ́n⌣jɛmíŋgɛn⌣nók⌢ (-n⌣n- < -d⌣n- §624) *after you cross the rails go to your right*.
-jó? (-ʲó? §§4271-2) *interrogative particle after* -o⌣, -u⌣ = -ó?
  X. álit⌣tǎran⌢ (-t⌣t- < -g⌣t- §707) *tell ɛáli to come*.
  Y. índojó? (-doʲó?) *here?*
jóm⌣ n. *day (not specially distinguishable from night, as nahár⌣, ugrɛ́s⌣ are)* [< يَوْم *id.*].
  obj. jómg(ɪ)⌣, -gɪ⌢.
  gen. jómn⌣v., jóm⌣c.
  pl. jómɪ⌣.
  mán⌣jómgɪ⌣tágomunan⌢ (§4665) *on that day they didn't come*.
  jóm⌣mɛ́w⌣bádɪr⌣bɪtárɪ⌢ (-m⌣m- < -m⌣w- §603, -m⌣b- < -rn⌣b- §595) *I shall come on the next day but one (the day after tomorrow), lit. ...after one day*.
  jóm⌣mɛ́w-wakkɪ⌣bɪtárɪ⌢ (-w-w- < -g-w- §719) *I shall come on the next day but one (the day after tomorrow), lit. ...omitting one day*.
  ásal⌣ánn⌣ór⌣uskɪkáttɪsɪn⌣jómun⌢ (-n⌣j- < -nn⌣j- §613) *tomorrow is the King's birthday, lit. ...is the day of-that-our-king-was-born*; ⌣ánn⌣ór⌣uskɪkáttɪsɪn⌣ *a noun-clause in the genitive* (§6156).
jóm⌣, like **nahár⌣**, *combines with the names of the days of the week to form noun-complexes; following the nominative (§4750):*
  kɪrágɛ⌣jóm⌣ *Sunday*.
  bǔš⌣jóm⌣ *Monday*.
  bušnóñ⌣jóm⌣ *Tuesday*.
  árbaha⌣jóm⌣ *Wednesday*.
  hamís⌣jóm⌣ *Thursday*.
  móšono⌣jóm⌣ *and*
  ğíma⌣jóm⌣ *Friday*.
  sámtɛ⌣jóm⌣ *Saturday*.
Also following the genitive (§4810):
  kɪrágɛn⌣jóm⌣ *Sunday*.
  bǔš⌣jóm⌣ (§862) *Monday*.
  bušnóñ⌣jóm⌣ (§839) *Tuesday*.
  árbahan⌣jóm⌣ *Wednesday*.
  hamís⌣jóm⌣ *Thursday*.
  móšonon⌣jóm⌣ *and*
  ğíman⌣jóm⌣ *Friday*.
  sámtɛn⌣jóm⌣ *Saturday*.
  kɪrágɛ⌣jóm⌣mónkon⌣ (-m⌣m- < -mn m- §825),
  kɪrágɛn⌣jóm⌣mónkon⌣,
  kɪrágɛ⌣jóm⌣bókkon⌣ (-m⌣b- < -mn b- §816) *and*
  kɪrágɛn⌣jóm⌣bókkon⌣ *till Sunday*.
  móšono⌣jómgɪ⌣tágoran⌢ *they came on Friday*.
  sámtɛn⌣jómgɪ⌣nókkoran⌢ *they went on Saturday*.
  tɛr⌣bǔš⌣jómɪrtōw⌣wándɪgómunun⌢ (-w⌣w- < -n⌣w- §720) *(s)he (it) has not appeared since Monday*.

jōmíjɛ — kắdd(ı)

jōmíjɛ (-jǎ⌣, -ja⌣) n. *daily wage* [< يَوْمِيَّة id.].
 obj. -jɛg⌣.
juhúdı⌣ (ğu-) n. (*a*) *Jew* [< يَهُودِيّ id.];
 (*b*, used as a term of abuse) *miser, avaricious person*.
 obj. -dıg⌣.
 pl. -dınč(ı)⌣.
 âıg⌣juhúdıg⌣ɛgó꙳ (s)*he (has) called me a miser*.

k⌣ (before a vowel § 1122) < kǎ⌣ *house*.
kǎ⌣ n. (*a*) *house* (*solid building of mud, brick or stone*); (*b*) *home*; (*c*) *receptacle*; (*d*) *hole or square* in the game síga⌣, q.v. [*RSN*, § 129, *TOB*, § 143, 77]—often enclitic (§ 1676) -kǎ⌣, and in composition kǎ-, kă-.
 obj. kǎg⌣.
 pl. kǎnč(ı)⌣ and kǎrı⌣ (§ 2440).
 téŋ⌣kǎ⌣sɛ́? *where is his (her) house?*
 kǎt⌣tubgéndıgır꙳ (-t⌣t- < -g⌣t- § 707) *sweep the house clean*.
 kǎr⌣ágın꙳ (s)*he is at (in) the house*.
 kǎ-wɛ́rr⌣ágın꙳ (s)*he's at (in) a (some) house* (-wɛ́rr⌣ < -wɛ́rro⌣ § 1122).
 kǎ-wɛ́rro⌣búgó꙳ (s)*he (it) was at (in) some house*.
 kǎn-tūr⌣ágın꙳ (s)*he's in the house*.
 kǎ-wēn-tūr⌣ágın꙳ (s)*he's in some house*.
 kǎr⌣nókkoran꙳ *they went (have gone) to the house*.
 kǎgaddı⌣nókkoran꙳ (s.v. -abd(ı)⌣) *they went (have gone) towards the house*.
 kǎk⌣kús꙳ *open the door*.
 kǎk⌣kóp꙳ *shut the door*.
 kǎk⌣kúsmɛŋgon⌣ğóm꙳ *knock at the door before you open it*.
 kǎn⌣ágıl⌣ *door-way of house*.
 kǎn-árrɛ⌣ (§ 2150) n. *neighbour*, lit. *neighbour of the house* [-árrɛ⌣ *neighbour* < *-ágrɛ⌣ (§ 669) < ág *squat* + intensive -r *many, often* + -ɛ⌣ of n. act., so **numerous or frequent squattings*, concrete...*squatters* § 2317].
 obj. -árrɛg⌣.
 pl. -árrɛnč(ı)⌣.
 kǎn⌣dógo and (§ 2363)
 kǎndógo⌣ *top of house, roof*.
 túrug⌣mátbahŋ kandogógı⌣sókkɛgon꙳ (-ógıs- § 512) *the wind (has) lifted off the roof of the kitchen*.
 †**kǎn-ğazma⌣** (§ 1681) *European slipper(s* § 4696*d*).
 kǎn⌣id⌣ and (§ 2363)
 kǎnid⌣ *inmate of house, householder*, s.v. íd⌣.
 pl. kǎn⌣írı⌣ and kǎnırı⌣.
 kǎnır⌣ágran꙳ *the inmates are at home*.
 kǎnırı⌣dámunan꙳ *the inmates aren't there*.
 kǎŋ⌣kóčč(ı)⌣ *house-top, roof*.
 kǎn⌣súmbud⌣ *foundation(s) of house*.
 kǎn⌣tu⌣ *interior of house* (§ 2363; s.v. tú⌣).
 obj. kǎn-tūg⌣, kǎn⌣tǔg⌣.
 gen. kǎn-tūn⌣, kǎn⌣tǔn⌣.
 kǎn-tu⌣dúlun꙳ *the interior of the house is large*.

 kǎn-tu-wɛ́rr⌣ágın꙳ (s)*he's inside some house*.
 kǎn-tu-wɛ́rro⌣bún꙳ (s)*he (it) is inside some house*.
 kǎn-tŭn-d(ı)⌣ (§ 5021) and
 kǎn-tŭn-d(ı)⌣ (§§ 2545 ff.) adj. *appertaining to the interior of the (a) house, indoor*.
 íškarı́ŋ-kǎ⌣ (§ 1676) *guests' quarters, guest-room*.
 obj. íškarıŋ⌣kǎg⌣.
 íškarıŋ⌣kǎr꙳ (s)*he (it) are (is) (they are) in the guest-room*.
 kǎndı́ŋ-kǎ⌣ *sheath of knife*.
 kǎñ-kǎ⌣ *stable*.
 koróm⌣kǎ⌣ and
 koróm-kǎ⌣ *spider's web, cobweb*.
 séllén-kǎ⌣ *central hole* in the game síga⌣ (q.v.).
 síwín-kǎ⌣ (-íŋ-k-; < -ídn-k- § 658) *sheath of sword, scabbard*.
 síwıŋ⌣kǎr꙳ *it's in the scabbard*.
 †**súfrán-kǎ⌣** (Eur.) *dining-room*.
 úññín-kǎ⌣ (§ 1676) *latrine, privy*.
 kǎn-d(ı)⌣ (§§ 2545 ff.) adj. *appertaining to the (a) house, etc., domestic*.

kán⌣ (< *ká-an- § 1111; § 3920) v.i. (*a*) *go to the house*, esp.; (*b*) *go to one's house, go home*.
 ind. pres. âı⌣kándi⌣, ɛr⌣kánın⌣ (-nī꙳, -nī꙳); fut. âı⌣bıkándi⌣ (⌣buk-); perf. âı⌣kánkori꙳.
 imperat. kán! (§ 952), pl. káwwɛ! (káwwɛ! § 720).
 subj. past âı⌣kánsı⌣ (⌣kássı⌣ § 680, -su-).
 def. perf. âı⌣kanóskori꙳.
 ɛŋ-kán! and
 kán! *go home!*
 ıŋ-káwwɛ! and
 káwwɛ! *go (pl.) home!*
 man⌣-kán! *go to that house!*
 man⌣-káwwɛ! *go (pl.) to that house!*
 âı⌣tɛŋ-kánkori꙳ and
 âı⌣tɛŋ⌣kǎr⌣nókkori꙳ *I went (have been) to his (her) house*.
 kanóskoran꙳ (*a*) *they have gone to the house*; (*b*) *they have gone home*.
 tıŋ-kanóskoran꙳ *they have gone home*.
 saíŋ-kándan꙳ *they go to Saɛ̣íd's house*.
 saíŋ-kánkoran꙳ *they went (have gone) to Saɛ̣íd's house*.
 bı-saíŋ-kándan꙳ *they will go to Saɛ̣íd's house*.
 sámıl-kánkoran꙳ *they went (have gone) to the sheikh's house*.
 âı-ōn⌣álıŋ-kánkiri, bıwɛ́tıddi꙳ *if I go to ɛ̣áli's house I shall tell him*.
 kǎm-bu-⌣ (§ 3960) v.i. stat. *be in a state of motion towards the (a) house, etc., be on one's way to the (a) house, etc., be going to the (a) house, etc.*
 âı⌣-kámbūri⌣ and
 âı⌣-kámbūri꙳ *I am on my way home*.
 ar⌣tɛŋ-kámbūru꙳ *we are on our way to his (her) house*.
 ar⌣man-kámbūru꙳ *we are on our way to that house*.
 *****kanɛdág-** *reported not in use*.
kábag⌣ n. *barge* (= sándal⌣) [< كَبَك id.].
 obj. kabágk(ı)⌣, -bákk(ı)⌣, -ki꙳.
 pl. kábagı⌣.

 bābúŋ⌣kábag⌣fadlɛ́gó꙳ (-ŋ-k- < -rn-k- § 659) *the steamer's barge (has) remained behind*.
kabbášı⌣ n. *Kabbáši* كَبَّاشِيّ, *one of the Kabābíš* كَبَابِيش.
 obj. -šıg⌣.
 pl. -šınč(ı)⌣.
kabbāšınčín-d(ı)⌣ (§§ 2545 ff.) adj. *appertaining to the Kabābíš*.
kǎbıd⌣ n. *small flat circular loaf* [< M. kabíd⌣ id. (*AZN* s.v.) < M. kabíd⌣ (*AZN*, p. 59 fin.) = D. kalíd⌣ *action of eating* § 2268].
 obj. kǎbıdk(ı)⌣, -bítk(ı)⌣, -bítt(ı)⌣ § 2462, -ki꙳, -ti꙳.
 pl. kǎb(ı)dı⌣.
kǎln⌣kǎbıd⌣ = kǎbıd⌣.
kabkáb⌣ (kapk-) n. *fever* [§ 2153; *RSN*, § 129].
 obj. -ábk(ı)⌣, -ápk(ı)⌣, -ki꙳.
 gen. -ábn⌣v⌣, -ám⌣c.
 kabkáb⌣âıg⌣árkó꙳ *fever (has) seized me*.
kabrınárt(ı)⌣, -ti꙳ n. *Kabrınarti* (on map), a small island east of Bádın Island, 3 miles below Kɛ́rma.
 obj. -tıg⌣.
kǎb-tód⌣ (kǎpt-, -tót⌣, -tó꙳) b. *Kabtot* (on map), a village on the left bank of the Nile about 4 miles below Urdi.
 obj. -tódk(ı)⌣, -tótk(ı)⌣, -tótt(ı)⌣ (§ 2462), -ki꙳, -ti꙳.
káčč(ı)⌣ (*a*) v.i. *play, sport*; (*b*) v.i. *jest, joke*; (*c*) v.t. *play at* [< كَجَّ id. § 2844].
 ind. pres. âı⌣káččıri꙳; perf. âı⌣káččıgori꙳ (N. -iko-, -iho-).
 imperat. káčči!
 sígak⌣káččıran꙳ (-k⌣k- < -g⌣k- § 569) *they play at síga* (q.v.).
 kuštɛnak⌣káččıran꙳ *they play cards*.
 zahárkı⌣káččıran꙳ *they play at dice*.
 gumárkı⌣káččıru꙳ (*a*) *let's gamble* (§ 5376); (*b*) *you (pl.) gamble*.
káččar⌣ (-čǎr⌣; §§ 2200 ff.) and
kaččíd⌣ (§§ 2256 ff.) n. *playing*, etc.
kaččıdk-ır-káčč(ı)⌣ (-ītkır-, -ītt- § 716; §§ 4156-60) v.i. and t. *have a great game (at), have a really good game (at)*.
 kaččídkırkáččıran꙳ *they have a really good game*.
kǎčč-an⌣ (§§ 3890 ff.) v.t. *tell to play*, etc., *let play*, etc.
kaččır-ɛ-ğu̯-bu-⌣ (§ 4069) v.i. and t. stat. *be on one's way (coming) to play*, etc.
kačč-ɛ-má-⌣ (§ 4036) and
kačč-ɛ-mǎ-⌣ (§ 4041) v.i. and t. *become unable to play*, etc.
kaččır-ɛ-nóg⌣ (§§ 4048 ff.) v.i. and t. *go to play*, etc.
kaččır-ɛ-nóg-bu-⌣ (-nóggu̯- § 546; § 4058) v.i. and t. stat. *be on one's way (going) to play*, etc.
kačč-ır-ɛ-tǎ⌣ (§§ 4060 ff.) v.i. and t. *come to play*, etc.
káčč(ı)⌣ obj. of kág⌣ *horse*.
káčč(ı)⌣ *investing tissue* s.v. kǎg⌣.
kǎdd(ı)⌣ n. *earthenware jar or pot* (of medium size, larger than súlɛ⌣, smaller than gǎlo⌣) [perhaps < κάδδιον *small jar*].

obj. -dɪgᴗ.
pl. -dɪnč(ɪ)ᴗ.
íččɪkᴗkáddɪnᴗtúrᴗmúgranᴗtérᴗmɛ́rɛlanɪmᴗmónkonᴖ *they leave the milk in the (a) jar until it becomes curdled.*
kádɛᴗ n. (*a*) *cloth*; (*b*) *garment.*
— with collective sg. (§ 4696*d*) [*RSN*, § 129].
obj. -dɛgᴗ.
pl. kadɛnč(ɪ)ᴗ.
kádɛnᴗníğɪlᴗ (-nᴗn- < -gᴗn- § 625) and kadénčɪnᴗníğɪlᴗ *tailor.*
kúmᴗkádɛᴗ (-mᴗk- < -bnᴗk- § 586) *sail(s).*
kádub (-dɪb) v.t. (*a*) *dig the surface of, dig on the surface of, hoe up;* (*b*) *dig, dig up, dig out* (= wáddᴗ(ɪ)) [perhaps contains √ká-*cut* (§ 4541); > Sudan Ar. كَدَّبَ *id.* (*a*)].
— wáddᴗ(ɪ) (that includes kádub) is said by some to be more commonly used of *digging deep.*
ind. pres. aɪᴗkádub(ɪ)riᴖ; perf. aɪᴗkadúbkoriᴖ (-úpk-).
arítkɪᴗkádupᴖ *dig up the ground.*
ógɪğᴗarítkɪᴗtúbrogɛkᴗkádubɪnᴖ(-kᴗk- < -dᴗk- § 568) *the man turns over the ground with a hoe.*
nógorɪᴗkadúbmunanᴖ *female slaves don't dig.*
gabúrkɪᴗkadúbkoranᴖ *they (have) dug the (a) grave.*
kádubarᴗ (-dɪb-, -bàrᴗ; §§ 2200ff.) and
kadubídᴗ (-dɪb-; §§ 2256ff.) n. *digging, etc.*
kádub-an (-dɪb-; § 3890ff.) v.t. *tell to dig, etc., let dig, etc.*
kádub-bŭ- (-dɪb-; § 3931β) v.i. stat. *be in a dug (etc.) state or condition.*
árɪdᴗkádubbūnᴖ *the soil is (has been) turned over.*
kúlᴗkádubbūnᴖ *a (the) hole is (has been) dug.*
kadubɛd-áğ- (-dɪb-; §§ 3877ff.) v.t. *be in the situation of having dug, etc.*
arídkɪᴗkadubɛdáğɪnᴖ *he has turned over the soil.*
kúlgɪᴗkadɪbɛdáğɪnᴖ *he has dug the (a) hole.*
kádub-kattɪ- (-dɪb-, -upk-, -ɪpk-; § 4093) v.p. *be dug, etc.*
árɪdᴗkadubkattóskóᴖ *the soil has been turned over.*
kúlᴗkádɪpkattɪgóᴖ *the hole was (holes were § 4647) (has been, have been) dug.*
kúlᴗdúl-lērᴗkadupkattóskóᴖ (-l-l- < -l-w- § 580) *a large hole has been dug.*
káğᴗ n. *snake* [§ 2054].
obj. kağk(ɪ)ᴗ, kákk(ɪ)ᴗ, -kiᴖ.
gen. kağnᴗv., kaŋᴗc.
pl. káğɪᴗ.
éssɪnᴗkáğᴗ and
éssɪn-tūŋᴗkáğᴗ *a Nile fish, of a dark colour, resembling an eel,* Polypterus sp. (*PF*, p. 97) [*water-snake*].
káğ-tod (káğtód-; § 2369) n. (*a*) *miserable snake, wretched snake;* (*b*) = káğᴗ.
obj. -tŏdk(ɪ)ᴗ, -tŏtk(ɪ)ᴗ, -tŏkk(ɪ)ᴗ, -tŏtt(ɪ)ᴗ (§ 2462), -kiᴖ, -tiᴖ.
gen. -tŏdnᴗv., -tŏnnᴗv.c., -tŏnᴗc.
pl. káğtonɪᴗ, kákt-.

káktodunᴖ *it's a miserable snake (…a 'beastly' snake).*
káktodᴗbɛlóskóᴖ *the 'beastly' snake has come (gone) out.*
kaŋ-tŏ́dᴗ (§ 2366) n. *young of snake;* with collective sg. (§ 4696*d*).
obj. -tŏdk(ɪ)ᴗ, -tŏtk(ɪ)ᴗ, -tŏkk(ɪ)ᴗ, -tŏtt(ɪ)ᴗ (§ 2462), -kiᴖ, -tiᴖ.
gen. -tŏdnᴗv., -tŏnnᴗv.c., -tŏnᴗc.
pl. káŋtonɪᴗ.
kaŋtódunᴖ *it's a young snake.*
kaŋtódᴗbɛlóskóᴖ *the little snake has come (gone) out.*
káŋ-d(ɪ)ᴗ (kaǵndɪᴗ, kaǵŋdɪᴗ, kaŋndɪᴗ § 643; §§ 2545ff.) adj. *appertaining to the (a) snake.*
káğ v.t. (*a*) *carry on one, have about one's person, carry, bear;* (*b*) *carry with one, bring along;* (*c*, a fast) *keep, observe* [§ 2054]; cp. ON. каѫк *bring, carry* GNT, s.v.; *RSN*, § 129].
ind. pres. aɪᴗkáğ(ɪ)riᴖ, ɛrᴗkáğɪnᴖ (-gíᴖ, -gíᴖ); perf. aɪᴗkáğkoriᴖ (ᴗkákkoriᴖ).
imperat. kák!
subj. past aɪᴗkáğsɪᴗ (ᴗkáksɪᴗ, -suᴗ).
árᴗdúŋɪkᴗkáğmunun̂ *we haven't the (any) money on us.*
áŋᴗkálgɪᴗkáğɪn̂ *(s)he carries (brings along) my (our) food.*
aɪᴗdértɪkᴗkáğriᴖ *I keep the fast.*
ramadáŋᴗkáğmunun̂ (-ŋᴗk- < -nᴗk- § 655; § 5541) *they don't keep Ramadán.*
káğarᴗ (-gàrᴗ; §§ 2200ff.) and
káğídᴗ (§§ 2256ff.) n. *carrying on one, etc.*
káčč(ɪ)ᴗ n. *investing tissue, rind, bark, skin, crust, shell, husk, pod;* with collective sg. (§ 4696*d*) [< *káğt(ɪ)ᴗ (§ 525) < káğ + -t of n. act. (§ 2325), concrete *what one carries on one* § 2228].
obj. -čɪgᴗ.
pl. -čɪnč(ɪ)ᴗ.
bérnᴗkáčč(ɪ)ᴗ and bérŋ-káčč(ɪ)ᴗ (*a*) *bark of trunk;* (*b*) *shaving(s).*
ğówwɪŋᴗkáčč(ɪ)ᴗ *bark of tree.*
hášamᴗkáččᴗ(ɪ)ᴗ (-mᴗk- < -bnᴗk- § 586) *shaving(s).*
kálnᴗkáčč(ɪ)ᴗ *crust(s) of bread.*
kúmbuŋᴗkáčč(ɪ)ᴗ *egg-shell(s).*
úguŋᴗkáčč(ɪ)ᴗ *bean-pod(s), bean-husk(s).*
kagákk(ɪ) v.i. *cluck* [onom.].
ind. pres. tɛrᴗkagákkɪn̂, perf. tɛrᴗkagákkɪgon̂ (-gŏᴖ, -góᴖ), N. -ɪkon̂, -kŏᴖ, -kóᴖ, -ɪhon̂, -hŏᴖ, -hóᴖ).
dúrmadɛᴗkagákkɪn, ténᴗsiᵘsíwɪgononᴗ ābbánnɪn̂ *the hen clucks, she is talking to her chickens.*
kagákkarᴗ (-kàrᴗ; §§ 2200ff.) and
kagákkídᴗ (§§ 2256ff.) n. *clucking.*
kagrúss(ɪ)ᴗ n. *irritating skin-disease, itch, mange* [< *kagɪrústᴗ(ɪ)ᴗ (§ 686) < √káğ- *get hot* (§ 4542) + -ɪr caus. (§ 3665) + -úsᴗ *evil* + -t dem. (§ 2324), so *that evil (thing that) heats* (§ 2319); *SMN*, p. 452 s.v. κακλ].
obj. -sɪgᴗ.
ínᴗhánuᴗkagrússɪkᴗkóᴖ *this donkey has the mange.*
káğᴗ n. (*a*) *horse* [*RSN*, § 200]; (*b*, in waterwheel, kólɛᴗ) *beam, with its ends engaged in the ground, and attached to*

the same buried cross-beams as the ends of the kómɛᴗ (q.v.); on the káğᴗ rests the end of the téwrɛᴗ (q.v.) near the vertical cog-wheel (árgadɛnᴗtódᴗ); on the end of the téwrɛᴗ is fixed the half-socket (bóččɪŋᴗkáloᴗ), the bearing on which the shoreward end of the horizontal axle (tórɛᴗ) turns; the vertical cog-wheel (árgadɛnᴗtódᴗ) rotates between the káğᴗ and the kómɛᴗ.
obj. káğk(ɪ)ᴗ, káčk(ɪ)ᴗ, káčč(ɪ)ᴗ § 523; -ğk-, -čk- § 323; -kiᴖ, -čiᴖ.
gen. káğnᴗv., káŋᴗc.
pl. káğlɪᴗ (§ 2433) and occ. káğɪᴗ.
kañ-bɪtánᴗ *foal, colt.*
káğnᴗɛ́uᴗ (*a*) *horse's tail;* (*b*) *comet.*
káñᴗhŏss(ɪ)ᴗ *horse's dung.*
káğlɪnᴗhŏss(ɪ)ᴗ *horses' dung.*
káñ-kāᴗ *stable (of mud or brick).*
kañ-kárr(ɪ)ᴗ *mare.*
káñ-kérr(ɪ)ᴗ *stable (of straw).*
káğnᴗónd(ɪ)ᴗ *stallion.*
kañ-súnt(ɪ)ᴗ *horse's hoof(s* § 4696*a).*
káñᴗtúndɪᴗ *horse-girth.*
káğɪbᴗbɛ́lᴗ (-bᴗb- < -gᴗb- § 519) n. *rainbow,* lit. *killer of horses.*
káğ-tod (káğt-, káčt-, -čt- § 324; § 2369) n. (*a*) *poor horse, wretched horse;* (*b*) = káğᴗ.
obj. káğtŏdk(ɪ)ᴗ, tŏtk(ɪ)ᴗ, -tŏkk(ɪ)ᴗ, -tŏtt(ɪ)ᴗ (§ 2462), -kiᴖ, -tiᴖ.
gen. -tŏdnᴗv., -tŏnnᴗv.c., -tŏnᴗc.
pl. káğtonɪᴗ.
káčtodunᴖ *it's a (wretched) horse.*
kañ-tŏ́dᴗ (§ 2366) n. *young of horse, foal, colt.*
obj. -tŏdk(ɪ)ᴗ, -tŏtk(ɪ)ᴗ, -tŏkk(ɪ)ᴗ, -tŏtt(ɪ)ᴗ (§ 2462), -kiᴖ, -tiᴖ.
gen. -tŏdnᴗv., -tŏnnᴗv.c., -tŏnᴗc.
pl. káñtonɪᴗ.
kañtódunᴖ *it's a foal (colt).*
káñ-d(ɪ)ᴗ (§§ 2545ff.) adj. *appertaining to the (a) horse, equine.*
káğbarᴗ n. *sand-column, etc.* = kašwárɛᴗ, q.v. [with káğ- cp. *SNK*, 299].
obj. kağbárk(ɪ)ᴗ, -kiᴖ.
pl. káğbarɪᴗ.
káğğ(ɪ) v.i. *ripen, etc.,* v.t. *testify, etc.* = kárğ(ɪ).
kahárt(ɪ)ᴗ adj. *warm* [< *kagárt(ɪ)ᴗ (§ 1017) < √káğ- *get warm* (§ 4542) + -ar gerundial -*ing* (§ 2200) + -t (§§ 2323ff.), so or. a noun *getting warm, *warmth*].
obj. -tɪgᴗ.
pl. -tɪnč(ɪ)ᴗ.
íŋᴗkahártɪnᴗ *this is warm.*
aɪᴗkahártᴗɛriᴖ *I am warm.*
ɛrᴗéssɪᴗkahártɪdᴗdólná? (-dᴗd- < -gᴗd- § 534) *do you want warm water?*
kahárt-an- (§ 3910α) v.i. *become warm.*
kahártam-bŭ- (§ 3949ff.) v.i. stat. *be in a state or condition of becoming warm.*
kahartan-ɛ-mă- (§ 4040) and
kahartand-ɛ-mă- (§ 4047) v.i. *become unable to get warm.*
aɪᴗkahartanɛmáğoriᴖ and N. aɪᴗkahartandɛmákoriᴖ *I couldn't get warm.*
kahártɪğ-ɪr (N. -ɪkɪr, -ɪhɪr; § 3701) (*a*) v.t. caus. *cause or allow to be warm;* (*b*) v.t. *render warm, warm.*

ind. pres. aɪ‿kahártɪgɪddɪ⌒, ˵˷˶.
íg‿aɪgɪ‿kahártɪgɪrɪn⌒ *the fire warms me.*
másɪl‿tékkɪ‿kahártɪgɪrɪn⌒ *the sun warms him (her, it).*
bóttɛ‿aɪgɪ‿kahartɪgírkó⌒ *the running (has) warmed me.*

†**káhk(ɪ)‿** n. *cake*; with collective sg. (§4696d) [< كَعْك *id.*].
obj. -kɪg‿.
pl. -kɪnč(ɪ)‿.
***káhkɪg-áu** (§3747α, b, 2) v.i. *make cake(s).*

káh(ɪ)lĭ‿ adj. *sharp, with keen edge* [< √káh- *get warm* (§4542) +l‿ participial (§2530) +-ĭ‿ adjectival (§2529); or perhaps < √ká- *cut* (§4541)].
obj. kah(ɪ)líg‿, káh(ɪ)lɪg‿ §§1698, 1154.
gen. kah(ɪ)lín‿, káh(ɪ)lĭn‿, -lɪn‿.
pl. kah(ɪ)línč(ɪ)‿, káh(ɪ)lɪnč(ɪ)‿.
ín‿kándɪ‿káhlɪn⌒ and ín‿kándɪ‿káhlín⌒ (cp. §1974) *this knife is sharp.*
ín‿kándɪ‿káhlín‿ín‿kahlímunun⌒ *this knife is sharp, that isn't.*
káhlɪg‿étta⌒ *bring the sharp one.*
káhlí-wɛg‿éttagorɪ⌒ *I (have) brought a sharp one.*

kah(ɪ)líkanɛ‿ (§§2295) n. *sharpness.*

kah(ɪ)líg-ɪr (N. -íkɪr, -íhɪr; §3701) (a) v.t. caus. *cause or allow to be sharp*; (b) v.t. *render sharp, sharpen.*
aɪ‿kándɪk‿kahlígɪddɪ⌒ *I sharpen the knife.*

kah(ɪ)lígɪr-an (N. -íkɪr-, -íhɪr-; §§3890ff., 3904) v.t. *tell to sharpen, let sharpen.*

kắɪ, kắj and **kắɪ̃** v.t. *fashion, form, shape, make, esp. out of wood or metal* [?contains √ká- *cut §4541].
ind. pres. aɪ‿kắɪrɪ⌒ (‿kắj(ɪ)rɪ⌒), ɛr‿kắjɪn⌒ (-jĭ⌒, -jí⌒); perf. aɪ‿kắɪkorɪ⌒.
imperat. kắɪ!
part. pres. kắɪl‿ *(one) that fashions, etc., fashioner, etc., fashioning, etc.*
bérkɪŋ‿kắɪl‿ *carpenter.*
šắrtɪk‿kắɪl‿ *blacksmith.*
kúbkɪ‿ǧöww‿urúmmɛrtoŋ‿kắɪran⌒ *they make the boat out of Acacia arabica.*
tábɪd‿šắ-wɛk‿kắɪkon⌒ *the smith (has) forged a spear.*

kắj-an (§§3890ff.) v.t. *tell to fashion, etc., let fashion, etc.*

kắjɛd-áǧ- (§3877ff.) v.t. *be in the situation of having fashioned, etc.*

kắɪ-kattɪ- (§4093) v.p. *be fashioned, etc.*

kájjo n. *scab, incrustation formed over wound in healing* [contains kál *cause itching to*; -o‿ §2306].
obj. -jog‿.
pl. -jonč(ɪ)‿.
kórn‿kájjo‿ *the scab of the wound.*

kắk! imperat. of kắg *carry, etc.*

kákkɛ v.t. *get warm at (in), warm oneself at (in), receive heat of* [< √kág- *get warm* §4542; -ɛ §2870; RSN, §129].
ind. pres. aɪ‿kákkɛrɪ⌒; perf. aɪ‿kákkɛgorɪ⌒ (N. -ɛko-, -ɛho-).
aɪ‿ígkɪ‿kákkɛrɪ⌒ *I warm myself at the fire.*
masílgɪ‿kákkɛgorɪ⌒ *I (have) got warm in the sun.*
íkkɪ‿kákkɛ⌒ *warm yourself at the fire.*

kákkɛrar‿ (-rɑ̆r‿; §§2200ff., 2210) and
kákkɛríd‿ (§§2256ff., 2263) n. *getting warm, warming oneself.*

kákkɛr-ɛ-mắ- (§§4016-17, 4036, 4041) v.t. *become unable to get warm at, etc.*
aɪ‿kákkɛrɛmắgorɪ⌒ *I couldn't get warm.*

kákkɪr v.t. *hatch* [< √kág- *get warm* (§4542) +-k obj. suff. +-ɪr caus. so render warm §3684].
ind. pres. tɛr‿kákkɪrɪn⌒ (-rĭ⌒, -rí⌒), tɪr‿kákkɪrran⌒ (-rã⌒, -rá⌒); perf. tɛr‿kákkɪrkon⌒ (-kŏ⌒, -kó⌒).
dúrmadɛ‿tén‿sɪsíwɪk‿kakkírkó⌒ *the hen (has) hatched out her chickens.*
káwɪrtɛ‿tém‿bɪtánɪk‿kakkɪróskó⌒ *the bird has hatched out her young.*
tín‿kumbúnčɪk‿kakkɪríddan⌒ *they hatch their eggs.*

kákkɪrar‿ (-rɑ̆r‿; §§2200ff., 2212) and
kakkɪríd‿ (§§2256ff., 2265) n. *hatching.*

kákkɪr-bŭ- (§3921β) v.i. stat. *be in a hatched state.*
kúmbu‿kákkɪrbūn⌒ *the egg is (eggs are §4696d, has, have been) hatched.*
kawírtɛm‿bɪtánɪ‿kakkírbūran⌒ *the bird's young are (have been) hatched.*

kakkɪrr-ɛg-áǧ- (§§4071ff.) v.t. = kakkɪrɛdól-.

kakkɪrr-ɛ-dól- (-rᵒd- §1178; §4022) and
kakkɪrr-ɛ-dól- (-rᵒd-; §4027) v.t. *be about to hatch.*
dúrmadɛ‿kúmbuk‿kakkɪrɛdólɪn⌒ *the hen is about to hatch the egg(s).*

kakkɪr-ɛ-mắ- (§4036) and
kakkɪrr-ɛ-mắ- (§4041) v.t. *become unable to hatch.*

kakkɪrɛd-áǧ- (§§3877ff.) v.t. *be in the situation of having hatched.*
dúrmadɛ‿kúmbuk‿kakkɪrɛdágɪn⌒ *the hen has hatched the egg(s).*

kál n. (a) *food*, esp.; (b) *bread*; (c) *loaf* [§2049].
obj. kálg(ɪ)‿, -gɪ⌒.
pl. kálɪ‿.
míssɪŋ‿kál‿ *mucus of the eye.*

kálg-ɪr (§3699) v.i. *make bread.*
ind. pres. aɪ‿kálgɪddɪ⌒ (‿kalgíddɪ⌒ §1806), ɛr‿kálgɪrɪn⌒ (-rĭ⌒, -rí⌒); perf. aɪ‿kalgírkorɪ⌒.

kálgɪr-an (§§3890ff., 3904) v.t. *tell to make bread, let make bread.*

kalgɪdd-ɛg-áǧ- (§§4071ff.) v.i. = kalgɪrɛdól-.

kalgɪd-ɛ-dól- (-rᵒd- §1178; §4025) and
kalgɪd-ɛ-dól- (-dᵒd-; §4033) v.i. *be about to make bread.*

kalgɪdd-ɛ-ǧŭ-bŭ- (§4069) v.i. stat. *be on one's way (coming) to make bread.*

kalgɪr-ɛ-mắ- (§4039) and
kalgɪdd-ɛ-mắ- (§4046) v.i. *become unable to make bread.*

kalgɪdd-ɛ-nóg (§§4048ff.) v.i. *go to make bread.*

kalgɪdd-ɛ-nóg-bŭ- (-nóggŭ- §546; §4058) v.i. stat. *be on one's way (going) to make bread.*

kalgɪdd-ɛ-tắ (§§4060ff.) v.i. *come to make bread.*

kalgɪrɛd-áǧ- (§§3877ff.) v.i. *be in the situation of having made bread.*

kál-kɪñ(ɪ)‿ (§§2536-7) adj. *foodless, without food, etc., devoid of food, etc., lacking food, etc.*
béndɪgɪl‿kálkɪññɪn⌒ *the beggar is without food.*
bélɛd‿kálkɪññɪn⌒ *the country is devoid of food.*

kálkɪññɪg-ɪr (˶˵˶˷; N. -ɪkɪr, -ɪhɪr; §§3703, 5708) (a) v.t. caus. *cause or allow to be foodless, etc.*; (b) v.t. *keep or leave without food, etc., starve.*
imperat. kálkɪññɪgɪr!

kál (α) v.i. *take food, feed, eat*; (β) v.t. (a) *eat, consume*; (b, of insect) *bite*; (c) *cause itching sensation to* [RMB s.v. kal; TOB, §143, 16; §2049].
ind. pres. aɪ‿kállɪn⌒, ɛr‿kálɪn⌒ (-lĭ⌒, -lí⌒); perf. aɪ‿kálkorɪ⌒.
imperat. kál!, pl. kálwɛ! (kálwé!).
def. (§§3789ff.) imperat. kálos! (kalós! §1890, kaló! §962); plur. kalóswɛ! (-óswé!, -ówwɛ! §724, -wé!, -óssɛ! §687, -sé!).
def. (§3789ff.) imperat. kálé! (˶˵, ˶˷ §965); pl. kaléwwɛ! (-ɛwwé!).
kalóskoran⌒ (a) *they have eaten (they have had their meal)*; (b, §5083) *they have eaten it (them).*
élɪm‿adémgɪ‿kálɪn⌒ *the crocodile eats human beings* (§4647).
íttɛ‿kádɛk‿kálɪn⌒ *(the) moth consume (the) cloth(es)*; §4696c, d.
mínd‿ékkɪ‿kálkó? *what bit (has bitten) you?*
ánn-i-aɪgɪ‿kálɪn⌒ *my hand itches (my hands itch §4696a).*

kallannắrt(ɪ)‿, -tɪ⌒ n. *Kalanarti (on map), an island near Bákɪr, about nineteen miles above Hándag* [Isle of Eating (§2961)].
obj. -tɪg‿.

kálar‿ (-lɑ̆r‿; §§2200ff.) and
kalíd‿ (§§2256ff.) n. *eating, consumption, etc.*

kálɛ‿ n. *cost, defrayed by bridegroom, of wedding-feast and refreshments provided by bride's parents* [lit. eating, what is eaten; -ɛ‿ of n. act. §2234ɛ].
obj. -lɛg‿.

kal-kátt(ɪ)‿ (§§2534-5b) adj. *gluttonous, greedy.*
obj. -tɪg‿.
pl. -tɪnč(ɪ)‿.

kál-an (§§3890ff.) v.t. *tell to eat, let eat.*

kal-bér (§3747ɛ') (a) v.i. *eat one's fill*; (b) v.t. *eat one's fill of.*

kalbér-an (§§3890ff., 3905) v.t. *tell to eat to repletion, let eat to repletion.*

kal-bŏrkɪr (§§4132, 5622) v.t. caus. *cause to fall down (etc. s.v. bŏr) by eating.*
nóɛ‿kák‿kalbórkɪran⌒ *the white ants* (§4696c) *bring a house down by consuming it.*

kál-bŭ- (§3931β) v.i. stat. *be in an eaten (etc.) state or condition.*
ím‿bér‿kálbūn‿kósɛ‿kálkó⌒ *this wood is eaten* (§6240), *insects have eaten it (this wood is worm-eaten).*

kall-ɛg-áǧ- (§§4071ff.) v.i. and t. = kalɛdól-.

kall-ɛ-dól- (-lᵒd- §1178; §4022) and
kall-ɛ-dól- (-lᵒd-; §4027) v.i. and t. *be about to eat, etc.*

kall-ɛ-ǧŭ-bŭ- (§4069) v.i. and t. stat. *be on one's way (coming) to eat, etc.*

kal-ɛ-má- (§4036) and
kall-ɛ-má- (§4041) v.i. and t. *become unable to eat, etc.*
kall-ɛ-nóg- (§§4048 ff.) v.i. and t. *go to eat, etc.*
kall-ɛ-nóg-bŭ- (-nóggŭ- §546; §4058) v.i. and t. stat. *be on one's way (going) to eat, etc.*
kall-ɛ-tá (§§4060 ff.) v.i. and t. *come to eat, etc.*
kalɛd-ág- (§§3877 ff.) v.t. *be in the condition of having eaten, etc.*
   mállek⌣kalɛdágran⌢ *they have eaten it (them §4950) all.*
kalg-ídd(ı) (N. kalkí-; §3725) (a) v.t. caus. *cause or allow to eat*; (b) v.t. *feed.*
   ind. pres. aı⌣kalgíddırı⌢; fut. aı⌣kalgíddırı⌢ (buk-); perf. aı⌣kalgíddıgorı⌢ (N. -iko-, -ıho-).
   imperat. kalgíddi!
   subj. past aı⌣kalgíddısı⌣ (-su⌣).
   ar⌣tírgı⌣kalgíddırıddu⌢ *we feed (each of §5456) them.*
   tɛr⌣tírgı⌣kalgíddırırın⌢ *(s)he feeds (each of) them.*
kalgíddar (N. -lkí-; -dár⌣; §§2200 ff., 2212) and
kalgıddíd⌣ (N. -lkı-; §§2256 ff., 2265) n. *causing or allowing to eat, feeding.*
kalgídd-an (N. -lkí-; §§3890 ff., 3904) v.t. *tell to feed, let feed.*
   álıh⌣hánuk⌣kalgíddandı⌢ (-h⌣h- < -g⌣h- §559) *I'll (§5369b) tell ɛáli to feed the donkey.*
kalgíddır-ɛg-ág- (N. -lkı-; §§4071 ff.) v.t. =kalgıddɛdól-.
kalgıdd-ɛ-dól- (N. -lkı-; -dᵒd- §1178; §4025) and
kalgıddır-ɛ-dól- (N. -lkı-; -rᵒd-; §4033) v.t. *be about to feed.*
kalgıddır-ɛ-ğŭ-bŭ- (N. -lkı-; §4069) v.t. stat. *be on one's way (coming) to feed.*
kalgıdd-ɛ-má- (N. -lkı-; §4039) and
kalgıddır-ɛ-má- (N. -lkı-; §4046) v.t. *become unable to feed.*
kalgıddır-ɛ-nóg- (N. -lkı-; §§4048 ff.) v.t. *go to feed.*
kalgıddır-ɛ-nóg-bŭ- (N. -lkı-; -nóggŭ- §546; §4858) v.t. stat. *be on one's way (going) to feed.*
   tíŋ⌣káğlık⌣kalgıddırɛnógbūran⌢ *they are going to feed their horses.*
kalgıddır-ɛ-tá (N. -lkı-; §§4060 ff.) v.t. *come to feed.*
kalgıddɛd-ág- (N. -lkı-; §§3877 ff.) v.t. *be in the situation of having fed.*
kál-katti- (§4093) v.p. *be eaten, etc.*
kálkattar (-dár⌣; §§2200 ff., 2213) and
kálkattíd⌣ (§§2256 ff., 2266) n. *being eaten, etc.*
kálkattı-bŭ- (kalkáttıbŭ- §1941; §4105) v.i. stat. *be in an eaten (etc.) state or condition.*
kal-ní (§3747ɛ') v.t. *drink while eating, eat and drink.*
   tır⌣kalnírá⌢ (=⌣kalníran⌢) *they eat and drink.*
   imperat. kalní!, pl. kalníwɛ! (-níwɛ́!).
kal-ní-an (§§3890 ff., 3905) v.t. *tell to eat and drink, let eat and drink.*
   kalnífá⌢ *tell him (her) to eat and drink (let it eat and drink).*
   wélgı⌣kalnífá⌢ *let the dog eat and drink.*
   kalníwanır⌢ and
   kalníwá⌢ (§5659) *tell them to eat and drink.*
kal-ni-bañ̃-ō-bán (cp. §3840, RN, §423) v.i. *eat, drink, talk, sing and dance.*
   bıkalnībáñ̃ōbándan⌢ *they will eat, drink, talk, sing and dance.*
kalos-ág (§§4180–4; -osgág, -ozg-, -ogg- §4185) v.i. and t. *squat (sit) after eating, remain squatting (sit on) after a meal.*
kálos-an (§§3890 ff., 3905) v.t. *tell to eat, let eat.*
kalos-tɛ́g (-ottɛ́g §714; §§4180–4; -osgıtɛ́g, -ozgı-, -oggı- §4185) v.i. and t. = kaloság.
kállɛ n. *dropping(s)*; with collective sg. (§4696c) [< √kál- *round (§4543)+-l⌣ det. or part (§§4558–9)+-ɛ⌣ of n. ess., so *that that is round §2234β].*
   obj. -lɛg⌣.
   bértıŋ⌣kállɛ *goat's droppings.*
   bértınčıŋ⌣kállɛ *goats' droppings.*
   ɛgén⌣kállɛ (-n⌣k- < -dn⌣k- §612) *sheep's droppings.*
   ɛgedıŋ⌣kállɛ *sheep's (pl.) droppings.*
   úrtıŋ⌣kállɛ and
   úrtınčıŋ⌣kállɛ *goat or sheep droppings.*
kálli *I eat* s.v. kál.
káll(ı) v.t. *push, press (oneself, one's hand) against.*
   ind. pres. aı⌣kállırı⌢, ɛr⌣kállın⌢ (-lí⌢, -lí⌢); perf. aı⌣kállıgorı⌢ (N. -ıko-, -ıho-).
   imperat. kálli!
   túrug⌣kobíttı⌣kállın⌢ *the wind presses against the door.*
kállar (-lár⌣; §§2200 ff.) and
kallíd (§§2256 ff.) n. *pushing, etc.*
kallidk-ır-káll(ı) (-ītkır-, -īttır- §716; §4156) v.t. *push (etc.) much, push heavily, give a powerful push to.*
káll-an (§§3890 ff.) v.t. *tell to push, etc., let push, etc.*
kálli-bŭ- (§3931β) v.i. stat. *be in a pushed (etc.) state or condition.*
kallɛd-ág- (§§3877 ff.) v.t. *be in the situation of having pushed, etc.*
kállı-kattı- (N. -iha-; §4093) v.p. *be pushed, etc.*
kallı-kus-os-tó (-ottó §714; §4189; -osgıtó, -ozgı-, -oggı- §4190) v.t. *enter (i.) after opening by pushing.*
   imperat. kallıkusostó!, -ottó!, -ósto!, -ótto! (§1958), -osgıtó!, -ósgıto!, etc. (§1959).
   kobíttı⌣kallıkusottógoran⌢ *pushing the door open they came (went) in.*
kalli-nál (§3747ɛ) v.t. *see (etc. s.v. nál) by pushing, etc.*
   imperat. kallınál! and ⌢ (§1871).
   kobídkı⌣tɛr-oŋ⌣kóbbugıŋ⌣kállınal⌢ *see by pushing it whether the door is shut.*
kallıfɛ́ (kɛl-) v.t. (a) *charge, command, enjoin, bid, order, direct*; (b) *cost* [< imperat. or imperf. stem of كلّف id. +-ɛ́ §3635].
   ind. pres. aı⌣kallıfɛ́rı⌢; perf. aı⌣kallıfɛ́gorı⌢ (N. -ɛ́ko-, -ɛ́ho-).
   imperat. kallıfɛ́!
   X. ɛr⌣mén⌣nókkó? *why did you go?*
   Y. tɛr⌣aıgı⌣kɛllıfɛ́gon⌢ *(s)he ordered me (to).*
   ím⌣míŋı⌣kɛllıfɛ́n? (-m⌣m- < -n⌣m- §604) *what does this cost?*
   ín⌣dúŋı⌣dıgrík⌣kallıfɛ́n? *this costs much money.*
   íŋgu⌣míŋı⌣kallıfɛ́goran? *what did (have) these cost?*
kálo⌣ n. *bearing, half-socket, half-collar,* in water-wheel (kólɛ⌣) [§2308].
   obj. -log⌣.
   pl. -lonč(ı)⌣.
   årɛn⌣kálo⌣ *inner bearing,* where river end of horizontal axle (tórɛ⌣) turns, resting on ɛssıkág⌣.
   bóččıŋ⌣kálo⌣ *outer bearing* on which shoreward end of horizontal axle turns; it is a small half-socket or half-collar, fixed on end of téwrɛ⌣ (q.v.) near vertical cog-wheel (árgadɛn⌣tód⌣).
   tórɛ⌣kálor⌣töróskon⌢ *the horizontal axle has gone into the bearing.*
   tórɛ⌣bóččıŋ⌣kálörtöŋ⌣kuttɛróskon⌢ *the horizontal axle has come (down) off the outer bearing.*
kám n. *camel* [< Beḍ. kam id. pl. §2391].
   obj. kámg(ı)⌣, -gi⌢.
   gen. kámn⌣v., kám⌣c. (§§816–31).
   pl. kámlı⌣ (§2433) and (less commonly) kámı⌣.
   kámm⌣dílt(ı)⌣ and kám⌣dílt(ı)⌣ *the camel's coat.*
   kám⌣ğɛr⌣ *the camel's back.*
   kám⌣hóss(ı)⌣ and kám⌣túr⌣ *camel's dung.*
   kám⌣míss(ı)⌣ *the camel's eye(s* §4696a).
   kámn⌣óss(ı)⌣ *the camel's leg(s* §4696a; *foot, feet).*
   kám⌣tŭ⌣ *the camel's belly.*
   kámlıg⌣fıwıl⌣ *camel herdsman.*
   gőrn⌣kám⌣ and occasionally gőrŋ⌣kám⌣ *large ant;* with collective sg. (§4696c).
kam-kárr(ı)⌣ *she-camel.*
kamn-ár⌣ (§4810) and
kamın-nár⌣ (§4817) n. *Kimnar* (on map), a village on the right bank of the Nile, east of centre of Argo Island [*Camel Shore*].
   obj. -árk(ı)⌣, -ki⌢.
   kamnárro⌣massınčíndıb⌣báñ̃ıran⌢ (-b⌣b- < -g⌣b- §519) *at Kamnár they talk Máḥasi.*
   úrdır⌣kamnárkı⌣kamınnárk⌣ɛrán⌢ *at El-Ordi they call Kamnár Kaminnár.*
kam-tód⌣ (§2366) *young camel.*
   obj. -tŏdk(ı)⌣, -tŏtk(ı)⌣, -tŏkk(ı)⌣, -tŏtt(ı)⌣ (§2462), -ki⌢, -ti⌢.
   gen. -tŏdn⌣v., -tŏnn⌣v.c., -tŏn⌣c.
   pl. kámtonı⌣.
   kamtódun⌢ *it's a young camel.*
kám-tod⌣ (§2369) (a) *rather poor camel, indifferent specimen of camel*; (b) =kám⌣.
   obj. kámtŏdk(ı)⌣, -tŏtk(ı)⌣, -tŏkk(ı)⌣, -tŏtt(ı)⌣ (§2462), -ki⌢, -ti⌢.
   gen. -tŏdn⌣v., -tŏnn⌣v.c., -tŏn⌣c.
   pl. kámtonı⌣.
   kámtodun⌢ *it's a (rather poor) camel.*
kám-d(ı)⌣ (§§2545 ff.) adj. *appertaining to the (a) camel, camel's.*
kămıl⌣ adj. *complete, whole, perfect* [< كامل id.].

kámıs — **kárğ(ı)**

obj. kāmílg(ı)⌣ (kămılg(ı)⌣ §1522), -gi⌒.
pl. kắmılı⌣.
kămıl-an- (§3910α) v.i. *become complete, etc.*
ğéllı⌣kămılaŋkó⌒ *the work is complete.*
kămılam-bŭ- (§§3949ff.) v.i. stat. *be in a state or condition of becoming complete, etc.*
kámıs⌣ n. *the day before yesterday* [perhaps contains أمس *yesterday* §2169].
obj. kamísk(ı)⌣, -ki⌒.
kamísk(ı)⌣, -ki⌒ (§4433) adv. *on the day before yesterday.*
kamísn⌣ŏwwéllo⌣ and
kamísn⌣ogóllo⌣ adv. *on the day before the day before yesterday (three days ago).*
kammăša⌣ n. *pincers, pliers, tongs* [< كمّاشة *id.*].
obj. -šag⌣.
pl. -šanč(ı)⌣.
kán *go to the house, etc.* s.v. kă⌣.
kānárrɛ⌣ *neighbour* s.v. kă⌣.
kándi⌣ *I go to the house, I go home* s.v. kă⌣.
kánd(ı)⌣ n. *knife* [< √ká- *cut (§4541) + -nd(ı)⌣ *appertaining to* (§§2545-6), so **appertaining to cutting* (§2301); RSN, §129 cps. كَنَدَ كَنَدً *secuit*; al. SMN, p. 451].
obj. -dıg⌣.
pl. -dınč(ı)⌣.
kándın⌣ád⌣ *handle of knife.*
kándın⌣ágıl⌣ *blade of knife.*
kándíŋ-kă⌣ *sheath of knife.*
kándın⌣kóčč(ı)⌣ *point of knife.*
kánd⌣átkıññı⌣nɛfɛ́munun⌒ *the (a) knife without a handle is useless.*
kánıd⌣ *inmate of house* s.v. kă⌣.
kánırı⌣ *inmates of house* s.v. kă⌣.
kanísse⌣ n. *dough* [kan-< kálın⌣ *of bread*, -íss-=(?)éss(ı)⌣ *water*, -ɛ⌣ of n. ess. (§2234β); §2292].
obj. -níssɛg⌣; s.v. átt(ı)⌣.
míssın⌣kanísse⌣ *rheum (mucous discharge) of the eye(s §4696a).*
kanísse-kırı⌣ (§§2539-40) adj. *resembling dough.*
kanísseκırın⌒ *it's like dough.*
kánnɛ⌣ n. *north.*
obj. kannɛg⌣.
íŋkɛ⌣kánnɛn⌒ *in this direction is north.*
kánnɛr⌣ágran⌒ *they live (etc. s.v. ág⌣) in the north.*
kannɛ́n-d(ı)⌣ (§§2545ff.) adj. *northern.*
dɛ́rıp⌣kannɛ́ndıgɛn⌣nókkoran⌒ (-n⌣- <-d⌣n- §624) *they went (have gone) by the northern track.*
kánn-an- (§3910β) v.i. *go to the north, go northwards.*
kannɛ̄gır-nóg (N. -ɛ̄kır-, -ɛ̄hır-; §4139) v.i. *go northwards.*
imperat. kannɛ̄gırnók!
kannɛ̄gırnókkoran⌒ *they went (have gone) northwards.*
kānún (§956a) n. (a) *receptacle for fire, fireplace, esp. for cooking* [< كانون *id.*]; (b) *lock (for fastening)* [< Sudan Ar. كانون *id.* = كانون AZA, p. 21].
obj. -úŋ(ı)⌣, -gi⌒.
pl. -únı⌣.

káñ⌣ c. gen. of káğ⌣ *horse.*
kañál⌣ adj. *bandy-legged.*
obj. -álg(ı)⌣, -gi⌒.
pl. -álı⌣.
tɛr⌣kañálun⌒ *(s)he is bandy-legged.*
ógığ⌣kañál-lɛ̄r⌣agóğın⌒ (-l-l- <-l-w- §580) *a bandy-legged man is carrying it (them).*
kaŋkaláb⌣, -áp⌒ n. *Kankalab (on map), an island 4 miles below Old Dóngola.*
obj. -ábk(ı)⌣, -ápk(ı)⌣, -ki⌒.
-karam⌣ (§4351) [< كَرَم *generosity*] and
⌣karám-ır (§4379) postp. (i) = prep. (§4288) *for, intended for, for the sake of, on behalf of, because of.*
— follow the genitive; predicative in pause (§§5858-60):
ín⌣ğawáb⌣níŋ-karam? (⌣níŋ⌣karámır?) *whom is this letter for? (to whom is it addressed?).*
ín⌣ğawáb⌣bustáŋ-karam⌒ *this letter is for the post.*
dúŋgíŋ-karam⌣aúkoran⌒ *they did (have done) it for (the sake of the) money.*
ín⌣áŋ-karam⌒ (⌣áŋ⌣karámır⌒) *this is for me.*
ín⌣έŋ-karam⌒ (⌣έŋ⌣karámır⌒) *this is for you.*
ín⌣tέŋ-karam⌒ (⌣tέŋ⌣karámır⌒) *this is for him (her, it).*
ín⌣áŋ-karam⌒ (⌣áŋ⌣karámır⌒) *this is for us.*
ín⌣íŋ-karam⌒ (⌣íŋ⌣karámır⌒) *this is for you (pl.).*
ín⌣tíŋ-karam⌒ (⌣tíŋ⌣karámır⌒) *this is for them.*
ín⌣áŋ-karámmunun⌒ *this is not for me (us).*
ín⌣έŋ-karamó? and
ín⌣έŋ-karámírɛ? *is this for you?*
ín⌣έŋ-karámmen? *isn't this for you?*
ín⌣óŋ-karam⌣nɛfɛ́munun, bagóndo⌣ nɛfɛ́n⌒ (⌣óŋ-k- <⌣ódn-k- §658) *this is of no use for the cold weather, it's useful in summer.*
έŋ⌣karámır⌣nókkoran⌒ *they went (have gone) on your behalf.*
dέrtıŋ⌣kăgar⌣dúllon⌣ tumbáŋ⌣karámır⌒ *keeping the fast is difficult because of tobacco (i.e. because tobacco is forbidden).*
-karam⌣ (§4352) and
⌣karámır (§4380) postp. (ii) = conj. (§4288) (a, constr. with pres. subj. gen.) *in order that*; (b, constr. with past subj. gen. or with pres. subj. gen. with past sense) *because* §§6211, 6214-16.
kobíttı⌣kús⌣tέr⌣tόŋ-karam⌣ and
kobíttı⌣kús⌣tέr⌣tόŋ-karámır⌒ *open the door that (s)he (it) may enter.*
kobíttı⌣kúskon⌣tír⌣toráŋ-karam⌣ and
kobíttı⌣kúskorı⌣tír⌣toráŋ-karámır⌒ *I opened the door that they might enter (I have opened the door that they may enter).*
tέr⌣dólmɛnín-karam⌣sókkɛrı⌒ *I take it (them) because (s)he doesn't want it (them).*
ar⌣sókkɛgoru⌣dólsun⌣karámır⌒ *we took it (away) because we liked (wanted) it.*
ar⌣sókkɛgoru⌣tír⌣kálmɛnsáŋ-karam⌒ *we took it (away) because they did not eat it.*

áı⌣ğăbɛmăgorı⌣ğúgr⌣έŋ-karam⌒ *I couldn't touch it because it was hot.*
kararέb⌣ n. *tripod* [sounds Bed.].
obj. -έbk(ı)⌣, -έpk(ı)⌣, -ki⌒.
pl. -έbı⌣.
károu v.i. *rattle, clatter, make a rattling or clattering noise* (= kórou, kúrub) [< kár-onom. +áu *make*, so *go kár! (§2863); cp. كَرْكَر *murmur, rumble*].
ind. pres. áı⌣kararúrı⌣, ɛr⌣károwın⌣ (-wí⌣, -wí⌒); perf. áı⌣karáukori⌒ (N. -áuho-).
áfɛš⌣kám⌣kóčči⌣károwın⌒ *the baggage rattles on the camel's back.*
tókkoŋ⌣karáumɛn⌒ *don't make a (that) rattling (etc.) noise.*
károwar⌣ (-wár⌣; §§2200ff.) and
karowíd⌣ (§§2256ff.) n. *rattling, etc.*
károu-bŭ- (§3931α) v.i. stat. *be in a rattling (etc.) state or condition.*
tăga⌣karáubun⌒ *the window is rattling.*
karowíŋ-ır (N. -íŋkır; §3688) v.t. caus. *cause or allow to rattle, etc.*
túruk⌣kobíttı⌣karawíŋırın⌒ *the wind makes the door (§4647) rattle.*
saháŋı⌣tókkoŋ⌣karawíŋırmɛn⌒ *don't make (let) the plates (§4647) clatter.*
kárɛ⌣ n. *fish*; with collective sg. (§4696d).
obj. -rɛg⌣.
pl. -rɛnč(ı)⌣.
kărɛg⌣ăbíl⌣ *(one) that nets fish, fisherman.*
áški⌣kárɛk⌣kálın⌒ *the monitor lizard eats fish.*
kărɛ-kal⌣ n. *heron (Ardea sp.), pelican* [lit. *eat-fish* §2381].
obj. kārɛkálg(ı)⌣, -gi⌒.
pl. kárɛkalı⌣.
kărɛ-kíññ(ı)⌣ (§§2536-7) adj. *devoid of fish.*
kărɛ́n-d(ı)⌣ (§§2545ff.) adj. *appertaining to fish.*
kárğ(ı) (káğğ(ı) §555) v.i. (a) *get ripe, ripen, mature*; (b) *get cooked*; (c) *get tanned* [RSN, §§129, 200].
ind. pres. tɛr⌣kárğın⌣ (-ğí⌣, -ğí⌒); perf. tɛr⌣kárğıgon⌣ (-gŏ⌒, -gó⌣, N. -ıkon⌣, -kŏ⌒, -kó⌣, -ıhon⌒, -hŏ⌒, -hó⌣).
part. pres. kárğıl⌣ (káğğıl⌣) *(one) that ripens, etc., ripening, etc.*
part. past kárğɛl⌣ (káğğɛl⌣) *(one) that ripened, etc., ripening, etc.*
márɛ⌣kárğıgó⌒ *the millet grew (has grown) ripe.*
ğăkud⌣kargóskŏ⌒ *the stew is (has got) cooked.*
áğın⌣ğúrtɛn⌣túr⌣kargóskó⌒ *the hide has got tanned in the (infusion of) pods of Acacia arabica.*
kárğar⌣ (káğğar⌣, -ğăr⌣, -ğɛr⌣; §§2200ff.) and
kargíd⌣ (káğğíd⌣; §§2256ff.) n. *becoming ripe, etc.*
kárğı-bŭ- (káğğı-; §3931α) v.i. stat. *be in a ripe (etc.) state or condition.*
kúsut⌣tɛr-óŋ⌣kăğğíbuğın⌣nălan⌒ (-t⌣t- <-g⌣t- §707) *tell him (her) to see whether the meat is done (cooked).*
áğın⌣kăğğíbun⌒ *the hide is dried (cured, tanned, ready for use).*
kárğıg-ır (káğğıg-, N. -ıkır-, -ıhır; §3682) (a) v.t. caus. *cause or allow to ripen, etc.*;

(b) v.t. *render ripe, etc., ripen, mature, cook (fully), tan.*
ind. pres. aı⌣kárǧıgıddı⌢ (⌣karǧıgíddı⌢ §1814).
kúsuk⌣kaǧǧıgıróskó⌢ *(s)he has (fully) cooked the meat.*
aǧíŋgı⌣ǧúrtɛgɛk⌣kárǧıgıddan⌢ (-k⌣k- < -d⌣k- §568) *they tan hides (§4647) with the pods (ib.) of Acacia arabica.*

kárǧıgırar⌣ (káǧǧı-, N. -ıkır-, -ıhır-; -rár⌣; §§2200ff., 2212) and

kárǧıgırı́d⌣ (kaǧǧı-, N. -ıkır-, -ıhır-; §§2256ff., 2265) n. *rendering ripe, etc.*

kárǧıgır-an (káǧǧı-, N. -ıkır-, -ıhır-; §§3890ff., 3904) v.t. *tell to cook (to tan), let cook (tan).*

karǧıgırɛd-áǧ- (kaǧǧı-, N. -ıkır-, -ıhır-; §§3877ff.) v.t. *be in the situation of having caused or allowed to ripen, etc.*
nóbıl⌣kárɛk⌣kaǧǧıgırɛdáǧın⌢ *the cook has cooked the fish.*
aǧíŋgı⌣karǧıgırɛdáǧrı *I have tanned the hide.*

kárǧ(ı) (káǧǧ(ı); §§5542–4) v.t. *testify (to), attest, bear witness to (of, that), state as (in) evidence* [specialized transitive use (§5342) of kárǧ(ı) i. *get ripe, etc.* quasi *bring to maturity, render definite, substantiate*].
Constructed with (a) direct object; (b) -ɛd⌣ (§4341); (c) clause in ⌣ɛg⌣, ⌣ɛg⌣ (§4339); (d) -(ı)r⌣, -*do⌣ (§4291).
When the simple verb kárǧ(ı) is used b and c form homophones (§5916); they are distinguished s.v. ákkárǧı-.
ind. pres. aı⌣kárǧırı⌢ (⌣káǧǧırı⌢), ɛr⌣kárǧın⌢ (⌣káǧǧın⌢, -ǧí⌢, -ǧí⌢); perf. aı⌣kárǧıgorı⌢ (⌣káǧǧı-, N. -ıko-, -ıho-).
part. pres. kárǧıl⌣ (káǧǧıl⌣) *(one) that testifies, etc., witness, testifying, etc.*; past kárǧɛl⌣ (káǧǧɛl⌣) *(one) that testified, etc., witness, testifying, etc.*; fut. bıkárǧıl⌣ (bu-, -káǧǧıl⌣) *(one) that will testify, etc., witness, testifying, etc.*
káǧǧılı⌣dıgrínčın⌢ *the witnesses are many.*
íŋgı⌣bıkárǧıran⌢,
íŋgɛb⌣bıkárǧıran⌢ (-b⌣b- < -d⌣b- §518) and
íŋg⌣éb⌣bıkárǧıran⌢ (íŋgɛb⌣...; -b⌣b- < -g⌣b- §519) *they will testify to this.*
ɛsmǎn⌣índ⌣agsíŋgı⌣káǧǧıran⌢,
ɛsmǎn⌣índ⌣agsíŋgɛk⌣káǧǧıran⌢ (-k⌣k- < -d⌣k- §568) and
ɛsmǎn⌣índ⌣agsíŋg⌣ék⌣káǧǧıran⌢ (⌣ɛk...; -k⌣k- < -g⌣k- §569) *they testify that ɛoθmǎn was there;* ⌣índ⌣índ⌣índ⌣índ⌣ (§1122), lit. *here,* i.e. *in witnesses' situation (cp. §6140).*
tɛr⌣íŋgı⌣káǧǧıgó⌢ *(s)he bore (has borne) witness to this.*
tɛr⌣íŋgon⌣íŋgonǧı⌣káǧǧıgó⌢ *(s)he bore (has borne) witness to this and that.*
álı⌣aı⌣ɛsmǎn⌣kár⌣tösúŋǧı⌣nálkor⌣égı⌣káǧǧıgó⌢ (⌣nálkor⌣ék⌣káǧǧıgó⌢) *ɛ álı (has) stated in evidence that he saw ɛoθmǎn enter the house.*
tɛr⌣álır⌣káǧǧıgó⌢ *(s)he gave (has given) evidence against ɛ álı.*
aı⌣sálumır⌣káǧǧıgorı *I gave (have given) evidence against Sálım.*

tɛr⌣áddo⌣káǧǧıgó⌢ *(s)he gave (has given) evidence against me (us).*
aı⌣téddo⌣káǧǧıgorı⌢ *I gave (have given) evidence against him (her).*
éddo⌣karǧóskoran⌢ *they have given evidence against you.*
múrsıgɛk⌣káǧǧın⌢ (-k⌣k- < -d⌣k- §568) *(s)he gives false evidence.*

kárǧar⌣ (káǧǧar⌣, -ǧar⌣, -ǧɛr⌣; §§2200ff.) and

karǧíd⌣ (kaǧǧíd⌣; §§2256ff.) n. *attestation.*

kárǧ-an (káǧǧan; §§3890ff.) v.t. *tell to testify, etc., let testify, etc.*

kárǧı-dɛn (káǧǧı-; §§3996–7) v.t. *testify (etc.) in favour of (the speaker), give evidence for (supporting, on behalf of the speaker).*
tɛr⌣aıǧı⌣káǧǧıdɛŋkó⌢ *(s)he gave (has given) evidence in my favour.*

kárǧı-tır (káǧǧı-; §§3998–9) v.t. *testify (etc.) in favour of (other than the speaker), give evidence for (supporting, on behalf of other than the speaker).*
aı⌣tékkı⌣káǧǧıtıkkorı⌢ *I gave (have given) evidence in his (her) favour.*

karǧır-ɛ-ǧú-bǔ- (kaǧǧır-; §4069) v.t. stat. *be on one's way (coming) to testify, etc.*

karǧır-ɛ-nóg (kaǧǧ-; §§4048ff.) v.t. *go to testify, etc.*

karǧır-ɛ-nóg-bǔ- (kaǧǧ-; -nóggǔ- §546; §4058) v.t. stat. *be on one's way (going) to testify, etc.*

karǧır-ɛ-tá (kaǧǧ-; §§4060ff.) v.t. *come to testify, etc.*

karǧɛd-áǧ- (kaǧǧɛd-; §§3877ff.) v.t. *be in the situation of having testified, etc.*

kárǧıg-ır (káǧǧıg-, N. -ıkır, -ıhır; §3682) v.t. caus. *cause or allow to testify, etc., call to witness, bring as witness.*
aı⌣ékkı⌣káǧǧıgıddı⌢ (...⌣kaǧǧıgíddı⌢ §1814) *I call you to witness.*
íŋg⌣áddo⌣káǧǧıgrı⌢ *bring witnesses to prove this against me (us); sc. if you can,* lit. *cause (someone, some persons) to testify this against me (us).*

kárǧı-kattı- (káǧǧı-; N. -ıha-; §4093) v.p. *be testified, etc.*
ıŋ⌣káǧǧıkattıgó⌢ *this was (has been) stated in evidence.*

kárr(ı)⌣ n. *female* [§2168, cp. Mīd. arr id. MZM, p. 338].
obj. -rıg⌣.
pl. -rınč(ı)⌣.
béntı⌣kárr(ı)⌣ *female date-palm.*
dúrmadɛ⌣kárr(ı)⌣ *hen.*
égɛd⌣kárr(ı)⌣ *ewe.*
hánu⌣kárr(ı)⌣ *she-ass.*
kam-kárr(ı)⌣ *she-camel.*
kañ-kárr(ı)⌣ *mare.*
kóddɛ⌣kárr(ı)⌣ *a prostrate herb,* Mollugo hirta, s.v. kóddɛ⌣.
múgdo⌣kárr(ı)⌣ *female post, weaker post, supporting lighter end of crossbeam (dfu⌣) in water-wheel (kólɛ⌣).*
sām-kárr(ı)⌣ *she-cat.*
wɛl-kárr(ı)⌣ *bitch.*

kárro⌣ n. *midrib of date-palm-branch* (جَرِيد);
with collective sg. (§4696b).
obj. -rog⌣.
pl. -ronč(ı)⌣.

kárum⌣ n. *fenugreek,* Trigonella faenugraecum, L. (BSP, 119).
obj. karúmg(ı)⌣, -gı⌢.

kás (a) v.t. *draw, bring (water) up or out;* (b) v.i. *draw water.*
ind. pres. aı⌣kásrı⌢; perf. aı⌣káskorı⌢.
subj. past aı⌣kássı⌣ (-su⌣).
part. pres. kásıl⌣ *(one) that draws, etc., drawer, etc., drawing, etc.*; past kásɛl⌣ *(one) that drew, etc., drawer, etc., drawing, etc.*
nóǧ⌣éssıg⌣úrurtöŋ⌣kásın⌢ *the female slave draws water from the river.*
éssıg⌣gówwırtöŋ⌣káskoran⌢ *they drew (have drawn) water from the well.*

kásar⌣ (-sár⌣; §§2200ff.) and

kasíd (§§2256ff.) n. *drawing, etc.*

kás-an (§§3890ff.) v.t. *tell to draw, etc., let draw, etc.*

káz-bǔ- (§727; §3931β) v.i. stat. *be in a drawn (etc.) state or condition.*
éssı⌣kázbún⌢ *the water is (has been) drawn.*

kasr-ɛg-áǧ- (§§4071ff.) v.i. and t. = kasɛdól-.

kas-ɛ-dól- (-s°d- §1178; §4022) and

kasr-ɛ-dól- (-r°d-; §4027) v.i. and t. *be about to draw, etc.*

kasr-ɛ-ǧú-bǔ- (§4069) v.i. and t. stat. *be on one's way (coming) to draw, etc.*

kas-ɛ-má- (§4036) and

kasr-ɛ-má- (§4041) v.i. and t. *become unable to draw, etc.*

kasr-ɛ-nóg (§§4048ff.) v.i. and t. *go to draw, etc.*

kasr-ɛ-nóg-bǔ- (-nóggǔ- §546; §4058) v.i. and t. stat. *be on one's way (going) to draw, etc.*

kasr-ɛ-tá (§§4060ff.) v.i. and t. *come to draw, etc.*

kasɛd-áǧ- (§§3877ff.) v.i. and t. *be in the situation of having drawn, etc.*

kásk-ır (§3683) v.t. caus. *cause or allow to draw, etc.*
aı⌣nógok⌣káskıddı⌢ *I send the female slave to draw water.*

kasıŋ-ır (⌢, N. -ŋkır; §3688) v.t. caus. *cause or allow to draw, etc.*

kás n. (a) *cup, esp.;* (b) *drinking-bowl cut out of rind of gourd* = kébɛ⌣ (b) [< Sudan Ar. كَاس < كَأْس *cup*].
obj. kásk(ı)⌣, -kı⌢.
pl. kásı⌣.
kás⌣kébɛrtöm⌣mérkattın⌢ *the kás is cut out of the gourd.*

kás n. *Nile fish of light colour,* Hydrocyon forskalii, H. lineatus, H. brevis (PF, p. 95) [= Sudan Ar. كاس id.].
obj. kásk(ı)⌣, -kı⌢.
pl. kásı⌣.

†kasaróna⌣ (kaza-, kozor-) n. *saucepan, cooking-pot* [< كسرونة < It. cassarola id.].
obj. -rónag⌣.
pl. -rónanč(ı)⌣.

kásır n. *turban* [§2286α; 'wol nominalform aus kas (FM) flechten' RNW s.v.].
obj. kasírk(ı)⌣, -kı⌢.
pl. kás(ı)rı⌣.

kášáu⌣ n. (a) *rattle to scare birds from crops, made by putting pebbles in a*

kåšɛ — kɛččınɛ́

gourd or tin (cp. *NSD*, p. 22) [< √káš- onom. of crepitation (§ 4545) + -áu *make, produce*, so **go-káš!*; cp. Sudan Ar. كَشْكُوش *id.*]; (*b*, in weaving) *peg in batten (sword tie CSW*, p. 31).
   obj. kašáug.
   pl. kašawínč(ı)⌣.

kåšɛ v.t. *stir (a liquid)* [§§ 2870 ff.; *RSN*, § 129].
   ind. pres. âı⌣kášɛrı⌢, ɛr⌣kášɛn⌢ (-šɛ́⌢, -šɛ́⌢); perf. âı⌣kášɛgorı⌢ (N. -ɛko-, -ɛho-).
   def. perf. âı⌣kášɛróskoskorı⌢ and more commonly âı⌣kášóskorı⌢.
   marákkı⌣kåšɛ⌢ *stir the broth*.
   ín⌣ǧakútkı⌣kåšɛgómunun⌢ *she did not stir (has not stirred) this stew* (in Dóngola the cook is a woman).

kåšɛrar (-rår⌣; §§ 2200 ff., 2210) and **kåšɛríd**⌣ (§§ 2256 ff., 2263) n. *stirring*.

kåšɛr-an (§§ 3890 ff., 3899) v.t. *tell to stir, let stir*.

kášše⌣ n. *finger*; with collective sg. (§ 4696 a) [< *kájsɛ < *kájsɛ < *kåı* *to fashion, form, shape* +-s dem. or dim. (§ 2319) + -ɛ⌣ of n. act. (§ 2234 δ), so **that (little) fashioner* § 2322].
   obj. -šɛg⌣.
   pl. -šɛnč(ı)⌣.
   ín⌣kášše⌣ (íŋ⌣káš-) *finger(s)*.
   ánn-íŋ⌣kášše⌣ *my finger(s)*.

kášš(ı)⌣ n. *refuse, waste, scrap(s), débris*, esp. *of crops or other vegetation*; with collective sg. (§ 4696 d); (=kawíš⌣) [< **kášt(ı)⌣ < √kåš- *crepitation* (§ 4545) sc. *of disturbed dry stalks*, etc. +-t dem. (§ 2324)].
   obj. -šıg⌣.
   pl. -šınč(ı)⌣.
   araŋ⌣kášš(ı)⌣ (-ŋk- < -gn- § 652) *débris of mustard-tree* (e.g. when attacked by termites).
   ašraŋkáññ⌣kášš(ı)⌣ *roots and stalks of beans*.
   bérn⌣kášš(ı)⌣ and bérn⌣kášš(ı)⌣ *fragment(s) of wood, shaving(s), sawdust*.
   hasénn⌣kášš(ı)⌣ (-énn⌣ká-, -éŋ⌣ká- § 658) *refuse of reaped crop, straw*.
   hášam⌣kášš(ı)⌣ (-m⌣k- < -bn⌣k- § 586) =bérn⌣kášš(ı)⌣.
   íllɛŋ⌣kášš(ı)⌣ *wheat stubble, wheat straw*.

kašwárɛ⌣ n. *whirling column of sand or dust travelling in eddy of wind* (=عصار), =kåǧbar⌣ [< **kaǧwárɛ < káǧ- *horse* + wár- *jump* +-ɛ⌣ of n. act. (§ 2234 γ), so *horse-jumping; káǧ- perhaps influenced by káš-ɛ *stir*; § 2350].
   obj. -wårɛg⌣.
   pl. kašwårénč(ı)⌣.

kát(¹)rɛ⌣ n. *wall* [cp. Eth. ቀጽር *id.* (*RSN*, § 129); -ɛ⌣ of n. ess. § 2234 β].
   obj. -rɛg⌣.
   pl. kat(¹)rénč(ı)⌣.
   kátrɛn⌣súmbud⌣ *foundation(s) of wall*.

kátter⌣hɛ̆rak⌣ (§ 1397) *thank you* [< كثر خيرك] addressed to one person.

katter-hɛ̆rak-an (§ 5665) v.t. *say 'thank you' to (one person), thank*.

katter-hɛ̆rak-aw-wɛ́-tır (§ 5692) v.t. *express thanks to (person not the speaker), thank*.

katter-hɛ̆rak-an-ǧu-wɛ́-tır (§ 5692) v.t. *go and express thanks to (person not the speaker), go and thank*.

-kátt(ı)⌣ adj. suffix, *given to, addicted to*, etc. § 2534.

-kattı- suffix forming passive § 4093.

kátt(ı) v.t. *wrap (a, object in covering) wrap up, envelop, swathe, roll up, wind*; (*b*, *covering round object*) *wrap round, roll round, wind round* [< **kánt(ı)*, cp. M. kánt(ı) *id.*; *AZN* has kånti D. *wickeln, winden*].
   ind. pres. âı⌣káttırı⌢; perf. âı⌣káttıgorı⌢ (N. -ıko-, -ıho-).
   dúŋık⌣kádɛgɛk⌣káttıgoran⌢ (-ɛk⌣k- < -ɛd⌣k- § 568) and dúŋık⌣kádɛr⌣káttıgoran⌢ *they (have) wrapped the money up in (a, the) cloth*.
   úlgı⌣káttın⌢ (s)*he winds the thread*.

káttar⌣ (-tår⌣; §§ 2200 ff.) and **kattíd**⌣ (§§ 2256 ff.) n. *wrapping*, etc.

kátt-an (§§ 3890 ff.) v.t. *tell to wrap*, etc., *let wrap*, etc.

káttı-bů- (§ 3931 β) v.i. stat. *be in a wrapped* (etc.) *state or condition*.
   gɛzåz⌣kádɛr⌣káttıbůn⌢ *the glass (bottle) is wrapped in the cloth*.

kattı-dígır (§ 4132) v.t. *tie* (etc. s.v. dígır) *after wrapping*, etc.

kattı-dıgır-ɛd-åg- (§§ 3877 ff.) v.t. *be in the situation of having tied* (etc.) *after wrapping*, etc.
   dúŋıt⌣téŋ⌣kádɛr⌣kattıdıgırɛdågın⌢ (-t⌣t- < -g⌣t- § 707) *he has the money wrapped and tied in his cloth (she has*, etc. *in her cloth)*.

kattɛd-åg- (§§ 3877 ff.) v.t. *be in the situation of having wrapped*, etc.

kattɛd-då- (§ 3990; -éggı-då-, occ. -édgıdå- §§ 3993-4) v.t. *be going along after wrapping*, etc., *carry (an object) along wrapped (up)*, etc.
   safd⌣kålgı⌣kádɛgɛk⌣kattɛddån⌢ (-k⌣k- < -d⌣k- § 568) *Safd is going along after wrapping the bread in a cloth*, i.e. *S. is carrying the bread along wrapped in a cloth*.

katteddår-an (-ɛggıdår-; §§ 3890 ff., 3905) v.t. *tell to carry along wrapped*, etc., *let carry along wrapped*, etc.
   ålıt⌣téŋ⌣kádɛgɛk⌣kattɛddåran⌢ (-t⌣t- < -g⌣t- § 707) *tell ɛáli to (let ɛáli) carry it (them) wrapped in his cloth*.

káttı-kattı- (N. -ıha-; § 4093) v.p. *be wrapped*, etc.
   tumbåg⌣wåragır⌣káttıkattın⌢ *(the) tobacco is wrapped in paper*.

kåůkåů⌣ adj. (*a*) *timid, shy*; (*b*) *cowardly* [§ 2507].
   obj. kåůkåůg(ı)⌣, -gı⌢.
   pl. kåůkåůnč(ı)⌣.
   búru⌣kåůkåůn, ógıǧ⌣kåůkåůmunun⌢ *the (a) girl is shy, the (a) man isn't*.
   ógıǧ⌣kåůkåůgı⌣dólmunan⌢ *they don't like a cowardly man*.

káwırtɛ⌣, **kåů(ı)rtɛ**⌣ n. *bird*; with collective sg. (§ 4696 c) [< k- prob. dem. (§ 2167) + åwır *wing* (§ 2148) + -tɛ⌣ (§ 2335); doublet of háwırtɛ⌣ *palm-frond*; see § 207; *RSN*, § 129].
   obj. -tɛg⌣.
   pl. -tɛnč(ı)⌣.

kawırtén-d(ı)⌣ (kåůır-, kåůr-; §§ 2545 ff.) adj. *appertaining to a bird, bird's*.

kawíš⌣ n. *débris of fields, dead leaves, litter, rubbish, refuse*; with collective sg. (§ 4696 d); (=kášš(ı)⌣) [?cp. Eg. Ar. كَوِّش *collect, gather*].
   obj. -íšk(ı)⌣, -kı⌢.
   pl. -íšı⌣.

káwwa⌣ n. *Kawa* (on map), *a village on the right bank of the Nile, about 2 miles above Urdi*.
   obj. -wag⌣.

káwwa⌣ adj. *broad, wide*.
   obj. -wag⌣.
   pl. -wanč(ı)⌣.
   dárıp⌣káwwán⌢ *the path is broad*.

káwwagıd⌣ n. *breadth, width* [§§ 2247-8].
   téŋ⌣káwwagıd⌣mıŋkottɛ́rré? *what is its breadth?*
   téŋ⌣kawwagíttı⌣nål⌢ *see what its width is*.

káww-an- (§ 3910 α) v.i. *become broad*, etc.

káwwam-bů- (§ 3949 ff.) v.i. stat. *be in a broadening* (i.) *state or condition*.

kawwanɛd-åg- (§ 3966 α) v.i. *be in the condition of having become broad*, etc.

káwwag-ır (N. -akır, -ahır; § 3701) v.t. caus. *cause or allow to be broad*, etc., *broaden, widen*.

kawwåñ adj. *deficient in one dimension, thin* (=Amh. ረቂቅ) [app. < káwwa *broad* +-ñ dim. § 4572].
   obj. -wåñg(ı)⌣, -gı⌢.
   pl. -wåñı⌣.
   íŋ⌣kådɛ⌣kawwáñun⌢ *this cloth is (too) thin*.
   wåråg⌣kawwáñun⌢ *the paper is (too) thin*.

kawwåñ-tod⌣ (§§ 2484, 2582) adj. *unsatisfactorily thin, wretchedly thin, miserably thin*.
   obj. -tŏdk(ı)⌣, -tŏtk(ı)⌣, -tŏkk(ı)⌣, -tŏtt(ı)⌣ § 2462, -kı⌢, -tı⌢.
   gen. -tŏdn⌣v., -tŏnn⌣v.c., -tŏn⌣c.
   pl. kawwåñtonı⌣.
   kådɛ⌣kawwåñtodun⌢ *the cloth is miserably thin*.

kawwåñ-an- (§ 3910 α) v.i. *become thin*.

kawwåñg-ır (N. -åñkır; § 3702) v.t. caus. *cause or allow to be thin, render thin, make thin*.

káwwɛ! *go (pl.) to the house!, go (pl.) home!*
   s.v. kå⌣.

kébɛ n. (*a*) *great gourd, Cucurbita maxima* (*BSP*, 209); (*b*) *drinking-bowl cut out of rind of fruit of* (*a*), =kås⌣ (*b*) [*RSN*, § 129].
   obj. kébɛg [> Sudan Ar. كبيق kɛbɛg⌣ *bowl* 2412].
   pl. kɛbénč(ı)⌣.
   éssın⌣kébɛ⌣ *gourd (drinking-bowl) for water*.
   kébɛgɛd⌣éssın⌣fıran⌢ (-n⌣n- < -g⌣n- § 625) *they drink (the) water from (out of*, lit. *by means of*, s.v. -ɛd⌣) *the (a) gourd*.

kɛččınɛ́ v.t. (*a*) *hate, dislike*; (*b*) *refuse* (= món *a*, *b*) [< imperat. or imperf. stem of Sudan Ar. كِشّن *id.* (*a*) +-ɛ́ § 3636].
   ind. pres. âı⌣kɛččınɛ́rı⌢; perf. âı⌣kɛččınɛ́gorı⌢ (N. -ɛ́ko-, -ɛ́ho-).
   imperat. kɛččınɛ́!

aı‿tíŋ‿kálgı‿kɛččınɛ́rı⌒ *I dislike their food.*
tɛr‿ín‿ırískı‿kɛččınɛ́n⌒ *(s)he (it) dislikes this smell.*
nográŋgı‿kɛččınɛ́gori⌒ *I (have) refused to go.*
tɛr‿áıgı‿dɛfɛ́raŋgı‿kɛččınɛ́gon⌒ *(s)he (has) refused to pay me.*

kɛččınɛ́rar (-rár‿; §§ 2200 ff., 2207) and
kɛččınɛ́rı́d‿ (§§ 2256 ff., 2260) n. *hating, etc.*

kɛččınɛ́-bŭ- (§ 3931 β) v.i. stat. *be in a hated (etc.) state or condition.*

kɛččınɛ́red-ág- (§§ 3877 ff.) v.t. *be in the situation of having refused, etc.*

kɛččınɛ́-katti- (N. -ɛ́ha-; § 4093) v.p. *be hated, etc.*

-kɛd- (*RN*, § 359) -kɛt⌒, -kɛ⌒) = -k- objective suffix + -ɛd s.v. *ɛ́d.*

kɛ́f n. *liking, fancy* [< كَيْف *id.*].
obj. kɛ́fk(ı)‿, -kı⌒.
ɛŋ‿kɛ́fkɛ́⌒ (s.v. -ɛd‿),
ɛŋ‿kɛ́fkɛ́⌒ (s.v. -r‿) and
ɛŋ‿kɛ́fun‿ *as you like,* lit. *it is* (§ 4229) *as you like.*

kɛfɛ́ v.i. *suffice, be enough* [< part of a stem of كَفَى *id.* +-ɛ́ § 3632].
ind. pres. aı‿kɛfɛ́rı⌒, ɛr‿kɛfɛ́n⌒ (-fɛ́⌒, -fɛ́⌒, -fɛ́⌒); perf. aı‿kɛfɛ́gori⌒ (N. -ɛ́ko-, -ɛ́ho-).
part. pres. kɛfɛ́l‿ *(one, quantity) that suffices, sufficient*; past kɛfɛ́rɛl‿ *(one, quantity) that sufficed, sufficient.*
kɛfɛ́n, aı‿tɛ́nnɛ‿dólmunun⌒ *it's enough, I don't want any more.*
(imperat.) kɛfɛ́! *enough of you!, stop!*
kɛfɛ́wɛ! *enough of you (pl.)!, stop!*

kɛfɛ́rar‿ (-rár‿; §§ 2200 ff., 2207) and
kɛfɛ́rı́d‿ (§§ 2256 ff., 2260) n. *sufficing.*

kɛfɛ́g-ır (N. -ɛ́kır, -ɛ́hır; § 3681) v.t. caus. *cause or allow to suffice.*

kɛffád‿ n. *upper arm;* with collective sg. (§ 4696a) [cp. كَفّة *palm* § 2397].
obj. -ádk(ı)‿, -átk(ı)‿, -átt(ı)‿ § 2462, -kı⌒, -tı⌒.
gen. -ádn‿v., -án‿c.
pl. -ádı‿.
kɛffám‿budúrt(ı)‿ (-m‿b- < -dn‿b- § 594) *shoulder-joint(s).*

-kɛgıd‿ s.v. -ɛ́n‿ *mother.*

kɛkkɛbɛrrúd‿ n. *a Nile fish that inflates itself; the body covered with spines, brownish, white underneath,* Tetrodon fahaka, *Steindachner (PF, p. 98).*
obj. -údk(ı)‿, -útk(ı)‿, -útt(ı)‿ § 2462, -kı⌒, -tı⌒.
pl. -údı‿.

kɛ́l n. *end, extremity, so (a) tip; (b) edge, border, boundary, frontier.*
— with collective sg. (§ 4696 d) [cp. ON. ⲕⲉⲗ *id.* ZNG s.v., *RSN*, § 129].
obj. kɛ́lg(ı)‿, gı⌒.
pl. kɛ́lı‿.
sárbɛŋ‿kɛ́l‿ *finger-tip(s), tip of toe (tips of toes).*
bɛlɛ́n‿kɛ́l‿ (-n‿k- < -dn‿k- § 612) *the boundary (-ries) of the district.*
kólɛŋ‿kɛ́l‿ *boundary (-ries) of estate irrigated by water-wheel.*

tır‿áñ¹raŋ‿kɛ́lgı‿bıǧíllɛran⌒ (-ŋ‿k- < -nn‿k- § 657; § 6156) *they will remember (him, her, it, them) as long as they live.*

kɛ́la‿ n. *(a) measure (vessel of standard capacity); (b)* ¹⁄₁₂ *árdɛbb* (ɛ́rdɛb‿), i.e. 16½ *litres* = 3·63 *gallons* = 0·454 *bushel* [< كَيْلَة *id.*].
obj. -lag‿.
pl. -lanč(ı)‿.
márɛk‿kɛ́lagɛd‿ásran⌒ and
márɛk‿kɛ́lagɛd‿abbırɛ́ran⌒ *they ascertain the amount of millet with a measure.*
ɛrdɛ́bır‿kɛ́la‿dımındówwı‿dábun⌒ *in an árdɛbb there are twelve kɛ́la.*
íuŋ‿kɛ́la‿ (§ 4685) *(a) the (a) measure(-ful) of grain (about 28 lb.); (b) the (a) measure for grain* = kɛ́l‿ıúnd(ı)‿.
béntıŋ‿kɛ́la‿ *(a) the (a) measure of dates; (b) the (a) measure for dates* = kɛ́la‿bɛntínd(ı)‿.
kɛ́la‿málw‿ídıw‿dábun⌒ *there are eight málwa in a kɛ́la‿.*
kɛ́la‿wɛr‿rátul‿arrídıwkırın⌒ *a kɛ́la is something like 28 lb.*
káǧ‿dórr‿íuŋ‿kɛ́lak‿kálkó⌒ *the horse ate (has eaten) a kɛ́la‿ of corn in a (the) week.*

kɛllıfɛ́ v.t. *charge (command), cost* = kallıfɛ́.

kɛ́lŭn‿ (§ 956a) n. *lock* [< كَيْلُون *id.*].
obj. -úŋ(ı)‿, -gı⌒.
pl. -úŋı‿.

kɛ́mıs‿ (§§ 2699, 2707) card. num. *four* [*RSN*, § 119; cp. ON. ⲕⲉⲙⲥⲟ *id. GNT* s.v.].
obj. kɛmísk(ı)‿, kɛ́m(ı)sk(ı)‿, -kı⌒.
gen. kɛ́msn‿, ızn‿ (§ 732).
pl. kɛ́msı‿.
kémız‿dán‿ (-z‿d- < -s‿d- § 729) *there are four.*
kɛ́m(ı)sun⌒ (-sŭ⌒, -sú⌒ §§ 939, 5232) and
tɛr‿kɛ́m(ı)sun⌒ (tɛr‿ § 5233) *it's (they're) four.*
kɛmsín⌒ (sı̆⌒, -sí⌒ § 5235) and
tír‿kɛmsín⌒ (tır‿ § 5236) *they're four.*
kɛ́mıs‿tágon⌒ and
kɛ́mıs‿tágoran⌒ *four came (have come;* § 5229).
tír‿kɛ́mıs‿nókkon⌒ and
tír‿kɛ́mıs‿nókkoran⌒ *the four of them went (have gone;* § 5245).
ógıč‿kɛ́mıs‿kúpk‿óččan⌒ and
ógıč‿kɛ́mıs‿kúpk‿óččıran⌒ *four men tow the boat* (§ 5239).
sǎ‿kɛ́m(ı)sun⌒ (-sŭ⌒, ‿kɛ́msú⌒) *it's four o'clock.*
sǎ‿kɛ́m(ı)sır‿ *at four o'clock.*
sǎ‿kɛ́m(ı)sır⌒ *it's at four o'clock* (§§ 5858–60).
sǎ‿kɛ́mız‿bókkon‿ (-z‿b- < -sn‿b- § 728) *till 4 o'clock.*

kɛmısn-d(ı)‿ (-ízn-; § 2737a) adj. *appertaining to four, of four, four's.*

kɛmsín-d(ı)‿ (§ 2737b) adj. = kɛmısnd(ı)‿.

kɛms-ínt(ı)‿ (kɛ́msınt(ı)‿; § 2740) ord. num. *fourth.*

kɛmsıntínd(ı)‿ (§ 2743) adj. *appertaining to the fourth.*

kɛmıŋgár‿ (§§ 2758, 5261–8) num. *the whole four, all four.*
obj. -árk(ı)‿, -kı⌒.

áŋgarɛn‿óssı‿kɛmıŋgár⌒ *they are the four feet of the Great Bear* (§ 5268).
tɛr‿kɛmıŋgárk‿ɛ́tta‿ *bring the four of them;* tɛr‿kɛmıŋgárk‿ a pronoun-complex (§ 5199).

kɛ́msırɛ‿ (§§ 2745) n. *¼, fourth part* [< kɛ́mıs- 4 + -ır *(action of) making* + -ɛ of n. ess., so *one of what makes into* 4 § 2287].
obj. kɛ́msırɛg‿.
pl. -rɛnč(ı)‿.
kɛ́msırɛd‿dɛ́n⌒ (-d‿d- < -g‿d- § 534) *give me a quarter.*
sáŋ‿kɛ́msırɛm‿bádkı‿tá⌒ *come in a quarter of an hour's time,* lit. *come after ¼ hour* = rúbu‿sǎm‿bádír‿ta⌒.

kɛmís-kırı‿ (-kíri‿ § 1532; § 2736) num. adj. *about four.*

kɛ́m(ı)s-an- (§ 2760) v.i. *become four.*

kɛ́m(ı)sam-bŭ- (§ 2761) v.i. stat. *be in a state or condition of becoming four.*

kɛmısk-ır (§ 2759) v.t. caus. *make into four.*

kɛmıskır-árbır (§ 4141) v.t. *fold in four.*

kɛmıskır-bág (§ 4138) v.t. *divide into four.*
imperat. kɛmıskırbák!

kɛmıskır-bagítte (§ 4140) v.t. *divide into four.*
ǧínɛk‿kɛmıskırbagíttɛgori⌒ *I (have) divided the pound into four.*

kɛndımɛ́r‿ n. *Kandamir* (on map), *ruins and a village on Tángas Island, about 7 miles above Old Dóngola.*
obj. -mɛ́rk(ı)‿, -kı⌒.

kɛ́rɛd‿, -ɛt⌒ n. *Kerat* (on map), *a village on the left bank of the Nile, about 3 miles below Ed-Débbaʰ.*
obj. kɛrɛ́dk(ı)‿, -ɛ́tk(ı)‿, -kı⌒.

kɛ́rɛñ‿ adj. *(a) curved, bent, crooked; (b) oblique, slanting* [§ 2509].
obj. kɛrɛ́ŋ(ı)‿, -gı⌒.
pl. kɛ́rɛñı‿.
íw‿wıččır‿kɛ́rɛñun⌒ (íw‿w- < ín‿w- § 720) *this stick is crooked.*
dábbar‿másıl‿kɛrɛ́ñun⌒ *at Ed-Débbaʰ the sun is slanting* (i.e. its apparent course from east to west is obliquely inclined to that of the Nile).

kérker v.i. *oscillate, vibrate, shake, rock, quiver, tremble* [onom. § 2851; *RSN*, §§ 129, 200].
ind. pres. aı‿kɛrkérrı‿, ɛr‿kɛ́rkɛrın⌒ (-rı̆⌒, -rí⌒); perf. aı‿kɛrkɛ́rkori⌒.
tɛ́nnı‿kɛ́rkɛrın⌒ *his (her) hand is (hands are* § 4696a) *unsteady.*

kɛ́rkɛrar‿ (-rár‿; §§ 2200 ff.) and
kɛrkɛ́ríd‿ (§§ 2256 ff.) n. *oscillation, etc.*

kɛrkɛrk-ídd(ı) (§ 3726) v.t. caus. *cause or allow to oscillate, etc.*
ind. pres. aı‿kɛrkɛrkíddırı⌒, ɛr‿kɛrkɛrkíddın⌒ (-dı̆⌒, -dí⌒); perf. aı‿kɛrkɛrkíddıgori⌒ (N. -ıko-, -ıho-).
imperat. kɛrkɛ́rkıddı!

kɛrkɛríŋ-ır (N. -ŋkır; ˊˊˊˊ; § 3688) v.t. caus. *cause or allow to oscillate, etc.*

kɛ́rma‿ n. *Kerma* (on map), *a small town on the right bank of the Nile above the third cataract, 6 miles below Argo Island* [perhaps < كُرْمَة *vine*].
obj. -mag‿.

kɛ́rrı‿ n. *(a) hut or shed built of straw, esp.; (b) stable, byre* [*RSN*, § 129].

kɛsbɛ́ — √kıññ-

obj. -rıg⌣ [> Sudan Ar. كَرِّيقة id. §2412].
pl. -rınč(ı)⌣.

kɛsbɛ́ v.t. gain, earn, acquire [< كَسَب gain + -ɛ́ §3616].
ind. pres. aı⌣kɛsbɛ́rı⌢; perf. aı⌣kɛsbɛ́gorı⌢ (N. -ɛ́ko-, -ɛ́ho-).

késɛl n. laziness, indolence [< كَسَل id.].
obj. kɛsélg(ı)⌣, -gi⌢.
kɛsɛl-kō (§4115) v.i. be lazy.
kɛsɛlkṓmunan⌢ they are not lazy.

késsɛ⌣ n. Kasea (on map), a village on the right bank of the Nile, about 3 miles above Old Dóngola.
obj. késsɛg⌣, késség⌣ (§1532).

kɛ́tta n. nest [< *kɛ́nta⌣ (§711); RSN, §129 s.v. kenti].
obj. -tag⌣.
pl. -tanč(ı)⌣.
káuırtɛŋ⌣kɛ́tta bird's-nest.

kɛ́u⌣, **kɛ́u**ʷ, **kɛ́w**⌣ n. cubit of 21 or 22 inches, from elbow to tip of middle finger plus width of hand (= dúra⌣ b).
obj. kɛ́ug(ı)⌣, -gi⌢.
pl. kɛ́wı⌣.
kádɛ⌣kɛ́ugɛd⌣áskattın⌢ and kádɛ⌣kɛ́ugɛd⌣abbırɛ́kattın⌢ cloth is measured by the cubit.

kíd⌣ n. bone; with collective sg. (§4696a) [< kíhid⌣ infra §971].
obj. kídk(ı)⌣, kítk(ı)⌣, kítt(ı)⌣ §2462, -ki⌢, -ti⌢.
gen. kídn⌣v., kínn⌣v.c., kín⌣c.
pl. kídı⌣.
bérıŋ⌣kíd⌣ rib(s).
tém⌣bérıŋ⌣kíd-dēg⌣gúššıgó⌢ (-d-d <-d-w- §533) (s)he (it) broke (has broken) one of his (her, its) ribs.
tém⌣bérıŋ⌣kíd-dēr⌣ǧúššıgó⌢ (§5341) one of his (her, its) ribs was (is) broken.
tém⌣bérıŋ⌣kíd⌣ówwıg⌣gúššıgó⌢ (s)he (it) broke (has broken) two of his (her, its) ribs.
tém⌣bérıŋ⌣kíd⌣ówwı⌣gúššıgó⌢ two of his (her, its) ribs were (are) broken.
kín-d(ı)⌣ (§§2545ff.) adj. appertaining to the bone, of the bone, bone's.

kím⌣ n. angle, corner.
obj. kímg(ı)⌣, -gi⌢.
pl. kímı⌣.
kímır⌣ (s.v. -r⌣) in the corner(s §4647).
kími-ko (§4120) v.i. have corners, be angular.
(part.) kími-kōl⌣ (§2577) adj. angular.

***kína**⌣ n. quinine [< كِينا id.].
obj. -nag⌣.

kīrındıwǎı⌣ (-wǎı⌣, -wǎi⌢, -wǎi⌢) n. Karendiwai (on map), a village on the right bank of the Nile, about 7 miles below Ed-Débbah [-wǎı⌣ ancient times].
obj. -wǎıg⌣, -wǎıg⌢.

kís⌣ n. bag, purse [< كِيس id.].
obj. kísk(ı)⌣, -ki⌢.
pl. kísı⌣.
kís-sēg⌣élkori⌢ (-s-s- < -s-w- §687) I (have) found a bag.

-k(ı)⌣, **-ki**⌢ adverbial (esp. objective) suffix §§2036ff.

kıbdád⌣ n. liver [apparently < *كِبْدَات a pl. of كِبْدَة id. §2397].
obj. -ádk(ı)⌣, -átk(ı)⌣, -átt(ı)⌣ §2462, ki⌢, -ti⌢.
gen. -ádn⌣v., -ánn⌣v.c., -án⌣c.

kıbríd n. match (for fire); with collective sg. (§4696d) [< كِبْرِيت sulphur, id.].
obj. -ídk(ı)⌣, -ítk(ı)⌣, -ítt(ı)⌣ §2462, -ki⌢, -ti⌢.
gen. -ídn⌣v., -ínn⌣v.c., -ín⌣c.
pl. -ídı⌣.

kídd(ı) v.i. (a) sink; (b) dive [§2868].
ind. pres. aı⌣kíddıri⌢, ɛr⌣kíddın⌢ (-dí⌢, -dí⌢); perf. aı⌣kíddıgori⌢ (N. -ıko-, -ıho-).
imperat. kíddi!, pl. kíddıwɛ! (-wɛ́!).
kúb⌣kíddıgó⌢ the boat sank (...has sunk).
unáttı⌣kıddóskon⌢ the moon has set.
kíddar⌣ (-dár⌣; §§2200ff.) and
kíddíd⌣ (§§2256ff.) n. sinking, etc.
kídd-an (§§3890ff.) v.t. let sink, tell to dive, let dive.
kíddı-bŭ- (§3931α) v.i. stat. be in a sunken (etc.) state or condition, lie sunk.
kúb⌣kíddıbūn⌢ the boat lies sunk.
kıddı-dí (§3747ɛ') v.i. die by sinking, drown, get drowned.
kıddır-ɛg-ág- (§§4071ff.) v.i. = kıddɛdól-.
kúb⌣kıddıregágkó⌢ the boat was about to sink.
kıdd-ɛ-dól- (-dᵒd- §1178; §4022) and
kıddır-ɛ-dól- (-rᵒd-; §4027) v.i. be about to sink, etc.
kúb⌣kıddıredólkó⌢ the boat was about to sink.
kıddɛd-ág- (§§3877ff.) v.i. be in the situation of having sunk, etc.
kíddıg-ır (N. -ıkır, -ıhır; §3682) v.t. caus. cause or allow to sink, etc.

kıhíd⌣ (kíhid⌣, kíhıd⌣ §1154) n. bone; with collective sg. (§4696a) [§2269; > kíd⌣ §971].
obj. -hídk(ı)⌣, -hítk(ı)⌣, -hítt(ı)⌣, -hídk(ı)⌣, -hítk(ı)⌣, -hítt(ı)⌣ §2462, -ki⌢, -ti⌢.
gen. -hídn⌣v., -hínn⌣v.c., -hín⌣c., -hídn⌣v., -hínn⌣v.c., -hín⌣c.
pl. kıhídı⌣, kíhıdı⌣.
bérıŋ⌣kıhíd⌣ rib(s).
kıhín-d(ı)⌣ (-hínd(ı); §§2545ff.) adj. appertaining to the bone, of the bone, bone's.

kílkıl⌣ n. tickle, tickling [imit. §§2151-2; cp. kál to itch; cp. Sudan Ar. كَلْكَل to tickle; RSN, §129 s.v. kíkili, TOB, §143, 206].
obj. kılkílg(ı)⌣, -gi⌢.
pl. kılkílı⌣.
tér⌣aık⌣kılkílg⌣áudɛnın⌢ (s)he (it) tickles me (⌣aík §515).
aı⌣tékkı⌣kılkílg⌣áutıddi⌢ I tickle him (her, it).

kím⌣ n. broad bracelet, worn by women [< Beḍ. kim (ABW, RBW s.v.) id.; §2088].
obj. kímg(ı)⌣, -gi⌢.
pl. kímı⌣.

kınísse⌣ n. thorn, prickle; with collective sg. (§4696b) [§2291].

obj. -sɛg⌣.
pl. -sɛnč(ı)⌣.
kınísse-wēr⌣aıgı⌣ǧómkō⌢ a thorn (has) wounded me.
abšóŋ⌣kınísse⌣ (-ŋ-k- < -gn-k- §652; -sé⌢ < -sɛn⌢ §§939, 4229) it's a hedgehog's prickle (porcupine's quill).

kınísse-kōl⌣ (§2579β) (a) adj. having thorns, thorny, prickly; (b) n. hedgehog, porcupine; (c) n. a grass, Pennisetum cenchroides, Rich. (BSP, 647) of which the seeds when ripe form troublesome burrs.
obj. -kólg(ı)⌣, -gi⌢.

N. **kínna**⌣ adj. (a) small, little (= S. kíñña⌣); (b) young (= S. kíñña⌣).
obj. -nag⌣.
pl. -narı⌣.
N. kínn⌣ɛ́sı⌣wɛkíttı⌣nókkori⌢ I went when I was young.

kínnēr⌣ ("", "" §1728; not confined to N.; §2682) indef. pron. a little, a few [< *kínn-wēr⌣ (§983) < √kínn- smallness (§4546) + -wēr⌣ a].
obj. kínnēg⌣ "", "", -gi⌢.
kínnēr⌣áŋkın (kínnɛ́ráŋkın)⌣ when a little (time) goes by, (in a little time, soon).
dúŋgı⌣kınnɛ́k⌣kóran⌢ they have a little money.

kınnɛ́g⌣, "", "", -gi⌢ (§5978) adv. a little, somewhat, rather.
kınnɛ́ǧ⌣góbbe⌢ wait a little.
énn-ı⌣kínnɛ́s⌣sɛrɛ́ré? (-s⌣s- < -g⌣s- §678) is your hand (are your hands §4696a) a little better?
énn-ur⌣kínnɛ́s⌣sɛráŋkomɛn? isn't your head a little better?

√kíññ- expresses lack, deficiency, smallness.

S. **kíñña**⌣ adj. (a) small, little; (b) young.
obj. -ñag⌣.
pl. kíññarı⌣.
ter⌣kíññán⌢ (§1970) (a) it is small; (b) (s)he (it) is young.
kíññ⌣ɛ́su⌣wɛkídkı⌣nógkori⌢ I went when I was young.

kíññakane⌣ (§2295) n. (a) smallness; (b) youngness, youth.

kíñña-tod⌣ (§2582) adj. unsatisfactorily (miserably, wretchedly) small.
obj. -tŏdk(ı)⌣, -tŏtk(ı)⌣, -tŏkk(ı)⌣, -tŏtt(ı)⌣ §2462, -ki⌢, -ti⌢.
gen. -tŏdn⌣v., -tŏnn⌣v.c., -tŏn⌣c.
pl. kíññatonı⌣.
kíññatodun⌣ it is miserably small.

kíññán-d(ı)⌣ (§§2545ff.) adj. appertaining to the (a) small (etc.) one.

kíññ-an- (§3910α) v.i. become small, etc., diminish, decrease.
kíññandan⌢ they diminish.

kíññam-bŭ- (§§3949ff.) v.i. stat. be in a diminishing (etc.) state or condition.

kíññanɛd-ág- (§3966α) v.i. be in a condition of having become small, etc., be in a diminished (etc.) condition.

S. **kíññag-ır** (§3701) (a) v.t. caus. cause or allow to be small, etc.; (b) v.t. render small, etc., diminish, decrease, reduce.
ind. pres. aı⌣kíññagıddi⌣, ɛr⌣kíñña-gırın⌣ (-rí⌢, -rí⌢).

-kíññ(ı) (§§1700, 2536-8) suffix forming adjectives -less, devoid of, lacking, with-

out [cp. ON. ᚱᛁᛈᛈᛁ id. GNT s.v., ZNG, §60].
obj. -kɪ́ññɪg⌣.
pl. -kɪ́ññɪnč(ɪ)⌣.
âɪ⌣dúŋgɪkɪ́ññɪ⌣érɪ⌢ I am penniless.
ɛ́r⌣dúŋgɪkɪ́ññɪn⌢ you are penniless.
tér⌣dúŋgɪkɪ́ññɪn⌣ (s)he is penniless.
ár⌣dúŋgɪkɪ́ññɪnč⌣éru⌢ we are penniless.
ír⌣dúŋgɪkɪ́ññɪnč⌣éru⌢ you (pl.) are penniless.
tír⌣dúŋgɪkɪ́ññɪnč⌣erán⌢ they are penniless.
gámb⌣ádkɪ́ññɪ⌣nɛfémunun⌢ the (an) axe without a handle is useless.
ágar⌣éssɪkɪ́ññɪd⌣dólmunan⌢ (-d⌣d- < -g⌣d- §534) they don't like (want) a waterless place.
ágarɪ⌣kultɪkɪ́ññɪ́nčɪt⌣tɛbéran⌢ (-t⌣t- < -g⌣t- §707) they search for (the) places free from flies.

-kɪ́ññɪr⌣ (§5860) postp. = prep. (§4287) without.
Suffixed to bare stem, and so forming adverbs (§4442):
âɪ⌣dúŋkɪ́ññɪr⌣ágrɪ⌢ I am (etc. s.v. ág) without money.
dúŋgɪkɪ́ññɪr⌣ággéllɪgāwɪn⌢ (s)he is working without money (i.e. wages).
óllɪkɪ́ññɪr⌣tókkon⌣âɪg⌣ógɪmɛn⌢ don't take me to a place without shade.

kíññɪg-ɪr (N. -ɪkɪr, -ɪhɪr; §3703) (a) v.t. caus. cause or allow to be devoid of, etc.; (b) v.t. deprive of, not give; (α) constructed with an object in the objective case, or (β) forming a complex with its object, that now bears no objective suffix (§§3747 α', b, 1, 5580, 5708).
dúŋgɪk⌣kíññɪgɪr and
dúŋgɪkɪ́ññɪgɪr (q.v.) cause or allow to lack money, not give money to.
âɪ⌣ɛ́kkɪ⌣kálgɪ⌣kɪ́ññɪgíddi⌢ and
âɪ⌣ɛ́kkɪ⌣kalkɪ́ññɪgíddɪ I do (shall §5369a) not give you food.
ár⌣tírgɪ⌣kálgɪ⌣kɪ́ññɪgɪ́ddu⌢ and
ár⌣tírgɪ⌣kalkɪ́ññɪgɪ́ddu⌢ we do (shall) not give them food.
tɪmbáb⌣tékkɪ⌣hâğak⌣kɪ́ññɪgɪ́rkó⌢ and
tɪmbáb⌣tékkɪ⌣hâğakɪ́ññɪgɪ́rkó⌢ his father didn't give (hasn't given) him anything (her father didn't give her anything).
âɪ⌣ɛ́kkɪ⌣mahîjakɪ́ññɪgíddi⌢ I shall (§5369a) pay you no wages.
âɪ⌣ɛ́kk⌣ɛm⌣mahîjakɪ́ññɪgíddi⌢ and
âɪ⌣ɛ́kk⌣ɛm⌣mahîjakɪ́ññɪgíddi⌢ I shall deprive you of your wages (...not pay you your wages).

kínja⌣ (§1034) = kíñña⌣ small, young.

-k-ɪr = -k- objective suffix (§908) + -ɪr causative suffix (§3665; RN, §348).

kɪrágɛ⌣ (-āhɛ⌣ §1017) n. Sunday [< Κυριακή id. RN, LN, AZN s.v., cp. ON. ᚴᛦᛈᛁᛆᚴᛂ id. GNT s.v., GCD, p. 11].
obj. -gɛg⌣.
pl. -gɛnč(ɪ)⌣.
ásal⌣kɪrágɛn⌣ (-ágɛ⌢, -ágé⌢) tomorrow is Sunday.
kɪrágɛ⌣jóm⌣ (§4750),
kɪrágɛn⌣jóm⌣ (§4810),
kɪrágɛ⌣nahár⌣ (⌣náh-, ⌣nɛh-; §4750) and
kɪrágɛn⌣nahár⌣ (§4810) Sunday.
kɪrágɛg⌣, -gɛgɪ⌣ (§4665),
kɪrágɛr⌣,
kɪrágɛ⌣jómg(ɪ)⌣, -gɪ⌢,
kɪrágɛ⌣jómɪr⌣,
kɪrágɛ⌣nahárk(ɪ)⌣, -kɪ⌢ and
kɪrágɛ⌣nahárro⌣ on Sunday.
kɪrágɛt⌣táran⌢ (-t⌣t- < -g⌣t- §707) they come on Sunday.
kɪrágɛb⌣bɪtáran⌢ (-b⌣b- < -g⌣b- §519) they will come on Sunday.
kɪrágɛ⌣jómgɪ⌣tágoran⌢ they came on Sunday.
kɪrágɛrtón⌣,
kɪrágɛ⌣jómɪrtón⌣ and
kɪrágɛ⌣nahárrotón⌣ since Sunday.
kɪrágɛm⌣mónkon⌣ and
kɪrágɛm⌣bókkon⌣ till Sunday.
kɪrágɛ⌣tál⌣ noun-complex (§4794) next Sunday (s.v. tá).
kɪrágɛ⌣tálnɪ⌣dór⌣ noun-complex (§4796) next Sunday week (دور الأحد (الجاي)).

kɪrāgén-d(ɪ)⌣ (-āhén-; §§2545ff.) adj. appertaining to Sunday, Sunday's.

kɪrâɪ⌣ n. payment for service, pay, wage, hire [< كِرَاءٌ id. (§1215a); cp. Amh. ነዶይ id.].
obj. -râɪg⌣.
pl. -râɪnč(ɪ)⌣.
ɛŋ⌣kɪrâɪg⌣ɛ́kkɪ⌣bɪtíddan⌢ they will give you your pay.

-kɪrɪ⌣ (-kírɪ §1701; §§2539-42, 5055-8) suffix forming adjectives like, resembling, similar to, -ish [< -k- obj. suff. (§907) + -ɪr- caus. suff. (§3665) + -ɪ⌣ adjectival (§2529), so or. making (part.)].
obj. -kɪrɪg⌣.
pl. -kɪrínč(ɪ)⌣ (§1702).
tɛr⌣gɪrídkɪrɪn⌢ (⌣gɪrídkírɪn⌢) (s)he (it) is like an ape.
tɪr⌣gɪrídkɪrɪnčɪn⌢ (-či⌢, -čí⌢; occ. -čɪn⌢, -či⌢, -čí⌢ §1162) they are like apes.
kúlu⌣kúmbukɪrɪ-wēn⌣nálkoran⌢ (-n⌣n- < -g⌣n- §625) they saw (have seen) a stone resembling an egg.
tɛr⌣âɪkírɪn⌢ (-rī⌢, -rí⌢) (s)he (it) is like me.
tɛr⌣ɛ́kkɪrɪn⌢ (-rī⌢, -rí⌢) (s)he (it) is like you.
tɛr⌣tékkɪrɪn⌢ (-rī⌢, -rí⌢) (s)he (it) is like him (her) it.
tɛr⌣árkɪrɪn⌢ (-rī⌢, -rí⌢) (s)he (it) is like us.
tɛr⌣írkɪrɪn⌢ (-rī⌢, -rí⌢) (s)he (it) is like you (pl.).
tɛr⌣tírkɪrɪn⌢ (-rī⌢, -rí⌢) (s)he (it) is like them.
âɪ⌣ɛ́kkɪr⌣érɪ⌢ I am like you.
ar⌣ɛ́kkɪr⌣éru⌢ we are like you.
tɪr⌣ɛ́kkɪr⌣erán⌢ (⌣erấ⌢, ⌣erá⌢) they are like you.
ar⌣ɛ́kkɪrɪnčɪn⌢ (-či⌢, čí⌢, occ. ⌣čɪn⌢, -či⌢, -čí⌢ §1162) we are like you.
tɪr⌣ɛ́kkɪrɪnčɪn⌢ (-či⌢, -čí⌢, occ. -čɪn⌢, -či⌢, -čí⌢ §1162) they are like you.
tínn⌣ó⌣iŋkírɪn⌢ their singing is like this (that).
iŋkírɪd⌣dóllɪ⌢ (-d⌣d- < -g⌣d- §534) (a) I like this kind; (b) I want him (her, it) like this.
tɛr⌣míŋkírɪré? what is (s)he (it) like?
díčkírɪg⌣ɛttágoran⌢ they (have) brought about five.

— suffixed to a noun-complex:
índo⌣jóm⌣dɪmíŋkɪrɪb⌣bɪñírran⌢ (-b⌣b- < -g⌣b- §519) they will stay here about ten days; -kɪrɪb⌣ is suffixed to ⌣jóm⌣dɪmín⌣ (§4783).
índon⌣ádɪr⌣sɪŋkám⌣bagóŋkírɪn⌢ (-m⌣b- < -dn⌣b- §594) the winter (of) here is like the summer at (lit. of) Sinkat; -kírɪn⌣ is suffixed to sɪŋkám⌣bagóŋ- (§4810).
íw⌣wélkɪrɪn⌢ (-w⌣w- < -n⌣w- §720) (a) this is like a dog; (b) it is like this dog; íw⌣wél- a noun-complex (§4866).
íw⌣wélkɪrɪmunun⌢ (a) this is not like a dog; (b) it is not like this dog.
inɪn⌣tûr⌣dáŋkɪrɪn⌢ (§5058) there seems to be some in this.

kísɪr⌣ n. guitar, lute [< κιθάρις id.; cp. LSG, p. 164, SNK, §12].
obj. kɪsírk(ɪ)⌣, -kɪ⌢.
pl. kís(ɪ)rɪ⌣.
kɪsɪ́rk⌣ággómɪn⌢ he is (keeps on) playing the guitar.
kɪsírn⌣kóɪ⌣,
kɪsɪrn⌣sílɪg⌣ and
kɪsɪrn⌣sílk(ɪ)⌣ string(s §4647) of guitar.

kɪsór⌣ n. scissors, shears [app. < كُسُور limbs].
obj. -órk(ɪ)⌣, -kɪ⌢.
pl. -órɪ⌣.

kɪštenér⌣ n. Kitchener [< Sudan Ar. كِشْتِنِير, kuštenér id.].
obj. -órk(ɪ)⌣, -kɪ⌢.

kɪtâb⌣ n. book [< كِتَاب id.].
obj. -ábk(ɪ)⌣, -ápk(ɪ)⌣, -kɪ⌢.
gen. -ábn⌣v., -ám⌣c.
pl. -ábɪ⌣ and kútub⌣ [< كُتُب].
obj. -ábɪg⌣, -gi⌢ and kutúbk(ɪ)⌣, -úpk(ɪ)⌣, -kɪ⌢.
gen. -ábɪn⌣ and kútubn⌣v., -um⌣c.
X. kɪtâbɪg⌣étta⌢ bring the books.
Y. kɪtâbɪn⌣nalkómunun⌢ (-n⌣n- < -g⌣n- §625) I haven't seen the books.

kɪtám-d(ɪ)⌣ (§§2545ff.) adj. appertaining to the (a) book, book's.

kɪtābín-d(ɪ)⌣ and
kutúm-d(ɪ)⌣ (§§2545ff.) adj. appertaining to (the) books, books'.

kíttɛ v.i. be silent [§§2870ff.].
ind. pres. âɪ⌣kíttɛrɪ; perf. âɪ⌣kíttɛgori⌢ (N. -ɛko-, -ɛho-).
imperat. kíttɛ!, ‶ (§1532), pl. kíttɛwɛ!,
part. pres. kíttɛ⌣ (one) that is silent, silent.
def. perf. (§3540) âɪ⌣kɪttɛróskori⌢ and âɪ⌣kɪttóskori⌢.
def. imperat. kíttɛros!, -rós!, -ró! §962); pl. kɪttɛroswɛ! (-róswɛ!, -rówwɛ! §724, -wé!, -rósse! §687, -sé!).
X. ólgon⌣ággáww⌣ná? is (s)he still brawling?
Y. wăraŋ⌣kɪttóskó⌢ no, (s)he has shut up.
áru⌣kɪttósko⌢ (⌣kɪttérosko⌢) the rain has ceased.

kíttɛrar⌣ (-rár⌣; §§2200ff., 2210) and
kɪttɛríd⌣ (§§2256ff., 2263) n. being silent, silence.

kítter-an (§§ 3890 ff., 3899) v.t. *tell to be silent, let be silent.*
jǎ⌣kítteraj⌣jǎ⌣nógá! (§939; -j⌣j- <-n⌣j- §567) *let him (her, it) either be silent or go away!*

kɪttɛ-dǎğɪ (§3747ᵉ) v.i. *walk about (etc. s.v. dǎğɪ) silently.*
sáb⌣kɪttɛdǎğɪn⌢ *the cat wanders silently about.*

kɪttɛ-tĕb (§3747ᵉ) v.i. *stand (etc. s.v. tĕb) silent.*
imperat. kɪttɛtĕp!

kɪttos-ǎg (§§4180-4; -osgǎg, -ozgǎg, -oggǎg §4185) v.i. *squat (etc. s.v. ǎg) silent, sit quiet, keep still.*
imperat. kɪttosǎk! (-osgǎk!, -ozg-, -ogg-).
kɪttosǎgran⌢ *they sit silent.*

kɪttos-nóg (-tonnóg §629; §§4180-4; -osgɪnóg, -ozgɪ-, -oggɪ- §4185) v.i. *go (etc. s.v. nóg) silently, go (etc.) quietly.*
imperat. kɪttosnók! (-tonnók!, -osgɪnók!, -ozgɪ-, -oggɪ-).
kɪttonnókkoran⌢ *they went (have gone) quietly away (they just went away,* Sudan Ar. راحَوا ساكت).

kɪttos-tĕb (-ottĕb §714; §§4180-4; -osgɪtĕb, -ozgɪ-, -oggɪ- §§4185-7) v.i. *stand etc. s.v. tĕb) silent, stand (etc.) quiet, stand (etc.) still.*
imperat. kɪttostĕp! (-ottĕp!, -osgɪtĕp!, -ozgɪ-, -oggɪ-).
kɪttottĕbran⌢ *they keep silent.*

kjátt(ɪ)⌣ adj. *(a) straight; (b) straight across, at right angles.*
obj. -tɪg⌣.
pl. -tɪnč(ɪ)⌣.
wɪččɪr⌣kjáttɪn⌢ *the stick is straight.*
dérɪb⌣kjáttɪmunun, kéreñun⌢ *the path is not straight, it's crooked.*
bér⌣kjáttɪmunun⌢ *the (piece of) wood (e.g. pole, beam) is not straight.*
hándagɪr⌣másɪl⌣kjáttɪn, dábbar⌣kéreñun⌢ *at El-Xándaq the sun is at right angles (i.e. its apparent course from east to west is at right angles to that of the Nile) at Ed-Débbáᵇ it is slanting (i.e. its apparent course is obliquely inclined to that of the Nile).*

†**klúb**⌣ n. *club, club-house* [< Eng. club].
obj. klúbk(ɪ)⌣, klúpk(ɪ)⌣, -ki⌢.
pl. klúbɪ⌣.

†**klúbb(ɪ)⌣** n. *club, club-house* [< Eng. club].
obj. -bɪg⌣.
pl. -bɪnč(ɪ)⌣.
mándo⌣klúbbɪr⌣ğélkori⌢ *I went and found him (her, it) over there at the club.*

kó⌣ n. *lion* [RSN, §200].
obj. kóg⌣.
pl. kónč(ɪ)⌣.

kōn-tŏd (§2366) n. *lion cub.*
obj. -tŏdk(ɪ)⌣, -tŏtk(ɪ)⌣, -tŏkk(ɪ)⌣, -tŏtt(ɪ)⌣ §2462, -ki⌢, -ti⌢.
gen. -tŏdn⌣v., -tŏnn⌣v.c., -tŏn⌣c.
pl. kóntonɪ⌣.
kōntŏdun⌢ *it's a lion cub.*

kó-tod (§2369) n. *(a) poor specimen of lion, wretched lion; (b) lion.*
obj. kótŏdk(ɪ)⌣, -tŏtk(ɪ)⌣, -tŏkk(ɪ)⌣, -tŏtt(ɪ)⌣ §2462, -ki⌢, -ti⌢.
gen. -tŏdn⌣v., -tŏnn⌣v.c., -tŏn⌣c.
pl. kótonɪ⌣.
kótodun⌢ *it's a (wretched) lion.*

kō v.t. *have, possess, own* [cp. ON. ĸo id. GNT s.v.]. See §§3565-6, 4109ff., 4672, 5545ff.
ind. pres. aī⌣kóri⌢, in complex also ⌣kōri⌢ "', ɛr⌣kón⌢ (⌣kŏ⌢, ⌣kóŏ⌢, ⌣kó⌢, ⌣kón⌢, ⌣kŏ⌢, ⌣kó⌢), in complex also ⌣kōn⌢ (etc.), ⌣kon⌢, ⌣kŏ⌢; perf. aī⌣kógori⌢ (N. ⌣kókori⌢, ⌣kóhori⌢ §1021).
imperat. kó!, pl. kówɛ!, "".
subj. past aī⌣kósɪ⌣ (-su⌣).
part. pres. kól⌣ *(one) that has, etc., possessor, having, etc.;* obj. kólg(ɪ)⌣.
kól⌣ *alone, etc.* s.v. kól⌣ *infra.*
part. past kórɛl⌣ *(one) that had, etc., possessor, having, etc.;* obj. kōrélg(ɪ)⌣.
neg. part. pres. kōmɛnɪl⌣ *(one) that does not have, etc., not having, etc.;* obj. kōmɛnɪlg(ɪ)⌣.
tɛr⌣hĕlgɪ⌣kón⌢ and tɛr⌣hĕl⌣kón⌢ *(s)he is energetic, lit. (s)he has energy.*
ín⌣ğakut⌣túllak⌣kŏ⌢ *this stew is smoked, lit.... has smoke.*
tɛr⌣habárkɪ⌣kón⌣ɛrán⌢ (§6142) *they say that (s)he has news.*
wɛlgɪ⌣kón⌢ *you have ((s)he has) the (a) dog.*
wɛlgɪ⌣kól⌣ *(one) that has a dog.*
ɪrískɪ⌣kó⌢ *it has a smell.*
ɪrískɪ⌣kómunun⌢ *it has no smell.*
ɪrískɪ⌣kól⌣míllɪn⌢ *that that has a smell is bad.*
ɪrískɪ⌣kōmɛnɪl⌣sérēn⌢ *that that has no smell is good.*
tɪr⌣éddo⌣mukóttɛk⌣kóran? *how much do you owe them?,* lit. *how much have they on you?* (s.v. -r⌣).
tɛr⌣éddo⌣míŋgɪ⌣kón? *what do you owe him (her)?*

kól⌣ (-kól; §§2543, 4943-8) adj. *unaccompanied, unassisted, unprompted; often to be rendered by an adverb(ial phrase) alone, only, by (of) oneself, of one's own accord* [a special use of kól⌣ part. of kō *have* §4944; RN, §148²].
obj. (-)kólg(ɪ)⌣, -gi⌢.
pl. -konɪ⌣, -kónɪ⌣.
kól⌣bɪtán⌢ *you (he, she, it) will come (back) by yourself (himself, herself, itself), alone, of your (his, her, its) own accord.*
X. tírgonon⌣uskúrkoná? *did (have) you put it with them?*
Y. kólgɪ⌣uskúrkori⌢ *I (have) put it by itself.*
kólgɪ⌣bán⌣ (<⌣buán⌣ s.v. bú) *let him (her, it) be by himself (herself, itself).*

— with a noun, forming a noun-complex (§4945):
kóbɪd⌣kól⌣kóbɪn⌢ *the door shuts of itself.*
šaī⌣kólg⌣áwan⌢ *tell him (her) to make (the) tea only.*
X. éssig⌣ɛttāgori⌢ *I (have) brought the (some) water.*
Y. éssi⌣kólgá? *(the) water only?*
íŋgɪ⌣kǎ⌣kóllo⌣dégri⌢ and íŋgɪ⌣kántu⌣kóllo⌣dégri⌢ *I wear this indoors only;* ⌣kǎ⌣kól- and ⌣kántu⌣kól- *noun-complexes.*
éndɪ⌣kólg⌣ɪšíŋkori⌢ *I (have) sent yours alone (...yours by itself);* éndɪ⌣kólg⌣ *a pronoun-complex (§5212) used as a noun-complex.*

— forming complex personal pronouns (§2619):
aī⌣kól⌣ *I alone, I by myself, I of my own accord.*
ɛk⌣kól⌣ *you alone, you by yourself, you of your own accord.*
tɛk⌣kól⌣ *(s)he (it) alone, etc.*
árkonɪ⌣ (árkónɪ⌣ §1532) *we alone, etc.*
írkonɪ⌣ (írkónɪ⌣) *you (pl.) alone, etc.*
tírkonɪ⌣ (tírkónɪ⌣) *they alone, etc.*
aī⌣kól⌣ǎgri⌣ *I am (live, etc. s.v. ǎg) alone, by myself.*
aī⌣kól⌣ɛri⌢ *I am alone, by myself.*
tɛk⌣kólun⌢ *(s)he (it) is alone.*
aī⌣kól⌣búgori⌢ *I was alone.*
árkonɪ⌣búgoru⌢ *we were alone.*
ɛk⌣kól⌣bɪnógná? *will you go alone?*
tɛk⌣kól⌣tǎgō⌢ *(s)he (it) came (has come) alone (by himself, etc.).*
X. sǎpk⌣ɛttǎlgɪ⌣gírɪš⌣dɪmíŋgɪ⌣bɪtíddi⌢ *I shall give ten piastres to the one that brings the cat.*
Y. tɛk⌣kól⌣bɪtán⌢ *it will come of its own accord.*
tírkonɪ⌣tǎgoran⌢ *they came (have come) alone (by themselves, etc.).*
aī⌣kólgɪ⌣mugó⌢ *leave me by myself.*
ɛk⌣kólgɪ⌣bɪmúgri⌢ *I shall leave you by yourself.*
tɛk⌣kólgɪ⌣bán⌣ *let him (her, it) be by himself (herself, itself).*
tɛk⌣kólg⌣úskur⌢ *put it by itself.*
árkonɪ⌣mugó⌢ (-m⌣m- <-g⌣m- §601) *leave us by ourselves.*
írkonɪ⌣bɪmúgru⌢ (-b⌣b- <-g⌣b- §519) *we shall leave you by yourselves.*
tírkonɪ⌣búwan⌢ *let them be by themselves.*
tírkonɪ⌣búwawwé⌢ *let (pl.) them be by themselves.*
tírkonɪ⌣g⌣úskur⌢ *put them by themselves.*

— a noun, instead of forming a complex with ⌣kól⌣, may be followed by ⌣tɛk⌣kól⌣ in apposition (§4947):
gezáz⌣kól⌣kúskó⌢ and
gezáz⌣tɛk⌣kól⌣kúskó⌢ *the bottle (has) opened by itself.*
šaīgɪ⌣tɛk⌣kólg⌣áwan⌢ *tell him (her) to make (the) tea only.*
kážkɪ⌣tɛk⌣kólg⌣ɛttāgoran⌢ *they (have) brought the horse only.*

kób *(a)* v.t. *shut, close; (b)* v.t. *shut in, shut up, confine, imprison; (c)* v.i. *shut (itself), close (itself)* (§5341).
ind. pres. aī⌣kób(!)ri⌢, ɛr⌣kóbɪn⌢ (-bī⌢, -bí⌢); perf. aī⌣kóbkori⌢ (⌣kópk-).
imperat. kóp!, pl. kóbwɛ! (-wé!, kóbbɛ! §517, -bɛ!).
subj. past aī⌣kóbsɪ⌣ (⌣kópsɪ⌣, -su⌣).
part. pres. kóbɪl⌣ *(one) that shuts, etc., shutter, etc., shutting, etc.,* obj. kobílg(ɪ)⌣, -gi⌢; past kóbɛl⌣ *(one) that shut, etc., shutter, etc., shutting, etc.,* obj. kobélg(ɪ)⌣ -gi⌢.

def. imperat. (§3789) kóbos! (kobós! §1890, kobó! §962); pl. kobóswɛ! (-bóswé!, -bówwɛ! §724, -wé!, -bóssɛ! §687, -sé!).
kóbrıá? (a) shall (§5369b) I shut it? (§5083); (b) shall I shut him (her, it) in (up)?
kǎk‿kópkori⁀ (-k‿k- < -g‿k- §569) I (have) shut the door, lit.... the house.
wélgı‿kópkoran⁀ they (have) shut the dog in (up).
kǎr‿kópkori⁀ I (have) shut him (her, it, them) up in the house.
án‿dɛ́ŋgı‿bıkóbri⁀ I shall pay my (our) debt.
án‿dɛ́nık‿kópkori⁀ I (have) paid my (our) debts.
án‿dɛ́nık‿kobırı́kkori⁀ I (have) paid (each of §5456) my (our) debts.
tín‿dɛ́ŋgı‿kóbran⁀ they pay their debt.
tín‿dɛ́nık‿kópkoran⁀ they (have) paid their debts.
tín‿dɛ́nık‿kobırı́kkoran⁀ they (have) paid (each of) their debts.
sandǔk‿kǒl‿kobóskó⁀ the box has shut by itself.
kóbar (-bår‿; §§2200ff.) and
kobı́d‿ (§§2256ff.) n. shutting, etc.
kóbıd‿ n. (a) = kobı́d‿; (b §2268) door.
obj. kobídk(ı)‿, -ítk(ı)‿, -ítt(ı)‿ §2462, -kı⁀, -tı⁀.
gen. -ídn‿v., -ín‿c., kóbıdn‿v., -ın‿c.
pl. kób(ı)dı‿.
míssıŋ‿kóbıd‿ eyelid; with collective sg. (§4696a).
kobídn‿í‿ door-handle.
kób-an (§§3890ff.) v.t. tell to shut, etc., let shut, etc.
álıs‿sandǔkkı‿kóbă⁀ (-s‿s- < -g‿s- §678) tell ɛ áli to shut the box.
imperat. kobmúk!
kób-bŭ- (§3931β) v.i. stat. be in a shut (etc.) state or condition.
part. pres. kóbbŭl‿ (one) that is in a shut (etc.) state or condition (a) n. prisoner; (b) adj. shut, closed; captive; obj. kóbbŭlg(ı)‿, -gı⁀.
part. past kóbbɛl‿ and (§3536), kób-bŭrɛl‿ (one) that was in a shut (etc.) state or condition; prisoner; shut, closed; captive.
kǎ‿kóbbŭn⁀ (a) the house is closed; (b) the door is shut.
tǎga‿kóbbŭgŏ⁀ the window was (had been) shut.
kǎ‿kobbǔmunun⁀ the house (door) is not closed.
úrtıncı‿máŋ‿kǎr‿kóbbŭran⁀ (the) goats (sheep) are (being kept) shut up in that house.
kób-bᵘ-an (-b(w)an; §§3962–3) v.t. have, or let be, in a shut (etc.) state or condition.
imperat. kóbbᵘan! (-b(w)an!, -b(w)ā!, -b(w)á!).
kobíttı‿kóbban⁀ let the door be (left, kept) shut.
sǎbkı‿kóbbá⁀ let the cat be shut up (in).
sǎbık‿kóbbŭwanır⁀ let (each of §5456) the cats be shut up (in).
kob(ı)r-ɛg-ǎg- (§§4071ff.) v.t. and i. = kobɛdól-.

māmǔr‿mágasık‿kobırıddɛgágın⁀ the mavmǔr is about to imprison (each of) the thieves.
kob-ɛ-dól- (-bᵒd- §1178; §4022) and
kob(ı)r-ɛ-dól- (-rᵒd-; §4027) v.t. and i. be about to shut, etc.
kob(ı)r-ɛ-ğŭ-bŭ- (§4069) v.t. stat. be on one's way (coming) to shut, etc.
kob-ɛ-mǎ- (§4036) and
kob(ı)r-ɛ-mǎ- (§4041) v.t. become unable to shut, etc.
kob(ı)r-ɛ-nóg (§§4048ff.) v.t. go to shut, etc.
tāgáncık‿kobırıddɛnogóskoran⁀ they have gone to shut (each of §5456) the windows.
kob(ı)r-ɛ-nóg-bŭ- (-nóggŭ- §546; §4058) v.t. stat. be on one's way (going) to shut, etc.
kob(ı)r-ɛ-tǎ (§§4060ff.) v.t. come to shut, etc.
kobɛd-ǎg- (§3877ff.) v.t. be in the situation of having shut, etc.
māmǔr‿sıgín-tūr‿kobɛdırǎgım‿mǎg-mendann‿íllar⁀ the mavmǔr has shut (each of) them up in prison, that they should not steal.
mágasık‿kobɛdágırırın⁀ he has imprisoned (each of) the thieves.
kobíŋg-ır ('‿‿, N. -ŋkır; §3688) v.t. caus. cause or allow to shut, etc.
kób-kattı- (kópk-; §4093) v.p. be shut, etc.
bǎp‿kópkattımunun⁀ the door is not (cannot be §5704) shut.
kobkáttı-bŭ- (kopk-; §4105) v.i. stat. be in a shut (etc.) state or condition.
kob-múg (§3747ɛ') v.t. leave after shutting, etc., leave shut (in, up).
imperat. kobmúk!
kobmugíŋ-ır (N. -ŋkır; §4212) v.t. caus. cause or allow to leave after shutting, etc.
ɛnnúrkı‿kobídkı‿kobmugíŋır⁀ make En-Nǔr leave the gate (door) shut.
kobos-gǔñčı-nál (-oggǔñ- §548; §4203; -osgıgǔñ-, -ozgı-, -oggı- §4205) v.t. after shutting, etc. look at carefully.
kobídkı‿koboggǔñčınal⁀ when you have closed the door look at it carefully.
kobos-káll(ı) (-okkál- §573; §§4180-4; -osgıkál-, -ozgı-, -oggı- §4185) v.t. push (etc. s.v. káll(ı)) after shutting.
kobídkı‿kobokkállı‿ press against the door after shutting it.
kobos-kallı-nál (-okkal-; §4203; -osgıkal-, -ozgı-, -oggı- §4205) v.t. after shutting see (i.e. try) by pushing.
kobídkı‿kobokkállınal⁀ (and ‿‿ˇ˘) see by pressing the door after shutting it (sc. whether it is properly shut).
kobos-óğı (§§4180-4; -osg-ó-, -ozgó-, -oggó- §4185) v.t. convey after shutting, etc.
kobos-mand-óğı (-omma- §609; -osgıma-, -ozgı-, -oggı- §5605) v.t. after shutting, etc. carry over there.
kob-úndur (§3769) v.t. put in after shutting, etc.
kóbbɛ! (§517) < kóbwɛ! shut! (pl.) s.v. kób.
kobódd(ı)‿, -dı⁀ n. Kabodi (on map), a village on the right bank of the Nile, about 6 miles below Kérma.
obj. -dıg‿.

kóčč(ı)‿ n. uppermost part, summit, top, upper surface [< *kógt(ı)‿ (§526) < √kóğ- *be above (§4548) + -t (§2325β); §2228].
obj. -čıg‿.
pl. -čıncı(ı)‿.
ílbɛŋ‿kóččım‿mérkori⁀ (-m‿m- < -gım- §601) I (have) cut the top of the tin.
kǎŋ‿kóčč(ı)‿ house-top, roof.
kándıŋ‿kóčč(ı)‿ point of knife.
síwın‿kóčč(ı)‿ (-ŋ‿k-; < -dn‿k- §658) point of sword.
kóččıg-ɛd (-ɛt⁀ §469; -ɛ́⁀ §966; §6007) adv. on (along, at, by, etc. s.v. -ɛd‿) the top.
kóččıgéd-dā- (§3988) v.i. be proceeding (etc. s.v. -dǎ-) on (etc.) the top.
ar‿gadím‿kóččıgeddágoru⁀ (-m‿k- < -bn‿k- §586) we were walking on the rails (§4696d) = ar‿gadím‿kóččıgen-nogbúgoru⁀.
kóččıged-ğŭ-bŭ (-ɛğğǔ-; §4219) v.i. stat. be in a state of motion (coming) on (etc.) the top.
kóččıgen-nóg (§4127) v.i. go on (etc.) the top.
imperat. koččıgɛnnók!
kóččıgen-nóg-bŭ- (-nóggǔ- §546; §4219) v.i. stat. be in a state of motion (going) on (etc.) the top.
kóččıget-tǎ (§4127) v.i. come on (etc.) the top.
kóččı-r (§6007) adv. on (in, at, to) the top.
kóččır⁀ (s)he (it) is (they are) on (the) top.
‿kóččır (§§5860, 5904) postp. (= prep. §4287) on top of, on.
— follows the genitive, of which -n‿ > -ŋ‿ or disappears (§2473; §4367):
tókkon‿íŋguŋ‿kóččır‿ténn‿uskúr-mɛn⁀ (‿ténn‿u- < ‿ténnɛ-u- §1122) don't put any more on top of these.
afɛ́ški‿kám‿kóččır‿kuğúrkoran⁀ (-m‿k- < -mn‿k- §598) they (have) put the baggage on the camel.
gókka‿kǎŋ‿kóččır‿ the pigeon is on (top of) the house.
gókkarı‿kǎŋ‿kóččır the pigeons are on the house.
tɛŋ‿kóččır‿úsuri⁀ I laugh at him (her, it).
kóččɛr‿ (§2682) indef. pron. some, a certain quantity or number [< kóčč-wɛ̄r‿ (§522) quasi an outstanding one].
obj. kóččɛg‿.
urtínčırtōŋ‿kóččɛr‿dabóskon⁀ some of the goats (sheep) have disappeared.
kóččɛg‿élkori, kóččɛg‿élkómunun⁀ some I found, some I didn't (some I have found, some I haven't).
kóččɛráŋkın‿ (-kĭ⁀, -kí⁀) adv. sometimes [lit. when it becomes some, -áŋkın‿ conditional of ‿án-].
tírgı‿kóččɛráŋkın‿nálli⁀ I sometimes see them.
ɛ́ssı‿kóččɛráŋkın‿dán, kóččɛráŋkın‿dámunun⁀ sometimes there is water, sometimes there isn't.
šɛtáŋ‿kóččɛráŋkıŋgon‿dǔlanı‿kóččɛ-ráŋkıŋgon‿kíññanın⁀ the fiend sometimes grows large and sometimes grows small.

kŏd v.t. *scrape, scratch.*
  ind. pres. āɪ⌣kódrɪ⌢; perf. āɪ⌣kódkorɪ⌢ (⌣kótk-).
  imperat. kót!
  sáb⌣āɪgɪ⌣kótkó⌢ *the cat (has) scratched me.*
kŏdar⌣ (-dàr⌣; §§ 2200 ff.) and
kōdíd⌣ (§§ 2256 ff.) n. *scraping, etc.*
kŏd-an (§§ 3890 ff.) v.t. *tell to scrape, etc., let scrape, etc.*
kŏd-bŭ- (§ 3931 β) v.i. stat. *be in a scraped (etc.) state or condition.*
  áğɪŋ⌣kódbūn⌢ *the skin (leather) has a scratch (scratches) on it (is scraped).*
kōdɛd-ág- (§§ 3877 ff.) v.t. *be in the situation of having scraped, etc.*
kŏd-kattɪ- (kŏtk-; § 4093) v.p. *be scraped, etc.*
kódde⌣ n. *name of two herbs growing on the river-bank.*
  obj. -dɛg⌣.
  pl. -dɛnč(ɪ)⌣.
kóddɛ⌣kárr(ɪ)⌣ *a prostrate herb,* Mollugo hirta, *C. B. Clarke (REM; BSP, 217),* lit. *female* kóddɛ⌣.
  kóddɛ⌣kárrɪg⌣úrtɪnčɪ⌣kállan⌢ (*the*) *goats (sheep) eat M. hirta.*
kóddɛn⌣ónd(ɪ)⌣ *a scented herb,* Ambrosia maritima, *Linn. (REM; BSP, 294),* lit. *male* kóddɛ⌣.
  kóddɛn⌣óndɪm⌣bɪtāŋg⌣urtɪnčɪ⌣kállan⌢ (*the*) *goats (sheep) eat the fruit of A. maritima.*
kóddɛ-kŏl⌣ n. *Kadakol* (on map), *a village on the right bank of the Nile about ten miles below Old Dóngola* [*possessing* kóddɛ⌣].
  obj. -kólg(ɪ)⌣, -gɪ⌢.
kŏdɛ n. *shaft, vertical passage from water-wheel* (kólɛ⌣) *to level of water* (SNK, 377 A 6) [< *kódɛ⌣ (§ 1069) < √kód- **depart vertically from the horizontal* (§ 4547, cp. §§ 5330–4) +-ɛ⌣ of n. act. specialized in concrete sense (§ 2234 δ), so *passage up and down*].
  obj. -dɛg⌣ [> Sudan Ar. كوديك, كوديك id.].
  pl. -dɛnč(ɪ)⌣.
  kódɛn⌣ɛu⌣ (⌣ɛu⌣) *channel from river to base of shaft.*
kodŏs⌣ n. *tobacco-pipe* [< Sudan Ar. كدوس id. < قادوس (κάδος, cadus, jar) *tube*].
  obj. -ósk(ɪ)⌣.
  pl. -ósɪ⌣.
  tér⌣kodósk⌣ännín⌢ *he is smoking (habitually smokes) a pipe.*
kógor⌣ adj. (*a*) *strong, muscular, powerful;* (*b*) *strong, hard, tough, solid* [< *kógor⌣ (§§ 1065, 1068) < *kógɪr⌣ (§ 1175) < kó-*have*, *hold* +-g suff. +-ɪr⌣ causative (§ 2496), so or. *causing to hold, tenacious-making* § 2563; cp. ON. коϒɪp *strengthen* GNT, s.v.].
  obj. kogórk(ɪ)⌣, -kɪ⌢.
  pl. kógor⌣.
  ógɪr⌣kógorun⌢ *the man is strong.*
  ín⌣hánu⌣kógorun⌢ *this donkey is strong.*
  bābŭr⌣kógorun⌢ *the steamer (engine) is powerful.*
  ím⌣bér⌣kógorun⌢ *this wood is strong (hard).*
  šártɪ⌣bɛ́rn⌣dógor⌣kógorun⌢ *iron is stronger than wood.*
kogórkanɛ⌣ (§ 2295) n. *strength, hardness, etc.*
kógor-an- (§ 3910 α) v.i. *become strong, etc.*
  ind. pres. āɪ⌣kógorandɪ⌢, ɛr⌣kógoranɪn⌢ (-nī⌢, -ní⌢); perf. āɪ⌣kógoraŋkorɪ⌢.
  subj. past āɪ⌣kógoransɪ⌣ (-assɪ⌣ § 680, -sʊ⌣).
kógoram-bŭ- (kogorámbŭ- § 1932 a; §§ 3949 ff.) v.i. stat. *be in a state or condition of becoming (having become) strong, etc.*
kogoraníŋg-ɪr (⌣⌣⌣⌣; N. -ŋkɪr; § 4213) v.t. caus. *cause or allow to become strong, etc.*
  ind. pres. āɪ⌣kogoraníŋgɪddɪ⌢, ⌣⌣⌣⌣.
kógork-ɪr (§ 3702) v.t. caus. *cause or allow to be or become strong, etc., render strong, etc., strengthen.*
  ind. pres. āɪ⌣kógorkɪddɪ⌢ (§ 1808).
  dóww⌣āɪg⌣kógorkɪrkó⌢ *the medicine (has) strengthened me.*
kóğɪr⌣ n. *peg;* with collective sg. (§ 4696 d) [< √kóğ- **be above* (§ 4548) +-ɪr⌣ *causation* (§ 2228), then concrete **what causes to be above,* *suspender*].
  obj. koğɪrk(ɪ)⌣, -kɪ⌢.
  pl. kóğ(ɪ)rɪ⌣.
  hɛ́man⌣kóğɪr⌣ *tent-peg(s).*
kóhɪl (kóɪl ́⌣ § 971) v.i. *limp, go lame.*
  ind. pres. āɪ⌣kó(h)íllɪ⌢, ɛr⌣kó(h)ɪlɪn⌢ (-lī⌢, -lí⌢); perf. āɪ⌣kó(h)ílkorɪ⌢.
kohíl-bŭ- (koíl-; § 3931 α) v.i. stat. *be in a limping state or condition, be lame.*
kŏɪ, **kŏɪ**⌣ n. (a) *tendon, sinew;* (b) *vein, artery;* (c, of guitar) *string.*
— with collective sg. (§ 4696 a) [RNW s.v.].
  obj. kóɪg(ɪ)⌣, kóɪg(ɪ)⌣, -gɪ⌢.
  pl. kóɪɪ⌣.
  kísɪn⌣kóɪ⌣ *guitar-string(s).*
kóɪd⌣ (́⌣) n. *a thorny shrub,* Zizyphus spina-christi, *Willd. (BSP, 105).*
  obj. koídk(ɪ)⌣, -ítk(ɪ)⌣, -ítt(ɪ)⌣ § 2462, -kɪ⌢, -tɪ⌢.
  gen. koídn⌣, -ín⌣c.
  pl. kóɪdɪ⌣.
kóɪl (́⌣) v.i. *limp* s.v. kóhɪl.
kójjɛ n. *Koya* (on map), *a village on the left bank of the Nile, opposite the northern end of Argo Island.*
  obj. kójjɛg⌣, kójjég⌣ (§ 1532).
kókɪr (kókur⌣ § 1175) n. *Kakur* (on map), *a village on the left bank of the Nile, about 5 miles below Ed-Débbah*.
  obj. kokírk(ɪ)⌣, -kɪ⌢.
  kokírro (s.v. -r⌣) *at (to) Kókɪr.*
  kokírro⌢ (§ 6007) *(s)he (it) is (they are) at Kókɪr.*
kókk(ɪ) v.i. and t. *knock* [imit.].
  ind. pres. āɪ⌣kókkɪrɪ⌢; perf. āɪ⌣kókkɪgorɪ⌢ (N. -ɪko-, -ɪho-).
  imperat. kókkɪ!
  kókkɪriá? *shall (§ 5369 b) I knock?*
  kobíttɪ⌣kókkɪgorɪ⌢ *I (have) knocked on (at) the door.*
  musmárkɪ⌣bɛ́rro⌣kókkɪgorɪ⌢ *I (have) knocked the nail into the wood.*
kókkar⌣ (-kàr⌣; §§ 2200 ff.) and
kokkíd⌣ (§§ 2256 ff.) n. *knocking.*
kókk-an (§§ 3890 ff.) v.t. *tell to knock, let knock.*
kókkɪ-bŭ- (§ 3931 β) v.i. stat. *be in a knocked state or condition.*
  musmăr⌣bɛ́rro⌣kókkɪbūn⌢ *the nail is (has been) knocked into the wood.*
kokkɪr-ɛ-nóg (§§ 4048 ff.) v.t. *go to knock.*
kókkɛd-ág- (§§ 3877 ff.) v.t. *be in the situation of having knocked.*
kókkɪ-kattɪ- (N. -ɪha-; § 4093) v.p. *be knocked.*
kokkɪ-síkk(ɪ) (§ 3747 ε') v.i. and t. *ask after knocking.*
  kokkɪsíkkɪrɪá? *shall (§ 5369 b) I knock and ask?*
kŏl⌣ (one) *that has* s.v. kŏ *have.*
kŏl, **-kŏl** *unaccompanied* s.v. kŏ *have.*
koláññ(ɪ)⌣ (§ 899) = koñáll(ɪ)⌣ *mirror.*
kólɛ n. (a) *water-wheel, wheel to raise water for irrigation;* (b) *area so irrigated, estate of irrigable land, irrigable fields* = ساقية (AESA, p. 424, SNK, 377 A, NSD, HESA s.v. *water-wheel*) [< √kól- **round* (§ 4543) +-ɛ⌣ of n. ess., so **what is round* § 2234 β; RSN, § 80].
  obj. -lɛg⌣.
  pl. kolɛnč(ɪ)⌣.
  kólɛ⌣wɛr⌣tí⌣ídɪwgɪ⌣dólɪn⌢ *one water-wheel requires eight head of cattle* (sc. to turn it in successive pairs).
  kólɛŋ⌣gɪrād⌣ $\frac{1}{24}$ *share of irrigable estate.*
  kólɛŋ⌣kɛ́l⌣ *boundary of estate irrigated by water-wheel.*
  tórbarɪ⌣márɛk⌣kólɛrtōŋ⌣gússančɪr⌣ ɛğğŭgoran⌢ *the labourers (have) carried the millet from the fields to the corn-bins.*
— parts of the water-wheel are:
  áglo⌣ *rung between cables* (álas⌣); the jars (bɛ́šɛnč(ɪ)⌣ are lashed, at intervals, to pairs of these rungs.
  álas⌣ *cable;* the two cables forming the belt passing over the wheel (átt(ɪ)⌣) raising water resemble with their rungs an endless ladder.
  alláğa⌣ *pad tilting-jar.*
  árɛ⌣ *interior* refers to *the river.*
  árɛn⌣ɛssɪn⌣írɪ⌣ *inner water rope, stay securing end of cross-beam* (dfu⌣) *near weaker post* (múgdo⌣kárr(ɪ)⌣) *to beam* (ɛssɪkág⌣) *under trough.*
  árɛŋ⌣kálo⌣ *bearing on which river end of horizontal axle* (tŏrɛ⌣) *turns.*
  árgadɛ⌣ *cog-wheel.*
  árgadɛŋ⌣gédɛ⌣ (a) *horizontal cog-wheel;* (b) *its rim.*
  árgadɛn⌣tŏd⌣ *vertical cog-wheel.*
  árgadɛn⌣tōŋ⌣gédɛ⌣ *rim of vertical cog-wheel.*
  átt(ɪ)⌣ *wheel raising water, vertical wheel over water.*
  áttɪn⌣sɛ́n⌣ *rope binding shoreward ends of* fášɛnč(ɪ)⌣ *and forming rim corresponding to* ğómbo⌣ *at their other ends.*
  bɛ́šɛ⌣ *jar;* the bɛ́šɛnč(ɪ)⌣ *discharge into the sáblo⌣.*
  bóčč(ɪ)⌣ *exterior,* refers to *the shore.*

bóččɪn‿έssɪn‿írɪ‿ *outer water rope*, stay securing end of cross-beam near weaker post in shoreward direction to a peg in the ground.

bóččɪŋ‿kǎlo‿ *bearing on which shoreward end of horizontal axle (tóre‿) turns.*

búgdo‿ *large upright post supporting cross-beam* = múgdo‿.

dálu‿ *channel receiving water from smaller trough (ǧaráttare‿).*

dára‿ *screen.*

dɪ́u‿ *cross-beam.*

dɪ́un‿úbbur‿ *hole under centre of cross-beam in which apex of vertical axle revolves.*

duŋgútt(ɪ)‿ *thick spoke of wheel raising water (átt(ɪ)‿).*

ɛlwɪ́l‿ *stay(s) extending from horizontal axle (tóre‿) to fǎšenč(ɪ)‿.*

ɛssɪkǎg‿ *beam supporting trough (sáblo‿) and horizontal axle towards its end.*

ɛssɪkǎgɪr‿ *block(s) resting on* ɛssɪkǎg‿ *and immediately supporting trough.*

ɛwɪrátt(ɪ)‿ *driver* = šúgɪl‿.

fǎše‿ *transverse limb at end of each spoke of wheel raising water; over these pass the cables (álasɪ‿).*

gawátt(ɪ)‿ *well under water-wheel.*

golmódd(ɪ)‿ *side-piece of yoke (íslam‿).*

ǧaráttare‿ *smaller trough through which water passes from* urówwa‿ *to* dálu‿.

ǧíbɪd‿ *platform on which track (mofs‿) is laid.*

ǧómbo‿ *rope binding ends of* fǎšenč(ɪ)‿ *nearest river and forming a rim corresponding to the* áttɪn‿šɛ́n‿.

íslam‿ *yoke.*

kǎg‿ *beam with ends in ground, supporting end of* tέwre‿ *near vertical cog-wheel.*

kǎlo‿ *bearing, half-socket, half-collar.*

kóde‿ *shaft, vertical passage up which water is drawn.*

kóden‿έu‿ *channel from base of shaft to river.*

kɔ́me‿ *beam with ends in ground; vertical cog-wheel rotates between this and* kǎg‿.

míšš(ɪ)‿ *vertical axle of larger cog-wheel (árgadeŋ‿géde‿).*

míššɪn‿úr‿ *apex of* míšš(ɪ)‿, *turning in hole in cross-beam (dɪ́u‿).*

míššɪn‿úsud‿ *bottom of* míšš(ɪ)‿, *turning in* sǎb‿.

mofs‿ *track, round which cattle working water-wheel walk counter-clockwise.*

múgdo‿ *large upright post supporting cross-beam* = búgdo‿.

múgdon‿ónd(ɪ)‿ *stronger post, supporting heavier end of cross-beam.*

múgdo‿kárr(ɪ)‿ *weaker post, supporting other end.*

ólos‿ *rope attaching yoke (íslam‿) to pole (túhum‿).*

sǎb‿ *small rectangular block, let into centre of platform, with shallow socket in which vertical axle (míšš(ɪ)‿) turns.*

sáblo‿ *larger trough, whence water flows through* urówwa‿ *to* ǧaráttare‿.

súlgade‿ *cog(s).*

šɛ́hɪr‿ (šέxɪr‿) *guiding rod, guide;* there are two, áren‿šɛ́hɪr‿ *inner guide*, inclined towards river, bóččɪn‿šɛ́hɪr‿ *outer guide*, inclined towards shore; they proceed from points near centre of wǎwɪr‿ and crossing each other reach the top right (as one faces the river) corners of the shaft (kóde‿); the álasɪ‿ ascend between them.

šúgɪl‿ *driver* = ɛwɪrátt(ɪ)‿.

tarántare‿ *thin spoke of wheel raising water.*

tέw(ɪ)re‿ *oblong block forming platform containing* sǎb‿.

tóre‿ *horizontal axle of wheel raising water (átt(ɪ)‿) and of smaller cog-wheel (árgaden‿tód‿).*

túhum‿ (túgum‿) *pole slanting from horizontal, drawn round by cattle working wheel; its upper end is fixed in the vertical axle (míšš(ɪ)‿); the driver sits on its forked lower end.*

tŭnd(ɪ)‿ (s.v. tŭ‿) *spoke of cog-wheel.*

urówwa‿ *small trough or channel between* sáblo‿ *and* ǧaráttare‿.

wǎwɪr‿ (-wᵘr‿) *beam fixed across shaft (kóde‿) under wheel raising water (átt(ɪ)‿).*

kolɛ-dúl‿ n. *upper of pair of water-wheels.*
  obj. -dúlg(ɪ)‿, -gi⌒.
  pl. -dúlɪ‿.

kolɛ-tód‿ (§ 2372) n. *lower of pair of water-wheels.*
  obj. -tŏdk(ɪ)‿, -tŏtk(ɪ)‿, -tŏkk(ɪ)‿, -tŏtt(ɪ)‿ § 2462, -ki⌒, -ti⌒.
  gen. -tŏdn‿v., -tŏnn‿v.c., -tŏn‿c.
  pl. kóletonɪ‿.
  kolɛdúl‿ám‿kóččɪr, kolɛtód‿ám‿ tógōr⌒ (-m‿ < -bn‿ § 586) *the upper wheel is on the top of the bank, the lower wheel is below the top of the bank.*

kólɛ-tod‿ (§ 2372) n. = kolɛtód‿.
  obj. kólɛtŏdk(ɪ)‿, -tŏtk(ɪ)‿, -tŏkk(ɪ)‿, -tŏtt(ɪ)‿ § 2462, -ki⌒, -ti⌒.
  gen. -tŏdn‿v., -tŏnn‿v.c., -tŏn‿c.
  pl. -tonɪ‿.
  kólɛtodun⌒ and
  kólɛtodun⌒ *it's a lower water-wheel.*

kolέn-d(ɪ)‿ (§§ 2545 ff.) adj. *appertaining to the (a) water-wheel, etc., of the (a) water-wheel, etc., water-wheel's, irrigable land's.*

kólod‿ (§§ 2699, 2707) card. num. *seven* [cp. ON. ⲕⲟⲗⲟⲧⲓ id. ZNG, § 113; RSN, § 121 cps. Eth. ሰባዕቱ 2].
  obj. kolódk(ɪ)‿, -ótk(ɪ)‿, -ótt(ɪ)‿ § 2462, -ki⌒, -ti⌒.
  gen. kolódn‿v., -ónn‿v.c., -on‿c., kolódn‿v., -ónn‿v.c., -ón‿c.
  pl. kólodɪ‿.
  kólodun‿ (-dū⌒, -dú⌒ § 939; § 5232) and tέr‿kólodun⌒ (tɛr‿ § 5233) *it's (they're) seven.*
  kolódín⌒ (-dī⌒, -dí⌒; § 5235) and tír‿kólodín⌒ (tɪr‿ § 5236) *they're seven.*
  ugrέs‿kólod‿fadlērósko⌒ *seven days are left* (§ 5239).
  sǎ‿kólodun⌒ *it's seven o'clock.*

kolón-d(ɪ)‿ (§ 2737 a) adj. *appertaining to seven, of seven, seven's.*

kolodín-d(ɪ)‿ (§ 2737 b) adj. = kolónd(ɪ)‿.

kolod-ínt(ɪ)‿ (kólodɪnt(ɪ)‿; § 2740) ord. num. *seventh.*

kolodɪntín-d(ɪ)‿ (§ 2743) adj. *appertaining to the seventh.*

kólodɪre‿ (§ 2745) n. $\frac{1}{7}$, *seventh part* [< kólod- 7 + -ɪr *(action of) making* + -e‿ of n. ess., so *one of what makes into 7 § 2287].
  obj. -rɛg‿.
  pl. -renč(ɪ)‿.

kolód-kɪrɪ‿ (-ótk-; -kírɪ‿ § 1532; § 2736) num. adj. *about seven.*

koloŋgǎr‿ (§§ 2758, 5261-7) num. *the whole seven, all seven.*
  obj. -ǎrk(ɪ)‿, -ki⌒.
  tɛr‿koloŋgǎrk‿étta⌒ *bring them all seven* (§ 5199).

kólod-an- (§ 2760) v.i. *become seven.*

kólodam-bŭ- (§ 2761) v.i. stat. *be in a state or condition of becoming seven.*

kolódk-ɪr (-ótkɪr, -óttɪr § 716; § 2759) v.t. caus. *make into seven.*

kolodkɪr-bǎg (-otkɪr-, -ottɪr-; § 4138) v.t. *divide into seven.*
  imperat. kolodkɪrbǎk!

kŏm‿ n. *heap, pile, stack* [< Sudan Ar. كوم kŏm id.].
  obj. kŏmg(ɪ)‿, -gi⌒.
  pl. kŏmɪ‿.

kóman‿ (§ 956 d) n. *shirt* [< √kóm- *envelop* (§ 4549) + -an‿ *utterance*, so *(what) says '(I) envelop'* § 2195].
  obj. kománg(ɪ)‿, -gi⌒.
  pl. kómanɪ‿.

kómbo‿ adj. (a, of animate objects) *stout, vigorous, fit, well, in good health;* (b, of animate objects) *stout, corpulent, fat;* (c, of inanimate objects) *strong, powerful* [§ 2561 γ; RSN, § 129].
  obj. -bog‿.
  pl. kómborɪ‿ and kómbonč(ɪ)‿.
  X. ɛr‿kómbomɛn? (-mɛ̃?, -mé?) *how are you?*, lit. *are you not well?* (§ 6249) i.e. *I hope you are well.*
  Y. hámdɪlɪllá! *praise be to God!*
  X. ɛr‿kómbomɛn? *how are you?*
  Y. (N.) ártoŋ‿έn‿hǎlgɪ‿serέkɪrel! (§ 6250) *God bless you!*, lit. *if God (is) causing your condition to be good* (sc. *I am well, like* si vales bene est, ego valeo).
  šǎrtɪ‿kómbon⌒ (the) *iron is strong.*
  túrug‿kómbó⌒ (§ 939) *the wind is strong.*

kómbokane‿ (§ 2295) n. *stoutness, vigour; corpulency; strength.*

kómb-an- (§ 3910) v.i. *become stout, etc.;* (after illness) *get better, recover.*
  ind. pres. aɪ‿kómbandɪ, ɛr‿kómbanɪn‿ (-ní⌒, -ní‿); perf. aɪ‿kómbaŋkori⌒.
  subj. past aɪ‿kómbansɪ‿ (-assɪ‿ § 680, -su‿).
  X. ɛr‿kómbaŋkomɛn? *have you not got better?* i.e. *I hope you have got better* (cp. § 5485).
  Y. hámdɪlɪllá? *praise be to God!*
  kómbaŋkoná? and
  kombanóskoná? *are you better?* (after illness).

kómɛ — kórou

bıkombámmunan⌒ *they will not get well, etc.*

kómbam-bŭ- (§§ 3949 ff.) v.i. stat. *be in a state or condition of becoming (having become) stout, etc., of getting (having got) better, etc.*

kombanɛd-ág- (§ 3966α) v.i. *be in the condition of having become stout, etc., of having got better, etc.*

kombaníŋg-ır (⌣́⌣⌣ ; N. -ŋkır; § 4213) v.t. caus. *cause or allow to become stout, etc., to get better, etc.*
 ind. pres. aı⌣kombaníŋgıddı⌒, ⌣⌣́⌣,
 ín⌣dáwa⌣kómbanıŋgırın⌒ *this medicine makes one get well.*

kómbog-ır (N. -okır, -ohır; § 3701) v.t. caus. *cause or allow to be or become stout, etc., render stout, etc., strengthen, fatten.*
 ind. pres. aı⌣kómbogıddı⌒, ɛr⌣kómbogırın⌒ (-rí⌒, -rí⌒).
 ín⌣dáwa⌣kómbogırın⌒ *this medicine makes one well.*

kómɛ n. (in water-wheel, kólɛ⌣) beam with its ends engaged in ground and fastened to same buried cross-beams as ends of káğ⌣; vertical cog-wheel (árgadɛn⌣ tód⌣) rotates between kómɛ⌣ and káğ⌣.
 obj. -mɛg⌣.
 pl. -mɛnč(ı)⌣.

kómɛ n. *Komi (on map), an island opposite Góld, ten miles above Hándag.*
 obj. kómɛg⌣, kómég⌣ (§ 1538).
 kōmɛnárt(ı)⌣ *the island of Kómɛ.*

kómıs v.t. *efface, erase, rub out, wipe out.*
 ind. pres. aı⌣kómısrı⌒, ɛr⌣kómısın⌒ (sí⌒, -sí⌒); perf. aı⌣komískorı⌒.
 báččık⌣komískoran⌒ *they (have) erased the writing.*

kómısar (-sɑr⌣; § 2200 ff.) and **komısíd** (§§ 2256 ff.) n. *effacement.*

kómıs-an (§§ 3890 ff.) v.t. *tell to efface, etc., let efface, etc.*

kómız-bŭ- (§ 3931β) v.i. stat. *be in an effaced (etc.) state or condition.*
 báččı⌣kómızbūn⌒ *the writing is (has been) effaced.*

komısɛd-ág- (§§ 3877 ff.) v.t. *be in the situation of having effaced, etc.*

kómıs-kattı- (§ 4093) v.p. *be effaced, etc.*

-k-on⌣ s.v. -on⌣.

kóndó⌒ (§ 1532; kóndo⌣c. § 1567, -dᵒ⌣v., -d⌣v. § 1122; § 4488) apocritic sentence-word *I don't know.*
 X. wélsɛ? *where is the dog?*
 Y. kóndó⌒ *I don't know.*
 X. ɛsmám⌣mén⌣támení? *why doesn't ǧoθmán come?*
 Y. kóndó⌒ *I don't know.*
 áli⌣kóndᵒ⌣egó⌒ (-d⌣egó⌒) ǧáli said he *didn't know.*

-konı⌣ pl. of **-kól⌣** alone s.v. kó.

-k-on-on⌣ *with, accompanying* s.v. -on-on⌣.

kóntɛ n. *(rigid) basket* (=sábad⌣) [< *kómtɛ⌣ < √kóm- *contain (§ 4549) + -t dem. (§ 4593) + -ɛ⌣ of n.v. concrete specialization (§ 2234δ), so *that container § 2235].
 obj. -tɛg⌣.
 pl. -tenč(ı)⌣.

kóñ⌣ n. (a) *face;* (b) *forehead;* (c) *front* [cp. ON. коp id. GNT s.v.; RSN, § 200].
 obj. kóñg(ı)⌣, -gi⌒.
 pl. kóñı⌣.
 X. ɛŋ⌣kóñır⌣kášši⌣dábun⌒ *there's a bit of something on your face.*
 Y. sɑ́ırɛ́? *where?*
 X. ɛn⌣tıbíllo⌒ *on your cheek.*
 sandúŋ⌣kóñır⌣báğbūn⌒ (-ŋ⌣k- < -gn⌣k- § 652) *it is written on the front of the box.*
 ártıŋ⌣kóñ⌒ *head or nose (up-stream extremity) of island.*

koñáll(ı)⌣ n. *mirror* [with -áll(ı)⌣ cp. ON. ⲁⲗⲗ *shine*(?), *appear*(?), GNT s.v.; RSN, § 129; perhaps < *koñnállı⌒ *I see (my) face* (cp. § 2381); § 2194].
 obj. -állıg⌣.
 pl. -állınč(ı)⌣.

kóp! imperat. of kób *shut, etc.*

kōr⌣ n. *wound;* with collective sg. (§ 4696d) [§ 4550; cp. ON. коp id. GNT s.v.].
 obj. kórk(ı)⌣, -ki⌒.
 pl. kórı⌣.
 ténn⌣óssı⌣kórun⌒ *his (her, its) foot (leg) is (feet, legs are) wounded* (§ 4719).
 áŋ⌣kór⌣ólgónun⌒ *my wound is still* (sc. unhealed).
 téŋ⌣kórkı⌣tágır⌣kúltı⌣téddo⌣támɛ-nınn⌣illár⌒ *cover his (her, its) wound(s) in order that the flies (§ 4696c) may not come on it (them).*

kōráb⌣ n. *loud cry, shout;* with collective sg. (§ 4696d) [app. a pronunciation of kōráğ⌣ id.].
 obj. -ábk(ı)⌣, -ápk(ı)⌣, -ki⌒.
 gen. -ábn⌣v., -ám⌣c.
 pl. -ábı⌣.
 kōrápkı⌣ğómran⌒ *they utter a loud cry (loud cries).*

kōráğ⌣ n. *loud cry, shout;* with collective sg. (§ 4696d) [onom., < Sudan Ar. كوراك kōrák id.].
 obj. -áğk(ı)⌣, -ákk(ı)⌣, -ki⌒.
 gen. -áğn⌣v., -áŋ⌣c.
 pl. -áğı⌣.
 kōrákk⌣áw'ran⌒ and kōrákkı⌣ğómran⌒ *they utter a loud cry (loud cries).*

kórbɛ n. *Korba (on map), a village on the left bank of the Nile, west of Argo Island, near its northern end.*
 obj. kórbɛg⌣, kórbég⌣ (§ 1532).

kórɛ n. *festival, feast,* now esp. *Bairam* [< κόρη (*feast of the*) *Virgin;* cp. ON. коpɛ, коpн id. GNT s.v.; § 2393].
 obj. kórɛg⌣.
 pl. korénč(ı)⌣.

— Greetings at Bairam (§§ 6262-3):
 X. kórɛg⌣áñnal! *live to see the feast!* sc. *again, often.*
 Y. áfjaŋ⌣kórɛŋgon⌣árgon⌣írgond⌣ árt⌣ɛttágoŋgıdd⌣ɛn! (⌣ɛttagoŋ-gıdd⌣ɛn!) *may it please God to have brought both health and the feast to both us and you (pl.);* -on⌣ ... ɛn! lit. *if (He) say,* i.e. *intend, will ...* sc. *we shall rejoice.*

The reply is often abbreviated to:
 áfjaŋ⌣kórɛŋgon⌣tágoŋgıdd⌣ɛn!; -ŋg- > -ŋŋ- (§ 662).

korén-d(ı)⌣ (§§ 2545 ff.) adj. *appertaining to the festival, etc., festive.*

kórı⌣ n. *whip (large or small)* [< √kór-

*break off (§ 4550) + -ı⌣ (§§ 2252-5), so *thing broken off;* cp. kuríččɛ⌣ *switch*].
 obj. kórıg⌣.
 pl. korínč(ı)⌣.

kórıs⌣ n. (a) *treadle of loom (CSW, p. 30);* (b) *cradle made of rope in which each jar (béšɛ⌣) of the water-wheel (kólɛ⌣) is attached to its rung (áglo⌣); the cradle has a pad (alláğa⌣) under its hinder end tilting it to the required angle.*

— with collective sg. (§ 4696d) [cp. K. id. (b), Schuh SNK, 377AII, MNK s.v.].
 obj. korísk(ı)⌣, -ki⌒.
 pl. kór(ı)sı⌣.
 duháŋ⌣kórıs⌣ *treadle of loom, loom treadle(s).*
 béšɛŋ⌣kórıs⌣ *cradle of jar, jar cradle(s).*

korkótt(ı)⌣ n. *cracked soil, dried mud* [< *korkórt(ı) (§ 713) < √kór- *break (§ 4550); the repeated syllable is descriptive (§ 2151); -t dem. (§ 2324); § 2330].
 obj. -tıg⌣.

kormokól⌣ n. *Karmako (on map), a village on the left bank of the Nile just above Ed-Débbaʰ.*
 obj. -kólg(ı)⌣, -gi⌒.
 kormokóllo (s.v. -r⌣) *at (to) K.*
 kormokóllo⌒ *(s)he (it) is (they are) at K.*

kórob⌣ n. *spider;* with collective sg. (§ 4696c).
 obj. koróbk(ı)⌣, -ópk(ı)⌣, -ki⌒.
 gen. koróbn⌣v., koróm⌣c., koróbn⌣v., kórom⌣c.
 pl. kórobı⌣.
 koróm⌣kå⌣ and koróm-kå⌣ (§ 2355) *spider's web(s), cobweb(s);* obj. koróm⌣kåg⌣, koróm-kåg⌣.
 koróm-ka⌣dıgrín⌒ *the cobwebs are numerous.*
 koróm⌣kå⌣dúlun⌒ (i) *the spider's web is large;* (ii) *it's a large cobweb* (§ 4744).
 koróm-kås⌣sókkɛ⌣ (-s⌣s- < -g⌣s- § 678) *clear away the cobweb(s).*

kórod⌣ n. *small stone, pebble;* with collective sg. (§ 4696c) *gravel* [< *kórıd⌣ (§ 1175) < √kór- *break up (§ 4550) + -id⌣ *making, formation (§§ 2256-7), so *what is broken up* § 2310a].
 obj. koródk(ı)⌣, -ótk(ı)⌣, -ótt(ı)⌣ § 2462, -ki⌒, -ti⌒.
 gen. koródn⌣v., -rón⌣c.
 pl. koródı⌣.

kórou v.i. *rattle, clatter, make a rattling (etc.) noise* (=káraū, kúrub) [onom., app. a pronunciation of káraū, or kórowın⌣ < kúrubın⌣ § 1015].
 ind. pres. aı⌣koróurı⌒, ɛr⌣kórowın⌒ (-wí⌒, -wí⌒); perf. aı⌣koróukorı⌒.
 S. dókkoŋ⌣koróumɛn⌣ *don't make a (that) rattling (etc.) noise.*

kórowar (-wɑr⌣; §§ 2200 ff.) and **korowíd** (§§ 2256 ff.) n. *rattling, etc.*

kórou-bŭ- (§ 3931α) v.i. stat. *be in a rattling (etc.) state or condition.*
 tága⌣kóroubūn⌒ *the window is rattling.*

korowíŋ-ır (N. -ŋkır; § 3688) v.t. caus. *cause or allow to rattle, etc.*
 túruk⌣tágak⌣korowíŋgırın⌒ *the wind makes the window(s* § 4647*) rattle.*
 S. saháŋgı⌣dókkoŋ⌣korowíŋgırmɛn⌣ *don't make (let) the plates (§ 4647) clatter.*

korráñ‿ n. *gecko*; with collective sg. (§4696c) [< korr- onom. of clicking sound + -án *say* + -ñ dim. §2304; *RSN*, §§129, 200].
   obj. -áñ(ı)‿, -gi⌒.
   pl. -áñı‿.
kórrɛ v.i. *snore* [lit. *say* 'kórr!' (§2874); cp. Amh. አንኰረፈ *id.*].
   ind. pres. aı‿kórrɛri⌒; perf. aı‿kórrɛgori⌒ (N. -ɛko-, -ɛho-).
   kórrɛrar‿ (-rȧr‿; §§2200 ff., 2210) and
   korrɛríd (§§2256 ff., 2263) n. *snoring*.
kórsɛ‿ n. *small frond of date-palm*, esp. of young plant; with collective sg. (§4696b) [< √kór- **break off* (§4550) + -s dim. (§2319) + -ɛ‿ of n. ess. (§2234), so **small breaking(s)-off* §2320].
   obj. -sɛg‿.
   pl. -sɛnč(ı)‿.
   írık‿kórsɛrtōn‿auran⌒ *they make rope from the small fronds of the date-palm*.
kórt(ı)‿, -ti⌒ n. *Korti* (on map), *a village on the left bank of the Nile about 44 miles above Ed-Débbah*.
   obj. -tıg‿.
   kórtır‿ *at (to) Kórti*.
   kórtır⌒ *(s)he (it) is (they are) at Kórti*⌒.
kōs‿ n. *shallow wooden bowl, deep wooden dish* (used for food) [§2053].
   obj. kósk(ı)‿, -ki⌒.
   pl. kósı‿.
   káln‿kósun⌒ and kál‿kósun⌒ (§809) *it's a (the) bowl for food*.
   kóskı‿húruǧırtōn‿auran⌒ *they make the kós‿ of (the wood of) Acacia albida*.
kōs v.i. *ferment, (of dough) rise* [§2053].
   ind. pres. tɛr‿kósın⌒ (-sí⌒, -sí⌒); perf. tɛr‿kóskon⌒ (-kō⌒, -kó⌒).
   mérsɛ‿kósın⌒ *the beer ferments*.
   kaníss‿ɛlgon‿kōskómunun⌒ *the dough has not yet risen*.
   kósar (-sȧr‿; §§2200 ff.) and
   kōsíd (§§2256 ff.) n. *fermenting, etc*.
   kōs-an (§§3890 ff.) v.t. *let ferment, etc*.
      aı‿kaníssɛk‿kósandi⌒ *I let the dough rise*.
   kōz-bū- (§727; §3931 α) v.i. stat. *be in a fermented (etc.) state or condition*.
      mérsɛ‿kōzbūn⌒ *the beer is in a fermented state*.
      kaníssɛ‿kōzbūn⌒ *the dough is risen*.
   kōsk-ir (§3683) v.t. caus. *cause or allow to ferment, etc*.
      ind. pres. aı‿kóskıddi⌒, ɛr‿kóskırın⌒ (-rí⌒, -rí⌒).
   kōsk-ıdd(ı) (§§1856, 3725) v.t. caus. = kóskır.
      ind. pres. aı‿kóskıddıri⌒.
      imperat. kóskıddi!
   kōsíŋ-ir ('—; N. -ŋkır; §3688) v.t. caus. = kóskır.
kósɛ‿ n. *small insect that consumes, small voracious insect, weevil*; with collective sg. (§4696c) [< **kóssɛ‿ < √1011) < √kós- **evil* (§4552) + -s dim. (§2319) + -ɛ‿ of n. ess. (§2234), so **evil little thing* §2320].
   obj. -sɛg‿.
   pl. kosɛnč(ı)‿.
   bérn‿kósɛ *small insect that eats wood*.

kósɛ‿béntıgon‿ağıŋgom‿bérkon‿šéji‿ málleɡoŋgı‿kálın‿ *the kósɛ‿ eats dates, hides, wood and everything*.
kóšɛ‿ n. *luxuriant growth* (of plant) [< **kóššɛ‿ < **kóñšɛ‿ < *kóñ face + -s dem. (§2319) + -ɛ‿ of n. ess. (§2234), so *that existence of a face §2322].
   obj. -šɛg‿.
   béntıŋ‿kóšɛ‿ *luxuriant growth of palm(s)*.
   ǧówwıŋ‿kóšɛ‿ *luxuriant growth of tree(s)*.
   téŋ‿kóšɛ‿dıgrín⌒ *it grows very luxuriantly*.
kótt(ı)‿ n. *quantity, amount, volume, bulk, size* [< **kódt(ı)‿ (§706) < √kód- **rise* (§4547) + -t of n. act. (§2325), so **rising, *ascension*; or < **kóft(ı)‿ (§713) < √kór- **break* (§4550) + -t, so **what is broken off*, like *frag-men, Bruch-teil*, §2325 β].
   obj. -tıg‿.
   pl. -tınč(ı)‿.
   ánn‿úrt‿énn‿úrtı‿kóttın⌒ (*AZN*, §56) *my (our) property is the size of yours*.
   kȧ‿kóttın⌒ *it's the size of a house, it's as big as a house* (§4750).
   hánu‿kóttın⌒ *it's as big as a donkey*.
   hánuı‿kóttınčın⌒ *they're as big as donkeys* (§4753).
   bértıkırın‿lákın‿tí‿kóttın⌒ *it's like a goat but it's the size of a cow*.
   ín‿ǧazm‿énn‿óssı‿kótté? *is this shoe (are these shoes §4696d) the size of your foot?*
   mám‿béled‿sōdáŋ‿kótté? *is that country as large as the Sūdán?*
kóttıg (-gi⌒ §4318) postp. (= conj. §4288) *as (so) long as, while, when*, lit. *during (for, in) the amount* (sc. of time) *that*—follows the bare subjunctive (§6196).
   S. aı‿ȧgʼrı‿kóttıd‿dókkon‿nógmen⌒ (-d‿d- < -g‿d- §534) *as long as I am here (there, present) don't go*.
   aı‿ȧgsı‿kóttık‿kíttegoran⌒ *as long as I was present they were silent*.
   ǧézma‿ǧȧwwur‿éŋ‿kóttıš‿šȧrtıg‿ úndur‿ (-š‿š- < -g‿š- §695) *while the shoe is (shoes are §4696 d) damp put the iron(s) in*.
   aı‿tékk‿ȧǧǧómrı‿kóttıd‿dígo⌒ (-d‿d- < -g‿d- §534) *while I was beating him (her, it) (s)he (it) died*.
   šúrbag‿ȧgáurı‿kóttık‿kúltı‿wēd‿dıgırtógo⌒ (-d‿d- < -g‿d- §537) *while I was making the soup a fly fell in*.
— following the negative subjunctive = *before (antequam, priusquam), until* with positive verb:
   gátır‿tȧmenıŋ‿kóttıt‿tȧ⌒ (-t‿t- < -g‿t- §707) *come before the train arrives*.
   másıl‿bélmenıŋ‿kóttít‿ta⌒ (§1742) *come before sunrise*.
   S. aı‿ékkı‿wētımmendı‿kóttıd‿dókkon‿aumen⌒ (-d‿d- < -g‿d- §534) *don't do (make) it until I tell you to*.
— this figure is often preceded by élgon‿ (ólgon‿):

ógıǧ‿élgon‿nógmenıŋ‿kóttıg‿índo‿ tȧ⌒ *come here before the man goes*.
   aı‿ólgon‿síkkımendı‿kóttıd‿déŋkoran⌒ (-d‿d- < -g‿d- §534) *before I asked they gave (it to me)*.
kúb‿ n. (*a*) *boat, ship, vessel*; (*b*, in weaving) *shuttle* (*CSW*, p. 35) [§4553; *RSN*, §§129, 200; Griffith cps. ON. ⲁⲟⲩⲡⲛⲓ *sailor GNT* s.v.].
   obj. kúbk(ı)‿, kúpk(ı)‿, -ki⌒.
   gen. kúbn‿v., kúm‿c.
   pl. kúblı‿ (§2433) and occ. kúbı‿.
   kúb‿sfwır‿būn⌒ *the boat lies on the sand*.
   kúb‿éssır‿tēbın⌒ *the boat floats* (lit. *stands*) *in the water*.
   múšraŋ‿kúb‿ *ferry-boat*.
   múšraŋ‿kúb‿ısȧıgɛt‿tēbın? *where does the ferry-boat wait?* (where is the ferry-boat stationed?).
   kúbır (s.v. -r‿) *in (on, to) the boat*.
   kúbır⌒ (§5858) *(s)he (it) is (they are) in the boat*.
   kúm‿tūr (s.v. tū) *inside the boat*.
   kúm‿tūr⌒ *(s)he (it) is (they are) inside the boat*.
   kúbn‿éndɛ‿ *mast*.
   kúm‿góñña and
   kúm‿kádɛ‿ *sail*, lit. *boat's cloth*.
   kúm‿góññan‿nígıl‿,
   kúm‿goññánčın‿nígıl‿,
   kúm‿kȧdén‿nígıl‿ and
   kúm‿kadénčın‿nígıl‿ *sail-maker*;
   -n‿n- < -g‿n- (§625; §5407).
   kúm‿ǧȧmb(ı)‿ and
   kúm‿ǧémb(ı)‿ *boat's (ship's) side*.
   kúm‿tȧraf *edge (top of side) of boat*.
   kúm‿tȧríf *ship's cable*.
kúb-tod‿ (kúptod‿; §2369) n. (*a*) *wretched boat, old boat*; (*b*) = kúbu‿.
   obj. kúbtōdk(ı)‿, kúpt-‿, -tōtk(ı)‿, -tōkk(ı)‿, -tōtt(ı)‿ §2462, -ki⌒, -ti⌒.
   gen. -tōdn‿v., -tōnn‿v.c., -tōn‿c.
   pl. kúbtonı‿, kúpt-.
   kúptodun⌒ *it's a (wretched) boat*.
kum-tód‿ (§2366) n. *small boat*.
   obj. -tōdk(ı)‿, -tōtk(ı)‿, -tōkk(ı)‿, -tōtt(ı)‿ §2462, -ki⌒, -ti⌒.
   gen. -tōdn‿v., -tōnn‿v.c., -tōn‿c.
   pl. kúmtonı‿.
   kumtōdun⌒ *it's a small boat*.
kúm-tu‿ (§2363) n. *interior of ship, hold*.
kúm-d(ı)‿ (§§2545 ff.) adj. *appertaining to the (a) boat, etc., boat's, ship's*.
   hílıb‿kúmdıd‿dabírkorandé? (-d‿d- < -g‿d- §534) *did they lose (have they lost) the ship's anchor?*
kubín-d(ı)‿ and
kublín-d(ı)‿ (§§2545 ff.) adj. *appertaining to (the) boats, etc., boats', ships'*.
kub(b)ȧıa‿ (-bȧıȧ‿, -bȧıɛ‿ §§1327, 1380) n. *drinking-glass, cup* [< كُبَايَة *id*.].
   obj. -bȧıag‿, -bȧıȧg‿, -bȧıɛg‿.
   pl. kub(b)ȧıančíı‿, -bȧıan‿, -bȧıɛn‿.
   kub(b)ȧıan‿í‿ *handle of cup*.
   kubȧı‿essínd(ı)‿ *glass for water, tumbler*.
   éssıŋ‿kubȧıa‿ (§4685) (a) *glass of water*; (b) = kubȧı‿essínd(ı)‿.
   kubȧıa‿šȧınd(ı)‿ *glass for drinking tea, tea-cup*.

kúbɛ⌣ — kúǧ

šáiŋ⌣kubáia⌣ (a) glass of tea, cup of tea; (b) =kubáia⌣šáind(ı)⌣.

kúbɛ⌣ n. (a, prop.) earthenware jar of the largest size; (b, applied to any) large jar [< √kúb- *vessel (§4553) +-ɛ⌣ of n. ess.; cp. Amh. ጎምቦ id.; RSN §§129, 200 s.v. gubē; §2234β].
obj. -bɛg⌣.
pl. kubénč(ı)⌣, kúbɛnč(ı)⌣ (§1597).
kúbɛ⌣mállen⌣dógor⌣dúlun⌢ the kúbɛ⌣ is the largest (§4968; jar) of all.
kúbɛ⌣dúlun, béntıgon⌣ı̌ugonn⌣íllɛr⌢ the kúbɛ⌣ is large, it's (§§5858–60) for dates and corn.

kúbrı⌣ n. bridge [< كبري id.].
obj. -rıg⌣.
pl. -rınč(ı)⌣.

kuččég v.t. ride s.v. kúǧ.

kúdde v.i. be clear, be transparent, be unclouded [§§2870ff.].
ind. pres. tɛr⌣kúddɛn⌢ (-dē⌢, -dé⌢); perf. tɛr⌣kúddɛgon⌢ (-gō⌢, -gó⌢), N. -ɛkon⌢, -kō⌢, -kó⌢, -ɛhon⌢, -hō⌢, -hó⌢).
part. pres. kúddɛ⌣ (one) that is clear, etc., clear, transparent, unclouded.
ólgon⌣sɛ́ma⌣kúddɛ́lun⌣ (§1966) the sky is still clear.

kúddɛrar⌣ (-rár⌣; §§2200ff., 2210) and
kuddɛríd⌣ (§§2256ff., 2263) n. clearness, etc.
sɛ́maŋ⌣kuddɛríd⌣ the clearness of the sky.

kúddɛ-bū- (§3931α) v.i. stat. be in a clear (etc.) state or condition.
ɛ́ssı⌣kúddɛbūn⌢ the water is clear.

kúddɛg-ır (N. -ɛkır, -ɛhır; ˵ §1532; §3679) v.t. caus. cause or allow to be clear, etc., render clear, etc., clarify.

kúdde v.i. get (partly or quite) burnt, get scorched [§§2870ff.].
ind. pres. aı̌⌣kúddɛrı⌢; perf. aı̌⌣kúddɛgori⌢ (N. -ɛko-, -ɛho-).

kúddɛrar⌣ (-rár⌣; §§2200ff., 2210) and
kuddɛríd⌣ (§§2256ff., 2263) n. getting burnt, etc.

kúdde-bū- (§3931α) v.i. stat. be in a burnt (etc.) state or condition.

kúddɛg-ır (N. -ɛkır, -ɛhır; ˵ §1532; §3679) v.t. caus. cause or allow to get burnt, etc., burn, scorch.
ind. pres. aı̌⌣kúddɛgıddı⌢.
X. ɛ́r⌣ǧawápkı⌣mín⌣áukon? what (mínɛ⌣ lit. how) have you done with (about) the letter?
Y. kuddɛgírkori⌢ I (have) burnt it.
aı̌⌣án⌣sárbɛk⌣kuddɛgírkori⌢ I (have) burnt (scorched) my finger(s), toe(s), §4696a.
ɛ́nn⌣ıǧ⌣íkkɛk⌣kúddɛgır⌢ (-k⌣k-, -d⌣k- §568) cauterize your hand(s), arm(s)), lit. burn your hand with fire.

kúddɛgırar⌣ (N. -ɛkır-, -ɛhır-; -rár⌣; §§2200ff., 2212) and
kuddɛgıríd⌣ (N. -ɛkır-, -ɛhır-; §§2256ff., 2265) n. burning, etc.

kúddɛgır-an (N. -ɛkır-, -ɛhır-; §§3890ff., 3904) v.t. tell to burn, etc., let burn, etc.

kuddɛgıdd-ɛg-ág- (§§4071ff.) v.t. =kuddɛgırɛdól-.

kuddɛgır-ɛ-dól- (N. -ɛkır-, -ɛhır-; -rᵒd- §1178; §4025) and

kuddɛgıdd-ɛ-dól- (-dᵒd-; §4033) v.t. be about to burn, etc.

kuddɛgıdd-ɛ-ǧŭ-bŭ- (§4069) v.t. stat. be on one's way (coming) to burn, etc.

kuddɛgır-ɛ-má- (N. -ɛkır-, -ɛhır-; §4039) and
kuddɛgıdd-ɛ-má- (§4046) v.t. become unable to burn, etc.

kuddɛgıdd-ɛ-nóg (§§4048ff.) v.t. go to burn, etc.

kuddɛgıdd-ɛ-nóg-bŭ- (-nóggŭ- §546; §4058) v.t. stat. be on one's way (going) to burn, etc.

kuddɛgıdd-ɛ-tá (§§4060ff.) v.t. come to burn, etc.

kuddɛgıred-ág- (N. -ɛkır-, -ɛhır-; §§3877ff.) v.t. be in the situation of having burnt, etc.

kúdd(ı)⌣, -di⌢ n. Kudi (on map), a village near the centre of Argo Island.
obj. -dıg⌣.

kúdɛ⌣ n. enclosure (formed by wall or fence) [RSN, §129].
obj. -dɛg⌣.
pl. kudénč(ı)⌣.
úrtınčıŋ⌣kúdɛ⌣ goats' (sheep's) enclosure.

kudrúkka⌣ n. Kudroka (on map), a village on Argo Island, south of its centre.
obj. -úkkag⌣, -úkkág⌣ (§1532).
kudrúkkar⌣áı̌⌣nógbūri⌢ I am on my way to K.

kúff(ı)⌣ n. penis.
obj. -fıg⌣.
pl. -fınč(ı)⌣.
kúffın⌣dílt(ı)⌣ pubes about penis.
kúffın⌣úr⌣ glans penis.
kúffın⌣úrn⌣áǧın⌣ prepuce.

kúffı-kıññ(ı)⌣ (§§2536-7) adj. without a penis.
tawwášıgol⌣lótıgon⌣kússagom⌣mállɛ⌣ kúffıkıññınčí⌢ (§939; -l⌣l- <-n⌣l- §581).

kuffın-d(ı)⌣ (§§2545ff.) adj. appertaining to the penis.

kug(u)lúg⌣ (kuk(u)-, -lúl⌣) n. cock [onom. §2154].
obj. -úgk(ı)⌣, -úkk(ı)⌣, -úlg(ı)⌣, -kı⌢, -gı⌢.
gen. -úgn⌣v., -úŋ⌣c., -úln⌣v., -úl⌣c., -úń⌣c.
pl. -úgı⌣, -úlı⌣.
kugulúŋ⌣dalál⌣ cock's wattle(s §4696a).

kugundára⌣ (kuhun- §1017) n. beetle; with collective sg. (§4696c) [< √kugun- *bend(s) (§4555) +-dá be present+gerundial -r (§§3548-56) +-a⌣ say (§2178), so (from its bent legs) *what says 'there are bends', i.e. *what exhibits bends].
obj. -rag⌣.
pl. -ranč(ı)⌣.

kugúnd(ı)⌣ n. elbow; with collective sg. (§4696a); (=kumúnd(ı)⌣) [< *kugúnnd(ı) (§613) + √kugun- *bend (§4555) +-nd(ı)⌣ appertaining to (§§2545ff.), so *what appertains to a bend, *angular part §2301].
obj. -dıg⌣.
pl. -dınč(ı)⌣.
ín⌣kugúnd(ı)⌣ (íŋ-k-) elbow(s).
óssıŋ⌣kugúnd(ı)⌣ ankle(s).

kúǧ v.i. be incumbent [<*kúdǧ (§2890) < √kúd- *be above (§4554)+-ǧ §§2880ff.; §2056].
— constructed with -r (-ro⌣, etc.).
ind. pres. tɛr⌣kúǧın⌢ (-ǧí⌢, ⌣kúǧí⌢); perf. tɛr⌣kúǧkon⌢ (⌣kúčk-, -ǧk-, -čk- §323; ⌣kúččon⌢ §523; -kō⌢, -kó⌢, -čō⌢, -čó⌢).
sálumır⌣kúǧın⌢ it's Sálım's duty (Sálım ought to do it).
ıň⌣álır⌣kúǧın⌢ this (that) is ɛ́ali's duty (ɛ́ali ought to do this (that)).
ím⌣mállɛ⌣samíllo⌣kúǧın⌢ all this (that) is the duty of the sheikh.
nógran⌣samíllo⌣kúǧın⌢ (nógran⌣ infinitive §2961) and
nogíd⌣samíllo⌣kúčkó⌢ the sheikh ought to have gone.
ín⌣áddo⌣kúǧın⌢ this is my (our) duty (I (we) ought to do this).
ín⌣ɛ́ddo⌣kúǧın⌢ you ought to do this.
ín⌣áddo⌣kúčkó⌢ I (we) ought to have done this.
ín⌣ɛ́ddo⌣kúčkó⌢ you ought to have done this.
dɛ́n⌣níddo⌣kúǧın? who ought to pay the debt?
ǧélli⌣téddo⌣kúǧıl⌣mállɛg⌣áwın⌢ (§4809) (s)he does all the work that (s)he ought to do.
ıň⌣ǧéll⌣áddo⌣kuǧíl-taran⌢ (§1976) this work is my (our) duty.

kúǧ n. (a) (bird's) crest, comb (=dírr(ı)⌣); (b) tuft (left on otherwise shaven head); (c) clitoris [nominal presentation of thing-meant by √kúǧ- rise, be above (§§2056, 4556), extension of √kúd- (§4554); §2250].
obj. kúǧk(ı)⌣, kúčk(ı)⌣, kúčč(ı)⌣ §523, -ǧk-, -čk- §323, -kı⌢, -či⌢.
pl. kúǧı⌣.
dúmmadɛŋ⌣kúǧ⌣ fowl's comb.
kugulúŋ⌣kúǧ⌣ cock's comb.
burúŋ⌣kúǧ⌣ clitoris.

kuǧ-ág (§3747ᵉ) v.i. squat (etc. s.v. ág) superimposed, squat (etc.) on.
imperat. kuǧák!
tɛ́r⌣kúrsıŋ⌣kóččır⌣kuǧágın⌢ (s)he sits on the (a) chair.
káwırtɛ⌣kăŋ⌣kóččır⌣kuǧágın⌢ the bird sits (birds sit §4647) on the house-top(s ib.).

kuǧág-an (§§3890ff., 3905) v.t. tell to squat (etc.) on, let squat (etc.) on.
bıtáŋ⌣áŋgarɛr⌣kuǧágan⌢ let the child sit on the bedstead.

kúǧ-bŭ- (kúǧǧŭ- §552; §3931α) v.i. stat. be in a superimposed state or condition, be upon, be on; be incumbent.
súlɛ⌣ígır⌣kúǧǧūn⌢ the pot is on the fire.
ǧákud⌣ígır⌣kúǧǧun⌢ the stew is on the fire.
X. ɛ́ssıg⌣ígır⌣kúǧur⌣ set the (some) water on the fire.
Y. kúǧbun⌢ it's on.
ín⌣téddo⌣kúǧbūn⌢ this is incumbent on him (her).
ín⌣téddo⌣kuǧbúmunun⌢ this is not incumbent on him (her).

kúǧ-bᵘ-an (-b(w)an; kúǧǧᵘan, -ǧ(w)an §552; §3962) v.t. tell to be upon, let be upon.

kúğğá!<kúğ-bⁿ-an! — kulwåhıd⌣

imperat. kúgbᵘan! (-b(w)an!, -b(w)ā!, -b(w)á!) and kúğğᵘan! (-ğ(w)an!, -ğ(w)ā!, -ğ(w)á!).
kádɛn⌣níbıdır⌣kúğğan⌢(-n⌣n-<-g⌣n- §625) the cloth is (clothes are §4696d) to be on the mat.

kuč-čɛ́g (§2861) v.t. mount, ride [< *kuğ-tɛ́g (§526) < kuğ- being on + -tɛ́g sit (§3747ᵉ)].
ind. pres. āı⌣kuččɛ́g(¹)ri⌢, ɛr⌣kuččɛ́gın⌢ (-gī⌢, -gí⌢); perf. āı⌣kuččɛ́gkori⌢ (-čɛ́kkori⌢).
imperat. kuččɛ́k!
hánuk⌣kuččɛ́gkó⌢ (s)he rode (has ridden) the (a) donkey.
gátır⌣mawaídk⌣uñurkógıri, bıkuččɛgóskori⌢ (-r⌣m-<-rn⌣m- §850; §6234κ) if I had known the train's times, I should have gone (come) by it, lit. ... I should have ridden.

kuččɛ́g-an (§§3890ff.) v.t. tell to mount, etc., let mount, etc.

kuččɛ́g-kattı- (-ɛ́kka-; §4093) v.p. be mounted, etc.
íŋ⌣kám⌣kuččɛ́kkáttımunun⌢ (§1939) this camel is not (cannot be §5704) ridden.

kúğ-ur (§3673) v.t. caus. cause or allow to be upon, place on, set upon [< *kúğ-ır §1189].
ind. pres. āı⌣kuğúrri⌢, ɛr⌣kúğurın⌢ (-rī⌢, -rí⌢).
barrádkı⌣kuğúrkon⌢ (s)he (has) put the kettle on (sc. the fire).
X. éssık⌣kuğúrkoná? did (has) (s)he (did, have you) put the water on? (sc. on the fire).
Y. ákkúğurın⌢ (s)he is putting it on.
kúsuk⌣kuğúrkoná? has (s)he (have you) put the meat on? (sc. to cook).
afɛ́škı⌣kám⌣kóččır⌣kuğur⌢ place the baggage on the (a) camel.
afɛ́škı⌣kúğur⌢ load the baggage (put the baggage on).
hodárkı⌣togógɛd⌣úskur, kúmbud⌣ dogógɛk⌣kúğur⌢ (-d⌣d-<-g⌣d- §534, -k⌣k-<-d⌣b §568) put the vegetables underneath, put the eggs on them on top.
tábak⌣kúğur⌢ put the (a) stamp on (sc. the letter).

kúğurar⌣ (-rár⌣; §§2200, 2212) and

kuğuríd (§§2256ff., 2265) n. (a) placing on, superimposition; (b) burden, load.
hánun⌣kuğurídmınéllé? what is the donkey's load?

kúğur-an (§§3890ff., 3904) v.t. tell to place on, etc., let place on, etc.

kuğurr-ɛg-ág- (§§4071ff.) v.t. = kuğurɛ-dól-.

kuğurr-ɛ-dól- (-rᵒd- §1178; §4025) and
kuğurr-ɛ-dól- (-rᵒd-; §4033) v.t. be about to place on, etc.

kuğurr-ɛ-ğŭ-bŭ- (§4069) v.t. stat. be on one's way (coming) to place on, etc.

kuğurr-ɛ-má- (§4039) and
kuğurr-ɛ-má- (§4046) v.t. become unable to place on, etc.

kuğurr-ɛ-nóg (§§4048ff.) v.t. go to place on, etc.

kuğurr-ɛ-nóg-bŭ- (-nóggŭ- §546; §4058) v.t. stat. be on one's way (going) to place on, etc.

kuğurr-ɛ-tá (§§4060ff.) v.t. come to place on, etc.

kuğurɛd-ág- (§§3877ff.) v.t. be in the situation of having placed on, etc.

kuğuríŋg-ır (ᵘ‿ , N. -ŋkır; §3691) v.t. caus. cause or allow to place on, etc.

kúğur-kattı- (ᵘ́‿‿ §1940; §4093) v.p. be placed on, etc.

kuğuros-tā (-ottá §714; §§4180-4; -osgıtá, -ozgı-, -oggı- §4185) v.t. come after placing on, etc., just (s.v. -tá) place on, etc., go and (§5713) place on, etc.
imperat. kuğurostá!, -osgıtá!, -ozgı-, -oggı-, -ósta!, -ósgıta!, -ózgı-, -óggı- (§1871).

kúğğá! < **kúğ-bⁿ-an!** let it be upon s.v. kúğ.

kuhundára (§1017) beetle = kugundára⌣.

kukkós⌣ n. cotton-seed; with collective sg. (§4696b); = gúlgul⌣ [< κόκκος kernel, berry §2393].
obj. -ósk(ı)⌣, -ki⌢.
pl. -ósı⌣.

kuk(u)lúg⌣ (-lúl⌣) cock = kug(u)lúg⌣.

kúl n. hole (in), cavity (differing from úb-bur⌣ hole through) [< √kúl- *round §4543; cp. MN. kọl Loch KBW s.v.].
obj. kúlg(ı)⌣, -gi⌢.
pl. kúlı⌣.
kúllo⌣ (s.v. -r⌣) in (to, into) the (a) hole.
kúllo⌢ (§5858) (s)he (it) is (they are) in the (a) hole.
kúll⌣úndur⌢ put him (her, it, them) into the hole.
índo⌣kúl-lēw⌣wáddi⌢ (-l-l-<-l-w- §580, -w⌣w-<-g⌣w- §719) dig a hole here.

kúl-kiññ(ı)⌣ (§§2536-7) adj. devoid of holes.
árıd⌣kúlkiññın⌢ the ground is devoid of holes.

kúl v.t. cause (a fixed object) to issue, put out, protrude, take out, extract.
ind. pres. āı⌣kúlli⌢, ɛr⌣kúlın⌢ (-lī⌢, -lí⌢); perf. āı⌣kúlkori⌢.
án⌣nétkı⌣kúlkori⌢ I (have) put my tongue out.
kártöm⌣bér-rēk⌣kúlkoran⌢ (-r-r-<-r-w- §672, -k⌣k-<-g⌣k- §569) they took (have taken) a (piece of) wood out of the house: the wood was a fixture; kártöm⌣bér-rēg-óskoran⌢ or kártöm⌣bér-rēs⌣sókkɛgoran⌢ (-s⌣s-<-g⌣s- §678) they took (have taken, moved, carried) a piece of wood out of the house: the wood was not a fixture.
gɛzáz-zēs⌣sandúğırtöŋ⌣kúlkori⌢ (-z-z-<-z-w- §737, -s⌣s-<-g⌣s- §678) I (have) got a bottle out of the case (sc. in which it was packed).

kúl-an (§§3890ff.) v.t. tell to put out, etc., let put out, etc.

kúlal⌣ n. ring [< √kúl- *round §4543; RSN, §§80, 129].
obj. kulálg(ı)⌣, -gi⌢.
pl. kúlalı⌣.

kuljómg(ı)⌣ (kulljó- §§804, 1396; -gi⌢) adv. every day [< كل يوم id. +-g(ı)⌣ §4476].
X. ıŋk⌣úskur⌢ put it like that (in this position, etc.).
Y. kuljómgá? (s.v. -á?) every day?

kúlma⌣ (kúrma⌣) n. one of the sorts of date growing in Dóngola; s.v. bɛ́nt(ı)⌣; with collective sg. (§4696b).
obj. -mag⌣.
pl. -manč(ı)⌣.

kúlt(ı)⌣ n. (a) fly; (b) small winged insect (larger ones are called fírrıl⌣).
— with collective sg. (§4696c) [§2329]:
obj. -tıg⌣.
pl. -tınč(ı)⌣.
asáln⌣kúlt(ı)⌣ (asán⌣kúlt(ı)⌣, asán⌣kúlt(ı)⌣ §656) bee(s).
kúltıgɛb⌣béran⌣ (-b⌣b-<-d⌣b §518; §§5452-3) n. fly-killer (s.v. bé).

kúltı-kiññ(ı)⌣ (§§2536-7) adj. devoid of flies.

kúltı-kırı⌣ (§§2539-40) adj. like a fly, like flies.

kultín-d(ı)⌣ (§§2545ff.) adj. appertaining to the fly, of the fly, fly's.

kúlu n. stone; with collective sg. (§4696d) [< √kúl- *round (§4543) + -u⌣ dem. §2337; cp. ON. ⲕⲟⲇⲗ rock GNT, s.v.; RSN, §§129, 200].
obj. kúlug⌣.
pl. kúlunč(ı)⌣.
X. tŭpkɛd⌣āggóñran⌢ they are building in brick.
Y. wáraŋ⌣kúlugédun⌢ no, it's in stone.

kúlu-kiññ(ı)⌣ (§§2536-7) adj. devoid of stones.
árıd⌣kúlukiññın⌢ the ground is devoid of stones.

kulum-mısíd⌣, -ít⌣ n. Kulumesid (on map), a village on the left bank of the Nile near the southern end of Argo Island [Stone Mosque; Sudan Ar.

مسيد < مسجد].

obj. -ítt(ı)⌣ (§716), -ti⌢.

kulún-d(ı)⌣ (§§2545ff.) adj. appertaining to stone(s), of stone(s), stone.
kúluŋ⌣kåg⌣āggóñran⌢ and (§4684) kå⌣kulúndıg⌣āggóñran⌢ they are building a house of stone.

kulún-tu⌣ Inside of the Stone(s; §2363), name of the district of the second cataract, just south of Wådi Ḥálfa = Sudan Ar. بطن الحجر Båṭn⌣ɛl-Ḥágar.
kulún-tūr⌣ágran⌢ they live in the Båṭn⌣ ɛl-Ḥágar.

kúlud⌣, -ut⌣ n. Kulud (on map), a village on the left bank of the Nile about 29 miles above Ed-Débbáʰ.
obj. kulúdk(ı)⌣, -útk(ı)⌣, -ki⌢.

kuludnárt(ı)⌣, -ti⌢ n. Kulud Island (on map).
obj. -tıg⌣.

kúlul⌣ n. hip; with collective sg. (§4696a) [< *kúlıl⌣ (§1189) < √kúl- *round (§4543) + -ıl⌣ determinative (§§2277ff.); §2343].
obj. kulúlg(ı)⌣, -gi⌢.
pl. kúlulı⌣.

kúlus⌣ n. Kulus (on map), a village on the right bank of the Nile, about ten miles above Ed-Débbáʰ.
obj. kulúsk(ı)⌣, -ki⌢.

kulwåhıd⌣ (kullwá- §§805, 1396; §2697) distr. pron. each one [< كل واحد id.].

kúm⌣ — kuríčč ɛ⌣

obj. -wăhídk(ɪ)⌣, -ítk(ɪ)⌣, -ítt(ɪ)⌣ §716, -ki⌢, -ti⌢.
kulwáhɪdk⌣kúlu⌣wɛwɛs⌣sókkɛgon⌢ (-s⌣s- < -g⌣s- §678) they took (have taken) up (away, s.v. sókkɛ) a stone each.
kulwahídkɪ⌣díčč ɪ⌣tíddi⌢ and kulwahídkɪ⌣díğ⌣díčč ɪ⌣tíddi⌢ I give them five each.
kulwahídkɪ⌣gírɪš⌣tóskɪt⌣tíddi⌢ (-t⌣t- < -g⌣t- §707) and kulwahídkɪ⌣gírɪš⌣tóskɪt⌣tíddi⌢ I give them three piastres each.
kulwăhíttu⌣ɛččɛnɛččɛn⌣tɛrkori⌢ I (have) planted each one separately.
kúm⌣c. gen. of kúb⌣ boat, etc.
kumáttɛ⌣ n. vulva [< *kumártɛ⌣ (§713) < kúm- protuberance + -ar⌣ nominal -ing (§§ 2200) + -t dim. (§ 2325 γ) + -ɛ⌣ of n. ess. (§ 2234β), so *what is a little protuberance; cp. mons Veneris; § 2226].
obj. -tɛg⌣.
pl. -tɛnč(ɪ)⌣.
kumáttɛn⌣dílt(ɪ)⌣ pubes about vulva.
kumáttɛn⌣ğɛmb(ɪ)⌣ labium; with collective sg. (§ 4696 a).
ɪnɛŋ⌣kumáttɛ! matris tuae vulva! (-ŋ⌣k- < -nn⌣k- § 657) and ɪnɛŋ⌣kumáttɛgi! matris tuae vulvam! (sc. ineo), a vulgar curse (كُسّ أُمَّك id.).
kumattɛn-d(ɪ)⌣ (§§2545 ff.) adj. appertaining to the vulva, vulvar.
kumáttɛn-tu⌣ uterus.
kumattɛn-tŭn-d(ɪ)⌣ (§5021) adj. appertaining to the uterus, uterine.
kúmbu⌣ n. egg; with collective sg. (§4696 d) [§§ 2299, 2337; cp. ON. ҡоумпот id. GNT s.v.].
obj. -bug⌣.
pl. -bunč(ɪ)⌣.
sorón⌣kúmbu⌣ (-ón⌣k- §651) testicle(s).
kúmbu-kɪrɪ⌣ (§§2539-40) adj. resembling the (an) egg, oval.
kumbúnčɪ-kɪrɪ⌣ (§§2539-40) adj. resembling (the) eggs.
kumbún-d(ɪ)⌣ (§§2545 ff.) adj. appertaining to the (an) egg, of the (an) egg, egg's.
kúmd⌣ boat's, etc. s.v. kúb⌣.
kúmmɛ-bŭ- (§§3927 ff.) v.i. stat. be in an insane state or condition, be possessed by an evil spirit (= ğániko-).
mán⌣ɛn⌣tɛkkól⌣ágkɪn⌣ténn⌣ágonon⌣ ābbánniŋ⌣kúmmɛbūn⌢ when that woman is alone she talks to herself, she is mad (§6240).
kummɛg(ɪ)ríd⌣ (§§2256 ff., 2265) n. insanity, possession by evil spirit.
tɛr⌣kummɛgrídkɪ⌣kúmmɛbūn⌢ (s)he is quite mad.
kumúnd(ɪ)⌣ n. elbow; with collective sg. (§4696 a); (= kugúnd(ɪ)⌣) [< √kúm- protuberance (§ 4556 a) + -u⌣ dem. (§ 4598) + -d(ɪ)⌣ appertaining to (§§ 2545 ff.), so *appertaining to that protuberance, that protuberant part §2301 α].
obj. -dɪg⌣.
pl. -dɪnč(ɪ)⌣.
ín⌣kumúnd(ɪ)⌣ (íŋ⌣k-) elbow(s).
óssɪŋ⌣kumúnd(ɪ)⌣ ankle(s).

kunús⌣ n. = kunúz⌣.
obj. kunúsk(ɪ)⌣, -ki⌢.
pl. kunúsɪ⌣.
kunús-d(ɪ)⌣ adj. = kunúznd(ɪ)⌣.
kunūsín-d(ɪ)⌣ adj. and n. = kunūzínd(ɪ)⌣.
kunúz⌣ n. Kénzi (كَنْزِي) [<] كُنُوز pl. (§ 2405) of كَنْزِي (one) of the بَنِي كَنْزِي a tribe whose name (LN, p. cxx, MAS, I, p. 150) was identified with that of the inhabitants of the Eg. kns-t das nördliche Nubien (EÆGl s.v.)].
obj. -núzk(ɪ)⌣, -núsk(ɪ)⌣, -ki⌢.
pl. -núzɪ⌣.
X. tén⌣tabbáh⌣dúŋgulārtōndέ? is his (her) cook from Dóngola?
Y. wáraŋ⌣kunúzun⌢ no, he's a Kénzi (§ 6240).
kunúzn-d(ɪ)⌣ (§§2545 ff.) adj. appertaining to the (a) Kénzi (كَنْزِي).
kunūzín-d(ɪ)⌣ (§§2545 ff.) (a) adj. appertaining to the Kunúz (كُنُوز); (b) n. language of the Kunúz, Kénzi Nubian.
kunūzíndɪb⌣bánniran⌢ (-b⌣b- < -g⌣b- § 519) and kunūzíndɪgɛb⌣bánniran⌢ (-b⌣b- < -d⌣b- § 518) they speak Kénzi.
kún v.i. (a) sink, descend; (b) be buried.
ind. pres. aī⌣kúñ(ɪ)ri⌢; perf. aī⌣kúñkori⌢.
subj. past aī⌣kúñ(ɪ)sɪ⌣ (-su⌣).
kúb⌣kuñóskō⌢ the boat has sunk.
síu⌣éssɪr⌣kuñóskó⌢ the sand has disappeared under the water (sc. as the river rose).
kát'rɛ⌣síwɪr⌣kuñóskō⌢ the wall has got buried under the sand.
úŋ⌣kuñóskon⌢ (-ŋ⌣k- < -n⌣k- §655) the moon has set.
tɛr⌣kúñɪm⌣bádɪr⌣béddɪran⌢ after (s)he is buried they pray.
kúñar⌣ (-ñár⌣; §§2200 ff.) and
kuñíd⌣ (§§2256 ff.) n. sinking, descent, being buried, burial.
kúñ-bŭ- (kúŋğŭ- §635; §3931 α) v.i. stat. be in a sunken (etc.) state or condition.
tém⌣míssɪ⌣kúñbūn⌢ his (her, its) eye is (eyes are §4696 a) bunged up.
kúñ-ur (§3673) v.t. bury.
ind. pres. aī⌣kuñúrri⌢; perf. aī⌣kuñúrkori⌢.
kúñurar⌣ (-rár⌣; §§2200 ff., 2212) and
kuñuríd⌣ (§§2256 ff., 2265) n. burying, burial.
kúñur-an (§§3890 ff., 3904) v.t. tell to bury, let bury.
kúñurwan⌢ tell them to bury him (her, it § 5083).
kuñúr-kattɪ- (‿‿ §1940; §4093) v.p. be buried.
kŭr n. a large Nile fish, dark in colour, Clarias anguillaris (PF, p. 90).
obj. kŭrk(ɪ)⌣, -ki⌢.
pl. kŭrɪ⌣.
kŭr⌣urúmmɛgoŋ⌣ɛnɪn⌣nosógoŋ⌣ɛnɪn⌢ Clarias anguillaris is black and long (s.v. -gɛn).
kŭr v.t. learn.
ind. pres. aī⌣kúrri⌢; ɛr⌣kúrɪn⌣ (-ri⌢, -rí⌢); perf. aī⌣kúrkori⌢.

subj. past aī⌣kúrsɪ⌣ (-su⌣).
part. pres. kúrɪl⌣ (one) that learns, learner, pupil, learning; obj. kúrɪlg(ɪ)⌣, -gi⌢; past kúrɛl⌣ (one) that learned, learner, learning; obj. kúrɛlg(ɪ)⌣, -gi⌢.
ólgoŋ⌣ğéllɪk⌣kúrkōmun⌢ (s)he hasn't learnt the work yet.
kúrar⌣ (-rár⌣; §§2200 ff.) and
kuríd⌣ (§§2256 ff.) n. learning.
kŭr-an (§§3890 ff.) v.t. tell to learn, let learn.
kŭr-bŭ- (§3938) v.i. stat. be in an instructed state or condition.
tímbɛs⌣mádrɑsár⌣séna⌣kɛmskɪ⌣tógon, ékkɛnɛ⌣kúrbun⌢ his (her) brother has been (s.v. tó) four years at school, he is now instructed.
kūrɛd-ág- (§§3877 ff.) v.t. be in the condition of having learnt.
búru⌣tɪnéndotōŋ⌣kūrɛdágɪn⌢ the girl has learnt (it) from her mother.
kúrk-ɪr (§3683) v.t. caus. cause or allow to learn, teach, instruct.
ind. pres. aī⌣kúrkɪddi⌢, ɛr⌣kúrkɪrɪn⌢ (-rī⌢, -rí⌢).
part. pres. kúrkɪrɪl⌣ (one) that teaches, teacher, teaching; past kúrkɪrɛl⌣ (one) that taught, teacher, teaching.
kúrkɪr-an (§§3890 ff., 3904) v.t. tell to teach, etc., let teach, etc.
kŭr-kattɪ- (§4093) v.p. be learnt.
goráŋ⌣kúrkattɪn⌢ the Coran is learnt (...can be learnt §5704).
kúra⌣ n. soft dates in mass (= ágwa⌣).
obj. -rag⌣ [> Sudan Ar. كُرِيق kurég id. §2412].
kúra⌣ n. ball [< Sudan Ar. كُورَة id., < كُرَة id.].
obj. -rag⌣.
pl. -ranč(ɪ)⌣.
kúragɛğ⌣ğómran⌢ (§§5452-3) n. instrument for hitting ball, bat, racquet, polostick, golf-club.
kúra⌣ n. bowl (basin) [< Sudan Ar. كُورَة id., < كُرَة sphere].
obj. -rag⌣.
pl. -ranč(ɪ)⌣.
kúríjɛ⌣ (-íjá⌣, -íja⌣) n. bowl (basin) [< Sudan Ar. كُورِيَّة id. < كُرِيَّة spherical].
obj. -jɛg⌣, -jág⌣, -jag⌣.
pl. -jɛnč(ɪ)⌣, -jánč(ɪ)⌣, -janč(ɪ)⌣.
kŭrɪ, -rɪ⌢ n. Kuri (on map), a village on the right bank of the Nile, about 34 miles above Ed-Débbá[h].
obj. -rɪg⌣.
kuríččɛ⌣ (-rúč- §1187) n. switch, esp. for driving cattle turning water-wheel (kólɛ⌣) [< *kúr(ɪ)gtɛ⌣ (§§ 526, 1518) < √kúr- *break off (§4557) + -ɪ- euph. + -ğ intensive (§2067) + -t dim. (§2325 γ) + -ɛ⌣ of n. ess. (§ 2234), so *little thing snapped off §2229].
obj. -čɛg⌣.
pl. -čɛnč(ɪ)⌣.
bɪtáŋ⌣kólɛn⌣gúrɪk⌣kuríččɛgɛš⌣šúgɪn⌢ (-š⌣š- < -d⌣š- §694) the boy drives the bulls of the water-wheel with a switch.

kúrma⌣ *sort of date* = kúlma⌣.
 obj. -mag⌣.
 pl. -manč(ı)⌣.
kúrsı⌣ n. *chair, stool* [< كُرْسِيّ *id.*].
 obj. -sıg⌣.
 pl. -sınč(ı)⌣.
kúrša⌣ n. *one of the better sorts of date growing in Dongola*; s.v. bént(ı)⌣; *with collective sg.* (§ 4696 b).
 obj. -šag⌣.
 pl. -šanč(ı)⌣.
kúrt(ı)⌣ n. *knee; with collective sg.* (§ 4696 a) [§ 2324].
 obj. -tıg⌣.
 pl. -tınč(ı)⌣.
 óssıŋ⌣kúrt(ı)⌣ *knee(s)*.
kůrt(ı)⌣, **-ti**⌒ n. *a village in the district of Awadánda on Argo Island*.
 obj. -tıg⌣.
kůrt(ı) v.t. *tangle, make tangled*.
 ind. pres. aī⌣kůrtırı⌒, ɛr⌣kůrtın⌒ (-tí⌒, -tí⌒); perf. aī⌣kůrtıgorı⌒ (N. -ıko-, -ıho-).
 ɛr⌣írık⌣kůrtóskon⌒ *you have tangled the rope*.
kůrtar⌣ (-tăr⌣; §§ 2200 ff.) and
kůrtíd⌣ (§§ 2256 ff.) n. *tangling*.
kůrtı-bŭ- (§ 3931 β) v.i. stat. *be in a tangled state or condition*.
 úl⌣kůrtıbūn⌒ *the thread is in a tangle*.
kůrtır-eg-åg- (§§ 4071 ff.) v.t. = kůrtɛdól-.
kůrt-ɛ-dól- (-t°d- § 1178; § 4022) and
kůrtır-ɛ-dól- (-r°d-; § 4027) v.t. *be about to tangle*.
kůrtɛd-åg- (§§ 3877 ff.) v.t. *be in the situation of having tangled*.
kůrtı-kattı- (N. -ıha-; § 4093) v.p. *be tangled*.
kúru⌣ n. *pigeon, dove* [< kúr- onom. + -u⌣ § 2337; *RSN*, § 200].
 obj. kúrug⌣.
 pl. kurúnč(ı)⌣.
kúrub⌣ n. *alluvium, alluvial earth* (= Sudan Ar. غُرير and includes gurúnt(ı)⌣ [either cogn. with √kárb(ı) *crumple (§ 4544) or contains √kúr- *break up (§ 4557) or < Sudan Ar. كَرَب *broken ground near river* (§ 1336)].
 obj. kurúbk(ı)⌣, -úpk(ı)⌣, -ki⌒.
 aŋgállɛr⌣kurúpk⌣undúddam⌣bássaranınn⌣íllar⌒ (-m⌣b- < -n⌣b- § 592) *they put alluvium into the lupines* (§ 4696 b) *that they may lose their bitterness*.
kúrub v.i. *rattle, clatter, make a rattling* (etc.) *sound* (= káraû, kórou) [onom.].
 ind. pres. aī⌣kúrubrı⌒, ɛr⌣kúrubın⌒ (-bí⌒, -bí⌒); perf. aī⌣kurúbkorı⌒ (-úpk-).
 šéjınč⌣sandúŋ⌣túr⌣kúrubran⌒ *the things rattle inside the box*.
kúrubar⌣ (-băr⌣; §§ 2200 ff.) and
kurubíd⌣ (§§ 2256 ff.) n. *rattling, etc.*
kurúb-bŭ- (§ 3931 α) v.i. stat. *be in a rattling* (etc.) *state or condition*.
 tåga⌣kurúbbūn⌒ *the window is rattling*.
kurubíŋ-ır (N. -ŋkır; § 3688) v.t. caus. = kurúbkır.
kurúbk-ır (-úpk-; § 3683) v.t. caus. *cause or allow to rattle, etc.*

kurúmb(ı)⌣ n. *cabbage; with collective sg.* (§ 4696 b) [< كُرُنْب *id.*].
 obj. -bıg⌣.
 pl. -bınč(ı)⌣.
kúruñ⌣ n. *hump* [§ 2304; *RSN*, § 129].
 obj. kurúñ(ı)⌣, -gi⌒.
 pl. kúruñ⌣.
 tíŋ⌣kúruñ⌣ *hump of cow* (... *of cattle* § 4647).
 kám⌣kúruñ⌣ (-m⌣k- < -mn⌣k- § 598) *hump of camel*.
kurúñ-kıñ̌ñ(ı)⌣ (§§ 2536-7) adj. *without a hump*.
 tí⌣kurúñkıñ̌ñ(ı)⌣ *cow without a hump (cattle without humps)*.
kuruñ-kȯl (§ 2600) adj. *with a hump, hunch-backed*.
 obj. -kȯlg(ı)⌣, -gi⌒.
 pl. kurúñkonı⌣.
kúrus⌣ adj. *old (not new), stale* [*RSN*, § 129].
 obj. kurúsk(ı)⌣, -ki⌒.
 pl. kúrusı⌣.
kurús-tod⌣ (§§ 2484, 2582) adj. *wretchedly old, terribly stale*.
 obj. kurústodk(ı)⌣, -tótk(ı)⌣, -tőkk(ı)⌣, -tȯtt(ı)⌣ § 2462, -ki⌒, -ti⌒.
 gen. -tȯdn⌣v., -tȯnn⌣v.c., -tȯn⌣c.
 pl. kurústonı⌣.
 dégır⌣kurústodun⌒ *the saddle is wretchedly old* (e.g. *old and worn out*).
kúrus-an- (§ 3910 α) v.i. *become old, etc.*
 káde⌣kúrusaŋkó⌒ *the cloth (has) got old*.
 máre⌣kúrusaŋkó⌒ *the millet (has) got stale*.
 kál⌣kúrusaŋkó⌒ *the bread (food) (has) got stale*.
kúrusam-bŭ- (§§ 3949 ff.) v.i. stat. *be in a state or condition of becoming old, etc., be advanced in the state of becoming old, etc.*
 béntı⌣kúrusambūn⌒ *the dates are getting old (stale)*.
kurusaned-åg- (§ 3966 α) v.i. *be in the condition of having become old, etc.*
kús (a) v.t. *open;* (b) v.t. *loose, unfasten, untie, undo;* (c) v.t. *release, set free;* (d) v.i. *open (itself), become unfastened, etc.* [cp. ON. коүсс, кıсс id. GNT s.v.; *RSN*, § 129].
 ind. pres. aī⌣kús(¹)rı⌒, ɛr⌣kúsın⌒ (-sí⌒, ⌣kúsí⌒); perf. aī⌣kúskorı⌒.
 imperat. kús!, pl. kúswɛ! (kúswé!, kússe! § 687, kússé!).
 subj. past aī⌣kússı⌣ (-su⌣).
 cond. pres. aī-oŋ⌣kúskırı⌣.
 part. pres. kúsıl⌣ *(one) that opens, etc., opener, etc., opening, etc.*, obj. kusílg(ı)⌣, -gi⌒; past kúsɛl⌣ *(one) that opened, etc., opener, etc., opening, etc.*, obj. kusélg(ı)⌣, -gi⌒.
 def. perf. aī⌣kusóskorı⌒.
 def. imperat. (§ 1890) kúsos! (kusós!, kusó!, occ. kúsó!); pl. kusóswɛ! (-sóswé!, -sówwé!, -wé!, -sóssɛ!, -sé!).
 kobídkı⌣kúskoran⌒ *they (have) opened the door (gate)*.
 kåk⌣kús *open the door*.
 kåk⌣kúsmɛŋgon⌣ǧóm⌒ *knock at the door before you open it*.
 írık⌣kúskoran⌒ *they (have) untied the rope*.
 kóbıd⌣kúskó⌒ *the door (has) opened*.

kúrma⌣ — **kús**

kóbıd⌣kȯl⌣kúskó⌒ *the door (has) opened by itself*.
kúsar⌣ (-săr⌣; §§ 2200 ff.) and
kusíd⌣ (§§ 2256) n. *opening, loosing, etc.*
kúšar⌣ (-šăr, -šɛr⌣ §§ 1036, 2216) n. *instrument for opening, etc., key* [> Sudan Ar. كُشَر *id.*].
 obj. kušárk(ı)⌣, -šăr-, -šér-, kúšark(ı)⌣, -šăr-, -šɛr-, § 1521, -ki⌒.
 pl. kúšarı⌣, -šărı⌣, -šɛrı⌣.
 kúšar⌣ɛlbénd(ı)⌣, -di⌒ and
 kúšar⌣ɛlbɛnčínd(ı)⌣, -di⌒ *tin-opener*.
kús-an (§§ 3890 ff.) v.t. *tell to open, etc., let open, etc.*
 X. álıb⌣bábkı⌣kúsā⌒ (-b⌣b- < -g⌣b- § 519) *let ɣáli open the door (gate)*.
 Y. kúzbūn⌒ *it's open*.
kúz-bŭ- (§§ 727, 3931 β) v.i. stat. *be in an open (etc.) state or condition*.
 X. kobítkı⌣kúskoná? *did you open (have you opened) the door?*
 Y. kúzbūgó⌒ *it was open*.
 íŋ⌣kóbbūn, éččel⌣kúzbūl-lēr⌣dán⌒ (-l-l- < -l-w- § 580) *this is shut (but § 6239) there is another, an open one*.
 írı⌣kúzbūn⌒ *the rope is (has been, has come) untied*.
kúz-bᵘ-an (-b(w)an; §§ 3962-3) v.t. *have, or let be, in an open (etc.) state or condition*.
 imperat. kúzbᵘan!, -b(w)an!, -b(w)ā!, -b(w)á!).
 X. tăgak⌣kúzbá⌒ *have the window (let the window be) open*.
 Y. aī⌣kúzbwandi⌒ *I will* (§ 5369 b).
kúz-dɛn (§§ 3996-7) v.t. *open to or for (the speaker)*.
 kåg⌣āıgı⌣kúzdɛndan⌒ *they open the door (lit. house) to (for) me*.
 kåg⌣āıgı⌣kuzdɛŋkoran⌒ *they opened the door to (for) me*.
kus(¹)r-eg-åg- (§§ 4071 ff.) v.t. and i. = kusɛdól-.
kus-ɛ-dól- (-s°d- § 1178; § 4022) and
kus(¹)r-ɛ-dól- (-r°d-; § 4027) v.t. and i. *be about to open, etc.*
kus(¹)r-ɛ-gŭ-bŭ- (§ 4069) v.t. stat. *be on one's way (coming) to open, etc.*
kus-ɛ-má- (§ 4036) and
kus-ɛ-mǎ- (§ 4041) v.t. *become unable to open, etc.*
kus(¹)r-ɛ-nóg (§§ 4048 ff.) v.t. *go to open, etc.*
kus(¹)r-ɛ-nóg-bŭ- (-nóggŭ- § 546; § 4058) v.t. stat. *be on one's way (going) to open, etc.*
kus(¹)r-ɛ-tá (§§ 4060 ff.) v.t. *come to open, etc.*
kusɛd-åg- (§§ 3877 ff.) v.t. *be in the situation of having opened, etc.*
 ál⌣dukkáŋgı⌣kusɛdágın⌒ *ɣáli has opened a shop*.
kus-ǧerrıbé (-rubé; § 3747ᵉ') v.t. *try to open, etc.*
kusíŋ-ır (*⌢⌢, N. -ŋkır; § 3688) v.t. caus. *cause or allow to open, etc.*
kús-kattı- (§ 4093) (a) v.p. *be opened, etc.;* (b) v.i. *be susceptible of being opened, etc.* (§§ 5704-5).
 bústam⌣máktáb⌣élgoŋ⌣kuskattıǧómunun⌒ *the post-office was not (has not been) opened yet*.

kuskáttɪ-bŭ- (§4105) v.i. stat. *be in an opened (etc.) state or condition.*
  X. álɪs⌣sandúkkɪ⌣kúsá↷ (-s⌣- < -g⌣s- §678) *let ɛáli open the box.*
  Y. kuskáttɪbūn↷ *it's opened.*

kus-múg (§3747ᵋ′) v.t. *leave after opening, etc., leave open, leave loose, leave unfastened, etc.*
  imperat. kusmúk!

kusmugíŋg-ɪr (N. -ŋkɪr; §4212) v.t. caus. *cause or allow to leave after opening, etc.*
  ennûrkɪ⌣tókkoŋ⌣kobídkɪ⌣kusmugɪŋgírmen↷ *don't let En-Núr leave the gate (door) open.*

kusos-tő (-ottő §714; §§4180-4; -osgɪtő, -ozgɪ-, -oggɪ- §4185) v.t. *enter after opening, etc.*
  imperat. kusostó! (-ottó!, -osgɪtó!, -ozgɪ-, -oggɪ-) and kusósto! (-ótto!, -ósgɪto!, -ózgɪ-, -óggɪ-).
  kobídkɪ⌣kusoggɪtógoran↷ *they (have) opened the door and entered.*

kus-šeŋkɪlέ (kuššɛn-; §3747ᵋ′) v.t. *after opening fasten with a hook, hook open.*

kuššeŋkɪlέr-an (kuššɛn-; §§3890ff., 3905) v.t. *tell to hook open, let hook open.*

kus-tέb (§3747ᵋ′) v.i. *stand (etc. s.v. tέb) open.*
  kóbɪd⌣kustέbɪn↷ *the door stands (remains) open.*

kustέb-an (§§3890ff., 3905) v.t. *let stand (etc.) open.*
  kobíttɪ⌣kustέbă↷ *let the door stand open.*

kustēbíŋg-ɪr (´⌣˘; N. -ŋkɪr; §4212) v.t. caus. *cause or allow to stand (etc.) open, keep open, leave open.*
  bábkɪ⌣kustēbɪŋgɪr↷ *keep the door open.*
  bábkɪ⌣kustēbɪŋgíddan↷ *they keep the door open.*
  kobíttɪ⌣tókkŏ⌣kustēbɪŋgírmέ, dímē⌣kóbbă↷ (§§939, 979) *don't let the door remain (don't keep, leave the door) open; it is always to be shut.*

kustēbíŋgɪr-an (´⌣˘; N. -ŋkɪr-; §§3890ff., 3905) v.t. *tell to keep open, etc., let keep open, etc.*
  álɪb⌣bábkɪ⌣kustēbɪŋgɪran↷ (-b⌣b- < -g⌣b- §519) *tell ɛáli to keep the door open.*

kús-tɪr (§§3998-9) v.t. *open to or for (other than the speaker).*
  kǎg⌣ɛkkɪ⌣bɪkústɪddan↷ *they will open the door to (for) you.*

kŭs n. *mug, large cup* = kŭz⌣ [<كوز id. §1300].
  obj. kúsk(ɪ)⌣, -ki↷.
  pl. kúsɪ⌣.
  έssɪŋ⌣kúsun↷ (§4685) (a) *it's the (a) mug of water;* (b) *it's the (a) mug for water.*
  kúsn⌣í⌣ *handle of mug.*

kússa⌣ (α) adj. (a) *weak, feeble,* (b) *lazy, idle, slack, indolent,* (c) *stupid,* (d) *effeminate;* (β) n. *sodomite.*
  obj. -sag⌣.
  pl. -sanč(ɪ)⌣ and -sarɪ⌣.
  bánnɪdɪr⌣kússan↷ *(s)he is a poor speaker.*

kúss-an- (§3910α) v.i. *grow weak, etc., become weak, etc., weaken.*

kússam-bŭ- (§§3949ff.) v.i. stat. *be in a weakening (etc., weakened) state or condition.*

kussanɛd-ág- (§3966α) v.i. *be in a weakened (etc.) state or condition.*

kússɛ! < **kúswɛ!** *open! (pl.),* etc. s.v. kús.

kúsu n. *flesh, meat* [§§2337-8; SMN, p. 452 s.v. ⲣⲁⲝ].
  obj. -sug⌣.
  pl. -sunč(ɪ)⌣.
  nέln⌣kúsu⌣ and
  nέl-kúsu⌣ (§809) (gum(s §4696a) = gírgɪd⌣.
  kús⌣ɛgεnd(ɪ)⌣ *mutton.*
  kúsu⌣gúmd(ɪ)⌣ and kúsu⌣tínd(ɪ)⌣ *beef.*
  kúsug⌣áu↷ *cook the meat.*
  kúsuk⌣kúğur↷ *put the meat on (sc. the fire).*

kusún-d(ɪ)⌣ (§§2545 ff.) adj. *appertaining to (the) flesh, etc., carnal.*

kúšar⌣ (-šăr⌣, -šɛr⌣) *key* s.v. kús.

kuštέna⌣ n. *playing-card(s), card(s);* with collective sg. (§4696d) [< Sudan Ar. كُشْتينة, كُشْتِينَة id. (§900)? < káčč(ɪ) play].
  obj. -nag⌣.
  pl. -nanč(ɪ)⌣.
  kuštέnak⌣káččɪn↷ *(s)he plays cards.*
  tέn⌣dúŋgɪk⌣kuštέnar⌣dábɪrɪn↷ *(s)he loses his (her) money at cards.*

kuttáb⌣ n. *primary school* [<كِتَاب id.].
  obj. -ábk(ɪ)⌣, -ápk(ɪ)⌣, -ki↷.
  gen. -ábn⌣v., -ám⌣c.
  pl. -ábɪ⌣.

kútte v.i. *descend* [< *kúdkɛ (§716) < √kúd- descend (§4554)+-k obj. suff.+-ɛ say §2870].
  ind. pres. aî⌣kúttɛrɪ↷; perf. aî⌣kúttɛgorɪ↷ (N. -ɛko-, -ɛho-).
  imperat. kútte!, pl. kúttɛwɛ! (-wέ!).
  def. perf. aî⌣kuttóskorɪ↷ and aî⌣kuttɛróskorɪ↷.
  ɛr⌣bukúttɛná? *shall you go (are you going to come) down?*

kúttɛr-an (§§3890ff., 3899) v.t. *tell to descend, let descend.*

kúttɛg-ɪr (N. -ɛkɪr, -ɛhɪr; §3679) (a) v.t. caus. *cause or allow to descend;* (b) v.t. *lower, bring down, let down;* (c) v.t. *unload (animal), unsaddle.*
  imperat. kúttɛgɪr! (kúttégɪr! §1532); pl. kúttɛgɪrwe! (kúttég-, -wέ!).
  hánuk⌣kuttɛgírkoran↷ *they took (have taken) the saddle (load) off the donkey.*

kúttɛgɪr-an (N. -ɛkɪr-, -ɛhɪr-; §§3890ff., 3904) v.t. *tell to lower, etc., let lower, etc.*
  káčkɪ⌣kúttɛgɪran↷ *tell him to unsaddle the horse.*

kútt(ɪ)⌣ n. (a) *mound, knoll;* (b) *high land, elevated ground* [< *kúdt⌣ (§706) < √kúd- rise (§4554)+-t dem. (§2325β); cp. ON. ⲕⲟϯⲧ *stand up* GNT s.v.].
  obj. -tɪg⌣.
  pl. -tɪnč(ɪ)⌣.
  tínn⌣árɪd⌣kúttɪn↷ *their land is high.*
  kúttɪn⌣dɛgíd⌣dúllon↷ *the irrigation of high land is difficult.*

kŭz⌣ (kŭs⌣) n. *mug, large cup* [<كوز id. §1300].
  obj. kŭzk(ɪ)⌣, kúsk(ɪ)⌣, -ki↷.
  pl. kŭzɪ⌣.
  έssɪŋ⌣kŭzun↷ *it's the (a) mug of (for §4685) water.*
  kŭzn⌣í⌣ *handle of mug.*

kŭzbŭ- *be open, etc.* s.v. kús.

kŭzdɛn *open to (the speaker)* s.v. kús.

lákɪn (§956a) conj. *but* [<لٰكِن id.].
  aî⌣tέkkɪ⌣nalkómunun, lákɪn⌣tέn⌣haddámgɪ⌣nálkorɪ↷ *I did not see him (her), but I saw his (her) servant.*

†lámba (-bă⌣) n. *lamp* [<لَمْبَة id < Eur.].
  obj. -bag⌣, -bág⌣.
  pl. -banč(ɪ)⌣, -bánč(ɪ)⌣, -bɛnč(ɪ)⌣ lámban⌣í⌣ *handle of lamp.*

lázɪm adj. *necessary* [<لازم id.].
  obj. lázɪmg(ɪ)⌣, -gi↷.
  pl. lázɪmɪ⌣.
  tέkkɪ⌣lázɪm⌣tɛbέl↷ (§6268) *you must search for him (her, it) till you find him (her, it).*

-lέ? *after* -l = -rέ?

lēmún (§956a) n. *lime, Citrus medica,* Linn. (BSP, 84); with collective sg. (§4696b) [<لَيْمُون id.].
  obj. -úŋg(ɪ)⌣, -gi↷.
  pl. -únɪ⌣.

líf n. *loofah, Luffa aegyptiaca, Miller* (BSP, 204) [<ليف id.].
  obj. lífk(ɪ)⌣, -ki↷.

lɪğám n. *bridle, bit* [<لِجَام id.].
  obj. -ămg(ɪ)⌣, -gi↷.
  pl. -ámɪ⌣.

-lo postp. *on, in, at, to, etc.* s.v. -r⌣.

†lokánda⌣ n. *inn, hotel* [<لُوكَنْدَة id. < It. locanda].
  obj. -dag⌣.
  pl. -danč(ɪ)⌣.

lón (§956a) n. *colour* [<لَوْن id.].
  obj. lóŋg(ɪ)⌣, -gi↷.
  pl. lónɪ⌣.

lóti⌣ *sodomite* = lúti⌣.

-lo-tŏn⌣ postp. *from, of* s.v. -r-tŏn⌣.

lúti⌣ (lótɪ⌣) n. *sodomite* [<لُوطِيّ id.].
  obj. -tɪg⌣.
  pl. -tɪnč(ɪ)⌣.

luzúm⌣ n. *necessity, need* [<لُزُوم id.].
  obj. -zŭmg(ɪ)⌣, -gi↷.
  ál⌣luzúm (-l⌣l- < -n⌣l- §581) *my (our) need.*
  tέl⌣luzúm⌣dán↷ *(s)he (it) is needed, lit. there is need of him (her, it).*
  ínɪl⌣luzúm⌣dáná? *is this necessary?*
  íl⌣luzúm⌣dógor⌣dúlun↷ (-m⌣d- < -mn⌣d- §817) *this is larger than necessary, lit. this is large above need.*
  aî⌣tέbrɪl⌣luzúm⌣dámunun↷ (-l⌣l- < -n⌣l- §581) *there is no need for me to stay (§6156).*

luzúm-kɪ́nn(ɪ)⌣ (§§2536-7) adj. *unnecessary, needless.*

luzúmkɪnnɪ́g-ɪr (¯⌣´⌣; N. -ɪkɪr, -ɪhɪr; §3703) v.t. caus. *render unnecessary;* in composition (§4137) *act unnecessarily.*

luzŭmkɪññɪgɪr-ābbód- (N. -ɪkɪr-, -ɪhɪr-; §5635) v.i. *be engaged in running (etc. s.v.* ābbód-) *unnecessarily.*
ɛr⌣luzŭmkɪññɪgɪrābbódɪn⌢ *you are (keep on) running unnecessarily.*

luzŭmkɪññɪgɪr-agŭkkɪ- (N. -ɪkɪr-,-ɪhɪr-; §5635) v.i. *be engaged in barking (etc. s.v.* āgŭkkɪ-) *unnecessarily.*
wélɪ⌣luzŭmkɪññɪgɪragŭkkɪran⌢ *the dogs are barking (constantly bark) unnecessarily.*
éw⌣wélɪ⌣luzŭmkɪññɪgɪragŭkkó⌢(-w⌣w- <-n⌣w- §720) *your dog was barking (constantly barked) unnecessarily.*

luzŭmkɪññɪgɪr-ăğğáŋgɪ- (N. -ɪkɪr-, -ɪhɪr-; §5635) v.t. *be engaged in filling (etc. s.v.* ăğğáŋgɪ-) *unnecessarily.*

luzŭmkɪññɪgɪr-āwwíg- (N. -ɪkɪr-, -ɪhɪr-; §5635) v.i. *be engaged in crying (etc. s.v.* āwwíg-) *unnecessarily.*
bɪtăn⌣luzŭmkɪññɪgɪrāwwígɪn⌢ *the child is (keeps on) howling needlessly (for no reason).*

-má⌢, -mă⌢ *that (yonder) s.v.* mán⌣.

mă- (§§3533, 3558, 3827) (a) v.i. *get tired, grow weary;* (b) v.i. *get bored, get afflicted by ennui;* (c) v.i. *get tired out, get exhausted;* (d) v.t. *become unable to, fail to* [< m- negative (§4561)+ăʾ *heart, so* *not (sc. have) *the heart* §2847].
ind. pres. āɪ⌣márɪ⌢, ɛr⌣mán⌢ (⌣mă⌢, ⌣máᵃ⌢ §337, ⌣mă⌢ §942); fut. āɪ⌣bɪmárɪ⌢ (⌣bum-); perf. āɪ⌣mágorɪ⌢ (N. ⌣máko-, ⌣máho-).
subj. past āɪ⌣másɪ⌣ (-su⌣).
part. pres. măl⌣ *(one) that gets tired, etc.*
part. past márɛl⌣ *(one) that got tired, etc.*
def. perf. āɪ⌣máróskorɪ⌢ *I am exhausted.*
— constructed with (a) infinitive (§§2961–3) +-do⌣ (s.v. -r⌣); (b) infinitive in objective case.

-ɛ-má- in complex (§§4035ff.) *become unable to.*
āɪ⌣nógrándo⌣mágorɪ⌢ (a) *I was too tired to go;* (b) *I failed to go, I couldn't go, lit. I at (-do⌣) going (⌣nógran-) was tired, etc.*
tāráŋgɪ⌣mágorɪ⌢, tărándo⌣mágorɪ⌢ and tărɛmágorɪ⌢ *I couldn't (became (have become) unable to, can't) come.*
ar⌣tāráŋgɪ⌣mágoru⌢, ar⌣tărándo⌣mágoru⌢ and ar⌣tărɛmágoru⌣ *we couldn't (can't) come.*
hán⌣iŋg⌣ɛğğŭráŋgɪ⌣măn⌢, hán⌣iŋg⌣ɛğğŭrándo⌣măn⌢ and hán⌣iŋg⌣ɛğğɛmán⌢ (s.v. éd) *the (a) donkey (becomes unable to, i.e.) cannot carry this.*
ín⌣hánu⌣kógorun, lákɪn⌣iŋg⌣ɛğğŭráŋgɪ⌣măn⌢ *this (that) donkey is strong, but it cannot carry this (that).*
ín⌣hán⌣āɪg⌣ɛğğŭrándo⌣măn⌢[1] *this (that) donkey is unable to carry me.*

---

[1] Reinisch (*RN*, §279 and s.v. *méu*) no doubt heard and wrote *măn, măn,* that subsequently he (or his printer) misread *meum, méun.*

márar⌣ (-rár⌣; §§2200ff., 2207) and
māríd⌣ (§§2256ff., 2260) n. *weariness, exhaustion, inability.*

mă-bŭ- (§3931α) v.i. stat. *be in a tired (etc.) state or condition.*
part. pres. măbŭl⌣ *(one) that is in a tired (etc.) state, tired, etc.*

măr-ɛ-ăg- (§§4071ff.) v.i. = mārɛdól-.

măr-ɛ-dól- (-rᵒd- §1178; §§4016–17, 4022, 4027) v.i. *be about to get tired, etc.*
mărɛdóllan⌢ *they are nearly exhausted.*

măg-ɪr (S. and N. §3686) (a) v.t. caus. *cause or allow to get tired, etc.;* (b) v.t. *tire, weary;* (c) v.t. *bore;* (d) v.t. *annoy, worry, vex, tease;* (e) v.t. *tire out, exhaust.*
ind. pres. āɪ⌣mágɪddɪ⌢; perf. āɪ⌣mágɪrkorɪ⌢.
kúlt⌣āɪg⌣mágɪrɪn⌢ *the flies* (§4696c) *worry me.*
ɛr⌣gɪrítkɪ⌣mágɪrkɪn⌣ékkɪ⌣báččɪn⌢ *if you tease the monkey it will bite you.*

măgɪrɛd-ăg- (§§3877ff., 3885) v.t. *be in the situation (attitude) of causing or allowing (or having caused or allowed) to be tired, etc.*
jóm⌣dɪgríg⌣árgɪ⌣măgɪrɛdákkó⌢ *(s)he (it) was (has been) annoying us for many days.*

maad(d)íjɛ⌣ *ferry, etc.* = mādíjɛ⌣.

mabsúd- (-út⌣ §1399) adj. *pleased, content, happy* [< مبسوط *id.*].
obj. -údk(ɪ)⌣, -útk(ɪ)⌣, -útt(ɪ)⌣ §2462, -kɪ⌢, -tɪ⌢.
pl. -údɪ⌣, -útɪ⌣.
tɛr⌣mabsúdun⌣ (-útun⌢ §1399) *(s)he (it) is pleased.*
āɪ⌣tíddotōm⌣mabsúd⌣érɪ⌣ *I am pleased with them.*

mabsúd-an- (§3910α) v.i. *become pleased, etc.*

mabsút-an- (§1399) v.i. = mabsúdan-.

mādíjɛ⌣ (māddí-, maadí-, maaddí-) n. (a) *ferry;* (b) *ferry-boat* [< معدية *id.*].
obj. -jɛg⌣.
pl. -jɛnč(ɪ)⌣.
mādíjɛ⌣ísáɪgɛt⌣tɛ́bɪn? *where does the ferry-boat wait? (where is the ferry-boat stationed?).*

măg v.t. (a) *take wrongfully, steal, rob* (stehlen); (b) *take wrongfully from, steal from, rob of* (bestehlen) [perhaps < neg. m- (§4561)+ ăg *be present, quasi* *not (sc. let) *be present, *away with* §2848; *RSN,* §§129, 200].
ind. pres. āɪ⌣măg(¹)rɪ⌢, ɛr⌣mágɪn⌢ (-gíʾ⌣, -gíʾ); perf. āɪ⌣mágkorɪ⌢ (⌣mákkorɪ⌣).
imperat. mák!
subj. past āɪ⌣mágsɪ⌣ (⌣máksɪ⌣, -su⌣).
part. pres. mágɪl⌣, obj. mágɪlg(ɪ)⌣, -gɪ⌢ *(one) that steals, etc., robber, thief, robbing, stealing;* past mágɛl⌣, obj. măgɛlg(ɪ)⌣, -gɪ⌢ *(one) that stole, etc., robber, thief, robbing, stealing.*
neg. imperat. tókkom⌣mágmɛn⌢ (-mé⌢, -mé⌢) and S. dókkom⌣mánnɛn⌢ (§661).
def. perf. āɪ⌣mágédkorɪ⌢ (-étk-) and āɪ⌣mágóskorɪ⌢.
án⌣dúŋgɪm⌣mágkó⌢ (-m⌣m- <-g⌣m- §601) *(s)he stole (has stolen) my (our) money.*

āɪg⌣mákkorā⌢ *they (have) robbed me.*
ánnartōn⌣án⌣dúŋgɪm⌣mágkoran⌢ *they stole (have stolen) my money from me (...our money from us).*
āɪg⌣án⌣dúŋgɪm⌣mágkoran⌢ *they (have) robbed me of my money.*

mágar⌣ (-gár⌣; §§2200ff.) and
māgíd⌣ (§§2256ff.) n. *theft, robbery.*

mágas⌣ (mágás⌣ §2060) n. *thief, robber* [§2220].
obj. magásk(ɪ)⌣, -kɪ⌢.
pl. mágasɪ⌣.

măg-kátt(ɪ)⌣ (măkkát-) adj. *given to stealing, etc., thievish* [§2534–5].
obj. -tɪg⌣.
pl. -tɪnč(ɪ)⌣.

mág-an (§§3890ff.) v.t. *tell to steal, etc., let steal, etc.*

mág-bŭ- (măggŭ- §546; §3931β) v.i. stat. *be in a stolen (etc.) state or condition.*
dúŋgɪ⌣măgbún⌢ *the money is (has been) stolen.*
āɪ⌣mágguɪɪ⌢ *I have been robbed.*

măg(¹)r-ɛg-ăg- (§§4071ff.) v.t. = mágɛdól-.

mág-ɛ-dól- (-gᵒd- §1178; §4022) and
măg(¹)r-ɛ-dól- (-rᵒd-; §4027) v.t. *be about to steal, etc.*

măg(¹)r-ɛ-gŭ-bŭ- (§4069) v.t. stat. *be on one's way (coming) to steal, etc.*

măg-ɛ-má- (§4036) and
măg(¹)r-ɛ-má- (§4041) v.t. *become unable to steal, etc.*

măg(¹)r-ɛ-nóg (§4048ff.) v.t. *go to steal, etc.*

măg(¹)r-ɛ-nóg-bŭ- (-nóggŭ- §546; §4058) v.t. stat. *be on one's way (going) to steal, etc.*

măg(¹)r-ɛ-tá (§§4060ff.) v.t. *come to steal, etc.*

măgɛd-ăg- (§§3877ff.) v.t. *be in the situation of having stolen, etc.*
dúŋgɪ⌣dɪgrím⌣mágɛdágran⌢ (-m⌣m- <-g⌣m- §601) *they have stolen much money.*
āɪg⌣dɪgrím⌣mágɛdágran⌢ *they have robbed me (of) a great deal.*

măgɛb-bód (§518; §§4169ff.; -gɛggɪbód §§4176–8) v.t. *run (away) after stealing, etc.*
dúŋgɪm⌣mágɛbbótkó⌢ *after stealing the money he (s)he ran away.*

măgɛd-dáb (§§4169ff.; -gɛggɪdáb §§4176–8) v.t. *disappear after stealing, etc.*
dúŋgɪm⌣mágɛddápkoran⌢ (-m⌣m- <-g⌣m- §601) *after stealing the money they disappeared.*

măg-kattɪ- (măkka-; §4093) v.p. *be stolen, etc.*
dúŋgɪ⌣măgkattɪgon⌢ *the money was (has been) stolen.*
āɪ⌣mágkattɪgorɪ⌢ *I was (have been) robbed.*

mágkattar⌣ (măkka-, -tár⌣; §§2200ff., 2213) and
măgkattíd⌣ (măkka-; §§2256ff., 2266) n. *being stolen, etc.*

mágos-nóg (-onnóg §629; §§4180–4; -osgɪnóg, -ozgɪ-, -oggɪ- §4185) v.t. *go (away) after stealing, etc.*
dúŋgɪm⌣măgonnogóskoran⌢ (-m⌣m- <-g⌣m- §601) *they have stolen the money and gone.*

mágal⌣ — málˈt(ı)⌣

mágal⌣ n. *Mágal, a village on the right bank of the Nile, about 13 miles above Kórti.*
 obj. magálg(ı)⌣, -gi⌢.
 magállo⌣ (s.v. -r⌣) *at (to) Mágal.*
 magállo⌢ *(s)he (it) is (they are) at Mágal.*
magásır⌣ n. *Magassir (on map), an island just south of Argo Island* [? < مَقَصَّر *Shortened* (§ 1380)].
 obj. magāsírk(ı)⌣, -ki⌢.
magáuda⌣ n. *Megauda (on map), a village on the right bank of the Nile, about eight miles below Old Dóngola.*
 obj. -gáudag⌣, -gaudág⌣ (§ 1538).
mággŭ- < **mágbŭ-** *be stolen, etc.* s.v. mág.
maggŭr⌣ n. *Magjur (on map), a small island four miles below Kérma* [? < مأجور *Hired*].
 obj. -ǧŭrk(ı)⌣, -ki⌢.
māgisse⌣ n. *a small herb, one of the Cyperaceae, (?) Fimbristylis dichostoma, Vahl.* (*BSP*, 631) REM.
 obj. -seg⌣.
maglúb⌣ *defeated, etc.* = mɛglúb⌣.
maháda⌣ < **makáda⌣** *maize.*
maháddā⌣ *cushion, etc.* = máhádda⌣.
máhal⌣ n. *famine* [< Sudan Ar. مَحَل *id.* § 1357].
 obj. mahálg(ı)⌣, -gi⌢.
 pl. máhalı⌣.
 ím⌣bɛlɛd⌣máhalun⌢ *this district is famine-stricken* (§ 4719).
maháll(ı)⌣ n. *place* = máháll(ı)⌣.
máhar⌣ n. *price of bride*, paid by bridegroom to her parents [< Sudan Ar. مَهْر *id.* < مَهْر *dowry*].
 obj. mahárk(ı)⌣, -ki⌢.
 pl. máharı⌣.
 ógıǧ⌣mahárk⌣āgéttān⌢ *the husband always brings the bride-price.*
mahátta⌣ n. *station* = máhátta⌣.
máhdı⌣ n. *the Máhdi* (= méhɛdı⌣) [< مَهْدِيّ *Guided* § 1389].
 obj. -dıg⌣.
mahdín-d(ı)⌣ (§§ 2545 ff.) adj. *appertaining to the Máhdi, Máhdist.*
mahdíjɛ⌣ (-jă⌣, -ja⌣) n. *time of the Máhdi* [< مَهْدِيَّة *id.*].
 obj. -jeg⌣.
mahíjɛ⌣ (-jă⌣, -ja⌣) n. *pay, salary, wage(s)* [< مَاهِيَّة *id.*].
 obj. -jeg⌣.
 pl. -jɛnč(ı)⌣.
 ém⌣mahíja⌣mukóttɛ́rɛ́⌢ *how much is your pay?*
mahíjɛ-kıññ(ı)⌣ (-jăk-, -jak-; §§ 2536-7) adj. *without pay, etc., unpaid.*
mahíjɛkıññıg-ır (-⌣-⌣-, N. -ıkır, -ıhır; § 3703) (a) v.t. caus. *cause or allow to be without pay, etc.*; (b) v.t. *deprive of pay, keep or leave unpaid.*
 āıg⌣mahíjakıññıgírkoran⌢ *they gave (have given) me no wages.*
 āıg⌣ám⌣mahíjak⌣kıññıgírkoran⌢ and
 āıg⌣àmmahìjakıññıgírkoran⌢ (§ 5708) *they (have) deprived me of my pay (they did not pay (have not paid) me my wages).*

mahkáma⌣ (§ 1575; máhkama⌣; măh-, -ká-, -mă⌣) n. *tribunal, court of law* [< مَحْكَمَة *id.*].
 obj. -mag⌣, -mág⌣.
 pl. -manč(ı)⌣, -mănč(ı)⌣, -mɛnč(ı)⌣.
mahkamán-d(ı)⌣ (§§ 2545 ff.) adj. *appertaining to a tribunal, etc.*
mahlán⌣ (§ 956 a) adj. *famished* [< Sudan Ar. مَحْلَان *id.*].
 obj. -ăng(ı)⌣, -gi⌢.
 pl. -ănı⌣.
 ín⌣ógıǧ⌣mahlánun⌢ *this (that) man is famished.*
máhzan⌣ (măxz-; § 956 a) n. *store, storeroom* [< مَخْزَن *id.*].
 obj. mahzáng(ı)⌣, -gi⌢.
 pl. máhzanı⌣.
 mahzándo⌣ (s.v. -r⌣) *in (into, to) the store.*
 mahzándo⌢ (§ 5858) *(s)he (it) is (they are) in the store.*
maín⌣ (§ 956 d) n. *left hand* [< ma- neg. (RSN, § 39) + ín⌣ *right hand* § 2171].
 obj. maíng(ı)⌣, -gi⌢.
 gen. maínn⌣v.
 ém⌣maínged⌣áu⌢ *do it with your left hand.*
 ém⌣maínged⌣ár⌢ *hold him (her, it) with your left hand.*
 ém⌣maínn⌣óssıs⌣sókkɛ⌢ (-s⌣s- < -g⌣s- § 678) *raise your left leg.*
 X. tır⌣sé? *where are they?*
 Y. ém⌣maínged⌢ (§ 966) *on your left.*
 maíngaddı⌣kálli⌢ *push him (her, it, them) towards the left.*
 maíngen⌣nókkoran⌢ (-n⌣n- < -d⌣n- § 624) *they went (have gone) to the left.*
maín-d(ı)⌣ (§§ 2545 ff.) adj. *appertaining to the left hand, left-hand.*
mák! imperat. of mág *steal.*
makáda⌣ (mahá- § 1027) n. *maize, Indian corn, Zea mays, L.* [< Sudan Ar. مَكَادَة *id.*].
 obj. -dag⌣.
 makádan⌣hágɛ⌣ *maize-stalk(s* § 4696 b).
mákwa⌣ (mák-) n. (a) *iron (for smoothing linen)* [< مَكْوَى *id.*]; (b) *place for ironing, laundry.*
 obj. -wag⌣.
 pl. -wanč(ı)⌣.
 ɛsmám⌣mákwak⌣kusɛdágın⌢ ɛoθmán *has opened a laundry.*
málága⌣ (-laga⌣) n. *spoon* [< مَعْلَقَة = مِلْعَقَة *id.*].
 obj. -lágág⌣, -lagag⌣.
 pl. -lágánč(ı)⌣, -gen-, -laganč(ı)⌣.
 málágan⌣í⌣ *handle of spoon.*
málɛ́š! interj. (a, *disregarding, overlooking*) *it doesn't matter, never mind, don't trouble about it, don't mention it;* (b, *apologizing*) *I beg your pardon, excuse me* [< ما عليش *id.*].
 X. (having involuntarily collided with Y.) málɛ́š!, āıı⌣ékki⌣nalkómunun⌢ *I beg your pardon, I didn't see you.*
 Y. málɛ́š! *don't mention it.*
málle⌣ (α) quantitative adj. *all*; (β) generic and distributive pronominal adj. *all,*

every; (γ, used as) indef. pron. *everyone, everybody, everything, the whole* [cp. ON. ⲘⲀⲖⲖⲈ *id.* GNT s.v.], §§ 4949-52.
 obj. -leg⌣.
 pl. -lɛnč(ı)⌣.
—pl. seldom heard except in a pronoun-complex (§ 5197):
 tır⌣mállɛnčı⌣tóran⌢ *they all enter* (= *every single one of them enters*).
 tır⌣málle⌣kă⌣wɛrro⌣tóran⌢ *they all (the whole lot of them) go into one house.*
 tér⌣mállɛk⌣kálkoran⌢ *they ate (have eaten) it all.*
 ír⌣mállɛb⌣bángısın⌢ (-b⌣b- < -g⌣b- § 519) *(s)he (it) will wake you all up.*
 sór⌣ár⌣mállɛm⌣bélɛdun⌢ (-m⌣b- < -n⌣b- § 592) *Sór is the village of all of us.*
 sǎb⌣kúsu⌣mállɛk⌣kalóskó⌢ *the cat has eaten up all the meat.*
 íngı⌣mállɛ⌣úñurın⌢ (§ 4626) and
 máll⌣íng⌣úñurın⌢ *everybody knows this (one).*
 ınnówwım⌣mállɛb⌣béttārı⌢ (-m⌣m- < -g⌣m- § 601, -b⌣b- < -g⌣b- § 519) *to-day I shall bring it all.*
 béndıgı⌣mállɛm⌣mínč⌣árın⌢ (-m⌣m- < -g⌣m- § 601) *every beggar is (all beggars are) hungry.*
 nahár⌣mállɛ⌣ (náh-, nɛh-) and
 ugrés⌣málle⌣ noun-complex (a) *all day, the whole day;* (b) *every day.*
 nahár⌣mállɛg, -gi⌢ adverb-complex (§ 6038) (a) *all day, the whole day;* (b) *every day.*
 ınnówwı⌣nahár⌣mállɛg⌣āgkó⌢ (§ 6042) *(s)he (it) has remained (s.v. āg) the whole of to-day.*
 nahár⌣mállɛg⌣āttāran⌢ and
 nahár⌣mállɛt⌣tăran⌢ (-t⌣t- < -g⌣t- § 707) *they come every day.*
 úgu⌣málle⌣ noun-complex (a) *all night, the whole night;* (b) *every night.*
 úgu⌣mállɛg, -gi⌢ adverb-complex (a) *all night, the whole night;* (b) *every night.*
 úgu⌣mállɛg⌣ākkorı⌢ and
 úgu⌣mállɛt⌣tékkorı⌢ (-t⌣t- < -g⌣t- § 707) *I (have) waited all night.*
 úgu⌣mállɛg⌣āttārı⌢ and
 úgu⌣mállɛt⌣tărı⌢ *I come every night.*
 kă⌣mállɛr⌣wēwɛg⌣úskur⌢ (§ 5187) *put one in each house.*
 án⌣dúngı⌣mállɛ-taran⌢ *my money has run out* (…*is finished, mein Geld ist alle*).
 šăı⌣mállɛ⌣té? *is the tea done with (finished)?*
 X. ím⌣mállɛ⌣té? (a) *is this all?;* (b) *is this at an end? (is this done with)?*.
 Y. éjjo, mállɛ-tánnan⌢ *yes, it is.*
mallén-d(ı)⌣ (§§ 2545 ff.) adj. *appertaining to all, etc., of all, etc.*
málˈt(ı)⌣ n. (a) *east*; (b) *right bank of the Nile* [< *más(ı)lt(ı)⌣ *place of the sun* § 2326; RSN, § 129 al.].
 obj. máltıg⌣.
 máltır⌣ (s.v. -r⌣) *in (to) the east, on (to) the right bank.*
 máltır⌢ (§ 5858) *(s)he (it) is (they are) in the east, on the right bank.*
 máltır⌣āgran⌢ *they live (etc. s.v. āg) in the east (…on the right bank).*

tɛŋ‿kǎ‿máltır⁀ *his (her) house is on the right bank.*
máltır‿nóguru⁀ *we (you pl.) go to the east (...to the right bank).*
máltírtōn‿tăgoran⁀ *they came (have come) from the east (...from the right bank).*
máltıg-ɛd‿ (-ɛt⁀, -ɛ́⁀ §966; §6007; s.v. -ɛd‿) *adv. on the east, by the eastern route, on (by) the right bank.*
máltıgen‿nókkoran⁀ (-n‿n- < -d‿n- §624) *they went (have gone) by the eastern route (...by the right bank).*
dúŋgula‿máltıgé⁀ *Old Dóngola is on the right bank.*
maltín-d(ı)‿ (§§ 2545 ff.) *adj. eastern, of the right bank.*
málˈt-an- (§§ 3910 ff.) *v.i. (a) go to the east; (b) become (part of) the right bank.*
ártı‿máltaŋkó⁀ *the island became (has become) part of the right bank.*
maltıgeb-bél (§ 4127) *v.i. issue (sc. from river, boat) on the right bank.*
imperat. maltıgebbél! and maltıgébbɛl! (§ 1871).
úrum‿múkkıgı‿maltıgébbɛl⁀ (-m‿m- < -g‿m- § 601) *crossing the river get out on the right bank;* ‿múkkıgı‿ § 5583.
maltıgebbél-an (§§ 3890 ff., 3905) *v.t. tell to issue on the right bank, let issue on the right bank.*
maltıgen-nóg (§ 4127) *v.i. go by the eastern route, by the right bank.*
imperat. maltıgennók! and maltıgénnok!
maltıgennókkoran⁀ = máltıgen‿nókkoran⁀ (*supra*).
maltıgennóg-an (§§ 3890 ff., 3905) *v.t. tell to go by the eastern route, etc., let go by the eastern route, etc.*
maltıgır-nóg (N. -ıkır-, -ıhır-; § 4139) *v.i. go eastwards, go to the right bank.*
N. maltıkırnókkoran⁀ *they went (have gone) eastwards (...to the right bank).*
maltıgırnóg-an (N. -ıkır, -ıhır-; §§ 3890 ff., 3905) *v.t. tell to go eastwards, tell to go to the right bank, let go eastwards, let go to the right bank.*
mált(ı)‿ *n. runnel, irrigation channel for water brought up by water-wheel* (kólɛ‿) [§ 2329].
obj. -tıg‿.
pl. -tınč(ı)‿.
máltin‿ónd(ı)‿ *main runnel,* جَدْوَل ذَكَر.
maltín-d(ı)‿ (§§ 2545 ff.) *adj. appertaining to the (a) runnel.*
mālúm‿ and " *adv. of course* [< مَعْلُوم id.].
X. símgı‿góllıgó⁀ *(s)he (it) swallowed (the) poison.*
Y. dígoná? *did (s)he (it) die?*
X. mālúm‿dígo⁀ *of course (s)he (it) died.*
málwa‿ *n. measure of capacity of 4⅛ litres =* ⅛ kɛ́la‿ [< مَلْوَة id.].
obj. -wag‿.
pl. -wanč(ı)‿.
kɛ́la‿wɛr‿málw‿ídıwun‿ *one kɛ́la‿ is eight málwa‿.*
ɛrdébır‿málwa‿tısaıŋgórıǧ‿dábun‿ *there are 96 málwa‿ in an ardébb.*

mǎman‿ (§§ 956d, 2644-5) *dem. pron. those (distant or absent), yonder; collective* (§§ 5125-6) [< *mán-man‿].
obj. māmáŋg(ı)‿, -gı⁀.
gen. mǎmanın‿.
pl. māmáŋgu‿, pl. obj. māmáŋgug‿.
mǎman‿tí‿ *yonder cattle.*
māmáŋgu‿nígu‿té? *who are those over there?*
māmanín-d(ı)‿ (§§ 2545 ff.) *adj. appertaining to those (etc.).*
māmaŋgún-d(ı)‿ (§§ 2545 ff.) *adj. appertaining to those (etc.).*
māmán-kırı‿ (‾‿‿, ‾‿‿; §§ 2539-40) *adj. resembling those (etc.).*
māmáŋgu-kırı‿ (§§ 2539-40) *adj. resembling those (etc.).*
māmanindı-kırı‿ (§ 2651) *adj. like that appertaining to those (etc.).*
māmaŋgúndı-kırı‿ (§ 2651) *adj. like that appertaining to those (etc.).*
māmanındínči-kırı‿ (§ 2651) *adj. like those appertaining to those (etc.).*
māmaŋgundínči-kırı‿ (§ 2651) *adj. like those appertaining to those (etc.).*
māmúr‿ *n. maʿmúr, prefect, administrative officer, esp. one in charge of a district* (mérkɛz‿) [< مَأْمُور *praefectus* (a rendering of Fr. *préfet*)].
obj. -úrk(ı)‿, -kı⁀.
pl. -múrı‿.
mán‿ (man‿ §§ 1721-2; §§ 956d, 2642, 2645) *dem. pron. that (distant, absent), yonder, that over there, that other* [< m- neg. (§ 4561) + √á- dem. of speaker (§ 4491) + -n‿ genitival, so *not of this; cp. ON. ᛘᛅᚾ id. GNT s.v.; RSN, §§ 72, 200].
obj. máŋg(ı)‿, -gı⁀.
gen. mánın‿.
pl. máŋgu‿, pl. obj. máŋgug‿.
— used substantivally and adjectivally (§§ 5120-1):
bābǔr‿nogóskon, mán‿tén‿túllan⁀ *the train (steamer) has gone, that (in the distance) is its smoke.*
mám‿bápkɛb‿béllan⁀ (-b‿b- < -d‿b- § 518) *they go (come) out by that (far, other) door.*
mán‿ádam‿ *that person* (§ 4866).
mán‿ádam‿ *those persons.*
mám‿béled‿ (§ 592) *that country (village).*
mán‿dúŋ(ı)‿ *that money.*
mán‿fānús‿, mám‿fānús‿ and máf‿fānús‿ (§ 542) *that lantern.*
máŋ‿gadíjɛ‿ (§ 646) *that lawsuit.*
mán‿ǧéll(ı)‿ *that work.*
mán‿hanu‿ *that donkey.*
mán‿kám‿ (§ 655) *that camel.*
mán‿kámlı‿ *those camels.*
mán‿lámbà‿ and mál‿lámba‿ (§ 581) *that lamp.*
mám‿már‿ (§ 604) *that village.*
mán‿níbıd‿ *that mat.*
mán‿rıjál‿ and már‿rıjál‿ (§ 670) *that dollar.*
mán‿sáfar‿ and más‿sáfar‿ (§ 680) *that journey.*
mán‿šábàkà‿ and máš‿šábàkà‿ (§ 698) *that net.*
mán‿tí‿ *that cow.*

máw‿wɛ́l‿ (§ 720) *that dog.*
mán‿zábıd‿ and máz‿zábıd‿ (§ 735) *that officer.*
— enclitic -man⁀ (-mā⁀, -má⁀ § 939) in:
tɛ́r-tarám-man⁀ *that's (s)he (it) over there.*
tɛ́r-tarám-mā, tɛ́n‿tírtıgonō‿nógbūn⁀ *that's (s)he over there, (s)he's walking with his (her) master.*
mán-do‿ (s.v. -r‿) (a) *on (in) that (yonder); (b) to that.*
mán-do‿ (§§ 4448-9, 6007) *adv.* (a) *over there, yonder* (remoter than téddo‿); (b) *thither (further than téddo‿).*
ógǧı‿mánd‿ágran⁀ *the men squat (etc. s.v. ǎg) over there.*
ɛ́nčı‿mándo‿nókkoran⁀ *the women went (have gone) over there.*
tɛr‿mándo‿ *(s)he (it) is over there.*
mándon‿ (mándō⁀, mándó⁀ § 939) *(s)he (it) is (they are) over there.*
tır‿mándončín⁀ *they are over there.*
X. tír‿mándoré? *are they there?*
Y. mándómunan⁀ *they are not (there).*
mándomen? *and*
mándomenın? *isn't (s)he (it) over there?*
mándomendan? *aren't they over there?*
mándo‿ *may form a genitive* (§ 4479):
mándon‿ádır‿ *the winter there, lit. ...of there.*
mandō̆n-d(ı)‿ (§§ 2545 ff., 2553) *adj. of yonder, of that place over there.*
mán-do-tōn‿ (s.v. -r-tōn‿; §§ 5858-60) *from that (distant, other, absent).*
mán-do-tōn‿ (§§ 4453, 6007) *adv. from over there, from yonder, from that other place.*
mándotōn⁀ (-tō⁀, -tō̆⁀, -tő⁀ § 939) *(s)he (it) is (they are) from over there, etc.*
máŋg-ɛd‿ (-ɛt⁀ § 469, -ɛ́⁀ § 966; §§ 5858-60) (a) *by (with, at, to, from, etc. s.v. -ɛd‿) that (distant, etc.);* (b) *adv.* (§§ 4462, 6007) *by (etc.) that (etc.), by that way, so.*
máŋgeb‿bıdágorandɛ? (-b‿b- < -d‿b- § 518) *did (have) they come (by) that way?*
ɛn‿dérıb‿máŋgé⁀ *your way is in that (other) direction.*
sandúg‿kártōm‿máŋgeb‿bún⁀ (§ 6031) *the box is on the other side of the house.*
maháttartōm‿máŋged‿dán‿ *there is some on that (far) side (on the other side) of the station.*
márrotōm‿máŋgen‿nókkoran⁀ (-n‿n- < -d‿n- § 624) *they went (have gone) beyond (to the other side of) the village.*
manín-d(ı)‿ (§§ 2545 ff.) *adj. appertaining to that (etc.), of that.*
maŋgún-d(ı)‿ (§§ 2545 ff.) *adj. appertaining to those (etc.), of those.*
máŋk-ɛ‿ (máŋkɛ́⁀ §§ 4414, 5940, 5957) *adv. in that (other) manner, like that (other, distant, absent), in that (etc.) position, posture or direction, so* [*having a tendency to that (other, etc.) < máŋk- obj. (§ 4410) + -ɛ́ *have a tendency to § 213].
máŋk‿áukattımunun; ıŋké! *it isn't (can't be § 5704) done like that; (showing) like this!*

mánk-ɛg⌣ (-gi⌒ §§4415, 5984) adv. = mánkɛ⌣.
mánkɛg⌣áukattımunun⌒ *it isn't (can't be) done in that way.*

mán-kırı⌣ (ᴧᴧᴠ, ᴧᴧᴧ; §§2539-40) adj. *resembling that (etc.), of that (etc.) kind.*

mángu-kırı⌣ (§§2539-40) adj. *resembling those (etc.).*

manı́ndı-kırı⌣ (§2651) adj. *like that appertaining to that (etc.).*

maŋgúndı-kırı⌣ (§2651) adj. *like that appertaining to that (etc.).*

manındínčı-kırı⌣ (§2651) adj. *like those appertaining to that (etc.).*

maŋgundínčı-kırı⌣ (§2651) adj. *like those appertaining to those (etc.).*

manám⌣ n. *dream* [< مَنام *id.*].
obj. -ámg(ı)⌣, -gi⌒.
pl. -ámı⌣.
manámgı⌣nálkori⌒ *I (have) had (lit. saw, have seen) a dream.*
manámır⌣nálkori⌒ *I saw (have seen) him (her, it, them) in a dream (in dreams §6288).*
manámır⌣nalíkkori⌒ *I saw (have seen) them in a dream (in dreams).*

mánd⌣ (before a vowel §1122) < mándo⌣ *there is* s.v. mán⌣.

mansúr⌣ *victorious, etc.* = mɛnsúr⌣.

máŋkɛ⌣ *so, etc.* s.v. mán⌣.

máŋŋɛn⌒ < mágmɛn⌒ s.v. mág *steal.*

már⌣ n. *village.*
obj. márk(ı)⌣, -ki⌒.
pl. márı⌣.
ám⌣már⌣urúp-taran⌒ *my (our) village is Urub.*
ám⌣márro⌣dámunun⌒ *there's none in my (our) village.*

márag⌣ (márag⌣) n. *broth, soup, gravy* [< مَرَق *id.*].
obj. marágk(ı)⌣, -ákk(ı)⌣, -ki⌒.
gen. marágn⌣v., -áŋ⌣c.

maragád⌣ (márag-, -akád⌣) *broth, etc.* = marragád⌣.

marawárt(ı)⌣, -ti⌒ n. *Marawarti (on map), a small island west of Argo Island near its northern end, opposite Gurúnti.*
obj. -tıg⌣.

márawı⌣, -wi⌒ n. *Merowe, a village on the left bank of the Nile now headquarters of Dóngola Province, 169 miles above Urdi (El-Ordi).*
obj. -wıg⌣.

márɛ⌣ (S. also máro⌣) n. *great millet, Sorghum vulgare,* Pers. (BSP, 663) [RSN, §80, RBW s.v. 'ár; cp. ON. ⲛⲁⲡⲡⲉ *id.,* ⲛⲁⲡⲟⲩ *bread* GNT s.v.; §2182].
obj. -rɛg⌣ [> Sudan Ar. مريق *id.* AESA s.v. Dura].
pl. marénč(ı)⌣.
márɛn⌣hábba *grain of great millet.*
márɛn⌣hágɛ *millet-stalk(s §4696b).*
márɛm⌣mɛrmétt(ı)⌣ *millet cut while still green.*

marén-d(ı)⌣ (§§2545 ff.) adj. *appertaining to great millet.*

márıs⌣ adj. *small in quantity or number, scanty, little, few;* §4953 [< marís-c. < *márıs (§1062) < má- *fail* (§2847) + -r ger. *ing* (§4585) + -ı- euph. (§484 β) + -s⌣ dem. (§2319), so **that failing,* *that failure].
obj. marísk(ı)⌣, -ki⌒.
pl. márısı⌣.
éssı⌣márisun⌒ (§4229) *the water is scanty.*
dúngı⌣márisun⌒ *the money is little.*
tínn⌣íčči⌣márisun⌒ *they have little milk,* lit. *their milk is little.*

márıs-an- (§3910α) v.i. *become scanty, etc.*

márisam-bŭ- (§3949 ff.) v.i. stat. *be in a state or condition of becoming scanty, etc.*

marısanɛd-ág- (§3966α) v.i. *be in a condition of having become scanty, etc.*

marís-sēr⌣ (§2682) indef. pron. *a little, a few* [< *marís-wēr §687].
obj. maríssɛg⌣, maríssēg⌣, ᴠᴧᴧ §1728.
ıčči⌣maríssēr⌣dá⌒ (§1786) *there is a little milk.*
marıssēd⌣dóllan⌒ (-d⌣- < -g⌣d- §534) *they want a little.*
éssı⌣maríssɛg⌣éttagoran⌒ *they (have) brought a little water.*
ékkɛn⌣ɛríd⌣maríssēr⌣fadlɛrósko, šɛllállou⌣nálkattın *few hippopotami (§4647) are left now; it (the h.) is seen in the cataract(s).*

marís-sŏd⌣ (§2583) adj. *(very) small in quantity or number, very little, very few, just a little, just a few* [< marís-tŏd⌣ §686].
obj. maríssŏdk(ı)⌣, -ŏtk(ı)⌣, -ŏtt(ı)⌣, -ŏkk(ı)⌣ §2462, -ki⌒, -ti⌒.
gen. -sŏdn⌣v., -sŏnn⌣v.c., -sŏn⌣c.
pl. maríssonı⌣.
maríssodun⌒ *there's just a little of it,* lit. *it is just a little.*

maríssŏd-dēr⌣ (ᴠ⁻ᴧᴧ, ᴠ⁻ᴧᴧ §2682) indef. pron. *a very little, just a few* [< *maríssŏd-wēr §533].
obj. maríssŏddɛg⌣, ᴠ⁻ᴧᴧ, ᴠ⁻ᴧᴧ.
íčči⌣maríssŏddēr⌣dá⌒ (§1786) *there is a very little milk.*
bér⌣maríssŏddéd⌣dá⌒ (-d⌣d- < -r⌣d- §537) *there is a very little wood.*
búm⌣maríssŏddéd⌣dóllan⌒ (-d⌣d- < -g⌣d- §534) *they want a very little coffee.*
íngurtóm⌣maríssŏddēr⌣sérɛn⌒ *just a few of these are good.*

maríssŏkk-ır- < *marísŏdk-ır- (§568).

marıssŏkkır-dɛn⌣ (§4139) v.t. *give very little, etc. (to the speaker).*

marıssŏkkır-tır (§4139) v.t. *give very little, etc. (to other than the speaker).*

markúb⌣ (már-, mɛr-) n. *slipper, shoe (native, not applied to European shoe ǧázma⌣);* with collective sg. (§4696d) [< مَركوب *id.*].
obj. -kúbk(ı)⌣, -kúpk(ı)⌣, -ki⌒.
gen. -kúbn⌣v., -kúm⌣c.
pl. -kúbı⌣.

S. **máro⌣** n. *great millet* = márɛ⌣.
obj. -og⌣.
pl. -onč(ı)⌣.
S. márog⌣ɛwírran⌒ *they grow great millet.*

S. **marón-d(ı)⌣** (§§2545 ff.) *appertaining to great millet.*

máro⌣ n. *manure from old sites* (SNK, 129, 376[85], NSD, p. 24 [< már⌣ *village* §§2306-7].
obj. -rog⌣ [> Sudan Ar. ماروق märóg⌣ *id.*].
pl. mărónč(ı)⌣, mărónč(ı)⌣.

marón-d(ı)⌣ (§§2545 ff.) adj. *appertaining to manure.*

márra⌣ (-rá⌣) n. *time, occasion* (Fr. *fois,* Ger. *Mal,* Sp. *vez*) = gır-; with collective sg. (§4696d) [< مَرّة *id.*].
obj. -rag⌣.
pl. -ranč(ı)⌣.

— used to form a numeral adverb-complex (§5270):
márra⌣tóskıg⌣, -gi⌒ *three times.*
márra⌣tóskıǧ⌣ǧómkori⌒ (-ǧ⌣ǧ- < -g⌣ǧ- §551) *I (have) struck him (her, it) three times.*
márra⌣digríg⌣, -gi⌒ *many times, often.*
márra⌣mıŋkottégi? *how many times?*
márra⌣mıŋkottɛn⌣nókkoran? (-n⌣n- < -g⌣n- §625) *how many times did they go (have they been)?*
márra⌣wéged⌣ (a) *at once, on the same occasion;* (b) *all at once, suddenly* = Sudan Ar. مَرّة واحدة.
tókkom⌣mállɛm⌣márra⌣wéges⌣sókkɛmɛn⌒ (-ɛm⌣m- < -ɛg⌣m- §601, -s⌣s- < -d⌣s- §677) *don't take it all (away) at once.*
tɛr⌣márra⌣wéget⌣tágon⌒ (-t⌣t- < -d⌣t- §706) *(s)he (it) came suddenly.*

marrága⌣ n. *Maragha (on map), a village on the left bank of the Nile just below Urdi* [< مَراغة *Wallowing-place*].
obj. -ágag⌣.

marragád⌣ (marag- §1000; már(r)ag-, -akád⌣, -ahád⌣ §§1027, 1273) n. *broth, soup, gravy* [< *مَرَقات a pl. of مَرَقة *id.* §2397].
obj. -ádk(ı)⌣, -átk(ı)⌣, -átt(ı)⌣ §2462, -ki⌒, -ti⌒.
kúsum⌣marragád⌣ *meat broth.*

⌣más⌣ (§4388) postp. *without* [app. or. a noun *absence (m- neg. §4561); ⌣másır⌣ *in absence] (α) follows -r⌣ (q.v.); (β) follows the genitive, of which -n > -m⌣; (γ) follows the genitive and receives -ır⌣ (§§5858, 5911); (δ) follows -r⌣ and receives -ır⌣.
dúŋgır⌣más⌣,
dúŋgır⌣más⌣,
dúŋgım⌣másır⌣ *without money.*
dúŋgır⌣másır⌣ and
dúŋgır⌣másır⌒ *(s)he (it) is (they are) without money.*
dúŋgır⌣másıré?,
dúŋgır⌣másıré?,
dúŋgım⌣másıró? and
dúŋgır⌣másıró? *(is (s)he (it), are they) without money?*
índo⌣más⌣,
ínım⌣más⌣,
ínım⌣másır⌣ and
índo⌣másır⌒ *without this (that).*
ínım⌣másır⌣ and
índo⌣másır⌒ *(s)he (it) is (they are) without this (that).*
éddo⌣más⌣ái⌣bınógmunun⌒,
ém⌣más⌣ái⌣bınógmunun⌒,
ém⌣másır⌣ái⌣bınógmunun⌒ and

éddo‿másır‿âi‿bınógmunun⌐ *I shall not go without you.*
ɛn‿tén‿tódır‿más‿tágon⌐, ɛn‿tén‿tóm‿más‿tágon⌐ (-m‿m- < -dn‿m- §606), ɛn‿tén‿tóm‿másır‿tágon⌐ and ɛn‿tén‿tódır‿másır‿tágon⌐ *the woman came (has come) without her child.*
tɛr‿ímmam‿másır⌐ *he is without a turban.*

masád‿ n. *residue after extraction of butter from curdled milk* [< *(what is left in the)* مساد *skin (in which butter is made)*].
 obj. -ádk(ı)‿, -átk(ı)‿, -átt(ı)‿ §2462, -kı⌐, -tı⌐.
 gen. -ádn‿v., -ánn‿v.c., -án‿c.
 pl. -ádı‿.
 íččı‿ğurrɛttakaddırundúddan; ıččı‿ tubbommɛrɛlanın; béñır‿undur-šákkıran, tén‿désk‿ósran; tém‿ fadlɛ́lgı‿masátt‿ɛrán⌐ *after drawing the milk (sc. from the cow, etc.) they bring and put it into a jar; the milk by standing (lit. lying) gets curdled; putting it into a skin they shake it and take out its butter; what remains of it they call masád*; s.v. ğurr(ı)‿.

másıl‿ n. (a) *sun*; (b) *sun's rays, sunshine* [cp. ON. ма́шаl *the sun* §2277].
 obj. masílg(ı)‿, -gı⌐.
 másıl‿bélkın‿ (§3013) *when the sun rises.*
 másıl‿tógın‿ *when the sun sets.*
 masílg‿ákkákkɛran⌐ *they are (make a practice of) warming themselves in the sun.*
 masíllo‿ (s.v. -r‿) *in the sun(shine).*
 masíllo⌐ (§5858) *(s)he (it) is (they are) in the sun(shine).*

másır‿ postp. *without* s.v. más‿.

mássı‿ n. *native of Máhas, Máhasi* [< مَحَسِي *id.*].
 obj. -sıg‿.
 pl. mássınč(ı)‿.
 mássınčín⌐ (-čí‿, -čí⌐ §939) *they are natives of Máhas.*
 mássınčım‿báññı‿ *the Máhasi dialect.*

massın-d(ı)‿ (§§2545ff.) adj. *appertaining to the (a) native of Máhas, of the (a) Máhasi.*

mássınčín-d(ı)‿ (§§2545ff.) (a) adj. *appertaining to (the) natives of Máhas, Máhasi;* (b) n. *the language of the natives of Máhas, Máhasi Nubian.*
 mássınčíndıb‿báññıran⌐ (-b‿b- < -g‿b- §519) and mássınčíndıgɛb‿báññıran⌐ (-b‿b- < -d‿b- §518) *they speak Máhasi.*

mássın-da‿ (⌐ §1675) n. *Máhas, a district on the Nile north of Dóngola from about 19° 45' to 20° 30' N. lat.* (دار المَحَس).
 obj. mássındag‿, mássındag‿, mássın‿ dág‿ §2482.
 mássındár‿ and mássın‿dár‿ *in (to) Máhas.*
 mássındár⌐ and mássın‿dár⌐ (§5858) *(s)he (it) is (they are) in Máhas.*
 mássındártōn‿tágoran⌐ *they came (have come) from Máhas.*

massındán-d(ı)‿ and

mássın‿dán-d(ı)‿ (§§2545ff.) adj. *appertaining to Máhas, of Máhas, Máhasi.*

mássın-dán- (§3923) v.i. *go to Máhas.*
 ind. pres. aı‿mássındándı⌐, ɛr‿mássın‿ dánın⌐ (-dání‿, -dání⌐); fut. âı‿bı‿ mássındándı⌐ (‿bum-); perf. aı‿mássındánkorı⌐.
 subj. past aı‿mássındánsı‿ (-dássı‿ §680, -su‿).

mássın-dámbū- (§3961) v.i. stat. *be in a state of motion towards Máhas, be on one's way to Máhas.*
 ind. pres. aı‿mássındámbūrı⌐.

másur‿ n. (a) *Egypt;* (b) *Cairo* [< مَصْر *id.* §1363].
 obj. masúrk(ı)‿, -kı⌐.
 masúrro‿ (s.v. -r‿) *in (to) Egypt (Cairo).*
 masúrro⌐ (§5858) *(s)he (it) is (they are) in Egypt (Cairo).*

masúrn-d(ı)‿ (§§2545ff.) adj. *Egyptian, Cairene.*

māsúra‿ n. *tube, pipe* [< مَأْسُورَة *id.*].
 obj. -rag‿.
 pl. -ranč(ı)‿.

mátbah‿ (mát-, -báh‿, -bax‿, -báx‿) n. *kitchen* [< مَطْبَخ *id.*].
 obj. matbáhk(ı)‿, -kı⌐.
 pl. mátbahı‿.

mawaíd‿ n. *appointed times* [< مَوَاعِيد *id.*].
 obj. -ídk(ı)‿, -ítk(ı)‿, -ítt(ı)‿ §2462, -kı⌐, -tı⌐.
 X. gátır‿adhɛrɛ́būná? *is the train late?* Y. wáran, tém‿mawaídrı⌐ *no, it's on time.*

máwın‿ (-wí⌐ §956) n. *assistant officer* [مُعَاوِن *id.*].
 obj. māwíng(ı)‿, -gı⌐.
 pl. máwını‿.

mádrása‿ (méd-, míd-, -rasa, -resa) n. *school* [< مَدْرَسَة *id.*].
 obj. mádrásag‿v., mádrásag‿c., mádrásagı §1574.
 pl. mádrásánč(ı)‿, mádrásánč(ı)‿.

mádrásán-d(ı)‿ (mɛd-, etc.; §2545ff.) adj. *appertaining to school.*

mádrás-an (méd-, etc.; §3910β) v.i. *go to school.*

mágas‿ *thief, robber* = mágas‿ s.v. mág‿.

máglūb‿ *defeated, etc.* = mɛglúb‿.

máhádda‿ (máxád-, mah-, maxád-) n. *cushion, pillow* [< مَخَدَّة *id.*].
 obj. -dag‿.
 pl. -danč(ı)‿.

máhall(ı)‿ (mah-, mɛhéll(ı)‿) n. *place* [< مَحَلّ *id.*].
 obj. -lıg‿.
 pl. -lınč(ı)‿.
 tém‿mɛhéllır‿uskúrkorı⌐ *I (have) put it in its place.*

máhallín-d(ı)‿ (mah-, mɛhɛl-; §§2545ff.) adj. *local.*

máhátta‿ (mah-, moh-, muh-, -tá‿) n. *station* [< مَحَطَّة *id.*].
 obj. -tag‿.
 pl. -tanč(ı)‿.

máhátt-an- (mah-, etc.; §3910β) v.i. *go to the station.*

máháttam-bū- (mah-, etc.; §3950β) v.i. stat. *be going to the station, be on one's way to the station.*

máhkáma‿ (máhkáma‿) *court, etc.* = mahkáma.

mákkı‿, -ki⌐ *Mékki* = mékkı‿.

máksab‿ (méksɛb‿) n. (a) *gain, profit* [< مَكْسَب *id.*]; (b) *interest (on money* = fáız‿).
 obj. máksabk(ı)‿, -ápk(ı)‿, -kı⌐.
 gen. máksabn‿v., -sám‿c.
 pl. máksábı‿.
 hawáğ‿árgı‿dúngım‿mɛksépkɛd‿ dɛnčırıkkó⌐ (-m‿m- < -g‿m- §601) *the merchant gave (has given) us (the) money at interest.*
 hawáğa‿tírgı‿dúngım‿máksápkɛt‿ tırıkkó⌐ *the merchant gave (has given) them (the) money at interest.*

máksáb-kíñ(ı)‿ (mɛksɛ́b-, -ápk-, -épk-; §§2536-7) adj. *devoid of gain, etc., without gain, etc.*
 hawáğ‿árgı‿dúngım‿máksápkıññır‿ dɛnčırıkkó⌐ *the merchant gave (has given) us (the) money free of interest.*

máktáb‿ (méktɛb‿) n. *place for writing, office, study* [< مَكْتَب *id.*].
 obj. máktábk(ı)‿, -tápk(ı)‿, -kı⌐.
 gen. máktábn‿v., -tám‿c.
 pl. máktábı‿.
 bústam‿máktáb‿ *post-office.*
 sílıg‿máktáb‿ (-g‿m- < -gn‿m- §793a), sílkım‿máktáb‿, tɛlɛgráf‿máktáb‿ (-f‿m- < -fn‿m- §789) and tɛlɛgrám‿máktáb‿ (-m‿m- < -fn‿m- §789) *telegraph-office.*
 ɛm‿bíba‿máktábır⌐ (§§1532, 5858) *your pipe is in the office.*

máktám-d(ı)‿ (mɛk-, tém-; §§2545ff.) adj. *appertaining to the (an) office, of the (an) office, official.*
 nogíd‿máktámdın‿dógor‿gɛ́nun⌐ *walking is better than being at the office, lit. ... than the office's.*

mánsūr‿ *victorious, etc.* = mɛnsúr‿.

márag‿ *broth* = márag‿.

márkaz‿ *government district, etc.* = mérkɛz‿.

márkūb‿ *slipper, etc.* = markúb‿.

mátbah‿ *kitchen* = mátbah‿.

mɛdɛ́ v.t. *sign, put one's signature to* [< mɛd- a stem of Sudan Ar. مَضَى عَلَى *id.* + -ɛ́ §3628].
 ind. pres. aı‿mɛdɛ́rı⌐; perf. aı‿mɛdɛ́gorı⌐ (N. -ɛ́ko-, -ɛ́ho-).
 imperat. mɛdɛ́!
 ɛr‿gawápkı‿mɛdɛ́goná? *did you sign (have you signed) the letter?*
 muféttıš‿gawápkı‿mɛdɛ́róskō⌐ *the inspector has signed the letter.*

mɛdɛrar‿ (-rár-; §§2200ff., 2207) and

mɛdɛríd‿ (§§2256ff., 2260) n. *signing, signature.*

mɛdɛ́r-an (§§3890ff., 3899) v.t. *tell to sign, let sign.*

mɛdɛ́-bū- (§3931β) v.i. stat. *be in a signed state or condition.*

mɛdébūlgɩ⌣nálkori⌢ (a) *I saw (have seen) the one that is signed;* (b) *I saw (have seen) that it was signed.*
— in *b* the direct object of ⌣nálkori⌢ is tékkɩ⌣ not expressed (§ 5083).
ğawáb⌣hitmébūn, mɛdébúmunun⌢ (§ 1930) *the letter is sealed, not signed.*
mɛdɛ́rɛd-ág- (§§ 3877 ff.) v.t. *be in the situation of having signed.*

médɩ⌣ (§ 2672) indef. pron. *very little, hardly anything, almost nothing* [< مَيدي *para*, $\frac{1}{40}$ *of piastre*].
obj. -dɩg⌣.
— used as object of negative verb (§§ 5169, 5476):
tɛɾ⌣mɛ́dɩg⌣íwmunun⌢ *(s)he hardly forgets the slightest thing.*
tɛɾ⌣mɛ́dɩg⌣uñúrmunū, lákɩn⌣tém⌣báññɩd⌣dɩgɾí⌢ *(s)he knows (lit. doesn't know) hardly anything, but (s)he talks much, lit. ....his (her) talk is much.*

médnɛ⌣ n. *Cairo* [< مَدينة *city*].
obj. médnɛg⌣.
médnɛɾ⌣nókkoran⌢ *they went (have gone) to Cairo.*
médn⌣áŋkoran⌢ *they went (have gone) to Cairo.*
médnɛɾtōn⌣tágoran⌢ *they came (have come) from Cairo.*

mɛdnɛ́n-d(ɩ)⌣ (§§ 2545 ff.) adj. *Cairene.*

médn-an- (§ 3910β) v.i. *go to Cairo.*
médnaŋkoran⌢ *they went (have gone) to Cairo.*

mɛdnam-bŭ- (§ 3950β) v.i. stat. *be in a state of motion towards Cairo, be on one's way to Cairo.*

mɛdnanɛd-ág- (§ 3966β) v.i. *be in the situation of having gone to Cairo.*

médrɛsa⌣ n. *school* = mádrasá⌣.

mɛglúb⌣ (mág-, mag-) (a) adj. *defeated, overcome* [< مَغْلوب id.]; (b) n. *defeated party, loser.*
obj. -úbk(ɩ)⌣, -úpk(ɩ)⌣, -ki⌢.
gen. -úbn⌣v., -úm⌣c.
pl. -úbɩ⌣.

méhɛdɩ⌣ n. *the Máhdi* = máhdɩ⌣ [< مَهْدِيّ *Guided* § 1389].
obj. -dɩg⌣.

mɛhɛdín-d(ɩ)⌣ (§§ 2545 ff.) adj. *appertaining to the Máhdi, Mahdist.*

mɛhɛdíjɛ⌣ (-já⌣, -ja⌣) n. *time of the Máhdi* [< مَهْدية id.].
obj. -jɛg⌣.

mɛhéla⌣ n. *El-Maheila (on map),* name of the desert track from Tɩmɛnáɾ to Mérowe [سِكّة المحيلة síkkat⌣elmɛhḗla].
obj. -lag⌣.
mɛhḗlagɛn⌣nókkoran⌢ (-n⌣n < -d⌣n- § 624) *they went (have gone) by the mɛhḗla.*

mɛhéll(ɩ)⌣ n. *place* = máháll(ɩ)⌣.

mékkɩ⌣ (mák-, -ki⌢) n. *Mékki,* a man's name [< مَكّي *Meccan*].
obj. -kɩg⌣.

mékseb⌣ n. *gain, profit* = máksáb⌣.
obj. mɛksébk(ɩ)⌣, -ɛ́pk(ɩ)⌣, -ki⌢.
gen. mɛksébn⌣v., -sɛm⌣c.
pl. mɛksébɩ⌣.

mékteb⌣ *place for writing, etc.* = máktáb⌣.

-mɛn (-mɛ̃, -mé⌢, -mɛn- § 4279) neg. particle *not,* used in forming neg. conjugation of verb (§§ 3087, 3075) [< m- negative (§ 4561) + -ɛn *is,* or. *it is not*].

-mɛn? (-mɛ̃?, -mé? § 951; §§ 4256-8) neg. interr. sign of predication *isn't it?* (*nonne...?, ἆρ' οὐ...; n'est-ce pas?*) [< m- neg. (§ 4561) + -ɛn? *is...?*].
— conjugated like the present tense of the verb (§ 2919 ff.):
-mɛndi? *am I not?*
-mɛnɩn? (-mɛní?, -mɛní?) *and -mɛn? (-mɛ̃?, -mé?) are you not?, is (s)he (it) not?*
-mɛndu? *are we not?, are you (pl.) not?*
-mɛndan? (-dã?, -dá?) *are they not?*
X. tágoná? *did (has) he come?*
Y. álɩmɛn? *(don't you mean)* ɛáli?, lit. *isn't it* ɛáli?
X. íŋgɩ⌣sókkɛ⌢ *take this.*
Y. telegráfmɛn? *(it's) a telegram (isn't it)?*
X. dɛn! *give it me.*
Y. mɩndílgɩmɛn? *(you mean give you?) the handkerchief (don't you?)*
X. kɩtápk⌣étta⌢ *bring the book.*
Y. gɛ́lɛmmɛ́? (-mm- < -gm- § 601) *(am I not to bring) the red one?*
kám⌣halármɛnɩn? *and* kám⌣halármɛn? *isn't the camel in the desert?*
kámlɩ⌣halármɛndan? *aren't the camels in the desert?*
X. ɾɩjál⌣goɾíččɛğ⌣ğantíkkoran⌢ (-ğ-ğ- < -d⌣ğ- § 550) *they (have) sold it for six dollars.*
Y. gálɩmɛnɩn? *isn't it dear?*

-mɛn? (-mɛ̃?, -mé?, -mɛn-? § 4280) neg. interr. particle *not?,* used in forming neg. interr. conjugation of verb (§§ 3118-19).

-mɛn-, -mɛ́n- and also as suffix **-mɛn⌣** conj. *but, on the contrary, however, yes but* (= بَل AZN, p. 31⁹) [< m- negative (§ 4561) + -ɛn? *is,* or. *it is not* sc. *as you say*].
— atonic (§ 1998), but can acquire stress (§ 1999);
— commonly infixed in future tense (§§ 6093-4) or suffixed to objective case (§§ 6095-6):
X. ɛsmán⌣sɛ́? *where's* ɛoθmán?
Y. bímɛntan⌢ (bɩmɛ́ntan⌢) *well, he'll come* (-mɛn- quasi *he's not here now but...*).
X. tágomɛn? *hasn't (s)he (it) come?*
Y. ólgonun, bímɛntān⌢ (bɩmɛ́ntān⌢) *and*
Z. ólgonun, búmɛntān⌢ *not yet, but (s)he will.*
X. tágoɾandɛ́? *have they come?*
Y. ólgónum⌣bímɛntaɾan⌢ *and*
Z. ólgónum⌣búmɛntaɾan⌢ *not yet; however, they will.*
X. nókkoɾandɛ́? *have they gone?*
Y. ólgónum⌣bímɛnnoɡɾan⌢ *and*
Z. ólgónum⌣búmɛnnoɡɾan⌢ *not yet, but they will.*

X. ɛ́ssɩ⌣ğugɾín⌢ *the water is (too) hot.*
Y. bɩmɛnoɾófɛlanɩn⌢ *yes, but it will get cool.*
X. tōɾáŋŋɩ⌣mónɩn⌢ (-ŋŋ- < -ŋg- § 2963) *(s)he (it) won't go (come) in.*
Y. bɩmɛ́ntōn⌢ *O yes (s)he (it) will.*
X. bɛlláŋgɩ⌣móndan⌢ *they won't go (come) out.*
Y. búmɛmbɛllan⌢ *O yes they will.*
X. ím⌣míllín⌢ *this is bad.*
Y. sɛɾɛ̄⌣bɩmɛ́ntān⌢ *however, the (some) good will come.*
X. ím⌣míllín⌢ *this is bad.*
Y. bɩmɛnsɛ́ɾanɩn⌢ *but it will improve.*
aɩ⌣ambɛ́skɩ⌣wɛgómunun, ɩmbɛ́skɩmɛw⌣wɛ́gori⌢ (-w⌣w- < -n⌣w- § 720) *I didn't say my brother but yours.*
tɛɾ⌣ɛ́m⌣baññítkɩ⌣dólmunun⌣eɛn⌣duŋgímmɛw⌣wɛ́ssɩn⌢ (< -gɩgmɛn⌣wɛ́ɾsɩn⌢ §§ 601, 720, 683) *(s)he doesn't want your remarks but (on the contrary wants) your money.*
X. tágoná? *has (s)he (it) come?*
Y. waɾan, dúhuɾaŋkímmɛn⌣tán⌢ *no, but (s)he (it) will come by noon.*

⌣mɛn...? *and* (infixed in verb-complex § 5605)

-mɛn-? (§§ 4423, 5962-3) adv. *why...?* [< √m- *what?* (§ 4560) + -ɛ́n *is;* cp. Amh. ምን 'ን id. AAE, s.v. ምን 'ን].
— always preceded by personal or demonstrative pronoun;
— constructed with positive verb or negative interrogative verb or interrogative sign of predication:
ɛɾ⌣mɛ́m⌣bódɩn? *why do you run?*
tɛɾ⌣mɛ́n⌣nógɩn? *why does (s)he (it) go?*
tíɾ⌣mɛ́n⌣nógɾan? *why do they go?*
tɛɾ⌣mɛ́n⌣nókkō? *why has (s)he (it) gone?*
tíɾ⌣mɛ́n⌣nókkoɾan? *why did they go? (why have they gone?).*
mám⌣mɛ́f⌣fadlɛ́gó? (-f⌣f- < -n⌣f- § 542) *why did that one yonder (that other one) stay (why has that one yonder (that other one) stayed) behind?*
ɛɾ⌣mɛ́n⌣āššákɩlɛ́n? *why are you (always) quarrelling?*
ɛɾ⌣mɛ́n⌣nógmɛnɩn? *why don't you go?*
ɩɾ⌣mɛ́n⌣nógmɛndu? *why don't you (pl.) go?*
ɛɾ⌣mɛ́n⌣nókkomɛnɩn? *why didn't you go? (why haven't you gone?).*
ɩɾ⌣mɛ́n⌣nókkomɛndu? *why didn't you (pl.) go? (why haven't you (pl.) gone?).*
álɩ⌣tɛɾ⌣mɛ́n⌣támɛnɩn? *why doesn't* ɛáli *come?*
ím⌣mɛ́n⌣ɩŋkóttēɾɛ́? *why is this so much (...in such a quantity)?*
tɛɾ⌣mɛ́n⌣āššɛkkɛ́n?, tɛɾ⌣āg-mɛ́n-šɛkkɛ́n? *and* tɛɾ⌣ammɛ́ššɛkkɛ́n? *why is (s)he (does (s)he keep on) complaining?*
— strengthened when preceded by míndɛ́...? (s.v. mín-):
míndɛ́⌣tíɾ⌣mɛ́n⌣tágoɾan? *why ever did (have) they come?*

-mɛndan?, -mɛndi?, -mɛndu? s.v. -mɛn?

mɛndíl⌣ *napkin, handkerchief* = mɩndíl⌣.

-mɛnɩn? (-mɛní?, -mɛní?) neg. interr. sign of predication *are you not?, is (s)he (it) not?* s.v. -mɛn?

mensûr~ (mán-, man-) (a) adj. *victorious, winning* [< مَنْصُور *id.*]; (b) n. *victor, winner.*
  obj. -úrk(ı)~, -ki⌒.
  pl. -úrı~.
  ɛr~éŋ~gadíjɛr~mɛnsúrrɛ? (-súrɛ́? §1003) *are you the winner in your lawsuit?*
mensûrkútt(ı)~, -ti~ n. *Mansurkotti* (on map), a village on the left bank of the Nile, about 28 miles above Ed-Débbā[h] [*Manṣûr Knoll*].
  obj. -tɪg~.
mɛr (a) v.t. *cut*; (b) v.t. *cut off, cut out, cut up, cut down*; (c) v.t. *circumcise*; (d) v.t. *cross, go across, traverse* (river, desert); (e) v.i. *get cut, tear, get torn, break, get broken, snap, slit* [cp. ON. *мер in мек-кı (§571) *scrap, small piece*, GNT s.v.; §2782; RSN, §129].
  ind. pres. āı~mérrı~, ɛr~mérın⌒ (~mérī⌒, ~mérí⌒); perf. āı~mérkori⌒.
  imperat. mér!, pl. mérwɛ! (-wɛ́!, mérrɛ! (§672), -rɛ́!).
  part. pres. mérıl~ *(one) that cuts, etc., cutter, etc., cutting, etc.*; past mérɛl~ *(one) that cut, etc., cutter, etc., cutting, etc.*
  pl.-obj. mérır.
  ind. pres. āı~mɛrı́ddi⌒, ɛr~mérırın⌒.
  ıŋgɛm~mér⌒ (-m~m-<-d~m- §600) (a) *cut it (them) with this (that)*; (b) *cut (some, off, out) here.*
  kádɛ~mɛróskon⌒ (-m~m-<-g~m- §601) *(s)he has (you have) cut the cloth.*
  kádɛ~mɛróskon⌒ *the cloth has torn (slit).*
  súlu~mɛrkúbkı~mérkó⌒ *the shoemaker (has) cut out the shoe(s §4696 d; sc. from a hide).*
  ǧówwım~mɛróskoran⌒ *they have cut down the tree(s §4696 b).*
  tónım~mérın⌒ (-m~m-<-g~m- §601) *he circumcises the boys.*
  úskar~búrum~mérın⌒ *the midwife circumcises the (a) girl.*
  úskar~búruı m~mérın⌒ *the midwife circumcises the girls.*
  úrum~mérkori⌒ *I crossed the river* (قطعت البحر).
  ágabam~mérkori⌒ (-m~m-<-g~m- §601) *I crossed the desert.*
  ın~ı́rı~kómbomunum~bumérın⌒ *this rope is not strong, it will break.*
  tómbıǧó, úl~mérkó⌒ *it broke, the thread snapped (it has broken, the thread has snapped.)*
mérar~ (-rár~; §§2200 ff.) and
mɛrı́d (§§ 2256 ff.) n. *cutting, etc., circumcision.*
mérɛ~ n. *pool* (more or less circular), *standing water* [lit. *cutting, what is cut*, or. sc. in sand by current and eddies of falling river; -ɛ~ of n. act. §2234ɛ].
  obj. mérɛg~.
  pl. mɛrɛ́nč(ı)~.
  kámlı~mérɛrtōn~nı́goran⌒ *the camels drank (have drunk) at (lit. from) the pool.*
mɛrméttı(ı)~ n. *sorghum cut while still green* [<*mɛrmért(ı)~ (§713) *cuttings*;

the repeated syllable is descriptive (§2151); -t dem. (§2324); §2330].
  obj. -tɪg~.
  márɛn~mɛrméttı(ı)~ and márɛm~mɛrméttı(ı)~ = mɛrméttı(ı)~.
mér-an (§§3890 ff.) v.t. *tell to cut, etc., let cut, etc.*
mér-bū- (§3931 β) v.i. stat. *be in a cut (etc.) state or condition.*
mɛrr-ɛg-ág- (§§4071 ff.) v.t. and i. = mɛrɛdól-.
mɛr-ɛ-dól- (-r°d- §1178; §4022) and
mɛrr-ɛ-dól- (-r°d-; §4027) v.t. and i. *be about to cut, etc.*
  kádɛ~mɛrɛdólın⌒ *the cloth is just going to tear.*
mɛrɪdd-ɛg-ág- (§§4071 ff.) v.t. = mɛrɪddɛdól-.
mɛrɪdd-ɛ-dól- (-d°d- §1178; §4030) v.t. *be about to cut, etc.* (more than one object).
mɛrr-ɛ-ǧŭ-bū- (§4069) v.t. stat. *be on one's way (coming) to cut, etc.*
mɛr-ɛ-má- (§4036) and
mɛrr-ɛ-má- (§4041) v.t. *become unable to cut, etc.*
mɛrr-ɛ-nóg (§§4048 ff.) v.t. *go to cut, etc.*
mɛrr-ɛ-nóg-bū- (-nóggū- §546; §4058) v.t. stat. *be on one's way (going) to cut, etc.*
mɛrr-ɛ-tá (§§4060 ff.) v.t. *come to cut, etc.*
mɛred-ág- (§§3877 ff.) (a) v.t. *be in the situation of having cut, etc.*; (b) v.i. *be in the condition of having got cut, etc.*
mér-kattı- (§4093) v.p. *be cut, etc.*
mɛros-áu (§§4180–84; -osgáu, -ozg-, -ogg- §4185; -áu, -áw) v.t. *make (etc. s.v. áu) after cutting, etc.*
  súlu~mɛrkúbkı~mɛroggáwın⌒ *the shoemaker cuts out and makes shoes* (§4696 d).
√**mér-** *ferment.*
mérɛl~ (a) adj. (of milk) *curdled, sour* [§2523 a]; (b) n. *curdled or sour milk.*
  obj. mɛrɛ́lg(ı)~, mɛrɛlg(ı)~ §1522, -gı~.
  ı́ččım~mérɛl~ (-m~m-<-n~m- §604) n. = mérɛl~.
mérɛl-an- (§3910α) v.i. *become curdled, etc., curdle, turn sour.*
mérɛlam-bū- (§§3949ᵅ) v.i. stat. *be in a curdling (curdled, etc.) state or condition.*
mérɛlanɛd-ág- (§3966α) v.i. *be in the condition of having curdled, etc.*
mérsɛ~ n. *beer* made from millet and dates [<*mérsɛ~ (§1048) < √mér- *ferment* +-s dem. +-ɛ of n. ess., so **that fermented thing*; less prob. < márɛ~ *millet* +éss(ı)~ *water* RNW s.v. mɛrísa; SMN, p. 451 s.v. mɛrísa; > Sudan Ar. مَرِيسَة *id.*].
  obj. -sɛg~.
  pl. -sɛ́nč(ı)~, mɛrɛsɛ́nč(ı)~.
  mérsɛn~nı́gori⌒ (-n~n-<-g~n- §625) *I drank (have drunk) (the) beer.*
mérkɛz~ (már-, -káz~) n. (a) *government district*; (b) *government district office, police-station, etc.* [<مَرْكَز *id.*].
  obj. mɛrkɛ́zk(ı)~, -ɛ́sk(ı)~, -ki⌒.
  pl. mérkɛzı~.
mɛrkúb~ *slipper, etc.* = markúb~.

mɛrméttı(ı)~ *sorghum cut while still green* s.v. mér.
mérsɛ~ *beer* s.v. √mér-.
mértaba~ n. *mattress* [<مَرْتَبَة *id.*].
  obj. -bag~.
  pl. -banč(ı)~.
mɛskín~ (§956 a) adj. (a) *poor*; (b) *humble, inoffensive* [<مِسْكِين *id.*].
  obj. -íŋ(ı)~, -gi⌒.
  pl. -íni~.
mɛ́u~, mɛ́w~ adj. *pregnant* (of woman or female animal).
  obj. mɛ́ug(ı)~, mɛ́wg(ı)~, -gi⌒.
  pl. mɛ́wı~.
  tıntınɛ́n~mɛ́wun⌒ *their mother is pregnant.*
  hánu~mɛ́ug~éttágoran⌒ *they (have) brought the (an) ass in foal.*
  tır~mɛ́wın⌒ *they are pregnant.*
mɛ́ukanɛ~ (mɛ́wk-; §2295) n. *pregnancy.*
mɛ́w-an- (§3910α) v.i. *become pregnant.*
  ind. pres. āı~mɛ́wandi⌒, ɛr~mɛ́wanın⌒ (-nī⌒, -ní⌒); fut. āı~bımɛ́wandi⌒ (~bum-); perf. āı~mɛ́waŋkori⌒.
  subj. past āı~mɛ́wansı~ (-assı~ §680), -su~).
mɛ́wam-bū- (§§3949α) v.i. stat. *be in a pregnant state or condition.*
  tɛr~mɛ́wambūn⌒ *she has become pregnant.*
mɛ́waned-ág- (§3966α) v.i. *be in the condition of having become pregnant.*
mɛ́wanıŋ-ır (and ⌃⌃; N. -ŋkır; §4213) v.t. caus. *cause or allow to become pregnant.*
  ind. pres. āı~mɛ́wanıŋgıddi⌒; perf. āı~mɛ́wanıŋgírkori⌒.
  subj. past āı~mɛ́wanıŋgırsı~ (-su~).
mɛ́ug-ır (mɛ́wgır; N. mɛ́ukır, -uhır, mɛ́wk-; §3701) (a) v.t. caus. *cause or allow to be pregnant*; (b) v.t. *render pregnant, impregnate.*
  ind. pres. āı~mɛ́ugıddi⌒, ɛr~mɛ́ugırın⌒ (-rī⌒, -rí⌒); perf. āı~mɛ́ugírkori⌒.
  subj. past āı~mɛ́ugırsı~ (-su~).
mínč(ı)~ n. *hunger* [<*mı́ñt(ı)~ (§901 a) <*mírñt(ı)~ (cp. §852) < mír *prevent* +-ñ dim. (§4572)+-t of n. act. (§2325α), so **little prevention* sc. of action, life, quasi **destitution*; §2228].
  obj. -čıg~.
  mínč~āıg~árī⌒ and (§4623)
  áıg~mínč~árī⌒ *hunger seizes me*, so (a) *I get hungry*; (b) *I am hungry.*
  tírgı~mínč~árırın⌒ *they get (are) hungry* (individually §5456).
  X. tér~sɛ́? *where is (s)he (it)?*
  Y. bɛ́lɛdır; mínč~árkım~bután⌒ *in the village; when (s)he (it) gets hungry (s)he (it) will come back.*
mír v.t. *hinder, impede, keep back, restrain, check, stop, not allow, prevent, cause not to* [< neg. m- (§4561)+í~ *hand* +-r *in*, so *not (sc. allow) in the hand, not make* (ír, q.v.) §2848 a].
  ind. pres. āı~mírri⌒; perf. āı~mírkori⌒.
  part. pres. mírıl~ *(one) that hinders, etc., hinderer, etc., hindering, etc.*; past mírɛl~ *(one) that hindered, etc., hinderer, etc., hindering, etc.*

tɛr‿aigɪ‿bắččɪrtōm‿mírɪn⌢ (s)he (it) hinders me from writing.
tén‿híss‿aigɪ‿bắččɪr‿mírɪn⌢ his (her) voice (its sound) hinders me in (my) writing.
éssɪm‿mírkoran⌢ (-m‿m- < -g‿m- §601) they (have) checked the flow of the water.
tɛlɛfṓŋgɛg‿gatírk‿ínnār‿mírw‿ɛgó⌢ (-g‿g- < -d‿g- §545) he (has) telephoned to them to keep the train back at their station, lit. he (has) said by telephone 'keep the train back with you'.
aigɪ‿mírkoran, zummárat‿tókkon‿ǧómmen‿ɛgi⌢ (-t‿t- < -g‿t- §707) they (have) stopped me, telling me not to play on the pipe.
tɛr‿aigɪ‿mírkó, tókkon‿súgammɛn‿ɛgi⌢ (s)he forbade (has forbidden) me to go to the market.
mírkori, tókkon‿aumɛn‿ɛgi⌢ I forbade (have forbidden) him (her) to do it.
ékkɪ‿mírkoná, tókkon‿nógmen‿ɛgi? did (s)he forbid (has (s)he forbidden) you to go?
míra‿ adj. barren, sterile [< mírar (§959) prevention specialized in passive adjectival sense prevented §2510; cp. ON. мıра id.].
obj. -rag‿.
pl. -ranč(ı)‿.
ɛ́n‿míran⌢ the woman is barren.
tí‿mírran⌢ the cow is barren.
kañ-kárrı‿míran⌢ the mare is barren.
mírar‿ (-rár‿; §2200 ff.) and
miríd‿ (§§2256 ff.) n. hindering, etc.
mír-an- (§3910 α) v.i. become barren, etc.
míram-bŭ- (§§3949 ff.) v.i. stat. be in the state or condition of becoming (having become) barren, etc.
ɛ́n‿mírámbūn⌢ the woman is past childbearing.
mír-an (§§3980 ff.) v.t. tell to hinder, etc., let hinder, etc.
mír-bŭ- (§3931 β) v.i. stat. be in a hindered (etc.) state or condition.
éssɪ‿mírbun⌢ the (flow of) water is cut off.
mir-ɛ-mắ- (§4036) and
mirr-ɛ-mắ- (§4041) v.t. become unable to hinder, etc.
mír-katti- (§4093) v.p. be hindered, etc.
mizắn (§956a) n. balance, scales, weighing-machine [< ميزان id.].
obj. -áŋg(ı)‿, -gi⌢.
pl. -án‿.
mɪzắnd‿úskur⌢ (-d‿ < -do‿ s.v. -r‿) put it (them) on the scales.
mídrasa‿ n. school = mádrasa‿.
mígrıb‿ n. sunset, dusk, early evening (= šárɛ‿) [< مَغْرِب id.].
obj. mɪgríbk(ı)‿, -ípk(ı)‿, -ki⌢.
pl. mígrıbı‿.
mill(ı)‿ adj. bad, of bad quality.
obj. -lıg‿.
pl. -lınč(ı)‿.
kúmbu‿míllın⌢ the egg is (eggs are §4696d) bad.
wílndı‿míll‿ɛgó⌢ yesterday's was bad.
míllımunun⌢ (s)he's (it's) not bad (i.e. fairly good).

míllıkanɛ‿ (§2295) n. badness.
mill-an- (§3910α) v.i. go bad, deteriorate, get worse.
ind. pres. tɛr‿míllanɪn⌢ (-nī⌢, -ní⌢);
fut. tɛr‿bɪmíllanɪn⌢ (‿bum-, -nī⌢, -ní⌢); perf. tɛr‿míllaŋkon⌢ (-kō⌢, -kó⌢).
kúsu‿míllanoskon⌢ the meat has (definitely) gone bad.
millam-bŭ- (§§3949 ff.) v.i. stat. be in a deteriorating (deteriorated) state or condition, be (getting) worse.
mılland-ɛg-ắg- (§3977) v.i. = mıllanɛdól-.
mılland-ɛ-dól- (-nᵒd- §1178; §3975) and
mılland-ɛ-dól- (-dᵒd-; §3978) v.i. be about to go bad.
íŋ‿kárɛ‿mıllandᵒdólın⌢ this (that) fish is about to go bad.
mıllanɛd-ắg- (§3966 α) v.i. be in the condition of having gone bad, be in a deteriorated condition, be worse.
mıllaníŋ-ır (‿‿‿; N. -ŋkır; §4213) v.t. caus. cause or allow to go bad.
mín...? (before a vowel §1122) < mínɛ...? how...?
mín-...? (only as declension-stem or in composition §2654) interr. pron. what...? [< √m- what? (§4560)+ín‿ this; cp. ON. мıɴ what? GNT s.v.; RSN, §75] nom. supplied by míndɛ...?, míndo...? infra.
obj. míŋ(ı)...?, -gi‿.
gen. mínın‿v....?, mınín‿c....?
(§1466).
ɛr‿íŋɪ‿mínun‿ándān? what do you think this is?
mín(¹)rɛ́? what is it?
tɛn‿ǧınsı‿mín¹rɛ? (a) what is his (her) tribe?; (b) what kind is it?
X. tıntımbáb‿mínrɛ? what is their father?
Y. tɛr‿hawwắdun⌢ he is a fisherman.
míŋ-gálıgın? what's it like?
míŋgɪ‿kálli? what am I (§5369b) to eat?
míŋgɪ‿dólın? what do you (does (s)he, it) want?
íŋgɪ‿míŋ‿ɛrán? what do they call this? (what's the name of this?).
mínın‿ıllár? on account of what?, because of what?, why?
tɛr‿mínín‿ǧéllıg‿ágáwın? what work (lit. the work of what) is (s)he doing?
mín-dɛ‿...? (§2654) interr. pron. what...? [i.e. mín-*dɛ‿...? §§889, 4275].
míndɛ‿nókkō? what went (has gone)?
míndɛ‿haslɛ́gon? what (has) happened?
‿min-dɛ́? (§§4244, 5797, mın-+interr. sign of pred. is what?, what is?
tɛr‿mindɛ́? what is the matter with him (her, it)?
mín-dé (in answer) used as sentence-word (§5796) whatever for? (= for what possible reason?), expressing surprise, indignation or contempt: what's the meaning of it! (cp. Amh. ም'ን'ጦ፡ id. AAE s.v. ም'ን).
X. súgaŋkoran⌢ they went (have gone) to the market.
Y. míndé? what ever for?
X. bınógmunan⌢ they won't go.
Y. míndé! what do they mean!

mín-dɛ...? used as adv. preceding and emphasizing ‿mén‿...? why...? (§5798).
míndɛ́‿tír‿mén‿nókkoran? why ever (on earth) did they go (have they gone)?
mínd‿aı‿mén‿nálmendi? why on earth don't I see him (her, it, them)?
mínd‿ɛr‿mén‿tắmenın? why on earth don't you come?
mínd‿ɛr‿mén‿tắgomenın? why ever didn't you come?
mín-do‿...? (§2654) interr. pron. what...?
míndo‿dán? and
míndo‿dắ? what is there? (qu'y a-t-il?, was giebt's?).
míndo‿nókkō? what went (has gone)?
míndo‿dabóskó? what has disappeared?
míndo‿haslɛ́gon? what (has) happened?
mín-do‿...? (s.v. -r‿) (a) on (in, to) what?; (b §§4450, 6007) adv. where?, whither?
míndo‿dán? and
míndo‿dắ? where is there some?
míndo‿bún? where does (s)he (it) lie? (where is it?).
mínd‿ắgın? where does (s)he (do you) live? (where is (s)he?).
ɛr‿míndo‿nókkon? and
míndo‿nókkō? where did you go (have you been) to?
míndo‿dabóskó? where has (s)he (it) disappeared to?
mín-dotŏn‿...? (-tō̃?, -tō?, -tṍ?; s.v. -rtŏn‿) (a) from what?, of what?; (b §§4454, 6007) adv. whence?
míndotŏn‿áukattın? what is it made of?
mín-ɛ‿...?, mín‿v....? (§§4416, 5958) adv. how? [lit. saying what?, being what? §213].
ɛr‿mínɛ‿wɛ́? what do you say?
hánum‿mínɛ‿wɛ́goran? (-m‿m- < -g‿m- §601) what did they say about the donkey?
mín‿auri! what shall I do! (expressing perplexity), what am I to do!
bɪ-mín-áuran? (§5384) what will they do? (expressing perplexity).
ɛr‿hánum‿mín‿áukon? what did you do (have you done) with (about) the donkey?
minɛg‿...?, -gi? (§§4417, 5985) adv. how?
ɛr‿mínew‿wɛ́gon? (-w‿w- < -g‿w- §719) what did you say?
X. tém‿báññıd‿sérēn⌢ what (s)he says is good.
Y. mínegi? how so?
‿mınéllé? (§§4245, 5799-800) what is...? [< mín- what? + -él being (part. of ‿é- be)+-*dé? is? (§4236) what is it that is?].
mınéllé? what is it?
pl. ‿mınélıré? what are...?
mınéllé? what is it?
mınélıré? what are they?
ím‿mınéllé? what is this (that)? (near).
mám‿mınéllé? what is that (over there)?
íŋgu‿mınélıré? what are these (those)? (near).
máŋgu‿mınélıré? what are those (over there)?

tέr⌣mɪnéllέ? *what is it?*
tír⌣mɪnélɪrέ? *what are they?*
— *usually of inanimate or impersonal animate objects, but also of persons:*
X. tέr⌣mɪnéllέ? *what is (s)he?*
Y. béndɪgɪlun⌢ *(s)he's a beggar.*
tén⌣ǵínsɪ⌣mɪnéllέ? *(a) what kind is it?; (b) what is his (her) tribe?*

mɪŋ-εd⌣...? (-εt? §469, -έ? §966; §§4463, 6007) *adv. by means of (etc. s.v. -εd*⌣*) what?, with what?, how?*
míŋgεk⌣káččɪran? (-k⌣k- < -d⌣k- §568) *what do they play with?*

mɪnin-d(ɪ)⌣...?, -di? (§§2545ff.) *interr. pron. adj. appertaining to what?, of what?*

míŋ-kɪrɪ⌣...?, -ri? (⌣, ⌣; §§2539-40) *interr. pron. adj. like what?*
míŋkɪrɪn? *what is (s)he (it) like?*

mɪŋ-kótt(ɪ)⌣...?, -ti? (mukót-, muhót-; §§2663, 5141, 5147-8, 5355) *interr. pron. how much?, how many?* [< mín-? *what...?* kótt(ɪ)⌣ *amount, quantity*].
obj. -kóttɪg⌣...?, -gi?
mɪŋkóttɪ⌣dán? *and*
mɪŋkóttɪ⌣dáran? *(a) how much is there?; (b) how many are there?*
sá⌣mɪŋkóttɪr? (s.v. -r⌣) *and*
sá⌣mɪŋkóttɪgi? (§4665) *at what time?*
X. aï⌣káčkεb⌣bɪǧúri⌢ (-b⌣b- < -d⌣b- §518) *I shall go on horseback.*
Y. kácčɪ⌣sá⌣mɪŋkóttɪd⌣dólɪn? (-d⌣d- < -g⌣d- §534 or < -r⌣d- §537) *at what time do you want the horse?*
gádas⌣sá⌣mɪŋkóttɪr⌣dólɪn? (-s⌣s- < -g⌣s- §678) *at what time do you (does (s)he) want lunch?*
mɪŋkóttɪrέ? (§5141) *(a) how much is it?; (b) how many are they?*
sá⌣mɪŋkóttɪrέ? *what's the time?* الساعة كم.

mɪŋkóttɪrε⌣...? (mukó-, muhó-; §§2664, 5144) *interr. pron. how much?, how many?* = mɪŋkótt(ɪ)⌣...?
kándɪ⌣mɪŋkóttɪrε⌣dán? *how many knives are there?*

mɪŋkótt-ēr⌣...? (mukót-, muhót-; §§2684, 5141, 5147-8, 5355) *interr. pron. adj. (about) how much?, (about) how many?* [< *mɪŋkótt-wēr...? (§717) *a how much?* كم واحد].
obj. mɪŋkóttēg⌣...?, mɪŋkóttεg⌣..., mɪŋkóttεg⌣...? (§1728), -gi?
εr⌣mɪŋkóttεg⌣εttágõ? *how much (many) did you bring (have you brought)?*
mɪŋkóttēk⌣kóran? *how much (many) have they (got)?*
tɪr⌣íddo⌣mɪŋkóttēk⌣kóran? *how much do you (pl.) owe them?* (s.v. -r⌣ *and* kó *have*).
ugrέs⌣mɪŋkóttēr⌣fadlεróskó? *how many days are left?*
tεr⌣séna⌣mɪŋkóttεg⌣índorέ? *how many years has (s)he (it) been here?* (§4666).
ógɪǧ⌣mɪŋkóttēr⌣nókkon? *and* (§5355)
ógɪǧ⌣mɪŋkóttēr⌣nókkoran? *how many men went (have gone)?*
sá⌣mɪŋkóttεrro⌣nókkoran? *at what time did they go?*
sá⌣mɪŋkóttεrr⌣undúddi? *at what time shall (§5369b) I put him (her, it, them, §5083) in?*

mɪŋkóttērré? *and* (§1004)
mɪŋkóttεré? *(a) how much is it?; (b) how many are they?*
mɪŋkóttērré? wεrrέ⌣wála⌣ówwᵘré? *and*
muhóttērré? wεrrέ⌣wáll⌣ówwɪré? *how many are they? one? or two?*
sá⌣mɪŋkóttεrré? *what's the time?*

mɪŋkóttērrε⌣...? (mukót-, muhót-, -tεrε⌣...?; §§2685, 5144) *interr. pron. adj. how much?, how many?*
ógɪǧ⌣mɪŋkóttεrrε⌣dábūn? *and* (§5355)
ógɪǧ⌣mɪŋkóttεrrε⌣dáburan? *how many men are there?*
kándɪ⌣mɪŋkóttεrrε⌣dán? *how many knives are there?*

mɪŋkótt-an-? (mukót-, muhót-; §2665) *v.i. become how much?, become how many?*
dúŋgɪ⌣mɪŋkóttaŋkó? *how much has the money become?, i.e. how much does the money amount to now?*

mɪŋkóttεr-an-? (mukot-, muhot-; §2686) *v.i.* = mɪŋkóttan-?

mɪndíl⌣ (mεn-) *n. napkin, handkerchief* [< منديل id.].
obj. -dílg(ɪ)⌣, -gi?
pl. -dílɪ⌣.

míndo⌣...? *what...?, where...?* s.v. mín-...?

mɪñmíñ *n. measles* [§2153; -ñ-, -ñ⌣ dim. §4572].
obj. -íñg(ɪ)⌣, -gi⌢.
bɪtám⌣mɪñmíñgɪ⌣kó⌢ *and*
bɪtám⌣mɪñmíñ-kó⌢ (§4119) *the child has measles.*

mɪráslɪ⌣ (mur-) *n. messenger* [< مراسلة id. §1348].
voc. -lī!
obj. -lɪg⌣.
pl. -lɪnč(ɪ)⌣.

mírɪg⌣ *n. (a) cross-beam supporting roof and resting on vertical beam (εndε⌣); (b) side-piece of frame of bedstead (áŋgarε⌣); with collective sg. (§4696d)* [> Sudan Ar. مرق id.].
obj. mɪrígk(ɪ)⌣, -ríkk(ɪ)⌣, -ki⌢.
gen. mɪrígn⌣v., -ríŋ⌣c.
pl. mírɪgɪ⌣.

mɪséka *n. a village in the district of Awadánda on Argo Island.*
obj. -kag⌣.
mɪsέka⌣massɪnčíndɪgεb⌣báññɪran⌢ (-b⌣b- < -d⌣b- §518) *at Mɪsέka they talk Máhasi.*

mɪsíd⌣ *n. (a) small mosque; (b) primary school, held in (a)* [< Sudan Ar. مسيد id. < مسجد].
obj. -fdk(ɪ)⌣, -ftk(ɪ)⌣, -ftt(ɪ)⌣ §2462, -ki⌢, -ti⌢.
gen. -ídn⌣v., -ín⌣c.
pl. -ídɪ⌣.

mɪsɪr *v.t. miss, fail to find, fail to reach, not obtain* [< *mɪsír (§1154) < neg. m- (§4561) +ɪs-? *where...?* +-ír *make*, so **not make where, not locate* §2849*].
ind. pres. aï⌣mɪsɪrrɪ⌢, εr⌣mísɪrɪn⌢ (-rí⌢, -rí⌢); perf. aï⌣mɪsírkori⌢.
gatírkɪ⌣mɪsírkoran⌢ *they (have) missed the train.*

mísɪrar⌣ (-rár⌣; §§2200ff.) *and*
mɪsɪríd⌣ (§§2256ff.) *n. missing, failure to find, etc.*

mísɪr-bŭ- (§3931β) *v.i. stat. be in a missed state or condition.*

mɪsɪrεd-ág- (§§3877ff.) *v.t. be in the situation of having missed.*
bābúrkɪ⌣mɪsɪrεdágran⌢ *they have missed the steamer (train).*

mísɪr-kattɪ- (§4093) *v.p. be missed.*

míslɪm *n. Moslem* [< مسلم id. §1348].
obj. mɪslímg(ɪ)⌣, -gi⌢.
pl. míslɪmɪ⌣.

mɪslím-d(ɪ)⌣ (§§2545ff.) *adj. appertaining to a Moslem, of a Moslem, Moslem.*

mɪslɪmín-d(ɪ)⌣ (§§2545ff.) *adj. appertaining to Moslems, of Moslems, Moslem.*

mɪsór⌣ *n. high Nile, inundation, time of the inundation* (= dεmírε⌣) [< Copt. ⲙⲉⲥⲱⲣⲏ *August*, RSN, §129; SNK, §335].
obj. -sór(ɪ)⌣, -ki⌢.
pl. -sórɪ⌣.

míssε *v.t. sprinkle, bespatter, splash* [§§2870ff., 2875].
ind. pres. aï⌣míssεri⌢; perf. aï⌣míssεgori⌢ (N. -εko-, -εho-).
arítk⌣έssɪgεm⌣míssεran⌢ (-m⌣m- < -d⌣m- §600) *they sprinkle the ground with water.*
agárkɪ⌣sfugεm⌣míssεgoran⌢ *they (have) sprinkled the place with sand.*
έkk⌣έssɪ⌣míssεn⌢ *the water splashes you.*

míssεrar⌣ (-rár⌣; §§2200ff., 2210),
mɪssεríd⌣ (§§2256ff., 2263) *and*
mɪssíd⌣ (§2264) *n. sprinkling, etc.*

mísεr-an (§§3890ff., 3899) *v.t. tell to sprinkle, etc., let sprinkle, etc.*

míssε-bŭ- (§3931β) *v.i. stat. be in a sprinkled (etc.) state or condition.*
árɪd⌣éssɪgεm⌣míssεbūn⌢ (-m⌣m- < -d⌣m- §600) *the ground is (has been) besprinkled with water.*

mɪssεd-ág- (§3540) *v.t.* = mɪssεrεdág-.

mɪssεrεd-ág- (§§3877ff.) *v.t. be in the situation of having sprinkled, etc.*
arítk⌣έssɪgεm⌣mɪssεrεdágran⌢ *they have sprinkled the ground with water.*

míssε-kattɪ- (N. -εha-; §4093) *v.p. be sprinkled, etc.*
árɪd⌣έssɪgεm⌣míssεkattɪn⌢ (-m⌣m- < -d⌣m- §600) *the ground is sprinkled with water.*

míss(ɪ)⌣ *n. (a) eye*, with collective sg. (§4696a), *and like* عين; *(b) the evil eye; (c) spring (of water)* [< *míns(ɪ)⌣ §680) < mɪn-? *what?* +-s dim., so **little (sc. means of seeing) what?* §2319].
obj. -sɪg⌣.
pl. -sɪnč(ɪ)⌣.
ám⌣míssɪgεn⌣nálkori⌢ (-m⌣m- < -n⌣m- §604, -n⌣n- < -d⌣n- §624) *I saw (have seen) him (her, it, them §5083) myself*, lit. *I saw...with my eye;* = Sudan Ar. شفته بعيني.
έm⌣míssɪn⌣tógortōn⌣nógram⌣bókkoŋ⌣gúnči⌢ *watch them until they are out of your sight*, lit. *...until they go from under your eye.*

míšano⌣ — mŏr

âı⌣míssıs⌣sándırı⌢ (-s⌣s- < -g⌣s-§678) *I fear the (evil) eye.*
ínım⌣míssırtōn⌣sándıran⌢ *they are afraid of this person's (evil) eye.*
míssıŋ⌣áğın⌣,
míssıŋ⌣kóbıd⌣ and
míssıŋ⌣tagídd(ı)⌣ n. *eyelid(s §4696a).*
míssıŋ⌣kál⌣,
míssıŋ⌣kanísse⌣ and
míssıŋ⌣nébed⌣ (⌣némed⌣) *rheum of the eye, mucous discharge of the eye.*

mıssín-d(ı)⌣ (§§2545ff.) adj. *appertaining to the (an) eye, etc.*

mıssıgéliñ⌣ (`"``` §§1521-2) n. *the largest Nile fish, of light colour, with red eyes,* Lates niloticus, *Cuv. and Val.* (*PF*, p. 96), (= sāmús⌣) [< míssı- *eye* + √gél- *red* (§4524) + -ñ⌣ dim., so *little red eye* §2304].
obj. -geliñg(ı)⌣, -gi⌢.
pl. -géliñ⌣.

míssı-kıññ(ı)⌣ (§§2536-7) adj. *without eyes.*

mıssı-wĕr-an- (§3910ff., 3913α, vi) v.i. *become of fixed opinion.*
ín⌣óğiğ⌣mıssıwĕraŋkó⌢ *this man is* (lit. *has become*) *of fixed opinion.*

mıssı-wĕk-kō (§4117) v.i. *have (only) one view, be of fixed opinion.*
ín⌣en⌣mıssıwĕkkōn⌢ *this (that) woman is of fixed opinion.*
part. pres. mıssıwĕkkōl⌣ (*one*) *that has (only) one view, etc.*

N. **míšano⌣** *Friday* = móšono⌣.

mišíndıl⌣ adj. *ugly* [< *mınsíndıl⌣ (§690) < mín-? *what?* +-s dem. (§2319) +-ı- euphonic +-nd- *appertaining to* (§2546) +-ıl⌣ participial, quasi **that that is appertaining to what?* §2532].
obj. mišındílg(ı)⌣, -gi⌢.
pl. mišíndıl⌣.
búru⌣mišíndılun⌢ (§1966) *the girl is ugly.*

mišındílkane⌣ (§2295) n. *ugliness.*

míšš(ı)⌣ n. (*a*) *door-post;* (*b*) *vertical axle of larger cog-wheel* (árgadeŋ⌣géde⌣) *of water-wheel* (kóle⌣).
obj. -šıg⌣ [> Sudan Ar. مشق míššıg⌣ id. (*b*)].
pl. -šınč(ı)⌣.
míššın⌣úr⌣ *apex of vertical axle, that turns in a hole in cross-beam* (dfu⌣).
míššın⌣úsud⌣ *bottom of vertical axle, that turns in in sáb⌣.*

mítar⌣ (tár⌣) n. *well supplying water-wheel* (*away from river*) [< مَتَرَة id. §§1334, 1394].
obj. mıtárk(ı)⌣, -ki⌢.
pl. mítarı⌣.
mıtárked⌣agewírran⌢ *they are* (*make a practice of*) *cultivating by means of* (*water from*) *a well.*

mohámmed⌣ (muh-, -màd⌣) n. *Muḥámmad, Mohammed, a man's name* [< محمد].
voc. -met!, -màt!
obj. mohammédk(ı)⌣, -étk(ı)⌣, -étt(ı)⌣, -ékk(ı)⌣ §2462; `"` §1522; -ki⌢, -ti⌢.
gen. mohammédn⌣v., -ménn⌣v.c., -mén⌣ c.; `"`; §§778-88.

mohámmen⌣báññıd⌣sérēn⌢ *Muḥámmad's (way of) speaking is good.*

mohammén-d(ı)⌣ (muh-, -mán-; §§2545ff.) adj. *appertaining to Muḥámmad, of Muḥámmad, Muḥámmad's.*

mohátta⌣ *station* = màhátta⌣.

moís⌣ n. *track round which cattle working water-wheel* (kóle⌣) *walk counter-clockwise; it is laid on a platform* (ğíbıd⌣) [(?) cp. Copt. ⲙⲟⲉⲓⲧ *way*].
obj. -ísk(ı)⌣, -ki⌢.
pl. -ísı⌣.
tínči⌣moísıɾ⌣nógran⌢ *the cattle walk on the track.*

mŏn (*a*) v.t. *hate, dislike;* (*b*) v.t. *refuse;* (*c*) v.i. *be unwilling* (*a, b* = kečči̇nɛ́) [< m- negative + √ŏn- *to like* (§4578), as ON. ⲙⲟⲛ id. < м- neg. + on *love* GNT s.vv.; *RSN*, §§129, 200].
ind. pres. âı⌣móndı⌢, er⌣mónın⌢ (-ní⌢, -ní⌢); perf. âı⌣mónkori⌢.
imperat. mŏn! (§952).
subj. past âı⌣mónsı⌣ (⌣mósı⌣ §974, -su⌣).
part. pres. mónıl⌣ (*one*) *that hates, etc., hater, etc., hating, etc.,* obj. mónílg(ı)⌣, -gi⌢; past mónel⌣ (*one*) *that hated, etc., hater, etc., hating, etc.,* obj. mōnélg(ı)⌣, -gi⌢.
er⌣mónná? and less commonly er⌣mónıná? *do you refuse?*
def. perf. âı⌣mónóskori⌢ *I have refused.*
X. nógan⌢ (§§3890ff.) *tell him (her) to go.*
Y. mōnóskō⌢ *(s)he won't,* lit. *(s)he has refused.*
ānús⌣ımbélkō, šugurráŋgı⌣mōnóskō⌢ *the lantern has gone up and one can't get it down,* lit.... *it has refused to descend.*
kúšar⌣dugállo⌣tōráŋŋı⌣mónın⌢ *the key won't go into the lock.*
áŋ⌣kŏr⌣gendıráŋŋı⌣mónın⌢ *my wound won't heal.*

mónar (-nár⌣; §§2200ff.) and

mōníd (§§2256ff.) n. *hatred, dislike; refusal; unwillingness.*

mōníd-am-mŏn-bū- (-mómbū-; §4166a) v.i. stat. *be in an intensely hated state or condition.*
mán⌣sámıl⌣mōnídammómbūn⌢ *that sheikh is very much hated.*

mōnídk-ır-mŏn (-ītkır-, -īttır-, §§4156-7) v.t. *hate (etc.) intensely, exceedingly, refuse absolutely.*
nográŋgı⌣mōnídkırmóŋkoran⌢ *they (have) absolutely refused to go.*

mŏn-bū- (mómbū-; §3931β) v.i. stat. *be in a hated (etc.) state or condition.*
ádemıg⌣gošší̇l⌣mómbūn⌢ *a cheat is disliked.*

mōn-ɛ-dól- (-nᵒd- §1178; §4022) and
mōnd-ɛ-dól- (-dᵒd-; §4027) v.t. *be about to hate, etc.*
bunóŋŋunum⌣mōnedólın⌢ *(s)he (it) won't go, (s)he (it) is going to refuse.*

mōned-áğ- (§§3877ff.) v.t. *be in the situation of having hated, etc.*
nográŋgı⌣mōnedáğran⌢ *they have refused to go.*

mŏn-kattı- (§4093) v.p. *be hated, etc.*
ím⌣móŋkattın⌢ *this (one) is hated.*

mōnos-bŏd (-obbód §521; §§4180-4; -osgıbód, -ozgı-, -oggı- §4185) v.t. *run away after refusing.*

mōnos-ğɛbɛlam-bŏd (-noğğeb- §556; -osgığeb-, -ozgı-, -oggı-; §§6296, 4185) v.t. *after refusing run away into the desert (mountains).*

⌣móŋkon⌣ (-kō⌢, -kó⌢, -ko §939) postp. (i = prep. §4287; §4383) (*a, in space*) *as far as, up to, down to, to;* (*b, in time*) *till, until* [a stereotyped verb-concretion (§5730) < *m-ón-k-on < m- neg. (§4561) + -ón- *like* (§4578) + -k obj. suff. + -on⌣ *like;* móŋk- is the object of -on⌣, so *(if you) like (if you) dislike,* *suppose that you don't suppose,* approx. *more or less].*
— follows the genitive, of which -n⌣ > -m⌣ (§604) or disappears (§§2473-4);
= ⌣bókkon⌣kám⌣móŋkon⌣tágoran⌢ *they came (have come) as far as the house.*
gúss⌣érdɛb⌣tóskım⌣móŋkos⌣sókken⌢ (-s⌣s- < -n⌣s- §680) *the corn-bin holds up to three* aràdıb (أرادب).
tém⌣béled⌣móŋkon⌣ (-d⌣m- < -dn⌣ m- §786),
tém⌣bélen⌣móŋkon⌣(-n⌣m- < -dn⌣ m- §612) and
tém⌣béled⌣móŋkon⌣ (-m⌣m- < -dn⌣ m- §606) *as far as his (her) village.*
ám⌣béledırtōn⌣tém⌣béled⌣móŋkos⌣sáŋ⌣kémsırén⌢ (-s⌣s- < -n⌣s- §680; §1972) *from my (our) village to his (her) village is a quarter of an hour.*
índotōn⌣hándaŋ⌣móŋkon⌣hánuges⌣sà⌣ówwín⌢ (§1970; -ŋm- < -gn⌣m- §659a, -s⌣s- < -d⌣s- §677) *from here to El-Xándaq by donkey is two hours.*
ékkenertŏ⌣sà⌣tóskım⌣móŋkō⌣ *from now till 3 o'clock.*

⌣móŋkon⌣ (-kō⌢, -kó⌢, -ko⌢) postp. (ii = conj. §4287; §4317) (*a*) *till, until;* (*b*) *as long as.*
— follows the subjunctive bare form (§§2943, 2951), that may be preceded by ⌣náman⌣ (§4483):
máŋg⌣élli⌣móŋkon⌣íŋgi⌣buskúddi⌢ *until I find that other I shall put this (one).*
ár⌣táru⌣móŋkon⌣tép⌢ *remain until we come.*
tàram⌣móŋkon⌣tébwe⌣ *remain (pl.) until they come.*
ar⌣táru⌣móŋkon⌣indo⌣ték⌢ and
ar⌣náman⌣táru⌣móŋkon⌣indo⌣ték⌢ *wait here till we come.*
âı⌣tàsı⌣móŋkon⌣tékkoran⌢ *they waited till I came.*
másıl⌣tŏm⌣móŋkon⌣ğóbbe⌣ *wait till the sun sets.*
tírg⌣er⌣nálım⌣móŋkon⌣gúñči⌢ *watch them as long as you (can §5377) see them.*
ter⌣nálkattım⌣móŋkon⌣gúñči⌢ *watch him (her, it) as long as (s)he (it) can (§5704) be seen.*

mŏr v.t. *bind, tie up, fasten* [§4564; *RSN*, §129].

ind. pres. āı͜mṓrrı͡; perf. āı͜mōrkori͡.
imperat. mṓr!, pl. mṓrwɛ! (-wé!, mṓrrɛ! §672, -rɛ́!).
ɛr͜káčči͜mōrkoná? *did you tether (have you tethered) the horse?*
mōrar (-rår-; §§ 2200ff.) and
mōríd͜ (§§2256ff.) n. *binding, etc.*
mōr-an (§§3890ff.) v.t. *tell to bind, etc., let bind, etc.*
ogíčkı͜mōrwan͡ and
ogíčči͜mōrran͡ *tell them to bind the man.*
mōr-bŭ- (§3931β) v.i. stat. *be in a bound (etc.) state or condition.*
part. pres. mōrbūl͜ *(one) that is bound, etc., prisoner, captive.*
káğ͜mōrbūn͡ *the horse is (has been) tethered.*
mōrr-ɛg-ág- (§§4071ff.) v.t. =mōrɛdól-.
mōr-ɛ-dól- (-rᵒd- §1178; §4022) and
mōrr-ɛ-dól- (-rᵒd-; §4027) v.t. *be about to bind, etc.*
mōrr-ɛ-ğŭ́-bŭ- (§4069) v.t. stat. *be on one's way (coming) to bind, etc.*
mōr-ɛ-má̆- (§4036) and
mōrr-ɛ-má̆- (§4041) v.t. *become unable to bind, etc.*
mōrr-ɛ-nóg (§§4048ff.) v.t. *go to bind, etc.*
mōrr-ɛ-nóg-bŭ- (-nóggŭ- §546; §4058) v.t. stat. *be on one's way (going) to bind, etc.*
mōrr-ɛ-tá̆ (§§4060ff.) v.t. *come to bind, etc.*
mōred-ág- (§§3877ff.) v.t. *be in the situation of having bound, etc.*
mōrk-ídd(ı) (§3725) v.t. caus. *cause or allow to bind, etc.*
ind. pres. āı͜mōrkíddırı͡.
imperat. mṓrkıddı!
āı͜tékki͜mōrkíddıgori͡ *I (have) made (let) him (her) tie him (her, it §5086) up.*
mōr-katti- (§4093) v.p. *be bound, etc.*
mōra n. *Mura (on map), a village on the right bank of the Nile about 38 miles above Ed-Débbá*ʰ.
obj. -rag͜.
mṓrɛ n. *Acacia ehrenbergiana, Hayne (BSP, 181).*
obj. mórɛg͜.
pl. morénč(ı)͜.
mṓro n. =mṓrɛ͜.
obj. mórog͜.
pl. morōnč(ı)͜.
mṓšono͜ (N. míšano͜) n. *Friday.*
obj. -nog͜.
pl. mošonṓnč(ı)͜.
móšono͜jóm͜ (§4750),
móšonon͜jóm͜ (§4810)
móšono͜nahǎr(nȧh-, nɛh-; §4750) and
móšonon͜nahǎr (§4810) *Friday.*
móšonog͜ (§4665),
móšonor͜,
móšono͜nahǎrk(ı)͜ and
móšono͜nahǎrro͜ *on Friday.*
móšonortōn͜ and
móšono͜nahǎrrotōn͜ *since Friday.*
móšonom͜mónkon͜ and
móšonom͜bókkon͜ *till Friday.*
ınnōẃwi͜móšonon͜ (-nō͡, móšonó͡ §939) *today is Friday.*
N. míšano͜jōmgı͜tákoran͡ *they came on Friday.*

mošonón-d(ı)͜ (N. mıšan-; §§2545ff.) adj. *appertaining to Friday, Friday's.*
mṓššo͜ n. *Mushu (on map), a village on the left bank of the Nile just north of Argo Island.*
obj. mōššog͜, móššóg͜ (§1532).
mottókk(ı)͜ (mut-) n. *Kénzi* [< *maltógk(ı)͡ (§§1175, 709, 569) <mált- east (q.v.)+ √óg- *be on (§4576)+-k adv. suff. (§2139), so *that is on the east; §2293; RSN, §129].
obj. -kıg͜.
pl. -kınč(ı)͜.
mottokkınčín-d(ı)͜ (mut-; §§2545ff.) (a) adj. *appertaining to the Kunúz, Kénzi;* (b) n. *Kénzi Nubian dialect, Kénzi.*
mōz͜ n. *banana, plantain (tree and fruit), Musa sapientium, Linn.* (BSP, 559); with collective sg. (§4696b) [< مَوْز id.].
obj. mōzk(ı)͜, mósk(ı)͜, -ki͡.
pl. mōzı͜.
mudág͜ (múdag͜) n. *pestle, instrument for pounding* [< Sudan Ar. مَدَق id. §1372].
obj. mudágk(ı)͜, -ák(ı)͜, -ki͡.
gen. -ágn͜v., -án͜c.
pl. mudági͜, múdagı͜.
múdfa͜ n. *cannon* [< Sudan Ar. مَدْفَع id.].
obj. -fag͜.
pl. -fanč(ı)͜.
mudír͜ n. *director, manager, governor* [< مُدِير id.].
obj. -ırk(ı)͜, -ki͡.
pl. -ırı͜.
múdul͜ n. *thumb* [§2343].
obj. mudúlg(ı)͜, -gi͡.
pl. múdulı͜.
mufétti š n. *inspector* [< مُفَتِّش id.].
obj. mufɛttíšk(ı)͜, -ki͡.
pl. mufɛttıšı͜.
mufɛttíšn-d(ı)͜ (§§2545ff.) adj. *appertaining to the (an) inspector.*
múg v.t. (a) *leave;* (b) *leave behind, abandon;* (c) *leave undisturbed, leave alone, let be;* (d) *leave unpunished, let off;* (e) *let, allow, permit;* (f, of bird, etc.) *lay (egg).*
ind. pres. āı͜múg(ı)rı͡; perf. āı͜múg-kori͡ (͜múkkori͡).
imperat. múk!, pl. múgwɛ! (-wé!, múggɛ! §547, -gé!).
subj. past āı͜múgsı͜ (͜múksı͜ §576; -su͜).
def. pres. āı͜mugósri͜; perf. āı͜mugóskori͜.
def. imperat. múgos! (mugós! §1890, mugó! §962); pl. mugóswɛ! (-góswé!; -gówwɛ! §724, -wé!; -gósse! §687, -sé!).
āı͜bımúgmunun͡ *I shall not leave (etc.) him (her, it, them §5083).*
X. tékki͜ğázɛgoná? *did he punish (has he punished) him (her)?*
Y. ınnōẃwim͜mugóskó͡ (-m͜m- <-g͜m- §601) *this time* (lit. *today) he has let him (her) off.*
aron͜gurápkı͜mukkógıru, kåkkı͜ bukálkon͜ (§6234κ) *if we had let it, the crow would have eaten the snake.*

ín͜sáb͜sandåmunun, wélg͜åbadam͜ múŋŋunun͡ (-ŋŋ- <-gm- §661) *this cat is not a coward, he never fails to attack a dog.*
dúrmadɛ͜kúmbum͜múkkon͡ (-m͜m- <-g͜m- §601) *the hen (has) laid an egg (some eggs §4696d).*
múgar (-gȧr͜; §§2200ff.) and
mugíd͜ (§§2256ff.) n. *leaving, etc.*
múg-an (§§3890ff.) v.t. *tell to leave, etc., let leave, etc.*
múg-bŭ- (múggŭ- §546; §3931β) v.i. stat. *be in a left (etc.) state or condition.*
mug(ı)r-ɛg-ág- (§§4071ff.) v.t. =mugɛdól-.
mug-ɛ-dól- (-gᵒd- §1178; §4022) and
mug(ı)r-ɛ-dól- (-rᵒd-; §4027) v.t. *be about to leave, etc.*
mug-ɛ-má̆- (§4036) and
mug(ı)r-ɛ-má̆- (§4041) v.t. *become unable to leave, etc.*
mugɛd-ág- (§§3877ff.) v.t. *be in the situation of having left, etc.*
mugk-ídd(ı) (mukk-; §3725) v.t. caus. *cause or allow to leave, etc.*
ind. pres. āı͜mugkíddıri͡.
imperat. múgkıddi!
āı͜tékki͜ıŋgi͜mukkíddıri͡ *I make (let) him (her, it) leave this.*
muging-ır (and ͜, N. -ŋkır; §3688) v.t. caus. *cause or allow to leave, etc.*
S. dókkon͜áıg͜án͜såm͜múgıŋgırmen͡ (-m͜m- <-g͜m- §601) *don't let me leave my watch behind.*
múg-katti- (múkka- §4093) v.p. *be left, etc.*
múgos-an (§§3890ff., 3905) v.t. *tell to leave, etc., let leave, etc.*
ádɛmıǧ͜ǧáwwɛm͜mugówwan͡ (§3900; -ǧ-ǧ- <-g͜ǧ- §551, -m͜m- <-g͜m- §601) *tell the persons to stop brawling.*
mugós-dɛn (-óddɛ̄n §538; §§4180-4, 3995ff.; -ósgıdɛn, -ózgı-, -óggı- §4185) v.t. *by leaving (etc.) give (to the speaker), leave for (the speaker).*
ıŋg͜áıgı͜mugóddɛn͡ *leave this for me.*
mugos-nɛdmɛ̆ (-onnɛ- §629; §§4180-4; -osgınɛ-, -ozgı-, -oggı- §4185) v.t. *regret after leaving, etc.*
sokkonnɛdmɛ̆giŋ͜génun͜mugonnɛdmɛ̆n͜dógor͡ (-n͜d- <-nn͜d- §833) *if you regret after taking it is better than if you regret after leaving behind* (a version of شيل أندم ولا تخلّي تَنْدَم).
mugos-nóg (-onnóg §629; §§4180-4; -osgınóg, -ozgı-, -oggı- §4185) v.t. *go after leaving, etc., go away from.*
mugonnók! *leave him (her, it, them §5083) and go away.*
mugosnóg-an (-onnóg-, -osgınóg-, -ozgı-, -oggı- §§3890ff., 3905) v.t. *tell to go after leaving, etc.*
mugos-tá̆ (-ottá̆ §714; §§4180-4; -osgıtá̆, -ozgı-, -oggı- §4185-7) v.t. *come after leaving, etc., leave, etc. and come, come away from.*
ind. perf. āı͜mugottá̆gori͡ (N. -áko-, -åho-), -oggıtá̆-.
imperat. sg. mugostá̆!, mugottá̆! and ͜, pl. mugottåwɛ!, -tåwé!

múgdo⌣ — murrɛ́

mugos-áıgonón-ta! (§5605) *leave him (her, it, them) and come with me!*
mugótt⌣ɛ́kkenɛ⌢ (§4627) *come away from him (her, it, them) now.*
mugostár-an (-ottár-, -osgıtár-, -ozgı-, -oggı-; §§3890ff., 3899, 3905) v.t. *tell to come away from, let come away from.*
tɛ́kkı⌣mugottáran⌢ and
tɛ́kkı⌣mugoggıtáran⌢ (§§5644ff.) *tell him (her) to leave him (her, it, them) and come, let him (her) leave him (her, it, them) and come, let him (her) come away from him (her, it, them).*
tírgı⌣mugottáran⌢ and
tírgı⌣mugoggıtáran⌢ *tell them to leave him (her, it, them) and come, let them leave him (her, it, them) and come, let them come away from him (her, it, them).*
mugòt-tɛ̀kkı-táran⌢ and
mugòggı-tɛ̀kkı-táran⌢ (§5603) *leave him (her, it) alone and let him (her, it) come.*
mugòt-tìrgı-táwan⌢ and
mugòggı-tìrgı-táwan⌢ *leave them alone and let them come.*
mugós-tır (-óssır §686; -óttır §714; §§4180-4, 3995ff.; -ósgıtır, -ózgı-, -óggı- §4185) v.t. *by leaving (etc.) give (to other than the speaker), leave for (other than the speaker).*
íngı⌣tírgı⌣mugóttırır⌢ *leave this for them.*
múgdo⌣ (búgdo⌣ §1014) n. *large upright post fixed in the ground, supporting cross-beam* (dfu⌣) *of water-wheel* (kólɛ⌣); *with collective sg.* (§4696d).
obj. -dog⌣.
pl.-donč(ı)⌣.
múgdon⌣ónd(ı)⌣ *male múgdo⌣ the stronger post (sometimes doubled) supporting the heavier end of the cross-beam; the múgdon⌣ónd(ı) is on one's left when one faces the river.*
múgdo⌣kárr(ı)⌣ *female múgdo⌣, the weaker post, supporting the lighter end of the cross-beam, on one's right as one faces the river.*
múggɛ! < múgwɛ! *leave!* (pl.), etc. s.v. múg.
muhátta⌣ *station* = mảhátta⌣.
muhótt(ı)⌣...?, muhóttɛ̄r⌣...? *how much?* = mıŋkótt(ı)⌣...?, mıŋkóttɛ̄r⌣...? s.v. mín-.
múk! imperat. of múg *leave*, etc.
mukáfa⌣ n. *reward, prize, gratuity, tip* [< مُكَافَأة id.].
obj. -fag⌣.
pl. -fanč(ı)⌣.
N. **múkk(ı)** v.t. *cut, cut down* (dates from palm) [< *múrk(ı) (§571) < √múr- *cut* (§4566) + -k §2853].
ind. pres. âı⌣múkkıri⌢; perf. âı⌣múkkıkori⌢ (-ıho-).
imperat. múkki!
ar⌣béntım⌣múkkıkoru⌢ (-m⌣- < -g⌣m- §601) *we (have) cut down the dates* (§4696b; = ar⌣béntıg⌣ğórkoru⌢).
múkk(ı) v.t. *cross, pass (go or come) across, pass over* [or. *cut*, like قَطَعَ البَحْرَ].
ind. pres. âı⌣múkkıri⌢; perf. âı⌣múkkıgori⌢ (N. -ıko-, -ıho-).

imperat. múkki!
úrub⌣bumúkkıri⌢ (-b⌣b- < g⌣b- §519) *I shall cross the river.*
úruk⌣kúpkɛm⌣múkkıgoran⌢ (-k⌣k- < -g⌣k- §569, -m⌣m- < -d⌣m- §600) *they (have) crossed the river by boat.*
mùkkı-màltıgɛb-bɛ́l (§5605) v.t. *after crossing issue (s.v. bɛ́l) on the east bank.*
imperat. mukkımaltıgébbɛl! (§1871).
úrum⌣mukkımaltıgɛbbɛlóskoran⌢ (-m⌣m- < -g⌣m- §601) *they have crossed the river and got out on the east bank.*
mùkkı-tıŋgàrkɛb-bɛ́l (§5605) v.t. *after crossing issue on the west bank.*
imperat. mukkıtıŋgárkɛ́bbɛl!
tır⌣mukkkıtıŋgárkɛbbɛlóskoran⌢ *they have crossed over and got out on the west bank.*
mukótt(ı)⌣...? (muhót- §1029, -ti?; §§2663, 5141, 5147-8, 5355) interr. pron. *how much?, how many?* = mıŋkótt(ı)⌣...? s.v. mín-.
obj. -kóttıg⌣..., -gi?
mukóttı⌣bınógın? and
mukóttı⌣bınógran? *how many will go?*
sả⌣mukóttır? (s.v. -r⌣) and
sả⌣mukóttıgi? (§4665) *at what time?*
mukóttırɛ́? (§5141) (a) *how much is it?;* (b) *how many are they?*
sả⌣mukóttırɛ́? *what's the time?*
mukóttırɛ...? (muhó-; §§2664, 5144) interr. pron. *how much?, how many?*
kándı⌣mukóttırɛ⌣dā́n? *how many knives are there?*
ógığ⌣mukóttırɛ⌣dā́n? *how many men are there?*
ógığ⌣muhóttırɛ⌣dápkó? *how many men (have) disappeared?*
mukóttɛ̄r⌣...? (muhót-; §§2684, 5141, 5147-8, 5355) interr. pron. adj. (about) *how much?, (about) how many?* = mıŋkóttɛ̄r⌣...?
obj. mukóttɛ̄g⌣...?, mukóttɛ́g⌣...? (§1728), -gi?
mukóttɛ̄g⌣ɛttári? *how much (many) shall (§5369b) I bring?*
gíriš⌣mukóttɛ̄r⌣dā́n? (§1786) *how many piastres are there?*
kándı⌣mukóttɛ̄r⌣dā́n? and
kándı⌣mukóttɛ̄r⌣dábun? *how many knives are there?*
tɛr⌣jṓm⌣mukóttɛ̄g⌣índ⌣ắkkon? *how many days was (s)he (it) here? (...has (s)he (it) been here? §4666).*
ógığ⌣mukóttɛ̄r⌣dā́n? and (§5355)
ógığ⌣mukóttɛ̄r⌣dắran? *how many men are there?*
sả⌣mukóttɛ̄rro⌣nógri? *at what time shall (§5369b) I go?*
mukóttɛ̄rɛ́? and
mukóttɛ̄rɛ́? (§1004) (a) *how much is it?;* (b) *how many are they?*
sả⌣mukóttɛ̄rɛ́? *what's the time?*
ín⌣séna⌣mukóttɛ̄g⌣índorɛ́? *how many years has this been here?*
mukóttɛ̄rrɛ⌣...? (muhót-, -tɛ̄rɛ⌣...?; §§2685, 5144) interr. pron. adj. *how much?, how many?*
ógığ⌣mukóttɛ̄rrɛ⌣dábun? and (§5355)
ógığ⌣mukóttɛ̄rrɛ⌣dáburan? *how many men are there?*

ógığ⌣mukóttɛ̄rrɛ⌣dápko? (...⌣dápkoran?) *how many men (have) disappeared? (...were (have been) lost?).*
kándı⌣mukóttɛ̄rrɛ⌣dā́n? *how many knives are there?*
mukótt-an-? (muhót-; §2665) v.i. *become how much?, become how many?*
dɛ́n⌣mukóttaŋkó? *how much has the debt become?, i.e. how much does it amount to now?*
mukóttɛ̄r-an-? (muhot-; §2686) v.i.= mukóttan-?
mulwắd⌣, -ắt⌢ n. *Mulwad (on map), a village on the right bank of the Nile about three miles below Hándag.*
obj. -ắdk(ı)⌣, -ắtk(ı)⌣, -ki⌢.
múmmud⌣ adj. *dumb* [< *múmmıd⌣ (§2340) <múmm- onom. of dumbness +-ıd⌣ *making* or *made* (§2256ff.); RSN, §§129, 200].
obj. mummúdk(ı)⌣, -útk(ı)⌣, -útt(ı)⌣ §2462, -ki⌣, -ti⌢.
pl. múmmudı⌣.
mummúdkanɛ⌣ (-útk-; ⌣⌣⌣; §2295) n. *dumbness.*
múmmud-an- (§3910α) v.i. *become dumb.*
-munun⌢ (-munũ, -munu⌢, -mun §§947-8, 1978-9) *negative suffix* (a) particle attached to parts of verb (§3077); (b) *sign of predication* (§§4252, 5824-9) *am not, (you sg.) are not, ((s)he, it) is not, (we, you pl.) are not.*
-munan⌢ (-munã, -muná⌢, -mun §§949, 1978-9) (a) attached in 3rd pers. pl. of verb; (b) (they) are not [-munun⌢ is either (a) < *-mɛn-un (§1175) <-mɛn- *not* (§4257)+-un⌢ *is, are* (§4229), or more probably (b) < -m- *not* (§4561) + -un-un *positive sign of predication repeated* §4253. -munan⌢ < -mun- (on analogy of -mun-un⌢) +-an⌢ (remains of or on analogy of -*dan⌢ §2919, -san §2947)].
âı⌣samílmunun⌢ *I am not the (a) sheikh.*
ɛr⌣ím⌣bɛléndımunun⌢ *you are not of this district.*
X. ín⌣hánurɛ́? *is this (that) the (a) donkey?*
Y. hánumunun⌢ *no, lit. it is not the (a) donkey.*
hánu⌣téndımun⌢ *the donkey is not his (hers).*
kám⌣halármunun⌢ *the camel is not in the desert.*
kámlı⌣halármunan⌢ *the camels are not in the desert.*
X. ní! *drink!*
Y. ɛ́kkɛnɛmunun⌢ *not now.*
X. índ⌣ɛttariá? *shall (§5369b) I bring it here?*
Y. indómunun⌢ *not here.*
múŋŋunun⌢ < múgmunun⌢ s.v. múg.
muráslı⌣ *messenger* = mıráslı⌣.
murrɛ́ v.i. *stroll, walk about, go for a walk, go on tour* [< مَرّ- *of imperfect of* مَرَّ *pass along* + ɛ́ §3623].
ind. pres. âı⌣murrɛ́ri⌢; perf. âı⌣murrɛ́gori⌢ (N. -ɛ́ko-, -ɛ́ho-).
imperat. murrɛ́!
murrɛ́rar (-rắr⌣; §§2200ff., 2207) and

murrĕríd (§§2256ff., 2260) n. *strolling, etc.*

murrɛ̄r-ɛ-nóg (§§4048ff.) v.i. *go to stroll, etc.*

murrɛ̄r-ɛ-nóg-bŭ- (-nóggŭ- §546; §4058) v.i. stat. *be on one's way (going) to stroll, etc.*

murrēren̄ógbūran⌒ *they are going for a stroll.*

múrs(ı)⌣ n. *lie, falsehood*; with collective sg. (§4696d) [< √múr- *bind* (§4565) +-s dim., so *little thing that binds* §2319].
 obj. -sıg⌣.
 pl. -sınč(ı)⌣.
 múrsıb⌣báññ(ı) (-b⌣b- < -g⌣b- §519) and
 múrsıw⌣wɛ́ (-w⌣w- < -g⌣w- §719) *tell a lie, tell lies.*
 tɛr⌣múrsıg⌣ǎbbáññın⌒ and tɛr⌣múrsıg⌣awwɛ́n⌒ (a) *(s)he is telling a lie (lies)*; (b) *(s)he habitually tells lies.*
 múrsıgek⌣karğıróskoran⌒ (-k⌣k- < -d⌣k- §568) *they have given false evidence.*

mursǎğ n. *liar* [-ǎğ contains -án *say, tell* §2190; RSN, §85].
 voc. -áč!
 obj. -ǎğk(ı)⌣, -áčk(ı)⌣, -áčč(ı)⌣ §523, -ki⌒, -či⌒.
 gen. -ǎğn⌣v., -áñ⌣c.
 pl. -ǎğı⌣.
 tɛr⌣mursǎğun⌒ *(s)he's a liar.*

murtıgád⌣ (-tᵘg- §1194) n. *knot* [< √múr- *tie* (§4565) + -tı- *thing* (§2325 β) + -g-
 obj. suff. + -ád⌣ **holder*, *holding* (§2061), so **holder (holding) of what is tied* §2186].
 obj. -ádk(ı)⌣, -átk(ı)⌣, -átt(ı)⌣ §2462, -ki⌒, -ti⌒.
 gen. -ádn⌣v., -ánn⌣v.c., -án⌣c.
 pl. -ádı⌣.
 murtıgátk⌣áukori⌒ *I (have) made a (the) knot.*
 murtıgád⌣sɛ́rɛ̄-wɛg⌣áukori⌒ *I (have) made a good knot.*

múruğ v.t. *cut off, detach by cutting, cut away, cut down* [< √múr- *cut* (§4566) + -u- euphonic (§1189) + -ğ intensive §2888].
 ind. pres. aı̄⌣muruğ(¹)ri⌣ (⌣múruğ(¹)ri⌣), ɛr⌣múruğın⌣ (-ğí⌣, -ğí⌣); perf. aı̄⌣muruğkori⌒ (-účk-).
 kándıgem⌣múruč⌣ (-m⌣m- < -d⌣m- §600) *cut it (them) off with a knife.*
 hétta-wēt⌣téddotōm⌣múruč⌣ (-t⌣t- < -g⌣t- §707, -m⌣m- < -n⌣m- §604) *cut a piece off from it.*

muruğ n. *piece cut off* [nominal presentation of thing-meant by múruğ §2056].
 obj. -úğ(ı)⌣, -účk(ı)⌣, -účč(ı)⌣ §523, -ki⌒, -či⌒.
 pl. -úğı⌣.

múruğar⌣ (-ğár⌣; §§2200ff., 2209) and
muruğíd⌣ (§§2256ff., 2262) n. *cutting off, etc.*

múruğ-an (§3890ff.) v.t. *tell to cut off, etc., let cut off, etc.*

muruğ-árk(ı) (-aríkk(ı); §3747ᵉ) v.t. *cutting off (etc.) throw, etc.* (s.v. árk(ı)).
 imperat. muruğárki! (-aríkki!).

wíččırn⌣kóččım⌣muruğárkıgó⌒ (-m⌣m- < -g⌣m- §601) *cutting off the top of the stick (s)he threw (has thrown) it away.*

muruğ-bŭ- (-úğğŭ- §552; §3931β) v.i. stat. *be in a cut off (etc.) state or condition.*
 ğówwı⌣muruğ́bun⌒ *the tree is (has been) cut down.*

muruğ-dɛn (§§3996-7) v.t. *cutting off (etc.) give (to the speaker), cut off (etc.) for (the speaker).*
 hétta-wɛ̄g⌣áıgı⌣muruğdɛ́ŋkon⌒ *(s)he (has) cut off a piece and gave (has given) it to me ((s)he (has) cut me a piece off).*

muruğed-áğ- (§§3877ff.) v.t. *be in the situation of having cut off, etc.*

muruğ-kattı- (-účk-; §4093) v.p. *be cut off, etc.*

muruğ-tır (-účt-; §§3998-9) v.t. *cutting off (etc.) give (to other than the speaker), cut off (etc.) for (other than the speaker).*
 hétta-wɛ̄t⌣tékkı⌣muručtır⌒ (-t⌣t- < -g⌣t- §707) *cut him (her, it) a piece off.*

musmǎr⌣ n. *nail* (clavus); with collective sg. (§4696d) [< مِسْمَار id.].
 obj. -árk(ı)⌣, -ki⌒.
 pl. -árı⌣.

músul n. *Musul* (on map), *a district and island at the head of the third cataract.*
 obj. musúlg(ı)⌣, -gi⌒.
 músuln⌣árt(ı) *the island of Músul.*
 musúllo (s.v. -r⌣) *at (to) Músul.*
 musúllo⌣ (§6007) *(s)he (it) is (they are) at Músul.*

mušémma⌣ n. *oil-cloth, waterproof, canvas* [< مُشَمَّع *waxed*, id.].
 obj. -mag⌣.
 pl. -manč(ı)⌣.

mušemmán-d(ı)⌣ (§§2545 ff.) adj. *appertaining to oil-cloth, etc., of oil-cloth, etc.*
 sandúğ⌣mušemmándır⌣ (§§5858-60) *it's (they're) in the canvas box.*

múšra⌣ n. *way to water, place where river is accessible, watering-place* [< Sudan Ar. مَشْرَع id.].
 obj. -rag⌣.
 pl. -ranč(ı)⌣.
 múšraŋ⌣kúb⌣ *ferry-boat.*
 múšraŋ⌣kúb⌣ısáır⌣tɛ́bın⌒ *where does the ferry-boat wait? (where is the ferry-boat stationed?).*

múšud n. *comb* (pecten) [Sudan Ar. مُشْط < مَشْط id. §1363].
 obj. mušúdk(ı)⌣, -útk(ı)⌣, -útt(ı)⌣ §2462, -ki⌒, -ti⌒.
 gen. mušúdn⌣v., mušún⌣c.
 pl. mušúdı⌣.

mutémma⌣ n. *small spherical crystalloid gold bead, combined with šólag⌣ in woman's necklace*; with collective sg. (§4696c) [< مُتَمَّة *completing*].
 obj. -mag⌣.
 pl. -manč(ı)⌣.

mútrag n. *necklace, worn by women* [< مُطْرَق id.].
 obj. mutrágk(ı)⌣, -ákk(ı)⌣, -ki⌒.

 gen. -ágn⌣v., -áŋ⌣c.
 pl. mútragı⌣.

mútt(ı) v.t. (a) *reap*; (b) *clip, cut short* [< *múrt(ı) (§713) < √múr- *cut* (§4566) + -t §2900; RSN, §§129, 200].
 ind. pres. aı̄⌣múttırı⌒, ɛr⌣múttın⌒ (-tí⌒, -tí⌒); perf. aı̄⌣múttıgori⌒ (N. -ıko-, -ıho-).
 imperat. mútti!
 part. pres. múttıl⌣ (*one*) *that reaps, etc., reaper, etc., reaping, etc.*; past múttɛl⌣ (*one*) *that reaped, etc., reaper, etc., reaping, etc.*
 íllɛm⌣múttıran⌒ (-m⌣m- < -g⌣m- §601) *they reap the wheat.*
 íllɛt⌣turúpkem⌣múttıran⌒ (-t⌣t- < -g⌣t- §707, -m⌣m- < -d⌣m- §600) *they reap the wheat with sickles* (§4647).
 undíltım⌣múttıl⌣ (-m⌣m- < -g⌣m- §601) *hair-cutter* (European style).
 án⌣sǎmak⌣kısőrkem⌣múttıri⌒ (-m⌣m- < -d⌣m- §600) *I clip my beard with scissors.*

múttar⌣ (-tǎr⌣; §§2200ff.) and
muttíd⌣ (§§2256ff.) n. *reaping, etc.*

mútt-an (§3890ff.) v.t. *tell to reap, etc., let reap, etc.*

mútti-bŭ- (§3931β) v.i. stat. *be in a reaped (etc.) state or condition.*
 ténn-ur⌣múttıbūn⌒ *his (her) hair* (lit. *head*) *is cut short.*

muttır-eg-áğ- (§§4071 ff.) v.t. = muttedól-.

mutt-ɛ-dól- (-tᵒd- §1178; §4022) and
muttır-ɛ-dól- (-rᵒd-; §4027) v.t. *be about to reap, etc.*

mutt-o-ğŭ-bŭ- (§4069) v.t. stat. *be on one's way (coming) to reap, etc.*

mutt-ɛ-má- (§4036) and
muttır-ɛ-má- (§4041) v.t. *become unable to reap, etc.*

muttır-ɛ-nóg (§§4048ff.) v.t. *go to reap, etc.*

muttır-ɛ-nóg-bŭ- (-nóggŭ- §546; §4058) v.t. stat. *be on one's way (going) to reap, etc.*

muttır-ɛ-tá- (§§4060ff.) v.t. *come to reap, etc.*

muttɛd-áğ- (§§3877ff.) v.t. *be in the situation of having reaped, etc.*
 ɛn⌣tímbes⌣dísınn-úrkı⌣muttedáğın⌒ *the woman, because her brother died, has cut her hair short with a knife*, lit. *...has reaped her head....*

múttı-kattı- (N. -ıha-; §4093) v.p. *be reaped, etc.*

muttókk(ı)⌣ Kénzi = mottókk(ı)⌣.

-n *genitival case-ending* (§4567).
-n⌒ (§§4229-31, 5770ff.) *positive sign of predication* is, are.
n⌣...? (before a vowel §1125) < **ní⌣...?** *who...?*
naál⌣ *sole, sandal* = nál⌣ [< نِعَال id. pl.].
naám n. *ostrich* [< نَعَام id.].
 obj. -ámg(ı)⌣, -gi⌒.
 pl. -ámı⌣.
nádd(ı)⌣ adj. (a) *sour*; (b) *bitter*; (c) *salt in taste* [< nárd(ı)⌣ (§537) id. LN, RN].

naddıfέ — nahár⌣

obj. -dıg⌣.
pl. -dınč(ı)⌣.
lēmŭn⌣déssı⌣náddın⌢ *an unripe lime is (unripe limes are §4696b) sour.*
gállo⌣náddın⌢ *an unripe date is (unripe dates are) sour.*
hál⌣náddın⌢ *(the) vinegar is sour.*
íŋ⌣gáhwa⌣náddın, sukkárkı⌣kómunun⌢ *this coffee is bitter, it has no sugar.*
šāi⌣náddın⌢ *the tea is bitter.*
kína⌣náddın⌢ *quinine is bitter.*
ín⌣έssı⌣náddın, umbúdkırın⌢ *this water is brackish, it's like salt.*

nádd-an- (§3910α) v.i. *become sour, etc.*

náddam-bŭ- (§§3949 ff.) v.i. stat. *be in a state of becoming (having become) sour, etc.*

naddıfέ (-dufέ) v.t. *clean* [< imperat. or imperf. stem of نَظَّفَ id. +-έ §3635].
ind. pres. āi⌣naddıfέri⌢; perf. āi⌣naddıfέgori⌢ (N. -έko-, -έho-).
imperat. naddıfέ!

naddıfέrar⌣ (-duf-, -rár-; §§2200 ff. 2207) and

naddıfέríd⌣ (-duf-; §§2256 ff., 2260) n. *cleaning.*

naddıfέr-an (-duf-; §§3890 ff., 3899) v.t. *tell to clean, let clean.*

naddıfέ-bŭ- (-duf-; §3931β) v.i. stat. *be in a cleaned state or condition.*

nadíf⌣ adj. *clean* [< نَظِيف id.].
obj. -ífk(ı)⌣, -ki⌢.
pl. -ífı⌣.

nadíf-an- (§3910α) v.i. *become clean.*

nadífam-bŭ- (§§3949 ff.) v.i. stat. *be in a state or condition of becoming (having become) clean, be getting (have got) clean.*

nadífk-ır (§3702) v.t. caus. *cause or allow to be clean, cleanse.*
ind. pres. āi⌣nadífkıddi⌢; perf. āi⌣nadífkírkori⌢.

náfεs⌣ (-fás⌣) *breath* = néfεs⌣.

náfıs⌣ *spirit, self* = néfıs⌣.

nágın? i.e. n⌣ágın? < ní⌣ágın? (§1125) *who is there?*

nágıs⌣ adj. *decreased, diminished; deficient, insufficient, incomplete, defective, short in measure, weight or amount* [< نَاقِص id.].
obj. nágısk(ı)⌣, -ki⌢.
pl. nág(ı)sı⌣.
fúkka⌣nágısun⌢ *the change is short.*
ɛr⌣áigı⌣dúŋgı⌣nágıskı⌣dέŋko⌢ *you gave (have given) me insufficient (short) money.*
— in fractions (§§2757, 5299-300, s.v. sá⌣) nágıs⌣ expresses *minus, less:*
X. wóggár⌣rátul⌣mıŋkóttı⌣dábun? (...⌣mıŋkóttɛr⌣dábun?) *how many rátul are there in (-r⌣) a wóggá?*
Y. tóskır⌣kέmsırɛ⌣nágıs⌢ *three less a quarter (2¾), lit. in three a quarter deficient.*
X. sá⌣mukóttέrrɛ? *what's the time?*
Y. tóskır⌣tóskırɛ⌣nágısun⌢ *2.40, lit. in three ⅓ is deficient.*
X. sıntákkı⌣tágoran? *when did they come?*
Y. sá⌣tóskır⌣tóskırɛ⌣nágısır⌢ *at 2.40.*

nāgısέ (nägsέ, näksέ,) v.i. *be decreased, etc., be short, etc.* [< نَاقِص *decreased* +-έ §3631].
ind. pres. tɛr⌣nāgısέn⌢ (nägs-, näks-, -sέ⌢, -sέ⌣, -sέ⌣); perf. tɛr⌣nāgısέgon⌢ (nägs-, näks-, -gŏ⌢, -gó⌢, N. -έkon⌢, -kŏ⌢, -kó⌢, -έhon⌢, -hŏ⌢, -hó⌢).

nāgısέg-ır (nägs-, näks-; N. -έkır, -έhır; §3681) (a) v.t. caus. *cause or allow to be decreased, etc.;* (b) v.t. *decrease, diminish, render deficient, etc.*
ind. pres. āi⌣nāgısέgıddi⌢.
íččın⌣nakséğırkó⌢ (-n⌣- < -g⌣n- §625) *(s)he (has) lessened (e.g. has given short measure of) the milk.*

nāgısέgırεd-ág- (nägs-, näks-; N. -έkır-, -έhır-; §§3877 ff.) v.t. *be in the situation of having caused or allowed to be decreased, etc.*
án⌣dúŋgın⌣nakséğıredágran⌢ (-n⌣- < -g⌣n- §625) *they have made my (our) money less (e.g. they have paid me (us) short).*

nāgısέgır-defέ (nägs-, etc.; §4137) v.t. *pay short, insufficiently, incompletely, not pay in full.*

nāgısέgır-defέ-dεn (nägs-, etc.; §§4142, 3996-7) v.t. *pay (to the speaker) insufficiently, etc.*
árgı⌣nakségırdefέdεnčırίkkó⌢ *(s)he did not pay (has not paid) us in full.*

nāgısέgır-defέ-dεned-ág- (nägs-, etc.; §§3877 ff.) v.t. *be in the situation of having paid (to the speaker) insufficiently, etc.*
árgı⌣nakségırdefέdεnčıredáğırırın⌢ *(s)he has not paid us in full.*

nāgısέgır-defέ-tır (nägs-, etc.; §§4142, 3998-9) v.t. *pay (to other than the speaker) insufficiently, etc.*
tírgı⌣nakségırdefέtırίkkó⌢ *(s)he did not pay (has not paid) them in full.*

nāgısέgır-defέ-tıred-ág- (nägs-, etc.; §§3877 ff.) v.t. *be in the situation of having paid (to other than the speaker) insufficiently, etc.*
tírgı⌣nakségırdefέtıredáğırırın⌢ *(s)he has not paid them in full.*

nāgısέŋ-ır (nägs-, näks-; N. -ŋkır; §3688) v.t. caus. = nāgısέgır.
ind. pres. āi⌣nāgısέŋgıddi⌢; perf. āi⌣nāgısέŋgírkori⌢.
ówwıt⌣tamámgır, tókkon⌣nagsέŋgırmεn⌢ (-t⌣t- < -g⌣t- §707) *make (it) exactly two, don't let it be less.*

⌣náhad (§4285δ; -nahad⌣ §4285γ; -at⌢) postp. (i = prep. §§4287, 4320) *like, as (epithet) as* [< نَحْت *nature, natural disposition, cast of constitution*].

— follows the undeclined stem (§4315):
íg⌣náhağ⌣ğúgurın⌢ (-ğ-ğ- < -d⌣ğ- §550) *it burns like fire.*
íg⌣nahağ⌣ğúgr⌣εgó⌢ *it was as hot as fire, lit. it was hot like fire.*
tɛr⌣wέl⌣náhad⌣úkkın⌢ *(s)he (it) barks like a dog.*
díbul⌣náhad⌣ırískı⌣kó⌢ *it has a smell like a corpse.*
búŋgı⌣wī-nahad⌣dólli⌢ *I want the coffee like yesterday's, lit.....like yesterday.*

⌣náhad⌣ (-nahad⌣, -at⌢) postp. (ii = conj. §§4287, 4321) *as.*
— follows the bare form of the subjunctive (§§2943, 2951):
búsın⌣náhad⌣úskur⌢ *set it as it was.*
āi⌣búsı-nahat⌣tέpkori⌢ *I (have) remained as I was.*

⌣naháď⌣ (-át⌢) postp. (i = prep. §4322) *like, as (epithet) as* = ⌣náhad⌣ [< نَحْت *nature, etc.* = نَحْت].
— follows the undeclined stem (§4315):
wέl⌣nahád⌣ağúkkın⌢ *(s)he (it) is (keeps on) barking like a dog.*

⌣nahád⌣ (-át⌢) postp. (ii = conj. §4323) *as.*
— follows the bare form of the subjunctive (§§2943, 2951):
tɛr⌣búsun⌣nahád⌣úskur⌢ *set it as it was.*

⌣nahádk(ı)⌣ (-hátk(ı)⌣, -hátt(ı)⌣ §716, -hákk(ı)⌣ §574⌣, -ki⌢, -ti⌢) postp. (i = prep. §4324) *like, as (epithet) as.*
— follows the undeclined stem (§4315):
íg⌣nahákkı⌣ğúgurın⌢ *it burns like fire.*

⌣nahádk(ı)⌣ (-hátk(ı)⌣, -hátt(ı)⌣ -hákk(ı)⌣ §574⌣, -ki⌢, -ti⌢) postp. (ii = conj. §4325) *as.*
— follows the bare form of the subjunctive (§§2943, 2951):
ár⌣ağsu⌣nahátti⌣tέkkoru⌢ *we remained as we were (sitting).*

⌣nahádk-εd (-átk⌢, -áttεd⌣, -ákkεd⌣, -εt⌢, -έ⌢; §§5858-60, 5889) postp. (i = prep. §4326) *like.*
— follows the undeclined stem (§4315):
íg⌣nahákkεğ⌣ğúgurın⌢ (-ğ-ğ- < -d⌣ğ- §550) *it burns like fire.*
ášk⌣έlum⌣nahákkεb⌣bówwın⌢ (-b⌣b- < -d⌣b- §518) *the Varanus lizard swims like a crocodile.*
tέr⌣wέl⌣nahákkεk⌣kōrábkı⌣ğómın⌢ (-k⌣k- < -d⌣k- §574) *(s)he (it) raises a loud cry like a dog.*
wέl⌣nahátté⌢ *it's like a dog.*

⌣nahádkεd (-átk⌢, -áttεd⌣, -ákkεd⌣, -εt⌢, -έ⌢) §§5858-60, 5889) postp. (ii = conj. §4327) *as.*
— follows bare form of subjunctive (§§2943, 2951):
āi⌣tέkkı⌣wέtıssu⌣nahákkεd⌣áukŏ⌢ *(s)he did (has done) as I told him (her).*
ar⌣έkkı⌣wέtıssu⌣nahákkέ⌢ *it's as we told you.*

nahár⌣ (náh-, nεh-) n. *day (as distinguished from night;* = ugrέs⌣) [< نَهَار id.].
obj. -árk(ı)⌣, -ki⌢.
pl. -árı⌣.
nahár⌣mállεg⌣, -gi⌢ (§§6038, 6043) adv.-complex (a) *all day, the whole day;* (b) *every day.*
nεhár⌣mállεg⌣índ⌣ağkoran⌢ *they (have) sat here all day.*
nahár⌣mállεg⌣ğáŋgi⌢ (-ğ-ğ- < -g⌣ğ- §551) *fill it every day.*
ınnówwı⌣nehár⌣ (§4750) and ınnówwın⌣nehár⌣ (§4810) noun-complex *today.*
ınnówwı⌣nehárro⌣tágoran⌢ *they came (have come) today.*
ınnówwın⌣nehárkı⌣nókkoran⌢ *they went (have gone) today.*

nahår⁀, like jóm⁀, combines with the names of the days of the week to form noun-complexes:
— following the nominative (§4750):
kɪrăgɛ⁀nahår⁀ *Sunday*.
bŭš⁀nahår⁀ *Monday*.
bušnóñ⁀nahår⁀ *Tuesday*.
árbaha⁀nahår⁀ *Wednesday*.
hamís⁀nahår⁀ *Thursday*.
móšono⁀nahår⁀ and
ğíma⁀nahår⁀ *Friday*.
sámtɛ⁀nahår⁀ *Saturday*.
— also following the genitive (§4810):
kɪrăgen⁀nahår⁀ *Sunday*.
bŭš⁀nahår⁀ (§864) *Monday*.
bušnóñ⁀nahår⁀ (§842) *Tuesday*.
árbahan⁀nahår⁀ *Wednesday*.
hamís⁀nahår⁀ (§859) *Thursday*.
móšonon⁀nahår⁀ and
ğíman⁀nahår⁀ *Friday*.
sámten⁀nahår⁀ *Saturday*.
kɪrăgɛ⁀nahår⁀móŋkon⁀ (-r⁀m- < -rn⁀m- §850),
kɪrăgɛ⁀nahår⁀móŋkon⁀,
kɪrăgɛ⁀nahårm⁀bókkon⁀ and
kɪrăgen⁀nahårm⁀bókkon⁀ *till Sunday*.
árbaha⁀nahårkɪ⁀tågoran⁁ *they came on Wednesday*.
móšonon⁀nahårro⁀nókkoran⁁ *they went on Friday*.
ar⁀bŭš⁀nahårroton⁀nalkómunun⁁ *we haven't seen him (her, it, them §5083) since Monday*.
nahårn-d(ɪ)⁀ (náh-, nɛh-; §§2545 ff.) *adj. appertaining to the day, of the day, the day's*.
nahås⁀ n. *copper, brass* [< نَحَاس *id.*].
obj. -åsk(ɪ)⁀, -kɪ⁁.
năksɛ́ *be decreased, etc.* = năgɪsɛ́⁁.
nál (a) v.t. *see*; (b) v.t. *look at, observe, watch*; (c) v.t. *look for, look out for*; (d) v.t. *see, learn by seeing, ascertain*; (e) v.i. *look* [cp. ON. ᚱᚨᛚ *id.* GNT s.v.; RSN, §§129, 200].
ind. pres. aı⁀nállı⁁, ɛr⁀nálın⁁ (-lí⁁, -lí⁁); perf. aı⁀nálkori⁁.
imperat. nál!, pl. nálwɛ! (nálwɛ́!).
part. pres. nálıl⁀ (*one*) *that sees, spectator, observer, seeing*; past nálɛl⁀ (*one*) *that saw, spectator, observer, seeing*.
pl.obj. imperat. nálır!, pl. nalírwɛ! (nalírwɛ!, nalíwwɛ! §723, -wɛ́!); nálırır!, pl. nalırírwɛ! (-ı́rwɛ́!, -íwwɛ!, -wɛ́!).
def. pres. aı⁀nálosrı⁁ (⁀nalósrı⁁ §1885); aı⁀nálɛdrı⁁ (⁀nalédrı⁁ §1895).
def. imperat. nálɛt! (nálɛ́!, ˘ˊ, ˘ˊ §1896); pl. nalédwɛ! (nalédwɛ́!, -léddɛ! §533, -dɛ́!).
áŋ⁀kăn⁀ıkkɪ⁀nálli *I see the light (fire) of my (our) house*.
ar⁀nalkómunun⁁ *we didn't see (haven't seen) him (her, it, them §5083)*.
íŋgun⁀nalıddi⁁ (-n⁀n- < -g⁀n- §625) and
íŋgun⁀nalíríddi⁁ *I('ll §5369b) look at (each of §5456) these*.
dúl-lɛn⁀nál⁀ (-l-l- < -l-w- §580, -n⁀n- < -g⁀n- §625) *look out for a large one*.
tékkı⁀nál⁀ *look for him (her, it)* = tékkı⁀tɛbɛnal⁀.
ɛr⁀ógıg̃⁀kı́sır⁀undúrsıŋgı⁀nálkoná? *did you see the man put it (them) into the bag?*
ɛr⁀tɛr⁀dúŋgıs⁀sókkɛsuŋgı⁀nálkoná? (-s⁀s- < -g⁀s- §678) *did you see him (her) take the money?*
tɛ́m⁀måktábkı⁀så⁀mıŋkóttɛrro⁀kusíŋgı⁀nál⁁ *see (i.e. ascertain) at what time he opens his office*.
éssit⁀tɛron⁀ğúgr⁀ɛgın⁀nál⁁ (-t⁀t- < -g⁀t- §707) *see whether the water is hot*.
N. kúlut⁀tɛrom⁀búkın⁀nál⁁ (-t⁀t- < -g⁀t-) *see whether the stone is there*.
nállı⁀tɛron⁀tågogın⁀ *I'll (§5369b) see whether (s)he (it) has come*.
X. bɛ́ntı⁀dåná? *are there any dates?* (§4696b).
Y. nállı⁁ *I'll (§5369b) see*.
nálar⁀ (-lår⁀; §§2200 ff.) and
nalíd⁀ (§§2256 ff.) n. *seeing, etc.*
káwɪrten⁀nálar⁀sɛ́rɛn⁁ and
káwɪrten⁀nalíd⁀sɛ́rɛn⁁ (a) *the bird's (birds' §4696c) sight is good, i.e. it sees well*; (b) *it is good to see the bird(s)*.
káwɪrten⁀nalíd⁀sɛrɛn⁀tɛrárkı⁀kálmɛndann⁀ıllår⁁ *it is good to watch the birds lest they eat the crops*.
nál-an (§§3890 ff.) v.t. *tell to see, etc., let see, etc.*
***nál-bŭ-** not heard.
nall-ɛg-ág- (§§4071 ff.) v.t. =nalɛdól-.
nal-ɛ-dól- (-lᵒd- §1178; §4022) and
nall-ɛ-dól- (-lᵒd-; §4027) v.t. *be about to see, etc.*
ar⁀nalıddᵒdóllu⁀ (§4030) *we are just going (about) to look at (for) them*.
nall-ɛ-ğŭ-bŭ- (§4069) v.t. stat. *be on one's way (coming) to see, etc.*
nal-ɛ-må- (§4036) and
nall-ɛ-må- (§4041) v.t. *become unable to see, etc.*
nall-ɛ-nóg (§§4048 ff.) v.t. *go to see, etc.*
nallɛnókkorandɛ́? *did they go (have they been) to see?*
kúbkɪ⁀nallɛnogóskoran⁁ *they have gone to look at (for) the boat*.
nall-ɛ-nóg-bŭ- (-nóggŭ- §546; §4058) v.t. stat. *be on one's way (going) to see, etc.*
X. hánun⁀nalóskorandɛ́? (-n⁀n- < -g⁀n- §625) *have they seen the donkey?*
Y. nallɛnógbŭran⁁ *they are going to have a look at (for) it*.
nall-ɛ-nog(ɪ)r-ɛg-ág- (§5700) v.t. =nallɛnogɛdól-.
nall-ɛ-nog-ɛ-dól- (-gᵒd- §1178; §5696) and
nall-ɛ-nog(ɪ)r-ɛ-dól- (-rᵒd-; §5698) v.t. *be about to go to see, etc.*
nall-ɛ-nog-ɛ-må- (§5697) and
nall-ɛ-nog(ɪ)r-ɛ-må- (§5699) v.t. *become unable to go to see, etc.*
nall-ɛ-tå- (§§4060 ff.) v.t. *come to see, etc.*
nalɛd-ág- (§§3877 ff.) v.t. and t. *be in the situation of having seen, etc.*
nalɛb-bél (§§4169 ff.; nalɛdgɪ-bél, -ɛggɪ- §§4176-8) v.t. *go (come) out on (after) seeing, etc.*
nalɛb-bél-bŭ- (§4220; -ɛdgɪ-, -ɛggɪ- §4221) v.t. stat. *be on one's way out on (after) seeing, etc.*
nalɛd-ɛttá (-ɛ́ttå, §4200; -ɛdgɛttá, -ɛggɛt-, -ɛdgɛ́ttå, -ɛggɛ́t- §4201) v.t. *bring (ɛttá s.v. ɛ́d) after seeing, etc.*
nalɛn-nóg (§§4169 ff.; nalɛdgɪ-nóg, -ɛggɪ- §§4176-8) v.t. *go (etc. s.v. nóg) on (after) seeing, etc.*
kúbkɪ⁀nalɛnnogóskoran⁁ *as soon as they saw the boat they were off*.
nalɛn-nóg-bŭ- (§4220; -ɛdgɪnóg-, -ɛggɪ- §4221; -nóggŭ- §546) v.t. stat. *be on one's way (going) on (after) seeing, etc.*
nalɛt-tá (§§4169 ff., 5723; -ɛdgɪ-tá, -ɛggɪ- §§4176-8) v.t. *come (back) on (after) seeing, etc., just go (§5713) and see, etc.*
imperat. nalétta!, -ɛ́dgɪta!, -ɛ́ggɪ-; pl. nalettáwɛ!, -ɛdgɪtá-, -ɛggɪ-, -tåwɛ́!
ğú⁀tɛron⁀ågkın⁀wáll⁀ågmɛŋkın⁀nalétta⁁ *go and see whether (s)he's there or not and come back (=just go and see whether (s)he's there or not)*.
nal-ɛttá (-ɛ́ttå §3855, §5723) v.t. *bring (ɛttá s.v. ɛ́d) on seeing, etc., bring after looking at, etc.*
imperat. nalétta!, pl. naléttáwɛ!, ˘́˘˘́.
nalɛt-tó (occ. -ɛdtó §§4169 ff.; -ɛdgɪ-tó, -ɛggɪ- §§4176-8) v.t. *go (come) in on (after) seeing, etc.*
aıgɪ⁀nalɛttógoran⁁ *as soon as they saw me they went (came) in*.
nalɛt-tó-bŭ- (occ. -ɛd-tó, §4220; -ɛdgɪtó-, -ɛggɪ- §4221) v.t. stat. *be on one's way in on (after) seeing, etc.*
nalɛd-wıdɛ-tá (-ɛwwı- §718; -wᵘdɛ- §4200; -ɛdgɪ-w-, -ɛggɪ- §4201) v.t. *come back on (after) seeing, etc.*
kólɛn⁀nalɛwwᵘdɛ́ta⁁ (-n⁀n- < -g⁀n- §625) *have a look at the water-wheel (etc. s.v. kólɛ⁀) and come back (=just go (§5713) and have a look, etc.)*.
nál-kattı- (§4093) v.p. *be seen, etc., be visible* (§5704).
nálkattar (-tår⁀; §§2200 ff., 2213) and
nalkattíd⁀ (§§2256 ff., 2266) n. *being seen, etc., visibility*.
nalkáttı-bŭ- (§§4105, 4107) v.i. stat. *be in a visible state or condition*.
ınnówwɪn⁀nalkattıbúmunun⁁ (-n⁀n- < -g⁀n- §625) *today (s)he (it) is not to be seen*.
nalos-bél (-obbél §521; §§4180-4; -osgɪ-bél, -ozgɪ-, -oggɪ- §4185) v.t. =nalɛbbél.
såbı⁀wɛ́lgı⁀nalobbélkoran⁁ *the cats on seeing the dog came (went) out*.
nalos-bél-bŭ- (-obbél-, -osgɪbél-, -ozgɪ-, -oggɪ- §§4222-3) v.t. stat. =nalɛbbélbŭ-.
nalos-sándı (§§4180-4; -osgɪsán-, -ozgɪ-, -oggɪ- §4185) v.t. *be afraid (of) on seeing*.
nalos-sandı-síg (§4203; -osgɪsan-, -ozgɪ-, -oggɪ- §4205) v.t. *be struck with fear and terror on seeing*.
aı⁀ğánın⁀naloggısandısíkkorı⁁ (-n⁀n- < -g⁀n- §625) *on seeing the fiend I was struck with fear and terror*.
nalos-tá (-ottá §714; §§4180-4; -osgɪtá, -ozgɪ-, -oggɪ- §4185) v.t. *come (back) on (after) seeing, etc.*
imperat. nalósta!, -ótta!, -ósgɪta!, -ózgɪ-, -óggɪ-; pl. naloståwɛ!, -ottá-, -ósgɪta!, -ozgɪ-, -oggɪ-, -wɛ́!
nalos-tó (-ottó §714; §§4180-4; -osgɪtó, -ozgɪ-, -oggɪ- §4185) v.t. *go (come) in on (after) seeing, etc.*
såbı⁀wɛ́lgı⁀nalottógoran⁁ *the cats on seeing the dog went (came) in*.

nál⌣ — nɛdmɛ́

nalos-úwɛ (§§4180-4; -osgú-, -ozgú-, -oggú- §4185) v.t. call on seeing.
    ar⌣áli⌣nnalosúwɛgoru⌢ (-n⌣n- < -g⌣n- §625) on seeing ɛáli we called him.
nalos-wɪdɛ-tá (-oww⌣ı- §724; §4203; -osgɪwɪ-, -ozgɪ-, -oggɪ- §4205; -wᵘdɛ-) v.t. come back on (after) seeing, etc.
    imperat. naloswídɛta!, -oww-, -osgɪwí-, -ozgɪ-, -oggɪ-, -wɪdɛta!, -wᵘdɛ́-.
    ar⌣kóle⌣nnaloggɪwᵘdɛtágoru⌢ (-n⌣n- < -g⌣n- §625) we (have) returned after looking at the water-wheel (etc. s.v. kólɛ⌣), i.e. we just went (have just been) and had a look at the water-wheel.
nál⌣ (naál⌣ §1350) n. sole, sandal; with collective sg. (§4696d) [< نَعْل id.].
    obj. nálg(ı)⌣, -gi⌢.
    pl. nálı⌣.
nālé (§1351) v.t. curse [< نَعَل imperf. stem of Sudan Ar. لَعَن < نَعَن id. +-ɛ́ §3619].
    ind. pres. aī⌣nālɛ́ri⌢; perf. aī⌣nālɛ́gori⌢ (N. -ɛ́ko-, -ɛ́ho-).
nálu n. sleep [§§2337-8; cp. ON. ралоγ id. GNT s.v.].
    obj. -lug⌣.
nalu-kátt(ı)⌣ (N. -uhá-) adj. addicted to sleep, lazy [§§2534-5].
    obj. -tɪg⌣.
    pl. -tɪnč(ı)⌣.
nálu-kɪññ(ı)⌣ (§§2536-7) adj. sleepless.
nálukɪññɪg-ɪr (‿‿‿‿, N. -ɪkɪr, -ɪhɪr; §§3703, 5708) v.t. caus. cause or allow to be sleepless.
nalun-ɛ́r⌣ n. sleepiness, drowsiness [< ná-lun⌣*ɛ́r⌣ intention (desire) of sleep §2244].
    obj. -ɛrk(ı)⌣, -ki⌢.
    aīg⌣nalunɛ́r⌣ārɪn⌢ and (§4626) nalunɛ́r⌣aīg⌣ārɪn⌢ I am sleepy.
⌣náman⌣ (§§4482-3) subord. conj.
    [< Sudan Ar. نامَن till] not in independent use, but optionally preceding a verb that is followed by ⌣bókkon or ⌣móŋkon; its omission does not change the sense (§§6194-5):
⌣náman...⌣bókkon and
⌣náman...⌣móŋkon (a) till, until; (b) while, as long as.
    tɪr⌣náman⌣tāram⌣bókkon⌣indo⌣tɛk⌢ wait here till they come.
    aī⌣náman⌣tārɪ⌣móŋkon⌣indo⌣tɛgwɛ́⌢ wait (pl.) here till I come.
    aī⌣náman⌣tanáll⌣bókkom⌣mugó⌢ leave him (her, it, them) till I come and look at him (her, it, them).
    aī⌣námam⌣bówwɪrɪ⌣bókkon⌣tókkon⌣tāmɛn⌢ don't come while I am bathing.
    tírgı⌣náman⌣ɛr⌣nāman⌣móŋkon⌣gúñči⌢ watch them as long as you (can §5377) see them.
năr n. side of river, river-bank, waterside (= ár⌣, gár⌣) [< ár id.; n- is the genitival -n⌣ of the preceding noun in everyday phrases such as éssɪn⌣ár⌣ waterside, úrun⌣ár⌣ river-bank (§4810) regarded as éssɪ⌣nár⌣, úru⌣nár⌣ (§4750); cp. ON. гар side, outside(?) GNT s.v.; §2171a].
    obj. nărk(ı)⌣, -ki⌢.
    pl. nărı⌣.

uru-năr⌣ (§2364) river-bank.
nărro⌣tɛ́p⌢ wait on the river-bank.
kúb⌣nărro⌣tɛ́bɪn⌢ the boat waits at the bank.
-năr⌣ (§§4304-5, 5858-60, 5874-6) postp. = prep. (a, rest) beside, by; (b, rest) with, at the dwelling of (παρά, apud, chez, bei, da, عِنْد); (c, rest) with, in the possession of (-ل, عِنْد); (d, motion) to, towards (not with place-names) commonly, but not exclusively, beside (etc.) a person, not a thing [unstressed, enclitic form of năr⌣ (water)side].
— suffixed to bare stem; with the personal pronouns -r-n- > -nn- (§628b).
    tăğír-năr⌣wɛ́rsɪngori⌢ I tried to get it (§5083) at the merchant's.
    án⌣năr⌣ta! (a) come to me!; (b) come to us!
    kă⌣năr⌣nógriá? shall (§5369b) I go to the house?
    tén⌣năr⌣tɛlɛgráfkı⌣ǧóm⌢ send him (her) a telegram.
-năr⌣, like -ل, عِنْد, may be rendered by have, have got.
    kúsar⌣búrunăr⌢ the girl has the key.
    kúsar⌣án⌣năr⌢ I have the key.
    kúsar⌣én⌣năr⌢ you have the key.
    kúsar⌣tén⌣năr⌢ (s)he has the key.
    kúsar⌣án⌣năr⌢ we have the key.
    kúsar⌣in⌣năr⌢ you (pl.) have the key.
    kúsar⌣tin⌣năr⌢ they have the key.
    X. én⌣sā⌣ǧɛdís⌣sɛ́? (-s⌣s- < -d⌣s- §677) where's your new watch?
    Y. án⌣năr⌢ I have it (I've got it).
    hánu⌣tín⌣năd⌣dā⌢ (§1786) -d⌣d- < -r⌣d- §537) they have the (a) donkey.
-năr accepts a sign of predication (§§4224ff.):
    kúsar⌣án⌣năru⌢ (§1966) I have the key.
    kúsar⌣én⌣năru⌢ you have the key, etc.
-năr + -rɛ́ > -nărɛ́ (§1009)
    kúsar⌣án⌣nărɛ́? have I (got) the key?
    kúsar⌣én⌣nărɛ́? have you (got) the key, etc.
-năr accepts the interrogative particle -ó? (§5845β i):
    kánd⌣én⌣nāró? have you the knife?
-năr-tōn⌣ (-năttōn §713; -tō⌢, -tō⌢, -tō⌢ §939; §§4311-2, 5858-60, 5881-4) postp. = prep. from (a person), away from, off.
    ambábnarton⌣néukori⌢ I (have) inherited it from my father.
    ár⌣íŋgɪ⌣tín⌣narton⌣ɛwɪrtɪrárkoru⌢ we (have) got this from them in exchange.
    aīg⌣dɪdɛdólɪn, aīg⌣ǧomɛdólɪn: án⌣nártom⌣mírwɛ! (s)he's just going to abuse me, (s)he's just going to hit me: keep (pl.) him (her) off me!
    ín⌣tén⌣narton⌢ this is from him (her).
    ín⌣tén⌣narton? (§5884) is this from him (her)?
-năr-tōn- accepts a sign of predication (§§4224ff.).
    ín⌣tén⌣nartónun⌢ this is from you.
    X. tín⌣nartōndɛ́? is (s)he (it) from them?
    Y. wăran, án⌣nartōn⌣ no, (s)he (it) is from me (us).
-năr-tōn- accepts -ó? (§5845β i):
    ín⌣tén⌣nartōnó? is this from him (her)?

nărd(ı)⌣ adj. sour, bitter, salt = nádd(ı)⌣.
năwɛ⌣ n. Naui (on map), a village on the right bank of the Nile, about 14 miles above Hándag.
    obj. năwɛk(ı)⌣, năwɛg⌣ (§1538).
náwud (náūud⌣) n. adze [< *náwɪd⌣ (§1202) < *nawíd⌣ (§1154) < -n⌣awíd⌣, i.e. genitival -n⌣ + awíd⌣ working (etc. s.v. áu) in some such common phrase as án⌣n⌣awíd⌣ my (sc. tool for) working taken as án⌣*nawíd⌣ my *tool; §2171a].
    obj. nawúdk(ı)⌣, -útk(ı)⌣, -útt(ı)⌣ §2462, -ki⌢, -ti⌢.
    pl. náwudı⌣, náūudı⌣.
    náūutkem⌣mérran⌢ (-m⌣m- < -d⌣m- §600) they cut it with an adze.
názɪr n. superintendent [< ناظِر id.].
    obj. názɪrk(ı)⌣ (§1521), -ki⌢.
    pl. názɪrı⌣.
    máhattan⌣názɪr⌣ station-master (ناظِر مَحَطَّة).
náfɛs⌣ (-fās⌣) breath = néfɛs⌣.
náfɪs spirit, self = néfís⌣.
náhār day = nahár⌣.
nébɛd n. cream = némɛd (§1014).
    obj. nɛbɛdk(ı)⌣, -ɛtk(ı)⌣, -étt(ı)⌣ §2462, -ki⌢, -ti⌢.
    gen. nɛbɛ́dn⌣v., nébɛn⌣c.
    íččɪn⌣nɛ́bɛd⌣ cream of milk.
    míssɪn⌣nébɛd⌣ rheum of the eye, mucous discharge of the eye.
nébɪ⌣ n. prophet (cp. ɛnnébɪ⌣) [< نَبِيء id.].
    obj. -bıg⌣.
    pl. nɛbínč(ı)⌣.
    nébɪ-wɛ́r⌣sɪnnarr⌣ɪmbɛlóskon⌢ a prophet has arisen in Sɛnnár.
nɛbíd n. wine (description of manufacture AZN s.v. [< نَبِيذ id.].
    obj. -bíd(ı)⌣, -bítk(ı)⌣, -bítt(ı)⌣ §2462, -ki⌢, -ti⌢.
    gen. -bídn⌣v., -bín⌣c.
    ɛnčɪ⌣nɛbítti⌣béntɪrtōn⌣āuran⌢ the women make wine from dates (§4696b).
néd⌣ n. tongue [RSN, §129].
    obj. nédk(ı)⌣, nétk(ı)⌣, néttı(ı)⌣ §2462, -ki⌢, -ti⌢.
    gen. nédn⌣v., nénn⌣v.c., nén⌣c.
    pl. nédı⌣.
nédn-d(ı)⌣ (nénn-d(ı)⌣, nén-d(ı)⌣; §§2545ff.) adj. appertaining to the tongue, tongue's, lingual.
nɛd-nosó-kōl⌣ (§2578) adj. impudent, insolent in speech, lit. having a long (-nosó-) tongue.
nɛdmɛ́ v.t. regret, be sorry about, repent of [< نِدم id. or نَدِم repentant + -ɛ́ §3616].
    ind. pres. aī⌣nɛdmɛ́ri⌢; perf. aī⌣nɛd-mɛ́gori⌢ (N. -ɛ́ko-, -ɛ́ho-).
    aī⌣íŋg⌣āusin⌣nɛdmɛ́ri⌢ (-n⌣n- < -g⌣n- §625) I regret that I did this (that).
nɛdmɛ́rar (-rár⌣; §§2200ff., 2207) and
nɛdmɛ́ríd (§§2256ff., 2260) n. regret, repentance.
nɛdmɛ́-bŭ (§3934) (a) v.i. stat. be in a regretted (etc.) state; (b) v.t. stat. be in a

150

regretting (etc.) state, be in a state of regret for.
aɪ‿nɛdmɛ́burɪ◠ *I am sorry.*

nɛdmɛ́g-ɪr (N. -ɛ́kɪr, -ɛ́hɪr; §3681) (*a*) v.t. caus. *cause or allow to regret, etc.*; (*b*) v.t. *render sorry, distress, grieve.*
ín‿āɪgɪ‿nɛdmɛ́gɪrɪn◠ *this distresses me.*

nɛdmɛ̄-kattɪ- (N. -ɛ̄ha-; §4093) v.p. *be regretted, etc.*

nɛdmɛ̄-káttɪ-bŭ- (N. -ɛ̄há-; §§4105, 4108) v.i. stat. *be in a regretted (etc.) state or condition.*

nɛfɛ́ v.i. *be useful* [< نَفْع *utility* + -ɛ́ §3620].
ind. pres. aɪ‿nɛfɛ́rɪ◠; perf. aɪ‿nɛfɛ́gorɪ◠ (N. -ɛ́ko-, -ɛ́ho-).
imperat. nɛfɛ́!
part. pres. nɛfɛ́l‿ (*one*) *that is useful, useful,* obj. nɛfɛ́lg(ɪ)‿, -gɪ◠; past nɛfɛ́rɛl‿ (*one*) *that was useful, useful,* obj. nɛfɛ́rɛlg(ɪ)‿, -gɪ◠.
neg. part. pres. nɛfɛ́mɛnɪl‿ (*one*) *that is not useful, useless,* obj. nɛfɛ́mɛnɪlg(ɪ)‿, -gɪ◠.
ím‿mɪ́ndo‿bɪnɛfɛ́n? *what will be the use of this?*
tollíd‿nɛfɛ́munun, kálli! kallíd‿nɛfɛ́n◠ *pulling is useless; push! pushing is of use (has some value, effect).*

nɛfɛ́rar‿ (-rár‿; §§2200ff., 2207) and
nɛfɛ̄ríd‿ (§§2256, 2260) n. *being useful, usefulness, utility, use.*

nɛfɛ́-bŭ- (§3931α) v.i. stat. *be in a useful state or condition.*

nɛfɛ́ŋg-ɪr (N. -ŋkɪr; §3688) v.t. caus. *cause or allow to be useful.*

néfɛs‿ (náf-, náf-, -fás‿ §1327) n. *breath* [< نَفَس id.].
obj. nɛfɛ́sk(ɪ)‿, -kɪ◠.
wárrɪrtōm‿bōdɛdágran, nɛfɛ́skɪ‿ kómunan◠ *they have run from a long way off, they are out of breath.*

néfɪs‿ (náf-, náf- §§1327, 1359) n. (*a*) *spirit, soul* [< نَفْس id.]; (*b*) *self;* (*c*) *person.*
obj. nɛfɪ́sk(ɪ)‿, -kɪ◠.
— *like* نَفْس, *supplies a reflexive pronoun* (§§2688-9, 2692, 5170):
ɛsmān‿tén-nɛfɪ́skɪ‿dúlgɪrɪn◠ ʕoθmán *is conceited (vain).*
aɪ‿án-nɛfɪ́skɪ‿'sérɛn‿ɛwɛ́gorɪ◠ *I said to myself 'good!' lit.... 'it is good'* (§6148).
án-nɛfɪ́skɪ‿béttarɪ◠ and
án-nɛfɪ́skɛb‿béttarɪ◠ (-b‿b- < -d‿b- §518) *I'll bring it (them) myself.*
aɪ‿án-nɛfɪ́skɛn‿nókkorɪ◠ (-n‿n- < -d‿n- §624) *I went (have been) myself.*
án-nɛfɪ́skɛw‿wɛ̄tíkkoru‿ (-w‿w- < -d‿w- §718) *we told him (her, them* §5083) *ourselves.*
aɪ‿án-nɛfɪ́skɛb‿bústar‿undúrkorɪ◠ (-b‿b- < -d‿b- §518) *I (have) put it (them) into the post myself.*
ɛ́n-nɛfɪ́skɛw‿āukonā? *did you do (have you done) it yourself?*
tɪmbábʊ‿tén-nɛfɪ́skɪ‿bɛ́gō◠ *his (her) father (has) killed himself.*
bɛnnáŋkolɛ‿nɛfɪ́s‿ówwɪd‿dólɪn◠ (-d‿d- < -g‿d- §534) *the cotton gin needs two persons (sc. to work it).*

ín‿ğéllɪ‿néfɪs‿tóskɪd‿dólɪn◠ *this work needs three persons.*
ín‿ğéllɪ‿néfɪs‿dɪgríd‿dólɪn◠ (-d‿d- < -g‿d- §534) *this work needs many persons.*

nɛfɪs-dúl-ko (§4120a) v.i. *be proud, conceited, vain.*
part. pres. nɛfɪsdúlkōl‿ (*one*) *that is proud, etc.,* obj. nɛfɪsdúlkōlg(ɪ)‿, -gɪ◠.
tɛr‿nɛfɪsdúlkó◠ (§939) (*s*)*he is proud (etc.).*

nɛhár‿ *day* = nahár‿.

‿nɛhéd-dé? (§§4246, 5801) interr. *sign of predication used of persons who are...?, who is...?, who (pl.) are...?* [‿nɛhéd- < نَحَت *carving, shaping, nature, constitution* (*a doublet of* ‿náhad‿); -dé? *are...?, is...?, are (pl.)...?* (s.v. -rɛ?)].
X. ɛ́r‿nɛhéddé? *who are you?*
Y. aɪ‿ɛnnúr-tará‿ *I'm En-Núr.*
X. ín‿nɛhéddé? *who is this?*
Y. ín‿áli-taran‿ *this is* ʕ*áli.*
X. tén‿tɪ́rtɪ‿nɛhéddé? *who is his (her, its) owner?*
Y. alíndɪn◠ (*s*)*he (it) is* ʕ*áli's (...belongs to* ʕ*áli).*
ír‿nɛhéddé? *who are you (pl.)?*
X. tɪr‿nɛhéddé? *who are they?*
Y. mohámmáttoṇ‿áhmáttɪn◠ (-tt- < -tk- < -dk- §716; s.v. -on‿) *Muḥammad and Áḥmad.*

nɛ́jj(ɪ) v.i. *swell.*
ind. pres. tɛr‿nɛ́jjɪn◠ (-jī◠, -jí◠); perf. tɛr‿nɛ́jjɪgon◠ (-gō◠, -gó◠; N. -ɪkon◠, -kō◠, -kó◠, -ɪhon◠, -hō◠, -hó◠).
ánn‿nɛjjɪ́óskó◠ *my hand has (hands have* §4696a) *swollen.*

nɛ́jjar‿ (-jár‿; §§2200ff.) and
nɛ́jjíd‿ (§§2256ff.) n. *swelling.*

nɛ́jjɪ-bŭ (§3931α) v.i. stat. *be in a swollen state or condition.*
tɛ́nn‿óssɪ‿nɛ́jjɪbūn◠ *his (her, its) leg (foot) is (legs, feet* §4696a) *are) swollen.*

nɛ́jjɪr-ɛg-ág- (§§4071ff.) v.i. = nɛjjɛdól-.

nɛ́jj-ɛ-dól- (-j°d- §1178; §4022) and
nɛ́jjɪr-ɛ-dól- (-r°d-; §4027) v.i. *be about to swell.*

nɛ́jjɛd-ág- (§§3877ff.) v.i. *be in the condition of having (become) swollen.*
tén-tu‿nɛ́jjɛdágɪn◠ *his (her, its) stomach is distended.*

nɛ́jjɪg-ɪr (N. -ɪkɪr, -ɪhɪr; §3682) (*a*) v.t. caus. *cause or allow to swell;* (*b*) v.t. *render swollen, swell.*
án-tūn‿nɛ́jjɪgɪrɪn◠ (-n‿n- < -g‿n- §625) *it distends my stomach.*

nɛ́jjɪ́ŋg-ɪr (nɛ́jjɪŋgɪr; N. -ŋkɪr; §3688) v. caus. ɪr = nɛ́jjɪgɪr.

nékk(ɪ)...?, *i.e.* n‿ɛ́kk(ɪ)‿ = nf‿ɛ́kk(ɪ)‿ (§1125), *who...you (obj.)?*
nékk‿íŋgɪ‿tíkkó? *who gave (has given) you this?*

nél n. (*a*) *tooth;* with collective sg. (§4696a) [*RSN,* §129 s.v. *nid*]; (*b*) = fíl‿nél‿ *ivory.*
obj. nélg(ɪ)‿, -gɪ◠.
pl. nélʊ‿.
nélṇ‿kúsʊ‿ and
nél‿kúsʊ‿ (§809) *gum(s* §4696a) = gírgɪd‿.
tén‿nél‿tóŋǧɪlū◠ *his (her, its) teeth are beautiful.*

tín‿nélɪ‿tóŋǧɪlī◠ *their teeth are beautiful.*

fíl-nél‿ (§2358; fílnɛl‿) *ivory.*
obj. fílnélg(ɪ)‿, -gɪ◠.
ín‿néllotōnun◠ (*a*) *this is from the tooth (teeth);* (*b*) *this is made of ivory.*

néln-d(ɪ)‿ (nén-d(ɪ)‿ §807; §§2545 ff.) adj. *tooth's, dental.*

némɛd n. *cream* = nébɛd‿ (§1014).
obj. nɛmɛ́dk(ɪ)‿, -ɛ́tk(ɪ)‿, -ɛ́tt(ɪ)‿ §2462, -kɪ◠, -tɪ◠.
gen. nɛmɛ́dn‿v., némɛn‿c.
íčč(ɪ)n‿némɛd‿ *cream of milk.*
míssɪn‿némɛd‿ *rheum of the eye, mucous discharge of the eye.*

nɛñ v.i. *lie (stand) in liquid, soak, become saturated.*
ind. pres. aɪ‿nɛ́ñ(ʊ)rɪ◠; perf. aɪ‿nɛ́ñkorɪ◠.
ğúrtɛ‿nɛ́ñɪn◠ *the pods (§4696b) of Acacia arabica soak.*
ğúrt‿ɛ́ssɪr‿nɛ́ñɪn◠ and
ğúrt‿ɛ́ssín‿tūr‿nɛ́ñɪn◠ *the pods of Acacia arabica soak in (the) water.*

nɛ́ñar‿ (-ñár‿; §§2200ff.) and
nɛ́ñíd‿ (§§2256ff.) n. *soaking, etc.*

nɛ́ñ-bŭ- (§3931α) v.i. stat. *be in a soaking or soaked (etc.) state or condition.*
áğɪn‿nɛ́ñbūn◠ *the hide is (has been) saturated.*
tɛ̄r‿ɛ́ssín‿tūr‿nɛ́ñbūn◠ (tɛ̄r‿ɛ́s- < tɛ̄rɪ‿ɛ́s- (§1122)) *the seed is soaking (has been soaked) in (the) water.*
tábbɛbūran, nɛñbúmunan◠ *they're wet, but not wet through.*
X. ɛr‿nɛ́ñbúgomen? *weren't you soaked?*
Y. wăran, aɪ‿nɛ́ñbúgómunun◠ (§1930) *no, I wasn't* (§5365).

nɛ́ñɛd-ág- (§§3877ff.) v.i. *be in the condition of having lain in liquid, etc.*

nɛ́ñg-ɪr (N. nɛ́ñkɪr; §3683) (*a*) v.t. caus. *cause or allow to lie in liquid, etc.;* (*b*) v.t. *soak, steep, saturate.*
ğúrtɛn‿nɛ́ñgɪddan◠ (-n‿n- < -g‿n- §625) *they soak the pods of Acacia arabica.*

nɛ́ñgɪrɛd-ág- (N. -ñkɪr-; §§3877ff.) v.t. *be in the situation of having caused or allowed to lie in liquid, etc.*
ağíŋgɪ‿nɛ́ñgɪrɛdágrɪ◠ *I have soaked the hide.*

nɛr v.i. (*a*) *sleep;* (*b*) *fall asleep, go to sleep* [*RSN,* §§129, 200].
ind. pres. aɪ‿nɛ́rrɪ◠, ɛr‿nɛ́rɪn◠ (-rī◠, -rí◠); perf. aɪ‿nɛ́rkorɪ◠.
part. pres. nɛ́rɪl‿ (*one*) *that sleeps, sleeper, sleeping,* obj. nɛ́rɪlg(ɪ)‿, -gɪ◠; past nɛ́rɛl‿ (*one*) *that slept, sleeper, sleeping,* obj. nɛ́rɛlg(ɪ)‿, -gɪ◠.
def. perf. nɛ́roskorɪ◠ (nɛ́róskorɪ), *I fell asleep* (§3805).
tókkon‿ténnɛ‿nɛ́rmɛn◠ *don't go to sleep again (i.e. don't fall asleep again).*

nɛ́rar‿ (-rár‿; §§2200ff.) and
nɛ̄ríd‿ (§§2256ff.) n. *sleeping, falling asleep.*

nɛ̄r-kátt(ɪ)‿, -tɪ‿ adj. *addicted to sleeping, lazy* [§§2534-5].

nɛ́r-bŭ- (§3931α) v.i. stat. *be asleep.*
ind. pres. aɪ‿nɛ́rbūrɪ◠, ɛr‿nɛ́rbūn◠ (-bū◠, -bū◠, -bŭ◠).
X. ɛ́r‿sáɪr‿ɛgó? *where were you?*
Y. aɪ‿nɛ́rbūgorɪ◠ *I was (have been) asleep.*

nɛššáb⌣ — ní⌣...?

nērr-ɛg-ág- (§§ 4071 ff.) v.i. = nēredól-.
nērr-ɛ-dól- (-rᵒd- § 1178; § 4022) and
nērr-ɛ-dól- (-rᵒd- § 4027) v.i. *be about to fall asleep.*
nērr-ɛ-ğŭ-bŭ- (§ 4069) v.i. stat. *be on one's way (coming) to sleep.*
nērr-ɛ-mă- (§ 4036) and
nērr-ɛ-mǎ- (§ 4041) v.i. *become unable to sleep.*
nērr-ɛ-nóg (§§ 4048 ff.) v.i. *go (away) to sleep, retire to sleep.*
nērr-ɛ-nóg-bŭ- (-nóggŭ § 546; § 4058) v.i. stat. *be on one's way (going) to retire to sleep.*
aı⌣nērrenógbūri↷ *I am on my way to bed.*
nērrenóggūran↷ *they are on their way to bed.*
nērr-ɛ-tă (§§ 4060 ff.) v.i. *come to sleep.*
nēríŋ-ır (nériŋgir; N. -ŋkır; § 3688) v.t. caus. = nɛ́rkır.
kúlt⌣ɛkkı⌣nēriŋgírmunun↷ *the flies* (§ 4696 c) *don't (won't* § 5369 a) *let you sleep.*
nɛ́rk-ır (§ 3683) v.t. caus. *cause or allow to sleep,* etc.
nɛššáb⌣ n. *arrow* [< Sudan Ar. نشّاب *id.* coll. § 1393].
 obj. -ábk(ı)⌣, -ki↷.
 pl. -ábı⌣.
nɛššigɛ́ v.t. *give snuff to* [< imperf. or imperat. stem of نشّق *id.* +-ɛ § 3636].
 ind. pres. aı⌣nɛššigɛ́ri↷; perf. aı⌣nɛššigɛ́-gori↷ (N. -ɛ́ko-, -ɛ́ho-).
 imperat. nɛššigɛ́!
 X. aıgı⌣nɛššigɛ́ró↷ (§ 962) *give me some snuff.*
 Y. N. aı⌣ɛkkı⌣nɛššigɛ́kori↷ *I gave (have given) you some.*
nɛšúg⌣ (nuš- § 1336) n. *snuff* [< نشوق *id.*].
 obj. -úgk(ı)⌣, -úkk(ı)⌣, -ki↷.
nɛ́u, nɛ́w, nɛ́u v.t. (a) *inherit;* (b) *be the heir of, inherit from* [RSN, § 129].
 ind. pres. aı⌣nɛ́w(ı)ri↷ (⌣nɛ́uri↷), ɛr⌣nɛ́wın(-wí↷, -wí↷); perf. aı⌣nɛ́ukori↷.
 part. pres. nɛ́wıl (one) *that inherits, heir, inheriting;* past nɛ́wɛl (one) *that inherited, heir, inheriting.*
 ɛr⌣kán⌣nɛ́ukoná? (-n⌣n- < -g⌣n- § 625) *did you inherit (have you inherited) the house?*
 ín⌣arítkı⌣bınɛ́uri↷ *I shall inherit this land.*
 aı⌣índın⌣arıttı⌣nɛ́ukori↷ *I (have) inherited my mother's land.*
 aríttı⌣índınarton⌣nɛ́ukori↷ *I (have) inherited the land from my mother.*
 aı⌣ambábkı⌣nɛ́ukori, índın⌣nɛ́ukori↷ (-n⌣n- < -g⌣n- § 625) *I inherited from my father and from my mother.*
nɛ́war⌣ (-wàr⌣; §§ 2200 ff., 2215) n. (a) *inheritance (what is inherited);* (b) *heir.*
 obj. nɛwárk(ı)⌣, -ki↷.
 aı⌣álin⌣nɛ́war⌣ɛri↷ *I am ɛáli's heir.*
nɛ́wíd⌣ (§§ 2256 ff.) n. (*act of*) *inheriting.*
nɛ́u-kattı- (§ 4093) v.p. *be inherited.*
nɛ́wɛ v.i. *breathe* [§§ 2870 ff., RSN, § 129].
 ind. pres. aı⌣nɛ́weri, ɛr⌣nɛ́wɛn (-wɛ↷, -wɛ́↷); perf. aı⌣nɛ́wegori↷ (N. -ɛko-, -ɛho-).
 def. imperat. nɛ́wos! (nɛ́wó! § 962); pl. nɛ̄wóswɛ! (-wóswɛ́!; -ówwɛ! § 724, -wɛ́!; -óssɛ! § 687, -sɛ́!).
 def. imperat. nɛ́wɛt! (nɛ́wɛ́! § 965), pl. nɛ̄wédwɛ! (-wɛ́!).
nɛ́wɛrar⌣ (-ràr⌣; §§ 2200 ff., 2210) and
nɛ̄wɛríd⌣ (§§ 2256 ff., 2263) n. *breathing.*
nɛwɛ́rt(ı)⌣, -ti↷ n. (a) *breathing, breath;* (b) *spirit, soul;* (c) *self* [§§ 2323 ff.].
 obj. -tıg⌣.
— like nɛ́fıs, supplies a reflexive pronoun (§§ 2691, 5170 γ iii):
án⌣nɛwɛ́rtı⌣dúkkın↷ *I am out of breath.*
nɛwɛrtı-dúkk(ı) (-d⌣d- < -g⌣d- § 534) v.i. *breathe deeply, sigh.*
 nɛwɛ́rtıd⌣dúkkıgó↷ *(s)he heaved a sigh.*
 tımbábt⌣ɛ́n-nɛwɛ́rtı⌣bɛ́gó↷ (-b⌣b- < -g⌣b- § 519) *his (her) father (has) killed himself.*
nɛ̄wɛ-dúkk(ı) (§ 3747 ɛ') v.i. *breathe deeply, sigh, utter unvoiced or voiced sigh (groan) while yawning.*
 ind. pres. aı⌣nɛ̄wɛdúkkıri↷; perf. aı⌣nɛ̄wɛdúkkıgori↷ (N. -ıko-, -ıho-).
nɛ̄wɛr-ɛ-mǎ- (§§ 4016-17, 4036, 4041) v.i. *become unable to breathe.*
 aı⌣nɛ̄wɛrɛmăgori↷ *I couldn't (can't) breathe.*

ní n. *last year.*
 obj. nígı⌣., níg⌣v.c. (§ 512), nígi↷.
 ín⌣nín⌣fun⌣ and
 ín⌣nín⌣fu-taran↷ *this is last year's grain.*
 nín⌣áru⌣dígr⌣ɛgó↷ *last year's rain was much.*
 nírtōn⌣índ⌣ágran↷ *they have been (lived) here since last year.*
nígı⌣., níg⌣v.c., nígi↷ (§ 4665) adv. *last year.*
 nígı⌣dífgon↷ and
 nfd⌣dífgon↷ (-d⌣d- < -g⌣d- § 534) *(s)he (it) died last year.*
 nígı⌣nókkoran↷ and
 nín⌣nókkoran↷ (-n⌣n- < -g⌣n- § 625) *they went last year.*
 nígı⌣tăgoran↷ and
 nít⌣tăgoran↷ (-t⌣t- < -g⌣t- § 707) *they came last year.*
 nígoŋgı⌣tăgoran↷ *they came last year too.*
nín-d(ı)⌣ (§§ 2545 ff.) adj. *last year's, of last year.*
 ín⌣fu⌣níndın⌣ (-dí↷, ⌣níndí↷) and
 ín⌣fu⌣nfndı-taran↷ (-tànnan↷) *this grain is last year's.*
 ín⌣fu⌣níndıré? *is this grain last year's?*
ní...? (n.v. § 1125; ní? § 1051; §§ 2652, 5131 ff.) interr. pron. *who?* [RSN, §§ 73-4, 164, TOB, § 115, 3].
 obj. níg⌣...?, nígi?
 gen. nín⌣...?
 pl. nígu⌣...?, nígu?
 pl. obj. nígug⌣...?, nígugi?
 pl. gen. nígun⌣...?
 X. bıdágó↷ *he has come.*
 Y. ní? ɛsmánó? *who?* ɛoθmán?
 X. nogóskon↷ *he has gone.*
 Y. ní? álió? *who?* ɛ áli?
 n⌣árg⌣agúwɛn? *who is calling us?*
 n⌣ɛkkı⌣tíkkó? *who gave (has given) it to you?*
 íŋgı⌣nǎukó? *who did (has done) this?*
 nín⌣nálkoran? (-n⌣n- < -g⌣n- § 625) *whom did they see? (whom have they seen?).*
 nít⌣tíddi? (-t⌣t- < -g⌣t- § 707) *whom shall I give it (them) to?*
 íŋgı⌣níg⌣ɛrán? (a) *what do they call this person?,* i.e. *what is this person's name?;* (b, = íŋgı⌣míŋ⌣ɛrán?) *what is this thing called?,* i.e. *what's the name of this?*
 ɛ́kkı⌣níg⌣ɛrán? *what is your name?*
 kašwárɛm⌣mássınčım⌣bannídkɛn⌣ níg⌣ɛrán? (-m⌣m- < -g⌣m- § 601; -m⌣b- < -n⌣b- § 592; -n⌣n- < -d⌣n- § 624) *what do they call a dust-column in the Máḥasi dialect?*
 ɛr⌣nín⌣hánug⌣ɛ́ttagon? *whose donkey did you bring (have you brought)?*
 X. wɛr⌣bıdágó↷ *someone has come.*
 Y. ní⌣té? ɛsmán⌣té! *who is he?* ɛoθmán?
 tɛ́r⌣ní⌣té? *who's that?, who is (s)he?*
 ír⌣nígu⌣té? *who are you (pl.)?*
 mám⌣bódılı⌣nígu⌣téddé? *who are those (over there) running?*
 ní⌣mándoré? (§ 5141) and
 ní⌣mándó? (§ 5142) *who is over there?*
— with -tɛ⌣...? (§ 5854):
 ní-tɛ⌣mán⌣ğúbūl? *who's that (over there) coming?* mán⌣ğúbūl a participle-complex (§ 5432).
 nígu-tɛ⌣mán⌣ğúbūli? *who are those (over there) coming?*
— ní⌣...? with -do⌣ is placed in the genitive and forms níddo⌣...? (§ 535):
 ín⌣níddo⌣kúğın? *whose duty is this?*
 dɛ́n⌣níddo⌣tɛ́bın? *who owes the (a) debt?*
— similarly with -dotōn⌣ (s.v. -rtōn⌣) ní⌣...? forms:
 níddotōn⌣...? and occasionally níndotōn⌣...? *from whom?*
 níddotōn⌣dıgrígırsándın? *whom are you (is (s)he, it) so much afraid of?*
nín-d(ı)⌣...? (-di?; § 2545 ff.) interr. pron. adj. *appertaining to whom?, of whom?, whose?*
 X. ín⌣hánu⌣níndıré? *whose is this donkey?*
 Y. ándín↷ *it's mine (ours).*
 X. hánug⌣ɛ́ttagoran↷ *they (have) brought the (a) donkey.*
 Y. níndıgi? *whose?*
níndı-kırı⌣...? (-ri?; §§ 2539-40) interr. pron. adj. *resembling that appertaining to whom?, like whose?*
nīgún-d(ı)⌣...? (-di?; §§ 2545 ff.) interr. pron. adj. *appertaining to whom (pl.)?, of whom (pl.)?, whose (pl.)?*
nīgúndı-kırı⌣...? (-ri?; §§ 2539-41) interr. pron. adj. *resembling that appertaining to whom (pl.)?, like whose (pl.)?*
nindínčı-kırı⌣...? (-ri?; §§ 2539-41) interr. pron. adj. *resembling those appertaining to whom?*
nıgundínčı-kırı⌣...? (-ri?; §§ 2539-41) interr. pron. adj. *resembling those appertaining to whom (pl.)?*
ní-rɛ⌣...? (§ 2653) interrog. pron. *who?* = ní⌣...?

ní‿bɪtabhɛ́n? *and*
nírɛ‿bɪtabhɛ́n? *who will cook?*
ní‿nálkon? *and*
nírɛ‿nálkon? *who saw (has seen him, her, it, them, §5083)?*
X. n‿éttagon? *and* nír‿éttagō? *who (has) brought him (her, it, them)?*
Y. aī⌒ I.
nírɛ‿tíddotōn‿tågomɛn? *who of them did (has) not come?*
gadíjɛr‿nírɛ‿mɛnsúrrɛ́? *who is the winner in the lawsuit?*
ní v.t. (a) *drink* [cp. ON. ɾei *id*. GNT s.v.; RSN, § 129]; (b, tobacco) *smoke*.
ind. pres. aī‿níri⌒; fut. aī‿bɪníri⌒ (‿bun-); perf. aī‿nígori⌒ (N. ‿níko-, ‿ního-).
imperat. ní! (occ. nḯ!), ní‿, pl. níwɛ! (níwɛ́!).
subj. past aī‿nísɪ‿ (-su‿).
part. pres. níl‿ *(one) that drinks, drinker, drinking*, obj. nílg(ɪ)‿; past nísɛl‿ *(one) that drank, drinker, drinking*, obj. niélg(ɪ)‿.
def. perf. aī‿nióskori⌒.
def. perf. aī‿niédkori⌒ (-étk-).
éssɪ‿kólgɪ‿nfri⌒ *I drink water only.*
nórɛn‿nígaŋ‿génun⌒ *it's good (a good thing) to drink (§ 5449) slowly*, i.e. *drinking slowly is a good thing.*
tumbákkɪ‿nírɛn⌒ *they smoke tobacco.*
sɪğárɛn‿níná‿wála‿kodóski? (-n‿n- < -g‿n- § 625) *does he (do you) smoke cigarettes (§ 4696 d) or a pipe?*
níar‿ (níàr‿, níɛr‿; §§ 2200 ff., 2215) n. (a) *drinking* = niíd‿; (b) *drink, something to drink, beverage, draught.*
obj. niárk(ɪ)‿, niár-, nfark(ɪ)‿, niárk(ɪ)‿, nfɛrk(ɪ)‿, -ki⌒.
pl. níar‿, níàr‿.
áskarɪ‿tågan‿éssɪn‿niárkɪ‿tírɪr⌒ *if (when) the soldiers come, give them (each) a drink of water.*
niíd‿ (§§ 2256 ff.) n. *drinking.*
ní-an (§§ 3890 ff.) v.t. *tell to drink, let drink.*
níwan⌒ (§ 3900) *let them drink.*
iŋgɪ‿tékkɪ‿tírɪ‿nían⌒ *give him (her, it) this to drink.*
iŋgɪ‿tírgɪ‿tírɪr‿níwan⌒ *give (each of) this to drink.*
ní-bŭ- (§ 3933) v.t. stat. *be in a state or condition of having drunk.*
tínč‿éssɪn‿níbūran⌒ (-n‿n- < -g‿n- § 625) *the cows have been watered.*
nir-ɛg-åg- (§§ 4071 ff.) v.t. *be about to drink.*
gáhwan‿nɪregåkkori⌒ *I was just going to drink (the) coffee.*
ni-ɛ-dól- (§ 4022) and
nir-ɛ-dól- (-rᵒd- § 1178; § 4027) v.t. = nīregåg-.
nir-ɛ-ğŭ-bŭ- (§ 4069) v.t. stat. *be on the way (coming) to drink.*
aī‿nɪregŭburi⌒ *I am coming to drink.*
ni-ɛ-må- (§ 4036) and
nir-ɛ-må- (§ 4041) v.t. *become unable to drink.*
nir-ɛ-nóg (§§ 4048 ff.) v.t. *go to drink.*
nir-ɛ-nóg-bŭ- (-nóggū- § 546; § 4058) v.t. stat. *be on one's way (going) to drink.*
nir-ɛ-tå (§§ 4060 ff.) v.t. *come to drink.*
aī‿bunɪretåri⌒ and
aī‿nɪrebutåri⌒ *I shall come to drink.*

niɛd-ág- (§§ 3877 ff.) v.t. *be in the condition of having drunk.*
tín‿gáhwan‿niɛdågran⌒ (-n‿n- < -g‿n- § 625) *they have drunk their coffee.*
niɛt-tå (§§ 4169 ff.; niɛdgɪ-tå, -ɛggɪ- §§ 4176-8) v.t. *come after drinking.*
imperat. niɛ́tta!, niɛ́dgɪta!, -ɛggɪ-.
aī‿niɛttåri⌒ and
aī‿niɛggɪtåri⌒ *I'll (§ 5369 b) come when I've had a drink.*
niɛt-ta-nóg (§ 4200; niɛdgɪtanóg, -ɛggɪ- § 4201) v.t. *come and go after drinking.*
šåigɪ‿niɛbbɪtanógri⌒ *I'll come and go as soon as I've drunk my tea.*
N. šåigɪ‿niɛggɪkkonombɪtanógr‿ɛkó⌒ (§ 5605) *(s)he said 'as soon as I've had my tea I'll come and go with you'.*
ní-kattɪ- (N. níha-; § 4093) v.p. *be drunk.*
níkattɪmunun⌒ (§ 1939) *it's undrinkable* (§ 5704).
níkattar‿ (N. níha-; -tår‿; §§ 2200 ff., 2213) and
nikattíd‿ (N. nīha-; §§ 2256 ff., 2266) n. *being drunk.*
nios-åg (§§ 3876, 4180-4; -osgág, -ozg-, -ogg- § 4185) v.t. *squat (sit) after drinking.*
tín‿gáhwan‿niosågran⌒ (-n‿n- < -g‿n- § 625) *they sit (remain sitting) after drinking their coffee.*
nios-tɛ́g (-ottɛ́g § 714; §§ 4180-4; -osgɪtɛ́g, -ozgɪ-, -oggɪ- §§ 4185-7) v.t. *squat (sit) after drinking.*
tín‿táhwan‿niottɛ́gran⌒ *they sit (remain sitting) after drinking their coffee.*
nírɛ...? *who?* = ní‿...?
nís v.t. *compress, press, squeeze, wring.*
ind. pres. aī‿nís(¹)ri⌒; perf. aī‿nískori⌒.
sɪmsímgɪ‿nísran‿zɛdk‿ósr‿égi⌒ (§ 6222) *they press (the) sesame in order to extract the oil.*
nógo‿šúkkɪl‿kádɛn‿nísɪn⌒ (-n‿n- < -g‿n- § 625) *the female slave that washes (wrings) the cloth(s, clothes § 4696 d).*
nísar‿ (-sår‿; §§ 2200 ff.) and
nisíd‿ (§§ 2256 ff.) n. *compression, etc.*
nís-an (§§ 3890 ff.) v.t. *tell to compress, let compress, etc.*
nίz-bŭ- (§ 3931 β) v.i. stat. *be in a compressed (etc.) state or condition.*
símsɪm‿nízbūn⌒ *the sesame is (has been) compressed.*
nísed-åg- (§§ 3877 ff.) v.t. *be in the situation of having compressed, etc.*
nís-kattɪ- (§ 4093) v.p. *be compressed, etc.*
nis-ós (§ 3747 ᵋ) v.t. *cause to issue (etc. s.v. ós) by compressing, etc., squeeze out.*
zɛ́dkɪ‿sɪmsímɪrtōn‿assáragɛn‿nisósran⌒ (-n‿n- < -d‿n- § 624) *they squeeze the oil from sesame with (-ɛd‿) an oil-press.*
nógorɪ‿kádɛrtōn‿éssɪn‿nisósran⌒ (-n‿n- < -g‿n- § 625) *the female slaves wring the water out of the cloth(s, clothes).*
níb v.t. *roast, grill.*
ind. pres. aī‿níb(¹)ri⌒, ɛr‿níbɪn⌒ (-bí⌒, -bí⌒); perf. aī‿níbkori⌒ (‿nípk-).

imperat. níp!, níb‿, pl. níbwɛ! (níbbɛ!, ⁻⁻).
subj. past aī‿níbsɪ‿ (‿nípsɪ‿, -su‿).
níbar‿ (-bår‿; §§ 2200 ff.) n. *roasting, etc.*
nɪbíd‿ n. (a, §§ 2256 ff.) = níbar‿; (b, § 2268) *roasted meat.*
obj. -ídk(ɪ)‿, -ítk(ɪ)‿, -ítt(ɪ)‿ § 2462, -ki⌒, -ti⌒.
gen. -ídn‿v., -ínn‿v.c., -ín‿c.
pl. níb‿.
níb-an (§§ 3890 ff.) v.t. *tell to roast, etc., let roast, etc.*
kúsun‿níbå⌒ (-n‿n- < -g‿n- § 625) *let him (her) roast the meat.*
níb-bŭ- (§ 3931 β) v.i. stat. *be in a roasted (etc.) state or condition.*
níb-kattɪ- (nípk- ; § 4093) v.p. *be roasted, etc.*
nɪbɛd-åg- (§§ 3877 ff.) v.t. *be in the situation of having roasted, etc.*
nɪbíŋ-ɪr (⁻⁻, N. -ŋkɪr; § 3688) v.t. caus. *cause or allow to roast, etc.*
níbk-ɪdd(ɪ) (nípk- ; § 3725) v.t. caus. *cause or allow to roast, etc.*
aī‿tékkɪ‿kúsun‿nípkɪddɪri⌒ (-n‿n- < -g‿n- § 625) *I make (let) him (her) roast the meat.*
nɪbos-kál (-okkál § 573; §§ 4180-4; -osgɪkál, -ozgɪ-, -oggɪ- § 4185) v.t. *eat after roasting, and*
mahádaŋ‿gáŋgarɛn‿nɪbokkállan⌒ *they roast and eat ears (§ 4696 b) of maize.*
níbɪd‿ n. *mat (made of palm-leaf fibre)* [RSN; § 129 cps. Eg. nbti (nbt *basket* GEG, p. 546) NEB† (opus contextum ex plexis palmis PLC s.v.); § 2088]
obj. nɪbídk(ɪ)‿, -ítk(ɪ)‿, itt(ɪ)‿ (§ 2462), -ki⌒, ti⌒.
pl. níb(¹)dɪ‿.
ɛ́nčɪ‿níbdɪh‿haúrtɛrtōn‿áwɪğran⌒ (-h‿h- < -g‿h- § 559) *(the) women make (the) mats out of palm-leaves.*
nič! imperat. of níğ *sew.*
níčč(ɪ)‿ *cloud* s.v. níğ.
níğ v.t. *sew.*
ind. pres. aī‿níğ(¹)ri⌒; perf. aī‿níğkori⌒ (‿níčk-, ‿níğk-, ‿níčk- § 323, ‿níččo- § 523).
imperat. nič!, pl. níğwɛ! (níğwé!, níğğɛ!, -gé!).
neg. imperat. tókkon‿níğmɛn! (-mɛ̃!, -mɛ́! § 939), tókkon‿níğñɛn! (-ñɛ̃!, -ñɛ́! § 557) and tókkon‿níññɛn! (-ñɛ̃!, -ñɛ́! § 639).
part. pres. níğɪl‿ *(one) that sews, sewer, tailor, sewing*, obj. nɪğílg(ɪ)‿, -gi⌒; past níğɛl‿ *(one) that sewed, sewer, tailor, sewing*, obj. nɪğélg(ɪ)‿, -gi⌒.
kádɛn‿níğɪl‿ (-n‿n- < -g‿n- § 625) and kadénčɪn‿níğɪl‿ *tailor.*
ğázman‿níğɪl‿ *cobbler.*
níğɪl-an (§ 3910 α) v.i. *become a tailor.*
ám‿bélɛdɪr‿ɛ́n‿níğmunun, ógɪğ‿ānníğɪn⌒ *in our (my) country the woman doesn't sew, the man (habitually) sews.*
níğar‿ (-ğår‿; §§ 2200 ff.) and
nɪğíd‿ (§§ 2256 ff.) n. *sewing.*
níčč(ɪ)‿ n. (a) *(action of) sewing* [< *níčt(ɪ)‿ < *níğt(ɪ)‿ §§ 526, 2325 α, 2228]; (b) *cloud, mist* [concrete specialization of a, *cloth, sc. that veils the scene*].

√nímın- — nódd(ı)

obj. -čıg◡.
pl. -čınč(ı)◡.
ınnówwıg◡ášai◡níččın⌒ today it is cloudy (§4719).
níččin-d(ı)◡ (§§2545ff.) (a) adj. appertaining to sewing; (b, §2301 α) n. pin (of wood or metal), skewer, awl.
obj. -dıg◡.
pl. -dınč(ı)◡.
ǧélli◡níččínd(ı)◡ sewing work.
níǧ-an (§§3890ff.) v.t. tell to sew, let sew.
níǧ-bŭ- (níǧǧŭ- §552; §3931 β) v.i. stat. be in a sewn state or condition.
níǧ-dĕn (§§3996-7) v.t. give (to the speaker) after sewing, sew for (the speaker).
níǧ(ˈ)r-eg-ág (§§4071 ff.) v.t. = níǧedól-.
níǧ-ε-dól- (-ǧºd- §1178; §4022) and
níǧ(ˈ)r-ε-dól- (-rºd-; §4027) v.t. be about to sew.
níǧ-ε-má- (§4036) and
níǧ(ˈ)r-ε-má- (§4041) v.t. become unable to sew.
níǧed-ág- (§§3877ff.) v.t. be in the situation of having sewn.
níǧíŋg-ır (˙˙˙; N. -ŋkır; §3688) v.t. caus. cause or allow to sew.
níǧ-kattı- (níčk-; §4093) v.p. be sewn.
níǧ-tır (níčt-; §§3998-9) v.t. give (to other than the speaker) after sewing, sew for (other than the speaker).
níǧǧŭ- < níǧbŭ- be sewn s.v. níǧ.
√nímın- vibrate with slight rapid motion, quiver [imit.].
nımínt(ı) and (§710)
nımítt(ı) v.i. move the eyelids, blink [< √nímın- +-t §2900].
ind. pres. ai◡nımíntırı⌒ (-ítti-); perf. ai◡nımíntıgori⌒ (-ítti-, N. -ıko-, -iho-).
imperat. nımínti! (-ítti!).
tém◡míssı◡nımíttın⌒ his (her, its) eye blinks (eyes blink §4696a).
nımíntíŋg-ır (-ítti-; ˙˙˙; N. -ŋkır; §3688) v.t. caus. cause or allow to blink, etc.
nımíntε◡ (-íttε◡) n. a small blood-sucking fly (Simulium griseicolle) that gets into the eye; with collective sg. (§4696c) [or. *blinking < nımínt + -ε◡ of n. act. §2234δ].
obj. -tεg◡.
pl. -tεnč(ı)◡.
nımíntε◡dúŋgular◡šíter◡dıgrí◡háli-sun⌒ S. g. occurs in Dóngola in winter in very great numbers.
nımíntε◡tékki◡nımıntíŋgırın⌒ the Simulia make him (her, it) blink.
nímnε◡ n. antimony (used for blacking eyelids) [< *nímınε◡ < √nímın- + -ε◡ of n. act., or. *quivering §2234δ].
obj. -εg◡.
nímır◡ n. leopard [<نمر id. §1359].
obj. nımírk(ı)◡, -ki⌒.
pl. nímˈ(ı)rí◡.
nímnε◡ antimony s.v. √nímın-.
◡níññεn! s.v. níǧ.
nıp! imperat. of níb roast.
nısid◡ n. year before last [< *nˈísid◡ (cp. §1125) < nˈ last year + ıs◡? where? + -ıd◡ *making (§2256), so *making last year where?, i.e. displacement of last year].

obj. nısídk(ı)◡, -ítk(ı)◡, -ítt(ı)◡ (§2462), -ki⌒, -ti⌒.
nısıdırıtön◡índ◡ágran⌒ they have been (lived) here since the year before last.
nısídk(ı)◡ (-ítk(ı)◡, -ítt(ı)◡, -ki⌒, -ti⌒ §4665) adv. the year before last.
nısítki◡nókkoran⌒ they went the year before last.
nısídn-d(ı)◡ (§§2545ff.) adj. of the year before last.
níšš(ı)◡ n. horn; with collective sg. (§4696a) [RSN, §129].
obj. -šıg◡.
pl. -šınč(ı)◡.
níššıgεǧ◡ǧóm (-ǧ◡ǧ- < -d◡ǧ- §550) v.t. butt.
nızéza◡ n. Nizeiza (on map), a village on the right bank of the Nile about 24 miles above Ed-Débbaʰ [< نَزِيزَة dim. of نَزّ water oozing from the ground].
obj. -zag◡.
nób◡ n. (a) Nubian, native of Nubia (in this sense not in general use in Dóngola, §§79, 81); (b) member of the Nubian tribes north of Dóngola, esp.; (c) Máhasi-speaking Nubian, native of Nubia between Dóngola and Dār-El-Kunúz [§2053; cp. Νοῦβαι, Νουβαῖοι, Νουβάδαι (RN, p. vii); Sudan Ar. نوبة nóba Nubians; ⲧⲁ-Ⲛⲟⲩⲃⲁⲧⲓⲁ, Ⲛⲟⲩⲃⲁⲧⲓⲁ, Ⲛⲟⲩⲃⲁⲝⲓⲁ, τὰ Νάπατα, αἱ Νάπαται, Napata (RN ib.); see MAS, I, pp. 12ff.; cp. núba◡ Nubian (language)].
voc. nóp!
obj. nóbk(ı)◡, nópk(ı)◡, -ki⌒.
gen. nóbın◡v., nóm◡c.
pl. nóbın◡.
nóm◡kåsé? where is the Nubian's (Máhasi's) house?
nóbım◡báññıt◡tóŋǧılun⌒ the (Máhasi) Nubians' language is beautiful.
nóm-d(ı)◡ (§§2545ff.) adj. appertaining to the (a) Nubian, etc.
nobín-d(ı)◡ (§§2545ff.) (a) adj. appertaining to the Nubians (etc., nóbı◡), Nubian, esp. of Máhas; (b) n. the language of the Nubians (etc.), esp. the Máhasi dialect (massınčínd(ı)◡).
nobíndıg◡uñúmmunun⌒ (s)he doesn't know (understand) Nubian (etc.).
nobíndıb◡báññıran⌒ (-b◡b- < -g◡b- §519) and
nobíndıgεb◡báññıran⌒ (-b◡b- < -d◡b- §518) they speak (Máhasi) Nubian.
nób v.t. (a) stew, cook; (b) beat up (stew) with nóbd(ı)◡. In the Nubian cuisine (a) includes (b) [§§2053, 2781; RSN, §129].
ind. pres. ai◡nóbrı⌒; perf. ai◡nóbkori⌒ (◡nópk-).
imperat. nóp!
part. pres. nóbıl◡ (one) that stews, etc., cook (n.), obj. nobílg(ı)◡; past nóbεl◡ (one) that stewed, etc., cook (n.), obj. nobélg(ı)◡.
def. imperat. nóbos!, nóbós!, nóbó!
έn◡ǧakútkı◡nóbın⌒ the woman cooks the stew.
marragátti◡nópkori⌒ I (have) made the (some) broth.
ǧakútti◡noboskori⌒ I have cooked the stew.

nóbd(ı)◡ n. cooking-stick, twirling-stick, stick about one foot long with cross-piece of about three inches near one end (✝); the end with the cross-piece is inserted in the stew (ǧákud◡) and the stick is twirled between the palms of the hands, the contents of the pot being thus stirred and beaten up [< nób beat up + -d of nomen instrumenti §2231].
obj. -dıg◡.
pl. -dınč(ı)◡.
nobódd(ı)◡ n. = nóbd(ı)◡ [< *nobósd(ı)◡ §538; §2231].
obj. -dıg◡.
pl. -dınč(ı)◡.
nóbar◡ (-bár◡; §§2200ff.) and
nobíd◡ (§§2256ff.) n. stewing, etc.
nób-an (§§3890ff.) v.t. tell to stew, etc., let stew, etc.
nobεd-ág- (§§3877ff.) v.t. be in the situation of having stewed, etc.
έn◡ǧakútti◡nobεdágın⌒ the woman has cooked the stew.
nób-kattı- (nópk-; §4093) v.p. be stewed, etc.
ǧákud◡nobkattóskó⌒ the stew has been cooked.
nob-tó (noptó; §3747 εˈ) v.i. enter (into a liquid) and become saturated and dissipated, enter and melt, melt in, lit. enter (as if) stewing (i.).
ágw◡íčči◡nobtón⌒ the soft dates melt in the milk.
ágwaǧ◡ǧúrumın◡íččır◡nobtónn◡ıllar⌒ (-ǧ◡ǧ- < -g◡ǧ- §551) (s)he kneads (a mass of) soft dates that they may melt in the milk.
ágwaǧ◡ǧogórran◡íččır◡noptóŋ-karam⌒ they squeeze the soft dates that they may melt in the milk.
nōbáštı◡ (§900) n. person on duty (= nō-bátši◡).
voc. -ti!
obj. -tıg◡.
pl. -tınč(ı)◡ (§1622).
ınnówwıg◡ai◡nobášt◡εri⌒ today I am on duty.
nōbátšı◡ n. person (employee of any kind) on duty [< نَوْبَتْجِي id.].
voc. -ši!
obj. -šıg◡.
pl. nōbatšínč(ı)◡ (§1623).
nōbátšıkanε◡ (§§2295-6) n. being on duty, time for being on duty, turn on duty.
ınnówwın◡nobátšıkanε◡sálεhndi⌒ (§939; -n◡n- < -g◡n- §625) today the turn on duty is Sálih's.
nóbrε◡ n. gold. Eg. nb, Copt. ⲛⲟⲩⲃ (RSN, §129 s.v. nábi), ON. ⲅⲁⲛ gold GNT, p. 69 (6); -r- intensive (§4586), -ε◡ of n. ess. (§2234β)].
obj. nóbreg◡, nóbrég◡, nobreǧ◡ (§1532).
nóbren◡ákaš◡ gold ear-ring(s §4696d).
nóbrén◡tábıd◡ goldsmith.
nóbrén-da◡ Home of Gold, name of a village near Sór (Suri on map) about six miles below Hándag.
nobrén-d(ı)◡ (§§2545ff.) adj. appertaining to gold, of gold, golden.
nódd(ı) v.t. (a) cut, cut up, cut into pieces; (b) cut off, cut down [< *nórd(ı) (RNW s.v.); nór- cogn. with nōr grind §2868).

ind. pres. aī‿nóddırı⌢; perf. aī‿nóddıgori (N. -ıko-, -ıho-).
imperat. nóddi!
part. pres. nóddıl‿ (one) that cuts, etc., cutter, cutting, obj. noddílg(ı)‿, -gi⌢; past nóddɛl‿ (one) that cut, etc., cutter, cutting, obj. noddélg(ı)‿, -gi⌢.
tumbákkı‿nóddıgó⌢ (s)he (has) cut up the tobacco.
ğówwın‿noddóskoran⌢ (-n‿n- < -g‿n- §625) they have cut down the tree.
nóddar‿ (-dàr‿; §§2200 ff.) and
nóddíd‿ (§§2256 ff.) n. cutting, etc.
nódd-an (§§3890 ff.) v.t. tell to cut, etc., let cut, etc.
nóddı-bŭ- (§3931 β) v.i. stat. be in a cut (etc.) state or condition.
tumbág‿nóddıbŭn⌢ the tobacco is (has been) cut up.
noddır-ɛg-ág- (§§4071 ff.) v.t. = noddɛdól-.
nodd-ɛ-dól- (-dᵒd- §1178; 4022) and
noddır-ɛ-dól- (-rᵒd-; §4027) v.t. be about to cut, etc.
noddır-ɛ-ğŭ-bŭ- (§4069) v.t. stat. be on one's way (coming) to cut, etc.
nodd-ɛ-má- (§4036) and
noddır-ɛ-má- (§4041) v.t. become unable to cut, etc.
noddır-ɛ-nóg (§§4048 ff.) v.t. go to cut, etc.
noddır-ɛ-nóg-bŭ- (-nóggŭ- §546; §4058) v.t. stat. be on one's way (going) to cut, etc.
noddır-ɛ-tá (§§4060 ff.) v.t. come to cut, etc.
noddɛd-ág- (§§3877 ff.) v.t. be in the situation of having cut, etc.
nóddı-kattı- (N. -iha-; §4093) v.p. be cut, etc.

nóg v.i. (a) go; (b) go along, travel, walk; (c) go away, depart [cp. ON. ᚱᚨᚴ id. ZNG s.v.; RSN, §200].
ind. pres. aī‿nóg(¹)ri⌢; perf. aī‿nógkori⌢ (‿nókko-).
imperat. nók!, pl. nógwɛ! (nógwé!, nóggɛ! §547, -gé!).
subj. past aī‿nógsı‿ (‿nóksı‿, -su‿).
part. pres. nógıl‿ (one) that goes, etc., goer, going, obj. nogílg(ı)‿, -gi⌢; past nógɛl‿ (one) that went, etc., goer, going, obj. nogélg(ı)‿, -gi⌢.
def. imperat. nógos! (nogós! §1890, nogó! §962), pl. nógoswɛ! (-wé!, -ówwɛ! §724, -wé!, -óssɛ! §687, -sé!).
tókkon‿nógmɛn! and
tókkon‿nóŋŋɛn! (§661) don't go (etc.).
tókkon‿nógmɛwwé!,
tókkon‿nógmɛndé! and
tókkon‿nóŋŋɛndé! don't (pl.) go (etc.).
masúrro‿bunóg⌢ (s)he (it) will go to Egypt (Cairo).
dúŋgular‿nogóskoran⌢ they have gone to (Old) Dóngola.
kàgaddı‿nógran⌢ they go towards the house.
nŏrɛn‿nógıl‿wárrı‿nógın⌢ he that goes slowly goes far.
sà‿nógın⌢ the clock (watch) goes.
kǎn‿áptır‿nógran⌢ they walk by (beside) the house.
tínn‿áttır‿nógri⌢ I walk beside them.

énčı‿sútɛ‿nógmunan⌢ (the) women don't walk fast.
ıškártınčı‿nókkan‿sawákınd‿ar‿bunógru⌢ when the guests go away we shall go to Suakin.
X. míŋgı‿gíğırın? what do you hear?
Y. gátır‿mán‿nogél-taran⌢ it's the train, that one that went off.
dállaná‿wála‿nogósri? and
dállaná‿wála‿nogósriá? is there anything (sc. for me) or shall (§5369 b) I go off?
nɛhǎr‿tóskı‿nogóskó, tóskı‿tɛbí⌢ three days have passed and (§6239) three are left.
nógar‿ (-gàr‿; §§2200 ff.) and
nogíd‿ (§§2256 ff.) n. going, walking, gait, departure.
tékkı‿tén‿nogídırtön‿uñúrkoran⌢ they knew him (her, it) by his (her, its) gait.
tŭn‿nogíd‿ diarrhœa.
úrun‿nogíd‿ current of the river.
nogíd-an-nóg (§§4161–3) v.i. (a) go at a great pace, go very rapidly; (b) go a long way, walk far; (c) go right away, go utterly, go for good.
nogídannóg-bŭ- (-nóggŭ- §546; §4166) v.i. stat. be in a state or condition of going at a great pace, etc., be on one's way off for good.
ír‿sogdándoton‿nogídannóggŭruá? are you (pl.) leaving the Sudan for good?
nogídk-ır-nóg (-ītkır-, -īttır- §716; §§4159–60) v.i. = nogídannóg.
nogídkır-nógbŭ- (-ītkır-, -īttır-; -nóggŭ- §546; §4165) v.i. stat. = nogídannógbŭ-.
nog-kátt(ı)‿ (nokkát- §569; §§2534, 2535 b) adj. good at walking, going (etc.) well.
ín‿hánu‿nokkáttın⌢ this donkey is a good goer.
nóg-an (§§3890 ff.) v.t. tell to go, etc., let go, etc.
ind. pres. aī‿nógandi⌢, ɛr‿nóganın⌢ (-ní⌢, -ní⌢); perf. aī‿nógaŋkori⌢.
imperat. nógan! (-gã!, -gá!).
def. imperat. noganós! (-nó!).
hánun‿nógan⌢ (-n‿n- < -g‿n- §625) let the donkey go.
nógwan⌢ (-gwǎ⌢, -gwá⌢; nóggan⌢ §547, -gã⌢, -gá⌢) let them go.
nog-bél (§§3747ᵉ, 3783) v.i. go (etc.) out.
imperat. nogbél!, nógbɛl! (§1871).
nóg-bŭ- (-nóggŭ- §546; §3931 α) v.i. stat. be in a state of motion (going, etc.), be in a going (etc.) state or condition, be on one's way (going, etc.), be going, etc.
sà‿nógbŭn⌢ the clock (watch) is going.
áŋ‿kǎr‿nógbŭri⌢ I am on my way to my (our) house.
tínnár‿aī‿nógbŭri⌢ I am on my way to them (their dwelling).
kannɛ́r‿nóggŭru⌢ we (you pl.) are travelling northwards.
ar‿súkkaddı‿nóggŭru⌢ we are on our way to the market.
nog(¹)r-ɛg-ág- (§§4071 ff.) v.i. = nogɛdól-.
nogrɛgákkoran⌢ they were just going to go.
nog-ɛ-dól- (-gᵒd- §1178; §4022) and
nog(¹)r-ɛ-dól- (-rᵒd-; §4027) v.i. be about to go, etc.
aī‿nogɛdólsı‿wekídkı‿tágoran⌢ they came when I was just going to go.

nog-ɛ-má- (§4036) and
nog(¹)r-ɛ-má- (§4041) v.i. become unable to go, etc.
aī‿nogɛmāróskori⌢ I have become unable to go (I was going and have broken down).
nog-ɛ-má-bŭ- (§4206) v.i. stat. be in a too tired (etc. s.v. má) state or condition to go, etc.
nogɛd-ág- (§§3877 ff.) v.i. be in the situation of having gone, etc.
nog-ğ-amínt(ı) (-ğ- < -ğu- §1111; §4147) v.t. after going along (-ğu-) show, go along and show.
ár‿tírgonom‿bınoggŭkágamıntırıddu⌢ (§5601) we shall go along with them and show them the house.
nog-ğ-ár (-ğ- < -ğu- §1111; §4147) v.t. after going along seize, go along and seize.
nog-ğ-éttä (-ğ- < -ğu- §1111; -éttä s.v. éd; §4206) v.t. go off and fetch, go along and bring.
imperat. nogğétta!
nog-ğ-ós (-ğ- < -ğu- §1111; §4147) v.t. after going along cause to issue (etc. s.v. ós), go along and bring (take) out.
noggŭsandŭkkós⌢ (§5601) go along and bring out the box.
nogğós-an (§§3890 ff., 3905) v.t. tell to go along and bring (take) out, let go along and bring (take) out.
tékkı‿noggŭsandŭkkósan⌢ (§5601) tell him (her) to go along and take out the box.
nog-ğŭ (§4092) v.i. go along, go onward, go on.
ind. pres. aī‿noggŭri⌢.
imperat. noggŭ!
nog-ğu-bédd(ı) (§4147) v.t. go along and entreat (...pray to).
nog-ğu-tɛkkonom-bédd(ı) (§5605) v.i. go along to pray with him (her), i.e. with one that has died (s.v. bédd(ı)), go to a funeral service.
índıkɛgıd‿dígon‿aī‿noggŭtɛkkonombéddıri⌢ my aunt has died, I am going to her funeral service.
nog-ğu-bél (§4147) v.i. issue after going along, go along out.
imperat. noggŭbél! ⁻ᵛ, ⁻ᵛ (§1953).
gadíbırtön‿noggŭbélım‿bádk‿ɛrın íŋgɛn‿nók⌢ (-ɛn‿n- < -ɛd‿n- §624) after you get clear of the rails go to your right.
nog-ğu-nál (§4147) v.t. see (etc. s.v. nál) after going along, go along and see (etc.).
imperat. noggŭnál! ⁻ᵛ, ⁻ᵛ (§1953).
moháttan‿nóggŭnal‿ go along to the station and ascertain.
moháttan‿nóggŭnal‿ (-n‿n- < -g‿n- §625) go along and look at (inspect) the station.
térom‿bélkogın‿nóggŭnal⌢ go along and see whether (s)he (it) has gone (come) out.
noggŭnálar‿ (-làr‿; §§2200 ff., 2213) and
noggŭnalíd‿ (§§2256 ff., 2266) n. going along and seeing (etc.).
noggŭnálàr‿nɛfén⌢ going along and seeing is useful.
noggŭnalíd‿sɛrén⌢ it's a good thing to go along and see.

noggunál-an (§§ 3890 ff., 3905) v.t. *tell to go along and see (etc.), let go along and see (etc.).*
wɛ́m⌣muháttar⌣noggǔnálaŋ⌣gátırōn⌣ tém⌣mawaídır⌣ɛ́gın⌢ (wɛ́m⌣m- < wɛ́g⌣m- § 601; § 6138) *send someone to the station to see whether the train is on time.*
noggunálwan⌢ *tell them to go along and see (etc.).*
nog-ǧu-nɛ́r (§ 4147) v.i. *sleep after going along, go along and sleep.*
 ind. pres. aî⌣noggunɛ́rrı⌢; perf. aî⌣noggunɛ́rkorı⌢.
nog-ǧu-sikk(ı) (§ 4147) v.t. *after going along ask, go along and ask.*
 imperat. noggusíkki!
nog-ǧ-úskur (-ǧ- < -ǧu- § 1111; § 4147) v.t. *put (down, etc. s.v. úskur) after going along, go along and put (down, etc.).*
nog-ǧu-tá (§ 4147) v.i. *come (back) after going along (off, away).*
 imperat. nogǧutá!, -ᵈ⌣, ⌣⌣, pl. noggutáwɛ!, -tắwé!
noging-ır (⌣⌣, N. -ŋkır; § 3688) v.t. caus. *cause or allow to go, etc.*
 tókkon⌣tírgı⌣nograŋgırímmɛn⌢ (§ 3690) *don't make (let, any of) them go.*
nógos-an (§§ 3890 ff., 3905) v.t. *tell to go, etc.*
 tírgı⌣nogóswan⌢ (-swā⌢, -swá⌢, -óssan⌢, -sā⌢, -sá⌢, -ówwan⌢, -wā⌢, -wá⌢, -óswanır⌢) *tell them to go.*
nogos-wıdɛ-tá (-owwı- § 724; § 4203; -osgıwı-, -ozgı-, -oggı- § 4205; -wᵘdɛ-) v.i. *return after going, etc.*
nógge! < **nógwɛ!** *go!* (*pl.*) s.v. nóg.
nóggǔ- < **nógbǔ-** *be going* s.v. nóg.
nógo⌣ n. *female slave* (app. < nóg *go*, as جَارِيَة id. < جَرَى *run*; but nóg- perhaps cogn. with núg- of núgud⌣ *male slave* (§ 2341); -o⌣ § 2306].
 obj. nógog⌣.
 pl. nógorı⌣.
nók! imperat. of nóg *go.*
nóŋga⌣, nóŋgɛ⌣, nóŋgo⌣ n. *chameleon* [2182; RSN, §§ 129, 200].
 obj. -gag⌣, -gɛg⌣, -gog⌣.
 pl. -ganč(ı)⌣, -gɛnč(ı)⌣, -gonč(ı)⌣.
nóŋŋɛn! < **nógmɛn!** *do not go!* s.v. nóg.
nóp! voc. of nób⌣ *Nubian,* imperat. of nób *stew.*
nǒr v.t. *grind* [§ 4571; RSN, § 129].
 ind. pres. aî⌣nǒrrı, ɛr⌣nǒrın⌢ (-rī⌢, -rí⌢); perf. aî⌣nǒrkorı⌢.
 part. pres. nǒrı⌣ (*one) that grinds, grinder, grinding,* obj. nǒrílg(ı)⌣, -gi⌢; past nǒrɛl⌣ (*one) that ground, grinder, grinding,* obj. nǒrɛlg(ı)⌣, -gi⌢.
 nógor⌣íllɛn⌣nǒrran⌢ (-r⌣í- < -rı⌣í-; -n⌣n- < -g⌣n- § 625) *the female slaves grind the corn.*
 nógo⌣ ǧuntókkɛn⌣nǒrın⌢ (-n⌣n- < -d⌣n- § 624) *the female slave grinds with the upper stone (i.e. has it in her hands).*
 ɛ́n⌣márɛr⌣raháɩɛgɛn⌣nǒrın⌢ (-r⌣r- < -g⌣r- § 669) *the woman grinds the millet in (-ɛd⌣ with) a hand-mill.*
nǒrar⌣ (-rắr⌣; §§ 2200 ff.) and
nǒríd⌣ (§§ 2256 ff.) n. *grinding.*

nǒrt(ı)⌣ n. *flour* [or. *grinding,* then *what is ground* § 2325 β].
 obj. -tıg⌣.
nǒr-an (§§ 3890 ff.) v.t. *tell to grind, let grind.*
nǒr-bǔ- (§ 3931 β) v.i. stat. *be in a ground state or condition.*
 íllɛ⌣nǒrbūn⌢ *the wheat is (has been) ground.*
 nǒrtı⌣nǒrbūn⌢ *the flour is (has been) ground.*
nǒrr-ɛg-ǎg- (§§ 4071 ff.) v.t. = nōrɛdól-.
nǒr-ɛ-dól- (-rᵒd- § 1178; § 4022) and
nǒrr-ɛ-dól- (-rᵒd-; § 4027) v.t. *be about to grind.*
nǒrr-ɛ-ǧǔ-bǔ- (§ 4069) v.t. stat. *be on one's way (coming) to grind.*
nǒr-ɛ-mǎ- (§ 4036) and
nǒrr-ɛ-mǎ- (§ 4041) v.t. *become unable to grind.*
nǒrr-ɛ-nóg (§§ 4048 ff.) v.t. *go to grind.*
nǒrr-ɛ-nóg-bǔ- (-nóggǔ- § 546; § 4058) v.t. stat. *be on one's way (going) to grind.*
nǒrr-ɛ-tá (§§ 4060 ff.) v.t. *come to grind.*
nǒrɛd-ág- (§§ 3877 ff.) v.t. stat. *be in the situation of having ground.*
nǒrk-ıdd(ı) (§ 3725) v.t. caus. *cause or allow to grind.*
 aî⌣nógon⌣nǒrkıddırı⌢ (-n⌣n- < -g⌣n- § 625) *I (I'll § 5369) make (let) the female slave grind (it).*
 nógom⌣márɛn⌣nǒrkıddóskoran⌢ (-m⌣m- < -g⌣m- § 601; -n⌣n- < -g⌣n- § 625) *they have made the female slave grind the millet.*
nǒr-kattı- (§ 4093) v.p. *be ground.*
nórɛ⌣ n. *termite, white ant;* with collective s.g. (§ 4696c) [< *nórrɛ (cp. §§ 1000 ff.) < *nógrɛ⌣ (§ 669) < nóg *go* + -r intensive (§ 4586) + -ɛ⌣ of n. act. (§ 2234), so *what goes in swarms* § 2317].
 obj. -rɛg⌣.
 pl. norɛnč(ı)⌣.
nǒrɛn⌣ (-rɛ̄⌢, nórɛ́ § 939) adv. *slowly, gently* [stereotyped sg. 3 of *nǒr-ɛ *be fine, in minute particles* §§ 4421, 4571, so or. quasi **it is little by little*].
 X. nǒrɛn⌣áû! *do it slowly!*
 Y. aî⌣nǒrɛn⌣baúrı⌢ *I will* (§ 5364).
 nǒrɛn⌣úndur⌢ *put him (her, it, them) in gently.*
 nǒrɛn⌣báññı⌢ *speak slowly.*
nǒrɛm-báññ(ı) (§ 4127) and emphasizing nǒrɛm-,
nǒrɛm-baññ(ı) (§ 1964) v.i. *speak slowly, speak gently.*
nǒrɛn-nóg (§ 4127) and emphasizing nǒrɛn-,
nǒrɛn-nog (§ 1964) v.i. *go (etc. s.v. nóg) slowly, gently.*
nǒrɛn-nóg-bǔ- (-nóggǔ- § 546; § 4217) v.i. stat. *be in a state of slow motion (going, etc.), be slowly on one's way (going, etc.).*
 bābǔr⌣nǒrɛnnógbugon⌢ *the steamer (train) was moving slowly.*
nǒrɛn! (nórɛ̄!, nórɛ́! § 3601) interj. and v. imperat. *slowly!, gently!, take care!*
 pl. nǒrɛwwɛ! (-wé!).
 nǒrɛ́! tókkon⌣sandúgır⌣wasáhat⌣ tóŋgırmɛ̄! (-t⌣t- < -g⌣t- § 707) *slowly! don't let (the) dirt get into the box!*
nǒro⌣ adj. *(a) fine-ground, powdered, in minute particles, fine; (b) cut fine, torn*

fine; (c) very small, minute; (d, in length) very short [§§ 2561 α, 4573].
 obj. -rog⌣.
 pl. -ronč(ı)⌣.
 nǒrtı⌣nǒro⌣ *fine-ground flour.*
 wárag⌣órığbǔlgı⌣nǒrog⌣ɛrán⌢ *they call torn-up paper nǒro⌣,* i.e. wárag⌣ nǒro⌣ = *little bits of paper* (§ 4696c).
 gór⌣nǒro⌣ *very small ant(s* § 4696c).
 núgun⌣díltı⌣nǒró⌢ (-n⌣d- < -dn⌣d- § 612; § 939) *the slave's hair is very short.*
nǒrokanɛ⌣ (§ 2295) n. *fineness, minuteness, etc.*
nǒro-tod (§ 2582) adj. *not satisfactorily fine-ground, etc.*
 obj. -tǒdk(ı)⌣, -tǒtk(ı)⌣, -tǒkk(ı)⌣, -tǒtt(ı)⌣ § 2462, -ki⌢, -ti⌢.
 gen. -tǒdn⌣v., -tǒnn⌣v.c., -tǒn⌣c.
 pl. nǒrotonı⌣.
 tén⌣díltı⌣nǒrotodun⌢ *his (her, its) hair is miserably short.*
nǒr-an (§ 3910α) v.i. *become fine-ground, etc.*
nǒram-bǔ- (§§ 3949 ff.) v.i. stat. *be in the state or condition of becoming or having become fine-ground, etc., be getting (have got) fine-ground, etc.*
nǒranɛd-ág- (§ 3966α) v.i. *be in the condition of having become fine-ground, etc., be in a fine-ground (etc.) condition.*
nǒrog-ır (N. -okır, -ohır; § 3701) (a) v.t. caus. *cause or allow to be fine-ground, etc.;* (b) v.t. *render fine-ground, etc.*
 ind. pres. aî⌣nǒrogıddı⌢.
nǒrogırg(ı) (N. -okır-, -ohır-; § 4467) adv. *fine, in (to, into) very small pieces.*
nǒrogır-bill(ı) (N. -okır-, -ohır-; § 4137) v.t. *pick to (into) very small pieces.*
nǒrogır-mér (N. -okır-, -ohır-; § 4137) v.t. *cut (etc. s.v. mér) fine, cut into very small pieces.*
nǒrogır-nódd(ı) (N. -okır-, -ohır-; § 4137) v.t. *cut up (etc. s.v. nódd(ı) fine, cut up into very small pieces.*
nósŏ⌣ adj. *(a) long (in space); (b, of persons,* like طَوِيل) *tall.*
 obj. nosóg⌣.
 pl. nosórı⌣ and nosónč(ı)⌣.
 úl⌣nósŏ⌣ *the (a) long thread.*
 sárbɛ⌣nósŏ⌣ *middle finger.*
 írı⌣nosón⌢ (-sŏ⌢, -sǒ⌢ § 939) and írı⌣nosón⌢ (-sŏ⌢, -só⌢) *the rope is (too) long.*
 írı⌣nosómunun⌢ *the rope is not long (enough).*
 ín⌣nosŏ⌢ *this is (too) long.*
 kắ⌣nosón⌢ (-sŏ⌢, -só⌢, -sŏ⌢, -só⌢) *the house is long.*
 kắ⌣nosón⌣álımunun⌢ *the house is long (but) not high.*
 ógığ⌣nósŏ⌣ *the (a) tall man.*
 ógığ⌣nosóm⌣bogómunun⌢ *the man is tall (but) not broad in build.*
 nósŏ-wɛd⌣dóllan⌢ (-d⌣d- < -g⌣d- § 534) *they want a long one.*
nósogıd n. *(a) length; (b, of person) tallness, height* [§§ 2247-9].
 obj. nosogídk(ı)⌣, -ítk(ı)⌣, -ítt(ı)⌣ (§ 2462), -ki⌢, -ti⌢.
 tén⌣nósogıd⌣mukóttɛ̄rrɛ́? *what is its length?*

tɛn‿nosogíttı‿nál⌒ *see what its length is.*
šan‿nósogıt‿kɛ́u‿tóskın⌒ *the length of the measuring-rod is three cubits.*

nós-an- (§ 3910α) v.i. *become long, lengthen, grow tall.*

nosám-bŭ- (§§ 3949 ff.) v.i. stat. *be in the state or condition of becoming or having become long, etc.*

nosanɛd-ág- (§ 3966α) v.i. *be in the condition of having become long, etc.*

nosóg-ır (N. -ókır, -óhır; § 3701) (a) v.t. caus. *cause or allow to be long, etc.*; (b) v.t. *lengthen.*

núba n. *Nubian, the Nubian language* [< نوبة *Nubians*, § 84].
 obj. -bag‿.
 ɛr‿núbag‿uñúnná? (-nn- < -rn- § 628) *do you know (understand) Nubian?*
 núbab‿báññi! (-b‿b- < -g‿b- § 519) and
 núbagɛb‿báññi! (-b‿b- < -d‿b- § 518) *talk Nubian!*

núbro‿ n. *spindle* (*CSW*, pp. 21, 22) [§§ 2306, 2308].
 obj. -rog‿.
 pl. -ronč(ı)‿.
 ɛ́nč‿núbrogɛb‿bɛnnákkı‿wédran⌒ (-b‿b- < -d‿b- § 518) *the women spin cotton with a spindle.*
 núbrom‿bér *pillar of spindle.*
 núbron‿dírr(ı) *notch of spindle.*
 núbroŋ‿gédɛ‿ *whorl of spindle.*
 núbroŋ‿gédɛ‿kɛbɛrtónun⌒ *the whorl of the spindle is (made) of gourd.*
 núbroŋ‿gól *top (notched end) of spindle.*
 núbroŋ‿šúš‿ *pillar of spindle.*

núd‿ n. *head, ear, spike (of cereal, spica);* with collective sg. (§ 4696 b) [< -n‿úd‿ < -n‿√ŭ*d‿ *head* (§ 4596 a); § 2171 a].
 obj. núdk(ı)‿, nútk(ı)‿, nútt(ı)‿ (§ 2462), -kı⌒, -tı⌒.
 pl. núdı‿.
 íllɛn‿núd‿ *ear(s) of wheat.*
 íun‿núd‿ *ear(s) of corn, head(s) of millet.*
 márɛn‿núd‿ *head(s) of millet.*

nuggára n. *drum, war-drum* [< Sudan Ar. نَقَّارَة *noggárà* id.].
 obj. -rag‿.
 pl. -ranč(ı)‿.
 nuggárag̈‿g̈óm⌒ (-g̈‿g̈- < -g‿g̈- § 551). *beat the drum.*

núgta‿ (núkta‿) n. *dot, point, spot;* with collective sg. (§ 4696 c) [< نُقْطَة id.]
 obj. -tag‿.
 pl. -tanč(ı)‿.

núgud‿ n. *(male) slave* [? cogn. Amh. ንግድ *trade;* or perhaps núg- cogn. with nóg- of nógo *female slave;* § 2340].
 voc. núgut!
 obj. nugúdk(ı)‿, -útk(ı)‿, -útt(ı)‿ § 2462, -kı‿, -tı‿.
 gen. núgudn‿v., -gun‿c.
 pl. núg(u)dı‿.

nugúdkanɛ‿ (-útk-; §§ 2295-6) n. *slavery.*
 obj. -nɛg‿.

nugún-d(ı)‿ (§§ 2545 ff.) adj. *appertaining to a (male) slave.*

núgud-an- (§ 3910α) v.i. *become a slave.*

núkta‿ < **núgta**‿ n. *dot, etc.*

númmɛ (nummé § 1532) v.i. *smell sweet, be sweet-scented* [< imperf. stem of نَمَّ id. + -ɛ § 3612].
 ind. pres. aı‿númmɛrı⌒ (‿nummérı⌒), ɛr‿númmɛn‿ (-mẽ‿, ‿nummén‿, -mɛ̃‿, -mɛ́⌒); perf. aı‿númmɛgorı⌒ (‿nummég-; N. -ɛko-, -éko-, -ɛho-, -ého-).
 part. pres. nummɛl‿ (nummél‿) (one) *that smells sweet, etc.*
 mámanı́gı‿nummɛlín⌒ (§§ 1161, 1972) *those flowers (over there) are sweet-scented.*

nŭr v.t. *thresh (by causing cattle to tread out).*
 ind. pres. aı‿nŭ́rrı⌒, ɛr‿nŭ́rın⌒ (-rĩ⌒, -rí⌒); perf. aı‿nŭ́rkorı⌒.
 part. pres. nŭ́rıl‿ (one) *that threshes, thresher, threshing,* obj. nŭ́rılg(ı)‿; past nŭ́rɛl‿ (one) *that threshed, thresher, threshing,* obj. nŭ́rélg(ı)‿.
 íllɛt‿tínčıgɛn‿nŭ́rran⌒ (-t‿t- < -g‿t- § 707, -n‿n- < -d‿n- § 624) *they thresh wheat by means of cattle.*

nŭ́rɛ‿ n. *threshing, treading out* [§ 2234 γ].
 obj. nŭ́rɛg‿ [> نَوْرَج *drag or sledge for threshing*].
 nŭ́rɛm‿bér *pole (planted upright in centre) of threshing-floor; a loop at the end of a rope passes round the pole; cattle are linked along the rope and driven round the pole over the corn* (*HWJ*; cp. *SNK*, 428).
 ín‿tínč‿íllɛn‿nŭ́rɛn‿íllɛr⌒ *these cattle are for treading out the corn.*
 márɛn‿nŭ́rɛm‿bérro‿šóndıran⌒ (-n‿n- < -g‿n- § 625) *they strew the (heads of) millet about the post in the threshing-floor.*

nŭr-an (§§ 3890 ff.) v.t. *tell to thresh, let thresh.*

nŭ́r-bŭ- (§ 3931 β) v.i. stat. *be in a threshed state or condition.*

nŭrr-ɛg-ág- (§§ 4071 ff.) v.t. = nŭrɛdól-.

nŭr-ɛ-dól- (-ʳod- § 1178; § 4022) and
nŭr-ɛ-dól- (-ʳod- § 4027) v.t. *be about to thresh.*

nŭrr-ɛ-ğŭ-bŭ- (§ 4069) v.t. stat. *be on one's way (coming) to thresh.*

nŭr-ɛ-má- (§ 4036) and
nŭrr-ɛ-má- (§ 4041) v.t. *become unable to thresh.*

nŭrr-ɛ-nóg (§§ 4048 ff.) v.t. *go to thresh.*

nŭrr-ɛ-nóg-bŭ- (-nóggŭ- § 546; § 4058) v.t. stat. *be on one's way (going) to thresh.*

nŭrr-ɛ-tá- (§§ 4060 ff.) v.t. *come to thresh.*

nŭrɛd-ág- (§§ 3877 ff.) v.t. *be in the situation of having threshed.*

nŭ́r-kattı- (§ 4093) v.p. *be threshed.*
 íllɛ‿nŭ́rkattın⌒ *the wheat is trodden out (teritur).*
 máro‿nŭrkattıgon, símsım‿ólgon‿ nŭrkattıgómunun⌒ *the millet has been trodden out, the sesame has not yet been trodden out.*

nušúg‿ (nɛš-) n. *snuff* [< نَشُوق id. § 1336].
 obj. -úgk(ı)‿, -úkk(ı)‿, -kı⌒.
 nušúkkı‿sórıñır‿undúkkó⌒ *he (has) put snuff up his nose.*

ñárr(ı) v.i. *(of dog) growl* [onom.].
 ind. pres. tɛr‿ñárrın⌒ (-rĩ⌒, -rí⌒), pl. tır‿ñárrıran⌒ (-rã⌒, -rá⌒); perf. tɛr‿ñárrıgon⌒ (-gõ⌒, -gó⌒); N. -ıkon⌒, -ıkõ⌒, -ıkó⌒, -ıhon⌒, -ıhõ⌒, -ıhó⌒).

ñúrr(ı) v.i. (a) *growl;* (b) *purr* [onom.].
 ind. pres. tɛr‿ñúrrın⌒ (-rĩ⌒, -rí⌒), pl. tır‿ñúrrıran⌒ (-rã⌒, -rá⌒); perf. tɛr‿ñúrrıgon⌒ (-gõ⌒, -gó⌒); N. -ıkon⌒, -ıkõ⌒, -ıkó⌒, -ıhon⌒, -ıhõ⌒, -ıhó⌒).
 kŏ‿sínnɛbūgıñ‿ñúrrın, dıgrígırsın‿nɛbūgın‿írrın⌒ (-ñ‿ñ- < -n‿ñ- § 640; § 1964) *when the lion is angry he growls, when he is very angry he roars.*
 sáb‿g̈úrrɛbūgıŋŋoñ‿ñúrrın‿sínnɛbūgıŋŋoñ‿ñúrrın⌒ *the cat purrs when it's pleased and growls when it's angry.*

ñúrrar‿ (-rár‿; §§ 2200 ff.) and
ñurríd‿ (§§ 2256 ff.) n. *growling; purring.*

-ŋŋon‿ < -ŋgon‿ (§ 662).

-ó! < -os! (§§ 962, 3801 ff.).
 kóp! *shut it* (in general).
 kobó! *shut it! (now).*

-ó⌒ (§ 5847) affirmative particle, approx. *well, at any rate* (zwar, quidem, μέν, γε).
 X. ál‿índo‿bıtúbbıná? tɛ́f‿férıs‿índo‿ būná? (-f‿f- < -n‿f- § 542) *will ɛ́áli sleep here? is his bed here?*
 Y. tɛ́f‿férıs‿índo‿bunó⌒ *well, his bed is here.*

-ó? *and always after* -o‿, *sometimes after* -u‿.

-jó? (-Jó) §§ 1986, 4267-72, 5844-6) deictic interrogative particle [a specialization of demonstrative -o § 4573; cp. Eth. -ʋ·ı (*DBCÆ*, § 161, 2 a) Gal. -ho? id. (*PHO*, p. 322)].
 (α) used in apocritic questions, suffixed to (a) the nominative of a noun, adjective, pronoun or numeral; (b) the bare form of the subjunctive of the verb (§§ 3057, 3122); (c) the conditional (§§ 3067, 3126); (d) an adverb-clause in -al (§ 6202); (e) a concretion in -on‿ (§ 5845 β iv).
 X. nókkon‿ (s)he (it) *went (has gone).*
 Y. ɛ́nó? *the woman?*
 X. tágon‿ (s)he (it) *came (has come).*
 Y. álıó? ɛáli?
 X. nogɛdólın⌒ (s)he (it) *is just going to go.*
 Y. gắdıó? *the judge?*
 X. nogóskoná? *has (s)he (it) gone?*
 Y. mıráslıó? *the messenger?*
 X. kánd‿ısé? *where is the knife?*
 Y. dúló? *the big one?*
 X. wăraŋ‿kíñña⌒ *no, the small one.*
 X. bıdígırın⌒ *you will fall.*
 Y. âı‿ıó? *I?*
 X. âıg‿ánnı‿óddın⌒ *my hand hurts (hands hurt § 4696 a) me.*
 Y. oŋgáró? *both?*
 Z. oŋgárré? *is it both?*
 X. wăran, wɛ́r⌒ *no, one.*
 W. šắnta‿ısé? *where is the valise?*
 X. âı‿sókkɛrıó? *the one I took?*
 Y. âı‿sókkɛsıó? *the one I took?*
 Z. âı‿sokkɛdágrıó? *the one I am carrying?,* lit. *the one I am in the situation of having taken?*
 V. kắg‿ʋsé? *where is the snake?*
 W. ɛr‿bɛ́sunó? *that you killed?*
 X. âı‿bɛ́sıó? *that I killed?*

ó͜ — óčč(ı)

Y. ár͜bɛ́sujó? *that we killed?*
Z. ír͜bɛ́suʲó? *that you (pl.) killed?*
X. bıwɛ́dɛndan͡ *they will tell me.*
Y. tăganó? *when they come?*
X. bótkon͡ *(s)he (it) ran (has run) away.*
Y. ɛr͜bɛlíŋgaló? *when you went (came) out?*
X. hánu͜tăróskó͡ *the donkey has come (back).*
Y. káčkonó? *and the horse?*

(β) **-ó**? renders a predicative adverb or adverb-complex interrogative, and the question may be anapocritic:
X. étta͡ *bring him (her, it, them).*
Y. máktåbıró? *to the office?*
X. mér! *cut it!*
Y. kándıgedó? *with a knife?*
álı͜kåró? *is ɣáli in the house?* (=álı͜ kåré?).
tɛr͜ódaró? *is (s)he (it) in the room?*
tır͜ódaró? *are they in the room?*
tír͜mándojó? *are they over there?*
ǧawắb͜bústán͜karamó? *and*
ǧawắb͜bústan͜ıllaró? *is the letter for the post?*
tɛr͜ímmam͜másıró? *and*
tɛr͜ímmam͜másıré? *is he without a turban?*

ó͜ n. *song*; with collective sg. (§ 4696d) [onom.; § 2049].
obj. óg͜.
pl. óńč(ı)͜.
aī͜óg͜uńúddi͡ *(a) I know the song; (b) I know (the) songs, i.e. I can sing.*

ó v.t. *sing* [onom.; § 2049].
ind. pres. aī͜óri͡, ɛr͜óń͡ (͜ó͡, ͜ó͡); fut. aī͜bóri͡; perf. aī͜ógori͡ (N. ͜óko-, ͜óho-).
imperat. ó!, ór͜., ó͜., pl. ówɛ! (ówɛ́!).
subj. past aī͜ósı͜ (͜ósu͜).
part. pres. ól͜ *(one) that sings, singer, singing,* obj. ólg(ı)͜, -gi͡; past órɛl͜ *(one) that sang, singer, singing,* obj. órɛlg(ı)͜, -gi͡.
def. perf. aī͜óróskori͡ and aī͜órédkori͡ (-étk-).
tínn͜óg͜óran͡ *they sing their song.*
tékk͜óran͡ (§ 6281) *they sing it.*

órar (órår͜; §§ 2200ff., 2207) and
ōríd͜ (§§ 2256ff., 2260) n. *singing.*

ór-an (§§ 3890ff., 3899) v.t. *tell to sing, let sing.*
tékk͜óran͡ (§ 6281) *tell him (her) to sing (it).*
tírg͜ówan͡ *tell them to sing (it).*

ōr-ɛg-ắg- (§§ 4071ff.) v.t. =ōrɛdól-.
ōr-ɛ-dól- (ōrºd- § 1178; §§ 4016-17, 4022, 4027) v.t. *be about to sing.*
ōr-ɛ-mắ- (§§ 4016-17, 4036, 4041) v.t. *become unable to sing.*
ōrɛd-ắg- (§§ 3877ff.) v.t. *be in the condition of having sung.*
óŋg-ır (N. óŋkır; § 3688) v.t. caus. *cause or allow to sing.*

ób v.i. *get inverted, get overturned, turn over, turn upside-down, upset* [cp. ON. **ovn** *id.*; *RSN*, § 129].
ind. pres. aī͜ób(ˡ)ri͡, ɛr͜óbın͡ (͜óbí͡, ͜óbí͡); fut. aī͜bób(ˡ)ri͡; perf. aī͜óbkori͡ (͜ópk-).
imperat. óp!
kúb͜ópkó͡ *the boat (has) upset.*
kúb͜óbóskon͡ *the boat has upset.*

ōbar͜ (óbår͜; §§ 2200ff.) and
ōbíd͜ (§§ 2256ff.) n. *getting inverted, etc., inversion.*

ób-an (§§ 3890ff.) v.t. *let become inverted, etc.*
ób-bū- (§ 3931 α) v.i. stat. *be in an inverted state or condition, be upside-down.*
sandúg͜óbbūn͡ *the box is (boxes are § 4647) upside-down.*
kúb͜óbbūn͡ *the boat is (has been) overturned (...is upside-down).*

ób-bᵘ-an (óbb(w)an; §§ 3962-3) v.t. *have, or let be, upside-down.*
tókkon͜sandúkk͜óbbammɛn͡ *don't let the box(es) be upside-down.*

ōb(ˡ)r-ɛg-ắg- (§§ 4071ff.) v.i. =ōbɛdól-.
kúb͜óbrɛgåkkó͡ *the boat was just going to upset.*
ōb(ˡ)r-ɛ-dól- (-rºd-; § 4027) v.i. *be about to get inverted, etc.*
kúb͜óbɛdólkon͡ and
kúb͜óbrɛdólkon͡ *the boat was just going to upset.*
ōb-ɛ-mắ- (§ 4036) and
ōb(ˡ)r-ɛ-mắ- (§ 4041) v.i. *become unable to get inverted, etc.*
ōbɛd-ắg- (§§ 3877ff.) v.i. *be in the condition of having got inverted, etc., be upside-down.*
kúb͜óbɛdågın͡ *the boat is upside-down.*

ób-ır (§ 3671) (a) v.t. caus. *cause or allow to get inverted, etc.;* (b) v.t. *invert, turn upside-down, overturn, upset.*
ind. pres. aī͜óbíddi͡ (͜óbıddi͡), ɛr͜óbırın͡ (-rí͡, -rí͡); fut. aī͜bōbíddi͡ (͜bóbıd-); perf. aī͜óbírkori͡ (͜óbır-).

óbırar (-rår͜; §§ 2200ff., 2212) and
ōbıríd͜ (§§ 2256ff., 2265) n. *inverting, etc., inversion.*

ōbıdd-ɛg-ắg- (§§ 4071ff.) v.t. =ōbıredól-.
túrug͜kúbk͜óbıddɛgågın͡ *the wind is just going to overturn the boat.*
ōbır-ɛ-dól- (-rºd- § 1178; § 4025) and
ōbıdd-ɛ-dól- (-dºd-; § 4033) v.t. *be about to invert, etc.*
túrug͜kúbk͜óbıredólkon͡ and
túruk͜kúpk͜óbıddɛdólkon͡ *the wind nearly upset the boat.*
ōbıdd-ɛ-ǧŭ-bū- (§ 4069) v.t. stat. *be on one's way (coming) to invert, etc.*
ōbır-ɛ-mắ- (§ 4039) and
ōbıdd-ɛ-mắ- (§ 4046) v.t. *become unable to invert, etc.*
ōbıdd-ɛ-nóg (§§ 4048, 4057) v.t. *go to invert, etc.*
ōbıdd-ɛ-nóg-bū- (-nóggŭ- § 546; § 4058) v.t. stat. *be on one's way (going) to invert, etc.*
ōbıdd-ɛ-tắ (§§ 4060, 4068) v.t. *come to invert, etc.*
ōbırɛd-ắg- (§§ 3877, 3883) v.t. *be in the situation of having inverted, etc.*
túruk͜kúpk͜óbırɛdågın͡ *the wind has overturned the boat.*

ōb-šúgur (ōpšú- §3747ᵋ') v.i. *descend after getting inverted, etc., descend upside-down.*
kúb͜óbšugúrkó͡ *the boat (has) upset and sank (has sunk).*

ōb-túrb(ı) (ōptúr- § 667 -túbb(ı); § 3747ᵋ') v.i. *lie inverted, lie prostrate, lie on one's stomach.*

óčč(ı) v.t. *drag, trail, tow* (=ošóšk(ı)) [perhaps cogn. with óǧı *convey*].
ind. pres. aī͜óččıri͡; fut. aī͜bóččıri͡; perf. aī͜óččıgori͡ (N. -ıko-, -ıho-).
imperat. óčči!
part. pres. óččıl͜ *(one) that drags, etc., dragger, etc. (and infra), dragging, etc.,* obj. oččílg(ı)͜.
máltın͜óččıl͜ (etc.) n. =óččıl͜ (infra).
tékkı͜kắn-tūrton͜óččıgoran͡ *they (have) dragged him (her, it) out of the house.*
kắǧkı͜kúllotōn͜oččétkoran͡ *they have dragged the snake out of the hole.*
kúpk͜óččıran͡ *they tow the boat.*
kúlum͜máltın͜tūr͜óččıran͜naddu-fɛ́rann͜ıllar͡ (-m͜m- <-g͜m- § 601) *they drag a stone (along) inside the runnel in order to clean it.*

óččar (-čår͜; §§ 2200ff.) and
oččíd͜ (§§ 2256ff.) n. *dragging, etc.*

óččıl͜ and (§ 1154)
óččıl͜ n. *runnel-cleaner, a large stone with rope attached, dragged along an irrigation runnel to clear it (NSD, p. 22).*
obj. oččílg(ı)͜, oččílg(ı)͜, -gi͡.
pl. óččılı͜, oččílı͜.
oččílgı͜máltın͜tūr͜óččıran͜naddu-fɛ́nn͜ıllar͡ *they drag the stone (along) inside the runnel that it may clean it.*

óčč-an (§§ 3890ff.) v.t. *tell to drag, etc., let drag, etc.*
óčči-bū- (§ 3931 β) v.i. stat. *be in a dragged (etc.) state or condition.*
ír͜óččıbūn͡ *the rope drags along.*
dárıb͜óččıbūn͡ *the road (in front of us) is long, lit. is dragged out, i.e. extends far.*

oččır-ɛg-ắg- (§§ 4071ff.) v.t. =oččɛdól-.
ōčč-ɛ-dól- (-čºd- § 1178; § 4022) and
ōčč-ɛ-dól- (-rºd-; § 4027) v.t. *be about to drag, etc.*
oččır-ɛ-ǧŭ-bū- (§ 4069) v.t. stat. *be on one's way (coming) to drag, etc.*
ōčč-ɛ-mắ- (§ 4036) and
oččır-ɛ-mắ- (§ 4041) v.t. *become unable to drag, etc.*
oččır-ɛ-nóg (§§ 4048ff.) v.t. *go to drag, etc.*
oččır-ɛ-nóg-bū- (-nóggŭ- § 546; § 4058) v.t. stat. *be on one's way (going) to drag, etc.*
oččır-ɛ-tắ (§§ 4060ff.) v.t. *come to drag, etc.*
kúpk͜óččırɛtågoran͡ *they came (have come) to tow the boat.*
oččɛd-ắg- (§§ 3877ff.) v.t. *be in the situation of having dragged, etc.*
kúpk͜óččɛdåkkoran͡ *they had towed the boat.*
oččɛd-dā- (§ 3991-; -ɛ́ggıdā-, occ. -ɛ́dgıdā- §§ 3993-4) v.t. *be going along dragging, etc., be dragging (etc.) along.*
tíg͜óččɛddåran͡ *they are dragging the cow along.*
kúpk͜óččɛddåran͡ *they are towing the boat along.*
oččɛn-nóg (§§ 4169ff.; oččɛ́ggınóg §§ 4176-8) v.t. *go (etc. s.v. nóg) dragging, etc., drag (etc.) away.*
imperat. oččɛnnók! (⁻⁻ § 1954).
tíg͜oččɛnnógın͡ *(s)he drags the cow away.*

očcı-gúšš(ı) (§3747ᵉ') (a) v.t. *break by (in) dragging, etc.*; (b) v.i. *break (get broken) by (in) dragging, etc.* (óčč(ı) alone reported not used intransitively §5341).
  kúpk⌣očči‿gúšš‿ıgoran⌢ *by dragging the boat they broke (have broken) it.*
  kúb⌣očči‿gúšš‿ıgó⌢ *the boat (has) dragged (i.e. scraped the bottom) and broke(n) (i.e. started a leak).*
óčči-kattı- (N. -ıha-; §4093) v.p. *be dragged, etc.*
  ír‿óččıkattın⌢ *the rope is dragged.*
-od⌣ (§6292) n. (α) *father-in-law* (a) = ɛn⌣ tımbáb⌣ *wife's father*, (b) = ógiñ⌣tımbáb⌣ *husband's father*; (β) *brother-in-law* (a) = ɛn⌣tímbɛs⌣ *wife's brother*, (b) = ógiñ⌣tímbɛs⌣ *husband's brother*, (c) = ɛssın⌣ógıǧ⌣ *sister's husband*.
  voc. -ot!
  obj. -ódk(ı)⌣, -ótk(ı)⌣, -ótt(ı)⌣ §2462, -ki⌢, -ti⌢.
  pl. -odı⌣.
  — always with a form of the possessive personal pronoun (§2626) prefixed:
  ánod⌣ *my father-in-law, etc.*
  ínod⌣ *your father-in-law.*
  tínod⌣ *his (her) father-in-law.*
  ántınod⌣ *our father-in-law.*
  íntınod⌣ *your (pl.) father-in-law.*
  tíntınod⌣ *their father-in-law.*
  (*ánnod⌣, *ínnod⌣, *tínnod⌣ not heard).
ód⌣ (§6292) n. *cold, cold weather* [§2061; ? < ádır *winter*, -r⌣ being taken as *in*].
  obj. ódk(ı)⌣, ótk(ı)⌣, ótt(ı)⌣ §2462, -ki⌢, -ti⌢.
  ınnów‿ódun⌢ *today is cold* (§4719).
  ınnówıg⌣ódun⌢ *today* (§4665) *it's cold.*
  kán-tūr⌣ágıl‿síkkın: 'bóčči‿ged⌣ód'rɛ́?' —bóčči‿ged⌣ágıl⌣ : 'ód dun'⌣ɛn⌢ *one that is (sits) in the house asks: 'is it cold outside?'—one that is outside says 'it is (cold)'.*
  ód⌣dámunun⌢ *it's not cold, lit. there is not (any) cold.*
  ód⌣áig⌣árın⌢ *and* (§4623) áig⌣ód⌣árın⌢ *I am cold, lit. the cold seizes me.*
  ót⌣tékk⌣árın⌢ *and* tékk‿ód⌣árın⌢ (s)*he (it) is cold.*
  X. ékk⌣ód⌣árná? *are you cold?*
  Y. áig⌣ód⌣ármunun⌣āi⌣kahárt⌣éri⌢ *I'm not cold, I'm warm.*
ód-an- (§3910α) v.i. *become cold (weather), turn cold.*
  ınnówıg⌣odanóskó⌢ *today it has turned cold.*
ódam-bŭ- (§§3949 ff.) v.i. stat. *be in a state of turning or having turned cold (weather).*
óda⌣ (ódà⌣) n. *room, apartment* [< وضة id.].
  obj. ódag⌣.
  pl. ódanč(ı)⌣.
ódd(ı) (a) v.i. *feel (receive the sensation of) pain, fall ill, become diseased*; (b) v.i. *feel (have the sensation of) pain, be ill, be diseased* = óddıbŭ-; (c) v.t. *become painful to, hurt*; (d) v.t. *be painful to, hurt* [? contains √ó*d *cold* (§4575) §2868; cp. ON. ⲟⲥⲏⲓ *sick* GNT s.v.; RSN, §129].
  ind. pres. āi⌣óddırı⌢; fut. āi⌣bóddırı⌢; perf. āi⌣óddıgori⌢ (N. -iko-, -iho-).
  part. pres. óddıl⌣ (a) *(one) that feels pain, etc., sick person, ill, diseased*; (b) *(one) that hurts, cause of pain, painful*, obj. oddílg(ı)⌣; past óddɛl⌣ (a) *(one) that felt pain, etc., sick person, ill, diseased*; (b) *(one) that hurt, cause of pain, painful*, obj. oddélg(ı)⌣.
  ɛsmán⌣óddın⌢ ɛoθmán *is ill.*
  súntınč⌣óddıran⌢ *the nails (hoofs, etc.) are diseased (painful).*
  āig⌣ám‿míss⌣óddın⌢ *my eye hurts (eyes hurt §4696a) me.*
  ánn-i‿āig⌣óddımunun⌢ *my hand does not (hands do not) hurt me.*
  án⌣nél⌣óddın⌢ *I have toothache.*
***óddar⌣** reported not used (§2214).
óddɛ⌣ n. *pain, illness, disease* [§2234γ].
  obj. -dɛg⌣.
  pl. -dɛnč(ı)⌣.
óddɛ-kō- (§4109) v.i. *have (a) pain, suffer pain.*
  ind. pres. āi⌣óddekōri⌢.
  part. pres. óddekōl⌣ *(one) that has a pain or pains, (one) suffering pain(s).*
oddíd⌣ (§§2256 ff.) n. (a) *feeling pain, falling ill, being in pain, etc.*; (b) *becoming or being painful, etc., painfulness.*
oddı-bɛ́jjı (§3747ᵉ') v.i. *start the morning (etc. s.v. bɛ́jjı) in pain, etc.*
  āi⌣oddıbɛ́jjıgori⌢ *I awoke this morning unwell.*
óddı-bŭ- (§3931α) v.i. stat. *be in a state or condition of pain, illness, etc., be in a diseased (etc.) state or condition.*
óddıg-ır (N. -ıkır, -ıhır; §3682) (a) v.t. caus. *cause or allow to feel pain, etc.*; (b) v.t. *make ill, render diseased, hurt.*
  úrk⌣óddıgırın⌢ (s)*he (it) gives one a headache.*
óg⌣ n. (a) *bosom, breast, upper front of body*; (b) *fathom measured between tips of middle fingers of laterally extended arms* [§4576; RSN, §129].
  obj. ógk(ı)⌣, ókk(ı)⌣, -ki⌢.
  pl. ógı⌣.
  óg⌣gɛr⌣kɛu⌣tóskın⌢ (-g⌣g- < -g⌣w- §547) *one fathom is three cubits.*
  ánn⌣ok⌣kɛu⌣tóskın⌣ *my fathom (sc. the one I make by extending my arms) is three cubits.*
  óg⌣mıŋkótter⌣dábūn? *how many fathoms are there?*
  bérk⌣ókkɛd⌣ásran⌢ *they measure timber by the fathom.*
óŋ-d(ı)⌣ (ógnd(ı)⌣, ógŋd(ı)⌣, óŋŋd(ı)⌣ §643; §§2545 ff.) adj. *appertaining to the bosom, etc.*
  šá⌣óŋd(ı)⌣ *and* (§1554) šā⌣óŋd(ı)⌣ *fathom rod.*
ógıǧ⌣ n. (a) *man (vir)*; (b) *husband*; (c, in measuring depth of well) *measure of about 5½ feet* (= Sudan Ar. راجل)
  [< √óg- *be above (§4576) + -ı- euph. + -ǧ intensive §2275; cp. ON. ⲟⲩⲓⲇ id. GNT s.v.; RSN, §129].
  voc. ógič!
  obj. ogíǧk(ı)⌣, -íčk(ı)⌣, -íčč(ı)⌣ (§523), -ǧk-, -čk- (§323), -ki⌢, -či⌢.
  gen. ógıǧn⌣v., ógıñ⌣. (§632).
  pl. óg(ı)ǧı⌣, voc. óg(ı)ǧi!
  — note the common stressing (§§1663–6) of
  ánn-ogıǧ⌣ *my husband.*
  ɛnn-ogıǧ⌣ *your husband.*
  ténn⌣ogıǧ⌣ *her husband.*
  ánn-ogíñ⌣tınɛ́n⌣ *my husband's mother* = ánnogo⌣ (s.v. -ogo⌣).
  ín‿ɛnn⌣ógıǧ⌣dióskon⌢ *this woman's husband has died.*
  ténn⌣ógıǧ⌣dióskon⌢ *and more commonly*
  ténn-ogıǧ⌣dióskó⌢ *her husband has died.*
  tínn⌣óǧǧı⌣ *their husbands.*
  ógıñ⌣dúru⌣ *old man.*
  gów‿ógıǧ⌣díǧun⌢ *the well is five men (deep), i.e. about 27½ feet.*
ogiñ-d(ı)⌣ (§§2545 ff.) adj. *appertaining to a (the) man, etc., of a (the) man, etc., a (the) man's, etc.*
  ıŋ‿kád⌣ogíñdın⌢ *this garment is a man's.*
ogiñdı-kırı⌣ (§2541) adj. *resembling that of a man, like a man's.*
ogǧin-d(ı)⌣ (§§2545 ff.) adj. *appertaining to (the) men, of (the) men, (the) men's.*
ogǧındı-kırı⌣ (§2541) adj. *like (the) men's.*
ogıč-čŏd⌣ (§2373) n. *male child up to about four years of age.*
  voc. -čŏt!, -čó!
  obj. -čŏdk(ı)⌣, -čŏtk(ı)⌣, -čŏtt(ı)⌣ §2462, -ki⌢, -ti⌢.
  gen. -čŏdn⌣v., -čŏnn⌣v.c., -čŏn⌣c.
  pl. ogıččonı⌣.
ogıččod⌣ (§2373) n. = ogıččŏd⌣.
  voc. -čot!, -čó!
  obj. ogíččodk(ı)⌣, -čŏtk(ı)⌣, etc.
  ogıččodn⌣⌢ *and*
  ogíččodn⌢ (§1966) *it's a little boy.*
  ín‿ánn‿ogíččódū⌢ *this is my (our) little boy.*
  ín‿tínn⌣ogíččódun⌢,
  ín⌣tínn⌣ogíččódun⌢ *and*
  ín‿tínn⌣ogíččódū⌢ *this is their little boy.*
ógıǧ-an- (§3910α) v.i. (a) *become a man, grow up*; (b) *become manly, become brave.*
  ind. pres. āi⌣ógıgandi⌢, ɛr⌣ógıǧanın⌢ (-ni⌢, -ní⌢); fut. āi⌣bógıǧandi⌢; perf. āi⌣ógıǧaŋkori⌢.
  subj. past āi⌣ógıǧansı⌣ (-assı⌣ §680, -su⌣).
  ogıǧanóskó⌢ (a) *he has grown up*; (b) *he has become brave.*
ógıǧam-bŭ- (§§3949 ff.) v.i. stat. *be in a growing up or grown up (man's) state, be grown up, be a grown man.*
ógıǧ⌣ gen. of ógıǧ⌣ *man.*
-ogo⌣ n. (α) *mother-in-law* (a) = ɛn⌣tınɛ́n⌣ *wife's mother*, (b) = ógiñ⌣tınɛ́n⌣ *husband's mother*; (β) *sister-in-law* (a) = ɛn⌣ tínness(ı)⌣ *wife's sister*, (b) = ógiñ⌣ tínnɛss(ı)⌣ *husband's sister*, (c) = -bésn⌣ ɛn⌣ *brother's wife* [< √óg- *be above (§4576+-o⌣ §2306].
  obj. -ogog⌣.
  pl. -ogorı⌣.
  — always with a form of the possessive personal pronoun (§2622) prefixed:
  ánnogo⌣ *my mother-in-law, etc.*
  ínnogo⌣ *your mother-in-law, etc.*

tínnogo‿ *his (her) mother-in-law, etc.*
antínnogo‿ *our mother-in-law, etc.*
ıntínnogo‿ *your (pl.) mother-in-law, etc.*
tıntínnogo‿ *their mother-in-law, etc.*

ógol‿ n. (a) *front part, foremost part, front;* (b) *earlier time, earliest time, beginning* [< *ógıl‿ (§1175) < óg‿ *upper front of body* + -ıl *determinative* (§2277)].
obj. ogólg(ı)‿, -gi⌒.
pl. ógol‿.

ogól-kırı‿ (-kírı‿ §1701; §§2539–40) adj. *like the front part, etc.*
X. έη‿kór‿mínε‿bún? *how is your wound?*
Y. marıssέg‿óddın, ogólkírımunun⌒ *it hurts a little, (but* §6239*) it's not like at first.*

ogóllo (§§4445, 6014) compl. adv. (a) *in front, ahead;* (b) *earlier, sooner, before, formerly, in (at) the beginning, at first.*
dérıb‿ogóllo‿tákkar‿εgó, ékkenε‿káww‿anóskó⌒ *at first (at its beginning) the path was (too) narrow, now it has got broad(er).*

ogóllo⌒ (§6007) pred. adv. *is (are) in front, etc.*
X. tér‿sé? *where is (s)he (it)?*
Y. ogólló⌒ (§1532) *he's (she's, it's) in front (ahead).*

‿ogól-lo‿ (§§4368, 5860, 5905) postp. (i = prep. §4288) (a) *in front of, ahead of, before;* (b) *in front of, before, in the presence of;* (c) *previously to, before.*
— follows the genitive:
tír-kăn‿ogóllo⌒ *they are in front of the house.*
tínn‿ogóllo‿nókkoran⌒ *they went (have gone) ahead of them.*
šăhıdın‿ogóllo‿wεtíkkori⌒ *I (have) told him (her) before (in the presence of) witnesses.*
tér‿ăıg‿gădın‿ogóllo‿kăǧǧıdεŋkó⌒ *(s)he gave (has given) evidence in my favour before the judge.*
wεrwέrn‿ogóllo‿ *in front of each other (one another), confronting each other (one another).*
ar‿sıgíddann‿ogóllo‿waddέru‿ (-nn‿ < -rn‿ §628a) *we perform ablutions before saying our prayers.*
árun‿ogóll‿addεráng‿dólli⌒ *I want to finish it before the rain.*

‿ogól-lo‿ (§§4369, 5860, 5905) postp. (ii = conj. §4288) *before.*
— follows the subjunctive genitive (§§2943, 2953):
tărann‿ogóllo‿dúŋgı‿dábın⌒ *before they come the money disappears.*
tăsann‿ogóllo‿dúŋgı‿dabóskó⌒ *before they came the money disappeared.*
bıtărann‿ogóllo‿dúŋgı‿bıdábın⌒ *before they come the money will disappear.*
ar‿nógrun‿ogóllo‿šahárkεb‿bıtăran⌒ (-b‿b- < -d‿b- §518) *they will come a month before we go.*
ín‿tír‿nógsann‿ogóllo⌒ *this was before they went.*

ogóln-d(ı)‿ (§§2545 ff.) and
ogónd(ı)‿ (§807) adj. (a) *appertaining to the foremost part, foremost, front, initial;* (b) *previous, former, earlier.*
ogóndın‿agárr‿úskur⌒ *put it in the place of the previous one.*

ogólndı-kırı‿ (ogón-; §2541) adj. *like the foremost, etc., like the previous, etc.*

ógol-an- (§3913β) v.i. *move (go, come) to(wards) the front part, etc., move forward(s), ahead, advance.*
ind. pres. ăı‿ógolandi⌒ (‿ogolándi⌒ §1926a); fut. ăı‿bógolandi⌒ (‿bogolándi⌒); perf. ăı‿ógolaŋkori⌒ (‿ogolaŋkori⌒ §1926a).
ógolammen? (-mẽ?, -mέ?) *do come on! (said by one ahead), lit. are you not going on?* (§5485).

ógolam-bŭ- (⁓́; §3950β) v.i. stat. *be in a state of forward motion, be on one's way ahead, etc., be advancing.*

ogolanεd-ăg- (§3966β) v.i. *be in the situation of having advanced.*

ogolan-nóg (§§3973, 4150) v.i. *go forwards, advance.*

ogolan-nóg-bŭ- (-nóggŭ- §546; §3974, 4153) v.i. stat. *be in a state of motion (going) forwards.*

ogólg-ır (N. -lkır; §3698) (a) v.t. caus. *cause or allow to be in front, etc.;* (b) v.t. *place in front, put ahead.*
íŋ‿ogólgır‿íŋ‿abákkır⌒ *put this in front and that at the back.*

ogolgır-óčč(ı) (N. -lkır-; §4136) v.t. *drag in front, drag forwards.*

ogolgır-tóllε (N. -lkır-; §4136) v.t. *pull in front, pull forwards.*

ogolgır-úskur (N. -lkır-; §4141) v.t. *put (etc. s.v. úskur) in front, ahead.*

óǧı v.t. (a) *convey, carry along,* and so, according to direction and the situation; (b) *take;* (c) *bring* [< éǧgu (§§992, 1181, 1196) < *εd-ǧú (§3853) *taking proceed, proceed with* (§5334); RNW s.v. *oji*].
ind. pres. ăı‿óǧ(ı)ri⌒ (‿óǧˈri⌒ §3562), ε‿óǧın⌒ (‿óǧı⌒, ‿óǧí⌒); fut. ăı‿bóǧ(ı)ri⌒ (-ǧˈri⌒); perf. ăı‿óǧıgori⌒ (N. -ıko-, -ıho-).
subj. past ăı‿óǧısı⌒ (-su‿).
def. perf. ăı‿óǧóskori⌒.
íŋı‿tín‿kăr‿óǧi⌒ *take this to their house.*
ăıgonom‿bóǧri⌒ *I'll take (bring) him (her, it, them) with me.*
mérkεzır‿óǧıruá? *shall we (you pl.) carry him (her, it, them) to the (government district) office?*
téŋ‿kăm‿mónkon‿óǧıgoru‿ (-m‿m- < -n‿m- §604) *we saw (have seen) him (her) home, lit. we took (have taken) him (her) as far as his (her) house.*
ín‿šém‿árgı‿mándo‿bóǧın⌒ *this candle will carry (i.e. suffice to light) us thither.*

óǧar‿ (óǧárˋ; §§2200 ff.) and
óǧíd (§§2256 ff.) n. *conveying, etc.*

óǧ-an (§3890 ff.) v.t. *tell to convey, etc., let convey, etc.*
hánuged‿óǧan⌒ *tell him (her) to convey him (her, it, them §5083) by donkey.*

óǧı-bŭ- (§3931β) v.i. stat. *be in a conveyed (etc.) state or condition.*

óǧı-dĕn (§3996–7) v.t. *give (to the speaker) after conveying, etc., convey (bring) to or for (the speaker).*

oǧ(ı)r-εg-ăg- (§4071 ff.) v.t. = oǧεdól-.

oǧ-ε-dól- (oǧºdól- §1178; §4022) and
oǧ(ı)r-ε-dól- (-rºd-; §4027) v.t. *be about to convey, etc.*

oǧ(ı)r-ε-ǧú-bŭ- (§4069) v.t. stat. *be on one's way (coming) to convey, etc.*

oǧ-ε-mắ- (§4036) and
oǧ(ı)r-ε-mắ- (§4041) v.t. *become unable to convey, etc.*

oǧ(ı)r-ε-nóg (§§4048 ff.) v.t. *go to convey, etc.*

oǧ(ı)r-ε-nóg-bŭ- (-nóggŭ- §546; §4058) v.t. stat. *be on one's way (going) to convey, etc.*

oǧ(ı)r-ε-tắ (§§4060 ff.) v.t. *come to convey, etc.*

oǧed-ắg- (§§3877 ff.) v.t. *be in the situation of having conveyed, etc.*
márεh‿hánuged‿oǧedágran⌒ (-h‿h- < -g‿h- §559) *they have conveyed the millet by donkey.*

oǧéd-dă- (§3991; oǧéggıdă-, occ. -έdgı- §§3993–4) v.t. *be going along while carrying, be carrying along.*

oǧen-nóg (§§4169 ff.; oǧeggınóg, occ. -εdgı- §§4176–8) v.t. *go (etc. s.v. nóg) while carrying, carry away, carry off.*

oǧet-tắ (§§4169 ff., 5723; oǧeggıtắ §§4176-8) v.t. *come conveying, come carrying, come with, bring along, go* (§5713) *and bring.*
imperat. oǧétta!, oǧέggıta!; pl. oǧεttăwέ!, -tăwέ!, oǧέggıtăwέ!, -tăwέ!

oǧ-εttắ (-έttă §3855; §5723) v.t. *bring* (εttắ s.v. έd) *conveying, bring along.*
imperat. oǧétta!, pl. oǧéttăwε!, ⁓́⁓έ.

oǧíŋ-ır (⁓́⁓; N. -ŋkır; §3688) v.t. caus. *cause or allow to convey, etc.*
ind. pres. ăı‿óǧıŋgıddi⌒ (N. -ıŋkıd-), ⁓́⁓, ⁓́⁓ §1812.

óǧı-tır (§§3998–9) v.t. *give (to other than the speaker) after conveying, etc., convey (take) to or for (other than the speaker).*
imperat. pl. oǧıtírwε!, -tírwε!, -tíwwε! (§723), -wέ!
έssı‿toddέg‿oǧıtir⌒ *take him (her, it) a little water.*
íŋgı‿samılg‿oǧıtir⌒ *take this to the sheikh.*
kálg‿oǧıtíkkori⌒ *I took (have taken) him (her, it, them §5083) the food (bread).*

óǧos-an (§§3890 ff., 3905) v.t. *tell to convey, etc., let convey, etc.*

oǧósw-an (-óssan §687; -ówwan §724; §3900) v.t. *tell (more than one person) to convey, etc., let (more than one person) convey, etc.*

oǧós-dĕn (-ódden §538; §§4180–4, 3995 ff.; -ósgıdĕn, -ózgı-, -óggı- §4185) v.t. *give (to the speaker) after conveying, etc., bring to or for (the speaker).*
imperat. oǧósdĕn! (-óddĕn!, -ósgıdĕn!, -ózgı-, -óggı-, -dĕ!, -dĕ!, -dĕ!).
ăı‿súgamburi, íŋg‿ăıg‿oǧóddεn⌒ *I am on my way to the market, carry this (that) for me.*

oǧos-tắ (-óttă §714; §§4180–4; -osgıtă, -ozgı-, -oggı- §4185) v.t. *come (after) conveying, etc., just* (s.v. -tắ) *carry away, go* (§5713) *and bring.*
íŋg‿ăı‿dólmunun, oǧótta! *I don't like (want) this: take it away and come (back),* (= *…just take it away*).

ar‿oğostågoru⌒,
ar‿oğottågoru⌒,
ar‿oğosgıtågoru⌒,
ar‿oğoggıtågoru⌒,
ar‿oğósgı‿tågoru⌒ (§ 5575) and
ar‿oğóggı‿tågoru⌒ (after) conveying it (them, him, her § 5083) we came (have come) (we (have) just carried it (etc.) away, came and took (have come and taken) it, etc., went (have been) and brought it, etc.).

oǧós-tır (-óttır § 714; -óssır § 686; §§ 4180-4, 3995 ff.; -ósgıtır, -ózgı-, -óggı- § 4185) v.t. *give* (to other than the speaker) *after conveying, etc., take or bring to or for* (other than the speaker).
oğostírkori⌒ (oğottír-, oğossír-, -íkkori⌒) and
oğosgıtírkori⌒ (oğoggıtír-, -íkkori⌒) *I took (have taken, brought) it (them) to him (her, it, them* § 5083).

oğostır-tá (-ottır-, -ossır-, -osgıtır-, -ozgı-, -oggı-; § 4195) v.t. *come after conveying to* (other than the speaker), *just carry to, go and take to* (other than the speaker).
X. ıŋ‿ahmétt‿oğottírta⌒ *just go and take this to Aḥmad.*
Y. (on returning) åı‿tékk‿oğottır-tågori⌒ *I've been and taken it to him.*

oğos-wıdɛ-tá (-owwı- § 724; § 4203; -osgı-wı-, -ozgı-, -oggı- § 4205; -wᵘdɛ-) v.t. *come back (after) conveying, etc., come back after carrying away, return after taking, just go* (s.v. -tá, § 5713) *and bring.*
imperat. oğoswídɛta!, -owwí-, -osgıwí-, -ozgı-, -oggı-, -wıdɛta!, -wᵘdɛ-.
ar‿oğoswᵘdɛtågoru⌒,
ar‿oğowwᵘdɛtågoru⌒,
ar‿oğosgıwᵘdɛtågoru⌒,
ar‿oğoggıwᵘdɛtågoru⌒,
ar‿oğósgı‿wᵘdɛtågoru⌒ (§ 5575) and
ar‿oğóggı‿wᵘdɛtågoru⌒ *after carrying it (them, him, her) away we came (have come) back.*

óı‿ n. *Hibiscus esculentus,* Linn., *edible hibiscus* (بامية ; BSP, 63).
obj. óıg‿.
pl. óınč(ı)‿.

ókk(ı)‿ n. *nail (clavus)* [< *óǧt(ı)‿ (§ 570) < √óg- *get or be on (§ 4576) + -t dim. (§ 2325γ), so **the little thing that gets (put) on; RSN,* § 129].
obj. -kıg‿.
pl. -kınč(ı)‿.

ólgon‿ (élgon‿ (§ 1177) q.v.; -gon‿, -gõ⌒, -gó⌒) adv. *(a) yet, still; (b) not yet* (so لسِّ, Amh. ገና•).
ólgon‿ seems to be commoner than élgon‿ in S.
ólgon‿ɛgéttınčín⌒ *they are still near.*
jŏm‿mɛ́r‿ólgónun⌒ (-m‿m- < -m‿w- § 603; § 1967) *it is one day more (...day longer).*
jŏm‿mɛ́r‿ólgon‿dån⌒ *there is one day more.*
X. ólgondé? (§ 5805) *is it still (going on)?*
Y. wåran, halás-taran⌒ *no, it's finished.*
X. ɛn‿zíkm‿ólgondé? *have you still got your cold?*

Y. ólgónun⌒ *yes,* lit. *it is still.*
ólgónun, tókkom‿betɛ́men⌒ *don't begin yet,* lit. *it's still* (sc. *too soon*), *don't begin.*
tɛr‿ólgom‿bɛlkómunũ⌒ *(s)he (it) hasn't gone (come) out yet.*
X. bústa‿nókkoná? *has the post gone?*
Y. ólgónun⌒ *not yet,* lit. *it is still.*
X. áša‿hådırun⌒ *dinner's ready.*
Y. åı‿ólgon‿éri, tágır⌒ *I'm not (ready) yet, cover it.*
X. ɛn‿táttı‿düróskó⌒ *your time on duty* (in cultivation by water-wheel) *is ended,* lit. *...has reached* (sc. *its end*).
Y. táttı‿ólgónun, dŭrkómunun⌒ *no, not yet,* lit. *the period is still* (sc. *unfinished, going on*), *it has not reached* (sc. *its end*).

ólgon‿ preceding the negative subjunctive (§ 6198), that may be followed by kóttıg = *before (antequam, priusquam)* with positive verb:
gåtır‿ólgon‿tåmenın‿índo‿tá⌒ and
gåtır‿ólgon‿tåmenŋ‿kóttıg‿índo‿tá⌒ *come here before the train arrives.*
ar‿ólgon‿síkkımendu‿kóttıs‿sókke-goran⌒ (-s‿s- < -g‿s- § 678) *they took it up (away) before we asked (them to).*

ólgon‿ preceding the negative subjunctive verb-concretion (§ 5744) = *before* with positive verb:
ɛr‿ólgon‿sókkemeŋgon‿åıg‿íddı⌒ (...sókkemeŋŋon‿... § 662) *ask me before you take it (them).*

óll(ı) n. *shadow, shade* [< *ó*dl(ı)‿ < √o*d *cold* (§ 4575) + -l‿ *determinative* (§ 2277), § 2298; *RSN,* § 129].
obj. -lıg‿.
pl. -lınč(ı)‿.
ín‿ğówwın‿óllı‿dıgrín⌒ *this (that) tree's shade is much, i.e. it affords plenty of shade.*
ténn‿óllı‿márısun⌒ *its shade is little.*
óllır‿bůgoran⌒ *they lay (have lain) in the shade.*
tır‿óllır‿ (§ 6007) *they are in the shade.*

ólli-kıññ(ı)‿ (§§ 2536–7) adj. *shadeless.*

ólos n. *rope attaching yoke* (íslam‿) *to pole slanting from horizontal* (túhum‿) *in water-wheel* (kólɛ‿) [app. a pronunciation of álas *cable*].
obj. olósk(ı)‿, -ki⌒.
pl. ólosı‿.

ómda n. *notable of village or district* [< عُمْدَة *id.*].
obj. -dag‿.
pl. -danč(ı)‿.

-on‿ (§§ 4398–400) *concretion-forming postposition suffixed to objective of noun or noun-equivalent* (a = adv.) *also, too, in addition, as well;* see §§ 4895β, 4896, 4900.
éssigon‿dåmunun⌒ *water, too, is lacking.*
súgır‿bíllegoŋ‿undúddan⌒ *they put* (pres.) *onions, too, into the cake* (s.v. súg‿).
ánn‿úrkon‿åıg‿óddın⌒ *my head, too, hurts me (I have a headache as well).*

éndıgon‿ådd́åbın⌒ *yours, too, is disappearing.*
åıgon‿ *I too, I also.*
ékkon‿ *you too, you also.*
tékkon‿ *(s)he (it) too, (s)he (it) also.*
árgon‿ *we too, we also.*
írgon‿ *you (pl.) too, you (pl.) also.*
tírgon‿ *they too, they also.*
X. ámbɛs‿dŭŋgıd‿dólın⌒ (-d‿d- < -g‿d- § 534) *my brother wants (the) money.*
Y. ékkon‿dólná? *do you also want it (some)?*
ékkon‿nók! *you go too!*
írgon‿nógwé! *you (pl.) go too!*
tékkow‿wɛ́run‿ (-w‿w- < -n‿w- § 720) *(s)he (it), too, is the same (...is one).*
írgon‿óğğıré? *and you, are you men?*
íŋgom‿bɛ́n‿ (íŋŋom‿bɛ́‿ §§ 662, 3530) *this (one), too, kills.*
ıŋgı‿sókkɛ: ıŋgóŋgı⌒ (§ 4627) *take this (away): and that.*
íččı‿toddĕgoŋgı‿tír *give him (her, it, them* § 5091) *a little milk also.*
wɛ́gom‿márısun‿ and
N. wɛ́kkom‿márısũ⌒ *and one is little (i.e. insufficient).*
dımíŋgon‿dıgrín⌒ *and ten is (too) much.*

-on‿ *takes the interrogative particle* -ó? (§ 5845β iv):
X. kåǧ‿tåróskon⌒ *the horse has come (back).*
Y. wélgonó? *the dog too?*

The noun-concretion in -on (§ 4895β) on receiving an adverb-forming postposition forms an adverb-concretion (§§ 6070 ff.):
kám‿ugúgoŋgı‿dábugŏ⌒ *the camel was present during the night also.*
N. ugúgoŋgı‿tåkoran⌒ *they came at night too.*
nígoŋgı‿nálkoran⌒ *they saw him (her, it, them) last year too.*

— a concretion in -on‿ may receive a predicative adverb-forming postposition (§ 6076):
hálagondo‿nálkattın⌒ *it is seen in the desert also.*
hálagondo⌒ *it is in the desert also.*
sıwítkoŋget‿tåmugın⌒ *he fights with the sword as well.*
sıwítkoŋgé⌒ *it is with the sword as well.*

— the adverb-forming postposition may be suffixed to the noun (-equivalent) inside the concretion (§ 6077):
sıŋkådırgon‿íŋkírı‿dån⌒ *at Sınkåt, too, there is some like this.*
sıwítketkon‿tåmugın⌒ *he fights with the sword also.*
íŋgekkoŋ‿kınnɛ́m‿mér⌒ (-kk- < -dk- § 574, -m‿m- < -g‿m- § 601) *cut a little off here as well.*

— here the objective suffix is -g or -k after the postposition -r (§ 908f):
índo‿dåŋ‿kårgon‿dån⌒ *there is some here and there is some in the house.*
kårgon‿dån⌒ *there is some in the house as well.*

-on‿...-on‿ (§§ 4401, 4901–2, 4906; = conj.) *both...and.*
oğíčkon‿ɛ́ŋgon‿nióskoran⌒ (... ‿nióskon‿ § 5362) *both the man and the woman have drunk.*

on — **ónd(ı)**

éssıgom márobe bɛ́rkıdd-dıran (... bɛ́rkıddın) (-b b- < -g b- §519) *the water and the sun make the millet sprout.*
âıgon ɛ́kkon uñúddu *both I and you know.*
tékkom béndıgılgow wɛ́run (-w w- < -n w- §720) *(s)he and a beggar are the same (thing).*
káčkon hánugow wɛ́lgon dabóskoran *the horse, donkey and dog have disappeared.*
— expressing addenda (§§ 5310–13):
kɛmískoŋ goríčkon dímınun 4+6 = 10.
tóskıgon tóskıgoŋ goríččɛ́ (§ 5312) 3+3=6.
goríǵkoŋ goríǵkon dımındówwıgɛ́ , goríčkoŋ goríčkon dımındówwıgɛ́ and goríččoŋ goríččon dımındówwıgɛ́ 6+6 = 12.
kolódkoŋ kolódkon dımındokɛmískɛ́ kolótkoŋ kolótkon dımındokɛmískɛ́ and kolóttoŋ kolótton dımındokɛmískɛ́ 7+7 = 14.
éssıgom bérkoŋ éttawan *and less commonly* (§ 4902)
éssıgoŋı bérkoŋ éttawan *tell them to bring both water and wood.*
kúbɛ máregom béntıgonn íllar (§ 6074) *the great jar (s.v. kúbɛ) is for millet and dates.*
hálagon úrun-túgondo nálkattın (§ 6085) *it is seen both in the desert and in the river.*
dárıg hálagon úrun-túgondo *the turtle is both in the desert and in the river.*
kámgon hánugoŋgɛt táran *they come both by camel and by donkey.*
íŋgɛkkoŋ kınnɛ́g íŋgɛkkoŋ kınnɛ́m mɛ́r (-kk- < -dk- § 574, -m m- < -g m- § 601) *cut a little both off here and off there.*

on (b, forming verb-concretions §§ 5725 ff. = subord. conj.) *while, though.*
— suffixed to subjunctive present sg. 3rd objective (§§ 2943, 5731 ff.); -ŋg- > -ŋŋ- (§ 662):
éssı dáŋgom marıssódun *though there is water, it's very little.*
N. áššı áččıŋgon adɛ́mgı kálmunun *though the monitor bites, it does not devour human beings.*
âı óddıbûŋgom bıkálmunun (-bûŋ-ŋom) *while I am ill I shall not eat.*
ɛr óddıbûŋgom bıkálmunun (-bûŋ-ŋom) *while you are ill you will not eat.*
tɛr óddıbûŋgom bıkálmunun (-bûŋ-ŋom) *while (s)he (it) is ill (s)he (it) will not eat.*
ar óddıbûŋgom bıkálmunun (-bûŋ-ŋom) *while we are ill we shall not eat.*
ır óddıbûŋgom bıkálmunun (-bûŋ-ŋom) *while you (pl.) are ill you (pl.) will not eat.*
tır óddıbûŋgom bıkálmunan (-bûŋ-ŋom) *while they are ill they will not eat.*

âı níǵıŋgon ágri (-ǵıŋŋon) *I am engaged in sewing.*
ɛr níǵıŋgon ágın (-ǵıŋŋon) *you are engaged in sewing, etc. s.v. ág.*
âı níǵıŋgon tɛ́gri (-ǵıŋŋon) *I am engaged in sewing, etc.*
ɛr níǵıŋgon tɛ́gın (-ǵıŋŋon) *you are engaged in sewing, etc. s.v. tɛ́g.*
âı níǵıŋgon ágsíddo (... tɛ̆gsíddo ; § 5742) *when I was engaged in sewing.*
— suffixed to negative subjunctive stem + -g- (§ 5743) *though, while* (-ŋg- > -ŋŋ- § 662):
tír dúŋgıg ármɛŋŋon ăǧǧélligáuran *though they get no money (for it) they are working (they are working without getting money).*
âı ólgon nógmɛŋgon ɛ́kkı bıtíddi (§ 5744) *before I go I shall give it (them § 5089) to you.*
— suffixed to conditional pres. sg. 3 + -g- (§ 5746) *while:*
šúgurkıŋgon súdun *while it goes down it is empty.*
— suffixed to negative imperative stem + -g- (§§ 5747–52) *...but (in next clause):*
tókkon árkımɛŋon âıg ıddi *don't throw (it away) but ask me, i.e. don't throw (it away) without asking me.*
S. dówwad dókkon ǧókkımɛŋŋoŋ gólli (-d d- < -g d- § 534) and
N. and S. dówwaǧ ǧókkımɛŋŋoŋ gólli (-ǧ ǧ- < -g ǧ- § 551) *don't chew the medicine but swallow it (swallow the medicine without chewing it).*
S. dówwad dókkon ǧókkımɛŋŋoŋ gólliwɛ́ and
N. and S. dówwaǧ ǧókkımɛŋŋoŋ gólliwɛ́ *don't (pl.) chew the medicine but swallow it.*

-on ...-on (§§ 5753–9 = subord. conj.) *both while...and while.*
— suffixed to subjunctive pres. sg. 3rd objective:
âı gɛrjɛ́ŋgom báǧıŋgon dólmunun *while I am reading and writing I do not want him (her, it, them).*
ɛr gɛrjɛ́ŋgom báǧıŋgon dólmunun *while you are reading and writing you do not want him (her, it, them).*
âı íriŋgon (-ıŋŋon) hásıbɛ́ŋgon (-ɛ́ŋŋon) tɛ́gri (ágri) *I am engaged in counting and reckoning.*
ɛr íriŋgon (-ıŋŋon) hásıbɛ́ŋgon (-ɛ́ŋŋon) tɛ́gın (ágın) *(s)he is engaged in counting and reckoning.*
tɛr íriŋgon (-ıŋŋon) hásıbɛ́ŋgon (-ɛ́ŋŋon) tɛ́gın (ágın) *(s)he is engaged in counting and reckoning.*
ar íriŋgon (-ıŋŋon) hásıbɛ́ŋgon (-ɛ́ŋŋon) tɛ́gru (ágru) *we are engaged in counting and reckoning.*
ır íriŋgon (-ıŋŋon) hásıbɛ́ŋgon (-ɛ́ŋŋon) tɛ́gru (ágru) *you (pl.) are engaged in counting and reckoning.*
tır íriŋgon (-ıŋŋon) hásıbɛ́ŋgon (-ɛ́ŋŋon) tɛ́gran (ágran) *they are engaged in counting and reckoning.*

√ **ŏn-** *to like* (§§ 4578–84).

-ŏn (occ. -ŏn, in formulae usually -ŏn, -ŏn, §§ 1990–3; §§ 4393–7) concretion-forming postposition, suffixable (without altering the sense) to the nominative case (subject) or objective case (object) or other adverbial complement before a verb in the conditional, quasi *for instance, to make the supposition, to assume,* but some lighter rendering is required (§ 4582). See §§ 4895 α, 4899 [a stereotyped verb *take (for instance), *consider, *admit, *include; cp. ON. on (a) v. *love*; (b) postp. = conj. *and*].
— If -ŏn is present it is suffixed to the subject, or if that is not expressed, to the object or other adverbial complement; if neither subject nor object is expressed, and there is no other adverbial complement, then -ŏn is absent:
âıon nálkıri, uñúddi and nálkıri, uñúddi *if (when) I see him (her, it, them § 5083) I know him (her, it, them).*
âıon nálkırı buñúddi and nálkırı buñúddi *if (when) I see him (her, it, them) I shall know him (her, it, them).*
ɛron ǧábɛgın ɛ́kk áččıran and ǧábɛgın ɛ́kk áččıran *if you touch them they bite you.*
ɛron ǧábɛgogın ɛ́kkı báččıgoran and ǧábɛgogın ɛ́kkı báččıgoran *if you had touched them they would have bitten you.*
ɛron tăgogın âı ɛ́kkı bıdɛfɛ́gori *if you had come I should have paid you.*
wɛ́lon úkkıgî mágǎs támunū *if (when) the dog barks the thief doesn't come.*
tıron tăgan âıgı wɛ́dɛn *if they come, tell me.*
mufɛ́ttıš ɛ́rŏn ăgkın gunál *go and see whether the new inspector is there.*
kobíttı tɛron kuzbúgın nál *see whether the door is open.*
tabbáhon íŋgı nŏrogırmɛ́rkogın, âı bıkálkori *if the cook had cut this up very small, I should have eaten it.*
nállı tɛron nókkogın *I'll see whether (s)he (it) has gone.*
árgon nálkıram bókkıran and árgon nálkam bókkıran *if they see us they hide.*
tírgŏn nalíkkım bókkın ,
tírgŏn nálkım bókkın ,
tírgı nalíkkım bókkın and
tírgı nálkım bókkın *if (when) (s)he (it) sees them (s)he (it) hides.*
éssı káron dámɛŋkıŋ gówwırtŏn étta *if there isn't water in the house fetch some from the well.*
— In formulae (§§ 6245 ff.) -ŏn (-ŏ̆n) precedes the subjunctive and participle: s.v. bārıkɛ́.

ónd(ı) n. *male* [< ogíñd(ı) , s.v. ógıǧ , stressed (§ 1521) § 2301; the resemblance to Amh. ወንድ *wond id.* (RSN, § 115⁵) is fortuitous.]
obj. -dıg .
pl. -dınč(ı) .
béntın ónd(ı) *male date-palm.*
káǧn ónd(ı) *stallion.*

kóddɛn‿ónd(ı)‿ *a scented herb, Ambrosia maritima*, s.v. kódda‿.

múgdon‿ónd(ı)‿ *male post, stronger post, supporting heavier end of crossbeam* (dίu‿) *in water-wheel* (kólɛ‿).

máltın‿ónd(ı)‿ *main runnel in irrigable estate* (kólɛ‿).

-on-on‿ (-onō⌢, -onó⌢, -ono⌢ §939; §4347) postp. (i = prep. §4288) *with, together with, accompanying* [i.e. -on‿ repeated §4584]—*attached to the objective:*

ar‿ahmétkonon‿tågoru⌢ *we came (have come) with Aḥmad.*

ténn‿askárkonon‿ısίŋkon⌢ *he (has) sent him (her, it, them §5089) with (...it, them by) his soldier (policeman).*

âıgonon‿ *with me.*

ékkonon‿ *with you.*

tékkonon‿ *with him (her, it).*

árgonon‿ *with us.*

írgonon‿ *with you (pl.).*

tírgonon‿ *with them.*

âıgonon‿tågoran⌢ *they came (have come) with me.*

âıgonón‿ta! (§1742) *come with me!*

ékkonom‿bıtåri⌢ *I shall (I'll §5383) come with you.*

tékkonon‿nókkori⌢ *I went with him (her, it).*

ar‿tékkonom‿béddıgoru⌢ *we (have) attended his (her) funeral service* (s.v. bédd(ı)).

sámıl‿ékkonom‿baññırángı‿dólın⌢ *the sheikh wishes to speak with (to) you.*

wɛrwégonon‿gɛndınógran⌢ *they go in step.*

-on-on‿ (onō⌢, -onó⌢, -ono⌢) postp. (ii = conj. §§4348, 6206) *as soon as, at the same time as.*

— suffixed to subjunctive objective (§§2943, 2953); -ŋg- > -ŋŋ- (§662):

árgı‿nallángonom‿bódran⌢ (-áŋŋo-) *as soon as they see us they run away.*

árgı‿nalsáŋgonom‿bótkoran⌢ (-áŋŋo-) *as soon as they saw us they ran away.*

hådıranίŋgonon‿éttaran⌢ (-ίŋŋo-) *they (will §5369a; tell him (her) to §6281) bring him (her, it) as soon as (s)he (it) is ready.*

hådırandáŋgonon‿éttaran⌢ (-áŋŋo-) *they (will) bring them as soon as they are ready.*

óñ (*a*) v.i. *weep aloud, wail, cry;* (*b*) v.t. *weep aloud (etc.) for, bewail* [onom., extension of ó *sing* §2895].

ind. pres. âı‿óñ(¹)ri⌢, ɛr‿óñın⌢ (‿óñί⌢, ‿óñί⌢); fut. âı‿bóñ(¹)ri⌢; perf. âı‿óñkori⌢.

dίɛlg‿oñóskoran⌢ *they have bewailed the deceased.*

óñar‿ (óñár‿; §§2200ff.) and

oñίd‿ (§§2256ff.) n. *weeping aloud, etc.*

óñ-kā‿ (§2384) n. *house of wailing,* i.e. house of a recently dead person, where the mourners assemble.

óñkár‿ågran⌢ *they are in the house of wailing.*

oñ-kátt(ı)‿ (*a*) adj. *weeping aloud, wailing;* (*b*) n. *mourner* [§§2534, 2535b].

obj. -tıg‿.

pl. -tınč(ı)‿.

mán‿ɛ́nč‿oñkáttınčín⌢ *those women (over there) are mourners.*

ógıǧ‿oñkáttɛnn‿ıllár‿ténn-urr‿ ɛskétt‿åbbógın⌢ *the man, because he is a mourner, is pouring dust on his head.*

óñ-mıssɛ‿ n. (§2386) *tear(-drop);* with collective sg. (§4696c).

obj. -sɛg‿.

pl. oñmıssɛ́nč(ı)‿.

óñ-bŭ- (§3931β) v.i. stat. *be in the state or condition of being wept aloud (etc.) for.*

dίɛl‿óñbūn⌢ *a (the) dead person is being bewailed.*

oñɛd-åg- (§§3877ff.) v.i. and t. *be in the situation of having wept aloud (for), etc.*

dίɛlg‿oñɛdågran⌢ *they have bewailed the deceased.*

óñ-kattı- (§4093) v.p. *be wept aloud for, etc.*

dίɛl‿óñkattın⌢ *a (the) dead person is bewailed.*

-óñ- only in būsn-óñ‿ *Tuesday* s.v. búš‿.

oŋår‿ both s.v. óww(ı)‿.

óŋgo‿ (óŋŋo‿ §662) n. *south* [§§2310, 4577; GCD, p. 28].

obj. oŋgo‿.

ίŋk‿óŋgon⌢ *in this direction is south.*

óŋgor‿ågran⌢ *they live (etc. s.v. åg) in the south.*

oŋgón-d(ı)‿ (oŋŋó-; §§2545ff.) adj. *southern.*

dérıb‿oŋgóndıgɛn‿nókkoran⌢ (-n‿n- < -d‿n- §624) *they went (have gone) by the southern track.*

óŋg-an- (óŋŋan-; §3910β) v.i. *go to the south, go southwards.*

ind. pres. âı‿óŋgandi⌢.

oŋgōgır-nóg (oŋŋó-; N. -ōkır-; §4140) v.i. *go southwards.*

oŋgōgırnógran⌢ *they go southwards.*

N. báŋganč‿oŋgōkırnókkoran, dıgrίnčıtaran⌢ *the locusts went (have gone) southwards, they are numerous* (§5791).

ór‿ n. *king* [§2389].

obj. órk(ı)‿, -ki⌢.

gen. óro‿.

pl. óruı‿, órwı‿ (§2432).

órn-d(ı)‿ (§§2545ff.) adj. *appertaining to the (a) king, royal.*

orwίn-d(ı)‿ (§§2545ff.) adj. *appertaining to kings, royal.*

órıg v.i. *get hungry* [RSN, §129].

ind. pres. âı‿órıg(¹)ri⌢, ɛr‿ór(¹)gın⌢ (-gi⌢, -gί⌢); fut. âı‿bórıg(¹)ri⌢; perf. âı‿orίgkori⌢ (-ίkko-).

imperat. órık!

subj. past âı‿órıgsı⌢ (-ıksı‿, -su‿).

part. pres. ór(¹)gıl‿ (*one*) *that gets hungry, hungry one, hungry;* obj. or(¹)gίlg(ı)‿; past ór(¹)gɛl‿ (*one*) *that got hungry, hungry one, hungry,* obj. or(¹)gélg(ı)‿.

or(¹)gίd‿ and

ór(¹)gıd‿ (§§2256ff.) n. *hunger.*

åıg‿órgıd‿ár(ı)n⌢ *I am hungry.*

éssın‿orgίd‿ (‿órgıd‿) *thirst.*

orıg-åg- (§3747ɛ') v.i. *sit (be, etc. s.v. åg) hungry.*

órıg-bŭ- (§3931α) v.i. stat. *be in a hungry state or condition.*

orıgίŋg-ır (⌢⌣⌣⌣; N. -ŋkır; §3688) v.t. caus. *cause or allow to get hungry.*

órıǧ (*a*) v.t. *tear up, tear to pieces;* (*b*) v.i. *get torn up, etc., tear up, etc.* [< ór- of órr(ı) *tear* + -ı- euphonic + -ǧ intensive or repetitive §2885].

ind. pres. âı‿órıǧ(¹)ri⌢, ɛr‿órıǧın⌢ (-ǧi⌢, -ǧί⌢); fut. âı‿bórıǧ(¹)ri⌢; perf. âı‿órıǧkori⌢ (-ίčk-).

imperat. órıč!

ǧawåpk‿orıǧóskó⌢ (s)*he has torn the letter up.*

ǧawåb‿orıǧóskó⌢ *the letter has got torn up.*

órıǧar‿ (-ǧár‿; §§2200ff.) and

orıǧίd‿ (§2256ff.) n. *tearing up, etc.*

órıǧ-an (§§3890ff.) v.t. *tell to tear up, etc., let tear up, etc.*

órıǧ-bŭ- (§3931β) v.i. stat. *be in a torn up (etc.) state or condition.*

wárag‿órıǧbūn⌢ *the paper is (has been) torn up.*

orıǧɛd-åg- (§§3877ff.) v.t. *be in the situation of having torn up, etc.*

warákk‿orıǧɛdågın⌢ (s)*he has torn the paper up.*

orıǧίŋg-ır (⌢⌣⌣⌣; N. -ŋkır; §3688) v.t. caus. *cause or allow to tear up, etc.*

órıǧ-kattı- (-ıčk-; §4093) v.p. *be torn up, etc.*

orófɛ, orófe, orófé (§§1794, 2878) v.i. *become cold, grow cold, cool* [§§2870ff.; contains √ó*d- cold §4575].

ind. pres. âı‿orófɛri⌢ (‿orófέri⌢, ⌣⌣⌣), ɛr‿orófɛn⌢ (-fɛ̄⌢, -fέ⌢, ‿orófɛ́n⌢, -fɛ̃⌢, -fé⌢, ‿orófɛ́n⌢, ‿orófɛ̃⌢); fut. âı‿borófɛri⌢ (‿borófέri⌢, ⌣⌣⌣); perf. âı‿orófɛgori⌢ (N. -ɛko-, -ɛho-; ⌣⌣⌣⌣).

def. perf. âı‿orofóskori⌢ (⌢⌣⌣⌣) *I have got cold.*

túrugır‿borófɛ⌢ (s)*he (it) will get cold in the wind.*

ίn‿éss‿orófémunun⌢ *this water does (will §5369a) not get cold.*

éss‿orofóskó⌢ *the water has got cold.*

(part. pres.) **orófɛl‿** (orófέl‿, orófɛ́l‿ §2524) adj. *cold, cool.*

éss‿orófɛlun⌢ (⌣⌣⌣⌢, ⌣⌣⌣⌣) *the water is cold.*

gålo‿dıgrίgır‿orófɛ́l-lēr‿ (-l-l- < -l-w- §580) *a very cool water-jar.*

orófɛrar‿ (⌢⌣⌣⌣, ⌣⌣⌣⌣; -rár‿; §§2200ff., 2210) and

orófɛrίd‿ (§§2256ff., 2263) n. *becoming cold, etc.*

orófɛl-an- (orófél-, orófɛ́l-; §3910α) v.i. *become cold, etc., cool.*

orófɛlam-bŭ- (orófél-, orófɛ́l-, orófɛlambŭ- §1932a; §§3949ff.) v.i. stat. *be in a cooling or cooled state or condition.*

éss‿orófɛlambūn⌢ *the water is getting cooled.*

orófɛlanɛd-åg- (§3966α) v.i. *be in a condition of having become cold, etc.*

orófɛ-bŭ- (orófé-, orófé-; §3931α) v.i. stat. *be in a cold state or condition.*

ind. pres. âı‿orófɛbūri⌢ (‿orófé-, ‿orófé-), ɛr‿orófɛbūn⌢ (‿orófé-, ‿orófé-, -bū⌢, -bū⌢, -bú⌢); perf. âı‿orófɛbúgori⌢ (N. -búko-, -búho-).

orófɛr-ɛg-åg- (§§4071ff.) v.i. = orófɛrɛdól-.

orōfɛr-ɛ-dól- (-r⁰d- §1178; §§4016-17, 4022, 4027) v.i. *be about to become cold, etc.*

orōfɛd-ág- (§§3877ff.) v.i. *be in a condition of having become cold, etc.*
  éss⏜orōfɛdágɪn⏜ *the water has become cold.*

orōfɛg-ɪr (N. -ɛkɪr, -ɛhɪr; orōfɛ́-, orōfɛ́-; §3680) (a) v.t. caus. *cause or allow to become cold, etc.*; (b) v.t. *cool.*
  ind. pres. âɪ⏜orōfɛgɪddɪ⏜ (⏜orōfɛ́gɪddɪ⏜, ˇˊˊˊ-, ˇˊˊˊ-, N. ⏜orōfɛkɪddɪ⏜, ˇˊˊ-, ˇˊˊ-ˊ⏜, ˇˊˊ-ˊ⏜).

orōfɛ́ŋ-ɪr (ˇˊˊˊ-, ˇˊˊ-; N. -ŋkɪr; §3688) v.t. caus. and v.t. = orōfɛgɪr.

órrɛ⏜ n. (a) *gram, chick-pea,* Cicer arietinum L. (BSP, 140); (b, applied to) *pea,* Pisum sativum L.
— with collective sg. (§4696b).
  obj. -rɛg⏜.
  pl. -rɛnč(ɪ)⏜.

orrɛ́n-d(ɪ)⏜ (§§2545ff.) adj. *appertaining to gram, etc.*

órr(ɪ) (a) v.t. *tear (from the edge);* (b) v.i. *get torn (etc.), tear (etc.).*
  ind. pres. âɪ⏜órrɪrɪ⏜; fut. âɪ⏜bórrɪrɪ⏜; perf. âɪ⏜órrɪgorɪ⏜ (N. -ɪko-, -ɪho-).
  imperat. órrɪ⏜.
  íŋ⏜kádɛg⏜órrɪgó⏜ *(s)he (it) tore (has torn) this cloth.*
  íŋ⏜kád⏜órrɪgó⏜ *this cloth (has) got torn (tore, has torn).*
— sometimes = órɪğ.
  X. ǧawâb⏜!sɛ́? *where is the letter?*
  Y. âɪ⏜órrɪgorɪ⏜ *I tore it up.*

órrar (-rár⏜; §§2200ff.) and **orríd** (§§2256ff.) n. *tearing, etc.*

órr-an (§§3890ff.) v.t. *tell to tear, etc., let tear, etc.*

órrɪ-bŭ- (§3931β) v.i. stat. *be in a torn (etc.) state or condition.*
  téŋ⏜kóman⏜órrɪbūn⏜ *his shirt is (has been) torn.*

orrɛd-ág- (§§3877ff.) v.t. *be in the situation of having torn, etc.*
  téŋ⏜komáŋ⏜orrɛdágɪn⏜ *(s)he has (you have) torn his shirt.*

órrɪ-kattɪ- (N. -ɪha-; §4093) v.p. *be torn, etc.*
  ín⏜órrɪkattɪn⏜ *this is (can be §5704) torn.*

-os (N. also -ōs §1103) forms a definitive conjugation (§§3789ff.) [< ós].

ṓs v.t. *cause to issue, so according to one's position* (a) *send forth, put out, give out, turn out, discharge;* (b) *bring out, get out, take out, produce;* (c) *dismiss from employment, discharge* [cp. ON. oc id. GNT s.v.; RSN, §129].
  ind. pres. âɪ⏜ós(¹)rɪ⏜, ɛr⏜ósɪn⏜ (⏜ósɪ́⏜, ⏜ósɪ́⏜); fut. âɪ⏜bós(¹)rɪ⏜; perf. âɪ⏜óskorɪ⏜.
  imperat. ós!, pl. óswɛ! (óswɛ́!, óssɛ! §687, óssɛ́!).
  subj. past âɪ⏜óssɪ⏜ (-su⏜).
  ɪw⏜wɛ́lg⏜ós⏜ (-w⏜w- < -n⏜w- §720) *send (take, bring) that dog out.*
  áŋgarɛh⏜hɛ́martōn⏜ósrɪá? (-h⏜h- < -g⏜h- §559) *shall (§5369b) I take (bring) the bedstead out of the tent?*
  ǧówwɪ⏜ténn⏜ígk⏜ōsóskon⏜ *the tree has put forth its blossoms* (§4696b).

  hukúm⏜amúrk⏜ōsóskon⏜ *the Government has issued an order.*
  X. mahzándo⏜mɪŋkóttɛ́r⏜dān? (§1786) *how many are there in the store?*
  Y. ɛddór⏜tóskɪn⏜ *I think (they are) three.*
  X. wɛ́g⏜ós⏜ *get out one.*
  téŋ⏜kándɪg⏜ōsóskó⏜ *he has got out his knife.*
  tínn⏜síwɪdɪg⏜óskoran⏜ *they drew (have drawn) their swords.*
  bɛnnáŋkolɛ⏜bɛnnágɪrtōŋ⏜kukkósk⏜ósɪn⏜ *the gin takes the seeds* (§4696b) *out of the cotton.*
  tén⏜tabbáhk⏜ōsóskó⏜ *(s)he has discharged his (her) cook.*

ósar (ósár⏜; §§2200ff.) and **ōsíd** (§§2256ff.) n. *causing to issue, etc.; discharge, dismissal.*

óss(ɪ)⏜ n. (a) *leg;* (b) *foot;* (c) *footprint, track.*
— with collective sg. (§4696a) [< *óst(ɪ)⏜ (§686) < *ōst(ɪ)⏜ (§1048) < ṓs *put forth* + -t of n. act., so *putting forth,* concrete *what is put forth,* *limb* §2319; cp. MN. otti id. MZM, p. 338]:
  obj. -sɪg⏜.
  pl. -sɪnč(ɪ)⏜.
  ínn⏜óss(ɪ)⏜ *right leg (foot).*
  maínn⏜óss(ɪ)⏜ *left leg (foot).*
  óss⏜ɛ́r⏜ *one leg s.v. wɛ́r*⏜.
  óssɪm⏜budúrt(ɪ)⏜ *joint(s) of leg (at hip, knee, ankle or of toe).*
  óssɪn⏜sárbɛ⏜ and ossɪs-sárbɛ⏜ (-s-s- < -n-s- §680; §2363) *toe(s).*
  áŋgarɛ⏜óssɪnč(ɪ)⏜ (a) *legs of bedstead;* (b) *the Great Bear.*
  ánn⏜ossɪs⏜šúkkɪrɪ⏜ (-š-š- < -g-š- §695) and
  ánn⏜ossɪnčɪš⏜šúkkɪrɪ⏜ *I('ll §5369b) wash my feet.*
  ténn⏜óssɪ⏜búdbūn⏜ *his (her, its) leg is dislocated (at hip, knee, ankle or of toe).*
  N. âɪ⏜ánn⏜óssɪgɛt⏜táhorɪ⏜ *I came (have come) on foot.*
  tínn⏜óssɪgɛt⏜tágoran⏜ *they came (have come) on foot.*
  ín⏜óssɪ⏜tīnčíndɪkɪrɪn⏜ *this track is (these tracks are) like those of cattle.*
  ɛ́nn⏜óssɪ⏜sɛrɛ̄n⏜ *you've brought us luck,* lit. *your foot is good* (cp. Isaiah 52⁷).

ossín-d(ɪ)⏜ (§§2545ff.) adj. *appertaining to the leg, etc., of the leg, etc., the leg's, etc.*

óssín-tu (§2363) n. *sole of foot;* with collective sg. (§4696a).
  obj. óssín-tūg⏜, óssɪn⏜tū́g⏜.
  gen. óssín-tūn⏜, óssɪn⏜tū́n⏜.

ossɪn-tū́n-d(ɪ)⏜ (§§2545ff.) adj. *appertaining to the sole of the foot.*

ṓs-an (§§3890ff.) v.t. *tell to cause to issue, etc., let cause to issue, etc.*
  álɪm⏜mám⏜bɛ́rtɪg⏜ósan⏜ (-m⏜m- < -g⏜m- §601) *let ɛ́áli turn (bring) that goat out.*

ōz-bŭ- (§727; §3931β) v.i. stat. *be in a sent forth (etc.) state or condition.*
  X. sandúkk⏜ōsóskoruá? *have you (pl.) taken (brought) the box out?*
  Y. ōzbūn⏜ *it has been taken (brought) out.*
  ámbɛs⏜tén⏜ǧɛllɪrtōn⏜ōzbūn⏜ *my brother has been dismissed from his job.*

ōs(¹)r-ɛg-ág- (§§4071ff.) v.t. = ōsɛdól-.

ōs-ɛ-dól- (ōs⁰d- §1178; §4022) and **ōs(¹)r-ɛ-dól-** (-r⁰d-; §4027) v.t. *be about to cause to issue, etc.*

ōs(¹)r-ɛ-ğŭ-bŭ- (§4069) v.t. stat. *be on one's way (coming) to cause to issue, etc.*

ōs-ɛ-má- (§4036) and **ōs(¹)r-ɛ-má-** (§4041) v.t. *become unable to cause to issue, etc.*

ōs(¹)r-ɛ-nóg (§§4048ff.) v.t. *go to cause to issue, etc.*

ōs(¹)r-ɛ-nóg-bŭ- (-nóggŭ- §546; §4058) v.t. stat. *be on one's way (going) to cause to issue, etc.*

ōs(¹)r-ɛ-tá (§§4060ff.) v.t. *come to cause to issue, etc.*

ōsɛd-ág- (§§3877ff.) v.t. *be in the situation of having caused to issue, etc.*

ṓs-kattɪ- (§4093) v.p. *be caused to issue, etc.*

ósmar⏜ n. *shoulder;* with collective sg. (§4696a) [§2198; RSN, §82].
  obj. osmárk(ɪ)⏜, -kɪ⏜.
  pl. ósmarɪ⏜.

ósmarn-d(ɪ)⏜ (§§2545ff.) adj. *appertaining to the shoulder.*

ṓssɛ! < **ṓswɛ!** *take (pl.) out!, etc.* s.v. ṓs.

óss(ɪ)⏜ *leg, foot,* s.v. ṓs.

óšog (ošóg §1752) v.t. (a) *shake;* (b) *shake down, shake level* (= óšoŋ) [freq. §2851].
  ind. pres. âɪ⏜ošóg(¹)rɪ⏜, ɛr⏜óšogɪn⏜ (⏜ošógɪn⏜, -gɪ́⏜, -gɪ́⏜); perf. âɪ⏜ošóg-korɪ⏜ (-ókko-).
  imperat. óšok! (ošók!).
  subj. past âɪ⏜ošógsɪ⏜ (-óksɪ⏜, -su⏜).
  ɛ́m⏜bítâŋg⏜óšogɪn⏜ *the woman shakes the child.*
  ǧówwɪg⏜óšográn⏜ *they shake the tree.*
  fun⏜asíddɪg⏜ošográn⏜ *they shake down the measure (measured amount) of grain.*

óšogar⏜ (ošóg-; -gár⏜; §§2200ff.) and **ošogíd** (§§2256ff.) n. *shaking, etc.*

óšog-an (ošóg-; §§3890ff.) v.t. *tell to shake, etc., let shake, etc.*

óšóg-bŭ- (-óggŭ- §546; §3931β) v.i. stat. *be in a shaken (etc.) state or condition.*
  asídd⏜ošóggūn⏜ *the measure is (has been) shaken down.*

ošogɛd-ág- (§§3877ff.) v.t. *be in the situation of having shaken, etc.*

ošogíŋ-ɪr (ˊˇˊˊ-; N. -ŋkɪr; §3688) v.t. caus. *cause or allow to shake, etc.*
  tókkon⏜ošogɪŋgírmɛn⏜ *don't make (let) him (her, it) shake him (her, it, them).*

óšóg-kattɪ- (-ókka-; §4093) v.p. *be shaken, etc.*

óšoŋ (ošóŋ §1752) v.t. (a) *shake;* (b) *shake down, shake level* (= óšog) [freq. §2851].
  ind. pres. âɪ⏜ošóŋrɪ⏜, ɛr⏜óšoŋɪn⏜ (⏜ošóŋɪn⏜, -ŋɪ́⏜, -ŋɪ́⏜); perf. âɪ⏜ošóŋkorɪ⏜.
  ɛ́n⏜tém⏜bítâŋg⏜óšoŋɪn⏜ *the woman shakes her child.*
  ǧówwɪg⏜ošóŋram⏜barámgɪ⏜šugúddɪr⏜égi; úrtɪ⏜kálɪn⏜ *they shake the acacias* (§4696b) *in order to bring down the blossoms (ib.); the goats (sheep, ib.) eat them.*
  fun⏜asíddɪg⏜ošóŋran⏜ *they shake down the measure (measured amount) of grain.*

óšoŋar⏜ (ošóŋ-; -ŋár⏜; §§2200ff.) and

ošoŋíd (§§2256ff.) n. *shaking, etc.*
óšoŋ-an (ošóŋ-; §§3890ff.) v.t. *tell to shake, etc., let shake, etc.*
ošóŋ-bŭ- (§3931β) v.i. stat. *be in a shaken (etc.) state or condition.*
  asíddˬošóŋbūnˀ *the measure is (has been) shaken down.*
ošoŋɛd-ág- (§§3877ff.) v.t. *be in the situation of having shaken, etc.*
  asíddɪgˬošoŋɛdágranˀ *they have shaken the measure down.*
ošoŋíŋ-ɪr (ˊˉˉ; N. -ŋkɪr; §3688) v.t. caus. *cause or allow to shake, etc.*
  tókkonˬošoŋɪŋgírmɛnˀ *don't make (let) him (her, it) shake him (her, it, them).*
ošóŋ-kattɪ- (§4093) v.p. *be shaken, etc.*
ošóšk(ɪ) v.t. *drag, trail, tow* (=óčč(ɪ)) [imit., freq. §2855)].
  ind. pres. āɪˬošóškɪrɪˀ; perf. āɪˬošóškɪgorɪˀ (N. -ɪko-, -ɪho-).
  imperat. ošóški!
  tíddotów-wɛrˬoččílgˬošóškɪnˀ (-w-w- <-n-w- §720) *one of them drags the runnel-cleaner* (s.v. óččɪl).
  túrugˬkúpkˬošóškɪnˀ *the wind drags the boat.*
  kúbkˬošóškɪranˀ *they tow the boat.*
ošóškar (-kár; §§2200ff.) and
ošóškíd (§§2256ff.) n. *dragging, etc.*
ošóšk-an (§§3890ff.) v.t. *tell to drag, etc., let drag, etc.*
ošóšk-bŭ- (§3931β) v.i. stat. *be in a dragged (etc.) state or condition.*
ošóškɪr-ɛg-ág- (§§4071ff.) v.t. =ošóškɛdól-.
ošóšk-ɛ-dól- (-kᵒd- §1178; §§4022-4) and
ošóškɪr-ɛ-dól- (-rᵘd-; §§4027-9) v.t. *be about to drag, etc.*
ošóškɪr-ɛ-ğŭ-bŭ- (§4069) v.t. stat. *be on one's way (coming) to drag, etc.*
ošóšk-ɛ-má- (§§4036-8) and
ošóškɪr-ɛ-má- (§§4041-3) v.t. *become unable to drag, etc.*
ošóškɪr-ɛ-nóg (§§4048ff.) v.t. *go to drag, etc.*
ošóškɪr-ɛ-nóg-bŭ- (-nóggŭ- §546; §4058) v.t. stat. *be on one's way (going) to drag, etc.*
  kúbkˬošóškɪrɛnóggūranˀ *they are on their way to tow the boat.*
ošóškɪr-ɛ-tá (§§4060ff.) v.t. *come to drag, etc.*
ošóškɛd-ág- (§§3877ff.) v.t. *be in the situation of having dragged, etc.*
  kúbkˬošóškɛdágranˀ *they have towed the boat.*
ošóškɛd-dā- (§3991; -ɛ́ggɪdā-, occ. -ɛ́dgɪ- §§3993-4) v.t. *be going along dragging, etc., be dragging (etc.) along.*
  ɛ́kkɛnˬɛgɛ́d-dɛ̌ğˬğánkó, nográŋgɪˬ mōnóskó, ošóškɛ́ddānˀ (-d-d- <-d-w- §533, -ğ-ğ-<-g-ğ- §551) *(s)he has now bought a sheep (and) it won't go (and) (s)he's dragging it along.*
ošóškɛn-nóg (§§4169ff.; -kɛggɪnóg §§4176-8) v.i. *go (etc. s.v. nóg) dragging, etc., drag (etc.) away.*
  imperat. ošóškɛnnók! (ˊˉˉ §1954).
  tígˬošóškɛnnógɪnˀ *(s)he drags the cow away.*
ošóškɪ-gúšš(ɪ) (§3747ᵋ') (a) v.t. *break by (in) dragging, etc.*; (b) v.i. *break (get broken) by (in) dragging, etc.* (ošóšk(ɪ) alone reported not used intransitively §5341).
  sandúkkˬošoškɪgúššɪgoranˀ *by dragging the box they broke (have broken) it.*
  kúbˬošoškɪgúššɪgóˀ *the boat (has) dragged (i.e. scraped the bottom) and broke (got broken, i.e. sprang (has sprung) a leak).*
ošóškɪ-kattɪ- (N. -ɪha-; §4093) v.p. *be dragged, etc.*
-ot! voc. of -od- *father-in-law, etc.*
ŏ́wwɛl (ŏ̄uwɛl, ówɛl, -wál, -wəl §§1041, 1332a, 1380) ord. num. *first* [<اوّل id.].
  obj. ŏ́wwɛ́lg(ɪ), -gi?
ŏ́wwɛ́lg-ɛd- (-ɛt? §469, -ɛ́? §966; §6007) adv. *at first.*
ŏ́wwɛlɛn (ŏ̄uwɛ-, etc.; §956a) adv. *firstly, at first* [<اوّل id.].
  ówwɛlɛnˬkíññˬɛgón, ɛ́kkɛnɛˬdúlanoskonˀ *at first (s)he (it) was small, now (s)he (it) has grown big.*
ŏ́wwɛ́l-lo (s.v. -r; §6007) adv. (a) *in the first place, first, in front, ahead;* (b) *at the first time, at first, firstly, earliest, soonest;* (c) *previously, earlier, sooner, before.*
  tɪrˬowwɛ́lloˀ *they are in the first place, etc.*
ŏ́wwɛ́llo (§§4370, 5860, 5906) postp. (=prep. §4287) (a, space) *before, in front of;* (b, time) *before, sooner than, earlier than.*
— *follows the genitive:*
  súgˬdúhurnˬowwɛ́lloˀ *the market is before noon.*
ŏ́wwɛ́ln-d(ɪ) (ŏ̄uwɛ́-, etc.; §2545ff.) adj. (a) *appertaining to the first, of the first, first, foremost;* (b) *former, previous.*
ŏ́ww(ɪ) (ŏ̄uw(ɪ), -wᵘ §§1041, 1202; ŏ́wᵘ §1012; -wiˀ, -wɪˀ §1165; §§2699, 2707) card. num. *two* [RSN, §115; cp. ON. ого, огог id. GNT s.v.].
  obj. -wɪg, -wᵘg, -giˀ
  pl. -wɪnč(ɪ), -čiˀ
  ówwɪˬtóskɪˬdánˀ *there are two or three.*
  ówwɪˬtóskɪnˀ *it's three twos.*
  ówwínˀ (-wíˀ, -wíˀ §§939, 1970, 5232) and
  tɛ́rˬówwɪnˀ (tɛr-, -wíˀ, -wíˀ §5233) *it's (they're) two.*
  ówwɪnčínˀ (-číˀ, -číˀ §5235),
  tírˬówwɪnčínˀ (tɪr-, §5236) and
  tɪrˬówwɪnˀ (-wíˀ, -wíˀ §5237) *they're two.*
  ówwɪˬtágonˀ and
  ówwɪˬtágoranˀ *two came (have come; §5229).*
  tɪrˬówwɪˬnókkonˀ and
  tɪrˬówwɪˬnókkoranˀ *the two of them went (have gone; §5245).*
  ógɪğˬówwɪˬkásɪnˀ and
  ógɪğˬówwɪˬkásranˀ *two men draw water* (§5239).
  X. mukóttɛ̌gɛğˬğánɛ́ttāgóˀ *at* (s.v. -ɛd-) *what price did you (he, she) buy (it, them)?*
  Y. rɪjálˬŏ́wᵘgɛ́ˀ *at two dollars.*
  gátɪrˬsǎˬŏ́wwɪrˀ *the train's at 2 o'clock.*
ŏ́wwín-d(ɪ) (ŏ̄uwí-; §2737a) adj. *appertaining to two, of two, two's.*
ŏ́wwɪnčín-d(ɪ) (ŏ̄uwɪ-; §2737b) adj. =ŏ́wwínd(ɪ).
ŏ́ww-ínt(ɪ) (ŏ̄uwí-, ŏ́wwɪnt(ɪ) ŏ̄uwɪ-; §2740) ord. num. *second.*
ŏ́wwɪntín-d(ɪ) (ŏ̄uwɪ-; §2743) adj. *appertaining to the second.*
oŋgǎr (§§2758, 5261-7) num. *the two, both* [< *ouŋgǎr < *owuŋgǎr (RNW s.v.) < ówwɪn of two+-g obj. suff. + -ár *seizure, so *comprehension of the two §2218].
  obj. -árk(ɪ), -kiˀ
  oŋgǎrˬwɛ́runˀ *they're both the same.*
  sǎbˬoŋgǎrˬtágonˀ and
  sǎbˬoŋgǎrˬtágoranˀ *both cats came (have come).*
  tínnˬoŋgǎrˬnókkonˀ,
  tínnˬoŋgǎrˬnókkoranˀ,
  tɪrˬoŋgǎrˬnókkonˀ and
  tɪrˬoŋgǎrˬnókkoranˀ *both of them went (have gone).*
  ɛrˬğawábˬoŋgǎrkɪˬsókkɛgoná? *did you take (have you taken) both letters?*
  ğawábˬoŋgǎrˬɛrˬāigɪˬdɛ́nsɪŋˬɛğğusandúgɪrundúrkoriˀ (§5605) *both of the letters you gave me I took (have taken) along and put into the box.*
  X. āigˬánnˬúlugˬóddɪnˀ *my ear hurts (ears hurt §4696a) me.*
  Y. oŋgǎró? *both?*
  Z. oŋgǎrré? *both?*
  X. wɛ̄rˀ *one.*
  ɛrˬtɛrˬoŋgǎrkɪˬnálkona?,
  ɛrˬtɪrˬoŋgǎrkɪˬnálkona? and
  ɛrˬtínnˬoŋgǎrkɪˬnálkona? *did you see (have you seen) them both?*
ŏ́wwɪ-kɪrɪ (§§2539, 2540d) num. adj. *about two, one or two, two or three.*
ŏ́ww-an- (§2760) v.i. *become two, become double.*
ŏ́wwam-bŭ- (§2761) v.i. stat. *be in a state or condition of becoming two, etc.*
ŏ́wwɪg-ɪr (ŏ́wwᵘgɪr, ŏ̄uw-; N. -ɪkɪr, -ɪhɪr; §2759) v.t. caus. *make into two.*
ŏ́wwɪg-árbɪr (-wᵘgɪr-, etc.) §4141) v.t. *fold in two.*
ŏ́wwɪgɪr-bág (§4138) v.t. *divide into two.*
  imperat. ŏ́wwɪgɪrbák!
  N. dúŋgɪgˬŏ́wwɪkɪrbákkóˀ *(s)he (has) divided the money into two.*
ŏ́wwɪgɪr-bagíttɛ (§4140) v.t. =ŏ́wwɪgɪr-bág.
ŏ́wwɪgɪr-gág (§4138) v.t. *split (etc. s.v. gág) in two.*
ŏ́wwɪgɪr-gásɪğ (§4140) v.t. *split (etc. s.v. gásɪğ) in two.*
ŏ́wwɪgɪr-gúšš(ɪ) (§4140) v.t. *break in two.*
  imperat. ŏ́wwɪrgúšši!
ŏ́wwɪgɪr-mɛ́r (§4138) v.t. *cut in two.*
ŏ́wwɪgɪr-órɪğ (§4140) v.t. *tear in two.*
  imperat. ŏ́wwɪgɪrórɪ́č!
ŏ́wwɪgɪr-órr(ɪ) (§4138) v.t. *tear in two.*
  imperat. ŏ́wwɪgɪrórri!
ŏ́wwɪgɪr-tómb(ɪ) (§4138) v.t. *break in two.*
  imperat. ŏ́wwɪgɪrtómbi!
ózbŭ- *be in a discharged (etc.) state* s.v. ós.

ps! (**psss**!) interj. to call a cat *puss!* [onom.].

-r⌣ (**-ɪr⌣, -ro⌣, -do⌣, -lo⌣**) postp. (i = prep. §§ 4291 ff.) (*a, rest*) *on, in, at, among*; (*b, motion*) *on, onto, into, to*; (*c, purpose*) *to, in order to obtain, for*; (*d*) *to the detriment of, against*, عَلَى [cp. M. -la⌣, -l⌣ ON. -λο, -λω, -ρο, -πο *id*., -ϫω, -ϫο *upon* (etc. *GNT* s.v.), ܠ, ܒ, ܠ, Eth. ለ- etc. § 4292; cp. *RSN*, § 100 a, *TOB*, § 99 a, p. 158].

-r⌒ (**-ɪr⌒, -ro⌒, -do⌒, -lo⌒**) may imply predication (§§ 5858–60).

-r is the form suffixed to vowels.
-do is the form suffixed to -n and to -r of personal pronouns.
-lo is the form suffixed to -l.
-ro is the form suffixed to -r except -r of personal pronouns.

— suffixed to the bare stem of a noun or noun-equivalent; but
 nf? *who?* is placed in the genitive, and so takes -do⌣, forming
 níddo? *on (etc.) whom?*
— **wĕr⌣** *one* takes -ro⌣ or -do⌣, forming
 wĕrro⌣ and
 wĕddo⌣ *on (etc.) one.*
 áddo⌣ (§ 2611) and
 N. âido⌣ *on (etc.) me.*
 éddo⌣ (§ 537) *on (etc.) you.*
 téddo⌣ *on (etc.) him (her, it).*
 áddo⌣ *on (etc.) us.*
 íddo⌣ *on (etc.) you (pl.).*
 tíddo⌣ *on (etc.) them.*

— to consonants other than -l, -n, -r the postp. -r⌣ is joined by -ɪ- (§ 484β), with the result that a series of homophones (§ 6288) is formed:
 bábɪr⌣ (*a*) *at the door*; (*b*) *at the doors.*
 gɪrbádɪr⌣ (*a*) *in the water-skin*; (*b*) *in the water-skins.*
 ğĕrífɪr⌣ (*a*) *on the foreshore*; (*b*) *on the foreshores.*
 súğɪr⌣ (*a*) *in the market*; (*b*) *in the markets.*
 káğɪr⌣ (*a*) *on the horse*; (*b*) *on the horses.*

— before -on⌣ -r takes either -k or -g (§ 908f):
 ínɪm⌣bádɪrkon⌣ and
 ínɪm⌣bádɪrgon⌣ *and after this, also after this.*
 kɪtáb⌣tarabézar⌣bún⌒ *the book is (lies) on the table.*
 kál⌣súfrar⌣bű⌒ *the food is on the table.*
 dárɪbɪr⌣élkori⌒ *I found him (her, it, them § 5083) on the road.*
 bún⌣súğɪr⌣dán⌒ *there is coffee in the market.*
 ĕn⌣súğɪr⌣ágɪn⌒ *the woman sits in the market.*
 ĕn⌣súğɪr⌒ *the woman is in the market.*
 téŋ⌣kár⌣ágɪn⌒ (*s)he is (lives s.v. ág) in his (her) house.*
 tér⌣kár⌒ (*s)he (it) is in the house.*
 tír⌣kár⌒ *they are in the house.*
 teššášar⌣nálkoran⌒ *they saw him (her, it, them) at the pedlars' place.*
 dúŋgular⌣ágran⌒ *they live at Old Dóngola (they live in Dóngola, s.v. dúŋgula⌣).*

masúrr⌣ágran⌒ (§ 1122) *they live in Egypt (Cairo).*
ásurro⌣tágoran⌒ *they came in the (late) afternoon.*
búšɪr⌣nókkoran⌒ and
búš⌣náhárro⌣nókkoran⌒ *they went on Monday.*
âi⌣masíllo⌣bɪtĕbmunun⌒ and (§ 4622)
masíll⌣âi⌣bɪtĕbmunun⌒ *I shall not remain in the sun.*
tɪr⌣sahándo⌒ *they are on the plate.*
tɪr⌣furúndo⌒ *they are in the oven.*
tér⌣báññɪdɪr⌣fálan⌒ (*s)he is clever at speaking (a good talker).*
ténn⌣úğr⌣ugrĕsɪr⌣gíríš⌣goríč-taran⌒ *his (her) pay is six piastres a day.*
šahárro⌣gín⌣ówwɪg⌣áddɛférán⌒ *they are paying (always pay s.v. ăddɛfĕ́) two pounds a month.*
ar⌣tárándo⌣mágoru⌒ (*a*) *we were too tired to come*; (*b*) *we couldn't come.*
táran⌣ inf. (§ 2961) of tá; lit. *we were unable at coming.*
íddo-wĕr⌣táwɛ! (§ 5359) *one of you come (here)!*
éssɪg⌣ígɪr⌣uskúrkori⌒ *I (have) set the water on the fire.*
súğɪr⌣nókkó⌒ (*s)he went (has gone) to the market.*
téŋ⌣kár⌣tōróskó⌒ (*s)he has entered his (her) house.*
dúŋgular⌣nogóskoran⌒ *they have gone to (Old) Dóngola (s.v. dúŋgula⌣).*
masúrro⌣nókkoran⌒ *they went (have gone) to Egypt (Cairo).*
tɛr⌣suwándo⌣bɪğű⌒ (*s)he (it) will go to Aswán.*
nŭrem⌣bérro⌣šóndɪran⌒ *they strew it about (round) the post in the threshing-floor.*
álɪg⌣íččɪr⌣ɪšɪndiá? *shall* (§ 5369 b) *I send ɛáli for (lit. to) the milk?*
bérr°⌣íšɪn⌒ (§ 1135) *send (him) for (to fetch) wood.*
ímⅈ⌣báğɪdɪr⌣sérēn⌒ *this is good (convenient) for writing.*

— expressing the multiplier (§§ 5317–18):
 ídɪw⌣ówwɪr⌣dɪmɪndogoríččé⌒ 8 × 2 = 16, quasi *eight in twos (is expressed) by sixteen.*
 díğ⌣góríğɪr⌣talatɪŋgé⌒ 5 × 6 = 30.
 góríğ⌣ídɪwɪr⌣arbaɪnídɪwgé⌒ 6 × 8 = 48.
 tóskɪ⌣dɪmíndo⌣talatɪŋgé⌒ 3 × 10 = 30.
 áddo⌣káğğɪran⌒ *they give evidence against me.*
 N. âido⌣kárğɪran⌒ *they give evidence against me.*
 éddo⌣káğğɪran⌒ *they give evidence against you.*
 téddo⌣káğğɪran⌒ *they give evidence against him (her).*
 áddo⌣káğğɪran⌒ *they give evidence against us.*
 íddo⌣káğğɪran⌒ *they give evidence against you (pl.).*
 tíddo⌣káğğɪran⌒ *they give evidence against them.*
 samíllo⌣káğğɪran⌒ *they give evidence against the sheikh.*
 âi⌣éddo⌣bɪkáğğɪri⌒ *I shall give evidence against you.*

ardahálg⌣édd⌣undúddi⌒ *I shall* (§ 5369 a) *put in a petition against you.*
dĕn⌣áddo⌣tĕbɪn⌒ *I (we) owe the (a) debt*, lit. *the (a) debt stands against me (us).*
dĕn⌣éddo⌣tĕbná? *do you owe the (a) debt?*
dĕnɪ⌣téddo⌣tĕb'ran⌒ (*s)he has debts.*
dĕn⌣téddo⌣kúğɪn⌒ (*s)he ought to pay the debt*, lit. *the debt is incumbent on him (her).*
álɪr⌣kúğɪn⌒ *it's ɛáli's duty (ɛáli ought to do it).*
ɛr⌣áddo⌣gínɛ⌣wĕk⌣kón⌒ (⌣kŏ⌒, ⌣kón⌒, ⌣kŏ⌒, ⌣kŏ⌒) *I (we) owe you one pound.*
tɛr⌣áddo⌣gínɛ⌣wĕk⌣kón⌒ (⌣kŏ⌒, ⌣kón⌒, ⌣kŏ⌒, ⌣kŏ⌒) *I (we) owe him (her) one pound.*
ɪr⌣áddo⌣gínɛ⌣wĕk⌣kóru⌒ (⌣kŏ⌒, ⌣kón⌒, ⌣kŏ⌒, ⌣kŏ⌒) *I (we) owe you (pl.) one pound.*
tɪr⌣áddo⌣gínɛ⌣wĕk⌣kóran⌒ (⌣kŏ⌒, ⌣kón⌒, ⌣kŏ⌒, ⌣kŏ⌒) *I (we) owe them one pound.*
âi⌣éddo⌣gínɛ⌣wĕk⌣kóri⌒ *you owe me one pound.*
âi⌣téddo⌣gínɛ⌣wĕk⌣kóri⌒ (*s)he owes me one pound.*
âi⌣íddo⌣gínɛ⌣wĕk⌣kóri⌒ *you (pl.) owe me one pound.*
âi⌣tíddo⌣gínɛ⌣wĕk⌣kóri⌒ *they owe me one pound.*
tɛr⌣éddo⌣mɪŋkóttĕk⌣kó? *how much do you owe him (her)?*
ɛr⌣téddo⌣mukóttĕk⌣kó? *how much does (s)he owe you?*
tɪr⌣éddo⌣míŋgɪ⌣kóran? *what do you owe them?*
ɛr⌣téddo⌣míŋgɪ⌣kó? *what do they owe you?*

— with signs of predication (§§ 5858–60):
-r does not take the positive sign of predication but may imply it,
-do, -lo, -ro may take it or imply it:
 săp⌣kár⌒ *the cat is in the house.*
 săbi⌣kár⌒ *the cats are in the house.*
 X. máhádda⌣sáiré⌒ *where is the cushion?*
 Y. áŋgárɛr⌒ *(it's) on the bedstead.*
 tír⌣kánčɪr⌒ and
 tír⌣kánčín⌒ *they are in the houses.*
 mágas⌣síğndón⌒ (-índon⌒, -índō⌒, -índo⌒, -índo⌒) *the thief is in prison.*
 fağírron⌒ (-rŏ⌒, -ró⌒, -ro⌒) *it is at dawn (etc. s.v. féğr⌣).*
 ogóllón⌒ (-lŏ⌒, -ló⌒),
 ogóllon⌒ (-lŏ⌒) and
 ogóllo⌣ *(s)he (it) is (they are) ahead (etc. s.v. ógol⌣).*
 ásurrón⌒ (-rŏ⌒, -ró⌒, asúr-),
 ásurro⌒ (asúrro⌒) *it is in the (late) afternoon.*
 X. wĕl⌣sɛ́? *where is the dog?*
 Y. dukkándon⌣ɛn⌒ (-do⌣ɛn⌒, -d'⌣ɛn⌒, -d⌣ɛn⌒ § 1135) *(s)he says it is in the shop.*

-r + -rĕ́? > -rĕ́? (§ 1007):
 gátɪr⌣máháttar⌒ *the train is at the station.*
 gátɪr⌣máháttaré? *is the train at the station?*

tér‿kăré? *is (s)he (it) in the house?*
— -r (**-do, -lo, -ro**) *also takes the interrogative particle* -ó?
kál‿kăr⌒ *the food is in the house.*
kál‿kăré? *and*
kál‿kăró? *is the food in the house?*
tér‿sɪɡ́índoré? *and*
tér‿sɪɡ́índojó? (-doló?) *is (s)he in prison?*
săp‿kărmunun⌒ *the cat is not in the house.*
săbɪ‿kărmunan⌒ *the cats are not in the house.*
săp‿kărmɛn? *isn't the cat in the house?*
săbɪ‿kărmɛndan? *aren't the cats in the house?*
dukkăndómunan⌒ *they are not in the shop.*
dukkăndomɛn? *and*
dukkăndomɛnɪn? *isn't (s)he (it) in the shop?*
sɪɡ́índomɛndan? *aren't they in prison?*

-do‿ *postp.* (ii = *conj.* §§ 4288, 4350) (*a*) *in the place that, where;* (*b*) *at the time that, when.*
— *suffixed to genitive of subjunctive* (§§ 2943, 2953), *and so* (§ 4293) *appears only in the form* -do‿.
— *original* -ndo *usually* > -ddo‿ (§ 535), *original* -nndo *always* > -ndo‿ (§ 620) *and is not further assimilated:*
ɛr‿ăgín‿ăk⌒ *and*
ɛr‿tɛ́gíndo‿tɛ́k⌒ *stay where you are (sitting), lit. sit where you sit.*
ír‿ăgrúdd‿ăgwɛ⌒ *and*
ír‿tɛgrúddo‿tɛgwɛ⌒ *stay (pl.) where you are (sitting).*
ɛr‿tɛbíndo‿tɛ́p⌒ *stay where you are (standing), lit. stand where you stand.*
ír‿tɛ́brúddo‿tɛ́bwɛ⌒ *stay (pl.) where you are (standing).*
tɛr‿ăgsínd‿ăkkó⌒ *(s)he (has) stayed where (s)he was (sitting).*
tɛr‿tɛ́gsíndo‿tɛ́kkó⌒ *(s)he (has) remained where (s)he was (sitting).*
tɛr‿tɛbsíndo‿tɛ́pkó⌒ *(s)he (has) stayed where (s)he was (standing).*
ár‿ăgsúddo‿tɛ́kkoru⌒ *we (have) stayed where we were (sitting).*
ar‿tɛ́bsúddo‿tɛ́pkoru⌒ *we (have) stayed where we were (standing).*
tɪr‿ăgsánd‿ăkkoran⌒ *they (have) stayed where they were (sitting).*
tɪr‿tɛ́bsándo‿tɛ́pkoran⌒ *they (have) stayed where they were (standing).*
tɛr‿ăgsínd‿ăgan⌒ (§ 5649) *let him (her) stay where (s)he was (sitting).*
tɛr‿tɛ́gsíndo‿tɛ́gan⌒ *let him (her) remain where (s)he was (sitting).*
tɛr‿tɛ́bsíndo‿tɛ́ban⌒ *let him (her) stay where (s)he was (standing).*
íŋɡɪ‿tɛr‿búndo‿bán⌒ (‿bắ⌒, ‿bá⌒, <‿bú-an⌒ § 1114) *leave this (that) where it is, lit. tell this to lie in (the place where) it lies.*
tɛr‿búsíndo‿bán⌒ (‿bắ⌒, ‿bá⌒) *leave it where it was.*
aɪ‿tăríddo‿ *when I come.*
ɛr‿tăndo‿ *when you come.*
tɛr‿tăndo‿ *when (s)he (it) comes.*
ar‿tărúddo‿ *when we come.*
ɪr‿tărúddo‿ *when you (pl.) come.*
tɪr‿tărándo‿ *when they come.*

aɪ‿tăsíddo‿ *when I came.*
ɛr‿tăsíndo‿ *when you came.*
tɛr‿tăsíndo‿ *when (s)he (it) came.*
ar‿tăsúddo‿ *when we came.*
ɪr‿tăsúddo‿ *when you (pl.) came.*
tɪr‿tăsándo‿ *when they came.*
-r *omitted before* -do‿ (§ 5927):
tír‿hartúmɪr‿ɛɡóran⌒ *they were at Khartoum.*
tír‿hartúm‿ɛsándo‿tăgori⌒ *I came when they were at Khartoum.*
ár‿mám‿bɛ́lɛdɪr‿bɪnógru⌒ *we shall go to that country.*
bɛ́lɛd‿ár‿bɪnógrúdd‿ín‿dɪgrín⌒ *in the country to which we shall go this is plentiful.*

-r-tŏn‿ *from, etc. s.v.* -r-tŏn‿.

ráha‿ *n. rest, ease* [< رَاحَة *id.*].
obj. -haɡ‿.

rahâɪɛ‿ (-âɪă‿, -âɪa‿) *n. mill turned by hand, hand-mill* [Sudan Ar. رِحَاية *id.*; < رَحاية *millstone*].
obj. -ɛɡ‿.
pl. -ɛnč(ɪ)‿.
rahâɪɛ‿ɡ́úɡon‿ɡ́ūntókkoŋ‿kó⌒ (§ 5545) *the mill has a nether and an upper stone.*
nóɡo‿rahâɪɛɡ́‿ɡ́óɡɪn⌒ (-ɡ́‿ɡ́- < -ɡ‿ɡ́- § 551) *the female slave turns the mill.*
nóɡ‿íllɛr‿rahâɪɛɡɛn‿nórɪn⌒ (-r‿r- < -ɡ‿r- § 669, -n‿n- < -d‿n- § 624) *the female slave grinds the wheat in (-ɛd with) the hand-mill.*

ráhâu‿ (rahâú‿, arráhâú‿, arrahâú‿) *n. crane, stork;* with *collective sg.* (§ 4696 *d*) [< رَهْو *id.* § 1357].
obj. -hâuɡ‿.
pl. ráhawɪ‿ (rahâwɪ‿).

rahís‿ (raxís‿) *adj. cheap* [< رَخِيص *id.*].
obj. -ísk(ɪ)‿, -ki⌒.
pl. -ísɪ‿.

rahís-an- (raxís-; § 3910 α) *v.i. become cheap, cheapen.*

rahísam-bŭ- (raxís-; §§ 3949 ff.) *v.i. stat. be in a cheapening or cheapened state or condition.*
márɛ‿rahísambūn⌒ *millet is getting (has got) cheap.*

ráhma‿ *n. mercy, pity* [< رَحْمَة *id.*].
obj. -maɡ‿.

rahmɛ́ *v.i. have mercy, have pity* [< رَحِمَ *id.* (or رَحْمَة *mercy* § 1393) + -ɛ́ § 3615].
ind. pres. aɪ‿rahmɛ́rɪ; perf. aɪ‿rahmɛ́-gori⌒ (N. -ɛ́ko-, -ɛ́ho-).
áddo‿rahmɛ́⌒ *have mercy on me (us).*
ɡâdɪ‿kóbbúllo‿rahmɛ́ɡó, tén‿ɡ́ízaš‿šóroɡɪrkó⌒ (-š‿š- < -ɡ‿š § 695) *the judge (has) had mercy on the prisoner, and* (§ 6239; *has*) *reduced his punishment.*

ramaḍán‿ *n. Ramaḍán, month of fasting* [< رَمَضَان *id.*].
obj. -âŋɡ(ɪ)‿, -ɡi⌒.
ramaḍándo‿ *in Ramaḍán.*
ramaḍándo⌒ (§ 6007) *it is (they are) in Ramaḍán.*
ramaḍán‿kăɡran⌒ (§ 5541) *they keep Ramaḍán.*

rasâs‿ *n.* (*a*) *lead* (metal) [< رَصَاص *id.*]; (*b*) *bullet;* with *collective sg.* (§ 4696 *d*) [< رَصَاصَة *id.* § 1393]; (*c*) *cartridge;* with *collective sg.* (§ 4696 *d*).
obj. -âsk(ɪ)‿, -ki⌒.
pl. -âsɪ‿.

rátul‿ *n. pound* (weight); with *collective sg.* (§ 4696 *d*) [< رَطْل *id.* § 1363].
obj. ratúlɡ(ɪ)‿, -ɡi⌒.
pl. rátulɪ‿.

ráddɛ́ (rɛd-) *v.i. answer* [رَدّ *n. answer* + -ɛ́ § 3623].
ind. pres. aɪ‿ráddɛ́rɪ; perf. aɪ‿ráddɛ́-gori⌒ (N. -ɛ́ko-, -ɛ́ho-).
imperat. ráddɛ!
mínɛ‿ráddɛ́rā? *what* (lit. *how do they*) *reply?*

rádd(ɪ)‿ (réd-) *n. asnwer* [< رَدّ *id.*].
obj. -dɪɡ‿.
pl. -dɪnč(ɪ)‿.

ráf‿ *n. shelf* [< رَفّ *id.* § 1370].
obj. ráfk(ɪ)‿, -ki⌒.
pl. ráfɪ‿.

ráff(ɪ)‿ *n. shelf* [< رَفّ *id.* § 1369].
obj. ráffɪɡ‿.
pl. ráffɪnč(ɪ)‿.

-rɛ...? (-*dɛ...?) §§ 879 ff., § 4275) *interrogative particle redundantly suffixed to interrogative pronouns:*
nírɛ‿tăɡon? *who came (has come)?* = ní‿tăɡon?
nírɛ‿bunóɡɪn? *who will go?* = ní‿bɪnóɡɪn?
mɪŋkóttɪrɛ‿dán?,
mukóttɪrɛ‿dán?,
mɪŋkóttɛ́(r)rɛ‿dán? *and*
mukottɛ́(r)rɛ‿dán? *how much is there? (how many are there?).*

-ré? (-*dé? §§ 879 ff.; §§ 4236 ff., 5792 ff.) *interrogative sign of predication am?, are?, is?, are (pl.)?* [*RSN*, § 50].
— *often attached to a final consonant by euphonic* -ɪ-, -ɪ́-:
-l-ré? > -llé?
-n-ré? > -ndé?
ín‿nóbrɛré? *is this gold?*
tɛr‿índoré? *and*
índoré? *is (s)he (it) here?*
ɛr‿ɪrɪɡré? *are you deaf?*
ódɪré? *is it* (sc. *the weather*) *cold?*
ín‿éndɪré? *is this yours?*
ím‿mɪnéllé?, tumbâɡɪré? *what's this?, tobacco?*
X. ɛsmân‿noɡóskó⌒ ɛ oθmán *has gone.*
Y. hánuɡedɪré? *by* (on *the*) *donkey?*
Z. hánuɡedó? *by* (on *the*) *donkey.*
tɛr‿orófɛllé? *is (s)he (it) cold?*
ɛr‿noɡíllé? *are you going* (one that goes)?
ín‿tínn‿uɡúllandé? *is this their fuel?*
ín‿šerífanārtōndé? *is this (one) from the Sherifa?*
— -ré? *usually ends the sentence, but occasionally a word follows:*
dukkándo‿mínɪn‿ɡ́ínsɪré‿dâl? *what kind is there (existing) in the shop?*
— *redundantly after interrogative pronouns:*
ní‿mándó? *and*
ní‿mándoré? *who is over there?*

rɛddɛ́ — rúbb(ı)‿

gadfjɛr‿nírɛ‿mɛglúbʰré? (§5145) *who is the loser in the lawsuit?*
mám‿mínın‿ğınısʰré? *(a) of what kind is that (yonder)?; (b) of what tribe is that person over there (that other)?* (s.v. ğínıs‿).
tır‿séna‿mukóttēg‿ındoré? *how many years have they been here?*
ín‿ısắırtōndé? *where is this (one) from?*
— -r‿+-ré? > -ré? when -ré? is suffixed to the postpositions -r‿ (§1007) and -när‿ (§1009):
 tɛr‿kắr⌒ and
 kắr⌒ *(s)he (it) is in the house.*
 tɛr‿kắré? and
 kắré? *is (s)he (it) in the house?*
 kál‿kúbıré? *is the food in the boat?*
 kám‿hálaré? *is the camel in the desert?*
 kúšar‿ɛ́nnaré? *have you got the key?*
— integral -r‿+-ré? usually > -rré?
 ín‿úrré? *is this the head?*
 tɛr‿tɛ́ŋ‿gadfjɛr‿mɛnsûrré? (but also... ‿mɛnsûré? §1003) *is (s)he the winner in his (her) lawsuit?*
— compounds in -wēr‿ (§1004) make -ērré? and -ēré?
 tɛr‿ıŋkóttērré? and
 tɛr‿ıŋkóttēré? *is it as much as this (that)?*
— repeated in alternative questions, and may lose stress when not pausal:
 tɛr‿índorɛ‿wálla‿mándoré? and
 tɛr‿índorɛ‿wálla‿mándoré? *is (s)he (it) here or over there?* (tɛr‿ commonly unstressed and omissible).
rɛddɛ́ v.i. *answer* = rắddɛ́.
rédd(ı)‿ n. *answer* = rắdd(ı)‿.
réıs‿ (réıs‿) n. *steersman, captain of ship* [< رَئِيس *id.*].
 obj. rɛísk(ı)‿, rɛísk(ı)‿, -kı⌒.
 pl. rɛísı‿, réısı‿, réısı‿.
rɛjjıhɛ́ v.t. *quiet, leave in quiet, set at rest, leave at rest* [< imperat. or imperf. stem of رَبَّى *id.* +-ɛ́ §3640].
 ind. pres. ãı‿rɛjjıhɛ́rı⌒; perf. ãı‿rɛjjıhɛ́-gorı⌒ (N. -ɛ́ko-, -ɛ́ho-).
 imperat. rɛjjıhɛ́!
 án-tod‿áıgı‿rɛjjıhɛ́munun, áıgı‿galabēn⌒ *my son doesn't let me rest, he wears me out.*
rɛjjıhɛ́rar- (-rằr‿; §§2200ff., 2207) and
rɛjjıhɛ́ríd‿ (§§2256ff., 2260) n. *quieting, etc.*
rɛjjıhɛ́r-an- (§§3890ff., 3899) v.t. *tell to quiet, etc., let quiet, etc.*
rɛjjıhɛ́-bŭ- (§3931β) v.i. stat. *be in a quieted (etc.) state or condition.*
rɛjjıhɛ́rɛd-ắg- (§§3877ff.) v.t. *be in the situation of having quieted, etc.*
rɛjjıhɛ́-kattı- (N. -ɛ́ha-; §4093) v.p. *be quieted, etc.*
rıjắl n. *dollar*; with collective sg. (§4696 *d*) [< رِيَال *id.* < Sp. *real*].
 obj. -ắlg(ı)‿, -gı⌒.
 pl. -ắlı‿.
 dúŋular‿gírıš‿ắrı‿rıjắl‿lɛ́run, sắuá-kíndo‿gírıš‿dímın‿rıjắl‿lɛ́run (-l‿l- <-l‿w- §580) *in Dóngola 20 piastres are one dollar, at Suắkın 10 piastres are one dollar.*

rıjắl‿ídıw‿gírıš‿kólod‿gírıš‿ímıl‿ sıttīnı‿kólodun⌒ *8 dollars and 7 piastres are 167 piastres.*
-ro‿ postp. *on, in, at, to, etc.* s.v. -r‿.
-r-tŏn‿ (-ır-tŏn‿, -ro-toŋ‿, -do-tŏn‿, -lo-toŋ‿; -tŏ⌒, -tŏ⌒, -tŏ́⌒ §939; §§4306-10) postp. (i = prep. §4288) *(a, space) from; (b, time) since; (c, partitive) from among, of; (d, partitive) of, made of, consisting of; (e, partitive) arising from, because of; (f, locative) by, at* [with -tŏn‿ cp. ON. -ⲇⲱⲛ, -ⲇⲟⲛ from GNT s.v.; RP, §47 fin., RSN, §§100*e*, 174*b*].
-r-tŏn‿ (-ır-tŏn‿, etc.) may imply predication (§§5858-60).
— lit. *from on* (etc.) s.v. -r‿, *since at, etc.*
— see variations of -r‿, that with -tŏn‿ produce -ırtŏn‿, -rotŏn‿, -dotŏn‿, -lotŏn‿.
— suffixed to the bare stem of a noun or noun-equivalent, but to genitive of nı̆‿...? *who...?*
 níddotŏn‿...? and occ. níndotŏn‿...? *from whom...?*
— with wíl‿ *yesterday.*
 wíldotŏn‿ *since yesterday* [app. < *wílndotŏn‿].
— with sıntắg‿...? *when?*
 sıntắgırrotŏn‿? and (§1008)
 sıntắgırotŏn? *since when?*
 kắrton‿tắgoran⌒ *they came (have come) from the house.*
 íŋ‿úrdırtōn‿ɛttarɛdắgrı⌒ *I have brought this from El-Órdi.*
 índotōn‿ *from this (from here).*
 índotōn⌒ *(s)he (it) is (they are) from this (from here).*
 mándotōn‿ *from that (yonder, from that other, from there).*
 mándotōn‿ *(s)he (it) is (they are) from that (yonder, from that other, from there).*
 ắddotŏn‿ *from me.*
 ɛ́ddotŏn‿ *from you.*
 téddotŏn‿ *from him (her, it).*
 ắddotŏn‿ *from us.*
 íddotŏn‿ *from you (pl.).*
 tíddotŏn‿ *from them.*
 hánu‿kırắgertōn‿nalkattıgómunun⌒ *the donkey has not been seen since Sunday.*
 éndıncˇırtów-wēg‿ɛ́tta⌒ (-w-w- < -n-w- §720) *bring one of yours.*
 téddotof‿fadlɛ́gon⌒ (-f‿f- < -n‿f- §542) *some of it was (is) left.*
 íccˇırtōm‿marıssoddɛ́d‿dɛ́ŋkoran⌒ (-d‿d- < -g‿d- §534) *they gave (have given) me a very little of the milk.*
 míndotōm‿ắukattıgon? *what was it (has it been) made of?*
 ãı‿téddotōn‿zālēbúgorı⌒ (-tōz‿zā- §735) *I was angry with him (her, at it).*
 tír‿ɛ́ddotōn‿howwılɛ́goran⌒ *they were surprised at you.*
 ɛr‿tíddotōm‿bastɛ́goná? and
 ɛr‿tíddotōm‿mabsûdʰré? *are you pleased with them?*
 ékk‿én‿nogídırton‿uñúrkorı⌒ *I knew you by your gait.*
 sandúkkı‿tógortōn‿ắrwé⌒ *grip (pl.) the box by its lower part, i.e. grip it underneath.*

kắ‿mằrrotōn‿ıŋgé⌒ *the house is on this side of (i.e. between us and) the village,* lit. *from the village the house is in this direction.*
 kólɛ‿mám‿mằrrotōm‿mắŋgé⌒ *the water-wheel (irrigable estate) is on the other side of that village.*
 béndıgıl‿ǵówwırtōm‿mắŋged‿ắgın⌒ *the beggar is on the other side of the tree,* lit. *...squats in that direction from the tree.*
 ɛ́ŋ‿kắrtōm‿mắŋged‿ắgın⌒ *the woman is (sitting) on the other side of the house.*
— with signs of predication (§5878):
 índotónun⌒ *(s)he (it) is from here (it is from this).*
 gússa‿síbertónun⌒ *the corn-bin is made of clay.*
 kádɛ‿bennắgırtónun⌒ *the cloth is made out of cotton.*
 ín‿óddɛ‿háwartónun‿ *this pain is due to (is the result of) the weather.*
 mándotōndé? *is (s)he (it) from over there?*
 háwartōndé? *is it from (due to) the weather?*
 tɛr‿ắm‿búttın‿ắm‿bélɛdırtōm-munun⌒ *he is of my age (but) not from my country.*
-do-tŏn‿ (-tŏn‿, -tŏn‿, -tŏ́⌒) postp. (ii = conj. §§4288, 4354) *(a) from the place that, from where; (b) from the time that, since.*
— suffixed to genitive of subjunctive (§§2943, 2953), and so appears only in the form -do-tŏn‿; -nd- usually > -dd- (§535), and -nnd- always > -nd- (§620); but not -dd- < -nnd-:
 ır‿ắgrúddotōm‿bɛltắwɛ⌒ *come (pl.) out from where you are (sitting).*
 tɛr‿ắgsíndotōm‿bɛltắgon⌒ *(s)he (it) came (has come) out from where (s)he (it) was (sitting).*
 ãı‿tékkı‿nalsíddotōn‿jóm‿tósk‿anóskó⌒ (-síndo-, -súddo-, -súndo-) *it's now* (lit. *it has become*) *three days since I saw him (her, it).*
 šáharı‿tósk‿anóskon‿ãı‿tékkı‿nalsíddotōn‿ *it's now three months since I saw him (her, it).*
 ãı‿uskursíddotōn‿sắn‿tốrtı-taran⌒ *it's half an hour since I put it.*
 tɛr‿tāsíndotōn‿jóm‿tóskı-taran⌒ *(s)he (it) came three days ago.*
 ar‿mánd‿uskursúddotōn‿sówwᵘgŏ⌒ *since we put it over there it has got dry.*
 ãı‿tékkı‿ıšınɛdắgríddotōn‿jóm‿tóskı-taran⌒ *it is three days since I sent him (her, it).*
 ãı‿tírgʷıšınɛdắgırıddíddotōn‿jóm‿tóskı-taran⌒ and
 ãı‿tírgʷıšınɛdırắgríddotōj‿jóm‿tóskı-tannan⌒ (§§5615-16) *it is three days since I sent them.*
rúbb(ı)‿ n. *measure of capacity of 8¼ litres* = ¼ kɛ́la [< رُبْع *id.* §1260].
 obj. -bıg‿.
 pl. -bınčˇ(ı)‿.
 kɛ́la‿wēr‿rúbb‿ówwın⌒ *1 kɛ́la* = *2 rúbbı*⌒.

kĕlar⌣rúbb⌣ówwı⌣dábun⁀ *there are two rúbbı⌣ in a kĕla⁀.*
rúbbı⌣wɛ́rı⌣málwa⌣kémsun⁀ *1 rúbbı⌣ = 4 málwa⌣.*
rúbbır⌣málwa⌣kémız⌣dábun⁀ *there are four málwa⌣ in a rúbbı⁀.*
ɛrdɛbır⌣rúbb⌣arrekémız⌣dábun⁀ *there are 24 rúbbı⌣ in an ardɛbb.*
rúbu⌣ n. (a) *quarter*, ¼ (=kémsirɛ⌣) [< رُبْع id. §1266]; (b) *measure of capacity* = ½ kĕla⌣ (= rúbb(ı)⌣).
   obj. -bug⌣.
   pl. rubúnč(ı)⌣.
   ír⌣rúbun⌣tórtin⁀ (-r⌣- < -n⌣- §670) (a) *this is* ½ *of* ¼; (b) *this is half a rúbu⁀ (measure).*
   să⌣ídıw⌣illa⌣rúbur⌣ *at 7.45*, lit. *at (-r⌣) eight less a quarter.*
   rúbu⌣săm⌣bádkı⌣tăgoran⁀ *they came a quarter of an hour later.*
   kĕlar⌣rúb⌣ówwı⌣dábun⁀ *there are two rúbu⌣ in a kĕla⁀.*
   rúbur⌣málwa⌣kémız⌣dábun⁀ *there are four málwa⌣ in a rúbu⌣.*
rúkun⌣ (§956a) n. *corner*, *angle* [< رُكْن id. §1363].
   obj. rukúŋg(ı)⌣, -gi⁀.
   pl. rúk(u)nı⌣.
   rukúndo⌣ (s.v. -r⌣) *in (to) the corner.*
   rúknır⌣ *in the corners.*
rúknı-ko- (§4120) v.i. *have corners, be angular.*
   ind. pres. tɛr⌣rúknıkon⌣ (-kõ⁀, -kó⁀).
   (part.) rúknıkōl⌣ (§2577) adj. *angular;*
   obj. ruknıkólg(ı)⌣, -gi⁀.
rŭmı⌣ (urúmı⌣, -mi⌣) n. *Rumi (on map) name of two villages on the left bank of the Nile, 15–17 miles above Hándag* [perhaps < رومي].
   obj. -mıg⌣.
   rŭmı⌣kánnɛ⌣ *Rúmi North.*
   rŭmı⌣óŋgo⌣ *Rúmi South.*
rutăna⌣ (-nà⌣) n. (a) *non-Arabic language,* esp. (b) *Nubian* [< Sudan Ar. رطانة *foreign language*].
   obj. -nag⌣.
   pl. -nanč(ı)⌣.
   rutănab⌣bánñi⁀ (-b⌣b- < -g⌣b- §519) and
   rutănagɛb⌣bánñi⁀ (-b⌣b- < -d⌣b- §518) *talk Nubian.*
rúzz(ı)⌣ n. *rice* [رُزّ id.].
   obj. -zıg⌣.

s⌣…? (before a vowel §1122) < sé⌣…? *where…?*
   s⌣áŋkon? (-kõ?, -kó?) (a) *where did you go (have you gone) to?*; (b) *where did (s)he (it) go (has (s)he (it) gone) to?*; (c) *what became (has become) of him (her, it)?*
   s⌣áŋkon! (-kõ!, -kó!) *goodness knows where (s)he (it) went (has gone) to!, goodness knows what became (has become) of him (her, it)!*
să⌣ n. (a) *hour*; with collective sg. (§4696d); (b) *watch, clock* [< ساعة id.].
   obj. săg⌣.
   pl. sănč(ı)⌣.
   săn⌣tórt(ı)⌣ *half an hour.*

săn⌣tóskirɛ⌣ *a third of an hour.*
săn⌣kémsirɛ⌣ *a quarter of an hour.*
săn⌣tórtıt⌣tépkoran⁀ (-t⌣t- < -g⌣t- §707; §4666) *they remained for half an hour.*
săn⌣tóskirem⌣bádkı⌣tăgoran⁀ *they came after a third of an hour, i.e. 20 minutes later.*
— so far as Nubians use numbered hours they now follow the European numbering, e.g. să⌣kólodır⌣ = *at 7 a.m. or at 7 p.m., not at 1 p.m.*
să⌣mıŋkóttíré?,
să⌣mıŋkóttērré? (-ērɛ́? §1004),
să⌣mukóttíré? and
să⌣mukóttērré? (-ērɛ́?) *what's the time?* (cp. wie viel Uhr ist's? كم الساعة, Amh. ስንት፡ሰዓት፡ነው።).
să⌣wɛrun⌣ (-rŭ⁀, ⌣wɛrú⁀ §939) *it's 1 o'clock.*
să⌣ówwın⁀ (-wĭ⁀, ⌣ówwí⁀) *it's 2 o'clock.*
să⌣tóskın⁀ (-kĭ⁀, ⌣tóskí⁀) *it's 3 o'clock.*
să⌣kém(ı)sun⁀ (-sŭ⁀, ⌣kém(ı)sú⁀) *it's 4 o'clock.*
să⌣dígun⁀ (-ğŭ⁀, ⌣dígú⁀) *it's 5 o'clock.*
să⌣gór(ı)ğun⌣ (-ğŭ⁀, ⌣gór(ı)ğú⁀) *it's 6 o'clock.*
să⌣kólodun⌣ (-dŭ⁀, ⌣kólodú⁀) *it's 7 o'clock.*
să⌣íd(ı)wun⁀ (-wŭ⁀, ⌣íd(ı)wú⁀) *it's 8 o'clock.*
să⌣ıskódun⁀ (-dŭ⁀, ⌣ıskódú⁀), *it's 9 o'clock.*
să⌣dím(ı)nun⁀ (-nŭ⁀, ⌣dím(ı)nú⁀) *it's 10 o'clock.*
să⌣dımındowɛrun⌣ (-rŭ⁀, -wɛrú⁀) *it's 11 o'clock.*
să⌣dımındówwın⁀ (⌣wĭ⁀, ówwí⁀) *it's 12 o'clock.*
ɛ́kkenɛ⌣să⌣wɛrun⁀ *it's now one o'clock.*
să⌣wɛrro⌣ *at 1 o'clock.*
să⌣ówwır⌣ *at 2 o'clock.*
să⌣tóskır⌣ *at 3 o'clock.*
să⌣kém(ı)sır⌣ *at 4 o'clock.*
să⌣dígır⌣ *at 5 o'clock.*
să⌣gór(ı)ğır⌣ *at 6 o'clock.*
să⌣kólodır⌣ *at 7 o'clock.*
să⌣íd(ı)wır⌣ *at 8 o'clock.*
să⌣ıskódır⌣ *at 9 o'clock.*
să⌣dımíndo⌣ *at 10 o'clock.*
să⌣dımındowɛrro⌣ *at 11 o'clock.*
să⌣dımındówwır⌣ *at 12 o'clock.*
să⌣wɛrro⁀ *it's at one o'clock.*
să⌣ówwır⁀ *it's at two o'clock, etc.* (§5858).
să⌣wɛrrón⌣ (-rŏ́⁀, -rŏ́⁀, -ron⁀, -rõ⁀, -ro⁀ §§939, 5868) *it's at one o'clock.*
să⌣wɛrro⌣tăgoran⁀ *they came at one o'clock.*
să⌣wɛrr⌣akkállan⌣ *they always eat at one o'clock.*
X. feğírro⌣să⌣kólodír⌣ta⌣ (§1742) *come in the morning at seven o'clock.*
Y. să⌣kólod⌣bédrın⌣ *seven o'clock is (too) early.*
să⌣ówwı⌣tamámır⌣ *it's at two o'clock precisely* (§5927a).
să⌣wɛrı⌣kémsirɛ⌣ (§5292) *an hour and a quarter.*
să⌣wɛrı⌣tóskirɛ⌣ *an hour and a third.*
să⌣wɛrı⌣tórt(ı)⌣ (§§5290–1) *an hour and a half.*
să⌣wɛrı⌣kémsiren⌣ (-rē⁀, ⌣kémsiré⁀) *it's 1.15.*

să⌣wɛrı⌣tóskiren⌣ (-rē⁀, ⌣tóskiré⁀) *it's 1.20.*
să⌣wɛrı⌣tórtın⌣ (-tĭ⁀, ⌣tórtí⁀) *it's 1.30.*
să⌣ówwır⌣tóskirɛ⌣nágıs⌣ (§5300) *an hour and two thirds.*
să⌣ówwır⌣tóskirɛ⌣nágısun⌣ (-sŭ⁀, ⌣ná⌣nágısú⁀) *it's 1.40.*
să⌣ówwır⌣kémsirɛ⌣nágısun⌣ (-sŭ⁀, ⌣nágısú⁀) *it's 1.45.*
să⌣wɛrı⌣kémsirɛ⌣nágısır⌣ *at 1.45.*
să⌣wɛrı⌣kémsirɛ⌣nágısır⌣ *it's at 1.45.*
să⌣wɛrı⌣kémsirer⌣tăgoran⌣ *they came at 1.15.*
să⌣wɛrı⌣tóskirer⌣tăgoran⁀ *they came at 1.20.*
să⌣wɛrı⌣tórtır⌣tăgoran⌣ *they came at 1.30.*
să⌣ówwır⌣tóskirɛ⌣nágısır⌣tăgoran⌣ *they came at 1.40.*
să⌣ówwır⌣kémsirɛ⌣nágısır⌣tăgoran⁀ *they came at 1.45.*
să⌣ówwı⌣kémsirer⌣nókkoran⌣ *they went at 2.15.*
să⌣ówwı⌣tórtın⌣ (-tĭ⁀, ⌣tórtí⁀) *it's 2.30.*
să⌣tóskı⌣tórtın⌣ (-tĭ⁀, ⌣tórtí⁀) *it's 3.30.*
să⌣kémsı⌣tórtın⌣ (-tĭ⁀, ⌣tórtí⁀) *it's 4.30.*
să⌣dígı⌣tórtın⌣ (-tĭ⁀, ⌣tórtí⁀) *it's 5.30.*
să⌣gór(ı)ğı⌣tórtın⌣ (-tĭ⁀, ⌣tórtí⁀) *it's 6.30.*
să⌣kólodı⌣tórtın⌣ (-tĭ⁀, ⌣tórtí⁀) *it's 7.30.*
să⌣íd(ı)wı⌣tórtın⌣ (-tĭ⁀, ⌣tórtí⁀) *it's 8.30.*
să⌣ıskódı⌣tórtın⌣ (-tĭ⁀, ⌣tórtí⁀) *it's 9.30.*
să⌣dím(ı)nı⌣tórtın⌣ (-tĭ⁀, ⌣tórtí⁀) *it's 10.30.*
să⌣dımındowɛrı⌣tórtın⌣ (-tĭ⁀, ⌣tórtí⁀) *it's 11.30.*
să⌣dımındówwı⌣tórtın⌣ (-tĭ⁀, ⌣tórtí⁀) *it's 12.30.*
să⌣dígı⌣dígun⁀ and
să⌣díğğı⌣dígun⁀ *it's 5.5* (⌣díğğı⌣ commoner in N. than in S.).
să⌣dígı⌣dím(ı)nun⁀ and
să⌣díğğı⌣dím(ı)nun⁀ *it's 5.10.*
să⌣dígı⌣dımındodígun⁀ and
să⌣díğğı⌣dımındodígun⁀ *it's 5.15.*
să⌣dígı⌣árın⁀ *it's 5.20.*
să⌣díğğı⌣arredígun⁀ *it's 5.25.*
să⌣dígı⌣talatínun⁀ and
să⌣díğğı⌣talatínun⁀ *it's 5.30.*
să⌣dígı⌣talatınıdígun⁀ and
să⌣díğğı⌣talatınıdígun⁀ *it's 5.35.*
să⌣dígı⌣arbaínun⁀ and
să⌣díğğı⌣arbaínun⁀ *it's 5.40.*
să⌣dígı⌣arbaınıdígun⁀ *it's 5.45.*
să⌣dígı⌣hamsínun⁀ and
să⌣díğğı⌣hamsínun⁀ *it's 5.50.*
să⌣dígı⌣hamsınıdígun⁀ and
să⌣díğğı⌣hamsınıdígun⁀ *it's 5.55.*
să⌣gór(ı)ğun⁀ *it's 6.*
să⌣górğı⌣dígun⁀ *it's 6.5.*
să⌣górğı⌣dím(ı)nun⁀ *it's 6.10.*
să⌣górğı⌣dımındodígun⁀ *it's 6.15.*
să⌣górğı⌣árın⁀ and
să⌣gór(ı)ğı⌣árın⁀ *it's 6.20.*
să⌣kémsı⌣dígun⁀ *it's 1.5.*
să⌣kémsı⌣dígun⁀ *it's 4.5.*
să⌣kólodı⌣dígun⁀ *it's 7.5.*
să⌣íd(ı)wı⌣dígun⁀ *it's 8.5.*
să⌣dímnı⌣dígun⁀ *it's 10.5.*
ɛ́kkenɛ⌣să⌣kémsı⌣tóskın⁀ *it's now 4.3.*
băbúr⌣să⌣kólodı⌣tórtırtōn⌣íd(ı)wı⌣kémsırem⌣móŋkon⌣attébın⁀ *the steamer (train) always waits from 7.30 to 8.15.*

sǎ⌣ídıwı⌣kémsırerton⌣ídıwı⌣tórtım⌣ bókkon⌣tĕpkó⌢ (s)he (it) waited from 8.15 to 8.30.
sǎ⌣tósk⌣ílla⌣tílıdun⌢ and
sǎ⌣tósk⌣ílla⌣tóskıren⌢ it's 2.40 = sǎ⌣tóskır⌣tóskırɛ⌣nǎgısun⌢.
sǎ⌣kéms⌣ílla⌣rúbun⌢ and
sǎ⌣kéms⌣ílla⌣kémsırɛn⌢ it's 3.45 = sǎ⌣kémsır⌣kémsırɛ⌣nǎgısun⌢.
sǎ⌣ıskódır⌣rúbu⌣nǎgısun⌢ it's 8.45.
sǎ⌣dımínd⌣ílla⌣rúbur⌣tǎgoran⌢,
sǎ⌣dımın⌣ílla⌣rúbur⌣tǎgoran⌢ and
sǎ⌣dımíndo⌣kémsırɛ⌣nǎgısır⌣tǎgoran⌢ they came at 9.45.
sǎ⌣kólod⌣ílla⌣rúbur⌣tǎgoran⌢,
sǎ⌣kólodır⌣ílla⌣rúbur⌣tǎgoran⌢,
sǎ⌣kólodır⌣ílla⌣kémsırɛr⌣tǎgoran⌢ and
sǎ⌣kólodır⌣kémsırɛ⌣nǎgısır⌣tǎgoran⌢ they came at 6.45.
dúhurn⌣ogóllo⌣ (s.v. -r⌣) before noon and
dúhurm⌣bǎdır⌣ after noon are only applied to hours near noon:
sǎ⌣wěrro⌣dúhurm⌣bǎdır⌣ at 1 p.m.
sǎ⌣ówwır⌣dúhurm⌣bǎdır⌣ at 2 p.m.
sǎ⌣tóskır⌣dúhurm⌣bǎdır⌣ at 3 p.m.
sǎ⌣kémsır⌣dúhurm⌣bǎdır⌣ at 4 p.m.
sǎ⌣díğır⌣mégrıbn⌣ogóllo⌣ at 5 p.m.
sǎ⌣gór(ı)ğır⌣mégríbır⌣ at 6 p.m.
sǎ⌣kólodır⌣mégrım⌣bǎdır⌣ at 7 p.m.
sǎ⌣ídıwır⌣urúğ(ı)⌣ (-gi⌢; §4665) and ugús⌣sǎ⌣ídıwır⌣ (-s⌣s- < -g⌣s- §678) at 8 p.m.
sǎ⌣ıskódır⌣ugúğ(ı)⌣ (-gi⌢) and ugús⌣sǎ⌣ıskódır⌣ at 9 p.m.
sǎ⌣wěrr⌣ugúğ(ı)⌣ (-gi⌢) and ugús⌣sǎ⌣wěrro⌣ at 1 a.m.
sǎ⌣ówwır⌣ugúğ(ı)⌣ (-gi⌢) and ugús⌣sǎ⌣ówwır⌣ at 2 a.m.
sǎ⌣tóskır⌣ugúğ(ı)⌣ (-gi⌢) and ugús⌣sǎ⌣tóskır⌣ at 3 a.m.
sǎ⌣kémsır⌣fěğır⌣ogóllo⌣ at 4 a.m.
sǎ⌣díğır⌣fěğır⌣ogóllo⌣ at 5 a.m.
sǎ⌣górğır⌣fěğırro⌣ at 6 a.m.
sǎ⌣kólodır⌣fěğırro⌣ at 7 a.m.
sǎ⌣íd(ı)wır⌣fěğırro⌣ at 8 a.m.
sǎ⌣ıskódır⌣fěğırro⌣ at 9 a.m.
sǎ⌣dımíndo⌣dúhurn⌣ogóllo⌣ at 10 a.m.
sǎ⌣dımındowěrro⌣dúhurn⌣ogóllo⌣ at 11 a.m.
duhúrro⌣ at noon.
X. sǎ⌣mukóttěré? what's the time?
Y. ékkɛnɛgá? now?[1]
X. éjjo⌢ yes.
Y. ídıwı⌣tórtın⌢ it's half-past eight.
sǎ⌣gɛddımén⌢ the watch (clock) gains.
gɛddımégon⌢ it (has) gained.
gɛddımērɛdágın⌢ it has gained.
géndıgır⌢ put it right, i.e. (a) set it correctly; (b) mend it; (c) clean it.
gɛddımēbūn⌢ it is fast.
gɛddımēbúmunun⌢ it is not fast.
ahhɛrēbūn⌢ it is slow.
ğáŋgi⌢ wind it up.
nógmɛn? (nógmɛnın?) doesn't (won't §5369b) it go?
nógın⌢ it goes.
nógná? does it go?
nógbūn (nóggūn⌢ §546) it's going.

---
[1] Those that have had dealings with Nubians will recognize this type of answer.

nógbūná? (nóggūná?) is it going?
nógmunun⌢ it doesn't go.
nogbúmunun⌢ it isn't going.
tébın⌢ it has stopped.
tépkó⌢ it had stopped.

sǎb⌣ n. (a) cat; with collective sg. (§4696d); (b, in water-wheel, kólɛ⌣) small rectangular block, with depression in its top, let into centre of platform (tewrɛ⌣) on which vertical axle (míšš(ı)⌣) stands; the bottom of the vertical axle (míssın⌣úsud⌣) pivots on the sǎb⌣.
obj. sǎbk(ı)⌣, sǎpk(ı)⌣, -ki⌢.
gen. sǎbn⌣v., sǎm⌣c.
pl. sǎbı⌣.
sǎbn⌣ónd(ı)⌣ male cat.
sǎm-kárr(ı)⌣ she-cat.
sǎbn⌣ágıl⌣ cat's mouth.
sǎm⌣dílt(ı)⌣ cat's fur.
sǎm⌣súnt(ı)⌣ cat's claw(s §4696a).
sǎm-tŏd⌣ (§2366) n. kitten.
obj. -tŏdk(ı)⌣, -tŏtk(ı)⌣, -tŏkk(ı)⌣, -tŏtt(ı)⌣ (§2462), -ki⌣, -ti⌢.
gen. -tŏdn⌣v., -tŏnn⌣v.c., -tŏn⌣c.
pl. sǎm-tonı⌣.
sǎb⌣ékkɛnɛ⌣sǎmtonık⌣kómunun⌢ (-k⌣k- < -g⌣k- §569) the cat has no kittens now.
ártın⌣sǎb⌣ tail (down-stream extremity) of island.
sǎm-d(ı)⌣ (§§2545 ff.) adj. appertaining to the (a) cat, feline.
sabaín⌣ (§956a) card. num. seventy [< سَبْعِين id.].
sabaín-d(ı)⌣ (§§2545 ff., 2738) adj. appertaining to 70, of 70, 70's.
sabaín-ínt(ı)⌣ (-ínınt(ı)⌣; §2742) ord. num. seventieth.
sabaíŋ-kırı⌣ (-kírı⌣ §1701; 2736) num. adj. about seventy.
sabbǎríje⌣ (-íją⌣, -íja⌣) n. one of the sorts of date growing in Dóngola, s.v. bént(ı)⌣; with collective sg. (§4696b) [< صَبَّارِيَّة id.].
obj. -jɛg⌣.
pl. -jɛnč(ı)⌣.
sábha⌣ (sápha⌣) n. side; with collective sg. (§4696a) [< صَفْحَة id.].
obj. -hag⌣.
pl. -hanč(ı)⌣.
án⌣sǎbh⌣áig⌣óddın⌢ I have a pain in my side(s), lit. my side hurts me.
kán⌣sábha⌣gúššıbūn⌣ the side of the house is broken (...sides...are...).
sáblo⌣ n. larger trough into which the jars (běšɛnč(ı)⌣) of a water-wheel (kólɛ⌣) discharge; the water flows from the sáblo⌣ (through the urówwa⌣, q.v.) to the smaller trough (ǧaráttarɛ⌣).
obj. -log⌣.
pl. -lonč(ı)⌣.
[obj. sáblog⌣ < Sudan Ar. سَبْلُوقَة sablóga id., and السَّبْلُوقَة ssabalóga the Trough, name of (sixth) cataract between Shendi and Khartoum (NSS, I, pp. 15, 16) called by Europeans Shabluka (šablúká)].
sabré⌣ (a) v.i. have patience, wait patiently, wait; (b) v.t. have patience with, endure, bear, stand, put up with, tolerate [< صَبَر patience + -ɛ §3615].
ind. pres. aı⌣sabréri⌢; perf. aı⌣sabrégori⌢ (N. -éko-, -ého-).
kınnés⌣sabré, tɛr⌣ahhǎsıbé⌢ (-s⌣s- < -g⌣s- §678) wait a little, (s)he's counting.
ím⌣mállɛs⌣sabrégoran⌢ they (have) endured all this.
aı⌣bısabrémunun⌢ I shall not put up with it.
sabrě́rar⌣ (-rȧr⌣; §§2200 ff., 2207) and
sabrěríd⌣ (§§2256 ff., 2260) n. patience, waiting, endurance, etc.
sabrě́r-an (§§3890 ff., 3899) v.t. tell to have patience, etc., let have patience, etc.
íŋ⌣ɛttarélgı⌣sabrěrá⌢ let him that brought this wait.
sabrěr-ɛ-mǎ- (§§4016–17, 4036, 4041) v.i. and t. become unable to have patience, etc.
aı⌣tím⌣bánňıd⌣dıgrís⌣sabrěrɛmǎgori⌢ (-s⌣s- < -g⌣s- §678) I couldn't endure their excessive talk.
sābún⌣ (§956a) n. soap [< صَابُون < σάπων, saponem].
obj. -búŋ(ı)⌣, -gi⌢.
N. sābúw-wēk⌣aı⌣físırtōs⌣sókkɛkori⌢ (-w-w- < -n-w- §2701, -s⌣s- < -n⌣s- §680) I took (have taken) a (piece of) soap from the pantry.
sǎda⌣ adj. pure, plain, neat, without admixture, esp. of coffee and tea [< سَادَه id.].
obj. -dag⌣.
pl. -danč(ı)⌣.
tókkon⌣súkkark⌣undúrmɛn: gáhwa⌣sǎdad⌣dén⌢ (-d⌣d- < -g⌣d- §534) don't put sugar in: give me coffee alone.
saddıgé⌣ v.t. believe, believe in, trust [< imperat. or imperf. stem of صَدَّق id. + -ɛ §3635].
ind. pres. aı⌣saddıgéri⌢, ɛr⌣saddıgén⌣ (-gé⌢, -gé⌢, -gé⌢); perf. aı⌣saddıgégori⌢ (N. -éko-, -ého-).
imperat. saddıgé!
habárkı⌣saddıgéran⌢ they believe the news.
ogíčkı⌣saddıgémunan⌢ they don't believe (in) the man.
saddıgér-ɛ-mǎ- (§§4016–17, 4036, 4041) v.t. become unable to believe, etc.
sādé⌣ v.t. help [< sād- < a stem of سَاعَد id. + -ɛ §3649].
ind. pres. aı⌣sādéri⌢, ɛr⌣sādén⌣ (-dé⌢, -dé⌢, -dé⌢); perf. aı⌣sādégori⌢ (N. -éko-, -ého-).
imperat. sādé!, pl. sādéwɛ! (-éwé!).
áıg⌣sādémunan⌢ they don't help me.
sāděr-an (§§3890 ff., 3899) v.t. tell to help, let help.
álıt⌣tékkı⌣sāděrá⌢ (-t⌣t- < -g⌣t-) let ɛáli help him (her, it).
álıs⌣sādéwan⌣ (-s⌣s- < -g⌣s- §678) tell them to help ɛáli.
sāděr-ɛ-mǎ- (§§4016–17, 4036, 4041) v.t. become unable to help.
sáfar⌣ n. journey, travelling [< سَفَر id.].
obj. safárk(ı)⌣, -ki⌢.
pl. sáfarı⌣.

safaré v.i. *travel* [< سفر *journey* + -έ §3621].
 ind. pres. aı‿safarέrıɔ, ɛr‿safarénɔ (-rέɔ, -rέɔ, -rέɔ); perf. aı‿safarέgoriɔ (N. -έko-, -έho-).
safarέrar‿ (-rár‿; §§2200ff., 2207) and **safarέríd**‿ (§§2256ff., 2260) n. *travelling*.
safarέ-bŭ- (§3931α) v.i. stat. *be in a state or condition of travelling, be on a journey*.
saffıré v.i. *whistle (with instrument), sound a whistle* [< imperat. or imperf. stem of صفر id. +-έ §3635].
 ind. pres. aı‿saffırέrıɔ, ɛr‿saffırénɔ (-rέɔ, -rέɔ, -rέɔ); perf. aı‿saffırέgoriɔ (N. -έko-, -έho-).
 imperat. saffıré!
 bābúr‿saffırέgın‿ *when (if) the (engine of the) steamer (train) whistles*.
 bābúr‿saffırērósko⁀ *the steamer (train) has whistled*.
saffırέrar‿ (-rár‿; §§2200ff., 2207) and **saffırέríd**‿ (§§2256ff., 2260) n. *whistling, etc.*
saffırέr-an‿ (§§3890ff., 3899) v.t. *tell to whistle, etc., let whistle, etc.*
 reíski‿saffırέran⁀ *let the steersman sound the whistle*.
saffırēr-ɛg-ág- (§§4071ff.) v.i. = saffırέrɛ-dól-.
saffırēr-ɛ-dól- (-rᵒd- §1178; §§4016-17, 4022, 4027) v.i. *be about to whistle, etc.*
saffırērɛd-ág- (§§3877ff.) v.i. *be in the situation of having whistled, etc.*
 bābúr‿saffırērɛdágın⁀ *the steamer (train) has whistled*.
ságar‿ (-gár‿) n. *rust* [< Sudan Ar. صقر ṣáǧar id.].
 obj. sagárk(ı)‿, -ki⁀.
saggıré v.i. *rust* [< imperf. stem of Sudan Ar. صقر id. +-έ §3635].
 ind. pres. ter‿saggırέn⁀ (-rέ⁀, -rέ⁀, -rέ⁀); perf. ter‿saggırέgon‿ (-έgó⁀, -έgó⁀, N. -έkon‿, -έkó⁀, -έkó⁀, -έhon‿, -έhõ‿, -έhó⁀).
 sártı‿saggırērósko⁀ *the iron has rusted*.
saggıré-bŭ- (§3931α) v.i. stat. *be in a rusty state or condition*.
 kándı‿saggırέbun⁀ *the knife is rusty*.
saggırég-ır (N. -έkır, -έhır; §3681) (a) v.t. caus. *cause or allow to rust*; (b) v.t. *render rusty, rust*.
 šártıs‿saggırέgırın‿(-s‿s- <-g‿s- §678) *it rusts the iron*.
ságı‿ (ség-) n. *roof* [< سقف id. §1359].
 obj. sagífk(ı)‿, -ki⁀.
 pl. ság(ı)fı‿.
sagírt(ı)‿ n. *short drawers (barely reaching the knee; worn by women under other garments, and by men for work in the fields, building, on boats, etc.), shorts* [< صغير *small* (§1048) + -t dem. §2333].
 obj. -tıg‿.
 pl. -tınč(ı)‿.
 tórbar‿tés‿sagírtıd‿dɛgɛdágın⁀ (-s‿s- <-n‿s- §680, -d‿d- <-g‿d- §534) *the (agricultural) labourer has put on his shorts*.
saháb‿ n. *cloud*; with collective sg. (§4696d) [< سحاب id.].

 obj. -ábk(ı)‿, -ápk(ı)‿, -ki⁀.
 gen. -ábn‿v., -ám‿c.
 pl. -ábı‿.
sahába n. *Sahaba (on map), a village on the left bank of the Nile, about 16 miles above Urdi*.
 obj. saháhag‿, sahábág‿ (§1538).
sáhan‿ (§956a) n. (a) *plate, dish* [< صحن id. §1357]; (b) *small basin*.
 obj. saháng(ı)‿, -gi⁀.
 pl. sáhanı‿.
sáı‿...? (sáı‿...?) *which?* = ısáı‿...?
 X. sáıg‿ɛttágoran? *which did they bring (have they brought)?*
 Y. káčkı⁀ *the horse*.
saíd n. *Saʿíd, a man's name* [< سعيد Felix].
 voc. -ít!
 obj. -ídk(ı)‿, -ítk(ı)‿, -ítt(ı)‿ §2462, -ki⁀, -ti⁀.
 gen. -ídn‿v., -ínn‿v.c., -ín‿c.
saín-d(ı)‿ (§§2545ff.) adj. *appertaining to Saʿíd, Saʿíd's*.
sáıkɛ‿...? (sáıkɛ‿...?, -kέ‿?) *in which (what) manner (position, direction)?, how?* = ısáıkɛ‿...?
sáır‿...? (sáır‿...?) *where?, whither?* = ısáır‿...?
saíré? (sáıré?) *where is?, where are?* = ısáıré?
sáıg‿ (sáıjıg‿) n. *goldsmith* [< صائغ id.].
 voc. sá(j)ık!
 obj. sá(j)ígk(ı)‿, -íkk(ı)‿, -ki⁀.
 gen. sá(j)ıgn‿v., -ıŋ‿c.
 pl. sá(j)ıgı‿.
sáım‿ (sáım‿) adj. *fasting* [< صائم id.].
 obj. -mg(ı)‿, -gi⁀.
 pl. -mı‿.
 aı‿sáım‿έrı⁀ *I am fasting*.
 ter‿sáımun‿ *(s)he is fasting*.
 ar‿sáım‿έru‿ (§1122) *we are fasting*.
 tır‿sáım‿ɛrán‿ *they are fasting*.
 ín‿óggı‿sáımín⁀ (§2444a) *these men are fasting*.
sáıs‿ n. *groom* [< سائس id.].
 obj. saísk(ı)‿, -ki⁀.
 pl. sáısı‿.
sakíba‿ (-ba‿, -ba‿) n. *sack* = sɛkíbɛ‿.
sákın (§956a) n. *resident* [< ساكن id.].
 obj. sáking(ı)‿, -gi⁀.
 pl. sákını‿.
†**sála** n. *reception-room, parlour* [< صالة It. *sala* id.].
 obj. -lag‿.
 pl. -lanč(ı)‿.
sálag‿ (-ak⁀) n. *Salagi (on map), a village on the left bank of the Nile, about five miles above Hándag*.
 obj. salágk(ı)‿, -ákk(ı)‿, -ki⁀.
 sálagır (s.v. -r‿) *at (to) S.*
 sálagır⁀ (§6007) *(s)he (it) is (they are) at S.*
salám‿ n. *greeting* [< سلام id.].
 obj. -ámg(ı)‿, -gi⁀.
 pl. -ámı‿.
 áıgı‿salámgı‿dέŋkoran⁀ *they greeted me* (s.v. dέn).

 tέkki‿salámgı‿tíkkoran⁀ *they greeted him (her; s.v. tír)*.
salám-aw-wέ-dɛn (§3909) v.t. *address (the speaker) by saying 'peace!', greet (the speaker)*.
 salámawwέdɛŋkó⁀ *(s)he greeted me*.
salám-aw-wέ-tır (§3909) v.t. *greet (other than the speaker)*.
sálέ! interj. *used (sung) by sailors when hauling, yoho!* [< صلوا عليه *bless Him!* (sc. the Prophet)].
 X. (hauling) sálέ!
 YY., ZZ. (hauling with X.) jálla!
 X. sálέ!
 YY., ZZ. jálla!
 da capo, ad lib.
sálɛh‿ n. *Ṣáliḥ, a man's name* [< صالح, صلح, Probus].
 obj. sálɛhk(ı)‿, -ki⁀.
sálɛhn-d(ı)‿ (§§2545ff.) adj. *Ṣáliḥ's*.
sálım‿ *Sálim* = sálum‿.
sálle‿ n. *Acacia seyal, Del. (BSP, 181); with collective sg. (§4696b)* [cp. طلح id., سيال A. spirocarpa].
 obj. -lɛg‿.
 pl. -lɛnč(ı)‿.
sállɛn-d(ı)‿ (§§2545ff.) adj. *appertaining to A. seyal*.
sallé v.i. (a) *pray (esp. aloud, according to Moslem ritual)*; (b) *chant (e.g. at work)* [< imperat. or imperf. stem of صلّى id. + -έ §3642].
 ind. pres. aı‿sallέrı⁀; perf. aı‿sallέgori⁀ (N. -έko-, -έho-).
 imperat. sallé!
sáll(ı)‿ (-lı‿) n. *Sali (on map), a village on the left bank of the Nile, about four miles below Hándag*.
 obj. -lıg‿.
 sállır (s.v. -r‿) *at (to) S.*
 sállır⁀ (§6007) *(s)he (it) is (they are) at S.*
sáll-an- (§3910β) v.i. *go to Sállı*.
sállam-bŭ- (§3950β) v.i. stat. *be in a state of motion towards Sálli*.
 sállambúrı⁀ *I am on my way to Sálli*.
sállɛd-ág- (§3966β) v.i. *be in the situation of having gone to Sálli*.
sálum‿ (-lım‿) n. *Sálim, a man's name* [< سالم *sound* §1342].
 obj. sálúmg(ı)‿, -gi⁀.
sálúm-d(ı)‿ (-lím-; §§2545ff.) adj. *appertaining to Sálim, Sálim's*.
sám‿ gen. of sáb‿ *cat*.
sám v.i. *become intoxicated, get drunk*.
 ind. pres. aı‿sámrı⁀, ɛr‿sámın⁀ (-mí⁀); perf. aı‿sámkori⁀
sámar‿ (-már‿; §§2200ff.) and **sámíd**‿ (§§2256ff., 2260) n. *intoxication, getting drunk*.
sám-bŭ- (§3931α) v.i. stat. *be in an intoxicated state or condition, be drunk*.
 part. pres. sámbul‿ *(one) that is drunk, drunken person*.
sámɛd-ág- (§§3877ff.) v.i. *be in the condition of having become intoxicated*.
 sámɛdágran‿ *they have got drunk*.

sămg-ɪr (N. -mkɪr; §3683) (a) v.t. caus. *cause or allow to become intoxicated, etc.;* (b) v.t. *intoxicate, make drunk.*
  ind. pres. āi⌣sámgɪddī⌣.
  mérsɛ⌣sámgɪrɪn⌣ *the beer is intoxicating.*
  mérsɛ⌣tírgɪ⌣sámgɪrkó⌣ *the beer (has) made them drunk.*
  mérsɛ⌣tírgɪ⌣sámgɪríkkó⌣ (§5458) *the beer (has) made (each of) them drunk.*

săma⌣ (**sắmɛ⌣**) n. (a) *beard, whisker(s);* (b) *chin* [RSN, §129].
  obj. -mag⌣, -mɛg⌣.
  pl. -manč(ɪ)⌣, -mɛn-.
  tén⌣sámag⌣ággáññɪn⌣ and sámag⌣ággáññɪn⌣ *he is shaving (habitually shaves) his beard.*

sámɛd⌣ n. *director of cultivation of irrigable estate* (NSD, pp. 21, 24) [< صَمَد *id.*].
  obj. samédk(ɪ)⌣, -étk(ɪ)⌣, -étt(ɪ)⌣ §2462, -kɪ⌣, -tɪ⌣.
  gen. sámedn⌣v., -ɛnn⌣v.c., -ɛn⌣c.
  pl. sámɛd⌣.
  éssɪn⌣sámed⌣ *overseer directing irrigation* (NSD, p. 21), lit. *overseer of the water.*

samén-d(ɪ)⌣ (§§2545 ff.) adj. *appertaining to the (a) director of cultivation.*

sámɪl⌣ n. *chief of village or district, sheikh* (شَيْخ) [§2277; cogn. sáma⌣ *beard*].
  obj. samílg(ɪ)⌣, -gɪ⌣.
  pl. sámɪl⌣.
  samíllo⌣bɪkággɪmunan⌣ *they will not give evidence against the sheikh.*

samíln-d(ɪ)⌣ (§§2545 ff.) adj. *appertaining to the (a) sheikh.*

sámtɛ⌣ n. *Saturday* [< السَّبْت ⌣ssábt *id.* + -ɛ⌣ of n. ess. §2236].
  obj. -tɛg⌣.
  pl. -tɛnč(ɪ)⌣.
  sámtɛ⌣jóm⌣ (§4750),
  sámtɛn⌣jóm⌣ (§4810),
  sámtɛ⌣nahár⌣ (⌣náh-, nɛh-; §4750) and
  sámtɛn⌣nahár⌣ (§4810) *Saturday.*
  sámtɛg⌣ (-gɪ⌣; §4665),
  sámtɛr⌣,
  sámtɛ⌣nahárk(ɪ)⌣ (-kɪ⌣) and sámtɛ⌣nahárro⌣ *on Saturday.*
  sámtertōn⌣ and sámtɛ⌣nahárrotōn⌣ *since Saturday.*
  sámtɛm⌣mónkon⌣ and sámtɛm⌣bókkon⌣ *till Saturday.*
  ɪnnówwɪ⌣sámtɛn⌣ (-tē⌣, ⌣sámté⌣ §939) *today is Saturday.*
  sámtɛn⌣nálkori⌣ (-n⌣n-<-g⌣n- §625) *I saw him (her, it, them) on Saturday.*
  sámtɛb⌣bɪnógri⌣ (-b⌣b-<-g⌣b- §519) *I shall go on Saturday.*

samtén-d(ɪ)⌣ (§§2545 ff.) adj. *appertaining to Saturday, Saturday's.*

sāmŭs⌣ n. *the largest Nile fish, of light colour,* Lates niloticus, Cuv. and Val. (PF, p. 96), (= mɪssɪgéliñ⌣).
  obj. -músk(ɪ)⌣, -kɪ⌣.
  pl. -mŭs⌣.

sán- *go where?* s.v. sé?

sándal n. *barge* (= kábag⌣) [صَنْدَل *id.* σάνδαλος].
  obj. sándalg(ɪ)⌣, -gɪ⌣.
  pl. sándal⌣.

sánd(ɪ) (ɪsán-, usán-; §5546) (a) v.i. *be afraid;* (b) v.t. *be afraid of, fear* [crystallization of (ɪ)sándi! *what will become of me!* s.v. ɪs-án- §2862].
  ind. pres. āi⌣sándɪri⌣; perf. āi⌣sándɪgori⌣ (N. -ɪko-, -ɪho-).
  imperat. sándi!
  part. pres. sándɪl⌣ (ɪs-, us-) *(one) that is afraid, etc., frightened person or animal, frightened,* obj. sandílg(ɪ)⌣, -gɪ⌣; past sándel⌣ (ɪs-, us-) *(one) that was afraid, etc., frightened person, etc.,* obj. sandélg(ɪ)⌣, -gɪ⌣.
  éssɪrtōn⌣sándɪran⌣, éssɪrtōs⌣sándɪran⌣ (-s⌣s-<-n⌣s- §680) and éssɪs⌣sándɪran⌣ (-s⌣s-<-g⌣s- §678) *they are afraid of (the) water.*
  āi⌣wéllotōs⌣sándɪri⌣ *I'm afraid of the dog(s §4647).*
  tɛr⌣álodɪs⌣sándɪn⌣ *(s)he (it) is afraid of the geese.*
  mágas⌣bɪtarangɛs⌣sándɪri⌣ (-s⌣s-< -d⌣s- §677) and āi⌣sándɪrɪ⌣mágas⌣bɪtarangé⌣ *I'm afraid of thieves' coming,* lit. ...*because thieves will come* (§6203).
  āi⌣mágas⌣tárann⌣íllar⌣sándɪri⌣ and āi⌣sándɪrɪ⌣mágas⌣tárann⌣íllar⌣ *I'm afraid of thieves' coming* (§6210).
  āi⌣sándɪrɪ⌣iškártɪnčɪ⌣támendann⌣íllar⌣ *I'm afraid that the guests may not come.*
  āi⌣sándɪrɪ⌣dúngɪ⌣támenɪnn⌣íllar⌣ *I'm afraid the money may not come.*
  sándɪrɪ⌣bugússɪn⌣égi⌣ (§§5341, 6229) *I'm afraid it will get broken.*
  — sometimes like *vereor, craindre:*
  āi⌣sándɪrɪ⌣bābúr⌣ahherɛmenɪnn⌣ íllar⌣ *I'm afraid the steamer (train) will be late,* lit. ...*that the steamer (train) may not be late.*

sandái⌣ (ɪs-, us-) n. *coward.*
  obj. -dáig(ɪ)⌣, -gɪ⌣.
  pl. -dáj⌣.
  sandáigɪ⌣dólmunan⌣ *they don't like (want) a coward.*

sándar (ɪs-, us-; -dár⌣; §§2200ff.) and
sandíd (ɪs-, us-; §§2256ff.) n. *being afraid, etc., fear.*

sandíd-an-sánd(ɪ) (§4161) v.i. and t. *be greatly afraid (of), fear exceedingly.*

sándɪ-bŭ- (ɪs-, us-; §3931 α) v.i. stat. *be in a state of fear, be afraid.*

sándɪg-ɪr (ɪs-, us-; N. -ɪkɪr, -ɪhɪr; §3682) (a) v.t. caus. *cause or allow to be afraid, etc.;* (b) v.t. *frighten, alarm.*
  ind. pres. āi⌣sándɪgɪddi⌣, ɛr⌣sándɪgɪrɪn⌣ (-rī⌣, -rí⌣).

sándɪgɪr-an (ɪs-, us-; N. -ɪkɪr, -ɪhɪr; §§3890ff., 3904) v.t. *tell to frighten, let frighten.*
  áli⌣wélgɪ⌣sándɪgɪran⌣ (-w⌣w-<-g⌣w- §719) *let ɛáli frighten the dog (away).*

sándɪ-sig (ɪs-, us-; §3747 ɛ') v.i. *be struck with fear and terror.*
  ar⌣sandɪsíkkoru⌣ *we were struck with fear and terror.*

sandos-bókk(ɪ) (-obbók- §521; §§4180-4; -osgɪbók-, -ozgɪ-, -oggɪ- §4185) v.i. and t. *being afraid (of) hide, hide in fear (of).*
  wél⌣magáskɪ⌣sandobbókkɪgó⌣ *the dog hid in fear of the thief.*

sándi? *where shall I go?* s.v. sé?

sandúg⌣ n. *box, chest, case* [< صَنْدُوق *id.*].
  obj. -úgk(ɪ)⌣, -úkk(ɪ)⌣, -kɪ⌣.
  pl. -úg⌣.
  sandúgn-í⌣ *handle* (§4696a) *of box.*
  sandúŋ⌣gúful⌣ *the lock of the box.*
  sandúŋ⌣kúšar⌣ *the key of the box.*

santád...? (-tát?, -tǎ⌣ §967),
santág...? (-tǎk? §469) and
santágk(ɪ)...? (-tǎkk-...?, -kɪ?) adv. *when?* = ɪsantád...?
  bābúr⌣santákkɪ⌣bɪmbélɪn? *when will the steamer (train) start?*

sángi? *go where?* (§5588).

sárbɛ⌣ n. *digit;* with collective sg. (§4696a) [cp. Eg. dbɛ (etc. EÆGl s.v.), ON. ⲥⲁⲡⲏⲏ *finger* ZNG, §56; ZUSA, p. 164[1]; RNW s.v., RSN, §129; §2389].
  obj. -bɛg⌣.
  pl. -benč(ɪ)⌣.
  ín⌣sárbɛ⌣ (ís⌣sárbɛ⌣ §680) *digit(s) of the hand(s), finger(s).*
  ánn-ín⌣sárbɛ⌣ *my finger(s).*
  óssɪn⌣sárbɛ⌣ (ossɪs-sárbɛ⌣ §680) *digit(s) of the foot (feet), toe(s).*
  sárbɛ⌣nósŏ⌣ *middle finger.*
  sárbɛŋ⌣kěl⌣ *finger-tip(s), tip of toe (tips of toes).*

sǎrɪ⌣ (sǎrrɪ⌣, sǎrrɛ⌣) n. *mast* = éndɛ⌣ (b) [< صَارِي *id.*].
  obj. -rɪg⌣, -rɛg⌣.
  pl. -rɪnč(ɪ)⌣, -rɛnč(ɪ)⌣.

sarráf⌣ (sǎr-) n. *cashier* [< صَرَّاف *id.*].
  obj. -áfk(ɪ)⌣, -kɪ⌣.
  pl. -áfɪ⌣.

sǎu, sǎw, sǎú v.i. *mingle, intermingle, mix, associate.*
  ind. pres. āi⌣sǎuri⌣, ɛr⌣sǎwɪn⌣ (-wī⌣, -wí⌣); perf. āi⌣sǎukori⌣.
  dáwag⌣essírro⌣šúlugran⌣sǎwɪnn⌣ íllar⌣ *they shake the medicine in the (a) bottle in order that it may mix.*
  álɪgon⌣esmǎngon⌣tírgonon⌣sǎukoran⌣ ɛáli and ɛoθmǎn *were (have been) mixed up with them.*
  āi⌣ǎrtɪn⌣írɪgonon⌣sǎukómunun⌣ *I did not associate with the people of the island.*
  égedɪ⌣bertínčɪgonon⌣sawóskoran⌣ *the sheep and the goats have mingled.*

sǎwar (-wǎr⌣; §§2200ff.) and
sǎwíd (§§2256ff.) n. *mingling, mixture.*

sǎw-an (§§3890ff.) v.t. *tell to mingle, etc., let mingle, etc.*

sǎu-bŭ- (§3931 α) v.i. stat. *be in a mingled (etc.) state or condition.*
  bértɪnč⌣ɛgedɪgonon⌣sǎuburan⌣ *the goats and sheep are mixed up.*

sǎw-ɪr (sǎw[u]r, sǎu(ɪ)r, sǎu[u]r; §3671) (a) v.t. caus. *cause or allow to mingle, etc.;* (b) v.t. *mingle, mix.*
  ind. pres. āi⌣sawíddi⌣ (-wírri⌣), ɛr⌣sǎwɪrɪn⌣ (-w[u]r⌣, ⌣sǎu(ɪ)r-, ⌣sǎu[u]r-, -rī⌣, -rí⌣); perf. āi⌣sawírkori⌣.
  pl.-obj. ind. pres. āi⌣sǎu(ɪ)ríddi⌣; perf. āi⌣sǎu(ɪ)rírkori⌣ (⌣sǎurríkkori⌣).
  ɪččɪgom⌣búngongɪ⌣sǎwɪr⌣ *mix the milk and the coffee.*

ábregon‿έssıgoŋgı‿sawíddan⌒ *they mix dried fermented bread with* (lit. *and*) *water.*
X. tékkı‿sawíddıá? *shall I mix it?*
Y. sέren, sáwᵘr⌒ *all right, mix it.*
X. oŋgárkı‿sawᵘríddıá? *shall I mix the two?*
Y. sέren, sáwᵘrır⌒ *all right, mix them.*

sǎwır-an (sǎwᵘr-, etc.; §§3890ff., 3904) v.t. *tell to mingle, etc., let mingle, etc.*

sǎwır-ǎu (sǎwᵘr-, etc.; §3764) v.t. *make by mingling, etc.*
áŋ‿kálgon‿tín‿ğahútkoŋgı‿saúraúkoran⌒ *by mixing our* (*my*) *bread and their stew they* (*have*) *made it* (sc. *the dish*).

sǎwıred-ǎg- (sǎwᵘr-, etc.; §§3877ff.) v.t. *be in the situation of having mingled, etc.*

sǎwır-εttǎ (sǎwᵘr-, etc.; -έttǎ §3855; §4142) v.t. *bring after mingling, etc.*
íččıgom‿búŋgoŋgı‿saúrétta⌒ *bring some milk and coffee mixed.*

sábab = **sέbeb** *cause, reason, motive.*
obj. sábábk(ı), -ápk(ı), -ki⌒.
gen. -ábn‿v., -ám‿c.
pl. sábábı.

sábad n. (*rigid*) *basket* (= kóntε) [< سَبَت id.].
obj. sábádk(ı), -átk(ı), -átt(ı) §2462, -kı⌒, -tı⌒.
pl. sábádı.

sakíbε (-bá, -ba) n. *sack* = sεkíbε.

saúákın n. *Suákin* [< سَواكِن < Beḍ. ó-sók-īb *at* (*to*) *the market* (sók < سُوق); *taken popularly as pl. of* سَاكِنة *female dweller; see E. M. Roper, SNR, XXII, II, pp. 293-4*].
obj. -ākíŋ(ı), -gi⌒.
saúakíndo (s.v. -r) *at* (*to*) *Suákin.*
saúakíndo⌒ (§§5858-60) (*s*)*he* (*it*) *is* (*they are*) *at Suákin.*

sε c. (§4418) adv. *where?, whither?* (see also s.v. ıs‿v.?) *unstressed and enclitic.*
X. έr‿sε‿kombáŋkomen? lit. *where have you not got better?, formula = I hope you are quite better* (§6254).
Y. hámdıllılá! *praise be to God!*

sέ? (§4249) locative interr. sign of pred. *where are?, where is?, where are* (*pl.*)?
[<¹sέ?, ısέ?] (= ısaíré?).
tέr‿sέ? *and*
tέs‿sέ? (§683) *where is* (*s*)*he* (*it*)?
tír‿sέ? *where are they?*
kǎ‿sέ? *where is the house?*
kušár‿sέ? *where is the key?*
X. έn‿hánu‿sέ? *where is your donkey?*
Y. ğănóskori⌒ *I've sold it.*
— *sometimes unstressed and enclitic* (§4250):
kušár‿sε? *where is the key?*
íŋ‿εttǎl‿sέ? *and*
íŋ‿εttǎl‿sε? *where is the bringer of* ((*s*)*he that brings*) *this?*
ğurnǎl‿índo‿búrέl‿sε? *where is the newspaper that lay here?*

s-án-? (§3915) v.i. *go where to?* (see §5588).
ind. pres.
sg. 1 aî‿sándi? *where do I* (*shall I, am I to* §5369*b*) *go to?*

2 εr‿sánın? (-nī?, sání?) *where do you* (*will you, are you to*) *go to?*
3 tεr‿sánın? (-nī?, sání?) *where does* (*s*)*he* (*it*) (*will* (*s*)*he* (*it*), *is* (*s*)*he* (*it*) *to*) *go to?*
pl. 1 ar‿sándu? *where do we* (*shall we, are we to*) *go to?*
2 ır‿sándu? *where do you* (*pl.*) (*will you* (*pl.*), *are you* (*pl.*) *to*) *go to?*
3 tır‿sándan? (-dǎ?, -dá?) *where do they* (*will they, are they to*) *go to?*
— *exclamatorily*:
(aî) sándi! *goodness knows what is to become of* (*will happen to*) *me!*
(εr) sánın! (-nī!, sání!) *goodness knows what is to become of* (*will happen to*) *you!*
(tεr) sánın! (-nī!, sání!) *goodness knows what is to become of* (*will happen to*) *him* (*her, it*)!
(ar) sándu! *goodness knows what is to become of* (*will happen to*) *us!*
(ır) sándu! *goodness knows what is to become of* (*will happen to*) *you* (*pl.*)!
(tır) sándan! (-dǎ!, -dá!) *goodness knows what is to become of* (*will happen to*) *them!*
perfect:
sg. 1 aî‿sáŋkori? *where did I* (*should I, was I to*) *go to?*
2 εr‿sáŋkon? (-kō?, -kó?) *where did you* (*should you, were you to*) *go to?*
3 tεr‿sáŋkon? (-kō?, -kó?) *where did* (*s*)*he* (*it*) (*should s*(*he*) (*it*), *was* (*s*)*he* (*it*) *to*) *go to?*
pl. 1 ar‿sáŋkoru? *where did we* (*should we, were we to*) *go to?*
2 ır‿sáŋkoru? *where did you* (*pl.*) (*should you* (*pl.*), *were you* (*pl.*) *to*) *go to?*
3 tır‿sáŋkoran? (-rǎ?, -rá?) *where did they* (*should they, were they to*) *go to?*
(tεr) sáŋkon! (-kō!, -kó!) *goodness knows what became* (*has become*) *of* (*happened to*) *him* (*her, it*)!
(tır) sáŋkoran! (-rǎ!, -rá!) *goodness knows what became* (*has become*) *of* (*happened to*) *them!*

sám-bŭ- (§§3949ff.) v.i. stat. *be going where?*
ind. pres. aî‿sámbŭri? *where am I going to?*; εr‿sámbŭn? (-bŭ?, -bú?) *where are you going to?*

sέbeb (sábab) n. *cause, reason, motive* [< سَبَب id.].
obj. sεbébk(ı), -έpk(ı), -ki⌒.
gen. sεbébn‿v., -έm‿c.
pl. sεbébı.

sεbéb-kıññ(ı) (-έpk-, sábábk-, -ápk-; §§2536-7) adj. *devoid of cause, etc.*

sεbébkıññı-r (§6007) adv. *without cause, etc.*
tέr‿sεbébkıññır‿sínnεbūn⌒ (*s*)*he is angry without a reason.*

sεbtέ (sεptέ) v.i. *be firm, be fixed, be steady, be still* [< ثَابِت *firm, etc.* + -έ §3631].
ind. pres. aî‿sεbtέri?; perf. aî‿sεbtέgori? (N. -έko-, -έho-).
imperat. sεbtέ!

áŋgarεn‿óssı‿sεptέn, kεrkέrmunun⌒ *the legs* (§4696*a*) *of the bedstead are firm, they don't wobble.*
hέmaŋ‿kóğırı‿sεbtέran, kεrkέrmunan⌒ *the tent-pegs are firmly fixed, they don't move.*

sεbtέrar (sεpt-, -rǎr; §§2200ff., 2207) and

sεbtέríd (sεpt-; §§2256ff., 2260) n. *firmness, etc.*

sεbtέr-an (sεpt-; §§3890ff., 3899) v.t. *tell to be firm, etc., let be firm, etc.*

sεbtέ-bŭ- (sεptέ-; §3931 α) v.i. stat. *be in a firm* (etc.) *state or condition.*

sεbtέ-bᵘ-an (sεpt-; -b(w)an; §§3962-3) v.t. *tell to be in a firm* (etc.) *state or condition, let be in a firm* (etc.) *state or condition.*
έnn-ıs‿sεptέban (-s- < -g- §678) *keep your hand*(*s* §4696*a*) *steady.*

sεbtέr-ε-mǎ- (sεpt-; §§4016-17, 4036, 4041) v.i. *become unable to be firm, etc.*

sέd n. *hunting* [< صَيْد id.].
obj. sέdk(ı), sέtk(ı), sέtt(ı) §2462, -ki⌒, -ti⌒.
gen. sέdn‿v., sέn‿c.
sεn-d(ı) (§§2545ff.) adj. *appertaining to hunting.*

sέgıf n. *roof* = ságıf.

séhem n. $\frac{1}{576}$th part, $\frac{1}{24}$ gírǎd (*square measure*) [< سَهْم id.].
obj. sεhémg(ı), -gi⌒.
pl. séhemı.

sεjjıdέ (sέjıdέ §1381) v.t. *hunt* [< a stem of Sudan Ar. اصيد تَصَيَّد id. + -έ §3652].
ind. pres. aî‿sεjjıdέri?; perf. aî‿sεjjıdέgori? (N. -έko-, -έho-).
imperat. sεjjıdέ!
gέlıs‿sεjjıdέran⌒ (-s- < -g- §678) *they hunt* (*the*) *gazelles.*

sεkíbε (sák-, sak-, -bá, -ba) n. *sack*
[< سَكِيبَة id.].
obj. -bεg.
pl. -bεnč(ı).

sεlgέ v.t. *boil* (*in a liquid*) [< سَلَق *boiling* + -έ §3616].
ind. pres. aî‿sεlgέri?; perf. aî‿sεlgέgori? (N. -έko-, -έho-).
imperat. sεlgέ!
N. kúmbus‿sεlgέkori⌒ (-s- < -g- §678) *I* (*have*) *boiled the egg* (§4696*d*).

sεlgέrar (-rǎr; §§2200ff., 2207) and

sεlgέríd (§§2256ff., 2260) n. *boiling.*

sεlgέr-an (§§3890ff., 3899) v.t. *tell to boil, let boil.*

sεlgέ-bŭ- (§3931 β) v.i. stat. *be in a boiled state or condition.*
kúmbu‿sεlgέbŭn⌒ *the egg is* (*has been, eggs are, have been*) *boiled.*

sεlgέ-dέn (§§3996-7) v.t. *after boiling give* (*to the speaker*), *boil for* (*the speaker*).
kúmbu‿ówwıs‿sεlgέdέn⌒ (-s- < -g- §678) *boil me two eggs.*

sεlgέ-kattı- (N. -έha-; §4093) v.p. *be boiled.*

sεlgέred-ǎg- (§§3877ff.) v.t. *be in the situation of having boiled.*
kúmbus‿sεlgέredágın⌒ (*s*)*he has boiled the eggs.*

sélgé-tır (§§3998-9) v.t. *after boiling give (to other than the speaker), boil for (other than the speaker).*
  kúmbu⌣tóskıs⌣sɛlgɛ́tır⌢ (-s⌣s- < -g⌣s- §678) *boil him (her) three eggs.*

séllɛ⌣ n. *centre* [RSN, §200].
  obj. -lɛg⌣.

sellɛnárt(ı)⌣ (-ti⌢) n. *Sellenarti (on map), a village on the left bank of the Nile about three miles below Old Dóngola* [Middle Island; *but now joined to the left bank*].
  obj. -tı⌣.

séllɛn-d(ı)⌣ (§§2545ff.) adj. *central.*

séllɛŋ-kă⌣ *central hole or square in the game síga* (q.v.).

séllɛr⌣ (§6007) adv. *in (to) the centre.*
  séllɛr⌢ (s)*he (it) is (they are) in the centre.*

sɛllımɛ́ (-lumɛ́) v.t. (a) *greet, salute* (= سَلَّمَ عَلَى); (b) *hand over, deliver* (= سَلَّمَ إِلَى); (c) *surrender* (= سَلَّمَ لِ) [< imperf. or imperat. stem of سَلَّمَ + -ɛ́ §3636].
  ind. pres. āı⌣sɛllımɛ́ri⌢; perf. āı⌣sɛllımɛ́gori⌢ (N. -ɛ́ko-, -ɛ́ho-).
  imperat. sɛllımɛ́!
  áskar⌣tɛ́n⌣zabídkı⌣sɛllımɛ́gon (...⌣tɛ́z⌣zabíttı⌣... §§736, 716) *the soldier (has) saluted his officer.*
  dúŋgıs⌣samílgı⌣tɛ́nn-ır⌣sɛllımɛ́gori⌢ (-s⌣s- < -g⌣s- §678) *I (have) delivered the money to the chief, into his hand.*
  bɛndɛ́rkı⌣sɛllımɛ́goran⌢ *they (have) surrendered the town.*

sɛllımɛ́rar⌣ (-lum-, -rár⌣; §§2200ff., 2207) and
sɛllımɛ́rid⌣ (-lum-; §§2256ff., 2260) n. *greeting, delivery, surrender.*

sɛllımɛ́r-an (-lum-; §§3890ff., 3899) v.t. *tell to greet, etc., let greet, etc.*

sɛllımɛ́-dɛ̆n (-lumɛ́-; §§3996-7) v.t. *give a greeting or salute to (the speaker), greet, salute.*

sɛllımɛ́-tır (-lumɛ́-; §§3998-9) v.t. *give a greeting or salute to (other than the speaker).*

séllım-kattı- (-lum-; §§4093, 4100) v.p. *be greeted, handed over, surrendered.*
  dúŋgı⌣tɛ́nnar⌣séllımkattın⌢ *the money is handed over to him (her).*

sɛ́llu̯⌣álɛ́! interj. *used (sung) by sailors when hauling, yoho!* (= sálɛ́!) [< صَلُّوا عَلَيْهِ *bless Him* (sc. *the Prophet*)].

sɛ́m⌣ n. *poison* (= símm(ı)⌣) [< سَمّ *id.* §1370].
  obj. sɛ́mg(ı)⌣, -gi⌢.
  pl. sɛ́mı⌣.
  sɛ́mgı⌣kő⌢ (a) (s)*he has (the) poison;* (b) *it is poisonous,* lit. *it has poison* = sɛ́mkő⌢.

sɛ́m-ko (§4119) v.i. *be poisonous.*
  ín⌣kăg⌣sɛ́mkő, ín⌣sɛ́mkómunū⌢ *this snake is poisonous, that isn't.*

sɛ́ma n. *sky* [< سَمَاء *id.*].
  obj. -mag⌣.

sɛmán-d(ı)⌣ (§§2545ff.) adj. *appertaining to the sky, of the sky.*

†sɛmafór⌣ n. *semaphore, railway signal* [< سيمافور < *sémaphore*].
  obj. -órk(ı)⌣, -ki⌢.
  pl. -óri⌣.

sɛ́n⌣ (§956d) n. *navel* [perhaps contains -ɛ́n⌣ *mother*].
  obj. sɛ́ŋ(ı)⌣.
  pl. sɛ́nı⌣.
  áttın⌣sɛ́n⌣ (*in water-wheel,* kólɛ⌣) *rope binding together the shoreward ends of all the transverse limbs* (fắsɛnč(ı)⌣) *of spokes of wheel raising water* (átt(ı)⌣); *it forms a* rim *corresponding to the* gŏmbo⌣ *that binds the riverward ends of the* fắsɛnč(ı)⌣.

sɛndɛ́ v.t. *support, prop up* [< imperat. or similar stem of سَانَدَ *id.* + -ɛ́ §3648].
  ind. pres. āı⌣sɛndɛ́ri⌢; perf. āı⌣sɛndɛ́gori⌢ (N. -ɛ́ko-, -ɛ́ho-).
  imperat. sɛndɛ́!

sɛndɛ́rar⌣ (-rár-; §§2200ff., 2207) and
sɛndɛ́rid⌣ (§§2256ff., 2260) n. *supporting, etc.*

sɛndɛ́-kattı- (N. -ɛ́ha-; §4093) v.p. *be supported, etc.*

sɛndɛ́r-an (§§3890ff., 3899) v.t. *tell to support, etc., let support, etc.*

sɛndɛ̄r-ɛ-mắ- (§§4016-17, 4036, 4041) v.t. *become unable to support, etc.*

sɛndɛ́rɛd-dā- (§3991; -ɛ́ggı-dā- occ. -ɛ́dgı- §§3993-4) v.t. *be going along supporting, etc., be supporting along.*
  duŋgúrkı⌣sɛndɛ́rɛddān⌢ (s)*he is supporting the blind (person) along.*

sɛ́na (-nă⌣) n. *year* [< سَنَة *id.*].
  obj. -nag⌣.
  pl. -nanč(ı)⌣.
  ɛr⌣sɛ́na⌣mukóttɛg⌣índorɛ́? *how many years have you been here?*

sɛ́nɛ⌣ (-nă⌣) n. *senna* = sɛnɛmɛ́kkɛ⌣.
  obj. sɛ́nɛg⌣.

sɛ̆nɛ n. *colossus, colossal statue;* with collective sg. (§4695) [cp. Eg. śn *Bruder,* śn *zwei EÆGr,* p. 23*, Copt. сннү *brothers SKG,* p. 77*].
  obj. -nɛg⌣.
  pl. -nɛnč(ı)⌣.
  heard in:
  árgo⌣sɛ̆nɛ⌣ (§2359), and as cpx. n. (§2361).
  argosɛ̆nɛ⌣ *the (two) Argo colossi* (BES, p. 755).
  árgo⌣sɛ̆nɛn⌣darípkɛd⌣āı⌣nókkori⌢ (*it was*) *by the way of (past) the Argo colossi (that) I went.*

sɛnɛmɛ́kkɛ⌣ (-nám-, -kă⌣) n. *true or Alexandrine* senna, *Cassia acutifolia, Del.* [< سَنَا مَكِّي *id.*] (BSP, 166).
  obj. -kɛg⌣.

sɛptɛ́ *be firm, etc.* = sɛbtɛ́.

sɛ́r⌣ n. *thong, strap* [< سَيْر *id.*].
  obj. sɛ́rk(ı)⌣, -ki⌢.
  pl. sɛ́rı⌣.

sɛ́r n. *gravel* [cogn. with sɛ́r *cut small* §2053].
  obj. sɛ́rk(ı)⌣, -ki⌢.
  pl. sɛ́rı⌣.

sɛ́r v.t. *chop, cut up, cut small* [cogn. with sɛ́r⌣ *gravel* §2053].
  ind. pres. āı⌣sɛ́rri⌢, ɛr⌣sɛ́rin⌢ (⌣sɛ́rí⌢, ⌣sɛ́rí⌢); perf. āı⌣sɛ́rkori⌢.
  part. pres. sɛ́rı⌣ (*one*) *that chops, etc., chopper, etc., chopping, etc.,* obj. sɛ́rılg(ı)⌣, -gi⌢; past sɛ́rɛl⌣ (*one*) *that chopped, etc., chopper, etc., chopping, etc.*
    obj. sɛ̄rɛlg(ı)⌣, -gi⌢.
  bíllɛs⌣sɛ́rkori⌢ (-s⌣s- < -g⌣s- §678) *I (have) cut up the onion(s* §4696b).
  ín⌣gŏwwıt⌣tír⌣mɛ́n⌣sɛ́rran? (-t⌣t- < -g⌣t- §707) *why do they chop these trees about?*

sɛ́rar⌣ (-rár⌣; §§2200ff.) and
sɛ́rid⌣ (§§2256ff.) n. *chopping, etc.*

sɛ́r-an (§§3890ff.) v.t. *tell to chop, etc., let chop, etc.*

sɛ́r-bóg (§3747ɛ') v.t. *pour (out) after chopping, etc.*

sɛ́r-bóg-bŭ- (§4216) v.i. stat. *be in a chopped (etc.) and poured (out) state or condition.*
  bíllɛ⌣súŋ⌣kóččır⌣sɛrbógbūn⌢ *the onions are (have been) cut up and poured over the cake (s.v.* súg⌣).

sɛ́r-bŭ- (§3931β) v.i. stat. *be in a chopped (etc.) state or condition.*
  bíllɛ⌣sɛ́rbūn⌢ *the onion is (has been, onions are, have been) cut up.*

sɛ̄rɛd-ág- (§§3877ff.) v.t. *be in the situation of having chopped, etc.*

sɛ̄rr-ɛg-ág- (§§4071ff.) v.t. = sɛ̄rɛdól-.

sɛ̄r-ɛ-dól- (-rᵒd- §1178; §4022) and
sɛ̄rr-ɛ-dól- (-rᵒd-; §4027) v.t. *be about to chop, etc.*

sɛ̄r-ɛ-mắ- (§4036) and
sɛ̄rr-ɛ-mắ- (§4041) v.t. *become unable to chop, etc.*

sɛ́r-kattı- (§4093) v.p. *be chopped, etc.*

sɛ́rɛ̆⌣ adj. (a) *good;* (b, like طَيِّب) *in good condition or health, well* (= kómbo⌣) [§§2520-1; RSN, §129].
  obj. -rɛ́g⌣.
  pl. -rɛ́ri⌣ and -rɛ́nč(ı)⌣.
  ısắı-tɛ⌣sɛ́rɛ? *which is the good (better, best) one.*
  sɛ́rɛ̆⌣hálısun (s)*he (it) is very good.*
  sɛ́rɛ̆⌣hálısun! *very good! (all right!).*
  sɛ́rɛn! (sɛ́rɛ̆!, sɛ́rɛ́! §1973) *good! (very well!, all right!),* lit. (*it) is good!*
  ín⌣sɛrɛ́m⌢ *this is good.*
  ín⌣sɛrɛ́munun⌢ *this is not good.*
  X. kărɛ⌣sɛr⌣ɛ́goná? *was the fish good?*
  Y. siɛ́l⌣ɛgő⌢ *it was stinking.*
  sɛrɛ́-wɛ̆g⌣ɛ́tta⌢ *bring a good one.*
  tımbáb⌣sɛrrɛ́? (a) *is his (her) father good? (pious, honest, kind, etc.);* (b) *is his (her) father well?* (= tımbáp⌣ kómborɛ́?).

sɛrɛ́gıd⌣ n. (a) *goodness, good condition, etc.;* (b) *virtue* [§§2247-8].
  obj. sɛrɛ̄gídk(ı)⌣, -ítk(ı)⌣, -ítt(ı)⌣ (§2462), -ki⌢, -ti⌢.

sɛrɛ́-kanɛ (§2295) n. = sɛrɛ́gıd⌣.
  obj. -nɛg⌣.
  ɛ́n⌣sɛrɛ́kanɛ⌣ (-n⌣s- < -nn⌣s- §613) (*the, a) woman's virtue.*

sɛ́r-an- (§3910α) v.i. *become good, etc., get well, improve, get better.*
  ind. pres. āı⌣sɛ́randi⌢, ɛr⌣sɛ́ranın⌢ (-ni⌢, -ní⌢).

sɛran- in composition often=*well, properly, satisfactorily.*

sɛran-ág- (§4151) v.i. *be (continuously) in good condition, etc., keep well* (=sɛrantɛ́b).
 W. ɛr⌣sɛranágmɛn? (-ǎŋŋɛn? §661, -mɛ̃?, -mé? §939) *how are you?*, lit. *are you not* (=*I hope you are*) *well?* (§3119).
 X. ártɪh⌣hamdɛ́ri!, sɛranágri⌒ (-h⌣h- <-g⌣h- §559) *I praise God!, I am well.*
 Y. hámdɪllá!, sɛranágri⌒ *praise be to God!, I am well.*
 Z. hámdɪlɪllá!, sɛranágri⌒ *praise be to God!, I am well* [sɛranágri⌒ often omitted].
 X. sɛranágmɛn? (-ǎŋŋɛn?, -mɛ̃?, -mé?) *how are you?*
 Y. árton⌣éh⌣hálgɪ⌣sɛrɛ́gɪrɪn! (-h⌣h- <-n⌣h- §560) *God bless you!* (§6247) i.e. *well, and I hope you are,* lit. *if God make your condition good, sc. I shall rejoice.*

sɛran-árk(ɪ) (§4151) v.i. *burn well.*
 íl⌣lámbà⌣sɛranárkĭ⌒ (-l⌣l- <-n⌣l- §581) *this lamp burns well.*

sɛram-bějjɪ (§4151) v.i. *start the morning (etc., s.v. bějjɪ) in good condition or health, be well on starting the morning, etc.*
 X. sɛrambějjɪgomɛn? (-mɛ̃?, -mé?) or N. sɛrambějjɪkomɛn? (-mɛ̃?, -mé?) *good morning,* lit. *have you* (=*I hope you have*) *started the morning well?*
 Y. âɪ⌣sɛrambějjɪgori⌒ (N. -ɪkori⌒), hámdɪlɪllá! *good morning!*, lit. *I have started the morning well, praise be to God!*
 X. sɛrambějjɪgomɛn? *good morning!*
 Y. árton⌣én⌣hálgɪ⌣sɛrɛ́gɪrɪn! and N. Z. árton⌣éh⌣hálgɪ⌣sɛrɛ́kɪrɪn! (-h⌣h- <-n⌣h- §560) *God bless you!*

sɛram-bíčč(ɪ) (§4151) v.i. *wake in good condition or health, be well on waking.*
 X. sɛrambíččɪgomɛn? *good morning!*, lit. *didn't you wake* (i.e. *I hope you woke*) *in good health?*
 Y. sɛrambíččɪgori, hámdɪlɪllá! *good morning!*, lit. *I awoke in good health, praise be to God!*

sɛram-bŭ- (§§3949ff.) v.i. stat. *be in an improving or improved state or condition, be getting better, be better.*

sɛranɛd-ág- (§3966α) v.i. *be in the condition of having become good, etc., be in an improved condition, be quite good or better.*

sɛraŋ-kóbbŭ- (§4153) v.i. stat. *be in a well shut (etc., s.v. kób) state or condition.*
 sandúgɪ⌣sɛraŋkóbbūrandɛ́? *are the boxes securely shut?*

sɛraŋ-kúzbŭ- (§4153) v.i. stat. *be in a well open (etc. s.v. kús) state or condition.*

sɛran-tɛ́b- (§4151) v.i. *be (continuously) in good condition, etc., keep well* (=sɛranág-).
 X. mínɛ⌣búran? *how are they?*
 Y. sɛrantɛ́bʰran⌒ *they keep well.*

sɛran-túrb(ɪ) (-túbb(ɪ) §520; §4151) v.i. *rest (etc. s.v. túrb(ɪ)) well.*
 X. sɛrantúbbɪ! *good-night!*

Y. ártɪn⌣hásɛbɪr! *good-night!*, lit. *in God's care!*
X. and Y. sɛrantúbbi! *good-night!*
Z. hɛ́rro⌣túbbɪwɛ́! (⌣túbbʷwɛ́!) *good-night!*, lit. *sleep in well-being!* (s.v. hɛ́r⌣).

sɛrɛ́g-ɪr (N. -ɛ́kɪr, -ɛ̃hɪr; §3701) (a) v.t. caus. *cause or allow to be good, etc.;* (b) v.t. *render good, etc., improve.*
ind. pres. âɪ⌣sɛrɛ́gɪddi⌒, ɛr⌣sɛrɛ́gɪrɪn⌒ (-rí⌒, -rí⌒).

sɛrɛ́gɪr⌣ (N. -ɛ́kɪr⌣, -ɛ̃hɪr⌣; §4466) and **sɛrɛ́gɪrg(ɪ)⌣** (N. -ɛ́kɪr-, -ɛ̃hɪr-; §4467) adv. *well, properly.*

sɛrɛ́gɪr- (N. -ɛ̄kɪr-, -ɛ̄hɪr-) in composition (§4989) *well, properly.*
 N. sɛrɛ̀kɪr⌣gɛ́llɪgāwanó⌒ and N. sɛrɛ̀kɪrgɪ-gɛ́llɪgāwanó⌒ *tell him (her) to work properly.*

sɛrɛ́gɪr-ámmɛr- (N. -ɛ̄kɪr-, -ɛ̄hɪr-; -ágmɛr-; §4142) v.t. *be engaged in cutting (etc., s.v. ámmɛr-) well, properly.*
sɛrɛ́gɪrámmɛrɪn⌒ (s)*he (it) is cutting well, etc.*=âssɛrɛ́gɪrmérɪn⌒, tɛ̄bsɛrɛ́gɪrmérɪn⌒.
 N. kánd⌣ɛ́kkɛnɛ⌣sɛrɛ̀kɪrámmɛrɪn⌒ *now the knife is cutting well.*

sɛrɛ́gɪr-áššuglɛ́- (N. -ɛ̄kɪr-, -ɛ̄hɪr-; -ágšu-; -šoglɛ́-, -šogolɛ́-; §4142) v.i. *be engaged in working (etc., s.v. áššuglɛ́-) well, properly.*

sɛrɛ́gɪr-áu (N. -ɛ̄kɪr-, -ɛ̄hɪr-; -áw, -áû; §4137) and emphasizing sɛrɛ́gɪr-.

sɛrɛ́gɪr-áu (N. -ɛ̄kɪr-, -ɛ̄hɪr-; -áw, -áû; §1964) v.t. *do (etc., s.v. áu) well, etc.*
gáhwas⌣sɛrɛ́gɪráû⌒ (-s⌣s- <-g⌣s- §678) *make some good coffee.*

sɛrɛ́gɪráw-an (N. -ɛ̄kɪr-, -ɛ̄hɪr-; §§3890ff., 3905) v.t. *tell to do well, etc., let do well, etc.*

sɛrɛ́gɪráwɛd-ág- (N. -ɛ̄kɪr-, -ɛ̄hɪr-; §§3877ff.) v.t. *be in the situation of having done well, etc.*
gɛ́llɪs⌣sɛrɛ́gɪráwɛdágran⌒ *they have done the work well.*

sɛrɛ́gɪr-áu-kattɪ- (N. -ɛ̄kɪr-, -ɛ̄hɪr-, -áuha-; §4142) v.p. *be done (etc.) well.*

sɛrɛ́gɪrɛd-ág- (N. -ɛ̄kɪr-, -ɛ̄hɪr-; §§3877ff.) v.t. *be in the situation of having caused or allowed to be good, etc.*

sɛrɛ́gɪr-gŭ́nč(ɪ) (N. -ɛ̄kɪr-, -ɛ̄hɪr-; -gŭ́nč(ɪ); §4137) v.t. (a) *look well at, watch well;* (b) *keep a good look-out for.*

sɛrɛ́gɪrgŭ́nč-an (N. -ɛ̄kɪr-, -ɛ̄hɪr-, -gŭ́nč-; §§3890ff., 3905) v.t. *tell to look well at, etc., let look well at, etc.*

sɛrɛ́gɪr-gɛ́llɪgau (N. -ɛ̄kɪr-, -ɛ̄hɪr-; -áw, -áû; §§4142-3) v.i. *work well, work properly.*

sɛrɛ́gɪrgɛ́llɪgáw-an (N. -ɛ̄kɪr-, -ɛ̄hɪr-; §§3890ff., 3905) v.t. *tell to work well, let work well.*

sɛrɛ́gɪr-kób (N. -ɛ̄kɪr-, -ɛ̄hɪr-; §4137) v.t. *shut (etc., s.v. kób) well, properly, securely.*
kóbidkɪ⌣sɛrɛ́gɪrkóp⌒ *shut the door well.*

sɛrɛ́gɪrkób-an (N. -ɛ̄kɪr-, -ɛ̄hɪr-; §§3890ff., 3905) v.t. *tell to shut (etc.) well, let shut (etc.) well, etc.*

sɛrɛ́gɪrkób-bŭ- (N. -ɛ̄kɪr-, -ɛ̄hɪr-; §4145) v.i. stat. *be in a well (etc.) shut (etc.) state or condition.*

sandúgɪ⌣sɛrɛ́gɪrkóbbūran⌒ *the boxes are securely shut.*

sɛrɛ́gɪrkobɛd-ág (N. -ɛ̄kɪr-, -ɛ̄hɪr-; §§3877ff.) v.t. *be in the situation of having shut (etc.) well, etc.*

sɛrɛ́gɪr-kób-kattɪ- (N. -ɛ̄kɪr-, -ɛ̄hɪr-; -kóp-k-; §4144) v.p. *be well (etc.) shut, etc.*

sɛrɛ́gɪr-kob-úndur (N. -ɛ̄kɪr-, -ɛ̄hɪr-; §4196) v.t. *put in after shutting (etc.) well, etc.*
sɛrɛ́gɪrkòb-gàlor-undúrkori⌒ (§5605) *after shutting it well I (have) put it into the water-jar.*

sɛrɛ́gɪr-kús (N. -ɛ̄kɪr-, -ɛ̄hɪr-; §4137) v.t. *open (etc., s.v. kús) well, completely.*

sɛrɛ́gɪrkús-an (N. -ɛ̄kɪr-, -ɛ̄hɪr-; §§3890ff., 3905) v.t. *tell to open (etc.) well, etc., let open (etc.) well, etc.*

sɛrɛ́gɪrkúz-bŭ- (N. -ɛ̄kɪr-, -ɛ̄hɪr-; §4145) v.i. stat. *be in a well (etc.) opened (etc.) state or condition.*

sɛrɛ́gɪrkusɛd-ág- (N. -ɛ̄kɪr-, -ɛ̄hɪr-; §§3877ff.) v.t. *be in the situation of having opened (etc.) well, etc.*

sɛrɛ́gɪr-kús-kattɪ- (N. -ɛ̄kɪr-, -ɛ̄hɪr-; §4144) v.p. *be well (etc.) opened, etc.*

sɛrɛ́gɪr-mér (N. -ɛ̄kɪr-, -ɛ̄hɪr-; §4137) v.t. *cut (etc., s.v. mér) well, etc.*

sɛrɛ́gɪrmér-an (N. -ɛ̄kɪr-, -ɛ̄hɪr-; §§3890ff., 3905) v.t. *tell to cut (etc.) well, etc., let cut (etc.) well, etc.*

sɛrɛ́gɪrmér-bŭ- (N. -ɛ̄kɪr-, -ɛ̄hɪr-; §4145) v.i. stat. *be in a well (etc.) cut (etc.) state or condition.*

sɛrɛ́gɪrmɛrɛd-ág- (N. -ɛ̄kɪr-, -ɛ̄hɪr-; §§3877ff.) v.t. *be in the situation of having cut (etc.) well, etc.*

sɛrɛ́gɪr-nál (N. -ɛ̄kɪr-, -ɛ̄hɪr-; §4137) v.t. *see (etc., s.v. nál) well, etc.*

sɛrɛ́gɪrnál-an (N. -ɛ̄kɪr-, -ɛ̄hɪr-; §§3890ff., 3905) v.t. *tell to see (etc.) well, etc., let see (etc.) well, etc.*

sɛrɛ́gɪrnalɛd-ág- (N. -ɛ̄kɪr-, -ɛ̄hɪr-; §§3877ff.) v.t. *be in the situation of having seen (etc.) well, etc.*
sɛrɛ́gɪrnalɛdágran⌒ *they have looked at him (her, it, them) thoroughly.*

sɛrɛ́gɪr-nódd(ɪ) (N. -ɛ̄kɪr-, -gɪnnó- §628; §4137) v.t. *cut up (etc., s.v. nódd(ɪ)) well, etc.*

sɛrɛ́gɪrnódd-an (N. -ɛ̄kɪr-, -ɛ̄hɪr-; §§3890ff., 3905) v.t. *tell to cut up (etc.) well, etc., let cut up (etc.) well, etc.*

sɛrɛ́gɪrnóddɪ-bŭ- (N. -ɛ̄kɪr-, -ɛ̄hɪr-; §4145) v.i. stat. *be in a well (etc.) cut up (etc.) state or condition.*

sɛrɛ́gɪrnoddɛd-ág- (N. -ɛ̄kɪr-, -ɛ̄hɪr-; §§3877ff.) v.t. *be in the situation of having cut up (etc.) well, etc.*

sɛrɛ́gɪr-šuglɛ́ (N. -ɛ̄kɪr-, -ɛ̄hɪr-; -šoglɛ́, -šogolɛ́; §4137) v.i. *work well, etc.*

sɛrɛ́gɪršuglɛ́r-an (N. -ɛ̄kɪr-, -ɛ̄hɪr-; §§3890ff., 3905) v.t. *tell to work well, etc., let work well, etc.*

sɛrɛ́gɪršuglɛ́rɛd-ág- (N. -ɛ̄kɪr-, -ɛ̄hɪr-; §§3877ff.) v.i. *be in the situation of having worked well, etc.*

sɛrɛ́gɪr-tɛ̄bmɛ́r- (N. -ɛ̄kɪr-, -ɛ̄hɪr-; §4142) v.t. *be engaged in cutting (etc., s.v. tɛ̄bmɛ́r-) well, etc.*

sérıñ — síkk(ı)

kánd ékkenɛ sɛrēgırtēbmérın now the knife is cutting well; =kánd ékkenɛ tēbsɛrēgırmérın.

sɛrēgır-úndur (N. -ēkır-, -ēhır-; §4141) v.t. *put in (etc., s.v. úndur) well, etc., put well in.*

sɛrēgırúndur-an (N. -ēkır-, -ēhır-; §§3890ff., 3905) v.t. *tell to put in (etc.) well, etc., let put in (etc.) well, etc.*

sɛrēgırundurɛd-ǎg- (N. -ēkır-, -ēhır-; §§3877ff.) v.t. *be in the situation of having put in (etc.) well, etc.*

sɛrēgır-úskur (N. -ēkır-, -ēhır-; §4141) v.t. *set (etc., s.v. úskur) well, etc.*

sɛrēgırúskur-an (N. -ēkır-, -ēhır-; §§3890ff., 3905) v.t. *tell to set (etc.) well, etc., let set (etc.) well, etc.*

sɛrēgıruskurɛd-ǎg- (N. -ēkır-, -ēhır-; §§3877ff.) v.t. *be in the situation of having set (etc.) well, etc.*

sérıñ n. *barley* [RSN, §129 cps. Eth. ሥርናይ wheat (<*ሥዕርናይ hirsutus cp. شعير barley, etc. DLÆ s.v. ሥዕርና, but 'vielleicht Lehnwort aus dem Hamitischen' PBÆ, 9) Beḍ. serám Sōm. sarén id.; AAE s.v. ስንደይ].
obj. sɛríñg(ı) (occ. approaches *sɛríng(ı) §647), -gı.
tín sɛríñg áddégran *they are watering their barley.*

sɛrsír n. *cockroach*, Blatta ægyptiaca; with collective sg. (§4696c) [صراصير id. pl. §§1310, 2405].
obj. -írk(ı), -kı.
pl. -írı.

sıɛ (sıé §2878) v.i. *stink* [<√sí- stink (§4588)+-ɛ §2870].
ind. pres. aı sıérı, ɛr sıén (sıé, sıé); pres. aı sıérı, ɛr sıén (sıé, sıé); perf. aı sıégorı (N. -ēko-, -ēho-), sıégorı (N. -éko-, -ého-).
subj. past aı sıésı (sıésı, -su).
part. pres. sıɛl (sıél) (one) that stinks, stinking object, stinking, fetid; obj. sıɛlg(ı), -gı.
kǎrɛ sıélun the fish is stinking.
ın sıémunun this does not stink.

sıɛrar (sıér-, -rǎr; §§2200ff., 2210) and **sıɛríd** (§§2256ff., 2263) n. *stinking, stink.*

sıɛl-an (sıélan-; §3910α) v.i. *become fetid.*

sıɛ-bŭ- (sıé-bŭ-; §3931α) v.i. stat. *be in a fetid state or condition.*
kǎrɛ sıɛbūn the fish is in a fetid condition.
kǎrón sıɛbūgın ɛǧǧárkı if the fish is in a fetid condition, take it and throw it away.

sıɛr-ɛg-ǎg- (§§4071ff.) v.i. =sıɛrɛdól-.

sıɛr-ɛ-dól- (-rᵒd- §1178; §§4016-17, 4022, 4027) v.i. *be about to stink.*
kǎrɛ sıɛredólın the fish is almost fetid.

síǧa n. *a game like draughts* [<سيجة id. DAG, p. 138].
obj. -gag.
síǧaj-jǎ korótkɛd jǎ kámlın tǔrkɛk káččıran (-j-j- <-g-j- §566, -k-k- <-d-k- §568) they play síǧa either with pebbles (§4696c) or with camel-dung.

síǧa kúl arrɛdíčkı kón, kúlık kárıg ɛrán, arrɛdígırtōn séllén-ka wákkıbūn; kórod arrɛkɛmískɛk káččıran, kórodıw wélıg ɛrán, kulwǎhıd wél dımındówwıgɛk káččın (-w-w- <-g-w- §719) síǧa has 25 holes, they call the holes houses, the middle house of the 25 is omitted; they play with 24 pebbles, they call the pebbles dogs, each plays with (i.e. each player has) 12 dogs.

síkk(ı) v.t. *loathe* [<√sí- stink (§4588)+-k(ı) §2853].
ind. pres. aı síkkırı; perf. aı síkkıgorı (N. -ıko-, -ıho-).
síɛlun, aı tékkı síkkırı *it is fetid, I loathe it.*

síkkar (-kǎr; §§2200ff.) and **sıkkíd** (§§2256ff.) n. *loathing.*

síkkıg-ır (N. -ıkır, -ıhır; §3682) (a) v.t. caus. *cause to loathe, nauseate;* (b) v.t. *nauseate, disgust.*
ín aıgı síkkıgırın this nauseates me.
aıgı síkkıgırkó it (has) nauseated me.

síni (a) adj. *china, of china* [<صيني id.]; (b) n. *china object, china;* with collective sg. (§4647).
obj. -nıg.
pl. -nınč(ı).
sáhan sínıg étta bring the (a) china plate.
sínıŋ kúra gúššıgó the china bowl (has) got broken.

síni-kırı (§§2539-40) adj. *like china.*

síu (síᵘ, síw) n. (a) *sand;* (b) *sand-bank, sand-dune;* with collective sg. (§4696d) [RSN, §129].
obj. síug.
pl. síwı.

síwır (§6007) adv. *on (in, into) the sand(s* §6288).
kúb síwır būn the boat lies on the sand.
síwır (s)he (it) is (they are) on the sand(s).

síⁿsíu (síws-, -síᵘ, -síw) n. *chick, young chicken;* with collective sg. (§4696c) [<Sudan Ar. سيوسيو síᵘsíu Amh. ሲውሲው id. AAE s.v. √ስውስው].
obj. -síug.
pl. -síwı.

síbɛ n. *mud, clay.*
obj. síbɛg.
pl. síbénč(ı).
síbɛrtónun (§5878) *it is made of clay.*
síbɛgɛg góñran (-g-g- <-d-g- §545) *they build in (lit. with) mud* (=gǎlúskɛg góñran s.v. gǎlús).

síbır n. *feather;* with collective sg. (§4696a) [RSN, §200].
obj. sıbírk(ı), -kı.
pl. síbrı.
káuırtɛn sıbírkı tén díltıg ɛrán they call a bird's feathers its dílti (hair).

sıg v.i. *get terrified, be struck with terror.*
ind. pres. aı sıgrı, ɛr sıgın (-gí, sıg); perf. aı sígorı (síkkorı).
gádı tékkı díárkɛh hokménǧal sıgóskó (-h-h- <-d-h- §558) *when the judge sentenced him to death he was struck with terror (...her to death she was...).*

sígar (-gǎr; §§2200) and **sıgíd** (§§2256ff.) n. *terror.*

síg-bŭ (síggŭ- §546; §3931α) v.i. stat. *be in a terrified state or condition.*
sígbūran they are in a state of terror.

sıgɛd-ǎg- (§§3877ff.) v.i. *be in the condition of having been terrified, etc.*
sıgɛdǎgran they are terror-struck.

sıgíŋ-ır ('--; N. -ŋkır; §3688) (a) v.t. caus. *cause or allow to get terrified, etc.;* (b) v.t. *terrify.*
ǧǎn aıgı sıgíŋırkó *the fiend terrified me.*

sıgídd(ı) v.i. *prostrate oneself in adoration, pray, say one's prayers* [<imperf. stem of سجد id. §2844].
ind. pres. aı sıgíddırı, ɛr sıgíddın (-dí, -dí); perf. aı sıgíddıgorı (N. -ıko-, -ıho-).
imperat. sıgíddı!

sıgíddar (-dǎr; §§2200ff.) and **sıgıddíd** (§§2256ff.) n. *praying, etc.*
sıgíddann ogóllo (-nn <-rn §628) and sıgíddaŋ gabúllo *before praying.*

sıgíddır-ɛg-ǎg- (§§4071ff.) v.i. =sıgıddɛdól-.

sıgıdd-ɛ-dól- (-dᵒd- §1178; §4022) and **sıgıddır-ɛ-dól-** (-rᵒd-; §4027) v.i. *be about to pray, etc.*

sıgíddır-ɛ-ǧǔ-bŭ- (§4069) v.i. stat. *be on one's way (coming) to pray, etc.*

sıgíddır-ɛ-nóg (§4048ff.) v.i. *go to pray, etc.*

sıgíddır-ɛ-nóg-bŭ- (-nóggŭ- §546; §4058) v.i. stat. *be on one's way (going) to pray, etc.*

sıgíddır-ɛ-tǎ (§§4060ff.) v.i. *come to pray, etc.*

sıgíddɛd-ǎg- (§§3877ff.) v.i. *be in the situation of having prayed, etc.*
sıgíddɛdǎgın *he has said his prayers.*

sıǧára n. (a) *cigarette;* (b, applied to) *cigar* with collective sg. (§4696d) [<سيجارة id. Eur.].
obj. -rag.
pl. -ranč(ı).

sıǧǧáǧa n. *rug, carpet* [<سجّادة id. §1238].
obj. -ǧag.
pl. -ǧanč(ı).

sıǧın (§956a) n. *prison* [<سجن id. §1359].
obj. sıǧıŋ(ı).
pl. síǧını.

sıǧíndo (s.v. -r; §6007) adv. *in prison.*
sıǧíndo dǎbugó (s)he was (has been) in prison.
tır sıǧíndo they are in prison.

síkkɛ n. *road, street* [<سكّة id.].
obj. -kɛg.
pl. -kɛnč(ı).

síkk(ı) (occ. ısíkk(ı) §1075) v.t. (a) *ask, inquire, question, ask of, inquire of;* (b) *ask for, request* (=íḍḍ(ı)) [see ısíkk(ı)].
ind. pres. aı síkkırı, ɛr síkkın (-kí, -kí); fut. aı bısíkkırı (bus-); perf. aı síkkıgorı (N. -ıko-, -ıho-).
imperat. síkki!

subj. past aî⁀síkkısı⁀ (-su⁀).
W. bābúr⁀tågoná⁀ has the steamer (train) come?
X. wɛs⁀síkk⁀ándi⁀ (-s⁀s- < -g⁀s- §678) I'll (§5369b) tell someone to ask.
Y. síkkandi⁀ I'll tell (him, someone §5339) to ask.
Z. aî⁀noggusíkkiri⁀ I'll go along and ask.
tírtıs⁀síkkıgoran⁀ (-s⁀s- < -g⁀s- §678) they (have) asked the owner.
éssıs⁀síkkıran⁀ they ask for water.
tírtıg⁀éssıs⁀síkkıgoran⁀ they (have) asked the owner for (some) water.
aî⁀bı-man-kánd⁀éssıs⁀síkkır⁀égi⁀ (§§5611, 6222) I shall go to that house to ask for water.
aî⁀tírgı⁀sıkkırríddi⁀ I('ll) ask (each of §5456) them.

síkkar (-kár⁀; §§2200ff.) and
sıkkíd⁀ (§§2256ff.) n. asking, inquiry, request.
án⁀sıkkít⁀tamám'ré? (-t⁀t- < -d⁀t- §706) is my question correct?

síkk-an (§§3890ff.) v.t. tell to ask, etc., let ask, etc.
álıs⁀síkkan⁀ (-s⁀s- < -g⁀s- §678) let ɛáli ask.
síkkıwan⁀ let them ask.

sıkked-åg- (§§3877ff.) v.t. be in the situation of having asked, etc.

síkkı-kattı- (N. -ıha-; §4093) v.p. be asked, etc.

sıkkı-nál (§3747ɛ') v.t. see (etc.), s.v. nál) by asking, etc., ascertain.
ind. pres. aî⁀síkkınálli⁀.
imperat. sıkkınál! and síkkınal! (§1871)

sıkkı-nal (§1964) v.t. see (etc.) by asking, etc., ask (etc.) so as to see, etc., ask (etc.) in order to see, etc. (§3783).
ind. pres. aî⁀síkkınalli⁀.

sıkkınál-an (síkkınalan §1872; §§3890ff., 3905) v.t. tell to ascertain, let ascertain.

sıkkır-ɛ-ğŭ-bŭ- (§4069) v.t. stat. be on one's way (coming) to ask, etc.

sıkkır-ɛ-nóg (§§4048ff.) v.t. go to ask, etc.
sıkkırɛnókkoran⁀ they went (have gone) to ask.

sıkkır-ɛ-nóg-bŭ- (-nóggŭ- §546; §4058) v.t. stat. be on one's way (going) to ask, etc.

sıkkır-ɛ-tá (§§4060ff.) v.t. come to ask, etc.

sıkkód⁀ (suk-, -ŏt⁀ §469) n. Sukkót, a district on the Nile from about 20° 30' to 21° 30' N. lat., north of Máḥas [' < sakluda < sa-kóloda 'die sieben gouverneure' RN s.v. Sakluda; but perhaps < sūgtŏd⁀ little market §570].
obj. -ŏdk(ı)⁀, -ŏtk(ı)⁀, -ŏtt(ı)⁀ §2462, -ki⁀, -ti⁀.
gen. -ŏdn⁀v., -ŏnn⁀v.c., -ŏn⁀c.
ısái-tɛ⁀sıkkót? which is Sukkót?
mán⁀sıkkódun⁀ and
mán⁀sukkódŭ⁀ that (yonder) is Sukkót.
sıkkódırtŏn⁀tågoran⁀ they came (have come) from Sukkót.

sıkkón-d(ı)⁀ (suk-; §§2545ff.) adj. appertaining to Sukkót, of Sukkót.

sıláde⁀ adj. round, circular [< √síl- *circle (§4589) +-åd⁀ *holding (§§2061, 2186) +-ɛ⁀ that says, that is (§2517), so or.

*that says 'holding a circle', *that is containing a circle].
obj. -dɛg⁀.
pl. -dɛnč(ı)⁀.
áda⁀sıláde⁀ circular tray.
sáhan⁀sıládén⁀ the plate is round.

sılátte⁀ n. fabric of coarse grass, rough matting [< *sılárte⁀ (§713) < √síl- *circle (§4589) +-ar⁀ nominal -ing (§2200) +-t dem. (§§2323ff.) +-ɛ⁀ of n. dic. or n. ess. (§2234), so what says (or is) 'encirclement', either from its uses, sılátte⁀ being employed as wind-screen for water-wheel, to build sheds for cattle, etc., or from the way it is made, the grass stems being tied, not plaited; §2226].
obj. -tɛg⁀ [> Sudan Ar. سلاتيك id. §2412].
pl. -tɛnč(ı)⁀.
sılátte⁀hamártertŏn⁀åukattın, awıč-káttımunun, dígırkattın⁀ sılátte⁀ is made of ḥálfa grass, it is not plaited, it is tied.
kólen⁀dára⁀hamártertŏn⁀sılátté⁀ (§4229) the screen of the water-wheel is sılátte⁀ made of ḥálfa grass.
kérrı⁀sıláttertŏn⁀åukattın⁀ the shed is made of sılátte⁀.

sílıg⁀ n. (a) wire; (b, of musical instrument) string; with collective sg. (§4696d); (c) telegraph, telegram =sílk(ı)⁀ (§1368) [< سلك id. §1359].
obj. sılígk(ı)⁀, -íkk(ı)⁀, -ki⁀.
gen. sílıgn⁀v., -ıŋ⁀c.
pl. síl(ı)g⁀.
kísır⁀sílıg⁀díčč⁀kó⁀ the guitar has five strings.
sílıg⁀máktáb⁀ (-g⁀m- < -gn⁀m- §793a) telegraph-office.

sílk(ı)⁀ n. wire, etc. =sílıg⁀ [< سلك id. §1359].
obj. -kıg⁀.
pl. -kınč(ı)⁀.
kísır⁀sílkı⁀díčč⁀kó⁀ the guitar has five strings.
sílkım⁀máktáb⁀ telegraph-office.

síll(ı)⁀ v.t. winnow, clean (grain) by passing (it) through wind.
ind. pres. aî⁀sílliri⁀; perf. aî⁀sílligori⁀ (N. -ıko-, -ıho-).
imperat. sílli!
énč⁀íllɛt⁀tabákkɛs⁀síllıran, íllɛ⁀tabá-gırton⁀árıdır⁀bŏgın, túrug⁀síltıs⁀ sókkɛn⁀ (-t⁀t- < -g⁀t- §707, -ɛs⁀s- < -ɛd⁀s- §677, -ıs⁀s- < -ıg⁀s- §678) (the) women winnow (the) wheat by taking (-ɛd⁀) a tray, the wheat pours down from the tray to the ground, the wind removes the chaff.

síllar (-lár⁀; §§2200ff.) and
sıllíd⁀ (§§2256ff.) n. winnowing, etc.

sílt(ı)⁀ n. chaff, fragments of straw, etc., winnowed from grain [§2325β].
obj. -tıg⁀.
pl. -tınč(ı)⁀.

síll-an (§§3890ff.) v.t. tell to winnow, etc., let winnow, etc.

síllı-bŭ- (§3931β) v.i. stat. be in a winnowed (etc.) state or condition.
márɛ⁀síllıbún⁀ the millet is (has been) winnowed.

sıllır-ɛg-åg- (§§4071ff.) v.t. =sıllɛdól-.
sıll-ɛ-dól- (-lᵒd- §1178; §4022) and
sıllır-ɛ-dól- (-rᵒd-; §4027) v.t. be about to winnow, etc.
sıll-ɛ-má- (§4036) and
sıllır-ɛ-má- (§4041) v.t. become unable to winnow, etc.
sıllɛd-åg- (§§3877ff.) v.t. be in the situation of having winnowed, etc.
sílli-kattı- (N. -ıha-; §4093) v.p. be winnowed, etc.

síllım n. (a) stair, step; with collective sg. (§4696d); (b) ladder [< Sudan Ar. سلّم id.].
obj. síllímg(ı)⁀, -gi⁀.
pl. síllımı⁀.

sílsıle⁀ n. chain [< سلسلة id.].
obj. -lɛg⁀.
pl. -lɛnč(ı)⁀.

símıd⁀ (-ıt⁀) n. Simit (on map), an island and district in Máḥas, at the head of the third cataract.
obj. símıdk(ı)⁀, -ítk(ı)⁀, -ítt(ı)⁀ §716, -ki⁀, -ti⁀.
símıdn⁀árt(ı)⁀ the island of S.
símıdır⁀ (s.v. -r⁀) in (to) S.
símıdır⁀ (§6007) (s)he (it) is (they are) in S.

símm(ı)⁀ n. poison (=sɛm⁀ §1370) [< Sudan Ar. سمّ id.].
obj. -mıg⁀.
pl. -mınč(ı)⁀.

símsım⁀ n. sesame, Sesamum indicum, DC. (BSP, 129) [< سمسم id.].
obj. sımsímg(ı)⁀, -gi⁀.
gen. símsımn⁀v., símsım⁀c.
símsım⁀dés⁀ and
símsım⁀zɛd⁀ sesame oil.
símsım⁀hábba⁀ grain(s) of sesame.

sína n. art, craft, skill [< صناعة id. §1353].
obj. -nag⁀.
pl. -nanč(ı)⁀.

sındála n. anvil [< Sudan Ar. سندالة id.].
obj. -lag⁀.
pl. -lanč(ı)⁀.

sınnár n. Sennár, a district on the Blue Nile [< سنار id.].
obj. -árk(ı)⁀, -ki⁀.
sınnárro⁀ (s.v. -r⁀) adv. in (to) Sennár.
sınnárro⁀ (§6007) (s)he (it) is (they are) in Sennár.

sínne v.i. get angry [§§2870ff.].
ind. pres. aî⁀sínnɛri⁀; perf. aî⁀sínnɛgori⁀ (N. -ɛko-, -ɛho-).
tékkonon⁀sínnɛri⁀ I (shall §5369a) get angry with him (her, it).

sínnɛrar⁀ (-rár⁀; §§2200ff., 2210) and
sınnɛríd⁀ (§§2256ff., 2263) n. anger, rage.
tén⁀sınnɛríd⁀dúllón⁀ his (her) anger is great, lit....heavy.

sínne-bŭ- (§3931α) v.i. stat. be in an angry state or condition.
tır⁀ékkonŏ⁀sínnɛbūrá⁀ they are angry with you.

sínnɛg-ır (N. -ɛkır, -ɛhır; §3679) (a) v.t. caus. cause or allow to get angry; (b) v.t. render angry, anger, vex.

sɪntåd⌣...? — sōkɛrɛ́

sɪnnɛrīd-an-sínnɛ (§4161) v.i. *get very angry*.

sɪnnɛrīdansínnɛ-bŭ- (§4166) v.i. stat. *be in a very angry state*.

sɪnnɛrīdk-ɪr-sínnɛ (-ītkɪr-, -īttɪr- §716; §4159) v.i. = sɪnnɛrīdansínnɛ.
  sɪnnɛrīdkɪrsínnégó⌒ *(s)he (has) got into a great rage*.

sɪnnɛrīdkɪrsínnɛ-bŭ- (-ītkɪr-, -īttɪr-; §4165) v.i. stat. = sɪnnɛrīdansínnɛbŭ-.

sɪntåd⌣...? (-tåt? §469, -tǎ?, ɪntǎ? §967),
sɪntåg⌣...? (-tǎk? §469) and
sɪntågkɪ⌣...? (-åkkɪ⌣...?, -ki?) adv. *when?*
= ɪsantåd⌣...? q.v.
  gátɪr⌣sɪntåd⌣ɪmbélɪn? *when does the train start?*
  ɛr⌣sɪntåb⌣bɪmbélɪn? (-b⌣b- < -d⌣b- §518 or < -g⌣b- §519) *when will you start?*
  ɪr⌣sɪntåd⌣ɪmbélkoru? *when did you (pl.) start?*
  sɪntån⌣nógru? (-n⌣n- < -d⌣n- §624 or < -g⌣n- §625) *when do we (you pl.) go?*
  tén⌣dukkåŋgɪ⌣sɪntåk⌣kóbɪn? (-k⌣k- < -d⌣k- §568 or < -g⌣k- §569) *when does he shut his shop?*
  tén⌣dukkåŋgɪ⌣sɪntåk⌣kusíŋgɪ⌣nál⌒ *see when (ascertain at what time) he opens his shop.*
  sɪntåg⌣góñkoran? (-g⌣g- possibly < -d⌣g- §545) *when did they build it?*
  X. bɪnógran⌒ *they will go.*
  Y. sɪntå? *when?*
  sɪntådɪrtōn?,
  sɪntågɪrrotōn? and (§1008)
  sɪntågɪrotōn? *since when?*
  ɛr⌣sɪntågɪrrotōn⌣índ⌣ågɪn? *how long have you been here?* lit. *since (s.v. -rtŏn⌣) when are you here?*

sɪŋkåd⌣ (-åt⌒ §469) n. *Sɪnkåt* [< سِنْكَات], name applied to ó-kwākw, a small town in the hills above Suákɪn.
  obj. -ådk(ɪ)⌣, -åtk(ɪ)⌣, -ått(ɪ)⌣ §2462, -ki⌒, -ti⌒.
  gen. -ådn⌣v., -ånn⌣v.c., -ån⌣c.
  sɪŋkådɪr (s.v. -r⌣; §6007) adv. *at (to) Sɪnkåt*.
  sɪŋkådɪr⌣ *(s)he (it) is (they are) at Sɪnkåt*.
  sɪŋkådn⌣éssɪ⌣míllɪn⌒ (-ånn⌣és-) *the water of Sɪnkåt is bad*.

-sɪr < **tɪ́r** *give* (q.v.) when suffixed to -s.

sɪtt(ɪ)⌣ n. *mistress, lady* [< سِتّ (< سَيِّدَة) id. §1369].
  voc. -ti!
  obj. -tɪg⌣.
  pl. -tɪnč(ɪ)⌣.

sɪttīn⌣ (§956a) card. num. *sixty* [< سِتّين id.].
  obj. -íng(ɪ)⌣, -gi⌒.

sɪttīn-d(ɪ)⌣ (§§2545ff., 2738) adj. *appertaining to 60, of 60, 60's*.

sɪttīn-ínt(ɪ)⌣ (-tínɪnt(ɪ)⌣; §2742) ord. num. *sixtieth*.

sɪttíŋ-kɪrɪ⌣ (-kírɪ⌣ §1701; §2736) num. adj. *about sixty*.

síwɪd⌣ n. *sword* [*RSN*, §129 cps. Eg. sft *knife* Copt. ⲥⲏϥⲉ سَيف (ξίφος *EÆGl*; *LSG*, p. 176) *sword*].
  obj. sɪwídk(ɪ)⌣, -ítk(ɪ)⌣, -ítt(ɪ)⌣ §2462, -ki⌒, -ti⌒.

gen. sɪwídn⌣v., -wínn⌣v.c., -wín⌣c., and -́-, -́́-

pl. síwɪdɪ⌣.
  sɪwídn⌣åd⌣ and
  sɪwídn⌣ɛ́ *hilt of sword*.
  sɪwídn⌣ågɪl⌣ *blade of sword*.
  síwín-kā⌣ and
  síwíŋ-kā⌣ (§658) *scabbard*.
  síwɪŋ⌣kóčč(ɪ)⌣ (-ɪŋ-k-) *point of sword*.

sóbɛ n. *wall* [*RSN*, §§80, 129, *ZNG* s.v. ⲥⲁⲣⲁⲧⲁⲛ].
  obj. -bɛg⌣.
  pl. sobénč(ɪ)⌣.
  sóbɛ⌣síbɛgɛg⌣góñgūn⌒ (-g⌣g- < -d⌣g- §545, -ñğ- < -ñb- §635) *the wall is (has been) built of mud*.

sōdán⌣ *the Sudan* = sūdán⌣.

sóg v.t. *accompany, go or come with (in attendance on), escort*.
  ind. pres. āi⌣sóg(ɪ)ri⌒, ɛr⌣sógɪn⌒ (-gi⌒, -gí⌒); perf. āi⌣sógkori⌒ (⌣sókko-).
  imperat. sók!
  subj. past āi⌣sógsɪ⌣ (⌣sóksɪ⌣, -su⌣).
  part. pres. sógɪl⌣ *(one) that accompanies, etc., accompanier, etc., accompanying, etc.*, obj. sogílg(ɪ)⌣, -gi⌒; past sógɛl⌣ *(one) that accompanied, etc., accompanier, etc., accompanying, etc.*; obj. sogélg(ɪ)⌣, -gi⌒.
  båm⌣bókkos⌣sókkori⌒ (-m⌣b- < -bn⌣b- §586, -s⌣s- < -n⌣s- §680) *I accompanied him (her, them) as far as the door.*
  X. ní⌣tékkɪ⌣sókkon? *who (has) accompanied him (her)?*
  Y. kól⌣nókkon, wɛr⌣tékkɪ⌣sokkómunun⌒ *(s)he went (has gone) alone, no-one (has) accompanied him (her).*

sógar⌣ (-går⌣; §§2200ff.) and
sogíd⌣ (§§2256ff.) n. *accompanying, etc*.

sóg-an (§§3890ff.) v.t. *tell to accompany, etc., let accompany, etc.*

sóg-bŭ- (sóggŭ- §546; §3931β) v.i. stat. *be in an accompanied (etc.) state or condition*.

sog(')r-ɛg-ág- (§§4071ff.) v.t. = sogɛdól-.

sog-ɛ-dól- (-g°d- §1178; §4022) and
sog(')r-ɛ-dól- (-r°d-; §4027) v.t. *be about to accompany, etc.*

sog(')r-ɛ-ğŭ-bŭ- (§4069) v.t. stat. *be on one's way (coming) to accompany, etc.*

sog(')r-ɛ-nóg (§§4048ff.) v.t. *go to accompany, etc.*

sog(')r-ɛ-nóg-bŭ- (-nóggŭ- §546; §4058) v.t. stat. *be on one's way (going) to accompany, etc.*

sog(')r-ɛ-tå (§§4060ff.) v.t. *come to accompany, etc.*

soged-åg- (§§3877ff.) v.t. *be in the situation of having accompanied, etc.*

sogéd-dá- (§3991; -éggɪdā-, occ. -édgɪ- §§3993-4) v.t. *be going accompanying, etc., be going along in attendance on, be escorting along.*
  samílgɪ⌣sogéddān⌒ *he is accompanying (is going in attendance on) the sheikh.*
  āi⌣tékkɪ⌣sogeddágori⌒ *I was (have been) accompanying (him, her).*

sogɛn-nóg (§§4169ff.; -ɛggɪnóg §§4176-8) v.t. *go accompanying, go with, go in attendance on.*

imperat. sogennók! (-́- §1954), pl. -nógwɛ!, -nógwɛ́!
  mufɛttíškɪ⌣sogennókkó⌒ *he went (has gone) with (in attendance on) the inspector.*
  tékkɪ⌣sogeggɪnók⌒ (-́- §1955) *accompany him (her).*

sogɛt-tá (§§4169ff., 5723; -ɛggɪtā §§4176-8) v.t. *come accompanying, come escorting.*
  imperat. sogétta!, sogéggɪta!, pl. sogéttāwɛ!, -́́-, sogéggɪtāwɛ!, -́́-.
  íŋgét-tɛ⌣sogettåri? (§5369b) *I escort him (her) by this way?*
  tékkɪ⌣sogéggɪtågoran⌒ *they came (have come) escorting him (her).*

sog-ɛttá (-éttā §3855; §5723) v.t. *bring* (ɛttá s.v. éd) *under escort.*
  imperat. sogétta!, pl. sogéttāwɛ!, -́-́.

sóg-kattɪ- (sókka-; §4093) v.p. *be accompanied, etc.*

sŏgdán⌣ (§956a) *the Sudan* = sūdán⌣.

sŏgdán⌣ (§956a) n. *Sogdan (on map)*, a small island near Kérma [< السُّودَان < ssūdán *the blacks* §1390].
  obj. -dåŋ(ɪ)⌣, -gi⌒.
  gen. -dånn⌣v., -dån⌣c.

sōkɛrɛ́ v.t. *register (at post-office)* [< سَوْكَر -sókår of مَسَوْكَر *registered* (based on It. *assicuro*) + -ɛ́ §3633].
  ind. pres. āi⌣sōkɛrɛ́ri⌒; perf. āi⌣sōkɛrɛ́gori⌒ (N. -éko-, -ého-).
  imperat. sōkɛrɛ́!

sōkɛrɛ́rar⌣ (-rár⌣; §§2200ff., 2207) and
sōkɛrɛ́ríd⌣ (§§2256ff., 2260) n. *registration*.

sōkɛrɛ́r-an (§§3890ff., 3899) v.t. *tell to register, let register.*
  álɪğ⌣ğawåpkɪ⌣sōkɛrɛ́rá⌒ (-ğ⌣ğ- < -g⌣g- §551) *let ɛáli register the letter.*

sōkɛrɛ́-bŭ- (§3931β) v.i. stat. *be in a registered state or condition.*
  ğawåb⌣sōkɛrɛ́būn⌒ *the letter is (has been) registered.*

sōkɛrɛ́red-åg- (§§3877ff.) v.t. *be in the situation of having registered, etc.*
  ğawåbkɪ⌣sōkɛrɛ́redágin⌒ *(s)he has registered the letter.*

sōkɛrɛ́-kattɪ- (N. -éha-; §4093) v.p. *be registered.*

sókkɛ v.t. (a) *take up, pick up, hoist, raise, lift, carry*; then like Lat. *tollere*; (b) *take away, remove*; (c) *carry, hold, contain* [cp. ON. ⲥⲟⲕⲕ id. *GNT* s.v.; §§2870ff.].
  ind. pres. āi⌣sókkɛri⌒, ɛr⌣sókkɛn⌒ (-kɛ̄⌒, -kɛ́⌒); perf. āi⌣sókkɛgori⌒ (N. -éko-, -ého-).
  subj. past āi⌣sókkɛsɪ⌣ (-su⌣).
  part. pres. sókkɛl⌣ *(one) that takes up, etc., taker up, etc., taking up, etc.*, obj. sokkɛ́lg(ɪ)⌣, -gi⌒; past sókkɛrɛl⌣ *(one) that took up, etc., taker up, etc., taking up, etc.*, obj. sokkɛ́rɛlg(ɪ)⌣, -gi⌒.
  pl.-obj. ind. pres. āi⌣sokkɛ́rɛdri⌒; perf. āi⌣sókkɛ́ddikori⌒ (-étkori⌒, -éttori⌒ §716).
  def. pres. āi⌣sókkɛ́srɪ⌒ (-́- -́- §§1883-4; ⌣sókkɛrosri⌒); perf. āi⌣sókkóskori⌒ (⌣sokkɛróskori⌒); imperat. sókkos! (sókkós! §1892, -kó! §962) and sókkɛros! (-ró!), pl. sokkóswɛ! (-kóswɛ́, -kówwɛ,

-wé!, -kósse! §687, -sé!) and sokkeróswe! (-róswé!, -równe!, -wé!, -rósse!, -sé!).
aı‿íŋgı‿dólli; er‿wéd‿dólkım‿máŋgı‿sókke⌒ (-d‿d- < -g‿d- § 534) *I want this; if you want one take that yonder.*
er‿bústan‿íllár‿g̑awǎpkı‿sókkegoná? *did you take (have you taken) the letter for the post?*
én‿gawǎpkı‿sókkegoná? índo‿búgō⌒ *did you take (have you taken) your letter? it was (lying) here.*
X. šántád‿dēn⌒ (§ 1743; -d‿d- < -g‿d- § 534) *give me the valise.*
Y. aı‿sókkesıgá? (§ 5838d) *the one I took?*
bērákkı‿sókke⌒ (a) *hoist the flag* (=‿dogōgırsókke⌒); (b) *remove the flag.*
X. tókkon‿íŋg‿índotōn‿sókkemen⌒ *don't take this away from here.*
Y. aı̂‿bısókkemun⌒ (§ 5364) *I won't,* lit. *I shall not remove.*
sandúg‿dıgrígır‿dúlun, ogíčči‿sókken⌒ *the box is very large, it holds a man.*
kúb‿erdeb‿mílgı‿sókken⌒ *the boat holds 100 árdebbs* (أردب).
ánn‿úbur‿erdeb‿goríčči‿sókken⌒ *my (our) grain-cache holds six arádıb.*
fātáhkı‿sókkegoran⌒ *they (have) recited the fátıha* (شالوا الفاتحة).
*sókkar‿, *sokkíd‿ reported not said.
sókkerar‿ (-rár‿; §§ 2200ff., 2210) and
sokkeríd‿ (§§ 2256ff., 2263) n. *taking up, etc.*
kúm‿sokkeríd‿mıŋkótterré? *what is the capacity of the boat?*
sókker-an (§§ 3890ff., 3899) v.t. *tell to take up, etc., let take up, etc.*
sokk-árk(ı) (-aríkk(ı); § 3747ε′) v.t. *after taking up (etc.) throw (etc., s.v. árk(ı)).*
kúlus‿sokkárkıgó⌒ (-s‿s- < -g‿s- § 678) and
kúlus‿sókkeg‿árkıgó⌒ (§ 5586) *(s)he (has) picked up a stone and threw (has thrown) it.*
ár‿mám‿málles‿sokkururárkıgoru⌒ (§ 5605) *we took all that (other) and threw it into the river (we have taken... and thrown...).*
sokk-ark-úndur (-arıkk-; § 4198) v.t. *throw in(to) after taking up, etc.*
aı̂‿kúlus‿sokkarıkkururundúddi⌒ (§ 5605) *I('ll 5369b) take up (away) the (a) stone and throw it into the river.*
kúlus‿sokkurarıkkundúrkori⌒ *I took up (away) the (a) stone and threw it into the river (I have taken... and thrown...).*
íŋgı‿sokkururbarıkkundúddi⌒ *after taking up (away) this I shall throw it into the river.*
ár‿íŋgı‿sokkururbarıkkundúddu⌒ *we shall take this away and throw it into the river.*
sokker-eg-ág- (§§ 4071ff.) v.t. = sokkeredól-.
sokker-e-dól- (-r°d- § 1178; §§ 4016-17, 4022, 4027) v.t. *be about to take up, etc.*
sokker-e-g̑u-bu- (§ 4069) v.t. stat. *be on one's way (coming) to take up, etc.*

sokker-e-mǎ- (§§ 4016-17, 4036, 4041) v.t. *become unable to take up, etc.*
ar‿kúlu‿dúlgı‿sokkeremágoru⌒ *we couldn't lift the large stone(s § 4696d).*
sokker-e-nóg (§§ 4048ff.) v.t. *go to take up, etc.*
sokker-e-nóg-bu- (-nóggu- § 546; § 4058) v.t. stat. *be on one's way (going) to take up, etc.*
sokker-e-tá- (§§ 4060ff.) v.t. *come to take up, etc.*
sokked-ág- (§§ 3540, 3877ff.) v.t. *be in the situation of having taken up, etc., be carrying.*
X. éw‿wıččírkı‿tókkon‿íwmen⌒ (-w‿w- < -n‿w- § 720) *don't forget your stick.*
Y. aı‿sokkedágri⌒ *I've taken it.*
X. šántád‿dēn⌒ *give me the valise.*
Y. aı̂‿sokkedágrıgá? *the one I am carrying?,* lit. *the one I am in the situation of having taken up?*
Z. aı̂‿sokkedágsıgá? *the one I was carrying?*
sokked-ág- (§§ 3540, 3877ff.) v.t. = sokkedág-.
sokked-árk(ı) (§§ 4169ff.; -keggár- §§ 4176-8; -aríkk(ı)) v.t. *throw (etc., s.v. árk(ı)) after taking up, etc.*
kúlus‿sokkedárkıgó⌒ (-s‿s- < -g‿s- § 678) and
kúlus‿sokkeggárkıgó⌒ *(s)he took up and threw (... has taken up and thrown) a (the) stone.*
kúlug‿úrur‿sokkedárkı⌒ (-keggár-) and (§ 5605)
kúlus‿sokkedururárkı⌒ (-keggur-) *pick up a (the) stone and throw it into the river.*
sokked-dā- (§ 3990; -kéggı-dā-, occ. -kédgı- §§ 3993-4) v.t. *be going along having taken up, etc., be carrying along.*
ind. pres. aı̂‿sokkeddári⌒, er‿sokkeddán⌒ (-éddá⌒, -éddá⌒).
X. berrád‿šándı‿tómbıbún⌒ *the teapot is broken.*
Y. ní‿sokkeddāsíŋgı‿nál⌒ (§ 6124) *see who was carrying it along.*
sokken-nóg (§§ 4169ff.; -keggınóg, occ. -kedgı- §§ 4176-8) v.t. *go (etc., s.v. nóg) after taking up, etc., go (off) with (λαβών), carry off.*
ír‿nókkıru, wıččır‿kómbos‿sokkennógwe⌒ (-s‿s- < -g‿s- § 678) *when you (pl.) go, take a strong stick with you,* lit.... *go taking a strong stick.*
dúŋgıs‿sokkennókkó⌒ *(s)he went (has gone) off with the money.*
sokke-sóg *accompany, etc., after taking up, etc. infra.*
sokkes-sóg (§§ 4169ff.; -keggısóg, occ. -kedgı- §§ 4176-8) v.t. *accompany (etc., s.v. sóg) after taking up, etc., accompany (etc.) with (λαβών).*
éw‿wıččírkı‿sokkessók⌒ (-w‿w- < -n‿w- § 720) *take your stick and accompany him (her, them § 5083); accompany him (her, them) with your stick).*
sokket-tá- (§§ 4169ff., 5723; -keggıtá, occ. -kedgı- §§ 4176-8) v.t. *come after taking up, etc., come carrying.*

ind. pres. aı̂‿sokkettári⌒, er‿sokkettán⌒ (-ettá⌒, -ettá⌒); perf. aı̂‿sokkettágori⌒ (N. -áko-, -áho-).
imperat. sokketta! (-kéggıta!), pl. sokkettáwe!, ⎯⎯́́, sokkeggıtáwe!, ⎯⎯́́.
íŋg‿aı̂gonos‿sokkétta! (-s‿s- < -n‿s- § 680) and
íŋg‿sókked-aı̂gonón-ta! (§§ 5605, 1742) *come with me (you) carrying this (take this and come with me).*
sokk-ettá (-ettá § 3855, § 5723) v.t. *bring (ettá s.v. éd) after taking up, etc., bring in one's hand(s) or arm(s).*
imperat. sokkétta!, pl. sokkéttáwe!, ⎯́⎯́.
sokke-g̑óm (§ 3747ε′) v.t. *strike (etc., s.v. g̑óm) after taking up, etc.*
tén‿zummáras‿sokkeg̑ómkó⌒ (-s‿s- < -g‿s- § 678) *he took up his pipe and played on it.*
téw‿wıččírkı‿sokkeg̑ómkó⌒ (-w‿w- < -n‿w- § 720) *taking up his stick he beat him (her, it, them § 5083).*
sókke-katti- (N. -eha-; § 4093) v.p. *be taken up, etc.*
sokkéŋ-ır (sókkeŋgır; N. -ŋkır; § 3688) v.t. caus. *cause or allow to take up, etc.*
ind. pres. aı̂‿sokkéŋgıddi⌒ (⎯⎯́, ⎯⎯́ § 1819).
tókkon‿álıg‿éssis‿sókkeŋgırmen⌒ (-s‿s- < -g‿s- § 678) *don't let (make) ε áli take the water away.*
S. íŋgı‿turúkkı‿dókkon‿sókkeŋgırmen⌒ *don't let the wind carry this (that) away.*
aı̂‿tírgı‿šéjı-wēb‿bısokkeraŋgırímmunun⌒ (-b‿b- < -g‿b- § 519) *I shall not let (anyone of § 5456) them take anything away;* aı̂‿tírgı‿ omissible (§§ 5078, 5083).
sokk-og̑os-tá- (-og̑ottá § 714; § 4189; -og̑osgıtá, -ozgı-, -oggı- § 4190) v.t. *come (back) after picking up and removing, just (s.v. -tá) take up and carry away.*
imperat. sokkog̑ósta! (-ótta!), sokkog̑ósgıta! (-ozgı-, -óggı-).
sókkos-an (§§ 3890ff., 3905) v.t. *tell to take up, etc., let take up, etc.*
sokkóswan! (-swá!, -swá!, -óssan!, -sá!, -sá!, -ówwan!, -wá!, -wá!; § 3900; -ánır! § 3901) *tell them to take it up, etc.*
sokk-ós (§ 3747ε′) v.t. *after taking up (etc.) take (bring s.v. ós) out, take up and out.*
sokkós-an (§§ 3890ff., 3905) v.t. *tell to take up and out, etc., let take up and out, etc.*
sokkos-nedmé (-onned- § 629; §§ 4180-4; -osgıne-, -ozgı-, -oggı- § 4185) v.t. *regret after taking up, etc.*
sokkonnedméran‿génun‿mugonnedméran‿dógor⌒ *to regret after taking is better than to regret after leaving behind* (a version of شيل أندم ولا تخلّي تندم).
sókkeros-an (§§ 3890ff., 3905) v.t. *tell to take up, etc., let take up, etc.*
sokkeróswan! (-swá!, -swá!, -óssan!, -sá!, -sá!, -ówwan!, -wá!, -wá!) *tell them to take it up, etc.*

sólıb⌣ — -ssŏd⌣

sokkɛ-sóg (§3747ε') v.t. *accompany (etc., s.v. sóg) after taking up, etc., accompany (etc.) with* (λαβών).
  fānúskı⌣sokkɛsók⌢ (§5596) *accompany him (her, them* §5083) *with a lantern.*
  ɛ́w⌣wıččírkı⌣sokkɛsók⌢ (-w⌣w- <-n⌣w- §720) *take your stick and accompany him (her, them).*

sokkɛ-sogɛn-nóg (§4179; -sogɛggı-nóg, occ. -ɛdgı- §4179b) v.t. *after taking up (etc.) go accompanying (etc., s.v. sogɛn-nóg), go accompanying with* (λαβών).
  fānúskı⌣sokkɛsogɛnnók⌢ *take the lantern and go with him (her, them).*

sokkɛs-sogɛn-nóg (§4196a) v.t. *go accompanying* (a person) *after taking up* (an object).
  wıččírkı⌣sokkɛssogɛnnók⌢ *take a stick and go with him (her, them).*

sokkɛ-wídɛgır (-wıdɛgír, -wᵘdé-, N. -ɛkır, -ékır, -ɛhır, -éhır; §4133a) v.t. caus. *cause to turn (etc., s.v. wídɛ) after taking up, etc.*

sólıb⌣ (-ıp⌢) n. *Saleb* (on map), *a village on the right bank of the Nile, about 9 miles below Ed-Débbá*ʰ [> صَلَب *crosses*].
  obj. solíbk(ı)⌣, -ípk(ı)⌣, -kı⌢.

sóll(ı) v.i. *get suspended, hang, become pendent, hang down.*
  ind. pres. āı⌣sóllırı⌢; perf. āı⌣sóllıgorı⌢ (N. -ıko-, -ıho-).
  imperat. sólli!
  ǵówwır⌣sóllıgorā⌢ *they hang on (up in, down from) the tree.*

sólli-bŭ- (§3931α) v.i. stat. *be in a state or condition of suspension, be hanging, etc.*
  fānús⌣ólgɛn⌣sóllıbūn⌢ *the lantern is still hanging up.*
  ǵówwır⌣sóllıburan⌢ *they are hanging on (etc.) the tree.*

sólli-bᵘ-an (-b(w)an; §§3962-3) v.t. *have, or let be, in a state of suspension, etc.*
  X. fānúskı⌣dógor⌣mugó⌢ *leave the lantern aloft.*
  Y. āı⌣sóllıbandı⌢ *I('ll* §5369b) *let it hang.*

sóllıg-ır (N. -ıkır, -ıhır; §3682) (a) v.t. caus. *cause or allow to get suspended, etc.;* (b) v.t. *suspend, hang, hang up.*
  ind. pres. āı⌣sóllıgıddı⌢, ɛr⌣sóllıgırın⌢ (-rī⌢, -rí⌢).
  fānúskı⌣sóllıgírkoran⌢ *they (have) hung the lantern up.*

sóllıgır-an (N. -ıkır-, -ıhır-; §§3890ff., 3904) v.t. *tell to suspend, etc., let suspend, etc.*
  álıf⌣fānúskı⌣sóllıgıran⌢ (-f⌣f- <-g⌣f- §540) *let ɣáli hang the lantern up.*

sollıgırɛd-ág- (N. -ıkır-, -ıhır-; §3877ff.) v.t. *be in the situation of having suspended, etc.*

sollıgıros-šákk(ı) (N. -ıkır-, -ıhır-; -oššák- §701; §§4180-4; -ıssıšák-, -ozgı-, -oggı- §4185) v.t. *shake after suspending.*
  íččım⌣béñgı⌣sollıgıroššákkıran⌢ *having suspended the skin of milk they shake it.*

sólli-kattı- (N. -ıha-; §4098) v.p. *be suspended.*
  fānús⌣sollıkattıráŋŋı⌣móŋkó⌢ (-ŋŋ- <-ŋg- §662) *the lantern couldn't*

(lit. *wouldn't) be hung up* (cp. Amh. ፋኑስ፡አልሰቀለም፡አለ። fānus⌣alıssáqqəlımm⌣álə. id. §§209, 236).

sór⌣ n. *Suri* (on map), *a village and district on the left bank of the Nile about 7 miles below Hándag.*
  obj. sórk(ı)⌣, -kı⌢.
  sórro⌣ (s.v. -r⌣) *at (to) Sór.*
  sórró⌢ (§§1532, 6007) *(s)he (it) is (they are) at Sór.*

sórtod⌣ (-ot⌢) n. *Sortot* (on map), *a village and district on the left bank of the Nile, about 8 miles above Urdi [Little Sór].*
  ín⌣sórtodun⌢ *this is Sórtod.*

sór-an- (§3910β) v.i. *go to Sór.*

sóram-bŭ- (§3950β) v.i. stat. *be in a state of motion towards Sór.*
  sórambūrı⌢ *I am on my way to Sór.*

sóranɛd-ág- (§3966β) v.i. *be in the situation of having gone to Sór.*

sóran-nog(¹)r-ɛg-ág- (§3980) v.i. =sórannogɛdól-.

sóran-nog-ɛ-dól- (-gᵒd- §1178; §3979) and
sóran-nog(¹)r-ɛ-dól- (-rᵒd-; §3981) v.i. *be about to go to Sór.*
  sórannogedóllı⌢ *I am just going to Sór.*

sóran-nog-ɛ-mā́- (§3982) and
sóran-nog(¹)r-ɛ-mā́- (§3983) v.i. *become unable to go to Sór.*
  sórannogɛmāgorı⌢ *I couldn't (haven't been able to) go to Sór.*

sórıñ⌣ n. *nose* [RSN, §129; TOB, §143, 309].
  obj. soríñg(ı)⌣ (-íng(ı)⌣ §647), -gı⌢.
  pl. sórıñı⌣.
  soríñı⌣éndɛ⌣ and
  soríñı⌣úmbu⌣ *bridge of the nose.*
  soríñı⌣tắr⌣ (-ñı̄t- <-ñn⌣t- §843) *in(side) the nose.*

soríñ-d(ı)⌣ (§§2545ff.) adj. *appertaining to the nose, nasal.*

sórod⌣ n. *scrotum.*
  obj. soródk(ı)⌣, -ótk(ı)⌣, -ótt(ı)⌣ §2462, -kı⌢, -tı⌢.
  gen. soródn⌣., -rón⌣c.
  pl. sórodı⌣.
  sorón⌣dílt(ı)⌣ *pubes on scrotum.*
  sorón⌣kúmbu⌣ (-óŋk- §651) *testicle(s* §4696a).

sorón-d(ı)⌣ (§§2545ff.) adj. *scrotal.*

soróğ⌣ (-óč⌣) n. *Sorog* (on map), *a village on the left bank of the Nile, west of Bádın Island near Kérma.*
  obj. -óčk(ı)⌣ (§523), -čı⌢.
  soróğır⌣ (s.v. -r⌣) *at (to) Soróğ.*
  soróğır⌢ (§6007) *(s)he (it) is (they are) at Soróğ.*

sóww(ı) v.i. *get dry, dry, dry up.*
  ind. pres. āı⌣sówwırı⌢; perf. āı⌣sówwıgorı⌢ (-wᵘg- §1202; N. -ıko-, -ıho-).
  ín⌣árıd⌣sútte⌣sówwın⌢ *this soil dries quickly.*
  éssı⌣bısówwın⌢ *the water will dry up.*
  éssı⌣sowwóskó⌢ *the water has dried up.*
  tɛr⌣sówwᵘgın⌣úndur⌢ *when it gets dry put it in.*
  aŋ⌣kóñ⌣sówwın⌢ *I am (we are) ashamed, lit. my (our) face dries.*

sówwar⌣ (-wăr⌣; §§2200ff.) and
sówwíd⌣ (§§2256ff.) n. *drying, desiccation.*

sóww-an (§§3890ff.) v.t. *let get dry, etc.*
  íŋ⌣kádɛs⌣sówwan⌢ (-s⌣s- <-g⌣s- §678) *let this cloth (etc., s.v. kádɛ⌣) dry.*
  íŋ⌣kadéncıs⌣sówwıwan⌢ (⌣sówwıwánırır⌢ §5456) *let these cloths (etc.) dry.*

sówwɛd⌣ (-wod- §1200) adj. (a) *dry;* (b) *avaricious, stingy* [§2522].
  obj. sówwɛdk(ı)⌣, -ɛ́tk(ı)⌣, -ɛ́tt(ı)⌣ §2462, -kı⌢, -tı⌢.
  pl. sówwɛdı⌣.
  úluk⌣sówwedun⌢ (-k⌣s- <-g⌣s- §576) *the leaf is (leaves are* §4696b) *dry (withered, dead).*
  hartúm⌣háwa⌣sówwódun⌢ (§1966) *the climate of Khartoum is dry.*
  tɛr⌣sówwɛd⌣én⌣úndur⌢ *when it's dry put it in.*

sówwɛd-an- (§3910α) v.i. *get dry, etc.*

sówwɛdam-bŭ- (§§3949ff.) v.i. stat. *be in a drying (up) or dried (up) state or condition.*

sówwɛ́dk-ır (-ɛ́tkır, -ɛ́ttır §716; §3702) (a) v.t. caus. *cause or allow to be dry, etc.;* (b) v.t. *render dry, dry, dry up.*
  ind. pres. āı⌣sówwédkıddı⌢.

sówwɛ́dkır-an (-ɛ́tkı-, -ɛ́ttı-; §§3890ff., 3904) v.t. *tell to or cause or allow to dry, etc.*

sówwı-bŭ- (-wᵘbŭ-; §3931α) v.i. stat. *be in a dry state or condition.*
  kál⌣íkkɛs⌣sówwıbūl⌣ (-s⌣s- <-d⌣s- §677) *bread that has been dried by means of fire* (e.g. the toast *that Europeans cause to be made).*

sóww-ídd(ı) (-wúd- §1201; §3721) (a) v.t. caus. *cause or allow to get dry, etc.;* (b) v.t. *render dry, dry, dry up.*
  ind. pres. āı⌣sówwíddırı⌢; perf. āı⌣sówwíddıgorı⌢ (N. -ıko-, -ıho-).
  sowwúddırıá? *shall* (§5369b) *I dry it?*
  énn-ıs⌣sowwíddı⌢ (-s⌣s- <-g⌣s- §678) *dry your hand(s* §4696a).
  ár⌣kálgı⌣furúndo⌣sowwíddıru⌣ sáfarn⌣íllār⌢ *we dry bread in the oven for a journey.*

sówwídd-an (-wúd-; §§3890ff., 3904) v.t. *tell to or let, cause or allow to get dry.*
  tékk⌣íŋ⌣kádɛs⌣sowwíddan⌢ (-s⌣s- <-g⌣s- §678) *let him (her, it) dry this cloth (etc., s.v. kádɛ⌣).*
  tékk⌣íŋ⌣kadéncıs⌣sówwıddíran⌢ *let him (her, it) dry these (various) cloths.*

sówwıddós-dɛn (-wud-; -óddɛn §538; §§4180-4, 3995ff.; -ósgıdɛn, -ózgı-, -óggı- §4185) v.t. *give (to the speaker) after drying, dry for (the speaker).*
  fu⌣toddém⌣mɛ́r⌣ígır⌣sowwuddóddɛn⌢ (-m⌣m- <-g⌣m- §601) *cut a little bread and when you have toasted it give it to me* (...and toast *it for me).*

sówwıddós-tır (-wud-; -óttır §714; -óssır §686; §§4180-4, 3995ff.; -ósgıtır, -ózgı-, -óggı- §4185) v.t. *give (to other than the speaker) after drying, dry for (other than the speaker).*

sówwıg-ir (-wug-; N. -ıkır, -ıhır; §3682) v.t. caus. and v.t. =sówwédkır.

sówwıgır-an (-wug-; N. -ıkır-, -ıhır-; §§3890ff., 3904) v.t. =sówwédkıran.

-ssŏd⌣ (§2368a) n. *sister's child, nephew, niece* = -ɛssın⌣tŏd⌣ [< *-stŏd⌣ (§686) < *-sstŏd⌣ < *-ɛss-tŏd⌣].

180

súd — súg

voc. -ssŏt!
obj. -ssŏdk(ı)⌣, -ssŏtk(ı)⌣, -ssŏkk(ı)⌣, -ssŏtt(ı)⌣ §2462, -kı⌢, -tı⌢.
gen. -ssŏdn⌣v., -ssŏnn⌣v.c., -ssŏn⌣c.
pl. -ssonı⌣.
— always with a form of the possessive personal pronoun (§2631) prefixed:
ássŏd⌣ *my sister's child* [a much worn-down form of ánnessın⌣tód⌣ *id*.].
íssŏd⌣ *your sister's child.*
tíssŏd⌣ *his (her) sister's child.*
ántıssŏd⌣ *our sister's child.*
íntıssŏd⌣ *your (pl.) sister's child.*
tíntıssŏd⌣ *their sister's child.*
súd v.t. *miss, fail to attain* [cp. súd⌣ *empty* §2495].
ind. pres. aï⌣súdri⌢; perf. aï⌣súdkori⌢ (⌣sútk-).
imperat. sút!
tɛr⌣bundúkkeğ⌣ğómkó⌢ súdkó⌢ (-ğ⌣ğ- < -d⌣ğ- §550) *he (has) fired and missed.*
X. dŭrkoná? *did you get (have you got) it?*
Y. súdkori⌢ *I (have) missed it.*
gókkas⌣sútkori⌢ (-s⌣s- < -g⌣s- §678).
gókkar⌣sútkori⌢ and
gókkartōn⌣sútkori⌢ *I (have) missed the pigeon.*
gɛ̈lgı⌣sútkó⌢,
gɛ̈llo⌣sútkó⌢ and
gɛ̈llotōn⌣sútkó⌢ *he (has) missed the gazelle.*
súdar (-dàr⌣; §§2200ff.) and
sudíd (§§2256ff.) n. *missing, failure to attain.*
súd-bŭ- (§3931 β) v.i. stat. *be in a missed (etc.) state or condition.*
gókka⌣súdbún⌢ *the pigeon has been missed.*
sudɛd-ág- (§§3877ff.) v.t. *be in the situation of having missed, etc.*
súd-kattı- (sútk-; §4093) v.p. *be missed, etc.*
súd⌣ (a) adj. *empty, vacant, bare, mere;* (b, used as n. §4954) *emptiness, vacancy, nothing* [cp. súd *miss* §2495].
obj. súdk(ı)⌣, sútk(ı)⌣, súdtt(ı)⌣ §2462, -kı⌢, -tı⌢.
gen. súdn⌣v., súnn⌣v.c., sún⌣c.
pl. súdı⌣.
ıbríg⌣súdk⌣ɛttágon⌢ *(s)he (has) brought the (an) empty pot.*
sandúg⌣súdun⌢ *the box is empty.*
ín⌣gáhw⌣éssı⌣súdun⌢ *this coffee is mere water.*
ím⌣béled⌣éskes⌣súdun⌢ (-s⌣s- < -d⌣s- §677) *this country is all dust,* lit. *is mere dust.*
ín⌣sún⌣dógor⌣génun⌢ *this is better than nothing* (دا أَحْسَن عَن ساكِت).
súd-ır (§4446) adv. *in vacancy, vacantly, merely, only, just.*
súdır⌣ágın⌢ *(s)he (it) just sits,* i.e. *is doing nothing, merely exists* (Sudan Ar. يَقعد ساكِت).
aï⌣súdır⌣ágri⌢ *I am unoccupied (at leisure).*
súdır⌣dán⌣ *(s)he (it) merely is present,* i.e. *is present and does nothing.*
súdn⌣ágar⌣ and
súdnagar⌣ n. *time or situation in which one has nothing to do, spare time, leisure.*
obj. súdn⌣agárk(ı)⌣, -kı⌢ and sūdnagárk(ı)⌣, -kı⌢.
ar⌣súdnagárkı⌣dóllu⌢ *we want (like) leisure.*
aï⌣súdnagárk⌣ɛlkómunun⌢ *I (have) found no leisure.*
súd-an- (§3910α) v.i. *become empty, etc.*
gırbád⌣súdaŋkó⌢ *the water-skin (has) got empty.*
súdam-bŭ (§§3949ff.) v.i. stat. *be in an emptying (i.) or empty state or condition.*
sūdan-túrb(ı) (-túbb(ı) §520; §4151) v.i. *lie empty.*
sūdantúrb-an (-túbb-; §§3890ff., 3905) v.t. *let lie empty.*
ín⌣agárkı⌣sūdantúbbá⌣ *let this place remain empty (keep this place clear).*
súdır-bŭ- (§3945) v.i. stat. *be in an empty (etc.) state or condition, lie vacant, lie idle.*
tér⌣árıd⌣súdırbú, bŭrú⌢ *that* (§5105) *land lies waste, it is uncultivated.*
tér⌣árıd⌣ɛwırbūlmunun, súdırbūltànnan⌢ *that land is not under cultivation, it is what is lying fallow.*
súdk-ır (sútk-; §3702) (a) v.t. caus. *cause or allow to be empty, etc.;* (b) v.t. *render empty, etc., empty.*
súdkır-an (§§3890ff., 3904) v.t. *tell to empty, let empty.*
sútte (sútté §4408) adv. *quickly, fast* [< *súdk-ɛ (§716) *saying emptiness, saying nothing, just acting*].
aï⌣sútte⌣báuri⌢ *I shall do it quickly.*
sútte⌣bınógri⌢ *I shall go quickly.*
súttɛ⌣ettá⌢ *bring him (her, it, them) quickly.*
súttɛ⌣ettáran⌢ *tell him (her) to bring him (her, it, them) quickly.*
súttɛ⌣tá! (súttɛ⌣ta! §1742) *come quickly!*
súttɛ⌣táwɛ! *come (pl.) quickly!*
sútté! (§3601) interj. and v. imperat. *quick!, be quick!, make haste!*
pl. sútte̋wɛ! (sútte̋wé!).
sutte-nóg (§4127) v.i. *go quickly.*
suttenóg-an (§§3890ff., 3905) v.t. *tell or allow to go quickly.*
sutte-tá (§4127) v.i. *come quickly.*
suttɛtár-an (§§3890ff., 3905) v.t. *tell or allow to come quickly.*
sutt-ɛttá (-éttă §3855) v.t. *bring quickly.*
suttɛttár-an (-éttaran; §§3890ff., 3905) v.t. *tell or allow to bring quickly.*
sūdán⌣ (sōdán⌣, sōgdán⌣; §956a) n. *the Sudan* [< السودان ssudán *the blacks*].
obj. -dáŋ(ı)⌣, -gi⌢.
gen. -dánn⌣v., -dán⌣c.
sūdándo⌣ (s.v. -r⌣; §6007) *in (to) the Sudan.*
sūdándo⌢ *(s)he (is) (they are) in the Sudan.*
sūdán-d(ı)⌣ (sōd-, sōgd-; §§2545ff.) adj. *appertaining to the Sudan, of the Sudan, Sudanese.*
obj. -dıg⌣.
pl. -dınč(ı)⌣.
suffára n. *whistle (instrument)* [< Sudan Ar. صَفَّارة *id.* §1336].
obj. -rag⌣.
pl. -ranč(ı)⌣.
bābŭr⌣suffárağ⌣ğómkó⌢ (-ğ⌣ğ- < -g⌣ğ- §551) *the steamer (train) (has) whistled.*
súfra (-rà⌣) n. *table (for meals)* [< سُفرة *id.*].
obj. -rag⌣.
pl. -ranč(ı)⌣.
†súfran⌣fúta⌣ (Eur.) *table-cloth.*
†súfráŋ-kă⌣ (Eur.) *dining-room.*
sufráğı⌣ (§1575) n. *table-waiter, waiter* [< سُفْرَجي *id.*].
obj. -ğıg⌣.
pl. sufrağınč(ı)⌣.
sufrağınčı⌣dámunan⌢ *there are no waiters (the waiters are absent).*
X. mınín⌣ğéllıg⌣ağáuran? *what work are they doing?*
Y. sufráğınčí⌣ *they are waiters.*
súg n. *large round flat loaf or cake, two or three inches thick and 20 inches or so in diameter, made esp. for use on journeys; with collective sg.* (§4696d) [§2049; cogn. Eth. Tĕ. Tña. Amh. ሥግ *food for journey* §2031].
obj. súgk(ı)⌣, súkk(ı)⌣, -kı⌢.
pl. súgı⌣.
súk⌣kóččérro⌣bíllɛgoŋ⌣undúddaŋ⌣ kóččérro⌣béntıgoŋ⌣undúddan⌢ *in some cakes they put onions* (§4696a) *as well* (s.v. -on⌣), *in others they put dates as well.*
súg⌣maróndı⌣dán⌣ıllén dı⌣dán⌣ *there is cake made of millet and* (§6239) *(cake) made of wheat.*
súgar n. *satchel, bag attached to the body* [< *súgár⌣ < súg- *cake* + -ár *hold*, so *cake-holder §2198].
obj. sugárk(ı)⌣, -kı⌢.
pl. súgarı⌣.
súg v.t. *bake, make (the cake called* súg⌣) [§2049].
ind. pres. aï⌣súgri⌢, ɛr⌣súgi⌢); perf. aï⌣súgkori⌢ (⌣súkkori⌢).
imperat. súk!
súkkı⌣déwır⌣súkkori⌢ *I (have) baked the cake on the bake-stone.*
kálgı⌣déwır⌣súkkori⌢ *I (have) baked the bread on the bake-stone.*
súgar⌣ (-gàr⌣; §§2200ff.) and
sugíd (§§2256ff.) n. *baking, etc.*
súg-an (§§3890ff.) v.t. *tell to bake, etc., let bake, etc.*
súg-bŭ- (súggŭ- §546; §3931β) v.i. stat. *be in a baked state or condition.*
kál⌣súggún⌢ *the bread is (has been) baked.*
suged-ág- (§§3877ff.) v.t. *be in the situation of having baked, etc.*
súg-kattı- (súkkat-; §4093) v.p. *be baked, etc.*
súg⌣ n. *market* [< سُوق *id.*].
obj. súgk(ı)⌣, súkk(ı)⌣, -kı⌢.
gen. súgn⌣v., sún⌣c.
pl. súgı⌣.
súgır⌣ (s.v. -r⌣; §6007) adv. *in (to) the market.*
súgır⌢ *(s)he (it) is (they are) in the market.*

súgır⌣nálkori⌢ I saw (have seen) him (her, it, them) in the market.
sŭŋ-d(ı)⌣ (súgnd(ı)⌣, súgŋd(ı)⌣, súŋŋd(ı)⌣ §643; §§2545 ff.) adj. *appertaining to the market, of or from the market.*
sŭ́g-an- (§3910β) v.i. *go to (the) market.*
  ind. pres. aī⌣súgandi⌢, ɛr⌣súganın⌢ (-nī⌢, -ní⌢); fut. aī⌣bısúgandi⌣ (⌣bus-); perf. aī⌣súgaŋkori⌢.
  subj. past aī⌣súgansı⌣ (-assı⌣ §680, -su⌣).
sŭ́gam-bŭ- (§3950β) v.i. stat. *be in a state of motion towards the market, be on one's way to (the) market, be proceeding to (the) market.*
sŭ́ganɛd-ág- (§3966β) v.i. *be in the situation of having gone to (the) market.*
sŭ́gan-nog(ı)r-ɛg-ág- (§3980) v.i. = sŭ́gan-nogɛdól-.
sŭ́gan-nog-ɛ-dól- (-gᵒd- §1178; §3979) and
sŭ́gan-nog(ı)r-ɛ-dól- (-rᵒd-; §3981) v.i. *be about to go off to (the) market.*
sŭ́gan-nog-ɛ-mă- (§3982) and
sŭ́gan-nog(ı)r-ɛ-mă- (§3983) v.i. *become unable to go off to (the) market.*
súgar⌣ satchel s.v. súg⌣.
súkkar⌣ (-kár⌣) n. *sugar* [< سُكَّر id.].
  obj. sukkárk(ı)⌣, -ki⌢.
súkk(ı) v.t. *chew (tobacco: distinguish from ğókk(ı) chew food)* [obj. case of súg⌣ cake stereotyped as verbal stem §2852].
  ind. pres. aī⌣súkkıri⌢; perf. aī⌣súkkıgori⌢ (N. -ıko-, -ıho-).
  imperat. súkki!
  tumbákkı⌣súkkıran⌢ *they chew tobacco.*
súkkar⌣ (-kár⌣; §§2200 ff.) and
sukkíd⌣ (§§2256 ff.) n. *chewing.*
  tumbág⌣súkkar⌣ *chewing (of) tobacco.*
súkk-an (§§3890 ff.) v.t. *tell to chew, let chew.*
súkkı-bŭ- (§3931β) v.i. stat. *be in a chewed state or condition.*
  tumbág⌣súkkıbūn⌢ *the tobacco is (has been) chewed.*
súkkı-kattı- (N. -ıha-; §4093) v.p. *be chewed.*
  ín⌣tumbág⌣súkkıkattın⌢ *this tobacco is (can be §5704) chewed.*
sukkṓd⌣ = sıkkṓd⌣ *Sukkōt.*
súlɛ n. *earthenware jar, pot* [< √súl- *round (§4589) + -ɛ *being, so *what is round §2234β].
  obj. súlɛg⌣.
  pl. sulɛ́nč(ı)⌣.
  súlɛ⌣síbɛrtōn⌣ (s.v. -rtōn⌣) *the (a) clay pot.*
  súlɛ⌣síbɛrtōn⌢ (§6007) *the pot is (made) of clay.*
  súl⌣éssıgon⌣ğakútkonon⌣ıllár⌢ *the súlɛ⌣ is both for (holding) water and for cooking.*
súlgadɛ n. *cog; with collective sg.* (§4696d) [< √súl- *circle (§4589) i.e. the (engaged) wheel + -g obj. suff. + -ad *seizure (§2184) + -ɛ of n. dic. or n. act. (§2234), so *what says 'I seize the wheel' or *what effects seizing the wheel §2187].
  obj. -dɛg⌣.
  pl. -dɛnč(ı)⌣.
sultānı́jɛ⌣ (-já⌣, -ja⌣) n. *bowl* [< سُلْطَانِيَّة id.].

obj. -jɛg⌣, -jág⌣, -jag⌣.
pl. -jɛnč(ı)⌣, -jánč(ı)⌣, -janč(ı)⌣.
súlu n. *(a) pedlar; (b) shoemaker, cobbler* [< √súl- *round (§4589) + -u⌣ dem., so *the one that goes round §§2337-8].
  obj. -lug⌣.
  pl. -luı⌣, súlwı⌣.
  súlu⌣mɛrkúbkı⌣mɛ́rın⌢ *the shoemaker cuts out shoes (sc. from a hide).*
sumárk(ı) v.i. *(a, of animate objects) be in a hurry, be eager to proceed; (b, of inanimate objects) be urgent, be pressing* [§2853] (zürnen, RN s.v. zumark, sich ärgern, verdrossen sein, AZN s.v. simárk, ärgerlich sein, LN s.v. simarke, not traced in D.).
  ind. pres. aī⌣sumárkıri⌢, ɛr⌣sumárkın⌢ (-kī⌢, -kí⌢); perf. aī⌣sumárkıgori⌢ (N. -ıko-, -ıho-).
  X. kınnég⌣ğóbbɛ⌢ (-ğ-ğ-< -g-ğ- §551) *wait a little.*
  Y. wăran, aī⌣sumárkıri⌢, bābúr⌣ımbɛlɛdólın⌢ *no, I'm in a hurry, the steamer (train) is just going to start.*
  ɛr⌣sumárkıná? *are you in a hurry?*
  ín⌣sumárkımunun⌢ *(a) this person is not in a hurry; (b) this matter is not urgent.*
  ín⌣ğawáb⌣sumárkın⌢ *this letter is urgent.*
  tárıd⌣sumárkıgó⌢ *the parcel was urgent.*
sumárkar⌣ (-kár⌣; §§2200 ff.) and
sumárkíd⌣ (§§2256 ff.) n. *hurry, urgency.*
sumárkı-nóg (§3747ε') v.i. *go (away) in haste.*
  imperat. sumárkınók!
sumárkı-tá (§3747ε') v.i. *come in haste.*
  imperat. sumárkıtá!, sumárkıta! (§1871).
súmbud⌣ n. *foundation; with collective sg.* (§4696d) [cp. ON. ⲥⲟⲙⲡⲟⲩⲧ id. ZNG s.v.; with súm- cp. Eg. śntj Grundriss, Copt. ⲥⲛⲧⲉ Grund, Basis, EÆGl; SKG, §99; -bud⌣ app. < *-buıd⌣ (§§2256-7, 2340) *lying n. verbi of bú lie].
  obj. sumbúdk(ı)⌣, -útk(ı)⌣, -útt(ı)⌣ §2462, -ki⌢, -tı⌢.
  gen. -údn⌣v., -únn⌣v.c., -ún⌣c.
  pl. súmbudı⌣.
  kán⌣súmbud⌣ *foundations of house.*
  kátrɛn⌣súmbud⌣ *foundations of wall.*
summára n. *pipe, flute* = zummára⌣.
sumúm⌣ *hot poisonous wind* [< سَمُوم id.].
  obj. -úmg(ı)⌣, -gi⌣.
  pl. -úmı⌣.
súndɛ (occ. súnnɛ §868b) v.t. *sniff, smell* [§§2870-4; RSN, §129].
  ind. pres. aī⌣súndɛri⌢; perf. aī⌣súndɛgori⌢ (N. -ɛko-, -ɛho-).
  tumbákkı⌣súndɛ *take snuff.*
  wırídkı⌣súndɛri⌢ *I smell the rose.*
súndɛrar (-rár⌣; §§2200 ff.) and
sundɛríd⌣ (§§2256 ff.) n. *sniffing, smelling.*
sundɛr-ɛ-dól- (-rᵒd- §1178; §§4016-17, 4022, 4027) v.t. *be about to sniff, etc.*
sundɛr-ɛ-mă- (§§4016-17, 4036, 4041) v.t. *become unable to sniff, etc.*
súndɛd-ág- (§§3877 ff.) v.t. *be in the condition of having sniffed, etc.*
súndɛ-kattı- (N. -ɛha-; §4093) v.p. *be sniffed, etc.*

súnnɛ v.t. *sniff, smell* = súndɛ.
  ind. pres. aī⌣súnnɛri⌢; perf. aī⌣súnnɛgori⌢ (N. -ɛko-, -ɛho-).
  tumbákkı⌣súnnɛ *take snuff.*
súnt(ı) n. *nail (unguis), claw, talon, hoof; with collective sg.* (§4696a) [< √súnpinch (§4590) + -t dem. (§2324) or dim. (§2325γ)].
  obj. -tıg⌣.
  pl. -tınč(ı)⌣.
  ín⌣súnt(ı)⌣ *finger-nail(s).*
  óssın⌣súnt(ı)⌣ *toe-nail(s).*
  săm⌣súnt(ı)⌣ (-m⌣s- < -bn⌣s- §586) *cat's claw(s).*
  kán⌣súnt(ı)⌣ (-ñ⌣s- < -ğn⌣s- §632) *horse's hoof(s).*
sunúkk(ı) v.t. *pinch* [< √sún- pinch (§4590); -k perhaps intensive §2853].
  ind. pres. aī⌣sunúkkıri⌢, ɛr⌣sunúkkın⌢ (-kī⌢, -kí⌢); perf. aī⌣sunúkkıgori⌢ (N. -ıko-, -ıho-).
  imperat. sunúkki!
sunúkkar (-kár⌣; §§2200 ff.) and
sunukkíd⌣ (§§2256 ff.) n. *pinching.*
sunúkk-an (§§3890 ff.) v.t. *tell to pinch, let pinch.*
sunúkkı-bŭ- (§3931β) v.i. stat. *be in a pinched state or condition.*
  ánn-i⌣sunúkkıbūn⌢ *my hand (arm) is (has been) pinched.*
sunukkɛd-ág- (§§3877 ff.) v.t. *be in the situation of having pinched.*
sunúkkı-kattı- (N. -ıha-; §4093) v.p. *be pinched.*
S. **sursúkk(ı)** v.i. *stagger, stumble* [imit. < *sursúrk(ı) §§571, 2855].
  ind. pres. aī⌣sursúkkıri⌢; perf. aī⌣sursúkkıgori⌢.
  sámbūl⌣sursúkkıran⌢ *drunken persons stagger.*
sursúkkar⌣ (-kár⌣; §§2200 ff.) and
sursukkíd⌣ (§§2256 ff.) n. *staggering, etc.*
sursúkkı-bŭ- (§3931α) v.i. stat. *be in a staggering (etc.) state or condition.*
  ógíğ⌣sursúkkıbūn⌢ *the man is in a staggering condition.*
sursúkkıg-ır (N. -ıkır, -ıhır; §3682) v.t. caus. *cause or allow to stagger, etc.*
N. **sursurúkk(ı)** v.i. *stagger, stumble* (= S. sursúkk()) [imit. < *sursurúrk(ı) §§571, 2855].
  ind. pres. aī⌣sursurúkkıri⌢; perf. aī⌣sursurúkkıkori⌢ (-ıho-).
  N. sámbūl⌣sursurúkkın⌢ *a (the) drunken person staggers.*
sursurúkkar⌣ (-kár⌣; §§2200 ff.) and
sursurukkíd⌣ (§§2256 ff.) n. *staggering, etc.*
sursurúkkı-bŭ- (§3931α) v.i. stat. *be in a staggering (etc.) state or condition.*
sursurúkkıg-ır (N. -ıkır, -ıhır; §3686) v.t. caus. *cause or allow to stagger, etc.*
  N. sámar⌣tékkı⌣sursurúkkıgırın⌢ *being drunk makes him (her) stagger.*
súruf⌣ n. *caterpillar; with collective sg.* (§4696c) [< سَرَف id. pl. §§1336, 2405].
  obj. surúfk(ı)⌣, -ki⌢.
  pl. súrufı⌣.
surúfn-d(ı)⌣ (§§2545 ff.) adj. *caterpillar's, larval.*
surwál⌣ n. *drawers (worn by either sex)* [< سِرْوَال id.].

obj. -wálg(ı)⌣, -gi⌒.
pl. -wálı⌣.
sút! imperat. of súd v.t. *miss.*
súttɛ́! *quickly!* s.v. súd⌣.
suwán n. *Aswán* [< أَصْوَان *id.* §1391].
obj. -áŋg(ı)⌣, -gi⌒.
suwándo⌣ (s.v. -r⌣) adv. *at (to) Aswán.*
suwándo⌣ (§6007) *(s)he (it) is (they are) at Aswán.*
suwándo⌣nók! *go to Aswán!*
suwán-an- (§3910β) v.i. *go to Aswán.*
ind. pres. aî⌣suwánandi⌣, ɛr⌣suwánaniın⌣ (-ní⌒, -ní⌒).
šá⌣ n. (a) *spear, lance;* (b) *measuring-rod of one fathom* = šá⌣óŋd(ı)⌣ [cp. ON. ɰа *id.*
(a) GNT s.v.; ? < *šar⌣ RSN, §129; cp. šár-t(ı)⌣ *iron*].
obj. -šág⌣.
pl. šánč(ı)⌣.
šá⌣óŋd(ı)⌣ and (§1554)
šá⌣óŋd(ı)⌣ *fathom rod*, s.v. óg⌣.
šák⌣kárrortōn⌣áuran⌒ *they make the fathom rod from the midrib of the date-palm-branch.*
árıd⌣šáged⌣áskattın⌒ *land is measured with a fathom rod.*
šabánɛ⌣ n. *Shabana* (on map), *a village on the left bank of the Nile, 7 miles above Hándag* [< شَبْعَانة *sated*].
obj. šabánɛg⌣, šabánɛg⌣ (§1538).
šabatúd⌣ (-út⌒) n. *Shebatot* (on map), *a village on the left bank of the Nile, just south of Hándag.*
obj. -údk(ı)⌣, -útk(ı)⌣, -ki⌒.
šāgúš⌣ *hammer, pickaxe* = šākúš⌣.
šáhar n. *month* [< شهر *id.* §1357].
obj. šahárk(ı)⌣, -ki⌒.
pl. šaharı⌣.
šahárro⌣ (s.v. -r⌣) adv. *in the month.*
šahárro⌣ (§6007) *it is in the month.*
šáhıd⌣ n. *witness* [< شاهد *id.*].
obj. šahídk(ı)⌣, -ítk(ı)⌣, -ítt(ı)⌣ §2462, -ki⌒.
gen. šáhıdı⌣v., -hınn⌣c., -hın⌣c.
pl. šáhıdı⌣.
šahín-d(ı)⌣ (§§2545ff.) adj. *appertaining to the (a) witness.*
šáı⌣ n. *tea* [< شاي *id.*].
obj. šáıgı⌣, -gi⌒; -g⌣ is usually not assimilated (§514a).
šáıgı⌣dullogıráu⌒ and less commonly
šáıd⌣dullogıráu⌒ *make the tea strong.*
X. šáıgı⌣sá⌣mıŋkóttır⌣éttari? *at what time shall (§5369b) I bring tea?*
Y. aî⌣tálabɛgıri⌒ (§3013) *when I ask (for it).*
šáın-d(ı)⌣ (§§2545ff.) adj. *appertaining to tea.*
bɛrrád⌣šáınd(ı)⌣ *tea-pot.*
šáıgɛ⌣ adj. and n. *Šáıgı* شايقي, (one) of the *Šáıgıja* شايقية, *an Arab tribe living south of Dóngola* [§2519].
obj. -gɛg⌣.
pl. -gɛnč(ı)⌣.
šáıgén-d(ı)⌣ (§§2545ff.) adj. *appertaining to the (a) Šáıgı.*
šáıgɛnčín-d(ı)⌣ (§§2545ff.) adj. *appertaining to the Šáıgıja.*

šākılɛ́⌣ (a) v.i. *quarrel;* (b) v.t. *quarrel with* (= šɛklɛ́⌣) [< *a stem of Sudan Ar.* اشاكل ıššákal *quarrel with one another* +-ɛ́ §3656].
ind. pres. aî⌣šākılɛ́rı⌣; perf. aî⌣šākılɛ́gori⌣ (N. -ɛ́ko-, -ɛ́ho-).
imperat. šākılɛ́!
aî⌣tékkonon⌣šākılɛ́rı⌒ *and*
aî⌣tékkı⌣šākılɛ́rı⌒ *I quarrel with him (her).*
tírgonon⌣šākılɛ́ran⌒ *they quarrel with them.*
šākılɛ́rar⌣ (-rár⌣; §§2200ff., 2207) *and*
šākılɛ́ríd⌣ (§§2256ff., 2260) n. *quarrelling.*
šākılɛ́-bū- (§3931α) v.i. stat. *be involved in a quarrel.*
aîgon⌣ɛsmáŋgon⌣šākılɛ́būru⌒ *I and ɛoθmán have a quarrel.*
šākılɛ́r-ɛg-ág- (§§4071ff.) v.i. and t. = šākılɛ́redól-.
šākılɛ́r-ɛ-dól- (-rᵒd- §1178; §§4016-17, 4022, 4027) v.i. and t. *be about to quarrel (with).*
šákk(ı)⌣ v.t. (a) *shake (milk) in a skin;* (b) *shake (skin containing milk);* (s.v. masád⌣) [imit.].
ind. pres. aî⌣šákkırı⌣; perf. aî⌣šákkıgori⌣ (N. -ıko-, -ıho-).
imperat. šákki!
íččıb⌣béŋır⌣šákkıran⌣désk⌣ósan⌣ɛgi⌒ (-b⌣- < -g⌣- §519; §6224) *they shake the milk in the skin in order to extract the butter, lit....intending (⌣ɛgi⌣) to say (-an⌣) 'extract the butter' (⌣désk⌣ós-).*
íččı⌣⌣béŋı⌣šákkıran⌣désk⌣ósır⌣ɛgi⌒ (§6223) *(s)he shakes the skin of milk in order to extract the butter.*
šákkar⌣ (-kár⌣; §§2200ff.) *and*
šákkıd⌣ (§§2256ff.) n. *shaking.*
šákkı-bū- (§3931β) v.i. stat. *be in a shaken state or condition.*
íččı⌣šákkıbūn⌣ *the milk is (has been) shaken.*
béŋ⌣šákkıbūn⌣ *the skin is (has been) shaken.*
šákkı-kattı- (N. -ıha-; §4093) v.p. *be shaken.*
šakšág⌣ n. *continuous rain, persistent rain, steady rain* [< *Sudan Ar.* شَكْشاكة *light continuous rain;* §§2151, 2153; cp. Amh. ችክችክ ይላል *id.*].
obj. -ágk(ı)⌣, -ákk(ı)⌣, -ki⌒.
ín⌣arun⌣šakšágun⌣ *this rain is persistent.*
ín⌣arun⌣šakšágun⌣ *this is persistent rain, lit. this is the persistent (one) of rain(s) (§4687).*
šakšág⌣arítkı⌣néŋırın⌒ *the persistent rain soaks the ground.*
déssɛ⌣šakšákkı⌣dólın⌒ *vegetation likes persistent rain.*
šakšág-an- (§3910α) v.i. *(of rain) become continuous, etc.*
áru⌣šakšágankó⌒ *the rain became (has become) persistent.*
šakšágam-bū- (§§3949ff.) v.i. stat. *(of rain) be in a state of continuity, be persistent.*
áru⌣šakšágambūn⌣ *the rain is persistent.*
šakúš⌣ (šāgúš⌣) n. (a) *hammer* [< شاكوش *id.*]; (b) *pickaxe.*

obj. -úšk(ı)⌣, -ki⌒.
pl. -úšı⌣.
šakúšn⌣ád⌣ *handle of hammer, etc.*
šākúš-kırı- (-kírı⌣ §1701; §§2539-40) adj. *like a hammer, etc.*
šánta⌣ *valise, etc.* = šántá⌣.
šárɛ⌣ n. *early evening, dusk, sunset* (= mígrıb⌣) [cp. MN. šare *Abend* KB, §100a].
obj. šárɛg⌣, šárɛgı⌣ ᴬᴰ, ᴸᴸ §1538.
šárɛg⌣ (§4665) adv. *in the early evening, at dusk.*
šárɛb⌣butáran⌒ (-b⌣- < -g⌣- §519) *they will come at dusk.*
álı⌣šárɛn⌣nókkō⌒ (-n⌣- < -g⌣- §625) *ɛáli went (away) at dusk.*
šárɛ-wıss(ı)⌣ (§2361) *evening star.*
šár-an- (§3910α) v.i. *become early evening, grow dusk.*
šárɛŋkó⌒ *(early) evening came (has come) on.*
šaríf⌣ (šár-, šɛr-) n. *nobleman, descendant of the Prophet* [< شريف *id.*].
obj. -ífk(ı)⌣, -ki⌒.
pl. -ífı⌣.
šarífa⌣ (šár-, šɛr-) n. *noblewoman, descendant of the Prophet* [< شريفة *id.*].
obj. -fag⌣.
pl. -fanč(ı)⌣.
šárkɛ⌣ (šɛr-) v.i. *be in good bodily condition, be in good health, be well.*
ind. pres. aî⌣šárkɛri⌣; perf. aî⌣šárkɛgori⌣ (N. -ɛko-, -ɛho-).
X. ɛsmán⌣ɛskıtámunun⌣ ɛoθmán *can't come.*
Y. tɛr⌣šárkɛmɛn? *isn't he well?*
X. óddıbūn⌣ *he's ill.*
šárkɛrar⌣ (šɛr-, -rár⌣; §§2200ff., 2210) *and*
šárkɛríd⌣ (šɛr-; §§2256ff., 2263) n. *good condition, good health.*
šárt(ı)⌣ n. (a) *iron;* (b) *iron object (instrument, box, etc.);* (c) *metal resembling iron* [< *šár (> šá⌣ *spear* RSN, §129) + -t(ı)⌣ §2326].
obj. -tıg⌣.
pl. -tınč(ı)⌣.
šártın⌣gɛ́lɛ⌣ *copper, brass.*
šártın⌣tábıd⌣ *blacksmith.*
šártık⌣kál⌣ *blacksmith.*
†šártın⌣hánu⌣ *bicycle, lit. ass of iron.*
šártín-d(ı)⌣ (§§2545ff.) adj. *appertaining to iron, etc., of iron, etc., iron.*
sandúg⌣šártíndırı⌒ (§6039) *it's (they're) in the iron box.*
šawál⌣ n. *sack* = šáwál⌣.
šábáka⌣ (šébɛkɛ⌣) n. *net* [< شَبَكة *id.*].
obj. -kag⌣, -kɛg⌣.
pl. -kánč(ı)⌣, -kɛnč(ı)⌣.
šántá⌣ (šán-, -ta⌣) n. *valise, portmanteau, trunk; portfolio* [< شنطة *id.*].
obj. -tág⌣, -tag⌣.
pl. -tánč(ı)⌣, -tanč(ı)⌣, -tɛnč(ı)⌣.
šántán⌣ *handle(s) of valise, etc.*
šáŋkál⌣ n. *hook* = šéŋkɛl⌣.
šáwál⌣ (šaw-, šǝw-) n. *sack* [< شَوَال *id.* §1346].
obj. -álg(ı)⌣, -gi⌒.
pl. -álı⌣.

šébɛkɛ⌣ net = šábȧkȧ⌣.
šég v.t. (a) implant, insert; (b) plant, plant out; (c) prick, pierce, puncture.
 ind. pres. āi⌣šég(¹)ri⌢, ɛr⌣šégɪn⌢ (-gī⌢, -gí⌢); perf. āi⌣šégkori⌢ (⌣šékkori⌢).
 imperat. šék!
  wıččírk⌣árıdır⌣šékkoran⌢ they (have) planted the stick in the ground.
  kınıssɛt⌣téddo⌣šékkó⌢ (-t⌣t-<-g⌣t- §707) (s)he (has) stuck the (a) thorn (thorns §4696b) into him (her, it).
  šetílgı⌣bišégri⌢ I shall plant out the young plant(s §4696b).
  šetlıb⌣bišégri⌢ (-b⌣b-<-g⌣b- §519) I shall plant out the young plants.
  šetlıb⌣bišegríddi⌢ I shall plant out the (various §5456) young plants.
  kınıss⌣áigı⌣šékkó⌢ the thorn(s) (has, have) pricked me.
  áigı⌣kınıssɛgeš⌣šékkó⌢ (-š⌣š-<-d⌣š- §694) (s)he (it) (has) pricked me with a (the) thorn (with thorns).
  kınıssɛ⌣šékkon⌣ɛn⌢ (s)he says that the (a) thorn(s) (has, have) pricked her (him).
šégar⌣ (-gȧr⌣; §§2200ff.) and
šegíd⌣ (§§2256ff.) n. implanting, etc.
šégɛ⌣ n. offshoot, esp. young plant at base of date-palm (that is taken and planted; = šetıl⌣); with collective sg. (§4696b) [lit. implanting, what is planted; -ɛ⌣ of n. act. §2234ɛ].
 obj. šégɛg⌣.
 pl. šegénč(ɪ)⌣.
  béntɪn⌣šégɛ⌣ young date-palm plant(s).
šég-an- (§§3890ff.) v.t. tell to implant, etc., let implant, etc.
šég-bŭ- (šéggŭ- §546; §3931β) v.i. stat. be in an implanted (etc.) state or condition.
  šetɪl⌣šégbūn⌢ the plant is (plants are §4696b, has (have) been) planted out.
šég(¹)r-ɛg-ág- (§§4071ff.) v.t. = šɛgɛdól-.
šég-ɛ-dól- (-gᵒd- §1178; §4022) and
šég(¹)r-ɛ-dól- (-rᵒd-; §4027) v.t. be about to implant, etc.
šégɛd-ág- (§§3877ff.) v.t. be in the situation of having implanted, etc.
šegíŋ-ɪr (šégɪŋɪr; N. -ŋkɪr; §3688) v.t. caus. cause or allow to implant, etc.
 ind. pres. āi⌣šegíŋɪddi⌢ (⌣šegɪŋgíddi⌢, §1812).
šég-kattɪ- (šékkat; §4093) v.p. be implanted, etc.
šégıg̃ v.t. implant (etc., s.v. šég) in several places, here and there [extension in -ıg̃ repetitive (§2883) of šég].
 ind. pres. āi⌣šégıg̃(¹)ri⌢, (⌣šegíg̃(¹)ri⌢); perf. āi⌣šégıg̃kori⌢ (-íčk-).
 imperat. šégıg̃č!
 pl.-obj. šégıg̃ırır.
  šetlıb⌣bišegíg̃ri⌢ (-b⌣b-<-g⌣b- §519) and
  šetlıb⌣bišegíg̃ríddi⌢ I shall plant out the young plants in various places.
  šetlıš⌣šegıg̃íríddi⌢ (-š⌣š-<-g⌣š- §695) they plant out the young plants in various places.
  abšǒg⌣áigı⌣šegıg̃óskó⌢ the hedgehog has pricked me in several places.
šégıg̃ar (-gȧr⌣; §§2200ff.) and
šégıg̃íd⌣ (§§2256ff.) n. implanting (etc.) in various places.

šégıg̃-an (§§3890ff.) v.t. tell to or let implant (etc.) in several places.
šegíg̃-bŭ- (§3931β) v.i. stat. be in the state or condition of being implanted (etc.) in several places.
  béntɪɛ⌣šegíg̃būn⌢ the date-palms are (have been) planted out in several places.
šegíg̃(¹)r-ɛg-ág- (§§4071ff.) v.t. = šɛgıg̃ɛdól-.
šegíg̃-ɛ-dól- (-gᵒd- §1178; §4022) and
šegíg̃(¹)r-ɛ-dól- (-rᵒd-; §4027) v.t. be about to implant (etc.) in several places.
šegíg̃ed-ág- (§§3877ff.) v.t. be in the situation of having implanted (etc.) in several places.
šegíg̃íŋ-ɪr (N. -ŋkɪr; §3688) v.t. caus. cause or allow to implant (etc.) in several places.
 ind. pres. āi⌣šegıg̃íŋgɪddi⌢.
šégıg̃-kattɪ- (-íčk-; §4093) v.p. be implanted (etc.) in several places.
šéh (šéx⌣) n. sheikh, chief of village, district or tribe [< شَيْخ id.].
 obj. šéhk(ɪ)⌣, -ki⌢.
 pl. šéhɪ⌣.
šéh-an- (šéxan-; §3910α) v.i. become (a) sheikh.
 ind. pres. āi⌣šéhandi⌢.
šéham-bŭ- (šéxam-; §§3949ff.) v.i. stat. be in the state of having become (a) sheikh.
šéhɪr⌣ (šéxɪr) n. (in water-wheel, kólɛ⌣) guiding-rod, guide; there are two: they proceed from points near the centre of the beam (wáwɪr) fixed across the shaft (kódɛ⌣) under the wheel raising water (átt(ɪ)⌣) and, crossing each other, extend to the upper right (as one faces the river) corners of the shaft; the ascending cables (álasɛ⌣) bearing the jars (béšenč(ɪ)⌣) pass between them and are thus kept in position [cp. K. šégɪr id. SNK, 377A¹⁷; pronunciation in D. app. from popular association with شَيْخ].
 obj. šéhírk(ɪ)⌣, -ki⌢.
 pl. šéhɪrɪ⌣.
  árɛn⌣šéhɪr⌣, inner šéhɪr⌣, the guiding-rod of which the top reaches the corner of the shaft nearer the river.
  bóččɪn⌣šéhɪr⌣, outer šéhɪr⌣, the guiding-rod of which the top reaches the corner of the shaft further from the river.
šéj(ɪ)⌣ (šéjj(ɪ)⌣) n. thing, object [< شَيْء id. §1217].
 obj. -jɪg⌣.
 pl. -jɪnč(ɪ)⌣, -jínč⌣ §1608.
  šéjɪ⌣wɛd⌣dɛŋkómunan⌢ (-d⌣d-<-g⌣d- §534) they didn't give (haven't given) me anything.
šɛkké (a) v.i. complain; (b) v.t. complain of, complain about [< a stem of Sudan Ar. تَشَكَّى = اتْشَكَّى id. +-ɛ́ §3654].
 ind. pres. āi⌣šɛkkɛ́ri⌢, ɛr⌣šɛkkɛ́n⌢ (-ɛ́⌢, -ɛ́⌢); perf. āi⌣šɛkkɛ́gori⌢ (N. -ɛ́ko-, -ɛ́ho-).
 imperat. šɛkké!

part. pres. šɛkkɛ́l⌣ (one) that complains, etc., complainant, complaining, obj. -ɛ́lg(ɪ)⌣, -gi⌢; past šɛkkɛ́rɛl⌣ (one) that complained, etc., complainant, complaining, obj. -ɛ́lg(ɪ)⌣, -gi⌢.
  āi⌣ɛkkɪ⌣šɛkkɛ́ri⌢ I (shall §5369a) complain of you.
šɛkkɛ́rar⌣ (-rȧr⌣; §§2200ff., 2207) and
šɛkkɛ́ríd⌣ (§§2256ff., 2260) n. complaint.
šɛkkɛ́r-an (§§3890ff., 3899) v.t. tell to complain, etc., let complain, etc.
šɛkkɛ́-bŭ- (§3931β) v.i. stat. be in the state or condition of being complained of, be the subject of complaint.
  ɛsmán⌣šɛkkɛ́būn⌢ ɛoθmán has been complained about.
šɛkkɛ́r-ɛg-ág- (§§4071ff.) v.i. and t. = šɛkkɛ́redól-.
šɛkkɛ́r-ɛ-dól- (-rᵒd- §1178; §§4016-17, 4022, 4027) v.i. and t. be about to complain (of).
šɛkkɛ́-kattɪ- (N. -ɛ́ha-; §4093) v.p. be complained of.
šɛkkɪré v.t. thank (= šɛkré) [< a stem of Sudan Ar. اتْشَكَّرَ = اشْكُرْ id. +-ɛ́ §3652].
 ind. pres. āi⌣šɛkkɪréri⌢; perf. āi⌣šɛkkɪrégori⌢ (N. -éko-, -ého-).
 imperat. šɛkkɪré!
  sítti⌣tímeg⌣ɛr⌣išínsunn⌣íllar⌣ɛkkɪ⌣šɛkkɪrén⌢ the lady thanks you for the water-melon you sent, lit....thanks you because you sent the water-melon.
šɛkkɪrérar⌣ (-rȧr⌣; §§2200ff., 2207) and
šɛkkɪrérid⌣ (§§2256ff., 2260) n. thanking.
šɛkkɪrér-an (§§3890ff., 3899) v.t. tell to thank, let thank.
šɛkkɪré-kattɪ- (N. -ɛ́ha-; §4093) v.p. be thanked.
šɛklé (a) v.i. quarrel; (b) v.t. quarrel with (= šákilé) [< a stem of Sudan Ar. اتْشَاكَل = اشَاكِل id. +-ɛ́ §3656].
 ind. pres. āi⌣šɛklɛ́ri⌢; perf. āi⌣šɛklɛ́gori⌢ (N. -éko-, -ého-).
 imperat. šɛklé!
  āi⌣tékkonon⌣šɛkléri⌢ and
  āi⌣tékkɪ⌣šɛkléri⌢ I quarrel with him (her).
šɛklɛ́rar⌣ (-rȧr⌣; §§2200ff., 2207) and
šɛklɛ́ríd⌣ (§§2256ff., 2260) n. quarrelling.
šɛklɛ́-bŭ- (§3931α) v.i. stat. be in a quarrelling state or condition.
šɛklɛ́r-ɛg-ág- (§§4071ff.) v.i. and t. = šɛklɛ́redól-.
šɛklɛ́r-ɛ-dól- (-rᵒd- §1178; §§4016-17, 4022, 4027) v.i. and t. be about to quarrel (with).
šɛkré v.t. thank (= šɛkkɪré) [< شاكر grateful or < a stem of شَكَرَ be grateful to +-ɛ́ §3631].
 ind. pres. āi⌣šɛkréri⌢; perf. āi⌣šɛkrégori⌢ (N. -éko-, -ého-).
 imperat. šɛkré!
šɛkrérar⌣ (-rȧr⌣; §§2200ff., 2207) and
šɛkrérid⌣ (§§2256ff., 2260) n. thanking.
šɛkrér-an (§§3890ff., 3899) v.t. tell to thank, let thank.
  álɪs⌣samílgɪ⌣šɛkréran⌢ (-s⌣s-<-g⌣s- §678) tell ɛáli to thank the sheikh.

šekrέ-kattı- (N. -έha-; §4093) v.p. *be thanked.*

šɛllál n. *cataract, rapid* [< شَلَّال id. 'der meroïtische Ortsname Sl'l' ZMS, p. 417γ].
 obj. -lálg(ı), -gi.
 pl. -láli.

N. **šέlog** v.t. and i. *shake* (=šúlug, q.v.) [imit.].
 ind. pres. aı̄šέlog(ı)ri; perf. aı̄šɛlókkori.
 imperat. šέlok!

N. **šɛlogíŋk-ır** (šέlogıŋkır; §3688) v.t. caus. *cause or allow to shake.*
 N. sandúkkı tókkon šɛlogıŋkírmɛn, tén tūr dábūl buhárbɛkattın *don't let the box get shaken, its contents will be spoiled.*

šéma n. (a) *wax*; (b) *candle*; with collective sg. (§4696d) [< شَمْع id. §1258].
 obj. -mag.
 pl. -manč(ı).

šɛmadán (§956a) n. *candlestick* [< شَمْعَدَان id.].
 obj. -áŋg(ı), -gi.
 pl. -áni.

šénɛb n. *moustache* [< شَنَب id.].
 obj. šɛnébk(ı), -épk(ı), -ki.
 gen. šɛnébn, šɛném c., ´-.
 pl. šénɛbi.

šɛníf n. *small fishing-net* (=ábɛ) [< شَنِيف *network sack*].
 obj. -ífk(ı), -ki.
 pl. -ífı.

šɛŋkɛl (šáŋkál) n. *hook* (to hold door, window, lid); with collective sg. (§4696) [< شَنْكَل id.].
 obj. šɛŋkélg(ı), -gi.
 pl. šέŋkɛli.

šɛŋkılέ (šáŋ-) v.t. *hook, fasten with a hook* [< imperat. or imperf. stem of شَنْكَل id. +-έ §3634].
 ind. pres. aı̄šɛŋkılέri; perf. aı̄šɛŋkılέgori (N. -έko, -έho-).
 imperat. šɛŋkılέ!

šɛŋkılέr-an (šáŋ-; §§3890 ff., 3899) v.t. *tell to hook, etc., let hook, etc.*

šɛríf
 šéh šɛríf n. *Sh. Sherif* (on map), a village on the left bank of the Nile, about five miles above Urdi [< شَيخ شَرِيف].
 obj. -ífk(ı), -ki.

šɛríg n. *partner* [< شَرِيك id.].
 obj. -ígk(ı), -íkk(ı), -ki.
 pl. -ígi.
 tér án šɛrígun *(s)he is my partner.*

šɛríg-an (§3910α) v.i. *become a partner.*
 šɛrígaŋkó *(s)he became (has become) a partner.*

šɛrıg n. (a) *east*; (b) *right bank of the Nile* [< شَرْق id. §1359].
 obj. šɛrígk(ı), -íkk(ı), -ki.
 gen. šɛrígn, -ıŋ c.
 šɛrıgı (s.v. -r) adv. *in (to) the east, on (to) the right bank (etc.).*
 šɛrıgır (§6007) *(s)he (it) is (they are) in the east (on the right bank, etc.).*
 šɛrıgır ágran *they live (etc. s.v. ág) in the east* (...*on the right bank, etc.*).
 téŋ ká šɛrıgır *his (her) house is on the right bank.*
 šέrıgırton tágoran *they came (have come) from the east (etc.).*

šɛrígk-ɛd (-íkkɛd; -kɛt, -kέ §966; §6007) adv. *on the east, by the eastern route, by (on) the right bank.*
 šɛríkkɛn nókkoran (-n- < -d- §624) *they went (have gone) by the eastern route* (...*by the right bank, etc.*).
 káwwa hannáŋ gɛbéllo šɛríkkɛ *Káwwa is opposite Hannág, (it's) on the east bank.*

šɛrín-d(ı) (-ígnd(ı), -ıgnd(ı), -ıŋnd(ı) §643; §§2545ff.) adj. *eastern, of the right bank, etc.*

šɛrıg-an (§§3910ff.) v.i. (a) *go to the east, etc.;* (b) *become (part of) the right bank.*
 hāmɛdnárt šɛrıgaŋkó *Ḥámıd's Island has become part of the right bank.*

šɛrıgkɛb-bél (-ıkkɛb-; §4127) v.i. *issue* (sc. from river, boat) *on the right bank.*
 imperat. šɛrıgkɛbbél! and šɛrıgkέbbɛl! (§1871).

šɛrıgkɛbbél-an (-ıkkɛb-; §§3890ff., 3905) v.t. *tell to issue on the right bank, let issue on the right bank.*

šɛrıgkɛn-nóg (-ıkkɛn-; §4127) v.i. *go by the eastern route, etc.*
 imperat. šɛrıgkɛnnók! and šɛrıgkέnnok!
 šɛrıkkɛnnókkoran = šɛríkkɛn nókkoran.

šɛrıgkɛnnóg-an (-ıkkɛn-; §§3890ff., 3905) v.t. *tell to go by the eastern route, etc., let go by the eastern route, etc.*

šɛrıgkır-nóg (-ıkkır-; §4139) v.i. *go eastwards, go to the right bank, etc.*
 šɛrıkkırnókkoran *they went (have gone) eastwards (etc.).*

šɛrıgkırnóg-an (-ıkkır-; §§3890ff., 3905) v.t. *tell to go eastwards, etc., let go eastwards, etc.*

šérkɛ *be well, etc.* = šárkɛ.

šɛrkέ v.t. *share, be a partner in* [< a stem of Sudan Ar. (في) اِشَّارَك id. +-έ §3657].
 ind. pres. aı̄šɛrkέri; perf. aı̄šɛrkέgori (N. -έko, -έho-).
 imperat. šɛrkέ!
 aı̄ıŋı tékkonon šɛrkέri *I share this with him (her) (I am a partner with him (her) in this).*

šɛrkέrar (-rár; §§2200ff., 2207) and
šɛrkέríd (§§2256ff., 2260) n. *partnership.*

šɛrkέr-an (§§3890ff., 3899) v.t. *tell to share, etc., let share, etc.*

šɛrk-áu (-áw, -áu; §3747ε') v.t. *do (etc. s.v. áu) jointly, share in doing, etc.*
 ğέlliš šɛrkáwwé (-š-<-g š- §695) *share (pl.) the work.*

šɛrkέ-bū- (§3931β) v.i. stat. *be in a shared state or condition.*
 dúŋgı šɛrkέbun *the money is jointly owned.*

šɛrkέrɛd-ág- (§§3877ff.) v.t. *be in the situation of having shared.*

šɛrkέ-kattı- (N. -έha-; §4093) v.p. *be shared.*
 dúŋgı šɛrkέkattın *the money is shared.*

šɛtán (§956a) n. (a, usual sense) *evil spirit, fiend, devil* [< شَيْطَان id.]; (b) *benevolent spirit.*
 obj. -áŋg(ı), -gi.
 pl. -áni.
 X. šɛtán šέrɛ dámunun *a good devil does not exist.*
 Y. šɛtán míllıgon dán sɛrέgon dán, tír dígrınčí *there are evil spirits* (§4647) *and good spirits, they are numerous.*

šɛtán-d(ı) (§§2545ff.) adj. *appertaining to an evil spirit, etc., fiendish, devilish.*

šɛtán-kırı (-kíri §1701; §§2539-40) adj. *like an evil spirit, etc.*

šɛtıl (-tul) n. *young plant; seedling; shoot* (=šέgɛ); with collective sg. (§4696b) [< شَتْل id. §1361].
 obj. šɛtílg(ı), -túl, -gi.
 pl. šέtlı, -tılı, -tulı.

šəwál n. *sack* = šáwál.

šīr v.t. (a) *plait*; (b) *haul in* [< *iššír (§403) < *ıššír (§1075) < *ınšír (§698) < *ınšír (§690) < ín- this +-s dem. (§2319) +-ír *make, so *make that (into) this §2859a].
 ind. pres. aı̄ šīrrı, ɛr šīrın (-rī, -rí); perf. aı̄ šīrkori.
 έnčı wɛrwén díltıš šīrran (-š-<-g š- §695) and έnčı wɛrwén úlı š šīrran *the women plait one another's hair.*
 hawwád úlgı šīrın *the fisherman hauls in the line.*
 hawwádı tínn úlı š šīrran (-š-<-g š- §695) *the fishermen haul in their lines.*

šīrar (-rár; §§2200ff.) and
šīríd (§§2256ff.) n. *plaiting, hauling in.*

šīr-an (§§3890ff.) v.t. *tell to plait, etc., let plait, etc.*

šīr-bū- (§3931β) v.i. stat. *be in a plaited (etc.) state or condition.*

šīrr-ɛg-ág- (§§4071ff.) v.t. = šīrɛdól-.

šīr-ɛ-dól- (-r°d- §1178; §4022) and
šīrr-ɛ-dól- (-r°d- §4027) v.t. *be about to plait, etc.*

šīr-ɛ-má- (§4036) and
šīrr-ɛ-má- (§4041) v.t. *become unable to plait, etc.*

šīrɛd-ág- (§3877ff.) v.t. *be in the situation of having plaited, etc.*

šīr-kattı- (§4093) v.p. *be plaited, etc.*

šıbbág n. *lattice, window* [< Sudan Ar. شُبَّاك id.].
 obj. -ágk(ı), -ákk(ı), -ki.
 gen. -ágn, -áŋ c.
 pl. -ági.

šıbır n. (flexible) *basket* [cp. Sudan Ar. كُونْشِبِر id. HSAT s.v.].
 obj. šıbírk(ı), -ki.
 pl. šíb(ı)rı.

šībır n. *span between extended ends of thumb and forefinger, approx. 7 inches* [< Sudan Ar. šībır id. < شِبْر id. §1359].
 obj. šībírk(ı), -ki.
 pl. šíb(ı)rı.

šıbšıbíllɛ (-la) n. *vulture* [< *šıbíl-šıbíll-ɛ (§2157) *(what) makes the sound 'šıbíl-šıbíll!'*, sc. with its wings; -ɛ (§2234α) and -a (§2178) of n. dic.; §2181].
 obj. -lɛg, -lag.
 pl. šıbšıbıllénč(ı), -lán-.
šídar (-dar-, -dɛr-, šítar-) n. *tree*; with collective sg. (§4696b) [< Sudan Ar. شَجَر > شدر *trees* §§867, 2403].
 obj. šídark(ı), -dár-, -dér-, šítark(ı), -kı.
 pl. šídarı, -dar-, -dɛr-, šítarı.
šídda (-dȧ) n. *energy, intensity, vehemence, violence, force, strength* [< شِدّة *id.*].
 obj. -dag, -dȧg.
 aı̊šíddak kŏmunun *I have no energy.*
šíddag-ɛd (-dȧg-; -ɛt, -ɛ́ §966) *with (etc., s.v. -ɛd) energy, etc.*
 — -ɛt, -ɛ́ may imply predication (§§5858–60):
 šíddagémmunun (-mm- < -dm- §600) *it is not by force (e.g. that it is to be done)* (s.v. -munun).
šíddagɛb-bód (-dȧg-; §§3745, 4167) v.i. *run with energy, etc., run hard.*
 imperat. šíddagɛbbót!, ¯´¯ (§1954a).
šíddagɛb-bóg (-dȧg-; §§3745, 4167) v.t. and i. *pour (etc., s.v. bóg) with energy, etc.*
 úru šíddagɛbbógın *the rain pours heavily (it pours heavily with rain).*
šíddagɛd-dā- (-dȧg-; §3988) v.i. *be going along with energy, etc.*
 bābu̇r šíddagéddān *the train (steamer) is travelling at a good rate.*
 bābu̇ron šíddagɛddȧgogın adam dıgríb bawwırɛ́gó (-b b- < -g b- §519) and N. bābu̇ron šíddagɛddȧhokın adam dıgríb buawwırɛ́kó *if the train (steamer) had been travelling fast, it would have injured many people.*
šíddagɛǧ-ǧóm (-dȧg-; §§3745, 4167) v.t. *strike (etc., s.v. ǧóm) with energy, etc., hit hard.*
 imperat. šíddagɛǧǧóm!, ¯´¯ (§1954a).
šíddagɛǧ-ǧŭ-bu̇- (-dȧg-; §4219) v.i. stat. *be in a state of energetic (etc.) motion (coming), be coming vehemently, etc.*
šíddagɛk-káll(ı) (-dȧg-; §§3745, 4167) v.t. *push (etc., s.v. káll(ı)) with energy, etc., push hard.*
 imperat. šíddagɛkkálli!
šíddagɛn-nóg (-dȧg-; §§3745, 4167) v.i. *go (etc., s.v. nóg) with energy, etc., go (etc.) impetuously.*
 mándotōm bıšíddagɛnnógran *they will rush away from there.*
šíddagɛn-nóg-bu̇- (-dȧg-; -nóggŭ- §546; §4219) v.i. stat. *be in a state of energetic (etc.) motion (going), be going hard.*
šíddagɛd-óčč(ı) (-dȧg-; §§3745, 4167) v.t. *drag (etc., s.v. óčč(ı)) with energy, etc.*
šíddagɛd-ošók(ı) (-dȧg-; §§3745, 4167) v.t. = šíddagɛdóčč(ı).
šíddagɛt-tá (-dȧg-; §§3745, 4167) v.i. *come with energy, etc., come vehemently, etc.*
šíddagɛt-tólle (-dȧg-; §§3745, 4167) v.t. *pull with energy, etc., pull hard.*

šíddagɛd-úndur (-dȧg-; §§3745, 4167) v.t. *insert (etc., s.v. úndur) with energy, etc.*
 tókkoš šíddagɛdundúrmɛn (-š š- < -n š- §698) *don't put him (her, it, them) in by force.*
šíddagɛd-úrr(ı) (-dȧg-; §§3745, 4167) v.t. *press (etc., s.v. úrr(ı)) with energy, etc., press hard, press tight.*
šídda-kíññ(ı) (-dȧk-; §§2536–7) adj. *devoid of vehemence, etc., gentle, mild.*
šíddakıññıg-ır (-dȧk-; ¯´¯ N. -ıkır, -ıhır; §§3703, 5708) (a) v.t. caus. *cause or allow to be devoid of vehemence, etc.*; (b) v.t. *render gentle, mild.*
šíg n. *side (part)* [< شَقّ *id.* §1372].
 obj. šígk(ı), šíkk(ı), -kı.
 pl. šígı.
 en šígır tép *keep to your side.*
 éš šíkkɛn nók (-š š- < -n š- §699, -n n- < -d n- §624), s.v. -ɛd) *your side.*
šírag n. *bolt (of lock, etc.)* [app. < شَرَك *trap*].
 obj. šırágk(ı), -ákk(ı), -kı.
 pl. šíragı.
šíre n. *tamarisk, Tamarix nilotica, Ehrenb.* (BSP, 47).
 obj. šírɛg.
 pl. šırénč(ı).
šítar (-tar-, -tɛr-; §1016) n. *tree* = šídar; with collective sg. (§4696b).
 obj. šítark(ı), -tár-, -tér-, -kı.
 pl. šítarı, -tarı, -tɛrı.
šítɛ n. *winter* [< شِتَاء *id.*].
 obj. -tɛg, -tɛgı.
šítɛg (§4665) adv. *in (the) winter.*
šíter (s.v. -r) adv. *in (the) winter.*
šíter (§6007) *it is (they are) in (the) winter.*
šítén-d(ı) (§§2545ff.) adj. *appertaining to winter, of winter.*
šít-an- (§3910α) v.i. *become winter.*
 šítaŋkó *it became (has become) winter.*
šítam-bu̇- (§§3949ff.) v.i. stat. *be in the state of becoming or having become winter, be winter.*
 šítambūn *winter is coming (has come) on.*
šítan-ɛ-dól- (-nᵒd- §1178; §3975) and
šítand-ɛ-dól- (-dᵒd- §3978) v.i. *be about to become winter.*
šoglɛ́ (šogolɛ́) v.i. *work, labour* = šuglɛ́.
šóka (-kȧ) n. *fork* [< شَوْكَة *id.*].
 obj. -kag, -kȧg.
 pl. -kanč(ı), -kȧn-, -kɛn-.
 šókan í *handle of fork.*
šókk(ı) v.t. *pound, batter* (= túkk(ı)) [imit.].
 ind. pres. aı̊šókkırı; perf. aı̊šókkıgorı (N. -ıko-, -ıho-).
 imperat. šókki!
 ǧúrtɛš šókkıran (-š š- < -g š- §695) *they pound the pods of Acacia arabica.*
 búŋgı šártıg fúndun tu̇r šókkıran (-f f- < -d f- §539) *they pound the coffee with a (the) piece of iron in a (the) mortar.*
šókkar (-kȧr- §§2200ff.) and
šókkíd (§§2256ff.) n. *pounding, etc.*
šókk-an (§§3890ff.) v.t. *tell to pound, etc., let pound.*
šókkı-bu̇- (§3931β) v.i. stat. *be in a pounded (etc.) state or condition.*

šokkɛd-åg- (§§3877ff.) v.t. *be in the situation of having pounded, etc.*
šókkı-kattı- (N. -ıha-; §4093) v.p. *be pounded, etc.*
šokk-os-nɛ́ŋ-ır (-on-nɛ́ñ- §629; §4202; -osgı-nɛ́ñ-, -ozgı-, -oggı- §4204; N. -nɛ́ñ-ır) v.t. *soak after pounding, etc.*
 ǧúrtɛš šokkosɛssırnɛ́ñgıddan (§5605; -š š- < -g š- §695) *after pounding the pods of Acacia arabica they steep them in water.*
šólag n. *cylindrical gold bead, combined with mutémma in woman's necklace*; with collective sg. (§4696c) [< Sudan Ar. شَوْلَق šólag *id.*].
 obj. šólágk(ı), -ákk(ı), -kı.
 pl. šólagı.
šólog v.t. and i. *shake* = šúlug.
šónd(ı) v.t. (a) *shake*; (b) *shake up, shake out, shake clean*; (c) *shake about, scatter, strew* [§2868].
 ind. pres. aı̊šóndırı; perf. aı̊šóndıgorı (N. -ıko-, -ıho-).
 nıbídkı šóndi *shake out the mat.*
 íllɛn nu̇rɛm bérro šóndıran (-n n- < -g n- §625) *they strew the (reaped heads of) wheat about the post in the threshing-floor.*
šóndar (-dȧr-; §§2200ff.) and
šóndíd (§§2256ff.) n. *shaking, etc.*
šónd-an (§§3890ff.) v.t. *tell to shake, etc., let shake.*
šóndı-bu̇- (§3931β) v.i. stat. *be in a shaken (etc.) state or condition.*
 níbıd šóndıbūn *the mat is (has been) shaken out.*
šondɛd-åg- (§§3877ff.) v.t. *be in the situation of having shaken, etc.*
 níbdıš šondɛdȧgran (-š š- < -g š- §695) *they have shaken out the mats.*
šóndı-kattı- (N. -ıha-; §4093) v.p. *be shaken, etc.*
šóro adj. (a) *light (not heavy)*; (b) *nimble, agile* [§2561β].
 obj. -rog.
 pl. -rorı and -ronč(ı).
 šaı̊šóro *weak tea.*
šórogıd n. *lightness, etc.* [§§2247–8].
šórokanɛ (§2295) n. *lightness, etc.*
šóro-tod (§2582) adj. *unsatisfactorily light.*
 obj. -tŏdk(ı), -tŏtk(ı), -tŏtt(ı) §2462, -kı, -tı.
 gen. -tŏdn v., -tŏnn v.c., -tŏn c.
 pl. šórotonı.
šór-an- (§3910α) v.i. *become light, etc., grow light, lose weight.*
šóram-bu̇- (§§3949ff.) v.i. stat. *be in a state or condition of growing or having grown light, etc.*
šóranɛd-åg- (§3966α) v.i. *be in the condition of having grown light, etc.*
šórog-ır (N. -okır, -ohır; §3701) (a) v.t. caus. *cause or allow to be light, etc.*; (b) v.t. *lighten, alleviate.*
 tén ǧízab bıšórogıddan (-b b- < -g b- §519) *they will reduce his (her) punishment.*
šórogır-åu (N. -okır-, -ohır-; §4137) v.t. *make lightly, keep light in making, make without allowing to be heavy.*

šōrogɪrǎw-an (N. -okɪr-, -ohɪr-; §§ 3890, 3905) v.t. *tell to make lightly, etc., let make lightly, etc.*
šăigɪ‿šōrogɪråwan⌒ *tell him (her) to make the tea weak.*

šǔg v.t. *(a) drive, drive along; (b) drive off, drive away.*
ind. pres. ai‿šúg(¹)ri⌒, ɛr‿šúgɪn⌒ (-gī⌒, -gí⌒); perf. ai‿šúgkori⌒ (‿šúkkori⌒).
imperat. šúk!, pl. šúgwɛ! (šúgwɛ́!, šúggɛ! § 547, -gɛ́!).
subj. past ai‿šúgsɪ‿ (‿šúksɪ‿, -su‿).
part. pres. šúgɪ‿ (one) that drives, etc., driver, etc., driving, etc.; in water-wheel (kólɛ‿) = ɛwɪrátt(ɪ)‿, obj. šūgílg(ɪ)‿, -gi⌒; past šúgɛl (one) that drove, etc., driver, etc., driving, etc., obj. šūgélg(ɪ)‿, -gi⌒.
def. perf. ai‿šūgóskori⌒.
bɪtăn‿tíncɪš‿šúgɪn⌒ (‿š‿š- < -g‿š- § 695) *a (the) boy drives the cattle (esp. of the water-wheel, kólɛ).*
wélɪš‿šúgɪrɪrɪn⌒ *he drives the (various § 5456) dogs off.*
tíncɪgɛš‿šúgran‿ (§ 5454; ‿š‿š- < -d‿š- § 694) n. *instrument for driving cattle, cattle-switch.*
šúgar‿ (-gár‿; §§ 2200 ff.) and
šūgíd‿ (§§ 2256 ff.) n. *driving, etc.*
šǔg-an (§§ 3890 ff.) v.t. *tell to drive, etc., let drive, etc.*
šǔg-bū- (šúggū- § 546; § 3931 β) v.i. stat. *be in a driven (etc.) state or condition.*
šǔg(¹)r-ɛ-ǎg- (§§ 4071 ff.) v.t. = šūgɛdól-.
šǔg-ɛ-dól- (-g°d- § 1178; § 4022) and
šǔg(¹)r-ɛ-dól- (-r°d- § 4027) v.t. *be about to drive, etc.*
šǔg(¹)r-ɛ-ǧǔ-bū- (§ 4069) v.t. stat. *be on one's way (coming) to drive, etc.*
šǔg-ɛ-mā- (§ 4036) and
šǔg(¹)-r-ɛ-mā- (§ 4041) v.t. *become unable to drive, etc.*
šǔg(¹)r-ɛ-nóg (§§ 4048 ff.) v.t. *go to drive, etc.*
urtíncɪš‿šǔg¹rɛnókkó⌒ (‿š‿š- < -g‿š- § 695) *(s)he went (has gone) to drive away the goats (sheep).*
šǔg(¹)r-ɛ-nóg-bū- (-nóggū- § 546; § 4058) v.t. stat. *be on one's way (going) to drive, etc.*
šǔg(¹)r-ɛ-tā́- (§§ 4060 ff.) v.t. *come to drive, etc.*
šǔgɛd-ǎg- (§§ 3877 ff.) v.t. *be in the situation of having driven, etc.*
šūgéd-dā- (§ 3991; -gɛ́ggɪdā-, occ. -ɛ́dgɪ-§§ 3993-4) v.t. *be going along driving, etc., be driving (etc.) as one goes along.*
urtíncɪš‿šūgɛddáran⌒ (‿š‿š- < -g‿š- § 695) *they are driving the goats (sheep) along.*
šūgɛn-nóg (§§ 4169 ff., 4193; -gɛggɪnóg, occ. -ɛdgɪ- §§ 4176-8) v.t. *go (etc., s.v. nóg) driving, go driving off, drive off with one, drive away with one.*
hánuš‿šūgɛnnókkó⌒ (‿š‿š- < -g‿š- § 695) *(s)he drove (has driven) the donkey off with him (her).*
hánuš‿šūgɛggɪnókkoran⌒ *they drove (have driven) the donkey off with them.*
šūgɛt-tā́ (§§ 4169 ff., 5723, 4193; -gɛggɪtā́, occ. -ɛdgɪ- §§ 4176-8) v.t. *come driving, etc.*

šǔg-ɛttā́ (-ɛ́ttā §§ 3855, 5723) v.t. *bring (ɛttā s.v. éd) driving.*
šūgos-nóg (-onnóg § 629; §§ 4180-4; -osgɪ-nóg, -ozgɪ-, -oggɪ- § 4185) v.t. *go (away) after driving away (§ 4193).*
hánuš‿šūhonnókkó⌒ (‿š‿š- < -g‿š-§ 695) *after driving away the donkey (s)he went (has gone) away.*
šūglɛ́ (šoglɛ́, šogolɛ́ § 1362) v.i. *work, labour* [< شغل n. *work* + -ɛ § 3617].
ind. pres. ai‿šūglɛ́ri⌒; perf. ai‿šūglɛ́gori⌒ (N. -ɛ́ko-, -ɛ́ho-).
imperat. šūglɛ́!, pl. šūglɛ́wɛ! (-lɛ́wɛ́!).
híttagɛš‿šūglɛ́goran⌒ (‿š‿š- < -d‿š-§ 694) *they (have) worked by the piece.*
šūglɛ́rar‿ (šog(o)l-, -rár‿; §§ 2200 ff., 2207) and
šūglɛ́ríd‿ (šog(o)l-; §§ 2256 ff., 2260) n. *working.*
šūglɛ́r-an (šog(o)l-; §§ 3890 ff., 3899) v.t. *tell to work, etc., let work, etc.*
šūglɛ́-bū- (šog(o)l-; §§ 3927 ff.) v.i. stat. *be in a worked (etc.) state or condition.*
ǧɛ́lli‿šūglɛ́būn⌒ *the work is in hand.*
šūglɛ́r-ɛg-ǎg- (šog(o)l-; §§ 4071 ff.) v.i. = šūglɛ́rɛdól-.
šūglɛ́r-ɛ-dól- (šog(o)l-; -r°d- § 1178; §§ 4016-17, 4022, 4027) v.i. *be about to work, etc.*
šūglɛ́r-ɛ-ǧǔ-bū- (šog(o)l-; § 4069) v.i. stat. *be on one's way (coming) to work, etc.*
šūglɛ́r-ɛ-mā- (šog(o)l-; §§ 4016-17, 4036, 4041) v.i. *become unable to work, etc.*
šūglɛ́r-ɛ-nóg (šog(o)l-; §§ 4048 ff.) v.i. *go to work, etc.*
šūglɛ́r-ɛ-nóg-bū- (šog(o)l-; -nóggū- § 546; § 4058) v.i. stat. *be on one's way (going) to work, etc.*
šūglɛ́r-ɛ-tā́- (šog(o)l-; §§ 4060 ff.) v.i. *come to work, etc.*
šūglɛ́rɛd-ǎg- (šog(o)l-; §§ 3877 ff.) v.i. *be in the situation of having worked, etc.*
šūglɛ́g-ɪr (šog(o)l-; N. -ɛ́kɪr, -ɛ́hɪr; § 3681) (a) v.t. caus. *cause or allow to work, etc.;* (b) v.t. *employ.*
bābúrkɪ‿šoglɛ́gírkoná? *did you make (have you made) the stove (etc., s.v. bābúr‿) work?*
šūgúdd(ɪ) *cause to descend s.v. šúgur.*
šúgum v.t. *(a) shake (vessel containing liquid) esp. in order to rinse; (b) rinse by shaking* [imit.].
ind. pres. ai‿šúgumri⌒, ɛr‿šúgumɪn⌒ (-mī⌒, -mí⌒); perf. ai‿šúgumkori⌒.
bɛ́ŋɪ‿šúgumɪn⌒ *(s)he shakes the skin (bag containing liquid).*
ánn‿agílgɪ‿šūgúmkori⌒ *I (have) rinsed my mouth.*
šúgumar‿ (-már‿; §§ 2200 ff.) and
šūgumíd‿ (§§ 2256 ff.) n. *shaking, etc.*
šúgum-an (§§ 3890 ff.) v.t. *tell to shake, etc., let shake, etc.*
šúgumɛd-ǎg- (§§ 3877 ff.) v.t. *be in the situation of having shaken, etc.*
šūgúm-kattɪ- (§ 4093) v.p. *be shaken, etc.*
šugum-úru (§ 3747 ɛ') v.t. *rinse by shaking.*
bɛ́ŋɪ‿šūgumurós⌒ *rinse out the skin by shaking it.*
šúgur (§ 2839) v.i. *descend, come (go) down* [cp. dígɪr *fall*, ON. ϲоτοϼ *Steigbügel* ZNG s.v.].

ind. pres. ai‿šugúrri⌒ (-gúddi⌒ §§ 3579, 6290), ɛr‿šúgurɪn⌒ (-rī⌒, -rí⌒); perf. ai‿šugúrkori⌒.
imperat. šúgur!, pl. šúgurwɛ! (šugúr-, -wɛ́!).
def. perf. ai‿šūguróskori⌒.
ógɪǧ‿ǧówwɪrtōn‿šugúrkon⌒ *the man came (has come) down from the tree.*
ógɪǧ‿ǧówwɪr‿šugúrkon⌒ *the man went (has gone) down the well.*
ɛ́ssɪr‿šugúrmunun, wɛ́dɪn⌒ *(s)he (it) doesn't sink in (the) water, (s)he (it) floats.*
šúgurar‿ (-rár‿; §§ 2200 ff.) and
šūguríd‿ (§§ 2256 ff.) n. *descent.*
šúgur-an (§§ 3890 ff.) v.t. *tell to descend, let descend.*
álɪš‿šúguran‿ (‿š‿š- < -g‿š- § 695) *tell ǧáli to go (come) down.*
šugúr-bū- (šúgurbū-; § 3931 α) v.i. stat. *be in a descending or descended state or condition.*
bɪtǎm‿béntɪrtōn‿šúgurbūn⌒ *the boy is on his way down the date-palm.*
ógɪǧ‿ǧówwɪr‿šugúrbūn⌒ *the man is on his way down the well.*
áru‿ǧɪbálló‿šugúrbūn⌒ *(the) rain is falling in the mountains.*
šugurr-ɛg-ǎg- (§§ 4071 ff.) v.i. = šugurɛ-dól-.
šugur-ɛ-dól- (-r°d- § 1178; § 4022) and
šugurr-ɛ-dól- (-r°d- § 4027) v.i. *be about to descend.*
šugur-ɛ-mā- (§ 4036) and
šugurr-ɛ-mā- (§ 4041) v.i. *become unable to descend.*
šugurɛd-ǎg- (§§ 3877 ff.) v.i. *be in the situation of having descended.*
šúgur-ǧɛrrɪbɛ́ (§ 3747 ɛ') v.i. *try to descend.*
šugúdd(ɪ) (a) v.t. caus. *cause or allow to descend;* (b) v.t. *bring (send, put, let, etc.) down, lower* [< *šugúrd(ɪ) < šúgur *descend* + -d caus. § 2865].
ind. pres. ai‿šugúddɪri⌒; perf. ai‿šugúddɪgori⌒ (N. -ɪko-, -ɪho-).
imperat. šugúddɪ! (§ 6290).
def. perf. ai‿šuguddóskori⌒.
šugúddar‿ (-dár‿; §§ 2200 ff.) and
šuguddíd‿ (§§ 2256 ff.) n. *bringing (etc.) down, lowering.*
šugúdd-an (§§ 3890 ff.) v.t. *tell to lower, etc., let lower, etc.*
šuguddɪr-ɛg-ǎg- (§§ 4071 ff.) v.t. = šugudd-ɛdól-.
šugudd-ɛ-dól- (-d°d- § 1178; § 4022) and
šuguddɪr-ɛ-dól- (-r°d- § 4027) v.t. *be about to lower, etc.*
šugudd-ɛ-mā- (§ 4036) and
šuguddɪr-ɛ-mā- (§ 4041) v.t. *become unable to lower, etc.*
šugudd-ɛd-ǎg- (§§ 3877 ff.) v.t. *be in the situation of having lowered, etc.*
šugúddɪ-kattɪ- (N. -ɪha-; § 4093) v.p. *be lowered, etc.*
šúk! imperat. of šúg *drive.*
N. šúk(ɪ) v.t. *wash* (= šúkk(ɪ)).
ind. pres. ai‿šúkɪri⌒; perf. ai‿šúkɪkori⌒ (occ. ‿šúkɪgori⌒ § 2981).
imperat. šúkɪ!
def. perf. ai‿šūkóskori⌒.
šúkɪkattɪ- (N. -ɪha-) v.p. and other derivatives as of šúkk(ɪ), with single -k- in N.

šúkk(ı) (N. šŭk(ı)) v.t. *wash* (used by some speakers only of washing inanimate objects) [< *šúgk(ı) < šŭg *drive out* sc. *the dirt from* + -k intensive §2853; *RSN*, §129].
  ind. pres. aı⌣šúkkırı⌢; perf. aı⌣šúkkıgorı⌢.
  imperat. šúkki!
  def. perf. aı⌣šúkkóskori⌢.
  part. pres. šúkkıʟ (*one*) *that washes, washer, washerman, washing*, obj. šúkkılg(ı)⌣, -gi⌢.
    kádɛš⌣šúkkıʟ (-š⌣š- < -g⌣š- §695) and kadénčıš⌣šúkkıʟ *washer of clothes, washerman*.
    washán⌣ɛgın⌣šúkkıran⌢ *if* (*when*) *it's* ((*s*)*he's, they're* §4647) *dirty they wash it* (*him, her, them*).
    gɛzázıš⌣šúkkosıʀ⌢ *wash* (*each of* §5456) *the bottles out*.
šúkkar⌣ (-kár⌣; §§2200 ff.) and
šúkkíd⌣ (§§2256 ff.) n. *washing*.
šúkkıdk-ır-šúkk(ı) (-ıtkır-, -ıttır-, §§4156, 4160) v.t. *wash thoroughly, completely*.
  ér⌣hodárkı⌣šúkkıtkır šúkkıgoná? *have you thoroughly washed the vegetables?*
šúkk-an (§§3890 ff.) v.t. *tell to wash, let wash*.
  áʟıg⌣ɛn⌣kádɛš⌣šúkkan⌣ (-š⌣š- < -g⌣š- §695) *let ɛáli wash his* (*own* §5670) *clothes*.
šúkkı-bŭ- (§3931β) v.i. stat. *be in a washed state or condition*.
  kádɛ⌣šúkkıbūn⌢ *the cloth is* (*has been*) *washed*.
šúkkır-ɛg-ág- (§§4071 ff.) v.t. = šúkkɛdól-.
šúkk-ɛ-dól- (-kᵒd- §1178; §4022) and
šúkkır-ɛ-dól- (-rᵒd- ; §4027) v.t. *be about to wash*.
šúkkır-ɛ-ğŭ-bŭ- (§4069) v.t. stat. *be on one's way* (*coming*) *to wash*.
šúkk-ɛ-má- (§4036) and
šúkkır-ɛ-má- (§4041) v.t. *become unable to wash*.
šúkk-ɛ-nóg (§§4048 ff.) v.t. *go to wash*.
šúkkır-ɛ-nóg-bŭ- (-nóggŭ- §546; §4058) v.t. stat. *be on one's way* (*going*) *to wash*.
šúkkır-ɛ-tá (§§4060 ff.) v.t. *come to wash*.
šúkkɛd-ág- (§§3877 ff.) v.t. *be in the situation of having washed*.
šúkkı-kattı- (§4093) v.p. *be washed*.
šúkkos-nís (-onnís §629; §§4180-4; -osgınís, -ozgı-, -oggı- §4185) v.t. *wring* (etc., s.v. nís).
  nógo⌣kádɛš⌣šúkkonnísın⌢ (-š⌣š- < -g⌣š- §695) *the female slave wrings the cloth(s* §4696 d) *after washing it* (*them*).
šúlug (šólog; N. šelog) (a) v.t. *shake, agitate, shake up* (esp. a liquid); (b) v.i. *shake, be agitated* [imit.].
  ind. pres. aı⌣šúlug(¹)ri⌢; perf. aı⌣šulúgkori⌢ (-úkko-).
  subj. past aı⌣šúlugsı⌣ (-uksı⌣, -su⌣).
  dówwaš⌣šúluk⌣ (-š⌣š- < -g⌣š- §695) *shake the medicine*.
  dówwag⌣ɛssírro⌣šúlug⌣sáwınn⌣íllár⌢ *shake up the medicine in the bottle for it to mix*.
  éssı bɛ́ñgɛš⌣šúlugran⌢ (-b⌣b- < -g⌣b- §519, -š⌣š- < -d⌣š- §694) *they shake* (*the*) *water in a* (*the*) *skin*.

éssı⌣bɛ́ñ⌣túr⌣šúlugın⌢ (-ñ⌣t- < -ñn⌣t §843) *the water shakes in the skin*.
šúlugar (-gár⌣; §§2200 ff.) and
šulugíd⌣ (§§2256 ff.) n. *shaking, etc., agitation*.
šúlug-an (§§3890 ff.) v.t. *tell to shake, etc., let shake, etc.*
šúlug-bŭ- (-uggŭ- §546; šulúg-; §3931β) v.i. stat. *be in a shaken* (etc.) *state or condition*.
  dáwa⌣šúlugbūn⌢ *the medicine is* (*has been*) *shaken*.
šulugíŋ-ır (šúlugıŋ-; N. šɛlogíŋkır, šélogıŋkır; §3688) v.t. caus. *cause or allow to shake, etc.*
šulúg-kattı- (-úka- ; §4093) v.p. *be shaken, etc.*
  dáwa⌣gɛzázır⌣šulúkkattın⌢ *the medicine is shaken in the bottle*.
  éssıgon⌣sɛ́rkon⌣ɛssírro⌣šulukkáttıgım⌣bıgéndın⌢ *if water and gravel are shaken in a* (*the*) *bottle it will get clean*.
šúna⌣ n. *heap, pile, stack* [contents of شونة *barn* §2409; *RSN*, §129].
  obj. -nag⌣.
  pl. -nanč(ı)⌣.
    tɛššáš⌣béntın⌣šúnan⌣tórtıǧ⌣ǧansókkɛgon⌢ (-ǧ⌣ǧ- < -g⌣ǧ- §551) *the* (*a*) *travelling merchant* (*has*) *bought and removed half of the heap of dates*.
    bérn⌣šúnanč ıb⌣bábúrn⌣íllɛr⌣agáuran⌢ (-b⌣b- < -g⌣b- §519) *they are making stacks of wood* (i.e. *fuel*) *for the steamer*.
    márɛn⌣šúnas⌣sokkóskoran, mahzánd⌣uskóskoram⌢ (-s⌣s- < -g⌣s- §678) *they have removed the heap of millet and put it into the store*.
    íllɛn⌣šúnak⌣kúbır⌣uskuróskoran⌢ *they have put the heap of wheat into the boat*.
šúnd(ı)⌣ n. *lip*; with collective sg. (§4696 a).
  obj. -dıg⌣.
  pl. -dınč(ı)⌣.
šúrba (-bá⌣, -bɛ) n. (a) *draught, dose of liquid*; (b) *soup* [< شربة id.].
  obj. -bag⌣.
  pl. -banč(ı)⌣.
†**šur(r)áb**⌣ n. *stocking, sock*; with collective sg. (§4696 d) [< شراب, شَرَاب id.].
  obj. -ábk(ı)⌣, -ápk(ı)⌣, -ki⌢.
  gen. -ábnv⌣., -ámc.
  pl. -ábı⌣.
  †šurábkɛs⌣sóllıgıddan⌢ (§5453; -s⌣s- < -d⌣s- §677) *what they hang up the sock(s) with, sock-suspenders*.
šurūd⌣ n. *contract, compact, bargain* [< شروط *stipulations*].
  obj. -údk(ı)⌣, -útk(ı)⌣, -útt(ı)⌣ §2462, -ki⌢, -ti⌢.
  šurútkɛd⌣ *according to the contract*.
šurūdk-áu (-útk-; §3747 a′, b, 2) v.i. *make a contract, etc.*
  šurūdkáuru⌢ *let us* (§5376) *make a contract*.
šurūdk-awos-áššuglɛ́ (-útk-; -osga-, -ozga-, -ogga-; cp. §§4207-8; s.v. áššuglɛ́) v.i. (a) *be engaged in working on contract*; (b) *habitually work on contract*.
  šurūtkawoggáššuglɛ́ran⌢ *they are working* (*habitually work*) *on contract*.

šúš⌣ n. *pillar* (of spindle, *CSW*, p. 21) [app. < شوشة *crest, tuft* §1394, §2409].
  obj. šúšk(ı)⌣, -ki⌢.
  pl. šúšı⌣.
    núbron⌣šúš⌣ *pillar of spindle*.

-**t**...? (before a vowel §1122) interrogative particle and sign of predication *is it that?, is?* = -tɛ⌣...?
tá v.i. *come*.
  ind. pres. aı⌣tári⌢, ɛr⌣tán⌢ (⌣tá⌣, ⌣tá⌢; occ. ⌢.⌣ta⌢ §944); fut. aı⌣bıtári⌢ (⌣but-); perf. aı⌣tágori⌢ (N. ⌣táko-, ⌣táho-).
  imperat. tá!, tá⌣c., tár⌣v., pl. táwɛ! (táwé!).
  subj. past aı⌣tásı⌣ (-su⌣).
  part. pres. tá ʟ (*one*) *that comes, comer, coming*, obj. tá lg(ı)⌣, -gi⌢; tá ln-d(ı)⌣ (tá nd(ı)⌣ §807; §5014) cpx. adj. *appertaining to the comer, of the coming*.
  part. past tárɛʟ (*one*) *that came, comer*, obj. tárélg(ı)⌣, -gi⌢; perf. tá gŏʟ (N. tá kŏʟ, tá hŏʟ) (*one*) *that came* (*has come*), *comer, having come*, obj. tá gŏlg(ı)⌣, -gi⌢; fut. bıtá ʟ (butá ʟ) (*one*) *that will come, comer, coming*, obj. -álg(ı)⌣, -gi⌢.
  neg. ind. pres. aı⌣támunun⌢ (-munū⌢, -munu⌢, -mun⌢ §947); perf. aı⌣tágomunun⌢ (-munū⌢, -munu⌢, -mun⌢).
  neg. interr. ind. pres. aı⌣támɛndi?; perf. aı⌣tágomɛndi?
  def. ind. pres. aı⌣tárosri⌢; perf. aı⌣táróskori⌢.
  def. imperat. sg. táré! (táré!, tárɛ!).
  índo⌣tá! (índó⌣ta! §1742) and tá⌣índo! *come here!*
  índo⌣táwɛ! (táwé!) *come* (pl.) *here!*
  ısáıgɛd⌣tán? and sáıgét⌣ta? (§944) *which way* (s.v. -ɛd⌣) *does* (*s*)*he* (*it*) *come?*
  mudír⌣ɛ́kkı⌣tár⌣ɛ́⌢ *the manager* (*governor*) *wants to see* (i.e. *has summoned*) *you*, lit. *the manager says* (⌣ɛ́⌢ < ⌣ɛ́n⌣ §939) *to you 'come!'* (cp. Amh. ሊብሏሻላሁ።).
  ékk⌣índo⌣tár⌣ɛgó⌢ (*s*)*he* (*has*) *called you*, lit. (*s*)*he* (*has*) *said 'come here!'* *to you*.
  kıráɡɛ⌣tá ʟ (§4794) n.-cpx. *next Sunday*, obj. kıráɡɛ⌣tá lg(ı)⌣, -gi⌢.
  kıráɡɛ⌣tá lg(ı)⌣, -gi⌢ (§4665) adv.-cpx. *on Sunday next*.
  kıráɡɛ⌣tállo (s.v. -r⌣) adv.-cpx. *on Sunday next*.
  kıráɡɛ⌣tállo⌢ (§6039) *it is* (*they are*) *on Sunday next*.
  kıráɡɛ⌣tálgı⌣bıtáran⌢ and
  kıráɡɛ⌣tállo⌣bıtáran⌢ *they will come next Sunday*.
  kágaddı⌣táróskoran⌢ *they have come towards the house*.
-**tá** as the verbal part (z §3744) of a verb-complex will sometimes be rendered by *go* or not rendered (§5713):
  súgırtōn⌣gutáru⌢ *we're just going to the market and back*.
  íŋ⌣oǧósta⌣ (⌣oǧótta⌢) *just take this away*, lit. *take this away and come* (*back*).

X. márɛ‿sɛ́? *where is the millet?*
Y. oğottågori⁀ *I have just removed it (je viens de l'enlever).*

tǎrar‿ (-rår‿; §§ 2200 ff., 2207),
tǎrǐd‿ and tǎrǐd‿ (-rɪd‿; §§ 2256 ff., 2260) n. *coming, arrival.*

— as ta- does not always > tār- before a vowel, and in view of their number, the following complexes are placed in their actual, rather than their etymological, alphabetical order:

ta-amínt(ı) (§§ 3866–7) v.t. *come and show.*
taamínt-an (§§ 3890 ff., 3905) v.t. *tell to come and show, let come and show.*
ta-ǎr (§§ 3866–7) v.t. *come and seize (etc., s.v. ǎr).*
taǎr-an (§§ 3890 ff., 3905) v.t. *tell to come and seize (etc.), let come and seize (etc.).*
ta-ǎu (-ǎw, -ǎu; tǎu § 1115a; §§ 3866–7) v.t. *come and do (etc., s.v. ǎu).*
taıŋgǎu! (§ 5601) *come and do this!*
taıŋgǎuwé! *come (pl.) and do this!*
ɛ́n‿takusugǎukon⁀ *the woman came and (has) cooked the meat.*
taǎw-an (§§ 3890 ff., 3905) v.t. *tell to come and do (etc.), let come and do (etc.).*
taıŋgǎwan! (-wǎ!, -wá!; § 5601) *tell him (her) to come and do this! (let him (her) come...).*
takusugǎwan! (-wǎ!, -wá!) *tell him (her) to come and cook the meat!*
ta-bág (§§ 3866–7) v.t. *come and distribute (etc., s.v. bág).*
imperat. tábak!, tabák! (§ 1912).
tabág-an (§§ 3890 ff., 3905) v.t. *tell to come and distribute (etc.), let come and distribute (etc.).*
ta-bǎg (§§ 3866–7) v.t. *come and divide (etc., s.v. bǎg).*
imperat. tábāk!, tabák! (§ 1913).
tabǎg-an (§§ 3890 ff., 3905) v.t. *tell to come and divide (etc.), let come and divide (etc.).*
ta-bagíttɛ (§§ 3866–7) v.t. *come and divide into shares.*
tabagíttɛr-an (§§ 3890 ff., 3905) v.t. *tell to come and divide, etc., let come and divide, etc.*
ta-bǎğ (§§ 3866–7) v.t. *come and write (etc., s.v. bǎğ).*
imperat. tábač!, tabáč! (§ 1913).
tabǎğ-an (§§ 3890 ff., 3905) v.t. *tell to come and write (etc.), let come and write (etc.).*
ta-bár (§§ 3866–7) v.t. *come and sort (etc., s.v. bár).*
imperat. tábar!, tabár! (§ 1912).
tabár-an (§§ 3890 ff., 3905) v.t. *tell to come and sort (etc.), let come and sort (etc.).*
ta-bɛ́ (§§ 3866–7) v.t. *come and kill, come and extinguish.*
imperat. tábɛ!, tabɛ́! (§ 1871).
íkkɪ‿tábɛ́⁀ *come and put the fire (light) out.*
tabɛ́r-an (§§ 3890 ff., 3905) v.t. *tell to come and kill, etc., let come and kill, etc.*
álɪg‿íkkɪ‿tabɛ́rá⁀ *let ɣáli come and put the fire (light) out.*
ta-bɛ́l (§§ 3866–7) v.i. *come and issue, come and pass out, come along out.*
tábɛl! (~́) *come along out!*
tabɛ́l-an (§§ 3890 ff., 3905) v.t. *tell to come and issue, etc., let come and issue, etc.*

ta-bɛtɛ́ (-bɛdɛ́; §§ 3866–7) v.t. *come and begin.*
tabɛtɛ́r-an (-ɛdɛ́-; §§ 3890 ff., 3905) v.t. *tell to come and begin, let come and begin.*
ta-bɛ́u (-bɛ́u; §§ 3866–7) v.t. *come and unravel (etc., s.v. bɛ́u).*
tabɛ́w-an (§§ 3890 ff., 3905) v.t. *tell to come and unravel (etc.), let come and unravel (etc.).*
ta-bír (§§ 3866–7) v.t. *come and transport.*
imperat. tábīr!, tabír!
tabír-an (§§ 3890 ff., 3905) v.t. *tell to come and transport, let come and transport.*
ta-bítt(ı) (§§ 3866–7) v.t. *come and pick up (etc. s.v. bítt(ı)).*
imperat. tabítti!
tabítt-an (§§ 3890 ff., 3905) v.t. *tell to come and pick up (etc.), let come and pick up (etc.).*
ta-bókk(ı) (§§ 3866–7) v.i. *come and hide (oneself).*
imperat. tabókki!
tabókk-an (§§ 3890 ff., 3905) v.t. *tell to come and hide, let come and hide.*
ta-bókk(ı) (§§ 3866–7) (a) v.t. *come and unload;* (b) v.i. *come and miscarry.*
imperat. tabókki!
tabókk-an (§§ 3890 ff., 3905) v.t. *tell to come and unload, let come and unload.*
ta-bókkır (§§ 3866–7) v.t. *come and conceal.*
tabókkır-an (§§ 3890 ff., 3905) v.t. *tell to come and conceal, let come and conceal.*
ta-bǒrkığ (§§ 3866–7) v.t. *come and demolish (etc., s.v. bǒr).*
tabǒrkığ-an (§§ 3890 ff., 3905) v.t. *tell to come and demolish (etc.), let come and demolish (etc.).*
ta-bǒrkır (§§ 3866–7) v.t. *come and fell (etc., s.v. bǒr).*
tabǒrkır-an (§§ 3890 ff., 3905) v.t. *tell to come and fell (etc.), let come and fell (etc.).*
ta-bǒww(ı) (§§ 3866–7) v.i. *come and bathe (i.), come and swim.*
imperat. tabǒwwi!
tabǒww-an (§§ 3890 ff., 3905) v.t. *tell to come and bathe, etc., let come and bathe, etc.*
ta-bǒwwídd(ı) (§§ 3866–7) v.t. *come and bathe (t.).*
imperat. tabǒwwíddi!
tabǒwwídd-an (§§ 3890 ff., 3905) v.t. *tell to come and bathe (t.), let come and bathe (t.).*
ta-dárr(ı) (§§ 3866–7) v.i. *come and ascend (etc., s.v. dárr(ı)).*
tadárr-an (§§ 3890 ff., 3905) v.t. *tell to come and ascend (etc.), let come and ascend (etc.).*
ta-dɛfɛ́ (§§ 3866–7) v.t. *come and pay.*
tadɛfɛ́r-an (§§ 3890 ff., 3905) v.t. *tell to come and pay, let come and pay.*
ta-dɛfɛ́dɛn (§§ 3866–7) v.t. *come and pay (the speaker).*
ǎıgɪ‿tadɛfɛ́dɛn⁀ *come and pay me.*
tadɛfɛ́dɛn-an (§§ 3890 ff., 3905) v.t. *tell to come and pay (the speaker), let come and pay (etc.).*
ta-dɛfɛ́tɪr (§§ 3866–7) v.t. *come and pay (other than the speaker).*
tadɛfɛ́tɪr-an (§§ 3890 ff., 3905) v.t. *tell to come and pay (other than the speaker), let come and pay (etc.).*

ta-dég (§§ 3866–7) v.i. and t. *come and cover one's loins (etc., s.v. dég).*
imperat. tádɛk!, tadɛ́k! (§ 1912).
hánut‿tádɛk‿ (-t‿t- < -g‿t- § 707) *come and saddle (load) the donkey.*
afɛ́škı‿tadégwɛ́⁀ *come (pl.) and load the baggage.*
tadég-an (§§ 3890 ff., 3905) v.t. *tell to come and cover the loins (etc.), let come and cover the loins (etc.).*
álɪh‿hánut‿tadégan⁀ (-h‿h- < -g‿h- § 559, -t‿t- < -g‿t- § 707) *let ɣáli come and saddle (load) the donkey.*
ta-děg (§§ 3866–7) v.t. *come and irrigate (etc., s.v. děg).*
imperat. tádɛ̌k!, tadɛ́k! (§ 1913).
tadɛ̌g-an (§§ 3890 ff., 3905) v.t. *tell to come and irrigate (etc.), let come and irrigate (etc.).*
ta-dɛ́n (§§ 3866–7) v.t. *come and give (to the speaker).*
imperat. tádɛn!, tádɛ́!, tádɛ̄!, tádɛ́!, tádɛn!, -dɛ́!, -dɛ̄!, -dɛ́! (§§ 1912–13).
tadɛ́n-an (§§ 3890 ff., 3905) v.t. *tell to come and give (to the speaker), let come and give (etc.).*
ta-dígır (§§ 3866–7) v.t. *come and tie (etc., s.v. díg-ır).*
tadígır-an (§§ 3890 ff., 3905) v.t. *tell to come and tie (etc.), let come and tie (etc.).*
ta-ɛrğɛ́ (taɛrɛğɛ́, -ɛrɛğğɛ́, -ɛrɪğɛ́; N. -ɛrɪğğɛ́; §§ 3866–7) v.i. and t. *come and wait (etc., s.v. ɛrğɛ́).*
taɛrğɛ́r-an (-rɛğ-, -rɛğğ-, -rɪğ-; N. -rɪğğ-; §§ 3890 ff., 3905) v.t. *tell to come and wait (etc.), let come and wait (etc.).*
ta-gɛddımɛ́ (-dumɛ́; §§ 3866–7) v.t. and i. *come and put forward, come and get ahead (etc., s.v. gɛddımɛ́).*
tagɛddımɛ́r-an (-dum-; §§ 3890 ff., 3905) v.t. *tell to come and put forward (etc.), let come and put forward (etc.).*
ta-gɛ́ddımkatt(ı) (-dum-; §§ 3866–7) v.i. *come and get ahead (etc., s.v. gɛddımɛ́).*
imperat. tagɛ́ddımkatti!
tagɛ́ddımkatt-an (-dum-; §§ 3890 ff., 3905) v.t. *tell to come and get ahead (etc.), let come and get ahead (etc.).*
ta-géndıgır (N. -ıkır, -ıhır; §§ 3866–7) v.t. *come and set right (etc., s.v. géndıgır).*
tagéndıgır-an (N. -ıkır, -ıhır; §§ 3890 ff., 3905) v.t. *tell to come and set right (etc.), let come and set right (etc.).*
ta-gığır (§§ 3866–7) v.t. *come and hear, come and smell (s.v. gığır).*
tagığır-an (§§ 3890 ff., 3905) v.t. *tell to come and hear, etc., let come and hear, etc.*
tǎgoŋ-ɪr (§ 3695) v.t. caus. *cause or allow to have come.*
árțɪ‿kórɛt‿tǎgoŋɪrɪn⁀ (-t‿t- < -g‿t- § 707) *God causes the feast to have come.*
árțɪ‿kórɛt‿tǎgoŋɪrkon⁀ *God (has) caused the feast to have come.*
tǎgan *tell to come and go, etc.* = tǎğuan.
ta-ğǎn (§§ 3866–7) v.t. *come and buy, come and sell (s.v. ğǎn).*
imperat. tǎğān!, tağǎn! (§ 1913).
tağǎn-an (§§ 3890 ff., 3905) v.t. *tell to come and buy (sell), let come and buy (sell).*

tá

ta-ǧóm (§§ 3866-7) v.t. *come and strike (etc., s.v. ǧóm).*
  imperat. táǧom!, taǧóm! (§ 1912).
taǧóm-an (§§ 3890 ff., 3905) v.t. *tell to come and strike (etc.), let come and strike (etc.).*
ta-ǧŏr (§§ 3866-7) v.t. *come and reap (etc., s.v. ǧŏr).*
  imperat. táǧōr!, taǧŏr! (§ 1913).
taǧŏr-an (§§ 3890 ff., 3905) v.t. *tell to come and reap (etc.), let come and reap (etc.).*
ta-ǧŭ (§§ 3866-7) v.i. *come and go, come and proceed.*
  imperat. táǧu!, taǧú! (§ 1912).
taǧŭ-an (-ǧuán, -ǧ^uán, -ǧwán, -ǧán; §§ 3858, 3905) v.t. *tell to come and go, etc., let come and go, etc.*
ta-ǧúgur (§§ 3866-7) v.t. *come and burn.*
taǧúgur-an (§§ 3890 ff., 3905) v.t. *tell to come and burn, let come and burn.*
ta-haddɪrɛ́ (§§ 3866-7) v.t. *come and make ready, come and prepare.*
tahaddɪrɛ́r-an (§§ 3890 ff., 3905) v.t. *tell to come and make ready, etc., let come and make ready, etc.*
ta-haddɪrɛ́gɪr (N. -ɛ́kɪr, -ɛ́hɪr; §§ 3866-7) v.t. = tahaddɪrɛ́.
tahaddɪrɛ́gɪr-an (N. -ɛ́kɪr, -ɛ́hɪr; §§ 3890 ff., 3905) v.t. = tahaddɪrɛ́ran.
ta-hallɪsɛ́ (taxal-; §§ 3866-7) v.t. *come and save, come and finish.*
tahallɪsɛ́r-an (taxal-; §§ 3890 ff., 3905) v.t. *tell to come and save, etc., let come and save, etc.*
ta-ír (§§ 3866-7) v.t. *come and count (etc., s.v. ír).*
taír-an (§§ 3890 ff., 3905) v.t. *tell to come and count (etc.), let come and count (etc.).*
ta-ɪdd(ɪ) (§§ 3866-7) v.t. *come and ask (etc., s.v. ɪ́dd(ɪ)).*
  imperat. taíddi!
taídd-an (§§ 3890 ff., 3905) v.t. *tell to come and ask (etc.), let come and ask (etc.).*
ta-ɪgídd(ɪ) (§§ 3866-7) v.t. *come and water (etc., s.v. ɪgídd(ɪ)).*
  imperat. taɪgíddi!
taɪgídd-an (§§ 3890 ff., 3905) v.t. *tell to come and water (etc.), let come and water (etc.).*
ta-índ(ɪ) (§§ 3866-7) v.t. *come and lift (etc., s.v. índ(ɪ)).*
  imperat. taíndi!
taínd-an (§§ 3890 ff., 3905) v.t. *tell to come and lift (etc.), let come and lift (etc.).*
ta-íñɪr (taíñir; §§ 3866-7) v.i. and t. *come and wait (for) (etc., s.v. íñɪr).*
taíñɪr-an (taíñiran; §§ 3890 ff., 3905) v.t. *tell to come and wait (for) (etc.), let come and wait (for) (etc.).*
ta-káčč(ɪ) (§§ 3866-7) v.i. *come and play (etc., s.v. káčč(ɪ)).*
  imperat. takáčči!
takáčč-an (§§ 3890 ff., 3905) v.t. *tell to come and play (etc.), let come and play (etc.).*
ta-kál (§§ 3866-7) v.t. *come and eat.*
  imperat. tákal!, takál! (§ 1912), pl. takálwɛ!, takálwɛ́!
  def. imperat. takálɛ!, pl. takálɛwwɛ!, takálɛwwɛ́!
  butakállan⌒ and tabukállan⌒ *they will come and eat (it, them).*

takál-an (§§ 3890 ff., 3905) v.t. *tell to come and eat, let come and eat.*
ta-kálgɪr (§§ 3866-7) v.i. *come and make bread.*
takálgɪr-an (§§ 3890 ff., 3905) v.t. *tell to come and make bread, let come and make bread.*
ta-kalgídd(ɪ) (N. -lkí-; §§ 3866-7) v.t. *come and feed (t.).*
  imperat. takalgíddi! (N. -lkí-).
takalgídd-an (N. -lkí-; §§ 3890 ff., 3905) v.t. *tell to come and feed (t.), let come and feed (t.).*
ta-kárǧ(ɪ) (-káǧǧ(ɪ); §§ 3866-7) v.t. *come and testify.*
  imperat. takárǧi!, -káǧǧi!
takárǧ-an (-káǧǧ-; §§ 3890 ff., 3905) v.t. *tell to come and testify, let come and testify.*
ta-kás (§§ 3866-7) v.t. and i. *come and draw (etc., s.v. kás).*
  imperat. tákas!, takás! (§ 1912).
takás-an (§§ 3890 ff., 3905) v.t. *tell to come and draw (etc.), let come and draw (etc.).*
ta-kób (§§ 3866-7) v.t. *come and shut (etc., s.v. kób).*
  imperat. tákop!, takóp! (§ 1912).
takób-an (§§ 3890 ff., 3905) v.t. *tell to come and shut (etc.), let come and shut (etc.).*
  álɪk⌣kóbdɪt⌣takóbɪran⌒ (-k⌣k- < -g⌣k- § 569, -t⌣t- < -g⌣t- § 707) *let ɛ áli come and shut (each of § 5456) the doors.*
ta-kúddɛgɪr (N. -ɛkɪr, -ɛhɪr; §§ 3866-7) v.t. *come and burn.*
takúddɛgɪr-an (N. -ɛkɪr, -ɛhɪr; §§ 3890 ff., 3905) v.t. *tell to come and burn, let come and burn.*
ta-kúǧur (§§ 3866-7) v.t. *come and place on (etc., s.v. kúǧur).*
takúǧur-an (§§ 3890 ff., 3905) v.t. *tell to come and place on (etc.), let come and place on (etc.).*
ta-kús (§§ 3866-7) v.t. *come and open (etc. s.v. kús).*
  imperat. tákus!, takús! (§ 1912).
takús-an (§§ 3890 ff., 3905) v.t. *tell to come and open (etc.), let come and open (etc.).*
ta-măg (§§ 3866-7) v.t. *come and steal (etc., s.v. măg).*
  imperat. támak!, tamák! (§ 1913).
tamăg-an (§§ 3890 ff., 3905) v.t. *tell to come and steal (etc.), let come and steal (etc.).*
ta-mér (§§ 3866-7) v.t. *come and cut (etc., s.v. mér).*
  imperat. támer!, tamér! (§ 1912).
tamér-an (§§ 3890 ff., 3905) v.t. *tell to come and cut (etc.), let come and cut (etc.).*
ta-mŏr (§§ 3866-7) v.t. *come and bind.*
  imperat. támor!, tamŏr! (§ 1913).
tamŏr-an (§§ 3890 ff., 3905) v.t. *tell to come and bind, let come and bind.*
ta-nál (§§ 3866-7) v.t. *come and see, come and look.*
  imperat. tánal!, tanál! (§ 1912).
tanál-an (§§ 3890 ff., 3905) v.t. *tell to come and see, etc., let come and see, etc.*
ta-nɛr (§§ 3866-7) v.i. *come and sleep.*
  imperat. tánɛr!, tanɛ́r! (§ 1913).

tanɛ́r-an (§§ 3890 ff., 3905) v.t. *tell to come and sleep, let come and sleep.*
ta-ní (§§ 3866-7) v.t. *come and drink.*
  imperat. táni! (occ. táni!), taní! (occ. taní!).
  aɪ⌣butanfri⌒ and (§ 5609)
  aɪ⌣tabunfri⌒ *I shall come and drink.*
taní-an (§§ 3890 ff., 3905) v.t. *tell to come and drink, let come and drink.*
ta-nóǧ (§§ 3866-7) v.i. *come and go.*
  imperat. tánok!, tanók!
  ékkonom⌣bɪtanógri⌒ *I shall (I'll § 5383) come (sc. to you) and go with you.*
tanóǧ-an (§§ 3890 ff., 3905) v.t. *tell to come and go, let come and go.*
  tékk⌣árgonon⌣tanógan⌒ *tell him (her) to come and go with us.*
táŋg-ɪr (N. -ŋkɪr; § 3688) (a) v.t. caus. *cause or allow to come;* (b) v.t. *send.*
  ind. pres. aɪ⌣táŋgɪddi⌒ (⌣́⌣ § 1806), ɛr⌣táŋgɪrɪn⌒ (-rí⌒, -rí⌒); fut. aɪ⌣bɪtáŋgɪddi⌒ (but-); perf. aɪ⌣táŋgɪrkori⌒.
  subj. past aɪ⌣táŋgɪrsɪ⌣ (-su⌣).
táŋg-an (N. -ŋkɪr-; §§ 3890 ff., 3904) v.t. *tell to cause or allow to come, let send.*
ta-ŏbɪr (§§ 3866-7) v.t. *come and invert (etc., s.v. ŏbɪr).*
taŏbɪr-an (§§ 3890 ff., 3905) v.t. *tell to come and invert (etc.), let come and invert (etc.).*
ta-óčč(ɪ) (§§ 3866-7) v.t. *come and drag (etc., s.v. óčč(ɪ)).*
  imperat. taóčči!
  kúbkɪ⌣taóččiwɛ́⌒ *come (pl.) and tow the boat.*
taóčč-an (§§ 3890 ff., 3905) v.t. *tell to come and drag (etc.), let come and drag (etc.).*
ta-óǧɪ (§§ 3866-7) v.t. *come and carry (etc., s.v. óǧɪ).*
taóǧ-an (§§ 3890 ff., 3905) v.t. *tell to come and carry (etc.), let come and carry (etc.).*
ta-ós (§§ 3866-7) v.t. *come and cause to issue (etc., s.v. ós).*
  íw⌣wélgɪ⌣taŏs⌒ (-w⌣w- < -n⌣w- § 720) *come and turn this dog out.*
taós-an (§§ 3890 ff., 3905) v.t. *tell to come and cause to issue (etc.), let come and cause to issue (etc.).*
ta-ošóšk(ɪ) (§§ 3866-7) v.t. *come and drag (etc., s.v. ošóšk(ɪ)).*
taošóšk-an (§§ 3890 ff., 3905) v.t. *tell to come and drag (etc.), let come and drag (etc.).*
tăr-an (§§ 3890 ff., 3899) v.t. *tell to come, let come.*
  imperat. tăran! (-rā!, tará!).
  tăwan⌒ *tell them to come (let them come).*
  índo⌣tārándɪá? (⌣tārandɪá?) *shall I (§ 5369b) tell him (her) to come here?*
  wɛ́t⌣tārandɪá? (-t⌣t- < -g⌣t- § 707) *shall I tell someone to come?*
  índo⌣tāwándɪá? (⌣tāwandɪá?) *shall I tell them to come here?*
  índo⌣tāwanɪríddɪá? *shall I tell (each of § 5456) them to come here?*
tăr-ɛg-ăg- (§§ 4071 ff.) = v.i. tăredól-.
tăr-ɛ-dól- (-r^odɪ- § 1178; §§ 4016-17, 4022, 4027) v.i. *be about to come.*
  ǧéksum⌣băšă⌣tăredólsuw⌣wekídkɪ⌣ gendɪgírkora⌒ (-w⌣w- < -n⌣w- § 720) *when Jackson Pasha was about to come they mended it, i.e. they mended it just before J.P. came.*

tār-ɛ-mǎ- (§§ 4016–17, 4036, 4041) v.i. *become unable to come.*
  tārɛmágoran⌢ *they couldn't (were unable to) come.*
tārɛd-ǎg- (§§ 3877 ff.) v.i. *be in the situation of having come.*
tǎros-an (§§ 3890 ff., 3905) v.t. *tell to come, let come.*
  tāróswan! (-swǎ!, -swá!, -óssan!, -sǎ!, -sá!, -ówwan!, -wǎ!, -wá! §§ 687, 724) *tell them to come!*
  tārόswanir! (-óssa-, -ówwa-) *tell (each of § 5456) them to come!*
tǎros-nóg (-onnóg § 629; §§ 4180–4; -osgi-nóg, -ozgi-, -oggi- § 4185) v.i. *come and go, go after coming.*
  tɛr⌣ékkɛnɛ⌣tāronnókkon⌢ *(s)he (it) has just been and gone.*
ta-sigídd(ı) (§ 3866–7) v.i. *come and pray.*
  imperat. tasıgíddi!
tasigídd-an (§§ 3890 ff., 3905) v.t. *tell to come and pray, let come and pray.*
ta-sóg (§§ 3866–7) v.t. *come and accompany (etc., s.v. sóg).*
  imperat. tások!, tasók! (§ 1912).
tasόg-an (§§ 3890 ff., 3905) v.t. *tell to come and accompany (etc.), let come and accompany (etc.).*
ta-sókkɛ (§§ 3866–7) v.t. *come and take up (etc. s.v. sókkɛ).*
tasόkkɛr-an (§§ 3890 ff., 3905) v.t. *tell to come and take up (etc.), let come and take up (etc.).*
ta-šǔg (§§ 3866–7) v.t. *come and drive (etc., s.v. šǔg).*
  imperat. tášūk!, tašúk! (§ 1913).
tašǔg-an (§§ 3890 ff., 3905) v.t. *tell to come and drive (etc.), let come and drive (etc.).*
ta-šuglɛ́ (-šog(o)lɛ́; §§ 3866–7) v.i. *come and work.*
  imperat. tašuglɛ́!, -šog(o)lɛ́!
tašuglɛ́r-an (-šog(o)l-; §§ 3890 ff., 3905) v.t. *tell to come and work, let come and work.*
ta-šǔkk(ı) (N. -šúk(ı); §§ 3866–7) v.t. *come and wash.*
  imperat. tašúkki! (N. -šúki!).
tašǔkk-an (N. -šúkan; §§ 3890 ff., 3905) v.t. *tell to come and wash, let come and wash.*
ta-tɛbɛ́ (§§ 3866–7) v.t. *come and seek (etc., s.v. tɛbɛ́).*
  imperat. tatɛbɛ́!
tatɛbɛ́r-an (§§ 3890 ff., 3905) v.t. *tell to come and seek (etc.), let come and seek (etc.).*
ta-tɛ́g (§§ 3866–7) v.i. *come and squat (etc., s.v. tɛ́g).*
  imperat. tátɛk!, tatɛ́k! (§ 1913).
tatɛ́g-an (§§ 3890 ff., 3905) v.t. *tell to come and squat (etc.), let come and squat (etc.).*
ta-tír (§§ 3866–7) v.t. *come and give (to other than the speaker).*
  imperat. tátır! (§ 1912), tatír! (§ 1948).
tatír-an (§§ 3890 ff., 3905) v.t. *tell to come and give (etc.), let come and give (etc.).*
ta-tó (§§ 3866–7) v.i. *come and enter, come along in.*
  imperat. táto!, tató! (§ 1871).
tatǒr-an (§§ 3890 ff., 3905) v.t. *tell to come and enter, etc., let come and enter, etc.*

ta-tóg (§§ 3866–7) v.t. *come and strike, come and beat.*
  imperat. tátōk!, tatók! (§ 1913).
tatόg-an (§§ 3890 ff., 3905) v.t. *tell to come and strike, etc., let come and strike, etc.*
ta-tóllɛ (§§ 3866–7) v.t. *come and pull.*
tatόllɛr-an (§§ 3890 ff., 3905) v.t. *tell to come and pull, let come and pull.*
ta-tómb(ı) (§§ 3866–7) v.t. *come and break.*
  imperat. tatómbi!
tatómb-an (§§ 3890 ff., 3905) v.t. *tell to come and break, let come and break.*
ta-túrb(ı) (-túbb(ı); §§ 3866–7) v.i. *come and lie down (etc., s.v. túrb(ı)).*
  imperat. tatúrbi!
tatúrb-an (-túbb-; §§ 3890 ff., 3905) v.t. *tell to come and lie down (etc.), let come and lie down (etc.).*
t-ǎu (§ 1115 a) v.t. *come and do (etc., s.v. ǎu) = taǎu.*
  íŋgı⌣tǎu⌢ *come and do this.*
  íŋgı⌣tǎuwé⌢ *come (pl.) and do this.*
  kúsut⌣tǎu⌢ (-t⌣t- < -g⌣t- § 707) *come and cook the meat.*
tǎw-an (§ 6290) v.t. *tell to come and do (etc.), let come and do (etc.).*
  kúsut⌣tǎwan⌢ *tell him (her) to come and cook the meat.*
ta-úll(ı) (§§ 3866–7) v.t. *come and kindle.*
  imperat. taúlli!
taúll-an (§§ 3890 ff., 3905) v.t. *tell to come and kindle, let come and kindle.*
ta-úndur (§§ 3866–7) v.t. *come and insert (etc., s.v. úndur).*
taúndur-an (§§ 3890 ff., 3905) v.t. *tell to come and insert (etc.), let come and insert (etc.).*
ta-úskur (§§ 3866–7) v.t. *come and set (etc., s.v. úskur).*
taúskur-an (§§ 3890 ff., 3905) v.t. *tell to come and set (etc.), let come and set (etc.).*
ta-wɛ́ (§§ 3866–7) v.t. *come and say (etc., s.v. wɛ́).*
tawɛ́r-an (§§ 3890 ff., 3905) v.t. *tell to come and say (etc.), let come and say (etc.).*
ta-wɛ́dɛn (§§ 3866–7, 3996–7) v.t. *come and tell (the speaker).*
  imperat. tawɛ́dɛn! (-dɛ̌!, -dɛ̃!, -dɛ́!, -dɛ! § 945).
  ǎıgı⌣tawɛ́dɛnó⌢ (§ 962) *come and tell me.*
  tǎıgı-wēdɛ́nos⌢ (-wēdɛ́nos⌢; § 5601) *come and tell me; tǎıgı- < ta-ǎıgı- (§ 1111).*
  N. bābúr⌣wǎndıkı⌣tǎıgıwēdɛ́nó⌢ *when the steamer (train) comes in sight come and tell me.*
tawɛ́dɛn-an (§§ 3890 ff., 3905) v.t. *tell to come and tell (the speaker), let come and tell (etc.).*
ta-wɛllɛ́ (§§ 3866–7) v.t. *come and kindle (etc., s.v. wɛllɛ́).*
tawɛllɛ́r-an (§§ 3890 ff., 3905) v.t. *tell to come and kindle, let come and kindle (etc.).*
ta-wɛ́tır (§§ 3866–7, 3998–9) v.t. *come and tell (other than the speaker).*
tawɛ́tır-an (§§ 3890 ff., 3905) v.t. *tell to come and tell (other than the speaker), let come and tell (etc.).*
  tírgı⌣tawɛ́tırıran⌢ *tell him (her) to come and tell (each of § 5456) them.*

tǎba⌣ n. *postage-stamp* [< طابع id. § 1258].
  obj. -bag⌣.
  pl. -banč(ı)⌣.
  tǎbag⌣úskur⌢ *put the stamp (sc. on the envelope).*
  tǎbak⌣kúǧur⌢ (-k⌣k- < -g⌣k- § 569) and
  tǎbaǧ⌣ǧóm⌢ (-ǧ⌣ǧ- < -g⌣ǧ- § 551) *put the stamp on (sc. the envelope).*
  tǎbaz⌣zárfır⌣kúǧur⌢ (-z⌣z- < -g⌣z- § 734) and
  tǎbaz⌣zárfır⌣ǧóm⌢ *put the stamp on the envelope.*
tǎbag n. *(a, prop.) very shallow circular basket, deep tray of basket-work; (b) tray (of any kind)* [< طبق id. (a)].
  obj. tabágk(ı)⌣, -ákk(ı)⌣, -ki⌢.
  gen. tábagn⌣v., -baŋ⌣c.
  pl. tábagı⌣.
  tábagı⌣hawírtertōn⌣níčkattıran, hǎuırt⌣ awıčkattın⌢ *tábagi are sewn out of (a strand of) palm-leaf, the palm-leaf is plaited.*
tabbǎh⌣ (tǎb-, -ǎx) n. *cook* [< طبّاخ id.].
  obj. -ǎhk(ı)⌣, -ǎxk(ı)⌣, -ki⌢.
  pl. -ǎhı⌣, -ǎxı⌣.
tabbǎhn-d(ı)⌣ (tǎb-, -ǎxn-; §§ 2545 ff.) adj. *appertaining to the (a) cook, (the) cook's.*
tábbɛ v.t. *moisten, wet* [§§ 2870 ff.].
  ind. pres. ǎı⌣tábberi⌣; perf. ǎı⌣tábbɛgori⌣ (N. -ɛko-, -ɛho-).
tábbɛrar (-rǎr⌣; §§ 2200 ff., 2210) and
tábbɛríd⌣ (§§ 2256 ff., 2263) n. *moistening.*
tábbɛr-an (§§ 3890 ff., 3899) v.t. *tell to moisten, etc., let moisten, etc.*
tábbɛ-bǔ- (§ 3931 β) v.i. stat. *be in a moistened (etc.) state or condition.*
tábbɛ-kattı- (N. -ɛha-; § 4093) v.p. *be moistened, etc.*
tabhɛ́ (tǎb-, -bxɛ́) v.i. and t. *cook* [< طبخ *cooking* + -ɛ́ § 3615].
  ind. pres. ǎı⌣tabhɛ́ri⌢ (occ. -hérı⌢ § 1073), ɛr⌣tabhɛ́n⌢ (-hɛ̌⌢, -hɛ⌢ § 939, occ. -hén⌢, -hɛ̌⌢, -hé⌢); perf. ǎı⌣tabhɛ́gori⌣ (N. -ɛ́ko-, -ɛ́ho-).
  imperat. tabhɛ́!
tabhɛ́rar (tǎb-, -bxɛ́-, -rǎr⌣; §§ 2200 ff., 2207) and
tabhɛ́rıd⌣ (tǎb-, -bxɛ́-; §§ 2256 ff., 2260) n. *cooking.*
tabhɛ́r-an (tǎb-, -bxɛ́-; §§ 3890 ff., 3899) v.t. *tell to cook, let cook.*
tábıd n. *smith* [*RSN,* § 129, 200; with -ıd⌣ cp. íd⌣ *man* (§ 2141); § 2270].
  obj. tabídk(ı)⌣, -ítk(ı)⌣, -ítt(ı)⌣ § 2462, -ki⌢, -tı⌢.
  gen. tábıdn⌣v., -bın⌣c.
  pl. tábdu⌣.
  nobrén⌣tábıd⌣ *goldsmith.*
  dúŋgın⌣tábıd⌣ *silversmith.*
  šǎrtın⌣tábıd⌣ *blacksmith.*
tábla n. *padlock* [< طبلة id.].
  obj. -lag⌣.
  pl. -lanč(ı)⌣.
tǎd⌣ (⌣tǎt⌢, ⌣tǎ⌣ § 963) postp. (=conj. §§ 4287, 4328) *when* [< *tǎ-ıd⌣ *coming, arrival, time when, deverbal n. in -ıd⌣ (§ 2257) of tǎ* come].

tág — takrŭrı‿

— follows the bare form of the subjunctive (§ 6200):
tékkı‿nálın‿tăd‿étta⌒ *when you see him (her, it) bring him (her, it).*
aı‿tékkı‿nálsı‿tăd‿úwegori⌒ *when I saw him (her) I called him (her).*
álı‿tăn‿tăd‿ékkı‿bıtírın⌒ *when ɛáli comes he will give you it (them §§ 5083, 5090).*
tér‿tăn‿tăb‿bısíkkırı⌒ (-b‿b- < -d‿b- § 518) *when (s)he comes I shall ask him (her).*
wăndın‿tăd‿aıgı‿wĕdĕn⌒ *when (s)he (it) comes in sight tell me.*
wăndın‿tăt‿tékkı‿wĕtır⌒ (-t‿t- < -d‿t- § 706) *when (s)he (it) comes in sight let him tell (her).*
ar‿úweru‿tăw‿wᵘdéta⌒ (-w‿w- < -d‿w- § 718) *when we call come back.*
aı‿ékkı‿úwerı‿tăt‿ta⌒ (§ 1742) *come when I call you.*
‿tăkk(ı)‿ (-ki⌒) postp. (= conj. §§ 4287, 4329) *when* (= ‿tăd‿) [< ‿*tădk(ı)‿ (§§ 574, 4665) *at the coming of*].
álı‿tăn‿tăkkı‿dúŋgıb‿bıtíddi⌒ (-b‿b- < -g‿b- § 519) *when ɛáli comes I shall (I'll § 5383) give him the money.*
băbúr‿wăndın‿tăkkı‿tékkı‿habárkıtır⌒ *when the steamer (train) comes in sight let him (her) know.*
‿tăkk-ɛd‿ (-ɛt‿, -έ⌒; §§ 5858–60, 4330) postp. *when* (= ‿tăd‿) [< ‿*tădk-ɛd‿ (§ 574) *at (on) the coming of*].
nógın‿tăkkɛd‿íŋgı‿sókkɛran⌒ *when (s)he (it) goes let him (her, it) take this.*
máŋg‿éllı‿tăkkɛd‿íŋgı‿bárkırı⌒ *when I find that other I shall throw this away.*
máŋg‿éllı‿tăkké⌒ *it's when I find that other.*
tág (tág § 1146) v.i. *acquire or receive a detachable or temporary cover, get covered, cover oneself, veil oneself* [cogn. with dég *cover one's loins* § 2781; cp. ON. ᴅᴀᴋ- *bedecken* ZNG s.v., ᴅᴇᴋᴋɪ *hide*].
ind. pres. aı‿tágrı⌒; perf. aı‿tágkori⌒ (‿tăkkori⌒).
imperat. tăk!, tág‿.
aıgı‿tág‿ɛgó⌒ *(s)he told me to veil myself.*
tínnɛssıt‿tág‿ɛgó⌒ (-t‿t- < -g‿t- § 707) *he told his (she told her) sister to veil herself.*
ɛn‿tén‿kádɛgɛt‿tágın‿tén‿kóñ‿nátkattımɛnınn‿íllɛr⌒ (-t‿t- < -d‿t- § 706) *the (a) woman is covered by her cloth(s) that her face may not be seen.*
tága n. *threshing-floor, place where cattle tread out corn, etc.* (s.v. nŭr) [< tágar‿ § 2177) *covered place*].
obj. -gag‿.
pl. tagánč(ı)‿.
tágar (tág-, -gár‿; §§ 2200ff.) and tagíd‿ (tág-; §§ 2256ff.) n. *getting covered, etc.*
tagídd(ı)‿ (tág-) n. *cover* [§ 2271].
obj. -dıg‿.
pl. -dınč(ı)‿.
ílban‿tagídd(ı)‿ *lid of tin (etc.).*
férıš‿tagídd(ı)‿ (-š‿t- < -šn‿t- § 865) *bed-spread, coverlet.*

míssın‿tagídd(ı)‿ *eyelid,* with collective sg. (§ 4696a).
tág-an (tág-; §§ 3890ff.) v.t. *tell to get covered, etc., let get covered, etc.*
tág-bŭ- (tággŭ- § 546; tág-; § 3931α) v.i. stat. *be in a covered (etc.) state or condition.*
áŋgarɛ‿kádɛgɛt‿tágbūn⌒ (-t‿t- < -d‿t- § 706; ‿tággūn⌒) *the bedstead is covered with (a, the) cloth.*
tém‿míssı‿tággūn⌒ *his (her, its) eye is (eyes are § 4696a) bunged up.*
tágbᵘ-an (tággᵘ-; tág-; -b(w)an; §§ 3962–3) v.t. *tell to be (let be) in a covered (etc.) state or condition.*
imperat. tágbᵘan! (-b(w)an!, -b(w)ă!, -b(w)á!, tággᵘan!, -g(w)an!, -g(w)ă!, -g(w)á!, tág-).
kórkı‿tággan⌒ *let the wound be (kept) covered.*
tagɛd-ág- (tág-; §§ 3877ff.) v.i. *be in the condition of having been covered.*
kór‿tagedágın⌒ *the wound has been (kept) covered.*
tág-ır (tág-; § 3671) (a) v.t. caus. *cause or allow to get covered, etc.;* (b) v.t. *provide with a detachable or temporary cover* (as distinguished from dóš), *cover, veil.*
ind. pres. aı‿tagírri⌒, ɛr‿tágırın‿ (-rí⌒, -rí⌒); perf. aı‿tagírkori⌒.
áŋgarɛk‿kádɛgɛt‿tagírran⌒ (-t‿t- < -d‿t- § 706) *they cover the bedstead with the (a) cloth (cloths § 4696d).*
ɛŋ‿kórkı‿tágır‿kúltı‿ğábɛmɛnınn‿íllar⌒ *cover your wound(s) in order that the flies should not touch it (them; § 4647).*
mám‿bɛrrăttı‿tén‿gútagɛt‿tagírkırı‿bógın⌒ *when I cover that other pot with its lid it leaks.*
tágır-an (tág-; §§ 3890ff., 3904) v.t. *tell to cover, let cover.*
tagırɛd-ág- (tág-; §§ 3877ff.) v.t. *be in the situation of having covered.*
kórkı‿tagırɛdágın⌒ *(s)he has covered the wound.*
šaıgı‿tagırɛdág¹rı⌒ *I have covered the tea* (e.g. *placed a cosy over the teapot*).
tága (-gá‿) n. *window* [< طاقة *id.*].
obj. tăgag‿.
pl. tăganč(ı)‿.
taggısĕ v.t. *depreciate, belittle* [< imperat. or imperf. stem of انتقص *id.* + -έ § 3660].
ind. pres. aı‿taggısĕri⌒; perf. aı‿taggısĕgori⌒ (N. -ého-, -ého-).
imperat. taggısĕ!
ğănărrăŋgı‿dólkan‿taggısĕran⌒ *when they want to buy (something) they depreciate (it).*
taggısĕrar (-rár‿; §§ 2200ff., 2207) and taggısĕríd‿ (§§ 2256ff., 2260) n. *depreciation.*
taggısĕr-an (§ 3890ff., 3899) v.t. *tell to depreciate, let depreciate.*
taggısĕ-bŭ- (§ 3931β) v.i. stat. *be in a depreciated state or condition.*
taggısĕ-kattı- (N. -ĕha-; § 4093) v.p. *be depreciated.*
tággŭ- < tágbŭ- *be in a covered state,* s.v. tág.

tágia (-gıa‿, tagía‿ §§ 1062, 1065, 1154) n. *cap* [< طاقيّة *id.*].
obj. tágiag‿, -gıag‿, tagíag‿.
pl. tagiánč(ı)‿, -giánč(ı)‿, tagfanč(ı)‿.
tăgın‿ (§ 956a) n. *shallow earthenware cooking-pan, frying-pan* [< طاجن *id.*].
obj. tăgıŋg(ı)‿, -gi⌒.
pl. tăgını‿.
tăgıŋgɛd-áu (-áu; § 4127) v.t. *cook in* (lit. *with* s.v. -ɛd‿) *the frying-pan, fry.*
tăgıŋgɛdáu-dĕn (-áu-; § 4000) v.t. *after frying give (to the speaker), fry for (the speaker).*
tăgıŋgɛdáu-tır (-áu-; § 4000) v.t. *after frying give (to other than the speaker), fry for (other than the speaker).*
kúmbut‿tăgıŋgɛdáutırır⌒ (-t‿t- < -g‿t- § 707) *fry them some eggs.*
tăgıŋ-ır-áu (N. -ŋkır-; -áu; § 4139) v.t. *fry.*
tăgıŋgıráu-dĕn (N. -ŋkır-; -áu-; § 4000) v.t. = tăgıŋgɛdáudĕn.
N. ıŋ‿kúmbut‿tăgıŋkıráudĕn⌒ *fry me the (some) eggs.*
tăgıŋgıráu-tır (N. -ŋkır-; -áu-; § 4000) v.t. = tăgıŋgɛdáutır.
tắgır‿ n. *merchant* [< تاجر *id.*].
obj. tăgırk(ı)‿, -ki⌒.
pl. tăgırı‿.
tāhúna n. *mill* [< طاحونة *id.*].
obj. -nag‿.
pl. -nanč(ı)‿.
bɛlédnırı‿tāhúnak‿kómunan, úrdır‿ıgrígınčı‿tāhúnánčık‿kóran⌒ *the people of the country have no mill, (but § 6239) at El-Ordi the Greeks have mills.*
tajjár‿ n. *strong current* [< تيّار *id.*].
obj. -árk(ı)‿, -ki⌒.
pl. -árı‿.
tajjár-an (§ 3910α) v.i. *become a strong current, run with a strong current.*
úru‿tajjáranın⌒ *the river runs with a strong current.*
tajjáram-bŭ- (§§ 3949ff.) v.i. stat. *be in a state of running with a strong current.*
tajjáranɛd-ág- (§ 3966α) v.i. *be in the condition of (having begun to run, and so) running with a strong current.*
úru‿tajjáranedágın⌒ *the river is running with a strong current.*
tắk! imperat. of tág *get covered.*
tắkkar‿ adj. *narrow* [cp. tăk *binden* RNW, -ar‿ gerundial *-ing* (§ 2200), so app. or. noun **tightening*].
obj. takkárk(ı)‿, -ki⌒.
pl. tăkkarı‿.
dárıp‿tăkkárun⌒ *the path is narrow.*
tắkkar (-kár‿) n. *Takkar (on map),* a village on the right bank of the Nile about 37 miles above Ed-Débbáʰ.
obj. takkárk(ı)‿, tăkkárk(ı)‿, -ki⌒.
tăkkar-an (§ 3910α) v.i. *become narrow.*
tăkkaram-bŭ- (§§ 3949ff.) v.i. stat. *be in the state or condition of becoming or having become narrow.*
‿tắkkɛd‿, ‿tắkk(ı)‿ *when* s.v. ‿tăd‿.
takrŭrı‿ n. (a, prop.) *Takrŭri, one of the Takárir* (تكارير) *or Takárna* (تكارنة NSS, I, p. 64) *a non-Arab tribe in*

Dārfūr (*MAS*, I, p. 82); then generally (b) *black person from the west or southwest* [< تَكْرُورِيّ *id.*].
obj. -rıgᴗ.
pl. -rınč(ı)ᴗ.

talabɛ́ (tálabɛ́) v.t. *demand, ask for* [< طَلَب n. *demand* +-ɛ́ §3621].
ind. pres. aı̄ᴗtalabɛ́ri⌒; perf. aı̄ᴗtalabɛ́gori⌒ (N. -ɛ́ko-, -ɛ́ho-).
imperat. talabɛ́!

talabɛ́rarᴗ (tálab-, -rár ᴗ; §§2200ff., 2207) and

talabɛ́rídᴗ (tálab-; §§2256ff., 2260) n. *demanding, etc.*

talabɛ́r-an (tálab-; §§3890ff., 3899) v.t. *tell to demand, etc., let demand, etc.*

talabēr-ɛg-ág- (tálab-; §§4071ff.) v.t. = talabēredól-.

talabēr-ɛ-dól- (tálab-; -rᵒd- §1178; §§4016-17, 4022, 4027) v.t. *be about to demand, etc.*

talabēr-ɛ-mǎ- (tálab-; §§4016-17, 4036, 4041) v.t. *become unable to demand, etc.*

talabēred-ág- (tálab-; §§3877ff.) v.t. *be in the situation of having demanded, etc.*

talabɛ́-kattı- (tálab-; N. -ɛ́ha-; §4093) v.p *be demanded, etc.*

talatínᴗ (§956a) card. num. *thirty* [< ثَلاثِين *id.* §1306].
obj. -íŋg(ı)ᴗ, -gi⌒.

talatín-d(ı)ᴗ (§§2545ff., 2738) adj. *appertaining to 30, of 30, 30's.*

talatin-ínt(ı)ᴗ (-tínınt(ı)ᴗ; §2742) ord. num. *thirtieth.*

talatíŋ-kırıᴗ (-kírıᴗ §1701; §2736) num. adj. *about thirty.*

táliñᴗ (§4437) adv. *with quick steps, stepping rapidly* [?cp. Amh. ፈጥኖ *quickly*; cp. *SNK*, §362].

táliñ! interj. *(walk) quickly!*

taliñ-nóg (§4127) v.i. *walk with quick steps, walk fast.*

tàliñ-táliñ (§4438b) adv. *with very quick steps, stepping very rapidly.*

tàliñ-táliñ! interj. *(walk) very quickly!*
tàliñ-táliñᴗnógın⌒ *(s)he (it) walks with very quick steps.*

taliñ-taliñ-nóg (§4127) v.i. *walk with very quick steps, walk very fast.*
taliñtaliñnógın⌒ *(s)he (it) walks very fast.*

tamámᴗ (tám-, tɛm-) (a) n. *completion* [<تَمام *id.*], obj. tamámg(ı)ᴗ, -gi⌒; (b) adj. *complete, correct, accurate, right,* obj. -ámg(ı)ᴗ, -gi⌒, pl. tamámıᴗ.
ínᴗtamámrɛ́? (-mⁱrɛ́?, -mırɛ́? §4238) *is this right?*
X. éndıᴗtamámırɛ́? *is yours all right?*
Y. tamámun ᴗ *yes* (§6104).
íŋguᴗtamámırɛ́? *are these correct?*

tamám-an- (tám-, tɛm-; §3910a) v.i. *become complete, etc.*
hısábᴗtámámáŋkó⌒ *the calculation (account) came (has come) right.*

tamáman-tá (tám-, tɛm-; §4151) v.i. *come out complete, etc., turn out correct, etc., work out correctly, work out right.*
hısábᴗtamámantágó⌒ *the calculation (has) worked out correct.*

fákkaᴗénnārᴗtámāmantágoná? *did you receive (have you received) the right change?*

tamámg-ır (tám-, tɛm-; N. -mkır; §3702) (a) v.t. caus. *cause or allow to be complete, etc.*; (b) v.t. *render complete, etc., complete, correct.*
tóskıtᴗtamámgır, tókkonᴗnagsɛ́ŋgırmɛn⌒ (-t ᴗt- <-g ᴗt- §707) *make (put, etc.) exactly three, don't let there be less.*

tamanínᴗ (§956a) card. num. *eighty* [< ثَمانِين *id.* §1306].
obj. -íŋg(ı)ᴗ, -gi⌒.

tamanín-d(ı)ᴗ (§§2545ff., 2738) adj. *appertaining to 80, of 80, 80's.*

tamanín-int(ı)ᴗ (-mínınt(ı)ᴗ; §2742) ord. num. *eightieth.*

tamaníŋ-kırıᴗ (-kírıᴗ §1701; §2736) num. adj. *about eighty.*

tambanárt(ı)ᴗ, **-ti**⌒ n. *Tambanarti (on map), an island about ten miles above Ed-Débbáʰ.*
obj. -tıgᴗ.

támug v.i. *fight, contend; quarrel* [*RSN*, §129].
ind. pres. aı̄ᴗtámug(¹)ri⌒, ɛrᴗtámugın⌒ (-gi⌒, -gí⌒); perf. aı̄ᴗtamúgkori⌒ (-úkko-).
imperat. támuk!
subj. past aı̄ᴗtámugsıᴗ (-uksıᴗ, -suᴗ).
arᴗtírgononᴗtámugru⌒ *we fight against them (we quarrel with them).*
bundúkkonᴗsıwítkoŋgetᴗtámugran⌒ (§4905) *they fight with gun and sword.*

támugarᴗ (-gárᴗ; §§2200ff.) n. *fighting, etc.*

tamugídᴗ (§§2256ff.) n. = támugar ᴗ.

támugıdᴗ (§2268) n. *fight, battle, war; quarrel.*
obj. tamugídk(ı)ᴗ, -ítk(ı)ᴗ, -ítt(ı)ᴗ (§2462), -kı⌒, -ti⌒.
gen. támugıdᴗv., -gınᴗc.
pl. támugıdın ᴗ.

támug-an (§§3890ff.) v.t. *tell to fight, etc., let fight, etc.*

tamug(¹)r-ɛg-ág- (§§4071ff.) v.i. = tamugɛdól-.

tamug-ɛ-dól- (-gᵒd- §1178; §4022) and

tamug(¹)r-ɛ-dól- (-rᵒd-; §4027) v.i. *be about to fight, etc.*

tamug-ɛ-mǎ- (§4036) and

tamug(¹)r-ɛ-mǎ- (§4041) v.i. *become unable to fight, etc.*

tamugíŋ-ır (ᵘ⌣; N. -ŋkır; §3688) v.t. caus. *cause or allow to fight, etc.*
ind. pres. aı̄ᴗtamugıŋgíddi⌒.

táncɛ v.t. *taste* [§§2870ff.]
ind. pres. aı̄ᴗtáncɛri⌒; perf. aı̄ᴗtáncɛgori⌒ (N. -ɛko-, -ɛho-).
def. perf. aı̄ᴗtancɛróskori⌒ and more commonly aı̄ᴗtancóskori⌒.
ɛrᴗmarákkıᴗtáncɛgoná? *did you taste (have you tasted) the broth?*

táncɛrarᴗ (-rárᴗ), **táncɛar**ᴗ (-cǎrᴗ; §§2200ff., 2211) and

táncɛrídᴗ, **tancíd**ᴗ (§§2256ff., 2264) n. *tasting.*

táncɛr-an (§§3890ff., 3899) v.t. *tell to taste, let taste.*
álıgᴗíŋgıᴗtáncɛrā⌒ *let ɛ áli taste this.*

tancɛd-ág- (§§3877ff.) v.t. *be in the situation of having tasted.*
marákkıᴗtancɛdágri⌒ *I have tasted the broth.*

táncɛ-kattı- (N. -ɛha-; §4093) v.p. *be tasted.*

-tánnan⌒ (-tànnǎ⌒, -tànná⌒ §939; §§4232-5, 5785-91) *deictic sign of predication it is* (commoner in S. than in N. = -taran) [< *-tàr-n-an⌒ (§628) < *-tàr-an-an⌒ <-tàr- *it* (=tɛrᴗ, M. tár, ON. тар) +-an⌒ *is* < *says* (§211) repeated like -ɛn-ɛᴗ, -un-unᴗ].
ɛ́n-tànnan⌒ *it's the woman.*
ɛ́nči-tànnan⌒ *it's (they're) the women.*
aı̄-tànnan⌒ *it's I.*
ɛr-tànnan⌒ *it's you.*
tɛ́r-tànnan⌒ *it's (s)he (it).*
ár-tànnan⌒ *it's we.*
ír-tànnan⌒ *it's you (pl.).*
tír-tànnan⌒ *it's they.*
tínᴗtód-tànnan⌒ *it's their child.* (tínᴗtódunᴗ *(s)he's their child.*)
ínᴗtínᴗtód-tànnan⌒ *this is their child* (= ínᴗtínᴗtódun⌒).
ámbɛsᴗáskar-tànnan⌒ *it's my brother the soldier.*
X. mámᴗmınɛ́llɛ́? *what's that (yonder)?*
Y. zäbınᴗğazmánči-tànnan⌒ *it's the officer's boots.*
dɛ́rtıᴗhalás-tànnan⌒ and
dɛ́rtıᴗxalás-sànnan⌒ (§686) *the fast is over.*

táŋgas n. *Tangussi (on map), a large island four miles above Old Dóngola.*
obj. taŋgásk(ı)ᴗ, -ki⌒.

taŋgasnárt(ı)ᴗ, **-ti**⌒ *the island of Táŋgas.*

tárᴗ v. imperat. of tá *come.*

tarabɛ́za (-záᴗ) n. *table* [<تَرابيزة < τράπεζα *id.*].
obj. -zagᴗ.
pl. tarabɛ́zanč(ı)ᴗ, -zán-, -zén-, -či⌒.

tárafᴗ (táráfᴗ) n. *edge, border* [< طَرَف *id.*].
obj. tarafk(ı)ᴗ, -ki⌒.
pl. tarafıᴗ.
kúmᴗtárafᴗ (-m ᴗt- < -bn ᴗt- §586) *edge (top of side) of boat.*

táragaᴗ n. *page, leaf (of book)* [< طَرَقة *one of series of successive things or of things overlying one another*].
obj. táragagᴗ.
pl. taragánč(ı)ᴗ.
kıtámᴗtáraga (-m ᴗt- < -bn ᴗt- §586) *leaf of book.*

-taran⌒ (-tarǎ⌒, -tará⌒ §939; §§4232-5, 5785-91) *deictic sign of predication it is* (= -tànnan⌒) [< *-tar- *it* (=tɛrᴗ, M. tar, ON. тар) +-an⌒ *is* < *says* (§211)].
ɛ́n-taran⌒ *it's the woman.*
ɛ́nči-taran⌒ *it's the women.*
aı̄-taran⌒ *it's I.*
ɛr-taran⌒ *it's you.*
tɛ́r-taran⌒ *it's (s)he (it).*
ár-taran⌒ *it's we.*
ír-taran⌒ *it's you (pl.).*
tír-taran⌒ *it's they.*
aı̄ᴗɛ́r-taranᴗandágori⌒ *I thought it was you.*
tínᴗtód-taran⌒ *it's their child.* (tínᴗtódunᴗ *(s)he's their child).*

tarántarɛ⌣ ín⌣tín⌣tód-taran⌢ *this is their child* (= ín⌣tín⌣tódun⌢).
ámbɛs⌣áskár-taran⌢ *it's my brother the soldier.*

tarántarɛ⌣ n. *thin spoke* of wheel raising water (átt(ı)⌣) in water-wheel (kólɛ⌣); there are four, alternating with the four thick spokes (duŋgúttınč(ı)⌣) [< *tǎr-an*! tǎr-ɛ! *say 'come!' say 'come!'* sc. as the wheel revolves].
obj. -rɛg⌣.
pl. tarantarénč(ı)⌣.

tǎrɛ! *come!* s.v. tǎ.

tarhǎd⌣ (-rxǎd⌣) n. *sandal* (=nǎl⌣); with collective sg. (§4696d) [?cp. طِراق *sole* (*AZN* s.v. tǎraka); §2397].
obj. -ǎdk(ı)⌣, -ǎtk(ı)⌣, -ǎtt(ı)⌣ (§2462), -ki⌢, -ti⌢.
pl. -ǎdı⌣.

tárıd⌣ n. *parcel* [< طرد *id.* §1359].
obj. tarídk(ı)⌣, -ítk(ı)⌣, -ítt(ı)⌣ (§2462), -ki⌢, -ti⌢.
pl. tár(ı)dı⌣.

tárıf⌣ (tár-, tér-) n. *thick rope, cable* [< Eg. Ar. طرف *id.* §1359].
obj. tarífk(ı)⌣, -ki⌢.
pl. tár(ı)fı⌣.
kúm⌣tárıf⌣ (-m⌣t- < -bn⌣t- §586) *ship's cable.*

tarkíñ n. (a) *a very small fish* appearing in great numbers just before the rising of the Nile; with collective sg. (§4696c); (b) *salt sauce and paste* made of (a) [-ñ dim. §2304].
obj. -íñg(ı)⌣, -gi⌢.
pl. -íñı⌣.

tartíb⌣ (tǎr-, tɛr-) n. *arrangement, disposition, order* [< ترتيب *id.*].
obj. -íbk(ı)⌣, -ípk(ı)⌣, -ki⌢.
pl. -íbı⌣.

tátt(ı)⌣ n. *watch, spell of duty*[1] averaging six hours in the cultivation of an irrigable estate (kólɛ⌣) [< *tǎtt(ı)⌣ (§1049) < *tǎdk(ı)⌣ (§716) obj. of tǎd⌣ (*coming, *time when* now postp.) when stereotyped as nominal stem §2139].
obj. -tıg⌣ [> Sudan Ar. تتّق *id.* (*HSA* s.v. water-wheel) §2412].
pl. -tınč(ı)⌣.
álın⌣tátti⌣halǎs-taran⌢ ɣáli's *turn of duty is ended.*
tén⌣tátti⌣dūróskon⌢ *his time on duty is ended.*
fɛǧın⌣tátti⌣fɛǧın-tǔrtōn⌣dúhur⌣móŋkon⌢ (-n⌣t- < -rn⌣t- §614, -r⌣m- < -rn⌣m- §850) *the forenoon watch is from day-break till noon;* ⌣móŋkon⌢ used predicatively (§5924a).
dúhurn⌣tátti⌣duhúrrotōn⌣šǎrɛm⌣móŋkon⌢ (-hun⌣tát- §852) *the (after)-noon watch is from noon till dusk.*
úgūn⌣tátti⌣šǎrɛrtōn⌣uguntórtırm⌣móŋkon⌢ *the night-watch is from dusk till midnight.*

---
[1] Misunderstood in *NSD*, p. 22; once a water-wheel starts there is, barring accidents, no interval till the cultivation is finished; it is as we run a ship from port to port.

fɛǧırfíjen⌣tátt⌣uguntórtırtōm⌣fɛǧım⌣móŋkon⌢ (-m⌣m- < -rn⌣m- §608) *the morning watch is from midnight till day-break.*
táttıd⌣dıfun⌣óllıgɛd⌣uñúddan⌢ (-d⌣d- < -g⌣d- §534) *they know the watch by the shadow of the cross-beam, e.g. they know when the shadow marks noon.*

tattúr⌣ n. *colocynth, bitter apple,* Citrullus colocynthis, Schrad. (*BSP*, 207) = úr⌣; with collective sg. (§4696b) [contains úr⌣ *id.*].
obj. -úrk(ı)⌣, -ki⌢.
pl. -úrı⌣.

tǎu < ta-ǎu *come and do,* etc. s.v. tǎ.

táwwa⌣ n. *frying-pan* [< طَوّة *id.*]
obj. -wag⌣.
pl. -wanč(ı)⌣.

tawwagɛd-ǎu (-ǎu; §4127) v.t. *cook in* (lit. *with* s.v. -ɛd⌣) *the frying-pan, fry.*

tawwagɛdǎu-dēn (-ǎu-; §4000) v.t. *after frying give* (to the speaker), *fry for* (the speaker).
kúmbut⌣tawwagɛdǎudēn⌢ (-t⌣t- < -g⌣t- §707) *fry me some eggs.*

tawwagɛdǎu-tır (-ǎu-; §4000) v.t. *after frying give* (to other than the speaker), *fry for* (other than the speaker).

tawwǎšı⌣ n. *eunuch* [< طواشي *id.* §1385].
obj. -šıg⌣.
pl. -šınč(ı)⌣.

tǎbbǎh⌣ (-ǎx⌣) n. *cook* = tabbǎh⌣.
tǎg, tǎgır = tǎg *get covered,* tǎgır *cover.*
tǎlǎbɛ́ v.t. *demand,* etc. = talabɛ́.
tǎl(l)ǎgrǎf⌣ n. *telegraph,* etc. = tɛlɛgrǎf⌣.
tǎmǎm⌣ *completion,* etc. = tamǎm⌣.
tǎrǎf⌣ n. *edge,* etc. = tɛb⌣.
tǎrıf⌣ *thick rope,* etc. = tárıf⌣.
tǎrtíb⌣ *arrangement,* etc. = tartíb⌣.

⌣tɛ́? (§§4247, 5808-16) *deictic interrogative sign of predication is it…?, is that…?, are (they)…?* (=⌣tɛ́ddɛ́?) [<⌣tɛ́r? §960].
tɛ́r⌣nı́⌣tɛ́? *is it (s)he? (is that it?).*
X. ín⌣tɛ́? *is this (s)he (it)?*
Y. éjjo, ín-tànnan⌢ *yes, it is,* lit. *yes, it's this.*
mǎn⌣ní⌣tɛ́? *who's that (over there)?*
ɛr⌣nı́⌣tɛ́? *who are you?*
ır⌣nı́gu⌣tɛ́? *who are you (pl.)?*
tír⌣nı́gu⌣tɛ́? *who are they?*
ıŋgu⌣nı́gu⌣tɛ́? *who are these?*
ın⌣nın⌣hǎnu⌣tɛ́? *whose donkey is this?*
tɛ́r⌣ısǎı⌣tɛ́? *which is (s)he (it)?*
jōm⌣mıŋkóttēr⌣tɛ́? *how many days is it?*
támugıd⌣halǎs⌣tɛ́? *is the war finished?,* lit. *the war is it finished?*
ín⌣ɛndí⌣tɛ́? *is this (that) yours?* = *ist das das deinige?*
(ín⌣ɛndírɛ́? *is this (that) yours?* = *ist das deines?*)

-tɛ⌣…? (*a,* attached to adverb §§4276, 5850-2) *interrogative particle is it that…? (est-ce que…?)* [enclitic form of ⌣tɛ́?].
ɛr⌣mǎktǎbír⌣tɛ⌣dólın? *do you want him (her, it, them §5083) in (at) the office?,* lit. *is it in the office (that) you want (him, etc.)?*
ɛr⌣ɛ́lgón-tɛ⌣nǎlın? *do you still see him (her, it, them)?,* lit. *is it still that you see?*

ír⌣ɛ́lgón-tɛ⌣nǎllu? *do you (pl.) still see him (her, it, them)?*
ólgón-tɛ⌣kǎllan? *do they still eat (it)?*
ɛ́nn-ur⌣ólgón-tɛ⌣óddın? *does your head still ache?*
ékkɛnɛ-tɛ⌣dólın? *do you (does (s)he) want him (her, it, them) now?*
tɛr⌣bursūdǎndo⌣kırǎgɛn⌣jōmgı-tɛ⌣nógın? *is it on Sunday that (s)he (it) goes to Port Sudan?*
ıŋ⌣índo-t⌣úskuddı⌣wǎlla⌣mǎnd⌣óǧıri? *shall* (§5369b) *I put this here or carry it over there?*
ıŋgugon-t⌣árgonon⌣ǎndandɛ́? *and these?, do they go with us?*

-tɛ⌣…? (*b,* attached to interr. pron. §5854) used as a sign of predication *is…?, are…?*
ní-tɛ⌣mǎm⌣bódıl? *who's that (over there) running?*
nígu-tɛ⌣mǎm⌣bódıli? *who are those (over there) running?*
ısǎı-tɛ⌣dúl? *which is the greater?* (…*greatest?,* etc., s.v. dúl⌣).

-tɛ⌣…? (*c,* occ. attached to interr. pron. followed by positive sign of predication §5854a):
ní-tɛ⌣nobátšın? *who is the man on duty?*

tɛ́b⌣ (§§3868-71, 5639-43) v.i. (a) *stand;* (b) *stand still, stop;* (c) *remain, stay, wait;* (d) *be in a situation, be continuously, remain, stay, keep;* (e) *remain (over), be left;* (f) *be, exist* [*RSN*, §129]—used indifferently of animate or inanimate objects:
ind. pres. aı̆⌣tɛ́b(¹)ri⌢; perf. aı̆⌣tɛ́bkori⌢ (tɛ́pk-).
imperat. tɛ́p!, pl. tɛ́bwɛ! (tɛ́bwɛ́!, tɛ́bbɛ! §517, tɛ́bbɛ́!).
subj. past aı̆⌣tɛ́bsı⌣ (⌣tɛ́psı⌣, -su⌣).
ékkɛn⌣ólgow⌣wıččír-rēd⌣dólım⌣bǎdkɛt⌣tɛkkól⌣but⌣ɛbın⌣ (-w⌣w- < -n⌣w §720, -r-r- < -r-w- §672, -d⌣d- < -g⌣d- §534) *(s)he now still needs a stick, but* (§6239) *later on (s)he will stand by himself (herself).*
urun⌣ǎrro⌣tɛ́bran⌢ *they stand on the river-bank.*
aı̆⌣wíríğ⌣tɛ́b'ri⌢ (-rıč⌣tɛ́b-) *I am naked* (=aı̆⌣wıríğğūri⌢) lit. *I stand naked.*
kúb⌣ɛ́ssır⌣tɛ́bın⌢ *the boat is* (i.e. *floats) in the water.*
sǎ⌣tɛ́bın⌢ *the watch (clock) has stopped (is not going),* lit. …*stands (still).*
ǎru⌣tɛ́bóskó⌢ *the rain has ceased.*
bǎbúr⌣índo⌣tɛ́pkómunun⌢ *the steamer (train) didn't stop here.*
dagíg⌣árıt⌣tɛ́pkoran⌢ (-t⌣t- < -g⌣t- §707; §4666) *they (have) waited (stayed) twenty minutes.*
mǎsıl⌣tɛ́pkım⌣bɛ̄rǎkkı⌣mǎsıl⌣tógım⌣fǎnúskı⌣sókkɛri⌢ *if the sun has not set* (lit. *remains) I('ll* §5369a) *take the flag, if it has set* (lit. *enters) I('ll) take the lantern.*
álı⌣tɛ́s⌣sǎmag⌣gǎññınǎ⌣wǎla⌣tɛ́bın? (-s⌣s- < -n⌣s- §681) *does ɣáli shave his beard or let it grow?,* lit. …*or does it remain?*
ɛ́lgon⌣úŋ⌣ówwıkırı⌣tɛ́bın⌢ *there are still about two months left* (⌣tɛ́bın⌣ = ⌣fadlɛ́n⌣).

nɛhắr‿dımındogórığ‿nogóskó, dımın-dokólot‿tɛ́bíⴰ 16 days have passed, 17 are left.
dɛ́n‿áddo‿tɛ́bın⌒ I (we) have got (owe) a debt.
dɛ́nı‿tíddo‿tɛ́b!ran⌒ they have got debts.

tḗb-an (§§ 3890 ff.) v.t. tell to stand, etc., let stand, etc.
ní‿mánd‿ännógın?, tḗban⌒ who's that walking (going) over there?, tell him (her) to stop.
íŋg‿ɛttarélgı‿tḗban⌒ tell him (her) that brought this to wait.
aî‿tékkı‿tḗbáŋkori⌒ I (have) told him (her) to wait.

tḗb-ăr- (§§ 3868–71) v.t. (a) be engaged in seizing (etc., s.v. ắr); (b) continually (habitually) seize (etc.).
ɛ́ssıt‿tḗbắrın⌒ (-t‿t- < -g‿t- § 707) (s)he (it) (a) is engaged in getting water; (b) continually (habitually) gets water.

tḗb-áttı- (§§ 3868–71) v.t. (a) be engaged in beating up (liquid dough) with the hand (s.v. átt(ı)); (b) continually (habitually) beat up, etc.
ɛ́ŋ‿kaníssɛt‿tḗbáttın⌒ (-t‿t- < -g‿t- § 707) the woman is beating (habitually beats) up (the) dough.

tḗb-awíddı- (§§ 3868–71) v.t. (a) be engaged in spreading (etc., s.v. awídd(ı)); (b) continually (habitually) spread (etc.).
síug‿aî‿tḗbawíddırı⌒ I am laying down (always lay down) sand (sc. on the floor).

tḗb-bŏd- (§§ 3868–71) v.i. (a) be engaged in running (etc., s.v. bŏd); (b) continually (habitually) run (etc.).

tḗb-bŏ́g- (§§ 3868–71) v.t. and i. (a) be engaged in pouring (etc., s.v. bŏ́g); (b) continually (habitually) pour (etc.).
áru‿tḗbbŏ́gın⌒ the rain is (keeps on) pouring.

tḗb-dáttı- (§§ 3868–71) v.i. (a) be engaged in walking stumblingly (etc., s.v. dátt(ı)); (b) continually (habitually) walk stumblingly (etc.).
báŋga‿tḗbdáttın⌒ the locust keeps on walking a few steps and stumbling.

tḗb-dí- (§§ 3868–71) v.i. be dying.

tḗb-ɛttă̆- and

tḗb-ɛttă̆- (§§ 3868–71) v.t. (a) be engaged in bringing (etc., s.v. ɛttă̆, s.v. éd); (b) continually (habitually) bring (etc.).
ɛskétkı‿tḗbéttäran⌒ they are bringing (continually bring) soil.

tḗb-gŭ̆ñčı- (§§ 3868–71) v.i. and t. (a) be engaged in looking (at) (etc., s.v. gŭ̆ñč(ı)); (b) continually (habitually) look (at) (etc.).

tḗb-ğăg- (§§ 3868–71) v.t. (a) be engaged in kneading (etc., s.v. ğăg); (b) continually (habitually) knead (etc.).
ɛ́ŋ‿kaníssɛt‿tḗbğăgın⌒ (-t‿t- < -g‿t- § 707) the woman is kneading (habitually kneads) (the) dough.

tḗb-ğăwwı- (-ğăuwı-, -wᵘ- § 1202; §§ 3868–71) v.i. (a) be engaged in brawling (etc., s.v. ğăww(ı)); (b) continually (habitually) brawl (etc.).

tēbíŋg-ır (-⁀-, N. -ŋkır; § 3688) v.t. caus. cause or allow to stand, etc.

(***tḗbk-ır**, = teb-kir RNW, s.v. Stellen, not heard.)

tēb-íñır (-íñír-; § 3871) v.i. and t. wait (for) by standing, etc.
tér‿ráddıt‿tēbíñır⌒ (-r‿r- < -n‿r- § 671, -t‿t- < -g‿t- § 707) stop and wait for his (her, its) answer.

tēb-íñır- (-iñír-; §§ 3868–71) v.i. and t. (a) be engaged in waiting (for) (etc., s.v. íñır); (b) continually (habitually) wait (for) (etc.).

tēb-kál- (tēpkál-; §§ 3868–71) v.t. (a) be engaged in eating (etc., s.v. kál); (b) continually (habitually) eat (etc.).

tēb-kás- (tēpkás-; §§ 3868–71) v.t. and i. (a) be engaged in drawing (etc., s.v. kás); (b) continually (habitually) draw (etc.).
nógo‿tēbkásın⌒ the female slave (a) is drawing water; (b) habitually draws water.

tēb-mér- (§§ 3868–71) v.t. (a) be engaged in cutting (etc., s.v. mér); (b) continually (habitually) cut (etc.).

tēb-nér- (§ 3869) v.i. be about to sleep = nēredól-.

tēb-ní- (§§ 3868–71) v.t. (a) be engaged in drinking; (b) continually (habitually) drink.

tēb-nóg- (§§ 3868–71) v.i. (a) be engaged in going (etc., s.v. nóg); (b) continually (habitually) go (etc.).

tēb-ŏ́- (§§ 3868–71) v.t. (a) be engaged in singing (etc., s.v. ŏ́); (b) continually (habitually) sing.

tēb-sɛrēgırmér- (tēp-sɛ-; §§ 3868–71) v.t. (a) be engaged in cutting well (etc., s.v. sɛrēgır-mér); (b) continually (habitually) cut well (etc.).
kánd‿ɛ́kkɛnɛ‿tēbsɛrēgırtēbmérın⌒ now the knife is cutting well; = kánd‿ɛ́kkɛnɛ‿sɛrēgırtēbmérın⌒ (§ 5642).

tēb-sıgíddı- (tēp-sı-; §§ 3868–71) v.i. (a) be engaged in praying, in saying one's prayers; (b) continually (habitually) pray.

tēb-síkkı- (tēp-sík-; §§ 3868–71) v.i. and t. (a) be engaged in asking (etc., s.v. síkk(ı)); (b) continually (habitually) ask (etc.).

tēb-tóg- (tēp-tóg-; §§ 3868–71) v.t. (a) be engaged in heating (etc., s.v. tóg); (b) continually (habitually) heat (etc.).

tēb-tŏ́g- (tēp-tŏ́g-; §§ 3868–71) v.t. (a) be engaged in striking (etc., s.v. tŏ́g); (b) continually (habitually) strike (etc.).

tēb-wáddı- (§§ 3868–71) v.t. (a) be engaged in digging (etc., s.v. wádd(ı)); (b) continually (habitually) dig (etc.).

tēb-wár- (§§ 3868–71) v.i. and t. (a) be engaged in jumping (etc., s.v. wár); (b) continually (habitually) jump (etc.).

tēb-wárĭğ- (§§ 3868–71) v.i. (a) be engaged in jumping about; (b) continually (habitually) jump about.
báŋga‿tēbwárığın⌒ the grasshopper keeps on jumping about.

tḗbbɛ! < **tḗbwɛ!** stand! (pl.), etc., s.v. tḗb.

tɛbɛ́ v.t. seek, search for, look for [< مصد or stem of نبع follow + -ɛ́ § 3620].
ind. pres. aî‿tɛbɛ́rı⌒; perf. aî‿tɛbɛ́gori⌒ (N. -ɛ́ko-, -ɛ́ho-).
imperat. tɛbɛ́!, pl. tɛbɛ́wɛ! (-bɛ́wɛ́!).

part. pres. tɛbɛ́l‿ (one) that seeks, seeker, seeking, obj. tɛbɛ́lg(ı)‿, -gi⌒; past tɛbɛ́rɛl‿ (one) that sought, seeker, seeking, obj. tɛbɛ́rɛlg(ı)‿, -gi⌒.
X. ɛllɛmágori⌒ I can't find him (her, it, them).
Y. tɛbɛ́gım‿bélın⌒ if you search you will find him (her, it, them).

tɛbɛ́rar (-rắr‿; §§ 2200 ff., 2207) and

tɛbɛ̄ríd (§§ 2256 ff., 2260) n. seeking, etc.

tɛbɛ́r-an (§§ 3890 ff., 3899) v.t. tell to seek, etc., let seek, etc.
tɛbɛ́wan⌒ (§ 3900) let them search.

tɛbɛ́r-ɛg-ă̆g- (§§ 4071 ff.) v.t. = tɛbɛ̄redól-.

tɛbɛ̄r-ɛ-dól- (-rᵒd- § 1178; §§ 4016–17, 4022, 4027) v.t. be about to seek, etc.

tɛbɛ̄r-ɛ-gŭ̆-bŭ̆- (§ 4069) v.t. stat. be on one's way (coming) to seek, etc.

tɛbɛ̄r-ɛ-mă̆- (§§ 4016–17, 4036, 4041) v.t. become unable to seek, etc.

tɛbɛ̄r-ɛ-nóg (§§ 4048 ff.) v.t. go to seek, go in search of.
ind. pres. aî‿tɛbɛ̄renógri⌒, ɛr‿tɛbɛre-nógın⌒ (-gi⌒, -nógí⌒).

tɛbɛ̄r-ɛ-nóg-bŭ̆- (-nóggŭ̆- § 546; § 4058) v.t. stat. be on one's way (going) to seek, etc.
ar‿ugulláŋgı‿tɛbɛ̄renóggŭ̆ru⌒ we are on our way to look for fuel.

tɛbɛ̄r-ɛ-tắ- (§§ 4060 ff.) v.t. come to seek, etc.

tɛbɛ̄-ɛ́l (tɛbɛ́l § 1113; § 3747ᵉ′) v.t. find on (after) seeking, etc.
sŭ̆gır‿tɛbɛ́ɛ́lkori⌒ on looking for him (her, it, them) I found him (her, it, them) in the market.

tɛbɛ́-kattı (N. -ɛ́ha-; § 4093) v.p. be sought, etc.

tɛbɛ̄-mísır (§ 3747ᵉ′) v.t. fail to find on (after) seeking, etc., seek (etc.) in vain (§ 3783).
sŭ̆gır‿gonísset‿tɛbɛ̄mısírkori⌒ (-t‿t- < -g‿t- § 707) I (have) looked for gum in the market and couldn't find it.

tɛbɛ̄-nál (§ 3747ᵉ′) v.t. see (etc., s.v. nál) by seeking, etc., ascertain by searching.
ind. pres. aî‿tɛbɛ̄nállı⌒.
imperat. tɛbɛ̄nál! and tɛbɛnal! (§ 1871).
wélom‿bélkogın‿tɛbɛ̄nállan⌒ they search to see whether the dog has gone out; wélom‿bélkogın‿ a noun-clause, object of -nállan⌒ (§ 6137).

tɛbɛ́-nal (§ 1964) v.t. see (etc.) by seeking, (etc.), seek (etc.) so as to see (etc.), seek (etc.) in order to see (etc.) (§ 3783), look about for.
ind. pres. aî‿tɛbɛ́nallı⌒.
tékkı‿tɛbɛ́nal⌒ look about for him (her, it).
wélgı‿tɛbɛ́nal⌒ look about for the dog.
térōm‿bélkogın, tɛbɛ́nal⌒ (§ 6234η) if (s)he (it) has gone (come) out, look about for him (her, it).

tɛbɛ̄-nóg (§ 3747ᵉ′) v.t. go seeking, etc., go in search of.
ind. pres. aî‿tɛbɛ̄nógri⌒, ɛr‿tɛbɛ̄nógın (-gi⌒, -gí⌒).
imperat. tɛbɛ̄nók! and tɛbɛ́nok! (§ 1871), pl. tɛbɛ̄nógwɛ! (-wɛ́!, -nóggɛ! § 547, -gɛ́!).

tɛbɛ̄ros-él (§§ 4180–4; -osgél, -ozg-, -ogg- §§ 4185–7) v.t. find by (on, after) seeking, etc.

⌣tɛ́ddɛ́? — tɛmmɛ́

⌣tɛ́ddɛ́? *is that...?, are (they)...?,* s.v. tɛr⌣.
tɛ́ddo⌣ *on him (her, it), to him (her, it), in it, there, thither,* s.v. tɛr⌣.
tɛ̄g (§3872) v.i. *(a) squat; (b) sit down, sit; (c) settle; (d) reside, live; (e) remain, stay, wait (not depart); (f) be in a situation, position or place, be continuously, remain, stay, keep (not change) position; (g) be present, be here, be there; (h) be* [§4591; cp. ON. тιк *sit* GNT s.v.; RSN, §§129, 200].
— *used of persons, like its synonym* åg.
ind. pres. aı⌣tɛ̄g(¹)ri⌢; fut. aı⌣bıtɛ̄g(¹)ri⌢ (⌣but-); perf. aı⌣tɛ̄gkori⌢ (⌣tɛ́kkori⌢).
imperat. tɛ̄k!, tɛ̄g⌣v., pl. tɛ̄gwɛ! (tɛ̄gwɛ́!, tɛ̄gge! §547, -gɛ́!).
subj. past aı⌣tɛ̄gsı⌣ (⌣tɛ́ksı⌣, -su⌣).
def. pres. aı⌣tɛ̄gosri⌢; perf. aı⌣tɛ̄góskori⌢.
def. imperat. tɛ̄gos! (tɛ̄gó! §962, tɛ̄gó!, tɛ̄go!), pl. tɛ̄goswɛ! (tɛ̄góswɛ!, -gówwɛ! §724, -wɛ́!, -góssɛ! §687, -sɛ́!).
níbıdır⌣tɛ̄k⌢ *squat on the mat.*
aı⌣tɛ̄g⌣ewɛ́ri⌢ *I say 'sit down'.*
ğɛn⌣wɛ̄g⌣góhdır⌣tɛ́kkori⌢ (ğɛn⌣nɛ̄g⌣ §627) *I remained (lived, have been) one year at Góhd.*
aı⌣tɛ̄grıá⌣wála⌣nógri? *shall* (§5369b) *I wait or go?*
aı⌣tɛ́nn⌣agárro⌣bıtɛ̄gri⌢ (a) *I shall sit (be) in his (her) place;* (b) *I shall wait (stay) instead of him (her).*
tókkon⌣ímbɛlmɛn, tɛ̄k⌢ *don't start, wait.*
tókkon⌣ímbɛlmɛn, tɛ̄gó⌢ *don't get up, sit down.*
aı⌣nínŋon⌣tɛ̄gri⌢ and
aı⌣nínŋon⌣tɛ̄gri⌢ (§5738) *I am (engaged in) drinking.*
aı⌣fɛttıšɛ́ŋgon⌣tɛ̄gın⌢ (-ɛ́ŋŋon⌣) *I am (engaged in) searching.*
ɛr⌣fɛttıšɛ́ŋgon⌣tɛ̄gın⌢ (-ɛ́ŋŋon⌣) *you are (engaged in) searching.*
tɛr⌣fɛttıšɛ́ŋgon⌣tɛ̄gın⌢ (-ɛ́ŋŋon⌣) *(s)he (it) is (engaged in) searching.*
ar⌣fɛttıšɛ́ŋgon⌣tɛ̄gru⌢ (-ɛ́ŋŋon⌣) *we are (engaged in) searching.*
ır⌣fɛttıšɛ́ŋgon⌣tɛ̄gru⌢ (-ɛ́ŋŋon⌣) *you (pl.) are (engaged in) searching.*
tır⌣fɛttıšɛ́ŋgon⌣tɛ̄gran⌢ (-ɛ́ŋŋon⌣) *they are (engaged in) searching.*
ar⌣nínŋon⌣tɛ́kkoru⌢ (⌣nínŋon⌣) *we were (have been) (engaged in) drinking.*
aı⌣nínŋon⌣kálıŋon⌣tɛ̄gri⌢ and
aı⌣nínŋon⌣kálıŋon⌣tɛ̄gri⌢ (§5756) *I am (engaged in) drinking and eating.*
aı⌣fɛttıšɛ́ŋgon⌣ısíkkıŋgon⌣tɛ̄gri⌢ (-ɛ́ŋŋ-, -ıŋŋ-) *I am (engaged in) searching and asking.*
ɛr⌣fɛttıšɛ́ŋgon⌣ısíkkıŋgon⌣tɛ̄gın⌢ (-ɛ́ŋŋ-, -ıŋŋ-) *you are (engaged in) searching and asking.*
tɛr⌣fɛttıšɛ́ŋgon⌣ısíkkıŋgon⌣tɛ̄gın⌢ (-ɛ́ŋŋ-, -ıŋŋ-) *(s)he is (engaged in) searching and asking.*
ar⌣fɛttıšɛ́ŋgon⌣ısíkkıŋgon⌣tɛ̄gru⌢ (-ɛ́ŋŋ-, -ıŋŋ-) *we are (engaged in) searching and asking.*
ır⌣fɛttıšɛ́ŋgon⌣ısíkkıŋgon⌣tɛ̄gru⌢ (-ɛ́ŋŋ-, -ıŋŋ-) *you (pl.) are (engaged in) searching and asking.*
tır⌣fɛttıšɛ́ŋgon⌣ısíkkıŋgon⌣tɛ̄gran⌢ (-ɛ́ŋŋ-, -ıŋŋ-) *they are (engaged in) searching and asking.*

ar⌣fɛttıšɛ́ŋgon⌣ısíkkıŋgon⌣tɛ́kkoru⌢ *we were (have been) searching and asking.*
tɛ̄g-an (§§3890 ff.) v.t. *tell to squat, etc., let squat, etc.*
tɛ̄g-båğ (§3747ɛ') v.t. *write (etc.,* s.v. båğ) *while squatting, etc.*
tɛ̄g(¹)r-ɛg-åg- (§§4071 ff.) v.i. = tɛ̄gɛdól-.
tɛ̄g-ɛ-dól- (-g°d- §1178; §4022) and
tɛ̄g(¹)r-ɛ-dól- (-r°d-; §4027) v.i. *be about to squat, etc.*
tɛ̄g-ɛ-må- (§4036) and
tɛ̄g(¹)r-ɛ-må- (§4041) v.i. *become unable to squat, etc.*
tɛ̄gɛd-åg- (§§3877 ff.) v.i. *be in the situation of having squatted, etc.*
tɛ̄g-íñır (-íñír; §3747ɛ') v.i. and t. *squat (etc.) waiting (for) (etc.,* s.v. íñır; §3783).
tɛ̄g-kál (tɛ̄kkál; §3747ɛ') v.i. and t. *squat (etc.) eating (etc.,* s.v. kál; §3783).
tɛ̄g-ní (§3747ɛ') v.i. and t. *squat (etc.) drinking* (§3783).
tɛ̄gos-íg (§§4180–4; -osgíg, -ozg-, -ogg- §4185) v.t. *tell (etc.,* s.v. íg) *after squatting, etc.*
tåwɛ, tɛ̄gosıgıdkíg¹ru⌢ (§5601) *come (pl.), let's* (§5376) *sit down and tell stories.*
tɛ̄gos-kál (-okkál §573; §§4180–4; -osgı-kál, -ozgı-, -oggı- §4185) v.i. and t. *eat (etc.,* s.v. kál) *after squatting, etc.*
árgonon⌣tɛ̄gokkál⌢ *sit down and eat with us.*
tɛ́gge! < tɛ̄gwɛ! *squat!* (pl.), *etc.* s.v. tɛ̄g.
tɛ̄k! imperat. of tɛ̄g *squat, etc.*
tɛ́kkɛ́⌢ < tɛ́kkɛt⌢ *with (etc.) it (etc.), there, etc.,* s.v. tɛr⌣.
tɛ́kkɛ⌣ < tɛ́kkɛg⌣ *thus, so, etc.,* s.v. tɛr⌣.
tɛ́kk(ı)⌣ *him, her, it, obj. of* tɛr⌣.
†tɛlɛfón (§956a) n. *telephone* [< تلفون *id.*].
obj. -óŋg(ı)⌣, -gi⌢.
tɛlɛgráf (tɛllɛ-, tál(l)åg-) n. (a) *telegraph* [< تَلْغْرَاف *id.*]; (b) *telegraph-office;* (c) *telegram.*
obj. -áfk(ı)⌣, -ki⌢.
gen. -áfn⌣v., -ám⌣c.
pl. -áfı⌣.
tɛlɛgráfn⌣úğrɛ⌣ *cost of telegram.*
tɛlɛgrám⌣bɛ́r⌣ *telegraph-pole.*
tɛlɛgrám⌣dáftár⌣ *telegraph-book, book of telegram-forms.*
tɛlɛgrám⌣máktáb⌣ and (§789)
tɛlɛgráf⌣máktáb⌣ *telegraph-office.*
tɛlɛgrám⌣mıráslı⌣ and (§789)
tɛlɛgráf⌣mıráslı⌣ *telegraph messenger.*
tɛlɛgráfkı⌣ğómkoran⌢ *they (have) sent a telegram* (s.v. ğóm).
aı⌣samílnár⌣tɛlɛgráfkı⌣ğómkori⌢ *I (have) sent a telegram to the sheikh.*
tɛlɛgráfkɛs⌣síkkıgori⌢ (-s⌣ < -d⌣s- §677) *I (have) inquired by telegram.*
tɛr⌣aıgı⌣tɛlɛgráfkɛw⌣wɛ́dɛ̄ŋkon⌢ (-w⌣w- < -d⌣w- §718) and
tɛr⌣aıgı⌣tɛlɛgráfkı⌣wɛ́dɛ̄ŋkó⌢ *(s)he (has) let me know by telegram.*
tɛ́kkı⌣tɛlɛgráfkɛb⌣bıwɛ́tıddi⌢ (-b⌣b- < -d⌣b- §518) and
tɛ́kkı⌣tɛlɛgráfkı⌣bıwɛ́tıddi⌢ *I shall let him (her) know by telegram.*

tɛlɛgráf-wɛ́-dɛ̄n (tɛllɛ-, tál(l)åg-; §5692) v.t. *inform (the speaker) by telegram.*
aıgı⌣tɛlɛgráfwɛ́dɛ̄ŋkoran⌢ *they (have) told me by telegram.*
tɛlɛgráf-wɛ́-tır (tɛllɛ-, tál(l)åg- §5692) v.t *inform (other than the speaker) by telegram.*
aı⌣tɛ́kkı⌣bıtɛlɛgráfwɛ́tıddi⌢ and (§5611)
aı⌣bı-tɛ́kkı-tɛlɛgráfwɛ́tıddi⌢ *I shall let him (her) know by telegram.*
tɛlɛ́wɛ v.i. *melt, become liquefied by heat* [§§2870 ff.].
ind. pres. tɛr⌣tɛlɛ́wɛn⌢ (-wɛ̄⌢, -wɛ́⌢); perf. tɛr⌣tɛlɛ́wɛgon⌢ (-gɔ̄⌢, -gó⌢), N. -ɛkon⌢, -ɛkɔ̄⌢, -ɛkó⌢, -ɛhon⌢, -ɛhɔ̄⌢, -ɛhó⌢).
šɛ́ma⌣masíllo⌣bıtɛlɛ́wɛn⌢ *the candle(s* §4696d) *will melt in the sun.*
tɛlɛ́wɛrar⌣ (-rår⌣; §§2200 ff., 2210) and
tɛlɛ́wɛríd (§§2256 ff., 2263) n. *melting, deliquescence.*
tɛlɛ́wɛ-bū- (§3931α) v.i. stat. *be in a melted (etc.) state or condition.*
dɛ́s⌣masíllo⌣tɛlɛwɛbū́n⌢ *the butter has got melted in the sun.*
tɛlɛ́wɛr-ɛg-åg- (§§4071 ff.) v.i. = tɛlɛ́wɛrɛ-dól-.
tɛlɛ́wɛr-ɛ-dól- (-r°d- §1178; §§4016–17, 4022, 4027) v.i. *be about to melt, etc.*
tɛlɛ́wɛg-ır (N. -ɛkır, -ɛhır; §3679) (a) v.t. caus. *cause or allow to melt, etc.;* (b) v.t. *melt.*
íg⌣dɛ́skı⌣tɛlɛ́wɛgırın⌢ *the fire melts the butter.*
tɛlɛ́wɛgıdd-ɛg-åg- (N. -ɛkı-, -ɛhı-; §§4071 ff.) v.t. = tɛlɛ́wɛgırɛdól-.
tɛlɛ́wɛgır-ɛ-dól- (N. -ɛkı-, -ɛhı-; -r°d- §1178; §4025) and
tɛlɛ́wɛgıdd-ɛ-dól- (N. -ɛkı-, -ɛhı-; -d°d-; §4033) v.t. *be about to cause to melt, etc.*
télığ⌣ n. *ice* [< تَلْج *snow,* and in Sudan Ar. *ice,* §1359].
obj. telíğk(ı)⌣, -íčk(ı)⌣, -íčč(ı)⌣ §523, -ki⌢, -či⌢.
gen. -líğn⌣v., -líñ⌣c.
télıñ⌣témɛn⌣ *the price of (the) ice.*
tɛlíñ-d(ı)⌣ (§§2545 ff.) adj. *appertaining to ice.*
tɛllɛgráf⌣ n. *telegraph, etc.* = tɛlɛgráf⌣.
tɛmám⌣ *completion, etc.* s.v. tamám⌣.
tɛmɛ́llı⌣, -li⌢ and
tɛmɛ́llıg⌣, -gi⌢ (§6000) adv. *constantly, continually, always* [< تَمَلِّي *id.*].
tɛmɛ́llın⌣nógran⌢ (-n⌣n- < -g⌣n- §625) *they always go.*
témɛn (§956a) n. *price* [< ثَمَن *id.*].
obj. tɛmɛ́ŋg(ı)⌣, -gi⌢ (s.v. -ɛd⌣(c.)).
tɛ́n⌣tɛ́mɛm⌣mukóttɛ̄rrɛ? *what's its price?*
tɛmmɛ́ (*tam-, *tám- not heard) v.t. *complete, finish, end* (= addɛ́) [< تَمّ *completion* + -ɛ́ §3623].
ind. pres. aı⌣tɛmmɛ́ri⌢; perf. aı⌣tɛmmɛ́-gori⌢ (N. -ɛ́ko-, -ɛ́ho-).
imperat. tɛmmɛ́!
ámbɛs⌣mádråsår⌣sɛ́na⌣tóskıt⌣tɛmmɛ́-gon⌢ (-t⌣t- < -g⌣t- §707) *my brother (has) completed three years at school.*
tɛr⌣ólgon⌣sɛ́nat⌣tɛmmɛgómunū̃⌢ *(s)he (it) hasn't completed a year yet.*

ğέllıt⌣tɛmmέgoran⌢ *they (have) finished the work.*
ğέllıt⌣tɛmmέgómunan⌢ *they did not finish (have not finished) the work.*

tɛmmέ-kattı- (N. -έha-; §4093) v.p. *be completed, etc.*

tén⌣, ténn⌣*v. of him (of her, of it), his (her, its)* gen. *of* tér⌣.

tént(ı)⌣ *his, hers, its* s.v. tér⌣.

tɛnnέ⌣*c.* (tɛnnέ⌣*c.*, ténn⌣*v.*, tɛnnέ⌢, ⌢́⌣́ §1995; §4469) adv. *again* [app. a back-formation (cp. *JL*, p. 173) from tɛnnέ-g⌣].
ténnɛ⌣bάññı⌢ *say it again.*
S. dókkon⌣ténn⌣aûmɛwwέ⌢ (a) *don't (pl.) do it again;* (b) *don't (pl.) make any more.*
kάlgı⌣ténn⌣étta⌢ and
ténnɛ⌣kάlg⌣έtta⌢ *bring some more food (bread).*
έssıt⌣ténn⌣έtta⌢ (-t⌣t- < -g⌣t- §707) *bring some more water.*
ténn⌣έssıg⌣έtta⌢ (a) *bring some more water;* (b, ténn⌣ gen. *of* tér⌣) *bring his (her, its) water.*
ɛr⌣ténnɛ⌣sάhanıd⌣dólnά? (-d⌣d- < -g⌣d- §534) *do you want some more plates?*
άdɛmı⌣ténnɛ⌣dígoran⌢ *more people (have) died.*

tɛnnέ-g⌣ (ténnέg⌣, ⌢́⌣́ §1995; -gı⌢; §§4470, 5981) adv. *again* [<*ténn⌣ wέg⌣ (§626b) *one (sc. more) of it*].
tɛnnέ⌣bıtάmunan⌢ and
tɛnnέb⌣bıtάmunan⌢ (-b⌣b- < -g⌣b- §519) *they will not come again.*
ténnɛ⌣naddufέ⌢,
tɛnnɛgı⌣naddufέ⌢ (§510) and
ténnɛn⌣naddufέ⌢ (-n⌣n- < -g⌣n- §625) *clean him (her, it, them) again.*
ténn⌣έtta⌢ and
tɛnnέg⌣έtta⌢ *bring some more (apporte encore).*
ténnɛ⌣wέg⌣έtta⌢ *bring another (one more, encore un).*

tɛnnέgon (ténnέgon⌣, ⌢́⌣́ §1995; §4471) adv. *again* = tɛnnέ⌣ [<*ténn⌣ wέg-on (§626b) *one of it also*].
tɛnnέgon⌣ágón⌢ *(s)he is (you are) singing again.*
tɛnnέgon⌣bάññı⌢ *say it again.*

tɛnnέgóng(ı)⌣ (⌢́⌣́, ⌢́⌣́ §1995; -gı⌢; §5981) adv. *again* = tɛnnέ⌣.
tɛnnɛgóngı⌣tάgoran⌢ *they came (have come) again.*

ténn-í⌣ *his (her) hand(s)* s.v. í⌣.

tɛnnúra⌣ n. *petticoat* [< تَنُّورَة id.].
obj. -rag⌣.
pl. -rančı⌣.

tɛnšíga⌣ n. *pinch of snuff;* with collective sg. (§4696d) [< Sudan Ar. تَنْشِيقَة tɛnšíga id.].
obj. -gag⌣.

tέp! imperat. of tέb v.i. *stand, etc.*

tér⌣ (tɛr⌣ §1718; §§2604 ff., 5076 ff.) pers. pron. *he, she, it* [§4591; cp. ON. ᚦᚨᛈ id. *GNT* s.v.].
obj. tέkk(ı)⌣ (<*térk(ı)⌣ §571b), -kı⌢.
gen. ténn⌣v. (<*térn⌣ §628b), ténn⌣c.
pl. tír⌣ q.v.
tɛr⌣ógığun⌢ *he's a man.*
tɛr⌣ogíč-taran⌢ *he's the man.*
tɛr⌣έnun⌢ *she's a woman.*
tɛr⌣έn-taran⌢ *she's the woman.*
tér⌣sέ? and tés⌣sέ? (§683) *where is (s)he (it)?*
tέkk⌣úwɛ⌢ *call him (her, it).*
tέkkı⌣nάllı⌢ *I see him (her, it).*
ténn-ă⌣ (§1671) *his (her, its) heart.*
ténn-ur⌣dúlun⌣ *his (her, its) head is large.*
ténn-úrkı⌣nάllı⌢ and
ténn-urkı⌣nάllı⌢ *I see his (her, its) head.*
ténn⌣άgıl⌣ *his (her, its) mouth.*
tém⌣bέlɛdun⌣ (§595) *it's his (her, its) country (village).*
tén⌣dúŋgı⌣sέ? *where is his (her) money?*
tén⌣fέrıš⌣, tém⌣fέrıš⌣ and tέf⌣fέrıš⌣ (§543) *his (her) bed-clothes.*
tέŋ⌣gadfjɛ⌣ (§648) *his (her) lawsuit.*
tén⌣ğέb⌣ *his (her) pocket.*
tén⌣hánu⌣ and téh⌣hánu⌣ (§561) *his (her) donkey.*
tén⌣kά⌣ (§659) *his (her) house.*
tén⌣luzúm⌣ and tél⌣luzúm⌣ (§583) *his (her, its) necessity.*
tém⌣míss(ı)⌣ (§608) *his (her, its) eye(s)* §4696a).
tén⌣nέd⌣ *his (her, its) tongue.*
tén⌣rάddı-taran⌢ and tér⌣rάddı-tάnnan⌢ (§671) *it's his (her, its) answer (it's the answer to it).*
tén⌣súkkar⌣ and tés⌣súkkar⌣ (§681) *his (her, its) sugar.*
tén⌣sάwάl⌣ and tés⌣sάwάl⌣ (§699) *his (her, its) sack.*
tén⌣tάbla⌣ *his (her, its) padlock.*
téw⌣wέl⌣ (§722) *his (her) dog.*
tén⌣zάbıd⌣ and téz⌣zάbıd⌣ (§736) *his (its) officer.*

— forming a complex with mάllɛ⌣ (§5195):
tér⌣mάllɛ⌣ *all of him (her, it).*
tér⌣mάllɛs⌣sókkɛgoran⌢ (-s⌣s- < -g⌣s- §678) *they took (have taken) it all.*

— forming a complex with a noun (§4843):
tér⌣ógığ⌣mάgasun⌢ *that man is a thief.*

— enclitic (§5104):
íčči-tarán-tɛr⌢ *that's the milk.*

-tèddɛ⌣...? (a, attached to adverb §§4277, 5853) interrogative particle *is it that...?*
ɛr⌣έlgon-tèddɛ⌣nάlın⌣? *do you still see him (her, it, them* §5083)?
ír⌣έlgon-tèddɛ⌣nάllu? *do you (pl.) still see him (her, it, them)?*

-tèddɛ⌣...? (b, attached to interr. pron. §5855) used as a sign of predication *is...?, are...?*
níʔ-tèddɛ⌣mán⌣ğúbūl? *who's that (over there) coming?*
nígu-tèddɛ⌣mán⌣ğúbuli? *who are those (over there) coming?*

⌣téddɛ́? (§§4248, 5808-16) deictic interrogative sign of predication *is it...?, is that...?, are (they)...?* (=⌣tέ?) [<⌣tér-*dέ? §537].
tér⌣ógığ⌣téddɛ́? *is that the man?*
tér⌣níʔ⌣téddɛ́? *who's that? (who is (s)he?).*
mämάŋgu⌣nígu⌣téddɛ́? *who are those yonder?*
ğέllı⌣halάs⌣téddɛ́? *is the work finished?*

X. ín⌣halάs⌣téddɛ́? *is this finished (at an end, done with)?*
Y. halάs-taran⌢ *yes* (§6104).

téddo⌣ (s.v. -r⌣; §4447) (a) *on (in, to, etc.) him (her, it);* (b) adv. *there (near);* (c) adv. *thither (near).*
téddo⌣ (§§5858-60) (s)he (it) is (they are) in him (her, it), (s)he (it) is there, they are there.
téddo⌣tōrɛdάgran⌢ *they have gone in there.*
téddo⌣bún⌣ *(s)he (it) lies (is) in there.*

tέkk-ɛ⌣ (tέkkέ⌣ §1532; §§4409, 5940, 5955) adv. *in that (this) manner, way, position, posture or direction, so, thus, like that (this)* [<tέkk- demonstrative (§5103) *that (this)* + -έ **have a tendency to* (§213), so **having a tendency to that (this)*].
tέkkɛ⌣bán⌣ (s.v. bú) *let him (her, it) be so (like this, like that).*
sɛrɛgıráu⌣, tέkkέ! *do it properly, like that!*

tέkk-ɛd⌣ (-ɛt⌣ §469, ⌢́⌣́ §1532, -έ⌢ §966; §§5858-60) adv. (a) *by (with, at, to, from, etc.,* s.v. -ɛd⌣); (b, §§4460, 6007) *in that (this) way, thereby, thus, so, there.*
X. (pointing to an instrument) tέkkɛk⌣kús⌢ (-k⌣k- < -d⌣k- §568) *open it with that.*
tέkkɛk⌣kúlub⌣bάlko! (-k⌣k- < -d⌣k-; -b⌣b- < -g⌣b- §519) and
kúlub⌣bάlko, tέkkέ! *mind the stone(s* §4696d) *there (in that place)!*
tέkkɛd⌣ɛsmάŋ⌣úwɛ⌢ and
ɛsmάŋ⌣úwɛ⌣tέkkέ⌢ *from there (where you are) call ɛoθmάn* (i.e. *don't go away to call him).*

tέkk-ɛg⌣, -gı⌢ (§§4409a, 5940, 5982) adv. = tέkkɛ⌣.
tέkkɛg⌣áu⌢ *do (etc.,* s.v. άu) *it in that way (etc.).*

tέk-kırı⌣ (-kírı⌣ §1701; §§2539-40, 2635) pers. pron. adj. *like him, like her, like it.*

tén-d(ı)⌣, -di⌢ (§2637) abs. poss. pron. *his, hers, its.*
obj. -dıg⌣.
pl. -dınέ(ı)⌣.
téndıg⌣έtta⌢ *bring his (hers, its).*

téndı-kırı⌣ (§2638) pers. pron. adj. *resembling that appertaining to him (her, it) like his (hers, its).*

tɛndínčı-kırı⌣ (§2638) pers. pron. adj. *resembling those appertaining to him (her, it), like his (hers, its).*

tέr v.t. *sow, plant.*
ind. pres. aı⌣tέrrı⌢, ɛr⌣tέrın⌢ (-rı⌢, -rí⌢); perf. aı⌣tέrkorı⌢ (-t⌣t- < -g⌣t- §707) *they sowed (have sown) (the) millet.*
márɛt⌣tέrkoran⌢ (-t⌣t- < -g⌣t- §707) *they sowed (have sown) (the) millet.*
innówıd⌣dúhurm⌣bάdır⌣máron⌣ tέrıb⌣bıtέru⌣ (-d⌣d- < -g⌣d- §534, -b⌣b- < -g⌣b- §519) *this afternoon we shall sow the millet (seeds).*
arídkıt⌣tέrran⌢ *they sow the land.*

tέrar⌣ (-rár⌣; §§2200ff.) n. (a) *sowing, tillage, cultivation;* (b) *(growing) crop.*
obj. tέrárk(ı)⌣, tέrark(ı)⌣, -rárk(ı)⌣, -kı⌢.
pl. tέrarı⌣.

tέrarn⌣árıd⌣ *sown ground, cultivated land.*

tɛ́rgıs⌣ — tin⌣

tɛ́n⌣ğɛ́llı⌣tɛ́rarun⌒ *his occupation is agriculture.*

údlañ⌣tɛ́ran⌣túr⌣bokkóskon⌒ (-n⌣t- <-rn⌣t- §852) *the hare has hidden in the crop.*

tɛríd⌣ (§§2256ff.) n. =tɛ́rar⌣ (a).

tɛ́rı⌣ n. (a) *seed;* with collective sg. (§4696b); (b) *semen.*
 obj. -rıg⌣.
 pl. -rınɛ́(ı)⌣.

tɛ́r-an- (§§3890ff.) v.t. *tell to sow, etc., let sow, etc.*

tɛ́r-bŭ- (§3931β) v.i. stat. *be in a sown (etc.) state or condition.*
 márɛ⌣tɛ́rbun⌒ *the millet is (has been) sown.*
 árıd⌣tɛ́rbun⌒ *the land is (has been) sown.*

tɛ̄rr-ɛg-ág- (§§4071ff.) v.t. =tɛ̄rɛdól-.

tɛ̄rr-ɛ-dól- (-rᵒd- §1178; §4022) and

tɛ̄rr-ɛ-dól- (-rᵒd-; §4027) v.t. *be about to sow, etc.*

tɛ̄rr-ɛ-má- (§4036) and

tɛ̄rr-ɛ-má- (§4041) v.t. *become unable to sow, etc.*

tɛ̄rɛd-ág- (§§3877ff.) v.t. *be in the situation of having sown, etc.*

tɛ́r-kattı- (§4093) v.p. *be sown, etc.*

tɛ́rgıs n. *Tergis* (on map), a village on the right bank of the Nile, about ten miles above Ed-Débbaʰ.
 obj. tɛrgísk(ı)⌣, -ki⌒.

tɛ́rıf *thick rope, etc.* =tárıf⌣.

tɛ́rıg⌣ adj. *deaf* [RN s.v. tɛ́rrig cp. طُرُش *be deaf*].
 obj. tɛrígk(ı)⌣, -íkk(ı)⌣, -ki⌒.
 pl. tɛ́r(ı)gı⌣.

tɛríg-kanɛ⌣ (-ikka-; §2295) n. *deafness.*
 obj. -nɛg⌣.

tɛ́rıg-an- (§3910α) v.i. *become deaf, grow deaf.*

tɛ́rıgam-bŭ- (tɛrıgámbŭ-; §§3949ff.) v.i. stat. *be in a state or condition of becoming or having become deaf.*
 tıntımbáb⌣tɛrıgambúgon⌒ *their father began (has begun) to grow (grew, has grown) deaf.*

tɛrıganɛd-ág- (§3966α) v.i. *be in the condition of having become deaf, be quite deaf.*

tɛrtíb⌣ *arrangement, etc.* s.v. tartíb⌣.

tɛ́s⌣sɛ́? (§683) <tɛ́r⌣sɛ́? *where is (s)he (it)?*

tɛswíra⌣ n. *picture, image* [<تَصْوِيرَة id.].
 obj. -rag⌣.
 pl. -ranɛ̌(ı)⌣.

tɛššáš⌣ n. *pedlar, travelling merchant* [<تَشَّاش id.].
 obj. -ášk(ı)⌣, -ki⌒.
 pl. -áši⌣.
 tímbɛs⌣tɛššášun⌒ *his (her) brother is a pedlar.*

tɛššáša⌣ n. (a) *place where pedlars assemble, pedlars' part of market* [<تَشَّاشَة id.]; (b) =tɛššáš⌣.
 obj. -šag⌣.
 pl. -šanɛ̌(ı)⌣.
 álıt⌣tɛššášar⌣nálkori⌒ (-t⌣t- <-g⌣t- §707) *I saw ɛáli at the pedlars' place.*
 tímbɛs⌣tɛššášan⌒ *his (her) brother is a pedlar.*

tɛ́tt(ı)⌣, -ti⌒ n. *Teiti* (on map), a village on the left bank of the Nile, about 15 miles below Hándag.
 obj. -tıg⌣.

tɛ́tt-an- (§3910β) v.i. *go to Tɛ́tti.*

tɛ́ttam-bŭ- (§3950β) v.i. stat. *be in a state of motion towards Tɛ́tti.*
 tɛ́ttambúran⌒ *they are on their way to Tɛ́tti⌒.*

tɛ́ttanɛd-ág- (§3966β) v.i. *be in the situation of having gone to Tɛ́tti.*

tɛ́w(ı)rɛ⌣ n. (in water-wheel, kólɛ⌣) *oblong block forming platform in centre of which is small block* (sáb⌣) *containing socket wherein vertical axle* (míšš(ı)⌣) *turns; on end near vertical cog-wheel* (árgadɛn⌣tód⌣) *is outer bearing* (bóɛ̌ɛ̌ıŋ⌣ kálo⌣) *in which shoreward end of horizontal axle* (tórɛ⌣) *turns.*
 obj. -rɛg⌣.
 pl. -rɛnɛ̌(ı)⌣.

tí⌣ n. (a) *head of cattle* (bull or cow); (b) *cow* [<*tíw<t- dem. (§4592)+-íw, -íu, -íᵘ tend at pasture;* cp. ON. ⲧⲟⲩⲉⲓ *cow* GNT s.v.; §2172; RSN, §§129, 200 al.].
 obj. -tíg⌣.
 pl. tínɛ̌(ı)⌣.
 tínɛ̌ıg⌣íwıl⌣ *neat-herd, cowherd.*
 kólɛn⌣tínɛ̌ık⌣kómunan⌒ *they haven't the cattle for (i.e. to turn) the water-wheel.*
 éssın⌣tí⌣, éssín-tı⌣ and éssıntí⌣ (§2355) *hippopotamus,* lit. *water-cow* (=ɛ̄rıd⌣) [>Sudan Ar. عِينِسْنْت ɛēsítt id.], obj. éssın⌣tíg⌣.
 úrun⌣tí⌣, urún⌣tí⌣ and urún-tī⌣ (§2355) *hippopotamus,* lit. *cow of the river* [>Sudan Ar. قِرِنْت gırínt id.], obj. úrun⌣tíg⌣.
 tínɛ̌ıgɛš⌣šúgran⌣ (§5454; -š⌣š- <-d⌣š- §694) n. *cattle-switch.*

tín-tŏd⌣ (§2366) n. *young of cow, calf, heifer;* with collective sg. (§4696d).
 obj. -tŏdk(ı)⌣, -tŏtk(ı)⌣, -tŏkk(ı)⌣, -tŏtt(ı)⌣ (§2462), -ki⌒, -ti⌒.
 gen. -tŏdn⌣v., -tŏnn⌣v.c., -tŏn⌣c.
 pl. tíntoni⌣.

tí-tod (§2369) n. (a) *cow of poor quality;* (b) =tí⌣.
 obj. títŏdk(ı)⌣, -tŏtk(ı)⌣, -tŏkk(ı)⌣, -tŏtt(ı)⌣ (§2462), -ki⌒, -ti⌒.
 gen. -tŏdn⌣v., -tŏnn⌣v.c., -tŏn⌣c.
 pl. títoni⌣.
 títodun⌒ *it's a (wretched) cow.*

tín-d(ı)⌣ (§§2545ff.) adj. *appertaining to the (a) cow (etc.), of the (a) cow, cow's, cattle's.*
 ın⌣íɛ̌ɛ̌ı⌣tíndıɛ́? *is this milk cow's?*
 kúsu⌣tínd(ı)⌣ *beef.*

tinɛ̌ín-d(ı)⌣ (§§2545ff.) adj. *appertaining to (the) cows (etc.), of (the) cows, cows', cattle's.*
 ın⌣íɛ̌ɛ̌ı⌣tinɛ̌índıɛ́? *is this milk cows'?*

tíŋ-gır (§2150) n. *path for cattle in an irrigated area* (kólɛ⌣) [tíŋ⌣gír⌣ *cattle's path;* K. gír=D. dárıb⌣.]
 obj. -gırk(ı)⌣, -ki⌒.
 pl. -gırı⌣.

tín⌣ n. *fig* [<Ar. تين id.].
 obj. tíŋg(ı)⌣.
 pl. tíni⌣.

tíbıl⌣ n. coll. (a) *temple* (of head); (b) *cheek* (=ğáham⌣) [RSN, §129].
 obj. tıbílg(ı)⌣, -gi⌒.
 pl. tíb(ı)lı⌣.

tíbıš⌣ n. *cucumber, Cucumis dipsaccus, Ehrenb.* (BSP, 206) [<Sudan Ar. تِبِش id. §1359].
 obj. tıbíšk(ı)⌣, -ki⌒.
 pl. tíb(ı)ši⌣.

tíddi⌣ *I give* s.v. tír.

tíddo⌣ *on* (etc., s.v. -r⌣) *them.*

tífıl⌣ n. *sediment, dregs* [<Eg. Ar. تَفْل id. =تُفْل §1359].
 obj. tıfílg(ı)⌣, -gi⌒.
 pl. tíf(ı)li⌣.

tığára⌣ n. *trade* [<تِجَارَة id.].
 obj. -rag⌣.

tílıd⌣ n. *third,* ⅓ [<Sudan Ar. tılt id. =تُلْت §1359].
 obj. tılídk(ı)⌣, -ítk(ı)⌣, -ítt(ı)⌣ (§2462), -ki⌒, -ti⌒.
 pl. tílıdı⌣.

tíllɛ v.i. *sweat, perspire* [§§2870ff., RSN, §129].
 ind. pres. aı⌣tíllɛri⌣, ɛr⌣tíllɛn⌒ (-lɛ̄⌣, -lɛ́⌒); perf. aı⌣tíllɛgori⌣ (N. -ɛko-, -ɛho-).

tíllɛrar⌣ (-rár⌣), **tíllar⌣** (-lár⌣; §§2200ff., 2211) and

tíllɛríd⌣, tıllíd⌣ (§§2256ff., 2264) n. *sweating, perspiration.*

tıllátt⌣, -ti⌣ n. *sweat, perspiration,* (concrete) [§§2222-3].
 obj. -tıg⌣.

tıllátt-an- (§3910α) v.i. *get into a sweating state or condition,* lit. *become sweat.*

tıllattam-bŭ- (§§3949ff.) v.i. stat. *be in a sweating state or condition.*

tíllɛ-bŭ- (§3931α) v.i. stat. *be in a state of perspiration, be in a sweating condition.*

tíllɛg-ır (N. -ɛkır, -ɛhır; §3679) v.t. caus. *cause or allow to sweat.*
 ín⌣áıgı⌣tíllɛgırın⌒ *this makes me sweat.*

tımbáb⌣ *his (her, its) father* s.v. -báb⌣.

tımbánɛss(ı)⌣ *his (her) paternal aunt* s.v. -báb⌣.

tımbánna⌣ *his (her) paternal uncle* s.v. -báb⌣.

tımbɛ́nna⌣ *his (her) paternal uncle* s.v. -bɛ́nna⌣.

tímbɛs⌣ *his (her) brother* s.v. -bɛs⌣.

tímɛ⌣ n. *water-melon, Citrullus vulgaris, Schrad.* (BSP, 207).
 obj. tímɛg⌣.
 pl. tımɛ́nɛ̌(ı)⌣.

tımɛn-ár n. *Tıminár* (on map), a village on the right bank of the Nile, about eight miles above Urdi [*Melon Shore*].
 obj. -árk(ı)⌣, -ki⌒.
 tımɛnár⌣sórton⌣gɛbéllo⌣máltigɛ̄⌒ (-ŋ-g- <-dn⌣g- §644) *Tımɛnár is opposite Sórtod, on the east bank.*

tímmɛn! <tírmɛn! *don't give!* s.v. tír *give.*

tímmunun⌒ <tírmunun⌒ *I (etc.) do not give* s.v. tír *give.*

tin⌣ n. (a) *west;* (b) *left bank of the Nile* (=gárıb⌣).

obj. tíng(ı)⌣, -gi⌒.
tíndo⌣ (s.v. -r⌣) adv. *in (to) the west, on (to) the left bank of the Nile.*
tíndo⌒ (§ 6007) *(s)he (it) is (they are) in the west (on the left bank of the Nile).*
tɛr⌣tíndó⌒ (§ 1532) *(s)he (it) is (a) in the west; (b) on the left bank.*
tır⌣tíndó⌒ *they are (a) in the west; (b) on the left bank.*
tínd⌣ágran⌒ *they live (etc. s.v. ág) (a) in the west; (b) on the left bank.*
tíndo⌣nókkoran⌒ *and*
tíndo⌣ğúgoran⌒ *they went (have gone) to the west.*
tíndotōn⌣táran⌒ *they come from the west.*

tín-d(ı)⌣, **-di**⌒ (§§ 2545 ff.) *adj. appertaining to the west, western, of the left bank.*

tín-an- (§§ 3910 ff.) *v.i. (a) go to the west, go to the left bank; (b) become (part of) the left bank.*
ártı⌣tınanóskó⌒ *the island has become part of the left bank (of the Nile).*

tıŋgár⌣ *n. (a) west; (b) prop.) left bank of the Nile* (=gárıb⌣) [<*tınŋgár⌣ (§ 646 a) < tínn⌣ *of the west* + gár⌣ *bank* § 2364]; tıŋgár ⌣is *now more commonly heard than* tín⌣ *both for a and b.*
obj. -árk(ı)⌣, -ki⌒.
tıŋgárro⌣ (s.v. -r⌣) *adv. in (to) the west, on (to) the left bank.*
tıŋgárro⌒ (§ 6007) *(s)he (it) is (they are) in the west (…on the left bank).*
tıŋgárr⌣ágran⌒ *they live (etc. s.v. ág) in the west (…on the left bank).*
tíŋ⌣ká⌣tıŋgárró⌒ (§ 1532) *their house is on the left bank.*
tıŋgárrotōn⌣tágoran⌒ *they came (have come) from the west (…from the left bank).*

tıŋgárk-ɛd⌣ (-ɛt⌒, -ɛ́⌒ § 966; § 6007) *adv. on the west, by the western route, by (on) the left bank.*
tıŋgárkɛn⌣nókkoran⌒ (-n⌣n- < -d⌣n- § 624) *they went (have gone) by the western route (…by the left bank).*
dábba⌣tıŋgárké⌒ *Ed-Débba*ᵇ *is on the left bank.*
hannák⌣káwwaŋ⌣gɛbéllo⌣tıŋgárké⌒ *Hannág is opposite Káwwa, it's on the west bank.*

tıŋgárn-d(ı)⌣, **-di**⌒ (§§ 2545 ff.) *adj. western, of the left bank.*

tıŋgár-an- (§§ 3910 ff.) *v.i. (a) go to the west, go to the left bank; (b) become (part of) the left bank.*
ártı⌣tıŋgáraŋkó⌒ *the island became (has become) part of the left bank.*

tıŋgárkɛb-bél (§ 4127) *v.i. issue (sc. from river, boat) on the left bank.*
úrum⌣múkkıgı⌣tıŋgárkébbɛl⌒ (-m⌣m- < -g⌣m- § 601; ⌣múkkıgı⌣ § 5583) *crossing the river get out on the left bank.*

tıŋgárkɛbbél-an (§§ 3890 ff., 3905) *v.t. tell to issue on the left bank, let issue on the left bank.*

tıŋgárkɛn-nóg (§ 4127) *v.i. go by the western route, by (on) the left bank.*
tıŋgárkɛnnókkoran⌒ = tıŋgárkɛn⌣nókkoran⌒ (*supra*).

tıŋgárkɛnnóg-an (§§ 3890 ff., 3905) *v.t. tell to go by the western route, etc., let go by the western route, etc.*

tıŋgárkır-nóg (§ 4139) *v.i. go westwards, go to the left bank.*
tıŋgárkırnókkoran⌒ *they went (have gone) westwards (…to the left bank).*

tıŋgárkırnóg-an (§§ 3890 ff., 3905) *v.t. tell to go westwards, etc., let go westwards, etc.*

tíŋg-ɛd⌣ (-ɛt⌒, -ɛ́⌒ § 966; § 6007) *adv. on the west, by the western route, by (on) the left bank.*
tíŋgɛn⌣nókkoran⌒ (-n⌣n- < -d⌣n- § 624) *and*
tíŋgɛǧ⌣ǧúgoran⌒ (-ǧ⌣ǧ- < -d⌣ǧ- § 550) *they went (have gone) (a) by the western route; (b) by the left bank.*
tíŋgɛt⌣tágoran⌒ (-t⌣t- < -d⌣t- § 706) *they came (have come) (a) by the western route; (b) by the left bank.*

tin⌣ *of them, their. gen. of* tír⌣ *they.*
tínda⌣ *his (her, its, their) home s.v.* dá⌣.
tínd(ı)⌣ *theirs s.v.* tír⌣.
tındımínd(ı)⌣, **-di**⌒ *adj. confused, mixed up, muddled,* [app. < tíndı⌣mınındín? *of what is theirs? i.e. what a muddle theirs is in!* § 2508].
obj. -dıg⌣.
áfɛš⌣tındımíndín, gɛ́ndıgır⌒ *the baggage is mixed up, put it in order.*
tém⌣báññıd⌣tındımíndín⌒ *what (s)he says is confused.*

tındımínd-an- (§ 3910α) *v.i. become confused, etc.*
ɛ́ssıgom⌣mérsɛgon⌣tındımındáŋkoran⌒ *the water and the beer (have) got mixed.*
ai⌣filfílgon⌣umbutkóŋgi⌣tındımındaníŋgi⌣dólmunun⌣ (§ 6131) ⌣umbútkon⌣tın- § 6134) *I don't like (want) the pepper and salt to get mixed;* ⌣filfílgon⌣umbutkóŋgı⌣ *a noun-concretion* (§§ 4913, 4901).

tındımíndıg-ır (N. -ıkır, -ıhır; § 3703) *(a) v.t. caus. cause or allow to be confused, etc.; (b) v.t. confuse, mix up, muddle.*
S. kadɛ́nčıd⌣dókkon⌣tındımíndıgırímmen⌒ (-d⌣d- < -g⌣d- § 534) *don't mix up the (various* § 5456) *cloths (clothes).*

tındımíndıgır-úskur (N. -ıkır-, -ıhır-; § 4140) *v.t. place (etc., s.v.* úskur) *confusedly, place (etc.) in confusion.*

tındımíndıgır-uskurɛd-ág- (N. -ıkır-, -ıhır-; §§ 3877 ff.) *v.t. be in the situation of having placed (etc.) confusedly, etc.*
ɛr⌣íŋgı⌣tındımíndıgıruskurɛdágın⌒ *and* (§ 5570)
ɛr⌣íŋgı⌣tındımíndıgırg⌣uskurɛdágın⌒ *you have put this down in a muddle.*

tınɛ́n⌣ *his (her, its) mother s.v.* -ɛ́n⌣.
tınɛ́ŋkɛgıd⌣ *his (her) maternal aunt s.v.* -ɛ́n⌣.
tínn⌣ *of them, their. gen. of* tír⌣.
tınná? < **tírná?** *do you (does (s)he, it) give? s.v.* tír.
tínnár⌣ < **tírnár**⌣ *beside them s.v.* -nár⌣.
tínnáu⌣ *his (her) grandmother s.v.* -áu⌣.
tínnɛss(ı)⌣ *his (her, its) sister s.v.* -ɛss(ı)⌣.
tínn⌣ɛ́ss(ı)⌣ *their water s.v.* ɛ́ss(ı)⌣.
tínn-i⌣ *their hands s.v.* i⌣.
tínnogo⌣ *his (her) mother-in-law s.v.* -ogo⌣.
tínnu⌣ *his (her) grandfather s.v.* -u⌣.

tínod⌣ *his (her) father-in-law s.v.* -od⌣.
tıntımbáb⌣ *their father s.v.* -báb⌣.
tıntımbánɛss(ı)⌣ *their paternal aunt s.v.* -báb⌣.
tıntımbánna⌣ *their paternal uncle s.v.* -báb⌣.
tıntımbénna⌣ *their paternal uncle s.v.* -bénna⌣.
tıntımbɛs⌣ *their brother s.v.* -bɛs⌣.
tıntınɛ́n⌣ *their mother s.v.* -ɛ́n⌣.
tıntınɛ́ŋkɛgıd⌣ *their maternal aunt s.v.* -ɛ́n⌣.
tıntınnáu⌣ *their grandmother s.v.* -áu⌣.
tıntınnɛss(ı)⌣ *their sister s.v.* -ɛss(ı)⌣.
tıntınnogo⌣ *their mother-in-law s.v.* -ogo⌣.
tıntınnu⌣ *their grandfather s.v.* -u⌣.
tıntınod⌣ *their father-in-law s.v.* -od⌣.
tıntıŋ(ı)⌣ *their maternal uncle s.v.* -g(ı)⌣.
tíntıssőd⌣ *their sister's child s.v.* -ssőd⌣.
tıŋgár⌣ *west, etc. s.v.* tín⌣.
tíŋ(ı)⌣ *his (her) maternal uncle s.v.* -g(ı)⌣.
tír (tır⌣ § 1718; §§ 2604 ff. 5076 ff.) *pers. pron. they* [§ 4591; cp. ON. ᛏᛖᛔ *id.* GNT s.v.].
obj. tírg(ı)⌣, -gi⌒.
gen. tínn⌣ *v.*, tínn⌣ *c.* (< *tírn⌣ § 628 b).
tír⌣tóskı⌣nókkon⌒ *and*
tír⌣tóskı⌣nókkoran⌒ *the three of them went (have gone;* § 5245).
tír⌣kémıs⌣tágon⌒ *and*
tír⌣kémıs⌣tágoran⌒ *the four of them came (have come).*
tínn-i⌣ (§ 1671) *their hands* (§ 4696 a).
tínn⌣ɛ́ss(ı)⌣ *their water.*
tím⌣béled⌣ (§ 595) *their country (village).*
tín⌣dúŋ(ı)⌣ *their money.*
tín⌣fádıl⌣, tím⌣fádıl⌣ *and* tíf⌣fádıl⌣ (§ 543) *their kindness.*
tíŋ⌣gadíjɛ (§ 648) *their lawsuit.*
tíŋ⌣ǧéll(ı)⌣ *their work.*
tín⌣hánu⌣ *their donkey.*
tíŋ⌣kám⌣ (§ 659) *their camel.*
tín⌣luzúm⌣ *and* tíl⌣luzúm⌣ (§ 583) *their necessity.*
tím⌣méksɛb⌣ (§ 608) *their profit.*
tín⌣nógo⌣ *their female slave.*
tín⌣rádd(ı)⌣ *and* tír⌣rádd(ı)⌣ (§ 671) *their answer.*
tín⌣sáfar⌣ *and* tís⌣sáfar⌣ (§ 681) *their journey.*
tín⌣šáwál⌣ *and* tíš⌣šáwál⌣ (§ 699) *their sack.*
tín⌣tórt(ı)⌣ *their half.*
tíw⌣wéli⌣ (§ 722) *their dogs.*
tín⌣zábid⌣ *and* tíz⌣zábıd⌣ (§ 736) *their officer.*
tíddo⌣ *on (etc. s.v.* -r⌣) *them.*

tín-d(ı)⌣ (§ 2637) *abs. poss. pron. theirs.*
obj. -dıg⌣.
pl. -dınč(ı)⌣.

tír-kırı⌣ (tírkírı⌒ § 1701; §§ 2539-40, 2635) *pers. pron. adj. like them.*

tíndı-kırı⌣ (§ 2638) *pers. pron. adj. resembling that appertaining to them, like theirs.*

tındínčı-kırı⌣ (§ 2638) *pers. pron. adj. resembling those appertaining to them, like theirs.*

tír *v.t. give (to other than the speaker)* [< *tír (§ 1154) < *deictic* t- (§ 4591) + í *hand* + -r *into, so* *(sc. *put) into that (not my) hand;* cp. ON. ᛏᛁᛔ *id.* GNT s.v.; § 2850].

tírt(ı)⌣ — tŏ

ind. pres. āı⌣tíddı⌢, ɛr⌣tírın⌢ (⌣tırí⌢, ⌣tírí⌢); fut. āı⌣bıtíddı⌢ (⌣but-); perf. āı⌣tírkorı⌢ (⌣tíkkorı⌣ §571a).
imperat. tír!, pl. tírwɛ! (tírwɛ́!, tíwwɛ! §723, -wɛ́!).
subj. past āı⌣tírsı⌣ (⌣tíssı⌣ §683, -su⌣).
cond. pres. āı-ŏn⌣tírkırı⌣ (⌣tíkkırı⌣ §571a).
part. pres. tírıl⌣ (one) that gives (etc.), giver, giving, obj. tırílg(ı)⌣, -gı⌢; past tírɛl⌣ (one) that gave (etc.), giver, giving, obj. tırélg(ı)⌣, -gı⌢.
pl. -obj. conjug. (§3037) tírır.
ind. pres. āı⌣tıríddı⌢, ɛr⌣tírırın⌢ (-rí⌢, -rí⌢); perf. āı⌣tırírkorı⌢ (⌣tıríkkorı⌢).
subj. past āı⌣tırírsı⌣ (⌣tıríssı⌣ §683, -su⌣).
interr. ind. pres. sg. 2nd and 3rd (t)ɛr⌣tírná? (§1083, ⌣tínná? §628).
neg. ind. pres. āı⌣tírmunun⌢ (⌣tímmunun⌢ §607, -munū⌢, -munu⌢, -mun⌢ §947).
neg. imperat. tókkon⌣tírmɛn! (⌣tímmɛn! §607, -mē!, -mé!); pl. tókkon⌣tírmɛwwɛ! (⌣tímmɛ-, -wɛ́!).
íŋgı⌣tír⌢ (§5091) and less commonly íŋgı⌣tékkı⌣tír⌢ give him (her, it) this.
tékk⌣íŋgı⌣tír⌢ give this to him (her, it; §4636).
tékk⌣íŋgút⌣tır⌢ (§1742; -t⌣t-<-g⌣t- §707) give these (this lot) to him (her, it).
tékk⌣íŋgut⌣tírır⌢ give these (various things) to him (her, it).
tírg⌣íŋgı⌣tírır and
tírg⌣íŋgı⌣tírır⌢ give this to them.
tírg⌣íŋgut⌣tır⌢ (-t⌣t-<-g⌣t- §707) and
tírg⌣íŋgút⌣tır⌢ give these (this lot) to them.
tírg⌣íŋgut⌣tírır⌢ give these (various things) to them.
ɛr⌣tékkı⌣dúŋgıb⌣bıtínná? (-b⌣b-< -g⌣b- §519) will you give him (her) the money?
ambésk⌣tíkkorı⌢ I gave (have given) it (them) to my brother.
tírgı⌣dúŋgıt⌣tıríkkoran⌢ (-t⌣t-<-g⌣t- §707) they gave (have given) (each of) them money.
āı⌣tékkı⌣tıróskorı⌢ and N. āı⌣tékkı⌣tıróskorı⌢ (§1103) I have given it (them) to him (her, it).
tír-an (§§3890ff.) v.t. *tell to give (to other than the speaker), let give (etc.).*
tıdd-ɛg-ág- (§§4071ff.) v.t. = tıredól-.
tır-ɛ-dól- (-r°d- §1178; §4022) and
tıdd-ɛ-dól- (-d°d-; §4027) v.t. *be about to give (to other than the speaker).*
tıdd-ɛ-ğŭ-bŭ- (§4069) v.t. stat. *be on one's way (coming) to give (etc.).*
tır-ɛ-má- (§4036) and
tıdd-ɛ-má- (§4041) v.t. *become unable to give (etc.).*
tıdd-ɛ-nóg (§§4048ff.) v.t. *go to give (to other than the speaker).*
dúŋgıt⌣tırıddɛnogóskoran⌢ (-t⌣t-< -g⌣t- §707) *they have gone to give (each of §5456) them money.*
tıdd-ɛ-nóg-bŭ- (-nóggŭ- §546; §4058) v.t. stat. *be on one's way (going) to give (etc.).*

tıdd-ɛ-tá (§§4060ff.) v.t. *come to give (etc.).*
tıred-ág- (§§3877ff.) v.t. *be in the situation of having given (to other than the speaker).*
āı⌣tékkı⌣dúŋgıt⌣tıredágrı⌢ (-t⌣t-< -g⌣t- §707) *I have given him (her) the money.*
tıros-an (§§3890ff., 3905) v.t. *tell to give (etc.), let give (etc.).*
tıróswan⌢ (-óswā⌢, -oswá⌢, -óssan⌢, -óssā⌢, -óssá⌢, -ówwan⌢, -ówwā⌢, -ówwá⌢) *tell them to give it (them).*
tıros-tá (-ottá §714; §§4180-4; -osgıtá, -ozgı-, -oggı- §§4185-7) v.t. *come after giving (to other than the speaker), (just) go (§5713) and give (etc.).*
imperat. tırósta (-óttá!, -ósgıta!, -ózgı-, -óggı-).
dúŋgıt⌣tırosírgı⌣bıtárı⌢ (§5582; -t⌣t- <-g⌣t- §707) *I shall come (back) after giving (each of §5456) them money, i.e. I'll (just) go and give them money.*
tıros-wídɛ (-owwí- §724; §§4180-4; -osgıwídɛ, -ozgı-, -oggı- §4185; -wídɛ, -wᵘdé) v.t. *return (i.) after giving (to other than the speaker), (just) go (§5714) and give (etc.).*
sálúmgı⌣tıroww°dé⌢ *give it to Sálım and come back, i.e. just go and give it to Sálım.*
tírt(ı)⌣, -tí⌢ n. *owner, master* [< *tírt(ı) (§1048) < deictic t- (§§4591-2) + -í- *hand* + -r- in +-t dem., so *he-in-(whose)-hand §§2172, 2332; RN, 292].
obj. tírtıg⌣.
pl. tírtınč(ı)⌣.
ɛ́ŋ⌣kán⌣tírtı-taran⌢ *the woman is owner of the house.*
tɛr⌣tírtık⌣kómunun⌢ *(s)he (it) has no owner.*
tırtín-d(ı)⌣ (§§2545ff.) adj. *appertaining to the owner.*
tírtı-kíñ̃(ı)⌣ (§§2536-7) adj. *without an owner, ownerless.*
tírtı-ko (§4118) v.i. *have an owner, belong to an owner.*
tɛr⌣tırtıkómunun⌢ *(s)he (it) has no owner.*
tısaín⌣ (-sáın⌣, -sɛín⌣ §956a) card. num. *ninety* [< تسعين id.].
obj. -íŋg(ı)⌣, -gı⌢.
tısaín-d(ı)⌣ (-sáın-, -sɛín-; §§2545ff., 2738) adj. *appertaining to 90, of 90, 90's.*
tısaín-int(ı)⌣ (-sáın-, -sɛín-, -ínınt(ı)⌣; §2742) ord. num. *ninetieth.*
tısaíŋ-kırı⌣ (-sáıŋ-, -sɛíŋ-; -kírı §1701; §2736) num. adj. *about ninety.*
tíss(ı)⌣ n. *afterbirth.*
obj. -sıg⌣.
pl. -sınč(ı)⌣.
ádam⌣tíssıg⌣úrur⌣undúddan, úru⌣ dámɛŋkın⌣árıdır⌣kuñúrran, úrtun⌣ tíssıš⌣šídarr⌣arkundúddan, wél⌣ kálmaın⌣íllárr (-m⌣t-<-mn⌣t- §2473; -š⌣š-<-g⌣š- §695) *they put the human afterbirth into the Nile; if the Nile is not there they bury it in the ground; the afterbirth of sheep (goats) they throw into trees; (all this) that the dogs (§4696d) should not eat it.*

tíssı⌣ < tírsı⌣ *(the fact, the one) that I gave* s.v. tír.
tíssŏd⌣ *his (her) sister's child* s.v. -ssŏd⌣.
tuššέ *lose one's way* = tuššέ.
tíšt(ı)⌣ n. *shallow metal pan, basin* [< طِشْت id.].
obj. -tıg⌣.
pl. -tınč(ı)⌣.
tıwέr⌣ n. *Tárgi* (تَرْقِي), *one of the Tawárıg* (تَوَارِق), *a distant tribe, members of which are met with in the desert west of Dóngola* [تَوَارِق *is regarded as a pl. objective* tıwέrıg §2406].
obj. -wέrk⌣, -kı⌢.
pl. -wέrı⌣.
tíwrı⌣ (§2377) n. *friend* (=áurı⌣) [< *tín-wrı⌣ §§2349, 2634].
obj. -rıg⌣.
pl. -rınč(ı)⌣ (tıwrínč(ı)⌣).
tíwrı-kíñ̃(ı)⌣ (§§2536-7) adj. *friendless.*
tíwwɛ! < **tírwɛ!** *give!* (pl.) s.v. tír.
-tŏ⌣ < **-tŏt⌢** *child, etc.* s.v. tŏd⌣.
tŏ v.i. *(a) enter, pass in*, and so *(b) come in; (c) go in; (d, of a heavenly body, like Amh. ገባ) go in (sc. to where it came from), i.e. set* [cogn. with tŭ⌣ *inside* §2059; §4594].
— constructed with -r⌣ (-ro⌣, etc.).
ind. pres. āı⌣tŏrı⌢, ɛr⌣tŏn⌢ (⌣tŏ⌢, ⌣tŏ⌢); perf. āı⌣tŏgorı⌢ (N. ⌣tŏkorı⌢, ⌣tŏhorı⌢).
imperat. tŏ!, tŏr⌣v., tŏ⌣c., pl. tŏwɛ!, tŏwé!
subj. past āı⌣tŏsı⌣ (-su⌣).
part. pres. tŏl⌣ (one) that enters, entrant, entering, obj. tŏlg(ı)⌣, -gı⌢; past tŏrɛl⌣ (one) that entered, entrant, entering, obj. tŏrélg(ı)⌣, -gı⌢.
kár⌣tŏgŏ⌢ *(s)he (it) (has) entered the house.*
sandúgır⌣tŏgon⌢ *it went (has gone) into the box.*
fɛğírro⌣tŏgŏ⌢ *(s)he (it) came (went) in at dawn (etc.), s.v. fɛ́gır⌣).*
āı⌣tékkı⌣tŏr⌣ɛgorı⌢ *I told him (her) to come (go) in.*
ékkɛnɛ⌣tŏróskŏ⌢ *now (s)he (it) has entered.*
kár⌣tŏróskoran⌢ *they have entered the house.*
X. tŏróskorandé? *have they entered?*
Y. tŏgomun⌢ *no* (§§949, 5364).
ámbɛs⌣mádrasár⌣séna⌣tŏskıt⌣ tŏgon⌢ (-t⌣t-<-g⌣t- §707; §4665) *my brother has been three years at school, lit.... entered the school three years (ago).*
másıl⌣tŏmɛnıŋ⌣kóttıt⌣tá⌢ (s.v. ⌣kóttıg⌣) *come before the sun sets.*
tŏrar⌣ (-rár⌣; §§2200ff., 2207) and
tŏríd⌣ (§§2256ff., 2260) n. *entrance, passing in, setting.*
tŏrɛ⌣ n. *(a, in water-wheel, kólɛ⌣) horizontal axle of wheel raising water* (átt(ı)⌣); *on its other end is the smaller cog-wheel* (árgadɛn⌣tŏd⌣); *(b, in loom, duhán⌣) cloth-beam, breast-beam* (CSW, p. 31) [< tŏ *enter* + gerundial -r (§3556)

+-ε⌣ of n. act. (§2234δ), or. *(act of) entering, entrance].
obj. -rɛg⌣ [> Sudan Ar. توريق tōrɛg id.].
pl. -rɛnč(ı)⌣.
tŏr-an (§§3890ff., 3899) v.t. tell to enter, etc., let enter, etc.
tŏwan⌒ let them come (go) in.
tŏ-bū- (§3931α) v.i. stat. be in a state of motion towards the interior, be on the (subject's) way in, be entering (=āttō a).
gátır⌣mohattar⌣tōbūn⌒ the train is on its way into the station.
tōr-ɛg-ág- (§§4071ff.) v.i. =tōrɛdól-.
tōr-ɛ-dól- (-rᵒd- §1178; §§4016-17, 4022, 4027) v.i. be about to enter, etc.
tōr-ɛ-má- (§§4016-17, 4036, 4041) v.i. become unable to enter, etc.
tōrɛd-ág- (§§3877ff.) v.i. be in the situation of having entered, etc.
to-ğú (§3747ε') v.i. after entering proceed (etc., s.v. ğú), go in and onward.
imperat. tŏğú!
to-ğú-bū- (§4216) v.i. stat. be in a state of motion in towards the speaker, be entering towards the speaker, be coming in here.
kăr⌣tŏğúbūran⌒ they are coming into the house (to me).
tŏŋg-ır (N. tŏŋkır; §3688) (a) v.t. caus. cause or allow to enter, etc.; (b) v.t. send in, let in.
ind. pres. aī⌣tŏŋgıddi⌒ (⌣tŏŋgíddi⌒ §1806), ɛr⌣tŏŋgırın⌒ (-rí⌒, -rí⌒).
íŋgı⌣tŏŋgíddıá? shall I send (let) this (one) in?
N. lókkuw⌣wɛkı⌣tŏŋkırmɛn⌒ (-w⌣w- <-ŋ-w- §720) don't let anyone in.
tŏ-tá (§3747ε') v.i. come along in.
ind. pres. aī⌣tŏtári⌒, ɛr⌣tŏtán⌒ (-tă⌒, -tă⌒); perf. aī⌣tŏtágori⌒ (N. -áko-, -áho-).
imperat. tŏta!, pl. tŏtáwɛ! (-táwé!).
tŏb⌣ n. (a) length of cloth, from 7 to 10 cubits; (b) outer cloth worn by either sex [< ثوب Sudan Ar. tōb id.].
obj. tŏbk(ı)⌣, tŏpk(ı)⌣, -kı⌒.
gen. tŏbn⌣v., tŏm⌣c.
pl. tŏbı⌣.
tŏm-d(ı)⌣ (§§2545ff.) adj. appertaining to a (the) length of cloth, etc.
tóbbe v.t. pat, tap [imit. §§2870ff., 2875].
ind. pres. aī⌣tóbbɛri⌒; perf. aī⌣tóbbɛgori⌒ (N. -ɛko-, -ɛho-).
ánn⌣osmárkı⌣tóbbɛgó⌒ (s)he tapped (patted) my shoulder.
wél⌣ténn⌣ɛugɛd⌣arídkı⌣tóbbɛgó⌒ the dog tapped the floor with its tail.
wél⌣ténn⌣ɛut⌣tóbbɛgó⌒ (-t⌣t-< -g⌣t- §707) the dog tapped its tail (against something).
tóbbɛrar⌣ (-rár⌣; §§2200ff., 2210) and
tobbɛríd⌣ (§§2256ff., 2263) n. patting, etc.
tobbɛrɛd-ág- (§§3877ff.) v.t. be in the situation of having patted, etc.
tócce v.i. crack (make sudden sharp noise) [imit. §§2870-4].
ind. pres. tɛr⌣tóccɛn⌣ (-čɛn, -čé⌒); perf. tɛr⌣tóccɛgon⌣ (-gŏ⌒, -gó⌒, N. -ɛkon⌣, -kŏ-, -kó⌒, -ɛhon⌣, -hŏ-, -hó⌒).
tén⌣sárbɛ⌣tóccɛgó⌒ his (her) finger cracked.

tóccɛrar⌣ (-rár⌣; §§2200ff., 2210) and
tóccɛríd⌣ (§§2256ff., 2263) n. cracking.
sárbɛn⌣toccɛríd⌣ cracking of finger(s §4696a).
tŏd⌣ n. (a) child, offspring, like bităn⌣, ولد, commonly; (b) male child, son; so (c) boy; (d, of animals) young [< *tŏ*d⌣ < √tŏ- *(be) inside (§4594) + -*d dem. or loc. (§§4506, 4508), so *(what is) inside sc. in the womb §2230; cp. Sudan Ar. بطن child AESA s.v. bear; cp. ON. тот id. GNT s.v.; RSN, §§129, 200].
voc. tŏt!
obj. tŏdk(ı)⌣, tŏtk(ı)⌣, tŏtt(ı)⌣, tŏkk(ı)⌣ §2462, -kı⌒, -tı⌒.
gen. tŏdn⌣v., tŏnn⌣v.c., tŏn⌣c.
pl. tŏnı⌣.
ín⌣tŏd'ré⌣wálla⌣búruré? is this a boy or a girl?
bértın⌣tŏd⌣ the (a) goat's kid.
hánun⌣tŏdun⌒ it's an ass's colt (foal).
kăŋ⌣tŏdkı⌣nálkoran⌒ (-ŋ⌣t- <-gn⌣t- §663) they saw (have seen) the snake's young one (... a young snake).
árgadɛn⌣tŏd⌣ vertical cog-wheel in water-wheel (kólɛ⌣, s.v. árgadɛ⌣.
tŏd⌣ in composition (§§2365ff.) > -tŏd⌣, -tŏt⌒, -tŏd⌣, -tŏt⌣, -tŏ⌒.
Compounds of the type bɛrtın⌣tŏd⌣ kid are resolved by some speakers into two words, each with its stress. This type expresses the young of animate objects and the diminutive of inanimate objects.
Compounds of the type bértı⌣tod⌣ unsatisfactory, poor or indifferent specimen of goat are diminutives in form but not necessarily in sense; many have the same sense, as regards size, as the noun without -tod⌣, but are depreciatives (taggısɛran⌒).
This type provides
(a) depreciatory nouns; these are also used as
(b) a sort of slang equivalent of the first noun; e.g. bértı⌣tod⌣ = bért(ı)⌣ goat.
(c) depreciatory adjectives: ɛsɛtod⌣ unsatisfactorily thin.
(d) a few diminutive nouns: bıtăn⌣tod⌣ small male child, búrtod⌣ little girl, ogíččod⌣ little boy.
tŏd-ágıl⌣ (§2361) n. large brownish Nile fish, Mormyrus caschive L., Mormyrus kannume (PF, p. 92) [child-mouth].
obj. tŏdagílg(ı)⌣, -gı⌒.
pl. tŏdág(ı)lı⌣.
tŏn-d(ı)⌣ (§§2545ff.) adj. appertaining to the (a) child, etc., juvenile.
tŏd-an- (§3910α) v.i. become a boy.
tŏddɛr⌣ (‾, ‾ §1728; §2682) indef. pron. a little, a few [< *tŏd-wɛr⌣ (§533) < tŏd⌣ little one + -wɛr⌣ a].
obj. tŏddɛg⌣, ‾‾, -gı⌒.
X. ɛssı⌣dólná? (-d⌣d- < -g⌣d- §534) do you want water?
Y. tŏddɛg⌣ɛtta⌣ bring a little.
íčcı⌣tŏddɛd⌣dólli⌣ I want (like) a little milk.
béntı⌣tŏddɛk⌣kísır⌣úndur⌣ put a few dates into the bag.

gáhwa⌣wázbūl⌣tŏddɛg⌣ɛttadɛn⌒ fetch me a little boiling coffee.
márɛm⌣mɛrmétti⌣tŏddɛgoŋg⌣ɛtta⌒ bring also a little green millet.
tŏdn-ɛ́n⌣ (tŏnnɛ́n⌣ §624) n. daughter-in-law.
obj. -ɛŋg(ı)⌣, -gı⌒.
pl. -ɛ́nč(ı)⌣.
tŏ́rt(ı)⌣, -tı⌒ (§2744) n. half [< *tŏd-t(ı)⌣ §§874, 2328].
obj. -tıg⌣, -tıgı⌒.
pl. -tınč(ı)⌣.
ugrɛsn⌣tŏrt(ı)⌣ n. (a) half the (a) day; (b) midday.
ugrɛsn⌣tŏrtıg⌣ (§4665) and
ugrɛsn⌣tŏrtır⌣ at midday.
ugrɛsn⌣tŏrtıt⌣tăgoran⌒ (-t⌣t-< -g⌣t- §707) they came at midday.
ugún⌣tŏrt(ı)⌣ n. (a) half the (a) night; (b) midnight.
ugún⌣tŏrtıg⌣ (§4665) and
ugún⌣tŏrtır⌣ at midnight.
ugún⌣tŏrtın⌣nókkoran⌒ (-n⌣n-< -g⌣n- §625) they went at midnight.
kándı⌣tŏrtır⌣gúššıbūn⌒ the knife is (has been) broken in half.
tŏ́rt-an- (§2760) v.i. become half, become reduced to a half, shrink to a half.
ɛ́ssı⌣tŏrtaŋkon⌒ the water (has) got reduced to a half.
íu⌣tŏrtanóskó⌒ the grain has got reduced to a half.
tŏ́rtam-bū- (§2761) v.i. stat. be in the state or condition of being or having been reduced to half.
ɛ́ssı⌣tŏrtambūn⌒ the water is reduced (has shrunk) to half.
tŏ́rtan-tŏ́mb(ı)⌣ (§4150) v.i. break into halves, break in half.
sáhan⌣tŏrtantómbᵘgó⌒ (§1192) the plate broke (has broken) in half.
tŏ́rtaŋ-gúšš(ı)⌣ (§4150) v.i. break into halves, break in half.
wíčcır⌣tŏrtaŋgúššıgó⌒ the stick broke (has broken) in half.
tŏ́rtıg-ır (N. -ıkır, -ıhır; §3697) v.t. (a) halve, divide into halves; (b) halve, reduce to a half.
ind. pres. aī⌣tŏrtıgıddi⌒ (§1813).
tɛr⌣ám⌣mahjat⌣tŏrtıgırkó⌒ (-t⌣t-< -g⌣t- §707) (s)he (has) reduced my pay to a half.
tŏ́rtıgır-bagítte (N. -ıkır, -ıhır-; §4136) v.t. divide into halves.
dúŋgı⌣tŏrtıgırbagíttɛgori⌒ (-t⌣t-< -g⌣t- §707) I (have) divided the money into halves.
tŏ́rtıgır-gúšš(ı) (N. -ıkır-, -ıhır-; §4136) v.t. break into halves.
wíčcırkı⌣tŏrtıgırgúššıgó⌒ (s)he (it) broke (has broken) the stick in half.
tŏ́rtıgır-tŏ́mb(ı) (N. -ıkır-, -ıhır-; §4136) v.t. break into halves.
aī⌣kálgı⌣tŏrtıgırtómbᵘgori⌒ I broke (have broken) the bread into halves.
toddán⌣ (§956d) n. share of crop produced on irrigable estate (kólɛ⌣) [< *tıddán⌣ (§§1185, 1071 Sudan Ar. تدّان id.) < *tıddán⌣ (§2413) < tíddan⌣ inf. of tír give, so giving, what is given (to each), share at harvest §2146].

tóg — tóllɛ

obj. -áŋg(ı)⌣, -gi⌒.
pl. -ánı⌣.
toddánıg⌣áuran⌒ *they make (out) the shares of the crop (divide the crop).*

tóg v.t. *heat, warm* [cp. ON. тoк *cook* GNT s.v.; *RSN*, §§ 129, 200].
ind. pres. âı⌣tógrı⌒, ɛr⌣tógın⌒ (-gĭ⌒, -gí⌒); perf. âı⌣tógkori⌒ (⌣tókkori⌒).
imperat. tók!, pl. tógwɛ! (tógwé!, tóggɛ! § 547, -gɛ́!).
subj. past âı⌣tógsı⌣ (⌣tóksı⌣, -su⌣).
ánn⌣íg⌣ígır⌣tókkori⌒ *I (have) warmed my hand(s* §4696a*) at the fire.*
kál⌣orófélgı⌣tókkoran⌒ *they (have) heated the cold food.*

tógar⌣ (-gàr⌣; §§ 2200 ff.) and
togíd (§§ 2256 ff.) n. *heating, etc.*

tóg-an (§§ 3890 ff.) v.t. *tell to heat, etc., let heat, etc.*

tóg-bŭ- (tóggŭ- § 546; § 3931 β) v.i. stat. *be in a heated (etc.) state or condition.*
kál⌣ígır⌣tógbūn⌒ *the food has been warmed at the fire.*
téŋ⌣kór⌣tóggŭ⌒ *his (her, its) wound has been warmed.*

tog-ettá (-ettă § 3855; § 4198) v.t. *bring after heating, etc.*
kálg⌣ígır⌣togétta⌒ *after warming it at the fire bring the food.*

tóg-kattı- (tókka-; § 4093) v.p. *be heated, etc.*
kŏr⌣ígır-ón⌣tókkattıgım⌣biwajjɛ́n⌒ *if the (a) wound (sore) is warmed at the fire it will get better (if wounds are warmed, etc.* § 4696d).

tőg (§§ 3132 ff.) v.t. *strike, beat* [*RSN*, §§ 129, 200].
ind. pres. âı⌣tőg(¹)rı⌒, ɛr⌣tőgın⌒ (⌣tőgĭ⌒, ⌣tőgí⌒); fut. âı⌣bıtőg(¹)rı⌒ (⌣but-); perf. âı⌣tőgkori⌒ (⌣tőkkori⌒).
imperat. tők!, pl. tőgwɛ! (tőgwé!, tőggɛ! §547, tőggɛ́!).
subj. past âı⌣tőgsı⌣ (⌣tőksı⌣, -su⌣).
part. pres. tőgıl⌣ (*one*) *that strikes, etc., striker, striking,* obj. tőgılg(ı)⌣, -gi⌒; past tőgel (*one*) *that struck, etc., striker, striking,* obj. tőgélg(ı)⌣, -gi⌒.

tőgar⌣ (-gàr⌣; §§ 2200 ff.) and
tőgíd (§§ 2256 ff.) n. *striking, etc.*

tőgıdk-ır-tőg (-ītkır-, -īttır- § 716; § 4156) v.t. *strike (etc.) heavily, give a sound beating to.*

tőgıdkırtőg-bŭ- (-ītkır-, -īttır-; -tőggŭ- § 546; § 4164) v.i. stat. *be in a heavily struck (well beaten) state or condition.*

tőg-an (§§ 3890 ff.) v.t. *tell to strike, etc., let strike, etc.*

tőg-bŭ- (tőggŭ- § 546; § 3931 β) v.i. stat. *be in a struck (etc.) state or condition.*

tőg(¹)r-ɛg-ág- (§ 4071 ff.) v.t. = tőgɛdól-.
tőg-ɛ-dól- (-gᵒd- § 1178; § 4022) and
tőg(¹)r-ɛ-dól- (-rᵒd-; § 4027) v.t. *be about to strike, etc.*
tőg(¹)r-ɛ-ğŭ-bŭ- (§ 4069) v.t. stat. *be on one's way (coming) to strike, etc.*
tőg-ɛ-mǎ- (§ 4036) and
tőg(¹)r-ɛ-mǎ- (§ 4041) v.t. *become unable to strike, etc.*
tőg(¹)r-ɛ-nóg (§§ 4048 ff.) v.t. *go to strike, etc.*

tőg(¹)r-ɛ-nóg-bŭ- (-nóggŭ- § 546; § 4058) v.t. stat. *be on one's way (going) to strike, etc.*
tőg(¹)r-ɛ-nog(¹)r-ɛg-ág- (§ 5700) v.t. = tőg(¹)rɛnogɛdól-.
tőg(¹)r-ɛ-nog-ɛ-dól- (-gᵒd- § 1178; § 5696) and
tőg(¹)r-ɛ-nog(¹)r-ɛ-dól- (-rᵒd-; § 5698) v.t. *be about to go to strike, etc.*
tőg(¹)r-ɛ-nog-ɛ-mǎ- (§ 5697) and
tőg(¹)r-ɛ-nog(¹)r-ɛ-mǎ- (§ 5699) v.t. *become unable to go to strike, etc.*
tőg(¹)r-ɛ-tǎ (§§ 4060 ff.) v.t. *come to strike, etc.*

tőgɛd-ág- (§§ 3877 ff.) v.t. *be in the situation of having struck, etc.*

tőg-kattı- (tókkattı-; § 4093) v.p. *be struck, etc.*

tőggŭ- < **tőgbŭ-** *be in a heated (etc.) state* s.v. tóg.

tőggŭ- < **tőgbŭ-** *be in a struck (etc.) state* s.v. tőg.

tógo⌣ n. *lower part, base, bottom* [§§ 2310, 4577; *RSN,* § 129].
obj. togóg⌣.
pl. togŏnč(ı)⌣.
ɛn⌣togóg⌣gūnčınók⌒ *watch (the ground) under you as you go.*

togóg-ɛd (-ɛt⌒, -ɛ́⌒ § 966; § 6007) adv. *by (etc., s.v. -ɛd⌣) the lower part, etc.*

togŏn-d(ı)⌣ (§§ 2545 ff.) adj. *appertaining to the lower part, etc., lower.*
obj. -dıg⌣.
pl. -dınč(ı)⌣.

togŏndı-kırı⌣ (§ 2541) adj. *resembling the lower.*

tógor⌣ (s.v. -r⌣) adv. *in (to) the lower part, etc., at (to) the bottom, below, underneath, down, downwards.*

tógor⌣ (§ 6007) (s)*he (it) is (they are) in the lower part, etc.*
tógor⌣úskur⌒ *put it (them) at the bottom, etc.*

⌣tógor⌣ (§§ 5860, 5907) postp. (= prep. § 4287; *of position and motion*) *below, beneath, under.*
— follows the genitive (§ 4371):
X. mánd⌣úskur⌒ *put it over there.*
Y. mánın⌣togóró? *under that yonder?*
ám⌣míssın⌣tógortón⌣nókkoran⌒ *they (have) passed out of my sight,* lit. ... *passed from under my eye.*

tóg-an- (§ 3913 β) v.i. *move (go, come) to(wards) the lower part, etc., move down(wards), descend.*

togám-bŭ- (§ 3952) v.i. stat. *be in a state of downward motion, be on one's way down, be descending.*

togánɛd-ág- (§§ 3965 ff.) v.i. *be in the situation of having descended.*

togan-nóg (§ 4150) v.i. *go down, descend.*

togánnóg-bŭ- (-nóggŭ- § 546; § 4153) v.i. stat. *be in a state of motion (going) downwards.*

togőg-ır (N. -őkır, -őhır; § 3697) (a) v.t. caus. *cause or allow to be or become the lower part, etc.;* (b) v.t. *lower.*
ind. pres. âı⌣togőgıddi⌒, ɛr⌣togőgırın⌒ (-rĭ⌒, -rí⌒).

togőgır- (N. -őkır, -őhır-) in composition *downwards, down.*

togőgır-tóllɛ (N. -őkır-, -őhır-; § 4140) v.t. *pull downwards, pull down.*

togőgır-úskur (N. -őkır-, -őhır-; § 4141) v.t. *set (etc., s.v. úskur) in the lower part, etc., put below.*
ind. pres. âı⌣togőgıruskúddi⌒, ɛr⌣togőgıruskurın⌒ (-rĭ⌒, -rí⌒).

togőgır-wár (N. -őkır-, -őhır-; § 4136) v.i. *jump downwards, jump down.*
ind. pres. âı⌣togőgırwarri⌒.

tók! imperat. of tóg *heat, etc.*

tők! imperat. of tőg *strike, etc.*

tókk(ı) v.i. *limp, go lame* [imit.].
ind. pres. âı⌣tókkıri⌒; perf. âı⌣tókkıgori⌒ (N. -ıko-, -ıho-).
imperat. tókki!
ín⌣hánu⌣tókkın⌒ *this donkey limps.*

tókkar⌣ (-kàr⌣; §§ 2200 ff.) and
tokkíd (§§ 2256 ff.) n. *limping.*

tókkı-bŭ- (§ 3931 α) v.i. stat. *be in a limping state or condition, be lame.*
ín⌣hánu⌣tókkıbūn⌒ *this donkey is lame.*

tókkıg-ır (N. -ıkır, -ıhır; § 3682) (a) v.t. caus. *cause or allow to limp;* (b) v.t. *render lame, lame.*

tókkon (S. also dók⌣, -kŏ⌒, -kó⌒ § 939; §§ 4468, 5477 ff.) adv. *usually (but not invariably) used with the negative imperative (§§ 3093-4), that it commonly precedes but occasionally follows* [< *tódk-on⌣ (§§ 574, 4895 β) *even a little, at all*].
tókkos⌣sókkɛmɛn⌒ (-s⌣s- < -n⌣s- § 680) and
sókkɛmɛn⌒ *don't take him (her, it, them) up (away);* occasionally
sókkɛmɛn⌣tókkon⌒.
tókkos⌣sókkɛmɛwwɛ⌒ (⌣sókkɛmɛw-wé⌒),
tókkos⌣sókkɛmɛndɛ⌒ (⌣sókkɛmɛn-dé⌒),
sókkɛmɛwwɛ⌒ (-wé⌒) and
sókkɛmɛndɛ⌒ (-dé⌒) *don't (pl.) take him (her, it, them) up (away);* occasionally
sókkɛmɛwwɛ⌣tókkon⌒ (-mɛndɛ⌣tók-⌣).
tókkõ⌣sándımɛ̃⌒ (§ 979) *don't be afraid.*
tókkon⌣íŋ⌣índotōn⌣sókkɛmɛn⌒ *don't take this (that) away from here.*
tókkon⌣tékkɛm⌣mérmɛn⌒ (-m⌣m- < -d⌣m- § 600) *don't cut him (her, it, them) (a) with it (that);* (b) *in that way* (s.v. tékkɛd⌣).
tókkon⌣énn⌣íged⌣ármɛn⌒ *don't take hold (of him, her, it, them) with your hand(s* § 4696a).
tókkon⌣íŋk⌣uskúrmɛn⌒ *don't put it like that.*

— with its verb omitted (§ 5482):
íŋk⌣úskur, tókkon⌣íŋkɛmɛn⌒ *put it like this, not like that.*

tóllɛ v.t. *pull, haul* [imit. §§ 2870 ff., 2875].
ind. pres. âı⌣tóllɛri⌒; perf. âı⌣tóllɛgori⌒ (N. -ɛko-, -ɛho-).
part. pres. tóllɛl⌣ (*one*) *that pulls, etc., puller, etc., pulling, etc.,* obj. tollɛ́lg(ı)⌣, -gi⌒; past tóllɛrɛl⌣ (*one*) *that pulled, etc., puller, etc., pulling, etc.,* obj. tollɛ-rɛ́lg(ı)⌣, -gi⌒.
def. perf. âı⌣tollɛróskori⌒ and ⌣tollóskori⌒.
kúpkı⌣tóllɛran⌒ *they tow the boat.*

tŏm⌣ — tósk(ı)⌣

— (in a boat) tóllɛ! *row!*, lit. *pull!*, pl. tóllɛwé!
bɛrákkı⌣tóllɛ! *hoist the flag*, lit. *pull the flag (up)*.
tóllɛrar⌣ (-rár⌣), **tóllar⌣** (-lár⌣; §§ 2200 ff., 2211) and **tollɛríd⌣tollíd⌣** (§§ 2256 ff., 2264) n. *pulling, etc.*
tollɛrídk-ır-tóllɛ (-ītkır-, -īttır- § 716; § 4156) v.t. *pull (etc.) forcibly, pull (etc.) violently*.
tóllɛr-an (§§ 3890 ff., 3899) v.t. *tell to pull, etc., let pull, etc.*
tollɛ-dígır (§ 4133a) v.t. *tie (etc.)*, s.v. dígır) *after pulling, etc.*
sɛ́rkı⌣tollɛdıgírkori⌢ *I (have) fastened the thong after pulling it (tight)*.
tollɛr-ɛg-ág- (§§ 4071 ff.) v.t. = tollɛrɛdól-.
tollɛr-ɛ-dól- (-rᵒd- § 1178; § 4016-17, 4022, 4027) v.t. *be about to pull, etc.*
tollɛr-ɛ-ğŭ-bŭ- (§ 4069) v.t. stat. *be on one's way (coming) to pull, etc.*
tollɛr-ɛ-má- (§§ 4016-17, 4036, 4041) v.t. *become unable to pull, etc.*
tollɛr-ɛ-nóg- (§§ 4048 ff.) v.t. *go to pull, etc.*
tollɛr-ɛ-nóg-bŭ- (-nóggŭ- § 546; § 4058) v.t. stat. *be on one's way (going) to pull, etc.*
tollɛr-ɛ-tá- (§§ 4060 ff.) v.t. *come to pull, etc.*
tollɛd-ág- (§§ 3540, 3877 ff.) v.t. = tollɛrɛd-ág-.
tollɛrɛd-ág- (§§ 3540, 3877 ff.) v.t. *be in the situation of having pulled, etc.*
tolléd-dā- (§ 3991; -ɛggıdá-, occ. -ɛdgı- §§ 3993-4) v.t. *be going along while pulling, etc., be pulling, etc. (as one goes) along*.
ɛgédkı⌣tolléddān⌢ *(s)he is pulling the sheep along*.
tolled-ğŭ-bŭ- (-ɛğğŭ- § 550; § 4220; -ɛggı-ğŭ-, occ. -ɛdgı- § 4221) v.t. stat. *be on one's way (coming) while pulling, etc., be approaching pulling, etc.*
tollɛn-nóg (§ 4169 ff.; -ɛggınóg, occ. -ɛdgı- §§ 4176-8) v.t. *go (etc., s.v. nóg) while (after having begun) pulling, etc., pull away*.
tollɛn-nóg-bŭ- (§ 4220; -ɛggınóg-, occ. -ɛdgı- § 4221; -nóggŭ- § 546) v.t. stat. *be on one's way (going) while pulling, etc., be pulling (etc.) away*.
tolled-tá (-ɛttá §§ 4169 ff., 5723; -ɛggıtá, occ. -ɛdgı- §§ 4176-8) v.t. *come after (while) pulling, etc., come pulling, etc.*
imperat. tollétta!, tolléggıta!
toll-ɛttá (-éttá §§ 3855, 5723) v.t. *bring (ɛttá s.v. éd) after (while, by) pulling, etc.*
tolléŋg-ır (⌣~; N. -ŋkır; § 3688) v.t. caus. *cause or allow to pull, etc.*
tóllɛ-kattı- (N. -ɛha-; § 4093) v.p. *be pulled, etc.*

tŏm⌣ n. *garlic* (= túm⌣) [< Eg. Ar. ثوم tŏm < ثوم id.].
obj. tŏmg(ı)⌣, -gi⌢.
gen. tŏmm⌣v., tŏmᵘ⌣.
tŏm-d(ı)⌣ (§§ 2545 ff.) adj. *appertaining to garlic, of garlic*.
tómb(ı) (a) v.t. *break*; (b) v.i. *break, get broken* (= gúšš(ı), *that is commoner*).
ind. pres. aı̌⌣tómbıri⌢; perf. aı̌⌣tómbıgori⌢ (-bᵘgo- § 1192, N. -bıko-, -bᵘko-).
imperat. tómbi!
subj. past aı̌⌣tómbısı⌣ (-su⌣).
part. pres. tómbıl⌣ (*one*) *that breaks, breaker, breaking*, obj. tombílg(ı)⌣, -gi⌢; past tómbɛl⌣ (*one*) *that broke, breaker, breaking*, obj. tombélg(ı)⌣, -gi⌢.
pl.-obj. tómbırır.
def. imperat. tómbos! (tombós! § 1890, tómbó! § 962), pl. tómbóswɛ! (-ówwɛ! § 724, -wé!, -óssɛ! § 687, -sé!).
ıŋgı⌣tómbᵘgó⌢ *(s)he (it) broke (has broken) this*.
ín⌣tómbᵘgó⌢ *this broke (has got broken)*.
tómbar⌣ (-bár⌣; §§ 2200 ff.) and
tombíd⌣ (§§ 2256 ff.) n. *breaking, fracture*.
tombíd-an-tómbı- (§ 4162) v.i. *get utterly broken, get completely broken, get smashed to pieces*.
tombídk-ır-tómb(ı) (-ītkır-, -īttır-; § 4156) v.t. *break completely, break to pieces*.
sât⌣tombídkırtómbıgó⌢ (-tᴗt- < -gᴗt- § 707) and
N. sât⌣tombíttırtómbıkó⌢ *(s)he (it) (has) smashed the watch to pieces*.
tómb-an (§§ 3890 ff.) v.t. (a) *tell to break (t.), let break (t.)*; (b) *let break (i.), let get broken*.
tombɛb-bél (§§ 4169 ff.; -ɛdgı-bél, -ɛggı- §§ 4176-8) (a) v.t. *issue (i.) by breaking (t.), break out through (of)*; (b) v.i. *break out*.
tombéd-ág- (§§ 3877 ff.) v.t. *be in the situation of having broken*.
tomb-ɛ-dól- (-bᵒd- § 1178; § 4022) and
tombır-ɛ-dól- (-rᵒd-; § 4027) v.t. and i. *be about to break*.
tombed-tó (commonly -ɛttó; §§ 4169 ff.; -ɛdgı-tó, -ɛggı- §§ 4176-8) (a) v.t. *enter (i.) by breaking (t.), break in through*; (b) v.i. *break in*.
kám⌣tombɛttósın⌣agárkı⌣géndıgır⌢ *repair the place (sc. in the fence) where the camel broke in (sc. into the enclosure)*.
tomb-ɛ-má- (§ 4036) and
tombır-ɛ-má- (§ 4041) v.t. *become unable to break*.
tombı-bél (§ 3747ɛ′) (a) v.t. *issue (i.) by breaking (t.), break out through (of)*; (b) v.i. *break out*.
tómbı-bŭ- (§ 3931 β) v.i. stat. *be in a broken state or condition*.
tómbı-kattı- (N. -ıha-; § 4093) v.p. *be broken*.
tómbıkattın⌢ *it is (gets) broken (rumpitur, se casse, wird zerbrochen)*.
tombıkáttıgon⌢ *it was (got) broken (has been broken, ruptum est, s'est cassé, ist zerbrochen worden)*.
tombır-ɛg-ág- (§§ 4071 ff.) v.t. and i. *be about to break*.
gɛzáz⌣tombırɛgákkó⌢ *the glass (bottle) was about to break*.
tombırıdd-ɛ-dól- (-dᵒd- § 1178; § 4031) v.t. *be about to break (more than one object)*.
tombırıdd-ɛg-ág- (§ 4077) v.t. = tombırıd-dɛdól-.
tombı-tó (§ 3747ɛ′) (a) v.t. *enter (i.) by breaking (t.), break in through*; (b) v.i. *break in*.
bértı⌣zɛ́rbɛt⌣tombıtógó⌢ (-tᴗt- < -gᴗt- § 707) *the goat (has) got in by breaking the fence (...goats (have) got... § 4696d)*.
tŏmd(ı)⌣ *appertaining to a length of cloth etc.*, s.v. tŏb⌣.
-tŏn⌣ (-tŏ⌣, -tŏ⌢) postp. *from, of*, suffixed to -r⌣ (-do⌣, etc.), -năr⌣, s.v. -r-tŏn⌣, -năr-tŏn⌣.
tŏnɛ n. *heel*; with collective sg. (§ 4696a) [§ 2235; RSN, § 200].
obj. -nɛg⌣.
pl. -nɛnč(ı)⌣.
tóŋğıl adj. *beautiful, handsome* [§ 2530].
obj. -tóŋğılg(ı)⌣, -gi⌢.
pl. tóŋğılı⌣.
tóŋğılkanɛ (§ 2295) n. *beauty*.
obj. tóŋğılkanɛg⌣.
tóŋğıl-an- (§ 3910α) v.i. *become beautiful, grow handsome*.
tóŋğılg-ır (N. -lkır; § 3702) (a) v.t. caus. *cause or allow to be beautiful, etc.*; (b) v.t. *render beautiful, etc., beautify, adorn*.
ind. pres. aı̌⌣tóŋğılgıddi⌢, ɛr⌣tóŋğıl-gırın⌢ (-rī⌢, -rí⌢).
ténn⌣agárkı⌣tóŋğılgırkon⌢ *(s)he (has) made his (her) place beautiful*.
tŏnı⌣ pl. of tŏd⌣ *child*.
tŏŋır *send in, let in* s.v. tŏ.
tórbar n. *agricultural labourer, agricultural peasant, field-hand* [< *túr(u)bār⌣ < túrub- sickle + ár hold, *sickle-holder*; cp. K. turbar, M. turba (AZN s.v.), ON. торпа (GCD, p. 14) id.; § 2198].
obj. torbárk(ı)⌣, -ki⌢ [torbár- > Sudan Ar. تربال id. § 2412].
pl. tórbarı⌣.
X. tórbarn⌣ŭğrɛ⌣šahárkı⌣mıŋkóttıré? *how much is a labourer's hire a month?*
Y. talatín⌣gírišun⌢ *it's thirty piastres*.
tŏrɛ⌣ *horizontal axle, cloth-beam* s.v. tŏ.
tŏrt(ı)⌣ *half* s.v. tŏd⌣.
tósk(ı)⌣, -ki⌢ (§§ 2699, 2707) card. num. *three* [RSN, § 116; cp. ON. тоѵско id. GNT s.v.].
obj. -kıg⌣.
pl. -kınč(ı)⌣.
tósk⌣ídwirɛ⌣ 3⅓.
tóskín⌢ (-kí⌢, -kí⌢ §§ 939, 1970, 5232) and
tér⌣tóskın⌢ (tɛr⌣, -kí⌢, -kí⌢ § 5233) *it's (they're) three*.
tóskınčín⌢ (-čí⌢, -čí⌢ § 5235),
tír⌣tóskınčín⌢ (tır⌣, -čí⌢, -čí⌢ § 5236) and
tır⌣tóskın⌢ (-kí⌢, -kí⌢ § 5237) *they're three*.
tósk⌣nókkon⌢ and
tóskı⌣nókkoran⌢ *three went (have gone; § 5229)*.
tír⌣tóskı⌣nógın⌢ and
tír⌣tóskı⌣nógran⌢ *the three of them go (§ 5245)*.
ógıč⌣tóskı⌣tébın⌢ and
ógıč⌣tóskı⌣tébran⌢ *three men wait (lit. ...stand; § 5239)*.
bābúr⌣sâ⌣tóskın⌢ *the steamer (train) is at 3 o'clock*.
tóska⌣ n. *the three stars in Orion's belt* [< tósk- *three* + -a⌣ *utterance, *what says 'three' § 2178].
obj. -kag⌣.

tóskan‿abáŋ-wıss(ı)‿ Sirius, lit. *the star of the back of tóska.*
toskín-d(ı)‿ (§2737a) adj. *appertaining to three, of three, three's.*
toskınčín-d(ı)‿ (§2737b) adj. = toskínd(ı)‿.
tosk-ínt(ı)‿ (tóskınt(ı)‿; §2740) ord. num. *third.*
toskıntín-d(ı)‿ (§2743) adj. *appertaining to the third.*
toskıŋgắr (§§2753, 5261-7) num. *the whole three, all three.*
  obj. -ărk(ı)‿, -ki⌒.
  tɛr‿toskıŋgắrk‿ɛ́tta⌒ *bring the three of them.*
  ɛr‿gawăb‿toskıŋgắrkı‿sókkɛgoná? *did you take (have you taken) all three letters?*
tóskırɛ‿ (§2745) n. ⅓, *third part* [< tósk- 3 +-ır *(action of) making + -ɛ‿* of n. ess., so *one of what makes into 3* §2287].
  obj. -rɛg‿.
  pl. -rɛnč(ı)‿.
tóski-kırı‿ (§2736) num. adj. *about three.*
tósk-an- (§2760) v.i. *become three, become treble.*
tóskam-bŭ- (§2761) v.i. stat. *be in a state or condition of becoming three, etc.*
toskıg-ır (N. -ıkır, -ıhır; §2759) v.t. caus. *make into three.*
toskıgır-árbır (N. -ıkır-, -ıhır-; §4141) v.t. *fold in three.*
  kádɛt‿toskıgırárbır⌒ (-t‿t- < -g‿t- §707) *fold the cloth in three.*
toskıgır-băg (N. -ıkır-, -ıhır-; §4138) v.t. *divide into three.*
  imperat. toskıgırbăk!
toskıgır-bagíttɛ (N. -ıkır-, -ıhır-; §4140) v.t. *divide into three.*
toskıgır-mɛ́r (N. -ıkır-, -ıhır-; §4138) v.t. *cut into three.*
  āı‿warákkı‿toskıgırmɛ́rri⌒ *I cut the paper into three.*
  súkkı‿toskıgırmɛ́rkori⌒ *I (have) cut the cake* (s.v. súg‿).
tósk(ı) v.i. *cough* [onom., cp. *tussire* id.].
  ind. pres. āı‿tóskırı⌒; perf. āı‿tóskıgori⌒ (N. -ıko-, -ıho-).
  imperat. tóski!
tóskar (-kăr‿; §§2200ff.) and
toskíd (§§2256ff.) n. *coughing.*
tóskıdɛ‿ n. *coughing, cough* [< tósk- *cough* + -ıd *gerundial -ing* (§§2256ff.) + -ɛ‿ of n. ess. §§2234β, 2273].
  obj. -dɛg‿.
  tóskıd‿āıg‿ărɛdắgın⌒ *I have a cough.*
  tóskıd‿āıg‿ɛ́lgom‿mukkómunun⌒ *the cough has not yet left me.*
tóskıg-ır (N. -ıkır, -ıhır; §3682) v.t. caus. *cause or allow to cough.*
  án‿zíkm‿āıg‿tóskıgırın⌒ *my cold makes me cough.*
tŏ́t! voc. of tód‿ *child.*
tŭ́‿, -tu‿, -tⁿv. n. (a) *inside, interior;* (b) *belly, stomach* [cp. ON ᛏᛟᚠ (GNT s.v.), MN. tǫ (KBW s.v.) tür (MZM, p. 338) id.; cogn. tǒ *enter* §2059; RSN, §129].
  obj. tŭ́g‿.
  pl. tŭ̆nč(ı)‿.
  ɛ́ssi‿māsúran‿tŭ́gɛn‿nógın⌒ (-n‿n- < -d‿n- §624) *the water passes through the pipe.*

Note the stress (§1671) of
án-tu‿ (§2374b) *my stomach*, obj. ántūg‿ and án‿tŭ́g‿, gen. ántūn‿ and án‿tŭ́n‿.
ɛ́n-tu‿ *your stomach*, obj. ɛ́ntūg‿ and ɛ́n‿tŭ́g‿, gen. ɛ́ntūn‿ and ɛ́n‿tŭ́n‿.
tɛ́n-tu‿ *his (her, its) stomach*, obj. tɛ́ntūg‿ and tɛ́n‿tŭ́g‿, gen. tɛ́ntūn‿ and tɛ́n‿tŭ́n‿;
but tín‿tŭ̆nč(ı)‿ *their stomachs.*
ántŭ́g‿ğómkon⌒ (-ğ‿ğ- < -g‿ğ- §551) *(s)he (it) (has) hit my stomach.*
ántu‿nógın⌒ *I have diarrhoea.*
tŭ̆n‿nógar‿ (-găr‿) and
tŭ̆n‿nogíd‿ *diarrhoea.*
-tᵘ‿, -tw before a vowel (§1135):
  ántᵘ‿āıg‿óddın⌒ (án|twāi|gód|dın⌒) *my stomach hurts me, I have a stomach-ache.*
ín-tu‿ *palm (of hand)* s.v. í‿.
kắn-tu‿ *interior of house* s.v. kắ‿.
kumáttɛn-tu‿ *uterus* s.v. kumáttɛ‿.
óssín-tu‿ *sole of foot* s.v. óss(ı)‿ s.v. ós.
tŭ́r‿ (s.v. -r‿) adv. *in (to) the interior, inside, in (to) the stomach.*
tŭ́r⌒ (§6007) *(s)he (it) is (they are) inside.*
‿tūr (§§4372, 5908) postp. (=prep. §4287) *inside, in, into.*
— follows the genitive; often unstressed and enclitic (§4373) (cp. Sudan Ar. فِي بَطْن).
N. márɛn-tūr‿tókoran⌒ *they went (have gone) into the (growing crop of) great millet* (= Sudan Ar. دَخَلُوا فِي بَطْن الْعَيْش).
kắn‿tūr‿ (kắn-tūr‿) adv.-complex *inside the house, indoors.*
kắn‿tūr‿ (§6039) *(s)he (it) is (they are) in the house.*
kắn-tūr‿ắkkoran⌒ *they were (sat, stayed, lived) in the house.*
kắn-tūr‿undúkkori⌒ *I (have) put him (her, it, them) inside the house.*
dárum‿tūr‿ (-m‿t- < -bn‿t- §586) *in (on) the path.*
dárum‿tūr‿ *(s)he (it) is (they are) on the path.*
dárum‿tūr‿ɛ́lkori⌒ *I found him (her, it, them) on the path.*
ɛ́rıd‿urún-tūr‿ắgın⌒ *the hippopotamus is (lives) in the river.*
íččín-tūr‿ɛ́ssı‿dắgon⌒ *there was water in the milk.*
fɛğın-tŭ́g‿ *at dawn, in the morning* s.v. fɛğır‿.
tŭ̆n-d(ı)‿ (§§2545ff.) (ʹα) adj. (a) *interior, inner;* (b) *appertaining to the belly, abdominal.* (β) n. (a) *girth (securing saddle);* (b, in water-wheel, kólɛ‿) *spoke of (either) cog-wheel;* (c) *woof, weft* (§2408).
  obj. -dıg‿.
  pl. -dınč(ı)‿.
  árgadɛn‿tŭ́ndınč(ı)‿ *spokes of cog-wheel.*
  kắñ‿tŭ̆nd(ı)‿ (-ñ‿t- < -ğn‿t- §632) n. *girth(s for saddle) of horse.*
  hánun‿tŭ̆nd(ı)‿ n. *girth(s for saddle) of donkey.*

tŭ̆-kŏ̄l‿ (§§2572ff.) adj. *obese.*
  obj. tūkŏ́lg(ı)‿, -gi⌒.
  pl. tŭ́kolı‿.
túb v.t. *sweep, brush.*
  ind. pres. āı‿tubrı⌒; perf. āı‿túbkori⌒ (túpk-).
  imperat. túp!, pl. tūbwɛ! (tŭ́bwɛ́!, tŭ̆bbɛ́! §517, -bɛ́!).
  def. imperat. túbos! (tubó! §962), pl. túbóswɛ! (-bówwɛ! §724, -wɛ́!, -bóssɛ! §687, -sɛ́!).
túbar (-băr‿; §§2200ff.) and
tubíd (§§2256ff.) n. *sweeping, etc.*
tubín-d(ı)‿ (§§2545ff.) (a) adj. *appertaining to sweeping, etc.;* (b) n. *sweepings, litter.*
  obj. -dıg‿.
  wasáha‿tubíndıs‿sókkeran⌒ (-s‿s- < -g‿s- §678) *let him (her) take away the sweepings of dirt, lit. … the dirt of sweeping.*
túb-an (§§3890ff.) v.t. *tell to sweep, etc., let sweep, etc.*
túb-bŭ- (§3931β) v.i. stat. *be in a swept (etc.) state or condition.*
tub-gɛ́ndıgır (N. -ıkır, -ıhır; §§4132, 5623) v.t. *set right by sweeping, etc., sweep (etc.) clean.*
  kắt‿tubgɛ́ndıgíddan⌒ (-t‿t- < -g‿t- §707) *they sweep the house clean.*
tubgɛ́ndıgır-an (N. -ıkır-, -ıhır-; §§3890ff., 3905) v.t. *tell to sweep (etc.) clean, let sweep (etc.) clean.*
tub-sókkɛ (§3747ɛ́) v.t. *take up (etc., s.v. sókkɛ) by sweeping, etc., up, sweep (etc.) away.*
  íŋgı‿bıtubsókkɛran⌒ *they will sweep this (that) away.*
tubsókkɛr-an (§§3890ff., 3905) v.t. *tell to sweep (etc.) up, etc., let sweep (etc.) up, etc.*
tub-šugúdd(ı) (§4132) v.t. *by sweeping (etc.) cause or allow to descend (etc., s.v. šugúdd(ı)), sweep (etc.) down.*
  wasáha‿mállɛt‿tubšugúddıgori⌒ (-t‿t- < -g‿t- §707) *I (have) swept down all the dirt.*
tubšugúdd-an (§§3890ff., 3905) v.t. *tell to sweep (etc.) down, let sweep (etc.) down.*
tŭ́b n. *brick (sun-dried)*, with collective sg. (§4696d) [< طُوب Copt. ⲧⲱⲃⲉ id. RSN, §129].
  obj. tŭ́bk(ı)‿, tŭ́pk(ı)‿, -ki⌒.
  gen. tŭ́bn‿., tŭ̆m‿.
  pl. tŭ́bı‿.
tŭ̆m-d(ı)‿ (§§2545ff.) adj. *appertaining to brick, of brick.*
tŭ́bbɛ! < tŭ́bwɛ! imperat. pl. of tŭ́b *sweep, etc.*
tubbɛ́ v.t. and i. *curse (at), swear (at)* (= čubbɛ́) [< tubb- < tább- in تَبَّاً *woe to…!, perish…!*, probably influenced by čubbɛ́, + -ɛ́ §3623].
  ind. pres. āı‿tubbɛ́rı⌒; perf. āı‿tubbɛ́gori⌒ (N. -ɛ́ko-, -ɛ́ho-).
  imperat. tubbɛ́!
  āıg‿tubbɛ́goran⌒ *they swore (have sworn) at me.*
  tókkon‿tubbɛ́mɛn⌒ *don't swear (at him, her, it, them §5083).*

túbb(ı) < túrb(ı) lie down.
túbro⌣ n. hoe [§§ 2306, 2308].
  obj. -rog⌣.
  pl. -ronč(ı)⌣.
  túbron⌣ád⌣ handle of hoe.
túff(ı) v.t. spit, spit out [imit., cp. ON. ⲧⲟⲩϕϕ id. GNT s.v.].
  ind. pres. aı⌣túffırı⌢, perf. aı⌣túffıgorı⌢ (N. -ıko-, -ıho-).
  imperat. túffi!
  ǧurúdkı⌣túffıgorı⌢ I spat out saliva.
túffar⌣ (-fár⌣; §§ 2200 ff.) and
tuffíd⌣ (§§ 2256 ff.) n. spitting, expectoration.
túffı-děn (§ 5690) v.t. spit at (the speaker), spit on.
  kág⌣áıgı⌣tuffıděŋkó⌢ the snake spat at me.
túffı-tır (§ 5690) v.t. spit at (other than the speaker), spit on.
  aı⌣tékkı⌣tuffıtíkkori⌢ I spat at him (her, it).
túgum⌣ and **túhum**⌣ (§ 1017) n. pole slanting from horizontal drawn round (counter-clockwise) by cattle working water-wheel (kólɛ⌣); its upper end is embedded in the vertical axle (míšš(ı) of the larger cog-wheel (árgadɛŋ⌣gédɛ⌣); its lower end, behind the oxen, is forked and provides a seat for the driver [طَقَم (< τάγμα DSA s.v.) harness § 1336; (> Sudan Ar. نَقَم id.)].
  obj. tugúmg(ı)⌣, -gı⌢.
  pl. túg(u)mı⌣.
  gúrıš⌣šúgıl⌣túhumır⌣áɡın⌢ (-š⌣š- < -g⌣š- 695) he that drives the bulls sits on the pole.
túhᵘmɛ⌣ large fishing-net = túkmɛ⌣.
túkk(ı) v.t. pound, thump, batter, beat (= šókk(ı)) [imit.].
  ind. pres. aı⌣túkkırı⌢; perf. aı⌣túkkıgorı⌢ (N. -ıko-, -ıho-).
  imperat. túkki!
  búŋgı⌣mudákkɛf⌣fúnduŋ⌣túr⌣túkkıran⌢ (-f⌣f- < -d⌣f- § 539) they pound (the) coffee with a (the) pestle in a (the) mortar.
túkkar⌣ (-kár⌣; §§ 2200 ff.) and
tukkíd⌣ (§§ 2256 ff.) n. pounding, etc.
túkk-an (§§ 3890 ff.) v.t. tell to pound, etc., let pound, etc.
túkkı-bǔ- (§ 3931 β) v.i. stat. be in a pounded (etc.) state or condition.
  ábug⌣túkkıbūn⌢ the wool is (has been) beaten.
tukkır-ɛg-áɡ- (§§ 4071 ff.) v.t. = tukkɛdól-.
tukk-ɛ-dól- (-kᵒd- § 1178; § 4022) and
tukkır-ɛ-dól- (-rᵒd-; § 4027) v.t. be about to pound, etc.
tukk-ɛ-má- (§ 4036) and
tukkır-ɛ-má- (§ 4041) v.t. become unable to pound, etc.
tukkɛd-ág- (§§ 3877 ff.) v.t. be in the situation of having pounded, etc.
túkkıg-ır (N. -ıkır, -ıhır; § 3682) v.t. caus. cause or allow to pound, etc.
  ind. pres. aı⌣túkkıgıddı⌢.
túkkı-kattı- (N. -ıha-; § 4093) v.p. be pounded, etc.

tukk-os-túŋg(ı) (-ot-túŋ- § 714; §§ 4180-4; -osgı-túŋ-, -ozgı-, -oggı- § 4185) v.t. tease out (card) after pounding.
  abúkkı⌣tukkostuŋgūrkɛttúŋgıran⌢ (§ 5605) after beating the wool they card it with a bow.
túkmɛ⌣ (túhᵘmɛ § 1027) n. large fishing-net [§ 2235].
  obj. -mɛg⌣.
  pl. -mɛnč(ı)⌣.
túlba n. (a) requisition, tax (whether paid in money, in kind, or in labour); with collective sg. (§ 4696 d); (b) working-party [< طُلْبَة id.].
  obj. -bag⌣.
  pl. -banč(ı)⌣.
  árın⌣túlba (-n⌣t- < -dn⌣t § 612) land-tax.
  X. ın⌣árıt⌣tén⌣túlba⌣mıŋkóttɛrrɛ́? how much is the tax on this land?
  Y. fɛddándo⌣rıjál⌣ówwın⌢ it's two dollars (on) the fɛddán.
  án⌣túlbad⌣dɛfɛ́goru⌣ (-d⌣d- < -g⌣d- § 534) we (have) paid our tax(es).
túlɛ v.i. stoop, bend down; bow oneself, bow; slant, slope; (= dɛrɛ́nɛ) [perhaps contains tǔ⌣ belly; §§ 2870 ff.].
  ind. pres. aı⌣túlɛrı⌢, ɛr⌣túlɛn⌢ (⌣túlɛ̃⌢, ⌣túlɛ̃⌢); perf. aı⌣túlɛgorı⌢ (N. -ɛko-, -ɛho-).
  def. perf. aı⌣túlóskori⌢ and aı⌣túlɛróskori⌢.
túlar⌣ (-lár⌣), **túlɛrar**⌣ (-rár⌣; §§ 2200 ff., 2211) and
tǔlíd⌣, **túlɛríd**⌣ (§§ 2256 ff.), 2264) n. stooping, bending down; bowing, bow, obeisance; downward slant, slope.
tūl-āb-bíttı- (-āgbít- § 519; §§ 4198, 5634) v.t. (a) be engaged in picking up (etc.), s.v. bíttı(ı) while stooping, etc.; (b) continually (habitually) pick up (etc.) while stooping, etc.
  tɛrıt⌣tūlābbíttıran⌢ (-n⌣t- < -g⌣t- § 707) they are (keep on) stooping and picking up (the) seed.
tūl-ās-sıgíddı- (-āgsı- § 679; §§ 4198, 5634-5) v.i. (a) be engaged in bowing in prayer (§ 3783); (b) continually (habitually) bow in prayer.
  tūlāssıgíddıran⌢ they are (keep on) bowing in prayer.
túlɛr-an (§§ 3890 ff., 3899) v.t. tell to stoop, etc., let stoop, etc.
túlɛ-bǔ- (§ 3931 β) v.i. stat. be in a stooping (etc.) state or condition.
túlɛg-ır (N. -ɛkır, -ɛhır; § 3679) v.t. caus. cause or allow to stoop, etc.
  ind. pres. aı⌣túlɛgıddı⌢.
tūlɛ-ǧáŋg(ı) (§ 3747ɛ') v.t. fill while stooping, etc.
  súlɛt⌣tūlɛǧáŋgıgó⌢ (-t⌣t- < -g⌣t- § 707) bending down (s)he (has) filled the pot.
tūlɛ-tēb-sıgíddı- (§§ 4198, 5643) v.i. = tūlāssıgíddı-.
  tūlɛtēbsıgíddıran⌢ they are bowing (habitually bow) in prayer.
túlla⌣ n. smoke [RSN, § 200].
  obj. -lag⌣.
tulúnč(ı) v.i. flash continually or continuously, glitter, sparkle, gleam, shine, be bright, be

túbb(ı) < túrb(ı) — túŋg(ı)

brilliant (= bılínč(ı), fılínč(ı)) [imit., -č intensive § 2864].
  ind. pres. tɛr⌣tulúnčın⌢ (-čı⌢, -čí⌢); perf. tɛr⌣tulúnčıgon⌢ (-gõ⌢, -gó⌢, N. -ıkon⌢, -ıkõ⌢, -ıkó⌢, -ıhon⌢, -ıhõ⌢, -ıhó⌢).
  másıl⌣tulúnčın⌢ the sun shines.
  unáttı⌣tulúnčın⌢ the moon shines.
  wíssı⌣tulúnčın⌢ the star glitters (...stars (§ 4696 d) glitter).
  íg⌣wárrırtōn⌣tulúnčın⌢ the fire (light) shines from afar.
  nóbrɛ⌣tulúnčın⌢ (the) gold is bright.
  búru⌣tulúnčın, tóŋıl⌣hálısun⌢ the girl is brilliant, she is very beautiful.
  tém⌣míssı⌣tulúnčın⌢ his (her, its) eyes (§ 4696 a) sparkle.
  gɛzáz⌣tulúnčın⌢ (the) glass glitters.
tǔm n. garlic (= tóm) [< Eg. Ar. نُوم <نُوم id.].
  obj. tǔmg(ı)⌣, -gı⌢.
  gen. túmn⌣., túm⌣c.
tǔm-d(ı)⌣ (§§ 2545 ff.) adj. appertaining to garlic, of garlic.
tumbág⌣ n. tobacco [< تُمْبَاك id.].
  obj. -ágk(ı)⌣, -ákk(ı)⌣, -kı⌢.
  gen. -ágn⌣., -áŋ⌣c.
  tumbákkı⌣nfran⌢ they smoke tobacco.
túmbura n. large drum [app. < Eg. Ar. طُمْبُورَة kind of guitar (SAE, s.v.) § 2408].
  obj. -rag⌣.
  pl. -ranč(ı)⌣.
túmbus⌣ n. Tumbus (on map), a village on the right bank of the Nile, about five miles north of Kérma.
  obj. tumbúsk(ı)⌣, -kı⌢.
  túmbusır⌣ (s.v. -r⌣) at (to) Túmbus.
  túmbusır⌢ (§ 6007) (s)he (it) is (they are) at Túmbus.
tǔnd(ı)⌣ girth, spoke, woof s.v. tǔ⌣.
√túŋg- twang, onom. of sound made on release by taut bow-string.
túŋg(ı) v.t. tease, tease out, card (with bow)[1] [onom.].
  ind. pres. aı⌣túŋgırı⌢; perf. aı⌣túŋgıgorı⌢ (N. -ıko-, -ıho-).
  imperat. túŋgi!
  part. pres. túŋgıl⌣ (one) that teases, etc., teaser, etc., teasing, etc., obj. tuŋgílg(ı)⌣, -gı⌢; past túŋgɛl⌣ (one) that teased, etc., teaser, etc., teasing, etc., obj. tuŋgɛ́lg(ı)⌣, -gı⌢.
  abúkkı⌣tuŋgúrkɛt⌣túŋgıran⌢ they card wool with a bow.
  bɛnnákkı⌣bɛnnáŋkóleged⌣ɛwírran, bádkı⌣tuŋgúrket⌣túŋgıran⌢ they gin the cotton with the machine, afterwards they tease it out with a bow.
túŋgar⌣ (-gár⌣; §§ 2200 ff.) and
tuŋgíd⌣ (§§ 2256 ff.) n. teasing out, etc.

---
[1] tease, card are unsatisfactory terms because they suggest teeth, and the bow (tuŋgúr⌣) has none. The taut string is released against the tangled cotton and teases it out very well. Until one sees it at work one would not believe that the string could tease so efficiently. Cotton is teased out in the same way with a bow in Syria.

túŋgul⌣ — tuššɛ́ (tıššɛ́)

†**tuŋgíl⌣** n. *bow (weapon)* = túŋgıl⌣.
 obj. -ílg(ı)⌣, -gi⌢.
 pl. -ílı⌣.

†**túŋgıl⌣** n. *bow (weapon).*
 obj. tuŋgílg(ı)⌣, -gi⌢.
 pl. túŋgılı⌣.

tuŋgŭr⌣ n. (a) *bow* (weapon: hardly known in this sense now, cp. *SNK*, 576); (b) *bow-shaped instrument for teasing (carding) cotton and wool.*
 obj. -úrk(ı)⌣, -ki⌢.
 pl. -úrı⌣.
 bɛnnåŋ⌣tuŋgŭrkı⌣kárrortōn⌣úlgɛd⌣ ǎuran, ténn⌣úl⌣bɛnnåŋırtōnun⌢ *they make the cotton-bow of a palm-leaf midrib with string; its string is of cotton.*

túŋ-an (§§ 3890ff.) v.t. *tell to tease, etc., let tease, etc.*

túŋı-bŭ- (§ 3931 β) v.i. stat. *be in a teased (etc.) state or condition.*
 bɛnnåg⌣túŋgıbūn⌢ *the cotton is (has been) teased out.*

tuŋgɛd-åg- (§§ 3877ff.) v.t. *be in the situation of having teased, etc.*

túŋı-katti- (§ 4093) v.p. *be teased, etc.*

túŋgul⌣ n. (a) *Old Dóngola* (on map) دَنْقَلَا اَلْعَجُوز, *a village on the right bank of the Nile, about 20 miles below Ed-Débbåʰ*; = dúŋgula⌣ (a); (b) *Túŋgul, name or title of eponymous king of* (a) (*RN* s.v. *wai*).
 obj. tuŋgúlg(ı)⌣, -gi⌢.
 tuŋgúllo⌣ (s.v. -r⌣) adv. *at (to) Old Dóngola.*
 tuŋgúllo⌢ (§ 6007) *(s)he (it) is (they are) at Old Dóngola.*
 tuŋgúll⌣ågın⌢ *(s)he is (lives) at Old Dóngola.*

tuŋgŭr⌣ n. *bow* s.v. túŋ(ı).

túp! imperat. of túb v.t. *sweep.*

túr v.t. *drive away, drive out, expel, chase away* [cp. ON. тоүа *vertreiben ZNG* s.v.].
 ind. pres. āı⌣túrrı⌢, ɛr⌣túrın⌢ (-rī⌢, -rí⌢); perf. āı⌣túrkori⌢.
 wɛ́l⌣såbkı⌣túrın⌢ *the dog drives the cat away.*

túrar⌣ (-ra̍r⌣; §§ 2200ff.) and
turíd⌣ (§§ 2256ff.) n. *driving away, expulsion, etc.*

túr-an (§§ 3890ff.) v.t. *tell to drive away, etc., let drive away, etc.*

turɛd-åg- (§§ 3877ff.) v.t. *be in the situation of having driven away, etc.*
 wɛ́l⌣såbıt⌣turɛdágırırın⌢ (-t⌣t- < -g⌣t- § 707) *the dog has chased the (various § 5456) cats away.*

túr-katti- (§ 4093) v.p. *be driven away, etc.*

tŭr⌣ n. *dropping(s) of camel;* with collective sg. (§ 4696 d) [< tŭ⌣ *belly* + -r⌣ *in,* so *(what is) in the belly, belly-contents*].
 obj. tŭrk(ı)⌣, -ki⌢.
 kám⌣tŭr⌣ (-n⌣t- < -mn⌣t- § 829) *camel's dung.*
 kámlın⌣tŭr⌣ *camels' dung.*

túrbɛ⌣ (-båa⌣, -ba⌣) n. *grave, tomb* [< تُرْبَة *id.*].
 obj. -bɛg⌣.
 pl. -bɛnč(ı)⌣.

túrb(ı) (tubb(ı) § 520) v.i. (a) *lie down;* (b) *lie down to rest, go to bed;* (c) *lie, rest, repose* ['compositum aus *tū-r-bū* auf dem bauche ligen' *RNW* s.v.].
 ind. pres. āı⌣túrbırı⌢ (tubbı-), ɛr⌣túrbın⌢ (túbbın⌢, -bī⌢, -bí⌢); perf. āı⌣túrbıgori⌢ (túbbı-, -bᵘgo- § 1194; N. -bıko-, -bᵘko-, -biho-, -bᵘho-).
 imperat. túrbi! (túbbi!), pl. túrbıwɛ! (túbb-, -bᵘwɛ!, -wɛ́!).
 X. hɛ́rro⌣túbbi! *good-night!,* lit. *lie down in well-being!*
 Y. ártın⌣hásɛbı! *good-night!,* lit. *(lie down) in God's care!*
 āı⌣turbóskori⌢ (tubbós-) *I have lain down (I have gone to bed).*
 tubbóskó⌢ *(s)he has gone to bed.*

túrbar⌣ (túbbar, -bår⌣; §§ 2200ff.) and
turbíd⌣ (tubbíd; §§ 2256ff.) n. *lying down, rest, repose.*

túrb-an (túbban; §§ 3890ff.) v.t. *tell to lie down, etc., let lie down, etc.*

turbır-ɛg-åg- (tubb-; §§ 4071ff.) v.i. = turbɛdól-.

turb-ɛ-dól- (tubb-; -bᵒd- § 1178; § 4022) and
turbır-ɛ-dól- (tubb-; -rᵒd-; § 4027) v.i. *be about to lie down, etc.*

turbır-ɛ-ğŭ-bŭ- (tubb-; § 4069) v.i. stat. *be on one's way (coming) to lie down, etc.*

turbır-ɛ-nóg (tubb-; §§ 4048ff.) v.i. *go to lie down, etc.*

turbır-ɛ-nóg-bŭ- (tubb-; -nóggŭ- § 546; § 4058) v.i. stat. *be on one's way (going) to lie down, etc.*

turbır-ɛ-tá (tubb-; §§ 4060ff.) v.i. *come to lie down, etc.*

turbɛd-åg- (tubb-; §§ 3877ff.) v.i. *be in the situation of having lain down, etc.*
 tubbɛdágri⌢ (§ 3880) (a) *I have lain down* (sc. *and am still lying down*), *I have gone to bed* (sc. *and am there*); (b) *I have rested* (sc. *and having done that* (-ɛd-) *am up again*).

turbos-gɛrjɛ́ (tubb-; -oggɛr- § 548; §§ 4180-4; -osgıgɛrjɛ́, -ozgı-, -oggı- § 4185; -gɛrɛ́) v.i. and t. *read after (while) lying down, read in bed.*
 ɛsmán⌣kıtápkı⌣kó⌢ tubbobbıgɛrjɛ⌢ (<-osbı- § 521) *ɛoθmán has a book; he will lie down and read.*

turbos-mɛrɛl-an- (tubb-; -ommɛ́- 609; -osgımɛ́-, -ozgı-, -oggı- § 5680) v.i. *(of milk) get curdled by lying* (Anglice *standing*).

turbos-nál (tubb-; -onnál § 629; §§ 4180-4; -osgınál, -ozgı-, -oggı- § 4185) v.t. *see (etc., s.v. nál) after lying down, etc.*
 āı⌣tékkı⌣tubboggınálkori⌢ *on lying (when I had lain) down I saw him (her, it).*

turráha⌣ n. *small fishing-net* [< Sudan Ar. طُرَّاحَة *id.*].
 obj. -hag⌣.
 pl. -hanč(ı)⌣.

túrub⌣ n. *sickle* [cp. tórbar⌣ *field-hand*].
 obj. turúbk(ı)⌣, -rúpk(ı)⌣, -ki⌢.
 gen. túrubn⌣v., -rum⌣c., túrubn⌣v., -rúm⌣c.
 pl. túr(u)bı⌣.
 túrubn⌣åd⌣ *handle of sickle.*
 íllɛt⌣turúpkɛğğórran⌢ (-t⌣t- < -g⌣t- § 707, -ğğ- < -dğ- § 550) and íllɛt⌣turúpkɛm⌣múttıran⌢ (-m⌣m- < -d⌣m- § 600; § 4647) *they reap (the) wheat with sickles.*
 mårɛt⌣turúpkɛğğórın⌢ (-t⌣t- < -g⌣t-) *he reaps (the) sorghum with a sickle.*
 béntı⌣turúpkɛğğórran⌢ (-ğğ- < -dğ-) *they cut down dates with a sickle.*

túrug⌣ n. *wind.*
 obj. turúgk(ı)⌣, -úkk(ı)⌣, -ki⌢.
 gen. túrugn⌣v., -ruŋ⌣c.
 pl. túrugı⌣.

†**turumbíl⌣** n. *motor-car* [< Sudan Ar. تُرُمْبِيل *id.* < Fr. *automobile*].
 obj. -ílg(ı)⌣, -gi⌢.
 pl. -ílı⌣.

tŭs v.t. *curse.*
 ind. pres. āı⌣tŭs(¹)ri⌢; perf. āı⌣tŭskori⌢.
 part. pres. tŭsıl⌣ *(one) that curses, curser, cursing,* obj. tŭsílg(ı)⌣, -gi⌢; past tŭsɛl⌣ *(one) that cursed, curser, cursing,* obj. tŭsɛ́lg(ı)⌣, -gi⌢.

tŭsar⌣ (-så̍r⌣; §§ 2200ff.) and
tŭsíd⌣ (§§ 2256ff.) n. *(action of) cursing.*

tŭss(ı)⌣, -si⌢ n. *curse;* with collective sg. (§ 4696 d) (< *tŭst(ı)⌣ § 686 < tŭs + -t of n. act. § 2319].
 obj. -sıg⌣.
 pl. -sınč(ı)⌣.

tŭz-bŭ- (§ 3931 β) v.i. stat. *be in an accursed state or condition.*

tŭs(¹)r-ɛg-åg- (§§ 4071ff.) v.t. = tūsɛdól-.

tŭs-ɛ-dól- (-sᵒd- § 1178; § 4022) and
tŭs(¹)r-ɛ-dól- (-rᵒd-; § 4027) v.t. *be about to curse.*

tŭsk-ır (§ 3683) v.t. caus. *cause or allow to curse.*

tŭsıŋg-ır (and ⌣⌢; N. -ŋkır; § 3688) v.t. caus. *cause or allow to curse.*

tŭs-katti- (§ 4093) v.p. *be cursed.*

tussába⌣ n. *mongoose, Herpestes albicauda F. Cuv.* (*KNH*, p. 39) [(a) prob. < *tuss-sáb-a⌣ < *tuss-* flatum ventris emittere (*RNW*; cp. Amh. ቱስ አለ *id.* senza rumore *GVA*) + -sáb- *cat* + -a⌣ *utterance* (§ 2178), so *(what) says the cat of the stench,* or (b) possibly < *tūr-sába⌣ (§ 683) < t- dem. (§ 4592) + -úr- *break wind* + -sáb- *cat* + -a⌣ *utterance* (§ 2172)].
 obj. -bag⌣.
 pl. -banč(ı)⌣.
 tussába⌣kåkkı⌣bēn⌢ *the mongoose kills snakes* (§ 4696 d).

tússa⌣ n. *(small) abscess, boil, tumour* [< Eg. Ar. طَشَّة *bubbling, ebullition* (*SAE²* s.v.) § 1336].
 obj. -šag⌣.
 pl. -šanč(ı)⌣.

tuššɛ́ (tıššɛ́) v.i. *lose one's way, stray* [< imperf. stem of Sudan Ar. طَشَّ ṭaššá, يِطِشّ jıṭíšš, jıṭýšš *id.* +-ɛ́ § 3623].
 ind. pres. āı⌣tuššɛ́ri⌢, perf. āı⌣tuššɛ́gori⌢ (N. -ɛ́ko-, -ɛ́ho-).
 sámıl⌣sándıgon⌣āı⌣tıššɛ́sun⌣íllɛr⌢ *the sheikh was alarmed because I got lost.*

tuššɛ́rar⌣ (tıš-, -rår⌣; §§ 2200ff., 2207) and

tuššĕríd‿ (tɪš-; §§2256ff., 2260) n. *straying*.

tuššɛ́-bŭ- (tɪš-; §3931α) v.i. stat. *be in a lost (etc.) state or condition*.
aı‿tɪššɛ́būrı⁀ *I have lost my way*.
hánu‿tɪššɛ́būn⁀ *the donkey (has strayed and) is lost*.

tuššɛ́g-ɪr (tɪš-, N. -ɛ́kɪr, -ɛ́hɪr; §3681) (a) v.t. caus. *cause or allow to lose one's way, etc.*; (b) v.t. *send astray, lead astray*.
tɪr‿árgɪ‿tuššɛ́gɪríkkoran⁀ *they (have) made (let) us lose our way*.

túšš(ɪ)‿, **-šɪ**⁀ n. *name of a plant* (not identified; small, with very narrow leaves of bitter taste and red blossom, eaten by cattle but not used otherwise; ? =tuššɪ‿ dárɪg).
obj. túššɪg‿ [>Sudan Ar. تُشِيك id. §2412].
túšš‿ígk‿ullóskó⁀ *the túšši has put forth blossoms*.
túššɪ‿dárɪg *deep-rooted heather-like undershrub, rooting where branches touch the ground*, Bergia suffruticosa, Fenzl. (BSP, 48).

-u‿ n. (a, prop.) *grandfather*; (b) *forefather, ancestor*.
obj. -ŭg‿.
pl. -ŭnč(ɪ)‿.
— always with a form of the possessive personal pronoun (§2622) prefixed:
ánnu‿ *my grandfather*.
ínnu‿ *your grandfather*.
tínnu‿ *his (her) grandfather*.
antínnu‿ *our grandfather*.
ɪntínnu‿ *your (pl.) grandfather*.
tɪntínnu‿ *their grandfather*.
tínnūn‿nálkorɪ⁀ (-n‿n-<-g‿n- §625) *I saw (have seen) his (her) grandfather*.
tínnūnčɪn‿nálkorɪ⁀ *I saw (have seen) his (her) grandfathers*.

úbb(ɪ) v.i. *get a hole (perforation), spring a leak* [<*úrb(ɪ), cp. RN, AZN s.v. urbur].
ind. pres. tɛr‿úbbɪn‿ (-bī‿, -bí⁀); perf. tɛr‿úbbɪgon‿ (-gõ⁀, -gó⁀, N. -ɪkon⁀, -ɪkõ⁀, -ɪkó⁀, -ɪhon⁀, -ɪhõ⁀, -ɪhó⁀).
ğɛrdɛ‿úbbɪgó⁀ *the bucket (has) got a hole*.
bɛ́ñ‿búbbɪn⁀ *the skin will get a hole*.
dál‿ubbóskó⁀ *the (well-)bucket (dálu‿ §1122) has developed a hole (...sprung a leak)*.

úbbar (-bár‿; §§2200ff.) and
ubbíd‿ (§§2256ff.) n. *getting a hole, etc.*

úbbɛd n. *hole (perforation), tear, rent* [§2242].
obj. ubbɛ́dk(ɪ)‿, -ɛ́tk(ɪ)‿, -ɛ́tt(ɪ)‿ (§2462), -kɪ⁀, -tɪ⁀.
pl. úbbɛdɪ‿.

úbbur n. *hole (perforation), tear, rent*; with collective sg. (§4696d) [<*úbbɪr‿ (§1189)<*úbbɪr‿ (§1154)<úbb- *get a hole*+-ír‿ **causation*, so **hole-causation §2344].
obj. ubbúrk(ɪ)‿, -kɪ⁀.
pl. úbburɪ‿.
ağɪnd‿ubbúrk‿āurɪ⁀ *I('ll §5369b) make a hole (holes) in the leather*.

úbbur‿ has the sense of kúl‿ in
dfun‿úbbur‿ *hole* or *socket under centre of cross-beam* (dfu‿) *of water-wheel* (kólɛ‿), *in which top of vertical axle* (míššɪn‿úr‿) *revolves*.

úbur‿ n. *large hole dug in the ground for storing grain, grain-cache* [<úbbur‿ §991].
obj. ubúrk(ɪ)‿, -kɪ⁀.
pl. úb(u)rɪ‿.
márɛn‿úbur‿ (S. also -ron‿ú-) *cache of (for) millet*.
íllɛn‿úbur‿ *cache of (for) wheat*.
S. gússan‿dógor‿máron‿úbur‿dɪgrí-gɪr‿dúlun; gúss‿ɛrdɛb‿tóskɪm‿ mónkos‿sókkɛn, úbur‿árɪm‿mónkos‿sókkɛn⁀ *an úbur for millet is much larger than a gússa‿ (corn-bin); a gússa‿ holds up to three arádɪb, an úbur‿ holds up to twenty*.

úbbɪ-bŭ- (-bᵘbū- §1194; §3931α) v.i. stat. *be in the state or condition of having a hole (aperture)*.
ğɛ́rdɛ‿úbbᵘbūn⁀ *the bucket has a hole in it*.
án‿ğɛ́b‿úbbɪbūn⁀ *my pocket has a hole in it*.
kúb‿úbbᵘbūgon⁀ *the boat had a leak*.

ubbɪr-ɛg-ág- (§§4071ff.) v.i. *be about to get a hole, etc.*
kúb‿ubbɪrɛgákkó⁀ *the boat had almost sprung a leak*.

ubb-ɛ-dól- (-bᵒd- §1178; §4022) and
ubbɪr-ɛ-dól- (-rᵒd-; §4027) v.i. *be about to get a hole, etc.*
gɪrbád‿ubbɛdólɪn⁀ *the water-skin is going to get a hole*.

úbbuğ (§2892) v.t. *make holes in, perforate (in several places)*.
ind. pres. aı‿ubbúğrɪ⁀, ɛr‿úbbuğɪn⁀ (ğī‿, -ğɪ⁀); perf. aı‿ubbúğkorɪ⁀ (-účk-).
ağɪng‿úbbuč⁀ *bore holes in the leather*.

úbbuğar (-ğár‿; §§2200ff., 2209) and
ubbuğíd‿ (§§2256ff., 2262) n. *perforation, etc.*

úbbuğ-an (§§3890ff., 3903) v.t. *tell to perforate, etc., let perforate, etc.*
aı‿tékk‿ağɪng‿úbbuğandɪ⁀ (§5369b) *tell him (her) to make holes in the leather*.

úbbuğ-bŭ- (úbbuğğŭ- §552; ubbúğbŭ-, -úğğŭ- §1522; §3931β) v.i. stat. *be in a perforated (etc.) state or condition*.
ağɪn‿ubbúğbūn⁀ *the leather has holes in it*.

ubbuğɛd-ág- (§§3877ff.) v.t. *be in the situation of having perforated, etc.*

ubbúğ-kattɪ- (-účk-; §4093) v.p. *be perforated, etc.*

úbbur (§3673) v.t. *make a hole through, tear a hole in, pierce, perforate*.
ind. pres. aı‿ubbúddɪ⁀, ɛr‿úbburɪn⁀ (-rī‿, -rí⁀); perf. aı‿ubbúrkorɪ⁀.
ɛr‿kádɛg‿ubbúrkon⁀ *you (have) made a hole in the cloth*.

úbburar (-rár‿; §§2200ff.) and
ubburíd‿ (§§2256ff.) n. *making a hole, etc.*

úbbur-an (§§3890ff., 3904) v.t. *tell to make a hole in, etc., let make a hole in, etc.*

úbbur-bŭ- (§3937) v.i. stat. *be in a pierced (etc.) state or condition*.

ubbudd-ɛg-ág- (§§4071ff.) v.t. =ubburɛ-dól-.

ubbur-ɛ-dól- (-rᵒd- §1178; §4022) and
ubbudd-ɛ-dól- (-dᵒd-; §4027) v.t. *be about to make a hole in, etc.*

ubburɛd-ág- (§§3877ff.) v.t. *be in the situation of having made a hole in, etc.*
kádɛg‿ubburɛdágrɪ⁀ *I have torn a hole in the cloth*.

ubburíŋ-ɪr (N. -ŋkɪr; §3692) v.t. caus. *cause or allow to make a hole in*.

úbbur-kattɪ- (§4093) v.p. *be pierced, etc.*

ubúrt(ɪ)‿, **-tɪ**⁀ n. *ash*; with collective sg. (§4696d) [perhaps <úbur‿ *hole*+-t dem. **what is in the hole §2329; RSN, §129].
obj. -tɪg‿.
pl. -tɪnč(ɪ)‿.
†ubúrtɪn‿dádɪ‿ *ash-tray*.

údlan‿ (§956d; -añ‿) n. *hare* [RSN, §§129, 200 s.v. Widla; -ñ dim. §4572].
obj. udláŋ(ɪ)‿, -áñ(ɪ)‿, -gɪ⁀.
pl. udlanɪ‿, -añɪ‿.

udúdɛ‿ n. *thunder* [<*ūd-úd-ɛ‿ (§2153) **utterance of 'úd! úd!'* §2234α].
obj. -dɛg‿.
pl. -dɛnč(ɪ)‿.
udúdɛ‿ğómkó⁀ *the thunder (has) sounded (it (has) thundered)*.
udúd‿āğğómɪn⁀ *it is (keeps on) thundering*.

√úff- onom. of sound of blowing, puffing.
úffɛ (a) v.i. *blow, puff, hiss*; (b) v.t. *blow, puff, blow up, blow about* [imit. §§2870-4, cp. Amh. ሃፍሃፍ id. RSN, §129].
ind. pres. aı‿úffɛrɪ⁀; perf. aı‿úffɛgorɪ⁀ (N. -ɛko-, -ɛho-).
def. perf. aı‿uffóskorɪ⁀ and aı‿uffɛró-skorɪ⁀.
kág‿úffɛn⁀ *the snake hisses*.
kág‿uffóskó⁀ *the snake has hissed*.
sáb‿úffɛn⁀ *the cat hisses*.
túrug‿ɛskédk‿úffɛn⁀ *the wind blows the dust up (about)*.
éskɛd‿úffɛn⁀ *the dust blows up (...blows about)*.

úffɛrar (-rár‿; §§2200, 2210) and
uffɛríd‿ (§§2256ff., 2263) n. *blowing, etc.*

úffɛr-an (§§3890ff., 3899) v.t. *tell to blow, etc., let blow, etc.*

úffɛ-bŭ- (§3931β) v.i. stat. *be in a blown (etc.) state or condition*.
éskɛd‿úffɛbūn⁀ *the dust is (has been) blown about*.

uffɛrɛd-ág- (§§3877ff.) v.i. and t. *be in the situation or condition of having blown, etc.*

uffɛr-ɛg-ág- (§§4071ff.) v.i. and t.=uffɛrɛdól-.

uffɛr-ɛ-dól- (-rᵒd- §1178; §§4016-17, 4022, 4027) v.i. and t. *be about to blow, etc.*

úffɛ-kattɪ- (N. -ɛha-; §4093) v.p. *be blown, etc.*

uff-ós (§3747ɛ') v.t. *cause to issue (etc., s.v. ós) by blowing, etc., blow out*.
ín‿ɛskédk‿uffós⁀ *blow this (that) dust out*.

uff-úndur (§3769) v.t. *put into by blowing, etc., blow into, blow in*.
túrug‿ɛskétt‿ám‿míssɪr‿uffundúkkó⁀

√úg- — úll(ı)

the wind blew (has blown) dust into my eye(s §4696a, ... our eyes).
háwag‿gırbådır‿uffundúddan‿tır‿úrugem‿mérr‿égi⌒ (-m‿m- < -g‿m- §601; §§6223, 5922) they blow air into the skins in order to cross the river by means of them.

ufúff(ı)‿, -fi⌒ n. lung; with collective sg. (§4696a); =fašfåš‿ [§§2151, 2153].
obj. -fıg‿.
pl. -fınč(ı)‿.

√úg- day (of 24 hours) [cp. ON. ⲟⲩⲕ id. (GNT s.v.), ŭg MD. Lebenszeit, Alter (AZN s.v.), i.e. days; RSN, §§129, 200; TOB, §143, 139, 141].

ugrɛ́s n. day (as distinguished from night =nahǻr‿, but also used like jóm‿); with collective sg. (§4696d) [< *ugurɛ́s‿ < ugur- (cp. ugur K. das Leben LN s.v., i.e. days, ON. ⲟⲩⲕⲟⲩⲡ day, time GNT s.v. ⲟⲩⲕ)+ɛ́s‿ early afternoon].
obj. -ɛ́sk(ı)‿, -ki⌒.
pl. -ɛ́sı‿.
ugrɛ́sn‿tṓrt(ı)‿ (a) half the (a) day; (b) midday (s.v. tŏ̌rt(ı)‿).
ugrɛ́s‿mukóttēr‿fadlēróskon? how many days are left?

ugrɛ́sk(ı)‿, -ki⌒ (§§4431-3) adv. (a) by day, in the day-time; (b) by the day, per day.
X. tém‿mahíje‿mınkóttēré? how much is his (her) pay?
Y. ugrɛ́skı‿gírıš‿dímnun⌒ it's ten piastres a day.
ugŭgon‿ugrɛ́skoŋgı‿šuglɛ́ran⌒ (§§6072-3) they work by night and by day.

ugrɛ́s‿málleg‿, -gi⌒ (§§6038, 6043) adv.-complex (a) all day, the whole day; (b) every day.
ınnówwıg‿ugrɛ́s‿málles‿šogolɛ́gori⌒ (-š‿š- < -g‿š- §695) today I have worked all day; ınnówwıg‿ is an adverb (§4433) and ugrɛ́s‿málleg‿ an adv.-complex.
ugrɛ́s‿málleg‿åttåran⌒ and ugrɛ́s‿mállet‿tåran⌒ (-t‿t- < -g‿t- §707) they come every day.
ugrɛ́s‿mállen‿nók⌒ (-n‿n- < -g‿n- §625) go every day.
ınnóww‿ugrɛ́s‿ (§4750) and ınnówwın‿ugrɛ́s‿ (§4810) n.-complex today.
ugrɛ́skı‿tågoran⌒ they came (have come) today.
ınnówwın‿ugrɛ́sır‿nókkoran⌒ they went (have gone) today.
ınnóww(ın)‿ugrɛ́s‿méllen‿nɛ́rbū-goran⌒ (-n‿n- < -g‿n- §625) they were (have been) asleep the whole of today; ınnóww(ın)‿ugrɛ́s‿málleg‿ an adv.-complex (§§6042, 6047a).

ugrɛ́s-an- (§3910α) v.i. become day.
ind. pres. ugrɛ́sanın⌒ (-nī⌒, -nī⌒); fut. bugrɛ́sanın⌒ (-nī⌒, -nī⌒); perf. ugrɛ́saŋkon⌒ (-kŏ⌒, -kó⌒).

ugrɛ́sam-bū- (§§3949ff.) v.i. stat. be in a state of becoming or having become day, be nearly day.

ugrɛ́san-ɛ-dól- (-nᵒd- §1178; §3975) and **ugrɛ́sand-ɛ-dól-** (-dᵒd-; §3978) v.i. be about to become day, be very nearly day.

úgu‿ n. age [i.e. number of one's days §§2337-8].
obj. úgug‿.
pl. úgunč(ı)‿.
âı‿ténn‿úgug‿uñúrmunun⌒ I don't know his (her, its) age.
ánn‿úgu‿ğɛ́n‿årın⌒ my age is 20 years.

úgŭ- n. night.
obj. ugŭ́g‿, -gi⌒.
pl. ugŭnč(ı)‿.
sámten‿úgu‿ the night of Saturday, i.e. (a) Saturday night; (b) ليلة السبت Friday night.

ugŭ́g‿, -gi⌒ (§§4431-3) adv. at night, in the night, by night.
ínn-ugŭ́g‿ (§4434) adv. tonight.
mán‿ugŭ́g‿ (§6050) adv.-complex on that night.
hán‿ugŭ́d‿dápkó⌒ (-d‿d- < -g‿d- §534) the donkey (has) disappeared in the night.
X. ålı‿bıtåná? will ɛ ålı come?
Y. ɛddór‿ínn-ugŭ́b‿bıtǻ⌒ (-b‿b- < -g‿b- §519) perhaps he will come tonight.
wíl‿ugŭ́t‿tågoran⌒ (-t‿t- < -g‿t- §707) they came last night.

úgu‿málleg, -gi⌒ (§6043) adv.-complex (a) all night, the whole night; (b) every night.
úgu‿málleg‿åkkoran⌒ and úgu‿mállet‿tɛ́kkoran⌒ (-t‿t- < -g‿t- §707) they (have) stayed all night.
kobíd‿úgu‿málleg‿åggŭ́ñč̌ıkópkoran⌒ they were (have been) shutting the door carefully every night.
N. úgu‿málleg‿åttåkoran⌒ and N. úgu‿mállet‿tåkoran⌒ (-t‿t- < -g‿t- §707) they came every night.
sǻ‿ıskódır‿ugŭ́g‿ and ugŭ́s‿sǻ‿ıskódır‿ (-s‿s- < -g‿s- §678) at 9 p.m.

ugŭ́n‿tŏ̌rt(ı)‿ n.-complex (§4810) (a) half the (a) night; (b) midnight.
ugŭn-tŏ̌rt(ı)‿ (§2354) n. midnight.
ugŭ́ntŏrtıg‿ (§4665) and ugŭntŏ̌rtır‿ at midnight.
ugŭntŏ̌rtıt‿tågoran⌒ (-t‿t- < -g‿t- §707) they came at midnight.
uguntŏ̌rtır‿åttågorá⌒ they used to come at midnight.

ugŭ́n-d(ı)‿ (§§2545ff.) adj. appertaining to the night, nocturnal.

úg-an- (§3910α) v.i. become night.
ind. pres. úganın⌒ (-nī⌒, -nī⌒); fut. búganın⌒ (-nī⌒, -nī⌒); perf. ugáŋkon⌒ (-kŏ⌒, -kó⌒).

ugám-bū- (§§3949ff.) v.i. stat. be in a state of becoming or having become night, be night.

ugan-ɛ-dól- (-nᵒd- §1178; §3975) and **ugand-ɛ-dól-** (-dᵒd-; §3978) v.i. be about to become night.

úgud‿, -ut⌒ n. bean, Dolichos lablab, Linn. (BSP, 154), Phaseolus vulgaris, Linn. (BSP, 149); with collective sg. (§4696b) [< *úgıd‿ (§1189) < √úg- day +-ıd‿ *making, so *daily (sc. food) §2340].
obj. ugúdk(ı)‿, -útk(ı)‿, -útt(ı)‿, -úkk(ı)‿ (§2462), -ki⌒, -ti⌒.

gen. úgudn‿v., úgunn‿v.c., úgun‿c.
pl. úgudı‿.
úguŋ‿kåč̌č̌(ı)‿ (-ŋ‿k- < -dn‿k- §651) bean-pod(s), husk(s) of bean(s).

ugún-d(ı)‿ (§§2545ff.) adj. appertaining to the bean.

ugúllan‿ (§956d) n. fuel [app. < úg(u)-night + -úll(ı)- kindle + -an‿ say, so *night says 'kindle', or *what says 'kindle (sc. me) (at) night'; ug- perhaps worn down from ugŭ́g- §2195].
obj. ugullåŋ(ı)‿, -gi⌒.
pl. ugullanı‿.
ğ‿ugullåŋgı‿tɛbɛ́⌒ (ğ‿ < ğu‿) go and look for fuel.
ugullåŋgı‿tɛbɛnókkoran⌒ they went (have gone) in search of fuel.

úğrɛ‿ (-rå‿, -ra‿) n. hire, pay, wages, rent [< أُجْرَة id.].
obj. úğrɛg, -råg‿, -rag‿.
ánn‿úğrå‿šahárro‿gínɛ‿tóskı-taran⌒ my pay is three pounds a month.
ténn‿úğrɛ‿šahárkı‿gín‿owwıtórtı-taran⌒ (§4668) his (her) pay (its hire) is two pounds and a half a month.
kån‿úğrɛ‿rıjål‿díğun⌒ (...‿díč̌-taran⌒ §5791) the rent of the house is five dollars.
bústan‿úğrɛ‿ the cost of the postage.
telegråfn‿úğrɛ‿ the cost of (sending) the telegram.

úkk(ı) v.i. (a) bark; (b) bawl=N. wŭ́kk(ı) [onom. §2853; 'ū machen' RN s.v. wel]
ind. pres. åı‿úkkıri⌒; fut. åı‿búkkıri⌒; perf. åı‿úkkıgori⌒ (N. -ıko-, -ıho-).
imperat. úkki!
wél‿úkkın⌒ the dog barks.
ɛr‿mén‿úkkın? why do you bawl?

úkkar‿ (-kår‿; §§2200ff.) and **ukkíd‿** (§§2256ff.) n. barking; bawling.

úkkıd‿ (§2256) n. barking, bark; bawling.
obj. ūkkídk(ı)‿, -ítk(ı)‿, -ítt(ı)‿ (§2462), -ki⌒, -ti⌒.
pl. úkkıdı‿.

úl‿ n. (a) thread; (b) string, cord, line (this sense not admitted by some that use dubára‿).
obj. úlg(ı)‿, -gi⌒.
pl. úlı‿.
úl‿bennånd(ı)‿ and bennånd‿úl‿ cotton thread.
hawwåd‿úlg‿åššírın‿ the fisherman is hauling the line in.

√úl- kindle [cp. ŭr anzünden AZN s.v.].

úll(ı) v.t. kindle, light, set fire to (=wɛllɛ́) §4599.
ind. pres. åı‿úllıri⌒; fut. åı‿búllıri⌒; perf. åı‿úllıgori⌒ (N. -ıko-, -ıho-).
imperat. úlli!
íkkı‿búllıri⌒ I shall light a (the) fire (light).
bérkı‿búllıri⌒ I shall set fire to the wood.

úllar‿ (-lår‿; §§2200ff.) and **ullíd‿** (§§2256ff.) n. kindling, etc.

úll-an (§§3890ff.) v.t. tell to kindle, etc., let kindle, etc.

úllı-bū- (§3931β) v.i. stat. be in a kindled (etc.) state or condition.
fg‿úllıbūn‿ the fire is alight.
bér‿úllıbūn‿åğğúgın⌒ the wood is alight, it's burning.

šɛm‿úllıbūn⌒ *the candle is (candles are §4647) alight.*
úlud‿úllıbūn⌒ *the charcoal is alight.*
íg‿bérr‿úllıbūn⌒ and (§4622) bérr‿íg‿úllıbūn⌒ *the fire has caught the wood, lit. the fire is alight in the wood.*
ullır-ɛg-ǎg- (§§4071 ff.) v.t. = ullɛdól-.
ull-ɛ-dól- (-lᵒd- §1178; §4022) and
ullır-ɛ-dól- (-rᵒd-; §4027) v.t. *be about to kindle, etc.*
ullır-ɛ-ğŭ-bŭ- (§4069) v.t. stat. *be on one's way (coming) to kindle, etc.*
ull-ɛ-má- (§4036) and
ullır-ɛ-má- (§4041) v.t. *become unable to kindle, etc.*
ullır-ɛ-nóg (§§4048 ff.) v.t. *go to kindle, etc.*
ullır-ɛ-nóg-bŭ- (-nóggŭ- §546; §4058) v.t. stat. *be on one's way (going) to kindle, etc.*
ullır-ɛ-tá- (§§4060 ff.) v.t. *come to kindle, etc.*
ullɛd-ǎg- (§§3877 ff.) v.t. *be in the situation of having kindled, etc.*
šɛmag‿ullɛdágın⌒ *(s)he has lit a (the) candle (candles §4647).*
úllıg-ır (N. -ıkır, -ıhır; §3682) v.t. caus. *cause or allow to kindle, etc.*
aı‿tékk‿íkk‿úllıgıddi⌒ *I'll (§5369b) make (let) him (her) light a (the) fire (light).*
aı‿tékkı‿lámbag‿ullıgírkori⌒ *I (have) made (let) him (her) light a (the) lamp.*
úllı-kattı- (N. -ıha-; §4093) v.p. *be kindled, etc.*
úlud‿ n. (a) *charcoal*, and applied to (b) *coal* [< *úlıd (§1189) < √úl- *kindle* +-ıd‿ *making* (§2256), so *(*action of*) *kindling*, then concrete **what makes or causes kindling* §2340].
obj. ulúdk(ı)‿, -útk(ı)‿, -útt(ı)‿ §2462), -ki⌒, -ti⌒.
gen. úludn‿v., úlunn‿v.c., úlun‿c.
pl. úlud‿.
ulún-d(ı)‿ (§§2545 ff.) adj. *appertaining to charcoal, etc.*
úlug‿ n. (a) *ear*; (b, of plant) *leaf*.
— with collective sg. (§4696a) [cp. ON. оүлυ *hear* GNT s.v.; RSN, §129 s.v. *ukki*].
obj. ulúgk(ı)‿, -úkk(ı)‿, -ki⌒.
gen. úlugn‿v., -uŋ‿c.
pl. úlugı‿.
déssɛn‿úlug‿ *a green leaf*, lit. *a leaf of green.*
ǵówwın‿ulúkkı‿kállan⌒ *they eat the leaves of the tree(s).*
úluk‿sowwétkı‿ǵınɛnartós‿sókkɛ-goran‿ (-k‿s- < -g‿s- §576, -s‿s- < -n‿s- §680) *they (have) removed the dry leaves from the garden*; úluk‿ sowwétkı‿ *a noun-complex* (§4760).
ulún-d(ı)‿ (-úgnd(ı)‿ §643; §§2545 ff.) adj. *appertaining to the ear, etc., of the ear, etc.*
umbílbıl (-búlbul- §1188) n. *beer (made from dates or millet)* [< Sudan Ar. اُمّ بِلْبِل *id.*].
obj. umbılbílg(ı)‿, -gi⌒.
pl. umbílbılı‿.
úmbu n. *palm-trunk (of date-palm and dōm-palm)*; with collective sg. (§4696b) [§2299].
obj. -bug‿.
pl. -bunč(ı)‿.
béntın‿úmbu‿ *trunk(s) of date-palm.*
hámbun‿úmbu‿ *trunk(s) of dōm-palm.*
soríñn‿úmbu‿ *bridge of the nose.*
béntım‿bérkon‿hámbum‿bérkoŋ‿ úmbug‿ɛrán⌒ *they call both the trunk of the date-palm and the trunk of the dōm-palm úmbu‿.*
úmbu‿gásıčkattın⌒ *the palm-trunk is (palm-trunks are) split in two.*
umbún-d(ı)‿ (§§2545 ff.) adj. *appertaining to the palm-trunk, of the palm-trunk.*
umbu-kǒl n. *Ambikol (on map), a village on the left bank of the Nile about four miles below Korti and 25 above Hambu-kǒl* [*having palm-trunks*].
obj. -kǒlg(ı)‿, -gi⌒.
umbukóllo‿ (s.v. -r‿) adv. *at (to) Umbukǒl.*
umbukóllo⌒ (§6007) *(s)he (it) is (they are) at Umbukǒl.*
úmbud‿ n. *salt* [< *úmmud‿ (§868) §2389; RSN, §129 s.v. *imid*].
obj. umbúdk(ı)‿, -útk(ı)‿, -útt(ı)‿ (§2462), -ki‿, -ti⌒.
gen. úmbudn‿v., -bunn‿v.c., -bun‿c.
pl. úmbud‿.
úmbun‿dád(ı)‿ *salt-bowl*, s.v. dádd(ı)‿.
umbún-d(ı)‿ (§§2545 ff.) adj. *appertaining to salt, of salt, saline.*
umbúššɛ‿ n. *tear(-drop)*; with collective sg. (§4696d) [< *umbúñše‿ < *-úñsɛ‿ < -*úññsɛ‿ < *umbúdñsɛ‿ < úmbud‿ *salt* +-ñ dim. (§4572) +-s dem. or dim. (§2319) +-ɛ‿ of n. ess. (§2234), so **that little existence of salt* §2322].
obj. -šɛg‿.
pl. umbuššénč(ı)‿.
umbúlbul (§1188) n. *beer* = umbílbıl‿.
obj. umbulbúlg(ı)‿, -gi⌒.
pl. umbúlbulı‿.
umdurmán (§956a) n. *Omdurmán* = búga‿ (a) [< اُمْ دُرْمان < اُمْ ...].
obj. -máŋ(ı)‿, -gi⌒.
umdurmándo‿ (s.v. -r‿) adv. *at (to) Omdurmán.*
umdurmándo⌒ (§6007) *(s)he (it) is (they are) at Omdurmán.*
umdurmán-an- (§3910β) v.i. *go to Omdurmán.*
umkarabığ‿, -ıč⌒ n. *Um Karabik (on map), a village on the right bank of the Nile, about five miles above Hándag* [< اُمّ كَرابيج *mother of whips*].
obj. -ığk(ı)‿, -íčk(ı)‿, -ğk-, -čk- (§323), -ki⌒.
úmur‿ n. *age* [< Sudan Ar. عُمُر = عُمْر *id.* §1363].
obj. umúrk(ı)‿, -ki⌒.
pl. úmurı‿.
ténn‿úmur‿mıŋkótterrɛ́? *how old is (s)he (it)?*
-un⌒ (-ū̃‿, -ú‿, -u‿ §939; §946; §§4229-31, 5770 ff.) *positive sign of predication is, are.*
-(u)n...-(u)n‿ *concretion-forming postposition both...and* (§4403).

— *suffixed to nom.*
álın‿ɛsmánun‿tǎgoran⌒ *ɛáli and ɛoθmán came (have come).*
ún‿ n. (a) *moon*; (b) *month* [cp. ON. оүн *id.* GCD, p. 11; ZNA, p. 194].
obj. úŋ(ı)‿, -gi⌒.
pl. únı‿.
ún‿ɛ́r‿ and
ún‿ɡɛdíd‿ *new moon.*
unátt(ı) n. *moon* [< *unárt(ı)‿ (§713) < ún‿ *moon* (§1062) +-ar‿ *nominal -ing* (§2200) +-t dem. (§§2323 ff.), so **that moon-(shin)ing*, **there being the moon* §2224].
obj. -tıg‿.
unátt‿ɛ́r‿ and
unáttı‿ɡɛdíd‿ *new moon.*
unátt‿ı‿bélsım‿bǎdır‿ *after the moon had risen.*
unátt‿ıtósıw‿wɛkítt(ı)‿ (-w‿w- < -n‿w- §720) *when the moon set.*
unáttıɡɛǧ‿ǧómbūn⌒ (-ǧ‿ǧ- < -d‿ǧ- §550) *(s)he is epileptic*, lit. *(s)he is moonstruck.*
únt(ı)‿ n. *dream* [§§2323, 2326].
obj. -tıg‿.
pl. -tınč(ı)‿.
úntın‿nálkori⌒ (-n‿n- < -g‿n- §625) *I (have) had (lit. saw, have seen) a dream.*
úntın‿nálkori‿ *I saw (have seen) him (her, it, them) in a dream.*
únčɛ‿ n. *pus, matter* [< *úññtɛ‿ (§901a) < úññ(ı)‿ *excrement* +-t. dem. or dim. (§§2323 ff.) +-ɛ‿ of n. ess. (§2234); §2239].
obj. -čɛg‿.
únč-an- (§3910α) v.i. *become pus, suppurate, fester.*
téŋ‿kŏr‿búnčanın⌒ *his (her, its) wound will fester.*
únčam-bŭ- (§§3949 ff.) v.i. stat. *be in a suppurating (etc.) state or condition.*
kŏr‿unčámbūn⌒ *the wound is festering.*
únčɛ-ko (§4119) v.i. *contain pus, be suppurating, be festering.*
íŋ‿kŏr‿únčɛkó⌒ *this wound contains pus.*
√únd- *be in or *put in (§4600).
und-ós (§3792) used as def. of úndur *put in, etc. (infra).*
ind. pres. aı‿undós(¹)ri⌒, ɛr‿undósın‿ (-sí⌒, -sí⌒); fut. aı‿bundós(¹)ri‿; perf. aı‿undóskori⌒.
imperat. undós! (undó! §962), pl. undóswɛ! (-ówwɛ! §724, -wé!, -óssɛ! §687, -sɛ́!).
subj. past aı‿undóssı‿ (-su‿).
ɛ́ŋ‿kálg‿undóskon⌒ *the woman has baked the bread.*
kálg‿undóskori, takalɛ́wwɛ́! *I have baked the bread, come (pl.) and eat!*
undós-dɛ̌n (-óddɛ̌n §538; §§4180-4, 3995 ff.; -ósgıdɛn, -ózgı-, -óggi- §4185) v.t. *give (to the speaker) after putting in, etc., put in (etc.) to or for (the speaker).*
undosdɛ̌n-ǧáŋg(ı) (-óddɛ̌n-, etc.; §4195) v.t. *fill by putting in for (the speaker).*
éssıg‿áıg‿undoddɛ̌ŋǧáŋgi‿ *fill it with water for me*, lit. *by putting water in for me fill (it).*

undílt(ı)‿ — úñur

undós-tır (-óttır §714, -óssır §686; §§4180-4, 3995 ff.; -ósgıtır, -ózgı-, -óggı- §4185) v.t. give (to other than the speaker) after putting in, etc., put in (etc.) to or for (other than the speaker).

undostır-ğáŋg(ı) (-ottır-, etc.; §4195) v.t. fill by putting in for (other than the speaker).
éssıt‿tékk‿undottırğáŋgıgoran⌢ (-t‿t- <-g‿t- §707) they (have) filled it with water for him (her).
éssıt‿tékk‿undossırğáŋgi⌢ fill it with water for him (her).
téŋ‿gírbag‿éssıt‿tékk‿undossırğáŋgıgori⌢ I (have) filled his (her) water-skin for him (her) with water.

únd-ur (§3675) v.t. (a) put in, introduce, insert; (b, put dough in dεur‿ on the bake-stone, that is placed on the fire, so) bake¹ [cp. ON. ουτουρ to place GNT s.v.].
ind. pres. aı‿undúddı⌢, εr‿úndurın⌢ (-rí⌢, -rí⌢); fut. aı‿bundúddı⌢; perf. aı‿undúrkori⌢ (-dúkko- §571a), εr‿undúrkon⌢ and εr‿úndurkon⌢.
imperat. úndur!, pl. úndurwε! (undúrwe! -dúwwε! §723; -wé!).
def. imperat. undurós! and more commonly undós!
désk‿éssırr‿undúddan⌢ they put (the) butter into a (the) bottle.
šaı‿tōddεg‿undúddıá? shall (§5369b) I put a little tea in?
ardahálgı‿tédd‿undúkkori⌢ I (have) put in a petition (sc. to the Government) against (-do‿) him (her).
kanıssε‿kóskın‿έn‿úndurın⌢ when the dough rises the woman bakes it.

úndurar (-ràr‿; §2200 ff., 2212) and
undurid (§§2256 ff., 2265) n. putting in, etc.

úndur-an (§§3890 ff., 3904) v.t. tell to put in, etc., let put in, etc.

únduran-dēn (§§5668-9) v.t. = undurεdēn.

únduran-tır (§§5668-9) v.t. = undurεtır.

únduran-ε-dēn (§§5668-9) v.t. = undurεdēn.

únduran-ε-tır (§§5668-9) v.t. = undurεtır.

úndur-dēn (undúrdēn; §§3995-7) v.t. put in for (the speaker), pass or hand in to (the speaker).
aıgı‿wawíddık‿kúbır‿undúrdēn⌢ give me the oar(s §4696d) into the boat.

úndur-tır (¯´˘; §§3995, 3998-9) v.t. put in for (other than the speaker), pass or hand in to (other than the speaker).
tékkı‿wawíddık‿kúbır‿undúrtır⌢ give him the oar(s §4696d) into the boat.

úndur-ε-dēn (§§5668-9) v.t. give (to the speaker) with instructions (-ε-) to put in, etc.

úndur-ε-tır (§§5668-9) v.t. give (to other than the speaker) with instructions (-ε-) to put in, etc.

undudd-εg-ág- (§§4071 ff.) v.t. = undurεdól-.

undur-ε-dól- (-rᵒd- §1178; §4022) and
undudd-ε-dól- (-dᵒd-; §4027) v.t. be about to put in, etc.

undudd-ε-ğŭ-bŭ- (§4069) v.t. stat. be on one's way (coming) to put in, etc.

undur-ε-má- (§4036) and
undudd-ε-má- (§4041) v.t. become unable to put in, etc.

undudd-ε-nóg (§§4048 ff.) v.t. go to put in, etc.

undudd-ε-nóg-bŭ- (-nóggŭ- §546; §4058) v.t. stat. be on one's way (going) to put in, etc.

undudd-ε-tá (§§4060 ff.) v.t. come to put in, etc.

undurεd-ág- (§§3877 ff.) v.t. be in the situation of having put in, etc.
índı‿kálg‿undurεdágın, takál⌢ my mother has baked (the) bread, come and eat.

undur-εlεū-bóg (§3765) v.t. after putting in (etc.) and rinsing pour out.
éssıd‿dádır‿undurεlεūbógó⌢ (§962; -d‿d- <-g‿d- §534) put water into the bowls (etc., s.v. dád(d)(ı)‿) and rinse them and pour it out.

undurεt-tá (§§4169 ff., 5723; undurεggı-tá §§4176-8) v.t. come (back) after putting in, etc., just go (§5713) and put in, etc.
imperat. undurεtta!, undurεggıta!

undur-εttá (-εttā §3855, §5723) v.t. bring (εttá s.v. έd) after putting in, etc.
imperat. undurεtta!
ínın‿tŭr‿undurέttāri⌢ I('ll §5369b) put it inside this and bring it.

undur-ğóğor (§3764) v.t. squeeze (etc., s.v. ğóğor) in (into).
N. áğwa‿tōddέk‿íččır‿undurğoğórkori⌢ I (have) squeezed a little of the soft dates in the milk.

undur-ğúrum (§3764) v.t. knead (etc., s.v. ğúrum) in (into).
áğwa‿tōddέg‿íččır‿undurğúrum⌢ knead a little of the soft dates in (the) milk.

unduríŋg-ır (˘´˘; N. -ŋkır; §3692) v.t. caus. cause or allow to put in, etc.
ind. pres. aı‿unduríŋgıddı⌢, ˘´˘˘˘

undurk-ídd(ı) (§3727) v.t. caus. cause or allow to put in, etc.
ind. pres. aı‿undurkíddıri⌢.
imperat. undúrkıddı!

undur-šákk(ı) (§3764) v.t. after putting (milk) in (a skin) shake (s.v. šákk(ı)).

undílt(ı)‿ hair of the head s.v. úr‿.

únt(ı)‿ n. dream s.v. ún‿.

úññ(ı)‿ n. excrement (of man, cat, dog); with collective sg. (§4696d) [<*usñ(ı)‿ <√ús- *crouch, *squat §4601)+-ñ‿ dim.].
obj. -ñıg‿.
pl. -ññč(ı)‿.
ádεm‿úññ(ı)‿ human excrement (of one person).
ádεmın‿úññ(ı)‿ human excrement (of more than one person).
sábın‿úññ(ı)‿ cat's excrement.
sábın‿úññ(ı)‿ cats' excrement.
wéln‿úññ(ı)‿ dog's excrement.
wéln‿úññ(ı)‿ dogs' excrement.
úññíŋ-kă- (§1676) latrine, privy.
obj. úññıŋ‿kăg‿.
úññıŋ‿kăr‿ in the latrine.

úñur v.t. (a) know; (b) understand [§2840].
ind. pres. aı‿uñúddı⌢ (⁻´´), εr‿úñurın⌢ (úñúrın⌢, ‿uñúrın⌢ §1539; -rí⌢, -rí⌢); perf. aı‿uñúrkori⌢ (-úkko- §571a).
subj. past aı‿uñúrsı‿ (-su‿).
part. pres. úñurıl‿ (one) that knows, etc., knower, etc., knowing, etc., obj. uñurílg(ı)‿, -gi⌢; past úñurεl‿ (one) that knew, etc., knower, etc., knowing, etc., obj. uñurέlg(ı)‿, -gi⌢.
pl.-obj. ind. pres. sg. 1 aı‿uñuríddi⌢.
árt‿úñurın⌢ God knows.
nı‿úñurın? and
nır‿uñúrın? who knows?
aı‿ısáır‿έrıg‿uñúddan⌢ they know where I am.
aı‿uñúrmun(un⌢) and
aı‿uñúmmun(un⌢ §§607, 947) I don't know (understand).
tεr‿núbag‿uñúmmunun⌢ (s)he doesn't know (understand) Nubian.
tεr‿bāg¹ráŋ‿uñúrna? and
tεr‿bāg¹ráŋ‿uñúnná? (§628a) can (s)he write?
óğğırtōm‿báččıg‿úñuríl-lēd‿dólli⌢ (-l-l- <-l-w- §580, -d‿d- <-g‿d- §534) I want one of the men that knows how to write.

úñurar (-ràr‿; §§2200 ff.) and
uñuríd (§§2256 ff.) n. knowledge, understanding.

uñur-áw (-áw, -áū; §3747ε') v.t. know how to do (etc., s.v. áu).
έm‿mérsεg‿uñuráwın⌢ the woman knows how to make beer.
gáhwag‿uñuraunā? do you (does (s)he) know how to make coffee?
írıg‿uñuráuri⌢ and (§5601)
uñurıgáuri⌢ I know how to make rope.

uñur-bág (§3747ε') v.t. know how to write, be able to write.
tεr‿uñurbáğná? can (s)he write?

uñúr-bŭ- (§3931β) v.i. stat. be in a known (etc.) state or condition.
massínčım‿báññıd‿índ‿uñúrbūn⌢ the Máhasi language is known here.

uñurεd-ág- (§§3877 ff.) v.t. be in the condition of having known, etc.

uñur-gεrjέ (-gεrέ; §3747ε') v.t. know how to read, be able to read.
ind. pres. aı‿uñurgεrjéri⌢ (occ. -jéri⌢ §1073), εr‿uñurgεrjén⌢ (-jě⌢, -jé⌢, -jé⌢, occ. -jén⌢, -jέ⌢, -jέ⌢).
εr‿íŋg‿uñurgεrjéná? can you read this?

uñur-ír (3747ε') v.t. (a) know how to count; (b) know how to make (rope) by rolling between the hands.
ind. pres. aı‿uñuríri⌢.
írıg‿uñurírran⌢ and
uñurıgírran⌢ they know how to make rope by rolling it between their hands.

uñurk-ídd(ı) (§3727) (a) v.t. caus. cause or allow to know, etc.; (b) v.t. teach, explain.
aı‿έkk‿íŋg‿uñurkíddıri⌢ I'll (§5369b) explain this to you.
uñúrkıddı! explain (him, her, it, them)!

uñúr-kattı- (§4093) v.p. be known, etc.

---
¹ Cp. our put the kettle (water, joint, etc.) on sc. the fire.

uñur-nǐǧ (§3747ε') v.t. *know how to sew, be able to sew.*

uñur-tabhɛ́ (-bxɛ́; §3747ε') v.t. *know how to cook, be able to cook.*
 ind. pres. āι‿uñurtabhɛ́riꞈ.
 perf. āι‿uñurtabhɛ́goriꞈ (N. -ɛ́ko-, -ɛ́ho-).

úŋgur‿ n. *Ungri (on map), a village on the right bank of the Nile, east of the centre of Argo Island.*
 obj. uŋgúrk(ι)‿, -kiꞈ.
 uŋgúrro‿ (s.v. -r‿) adv. *at (to) Uŋgur.*
 uŋgúrroꞈ (§6007) *(s)he (it) is (they are) at Uŋgur.*

úr n. *head* [√ú*d §4596a; RSN, §129 s.v. ör; cp. ON. ourp *id.* GNT s.v.; cogn. ór‿ *king*].
 obj. úrk(ι)‿, -kiꞈ.
 pl. úrι‿.
 — enclitic (§1671) in
 ánn-ur‿ *my head.*
 ɛ́nn-ur‿ *your head.*
 ténn-ur‿ *his (her, its) head.*
 tínn-urι‿ *their heads.*
 ánn-ur‿ā́ιg‿óddιnꞈ *my head hurts me, I have a headache.*
 tínn-ur‿tírg‿óddιnꞈ (§4647) and
 tínn-urι‿tírg‿óddιranꞈ *their heads ache.*
 ténn-urk‿āššírιnꞈ *she is plaiting her (another woman's) hair.*
 weǧádked‿eskédkι‿tínn-urro‿bōge-dágranꞈ *they have poured earth on their heads as a sign of mourning.*
 ténn-ur‿múttιbūn‿ *his (her) hair is (has been) cut short.*
 úrkι‿ǧáññιl‿ *one that shaves the head, barber.*
 kúffιn‿úr‿ *glans penis.*
 úr-ro‿ (a) on (in, to, s.v. -r‿) *the head;* (b) *in respect of animals) (reckoning) by the head.*
 ám‿bértιnč‿úrro‿díǧιnꞈ *my goats are five head.*
 bért‿úrro‿díččι‿kóriꞈ *I have five head of goats.*
 úrro‿ (§6007) *it is (they are) on (in) the head.*

úm-d(ι)‿ (§§2545ff.) adj. *appertaining to the head, of the head, the head's.*

undílt(ι)‿ n. *hair of the head; with collective sg.* (§4696a) [< *urndílt(ι)‿ (§621) < úrn‿dílt(ι)‿ §2150].
 obj. -tιg‿.
 pl. -tιnč(ι)‿.

úrt(ι)‿ (-tu‿ §1189) n. *with collective sg.* (§4696d) (a) *possession, thing that one has,* collective sg. *belongings, property,* esp. (b) *goat, sheep,* collective sg. *flock,* (like κτῆνος, Amh. ከብት) [< úr‿ *head* + -t dem. (§2326); cp. our *chattel, cattle* < Lat. *capitale what is counted by the head*; cp. ON. ourpti *id.* ZNA, p. 189].
 obj. -tιg‿, -tug‿.
 pl. úrtιnč(ι)‿, -tun‿, urtínč(ι)‿, -tún-.
 úrtι‿mɛ́rerton‿nígonꞈ and
 úrtι‿mɛ́rerton‿nígoranꞈ *the flock drank (have drunk) at (lit. from) the pool.*
 úrtιg‿íwιl‿ (-tug‿í-) *goatherd, shepherd.*
 urtúnčιrtów-wɛr‿dabóskóꞈ (-w-w- < -n‿w- §720) *one of the goats (sheep) has disappeared.*
 úrtιk‿kóranꞈ *they have (the) goats (sheep).*

úrtι-kιñ́ñ(ι)‿ (-tuk-; §§2536-7) adj. *without goats or sheep.*

úrtι-kō (-tuk-; §4115) v.i. *have goats (sheep).*
 part. úrtιkōl‿ (-tuk-) *(one) that has goats (sheep),* obj. urtιkōlg(ι)‿ (-tuk-), -giꞈ.
 úrtιkōranꞈ *they are goat-owners (sheep-owners).*

urtιn-d(ι)‿ (-tún-; §§2545ff.) adj. *appertaining to goats or sheep.*

urtιnčín-d(ι)‿ (-tun-; §§2545ff.) adj. *appertaining to goats (sheep), of the goats (sheep), goats', sheep's.*
 ín‿ιčč‿urtιnčíndín, tíndímununꞈ *this milk is goats', not cow's.*

úr n. *colocynth, bitter apple,* Citrullus colocynthis, Schrad. (BSP, 207), = tattúr‿ [§2053].
 obj. úrk(ι)‿, -kiꞈ.
 pl. úrι‿.

úr v.i. *break wind inaudibly* [§2053].
 ind. pres. āι‿úrri‿, ɛr‿úrιn‿ (‿úri‿, ‿úriꞈ); perf. āι‿úrkoriꞈ.

úrar‿ (úrár‿; §§2200ff.) and
úrid (§§2256ff.) nom. act.

úrιǧ v.i. *break wind audibly* [< úr + -ι- euphonic (§483β) + -ǧ intensive §2884].
 ind. pres. āι‿úrιǧriꞈ, ɛr‿úr(ι)ǧιnꞈ (-ǧiꞈ, -ǧiꞈ), perf. āι‿úrιǧkoriꞈ (-íčk-, úrǧk-, úrčk-, -gk-, -čk-).

úrǧar‿ (-ǧár-; §§2200ff.) and
urǧíd (§§2256ff.) nom. act.
 ūríd‿ulúkkeg‿gιǧιrkáttιmunun, urǧíd‿gíǧιrkáttιnꞈ (-g‿g < -d‿g §545)
 ūríd‿*is not perceived by the ear,* urǧíd *is perceived.*

úrd(ι)‿, -dιꞈ n. *El-Ordi (on map), the town on the left bank of the Nile now officially called Dongola* (دنقلا, دنقله [< اوردي camp §1389].
 obj. -dιg‿.

úrd-an- (§3910β) v.i. *go to El-Ordi.*
 ind. pres. āι‿úrdandi‿, ɛr‿úrdanιn‿ (-ní‿, -níꞈ); fut. āι‿búrdandiꞈ; perf. āι‿úrdaŋkoriꞈ.
 subj. past āι‿úrdansι‿ (-assι‿ §680, -su‿).

úrdam-bŭ- (§3950β) v.i. stat. *be in a state of motion towards El-Ordi, be on one's way to El-Ordi, be going to El-Ordi.*
 ind. pres. āι‿úrdambūriꞈ.

urdanɛd-ág- (§3966β) v.i. *be in the situation of having gone to El-Ordi.*

urdan-nog(¹)r-ɛg-ág- (§3980) v.i. =urdannogɛdól-.

urdan-nog-ɛ-dól- (-gºd- §1178; §3979) and
urdan-nog(¹)r-ɛ-dól- (-rºd-; §3981) v.i. *be about to go off to El-Ordi.*
 ar‿urdannogredóllu‿ *we are just going to go off to El-Ordi.*

urdan-nog-ɛ-mǎ- (§3982) and
urdan-nog(¹)r-ɛ-mǎ- (§3983) v.i. *become unable to go off to El-Ordi.*
 āι‿urdannogemágoriꞈ *I couldn't (was, have been, unable) to go off to El-Ordi.*

úrιǧ s.v. úr.

urówwa‿ n. *small trough or channel in water-wheel* (kólε‿); *the water flows from the larger trough* (sáblo‿) *through the urówwa‿ to the smaller trough* (ǧaráttarε‿); *the urówwa‿ is sometimes omitted* [< *uróswa‿ (§724) < úr(u)- *stream*, i.e. *water* + ósw(ε) *take* (pl.) *out* + -a(n) *say*, so *(what) says 'take (pl.) out the water'*; or urów- may be imperat. pl. of urós *rinse out* (def. of úru *rinse* §2178].
 obj. -wag‿.
 pl. -wanč(ι)‿.

úrr(ι) v.t. *press, press down, compress, squeeze* (= ǧákk(ι) a).
 ind. pres. āι‿úrrιri‿; perf. āι‿úrrιgoriꞈ (N. -ιko-, -ιho-).
 lēmúŋg‿úrri‿ *squeeze the lime(s) §4696b).*
 tɛr‿ánn-ιg‿úrrιgonꞈ *(s)he squeezed my hand(s §4696a).*

úrrar‿ (-rár‿; §§2200ff.) and
urríd (§§2256ff.) n. *pressure, etc.*

úrr-an (§§3890ff.) v.t. *tell to press, etc., let press, etc.*

úrrι-bŭ- (§3931β) v.i. stat. *be in a pressed (etc.) state or condition.*
 wíččιr‿kúlu‿dúl‿tógor‿úrrιbūn‿ (-l‿t- < -ln‿t- §813) *the stick is (being) pressed under a large stone* (sc. *to get straightened*).

urrɛd-ág- (§3877ff.) v.t. *be in the situation of having pressed, etc.*

úrrι-kattι- (N. -ιha-; §4093) v.p. *be pressed, etc.*

úrsε‿ n. *root;* with collective sg. §4696b) [RSN, §129].
 obj. -sεg‿.
 pl. -senč(ι)‿.
 ǧówwιn‿úrsε‿ *the root(s) of the tree.*
 ténn‿úrs‿óddιn‿ and
 ténn‿úrs‿óddιbūnꞈ *its roots are diseased.*

ursɛ́n-d(ι)‿ (§§2545ff.) adj. *appertaining to the root, of the root.*

úrta (-tá‿) n. *battalion* [< ارطة *id.*].
 obj. -tag‿, -tåg‿.
 pl. -tanč(ι)‿, -tǎn-.
 urtán-d(ι)‿ (§§2545ff.) adj. *appertaining to the (a) battalion, the (a) battalion's.*

úrt(ι)‿ *possession, goat, sheep,* s.v. úr‿.

úrtιna‿ (-tuna‿ §1189) adj. *short.*
 obj. -nag‿.
 pl. -nanč(ι)‿.
 ír‿úrtιnánꞈ (§1972) *the rope is short.*
 ógιǧ‿úrtιnan‿nálkoriꞈ (-n‿n- < -g‿n- §625) *I saw (have seen) the short man.*
 wɛ́kιd‿úrtιnánꞈ *the time is short.*

urtιna-tod (-tún-; §§2484, 2582) adj. *unsatisfactorily short.*
 voc. -tot!, -tó!
 obj. -tŏdk(ι)‿, -tŏtk(ι)‿, -tŏkk(ι)‿, -tŏtt(ι) §2462, -kiꞈ, -tiꞈ.
 gen. -tŏdn‿v., -tŏnn‿v.c., -tŏn‿c.
 pl. urtínatonι‿, -tún-.
 urtúnatodun‿ *(s)he (it) is wretchedly short.*

úrtιn-an- (-tun-; §3910α) v.i. *become short.*
 wɛ́kιd‿urtιnáŋkoꞈ *the time (has) got short.*

úru⌣ — úsk(ı)

úrtınam-bŭ- (-tun-; §§ 3949 ff.) v.i. stat. *be in a state of becoming or having become short.*
  wékıd⌣urtunámbūn⌢ *the time has got short.*
urtınág-ır (-tun-; N. -ákır, -áhır; §3701) (a) v.t. caus. *cause or allow to be short;* (b) v.t. *shorten.*
  írıg⌣urtınagíddı⌢ *I('ll §5369b) shorten the rope.*
úru⌣ n. (a) *great water, river,* esp. (b) *Nile* [cp. Eg. *ı͗trw* Strom *ÆGl*, Copt. єιοορ, єιєρο Fluss *SKG*, §§ 71*, 76*, 114*; *RSN*, §§ 129, 200, W. Till in *WZKM*, 36, p. 189].
  obj. úrug⌣.
  pl. úrunč(ı)⌣.
  umbúdn⌣úru⌣ *the sea* [cp. بَحْرُ المَالِحِ *id.*].
  ıŋɛ́ŋg⌣úru⌣dúlun⌢ *this year the Nile is high, lit. ...is great.*
  úrun⌣tí⌣, úrún⌣tí⌣ and urún-tı⌣ (§2355) *hippopotamus,* lit. *cow of the river* [> Sudan Ar. قِرِنْت *gırínt id.*].
  obj. úrun⌣tíg⌣.
  úrugeb⌣bówwıran⌣ (-b⌣b- < -d⌣b- §518; §§ 5452-3) *instrument for swimming in the river,* i.e. *inflated skin(s).*
uru-nắr (§2364) n. *river-bank* = úrun⌣ắr⌣.
urún-d(ı)⌣ (§§ 2545 ff.) adj. *appertaining to the (a) great water, etc.*
úru v.t. *wash out, rinse* [§2049].
  ind. pres. aı⌣úruri⌢, er⌣úrun⌣ (⌣úrū⌣, ⌣úrú⌣); perf. aı⌣úrugori⌢ (N. -uko-, -uho-).
  def. urós.
  ánn⌣agílg⌣úrugori⌢ *I (have) rinsed my mouth.*
úrub⌣, -up⌢ n. *Urbi* (on map), a village on the left bank of the Nile, about ten miles below Hándag.
  obj. urúbk(ı)⌣, -úpk(ı)⌣, -ki⌢.
  úrubır⌣ (s.v. -r⌣) adv. *at (to) U.*
  úrubır⌣ (§6007) *(s)he (it) is (they are) at U.*
úruğ⌣ = húruğ⌣ *Acacia albida.*
úrum⌣ n. *black substance* [*RSN*, §§ 129, 200].
  obj. urúmg(ı)⌣, -gi⌢.
  pl. urumı⌣.
  ígn⌣urum⌣ *soot.*
urúmmɛ⌣ adj. (a) *black;* (b) *dark, without light;* (c) *dark-coloured,* e.g. *dark blue* [§§ 2517-18].
  obj. -mɛg⌣.
  pl. urúmmɛr⌣ and urumménč(ı)⌣.
  urúmmɛ⌣ (-mɛ⌢, urúmmɛ́⌢ §939) *(s)he (it) is black;* etc.
  ğóww⌣urúmmɛ⌣ *Acacia arabica, Willd.* (*BSP*, 181).
urúmmɛ-kırı⌣ (§§ 2539-40) adj. *blackish, rather dark, dusky.*
urámm-an- (§3910α) v.i. *become black, etc.*
  ind. perf. tɛr⌣urúmmaŋkon⌣ (-kŏ⌢, -kó⌢).
  gŭ⌣urúmmaŋkogın⌣kắr⌣ğuráŋg⌣ısándırı⌢ *when it has got dark I am afraid to go to the house.*

urúmmɛg-ır (N. -ɛkır, -ɛhır; §3701) (a) v.t. caus. *cause or allow to be black, etc.;* (b) v.t. *blacken, darken.*
urúmı⌣, -mi⌢ (rúmı⌣) n. *Rumi* (on map) name of two villages on the left bank of the Nile, 15-17 miles above Hándag.
  obj. -mıg⌣.
  urúmı⌣kánnɛ⌣ *Urúmi North.*
  urúm⌣óŋgo⌣ *Urúmi South.*
urúttɛ v.i. *wink* [cp. K. *úru* sehen, betrachten *AZN* s.v., *SNK*, 197; §§ 2870 ff.].
  ind. pres. aı⌣urútterı⌢; perf. aı⌣urúttɛgori⌢ (N. -ɛko-, -ɛho-).
ús⌣ adj. (a) *bad;* (b, of persons) *of bad character, evil, wicked* [< *low, *base, *inferior,* cogn. √ús- *crouch* §4601; *RSN*, § 129].
  obj. úsk(ı)⌣, ki⌢.
  pl. úsı⌣.
  nél⌣úsun⌢ *the tooth is bad.*
  ín⌣ógığ⌣úsun⌢ *this man is bad.*
  ɛn⌣ógıñ⌣dógor⌣úsun⌢ (-ñ⌣d- < -ğn⌣d- §632) *the woman is worse than the man.*
ús-an- (§3910α) v.i. *become bad, deteriorate.*
  ind. pres. aı⌣úsandı⌢; perf. aı⌣úsaŋkori⌢.
úsam-bŭ- (§§ 3949 ff.) v.i. stat. *be in a state of becoming or having become bad, be in a deteriorating (-ated) state or condition.*
usánd(ı) (isán-, sán-; § 5546) (a) v.i. *be afraid;* (b) v.t. *fear* = sánd(ı), q.v.
  ind. pres. aı⌣usándırı⌣; fut. aı⌣busándırı⌣; perf. aı⌣usándıgori⌢ (N. -ıko-, -ıho-).
úskadɛ⌣ (úskádɛ⌣ §1532) n. *catarrh in nose or throat* = ískıdɛ⌣ (§§ 1151, 1171).
  obj. -dɛg⌣.
  ín⌣úskadé-taran⌢ *this is catarrh.*
  úskad⌣áıg⌣ārɛdágın⌢ *I have a cold in the head.*
úsk(ı) (a) v.i. *bear, have a child, produce young;* (b) v.t. *bear, give birth to* [< √ús- *crouch,* *sit §4601 (עַל־הָאָבְנַיִם) Ex. 1¹⁶ *GBH* s.v. אָבֵן) + -k(ı) §§ 2853-4; -k(ı) app. intensive in a, causative in b].
  ind. pres. aı⌣úskırı⌢; fut. aı⌣búskırı⌢; perf. aı⌣úskıgori⌢ (N. -ıko-, -ıho-).
  def. perf. aı⌣uskóskori⌢.
  ténn⌣ɛn⌣uskóskon⌢ *his wife has had a child.*
  X. ɛnn⌣ɛn⌣míŋg⌣úskıgó? *what child did your wife have?* (...*has your wife had?*).
  Y. barsínčıgı⌣ *twins.*
  tí⌣bárs⌣ówwıg⌣uskóskó⌢ *the cow has had twin calves.*
  sáb⌣bıtáŋ⌣kemísk⌣uskóskó⌢ *the cat has had four kittens.*
úskar⌣ (-kár⌣; §§ 2200 ff., 2217) n. *midwife.*
  obj. uskárk(ı)⌣, -ki⌢.
  pl. úskarı⌣.
úskıd (-kıd⌣; §§ 2256 ff.) n. *parturition.*
  obj. uskídk(ı)⌣, -kítk(ı)⌣, -kítt(ı)⌣ §2462, -kíd-, -kít-, -ki⌢, -ti⌢.
  pl. úskıdı⌣, -kıdı⌣.
úskı-bŭ- (§3931β) v.i. stat. *be in a born state or condition.*

  tém⌣bıtán⌣úskıbūn⌢ *his (her) child is (has been) born.*
uskır-ɛg-ág- (§§ 4071 ff.) v.i. and t. = uskɛdól-.
usk-ɛ-dól- (-kᵒd- §1178; §4022) and
uskır-ɛ-dól- (-rᵒd- §4027) v.i. and t. *be about to bear, etc.*
  ténn⌣ɛn⌣uskɛdólın⌢ *his wife is about to have a child.*
úski-kattı- (N. -ıha-; §4093) v.p. *be born.*
úsk-ur (§3685) v.t. (a) *set, place, put, lay;* (b) *set down, put down, lay down;* (c) *pay (price, cost)* [< *úskır (§1189) < √ús- *sit (§4601) + -k- obj. suff. + -ır causative; cp. ON. ονсκονρ *id. GNT* s.v.].
  ind. pres. aı⌣uskúddı⌢, ɛr⌣úskurın⌣ (-rǐ⌢, -rí⌢); fut. aı⌣buskúddı⌢; perf. aı⌣uskúrkori⌢.
  imperat. úskur!, pl. uskúrwɛ! (úskurwɛ́!, -úwwɛ! §723, -wɛ́!).
  subj. past aı⌣uskúrsı⌣ (⌣‒̑́⌣ §1806; -ússı⌣ §683, -su⌣).
  neg. imperat. tókkon⌣uskúrmɛn! (mɛ̃!, -mé!), pl. tókkon⌣uskúrmɛwwɛ! (-wɛ́!).
  pl.-obj. ind. pres. aı⌣uskurıddı⌢.
  def. perf. aı⌣uskuróskori⌢ and (wrongly used) aı⌣uskóskori⌢.
  X. (giving Y. a letter to post) tábag⌣ úskur⌢ *put the stamp* (sc. *on the letter*).
  Y. uskúddi⌢ *I will* (§§ 5364, 5369b).
  šántag⌣áŋgárɛŋ⌣kóččır⌣uskúrkoran⌢ *they (have) placed the valise on the bedstead.*
  íŋg⌣íŋın⌣kóččır⌣úskur⌢ *put this on that.*
  márɛm⌣mahzánd⌣uskuróskoran⌢ (-m⌣m- < -g⌣m- §601) and márɛm⌣mahzánd⌣uskóskoran⌢ *they have put the millet into the store.*
  ar⌣šahárro⌣gín⌣ówwıb⌣buskúddu⌣ (-b⌣b- < -g⌣b- §519) *we shall pay two pounds a month.*
úskurar⌣ (-rár⌣; §§ 2200 ff., 2212) and
uskuríd⌣ (§§ 2256 ff., 2265) n. *setting, etc.*
úskur-an (§§ 3890 ff., 3904) v.t. *tell to set, etc., let set, etc.*
***úskur-bŭ-** said by many not to be in use.
uskúr-dɛn (úskurdɛ̌n; §§ 3996-7) v.t. *set (etc.) for (the speaker).*
  índ⌣uskúrdɛn⌣ *put it (them) here for me.*
uskudd-ɛg-ág- (§§4071 ff.) v.t. = ⌣uskurɛdól-.
uskur-ɛ-dól- (-rᵒd- §1178; §4025) and
uskudd-ɛ-dól- (-dᵒd- §4033) v.t. *be about to set, etc.*
uskudd-ɛ-gŭ́-bŭ- (§4069) v.t. stat. *be on one's way (coming) to set, etc.*
uskur-ɛ-má- (§4039) and
uskudd-ɛ-má- (§4046) v.t. *become unable to set, etc.*
uskudd-ɛ-nóg (§§ 4048, 4057) v.t. *go to set, etc.*
  ind. pres. aı⌣uskuddɛnógrı⌢.
uskudd-ɛ-nóg-bŭ- (-nóggŭ- § 546; §4058) v.t. stat. *be on one's way (going) to set, etc.*
uskudd-ɛ-tá- (§4060, 4068) v.t. *come to set, etc.*
uskurɛd-ág- (§§ 3877, 3883) v.t. *be in the situation of having set, etc.*

uskuríŋ-ɪr (⁓; N. -ŋkɪr; §3692) v.t. caus. *cause or allow to set, etc.*
ind. pres. aı⏜uskuríŋgıddı⏜, ⁓,

uskúr-kattı- (uskúrkattı-; §4093) v.p. *be set, etc.*

uskúr-tɪr (úskurtɪr; §§3998-9) v.t. *set (etc.) for (other than the speaker).*

uskuroğ-ğammɛ-nóg (§556; §4203; -osgı-, -ozgı-, -oggı §4205; -ğammɛ-nog (§1964) emphasizing -ğammɛ-together) v.t. *after setting (object §5592) go together.*

uskuros-nóg (-onnóg §629; §§4180-4; -osgınóg, -ozgı-, -oggı §4185) v.t. *go (away) after setting, etc.*

uskuros-tá (-ottá §714; §§4180-4; -osgıtá, -ozgı-, -oggı §4185) v.t. *come after setting, etc., just (s.v. -tá) set, etc., go (§5713) and set, etc.*
íŋ⏜uskurótta⏜ *come when you've put that down (= go and put that down).*

úss(1) (a) v.i. *evacuate the bowels, defecate;* (b) v.t. *evacuate from the bowels* [√ús- *crouch §4601*].
ind. pres. aı⏜ússırı⏜; perf. aı⏜ússıgorı⏜ (N. -iko-, -iho-).
imperat. ússı!
def. perf. aı⏜ussóskorı⏜.

ússar⏜ (-dȧr; §§2200ff.) and
ussíd⏜ (§§2256ff.) n. *defecation.*

ussɪr-ɛ-nóg (§§4048ff.) v.i. and t. *go to defecate, etc.*
ind. pres. aı⏜ussırenógrı⏜.

ussɛd-ȧg- (§§3877ff.) v.i. and t. *be in the condition of having defecated, etc.*

ussíŋ-ɪr (ússıŋɪr; N. -ŋkɪr; §3688) (a) v.t. caus. *cause or allow to defecate, etc.;* (b) v.t. *purge.*
ín⏜dáw⏜ússıŋgırın⏜ *this medicine is laxative.*

ústa⏜ n. *craftsman, artisan* [< أُسْطَى id. < أُسْتَاذ *master craftsman*].
obj. -tag⏜.
pl. tanč(ı)⏜.

úsu v.i. *laugh.*
ind. pres. aı⏜úsurı⏜, ɛr⏜úsun⏜ (⏜úsú⏜, ⏜úsú⏜); perf. aı⏜úsugorı⏜ (N. -uko-, -uho-).
subj. past aı⏜úsusı⏜ (-su⏜).
tén⏜kóččır⏜úsuran⏜ *they laugh at him (her, it).*

úsud-, **-ut**⏜ n. (a) *buttock;* with collective sg. (§4696a); (b) *anus* [< *úsıd- (§1189) < √ús- **squat (§4601)+ -ıd- *making, causation (§2256), so *(action of) squatting, then concrete (§2268) §2340); popularly identified with أُسْت id.*].
obj. usúdk(ı)⏜, -útk(ı)⏜, -útt(ı)⏜ §2462, -kı⏜, -tı⏜.
gen. úsudn⏜v., úsunn⏜v.c., úsun⏜c.
pl. úsudı⏜.
ɪmbábn⏜úsut! *patris tui anus!* and
ɪmbábn⏜úsutti! *patris tui anum! (sc. ineo RN s.v. Usut), a vulgar curse* (cp. طِيز أَبُوك *id.*).
mán⏜ɛn⏜ténn⏜úsudı⏜dúlınčín⏜ (§4881) *that woman's buttocks are large.*

usús⏜ n. (a) *whistle (natural sound), whistling;* (b, *of bird*) *piping, song* = ɪsís⏜ [onom. §2153].
obj. -úsk(ı)⏜, -kı⏜.
pl. -úsı⏜.
tód⏜usúskı⏜ğómın⏜ *the boy whistles.*
káwɪrtɛ⏜usúskı⏜ğómın⏜ *the bird sings (the birds sing §4647).*

úwɛ v.t. *call, summon* [< √úw- onom. (§4602) + -ɛ *say* (§§2870ff.), *say 'úw!' to;* cp. ON. ᚢᛋᚢᛆ *cry out* GNT s.v.].
ind. pres. aı⏜úwɛrı⏜, ɛr⏜úwɛn⏜ (⏜úwɛ̃⏜, ⏜úwé⏜); fut. aı⏜búwɛrı⏜; perf. aı⏜úwɛgorı⏜ (N. -ɛko-, -ɛho-).
imperat. úwɛ!, pl. úwɛwɛ! (-wé!).
subj. past aı⏜úwɛsı⏜ (-su⏜).
part. pres. úwɛl⏜ (one) *that calls, etc., caller, calling,* obj. ūwɛlg(ı)⏜, -gi⏜;
past úwɛrɛl⏜ (one) *that called, etc., caller, calling,* obj. ūwɛrɛlg(ı)⏜, -gi⏜.
úwɛgoná? *did you (he, she) call?*
māmúr⏜tírgı⏜búwɛrırın⏜ *the district officer (mavmúr) will summon (each of §5456) them.*

úwɛrar⏜ (-dȧr⏜; §§2200ff., 2210) and
ūwɛríd⏜ (§§2256ff., 2263) n. *calling, summons.*

úwɛr-an (§§3890ff., 3899) v.t. *tell to call, etc., let call, etc.*

úwɛ-bū- (§3931β) v.i. stat. *be in a called (etc.) state or condition.*
aı⏜mérkɛzɪr⏜úwebūrı⏜ *I am (have been) summoned to the government office.*

úwɛr-ɛg-ȧg- (§§4071ff.) v.t. = ūwɛrɛdól-.

úwɛr-ɛ-dól- (-rºd- §1178; §§4016-17, 4022, 4027) v.t. *be about to call, etc.*

úwɛr-ɛ-ğŭ-bū- (§4069) v.t. stat. *be on one's way (coming) to call, etc.*

úwɛr-ɛ-má- (§§4016-17, 4036, 4041) v.t. *become unable to call, etc.*

úwɛr-ɛ-nóg (§§4048ff.) v.t. *go to call, etc.*

úwɛr-ɛ-nóg-bū- (-nóggū- §546; §4058) v.t. stat. *be on one's way (going) to call, etc.*

úwɛr-ɛ-tá (§§4060ff.) v.t. *come to call, etc.*

úwɛg-ɪr (N. -ɛkɪr, -ɛhɪr; §3679) v.t. caus. *cause or allow to call, etc.*
māmúrk⏜aı⏜tékkı⏜úwɛgıddı⏜ *I (shall §5369a) get the district officer (mav-múr) to summon him (her).*

úwɛ-kattı- (N. -ɛha-; §4093) v.p. *be called, etc.*

ūwɛ-mísɪr (§3747ɛ') v.t. *after calling fail to find (etc., s.v. mísɪr).*

wád (a) v.t. *bleed, draw blood from;* (b) v.i. *have oneself bled, be bled.*
ind. pres. aı⏜wád(!)rı⏜, ɛr⏜wádın⏜ (-dí⏜, -dí⏜); perf. aı⏜wádkorı⏜ (⏜wátk-).
imperat. wát!

wádar⏜ (-dȧr⏜; §§2200ff.) and
wadíd⏜ (§§2256ff.) n. *blood-letting.*

wád-an (§§3890ff.) v.t. *tell to bleed, let bleed, etc.*

wád-bū- (§3931β) v.i. stat. *be in a bled state or condition.*
ádɛm⏜wádbūn⏜ *the man (woman) has been bled.*

wadɛd-ȧg- (§§3877ff.) v.t. *be in the situation of having bled, etc.*

aı̄gı⏜wadɛdágın⏜ *he has bled me.*

wád-kattı- (wátk-; §4093) v.p. *be bled.*

wádag n. *animal fat, grease* [< وَدَك *id.*].
obj. wadágk(ı)⏜, -ákk(ı)⏜, -ki⏜.
gen. wadágn⏜v., wadán⏜c., ⏜.
pl. wádagı⏜.

wádah adj. *clear, plain, intelligible* [< وَاضِح *id.* §1340].
obj. wādáhk(ı)⏜, -ki⏜.
pl. wádahı⏜.
tém⏜báñnıd⏜wádahun⏜ *his (her) language is clear.*

waddɛ́ v.i. *perform ablutions (before prayer)* [< *a stem of Sudan Ar.* اِتْوَضَّأ *id.* + -ɛ́ §3653].
ind. pres. aı⏜waddɛ́rı⏜; perf. aı⏜waddɛ́gorı⏜ (N. -ɛ́ko-, -ɛ́ho-).
imperat. waddɛ́!, pl. waddɛ́wɛ! (-dɛ́wɛ́!).
sıgíddann⏜ogóllo⏜waddɛ́ran⏜ *they perform ablutions before saying their prayers.*

waddɛ́rar⏜ (-rȧr⏜; §§2200ff., 2207) and
waddɛ́ríd⏜ (§§2256ff., 2260) n. *performance of ablutions (etc.).*

waddɛ́r-an (§§3890ff., 3899) v.t. *tell to perform ablutions (etc.).*

waddɛ́-bū- (§3931α) v.i. stat. *be in the state or condition of having performed ablutions (etc.).*

waddɛ́-kattı- (N. -ɛ́ha-; §5707) v.p. impersonal.
waddɛ́kattın⏜ *ritual ablutions are (can be §5704) performed.*

wádd(1) v.t. *dig, dig up, dig out, excavate* (o.v. kúdub) [§2868].
ind. pres. aı⏜wáddırı⏜; perf. aı⏜wáddıgorı⏜ (N. -iko-, -iho-).
imperat. wáddi!
part. pres. wáddıl⏜ (one) *that digs, etc., digger, etc., digging, etc.,* obj. waddılg(ı)⏜, -gi⏜; past wáddɛl⏜ (one) *that dug, etc., digger, etc., digging, etc.,* obj. waddɛlg(ı)⏜, -gi⏜.
ógığ⏜arítkı⏜túbrogɛw⏜wáddın⏜ (-w⏜w- < -d⏜w- §718) *the man digs up the earth with a hoe.*
nógorı⏜wáddımunan⏜ *female slaves don't dig.*
kúl⏜dúlgı⏜waddóskó⏜ *he has dug a large hole.*

wáddar⏜ (-dȧr⏜; §§2200ff.) and
waddíd⏜ (§§2256ff.) n. *digging, etc.*

wádd-an (§§3890ff.) v.t. *tell to dig, etc., let dig, etc.*

wáddı-bū- (§3931β) v.i. stat. *be in a dug (etc.) state or condition.*
kúl⏜wáddıbūn⏜ *the (a) hole is (has been) dug.*

waddɛd-ȧg- (§§3877ff.) v.t. *be in the situation of having dug, etc.*
kúlgı⏜waddɛdágın⏜ *he has dug the (a) hole.*

wadd-él (§3747ɛ') v.t. *find after (on, by) digging, etc.*
kúlu⏜kúmbukırı⏜dúl-lēw⏜waddél-koran⏜ (-l-l- < -l-w- §580, -w⏜w- < -g⏜w- §719) *on digging they (have) found a large oval stone.*

wáddı-kattı- (N. -ıha-; §4093) v.p. *be dug, etc.*

wádın — ⌣wála⌣ . . . ?

kúl⌣wáddıkattın⌢ *the (a) hole is dug.*
N. kúl⌣dŭl-lɛ̄r⌣waddıhattóskó⌢ (§ 1030; -l-l- < -l-w- § 580) *a large hole has been dug.*

wádıñ v.i. and t. *kick* [? < √wá*d- *apart* (§ 4604) + euphonic -ı- + -ñ, as we say *to let out* § 2895].
ind. pres. aı̄⌣wadıñrı⌢, ɛr⌣wádıñın⌢ (-ñí⌢, -ñí⌢); perf. aı̄⌣wadıñkori⌢.
kám-mɛ̄r⌣tékkı⌣wadıñóskó⌢ (-m⌣m- < -m⌣w- § 603) *a camel has kicked him (her, it).*

wadıñar⌣ (-ñɑr⌣; §§ 2200 ff.) and
wadıñíd⌣ (§§ 2256 ff.) n. *kicking.*

wádıñ-bŭ- (§ 3931 β) v.i. stat. *be in a kicked state or condition.*
ógığ⌣wádıñbūn⌢ *the man has been kicked.*

wadıñ-ɛg-ág- (§§ 4071 ff.) v.i. and t. = wadıñɛdól-.

wadıñ-ɛ-dól- (-ñ°d- § 1178; § 4022) and
wadıñɛ-ɛ-dól- (-r°d-; § 4027) v.i. and t. *be about to kick.*

wadıñɛd-ág- (§§ 3877 ff.) v.i. and t. *be in the situation of having kicked.*
káğ⌣aı̄gı⌣wadıñɛdágın⌢ *the horse has kicked me.*

wadıñ-ğóm (§ 3747 ε') v.t. *strike by kicking, kick.*
hánu⌣bıtáŋgı⌣wadıñğómkó⌢ *the donkey gave (has given) the child a kick.*

wádu⌣ n. *water for ritual ablutions* [< وَضوء id.].
obj. -ug⌣.

wadún-d(ı)⌣ (§§ 2545 ff.) adj. *appertaining to water for ritual ablutions.*
ıbríg⌣wadúnd(ı)⌣ *pot for water for ritual ablutions.*

waffıré v.i. and t. *save, husband, lay by* [< imperat. or imperf. stem of وَقَر id. + -έ § 3635].
ind. pres. aı̄⌣waffırέri⌢; perf. aı̄⌣waffırέ-gori⌢ (N. -έko-, -έho-).
imperat. waffıré!
aı̄⌣án⌣dúngıb⌣bıdabírmunun, bımew⌣waffırέri⌢ (§ 6093; -b⌣b- < -g⌣b- § 519, -ww- < -nw- § 721) *I shall not spend my money but (-mɛn-) shall save it.*
dúngıw⌣waffırέgan⌣génun⌢ (-w⌣w- < -g⌣w- § 719; § 5449) *saving money is good.*

waffırέrar⌣ (-rɑr⌣; §§ 2200 ff., 2207) and
waffırέríd⌣ (§§ 2256 ff., 2260) n. *saving, etc.*

waffırέr-an (§ 3890 ff., 3899) v.t. *tell to save, etc., let save, etc.*

waffıré-bŭ- (§ 3931 β) v.i. stat. *be in a saved (etc.) state or condition.*
dúngı⌣waffırέbun⌢ *the money is (has been) saved.*

waffırέr-ɛ-má- (§§ 4016–17, 4036, 4041) v.i. and t. *become unable to save, etc.*

waffırέrɛd-ág- (§§ 3877 ff.) v.i. and t. *be in the situation of having saved, etc.*

waffırέ-kattı- (N. -έha-; § 4093) v.p. *be saved, etc.*

wahag-, wȧhag- n. *omission* [< وَعْك *prostration, diminution* § 1264].
obj. wahágk(ı)⌣, wȧh-, -hákk(ı)⌣, -ki⌢ [> wákk(ı) *omit*].
gen. wahágn⌣, wȧh-.
asál⌣wȧhágn⌣έss(ı)⌢ *the water of (i.e. to be brought, given, etc.) the day after tomorrow.*

⌣wahágk(ı)⌣ (⌣wȧh-, -hákk(ı)⌣) postp. (= prep. § 4356) *with the omission of, omitting,* in asál⌣wahákk(ı)⌣ (-l⌣w- < -ln⌣w- § 815) adv. (*on*) *the day after tomorrow,* lit. *with the omission of tomorrow.*
asál⌣wahákkı⌣bıtaran⌢ *they will come the day after tomorrow.*

wȧhaš⌣ n. *wild beast;* with collective sg. (§ 4696 d) [< وَحْش id. § 1357].
obj. wahášk(ı)⌣, -ki⌢.
pl. wȧhašı⌣.

wȧ̆i⌣ (wȧi⌣) n. *distant past time, antiquity, ancient times* [< *wȧri⌣ < √wá*d- *distant, remote* (§ 4604) + -i⌣ § 2253 β].
obj. wȧig⌣, wȧ̆ig⌣.

wȧ̆in-d(ı)⌣ (wȧind(ı)⌣; §§ 2545 ff.) adj. *appertaining to antiquity, ancient.*

wȧ̆ig⌣ (wȧ̆ig⌣, -gi⌢; § 4431) adv. *in ancient times.*
wȧ̆iŋ⌣kúlukırın⌢ (-ŋ-k- < -n⌣k- § 655; § 5056) *it's like an ancient stone.*

wȧ̆ikıd⌣ (wȧik-) n. = wȧ̆i⌣ [< wȧ̆ik- app. older obj. case of wȧ̆i⌣ + -ıd⌣ **making*, *formation*, so or. *antiquity-formation § 2260 a].
obj. wȧ̆ikídk(ı)⌣, wȧ̆ik-, -ítk(ı)⌣, -ítt(ı)⌣ § 2462, -ki⌢, -ti⌢.
wȧ̆ikıŋ⌣kúlu⌣ (-ŋ-k- < -dn⌣k- § 651) (*the*) *ancient stone(s § 4696 d).*

wȧ̆ikídk(ı)⌣, wȧ̆ik-, etc. (§ 4431) adv. *in ancient times.*

wajjé v.i. *recover, get well, get better, heal* [< وَعي *recovery* + -έ §§ 1263, 3629].
ind. pres. aı̄⌣wajjέri⌢, ɛr⌣wajjέn⌣ (-jέ⌢, -jέ⌢); perf. aı̄⌣wajjέgori⌢ (N. -έko-, -έho-).
imperat. wajjé!
def. pres. aı̄⌣wajjɛ̄róskori⌢.
kór⌣bıwajjέn⌢ *the wound will get better.*
wajjέroskoran⌢ *they have recovered.*
áŋ⌣kór⌣wajjέroskó⌢ *my wound has healed.*

wajjέrar⌣ (-rɑr⌣; §§ 2200 ff., 2207) and
wajjέríd⌣ (§§ 2256 ff., 2260) n. *recovery, healing.*

wajjέ-bŭ- (§ 3931 α) v.i. stat. *be in a recovered state or condition.*
wajjέbūran⌢ *they have recovered (they are better).*

wajjέrɛd-ág- (§§ 3877 ff.) v.i. *be in the condition of having recovered, etc.*

wajjέr-ɛg-ág- (§§ 4071 ff.) v.i. = wajjέr-ɛdól-.

wajjέr-ɛ-dól- (-r°d- § 1178; §§ 4016–17, 4022, 4027) v.i. *be about to recover, etc.*
wajjɛ̄rέdólın⌢ *(s)he (it) is nearly well again.*

wajjέg-ır (N. -έkır, -έhır; § 3681) (a) v.t. caus. *cause or allow to recover, etc.;* (b) v.t. *cure.*
ind. pres. aı̄⌣wajjέgıddi⌢.
hakím⌣tékkı⌣wajjέgırkó⌢ *the doctor (has) cured him (her).*
hakím⌣áŋ⌣kórkı⌣wajjέgıróskó⌢ *the doctor has healed my wound.*

wakíl⌣ (wȧk-, wɛk-) n. *agent, representative, local manager, postmaster, stationmaster* [< وَكيل id.].
obj. -kílg(ı)⌣, -gi⌢.
pl. -kílı⌣.
bústan⌣wakíl⌣ (-aw⌣wa- § 720) *postmaster.*

wákk(ı) v.t. *omit, leave out, miss out, pass over* [< wahákk(ı)⌣ s.v. wahag- § 2852; but Schäfer *SNK*, 762 includes K. *wakke lassen* among Nubian verbs, i.e. those not of Arabic origin].
ind. pres. aı̄⌣wákkıri⌢; perf. aı̄⌣wákkıgori⌢ (N. -ıko-, -ıho-).
imperat. wákki!
tóskıt⌣talabέgori, ówwıg⌣ıšínkó, wɛw⌣wákkıgó⌢ (-t⌣t- < -g⌣t- § 707, -w⌣w- < -g⌣w- § 719) *I (have) asked for three, (s)he has sent two and left one out.*
íŋgı⌣wákkı⌣mángɛn⌣nók⌢ (-n⌣n- < -d⌣n- § 624) *pass by this (turning, etc. and) go by (-ɛd⌣) that (other way).*
X. ékkı⌣míŋgı⌣tíkkó? *what did (s)he give (has (s)he given) you?*
Y. aı̄gı⌣wákkıgon, šέjı⌣wέd⌣dέŋkó⌣munun⌢ (-d⌣d- < -g⌣d- § 534) *(s)he (has) passed me over, (s)he didn't give (hasn't given) me anything.*
Z. wakkóskon, aı̄gı⌣dέŋkon⌣dámunun⌢ *(s)he has passed (me) over, (s)he didn't give (hasn't given) me anything.*

-wakk(ı)⌣, -ki⌢ (§ 4345) postp. (= prep. § 4287) *omitting, leaving out, except, but, less* [unstressed, enclitic form of wákk(ı)] suffixed to the objective:
káččı⌣wakkı⌣mállɛğ⌣ğántíkkori⌢ (-ğ⌣ğ- < -g⌣ğ- § 551) *I (have) sold everything but the horse.*
dúngı⌣mállɛr⌣rıjál⌣kɛmískı⌣wakkı⌣defέgoran⌢ (-r⌣r- < -g⌣r- § 669) *they (have) paid all the money but four dollars.*
dúngır⌣rıjál⌣lέw⌣wakkı⌣defέgoran⌢ (-r⌣r- < -g⌣r- § 669, -l⌣l- < -l⌣w- § 580, -ww- < -gw- § 719) *they (have) paid the money less one dollar.*
jóm⌣mέw⌣wakkı⌣tȧgoran⌢ (-m⌣m- < -m⌣w- § 603, -ww- < -gw- § 719) *they came on the next day but one.*
ún⌣wέw⌣wakkı⌣bıtaran⌢ *they will come the month after next.*
nahár⌣wέw⌣wakkı⌣ówwıntír⌣ (-ww- < -gw- § 719; § 1532) and with -g⌣ (§ 4346).
nahar⌣wέw⌣wakkıg⌣ówwıntír⌣ *on every second day.*

wákkı-bŭ- (§ 3931 β) v.i. stat. *be in an omitted (etc.) state or condition.*

wakkɛd-ág- (§§ 3877 ff.) v.t. *be in the situation of having omitted, etc.*
aı̄gı⌣wakkɛdágran⌢ *they have left me out.*

wákkı-kattı- (N. -ıha-; § 4093) v.p. *be omitted, etc.*
mósono⌣wákkıkattın⌢ *Friday is left out.*

⌣wála⌣ . . . ? and

⌣wálla⌣...? (§4483) conj. in questions ... or...? [< وَلاَ, Sudan Ar. وَلَّا id.].
ká⌣dúllέ⌣wála⌣kíññaré? is the house large or small?
mám⌣bέrtɪrέ⌣wáll⌣εgεd¹rέ? (-m⌣b- < -n⌣b- §592) is that yonder the (a) goat or the (a) sheep?
bέrtɪd⌣dólná⌣wáll⌣εgétki? (-d⌣d- < -g⌣d- §534) do you want the goat or the sheep?
índo⌣tέgrɪá⌣wálla⌣kándi? shall (§5369b) I stay here or go home?
wála⌣...wála (§4483) conj. neither...nor [< وَلاَ...وَلاَ id.] with negative verb:
tímbεs⌣wála⌣gɪǧírmunun⌣wála⌣báññɪ-munun⌢ his (her) brother can (§5377) neither hear nor speak.
wál⌣íččıw⌣wála⌣sukkárkɪ⌣dólmunun, gáhwa⌣sádad⌣dólli⌢ (-w⌣w- < -g⌣w- §719, -d⌣d- < -g⌣d- §534) I want neither milk nor sugar, I want plain coffee.
X. káčči⌣dólná⌣wálla⌣hánugi? do you want the horse or the donkey?
Y. wála⌣káčči⌣wála⌣hánugi⌢ (I want §4663) neither the horse nor the donkey.
wálag (wέlεg, N. wέlεŋ) v.t. wave, wave about, brandish, flourish [imit.].
ind. pres. aī⌣wálag(¹)ri⌢, εr⌣wálagin⌢ (-gī⌢, -gí⌢); perf. aī⌣walágkori⌢ (-ákko-).
imperat. wálak!
subj. past aī⌣wálagsı⌣ (-aksı⌣, -su⌣).
tέn⌣sıwídkı⌣walágkon⌢ he (has) brandished his sword.
tókkos⌣sáw⌣walágmεn⌢ (-s⌣s- < -n⌣s- §680, -w⌣w- < -g⌣w- §719, ⌣waláŋ-ŋεn⌢ §661) don't wave the watch (clock) about.
wálag-an (§§3890ff.) v.t. tell to wave, etc., let wave, etc.
wálag-bŭ- (walágbŭ-; §3931β) v.i. stat. be in a waved (etc.) state or condition.
mındíl⌣túrugır⌣wálagbūn⌢ the handkerchief is fluttering in the wind.
wálag-kattı- (-akka-; §4093) v.p. be waved, etc.
⌣wálla⌣...? conj. ...or...? s.v. ⌣wála⌣...?
wambánessi! O my aunt! s.v. wó⌣c....!
wambánna! (-bέn-) O my uncle! s.v. wó⌣c....!
wambáp! O my father! s.v. wó⌣c....!
wámbes! O my brother! s.v. wó⌣c....!
wámburu! O my daughter! s.v. wó⌣c....!
wănd(ı) v.i. appear, become visible, come in sight [§2868].
ind. pres. aī⌣wăndıri⌢, εr⌣wăndın⌢ (-dī⌢, -dí⌢); perf. aī⌣wăndıgori⌢ (N. -ıko-, -ıho-).
subj. past aī⌣wăndısı⌣ (-su⌣).
bābúr⌣wăndıgım⌣bıtări⌢ when the steamer (train) comes in sight I shall come.
mufέttiš⌣wăndóskon⌢ the inspector has come in sight.
X. wέl⌣sáıré? where is the dog?
Y. wăndımunun⌢ it is not to be seen, lit. it does not appear.
íw⌣wárrırtów⌣wăndın⌢ (-w⌣w- < -n⌣w- §720) this can be seen at a distance, lit. this appears from afar.
wăndar⌣ (-dàr⌣; §§2200ff.) and

wăndíd⌣ (§§2256ff.) n. appearance, etc.
wăndı-bŭ- (§3931α) v.i. stat. be in a visible state or condition.
bābúr⌣wăndıbūn⌢ the steamer (train) is in sight.
wăndır-εg-ág- (§§4071ff.) v.i.=wăndε-dól-.
wănd-ε-dól- (-dᵒd- §1178; §4022) and
wăndır-ε-dól- (-rᵒd-; §4027) v.i. be about to appear, etc.
wăndıg-ır (N. -ıkır, -ıhır; §3682) (a) v.t. caus. cause or allow to appear, etc.; (b) v.t. produce, show, exhibit.
tεr⌣tέn⌣dúŋgıw⌣wăndıgírmunun⌢ (-w⌣w- < -g⌣w- §719) he doesn't let his (she doesn't let her) money appear.
ǧówwı⌣tέnn⌣ígki⌣wăndıgírın⌢ the tree produces its (trees produce their §4696b) blossoms (ib.).
wánnεn! O my wife! s.v. wó⌣c....!
wánnessi! O my sister! s.v. wó⌣c....!
wánnogič! O my husband! s.v. wó⌣c....!
wántó! O my son! s.v. wó⌣c....!
-wan-g-al s.v. -al⌣.
wáŋgi! O my uncle! s.v. wó⌣c....!
wár v.i. jump, leap, spring [§4604].
ind. pres. aī⌣wárri⌢, εr⌣wárın⌢ (⌣wári⌢, ⌣wári⌢); perf. aī⌣wárkori⌢.
úrur⌣wárkoran⌢ they (have) jumped into the river.
wárar⌣ (-ràr⌣; §§2200ff.) and
waríd⌣ (§§2256ff.) n. jumping, etc.
wár-an (§§3890ff.) v.t. tell to jump, etc., let jump, etc.
war-bél (§3747ε') v.i. issue by jumping, etc., jump (etc.) out.
kárε⌣kúbırtów⌣warbélkó⌢ (-w⌣w- < -n⌣w- §720) the fish (has) jumped out of the boat.
warr-εg-ág- (§§4071ff.) v.i.=warεdól-.
war-ε-dól- (-rᵒd- §1178; §4022) and
warr-ε-dól- (-rᵒd-; §4027) v.i. be about to jump, etc.
war-ε-má- (§4036) and
warr-ε-má- (§4041) v.i. become unable to jump, etc.
war-tó (§3747ε') v.i. enter by jumping, etc., jump (etc.) in.
kúbır⌣wartógori⌢ I jumped into the boat.
wárag (wărág⌣) n. paper, piece of paper, document; with collective sg. (§4696d) [< ورق id.].
obj. warágk(ı)⌣, -ákk(ı)⌣, -kı⌣.
gen. wárag̊n⌣v., wárag̊⌣c.
pl. wáragı⌣.
wăran⌢ (-rā⌢, wărá⌢ wăra⌢ §939; wăran⌣; §4488) apocritic sentence-word no [<*wăran⌢ (-á->§1069) < √wá*d (§4604) far+-an⌢ say, so *let (sc. what you say) be far.
X. fadlέgorandé? did they stop (have they stopped) behind?
Y. wăram⌣bıdágoran⌢ no, they came (have come) on.
wărang⌣εgóran⌢ and (§6107)
wărang⌣εgóran⌢ they (have) said 'no'.
wărang⌣tókkow⌣wέmεn⌢ (-w⌣w- < -n⌣w- §720) don't say 'no'.
wărı̆g v.i. jump (etc., s.v. wár) continually, jump (etc.) about [< wár- jump+-ı-euphonic+-ǧ intensive §2883].

ind. pres. aī⌣wárıg(¹)ri⌢, εr⌣wárıg̊ın⌢ (-gī⌢, -gí⌢); perf. aī⌣warígkori⌢ (-íčk-).
imperat. wárič!
wárıg̊ar⌣ (-gàr⌣, -gεr⌣; §§2200ff.) and
warıǧíd⌣ (§§2256ff.) n. continual jumping, etc.
wárıs v.t. stretch, stretch out, extend [app. by dissimilation <*wárır (§866) < √wá*d--apart, distant (§4604)+-ır caus. (§3665), cause to be apart, render distant §2894].
ind. pres. aī⌣warísri⌢, εr⌣warísın⌢ (-sī⌢, -sí⌢); perf. aī⌣warískori⌢.
ánn⌣íŋgı⌣warískori⌢ I (have) stretched out my right arm (hand).
έnn⌣ínn⌣óssıw⌣wárıs⌢ (-w⌣w- < -g⌣w- §719) stretch out your right leg.
wárısar⌣ (-sàr⌣; §§2200ff.) and
warısíd⌣ (§§2256ff.) n. stretching, extension.
wáris-an (§§3890ff.) v.t. tell to stretch, etc., let stretch, etc.
warís-kattı- (§4093) v.p. be stretched, etc.
wárrı⌣ (a) n. distance, remoteness; (b, used as predicative §4721) adj. distant, remote, far away [stereotyped form of wárrı⌣ subj. pres. of wár (the supposition that) I jump §2144].
obj. -rıg⌣.
pl. -rıŋč(ı)⌣.
wárrırtōn⌣nálkattıran⌢ they are (can be §5704) seen at (lit. from) a distance.
wárrıg⌣εskınálmunan⌢ they cannot see the distant one(s §4647).
wárrırέ? is (s)he (it, are they) far?
índotōw⌣wárrıré? (-w⌣w- < -n⌣w- §720) is (s)he (it, are they) far from here?
wárrır⌣ (s.v. -r⌣) adv. at a distance, far away, far off.
wárrır⌣ (§6007) (s)he (it) is (they are) at a distance, far away, far off.
⌣wárrır (§§4374, 5860, 5909) postp. (=prep. §4288) at a distance (etc.) from.
— follows the genitive:
έn⌣wárrır⌣ and (§722)
έw⌣wárrır⌣ far away from you.
έn⌣wárrır⌢ (έw⌣wár-) (s)he (it) is (they are) far away from you.
warrín-d(ı)⌣ (§§2545ff.) adj. distant, remote, further.
wárr-an (§3913β) v.i. become distant, recede.
wárram-bŭ- (§3950β) v.i. stat. be in a receding state or condition.
warranε-ág- (§§3965ff.) v.i. be in the situation of having become distant, etc.
warran-nóg (§§3973, 4150) v.i. go far (further) away.
imperat. warrannók!
warran-nóg-bŭ- (-nóggŭ- §546; §§3974, 4153) v.i. stat. be in a state of motion (going) far (further) away.
wárrır-bŭ- (§§3947-8, 1931) v.i. lie at a distance, be far away.
ind. pres. aī⌣warrırbúri⌢.
imperat. warrírbu!, wárrırbu!
εgέttırbúlgı⌣sókkεgoran, wárrırbúlg⌣έttágoran⌢ they (have) removed what was near and brought what was distant.

wás — wέ

wárrıg-ır (N. -ıkır, -ıhır; §3697) (a) v.t. caus. *cause or allow to be distant, etc.*; (b) v.t. *remove, put (take, keep) away.*
  ind. pres. aī⌣wárrıgıddi⌢, εr⌣wárrıgırın⌢ (-rī⌢, -rí⌢).
warrıgır-úskur (N. -ıkır-, -ıhır-; §4141) v.t. *set at a distance, place far off.*
  ind. pres. aī⌣warrıgıruskúddi⌢, εr⌣warrıgıruskurın⌢ (-rī⌢, -rí⌢).
wás v.i. *boil, come to the boil.*
  ind. pres. tεr⌣wásın⌢ (-sī⌢, -sí⌢); perf. tεr⌣wáskon⌢ (-kŏ⌢, -kó⌢).
  part. pres. wásıl⌣ (*liquid*) *that boils, boiling,* obj. wāsílg(ı)⌣, -gi⌢.
  έssı⌣wásın⌢ *the water boils.*
  έssı⌣wásná? *does the water boil?*
  έssı⌣wáskın⌣ *when the water boils.*
  έssı⌣wásóskó⌢ *the water has come to the boil.*
wásar⌣ (-dɑ̀r⌣; §§2200ff.) and
wāsíd⌣ (§§2256ff.) n. *boiling, ebullition.*
wǎz-bŭ- (§§927, 3931α) v.i. stat. *be in a boiling state or condition.*
  X. έssı⌣wǎzbūllέ? (s.v. -rέ?) *is the water boiling?*
  Y. wǎzbūn⌢ *it is* (§5364).
  έssı⌣wǎzbúgın⌣ *if (when) the water is boiling.*
  έssı⌣wǎzbúmεŋkın⌣ *if (when) the water is not boiling (unless the water is boiling).*
wās(ˡ)r-εg-ǎg- (§§4071ff.) v.i. = wāsεdól-.
  έssı⌣wāsˡrεgágın⌢ *the water is just going to boil.*
wás-ε-dól- (-sᵒd- §1178; §4022) and
wās(ˡ)r-ε-dól- (-rᵒd-; §4027) v.i. *be about to boil.*
wāsεd-ǎg- (§§3877ff.) v.i. *be in the condition of having come to the boil.*
  έssı⌣wāsεdǎgın⌢ *the water is at the boil.*
wǎsk-ıdd(ı) (§§1856, 3725) (a) v.t. caus. *cause or allow (a liquid) to boil;* (b) v.t. *render boiling, bring to the boil, boil;* (c) v.t. *boil (in a liquid) =* sεlgέ.
  ind. pres. aī⌣wǎskıddıri⌢; perf. aī⌣wǎskıddıgori⌢ (N. -ıko-, -ıho-).
  imperat. wǎskıddi!
  íg⌣έssıw⌣wǎskıddın⌢ (-w⌣w- < -g⌣w- §719) *the fire brings the water to the boil.*
  aī⌣έssıw⌣wǎskıddıgori⌢ *I (have) boiled the (some) water.*
  hodárkı⌣wǎskıddıgó⌢ *(s)he (has) boiled the (some) vegetables.*
wǎskıdd-an ("⌣"; §§3890ff., 3904) v.t. *tell to boil, let boil.*
  έssıw⌣wǎskıddá⌢ (-w⌣w- < -g⌣w- §719) *let him (her) boil the (some) water.*
  kúmb⌣ówwıw⌣wǎskíddan⌢ *tell him (her) to boil two eggs.*
wǎskıddar⌣ (-dɑ̀r⌣; §§2200ff., 2212) and
wǎskıddíd⌣ (§§2256ff., 2265) n. *causing or allowing to boil.*
wásah⌣ (a) adj. *dirty, soiled;* (b) n. *dirt* [< وسخ id. (a) §§1340, 1235].
  obj. wasáhk(ı)⌣, -ki⌢.
  pl. wásahı⌣.
  kádε⌣wásah⌣nεfέmunun⌢ *a (the) dirty cloth is useless.*
  ín⌣wásahun⌢ and (§720)

íw⌣wásahun⌢ (a) *this is dirty;* (b) *this is dirt.*
wasáhkı⌣mín⌣ósri? *how (⌣mínε §1122) am I to (shall I §5369b) take out the dirt?*
tέn⌣wásah⌣dıgrín⌢ (tέw⌣wásah⌣§722) *(s)he (it) is very dirty,* lit. *his (her, its) dirt is much.*
wasáha⌣ n. *dirtiness, dirt* [< وسٰخة id.].
  obj. -hag⌣.
  wasáha⌣dıgríg⌣índ⌣áukoran⌢ *they (have) made a lot of dirt here.*
  wasáham⌣mín⌣ósri? (-m⌣m- < -g⌣m- §601) *how (⌣mínε⌣) am I to take out the dirt?*
washǎn (-sxǎn⌣ §1397) adj. *dirty, soiled* [< وسخان id.].
  obj. -hăng(ı)⌣, -gi⌢.
  pl. -hǎnı⌣.
washǎŋ-ır (-sxǎ-; N. -ŋkır, §3702) (a) v.t. caus. *cause or allow to be dirty, etc.;* (b) v.t. *render dirty, etc., dirty, soil, defile.*
  ind. pres. aī⌣washǎŋgıddi⌢.
  fútaw⌣wasxǎŋgırın⌢ (-w⌣w- < -g⌣w- §719) *(s)he (it) soils (you soil) the cloth.*
wásıl⌣ *receipt* = wέsıl⌣.
wassāhέ (a) v.t. *defile, dirty, soil;* (b) v.i. *make dirt, make a mess* usually wassahέ; wassahέ probably due to influence of wasáha⌣ [< a stem of وسّخ id. +-έ §3643].
  ind. pres. aī⌣wassahέri⌢; perf. aī⌣wassahέgori⌢ (N. -έko-, -έho-).
  íŋgı⌣wassahέgon⌢ *(s)he (it) (has) (you have) dirtied this.*
  wassahέróskó⌢ *(s)he (it) has (you have) (a) dirtied it* (§§5078, 5083); (b) *made a mess.*
wǎsu⌣ n. *leveller, toothless rake (for levelling and smoothing ground for irrigation; larger than* έlbıl⌣; SNK, 376, 53) [§2337].
  obj. wǎsug⌣ [> Sudan Ar. واسوق id.].
  pl. wǎsunč(ı)⌣.
wǎu, wǎw, wǎu v.t. *row, paddle.*
  ind. pres. aī⌣wǎuri⌢ (⌣wǎw(ˡ)ri⌢), εr⌣wǎwın⌢ (-wī⌢, -wí⌢); perf. aī⌣wǎukori⌢.
  imperat. wǎu!, pl. wǎwwε! (-wέ!).
  kúbkı⌣wǎuran⌢ *they row the (a) boat.*
wǎwar⌣ (-wɑ̀r⌣; §§2200ff.) and
wǎwíd(ı)⌣ (§§2256ff.) n. *rowing, etc.*
wǎwıdd(ı)⌣ n. *oar;* with collective sg. (§4696d) [§2271].
  obj. -dıg⌣.
  pl. -dınč(ı)⌣.
wǎw-an (§§3890ff.) v.t. *tell to row, etc., let row, etc.*
wǎw-ε-má- (§4036) and
wǎur-ε-má- (wǎw(ˡ)r-; §4041) v.t. *become unable to row, etc.*
wǎwır (-wᵘr) n. *(in water-wheel,* kólε⌣) *beam fixed across shaft* (kódε⌣) *underneath wheel raising water* (átt(ı)⌣); *from points near its centre two rods* (šέhrı⌣) *proceed, crossing each other, to upper right (as one faces river) corners of shaft.*

obj. wǎwírk(ı)⌣, -ki⌢.
pl. wǎw(ı)rı⌣, -wᵘrı⌣.
wǎzbŭ- *be boiling* s.v. wǎs.
wázın⌣ (wáz-, wέz-; §956a) n. *weight* [< وزن id. §1359].
  obj. wazíng(ı)⌣, -gi⌢.
  X. íni⌣wázın⌣mukóttērré? (-w⌣w- < -n⌣w- §720) *what is the weight of this (that)?*
  Y. tέw⌣wέzın⌣rátul⌣dımıŋkólodı⌣ toski-tόrt⌣áŋkon⌢ *it weighs 73½ lb.,* lit. *its weight went to (i.e. was found to be) 73½ lb.*
  aī⌣tέw⌣wazíŋg⌣unúrmunun⌢ *I don't know his (her, its) weight.*
waznέ (wàz-, wεz-) v.t. *weigh* [< وزن id. *weighing* +-έ §3615].
  ind. pres. aī⌣waznέri⌢; perf. aī⌣waznέgori⌢ (N. -έko-, -έho-).
  imperat. waznέ!
waznέrar⌣ (-rɑ̀r⌣; §§2200ff., 2207) and
waznέríd⌣ (§§2256ff., 2260) n. *weighing.*
waznέr-an (§§3890ff., 3899) v.t. *tell to weigh, let weigh.*
waznέ-bŭ- (§3931β) v.i. stat. *be in a weighed state or condition.*
  sandúg⌣dúlnd⌣waznέbūn, lákın⌣ sandúk⌣kıññánd⌣waznεbúmunun⌢ *that of the large box has been weighed, but that of the small box has not.*
waznέ-katti- (wàz-, wεz-; N. -έha-; §4093) v.p. *be weighed.*
  tεr⌣weznέkattın⌣ *(s)he (it) is weighed.*
  aī⌣waznέkáttıgori⌢ *I (have) got weighed.*
wàhag- = wahag- *omission.*
wáhıd⌣ (§1027) *time* < wákıd⌣ = wέkıd⌣.
wakíl⌣ *agent, etc.* = wakíl⌣.
wárag⌣ *paper* = wárag⌣.
wásıl⌣ *receipt* = wέsıl⌣.
wázın⌣ *weight* = wázın⌣.
wέ v.t. (a) *say* (= ⌣έ-); (b) *say of, say about;* (c) *call, name, term;* (d) *say to, tell, bid* [RSN, §129].
— constr. with (a) *noun (pronoun) in objective (acc. or dat.);* (b) *adverb;* (c) *adverb and objective;* (d) *sentence (noun-clause §6140) without obj. suff.;* (e) *double objective* (§6151).
  ind. pres. aī⌣wέri⌢ (occ. ⌣wέri⌢ §1059), εr⌣wέn⌢ (⌣wέ⌢, ⌣wέ⌢; §942, occ. ⌣wέn⌢, ⌣wέ⌢, ⌣wέ⌢); perf. aī⌣wέgori⌢ (N. ⌣wέko-, ⌣wέho-).
  imperat. wέ!, pl. wέwε! (wέwέ!).
  part. past wέrεl⌣ (*one*) *that said, etc.,* obj. wέrεlg(ı)⌣, -gi⌢.
  tεr⌣múrsıw⌣wέgon⌢ (-w⌣w- < -g⌣w- §719) *(s)he (has) told a lie* (...*lies* §4696d).
  íŋgı⌣wέmunan⌢ *they don't say this (that).*
  tέnn-āw⌣wέgó⌢ (s.v. ǎ⌣; -w⌣w- < -g⌣w- §719) *he said it to himself (she said it to herself).*
  íŋkε⌣wέgori⌢ *I said so.*
  εr⌣íŋkε⌣wέgon⌢ *you said so.*
  tεr⌣íŋkε⌣wέgó⌢ *(s)he said so.*
  tókkon⌣íŋkε⌣wέmεn⌣ (-mέ⌢, ⌣wέmέ⌢) *don't say so.*
  mínε⌣wέn? *what* (lit. *how do you* (...*does (s)he) say?*

mínɛ‿wɛ́gon? *what did you (...(s)he) say?*
dúŋgɪm‿mínɛ‿wɛ́gon? (-m‿m- < -g‿m- §601) *what did (s)he say about the money?*
āı‿tókkon‿nógmɛw‿wɛ́gorıⁿ (-w‿w- < -n‿w- §720) *I said 'don't go'.*
āı‿ɛ́kkı‿tókkon‿nógmɛw‿wɛ́gorıⁿ *I told you not to go.*
nugúdk‿ám‿bélɛdır‿hasáŋgı‿wɛ́mu-nunⁿ *in my (our) country we do not name a slave Ḥásan.*
— with redundant án *say*:
āı‿nóg‿áŋgı‿wɛ́gorıⁿ and
N. āı‿nóg‿áŋgı‿wɛ́korıⁿ *I said 'go'*, lit. *I said saying 'go'*; a resolution (§5582) of the complex awwɛ́, q.v. s.v. án *say*.
wɛ́rar (-rɑ̀r‿; §§2200 ff., 2207) and
wɛrɪ́d‿ (§§2256 ff., 2260) n. *(act of) saying*, etc.
wɛ́rɛ‿ n. *what is said, saying, statement, remark, report, news*; with collective sg. (§4696d) [§2234ɛ].
obj. -rɛg‿.
pl. -rɛnč(ı)‿.
ɛr‿íw‿wɛ́rɛs‿sáır‿gıɣírkó? (-w‿w- < -n‿w- §720, -s‿s- < -g‿s- §678) *where did you hear this said?*
wɛ́r-an (§§3890 f., 3899) v.t. *tell to say, etc., let say, etc.*
wɛ́-bŭ- (§3931 β) v.i. stat. p. *be in a said (etc.) state or condition.*
ím‿báññɪd‿wɛ́būnⁿ *this expression is in use.*
wɛ́-dɛ̄n *tell* infra.
wɛ̄r-ɛg-ág- (§§4071 ff.) v.t. = wɛ̄rɛdól-.
wɛ̄r-ɛ-dól- (-rᵒd- §1178; §§4016-17, 4022, 4027) v.t. *be about to say, etc.*
wɛ̄r-ɛ-ǧŭ-bŭ- (§4069) v.t. stat. *be on one's way (coming) to say, etc.*
wɛ̄r-ɛ-má- (§§4016-17, 4036, 4041) v.t. *become unable to say, etc.*
wɛ̄r-ɛ-nóg (§§4048 ff.) v.t. *go to say, etc.*
wɛ̄r-ɛ-nóg-bŭ- (-nóggū- §546; §4058) v.t. stat. *be on one's way (going) to say, etc.*
wɛ̄r-ɛ-tá (§§4060 ff.) v.t. *come to say, etc.*
wɛ̄rɛd-ág- (§§3877 ff.) v.t. *be in the situation of having said, etc.*
íŋkɛ‿wɛ̄rɛdágɪnⁿ *(s)he has said so.*
wɛ́-kattɪ- (N. wɛ́ha-; §4093) v.p. *be said, etc.*
ím‿báññɪd‿wɛ́kattɪnⁿ *this (that) expression is used.*
íw‿wɛ́kattɪmununⁿ (-w‿w- < -n‿w- §720) *this (that) is not said.*
wɛ́-dɛ̄n (§§3996-7) v.t. *say to (the speaker), inform, tell, bid, instruct (the speaker).*
ind. pres. ɛr‿wɛ́dɛnɪnⁿ (-nīⁿ, -níⁿ); perf. āı‿wɛ́dɛ̄ŋkonⁿ (‿wɛ́dɛ̄ŋkonⁿ §1935; -kŏⁿ, -kóⁿ).
imperat. wɛ́dɛn! (wɛ́dɛ̄!, wɛ́dɛ̄!, wɛ́dɛ́!, wɛ́dɛ! §945).
subj. past ɛr‿wɛ́dɛ̄nsɪnⁿ (-sunⁿ, ˜⁻ˇ).
árgı‿wɛ́dɛ̄nčɪrɪrⁿ *tell us.*
tɛlɛgráfkɛw‿wɛ́dɛ̄nⁿ (-w‿w- < -d‿w- §718) *inform me by telegram.*
wɛdɛ̄n-an (§§3890 ff., 3905) v.t. *tell to tell, etc. (the speaker), let tell, etc. (the speaker).*
āıgı‿wɛ̄dɛ̄nanⁿ *tell him (her) to tell me.*
wɛ̄dɛ̄nd-ɛg-ág- (§§4071 ff.) v.t. = wɛ̄dɛ̄nɛ-dól-.

wɛ̄dɛ̄n-ɛ-dól- (-nᵒd- §1178; §4022) and
wɛ̄dɛ̄nd-ɛ-dól- (-dᵒd-; §4027) v.t. *be about to tell, etc. (the speaker).*
wɛ̄dɛ̄nd-ɛ-ǧŭ-bŭ- (§4069) v.t. stat. *be on his (her, your, their) way (coming) to tell, etc. (the speaker).*
wɛ̄dɛ̄n-ɛ-má- (§4036) and
wɛ̄dɛ̄nd-ɛ-má- (§4041) v.t. *become unable to tell, etc. (the speaker).*
āıgı‿wɛ̄dɛ̄nɛmágoranⁿ and
āıgı‿wɛ̄dɛ̄ndɛmágoranⁿ *they couldn't tell me.*
wɛ̄dɛ̄nd-ɛ-tá (§§4060 ff.) v.t. *come to tell, etc. (the speaker).*
wɛ̄dɛ̄nɛd-ág- (§§3877 ff.) v.t. *be in the situation of having told, etc. (the speaker).*
āıgı‿wɛ̄dɛ̄nɛdágɪnⁿ *(s)he has told me.*
wɛ́-tɪr (§§3997-8) v.t. *say to (other than the speaker), tell, inform, instruct (other than the speaker).*
ind. pres. āı‿wɛ́tɪddɪⁿ, ɛr‿wɛ́tɪrɪnⁿ (-rīⁿ, -ríⁿ); perf. āı‿wɛ́tɪrkorıⁿ (-tɪkko-; ˜⁻ˇ §1946).
subj. past āı‿wɛ́tɪrsɪ‿ (-tɪssı‿, -tɪrsu‿, -tɪssu‿).
bɛlóskoraw‿wɛ́tɪrⁿ (-w‿w- < -n‿w- §720) *say to him (her, them) 'they have gone out'.*
tɛ́kk‿ím‿mállɛw‿wɛ́tɪkkorıⁿ (-w‿w- < -g‿w- §719) *I (have) told him (her) all this (that).*
íŋg‿āı‿ɛ́kkı‿wɛ́tɪmmɛndı‿kóttɪt‿tók-kon‿sókkɛmɛnⁿ (-t‿t- < -g‿t- §707) *don't take this away till I tell you to.*
— with redundant -an *say.*
wɛ́tɪrɪr‿nógwanⁿ (‿nóggan‿) *tell (each of §5456) them to go* —nógw‿awwɛ́-tɪrɪrⁿ (s.v. án *say*).
wɛ́tɪr-an (§§3890 ff., 3905) v.t. *tell to tell, etc., let tell, etc. (other than the speaker).*
tɛ́kkı‿wɛ́tɪranⁿ *tell him (her) to tell him (her).*
ɛsmáŋgı‿wɛ́tɪranⁿ (a §6291) *tell him (her) to tell ɛθmán*; (b §6291) *tell ɛoθmán to tell him (her).*
wɛ̄tɪdd-ɛg-ág- (§§4071 ff.) v.t. = wɛ̄tɪrɛ dól-.
wɛ̄tɪr-ɛ-dól- (-rᵒd- §1178; §4022) and
wɛ̄tɪdd-ɛ-dól- (-dᵒd-; §4027) v.t. *be about to tell, etc. (other than the speaker).*
wɛ̄tɪdd-ɛ-ǧŭ-bŭ- (§4069) v.t. stat. *be on one's way (coming) to tell, etc. (other than the speaker).*
wɛ̄tɪr-ɛ-má- (§4036) and
wɛ̄tɪdd-ɛ-má- (§4041) v.t. *be unable to tell, etc. (other than the speaker).*
wɛ̄tɪdd-ɛ-nóg (§§4048 ff.) v.t. *go to tell, etc. (other than the speaker).*
wɛ̄tɪdd-ɛ-nóg-bŭ- (-nóggū- §546; §4058) v.t. stat. *be on one's way (going) to tell, etc. (other than the speaker).*
wɛ̄tɪdd-ɛ-tá (§§4060 ff.) v.t. *come to tell, etc. (other than the speaker).*
wɛ̄tɪrɛd-ág- (§§3877 ff.) v.t. *be in the situation of having told, etc. (other than the speaker).*
wɛ́d v.i. *float.*
ind. pres. āı‿wɛ́d(¹)rıⁿ, ɛr‿wɛ́dɪnⁿ (-dīⁿ, -díⁿ); perf. āı‿wɛ́dkorıⁿ (‿wɛ́tk-).
fúllanč‿ɛ́ssɪr‿wɛ́d¹ranⁿ *(the) corks float in (the) water.*
S. dókkoš‿šúgurmɛn, wɛ́t! (-š‿š- < -n‿š- §698) *don't go under, float.*

wɛ́dar (-dɑ̀r‿, -dɛr‿; §§2200 ff.) and
wɛdíd‿ (§§2256 ff.) n. *floating.*
wɛ́d-an (§§3890 ff.) v.t. *tell to float, let float.*
wɛ́d-bŭ- (§3931 α) v.i. stat. *be in a floating state or condition.*
bɛ́r‿ɛ́ssɪr‿wɛ́dbunⁿ *the wood is floating in the water.*
wɛ́dk-ɪdd(ı) (wɛ́tk-; §3725) v.t. caus. *cause or allow to float.*
háwa‿gɪrbátkı‿wɛ́tkɪddɪnⁿ *the air causes the skin to float.*
háwa‿gɪrbádɪr‿uffundúddan, háwa‿gɪrbádɪw‿wɛ́tkɪddɪnⁿ (-w‿w- < -g‿w- §719) *they blow air into the skins, the air makes the skins float.*
wɛ́d v.t. *spin* [RSN, §200].
ind. pres. āı‿wɛ́d(¹)rıⁿ, ɛr‿wɛ́dɪnⁿ (-dīⁿ, -díⁿ); perf. āı‿wɛ́dkorıⁿ (‿wɛ́tk-).
imperat. wɛ́t!
ɛ́nčı‿bɛnnáukkı‿wɛ́d¹ranⁿ *(the) women spin (the) cotton.*
ɛ́n‿úlgı‿bɛnnáugɪrtów‿wɛ́dɪnⁿ (-w‿w- < -n‿w- §720) *the woman spins (the) thread from (the) cotton.*
wɛ́dar (-dɑ̀r‿, -dɛr‿; §§2200 ff.) and
wɛdíd‿ (§§2256 ff.) n. *spinning.*
wɛ́d-an (§§3890 ff.) v.t. *tell to spin, let spin.*
wɛ́d-bŭ- (§3931 β) v.i. stat. *be in a spun state or condition.*
úl‿wɛ́dbūnⁿ *the thread is (has been) spun.*
bɛnnáu‿wɛ́dbūnⁿ *the cotton is (has been) spun.*
wɛ́dk-ɪdd(ı) (wɛ́tk-; §3725) v.t. caus. *cause or allow to spin.*
ind. pres. āı‿wɛ́dkɪddɪrɪⁿ.
tɪnɛ́n‿tɛ́m-burub‿bɛnnákkı‿wɛ́tkɪd-dɪnⁿ (tɛ́m-buru‿ s.v. búru‿; -b‿b- < -g‿b- §519) *the mother makes her daughter spin cotton.*
wɛ́d-kattɪ- (wɛ́tk-; §4093) v.p. *be spun.*
úl‿bɛnnágɪrtów‿wɛ́dkattɪnⁿ (-w‿w- < -n‿w- §720) *(the) thread is spun from (the) cotton.*
wɛ́gga‿ (wóg-, -gɑ̀‿) n. *weight of 2¾ lb.*; with collective sg. (§4696d) [< وَقّة *id.*].
obj. -gag‿.
pl. -ganč(ı)‿.
wɛ́ga- (wɑ́ga-) [< وَجَع *pain* §1258].
wɛǧád‿ (wàǧ-) n. *mourning* [? < وَجَعَات *dolore correptae (mulieres)*, or وَجَعَات a pl. of وَجَع *pain* §2397].
obj. -ádk(ı)‿, -átk(ı)‿, -átt(ı)‿ §2462, -kı‿, -tıⁿ.
ógıg‿wɛǧádn‿ıllɑ̀r‿ténn-urr‿ɛskédkı‿bóginⁿ *the man pours earth on his head for (as a sign of) mourning.*
(***wɛ́ǧ-an-** not heard.)
wɛ̌ǧ-am-bŭ- (wɑ́ǧ-; §3958) v.i. stat. *be in a state or condition of pain.*
āı‿wɛǧamburiⁿ *I am in pain.*
wɛ́ga-kattɪ- (wɑ́ga-; N. -aha-, §1030; §4102) (a) v.i. *be sad, be distressed, grieve*; (b) v.t. *be sad at (because of), grieve over, deplore.*
imperat. wɛ́ǧakattɪ!
N. álı‿wɛ́ǧahattɪnⁿ *ɛáli is distressed.*

wéhɪd‿ < wékɪd‿ — wénɛs‿

tɪr‿méw‿wéǧakattıran? (-w‿w- < -n‿w- §720) *why are they sad?*
X. ɛr‿méw‿wéǧakattın? *why are you sad?*
Y. âi‿ambâb‿dísıŋgı‿wéǧakattıri⌒ *I am sad because my father (has) died.*

wéǧakattı-bŭ- (wáǧ-, N. -aha-; §4106) v.i. stat. *be in a state of sadness, be sad.*
tén‿nogítkɛw‿wéǧakattıbúran⌒ (-w‿w- < -d‿w- §718) *they are sad at his (her) going.*
ɛn‿wéǧakáttıbúl-lɛ̄n‿nálkori⌒ (-l-l- < -l-w- §580, -n‿n- < -g‿n- §625) *I saw (have seen) a woman grieving.*

wéhɪd‿ < wékɪd‿ *time.*
wekíl‿ *agent, etc.* = wákıl‿.
wékɪd‿ (wák-; wéhɪd‿, wáhɪd‿ §1027) n. *time, occasion* [< وَقْت id. §1359].
obj. wekídk(ı)‿, -ítk(ı)‿, -ítt(ı)‿ §2462, -ki⌒, -ti⌒.
gen. wékıdn‿v., -kınn‿v.c., -kın‿c.
pl. wékıdı‿.

‿wekídk(ı)‿ (‿wàk-, etc.; §4665) postp. (= conj. §4287) *at the time that, when.*
— *follows the bare subjunctive* (§4331):
âi‿tári‿wekídk(ı)‿ *at the time that I come,* i.e. *when I come.*
âi‿tási‿wekídk(ı)‿ *when I came.*
âi‿tírgı‿nálsı‿wekíttı‿uŋúrkori⌒ *when I saw them I knew them.*
kúp‿kıddedólsı‿wekíttı‿úrur‿wárkoran⌒ (-w‿w- < -n‿w- §720) *when the boat was on the point of sinking they jumped into the river.*

wékɪd-an- (wák-, etc.; §3910α) v.i. *become time.*
wékıdaŋkon⌒ (-kõ⌒, -kó⌒) *it became (has become, is) time.*
tá!, ar‿nógrun‿wékıdaŋkó⌒ (-ruw‿ wɛ- §720) *come!, it's time we went,* lit. *it has become (is) the time of (that) we go* (§6156).
nógru!, wékıdaŋkó⌒ *let's go!* (§5376), *it's time* (sc. *to go*).

wékɪdam-bŭ- (§§3949ff.) v.i. stat. *be in the state or condition of becoming or having become time.*
wékıdambūn⌒ *it's time* (= wékıdaŋkon⌒, wékıdanóskon⌒).

N. wékk(ı)‿, wék(ı)‿ obj. of wɛr‿ *one.*

wél‿ n. (a) *dog;* (b) *piece in the game of* síǧa (q.v.).
— *with collective sg.* (§4696d) [< *u-él‿ (one) *that says 'u!', barker* (RN s.v.) -él‿ *part. of* ɛ *say;* §2147].
obj. wélg(ı)‿, -gi⌒.
pl. wéli‿.
wél‿úkkın⌒ *the dog barks.*
wél‿wígın⌒ *the dog whines (howls).*
wél‿kárr(ı)⌒ *bitch.*
wéln‿dílt(ı)‿ and (§806) wél‿dílt(ı)‿ *dog's coat (fur).*
síǧak‿káččıgan, kulwáhıd‿wél‿dımındówwıgɛk‿káččın⌒ (-ak‿k- < -ag‿k- §569, -ɛk‿k- < -ɛd‿k- §568) *when they play síǧa, each plays with* (-ɛd) *12 pieces.*

wél-kırı‿ (wélkírı‿ §1701; §§2539-40) adj. *resembling a dog, doglike.*
wéln-d(ı)‿ (§§2545 ff.) adj. *appertaining to the (a) dog, canine.*

wél-kōl‿ (§§2572-4) adj. *having a dog or dogs, with a dog or dogs.*
ógıǧ‿wélkōl‿nogóskó⌒ *the man with the dog(s) has gone.*
ógıǧ‿wélkōlgı‿nálkori⌒ *I saw (have seen) the (a) man with the (a) dog (dogs).*

wɛln-tŏd‿ (wélntŏd‿ §1684; wɛltŏd‿, ⁓, §813; wɛntŏd‿, ⁓ §814; §2366) n. (a) *young of dog, puppy;* with collective sg. (§4696d); (b, *term of abuse*) *son of a dog* ابْن اَلْكَلْب , ابْن كَلْب , Sudan Ar.
also ود اَلْكَلْب .
voc. -tŏ̆t!, -tó!
obj. -tŏdk(ı)‿, -tŏtk(ı)‿, -tŏkk(ı)‿, -tŏtt(ı)‿ §2462, -ki⌒, -ti⌒.
gen. -tŏdn‿v., -tŏnn‿v.c., -tŏn‿c.
pl. wélntonı‿, wélt-, wént-.
pl. voc. -ni!
wɛlntŏ́dun⌒ (a) *it's a puppy;* (b) *he's a son of a dog.*

wɛntó! *O son of a dog!* (يَا ابْن اَلْكَلْب).
âigı‿wɛntókk‿ɛgó⌒ (s)*he (has) called me a son of a dog.*
tékki‿wɛntókk‿ɛgó⌒ (s)*he (has) called him a son of a dog (...her a bitch).*

wél-tod‿ (§2369) n. (a) *poor, indifferent or unsatisfactory specimen of dog;* (b) = wél‿.
voc. wéltot!, wéltó!
obj. wéltŏdk(ı)‿, -tŏtk(ı)‿, -tŏkk(ı)‿, -tŏtt(ı)‿; -tŏdk(ı)‿, etc.; -ki⌒, -ti⌒.
gen. -tŏdn‿v., -tŏnn‿v.c., -tŏn‿c.
pl. wéltonı‿.
pl. voc. -ni!
wéltodun⌒ *it's a (miserable) dog.*

wéleg‿ (N. -lɛŋ) v.t. *wave (about), brandish, flourish* (= wálag).
ind. pres. âi‿wéleg(¹)ri⌒, ɛr‿wélegin‿ (-gi⌒, -gí⌒); perf. âi‿wélégkori⌒ (-ékko-).
imperat. wélek!
subj. past âi‿wélegsı‿ (-ɛksı‿, -su‿).
ɛnči‿tím‿mındflıw‿wélegran⌒ (-m‿m- < -n‿m- §608, -w‿w- < -g‿w- §719) *the women wave their handkerchiefs.*
tén‿sıwítkı‿wélékkó⌒ *he (has) brandished his sword.*
wél‿ténn‿ɛuw‿wélékkó⌒ (-w‿w- < -g‿w- §719) *the dog wagged its tail.*

wéleg-an‿ (§3890ff.) v.t. *tell to wave, etc., let wave, etc.*
N. wélɛŋ‿ v.t. *wave, etc.* = wéleg.
ind. pres. âi‿wélɛŋ(¹)ri⌒, ɛr‿wélɛŋın‿ (-ŋi⌒, -ŋí⌒); perf. âi‿wéléŋkori⌒.
N. tés‿sıwíttı‿wéléŋkó⌒ (-s‿s- < -n‿s- §681) *he (has) brandished his sword.*

wɛlése, wɛlése and wɛlésé (§§1794, 2878) v.t. (a) *leave, leave alone, let be;* (b) *leave, leave behind, abandon* [§§2870ff.].
ind. pres. âi‿wɛléseri⌒ (⁓, ⁓), ɛr‿wɛlésen‿ (-sé‿, -sé‿, ⁓, -sé‿, ⁓, -sé‿); perf. âi‿wɛlésegori⌒ (N. -éko-, -ého-; ⁓).
wɛlése! (⁓, ⁓) (a) *leave (etc.) him (her, it, them)!;* (b) *never mind!* (بلاش).

imperat. pl. wɛlésɛwɛ! (-lésɛwé!, -lésɛwé!, -lésɛwé!).

wɛlésɛrar‿ (wɛlésér-; -rár‿; §§2200ff., 2210) and
wɛlésɛríd‿ (§§2256ff., 2263) n. *leaving, leaving alone, leaving behind.*
wɛléser-an‿ (wɛlésér-; §§3890, 3903) v.t. *tell to leave, etc., let leave, etc.*
wɛlése-bŭ- (wɛlésé-; §3931β) v.i. stat. *be in a left (etc.) state or condition.*
wɛlésed-ág- (§§3877ff.) v.t. *be in the situation of having left, etc.*
wɛléseg-ır (N. -ɛkır, -ɛhır; ⁓, ⁓; §3680) v.t. caus. *cause or allow to leave, etc.*
âi‿tékk‿íŋgı‿wɛlésegıddi⌒ *I make (let) him (her, it) leave (etc.) this (that).*
wɛlésegıred-ág- (N. -ɛkır-, -ɛhır-; §§3877ff.) v.t. *be in the situation of having caused or allowed to leave, etc.*
âi‿tékk‿íŋgı‿wɛlésegıredágri⌒ *I have made (let) him (her, it) leave (etc.) this (that).*
wɛlése-kattı- (-lésekat-; N. -ɛha-, -éha-; §4093) v.p. *be left, etc.*

wellé v.t. *kindle, set fire to, light* (= úll(ı)‿) [< imperat. or imperf. stem of ولع id. +-é §3641].
ind. pres. âi‿wellɛ́ri⌒; perf. âi‿wellégori⌒ (N. -éko-, -ého-).
imperat. wellé!
íkkı‿wellégoran⌒ *they (have) lit a fire.*
fānúskı‿wellɛría? *shall* (§5369b) *I light the lantern?*

wellɛrar‿ (-rár‿; §§2200ff., 2207) and
wellɛríd‿ (§§2256ff., 2260) n. *kindling.*
wellɛr-an‿ (§3890ff., 3899) v.t. *tell to kindle, etc., let kindle, etc.*
wellé-bŭ- (§3931β) v.i. stat. *be in a kindled (etc.) state or condition, be alight.*
fānús‿wellébūn⌒ *the lantern is alight.*
wellɛr-eg-ág- (§§4071ff.) v.t. = wellɛredól-.
wellɛr-e-dól- (-rᵒd- §1178; §§4016-17, 4022, 4027) v.t. *be about to kindle, etc.*
wellɛr-e-ǧŭ-bŭ- (§4069) v.t. stat. *be on one's way (coming) to kindle, etc.*
wellɛr-e-má- (§§4016-17, 4036, 4041) v.t. *become unable to kindle, etc.*
wellɛr-e-nóg (§§4048ff.) v.t. *go to kindle, etc.*
wellɛr-e-nóg-bŭ- (-nóggŭ- §546; §4058) v.t. stat. *be on one's way (going) to kindle, etc.*
wellɛr-e-tá (§4060ff.) v.t. *come to kindle, etc.*
wellɛred-ág- (§§3877ff.) v.t. *be in the situation of having kindled, etc.*
wellég-ır (N. -ékır, -éhır; §3681) v.t. caus. *cause or allow to kindle, etc.*
wellé-kattı- (N. -éha-, §4093) v.p. *be kindled, etc.*

wɛlwétt(ı)‿ n. *cool wind, cool air* [< *wɛl-wél-t(ı)‿ §2330, RSN, §129].
obj. -tıg‿.
pl. -tınč(ı)‿.

wénes‿ n. (a) *social intercourse;* (b) *conversation, talk, chat* [< Sudan Ar. وَنَس= أُنْس id.].
obj. wenésk(ı)‿, -ki⌒.
pl. wénesı‿.

wénnɪs-katt(ɪ) (§4102) v.i. (*a*) *associate, have intercourse*; (*b*) *converse, talk together, chat* [cp. Sudan Ar. اِتْوَنَّسَ *id.*].
ind. pres. āɪ‿wénnɪskattɪrɪ⌒.
imperat. wénnɪskatti!
ír‿wɛnnɪskáttɪgɪrᵘ‿āī‿mínɛ‿bắgri? (§5369*b*) *if you* (*pl.*) *talk together how am I to write?*
wentó! *O son of a dog!* s.v. **wél**‿.
wɛ̆r‿ (§§2699-2706) (i) card. num. *one* [<*gwar *RSN*, §114; cp. ON. ονερ *id. GNT* s.v.].
obj. wɛ̆g‿, wɛ̆gɪ⌒, N. also wɛ̆kk(ɪ)‿, wɛ̆k(ɪ)‿, wɛ̆k(k)i⌒.
gen. wɛ̆rn‿v., wɛ̆nn‿v., wɛ̆n‿v.c.
pl. wɛ̆rɪ‿.
‿w- may assimilate a preceding -n‿, but most other preceding consonants assimilate ‿w-; -g‿ of wɛ̆g‿ is assimilated by a following consonant, so that of ‿wɛ̆g‿ only -ɛ̆- may remain unchanged:
íŋgurtōw‿wɛ̆r‿dábkon⌒ (-w‿w-<-n‿w- §720) *one of these* (*has*) *disappeared*.
tíddotōw‿wɛ̆g‿étta⌒ *bring one* (*unum, unam,* ἕνα, μίαν, ἕν) *of them*.
tékk‿árɪd‿gédem‿wɛ̆t‿tɪddáŋgɪ‿dólmunan⌒ (-d‿g- < -dn‿g- §781, -t‿t- < -g‿t- §707) and
tékk‿árɪŋ‿gédem‿wɛ̆t‿tɪddáŋgɪ‿dólmunan⌒ (-ŋ‿g- < -dn‿g- §644, -m‿m- < -m‿w- §603) *they don't want to give him (her) a single (square) foot of land*.
ógɪğ‿ğɛ̆rn‿úğrɛ‿ (-ğ‿ğ- < -ğ‿w- §553) *one man's wages*.
wɛ̆rɪ‿kémsɪrɛ‿ (§2722β) 1¼.
wɛ̆gon‿wɛ̆gon‿ówwɪgɛ́⌒,
wɛ̆gow‿wɛ̆gon‿ówwɪgɛ́⌒ (-w‿w-<-n‿w- §720) and
N. wɛ̆kkow‿wɛ̆kkon‿ówwɪgɛ́⌒ (§§5310, 5312) *1 + 1 = 2*.
wɛ̆rro‿ and
wɛ̆ddo‿ *on* (*in, at* s.v. -r‿) *one* (§§5858-60).
ténn‿óss‿ɛrro‿tɛ́bɪn⌒ (§984) (*s*)*he* (*it*) *stands on one leg*, lit....*on his* (*her, its*) *one leg*.
wɛ̆r‿ (ii) pron. used in predicate *one, the same*.
X. gáhwad‿dólná‿wála‿šắigi? (-d‿d- < -g‿d- §534) *do you want coffee or tea?*
Y. mállɛ‿wɛ̆run⌒ *it's all one (the same, immaterial).*
íw‿wɛ̆run‿íŋgow‿wɛ̆run⌒ (-w‿w-<-n‿w- §720) *this is one and this* (*that*) *is one (the same).*
wɛ̆r‿ (iii) (§2670) indef. pron. *somebody, someone, anybody, anyone, one*, pl. *some*.
émkɪn‿tékkɪ‿wɛ̆r‿mắkkon⌒ *perhaps someone stole (has stolen) him (her, it).*
X. kắg‿índo‿dắná? *are there snakes* (§4696*d*) *here?*
Y. wílgɪ‿wɛ̆b‿bɛ̆goru⌒ (-b‿b- < -g‿b- §519) *we killed one yesterday*.
X. súgɪr‿dắná? *is there any in the market?*
Y. wɛ̆s‿síkkandi⌒ (-s‿s- < -g‿s- §678) *I'll* (§5369*b*) *tell someone to ask.*
ğu‿wɛ̆gɪ‿índ‿ɪšín⌒ and
N. ğu‿wɛ̆kɪ‿índ‿ɪšín⌒ *go and send one (someone) here.*
āī‿wɛ̆gɪ‿dólmunun⌒ and
āī‿wɛ̆d‿dólmunun⌒ *I don't want one (any, anybody, anything).*
āī‿wɛ̆r‿bɛlíŋgɪ‿dólmunun⌒ *I don't want anybody to come (go) out*; ‿wɛ̆r‿bɛlíŋgɪ‿ (§1622) is the object of ‿dólmunun⌒.
X. mám‿mɪnɛ́llɛ́? *what's that over there?*
Y. tíddotōw‿wɛ̆rn‿ɛ́gedun⌒ (-w‿w-<-n‿w- §720) *it's a sheep of one of them.*
íŋgurtōw‿wɛ̆rɪ‿dábkoran⌒ *some of these (have) disappeared.*
wɛ̆rⁱ‿úrur‿undúddan, wɛ̆rⁱ‿árɪdɪr‿kuñúrran⌒ *some put it (them) into the river, some bury it (them) in the ground.*
wɛ̆r‿wɛ̆g‿ábbɛ́n⌒ *one (person, animal, etc.) is killing another.*
-wɛ̄r (iv) enclitic, unstressed or with secondary stress (§§2674-9, 4932-4) indef. pronom. adj. *a, some, one, a one, a... one.*
hánu-wɛ̄r‿áhhóŋgɪn⌒ *a (some) donkey is braying.*
ğówwɪ-wɛ̄rn‿óllɪr‿ (§§5858-60) *in the shade of some (a) tree.*
ğówwɪ‿dúl-lɛ̄rn‿óllɪr‿ (-l-l- < -l-w- §580) *in the shade of some (a) large tree.*
dúl-lɛ̄b‿bɛ̆gori⌒ (-b‿b- < -g‿b- §519) *I (have) killed a big one.*
ín‿ódd‿ɛ‿dɪgrí-wɛ̄b‿bɛ̆gó⌒ *this disease (has) killed many a one.*
kándɪ-wɛ̄rɪg‿éttarɪr‿ *bring some knives.*
tɛr‿kán-tu-wɛ̄ro‿bŭgó⌒ (*s*)*he* (*it*) *was* (*has been*) *inside some house.*
-wɛ̄r‿ (v) enclitic, unstressed or with secondary stress, indef. pron. *somebody, etc.* (=iii); this is really iv used substantivally in the sense of iii:
tókków-wɛ̄t‿tắŋgɪrmɛn⌒ (-w‿w- < -n‿w- §720, -t‿t- < -g‿t- §707) *don't let one (anyone) come.*
tíddotōw-wɛ̄g‿étta⌒ *bring (some)one (aliquem, aliquam, aliquid,* τινα, τι*) of them.*
-wɛ̄r‿ (vi) enclitic, unstressed (§2491) indef. article *a.*
fɪríčči-wɛ̄r‿índo‿dán⌒ and
fɪríčč-ɛ̄r‿índo‿dá⌒ *there is a mason wasp here.*
ámbɛs‿ɛgéd-dɛ̄g‿goğedágɪn⌒ (-d‿d-< -d-w- §533) *my brother has slaughtered a sheep.*
dúrmadɛ‿kúmbu-wɛ̄m‿múkkó⌒ (-m‿m-<-g‿m- §601) *the hen (has) laid an egg.*
sắb‿ğɪgír-rɛ̄k‿kálkō⌒ (-r-r- < -r-w- §672, -k‿k- < -g‿k- §569) *the cat ate (has eaten) a mouse.*
írís-sɛ̄r‿dắgon⌒ (-s-s- < -s-w- §687) *there was (has been) a smell.*
bɪtắw-wɛ̄r‿ɛttắgo⌒ (-w-w- < -n‿w- §720) *a child (has) brought it (them).*
-wɛ̄r‿ may acquire stress by bearing a suffix (§1565):
ógğɪ‿kúb-bɛ̆rro‿dábugoran⌒ (-b-b- < -b-w- §517) and
ógğɪ‿kúb-bɛ̆ddo‿dábugoran⌒ *the men were in a boat.*
kắ-wɛ̆dd‿ắgɪn⌒ (*s*)*he lives in a house.*
wɛ̆n-d(ɪ)‿ (§2737*a*) adj. *appertaining to one, of one, one's.*
wɛ̆rín-d(ɪ)‿ (§2737*b*) adj. *appertaining to some, of some.*

wɛ̆r-an- (§2760) v.i. *become one, unite, coalesce.*
wɛ̆ram-bŭ- (§2761) v.i. stat. *be in a uniting* (*i.*) *or united state or condition.*
***wɛ̆raned-ắg-** not heard.
wɛ̆r-wɛ̆r-, wɛ̆r-wɛ̆- (§§2695, 5172-82) reciprocal pron. *one another, each other.*
obj. wɛ̆rwɛ̆g‿.
gen. wɛ̆rwɛ̆rn‿v., wɛ̆rwɛ̆nn‿v., wɛ̆rwɛ̆n‿v.c.
wɛrwɛ̆g‿ábbɛ́ran⌒ *they are killing one another* (...*each other*).
wɛrwɛ̆d‿dóllan⌒ (-d‿d- < -g‿d- §534) *they love each other* (...*one another*).
ɛ́nči‿wɛrwɛ̆m‿móndan⌒ (-m‿m-<-g‿m- §601) (*the*) *women hate each other* (...*one another*).
wɛrwɛ̆g‿gáligɪlɪn⌒ (part. pl. §2960+ -n‿ §4229) *they resemble each other* (...*one another*).
ɛ́nči‿wɛrwɛ̆n‿díltɪg‿awíčkoran⌒ *the women* (*have*) *plaited each other's* (...*one another's*) *hair.*
áŋ‿kắgon‿téŋ‿kắgow‿wɛrwɛ̆n‿ɛgéttɪnči⌒ (-w‿w- < -n‿w- §720) *my* (*our*) *house and his* (*her*) *house are near each other* (§5179).
wɛrwɛ̆gonon‿gɛndɪnógran⌒ *they walk in step.*
āīgon‿tékkow‿wɛrwɛ̆n‿tínnɛss‿ówwɪg‿ɛdedágru⌒ (-w‿w- < -n‿w- §720) *I and he are married to two sisters*, lit. ...*are in the situation of having married two sisters each* (*sister*) *of the other* (*sister*); (§5181).
wɛrwɛ̆rn‿ogóllo‿,
wɛrwɛ̆nn‿ogóllo‿ and
wɛrwɛ̆n‿ogóllo‿ (s.v. -r‿) *in front of each other, one confronting the other.*
wɛrwɛ̆rn‿ogóllo‿ (§§5858-60) *they are in front of each other.*
wɛ̄r-wɛ̄-, wɛ̄-wɛ̄- (§§2695-6, 5183-9) distributive pron. *one each.*
obj. wɛ̆rwɛ̆g‿, wɛ̄wɛ̆g‿ and exceptionally in N. wɛ̄gwɛ̆g‿.
kálgɪ‿wɛ̄wɛ̆k‿kálkoran⌒(-k‿k- < -g‿k- §569) *they ate (have eaten) a loaf each.*
fɪŋğắn‿wɛ̄wɛ̆n‿níran⌒ (-n‿n- < -g‿n- §625) *they drink a cup each.*
N. fɪŋğắn‿wɛ̄gwɛ̆n‿níhoran⌒ *they drank* (...*have drunk*) *a cup each.*
ar‿wɛ̄wɛ̆f‿fɪŋğắŋgɪ‿tíkkoru⌒ (-f‿f- < -g‿f- §540) *we gave* (*have given*) *them a cup each.*
wɛ̄wɛ̆t‿tóskɪt‿tíddi⌒ (-t‿t- < -g‿t- §707) and
wɛ̄wɛ̆t‿tóskɪt‿tóskɪt‿tíddi⌒ *I*('*ll* §5369) *give them three each.*
wɛ̄wɛ̆g‿gírɪš‿tóskɪt‿tíddi⌒ and
wɛ̄wɛ̆g‿gírɪš‿tóskɪt‿tóskɪt‿tíddi⌒ *I*('*ll*) *give them three piastres each.*
werwɛ̆get‿tắgoran⌒ (-t‿t- < -d‿t- §706) *they came* (*have come*) *one by one.*
werwɛ̆ged‿dúkkɪgō⌒ (*s*)*he* (*has*) *pulled them out one by one.*
ɛ́n‿díltɪw‿werwɛ̆ged‿dúkkɪgon⌒ (-w‿w- < -g‿w- §719) *the woman* (*has*) *pulled out the hairs* (*feathers* §4696*d*) *one by one.*
wɛrsɛ́ v.t. (*a*) *inherit*; (*b*) *be the heir of*

wérs(ı) — **wídɛ, wɪdé, wᵘdé**

[< وارث *heir* or ورث *inheritance* +-έ §3631].
ind. pres. aî⌣wersέriᐱ; perf. aî⌣wersέ-goriᐱ (N. -έko-, -έho-).
in⌣arítt⌣ambábırtōw⌣wersέgoriᐱ (-w⌣w- < -n⌣w- §720) *I (have) inherited this land from my father.*
ambábkı⌣wersέgoriᐱ *I (have) inherited from my father.*
wersέrar⌣ (-rár⌣; §§2200 ff., 2207) and **wersέríd⌣** (§§2256 ff., 2260) n. *inheriting.*
wersέ-kattı- (N. -έha-; §4093) v.p. *be inherited.*

wέrs(ı) (wέss(ı) §683; §2827) v.t. (a) *wish for, want*; (b) *seek, try to obtain*; (c) *seek as wife, woo.*
ind. pres. aî⌣wέrsırıᐱ; perf. aî⌣wέrsıgoriᐱ (N. -ıko-, -ıho-).
imperat. wέrsi!
aî⌣ɛkkı⌣tablánčıt⌣tírkır⌣ér⌣tíddotōw⌣wersíngı⌣sókkɛᐱ (-t⌣t- < -g⌣t- §707, -w⌣w- < -n⌣w- §720) *if I give you the padlocks you (can §5377) take from them what you want.*
íngı⌣tägírnár⌣bıwέrsıriᐱ *I shall try to get this at the merchant's.*
ím⌣búruw⌣wέrsıri⌣tέkkı⌣dóllıgέᐱ (-w⌣w- < -g⌣w- §719; s.v. -ɛd⌣ ii) *I woo this girl because I love her.*
wέrsar⌣ (-sár⌣; §§2200 ff.) and **wersíd⌣** (§§2256 ff.) n. *wishing for, etc.*
wέrs-an (§§3890 ff.) v.t. *tell to seek, etc., let seek, etc.*
wέrsı-bŭ- (§3931β) v.i. stat. *be in a wanted (etc.) state or condition.*
wɛrsır-ɛg-ág- (§§4071 ff.) v.t. = wɛrsɛdól-.
wɛrs-ɛ-dól- (-sᵒd- §1178; §4022) and **wɛrsır-ɛ-dól-** (-rᵒd-; §4027) v.t. *be about to seek, etc.*
aî⌣mám⌣búrut⌣tımbábnár⌣wɛrsɛ-dólliᐱ (-t⌣t- < -g⌣t- §707) *I am about to ask for that girl from her father.*
wersɛd-ág- (§§3877 ff.) v.t. *be in the situation of having wanted, etc.*
ím⌣bób⌣ím⌣búruw⌣wɛrsɛdágınᐱ (-w⌣w- < -g⌣w- §719) *this (that) young man has asked the hand of this (that) girl.*
wέrsı-kattı- (N. -ıha-; §4093) v.p. *be wanted, etc.*
wĕrwέ- *one another, one each* s.v. wĕr⌣.
wésıl⌣ (wás-, wás-) n. *(written acknowledgment of) receipt* [< وصل id. §1359].
obj. wɛsílg(ı)⌣, -giᐱ.
pl. wέsılı⌣.
wέss(ı) < **wέrs(ı)** *wish for, etc.*
wέšš(ı)⌣ n. *face, front* [< Sudan Ar. وشّ id. = وجه].
obj. -šıg⌣.
pl. -šınč(ı)⌣
έw⌣wέššı⌣washánunᐱ (-w⌣w- < -n⌣w- §722) *your face is dirty.*
X. έrrı⌣sáır⌣bággun? *where is the name written?*
Y. sandúŋ⌣wέššırᐱ (-ŋ⌣w- < -gn⌣w- §642) *on the front of the box.*
wέt! imperat. of wέd *float, spin.*
wĕwέg⌣ *one each* s.v. wĕr⌣.
wézın⌣ *weight* = wázın⌣.

wíd v.i. *wander, roam, ramble, stroll.*
ind. pres. aî⌣wíd(¹)riᐱ, ɛr⌣wídınᐱ (-dīᐱ, -díᐱ); perf. aî⌣wídkoriᐱ (wítk-).
imperat. wít!
tókkow⌣wídmɛwwέ⌣, índ⌣ágwέᐱ (-w⌣w- < -n⌣w- §720) *don't (pl.) wander about, sit down here.*
wídar⌣ (-dár⌣; §§2200 ff.) n. *wandering.*
wíd-kátt(ı)⌣ (wítk-) adj. *given to wandering, etc., apt to wander, etc.* [§§2534, 2535b].
obj. -tıg⌣.
pl. -tınč(ı)⌣.
wid(¹)r-ɛ-nóg (§§4048 ff.) v.i. *go to wander, etc.*
wid(¹)r-ɛ-nóg-bŭ- (-nóggŭ- §546; §4058) v.i. stat. *be on one's way (going) to wander, etc.*
aî⌣kınnéw⌣wíd¹rɛnógbūriᐱ (-w⌣w- < -g⌣w- §719) *I am going for a little stroll.*

wíg v.i. (a) *cry, scream, howl*; (b) *low, bleat, squeal, whine, mew, crow, chirp, twitter, etc.* [onom.].
ind. pres. aî⌣wíg(¹)riᐱ, ɛr⌣wígınᐱ (-gīᐱ, -gíᐱ); perf. aî⌣wígkoriᐱ (⌣wíkko-).
imperat. wík!
subj. past aî⌣wígsı⌣ (⌣wíksı⌣, -su⌣).
bıtăn⌣wígınᐱ (-tăw⌣wí- §720) *the child howls.*
tí⌣wígınᐱ *the cow lows.*
έgɛd⌣wígınᐱ *the sheep bleats.*
hallúf⌣wígınᐱ *the pig squeals.*
wέl⌣wígınᐱ *the dog whines (howls).*
sáb⌣wígınᐱ *the cat mews (howls).*
dúrmadɛ⌣wígınᐱ *the cock crows.*
kám⌣wígınᐱ *the camel gurgles (grunts, whines).*
hánu⌣hóŋgın⌣wígınᐱ *the donkey brays and* (§6239) *squeals.*
fóğa⌣fɛğínn⌣ogóllo⌣wígınᐱ *the little birds* (§4696d) *twitter (chirp) before day-break.*
gırgíttɛ⌣wígınᐱ *the cricket chirps (the crickets chirp).*
wígar⌣ (-gár⌣; §§2200 ff.) and **wígıd⌣** (§§2256 ff.) n. *crying, lowing, etc.*
wig-kátt(ı)⌣ (wıkkát-) adj. *given to crying, lowing, etc.* [§§2534, 2535b].
obj. -tıg⌣.
pl. -tınč(ı)⌣.
wík! imperat. of wíg *cry, etc.*
wíl⌣ n. *yesterday (dies hesternus)* [RSN, §§129, 200].
obj. wílg(ı)⌣, -giᐱ.
íw⌣wíln⌣έssınᐱ (-w⌣w- < -n⌣w- §720) *this is yesterday's water.*
wíln⌣kálunᐱ and
wíl-kálunᐱ (§809) *it's yesterday's bread (food).*
ınn⌣ówwı⌣wín⌣dógor⌣oróféluñᐱ (-n⌣d- < -ln⌣d- §619) *today is colder than yesterday.*
wíldotōn⌣dámunanᐱ (s.v. -r-tōn⌣) *they have been absent (there haven't been any) since yesterday.*
wíldotōn⌣ágınᐱ *(s)he has been (sitting here) since yesterday.*
wílg(ı)⌣, -gi⌣ (§4431) adv. *yesterday (heri).*
wílgı⌣nókkoranᐱ *they went yesterday.*

wíl-ugúg⌣, -gi⌣ (§6041) adv.-complex *last night.*
wíl⌣ugún⌣nálkoriᐱ (-n⌣n- < -gn- §625) *I saw him (her, it, them) last night.*
wíln-d(ı)⌣ (§§2545 ff.) adj. *appertaining to yesterday, yesterday's.*
wílndıg⌣ɛttāgómunanᐱ *they didn't bring (...haven't brought) yesterday's.*
wílndı-kırı⌣ (§2541) adj. *resembling yesterday's.*
wílndıkırınᐱ *it's like yesterday's.*
wíččır⌣ (-čír⌣) n. *stick* [< *wıgtír⌣ (§§525, 1154) < wíg (to) *cry*+-t of n. act. (§2325α)+-ír⌣ *causation, so or. *crying-causation, then specialized in concrete sense as n. instr. §§2283-5].
obj. wıččírk(ı)⌣, -čír-, -kiᐱ.
pl. wíččıru⌣, -čırı⌣, -ᵘ (§1532).

wídɛ, wɪdé (§1794) and **wᵘdé** (§1202; §2878) v.i. (a) *turn (in any direction, so)* (b, *of body at rest*) *turn, turn round, turn over*; (c, *of body in linear motion*) *turn, turn round, turn back, return* [cp. ON. ⲟⲣⲉⲓⲁ- id. ZNG s.v.; RSN, §129 s.v. wíd].
ind. pres. aî⌣wíderi⌣, ɛr⌣wídɛn⌣ (-dɛ̄ᐱ, ⌣wídέᐱ), aî⌣wıdέriᐱ (⌣wᵘd-, ⌣wᵘdέᐱ, -dέᐱ, -dέᐱ); perf. aî⌣wídɛgoriᐱ (N. -ɛko-, -ɛho-), aî⌣wıdέgoriᐱ (⌣wᵘd-, N. -έko-, -έho-).
def. perf. aî⌣wıdɛróskoriᐱ.
wídɛrar⌣ (wıdέr-, wᵘdέr-, -rár⌣; §§2200 ff., 2210) and
wídɛríd⌣ (wᵘd-; §§2256 ff., 2263) n. *turning, etc.*
wídɛr-an (wıdέr-, wᵘdέr-; §§3890 ff., 3899) v.t. *tell to turn, etc., let turn, etc.*
wídɛ-bél (wᵘdɛ-; §§3873-4) v.i. *issue after (by, in) turning, go (come) back out, go (come) out again.*
imperat. wıdɛbél! and wıdέbél! (wᵘd-).
wídɛ-bıdá (wᵘdɛ-; §§3873-4) v.i. *come after turning, come back, come back again, return.*
ind. pres. aî⌣wıdɛbıdáriᐱ.
imperat. wıdέbıda!
wídɛ-bŭ- (wıdέ-, wᵘdέ-; §3931α) v.i. stat. *be in a turning (etc.) state or condition.*
aî⌣sámtɛ⌣nɛhárkı⌣wᵘdέbūriᐱ *I am returning on Saturday.*
wídɛr-ɛg-ág- (wᵘd-; §§4071 ff.) v.i. = wıdɛrɛdól-.
wídɛr-ɛ-dól- (wᵘd-, -rᵒd- §1178; §§4016-17, 4022, 4027) v.i. *be about to turn, etc.*
wídɛr-ɛ-má- (wᵘd-; §§4016-17, 4036, 4041) v.i. *become unable to turn, etc.*
wídɛrɛd-ág- (wᵘd-; §§3877 ff.) v.i. *be in the situation of having turned, etc.*
wídɛg-ır (wıdέg-, wᵘdέg-; N. -ɛkır, -ɛhır, -έkır, -έhır; §3680) (a) v.t. caus. *cause or allow to turn (i.)*; (b) v.t. *turn*; (c) v.t. caus. *cause or allow to turn (i.) round or over*; (d) v.t. *turn round or over, reverse, invert*; (e) v.t. caus. *cause or allow to turn back (i.)*; (f) v.t. *turn back, send back, put back, return.*
ind. pres. aî⌣wídɛgıddıᐱ, ⌣wıdɛgíddıᐱ (⌣wᵘd-), ⌣wıdɛgíddı⌣ (⌣wᵘd-); N. aî⌣wídɛkıddıᐱ (-ɛhı-), ⌣wıdέkıddı⌣

wígıd⌣ — zábıd⌣

(⌣wᵘd-, -ɛ́hı-), ⌣wıdɛkíddi⌒ (⌣wᵘd-, -ɛ́hí-), ɛr⌣wídɛgırın⌒ (-rĩ⌒, -rí⌒), ⌣wıdɛ́gırın⌒ (⌣wᵘd-, -rĩ⌒, -rí⌒); N. ɛr⌣wídɛkırın⌒ (-ɛhı-, -rĩ⌒, -rí⌒), ⌣wídɛ́kırın⌒ (⌣wᵘd-, -ɛ́hı-, -rĩ⌒, -rí⌒). tókkow⌣wᵘdɛ́gırmɛn⌒ (-w⌣w- < -n⌣w- §720) *don't cause (allow) him (her, it) to turn, etc.*
kıtábkı⌣tɛ́nn⌣agárro⌣wᵘdɛgírkori⌒ *I (have) put the book back in its place.*

wıdɛgır-dɛ́n(wᵘd-, N.-ɛ́kır-, -ɛ́hır-; §§4135, 3996-7) v.t. *(a) give back, return* (to the speaker); *(b) give in exchange* (to the speaker); *(c) answer* (to the speaker).
íngı⌣wᵘdɛgırdɛ́ŋkoran⌒ *they gave (have given) me this (α) back (β) in exchange.*
íŋkɛw⌣wıdɛ́gırdɛŋkó⌒ (-w⌣w- < -g⌣w- §719) *(s)he answered me in this way.*
âı⌣síkkıgori, âıgı⌣wıdɛgırdɛŋkómunan⌒ *I (have) asked, (but) they didn't answer me.*

wıdɛgır-ɛttá (wᵘd-; N. -ɛkır-, -ɛhır-; -ɛ́ttá §3855, §4142) v.t. *(a) bring back; (b) bring in return, in exchange.*
tırôn⌣ákkan⌣tír, tırôn⌣dámɛŋkaw⌣wᵘdɛgıréttá⌒ (-w⌣w- < -n⌣w- §720) *if they are there, give it to them; if they are not there, bring it back.*

wıdɛgır-oǧostá (wᵘd-; N. -ɛkır-, -ɛhır-; -ottá, etc. s.v. óǧı; §4142) v.t. *come after carrying back, just* (s.v. tá) *carry back.*
íŋg⌣âı⌣dólmunun, wᵘdɛgıroǧóttá⌒ *this I don't want (like): after carrying it back come (back) (=...just take it back).*

wıdégır-tır (wᵘd-; N. -ɛ́kır-, -ɛ́hır-; §§4135, 3998-9) v.t. *give back, etc.* (to other than the speaker).
âı⌣ɛ́kkı⌣míŋgı⌣wıdɛgırtíddi? *what do I (am I for, shall I §5369b) give you (α) back?* (β) *in exchange?*
âı⌣ɛ́kkı⌣mínɛ⌣wᵘdɛgırtíddi? *what (lit. how) do I answer you?*

wıdɛgır-úskur (wᵘd-; N. -ɛkır-, -ɛhır-; §4141) v.t.
(a) set after turning (t.), etc., place in a reversed or inverted position.
(b) return to its place, put back.

wıdɛ-nóg (wᵘd-; §§3873-4) v.i. *go (away) after turning, go back (again), return.*
imperat. wıdɛnók!, wᵘd-, ̋, ̈

wıdɛ-tá (wᵘd-; §§3873-4) v.i. *come after turning, come back (again), return* (see naloswıdɛtá, oǧoswıdɛtá).
imperat. wıdɛta!, wídɛta!, wᵘdɛta!
ɛr⌣tɛ́kkı⌣nálın⌣tâw⌣wᵘdɛ́ta⌒ (-w⌣w- < -d⌣w- §718) *when you see him (her, it) come back.*

wıdɛ-tó (wᵘd-; §§3873-4) v.i. *enter after (by, in) turning, go (come) back in (again).*
imperat. wıdɛto!, wıdɛtó!, wᵘdɛto!

wıdɛ́ŋır (wᵘd-, wídɛŋır, N. -ŋkır-; §3688) v.t. caus. and v.t.=wídɛgır.
S. dókkow⌣wıdɛ́ŋırmɛn⌒ (-w⌣w- < -n⌣w- §720) *don't cause (allow) him (her, it) to turn, etc.*
íŋkɛw⌣wıdɛŋírkoran⌒ (-w⌣w- < -g⌣w- §719) *they (have) answered thus.*

wıdɛros-nóg (wᵘd-; -onnóg §629; §§4180-4, -osgınóg, -ozgı-, -oggı- §4185) v.i. *go after turning, go back, return.*

wıdɛros-tá (wᵘd-; -ottá §714; §§4180-4; -osgıtá, -ozgı-, -oggı- §4185) v.i. *come after turning, come back, return.*

wıd-ımbɛl-bél (wᵘd-; §§3873-4, 3766) v.i. *after turning (etc.) start out.*
imperat. wıdímbɛlbɛl! (wᵘd-).

wígıd⌣ n. *worm, larva;* with collective sg. (§4696c).
obj. wıgídk(ı)⌣, -ítk(ı)⌣, -ítt(ı)⌣ §2462, -kı⌒, -tı⌒.
gen. wígıdn⌣v., -gınn⌣v.c., -gın⌣c.
pl. wígıdı⌣.
íw⌣wígıdun⌒ (-w⌣w- < -n⌣w- §720) *this is a worm (these are worms).*

wıgín-d(ı)⌣ (§§2545 ff.) adj. *appertaining to a worm, of a worm, of worms.*

wígıd-an- (§3910α) v.i. *turn into a worm (...into worms), become a worm, become worms.*
índo⌣wasáhag⌣ɛrom⌣múkkım⌣bıwígıdanın⌒ *if you leave dirt here it will turn into (i.e. breed) worms.*

wígıdam-bŭ- (§§3949 ff.) v.i. stat. *be in the state or condition of turning (having turned) into worms.*

wıll(ı) v.t. *demolish, pull down, take down, take to pieces.*
ind. pres. âı⌣wíllıri⌒; perf. âı⌣wíllıgori⌒ (N. -ıko-, -ıho-).
imperat. wíllı!
kérrıw⌣wíllıran⌒ (-w⌣w- < -g⌣w- §719) *they demolish the shed.*
kólɛw⌣wıllóskoran⌒ (-w⌣w- < -g⌣w- §719) *they have taken down the waterwheel.*

wíllar⌣ (-lár⌣; §§2200 ff.) and
wıllíd⌣ (§§2256 ff.) n. *demolition, etc.*

wıll-an (§§3890 ff.) v.t. *tell to demolish, etc., let demolish, etc.*

wıllı-bŭ- (§3931β) v.i. stat. *be in a demolished (etc.) state or condition.*
kólɛ⌣wıllıbún⌒ *the water-wheel is (has been) taken down.*

wıllır-ɛg-ág- (§§4071 ff.) v.t. =wıllɛdól-.
wıll-ɛ-dól- (-lᵒd- §1178; §4022) and
wıllır-ɛ-dól- (-rᵒd-; §4027) v.t. *be about to demolish, etc.*

wıllɛd-ág- (§3877 ff.) v.t. *be in the situation of having demolished, etc.*
kólɛw⌣wıllɛdágran⌒ (-w⌣w- < -g⌣w- §719) *they have taken the water-wheel down.*

wıllı-kattı- (N. -ıha-; §4093) v.p. *be demolished, etc.*

wíndi! *O my mother!* s.v. wó⌣c....!
wíndıkɛgıt! *O my aunt!* s.v. wó⌣c....!

wírda⌣ (-dá⌣, -dɛ⌣) n. *fever* [< وَرْد id.].
obj. -dag⌣.
pl. -danč(ı)⌣.

wírıd⌣ n. *(a, prop.) rose; (b) flower, blossom.*
— with collective sg. (§4696b) [< وَرْد id. §1334].
obj. wırídk(ı)⌣, -ítk(ı)⌣, -ítt(ı)⌣ §2462, -kı⌒, -tı⌒.
gen. wírıdı⌣, -ın⌣c.

wírıǧ⌣ adj. *naked, bare* [RSN, §129].
obj. wírıǧk(ı)⌣, -íčk(ı)⌣, -íčč(ı)⌣ §523, -kı⌒, -či⌒.
gen. wírıǧn⌣v., -rıñ⌣c. §632.

pl. wír(¹)ǧı⌣.
tɛr⌣wírıǧun⌒ *(s)he is naked (it is bare).*

wírıǧ-an- (§3910α) v.i. *become naked, etc.*

wírıǧam-bŭ- (§§3949 ff.) v.i. stat. *be in the state or condition of becoming or having become naked, etc.*

wırıǧanɛd-ág- (§3966α) v.i. *be in the condition of having become naked.*

wírıǧ-bŭ- (-íǧǧŭ- §552; §3945) v.i. stat. *be in a naked (etc.) state or condition.*
wırígbúran⌒ (-íǧǧŭ-) *they are naked.*

wısáda⌣ (wᵘs- §1202) n. *wooden support for sleeper's head* (used by Haḍ'ɛ́ndawa, not by Nubians; described *RBW* s.v. *metár'as*; cp. *SNK*, 655) [< وِسَادَة id.].
obj. -dag⌣.
pl. -danč(ı)⌣.

wıss(ı)⌣ n. *star;* with collective sg. (§4696d) [< *wíns(ı)⌣ §680 < *w¹ns(ı)⌣ < *úns(ı)⌣ < ún⌣ moon +-s dim. §2319; cp. ON. ⲟⲩⲉⲓϣⲉⲓ id. *GNT* s.v.; *RSN*, §129 s.v. *wínji*].
obj. -sıg⌣.
pl. -sınč(ı)⌣.
wíssı⌣gɛ́lɛ⌣ *the red star, Mars.*

wíssi-kıñ́ñ(ı)⌣ (§§2536-7) adj. *without stars.*
úgu⌣wíssıkıñ́ñ(ı)⌣ *a night without stars.*

wó⌣c....! (wó⌣c., wᵒv., w⌣v.; §2450) interjectional particle *O...!* for calling to or addressing persons; wó⌣ (etc.) is followed by the vocative, and does not stand alone:
wó⌣mohámmɛt! *O Muḥámmad!*
wó⌣sáłum! *O Sáłim!*
wó⌣safт́! *O Saʿíd!*
wó⌣bı́rnı! *O girl!*
wó⌣tót! *O boy!*
wº⌣ɛnnúr! and w⌣ɛnnúr! *O En-Núr!*
wº⌣ambáp! and wambáp! *O my father!*
wº⌣índi! and wíndi! *O my mother!*
wántó! *O my son!*
wº⌣amburu! and wámburu! *O my daughter!*
wº⌣ámbɛs! and wámbɛs! *O my brother!*
wº⌣ánnɛssi! and wánnɛssi! *O my sister!*
wambánna! (-bɛ́n-) *O my uncle!*
wáŋgi! *O my uncle!* (s.v. -g(ı)⌣).
wambánɛssi! *O my aunt!*
wíndıkɛgıt! *O my aunt!* (s.v. índ(ı)⌣).
wánnɛn! *O my wife!*
wánnogič! *O my husband!*

wógga⌣ (wég-, -gá⌣) n. *weight of 2¾ lb.;* with collective sg. (§4696d) [< وِقَّة id.].
obj. wóggag⌣.
pl. wóggančı)⌣.

wᵘdɛ́ *turn, etc.* = wídɛ.

N. **wŭkk(ı)** v.i. *(a) bark; (b) bawl* = úkk(ı) [onom.].
ind. pres. âı⌣wŭkkıri⌒; perf. âı⌣wŭkkıkori⌒ (-ıho-).
imperat. wŭkki!

wᵘsáda⌣ *wooden support for head of sleeper* = wısáda⌣.

zábıd⌣ n. *officer* [< ضَابِط id.].
obj. zábıdk(ı)⌣, -ítk(ı)⌣, -ítt(ı)⌣ §2462, -kı⌒, -tı⌒.
gen. zábıdn⌣v., -ınn⌣v.c., -ın⌣c.

zábar‿ — zummára‿

pl. zắbɪdɪ‿.
zābín-d(ɪ)‿ (§§ 2545 ff.) adj. *appertaining to the (an) officer, (the) officer's.*
zăbtíje‿ (zăpt-, -íja‿, -íja‿) n. *police-station* [< ضَبْطِيَّة *id.*].
  obj. -ɛg‿.
  pl. -ɛnč(ɪ)‿.
  zaptíjar‿óğɪruá? *shall (§ 5369b) we carry him (her, it, them) to the police-station?*
záhar‿ n. *die (dice);* with collective sg. (§ 4696d) [< زَهْر *id.* § 1357].
  obj. zaháŕk(ɪ)‿, -kiᴖ.
  pl. záharɪ‿.
  zaháŕkɪ‿káččɪranᴖ *they play at dice.*
  tɛn‿dúŋgɪz‿zahárro‿dábɪrinᴖ (-z‿z- <-g‿z- § 734) *he loses his money at dice.*
zăl‿ n. (a) *anger, rage, vexation, irritation* [< زَعَل *id.* § 1352]; (b) *grief, sorrow, regret.*
  obj. zălg(ɪ)‿, -giᴖ.
  tɛn‿zăl‿dúllónᴖ *his (her) anger (etc.) is great, lit. ... heavy.*
zălé‿ v.i. (a) *get angry, vexed, annoyed, irritated;* (b) *become grieved, sorry, depressed* [< زَعَل imperf. stem of زَعَل *id.* +-ɛ́ § 3619].
  ind. pres. aī‿zālɛ́riᴖ; perf. aī‿zālɛ́goriᴖ (N. -ɛ́ko-, -ɛ́ho-).
  imperat. zālɛ́!
  tɪr‿áddotōn‿zālɛ́goranᴖ *they (have) got angry with me (us).*
zălɛ́rar‿ (-răr‿; §§ 2200ff., 2207) and
zălɛ́ríd‿ (§§ 2256ff., 2260) n. *getting angry, etc.*
zālɛ́-bŭ- (§ 3931α) v.i. stat. *be in a state of getting or having got angry, etc.*
  tɪr‿éddotōn‿zālɛ́bŭgoranᴖ *they were getting (had got) angry with me.*
zālɛ̄r-ɛg-ắg- (§§ 4071ff.) v.i. = zālɛ̄redól-.
zălɛ̄r-ɛ-dól- (-ʳᵒd- § 1178; §§ 4016-17, 4022, 4027) v.i. *be about to get angry, etc.*
zălɛ̄g-ɪr (N. -ɛ́kɪr, -ɛ́hɪr; § 3681) (a) v.t. caus. *cause or allow to get angry, etc.;* (b) v.t. *anger, vex, anno; grieve, depress.*
zamán‿ (zăm-, zɛm- § 956a) n. *time, long time* [< زَمَان *id.*].
  obj. zamăŋ(ɪ)‿, -giᴖ.

pl. zamănɪ‿.
  zɛmándotōn‿ *since long ago, for a long time* (مِن زَمَان).
  zămándotōn‿índ‿ăginᴖ *(s)he (it) has been (sitting, living, etc., s.v. ăg) here a long time.*
zamăŋ(ɪ)‿, -giᴖ (§ 4431) adv. (a) *long ago, long since;* (b) *previously, formerly.*
  zamăŋ‿išíŋkoranᴖ *they (have) sent him (her, it, them) long ago.*
zamắn-d(ɪ)‿ (zăm-, zɛm-; §§ 2545ff.) adj. (a) *of long ago, ancient;* (b) *previous, former.*
zamānín-d(ɪ)‿ (zăm-, zɛm-; §§ 2545ff.) adj. = zamắnd(ɪ)‿.
†**zaráf‿** n. *giraffe* [< زَرَاف *id.* coll. §§ 1393, 2403].
  obj. -áfk(ɪ)‿, -kiᴖ.
  pl. -áfɪ‿.
zárɪf‿ n. *envelope* [< ظَرْف *id.* § 1359].
  obj. zarífk(ɪ)‿, -kiᴖ.
  pl. zár(ɪ)fɪ‿.
  zárfɪr‿úndur‿ *put it (them) into the (an) envelope.*
zawaráḍ‿ (-ăt‿) n. *El Zawarat (on map), a village on the left bank of the Nile, near the southern end of Argo Island.*
  obj. -ăţt(ɪ)‿ (§ 716), -tiᴖ.
zárbɛ‿ n. *fence* = zɛ́rbɛ‿.
zɛ́d‿ n. *(vegetable) oil* [< زَيْت *id.*].
  obj. zɛ́dk(ɪ)‿, zɛ́tk(ɪ)‿, zɛ́tt(ɪ)‿ § 2462, -kiᴖ, -tiᴖ.
  gen. zɛ́dn‿v., zɛ́nn‿v.c., zɛ́n‿c.
  símsɪm‿zɛ́d‿ *sesame oil.*
zɛ́mb(ɪ)‿ n. *crime, offence, sin* [< ذَنْب *id.*].
  obj. -bɪg‿.
  pl. -bɪnč(ɪ)‿.
†**zɛnóbja‿** n. *cigar;* with collective sg. (§ 4696d) [< Sudan Ar. زنوبيا *id.* AESA s.v.].
  obj. -jag‿.
  pl. -janč(ɪ)‿.
  [In 1901 Zenobia (Ζηνοβία) was the only brand of cigar to be had at Angelo Capato's shop in Omdurman; our Nubian servants spread the name all over the Sudan.]
zɛ́rbɛ‿ (zăr-) n. *fence of thorn-bushes, fenced enclosure* [< زَرْب *id.* + -ɛ‿ of n. ess. § 2236].

  obj. -bɛg‿.
  pl. -bɛnč(ɪ)‿.
  zɛ́rbɛn‿ágɪl‿ *opening of (gate in) fence.*
zɛríbɛ‿ n. = zɛ́rbɛ‿ [< زَرِيبَة *id.*].
  obj. -bɛg‿.
  pl. -bɛnč(ɪ)‿.
zɛrzúr‿ n. *sparrow, Passer rufidorsalis Brehm (KNH, p. 41);* with collective sg. (§ 4696c) [< زُرْزُور *id.*].
  obj. -zúrk(ɪ)‿, -kiᴖ.
  pl. -zúrɪ‿.
zīdɛ́‿ v.t. *increase* [< imperf. stem of زَاد يَزِيد *id.* +-ɛ́ § 3625].
  ind. pres. aī‿zīdɛ́riᴖ; perf. aī‿zīdɛ́goriᴖ (N. -ɛ́ko-, -ɛ́ho-).
  kɪnnɛz‿zīdɛ́ᴖ (-z‿z- <-g‿z- § 734) *increase (it) a little.*
  bíllɛk‿kɪnnɛz‿zīdɛ́ᴖ *put a little more onion.*
zīdɛ́rar‿ (-răr‿; §§ 2200ff., 2207) and
zīdɛ́ríd‿ (§§ 2256ff., 2260) n. *increasing.*
zīdɛ́r-an (§§ 3890ff., 3899) v.t. *tell to increase, let increase.*
zīdɛ̄r-ɛ-mắ- (§§ 4016-17, 4036, 4041) v.t. *become unable to increase.*
zīdɛ́g-ɪr (N. -ɛ́kɪr, -ɛ́hɪr; § 3681) v.t. caus. *cause or allow to increase.*
  ind. pres. aī‿zīdɛ́gɪddiᴖ.
zɪáda‿ (a) n. *increase, excess, addition* [< زِيَادَة *id.*]; (b) adj. *more, additional.*
  obj. -dag‿.
  pl. -danč(ɪ)‿.
  ár‿ɛskɛz‿zɪádagoŋ‿undúrkoruᴖ (-z‿z- <-d‿z- § 733) *we (have) also put in some more earth* = ɛskɛ́tkɪ‿ ténnɛgon‿undúrkoruᴖ.
zíkmɛ‿ (-mắ‿, -ma‿) n. *catarrh in nose or throat, cold in the head* (= ískɪdɛ‿, úskadɛ‿) [< زُكْمَة *id.*].
  obj. -mɛg‿.
zɪmmăr‿
  hăğ‿zɪmmár‿ n. *Hag Zumar (on map), a village on Argo Island, south of its centre.*
  obj. -ărk(ɪ)‿, -kiᴖ.
zummára‿ (su-) n. *pipe, flute* [< Sudan Ar. زَمَّارَة *id.* = زَمَارَة *id.*].
  obj. -rag‿.
  pl. -ranč(ɪ)‿.
  zummárag‿ağğóminᴖ *he is playing (habitually plays § 3832) on the (a) pipe.*

ENGLISH–NUBIAN

a indef. article -wēr‿ (§§ 2491, 4932–4): *I want a towel*: fúta-wēd‿dólli◠.
 a is often not to be rendered (§§ 4689–92): *Give him a piastre*: gıríški‿tír◠.
abandon v.t. wɛlɛ́sɛ (wɛlēsé, ˇˊˊ §§ 1794, 2878); múg.
able, be (=*can* q.v.) v. aux. ɛ́sk(ı) (ísk(ı)). *They weren't able to spoil it*: harbēɛ‿mågoran◠.
ablutions (ritual), perform v.i. waddɛ́.
ablutions (ritual), water for n. wádu‿.
about prep.
 What did he say about the horse? káčči‿ mínɛ‿wɛ́gon?
 What did you do about the saddle? ɛr‿ dɛgírkı‿mín‿áukon?
 I shall stop here about three days: índo‿ jōm‿tóskıkırıb‿biñírri◠.
 He died about five years ago: tɛr‿dīsíndotōn‿ğɛ́n‿díčkırı-taran◠.
above adv. dógōr‿ (§ 6007).
above prep. —n‿dógōr‿ (§ 5898).
 above the house: kån‿dógōr‿.
Abraham n. abrahín‿.
abscess n. amğulúd‿; bɛ́lt(ı)‿; (*small*) tússa‿.
absent adj. ǎgmɛnıl‿ (§ 3112); tɛ́gmɛnıl‿; dámɛnıl‿; búmɛnıl‿.
 Are the inmates of the house absent? (a) kånır‿ǎgmɛndan? (b) kånırı‿dámɛndan?
abundant adj. dígrĭ‿ (dıgrí‿).
abuse n. (*reviling*) dídar‿ (-dår‿); dıdíd‿; dídt(ı)‿ (dítt(ı)‿).
abuse v.t. (*revile*) díd.
 Don't abuse him: tókkon‿dídmɛn◠.
Abyssinian n. hábáši‿ (-baši‿, -beši‿).
Acacia albida n. húruğ‿ (úruğ‿).
Acacia arabica n. ğǒww‿urúmmɛ‿; ğǒww(ı)‿.
 pod(s) of Acacia arabica: ğúrtɛ‿.
Acacia ehrenbergiana n. mórɛ‿.
Acacia seyal n. sállɛ‿.
Acacia spirocarpa n. gándɛ‿.
accompany v.t. (*go with*) sóg; sogédda-.
according to prep. -ɛd‿.
 Does he decide according to law? hákkɛd‿ ähhokmɛ́ná?
account n. (*reckoning*) hısáb‿.
accurate adj. tamám‿ (tåm-, tɛm-).
ache n. óddɛ‿.
ache v.i. ódd(ı); óddıbŭ-.
 My head aches: ánn-ur‿åıg‿óddın◠.
Acheta sp. n. bángа‿.
acquire v.t. kɛsbɛ́.
acre n. fɛddán‿.
across, come (go) v.t. múkk(ı).
act v.i. åu (åw, åu).
action n. áwar‿ (áwår‿); áwíd‿.
Adam's apple n. gőz‿ (gős‿).

addition n. (*increase*) zıáda‿.
additional adj. zıáda‿.
adhesive adj. ǧóndo‿.
adolescent n. bób‿.
adore v.t. abdɛ́.
adorn v.t. tónǧılgır.
adroit adj. fála‿.
advance v.i. ógolan-; gɛddımɛ́ (-dumɛ́); gɛ́ddımkatt(ı) (-dum-).
advantage n. fåıda‿ (fåıda‿); faıdåd‿.
advantageous adj. faıdakól‿ (fåıdakól‿).
adze n. náwud‿ (náuud‿).
afar adv. wárrı‿.
affair n. ğɛ́lli‿; håğá‿.
affection n. dólar‿ (-dår‿); dolíd‿; dólt(ı)‿.
afraid, be v.i. sándı (ısán-, usán-; § 5546); åssándı (ågsán-, åksán-); sándıbŭ- (ısán-, usán-).
 (S)*he (it) is afraid*: tɛr‿ısándın◠, pl. tır‿ ısándıran◠.
 Don't be afraid: tókkon‿sándımɛn◠, pl. tókkon‿sándımɛwwɛ́◠.
 What are you so much afraid of? míndotōn‿dıgrı́gırsándın?
 Are you afraid of him (her, it)? (a) ɛr‿ tɛ́kkı‿sándıná? (b) ɛr‿tɛ́ddotōn‿sándıná?
 Are you afraid of thieves' coming? ɛr‿ mágası‿bıtárangɛs‿sándıná?
 Are they afraid of the dog? (a) wɛ́lgı‿sándırandɛ́? (b) wɛ́llotōn‿sándırandɛ́?
after conj. ‿bådır‿ (§ 5910); ‿bádk(ı)‿ (‿båtk(ı)‿, ‿bátt(ı)‿; § 4386); ‿ahírro‿.
 Do it after I go out: åı‿bɛ́llım‿bådır‿áu◠.
 after the man comes: ógıǧ‿tåm‿bådır‿.
 after the man came: ógıǧ‿tåsım‿bådır‿.
 after the man goes: ógıǧ‿nógım‿bådır‿.
 after the man went: ógıǧ‿nógsım‿bådır‿.
 After Sålim comes let ɣáli go: sálum‿ tåm‿bådır‿ålın‿nógan◠.
 After you get clear of the railway go to your left: gadíbırtōn‿noggúbɛ́lım‿bådk‿ ɛ́m‿maıŋgɛn‿nók◠.
after prep. (*of time*) —m‿bådır‿ (§ 4376). (*of place and time*) —m‿bådk(ı)‿ (-m‿ båtk(ı)‿, -m‿bått(ı)‿ § 4356); —n‿ abåğır‿ (§ 4358); —n‿abågkɛd‿ (-åkk-, -kɛt◠, -kɛ́◠ § 4380a).
 after dinner: áṣam‿bådır‿.
 Come after me: ánn‿abåğír‿ta◠.
afterbirth n. tíss(ı)‿.
aftermath n. búttɛ‿.
afternoon n. (*early*) ɛ́s‿; (*late*) ásur‿.
 in the afternoon: dúhurm‿bådır‿.
 this afternoon: ınnówwı‿dúhurm‿bådır‿.
 tomorrow afternoon: asálgı‿dúhurm‿ bådır‿.
afterwards adv. bådır‿; bådk(ı)‿ (båtk(ı)‿, bátt(ı)‿, -kı◠, -tı◠); bådkɛd‿ (båtk-,

bått-; -ɛt◠, -ɛ́◠); abåğır‿; abågkɛd‿ (-åkk-; -ɛt◠, -ɛ́◠).
 Do this afterwards: ıŋgı‿bådkɛd‿áu◠.
again adv. tɛnnɛ́‿ (tɛ́nnɛ́‿; tɛnnɛ́◠, ´˜, ˊˊ); tɛnnɛ́g‿; tɛnnɛ́gon‿.
 Say it again: tɛ́nnɛ‿wɛ́◠ (tɛ́nnɛ‿wɛ◠); tɛnnɛ‿báññi◠ (tɛ́nnɛ́b‿báññi◠).
 He will not go again: tɛnnɛ́b‿ınógmunun◠.
 He will not come again: tɛnnɛ́b‿bıtámunun◠.
 Do it again: tɛnnɛ́gon‿áu◠.
 Don't do it again: tókkon‿tɛ́nn‿áumɛn◠.
against prep. -r‿ (-ır‿, -ro‿, -do‿, -lo‿ §§ 4291 ff.).
 Did you give evidence against him? ɛr‿ tɛ́ddo‿kárǧıgoná?
 Has he put in a petition against you? ardahålg‿ɛ́dd‿undúrkoná?
age n. úgu‿; úmur‿. *old age*: dúrukanɛ‿.
 What is your age? ɛ́nn‿úgu‿mukóttɛ́rrɛ́? ; ɛ́nn‿úmur‿mıŋkóttɛ́rrɛ́?
aged adj. dúru‿.
agent n. wakíl‿ (wåk-, wɛk-).
agile adj. šóro‿.
ago adv.
 I sent it long ago: zamåŋg‿ıšíŋkori◠.
 I saw him three days ago: åı‿tɛ́kkı‿nalsúddotōn‿jōm‿tóskı-taran◠.
agree v.i. (*consent*) ɛrdɛ́.
agriculture n. tɛrar‿ (-rår‿); tɛríd‿.
ahead adv. ogóllo‿.
 Go (on) ahead: ogóllo‿nók◠, pl. ...‿nógwɛ◠.
ahead, move (go, come) v.i. ógolan; gɛddımɛ́ (-dumɛ́); gɛ́ddımkatt(ı) (-dum-).
ahead of prep. —n‿ogóllo‿; —n‿ōwwɛ́llo‿.
 Go ahead of us: ánn‿ogóllo‿nók◠.
ailment n. óddɛ‿.
air n. (*atmosphere*) háwa‿.
alarm v.t. sándıgır (ıs-, us-).
alight, be v.i. ǧugbŭ-.
alight, set v.t. ǧúgur.
alive, be v.i. áñ; áñbŭ-.
 Is (s)he (it) alive? áññá?
 (S)*he (it) is not alive*: áñmunun◠.
all adj. mállɛ‿.
 Bring it all: mállɛg‿ɛ́tta◠.
 All four of them came: (a) tɛr‿kɛmıŋgår‿ tågon◠ (...‿tågoran◠); (b) tíñ‿kɛmıŋgår‿tågon◠ (...‿tågoran◠); (c) tır‿ kɛmıŋgår‿tågoran◠.
 Take all six of them away: tɛr‿gorıŋgårkı‿sókkɛ◠ (tíñ‿go-).
 Is that all? (is that the lot?): gɛ́dır‿tɛ́?
 Pick up all the small ones: kíñña‿kíññab‿ bítti◠.
all day adv. ugrɛ́s‿mállɛg‿; nahár‿mállɛg‿.

allow —Arabic

The wind blows all day: túrug⌣ugrɛ́s⌣ málleg⌣úffen⌢.
We stayed all night: ar⌣úgu⌣málleg⌣ ákkoru⌢; ar⌣úgu⌣mállet⌣tɛ́kkoru⌢.
Don't touch it at all! ɛ́bɛdɛn⌣tókkon⌣ ğábɛmɛn!
All right! sɛ́rɛ́n! (and s.v. *right*).

allow v.t. múg. To allow the action or state of a verb is expressed by its causative stem (§§ 3663 ff.):
Don't allow him to go to the market: súgɪr⌣tókkon⌣nógɪŋgɪrmɛn⌢.

alluvial, *newly-formed alluvial land:* gu-rúnt(ɪ)⌣.

aloft adv. dógŏr⌣.

alone adv. kól⌣ (-kól⌣ §§ 4943–8).
Has he come alone?: kól⌣tágoná?
I shall go alone: ãikól⌣bɪnógrɪ⌢.
Go alone: ɛkkól⌣nók⌢, pl. írkonɪ⌣nógwɛ⌢.
Let him go alone: tɛkkólgɪ⌣nógan⌢.
See whether he is alone: tɛkkól⌣ăgkɪn⌣ nál⌢.
Bring the horse alone: káčkɪ⌣tɛkkólg⌣ étta⌢.

along
Who was carrying it along?: ní⌣sokkɛd-dágon?

alongside prep. —n⌣ábtɪr⌣ (⌣áptɪr⌣, ⌣áttɪr⌣; §§ 4375, 5894).
alongside the path: darúbn⌣áttɪr⌣.

also adv. -on⌣ suffixed to objective (§§ 4398–400).
He is to come, and you also: tɛ́kkɪ⌣tăran, ɛ́kkon⌢.
Bring mine also: ándɪgoŋg⌣étta⌢.
Do it now and after lunch also: ɛ́kkɛnɛg⌣ áu⌣gádam⌣bádɪrgon⌣áu⌢ (-dɪrkon⌣ áu⌢).

alter v.i. ɛ́ččɛlan.

alter v.t. gajɪrɛ́; ɛččɛ́lgɪr.
Don't alter it: tókkoŋ⌣gajɪrɛ́mɛn⌢.

alternate
Water it on alternate days: jóm⌣mɛ́w-wakkɪg⌣ówwɪntɪr⌣dɛ́k⌢.

always adv. dímɛ⌣; dímɛg⌣ (-gi⌢); dímɛn⌣ (-mɛ̃n⌣, -mɛ́⌢); dímɛŋg(ɪ)⌣ (-gi⌢); tɛmɛ́llɪ⌣ (-li⌢); tɛmɛ́llɪg⌣ (-gi⌢).

Amaranthus blitum n. goglådɛ⌣.

amazed, be v.i. hŏwwɪlɛ́.
I am amazed at it: (a) ãi⌣tɛ́ddoton⌣ howwɪlɛ́ri⌢; (b) ãi⌣tɛ́kkɪ⌣howwɪlɛ́ri⌢.

Ambrosia maritima n. kóddɛn⌣ónd(ɪ)⌣.

among prep. —m⌣bárrɛr⌣ (§§ 4361, 5897).
It is among the stones: kúlum⌣bárrɛr⌢.

amount n. kótt(ɪ)⌣; gédɪr⌣.
What amount does he want?: tɛ́r⌣mɪŋkót-tɛ̄d⌣dólɪn?
Do you know the amount of it?: ɛr⌣tɛ́ŋ⌣ gɛdírk⌣uñúrná?

ample adj. (*that suffices*) kɛfɛ́l⌣; (*that sufficed*) kɛfɛ́rɛl⌣.

ancestors n. -ūnč(ɪ)⌣ (s.v. -u⌣).

anchor n. hílɪb⌣.

ancient adj. zamånd(ɪ)⌣ (zám-, zɛm-); zamānínd(ɪ)⌣ (zám-, zɛm-); wåɪnd(ɪ)⌣ (wåɪn-); gɛdím⌣.
ancient times: wåɪ⌣ (wåi⌣); wåɪkɪd⌣ (wåɪk-).
Is it like an ancient stone? wåɪŋ⌣kúlukɪ-rɪrɛ́?
Are there any ancient stones here? kúlu⌣ wåɪnd⌣índo⌣dåná?

Are there any more ancient stones in this district? tɛ́nnɛ⌣kúlu⌣wåɪnd⌣ím⌣bɛ́lɛ-dɪr⌣dåná?

and conj. -on⌣...-on⌣ suffixed to objective (§§ 4401, 4901-2, 4906); -dãn⌣ (-dä⌣, -dã⌣)...-dãn⌣ (-dä⌣, -dã⌣) suffixed to nominative (§ 4402); -(u)n⌣...-(u)n⌣ suffixed to nom. (§ 4403).
Two and two are four: ówwɪgon⌣ówwɪgoŋ⌣ kɛmískɛ⌢.
ʕoθmấn and ʕáli came: (a) ɛsmáŋgon⌣ álɪgon⌣tågoran⌢; (b) ɛsmấn-dãn⌣álɪ-dãn⌣tågoran⌢; (c) ɛsmấnun⌣álɪn⌣ tågoran⌢.
I want bread and butter: (a) kálgon⌣ déskoŋgɪ⌣dólli⌢; (b) kál-dãn⌣dés-dãŋgɪ⌣dólli⌢; (c) kálun⌣dɛsúŋgɪ⌣ dólli⌢.
Have they brought wood and water? (a) ugúlláŋgon⌣éssɪgoŋg⌣ɛttāróskorandɛ́? (b) ugúllan-dãn⌣éssɪ-dãŋg⌣ɛttāróskorandɛ́? (c) ugúllanun⌣éssíŋg⌣ɛttārós-korandɛ́?
Take this away: and this: íŋgɪ⌣sókkɛ: ɪŋgóŋgi⌢.
X. *Has the master come?* tírtɪ⌣tågoná?
Y. *Yes:* ɛ́jjo⌢.
X. *And the guest?* ɪškártɪgoná?
X. *Did he take the parcel?* tarídkɪ⌣sókkɛ-goná?
Y. *Yes:* sókkɛgon⌢.
X. *And the letter?* ğawápkoŋgá?
Open and I'll come in: kús, ãi⌣tóri⌢.
He went out and has not returned: bɛ́lkon, tågomunun⌢.
I looked for it and couldn't find it: tɛbēmɪsírkori⌢ (§ 3784).
Knock and ask: kokkɪsíkki⌢.
Come and take it away: tasókkɛ⌢.
Take it away and come back: sokkɛw⌣dɛta⌢.
Come and see: tánal⌢.
Put it down and go: uskuronnók⌢.
Go and put it down: noggúskur⌢.

anger n. sínnɛrar⌣ (-rár⌣); sɪnnɛríd⌣; zál⌣.

anger v.t. sínnɛgɪr; zālɛ́gɪr.

angle n. kím⌣; rúkun⌣.

angry, be v.i. sínnɛbū-; zālɛbū-.
I am angry with you: (a) ãi⌣ɛ́kkonon⌣ sínnɛbúri⌢; (b) ãi⌣ɛ́ddoton⌣zālɛbúri⌢.

angry, get v.i. sínnɛ; zālɛ́.

angular adj. kímɪkól⌣; rúknɪkól⌣.

animal n. (*wild*) wáhaš⌣.

ankle n. óssɪŋ⌣kugúnd(ɪ)⌣; óssɪŋ⌣ku-múnd(ɪ)⌣.

anklet n. híğɪl⌣.

annoy v.t. (*anger*) sínnɛgɪr, zālɛ́gɪr; (*harass*) mágɪr.
Don't annoy him (her, it): tókkon⌣tɛ́kkɪ⌣ sínnɛgɪrmɛn⌢.

annoyed, get v.i. sínnɛ; zālɛ́.

another pron. and adj.
Bring another (*one more*): tɛ́nnɛ-wɛ̄g⌣ étta⌢.
Bring another (*a different one*): ɛččɛ́l-lēg⌣ étta⌢.
Bring another (*an additional*) *chair:* tɛ́nnɛ⌣ kúrsɪg⌣étta⌢.
Bring another (*a different*) *chair:* kúrs⌣ ɛččɛ́l-lēg⌣étta⌢.
Is there another (*additional*)? tɛ́nnɛ⌣ dåná?

Is there another (*different*)? ɛččɛ́l-lēr⌣ dåná?
Is there another like this? tɛ́nn⌣íŋkírɪ-wɛ̄r⌣ dåná?
Is there another kind? ğíns⌣ɛččɛ́l-lēr⌣ dåná?

answer n. rádd(ɪ)⌣ (rɛ́d-).
Bring back an answer: ráddɪg⌣ārétta⌢.
Has he (have you) brought back an answer? ráddɪg⌣āréttagona?
Where is the answer to my note? án⌣ ğawåm⌣ráddɪ⌣sɛ́?
He is to bring back an answer: ráddɪg⌣ āréttaran⌢.
Let him wait and bring the answer: ráddɪg⌣ iñréttaran⌢.
If there is an answer, bring it: ráddōn⌣ dågɪn⌣étta⌢.

answer v.i. ráddɛ́ (rɛddɛ́).

answer v.t. wɪdɛ́gɪr (wɪdɛ́g-, wᵘdɛ́g-); wɪdɛ́ŋgɪr (wᵘd-, wɪ́dɛŋgɪr); (*to the speaker*) wɪdɛ́gɪrdɛ̄n (wᵘdɛ́-); (*to other than the speaker*) wɪdɛ́gɪrtɪr (wᵘdɛ́-).
What does he answer? míŋgɪ⌣wᵘdɛ́ŋgɪrɪn?
Have you told him? What did he answer? wɛtíkkoná? míŋgɪ⌣wɪdɛ́gɪrkó?
What do I (how am I to) answer you? ãi⌣ɛ́kkɪ⌣mínɛ⌣wᵘdɛgɪrtíddi?
Don't answer me in that manner: tókkon⌣ íŋkɛw⌣wᵘdɛgɪrdɛ́mmɛn⌢.

ant n. gŏr⌣. *large ant:* gŏrn⌣kám⌣. *white ant* (*termite*): nórɛ⌣.

antelope n. gɛ́l⌣.

antimony n. nímnɛ⌣.

antiquity n. (*ancient times*) wåɪ⌣ (wåi⌣); wåɪkɪd⌣ (wåɪk-).

anxious, be v.i. hɛmmɛ́.
I am anxious about ʕáli: álɪn⌣íllɛr⌣ hɛmmɛ́ri⌢.

anus n. úsud⌣.

anvil n. sɪndåla⌣.

any pron. and adj.
If there is any, bring it: dågɪn, étta⌢.
Was any of it left? tɛ́ddotŏf⌣fadlɛ́gona?
Have you (got) any eggs? kúmbuk⌣kóná?

any one = **anybody**.
I don't want any one (to be) here: índo⌣ wɛ̄d⌣dólmunun⌢.

anybody indef. pron. wɛ̄r⌣.
Don't tell anybody: tókkow⌣wɛ́w⌣wɛ́tɪr-mɛn⌢.
Don't let anybody take it away: tókkow⌣ wɛ́s⌣sókkɛŋgɪrmɛn⌢.

anything indef. pron. šɛ́ji-wɛ̄r⌣.
Did he give you anything? ɛ́kkɪ⌣šɛ́ji-wɛ̄t⌣ tíkkoná?
X. *What has he brought?* míŋg⌣ɛ́ttagon?
Y. *He hasn't brought anything:* ɛ́ttagon⌣ dámunun⌢ (§ 6118).

apartment n. óda⌣ (ódɑ⌣).

ape n. abalãñ⌣; gírid⌣.

aperture n. úbbɛd⌣; úbbur⌣; ágɪl⌣.

apoplexy n. fatfåd⌣; fátterar⌣ (-rár⌣); fatteríd⌣.

appear v.i. (*come in sight*) wånd(ɪ)⌣.

apprentice n. kúrɪl⌣.

approach v.i. ɛgɛ́ttan-.

Arab n. árab⌣.

Arabic (**Arabian**) adj. arabínd(ɪ)⌣.

Arabic n. árabɪ⌣; arabínd(ɪ)⌣.

Talk Arabic: (a) árabıbꜱbáññıↄ; (b) arabíndıbꜱbáññıↄ; (c) árabıgebꜱbáññıↄ; (d) arabíndıgebꜱbáññıↄ.
Don't talk Arabic: (a) tókkonꜱárabıbꜱbáññımɛnↄ; (b) tókkonꜱarabíndıbꜱbáññımɛnↄ; (c) tókkonꜱárabıgebꜱbáññımɛnↄ; (d) tókkonꜱarabíndıgebꜱbáññımɛnↄ.
***Ardea* sp.** n. kárɛkalꜱ.
árdebb (اَرْدَبّ) n. érdɛbꜱ.
area irrigated by water-wheel n. kólɛꜱ.
argue v.i. gálıté.
Aristolochia bracteata n. ıččín-bɛrꜱ (-ím-bɛr-).
arm n. íꜱ, -iꜱ (§2374b).
upper arm: kɛffádꜱ.
forearm: ğɛrídꜱ; dúraꜱ.
arm-pit n. áuuntogoꜱ.
army n. áskarıꜱ.
The king of the Abyssinians sent his army: habɛšínčınꜱórꜱténnꜱáskarıgꜱıšíŋkóↄ.
arrangement n. tartíbꜱ (tár-, tɛr-).
arrival n. tárarꜱ (-rár-); tārídꜱ (tárīdꜱ, -rıdꜱ).
arrive v.i. (where the speaker is) tá; (elsewhere) ğú.
Has (s)he (it) arrived (here)? tágoná?
Have they arrived (here)? tágorandé?
Ask whether (s)he (it) has arrived in Khartoum: hartúmırꜱğúgogınꜱsíkkıↄ.
arrow n. nɛššábꜱ.
art n. sínaꜱ.
artery n. kóıꜱ (kóȋꜱ).
artisan n. basírꜱ; ústaꜱ.
as conj. ꜱnáhad (§4285δ; ꜱnahad §4285γ; §4321); ꜱnahádꜱ (§4323); ꜱnahádk(ı)ꜱ (-átk(ı)ꜱ, -átt(ı)ꜱ, -ákk(ı)ꜱ §4325); ꜱnahádkɛdꜱ (-átk-, -áttɛd-, -ákkɛd-, -ɛtↄ, -éↄ; §§5858–60, 4327, 5889).
Put it as it was: tɛrꜱbúsınꜱnáhadꜱúskurↄ.
Place it as I placed it: áiꜱtékkꜱúskursıꜱnahákkedꜱúskurↄ.
Do as I told you: áiꜱékkıꜱwétıssıꜱnahákkedꜱáuↄ.
as big (*large*) **as:** kótt(ı)ꜱ.
It's as big as a date-palm: béntıꜱkóttınꜱ.
as far as prep. —mꜱbókkonꜱ (-kõↄ, -kóↄ; §4381); —mꜱmónkonꜱ (-kõↄ, -kóↄ; §4383).
from here as far as the house: índotoŋꜱkámꜱbókkonꜱ.
as long as conj. (*during the time that*) kóttıgꜱ.
As long as I am here don't (*pl.*) *talk:* áiꜱíndꜱágrıꜱkóttıtꜱtókkomꜱbáññımɛwwéↄ.
as much as
It is as much as this: tɛrꜱıŋkóttɛrunↄ.
as soon as conj. -onoꜱ suffixed to subjunctive objective (§§4348, 6206).
Bring it as soon as it's ready: hádıranıŋgononꜱéttaꜱ (-ıŋŋo-).
As soon as I've had a bath I'll come: áiꜱbōwwettárıꜱ.
As soon as I see it I shall come in: nalɛbbıtórıↄ.
as well adv. (*in addition*) -onꜱ suffixed to objective (§§4398–4400).
Let him come as well: tékkoŋgıꜱtáranↄ.
Let them come as well: tírgoŋgıꜱtáwanↄ.
ascend v.i. dárr(ı); dógan-; ɛgéččɛ.

ascertain v.t. sıkkınál.
ash (**ashes**) n. ubúrt(ı)ꜱ.
ashamed, be v.i.
He is ashamed: téŋꜱkóñꜱsówwınↄ.
They are ashamed: tíŋꜱkóñꜱsówwınↄ.
ashore adv. bárrırꜱ.
ashore, go v.i. bárran-.
ash-tray n. ubúrtınꜱdád(ı)ꜱ (ꜱdádd(ı)ꜱ); ubúrtınꜱsáhanꜱ.
Bring an ash-tray: (a) ubúrtınꜱdádıgꜱéttaꜱ; (b) ubúrtınꜱsaháŋꜱéttaꜱ.
ask v.t. ídd(ı); síkk(ı) (ısíkk(ı)).
Ask the sheikh: (a) samílgꜱíddıↄ; (b) samílgꜱsíkkıↄ.
Ask the lady: (a) síttıgꜱíddıↄ; (b) síttısꜱsíkkıↄ.
Ask me before you go: ɛrꜱólgonꜱnógmɛŋgonꜱáigꜱíddıↄ.
Ask the station-master at what time the train will come: máháttanꜱnázırkıꜱgátırꜱsáꜱmıŋkóttɛrroꜱbítáŋgıꜱsíkkıↄ.
Have you been to ask? ɛrꜱsıkkırɛnókkoná?
Tell someone to go and ask about the train: wɛnꜱnóğğu-gatírkı-síkkanↄ.
He asked what he was to do: míŋꜱáurıꜱɛgóↄ.
We'll go to that house to ask for some water: (a) árꜱmaŋ-kándꜱéssıgꜱíddırꜱégıↄ; (b) árꜱmaŋ-kándᵘꜱéssısꜱsíkkırꜱégıↄ.
ask for v.t. talabé.
Ask for water: éssıtꜱtalabéↄ.
asleep, be v.i. ánnɛ́r- (ágnɛ́r-); nɛ́rbŭ-.
You were asleep: ɛrꜱnɛ́rbúgōↄ.
They are asleep, don't talk: nɛ́rbūran, tólkkomꜱbáññımɛnↄ.
ass n. hánuꜱ.
she-ass: hánuꜱkárr(ı)ꜱ.
assemble v.i. ğámmɛ.
assemble v.t. ğámmɛgır.
assist v.t. sádɛ; ássádɛ.
associate v.i. sáu (sáw, sáu); wénnıskatt(ı).
astonish v.t. ağabɛ́gır.
astonished, be v.i. ağabɛ́; hówwılɛ́.
I am astonished at this: (a) áiꜱíŋꜱağabɛ́rıↄ; (b) áiꜱíŋgıꜱhowwılɛ́rıↄ; (c) áiꜱíndotōnꜱhowwılɛ́rıↄ.
Aswán n. suwánꜱ.
at Aswán: suwándoꜱ.
at prep. -rꜱ after a vowel; -ırꜱ after a consonant, but -roꜱ after -r (except of personal pronouns); -loꜱ after -l; -do after -n and personal pronouns; see §§4291 ff. (*chez*) -nárꜱ (§§4304–5). (*of price*) -ɛdꜱ (-ɛtↄ, -é.ꜱ; §§4341–3).
at dinner: ášarꜱ.
He threw a stone at the goats: bértınčırꜱkúlu-wɛğꜱárkıgonↄ.
at the market: súgırꜱ.
at breakfast: futúrroꜱ.
He threw a stone at the dog: wélloꜱkúlu-wɛğꜱárkıgóↄ.
at Port Sudan: bursūdándoꜱ.
He threw a stone at him: téddoꜱkúlu-wɛğꜱárkıgōↄ.
Try to get it at the merchant's: táğırnárꜱwérsıↄ.
He sells it at ten piastres: gírıšꜱdımíŋgɛğꜱğántırınↄ.
I was surprised at that: áiꜱíndotonꜱhowwılɛ́gorıↄ.

at all adv. (with negative) ábadanꜱ; (with negative) abadáŋ(ı)ꜱ; (with negative) ɛbɛdɛnꜱ; (with negative) ɛbɛdéŋ(ı)ꜱ.
Don't bring it at all: ábadanꜱtókkonꜱéttamɛnↄ.
There isn't any at all: abadáŋgıꜱdámununↄ.
attain v.t. dúr.
attempt v.t. ğɛrrıbɛ́ (-rubɛ́).
attend v.i.
Attend to me: ɛ́mꜱbálgꜱáddoꜱdáranↄ.
attention n. (*mind*) bálꜱ; (*care*) hásabꜱ.
attention to, pay v.t. bálko.
Pay attention to this: íŋgıꜱbálkoↄ, pl. íŋgıꜱbálkowɛↄ.
attest v.t. kárğ(ı) (kágğ(ı)).
aunt n. (*paternal*) -bánɛss(ı)ꜱ; (*maternal*) -éŋkɛgıdꜱ.
Always with a form of the poss. pers. pron. (§2629) prefixed:
my paternal aunt: ambánɛss(ı)ꜱ.
your paternal aunt: ımbánɛss(ı)ꜱ.
his (*her*) *paternal aunt:* tımbánɛss(ı)ꜱ.
our paternal aunt: antımbánɛss(ı)ꜱ.
your (*pl.*) *paternal aunt:* ıntımbánɛss(ı)ꜱ.
their paternal aunt: tıntımbánɛss(ı)ꜱ.
my maternal aunt: índıkɛgıdꜱ.
your maternal aunt: ıŋɛ́ŋkɛgıdꜱ.
his (*her*) *maternal aunt:* tıŋɛ́ŋkɛgıdꜱ.
our maternal aunt: antıŋɛ́ŋkɛgıdꜱ.
your (*pl.*) *maternal aunt:* ıntıŋɛ́ŋkɛgıdꜱ.
their maternal aunt: tıntıŋɛ́ŋkɛgıdꜱ.
authentic adj. alɛ́ꜱ.
automobile n. turumbílꜱ.
avaricious adj. sówwɛdꜱ (sówwodꜱ).
await v.t. íñır (ıñír); ɛrğɛ́ (ɛrɛğɛ́, ɛrɛğğɛ́, ɛrığɛ́).
awake, be v.i. bíččıbŭ-.
away adv. wárrırꜱ.
Place it away from the door: bábırtōwꜱwarrıgırúskurꜱ, pl. … warrıgıruskúrwɛↄ.
away, keep v.i. bái (bāi).
Keep away from ɣáli: álırtōmꜱbáiↄ, pl. álırtōmꜱbáiwɛↄ.
away, keep v.t. bájıŋgır (bajíŋgır).
Keep the cook away from the beer: ğakútkꜱáwılgꜱmérsɛrtōmꜱbajíŋgırↄ.
away, take v.t. sókkɛ; árɛnnóg; ındɛnnóg.
Take it away: sókkɛↄ, pl. sókkɛwɛↄ.
Don't take it away: tókkonꜱsókkɛmɛnↄ, pl. tókkonꜱsókkɛmɛwwɛↄ.
awl n. ničínd(ı)ꜱ.
axe n. gámbuꜱ; fásꜱ.
handle of axe: gámbunꜱádꜱ; fásnꜱádꜱ.
axle n. (in water-wheel, *horizontal*) tórɛꜱ; (in water-wheel, *vertical*) míšš(ı)ꜱ.

baboon n. gírıdꜱ.
baby n. bıtāntódꜱ (bıt-).
back adj. (*hinder*) abáŋd(ı)ꜱ.
back n. ğérꜱ.
on my back: ánꜱğérroꜱ.
Lie on your back: (a) énꜱğérkɛtꜱtúbbıↄ; (b) ɛgɛččɛtúrbıↄ.
back part n. ákkaꜱ.
back, put v.t. (*return*) wídɛgır (wıdɛ́g-, wᵘdɛ́g-), wídɛŋgır (wᵘd-, wídɛŋgır); (*put behind*) abágkır (-ákkır).
Put it back in its place: ténnꜱagárroꜱwᵘdégırↄ.
backwards, go v.i. abágannóg.
backwards, move v.i. abágan-.

bad — be

bad adj. míll(ı)‿; ús‿; (*inferior*) bárɛd‿.
  It's bad: míllın⌒.
  It's the bad one: míllı-taran⌒.
  The man is bad: ógıǧ‿úsun⌒.
  The fish is bad: kårɛ‿míllın⌒.
bad, go v.i. míllan-.
  It's going bad: míllambūn⌒.
  This has gone bad: ím‿míllanoskon⌒.
bag n. gárar‿; kís‿; (*skin*) dábja‿.
  Put it into the bag: garárr‿úndur⌒.
  Put them into the bag: garárr‿úndurır⌒.
  A bag is lying on the table: kís-sēr‿tara-bĕzaŋ‿kóččır‿būn⌒.
baggage n. áfɛš‿.
Bagrus bayad n. dáško‿.
bake v.t. súg; úndur.
  Has he baked the bread? tér‿kálg‿undós-koná?
bake-house n. dĕuŋ‿ká‿.
bake-stone n. dĕuŋ‿ (dĕu‿).
balance n. (*for weighing*) mīzán‿.
Balanites aegyptiaca n. hıǧlíd‿.
bald adj. fṓǧ‿.
ball n. kŭra‿.
banana n. mṓz‿.
band n.
  band suspending drawers: díkkɛ‿.
bandy-legged adj. kañál‿.
bank n. (*of river*) ár‿; går‿; når‿; urunår‿.
  on the bank: árro‿.
  steep bank: ábol‿.
  top of bank: áb‿.
  right bank: (*a*) mált(ı)‿ (lit. *east*); (*b*) šérıg‿ (lit. *east*).
  left bank: (*a*) tıŋgár‿ (lit. *west*); (*b*) gárıb‿ (lit. *west*).
  These terms, that are true where the Nile flows northward, are also used where it flows in other directions, where they are not true; e.g. at Merowe the right bank, that there is the west bank, is called mált(ı)‿ (šérıg‿), and the left bank, that there is the east bank, is called tıŋgár‿ (gárıb‿).
  X. Where are the camels? kámlı‿sέ?
  Y. On the right bank: máltır⌒.
barber n. gáññıl‿.
Barbus bynni n. bınníjɛ‿.
bare adj. wírıǧ‿.
  bare ground: bŭd‿.
bargain n. šurŭd‿.
bargain v.i. gāwılέ.
  Bargain with him: tékkonoŋ‿gāwılέ⌒.
barge n. kábag‿; sándal‿.
bark n. (*of dog*) úkkar‿ (-kár‿), ūkkíd‿ (úkkıd‿); (*of tree*) káčč(ı)‿, gábad‿.
bark v.i. úkk(ı).
barley n. sérıñ‿.
barren adj. míra‿.
basin n. (*small*) sáhan‿; (*large*) tíšt(ı)‿.
basket n. (*flexible*) šíbır‿; (*rigid*) kóntɛ‿, sábad‿.
  basket-work tray (*plate*): áda‿.
bat n. (*animal*) fíčč(ı)‿; (*instrument*) kŭra-gɛǧ‿ǧómran‿.
bath n. hammám‿.
  I am going to (=shall) have a bath: āı‿bıbówwıri⌒.
  I'm just going to have a bath: āı‿bowwɛ-dólli⌒.
  How am I to have a bath in this draught? ín‿túrugır‿mín‿bówwiri?

bathe v.i. bŏww(ı).
  I am going to bathe in the river: úrur‿bıbówwıri⌒.
bathe v.t. bŏwwídd(ı).
battalion n. úrta‿.
batter v.t. šókk(ı); túkk(ı).
battle n. támugıd‿.
bawl v.i. úkk(ı).
  Don't bawl: tókkon‿úkkımɛn⌒.
bawling n. úkkar‿ (-kár‿); ūkkíd‿ (úkkıd‿).
be v.i. ‿έ- (‿ɛ- §§ 1790–1; §§ 2803, 3500ff., 5509ff.).
  (after adjective-concretions and verb-concretions) -gen (§§ 3596–7, 5520–7) often rendered by a sign of predication (§§ 4224–58, 5760–5836) or implied in a predicative postposition (§§ 5858ff.) or adverb (§§ 6007ff.).
  (*be situated, exist*) bŭ (lit. *lie*).
  (*be in a state or condition*) complex in -bŭ- (§§ 3927ff.).
  (*be present, exist*) dǎ-.
  (*be present, exist*) dábŭ-.
  (*exist continuously*) ág (lit. *sit*).
  (*exist continuously*) tĕb (lit. *stand*).
  (*forming the passive*) complex in -kattı- (§§ 4093–4104, 5703–7).
  I am rich: āı‿ırǧέn‿έri⌒ (‿ɛri⌒).
  You are rich: ɛr‿ırǧέnun⌒ (-nū⌒, -nú⌒, -nu §939).
  (S)he is rich: tɛr‿ırǧέnun⌒ (-nū⌒, -nú⌒, -nu §939).
  We are rich: ar‿ırǧέn‿έru⌒ (‿ɛru⌒) and ar‿ırǧέnın‿ (-nī⌒, -ní⌒, -nı⌒, -nin⌒, -nı⌒, -nı́⌒, -ni⌒).
  You (pl.) are rich: ır‿ırǧέn‿έru⌒ (‿ɛru⌒) and ır‿ırǧέnın⌒ (-nī⌒, -ní⌒, -nı⌒, -nin⌒, -nı⌒, -nı́⌒, -ni⌒).
  They are rich: tır‿ırǧέn‿έran⌒ (‿ɛrán‿, ‿ɛran⌒, ‿ɛrán⌒, ‿ɛrá⌒, ‿ɛran⌒, ‿ɛrã⌒, ‿ɛra⌒) and tır‿ırǧέnın⌒ (-nī⌒, -ní⌒, -nı⌒, -nin⌒, -nı⌒, -nı́⌒, -ni⌒).
  I am near: āı‿ɛgétt‿έri⌒.
  You are near: ɛr‿ɛgéttín⌒.
  (S)he (it) is near: tɛr‿ɛgéttín⌒.
  We are near: ar‿ɛgétt‿έru⌒.
  You (pl.) are near: ır‿ɛgétt‿έru⌒.
  They are near: tır‿ɛgétt‿έran⌒.
  We are near: (*a*) ar‿ɛgétt‿έru⌒; (*b*) ar‿ɛgéttınčín⌒; (*c*) ar‿ɛgéttínčı-taran⌒; (*d*) ar‿ɛgéttínčı-tànnan⌒.
  I am not rich: āı‿ırǧέmmunun⌒ (-munū, -munu, -mun §947).
  You are not rich: ɛr‿ırǧέmmunun⌒ (-munū⌒, -munu⌒, -mun⌒ §947).
  (S)he is not rich: tɛr‿ırǧέmmunun⌒ (-munū⌒, -munu⌒, -mun⌒ §947).
  We are not rich: ar‿ırǧέmmunun⌒ (-munū⌒, -munu⌒, -mun⌒ §947).
  You (pl.) are not rich: ır‿ırǧέmmunun⌒ (munū⌒, -munu⌒, -mun⌒ §947).
  They are not rich: tır‿ırǧέmmunan⌒ (-munã⌒, -muná⌒, -muna⌒, -mun⌒ §949).
  Am I not rich? āı‿ırǧέmmɛndi?
  Are you not rich? ɛr‿ırǧέmmɛnın? (-mɛnî?, -mɛní?, -men?, -mε̃?, -mέ? §951).
  Is (s)he not rich? tɛr‿ırǧέmmɛnın? (-mɛnî?, -mɛní?, -men?, -mε̃?, -mέ? §951).
  Are we not rich? ar‿ırǧέnımɛndu?

  Are you (pl.) not rich? ır‿ırǧέnımɛndu?
  Are they not rich? tır‿ırǧέnımɛndan? (-dã?, -dá?).
  Am I deaf? āı‿térıǧ‿έrıá?
  Are you deaf? ɛr‿térıgrέ?
  Is (s)he (it) deaf? tɛr‿térıgrέ?
  Are we deaf? ar‿térıǧ‿έruá?
  Are you (pl.) deaf? ır‿térıǧ‿έruá?
  Are they deaf? tır‿térıǧ‿ɛrándέ?
  Am I near? āı‿ɛgétt‿έrıá?
  Are you near? ɛr‿ɛgéttırέ?
  Is (s)he (it) near? tɛr‿ɛgéttırέ?
  Are we near? ar‿ɛgétt‿έruá?
  Are you (pl.) near? ır‿ɛgétt‿έruá?
  Are they near? tır‿ɛgétt‿ɛrándέ?
  When I was here I saw it: āı‿índ‿έsı‿wɛkíttı‿nálkori⌒.
  When you were here you saw it: ɛr‿índ‿έsıw‿wɛkíttı‿nálkon⌒.
  When (s)he (it) was here (s)he (it) saw it: tɛr‿ínɛ‿έsıw‿wɛkíttı‿nálkon⌒.
  When we were here we saw it: ar‿índ‿έsu‿wɛkíttı‿nálkoru⌒.
  When you (pl.) were here you saw it: ır‿índ‿έsu‿wɛkíttı‿nálkoru⌒.
  When they were here they saw it: tır‿índ‿έsaw‿wɛkíttı‿nálkoran⌒.
  It was like (resembled) this: ıŋkır‿ɛgó⌒.
  Where was (s)he (it)? såır‿ɛgṍ?
  Where have you been? ɛr‿ısåır‿ɛgó?
  It is large and handsome: dŭlgoŋgɛnın‿tóŋılgoŋgɛnın⌒.
  They are large and handsome: dūlínčıgoŋ-gendan‿tóŋılgoŋgɛndan⌒.
  Is (s)he (it) here? indorέ?
  Is (s)he (it) here or over there? indorɛ‿wálla‿mándorέ?
  Where are we? (*a*) ar‿ᴵsáırέ?; (*b*) ár‿sέ?
  ʕáli is in the kitchen: (*a*) álı‿matbáhır⌒; (*b*) álı‿dĕuŋ‿kår⌒.
  X. Is ʕáli in the kitchen? (*a*) álı‿matbáhırέ? (*b*) álı‿matbáhıró? (*c*) álı‿matbá-hıró? (*d*) álı‿dĕuŋ‿kårέ? (*e*) álı‿dĕuŋ‿kårέ? (*f*) álı‿dĕuŋ‿kåró?
  Y. No, he's in the market: wåran, súgır⌒.
  Is the cat in the room? (*a*) sáb‿ódar? (*b*) sábı‿ódaré?
  Are the cats in the room? (*a*) sábı‿ódar? (*b*) sábı‿ódaré? (*c*) sábı‿ódaró?
  Two and three are five: őwwıgon‿tóskı-gon‿díčkέ⌒ (§ 5312).
  This is from me: (*a*) ín‿ánnartōn⌒; (*b*) ín‿annartōnun⌒.
  Is this from you? ín‿énnartōndέ?
  Is it from him (her)? ténnartōndέ?
  This is from us: ín‿ánnartōn⌒ (-tōnun⌒).
  Is it from you (pl.)? ínnartōndέ?
  Is this from them? ín‿tínnartōndέ?
  This is not from me: ín‿annartómmunun⌒.
  These are not from me: íŋg‿annartóm-munan⌒.
  X. Where is he? tér‿sέ?
  Y. He's in his house: téŋ‿kår⌒.
  Where are the camels? kámlı‿sέ?
  Is (s)he (it) here? tɛr‿indorέ?
  Are they here? tır‿indorέ?
  He says it is in the train: gatírron‿ɛn⌒ (-rr°‿ɛn⌒, -rr‿ɛn⌒ § 5868).
  Tomorrow is Monday: (*a*) ásal‿bŭ́sun⌒; (*b*) ásal‿bŭ́š-taran⌒; (*c*) ásal‿bŭ́š-tànnan⌒.
  It's white: arṓn⌒ (árōn⌒ § 1973).

Is it white? aróré?
It's not white: arómunun⌒.
Isn't it white? arómenın? (-men?).
It's the white one: (a) aró-taran⌒; (b) áro-tànnan⌒.
The meat is raw: kúsu⌣déssın⌒.
It's the raw meat: kúsu⌣déssı-taran⌒.
His brother is a soldier: tímbes⌣áskarun⌒.
His brother is not a soldier: tímbes⌣áskár-munun⌒.
Is his brother a soldier? tímbes⌣áskarré?
Isn't his brother a soldier? tímbes⌣áskár-menın? (-men?).
It's his brother the soldier: (a) tímbes⌣askár-taran⌒; (b) tímbes⌣áskar-tànnan⌒.
He's her son: tén⌣tódun⌒.
It's her son: (a) tén⌣tód-taran⌒; (b) tén⌣tód-tànnan⌒.
You are a Moslem: er⌣míslımun⌒.
You are not a Moslem: er⌣mıslímmunun⌒.
Are you a Moslem? er⌣míslım(¹)ré?
Are you not a Moslem? er⌣mıslímmen?
You are the owner: er⌣tírtımun⌒.
You are not the owner: er⌣tírtímunun⌒.
Are you the owner? er⌣tírtıré?
Are you not the owner? er⌣tírtımen?
This is the owner: (a) ın⌣tírtı-taran⌒; (b) ın⌣tírtı-tànnan⌒.
This isn't the owner: ın⌣tírtímunun⌒.
Is this the owner? ın⌣tírtıré?
Isn't this the owner? ın⌣tírtımenın? (-men?).
It's mine: ándín⌒.
They're mine: ándınčín⌒.
It's not mine: ándımunun⌒.
They're not mine: andínčımunan⌒.
Is it yours? éndıré?
Are they yours? éndınčıré?
Isn't it yours? éndımen?
Aren't they yours? endínčımendan?
It isn't this; bring the other: ímmunun; eččélg⌣étta⌒.
X. Is that (near) Mohammed? ím⌣mohámmet⌣té?
Y. Yes, it is: mohámmét-taran⌒.
X. What's this? (...that?) ím⌣mınéllé?
Y. It's a bat: fíččin⌒.
Isn't that (yonder) one of our people? mán⌣ándınčırtów⌣wérmen?
This is Sam's place: ın⌣sémn⌣ágár-taran⌒.
Is it on Monday that he comes? búš⌣jómgı-te⌣tắn?
Is it ɣáli? tér⌣áli⌣té?
X. Is that (yonder) ɣáli? mán⌣áli⌣té?
Y. No, it is not: wăran, térmunun⌒.
Is that (s)he (it) over there? mán⌣ıker⌣té?
Whose horse is this? ın⌣ín⌣kắg⌣té?
X. Where is Sálım? sălum⌣sáıré?
Y. He is here: índo⌣bún⌒.
What is in the store? mahzándo⌣míndo⌣bún?
This was (found, lying) in the basket: ın⌣sábădır⌣búgŏ⌒.
It wasn't (disposed, arranged) like this: ínke⌣búgómunun⌒.
Is there one (does one exist)? wér⌣búná?
Where is the tobacco that was there? (a) tumbág⌣téddo⌣bél⌣sé? (b) tumbág⌣téddo⌣búrel⌣sé?

The tobacco is to be here: tumbákk⌣índo⌣bán⌒ (lit. *tell the tobacco to lie here* §5661).
It is not to be here: tókkon⌣índo⌣bámmen⌒.
He is naked: (a) wırígbun⌒ (-ígğun⌒); (b) wírığ⌣tébın⌒ (-ıč⌣té-).
This is not clean: íŋ⌣gendıbúmunun⌒.
Where was (s)he (it)? sáır⌣dắgon? and sáid⌣dắgon?
Where has (s)he (it) been? sáır⌣dắgon? and sáid⌣dắgon?
There are eight men: ógığ⌣ídıw⌣dắn⌒.
There is some: dắn⌒.
There isn't any: dắmunun⌒.
Isn't there any? dắmen?
Are there any onions today? ınnówwıb⌣bílle⌣dắná?
Aren't there any onions? bílle⌣dắmen?
If there is another water-wheel let me see it: kól⌣eččélon⌣dắgın⌣amínti⌒.
Where is ɣáli (to be found)? áli⌣sáır⌣dắn?
X. Is there any water? éssı⌣dắná?
Y. Yes, there is some in the house: dắn⌣kár⌣dắbun⌒.
X. Is there any milk? íčči⌣dắná?
Y. Yes, there is (some); it is in the pantry: éjjo, dắn; físır⌣bún⌒.
There is some sand in my shoe: án⌣ğázman⌣túr⌣sfu⌣dắbun⌒.
(S)he (it) was not here: índo⌣dắbugómunun⌒.
Let him (tell him to) stay where he is: tér⌣ágíndo⌣tégan⌒.
Let him stay (leave him) where he is: tér⌣ágíndo⌣múk⌒.
Stay where you are (sitting): er⌣ágíndo⌣ték⌒.
Stay where you are (standing): er⌣tébíndo⌣tép⌒.
Stay (pl.) where you are (sitting): ır⌣ágrúddo⌣tégwe⌒.
Stay (pl.) where you are (standing): ır⌣tébrúddo⌣tébwe⌒.
We shall stay where we are: ár⌣ágrúddo⌣bıtégru⌒.
They are without money: dúŋgıkíññır⌣ágran⌒.
He is without water: éssım⌣más⌣ágın⌒.
Leave the donkey where it is (stands): hánut⌣tér⌣tébíndo⌣mugó⌒.
Leave the donkey where it is (lies): hánut⌣tér⌣búndo⌣mugó⌒.
Leave the boat where it is (afloat): kúpkı⌣tér⌣tébíndo⌣mugó⌒.
Leave the boat where it is (aground): kúpkı⌣tér⌣búndo⌣mugó⌒.
This wood is not split (is unsplit, ist nicht gespalten, non diffissum est): ím⌣bér⌣gágbúmunun⌒.
This wood is not split (wird nicht gespalten, non diffinditur): ím⌣bér⌣gágkattımunun⌒.
What is there to be seen? míndo⌣nálkattın⌒.
Let him (her it) be: (a) welése⌒, pl. welésewe⌒; (b) mugó⌒, pl. mugówwe⌒.
(S)he (it) is to go: nógan⌒ (§§3890ff.).
They are to go: nógwan⌒.
be = *come* tắ.
He hasn't been here since Sunday: kıráherton⌣índo⌣tágómunun⌒.

I shall be here: índo⌣bıtắri⌒.
I shall (still) be here: índo⌣bıtégri⌒.
be = *go* nóg.
Have you been to Omdurman? er⌣búgar⌣nókkoná?
Where have you been to today? er⌣ınnówwıg⌣sáır⌣nókkon?
Where have you (pl.) been (to)? ır⌣sáır⌣nókkoru?
be present v.i. (*of persons*) ág; (*of persons or things*) dá-, dắbŭ-.
Is ɣoθmắn present? esmắn⌣ágná?
bead n. hábba⌣; háb⌣.
(*small*) aríñče⌣.
(*gold, cylindrical*) šólag⌣.
(*gold, spherical*) mutémma⌣.
beam n. bér⌣.
(*vertical*) énde⌣.
(*cross-beam resting on* énde⌣) mírıg⌣.
(*beam(s) lying across* mírıg⌣) féleg⌣.
(*fixed across shaft* under water-wheel) wăwır⌣ (-wᵘr⌣).
cloth-beam (*in loom*) tóre⌣.
bean n. (*Vicia faba*) fúl⌣.
(*Dolichos lablab*) úgud⌣.
(*Phaseolus vulgaris*) úgud⌣.
(*Phaseolus mungo*) ašránke⌣.
Bear, the Great n. áŋgare⌣; áŋgaren⌣óssınč(ı)⌣.
bear v.t. (*carry*) óğı; sókke.
(*have about one's person*) kág.
(*give birth to*) úsk(ı).
(*tolerate*) sabré.
beard n. sáma⌣ (sáme⌣).
He has a large beard: tén⌣sáma⌣dúlun⌒.
bearer n. (*one that brings*) éttăl⌣; (*one that brought*) éttărel⌣.
Is the bearer waiting? éttărel⌣ágná?
bearing n. (*half-socket, half-collar*) kălo⌣.
beast n. (*wild*) wáhaš⌣.
beat v.t. ğóm; šókk(ı); túkk(ı).
Don't beat him (it): tókkon⌣ğómmen⌒, pl. tókkon⌣ğómmewe⌒.
He beats a drum: nuggăragˇ⌣ğómın⌒.
They beat (have beaten) him (it) to death: ğombégoran⌒.
beautiful adj. tóŋıl⌣.
beautify v.t. tóŋılgır.
beauty n. tóŋılkane⌣.
because conj. -ed (-et⌒, -é⌒) suff. to obj. (§4344); ⌣ıllar⌣ (-lár⌣, -ler⌣) following gen. (§4378); -karam⌣ suff. to gen. (§4352); ⌣karámır⌣ following gen. (§4380).
He doesn't like it because it's hot: gúgr⌣éŋged⌣dólmunun⌒.
He dislikes it because it is bitter: nádd⌣éŋgem⌣mónın⌒.
He is telling lies because he is afraid: tér⌣sándíŋgem⌣múrsıg⌣áwwén⌒.
X. Why does that one over there run away? mám⌣mém⌣bódın?
Y. Because he is afraid: ısándıŋgé⌒.
You are ill because you drank it: er⌣nísunum⌣íllár⌣óddıbŭn⌒.
Because we took this away, he did not come: íŋgı⌣sókkesun⌣íller⌣tágomunun⌒.
because of prep. —n⌣íllar⌣ (-lár⌣, -ler⌣; §4377); —ŋ⌣karam⌣ (§4351); —ŋ⌣karámır⌣ (§4379).
because of the rain: árun⌣íllar⌣.

become v.i. ⌣án- (§§ 3888-9, 5492-6); complex in -an- (§§ 3910 ff.).
What has become of him (her, it)? s⌣áŋkó?, lit. *Where has (s)he (it) gone?*
Goodness knows what has become of him (her, it)! ɪsáŋkon! (-kŏ!, -kó!).
(S)he (it) has become deaf: tɛ́rɪgaŋkon⌢.
bed n. férɪš⌣.
Is my bed here? áf⌣férɪš⌣índo⌣búná?
He has gone to bed: turbóskon⌢ (tubbóskó⌢).
Is he (already) in bed? turbóskoná?
Has he gone to bed? ğuturbóskoná?
Have they gone to bed? ğuturbóskorandɛ́?
I shall read (it) in bed: tubbobbɪgɛrjɛ́rɪ⌢.
bed-clothes n. férɪš⌣.
bedroom n. nálun⌣óda⌣ (⌣óda⌣).
Put these into the bedroom: íŋgun⌣nálun⌣ódar⌣úndurɪr⌢.
This is my bedroom: ɪn⌣āɪ⌣nérrɪn⌣ódátaran⌢.
Put it into my bedroom: nérrɪn⌣ódar⌣úndur⌢.
It is in my bedroom: āɪ⌣nérrɪn⌣ódar⌣bún⌢.
It is in his bedroom: tɛr⌣nérɪnn⌣ódar⌣bún⌢.
It is in our bedroom: ar⌣nérrun⌣ódar⌣bún⌢.
Bring me a handkerchief from my bedroom: nérrɪn⌣ódártōn⌣mɛndíl-lēg⌣éttadēn⌢.
Open my bedroom windows: āɪ⌣nérrɪn⌣ódar⌣táğančík⌣kus⌢.
bed-spread n. férɪš⌣tagídd(ɪ)⌣.
bedstead n. áŋgarɛ⌣ (-gárɛ⌣).
Bring the bedstead: áŋgarɛg⌣étta⌢.
Bring (pl.) the bedstead: áŋgarɛg⌣éttawé⌢.
Bring the bedsteads: aŋgarénčɪg⌣éttarɪr⌢.
Bring (pl.) the bedsteads: aŋgarénčɪg⌣éttaríwwé⌢.
Put my bedstead into the room: ánn⌣áŋgarɛg⌣ódar⌣úndur⌢.
Put it on the bedstead: áŋgarɛŋ⌣kóččɪr⌣úskur⌢.
It's on the bedstead: áŋgarɛŋ⌣kóččɪr⌣bún⌢.
bee n. asáln⌣kúlt(ɪ)⌣ (asán⌣k-, asáɲ⌣k-).
beef n. kúsu⌣tínd(ɪ)⌣; kúsu⌣gúrnd(ɪ)⌣.
beer n. *(made from dates or millet):* umbílbɪl⌣; umbúlbul⌣.
(made from dates and millet): baggāníjɛ⌣; mérsɛ⌣.
(European) †bíra⌣.
beetle n. kugundára⌣ (kuhun-).
before adv. *(of place and time)* ŏwwéllo⌣; ogóllo⌣.
(of time) gabúllo⌣.
before conj. ⌣ogóllo⌣ (§ 4369); use negative subjunctive (§ 6188), that is often preceded by élgon⌣ (ólgon⌣; § 6189) and may be followed by ⌣kóttɪg⌣ (§§ 6197-8); élgon⌣ (ól-) with negative subjunctive verb-concretion (§ 5744).
before I go: nógrɪn⌣ogóllo⌣.
before I went: nógsɪn⌣ogóllo⌣.
Come before the sun rises: másɪl⌣bélmɛnín⌣ta⌢.
Don't come in before I am dressed: āɪ⌣dɛgɛdágmɛndɪ⌣tókkon⌣tŏmɛn⌢.
Before I saw him he disappeared: āɪ⌣élgon⌣nálmɛndɪ⌣dabóskon⌢.
Before I had seen him he had disappeared: āɪ⌣élgon⌣nálkomɛndɪ⌣dabóskogon⌢.
Bring it before I ask for it: āɪ⌣ólgon⌣síkkɪmɛndɪ⌣kóttɪg⌣étta⌢.
Don't bring it before I ask you for it: āɪ⌣ékk⌣ólgon⌣síkkɪmɛndɪ⌣kóttɪt⌣tókkon⌣éttāmɛn⌢.
Before I go I shall pay you: āɪ⌣ólgon⌣nógmɛŋgon⌣ékkɪ⌣bɪdɛfétɪddi⌢.
Before we go we shall pay you: ar⌣ólgon⌣nógmɛŋgon⌣ékkɪ⌣bɪdɛfétɪddu⌢.
Before I eat I shall drink: āɪ⌣élgoŋ⌣kálmɛŋŋom⌣bunfri⌢.
Put out the light before you go: ɛr⌣ólgon⌣nógmɛŋgon⌣íkkɪ⌣bé⌢.
before prep. *(of place and time)* —n⌣ogóllo⌣; —n⌣ŏwwéllo⌣.
(of time) —ŋ⌣gabúllo⌣.
before dinner: ášan⌣ogóllo⌣.
Put it on the table before the food: súfraŋ⌣kóččɪr⌣káln⌣ogóll⌣úskur⌢.
beg v.t. bédd(ɪ); *(ask alms)* béndɪg.
beggar n. béndɪgɪl⌣.
begin v.t. betɛ́ (bɛdɛ́).
beginning n. ógol⌣.
in (at) the beginning: ogóllo⌣.
behalf
He did it on your behalf: éŋ-karam⌣áukon⌢.
Let him write a petition on your behalf: ardahálg⌣énn⌣íllar⌣bāğan⌢.
behave v.i. áu (áw, áu).
behind adv. abáğɪr⌣; abáğkɛd⌣ (-ákk-, -ɛt⌢, -ɛ́⌢).
behind prep. —n⌣abáğɪr⌣ (§ 4358); —n⌣abáğkɛd⌣ (-ákk-, -ɛt⌢, -ɛ́⌢; § 4380 a); —n⌣ğérro⌣ (§ 4366); —n⌣ğérkɛd⌣ (-ɛt⌢, -ɛ́⌢; § 4380 a).
It's behind the door: bábn⌣abáğɪr⌣bún⌢.
It's behind the house: kán⌣ğérro⌢.
Sálɪm is behind the house: sálum⌣kán⌣ğérkɛ⌢.
behind, place v.t. abáğkɪr⌣ (-ákk-).
behind, stay v.i. fadlɛ́ (s.v. *stay behind*).
belch v.i. éšɛ.
believe v.t. saddɪgɛ́; *(suppose that)* andá-, edá-.
I don't believe him (her, it): āɪ⌣saddɪgɛ́munun⌢.
believe in v.t. *(trust)* āmɪnɛ́.
I don't believe in him (her, it): āɪ⌣tékk⌣āmɪnɛ́munun⌢.
bell n. ğáras⌣ (ğáras⌣, ğérɛs⌣).
Ring the bell: ğaráskɪ⌣ğóm⌢.
belly n. tú⌣ (-tu⌣ § 1671).
belong v.i.
X. *Whose is that dog over there?* máw⌣wél⌣níndɪré?
Y. *It belongs to the Arabs:* arabíndín⌢.
Does (s)he (it) belong here? ɪndóndɪré?
belongings n. áfɛs⌣.
below adv. tágor⌣.
Put it below: tógor⌣úskur⌢.
Bring it below: tógor⌣étta⌢.
below prep. —n⌣tógor⌣ (§ 5907).
belt n. hɪzām⌣; gáš⌣.
bend down v.i. túlɛ; dɛréñɛ.
beneath adv. tógor⌣.
beneath prep. —n⌣tógor⌣ (§ 5907).
benefit n. fáɪda⌣ (fáɪda⌣); faɪdád⌣.
bent adj. kérɛñ⌣.
Bergia suffruticosa n. túššɪ⌣dárɪg⌣.
beside prep. —n⌣ábtɪr⌣ (-n⌣áptɪr⌣, -n⌣áttɪr⌣).
Put the chair beside the bedstead: kúrsɪg⌣áŋgarɛn⌣áttɪr⌣úskur⌢.
besides prep. —ŋ⌣gɛ́r⌣ (§§ 5167-8).
bespatter v.t. míssɛ.
best adj. áhsɛn⌣.
Bring the best of them: tídd⌣áhsɛŋ⌣étta⌢.
bet n. dígar⌣; dɪgíd⌣.
There is a bet of 20 piastres on it: gírɪš⌣árɪgɛd⌣dígbūn⌢.
bet v.t. díg (constr. with -ɛd⌣).
betrothed n. hatíb⌣.
better adj. áhsɛn⌣.
Is your wound better? ɛŋ⌣kŏr⌣áhsɛndɛ́?
Are you better? (a) ɛr⌣kómbaŋkoná? (b) ɛr⌣kombanóskoná?
This is better than that (near): ɪn⌣ínɪn⌣dógor⌣génun⌢.
better, get v.i. *(improve)* séran-; *(after illness)* kómban-, wajjɛ́.
It has got a little better: kɪnnɛ́s⌣sɛranóskó⌢.
I am getting better: āɪ⌣kómbandi⌢.
(S)he has got a little better: kɪnnɛ́k⌣kombanóskó⌢.
between prep. —m⌣bárrɛr⌣.
between you and me: ékkon⌣āɪgom⌣bárrɛr⌣.
Put it between them: tím⌣bárrɛr⌣úskur⌢.
It's between them: tím⌣bárrɛr⌢.
bewail v.t. óñ.
beware v.i. bálko.
Beware of the dog: wéllotōn⌣énn-āb⌣bálko⌢.
beyond prep. —rtōm⌣máŋgɛd⌣ (-gɛt⌢, -gɛ́⌢; § 6068).
He (it) went beyond the tree: ğówwɪrtōm⌣máŋgɛn⌣nókkon⌢.
bicycle n. šártɪn⌣hánu⌣.
bid v.t. *(command)* kallɪfɛ́ (kɛl-).
big adj. dúl⌣.
I don't want a big one: āɪ⌣dúl-lēd⌣dólmunun⌢.
The steamer's as big as a house: bābúr⌣ká⌣dúl⌣kóttɪn⌣⌣.
bile n. étt(ɪ)⌣.
bin n. gússa⌣.
bind v.t. dígɪr; mór.
bird n. káwɪrtɛ⌣ (káurtɛ⌣, káurtɛ⌣); *(small)* fóğa⌣.
birth n. úskɪd⌣ (-kɪd⌣).
birth to, give v.t. úsk(ɪ).
birthday
Monday is the King's birthday: búš⌣ánn⌣ór⌣úskɪkáttɪsun⌣jŏmun⌢.
bit n. *(piece)* hítta⌣ (hétta⌣); *(of bridle)* lɪgám⌣.
bitch n. wɛl-kárr(ɪ)⌣.
bite v.t. áčč(ɪ); *(of insect)* kál.
It will bite you: ékkɪ⌣báččɪn⌢.
X. *Are you afraid of it?* ɛr⌣tékkɪ⌣sándɪná?
Y. *No, it doesn't bite:* wǎran, adémg⌣áččɪmunun⌢.
What has bitten him (her, it)? míndo⌣tékkɪ⌣kálkó?
bitter adj. nádd(ɪ)⌣.
bitter apple n. úr⌣; tattúr⌣.
black adj. urúmmɛ⌣.
blacksmith n. šártɪk⌣kál⌣; šártɪn⌣tábɪd⌣.

blade n. ágıl‿.
　blade of knife: kándın‿ágıl‿.
　blade of sword: sıwídn‿ágıl‿.
blandish v.t. ğǎškır.
blanket n. battānı́jɛ‿ (jȧ‿, -ja‿).
Blatta aegyptiaca n. sɛrsı́r‿.
bleat v.i. béjj(ı); wı́ğ.
bleed v.i. gɛ̌wan-.
bleed v.t. wád.
bless v.t. bédd(ı).
blind adj. dúŋgur‿.
blindness n. duŋgúrkanɛ‿.
blink v.i. nımı́nt(ı) (-mı́tt(ı)).
blood n. gɛ́u‿ (gɛ́u, gɛ̌w‿, gɛ́u‿).
　Are you passing blood from your bowels? ɛr‿gɛ́ug‿āgússıná?
　Are you passing blood from your bladder? ɛr‿gɛ́ug‿āgɛ́kkıná?
blood-money n. (*compensatory*) díjɛ‿.
blossom n. íǧ‿; ǧówwın‿íǧ‿; šídȧrn‿íǧ‿; wírıd‿.
blow v.t. úffɛ.
blow one's nose v.i. fúčɛ.
blue adj. (*light*) dɛ́ssɛ‿; (*dark*) urúmmɛ‿.
blunt adj. díɛl‿.
　The knife is blunt: kándı‿díélun⌢.
　I don't want a blunt knife: kándı‿diélg‿ âi‿dólmunun⌢.
boar n. hallúf‿.
boat n. kúb‿, pl. kúblı‿ and kúbı‿; (*small*) kumtŏd‿, búll(ı)‿.
　Who is in that boat? máŋ‿kúbır‿ nȧğın?
body n. ǧísım‿; ǧídda‿ (ǧítta‿).
boil n. (*tumour*) amǧulúd‿, bɛ́lt(ı)‿; (*small*) tússȧ‿.
boil v.i. wȧ́s.
　Is the water boiling? ɛ́ssı‿āwwȧ́sná?
　Bring some boiling water: ɛ́ssı‿wȧ́zbūlg‿ éttȧ⌢.
　Pour in a little boiling water: ɛ́ssı‿wȧ́zbūl‿ tŏddɛ́b‿bŏgúndur⌢.
　Put a little (of the) boiling water in: ɛ́ssı‿ wȧzbúllotŏŋ‿kınnɛ́ǧ‿úndur⌢.
boil v.t. (a liquid or in a liquid) wȧ́skıdd(ı); (in a liquid) sɛlgɛ́.
　Boil some water: ɛ́ssıw‿wȧ́skıddı⌢.
　Have you boiled the water? ɛ́ssıw‿wȧ́skıddıgoná?
　Boil the eggs: (*a*) kúmbuw‿wȧ́skıddı⌢; (*b*) kúmbus‿sɛlgɛ́⌢.
bolt n. (*of lock, etc.*) šírag‿.
bone n. kıhíd‿ (kíhid‿, kíhid‿, kíd‿).
book n. kıtáb‿; (*for writing in*) dȧ́ftar‿ (dȧ́ftar‿, dɛ́fter‿).
　Don't put it on the book: kıtȧ́m‿kŏ́ččır‿ tókkon‿úskurmɛn⌢.
　If water comes on books it spoils them: ɛ́ssı‿kıtābíŋ‿kŏ́ččır‿bŏkkıŋ‿kıtābíh‿ harbɛ̌‿.
boot n. ǧȧzma‿ (ǧȧ́z-, ǧɛ́z-, -mȧ‿).
border n. (*edge*) tȧ́raf‿ (tȧ́rȧ́f‿); kɛ́l‿.
bore v.t. (*weary*) galabɛ́; mȧ́gır.
bore a hole (holes) in v.t. úbbuǧ.
bored, be v.i. mȧ́; mȧbū-.
borrow v.t. asíkk(ı).
bosom n. óg‿.
both pron. adj. oŋgȧ́r‿.
　Did you take both of them? (*a*) ɛr‿tɛr‿ oŋgȧ́rkı‿sókkɛgoná? (*b*) ɛr‿tır‿oŋ- gȧ́rkı‿sókkɛgoná? (*c*) ɛr‿tínn‿oŋgȧ́rkı‿ sókkɛgoná?

X. My eye hurts me: âig‿ȧ́m‿míss‿ óddın⌢.
Y. One? wɛ́ró?
X. No, both do: wȧ́ran, oŋgȧ́r⌢.
　Did you see both horses? kȧ́ǧ‿oŋgȧ́rkı‿ nȧ́lkoná?
bottle n. ɛ́ssır‿; (*glass*) gȧzȧ́z‿ (gɛz-, gız-).
bottom n. bún‿; tógo‿; úsud‿.
　at the bottom: tógor‿.
　Hit the box on its bottom: sandúgk‿úsudır‿ ǧŏ́m⌢.
boundary n. kɛ́l‿.
bow n. (*weapon*) tuŋgǔ́r‿.
　(*obeisance*) tǔ́lɛrar‿ (-rȧ́r‿); tūlɛríd‿.
　bow of boat: kúm‿gól‿.
bow v.i. tǔ́lɛ.
bowels n. dúgus‿ (dúŋus‿).
　evacuate bowels: úss(ı).
bowl n. (*basin*) sultānı́jɛ‿ (-jȧ‿, -ja‿); kúrȧ‿; kūríjɛ‿ (-jȧ‿, -ja‿); dȧ́d(ı)‿ (dȧ́dd(ı)‿).
　(*ball*) kúrȧ‿.
box n. sandúg‿; (*small*) ílbɛ‿ (ɛ́l-, -bȧ‿, -ba‿).
　handle of box: sandúgn‿í‿.
　Put it into the box: sandúgır‿úndur⌢.
　Put it inside the box: sandúŋ‿tǔ́r‿úskur⌢.
boy n. bıtȧ́n‿ (bıt-), tŏ́d‿; (*little*) ogıčč̌ŏ́d‿.
　Is this your little boy? ín‿ɛnn‿ogıčč̌ŏ́dıré?
bracelet n. bír‿; ǧɛ́rt(ı)‿; (*broad*) kím‿.
branch n. ȧ́ss(ı)‿; ȧ̂ur‿(ȧ̂u‿r‿, ȧ̂uır‿, ȧ́wır‿).
brandish v.t. wɛ́lɛg.
　They brandished their swords: tín‿síwıdıw‿ wɛlɛ́kkoran⌢.
brass n. šȧ́rtı‿gɛ́lɛ‿; nahȧ́s‿.
brave, become v.i. ógıǧan-.
brawl n. ǧȧ́wwɛ‿ (ǧȧ́uwɛ‿).
brawl v.i. ǧȧ́ww(ı) (ǧȧ́uw(ı), -wᵘ).
　Don't brawl: tókkon‿ǧȧ́wwmɛn⌢, pl. ...‿ǧȧ́wwᵘmɛwwɛ⌢.
　He keeps on brawling: tɛr‿ȧ̌ǧǧȧ́wwᵘn⌢.
brawler n. ǧȧ́wwıkȧ́tt(ı)‿ (ǧȧ́uwı-, -wᵘk-).
bray v.i. hŏ́ŋ(ı).
　This donkey brays too much: ín‿hȧ́nu‿ dıgrı́gırhŏ́ŋgın⌢.
bread n. kȧ́l‿; íu‿ (íᵘ‿, íw‿).
　new bread: íu‿ǧɛdíd‿.
　stale bread: kȧ́l‿kúrus‿.
breadth n. kȧ́wwagıd‿; bóǧogıd‿; boǧŏ́- kanɛ‿.
　What is its breadth? tɛ́ŋ‿kȧ́wwagıd‿ mıŋkóttɛ̄rré?
break v.i. tómbıkatt(ı) (-buk-); gúšš(ı); tómb(ı)‿; mɛ́r.
　It will break (...get broken): bıtómb- bıkattın⌢.
　The cup broke: fıŋǧȧ́ŋ‿gúššıgon⌢.
　Yesterday the rope broke: wílg‿írı‿ mɛrkó⌢.
break v.t. gúšš(ı); tómb(ı).
　You will break it: ɛr‿bıgúššın⌢, pl. ır‿ bıgúššıru⌢.
　Don't break it: tókkon‿gúššımɛn⌢, pl. ...‿gúššımɛwwɛ⌢.
　He broke the cup: fıŋǧȧ́ŋı‿gúššıgon⌢.
　What is (...has been) broken? míndo‿ tómbıkattıǧó?
break in v.i. tombɛdtó (-ɛttó).
break wind v.i. ȧ́r; úrıǧ.
breakfast n. futǔ́r‿.
　Bring breakfast: futúrk‿éttȧ⌢.
　Has (s)he had breakfast? fattırɛ̄rédkoná?

I shall eat this for breakfast: ıŋı‿futúrro‿ bıkȧ́llı⌢.
breakfast v.i. fattırɛ́.
breaking out n. (of rash, etc.) bɛ́lt(ı)‿.
breast n. (*pectus*) óg‿; (*mamma*) ɛ́rt(ı)‿.
breath n. nɛwɛ́rt(ı)‿; nɛ́fɛs‿ (nȧ́f-, nȧ́f-, -fȧs‿).
　He is out of breath: tɛ́ŋ‿nɛwɛ́rtı‿dúkkın⌢.
breathe v.i. nɛ́wɛ.
　There's no air here: I can't breathe: índo‿ hȧ́wa‿dȧ́munun‿: âi‿ɛskınɛ́wɛmunun⌢.
breeze n. túrug‿; hȧ́wa‿.
brick n. túb‿.
bridge n. kúbrı‿.
　bridge of the nose: (*a*) soríñn‿éndɛ‿; (*b*) soríñn‿úmbu‿.
bridle n. lıǧȧ́m‿.
brigand n. mȧ́gas‿ (mȧ́gȧs‿).
bright (brilliant), be v.i. bılíŋč(ı); fılítt(ı) (fılȧ́tt(ı), fılíŋč(ı)); tulúŋč(ı).
bring v.t. ɛttȧ́; §3855); ɛbbıdȧ́ (§3851); ındɛ́ttȧ (ındɛ́ttȧ, §5723).
　Bring him (her, it) here: índ‿ɛ́ttȧ⌢, pl. índ‿ɛ́ttȧwɛ⌢.
　Bring them here: índ‿ɛ́ttȧrır⌢, pl. índ‿ ɛttȧ́rıwwɛ⌢.
　Don't bring him (her, it): tókkon‿ɛ́ttȧmɛn⌢, pl. tókkon‿ɛ́ttȧmɛwwɛ⌢.
　What has (s)he (it) brought? tɛr‿míŋ‿ ɛ́ttagon?
　What did they bring? míŋ‿ɛ́ttagoran?
　Have you brought it? ɛr‿ɛ́ttȧgoná?
　Has he brought some water? tɛr‿ɛ́ssıg‿ ɛ́ttagoná?
　Let him bring it: ɛ́ttaran⌢.
　Let him bring some water: ɛ́ssıg‿ɛ́ttaran⌢.
　Let ɛ́li bring some water: ȧ́lıg‿ɛ́ssıg‿ ɛ́ttaran⌢.
　Who brought this? n‿íŋ‿ɛ́ttagon?
　Who brings the bread? kȧ́lgı‿n‿ɛ́ttan?
　(S)he is bringing him (her, it): ɛǧǧúbun⌢.
　Is (s)he bringing him (her, it)? ɛǧǧúbuná?
　Bring that chair: máŋ‿kúrsıg‿ındɛ́ttȧ⌢.
　Bring some more: (*a*) tɛ́nn‿ɛ́ttȧ⌢; (*b*) tɛn- nɛ́g‿ɛ́ttȧ⌢.
　Bring some more butter: (*a*) dɛ́sk‿tɛ́nn‿ ɛ́ttȧ⌢; (*b*) tɛ́nnɛ‿dɛ́sk‿ɛ́ttȧ⌢.
　Bring (pl.) some more chairs: tɛ́nnɛ‿ kúrsıncıǧ‿ɛ́ttȧwɛ⌢.
　I haven't brought it with me: âigonon‿ ɛttȧ́gomunun⌢.
　Aren't you going to bring it? béttȧmɛn?, pl. béttȧmɛndu?
bring back v.t. ɛttȧ́ (ɛ́ttȧ).
bring out v.t. ós.
　Bring out a chair from the tent: kúrsı- wɛh‿hɛ́marton‿ós⌢.
bring to (for) v.t. (the speaker) ɛttadɛ́n (§4000); (other than the speaker) ɛ́ttatır (§4000).
bring together v.t. (*assemble*) ǧȧ́mmɛgır.
bring up v.t. (*rear*) dŏ́ñ.
　Where were you brought up? ɛr‿sȧ́ır‿ dŏ́ñkattıgon?
　Did they bring this boy up? ín‿tŏ́d‿tín‿ dŏ́ñɛd¹ré?
broad adj. kȧ́wwa‿; bóǧŏ‿.
　The man is broad in build: ógıǧ‿bóǧŏn⌢.
broken adj. gúššɛd‿.
　This is broken: ıŋ‿gúššɛdun⌢.
　Is it broken? gúššɛd¹ré?
broken, be v.i. gúššıbū-; tómbıbū-.

broom n. bírd(ı)‿.
broth n. márag‿ (márag‿); mar(r)agád‿ (mar(r)agád‿).
brother n. -bɛs‿; always with a form of the possessive personal pronoun (§2629) prefixed:
  my brother: ámbɛs‿.
  your brother: ímbɛs‿.
  his (her, its) brother: tímbɛs‿.
  our brother: antímbɛs‿.
  your (pl.) brother: ıntímbɛs‿.
  their brother: tıntímbɛs‿.
brother-in-law n. (in general) -od‿ (= *father-in-law*).
  (*wife's brother*) ɛn‿tímbɛs‿ (s.v. -bɛs‿).
  (*husband's brother*) ógıñ‿tímbɛs‿ (s.v. -bɛs‿).
  (*sister's husband*) -ɛssın‿ógığ‿ (s.v. -ɛss(ı)‿).
brown adj. (*reddish*) gɛ́lɛ‿.
brush n. fúrša‿.
brush v.t. túb; fúršagɛğ‿ğóm; fúršagɛg‿géndıgır; fúršagɛn‿naddıfɛ́.
  Brush your clothes: (a) ɛŋ‿kádɛt‿túp⌢; (b) ɛŋ‿kádɛf‿fúršagɛğ‿ğóm⌢.
buck n. (*antelope*) gɛ́l‿; gɛ́lm‿búttul‿.
buck v. (*slang*)
  '*Buck up!*' ɛŋ‿hɛ́lg‿ŭ́ñgır!
bucket n. ğɛ́rdɛl‿; (*well-*) dálu‿.
  handle of bucket: ğɛ́rdɛln‿í‿.
  Pour it into the bucket: ğɛrdɛ́llo‿bók⌢.
bug n. (***Cimex*** **sp.**) bágg(ı)‿.
build v.t. góñ.
  When did they build this? ıŋgı‿sıntåg‿góñkoran?
  Do they build boats? kúblıg‿ākkāırıd-dandɛ́?
builder n. kåg‿góñıl‿; góñıl‿.
bulk n. kótt(ı)‿.
bull n. gúr‿.
bullet n. rasás‿.
bulrush millet n. éndɛ‿.
bunged up, be v.i. (*of eye*) kúñbŭ-; tágbŭ-.
  Why is your eye bunged up? (a) ém‿míssı‿mɛ́ŋ‿kúñbūn? (b) ém‿míssı‿mɛ́n‿tágbūn?
burden n. dɛ́gar‿ (-går‿); dɛgíd‿; kúğurar‿ (-rår‿); kuğurfíd‿.
burn v.i. ğúg; årk(ı).
  This wood doesn't burn: ím‿bɛ́r‿ğúgmunun⌢.
  This lamp doesn't burn well: íl‿lámbå‿sɛranárkımunun⌢.
burn v.t. ğúgur; kúddɛgır.
burst v.i. and t. gág.
  It will burst: bıgágın⌢.
bury v.t. kúñur.
  Bury him (her, it) deep: dollıgırkúñur⌢, pl. dollıgırkuñúrwɛ⌢.
bush n. (*shrub*) ğŏww(ı)‿, šídår‿; (*uninhabited country*) hála‿.
business n. ğɛ́llı‿.
busy adj. ğɛ́llıkŏl‿.
  I am busy: (a) ğɛll‿ánnår‿dān⌢; (b) âı‿ğɛ́llıkōri⌢.
  Are you busy? ɛr‿ğɛ́llıkōnå?
  Is he busy? tɛr‿ğɛ́llıkōnå?
  I am busy writing: âı‿båč̌čır‿tɛ́grı⌢.
  I'm busy shaving: âı‿ággåñ́ñırı⌢.
but conj. låkın; -mɛn- (-mɛ́n-, -mɛn‿§§6093-6).
  X. *Hasn't* ɛ *áli gone?* álı‿nókkomɛn?
  Y. *Not yet, but he will*: ólgónum‿bímɛnnogın⌢.
  It's like this but smaller: ıŋkır‿ɛ́ŋgoŋ‿kíññan⌢.
  He hears, but he cannot speak: gíğırın, ɛskıbáññımunun⌢.
  We looked for it but couldn't find it: tɛbēmısírkoru⌢.
but prep. (*omitting*) (obj. case)—wakk(ı)‿ (§4345), ílla‿ (§4282); (*besides*) —ŋ‿gɛ́r‿ (§§5167-8).
  I have sold everything but the house: kåwwakkı‿mállɛğ‿ğåntíkkori⌢.
  He sold me everything but the horse: kåč̌č̌ıwakkı‿mállɛğ‿ğåndēŋkon⌢.
  I paid all the money but one dollar: dúŋgı‿mållɛr‿rıjål‿lɛ́wwakkı‿dɛfɛ́gori⌢.
  Nobody but you has come: ɛŋ‿gɛ́r‿tågomunun⌢.
  I saw nobody but you: ɛŋ‿gɛ́rkı‿nalkómunun⌢.
butcher n. ğɛzzár‿.
butt v.t. nıššıgɛğ‿ğóm.
butter n. dɛ́s‿; fúrsa‿ (-så‿).
  clarified butter: ísın‿.
butterfly n. fírrıl‿ (-rīl‿).
buttock n. abåg‿; ğåbåd‿; úsud‿.
buy v.t. ğån(q.v.); ğånår ğånɛttå (-ɛ́ttă §5723).
  X. *Who gave you that knife?* íŋ‿kándın‿n‿ɛ́kkı‿tíkkon?
  Y. *I bought it*: ğåŋkori⌢.
  I want to buy a horse: kåğ‿gɛ́ğ‿ğåndåŋgı‿dólli⌢.
  I bought the horse: kåč̌čı‿ğånårkori⌢.
  I shall buy the camel: kámgı‿bığånårri⌢.
  I buy, I don't sell: âı‿ğånårri, âı‿ğåntímmunun⌢.
  Buy some coffee: búŋgı‿ğånɛtta⌢.
  I have bought all this for a piastre: ím‿mállɛğ‿gírıš‿šɛ́gɛğ‿ğånåróskori⌢ (‿šɛ́gɛğ‿ < ‿wɛ́g-ɛd‿ §§704, 550 for one).
by prep. (*by means of*) -ɛd‿ (-ɛt⌢, -ɛ́⌢) suffixed to objective (§4341); (*beside, near*) —n‿åbtır‿ (-n‿åpt-, -n‿ått- §4375); (*agent*) —n‿íged‿ (-ɛt⌢, -ɛ́⌢ §5706).
  Whom did you send the letter by? ɛr‿ğawåpkı‿nígɛd‿íšíŋkon?
  X. *He's come*: tågó⌢.
  Y. *By donkey?* hánugɛdıré?
  Z. *By donkey?* hánugɛdó?
  From here to El-Xándaq is two hours by donkey: índotōn‿hándaŋ‿bókkon‿hánugɛs‿så‿ówwın⌢.
  I crossed the river by boat: úruk‿kúpkɛm‿múkkıgori⌢.
  Take it out by that door: mám‿båpkɛd‿ós⌢.
  He works by the piece: híttagɛš‿šuglɛ́n⌢.
  Wait for me by the well: gówwın‿åttır‿åıg‿ɛrğɛ́⌢.
  He was killed by the Arabs: árabın‿íged‿dígon⌢.
  We shall travel by night, not by day: ugúb‿bısafarɛ́ru, ugréskımunun⌢.
  I know him by his gait: tɛ́kkı‿tɛ́n‿nogí-dırtōn‿uñúddi⌢.
  Hold it by the lower part: tógortōn‿år‿.
  It will be finished by noon: (a) dúhur‿åŋkım‿bıhalásanın⌢; (b) dúhuraŋkım‿bıhalåsanın⌢.
  If we are not back by sunset, send the lantern: másıl‿tóm‿bókkon‿år‿tåmɛŋkıru, fånúsk‿ıšín⌢.
  He broke it by squeezing it: ğogortóm‿bıgon⌢.
  They came out one by one: wɛrwɛ́gɛb‿bɛ́lkoran⌢.
byre n. kɛ́rr(ı)‿.

cabbage n. kúrumb(ı)‿.
cable n. (*thick rope*) tárıf‿ (tár-, tɛ́r-); álas‿.
cache n. (*for grain*) úbur‿.
Cairo n. másur‿; médne‿.
cake n. súg‿; (*European*) †kákk(ı)‿.
calculate v.t. håsıbɛ́.
calculation n. hısåb‿.
calf n. (*young of cow*) gurtŏd‿.
call v.t. (*summon*) úwɛ; (*name*) ‿ɛ́-.
  Call him (her, it): tɛ́kk‿úwɛ⌢.
  Don't call him (her, it): tókkon‿tɛ́kk‿úwɛmɛn⌢.
  Call ɛ *áli*: álıg‿úwɛ⌢.
  Call Aḥmad: áhmådk‿úwɛ⌢.
  Call them: úwɛrır⌢.
  Don't call them: tókkon‿ūwɛrímmɛn⌢.
  I did not call: âı‿ūwɛgómunū⌢.
  Why have you come? I did not call you: ɛr‿mɛ́n‿tågō? âı‿ɛ́kk‿ūwɛgómunū⌢.
  Wait till I call you: âı‿ɛ́kk‿úwɛrı‿bókko‿ğóbbɛ⌢ (§979).
  Don't come unless I call: âı‿úwɛmɛŋkırı‿tókkon‿tåmɛn⌢, pl. ...‿tåmɛwwɛ⌢.
  The lady is calling you: sítt‿ɛ́kk‿úwɛ⌢.
  What do they call this? ıŋgı‿míŋ‿gɛran?
Calotropis procera n. håbıd‿.
camel n. kám‿.
  she-camel: kám‿kárr(ı)‿.
  young camel: kamtŏd‿.
  camel-dung: kám‿tŭr‿; kám‿hŏss(ı)‿.
  Bring the camel: kámg‿ɛ́tta, pl. ...‿ɛ́ttāwɛ⌢.
  Bring the camels: kámlıg‿ɛ́ttarır⌢, pl. ...‿ɛttaríwwɛ⌢.
  Where is the camel? kám‿ısåıré?
  Where are the camels? kámlı‿såıré?
can v. aux. (*be able to*) ɛ́sk(ı) (ísk(ı)‿); (*know how to*) úñur.
  I can: âı‿ɛ́skıri⌢.
  You can: ɛr‿ɛ́skın⌢ (-kī⌢, -kí⌢).
  (S)he (it) can: tɛr‿ɛ́skın⌢ (-kī⌢, -kí⌢).
  We can: ar‿ɛ́skıru⌢.
  You (pl.) can: ır‿ɛ́skıru⌢.
  They can: tır‿ɛ́skıran⌢ (-rā⌢, -rá⌢).
  I cannot: âı‿ɛ́skımunun⌢ (‿ɛ́skí- §1979; -munū, -munu⌢, -mun⌢).
  You cannot: ɛr‿ɛ́skımunun⌢ (‿ɛ́skí- §1979; -munū, -munu⌢, -mun⌢).
  (S)he (it) cannot: tɛr‿ɛ́skımunun⌢ (‿ɛ́skí- §1979; -munū, -munu⌢, -mun⌢).
  We cannot: ar‿ɛ́skımunun⌢ (‿ɛ́skí- §1979; -munū, -munu⌢, -mun⌢).
  You (pl.) cannot: ır‿ɛ́skımunun⌢ (‿ɛ́skí- §1979; -munū, -munu⌢, -mun⌢).
  They cannot: tır‿ɛ́skımunan⌢ (ɛ́skí-, -munā⌢, -muná⌢) and s.v. må-.
  Can I? âı‿ɛ́skıriá?
  Can you? ɛr‿ɛ́skınå?
  Can (s)he (it)? tɛr‿ɛ́skınå?
  Can we? ar‿ɛ́skıruá?
  Can you (pl.)? ır‿ɛ́skıruá?

candle — circumcision

Can they? tɪrⴑéskɪrandé?
Cannot I? āɪⴑéskɪmɛndi?
Cannot you? ɛrⴑéskɪmɛn?
Cannot (s)he (it)? tɛrⴑéskɪmɛn?
Can we? arⴑéskɪmɛndu?
Can you (pl.)? ɪrⴑéskɪmɛndu?
Can they? tɪrⴑéskɪmɛndan?
Can you carry it? ɛrⴑɛskɪsókkɛná?
Can you hear? ɛrⴑɛskɪgɪğírná?
Can you see (him, her, it, them)? ɛrⴑɛskɪnálná?
Can you walk? ɛrⴑɛskɪnógná?
I cannot go: āɪⴑnogɛmắriᴖ.
I cannot see (him, her, it): āɪⴑnalɛmắriᴖ.
Can't you walk? (a) ɛrⴑɛskɪnógmɛn? (b) ɛrⴑnogɛmắná? (c) ɛrⴑnogɛmắbūná?
Can't you see? (a) ɛrⴑɛskɪnálmɛn? (b) ɛrⴑnalɛmắná?
Can't you carry it? (a) ɛrⴑɛskɪsókkɛmɛn? (b) ɛrⴑsokkɛrɛmắná?
I couldn't (was unable to) ask for it: āɪⴑtalabɛrɛmắgoriᴖ.
Couldn't you (were you unable to) pay? ɛrⴑdɛfɛrɛmắgoná?
They could not cut the wood: bɛ́rkɪⴑmɛrɛmắróskoranᴖ.
Can you read? ɛrⴑuñurgɛrjɛ̌ná?
Can you cook? (a) ɛrⴑuñurtabhɛ̌ná? (b) ɛrⴑğakútkⴑuñuráuná?
Can you cook this? (a, do you know how to…?) ɛrⴑíŋgⴑuñurtabhɛ̌ná? (b, have you the means of cooking this?) ɛrⴑíŋgⴑɛskɪtabhɛ̌ná?
It can be seen: nálkattɪnᴖ, pl. nálkattɪranᴖ.
It cannot be seen: nálkattɪmununᴖ, pl. -munanᴖ.
(S)he (it) cannot be found: élkattɪmununᴖ, pl. -munanᴖ.
Can't (s)he (it) be found? élkattɪmɛn?, pl. -mɛndan?
candle n. šémaⴑ.
candlestick n. šɛmadánⴑ.
cannon n. múdfaⴑ.
The cannon has gone off: múdfaⴑ ğomóskóᴖ.
cantár (قنطار) n. guntárⴑ.
canvas n. mušémmaⴑ.
cap n. tágia ⴑ (-gɪaⴑ, tagĭaⴑ).
Capparis aphylla n. gámrɛⴑ.
captain n. (*of ship*) réīsⴑ (réɪsⴑ).
captive adj. and n. (*confined*) kóbbūlⴑ; (*bound*) mórbūlⴑ.
capture v.t. ắr.
car n. (*motor-*) turumbílⴑ.
card n. (*playing-*) kuštɛ̌naⴑ.
card v.t. túŋg(ɪ).
care n. (*attention*) bálⴑ; hásabⴑ (-sɛbⴑ).
Take care! (*pay attention!*) bálko!, pl. bálkowɛ! (*slowly!*) nɔ́rɛn! (-rɛ̄!), pl. nɔ́rɛwwɛ!
care of, take v.t. bálko.
Take care of this: íŋgɪⴑbálkoᴖ.
Tell him to take care of it: tékkɪⴑbálkoranᴖ (§ 5647).
careless adj. kússaⴑ.
caress v.t. ğáškɪr.
carpenter n. bɛ́rkɪⴑkắɪlⴑ; basírⴑ.
carpet n. sɪğğắğaⴑ.
carriage n. arabíjɛⴑ (-jáⴑ, -jaⴑ).
carrion n. fatísⴑ.
carry v.t. óğɪ; sókkɛ; (*have about one's person*) kắg.

What are you carrying? ɛrⴑmíŋgⴑagóğɪn?
Let ɣáli carry my helmet: álɪgⴑắmⴑ burnɛ́tagⴑóğanⴑ.
carry away (off) v.t. ārɛnnóg; ɪndɛnnóg; ɪndɛğğǔ; sókkɛ.
cart n. arabíjɛⴑ (-jáⴑ, -jaⴑ).
cartridge n. bārúdⴑ; rasásⴑ.
case n. (*box*) sandúgⴑ; (*legal*) gadíjɛⴑ (-jáⴑ, -jaⴑ).
cashier n. sarráfⴑ (sár-).
Cassia acutifolia n. sɛnɛmékkɛⴑ (-nám-, -káⴑ); sénɛⴑ (-náⴑ).
Cassia obovata n. abúrrɛⴑ.
cast v.t. árk(ɪ); aríkk(ɪ).
castle n. díbⴑ.
castor-oil plant n. ábkoñⴑ (ápk-).
cat n. sábⴑ.
she-cat: sām-kárr(ɪ)ⴑ.
Give this to the cat: íŋgɪⴑsábkɪⴑtírᴖ.
cat, interj. *to call:* ps! (pss!).
cat, interj. *to drive away:* bíss!; físs!
cataract n. (*rapid*): šɛllálⴑ.
catarrh n. (*in nose or throat*): ískɪdɛⴑ (úskadɛⴑ); zíkmɛⴑ (-máⴑ, -maⴑ).
catch v.t. áb; ár; (*with net*) áb; (*overtake*) dúr.
He caught the ball: kúragⴑápkonᴖ.
X. *Catch!* áp!
Y. *Throw it!* árki!
The cat caught the mouse: sábⴑğɪgírkⴑárkonᴖ.
Do they catch (net) fish? kárɛgⴑábrandé?
He ran after him but couldn't catch him: ténnⴑabáğɪrⴑbódkon, dúrkómununᴖ.
Did you ((s)he (it)) catch the post? bústadⴑdúrkoná?
caterpillar n. súrufⴑ.
catfish n. (*Bagrus bayad, Forskal*): dáškoⴑ.
cattle, head of n. tíⴑ.
cattle (pl.) tínč(ɪ)ⴑ.
Have they got cattle? tínčɪkⴑkórandé?
Has he cattle for (to turn) the water-wheel? kólɛnⴑtínčɪkⴑkóná?
cattle-shed n. kérr(ɪ)ⴑ.
cause n. sébɛbⴑ (sábábⴑ).
cave n. ğárⴑ.
cavity n. kúlⴑ.
central adj. sɛllénd(ɪ)ⴑ; (*intervening*) barrénd(ɪ)ⴑ.
centre n. séllɛⴑ (s.v. *middle*).
in the centre: séllɛrⴑ.
certain adj. (*authentic*) alɛ́ⴑ.
Is the news certain? hábarⴑalɛ́ré?
chaff n. sílt(ɪ)ⴑ.
chain n. ğɛnzírⴑ; sílsɪlɛⴑ.
chair n. kúrsɪⴑ.
chamber-pot n. ɛkkédnⴑɪbrígⴑ.
chameleon n. nóŋgaⴑ (-gɛⴑ, -goⴑ).
change n. (*small coin*) fákkắⴑ (fákⴑ, fɛ́k-, -kaⴑ, -kɛⴑ).
change v.i. éččɛlan-.
change v.t. (*alter, replace*) gajír̃; éččɛlgɪr.
(*exchange*) éwɪr.
(*into smaller coin*) éwɪr; fɛkké (fákⴑ, fak-); fékkagɪr (fák-, fak-).
Change (alter, replace) this: íŋgɪⴑgajírɛ̌.
Don't change (alter) this: tókkonⴑíŋgɪⴑgajírɛ̌mɛnⴑ.
Change this for another: íŋgⴑéččɛllɛ̌gɛdⴑéwɪrᴖ.
I want to change my clothes: áŋⴑkádɛgⴑgajɪrɛ̄ráŋgɪⴑdólliᴖ.

Go and change this pound: íŋⴑgínɛgⴑɛwɪréttaᴖ lit. *after changing this pound come.*
Go and change this: íŋgɪⴑfɛkkagɪréttaᴖ lit. *after changing bring this.*
Have you changed the pound? gínɛgⴑɛwírkoná?
Let him change this pound: íŋⴑgínɛfⴑfɛkkɛ́ranᴖ.
channel n. (*runnel*) málťi)ⴑ.
(*in water-wheel, from river to base of shaft*) kódɛnⴑɛ́uⴑ.
(*in water-wheel, between troughs*) urɔ́wwaⴑ.
(*in water-wheel, from smaller trough to runnel*) dáluⴑ.
charcoal n. úludⴑ.
charge v.t. (*enjoin*) kallɪfɛ́ (kɛl-).
charge of, take v.t. ɪstɛlɛmɛ́.
chase away v.t. túr.
chat n. wénɛsⴑ.
chat v.i. wénnɪskattɪ.
They chat: wénnɪskattɪranᴖ.
cheap adj. rahísⴑ.
cheat v.t. goššɛ̌.
He was cheating me: āɪgⴑaggoššɛ̌gonᴖ.
He was cheating us: árgɪⴑaggoššɛ̌ríkkonᴖ.
He has cheated me: āɪgɪⴑgoššɛ̌rɛdágɪnᴖ.
He has cheated us: árgɪⴑgoššɛ̌rɛdágɪrɪrɪnᴖ.
They have cheated us: árgɪⴑgoššɛ̌rɛdāgɪríddanᴖ.
Don't cheat! tókkonⴑgoššɛ́mɛn!, pl. tókkonⴑgoššɛ́mɛwwɛ́!
check v.t. mír.
cheek n. ğáhamⴑ (ğắh-, ğɛ́h-); tíbɪlⴑ (also = *temple*).
cheese n. ğíbnaⴑ (-náⴑ); ğíbɪnⴑ.
chest n. (*box*) sandúgⴑ; (*breast*) úgⴑ.
chew v.t. (*food*) ğókk(ɪ)ⴑ; (*tobacco*) súkk(ɪ).
chicken n. dúrmadɛnⴑtódⴑ; (*young*) siᵘsíuⴑ (siwsⴑ, -síwⴑ).
chick-pea n. órrɛⴑ.
chief n. (*of village, district*) sámɪlⴑ; šɛ́hⴑ (šɛ́xⴑ).
child n. bɪtánⴑ (bɪt-, but-); tódⴑ; (*little male*) ogɪččódⴑ (ogíččodⴑ); (*little female*) búrtodⴑ.
Were your brother's children there? ímbɛstonɪⴑdábugorandé?
Have any more children died? bɪtánɪⴑténnɛⴑdióskorandé?
These children are like flies: ímⴑbɪtánɪⴑkúltɪkɪríncínⴑ.
Let the child go away: bɪtáŋɪⴑnóganⴑ.
She is going to have a child: uskɛdólɪnᴖ.
chin n. sámaⴑ (-mɛⴑ).
china adj. and n. sínɪⴑ.
I want a china cup: fɪŋğánⴑsínɪdⴑdólliᴖ.
chirp v.i. wíg.
choke v.t. gíd; (*to death*) gɪdbɛ́.
choose v.t. bár.
Choose one: wɛ̄bⴑbárᴖ.
chop v.t. sɛ̌r; nódd(ɪ).
cicatrice n. kájjoⴑ.
Cicer arietinum L. n. órrɛⴑ.
cigar n. zɛnóbjaⴑ.
cigarette n. sɪğáraⴑ.
circle n. gédɛⴑ.
circular adj. gɪrídɛbūlⴑ; sɪládɛⴑ.
circumcise v.t. mɛ́r.
circumcised, be v.i. mérbū-; v.p. mérkatt(ɪ).
circumcision n. mérarⴑ (-rắrⴑ); mɛrídⴑ.

Citrullus colocynthus n. úr‿; tattúr‿.
Citrullus vulgaris n. tímɛ‿.
Clarias anguillaris n. kŭr‿.
clasp v.t. gắrɛ.
class n. (*sort*) ğíns(ı)‿; ğínıs‿.
classify v.t. bár.
clatter v.i. káraŭ; kórou; kúrub.
claw n. súnt(ı)‿.
clay n. síbɛ‿.
clean adj. nadíf‿.
clean v.t. naddıfɛ́ (-dufɛ́); nadífkır; géndıgır.
  Have you cleaned it? (a) ɛr‿naddıfɛ́goná?
  (b) ɛr‿nadífkírkoná? (c) ɛr‿gendıgírkoná?
  Has he cleaned it? tɛr‿naddıfɛ́goná?
  You have not cleaned it: ɛr‿gendıgırkómunŭ‿.
  (*S*)*he has not cleaned it:* tɛr‿gendıgırkómunŭ‿.
  Clean it and bring it (*back*): gendıgırɛ́tta‿.
  Clean up (*pl.*) *the whole place:* ágar‿
  mállen‿nadífkırwɛ‿.
clean, be v.i. naddıfɛ́bŭ-.
  (*S*)*he* (*it*) *is clean:* naddıfɛ́bŭn‿.
clear adj. (*plain*) wådah‿.
clear (not opaque), be v.i. kúddɛ; kúddɛbŭ-.
clear (not opaque), render v.t. kúddɛgır ($^{\prime\prime\prime}$).
clerk n. båğıl‿.
clever adj. fåla‿.
  (*S*)*he is clever:* fålan‿.
  (*S*)*he is not clever:* tɛr‿fålamunun‿.
cliff n. ábol‿.
climate n. háwa‿.
climb v.i. dárr(ı); ɛgɛ́čɛ.
clip v.t. mútt(ı).
clitoris n. kúğ‿; burúŋ‿kúğ‿.
cloak n. abåĭa‿ (ıb-).
clock n. så‿ (s.v. *watch*).
close v.t. kób.
cloth n. kádɛ‿; (*native*, دمور) góñña‿;
  (*for wiping*) fúta‿.
  cloth-beam (in loom): tórɛ‿.
clothes n. pl. kádɛ‿ (§4696d); kadɛ́nč(ı)‿.
clothes-moth n. íttɛ‿.
cloud n. níčč(ı)‿; sahåb‿.
clouded, become v.i. dúg.
club n. (*stick*) wíččır‿ (-čır‿); (*at golf*)
  kŭragɛǧ‿ǧómran‿; (-*house*) klúb‿,
  klúbb(ı)‿.
cluck v.i. kagákk(ı).
cluster n.
  cluster of leaves at top of date-palm:
  béntıŋ‿gól‿.
coarse adj. (*large in grain*) bárığ‿.
coat n. ǧak(k)ɛ́ta‿; (*of animal*) dílt(ı)‿.
coax v.t. gåškır.
cobbler n. súlu‿; ǧazmán‿nígıl‿.
cobweb n. koróm-kå‿.
cock n. kug(u)lúǧ‿ (kuk(u)-, -lúl‿).
cockroach n. sɛrsír‿.
coffee n. (*bean and drink*) bún‿, búnn(ı)‿;
  (*drink*) gáhwa‿.
  Would you like some coffee? gáhwad‿dólná?
  Make some coffee: gáhwag‿åŭ‿.
  Tell him to make some coffee: gáhwag‿åwan‿.
  Tell him to make a little good coffee:
  gáhwa‿sɛ́rɛ‿toddɛ́g‿åwan‿.
  Bring my coffee: áŋ‿gáhwag‿ɛ́tta‿.

cog n. súlgadɛ‿.
cog-wheel n. árgadɛ‿.
coin n. dúŋg(ı)‿.
  Bring coin, not paper: dúŋgıg‿ɛ́tta,
  warákkı‿tókkon‿ɛ́ttamen‿.
cold adj. orófɛl‿ ($^{\prime\prime\prime}$, $^{\prime\prime\prime}$).
  (*S*)*he* (*it*) *is cold:* orófɛlun‿.
  (*S*)*he* (*it*) *is very cold:* dıgrígıroróf ɛlun‿.
  I am cold: åĭ‿orófɛbúrı‿.
  I've got cold: åĭ‿orófɛdágrı‿.
  Is the water cold? ɛ́ss‿orófɛ́lɛ́?
  The water is not cold: ɛ́ss‿orófɛlmunun‿.
  Bring a cold one: orófɛ́l-lɛ̌g‿ɛ́tta‿.
  Don't let it get cold: (a) tókkon‿orófɛgírmen‿ (b) tókkon‿orófɛŋgírmen‿.
cold n. (*of weather*) ód‿; (*in the head*) ískıdɛ‿
  (úskadɛ‿), zíkmɛ‿ (-må‿, -ma‿).
  It (*the weather*) *is cold today:* ınnów‿‿
  ódun‿.
  Has he still got his cold? tɛ́n‿zíkm‿
  ólgondɛ́?
cold, be v.i. orófɛbŭ- ($^{\prime\prime\prime}$, $^{\prime\prime\prime}$).
  I am cold: åĭ‿orófɛ́búrı‿.
cold, become (get) v.i. orófɛ ($^{\prime\prime\prime}$, $^{\prime\prime\prime}$).
  I am getting cold: åĭ‿orófɛrı‿.
  I have got cold: åĭ‿orófóskorı‿.
  It does not get cold: orófɛmunun‿.
collapse v.i. bőr.
collect v.i. (*come together*) ǧámmɛ.
collect v.t. ǧámmɛgır.
colocynth n. úr‿; tattúr‿.
colossus n. s.v. sɛ́nɛ‿.
colour n. lón‿.
  What colour is it? tɛl‿lón‿mínˈrɛ́?
colt n. (*young*) kañ-bıtán‿; kañ-tód‿.
comb n. (*pecten*) múšud‿, bɛ́sır‿; (*crista*)
  dírr(ı)‿, kúǧ‿; *cock's comb:* (a) kugulúŋ‿dírr(ı)‿; (b) kugulúŋ‿kúǧ‿.
comb v.t. bɛs.
come! interj. (urging, inciting, encouraging)
  jálla!
  Come, leave him (*her, it*) *alone!* jálla!
  mugó!
come v.i. tå; bıdá; ǧŭ (§ 5332).
  Come here! índo‿tá! índo‿tårɛ́! pl. índo‿
  tåwɛ́!
  Come with me: (a) åĭgonón‿ta‿, pl.
  åĭgonon‿tåwɛ‿; (b) åĭgonom‿bída‿,
  pl. åĭgonom‿bıdåwɛ‿.
  Are you coming? (= *will you come?*) ɛr‿
  bıtáná?, pl. ır‿bıtáruá?
  Is (*s*)*he* (*it*) (*now*) *coming?* tɛr‿tåná?, pl.
  tarandɛ́?
  Is (*s*)*he* (*it*) *coming?* (= *will* (*s*)*he* (*it*) *come?*):
  tɛr‿bıtáná?, pl. bıtárandɛ́?
  I'm just coming: åĭ‿tårɛdóllı‿.
  Hasn't (*s*)*he* (*it*) *come?* tågomɛn?, pl.
  tågomɛndan?
  (*S*)*he* (*it*) *hasn't come yet:* ólgon‿tågomunun‿.
  Who has come? ní‿tágon?
  Who came? ní‿tágon?
  Let him (*her, it*) *come:* tåran‿.
  Let them come: tåwan‿.
  Don't let him (*her, it*) *come:* tókkon‿
  tåŋgırmen‿.
  Don't let them come: tókkon‿tåraŋgırmen‿.
  Don't let anybody come: tókkow‿wɛ́t‿
  tåŋgırmen‿.
  Tell him (*her*) *to come to me:* ánnar‿
  tåran‿.

  Let ε åli come to me: álıg‿ánnar‿tåran‿.
  When (*s*)*he* (*it*) *comes let me know:* tɛr‿
  tån‿tåd‿åıg‿wɛ́dɛn‿.
come ahead v.i. ógolan-.
come back v.i. wıdɛtå (wᵘd-); wıdɛbıdå
  (wᵘd-).
  (*S*)*he* (*it*) *will come back:* buwıdɛtån‿.
  They have come back: wıdɛbıdågoran‿.
come down v.i. šúgur.
come in v.i. tó; tótå.
  Come in! (*a*) tó!, pl. tówɛ́! (*b*) tóta!, pl.
  totåwɛ́! (*c*, welcoming a guest) faddılɛ́!,
  pl. faddılɛ́wɛ́!
  I don't want anybody to come in: åĭ‿wɛ́r‿
  tóŋgı‿dólmunun‿.
come in sight v.i. wånd(ı).
  Tell me when (*s*)*he* (*it*) *comes in sight:*
  wåndın‿tåd‿åıg‿wɛ́dɛn‿.
come on (ahead) v.i. ógolan-.
come out v.i. bɛ́l; bɛltå.
  Come out of it (*of that*): tɛ́ddotóm‿bɛ́lta‿.
  Come out with me: åĭgonon‿ǧubɛ́l‿, lit.
  go along out with me.
  An order came out: ámur‿bɛ́lkon‿.
come together v.i. (*one to another*):
  ǧámmɛ; (*one with another*): ǧámmɛtå.
come up v.i. dárr(ı); ɛgɛ́čɛ; (*rise*) ımbɛ́l
  ($^{\prime\prime}$).
comet n. kåǧn‿ɛ́u‿.
command n. ámur‿.
command v.t. (*bid*) kallıfɛ́ (kɛl-).
commence v.t. betɛ́ (bɛdɛ́).
compact n. šurúd‿.
company n. ǧamánč(ı)‿.
complain v.i., complain of v.t. šɛkkɛ́.
  Whom are you complaining about? (a) ɛr‿
  níg‿åššɛkkɛ́n? (b) ɛr‿ån-nís̆-šɛkkɛ́n?
  (§ 5601)
  What do you complain of? ɛr‿míŋgı‿
  šɛkkɛ́n?
  What's the matter with him (*her*)? *Why is*
  (*s*)*he complaining?* tɛr‿míndɛ́? tɛr‿
  mɛ́n‿åššɛkkɛ́n?
complaint n. šɛkkɛ́rar‿ (-rår‿); šɛkkɛ́rí d‿.
complete adj. tamåm‿ (tåm-, tɛm-);
  kåmıl‿.
complete v.t. addɛ́; tɛmmɛ́; hallıs̆ɛ́.
completion n. tamåm‿ (tåm-, tɛm-).
comprehend v.t. (*grasp mentally*) år;
  fɛhmɛ́.
compress v.t. árr(ı); ǧákk(ı); ǧógor.
conceal v.t. bókkır.
conceited, be v.i. nɛfısdúlko.
  He is conceited: nɛfısdúlkon‿.
concerned, be v.i. (*be anxious*) hɛmmɛ́.
  I am concerned at (*about*) *this:* ının‿ıllɛr‿
  hɛmmɛ́rı‿.
condemn v.t. hokmɛ́ (huk-).
  The court condemned them to death: mahkáma‿diárkɛh‿hokmɛríkkon‿.
condemnation n. hókum‿ (húkum‿,
  hókom‿).
condition n. (*state*) hål‿.
  This is in good condition: íŋ‿génun‿.
  This is not in good condition: íŋ‿gémmunun‿.
conditions (of contract) n. šurúd‿.
confuse v.t. tındımíndıgır; halbıtɛ́ (xal-).
confused adj. tındımínd(ı)‿.
  What they say is confused: tím‿båññıd‿
  tındımíndın‿.

congratulate v.t. (the speaker) bārıkɛ́dĕn, gúrrɛdĕn; (other than the speaker) bārıkɛ́tır, gúrrɛtır.
They congratulated me: (āigı⌣) bārıkɛ́dɛ̆ŋkoran⌢.
He congratulated me: āigı⌣gurrɛdɛ́ŋkon⌢.
I congratulate you: āi⌣ɛ́kkı⌣bārıkɛ́tıddi⌢.
I congratulate you on this: āi⌣ɛ́kk⌣ínın⌣íllɛr⌣gúrrɛtıddi⌢.
They congratulated them: bārıkɛ̄tıríkkoran⌢.
consent v.i. ɛrdɛ́.
conspiracy n. fítnɛ⌣.
constantly adv. dímɛ⌣; dímɛg⌣ (-gi⌢); dímɛn⌣ (-mē⌢, -mé⌢); dímɛŋ(ı)⌣ (-gi⌢); tɛméllı⌣ (-li⌢); tɛméllıg⌣ (-gi⌢).
construct v.t. åu (åw, åú).
construction n. åwar⌣ (åwår⌣); āwíd⌣.
consume v.t. kál.
contain v.t. (*potentially*) sókkɛ.
It contains three arādıb (أرادب): (*a, potentially*) ɛ́rdɛb⌣tóskıs⌣sókkɛn⌢; (*b, actually*) tɛ́n⌣tŭr⌣ɛ́rdɛb⌣tóskı⌣dǎ́n⌢.
contemporary n. (*equal in age*) bútt(ı)⌣.
content(ed) adj. mabsúd⌣.
continually adv. dímɛ⌣, etc. s.v. *constantly*.
continue v.t. āg-complex (§§ 3831 ff.).
They continue dancing all night: úgu⌣ mállɛg⌣ābbándan⌢.
contract n. šurúd⌣.
contract v.i. (*bargain*) gāwıĺɛ́.
contract, be engaged under v.i. gāwıĺɛ̄rɛdǎ́g.
contradict v.t. gālıtɛ́.
contrary, on the adv. -mɛn- (-mén-, -mɛn- §§ 6093-6).
conversation n. wɛ́nɛs⌣.
converse v.i. wɛ́nnıskattı.
convey v.t. bír; óǧi.
cook n. nóbıl⌣; ǧakúdk⌣åwıl⌣; tabbáh⌣.
If the cook wearies the lady I shall turn him out: tabbáh⌣síttım⌣mǎgırkım⌣ bóşri⌢.
cook v.i. ǧakúdk⌣åu (⌣åw, ⌣åú); v.i. and t. tabhɛ́ (-bxɛ́); v.t. kárǧıgır (káǧǧı-).
Who will cook? (a) nírɛ⌣ǧakúdkı⌣båwın? (b) nírɛ⌣bıtabhɛ́n?
Do you know how to cook? (a) ɛr⌣uñurtabhɛ́ná? (b) ɛr⌣ǧakútk⌣uñuråuná?
Can he cook? tɛr⌣ɛskıtabhɛ́ná?
Has he cooked the stew? (a) tɛ́r⌣ǧakútt⌣ åukoná? (b) tɛr⌣ǧakútt⌣nópkoná?
Has he cooked the meat? (a) kúsug⌣awóskoná? (b) kúsug⌣åukarǧıgıróskoná?
This is not cooked, it is raw: íŋ⌣karǧıbugómunū, dɛ́ssi⌢.
cooking-pot n. (*European*) kasaróna (kaza-, kozor-); (*native earthenware*) súlɛ⌣.
cool adj. orófɛl⌣ (⌣⌣⌣, ⌣⌣⌣; s.v. *cold*).
cool wind: wɛlwétt(ı)⌣.
cool v.i. orófɛ (⌣⌣⌣, ⌣⌣⌣).
Let it cool: oróférán⌢.
cool v.t. oroféǧır (⌣⌣⌣, ⌣⌣⌣).
Cool this: íŋ⌣orófɛǧırɔ⌣.
copper n. nahás⌣; šarti⌣gɛ́lɛ⌣.
coquet v.i. gåš.
coquetry n. gåšar⌣ (-šår⌣); gāšíd⌣.
cord n. úl⌣.
cork n. (*stopper*) fúlla⌣.

corn n. (*single grain*) hábba⌣, háb⌣; (*collective, esp. sorghum*) íu⌣ (íu⌣, íw⌣); (*collective, wheat*) íllɛ⌣.
corn-bin n. gússa⌣.
corner n. kím⌣; rúkun⌣.
(S)he (it) is in the corner: kímır⌣bún⌢.
Put it in the corner: kímır⌣úskur⌢, pl. …⌣uskúrwɛ⌢.
corpulent adj. túkol⌣; kómbo⌣.
correct adj. tamám⌣ (tám-, tɛm-).
cost n. (*price*) témɛn⌣; (*expense*) úǧrɛ⌣ (-rá⌣, -ra⌣).
cost v.t. kallıfɛ́ (kɛl-).
What do these cost? íŋgu⌣míŋgı⌣kallıfɛ́ran?
What did this cost? ím⌣míŋgı⌣kɛllıfɛ́gó?
cotton n. (-*plant, -wool, thread and cloth*) bɛnnág⌣; bɛnnáug⌣.
cotton-seed n. kukkós⌣; gúlgul⌣.
couch-grass n. gǒrɛ⌣.
cough n. tóskıdɛ⌣.
You have a cough: tóskıd⌣ɛ́kk⌣āredágın⌢.
cough v.i. tósk(ı).
count v.t. ír; hāsıbɛ́; (*by looking at*) írnal, hāsıbɛ́nal.
Have you counted the money? (a) dúŋıg⌣ írkoná? (b) dúŋıh⌣hāsıbɛ́goná?
Count the eggs: kúmbug⌣írnal⌢.
Count the sheep: ɛ́gɛdıg⌣írnal⌢.
Count the sacks: (a) gárarıg⌣ír⌢; (b) gárarıg⌣írnal⌢.
Have they counted the camels? kámlıg⌣ írkorandɛ́?
country n. bélɛd⌣; (*uninhabited*) hála⌣.
countryman n. bélɛdn⌣íd⌣ (bɛlɛ́dnıd⌣).
course, of adv. malúm⌣.
court n. (*tribunal*) mahkáma (máh-, -ká-, -má⌣).
courtyard n. hǒš⌣.
cousin n. (*father's brother's son*) -bǎnnantód⌣; -bēnnan-tód⌣; -dabíss(ı)⌣.
(*father's brother's daughter*) -bǎnnámburu⌣ (-ámburu⌣); -bēnnám-buru⌣ (-ámburu⌣); -dabíss(ı)⌣.
(*father's sister's son*) -banɛssın-tód⌣.
(*father's sister's daughter*) -bānɛssím-buru⌣ (-ímburu⌣).
(*mother's brother's son*) -gın-tód⌣ (-gíntód⌣).
(*mother's brother's daughter*) -gím-buru⌣ (-gímburu⌣).
(*mother's sister's son*) -ɛŋkɛgın-tód⌣.
(*mother's sister's daughter*) -ɛŋkɛgím-buru⌣ (-gímburu⌣).
Always with a form of the poss. pers. pron. (§§ 2622 ff.) prefixed:
my father's brother's son: ambǎnnan-tód⌣.
your father's brother's son: ımbǎnnan- tód⌣.
his (her) father's brother's son: tımbǎnnantód⌣.
our father's brother's son: antımbǎnnantód⌣.
your (pl.) father's brother's son: ıntımbǎnnan-tód⌣.
their father's brother's son: tıntımbǎnnantód⌣.
my father's brother's daughter: ambǎnnámburu⌣ (-búru⌣); ambēnnám-buru⌣ (-búru⌣); andabíss(ı)⌣.
your father's brother's daughter: ımbǎnnám-buru⌣ (-búru⌣); ımbēnnámburu⌣ (-búru⌣); ındabíss(ı)⌣.

my mother's brother's son: aŋgıntód⌣ (aŋgíntód⌣).
your mother's brother's son: ıŋgıntód⌣ (ıŋgíntód⌣).
our mother's brother's daughter: antıŋgímburu⌣ (-búru⌣).
your (pl.) mother's sister's son: ıntınɛ̄ŋkɛgıntód⌣.
their mother's sister's daughter: tıntınɛ̄ŋkɛgím-buru⌣ (-búru⌣).
cover n. tagídd(ı)⌣; gúta⌣ (gáta⌣, gáta⌣).
cover v.t. (*put detachable or temporary cover on*) tágır; (*put fixed or permanent cover on*) dǒš.
Cover the wound lest the flies come on it: kǒrkı⌣tágır⌣kúltı⌣téddo⌣tåmɛnın⌣ illár⌢.
Cover the tea-pot so that it may not get cold: šåim⌣bɛrrádkı⌣tágır⌣orófɛmɛnın⌣illár⌢.
Cover over the runnel so that the path may pass over it: máltıd⌣dǒš⌣dérıb⌣téŋ⌣ kóčč́ıgɛg⌣gašɛ́nn⌣illár⌢.
covered, be v.i. tág.
coverlet n. férıš⌣tagídd(ı)⌣.
cow n. tí⌣.
cow-dung: (a) tín⌣hóss(ı)⌣; (b) tínčın⌣ hóss(ı)⌣.
cow-house: kérr(ı)⌣.
I want cow's milk: tín⌣íčč́ıd⌣dólli⌢.
coward n. sandǎí⌣; kǎuk⌣.
He is a coward: sandájun⌢.
They are cowards: sandajín⌢.
cowherd n. tíncıg⌣íwıl⌣.
crack n. gágar⌣ (-går⌣); gagíd⌣.
There's a large crack here: índo⌣gagíd⌣ dúl⌣lɛr⌣dǎ́n⌢.
crack v.i. (*split*) gág; (*make noise*) tóčč́ɛ.
crack v.t. tóčč́ɛ.
cracked adj. gágbūl⌣ (gággūl⌣).
This is cracked: íŋ⌣gágbun⌢.
craft n. (*art*) sína⌣.
craftsman n. basír; ústa⌣.
crane n. (*Grus sp.*) arraháu⌣ (árraháu⌣); raháu⌣ (ráháu⌣).
cream n. nébɛd⌣ (némɛd⌣).
credulous adj. gaším⌣.
crest n. (*of bird*) kúǧ⌣.
cricket n. (*Acheta sp.*) bánga; **Gryllus sp.** gırgíttɛ⌣.
crime n. ǧınáǰɛ⌣ (-ǰå⌣, -ǰa⌣); zémb(ı)⌣.
crocodile n. élım⌣ (élum⌣).
crooked adj. kérɛñ⌣.
This is crooked: íŋ⌣kérɛñun⌢.
crop n. (*growing*) tɛ́rar⌣ (-rår⌣); dɛ́ssɛ⌣.
cross v.t. (*go or come across*) múkk(ı); gǎšɛ́.
I crossed the river: (a) úrum⌣múkkıgori⌢; (b) úrum⌣mérkori⌢.
Did you cross the railway? ɛr⌣gadíbkı⌣ gašɛ́goná?
The runnel crosses the road: máltı⌣derıbkı⌣ gašɛ́n⌢.
cross-beam n. (*supporting roof*) mírıg⌣; (*in water-wheel*) díu⌣ (díw⌣).
crow n. guráb⌣.
crow v.i. wíg.
crumple v.i. ǧógor.
crust n. káčč́(ı)⌣.
cry n. (*loud*) kǒrág⌣.
cry v.i. wíg; (*weep aloud*) óñ.
Don't cry: tókkon⌣óñmɛn⌢.

cubit n. (*21–22 inches*) kɛ́u⌣ (kɛ́ᵘ⌣, kɛ́w⌣); dúra⌣.
Cucumis dipsaceus n. tíbıš⌣.
Cucumis melo n. găwŭn⌣ (gău͡ŭn⌣).
Cucurbita maxima n. kɛ́bɛ⌣.
cultivate v.t. éwır.
   X. *What are you doing now?* ɛr⌣ékkɛnɛ⌣ míng⌣ăgăwın?
   Y. *I am cultivating an (irrigated) estate:* kólɛg⌣ăgɛwírri⌢.
cultivation n. tɛ̆rar⌣ (-rắr⌣); tɛ̄ríd⌣.
cup n. kŭ́z⌣ (kŭ́s⌣); kắs⌣; kub(b)ắi͡a⌣ (-ắi͡a⌣); (*small*) fıngắn⌣.
   handle of cup: kŭ́zn⌣í⌣ (kŭ́sn⌣í⌣); kub(b)ắi͡an⌣í⌣.
   handle of small cup: fıngắnn⌣í⌣.
   coffee-cup: gáhwan⌣fıngắn⌣.
   tea-cup: šắiŋ⌣kubắi͡a⌣; šắin⌣fıngắn⌣.
cupboard n. dōlắb⌣.
   in the cupboard: dōlắbır⌣.
   Pit it (them) into the cupboard: dōlắbır⌣ úndur⌢.
curdle v.i. mɛ́rɛlan-.
   curdled milk: mɛ́rɛl⌣.
cure v.t. wajjɛ́gır.
current n. nogíd⌣; (*strong*) tajjắr⌣.
   The river is running with a strong current: (a) úru⌣tajjắrambūn⌢; (b) úru⌣tajjăranɛdắgın⌢; (c) úru⌣gŭ́rrın⌢.
curse n. tŭ́ss(ı)⌣.
curse v.t. tŭ́s; nālɛ́; (*at*) čubbɛ́, tubbɛ́.
curved adj. kɛ́rɛl⌣.
cushion n. máhádda⌣ (mah-).
cut v.t. mɛ́r; (corn, grass) gŏr.
   Don't cut the rope: írıt⌣tókkom⌣mɛ́rmɛn⌢.
   Cut down the tree: gŏwwım⌣mɛ́r⌢.
   Cut the grass: gídkı⌣gŏr⌢.
   Go and cut some grass: gíd⌣toddɛ́gˇ⌣ gŏrétta⌢, lit. *after cutting bring a little grass*.
cut off v.t. múrugˇ.
cut short v.t. mútt(ı).
cut up v.t. nódd(ı); sɛ́r.
   Cut this up: íŋı⌣nóddi⌢.
Cynodon dactylon n. gŏrɛ⌣.

daily wage n. jōmíjɛ⌣ (-jă⌣, -ja⌣).
damn! interj. čúpp!
damp adj. gˇắwwur⌣ (gˇău͡wur⌣).
damp v.t. tắbbɛ.
dance v.i. bắn.
dark adj. urúmmɛ⌣.
   It's dark (there is no light): gŭ́⌣urúmmɛn⌢.
   It will get dark: búganın⌢ (s.v. úgu⌣).
   when it gets dark: gŭ́⌣urúmmaŋkın⌣.
   When it gets dark, go: ắšăi⌣urúmmaŋkın⌣ nók⌢.
date n. (*tree and fruit*) bɛ́nt(ı)⌣.
   soft dates in mass: (a) kúra⌣; (b) ắgwa⌣.
   unripe date: (a) gállo⌣; (b) díffɛ⌣.
   date-stone: (a) fắs⌣; (b) bɛ́ntın⌣fắs⌣.
   small frond of date-palm: kórsɛ⌣.
daughter n. búru⌣.
   Is this your daughter? ín⌣ém-bururɛ́?
daughter-in-law n. tōdnɛ́n⌣ (tōnnɛ́n⌣).
dawn n. fắgˇır⌣ (fɛ́gˇ-).
   at dawn: (a) făgírk(ı)⌣; (b) făgírro⌣.
   Come at dawn: fɛgˇírro⌣tá⌢ (⌣tắrɛ⌢), pl. …tắwɛ⌢.

day n. ugrɛ́s⌣; nahắr⌣ (nắh-, nɛh-); jóm⌣.
   all day adv. (a) ugrɛ́s⌣mállɛg⌣; (b) nahắr⌣ mállɛg⌣.
   every day adv. (a) ugrɛ́s⌣mállɛg⌣; (b) nahắr⌣mállɛg⌣; (c) kul(l)jóm͡g(ı)⌣.
   Does (s)he (it) come every day? (a) ugrɛ́s⌣ mállɛt⌣tăná? (b) nahắr⌣mállɛt⌣tăná? (c) kuljómgı⌣tăná?
   I gave it to you that day: mán⌣jómg⌣ ɛ́kki⌣tíkkori⌢.
   I gave it you three days ago: ăi⌣ɛ́kkı⌣ tırsíddotōn⌣jóm⌣tóski-taran⌢.
   Open it at night; shut it by day: ugŭ́k⌣kŭ́s, ugrɛ́ski⌣kóp⌢.
   It's nearly day: ugrɛ́sanɛdólın⌢.
dead adj. (a) díbūl⌣; (b) díɛl⌣.
   (S)he (it) is dead: díɛlun⌢.
   Clear away the dead leaves: úlug⌣díbūlgı⌣ sókkɛ⌢.
dead, be v.i. díbū-.
   (S)he (it) is dead (= lies dead): díbūn⌢.
   (S)he (it) is dead (= has died): dígon⌢.
   (S)he (it) is not dead (= is not lying dead): díbūmunun⌢; (= has not died): dígomunun⌢.
deaf adj. tɛ́rıg⌣.
   I am deaf: ăi⌣tɛ́rıg⌣ɛ́ri⌢.
   I am not deaf: ăi⌣tɛ́rıgmunun⌢.
   Are you deaf? ɛr⌣tɛ́rıgrɛ́?
   (S)he (it) is deaf: tɛr⌣tɛ́rıgun⌢.
   (S)he (it) is not deaf: tɛr⌣tɛ́rıgmunun⌢.
   Is (s)he (it) deaf? tɛr⌣tɛ́rıgrɛ́?
dear adj. (*costly*) gălı⌣.
   It is (too) dear: gălın⌢.
death n. díar⌣ (díắr⌣, díɛr⌣).
débris n. (*refuse*) kắšš(ı)⌣; kawíš⌣.
debt n. dɛ́n⌣.
   Have you got debts? dɛ́n⌣ɛ́ddo⌣tɛ́brandɛ́?
   Have you paid your debt? ɛr⌣ɛ́n⌣dɛ́ŋgı⌣ kópkoná?
   Has he paid his debts? (a) tɛr⌣tɛ́n⌣dɛ́nık⌣ kópkoná? (b) tɛr⌣tɛ́n⌣dɛ́nık⌣kobırík-koná?
deceive v.t. gošš̆ɛ́.
   They have deceived me: ăigı⌣goššɛ́rɛ-dăgran⌢.
   I was deceived: ăi⌣goššɛ́kattıgori⌢.
decision n. (*judicial*) hókum⌣ (húkum⌣, hókom⌣).
decrease v.i. kíññan-; năgısɛ́ (năgsɛ́, nắksɛ́).
decrease v.t. kíññagır; năgısɛ́gır (năgsɛ́-, nắksɛ́-).
decreased adj. năgıs⌣.
deed n. ăwar⌣ (ăwắr⌣); ăwíd⌣.
deep adj. dóll(ı)⌣.
   The ravines are deep: hŏrı⌣dóllınčí⌢.
deepen v.t. dóllıgır.
defecate v.i. ŭ́ss(ı).
deficient adj. năgıs⌣.
deficient, be v.i. năgısɛ́ (năgsɛ́, nắksɛ́).
   The money is deficient: dúŋgı⌣năgısɛ́n⌢.
defile v.t. ɛ́rtıgır; wassahɛ́.
delay v.t. ắhhɛrɛ́gır; attılɛ́.
   Don't delay him (her, it): tókkon⌣ahhɛrɛ́-gırmɛn⌢.
delayed, be v.p. ắhhɛrɛ́; ắhhɛrkattı-; ắttılkattı-.
delight v.t. bastɛ́gır.
deliver v.t. (*save*) hallısɛ́; (*hand over*) sɛllımɛ́ (-lumɛ́).
demand v.t. talabɛ́.

demolish v.t. bŏrkıgˇ; wíll(ı).
demon n. gˇắnı⌣; ıblís⌣.
Demostachya cynosuroides n. hamắrtɛ⌣.
depart v.i. nóg.
departure n. nógar⌣ (-gắr⌣); nogíd⌣.
deplore v.t. wɛ́gˇakatt(ı) (wắgˇ-).
depreciate v.t. taggısɛ́.
depress (*mentally*) v.t. zālɛ́gır.
depressed (mentally), become v.i. zālɛ́.
depth n. dóllıgıd⌣.
   What is its depth? tɛ́n⌣dóllıgıd⌣mukót-tɛ̄rrɛ́?
   What is the depth of the well? gŏwwın⌣ dóllıgıd⌣mukóttɛ̄rrɛ́?
dervish n. dɛrɛwíš⌣.
descend v.i. šúgur, kútte; (*sink*) kídd(ı), kúñ.
desert n. hála⌣; ắgaba⌣.
   in the desert: hálar⌣.
desire n. dólar⌣ (-lắr⌣); dolíd⌣; dólt(ı)⌣.
desire v.t. dól; (*want*) wɛ́rs(ı).
destitute adj. hắgˇakıññ(ı)⌣ (-gˇăk-, -gˇɛk-).
destroy v.t. harbɛ́.
detain v.t. attılɛ́.
devil n. ıblís⌣; gˇắnı⌣; šɛ̆tắn⌣.
   sand-devil (column of sand or dust): (a) kắgˇbar⌣; (b) kašwắrɛ⌣.
   Let him (her, it) go to the devil! gˇúkuñan!
   The devil is in this lock: (a) ín⌣dúgal⌣ gˇắnık⌣kó⌢; (b) ín⌣dúgal⌣gˇắnık⌣kó⌢.
devilish adj. gˇănínd(ı)⌣.
dialect n. bắññıd⌣.
diarrhoea n.
   (S)he has diarrhoea: tɛ́n-tu⌣nógın⌢.
die n. (*one of dice*) záhar⌣.
die v.i. dí.
   Did (s)he (it) die? dígoná?
   Did they die? dígorandɛ́?
   Have any more people died? ắdắmı⌣tɛ́nnɛ⌣ dióskorandɛ́?
different adj. ɛ́ččɛl⌣.
   I want a different one: ɛ́ččɛl-lɛ̄d⌣dólli⌢.
   That country is different from this: mám⌣ bɛ́lɛd⌣ínın⌣dógor⌣ɛ́ččɛlun⌢.
difficult adj. dúllo⌣.
dig v.t. wắdd(ı).
   X. *Have they dug the hole?* kúlgı⌣wắddıgorandɛ́?
   Y. *They are digging it:* tɛ̄bwắddıran⌢.
digit n. sắrbɛ⌣.
diligent adj. gˇɛllıgˇău͡kátt(ı)⌣.
diminish v.i. kíññan-; năgısɛ́ (năgsɛ́, nắksɛ́).
diminish v.t. kíññagır; năgısɛ́gır (năgsɛ́-, nắksɛ́-).
diminished adj. năgıs⌣.
dining-room n. súfraŋ⌣kắ⌣ (-raŋ⌣).
   Put it into the dining-room: súfraŋ⌣kắr⌣ úndur⌢.
dinner n. ắša⌣.
   Is dinner ready? ắša⌣hắdırrɛ́?
   Bring dinner: ắšag⌣ɛ́tta⌢.
Dipus aegypticus n. burúkk(ı)⌣.
direct v.t. (*enjoin*) kallıfɛ́ (kɛl-).
direction n. árıg⌣.
director n. mudír⌣.
dirt n. wasắha⌣.
dirty adj. ɛ́rt(ı)⌣; wắsah⌣; wăšắn⌣.
   Take away the dirty ones: (a) ɛrtíncıs⌣ sókkɛ⌢; (b) wắsahıs⌣sókkɛ⌢; (c) wăhắnıs⌣sókkɛ⌢.
   He is dirty: tɛ́n⌣gˇísım⌣ɛ́rtín⌢, lit. *his body is dirty*.

dirty v.t. ɛ́rtɪgɪr; wassahɛ́.
disabled adj. ắğɪz◡.
disappear v.i. dáb.
discharge v.t. (*from employment*) ós.
disease n. óddɛ◡.
diseased adj. (*now*) óddɪl◡; (*before now*) óddɛl◡.
disentangle v.t. bɛ́u (bɛ́w, bɛ́u).
disgust v.t. sɪ́kkɪgɪr.
dish n. (*vessel*) sáhan◡, dắd(ɪ)◡ (dắdd(ɪ)◡); (*food*) ğákud◡, kál◡.
dislike v.t. (*a*) mőn; (*b*) kɛččɪnɛ́.
 I dislike this: íŋgɪ◡móndi◠.
 They dislike this: íŋgɪ◡móndan◠.
dislocated, be v.i. búdbŭ-.
 Your shoulder is dislocated: ɛ́nn◡ósmar◡ búdbūn◠.
dislocated, become v.i. búd.
dislocation n. búdar◡ (-dár◡); budɪ́d◡.
 dislocation of the knee: kúrtɪm◡búdar◡.
dismiss n. (*off duty*) dɛstúr◡.
 Dismiss! dɛstúrk◡ắu!, pl. dɛstúrk◡ắuwɛ!
 Tell him to dismiss: dɛstúrk◡ắuan◠.
 Tell them to dismiss: dɛstúrk◡ắuwan◠.
dismiss v.t. (*tell to go*) nógan; (*discharge from employment*) ós.
displeased adj.
 I am displeased with him (her, ...at it): aī◡tɛ́ddotōm◡mabsúdmunun◠.
disposition n. (*arrangement*) tartíb◡ (tár-, tɛr-).
dispute v.t. gālɪtɛ́.
dissolve v.t. and i. ğŭ́dɛ.
distant adj. wárr(ɪ)◡; warrínd(ɪ)◡; bájɛl◡.
 I can't see the distant one: warríndɪg◡ ɛskɪnálmunun◠.
distant, be v.i. bắɪ (báj, bắɪ).
distend v.t. nɛ́jjɪgɪr.
distressed, be (*grieve*) v.i. wɛ́ğakattɪ- (wắğ-).
 Why is (s)he distressed? tɛr◡méw◡wɛ́ğakattɪn?
distribute v.t. bág.
 Distribute the money: dúŋgɪb◡bák◠.
 Distribute the money to them: tírgɪ◡ dúŋgɪb◡bágɪrɪr◠.
 Distribute this among them: tírg◡iŋgɪ◡ bágɪrɪr◠.
 Let him distribute this: íŋgɪ◡bágan◠.
district n. bɛ́lɛd◡; (*administrative*) mɛ́rkɛz◡.
 district officer (*maᵛmŭr*): māmúr◡.
dive v.i. kídd(ɪ).
divide into shares v.t. bág; bagíttɛ.
divorce v.t. bắğ.
 Has he divorced his wife? ténn◡ɛ́ŋgɪ◡ bắğóskoná?
do v.t. áu (ắw, ắu).
 Who did this (that)? íŋgɪ◡n◡ắukó?
 Do this (that): íŋg◡áu◠.
 Do (pl.) this (that): íŋgɪ◡ắuwɛ◠.
 Come and do this: (a) ta-ɪŋg◡áu◠ (§5601); (b) íŋgɪ◡tắu◠.
 Come (pl.) and do this: (a) ta-ɪŋg-áuwɛ́◠ (§5601); (b) íŋgɪ◡tắuwɛ́◠.
 Don't do this (that): tókkon◡íŋg◡áumɛn◠.
 Don't (pl.) do this (that): tókkon◡íŋg◡ ắumɛwwɛ◠.
 Don't do it like that: you'll break it: íŋkɛt◡tókkon◡áumɛn: bɪtómbɪn◠.
 The cat washes its face, the dog doesn't: sáb◡tén◡kóñgɪ◡šúkkɪn, wɛ́l◡šúkkɪmunun◠.

Does he shave his beard? tén◡sámag◡ gáññɪná?
 X. *Did they come?* tắgorandɛ́?
 Y. *Some did, others didn't*: wɛ̌rɪ◡tắgoran, wɛ̌rɪ◡tắgomunan◠.
What have they done with the money? dúŋgɪm◡mín◡ắukoran? (also = *what have they done about the money?*).
What will you do! (expressing perplexity): bɪ-mín◡ắwɪn? (lit. *how will you do?*).
This is done with: ím◡mállɛ-taran◠.
 X. *Is this done with?* ím◡mállɛ◡tɛ́?
 Y. *Yes, it is*: ɛ́jjo, mállɛ-taran◠.
Do come in: tómɛn?, pl. tómɛndu?
doctor n. hakím◡.
document n. wárag◡ (wárăg◡).
dog n. wɛ́l◡.
 Let the dog out: wɛ́lgɪ◡bɛ́lan◠.
 Turn the dog out: wɛ́lg◡ós◠.
 Does this dog bite? íw◡wɛ́l◡ádamɪg◡ áččɪná?
dog-star, the n. tóskan◡abáŋ-wɪss(ɪ)◡.
Dolichos lablab n. úgud◡.
dollar n. rɪjál◡.
dōm-palm n. hámbu◡.
 seed of dōm-palm: gúll(ɪ)◡.
dome n. gúbba◡.
Dóngola n. (*the country*) dúŋgula◡; (*the town: Old*) dúŋgula◡, túŋgul◡; (*the town: New*) úrd(ɪ)◡.
Dongolese adj. duŋgulánd(ɪ)◡.
Dongolese n. (*person*) duŋgulăwɪ◡, bɛ́rbɛrɪ◡, bárbarɪ◡; (*language*) duŋgulánd(ɪ)◡, rutána◡, índ(ɪ)◡ (s.v. *ír*◡). S.v. *Nubian*.
donkey n. hánu◡.
 Have you ever seen a greater donkey than him? ɛr◡ún◡dógor◡hánun◡nálkoná?
 You are a donkey: ɛr◡hánun◠.
 He is a donkey: tɛr◡hánun◠.
door n. kóbɪd◡; báb◡.
 Shut the door (*of a room* or *house*): kák◡ kóp◠.
 Open the door (*of a room* or *house*): kák◡ kús◠.
 (S)he (it) is not to come past my door: tókkon◡ám◡bábkɪ◡gašɛ́mɛnan◠.
 They are not to come past my door: tókkon◡ ám◡bábkɪ◡gašɛ́mɛwwan◠.
door-handle n. kobídn◡í◡; bábn◡í◡.
door-post n. míšš(ɪ)◡.
dot n. núgta◡ (núkta◡).
dough n. kanísɛ◡.
dove n. kúru◡; gókka◡.
down adv. tógor◡.
down, bring (send, put, etc.) v.t. šu-gúdd(ɪ)◡; kúttɛgɪr.
down, come (go) v.i. šúgur◡; kúttɛ.
 Has (s)he (it) come down? šugúrkoná?
 Hasn't (s)he (it) come down? šugúrkomɛn?
down to prep. —m◡bókkon◡ (-kō◠, -kó◠); —m◡móŋkon◡ (-kō◠, -kó◠).
drag v.t. óčč(ɪ); ošóšk(ɪ).
draught n. (*of air*) túrug◡; (*of liquid*) níar◡ (níăr◡, níɛr◡); šúrba◡ (-bắ◡, -bɛ◡).
draw v.t. (*pull*) tóllɛ; (*pull out*) ós; (*water*) kás.
 Did he draw his knife? tén◡kándɪg◡ óskoná?
 Did they draw their swords? tín◡síwɪdɪg◡ óskorandɛ́?
drawers n. (*garment of either sex*) surwắl◡. (*short*) sagírtɛ◡.

drawing-room n. sála◡.
dream n. únt(ɪ)◡; manắm◡.
dregs n. tífɪl◡.
dress (oneself) v.i. kádɛd◡dɛ́g; dɛ́g.
 I am going to dress: áŋ◡kádɛd◡dɛgɛdólli◠.
 Dress yourself (*put your clothes on*): ɛ́ŋ◡ kádɛd◡dɛ́k◠.
 I am dressed: aī◡dɛgɛdắgri◠.
 I am not dressed: aī◡dɛgɛdắgmunun◠.
 He is dressing: áddɛgɪn◠.
 Did he dress your wound? ɛŋ◡kórkɪ◡ gɛndɪgírkoná?
drink n. (*beverage*) níar◡ (níăr◡, níɛr◡).
drink v.t. ní.
 What shall I drink out of? míŋgɛn◡nɪ́ri?
 Has (s)he (it) drunk? nɪ́óskoná?
 Have they drunk? nɪ́óskorandɛ́?
drip v.i. déttɛ.
drive (along) v.t. šúg.
 It dropped from the tree: ğówwɪrtōn◡ dɪgírkon◠.
drive away v.t. túr; šúg.
 Let him drive it away: túran◠; šúgan◠.
 Let him drive them away: túrɪran◠; šúgɪrɪran◠.
driver n. šúgɪl◡; (*of water-wheel*) ɛwɪrátt(ɪ)◡.
drop v.i. dígɪr.
 It dropped from the tree: ğówwɪrtōn◡ dɪgírkon◠.
drop v.t. (*throw down*) árk(ɪ), arík(ɪ); (*let fall*) (dɪgɪ́rkɪr, díg(ɪ)rɪŋgɪr (͞ ͝ ͝, - ͝ ͝).
 Drop it: árki◠, pl. arík◠.
 Don't drop it: (a) tókkon◡tɛ́kk◡árkɪmɛn◠; (b) tókkon◡dɪgírkɪrmɛn◠ (͞ ͝ ͝); (c) tókkon◡díg(ɪ)rɪŋgɪrmɛn◠ (͞ ͝ ͝ ͝, ͝ ͝ ͝ ͞).
 Don't (pl.) drop it: (a) tókkon◡tɛ́kk◡ árkɪmɛwwɛ́◠; (b) tókkon◡dɪgírkɪrmɛwwɛ́◠ (͞ ͝ ͝ ͝); (c) tokkon◡dígɪrɪŋgɪrmɛwwɛ́◠ (͞ ͝ ͝ ͝, ͝ ͝ ͝ ͞).
droppings n. (*of animal*) hóss(ɪ)◡; (*of cattle, horse, donkey*) hóss(ɪ)◡; (*of goat, sheep*) kállɛ◡; (*of camel*) túr◡.
drown v.i. kɪddɪdí.
drowsiness n. nalunɛ́r◡.
drowsy
 (S)he (it) is drowsy: tɛ́kkɪ◡nalunɛ́r◡ắrɪn◠.
drum b. nuggára◡; túmbura◡.
drunk, be v.i. sámbŭ-.
 Is (s)he drunk? tɛr◡sámbūná?
drunk, get v.i. sắm.
 Don't get drunk: tókkon◡sámmɛn◠.
drunk, make v.t. sắmgɪr.
 It will make you drunk: ɛ́kkɪ◡bɪsámgɪrɪn◠.
 The beer will make me drunk: mɛ́rs◡aīgɪ◡ bɪsámgɪrɪn◠.
drunkenness n. sămar◡ (-már◡); sámíd◡.
dry adj. sówwɛd◡ (-wod◡).
 It is dry: sówwɛdun◠.
 It isn't dry: sowwɛ́dmunun◠.
dry v.i. sóww(ɪ).
 It has dried (up): sowwóskon◠.
dry v.t. sówwídd(ɪ); sówwɪgɪr.
 Have you dried your hands? ɛnn◡ís◡ sowwíddɪgoná?
dug adj. ɛ́rt(ɪ)◡.
dull adj. (*ponderous*) dúllo◡; (*stupid*) ɛrɪkkómɛnɪl◡, ɛrɪkkattɪbúmɛnɪl◡.
dumb adj. múmmud◡.
dung n. ɛ́kkɛd◡; (*of animals*) hóss(ɪ)◡; see *droppings*.
dupe v.t. goššɛ́.
 Is (s)he easily duped? tɛr◡gašímrɛ́?

during
  (S)he (it) disappeared during the night: ugúd‿dápkon⌢.
dusk n. (twilight) šárɛ‿; mígrıb‿.
  at dusk: šárɛg‿, -gi⌢.
dusky adj. urúmmɛkırı‿.
dust n. éskɛd‿; (in commotion) gubår‿, gutår‿.
dust-devil (column of dust) n. kašwårɛ‿; kåğbar‿.
dust-storm n. gutår‿.
duty
  This is your duty: ín‿éddo‿kúğın⌢.
  This was your duty: ín‿éddo‿kúčkon⌢.
duty, person on, n. nŏbátšı‿.
  Who is the man on duty? ní-tɛ‿nobátšın?
dwell v.i. åg; tĕg.

each (each one) distr. pron. kulwáhıd‿ (kullw-).
  Each man gives a piastre: óggı‿gírıš‿ wɛwɛ́t‿tíddan⌢.
  Put one into each boat: kúb‿mállɛr‿ wɛwɛ́g‿úndur⌢.
ear n. úlug‿; (spica) núd‿, ɹuŋ‿gól‿; (spica nearly ripe) gáŋgarɛ‿ (-rı‿).
earlier adj. ogólnd(ı)‿ (ogónd(ı)‿).
earlier adv. ŏwwéllo‿; ogóllo‿.
earlier than prep. —n‿ŏwwéllo‿; —n‿ogóllo‿.
early adv. bédrır‿.
  very early: fɛğıntúg‿.
  Bring it early tomorrow: asálgı‿bɛdrı‿girétta⌢.
  I wish to wake early: åi‿bɛddırēbıčči‿rángı‿dólli⌢.
  Tell him (her) to come early: bɛdrıgır‿táran⌢.
earn v.t. kɛsbɛ́.
ear-ring n. ákaš‿; (solid) bíblığ‿.
  gold ear-ring: nóbrɛn‿ákaš‿.
  silver ear-ring: dúŋgın‿ákaš‿.
earth n. (ground) gú‿; (soil, ground) árıd‿; (loose) éskɛd‿.
  Clean it with earth: ɛskɛ́dkɛn‿naddıfɛ́⌢.
ease n. råha‿.
ease nature v.i. (evacuate bowels) úss(ı).
east n. mált(ı)‿; šérıg‿.
eastwards adv. máltır‿; šérıgır‿.
easy adj. héjjın‿.
  (to a rower) Easy! tĕp!, pl. tĕbwé!
eat v.t. kál.
  I shall not eat this: åi‿ıŋgı‿bıkálmunun⌢.
  X. I want something to eat: åi‿šɛ́jı-wɛk‿ kállaŋgı‿dólli⌢.
  Y. Eggs or vegetables? kúmbugá‿wálla‿hodárki?
  If I don't eat at night I sleep well: åion‿ugúk‿kálmɛŋkırı‿sɛrɛgırnɛ́rri‿.
  If there's nothing else I'll eat this: ɛ́ččɛlon‿ dámɛŋkın‿íŋgı‿bıkálli⌢.
edge n. (border) táraf (tåråf‿); kɛ́l‿.
  Put it on the edge of the plate: sáhan‿ táraɹır‿úskur⌢.
  river's edge: urunår‿.
efendi n. ɛfɛ́ndı‿.
  I want one of the efendiyya: ɛfɛndínčırtów‿wɛd‿dólli⌢.
efface v.t. kómıs.
egg n. kúmbu‿.
  boiled eggs: kúmbu‿sɛlgɛbūl‿.
  fried eggs: kúmb‿asílbūl‿.
  poached eggs: kúmbu‿téŋ‿káččım‿másır‿sɛlgɛbūl‿.
  I want two eggs: kúmb‿ówwıd‿dólli⌢.
  When the eggs are boiled, bring them: kúmbunčı‿wázburan‿tád‿étta⌢.
  This egg is not fresh: íŋ‿kúmb‿ɛ́rmunun⌢.
  This egg is stale: íŋ‿kúmbu‿kúrusun⌢.
  I don't want old eggs: kúmbunčı‿kúrusıd‿dólmunun⌢.
  I want some fresh eggs: kúmbunč‿ɛ́rı‿wɛ́rıd‿dólli⌢.
  The egg is (eggs are §4696d) to be soft (-boiled): kúmbuğ‿ğagādéban⌢.
  The egg is (eggs are) to be hard(-boiled): kúmbud‿dɛŋgelámban⌢.
  Boil me two eggs hard: kúmb‿ówwıd‿dɛŋgɛgırsɛlgɛ́dēn⌢.
  Boil me the egg(s) soft: kúmbuğ‿ğagādɛ‿gırsɛlgɛ́dēn⌢.
egg-shell n. kúmbuŋ‿káčč(ı)‿.
Egypt n. másur‿.
eight card. num. ídıw‿.
eighteen card. num. dımındídıw‿.
eighth ord. num. ıd(ı)wínt(ı)‿ (íd(ı)-wınt(ı)‿).
eighty card. num. dımınídıw‿; tamanín‿.
either…or conj. já‿…já‿; (after a negative) wála‿…wála‿.
  Tell either Muḥámmad or Sålım to go: já‿mohammétkı‿já‿sålımgı‿nógan⌢.
  X. Do you want it now or later? ékkɛnɛ-tɛ‿dólın‿wálla‿bádké⌢?
  Y. I don't want it either now or later: wál‿ékkɛnɛ‿dólmunun‿wála‿bádké⌢.
elbow n. kugúnd(ı)‿; kumúnd(ı)‿.
elephant n. fíl‿.
eleven card. num. dımındowɛ́r‿.
eleventh ord. num. dımındówwɛl‿ (-wəl‿, -wəl‿).
else
  I don't want anything else: šɛ́j‿ɛččɛ́lgı‿dólmunun⌢.
embrace v.t. gårɛ.
emerge v.i. bél.
empty adj. súd‿; fádı‿.
  This is empty, take it away: ín‿súdun, sókkɛ⌢.
  Bring the empty bucket: ğɛ́rdɛl‿súdk‿étta⌢.
empty v.t. súdkır (sútk-).
  Empty this: íŋgı‿sútkır⌢.
enclosure n. (fence) zɛ́rbɛ‿; (formed by fence or wall) kúdɛ‿; (court) hóš‿.
end n. (extremity) kɛ́l‿; åhır‿ (áxır‿); (latter part) abág‿.
  finger-end: sárbɛŋ‿kɛ́llo‿.
  at the end of the finger: sárbɛŋ‿kɛ́llo‿.
  at the end: abågır‿.
  at the end of the job: ğɛllın‿abágır‿.
  It is at an end: halás-taran⌢.
end v.t. (complete) addɛ́; tɛmmɛ́.
endurance n. sabrɛ́rar‿ (-rår‿); sabrɛ̄ríd‿.
endure v.t. sabrɛ́.
enemy n. ádu‿.
energy n. hél‿; šídda‿ (-dá‿).
engaged part. (busy) ğɛllıköl‿.
engaged, be v.i. (be busy) ğɛllıkŏ-.
  Is (s)he engaged? tɛr‿ğɛllıkoná?
English adj. ıŋglízı‿; ıŋglīzínd(ı)‿.
English n. (the language) ıŋglízı‿.
  Does (s)he know English? tɛr‿ıŋglízıg‿uñúrná?
  Did (s)he talk English? (a) ıŋglízıb‿báññıgoná? (b) ıŋglízıgɛb‿báññıgoná?
Englishman n. ıŋglíz‿.
  Did an Englishman come? ıŋglíz-zēr‿tågoná?
  Have you seen an Englishman? ıŋglíz-zēn‿nálkoná?
enjoin v.t. kallıfɛ́ (kɛl-).
enlarge v.t. dúlgır.
enough adj. (that suffices) kɛfɛ́l‿; (that sufficed) kɛfɛ́rɛl‿.
  It's not long enough: nosómunun⌢ (enough implied).
enough, be v.i. kɛfɛ́.
  That (this) is enough: íŋ‿kɛfɛ́n⌢.
  It's not enough: kɛfɛ́munun⌢.
  Is it enough? kɛfɛ́ná?
  Isn't it enough? kɛfɛ́mɛn?
enough, have v.i. and t. bɛ́r.
  I have had enough: åi‿bɛ́rburi⌢.
  I want the vegetables to have enough water. hodárk‿éssıb‿bēríŋgı‿dólli⌢.
enrage v.t. sínnɛgır.
enter v.i. tó.
entrails n. dúgus‿ (dúñus‿).
entreat v.t. bédd(ı).
envelop v.t. kátt(ı).
envelope n. zárıf‿.
epilepsy n. fatfád‿; fátterar‿ (-rår‿); fatteríd‿.
epileptic n. unáttıgɛğ‿ğómbul‿.
  Is (s)he an epileptic? unáttıgɛğ‿ğómbuná?
equitable adj. haggánı‿.
erase v.t. kómıs.
eruption n. (of rash, etc.) bélt(ı)‿.
escape v.i. bód; bɛlbód.
escort v.t. sóg.
especially adv. husúsan‿ (xu-).
estate n. (irrigable area) kólɛ‿.
eunuch n. tawwåšı‿.
European adj. and n. afráŋı‿.
evening n. (early) šárɛ‿; mígrıb‿.
  in the early evening: šárɛg‿.
evening star n. šárɛ-wıss(ı)‿.
ever adv. (with negative) ábadan‿; abadáŋ(ı)‿; ébɛdɛn‿; ɛbɛdɛ́ŋ(ı)‿.
  I haven't ever seen him (her, it, them): abadáŋı‿nalkómunun⌢.
  I don't ever drink it: åi‿tékk‿ánnímunun⌢.
every adj. mállɛ‿.
  (S)he goes every day: (a) ugrɛ́s‿mállɛg‿ánnógın‿; (b) ugrɛ́s‿mállɛn‿nógın‿.
  We went every night: (a) úgu‿mállɛg‿ánnókkoru‿; (b) úgu‿mállɛn‿nókkoru⌢.
  It's on every second day: ugrɛ́s‿wɛ́wwakk‿ówwıntır⌢.
  Give him (her, it, them) every good one: sérɛ‿sɛrɛ́t‿tír⌢.
evidence
  (S)he gave false evidence: múrsıgɛk‿kárğıkon⌢.
evidence, state in v.t. kárğ(ı) (káğğ(ı)).
evident adj. wådah‿.
evil adj. ús‿.
ewe n. égɛd‿kárr(ı)‿.
examine v.t. gúñč(ı); fɛttıšɛ́.
  Examine this well: íŋgı‿sɛrēgırgúñči⌢.
excavate v.t. wádd(ı).

exceedingly adv. désɛn‿ (-sɛ̃⌒, -sé⌒); dɪgríg‿; dɪgrígɪrg(ɪ)‿; hálɪs‿ (xă-).
(S)he (it) is exceedingly tired: désɛm‿ măbūn⌒.
except prep. *(omitting)* (obj. case) -wakk(ɪ)‿ (§ 4345), ílla‿ (§ 4282); *(besides)* —ŋ‿ gɛ́r‿ (§§ 5167-8).
X. Has the baggage come? áfɛš‿tågoná?
Y. It's all come except the lantern: fănúskɪ-wakkɪ‿málɛ‿tågon⌒.
excess n. zɪăda‿.
exchange v.t. éwɪr.
Exchange this for a good one: íŋgɪ‿sɛrɛ́-wɛ̄gɛd‿éwɪr⌒.
Go and exchange this: íŋg‿ɛwɪrétta⌒ (§ 5713).
exchange, give in v.t. (to the speaker) ɛwɪrósdɛn (-óddɛn, -ósgɪdɛn, -ózgɪ-, -óggɪ-), wɪdɛ́gɪrdɛn (wᵘdɛ́-); (to other than the speaker) ɛwɪróstɪr (-óttɪr, -ósgɪtɪr, -ózgɪ-, -óggɪ-), wɪdɛ́gɪrtɪr (wᵘdɛ́-).
Give me this in exchange: ăɪg‿íŋg‿ɛwɪrógg-ɪdɛn⌒.
I shall give you this in exchange: ăɪ‿ɛ́kk‿íŋg‿ɛwɪrobbɪtíddɪ⌒.
I gave him (her) another in exchange: ăɪ‿tɛ́kk‿ɛ́čč́ɛ́l-lɛ̄g‿ɛwɪrottíkkorɪ⌒.
excrement n. *(human)* úńń(ɪ)‿; *(animal)* hŏss(ɪ)‿; *(of cat, dog)* úńń(ɪ)‿; *(of cattle, horse, donkey)* hŏss(ɪ)‿; *(of goat, sheep)* kállɛ‿; *(of camel)* túr‿.
human excrement: (of one person) ádɛmn‿úńń(ɪ)‿; (of more than one person) ádɛmɪn‿úńń(ɪ)‿.
excreta n. *(human and animal)* ɛ́kkɛd‿.
human excreta: (of one person) ádɛmn‿ɛ́kkɛd‿; (of more than one person) ádɛmɪn‿ɛ́kkɛd‿.
camel's excreta: kámn‿ɛ́kkɛd‿.
excuse
Excuse me: (apologizing for involuntary action) mălɛ́š!
exhaust v.t. *(tire)* galabɛ́; măgɪr.
exhausted, be v.i. *(be tired)* mă-; măbŭ-.
exhibit v.t. wăndɪgɪr; amínt(ɪ).
exist v.i. bŭ; *(continuously)* ăg; *(be present)* dă-, dăbŭ-.
expect v.t. ɛrg̊ɛ́ (ɛrɛg̊ɛ́, ɛrɛǧ̊ɛ́, ɛrɪǧ̊ɛ́); íńɪr (ɪńɪr).
Whom do they expect (to come)? níg‿ɪńɪrran?
expel v.t. túr.
expense n. *(cost)* úgrɛ‿ (-ră‿, ra‿).
explain v.t. uńurkídd(ɪ); fɛhmɛ́gɪr.
Explain this to me: (a) íŋg‿ăɪg‿uńúr-kɪddɪ⌒; (b) íŋg‿ăɪgɪ‿fɛhmɛ́gɪr⌒.
explanation n. ɪbăr‿.
explode v.i. and t. gág.
The gun exploded: búndug‿gákkon⌒.
extend v.t. wărɪs.
exterior (external) adj. bočč́índ(ɪ)‿.
exterior n. bóčč́(ɪ)‿.
extinguish v.t. bɛ́.
extinguished, be v.p. df.
extract v.t. ós; dúkk(ɪ).
extremity n. *(end)* kɛ̆l‿; ăhɪr‿ (ăxɪr‿).
eye n. míss(ɪ)‿.
Keep an eye on this: íŋgɪ‿bálko⌒.
Keep an eye on the path as you go: daríbkɪ‿gūńč́ɪnók⌒.
eyebrow n. håǧɪb‿; míssɪn‿håǧɪb‿.

eyelid n. míssɪŋ‿kóbɪd‿; míssɪn‿tagídd(ɪ)‿; míssɪn‿ăǧɪn‿.

face n. kóń‿; wɛ́šš(ɪ)‿.
fade v.i. *(lose colour)* bótt(ɪ).
Fad**l** n. fádɪl‿ (fád-).
faeces n. ɛ́kkɛd‿; úńń(ɪ)‿.
fail v.i. mă-; ɛ́sk(ɪ) (ísk(ɪ)) in negative.
fair adj. *(equitable)* haggănɪ‿; *(beautiful)* tóŋǧɪl‿.
That's not fair: ín‿haggănɪmunun⌒.
fall v.i. dɪ́gɪr; *(collapse)* bŏr.
You will fall: ɛr‿bɪdígɪrɪn⌒, pl. ɪr‿bɪdɪgírru⌒.
(S)he (it) has fallen down: dɪgróskon⌒.
What fell down? míndo‿dɪgírkō?
What has (just) fallen down? míndɛ‿dɪgíróskō?
If it is (put, left) like that it will fall (down): íŋkɛ‿búǧɪm‿bɪdígɪrɪn⌒.
Here it will not fall (down): índo‿bɪdɪgírmunun⌒.
X. (S)he (it) will fall (down): bɪdígrɪn⌒.
Y. No, (s)he (it) won't: wăran, bɪdɪgírmunun⌒.
The tree is falling down: g̊ŏww‿abbŏrɪn⌒.
The house is falling down: kă‿abbŏrɪn⌒.
Don't let him (her, it) fall: (a) tókkon‿dɪgɪrkírmɛn⌒; (b) tókkon‿dɪgɪrɪŋgírmɛn⌒.
fall in (into) v.i. dɪgɪrtŏ.
(S)he (it) has fallen into the river: úrur‿dɪgɪrtŏróskon⌒.
family n. ăɪla‿.
famine n. măhal‿.
fancy n. (كيف) kɛ́f‿.
far (off) adj. and adv. wárr(ɪ)‿.
Is it far? wárrɪrɛ́?
Is it far from here? índotōw‿wárrɪrɛ́?
How far is it from El-Xándaq to Ed-Débbă? hándagɪrtōn‿dábbam‿móŋkom‿mukóttɛ̄rrɛ́?
far away (far off) adv. wárrɪr‿.
far (away), be v.i. băɪ (băj, băɪ).
fashion v.t. ău (ăw, ău); *(out of wood or metal)* kăɪ (kăj, kăɪ).
fast adj. bŏdkátt(ɪ)‿.
Is the horse fast? kăǧ‿bŏdkáttɪrɛ́?
Your watch is fast: ɛn‿să‿gɛddɪmɛ́būn⌒.
fast adv. súttɛ‿.
Walk very fast: (a) bagăšɛbagăšɛnók⌒; (b) taĺɪnt́alɪńnók⌒.
fast n. dɛ́rt(ɪ)‿.
fast v.i. dɛ́rtɪk‿kăg.
Are you fasting? ɛr‿dɛ́rtɪg‿ăkkăgná?
fasten v.t. dɪ́gɪr; mŏr.
fasting adj. săɪm‿ (săɪm‿).
Are you fasting? ɛr‿săɪmrɛ́?
Is (s)he fasting? tɛr‿săɪmrɛ́?
fat adj. *(corpulent)* túkŏl‿; kómbo‿.
fat n. *(of animal)* wádag‿.
father n. -băb‿; always with a form of the possessive personal pronoun (§ 2629) prefixed, thus:
my father: ambăb‿.
your father: ɪmbăb‿.
his (her, its) father: tɪmbăb‿.
our father: antɪmbăb‿.
your (pl.) father: ɪntɪmbăb‿.
their father: tɪntɪmbăb‿.

father-in-law n.-od‿; always with a form of the poss. pers. pron. (§ 2626) prefixed, thus:
my father-in-law: ánod‿.
your father-in-law: ínod‿.
his (her) father-in-law: tínod‿.
our father-in-law: ántɪnod‿.
your (pl.) father-in-law: íntɪnod‿.
their father-in-law: tíntɪnod‿.
fathom n. óg‿.
rod a fathom in length: šă‿.
Fátɪma n. fătna‿.
favour n. *(kindness)* fádɪl‿.
favour, do the v.i. faddɪlɛ́.
fear n. sándar‿ (ɪs-, us-, -dăr‿); sandíd‿ (ɪs-, us-).
fear v.t. sánd(ɪ) (ɪsán-, usán-; § 5546).
Do they fear him (her, it)? (a) tɛ́kkɪ‿sándɪrandɛ́? (b) tɛ́ddotōn‿sándɪrandɛ́?
feast n. *(festival)* kórɛ‿.
feather n. síbɪr‿.
the bird's feathers: (a) kăᴜɪrtɛn‿síbɪr‿; (b) kăᴜɪrtɛn‿dílt(ɪ)‿.
feeble adj. kússa‿; ăǧɪz‿.
feed v.i. kăl.
feed v.t. kalgíd(ɪ).
Tell him (her) to feed the horse: kăč́č́ɪ‿kalgíddan⌒.
X. Feed the horse: kăč́č́ɪ‿kalgíddɪ⌒.
Y. All right, I will: sɛ́rɛ̄n, ăɪ‿bukalgíddɪrɪ⌒.
X. Feed the horses: kăǧɪk‿kalgíddɪrɪr⌒.
Y. All right, I will: sɛ́rɛ̄n, ăɪ‿bukalgɪd-díddɪ⌒.
If you had fed him (her, it), (s)he (it) would not have died: ɛroŋ‿kalgɪddɪgógɪn, tɛr‿bɪdɪgómunun⌒.
Feed him (her, it) well: tɛ́kk‿ɛ́šan⌒.
feel v.t. *(touch)* ǧăbɛ; *(perceive)* hɪssɛ́.
fell v.t. bŏrkɪǧ.
female n. kárr(ɪ)‿.
fence n. zɛ́rbɛ‿.
fenugreek n. kárum‿.
ferment v.i. kŏs.
ferry n. măddíjɛ‿ (măddí-, maadí-, maadí-).
Where is the ferry? măddíjɛ‿sɛ́?
ferry-boat n. múšraŋ‿kúb‿.
Where is the ferry-boat stationed? múšraŋ‿kúb‿săɪgɛt‿tɛ́bɪn⌒?
fester v.i. úńcan-.
It will fester: búńcanɪn⌒.
festival n. kórɛ‿.
fetch v.t. ɛttă (ɛ́ttă; § 3855); ɛbbɪdă (§ 3851); ɪndɛttă (ɪndɛ́ttă; § 5723).
Go and fetch some water: ɛ́ssɪn‿nog-ǧɛ́tta⌒, pl. ...ǧɛ́ttawɛ⌒.
Did it fetch a good price? dúŋgɪ‿dɪgríd‿dúrkoná?
fetid adj. sɪɛ́l‿ (sɪɛ́l‿).
It is fetid: sɪɛ́lun⌒.
fever n. kabkăb‿; wírda‿ (-dă‿, -dɛ‿); húmma‿ (-mă‿).
few, a indef. pron. kínnɛr‿ (˘˘, ˘˘˘ § 1728); marɪ́ssɛ̄r‿; tŏddɛ̄r‿ (˘˘, ˘˘˘ §§ 1728, 2682).
Give him a few dates: bɛ́ntɪ‿marɪssɛ́t‿tɪr⌒.
Give me a few dates: bɛ́ntɪ‿marɪssɛ́d‿dɛn⌒.
Bring a few eggs from the market: kúmbu‿toddɛ́s‿súgɪrtōn‿ɛ́tta⌒.
fibre n. *(of bark)* hăšma‿ (occ. ăšma‿); *(of leaf)* awíčč́ɛ‿.

Ficus sycomorus n. ğɪmbɛ́z⌣.
fields, irrigable n. kólɛ⌣.
fiend n. ɪblís⌣; ğắnɪ⌣.
fiendish adj. ğănínd(ɪ)⌣.
fifteen card. num. dɪmɪndodíğ⌣.
fifth ord. num. dɪğínt(ɪ)⌣ (díğɪnt(ɪ)⌣).
fifty card. num. dɪmɪndíğ⌣; hamsín⌣.
fig n. tín⌣.
fight n. támugɪd⌣.
fight v.i. támug.
fig-tree, sycamore n. ğɪmbɛ́z⌣.
fill v.t. ğắŋg(ɪ).
Fill the small jug with water: ɪbríg⌣kíññag⌣ éssɪğ⌣ğắŋgi⌢.
Fill this and take it away: íŋgɪ⌣ğaŋgɪ-sókkɛ⌢.
Fimbristylis dichostoma(?) n. măgíssɛ⌣.
find v.t. él.
I have found it: ɛlóskori⌢.
Have you found it? élkoná?
If you find it, tell me: ɛɾ⌣tékk⌣élkɪn⌣ áɪgɪ⌣wédɛn⌢.
If you don't find him (her, it, them), come back: ɛɾon⌣élmɛŋkɪw⌣wɪdé⌢.
If you find it I'll give you ten piastres: ɛɾon⌣élkɪŋ⌣gírɪš⌣dɪmíŋgɪ⌣butíddi⌢.
I searched for him (her, it, them) but couldn't find him (her, it, them): tɛbɛ̄mɪ-sírkori⌢.
Perhaps I shan't find him (her, it, them): ɛddór⌣bɪmɪsírri⌢.
Perhaps you will find some, perhaps you won't: ɛddór⌣bélɪn, ɛddór⌣bɪmísɪ-rɪn⌣.
fine adj. (*in small particles*) nóro⌣.
fine n. garắma⌣.
He punished him (her) with a fine: tékkɪ⌣ garắmagɛğ⌣ğăzégon⌢.
finger n. kắššɛ⌣; sắrbɛ⌣.
middle finger: sắrbɛ⌣nósŏ⌣.
finger-nail n. ín⌣súnt(ɪ)⌣.
finish v.t. (*complete*) addɛ́; tɛmmɛ́; hallɪsɛ́.
Have they finished the work? ğéllɪt⌣ tɛmmɛ́gorandɛ́?
When you have finished this work, come to me: ín⌣ğéllɪg⌣addɛ́m⌣bắdk⌣ánnắr⌣ ta⌢.
finished part.
The tea is finished (done with): šăĭ⌣mắllɛ-taran⌢.
fire n. íg⌣.
Light a (the) fire: íkk⌣úlli⌢, pl....⌣úl-lɪwɛ⌢.
Put the fire out: íkkɪ⌣bɛ́⌢, pl....⌣bɛ́wɛ⌢.
Don't let the fire go out: tókkon⌣ígkɪ⌣ díŋgɪrmɛn⌢.
Is the water on the fire? éss⌣íŋ⌣kóččɪr⌣ búná?
fire v.i. (*with gun*) bundúkkɛğ⌣ğóm.
He fired at and hit him (her, it): bundúk-kɛğ⌣ğómkon, dúrkon⌢.
fire, be on v.i. ğúgbŭ-.
fire, set on v.t. ắrkɪr; úll(ɪ); wɛllɛ́.
fire-place n. kănún⌣.
firewood n. ugúllan⌣.
firm adj. (*hard*) dɛ́ŋgɛl⌣.
first ord. num. ṓwwɛl⌣ (ṓuwɛl⌣, ṓwɛl⌣, -wăl-, -wəl-); ṓwwélnd(ɪ)⌣ (ṓuwɛ́-, ṓwɛ́-, -wắl-, -wə́l-).
at first: ṓwwélgɛd⌣; ṓwwɛlɛn⌣.
fish n. kắrɛ⌣.
fisherman n. kắrɛg⌣ắbɪl⌣; hawwắd⌣.

fish-hook n. ğắkar⌣ (ğắhar⌣; N. ğắkkar⌣).
fit n. (*epileptic, apoplectic*) fatfắd⌣.
(S)he fell in a fit: dɪgɪrfắttɛgon⌢.
fit, have a v.i. fắttɛ.
five card. num. díğ⌣.
flag n. bɛ́rag⌣.
flame n. íg⌣.
flash v.i. bɪlínč(ɪ); fɪlínč(ɪ) (fɪlítt(ɪ), fɪlắtt(ɪ)); tulúnč(ɪ).
flea n. bargúd⌣.
fleet adj. bŏdkắtt(ɪ)⌣.
flesh n. kúsu⌣.
flirt v.i. ğắš.
float v.i. wéd.
It floats in (on) water: éssɪr⌣wédɪn⌢.
flock n. (*sheep or goats*) úrt(ɪ)⌣.
floor n. ắrɪd⌣; gŭ́⌣.
on the floor: ắrɪdɪr⌣.
Put it on that, not on the floor: mắnɪŋ⌣ kóččɪr⌣úskur, arɪdírmunun⌢.
flour n. nŏ́rt(ɪ)⌣.
flower n. íg⌣; ğŏ́wwɪn⌣íg⌣; šídam⌣íg⌣; wírɪd⌣.
flute n. zummắra⌣.
fly n. kúlt(ɪ)⌣.
There are very many flies here: kúlt⌣índo⌣ dɪgrín⌢.
fly v.i. fírr(ɪ).
fly-killer n. kúltɪgɛb⌣bɛ́ran⌣; kúltɪgɛğ⌣ ğómran⌣.
Bring the fly-killer: kúltɪgɛb⌣bɛ̄ráŋg⌣ étta⌢.
foal n. (*mare's*) kañ-bɪtắn⌣; kañ-tŏ́d⌣.
ass's foal: hanun-tŏ́d⌣.
foam n. gúmmud⌣.
fold v.t. árbɪr.
Don't fold it: tókkon⌣árbɪrmɛn⌢.
follow
Follow them: tínn⌣abắgɪr⌣nók⌢.
fond, be v.i. hɛnnɛ́ (hɪn-).
He is fond of his son: tén⌣tŏ́dɪr⌣hɛnnɛ́n⌢.
I am fond of him (her): ăĭ⌣téddo⌣hɛnnɛ́ri⌢.
fondle v.t. ğắškɪr.
food n. kắl⌣; ắkɪl⌣.
Have they had (some, their) food? kalós-korandɛ́?
fool n. and
foolish adj. ɛɾɪkkómɛnɪl⌣; ɛɾɪkkattɪbŭ̆mɛ-nɪl⌣.
(S)he is a fool: tɛ́r⌣ɛɾɪkkómunun⌢.
foot n. óss(ɪ)⌣; (*linear measure*) gédɛm⌣.
Did you come on foot? ɛr⌣énn⌣óssɪgɛt⌣ tắgoná?
Did they come on foot? tínn⌣óssɪgɛt⌣ tắgorandɛ́?
Go on foot: énn⌣óssɪgɛn⌣nók⌢, pl. ínn⌣ óssɪgɛn⌣nógwɛ⌢.
footprint n. átar⌣; óss(ɪ)⌣.
for prep. (*intended for, because of, for the purpose of*) —n⌣íllắr⌣ (-lar⌣, -lɛr⌣; §4377).
(*intended for, for the sake of*) —ŋ-karam⌣ (§4351); —ŋ⌣karamír⌣ §4379).
(*because of and of price*) -ɛd⌣ (-ɛt⌢, -ɛ́⌢; §4341).
X. This letter is not for me: ín⌣ğawắb⌣ ắnn⌣ɪllắrmunun⌢.
Y. Whom is it for? tɛ́r⌣nín⌣ɪllar?
Whom is it (intended) for? (a) tɛ́r⌣níŋ-karam? (b) tɛ́r⌣níŋ⌣karamír?
Is it for me? (a) tɛr⌣ắnn⌣ɪllaró? (b) tɛr⌣ ắŋ-karamó? (c) tɛr⌣ắŋ⌣karamɪré?

This is for milk; that's for water, not for milk: ín⌣íččɪn⌣íllɛr; ín⌣éssɪn⌣íllɛr, íččɪn⌣ɪllɛ́rmunun⌢.
Do they do it for (the sake of) money? dúŋgíŋ-karam⌣ắurandɛ́?
I can't work for (because of) the flies: ăĭ⌣kúltɪgɛd⌣ɛskɪšuglɛ́munun⌢.
X. For how much did you buy this (object of yours, s.v. ğắn)? íŋgɪ⌣mukóttɛ́gɛğ⌣ ğắŋkon?
Y. For three dollars: rɪjắl⌣tóskɪgɛ́⌢.
I have sent him (her) for (to fetch) milk: íččɪr⌣ɪšíŋkori⌢.
What can I do for you? ăĭ⌣ékkɪ⌣míŋg⌣ ăŭtɪddi?
Go and fetch it for me from the steamer: băbŭ́rrotōn⌣ắrɛttádɛn⌢ (*go* implied in -ɛltá- §5713).
forbid v.t. hağğɪrɛ́.
I forbade him (her) to go to the market: mírkori, tókkon⌣súgammɛn⌣égi⌢.
Did (s)he forbid you to do it? ékkɪ⌣mírkoná, tókkon⌣ắumɛn⌣égi?
force n. (*vehemence*) šídda⌣ (-dắ⌣).
Don't do it by force: tókkon⌣šíddagɛd⌣ ắumɛn⌢.
forceps n. (*large*) kammắša⌣; (*small*) bắskal⌣.
forearm n. ğɛríd⌣; dúra⌣.
forefathers n. -ŭ̆nč(ɪ)⌣ (s.v. -u⌣).
forehead n. kón⌣.
foremost adj. ṓwwélnd(ɪ)⌣; ogólnd(ɪ)⌣ (ogónd(ɪ)⌣).
foreshore n. ğérɪf⌣ (ğéruf⌣).
forest n. gắba⌣.
forget v.t. fu (í ͧ, íw).
I shall not forget: ăĭ⌣bí ͧmunun⌢.
I have forgotten: f ͧkori⌢.
Have you forgotten? ɛr⌣íwkoná?
Don't forget: tókkon⌣f ͧmɛn⌢.
forgive v.t. ăfɛ́.
Forgive him (her): tékk⌣ăfɛ́ró⌢.
X. Forgive me! ăĭg⌣ăfɛ́ró!
Y. Very well, I forgive you: sɛ́rɛ̄n, ékk⌣ ăfɛ́gori, lit....*I have forgiven you.*
fork n. šóka⌣ (-kă⌣).
handle of fork: šókan⌣í⌣.
Bring a fork: šóka-wɛg⌣étta⌢.
Bring some forks: šóka-wɛrɪg⌣éttarɪr⌣.
form v.t. ắu (ắw, áu).
(*out of wood or metal*) kắi (kắj, kắi).
formation n. ắwar⌣ (ắwăr⌣); ắwfɪd⌣.
former adj. ogólnd(ɪ)⌣ (ogónd(ɪ)⌣); ṓw-wélnd(ɪ)⌣; gɛdím⌣; zamánd(ɪ)⌣ (zắm-, zɛm-, -mănínd(ɪ)⌣).
formerly adv. ogóllo⌣; ṓwwéllo⌣; gabúllo⌣; zamắŋ(ɪ)⌣ (zắm-, zɛm-).
forth n. (*latrine*) úññíŋ-kă⌣.
fortress n. díb⌣.
forty card. num. dɪmɪŋkémɪs⌣; arbaín⌣.
forward, move (go, come) v.i. ógolan-; gɛddɪmɛ́ (-dumɛ́); géddɪmkatt(ɪ) (-dum-).
forward, put v.t. gɛddɪmɛ́ (-dumɛ́).
foul v.t. ɛ́rtɪgɪr; wassahɛ́.
foundation n. súmbud⌣.
four card. num. kémɪs⌣.
fourteen card. num. dɪmɪndokémɪs⌣.
fourth ord. num. kɛmsínt(ɪ)⌣ (kémsɪnt(ɪ)⌣).
fowl n. dúrmadɛ⌣ (dúmmadɛ⌣).
fox n. ɛ́ukol⌣ (ɛúkkŏl⌣).
free adj. húrr(ɪ)⌣.

Look for a place free from flies: ágar⌣kúltıkıñññıt⌣tɛb ɛ͡.
freedom from care n. fadabál⌣.
fresh adj. ɛ́r⌣; ğɛdíd⌣.
Friday n. móšono⌣; ğíma⌣.
  on Friday: (a) móšonog⌣ (-gi͡); (b) ğímag⌣ (-gi͡).
  (S)he (it) will come on Friday: (a) móšonob⌣bıtán͡; (b) ğímab⌣bıtán͡.
friend n. áwr(ı)⌣ (áur(ı)⌣); tíwr(ı)⌣.
frighten v.t. sándıgır (ıs-, us-); halɛ́.
  Don't frighten him (her, it): tókkon⌣sandıgírmɛn͡, pl. tókkon⌣sandıgírmɛwwɛ͡.
  Don't frighten them: tókkon⌣sandıgírímmɛn͡, pl. tókkon⌣sandıgírímmɛwwɛ͡.
frightened, be v.p. hálɛhattı- (-ləh-, hálha-).
frizzly adj. gúrgud⌣.
frog n. góglatt(ı)⌣.
from prep. -rton⌣ after a vowel; -ırton⌣ after a consonant, but -roton⌣ after -r; -loton⌣ after -l; -doton⌣ after -n⌣; (a person) -nārtŏn⌣.
  Where have you come from? ɛr⌣ısáırtōn⌣tågon?
  Where has (s)he (it) come from? tɛr⌣ısáırton⌣tågon?
  What's this? Is it from (due to) the water? ím⌣mınɛ́llɛ́? ɛ́ssırtōná?
  Has (s)he (it) come from the office? máktabırton⌣tågoná?
  Has (s)he (it) gone from the village? mårroton⌣nókkoná?
  Has (s)he (it) come from the sheikh? samílloton⌣tágona?
  It can't be seen from here: índoton⌣nalkáttımunun͡.
  This is from them: ín⌣tínnarton͡.
  This lamp is different from that one: íl⌣lámb⌣ínın⌣dógor⌣ɛ́ččɛlun⌣.
frond n.
  small frond of date-palm: kórsɛ⌣.
front adj. ogólnd(ı)⌣ (ogónd(ı)⌣).
front n. ógol⌣; (*face*) kóñ⌣, wɛ́šš(ı)⌣; *in front:* ogóllo⌣.
front of, in prep. —n⌣ogóllo⌣; —n⌣ówwɛ́llo⌣.
  (S)he sits in front of the house: kán⌣ogóll⌣ågın͡.
  It is in front of you: ɛ́nn⌣ogóllo⌣bún⌣.
  Go in front (ahead) of us: ánn⌣ogóllo⌣nók͡, pl. ...⌣nógwɛ͡.
frontier n. kɛ́l⌣.
fruit n. (*seed*) bıtán⌣ (bıt-).
  Do they eat the fruit of this tree? ín⌣ğówwım⌣bıtángı⌣kállandɛ́?
fry v.t. ásıl; gɛ́lɛgır; tawwagɛdáu; tāğıngɛdáu.
  Fry the fish in butter: kárɛd⌣dɛ́skɛd⌣ásıl͡.
  Fry the onions in butter: bíllɛd⌣dɛ́skɛg⌣gɛ́lɛgır͡.
  Tell him (her) to fry two eggs: kúmb⌣ówwıg⌣ásılan͡.
  Fry him (her) some eggs: kúmbut⌣tawwagɛdáutır͡.
  Fry me some eggs: kúmbut⌣tāğıngɛdáudɛn͡.
frying-pan n. tåğın⌣; táwwa⌣.
fuel n. ugúllan⌣.
full adj. ğáŋgıbūl⌣.
  Is it full? ğáŋgıbūná?
  It was full: ğáŋgıbūgon͡.
  It was full of water: ɛ́ssı⌣ğáŋgıbūgon͡.
  Bring a bucket of water: ğɛrdɛ́l-lēg⌣ɛ́ssığ⌣ğaŋğɛ́tta͡.
  The camel is full up with water: (a, *is fully laden with water*): kám⌣ɛ́ssıgɛğ⌣ğáŋgıbūn͡; (b, *has drunk its fill*): kám⌣ɛ́ssıgɛb⌣bɛ́rbūn͡.
funeral
  They went to his (her) funeral: tɛ́kkonom⌣bɛ́ddıgoran͡.
fur n. dílt(ı)⌣.
further adj. warrínd(ı)⌣.

gain n. máksåb⌣ (mɛ́ksɛb⌣).
gain v.t. kɛsbɛ́.
gait n. nogíd⌣.
gall n. ɛ́tt(ı)⌣.
gambling n. gumár⌣.
gape v.i. gāñgıdd(ı).
garden n. ğınɛ́na⌣ (-ná⌣).
  in the garden: (a) ğınɛ́nar⌣; (b) ğınɛ́nan⌣tūr⌣.
garlic n. tóm⌣.
garment n. kádɛ⌣.
gate n. kóbıd⌣; báb⌣.
gather v.i. (*come together*) ğámmɛ.
gather v.t. (*bring together*) ğámmɛgır; (*pick up*) bítt(ı).
gazelle n. gɛ́l⌣.
gecko n. korráñ⌣.
generosity n. hɛ́r⌣.
gentle adj. šíddakıñ̃ñ(ı)⌣ (-dåk-).
gentleman n. ɛfɛ́ndı⌣; (*non-Moslem*) hawáğɛ⌣ (xa-, -ğú⌣, -ğa⌣).
gently adv. nórɛn⌣ (-rɛ̄⌣, nórɛ͡).
  Take it and lower it gently: nórɛn⌣ārkúttɛgır͡.
genuine adj. alɛ́⌣.
get v.i. (*become*) complex in -an- (§§3910ff.).
  It's got larger: dúlaŋkó͡.
  It has got cut: mɛróskon͡.
get v.t. (*obtain*) ɛ́l; dúr.
  Did you get it? ɛ́lkoná?
  Have you got a knife? (a, *in general*) kándı-wɛ̄k⌣kóná? (b, *at hand*) kándıwɛ̄r⌣ɛnnarɛ́?
  Have you got some string? (a, *in general*) úl-lɛ̄k⌣kóná? (b, *at hand*) úl-lɛ̄r⌣ɛnnarɛ́?
  Have you got the money? dúŋg⌣ɛnnarɛ́?
  Have we got paper? wárag⌣ánnarɛ́?
  X. I'll give you the key: āı⌣ɛ́kkı⌣kušárkı⌣bıtíddı͡.
  Y. I've got it: ánnar͡.
  What has (s)he got? míndɛ⌣tɛ́nnad⌣dán?
  What pay does (s)he get? tɛ́m⌣mahíjɛ⌣mukóttɛ́rrɛ́?
get ahead v.i. ógolan-.
get better v.i. (*improve*) sɛran-; (*after illness*) kómban-, wajjɛ́.
get in v.i. tó.
  (S)he (it) can't get in: ɛskıtómunun͡.
get on (ahead) v.i. ógolan-.
get up v.i. ımbɛ́l (ímbɛl).
  Don't get up: tókkon⌣ímbɛlmɛn͡, pl. tókkon⌣ímbɛlmɛwwɛ͡.
get well v.i. kómban-; wajjɛ́.
giddy, get v.i. dōhɛ́ (dōxɛ́).
gift n. hadíjɛ⌣ (-já⌣, -ja⌣).

gin n. (*to remove seeds from cotton*) bɛnnáŋkolɛ⌣.
gin v.t. ɛ́wır.
giraffe n. zarɛ́f⌣.
girl n. búru⌣; (*little*) búrtod⌣.
  Is this your little girl? ın⌣ɛm⌣burtódırɛ́?
girth n. dɛ́gırn⌣hızám⌣ (-gın⌣hı-); hızám⌣; tünd(ı)⌣.
  horse-girth: káñ⌣hızám⌣; káñ⌣tünd(ı)⌣.
  donkey-girth: hánun⌣hızám⌣; hánun⌣tünd(ı)⌣.
give v.t. (*to the speaker*) dɛ́n (§§3584-92, 5534); (*to other than the speaker*) tír; (*hand, pass*) ɛttå (ɛ́ttā; §3855), ɛbbıdå (§3851).
  Give it me: dɛ́n͡.
  Give me this (that): íŋgı⌣dɛ́n͡.
  Give me these (those): íŋgud⌣dɛ́n͡.
  Don't give me this: íŋgı⌣tókkon⌣dɛ́mmɛn͡.
  Give me that other (yonder): máŋgı⌣dɛ́n͡.
  Give us these: árgı⌣íŋgud⌣dɛ́nčır͡.
  Give us those (others): árgı⌣máŋgud⌣dɛ́nčır͡.
  Give it to him (her, it): tír͡.
  Shall I give it to him (her, it)? tíddıá?
  Don't give it to him (her, it): tókkon⌣tímmɛn͡, pl. tókkon⌣tímmɛwwɛ͡.
  Don't give him (her, it) this: íŋgı⌣tókkon⌣tímmɛn͡, pl. ...⌣tímmɛwwɛ͡.
  Don't give them this: íŋgı⌣tókkon⌣tırímmɛn͡, pl. ...⌣tırímmɛwwɛ͡.
  Give it to the lady: síttıt⌣tír͡, pl. síttıt⌣tírwɛ͡.
  Give these to the lady: ıŋgus⌣síttıt⌣tír͡ (§1742).
  Give it (them) to the ladies: síttınčıt⌣tírır͡, pl. síttınčıt⌣tírıwwɛ͡.
  (S)he give them the money: tírgı⌣dúŋgıt⌣tıríkkon͡.
  Who gave it you? (a) n⌣ɛ́kkı⌣tíkkon? (b) nír⌣ɛ́kkı⌣tíkkon?
  Whom did you give it to? ɛr⌣nít⌣tíkkon?
  Did you give it (them) to them? ɛr⌣tírgı⌣tıríkkoná?
  X. What did (s)he give you? míŋg⌣ɛ́kkı⌣tíkkon?
  Y. A parcel: tarítkı⌣dɛ́ŋkon͡.
  I am going to the post: give me the letters: āı⌣bústar⌣nógburi; ğawábıg⌣ɛ́tta͡.
give back v.t. (*to the speaker*) wıdɛ́gırdɛn (wᵘdɛ́); (*to other than the speaker*) wıdɛ́gırtır (wᵘdɛ́).
  Don't give me this back: tókkon⌣íŋgı⌣wıdɛgırdɛ́mmɛn͡.
  Give it back to him (her): wıdɛ́gırtır͡.
give up v.t. (*abandon*) wɛlɛ́sɛ (wɛlɛsɛ́, ˋˋˋ); múg.
glad, be v.i. bastɛ́; gúrrɛ.
  (S)he will be glad to see us: árgı⌣nálkım⌣bıbastɛ́n͡.
glass n. (*substance*) gåzåz⌣ (gaz-, gɛz-, gız-); (*drinking-*) kub(b)åıa⌣ (-båıå⌣, -båıɛ⌣).
gleam (glitter) v.i. bılínč(ı)⌣; fılínč(ı)⌣ (fılítt(ı), fılátt(ı)); tulúnč(ı).
glutinous adj. ğóndo⌣.
gluttonous adj. kalkátt(ı)⌣.
gnaw v.t. gór.
go v.i. nóg, constr. with -r⌣; án-, constr. without a postp. and usually forming a complex (§3910β); ğắ-.

go — Grus sp.

Go! nók!, pl. nógwɛ!
Go along (on, off, away)! nogó!, pl. nogówwɛ.
Don't go: tókkon⌣nógmɛn⌢, pl. tókkon⌣nógmɛwwɛ⌢.
Go away from here: índotōn⌣nók⌢.
I shall go to Khartoum: (a) hartůmır⌣bınógri⌢; (b) âı⌣bıhartůmandi⌢.
(S)he went to Dóngola: (a) dúŋgular⌣nókkon⌢; (b) dúŋgulaŋkon⌢.
(S)he has gone to Dóngola: (a) dúŋgular⌣nogóskon⌢; (b) duŋgulanóskon⌢.
Go on (ahead), I'm coming: nóg⌣âı tåri⌢.
Go and sit down: ǧutḗgó⌢, pl. ǧutēgówwɛ⌢.
Go along and come back quickly! (a) ǧusúttɛ-ta!, pl. ǧu-súttɛ-tåwɛ! (b) súttɛ nóǧǧuta!, pl. súttɛ⌣noǧǧutåwɛ!
Go to him (her): tɛ́nnar⌣nók⌢.
(S)he is to go to him (her): tɛ́nnar⌣nógan⌢.
Go to the lady: síttınar⌣nók⌢.
Tell him (her) to go to the lady: síttınar⌣nógan⌢.
Where are you going to? såir⌣nóggūn?, pl. såir⌣nóggūru?
Where is (s)he (it) going to? såir⌣nóggūn?, pl. såir⌣nóggūran?
Where will (s)he (it) go to? såir⌣bınógın?
I am going to the house: âı⌣kámbūri⌢.
Go and change this pound: íŋ⌣gínɛffɛkkagırétta⌢, lit. *after changing it bring this pound* (§ 5713).
Shall I go and buy a little milk? âı⌣íččı tóddḗǧ⌣ǧānéttāriá?, lit. *am I to buy and bring...?*
It has gone bad: mıllanósko⌢.
go ahead v.i. ógolan-.
go ashore v.i. bárran-.
go back v.i. wıdɛnóg (wᵘd-).
go bad v.i. míllan-.
go down v.i. šúgur, kúttɛ; *(sink)* kídd(ı), kúñ.
Tell me when the signal goes down: sɛmafōr⌣šugúrkın⌣âıgı⌣wḗdɛn⌢.
Did the boat go down? kúb⌣kíddıgoná?
Don't do it now, wait till the sun goes down: tókkon⌣ɛ́kkɛn⌣åumɛn, másıl⌣tóm⌣bókkon⌣ǧóbbɛ⌢.
go in v.i. tó.
(S)he (it) has gone in: tōróško⌢.
go on (ahead) v.i. ógolan-.
go out v.i. *(issue)* bɛ́l, bóččan-; *(be extinguished)* df.
I'm going out: âı⌣bóččandi⌢.
I'm just going out: âı⌣bɛlɛdólli⌢.
(S)he (it) has gone out: (a) bɛlóško⌢; (b) boččanóskó⌢; (c) boččanɛdágın⌢.
The fire (light) has gone out: íg⌣díoškon⌢.
If anyone comes, say that we have gone out: wɛ̌r⌣tǎn⌣tá, bɛ́lkoran⌣an⌢ lit. ...*say 'they have gone out'.*
go together v.i. *(assemble)* ǧámmɛ; *(go one with another)* ǧammɛnóg.
go up v.i. dárr(ı); ɛǧɛ́ččɛ.
go with v.t. *(accompany)* sóg; sogɛnnóg.
Go with him (her): tékkı⌣sók⌢; tékkı⌣sogɛnnók⌢.
goat n. bɛ́rt(ı); *he-goat:* búttul; *she-goat:* bɛ́rt(ı).
goatherd n. úrtıg⌣íwıl (-tug⌣í-); bɛrtínčıg⌣íwıl.

God n. árt(ı).
God knows: árt⌣úñurın⌢.
goer n. nogkátt(ı) (nokká-).
This donkey is not a good goer: ín⌣hánu nogkáttımunun⌢.
gold n. nóbrɛ.
goldsmith n. nobrén⌣tábıd; så(j)ıg.
golf n. kúra.
golf-club n. kůrageǧ⌣ǧómran.
good adj. sɛ́rɛ̌; gɛ́n.
This is good: íŋ⌣sɛ́rɛn; íŋ⌣gɛ́nun⌢.
It's very good: sɛ́rɛ⌣hålısun⌢.
This is not good: íŋ⌣sɛrɛ́munun⌢; íŋ gɛ́mmunun⌢.
The fish is not good: kárɛ⌣sɛrɛ́munun⌢.
X. *Good morning!* sɛrambḗjjıgomɛn!
Y. *Good morning!* sɛrambḗjjıgori, hámdılıllá!
X. *Good morning!* sɛrambíččıgomɛn!
Y. *Good morning!* sɛrambíččıgori, hámdılıllá!
X. *Good-night!* hḗrro⌣túbbi!
Y. *Good-night!* ɛ́kkon⌣hḗrro⌣túbbi! — S.v. *night*, hḗr.
X. *Good-night!* hḗrro⌣túbbi!
Y. *Good-night!* ártın⌣håsɛbır!
X. *Good-night!* sɛrantúrbi!
Y. *Good-night!* ártın⌣håsɛbır!
We are leaving the Sudan for good: ársogdåndotōn⌣nogídannógbūru⌢.
good! interj. sérɛn!
good-bye! interj. hḗrró! (to which the reply is) ártın⌣håsabır! (-sɑ̀b-, -sɛb-).
goodness n. sɛrɛ́kanɛ.
Goodness knows what is to become of me! ısándi!
Goodness knows what is to become of you! ɛr⌣ısánın!
goods n. budáɛ (-dǎ́ɑ̀, -dǎ́ɑ⌣); budáɛnč(ı).
goose n. álod.
Gordon n. gardón.
Gordon Pasha: gardóm⌣båša.
gourd n. kébɛ.
govern v.t. hokmḗ (huk-).
government n. hukúma (-mɑ̀); *(rule)* hókum (húkum, hókum).
governor n. håkum; *(local)* mudír.
grain n. *(single)* hábba, háb; *(coll. esp. millet)* fu (fᵘ, fw); *(coll. wheat)* íllɛ.
gram n. órrɛ.
grandchild n. *(son's son)* bitāntód (bıt-, but-).
(son's daughter) bitámburu (bıt-, but-; ⁓̆).
(daughter's son) buruntód.
(daughter's daughter) burúmburu (⁓̆).
grandfather n. -u; only with a form of the poss. pers. pron. (§2622) prefixed:
my grandfather: ánnu.
your grandfather: ínnu.
his (her) grandfather: tínnu.
our grandfather: antínnu.
your (pl.) grandfather: ıntínnu.
their grandfather: tıntínnu.
I saw your grandfather: ínnūn⌣nålkori⌢.
grandmother n. -åu; only with a form of the poss. pers. pron. (§2622) prefixed:
my grandmother: ánnåu.
your grandmother: ínnåu.
his (her) grandmother: tínnåu.

our grandmother: antínnåu.
your (pl.) grandmother: ıntínnåu.
their grandmother: tıntínnåu.
I saw their grandmother: tıntínnåun nålkori⌢.
I saw their grandmothers: tıntınnåwın nålkori⌢.
grasp v.t. år.
grass n. gíd; *(couch-)* górɛ.
grasshopper n. dódɛ; báŋgan⌣dódɛ.
gratuity n. mukåfa.
grave n. gábur; túrbɛ (-bɑ̀, -ba).
gravel n. sɛ̌r; kórod.
gravy n. márag (márág); mar(r)agád (mår(r)åg-).
graze v.i. kál.
The sheep grazes: ɛ́gɛd⌣kålın⌢.
graze v.t. fu (fᵘ, fw).
The boy grazes the sheep (pl.): bıtǎn ɛ́gɛdıg⌣íwırırın⌢.
grease n. wådag.
great adj. dúl.
Great Bear, the n. áŋgarɛ; áŋgarɛn óssınč(ı).
great millet n. máro.
greedy adj. kalkátt(ı).
Greek n. and adj. ıgrígı.
green adj. dɛ́ssɛ.
greens n. dɛ́ssɛ; hodár (xo-).
greet v.t. sɛllımḗ (-lumḗ); *(the speaker)* salåmgı⌣dḗn; *(other than the speaker)* salåmgı⌣tír.
They greeted me: salåmg⌣âıgı⌣dḗŋkoran⌢.
Greet him (her): salåmgı⌣tír⌢.
Greet them: salåmgı⌣tírır⌢.
greeting n. salåm.
(S)he gave me many greetings: âıgı dıgrīgırsɛllımḗgon⌢.
grief n. zål.
grieve v.i. *(grieve over* v.t.) wɛ́ǧakattı (wåǧ-, -ahat-).
grieve v.t. zālḗgır.
grieved, become v.i. zālḗ.
grill v.t. níb.
grilled meat: nıbíd.
grind v.t. ǧǒg; nór.
grip v.t. år.
groom n. såıs.
ground n. gǔ; árıd.
bare ground: bůd.
on the ground: árıdır.
group n. ǧamánč(ı).
grow v.i. dúlan.
(S)he (it) will grow: tɛr⌣bıdúlanın⌢.
(S)he (it) has grown: dúlaŋkon⌢.
(S)he (it) is still growing: ólgon⌣āddúlanın⌢.
grow v.t. ɛ́wır.
Have you grown corn? ɛr⌣íllɛg⌣ɛwıróskoná?
What are you growing? ɛr⌣míŋ⌣āgɛ́wırın?
What are you (pl.) growing? ír⌣míŋ ågɛwírru?
What is (s)he growing? tɛr⌣míŋ⌣āgɛ́wırın?
What are they growing? tír⌣míŋ ågɛwírran?
growl v.i. ñúrr(ı); *(of dog)* hárr(ı), ñárr(ı).
growth, luxuriant (of plant) n. kóšɛ.
Grus sp. n. arrahåu (árrahåu).

***Gryllus* sp.** n. gɪrgíttɛ‿.
guest n. ɪškárt(ɪ)‿.
guest-room n. íškaríŋ-kă‿; íškarɪŋ‿óda‿.
  Clean out the guest-room: íškarɪŋ‿kån‿ naddufé⁀.
guide n. habír‿.
guiding-rod n. (in water-wheel) šḗhɪr‿ (šḗxɪr‿).
guitar n. kísɪr‿.
gullible adj. gaším‿.
gum n. (*of teeth*) gírgɪd‿, nέln‿kúsu‿ (nέl‿kúsu‿); (*of tree*) goníssɛ‿.
gummiferous adj. goníssɛkōl‿.
gun n. búndug‿.
gunpowder n. bārúd‿.
gut n. dúgus‿ (dúnus‿).

hair n. dílt(ɪ)‿.
hairdresser n. (*hair-cutter*) undíltɪm‿ múttɪl‿; (*head-shaver*) úrkɪ‿gáññɪl‿.
half n. tŏ́rt(ɪ)‿.
  Where is the other half? tŏ́rt‿ōwwíntɪ‿sέ?
  Divide this into halves: íŋgɪ‿tŏ́rtɪgɪrbagíttɛ‿.
  I shall reduce his (her) pay to half: āi‿tém‿ mahíjab‿bɪtŏ́rtɪgɪddi⁀.
  (S)he broke the stick in half: wɪččírkɪ‿ tŏ́rtɪgɪrtómbɪgon⁀.
  The stick broke in half: wɪččɪr‿tŏ́rtantómbɪgon⁀.
ḥalfa (حَلْفَاء) *grass* n. hamárte‿.
halve v.t. (*reduce to a half*) tŏ́rtɪgɪr; (*divide into halves*) tŏ́rtɪgɪrbagíttɛ.
hammer n. šakúš‿.
  handle of hammer: šăkúšɛ̆n‿åd‿.
hand n. í‿, -i‿ (§ 2374 *b*).
  Give it into his (her) hand: ténn‿ír‿tír⁀.
  Did you give it into his (her) hand? ténn‿ír‿tíkkoná?
  My hands are dirty: ánni‿értín⁀.
  Are your hands clean? énni‿nadíf'ɪré?
  I want to wash my hands: (*a*) ánn‿ig‿ έuraŋgɪ‿dólli⁀; (*b*) ánn‿ɪš‿šúkkɪraŋgɪ‿dólli⁀.
  Have you washed your hands? (*a*) énn‿ig‿ έukoná? (*b*) énn‿ɪš‿šúkkɪgoná?
  They waved their hands: tínn‿ɪw‿wɛlέkkoran⁀.
hand v.t. ettá (έttă̆, § 3855); ɛbbɪdá (§ 3851).
  Hand me that: (*a*) íŋg‿εtta⁀; (*b*) íŋg‿εbbída⁀.
hand in v.t. (*to speaker*) úndurdĕn; (*to other than speaker*) úndurtɪr.
hand over v.t. sɛllɪmέ (-lumέ).
handkerchief n. mɪndíl‿ (mɛn-).
  Bring me a handkerchief: mɛndíl-lɛg‿ έttadēn⁀.
handle n. í‿; (*helve of wood or substitute*) åd‿.
  handle of box: sandúgn‿í‿.
  handle of bucket: ǧɛ́rdɛln‿í‿.
  handle of cup: kúzn‿í‿; kúsn‿í‿; kub(b)åian‿í‿.
  handle of small cup: fɪŋgánn‿í‿.
  handle of door: kobídn‿í‿; bábn‿í‿.
  handle of fork: šókan‿í‿.
  handle of jug: ǧákkɪn‿í‿; ǧágn‿í‿.
  handle of lamp: lámban‿í‿.
  handle of lantern: fānúsn‿í‿.
  handle of spoon: målagan‿í‿.
  handle of tea-pot: bɛrrådn‿í‿.
  handle of valise: šánt̃an‿í‿.
  handle of axe: fåsn‿åd‿; gámbun‿åd‿.
  handle of hammer: šakúšn‿åd‿.
  handle of hoe: túbron‿åd‿.
  handle of knife: kándɪn‿åd‿.
  handle of pen (*penholder*): gálamn‿åd‿.
  handle of sickle: túrubn‿åd‿.
handle v.t. ǧábɛ.
hand-mill n. rahāiɛ‿ (-āià‿, -āia‿).
handsome adj. tónǧɪl‿.
hang v.i. (*be suspended*) sóll(ɪ); sóllɪbŭ-.
  It is hanging up: sóllɪbūn⁀.
hang (**up**) v.t. sóllɪgɪr.
happen v.i. has(ɪ)lέ; ǧɪrέ.
  It happens in this way: íŋkɛ‿haslέn⁀.
happiness n. gúrrebūrar‿ (-rár‿).
happy adj. mabsúd‿.
happy, be v.i. bastέ; gúrrɛ.
harass v.t. måǧɪr.
hard adj. (*firm*) dέŋgɛl‿, kógor‿; (*difficult*) dúllo‿.
  The wood is not hard: bέr‿kogórmunun⁀.
hard adv. šíddagɛd‿ (-dåg-; -gɛt⁀, -gέ⁀).
  Don't hit him (her, it) hard: tókkon‿ šɪddagɛǧǧómmɛn⁀.
hard-working adj. ǧɛlligāukátt(ɪ)‿.
hare n. údlan‿ (-añ‿).
harlot n. dɛññára‿.
Hásan n. hásɛn‿ (-san‿).
haste
  Make haste! súttɛ!, pl. súttɛwέ!
hat n. burnέta‿.
hatch v.t. kákkɪr.
hatchet n. gámbu‿; fås‿.
  handle of hatchet: gámbun‿åd‿; fåsn‿åd‿.
hate v.t. món‿; kɛččɪnέ.
  I hate this: íŋgɪ‿móndi⁀.
  They hate this: íŋgɪ‿móndan⁀.
haul v.t. tóllɛ.
haul in v.t. šír.
  Haul in the line: úlgɪ‿šír⁀.
haunch n. ǧåbåd‿.
have v.t. (*possess*) kó; (*have at hand*) s.v. -năr‿.
  I have money: dúŋg‿ánnar⁀.
  You have money: dúŋg‿έnnar⁀.
  (S)he has money: dúŋgɪ‿ténnar⁀.
  We have money: dúŋg‿ánnar⁀.
  You (pl.) have money: dúŋg‿únnar⁀.
  They have money: dúŋgɪ‿tínnar⁀.
  Has (s)he the parcel? tárɪt‿ténnaré?
  Have they the donkey? hánu‿tínnaré?
  Have you a knife? έnnar‿kándɪ‿dåná?
  Last night I had it in my hand: wīl‿ugúg‿ ánnɪr‿dåbugon⁀.
he pers. pron. tέr‿ (tɛr‿).
  Is it he? tέr‿té?
head n. úr‿; (*of millet, etc.*) núd‿.
headache
  I have a headache: āig‿ánn-ur‿óddin⁀.
  It gives one a headache: úrk‿óddɪgɪrɪn⁀.
headman n. (*of village, district*) sámɪl‿; šέh‿ (šέx‿).
heal v.i. gέnd(ɪ); (*completely*) wajjέ.
heal v.t. wajjέgɪr.
heap n. súna‿; kóm‿.
hear v.t. gíǧɪr.
  I hear him (her, it, them): āi‿gɪǧírri⁀.
  I don't hear him (her, it, them): āi‿ gɪǧírmunun⁀.
  Do you hear him (her, it, them)? gɪǧɪrná?, pl. gɪǧɪrruá?
  Don't you hear him (her, it, them)? gíǧɪrmɛn⁀, pl. gɪǧɪrmɛndu?
  Did you hear a camel? (α, *moving*) kám‿ harákkɪ‿gɪǧɪrkoná? (β, *its voice*) (*a*) kám‿hískɪ‿gɪǧírkoná? (*b*) kám‿híssɪg‿ gɪǧírkoná?
  Didn't you hear? gɪǧɪrkomɛn?
  Can't you hear me? έr‿āig‿ɛskɪgíǧɪrmɛn?
heart n. å‿ (‿å̆ § 1066, -å‿).
  Does your heart hurt you? έnna‿ɛ́kk‿ óddɪná?
heat n. ǧugrɪgɪd‿.
  I can't stand the heat: ǧugrɪgítkɪ‿móndi⁀.
heat v.t. ǧugrɪgɪr; tóg.
heavy adj. dúllo‿.
  This is heavy: ɪn‿dúllon⁀.
  It's not heavy: dúllomunun⁀.
  These are heavy: íŋgu‿dúllončín⁀.
  These are not heavy: íŋgu‿dúllončímunan⁀.
  Is it heavy? dúlloré?
  Are they heavy? (*a*) dúllončɪré? (*b*) dúllorɪré?
heddle n. bεsír‿ (bέsɪr‿).
hedgehog n. kɪnɪssɛkōl‿; abšóg‿.
heed v.t. bålko.
heel n. tónɛ‿.
he-goat n. búttul‿.
heifer n. tɪntŏ́d‿.
height n. (*of person*) nósogɪd‿.
  What is his (her) height? tén‿nósogɪd‿ mɪŋkóttɛrré?
heir n. néwar‿ (-wår‿).
hell n. ǧɛhénnɛb‿.
hellish adj. ǧɛhɛnnémd(ɪ)‿.
helmet n. burnέta‿.
help v.t. sådέ; åssådέ.
  Help me: åig‿‿sådέ⁀, pl. ...‿sådēwέ⁀.
helve n. åd‿.
hen n. dúrmadɛ‿ (dúmmadɛ‿).
hence adv. índotōn‿.
her poss. pron. ténn‿v., ténn‿c.
  her money: tén‿dúŋ(ɪ)‿.
  her house: tén‿kå‿.
  her child: tém‿bɪtån‿.
  her head: ténn-ur‿.
herdsman n. íwɪl‿.
  camel herdsman: kámlɪg‿íwɪl‿.
here adv. índo‿.
  Come here: (*a*) índo‿tá⁀; (*b*) índo‿tåré⁀; pl. índo‿tåwɛ⁀.
  (S)he (it) is here: índón⁀ (> índő > índó⁀).
  X. Where is it? tέr‿sέ?
  Y. Here: índo⁀.
  Here it is: índó⁀.
  (S)he (it) is not here: índómunun⁀.
hereby adv. íŋgɛd‿ (-gɛt⁀, -gέ⁀).
heron n. kårɛkal‿.
hers abs. poss. pron. ténd(ɪ)‿.
  It's hers: téndín⁀.
  Is it hers? téndɪré?
  It's not hers: téndɪmunun⁀.
  Isn't it hers? téndɪmɛn?
  They're hers: téndɪnčín⁀.
  Are they hers? téndɪnčɪré?
  They're not hers: tɛndɪnčɪmunan⁀.
  Aren't they hers? tɛndɪnčɪmɛndan?
  Is this (that) hers? (*a*) ɪn‿téndɪrέ? (*b*) ɪn‿ téndɪté? (*is this the one that is hers?*)
  Are these (those) hers? íŋgu‿téndɪnčɪré?

hey!, hi!, interj. hóı! (hóı!); hế!
Hibiscus esculentus n. ólᴗ.
hidden, be v.i. bókkıbū-.
　(S)*he (it) is hidden:* bókkıbūnᴖ.
hide n. ăǧınᴗ.
hide v.i. bókk(ı).
　(S)*he (it) has hidden:* bokkóskonᴖ.
hide v.t. bókkır.
　Don't hide him (her, it, them): tókkomᴗ bókkırmenᴖ.
high adj. álıᴗ.
　The house is high: kăᴗálınᴖ.
　The mountain is not high: ǧébɛlᴗálımununᴖ.
hill n. ǧébɛlᴗ.
hilt n. ádᴗ; fᴗ.
　hilt of sword: (a) sıwídnᴗádᴗ; (b) sıwídnᴗfᴗ.
hinder adj. abắŋd(ı)ᴗ.
　hinder part: abắgᴗ.
hinder v.t. attılế; mír.
　Don't hinder me: tókkonᴗấıgᴗattılếmɛnᴖ.
hip n. kúlulᴗ.
hippopotamus n. ɛ́rıdᴗ; ɛ́ssınᴗtíᴗ (ɛ́ssíntīᴗ).
hire n. úǧrɛᴗ (-rȧᴗ, -ra); kırắıᴗ.
hire, grant on v.t. bǻıdĕn (bắı-) (to the speaker); aǧǧırɛ́dĕn (to the speaker); bǻıtır (bắı-) (to other than the speaker); aǧǧırɛ́tır (to other than the speaker).
hire, procure on v.t. bắı (bắj, bắı); aǧǧırɛ́.
　I shall hire one: wēbᴗbaǧǧırɛ́rıᴖ.
　I want to hire a house: kă-wēbᴗbắırắŋgıᴗdóllıᴖ.
　He will hire a house in the town: bélɛnᴗtúrᴗkă-wēbᴗbaǧǧırɛ́nᴖ.
his abs. poss. pron. ténd(ı)ᴗ.
　It's his: téndínᴖ.
　Is it his? téndırɛ́?
　It's not his: téndımunᴖ.
　Isn't it his? téndımɛn?
　They're his: téndınčínᴖ.
　Are they his? téndınčırɛ́?
　They're not his: tendínčımunanᴖ.
　Aren't they his? tendínčımɛndan?
　Is this (that) his? (a) ínᴗténdırɛ́? (b) ínᴗténdıᴗtế? (*is this the one that is his?*).
　Are these (those) his? íŋgᴗténdınčırɛ́?
his poss. pron. ténnᴗᴗ, ténᴗc.
　his money: ténᴗdúŋg(ı)ᴗ.
　his house: ténᴗkắᴗ.
　his country: témᴗbélɛdᴗ.
　his hand: ténnᴗīᴗ.
hiss v.i. úffɛ.
hit v.t. ǧóm.
　Don't hit him (her, it)! tókkonᴗǧómmɛn!, pl. tókkonᴗǧómmɛwɛ́!
　Don't hit the donkey: tókkohᴗhánuǧᴗǧómmɛ́ᴖ.
　Don't hit the donkey on the head: tókkohᴗhánutᴗténnᴗúrroᴗǧómmɛ́ᴖ.
hither adv. índoᴗ.
hoe n. túbroᴗ.
　handle of hoe: túbronᴗádᴗ.
hoist v.t. sókkɛ; dogōgırsókkɛ; dogōgırtóllɛ.
　Hoist the flag: bērákkıᴗdogōgırtóllɛᴖ.
hold n. (*of ship*) kúmtuᴗ.
hold v.t. (*grasp*) ǻr; (*contain*) sókkɛ.
　It holds two árdɛbb (اردبين): (a, potentially) ɛ́rdɛbᴗṓwwısᴗsókkɛnᴖ; (b, actually) ténᴗtūrᴗɛ́rdɛbᴗṓwwıᴗdắnᴖ.
hold of, take (catch) v.t. ǻr.
　Catch hold of this: íŋgᴗǻrᴖ.
hole n. (*perforation, aperture*) úbbɛdᴗ; úbburᴗ, ágıᴗ; (*cavity*) kúlᴗ.
　Has your pocket got a hole in it? ɛ́nᴗǧɛ́bᴗúbbıbūná?
　Put it into the hole: kúllᴗúndurᴗ.
　Dig the hole here: kúlgᴗíndoᴗwáddıᴖ, pl. ....wáddıwɛᴖ.
home n. (*house*) kắᴗ; (*district*) dắᴗ (-da).
　Go home: (a) kắnᴖ, pl. káwwɛᴖ; (b) ɛŋkắnᴖ, pl. ıŋ-káwwɛᴖ; (c) ındắnᴖ, pl. ındáwwɛᴖ.
　I'm going (= shall go) home: ắıᴗbıkándıᴖ.
　I'm on my way home: (a) ắıᴗaŋ-kámbūrıᴖ; (b) ắıᴗkámbūrıᴖ.
　(S)he has gone home: (a) tɛŋ-kanóskonᴖ; (b) ténᴗkắrᴗnogóskonᴖ; (c) tɛŋᴗkắrᴗǧuóskonᴖ.
　Go home: (a) ɛ́ŋᴗkắrᴗnókᴖ, pl. íŋᴗkắrᴗnógwɛᴖ; (b) ɛ́nᴗdắrᴗnókᴖ, pl. ínᴗdắrᴗnógwɛᴖ.
　Has (s)he gone home? tɛŋ-kanóskoná?
　Did they see him (her) home? tɛ́ŋᴗkắmᴗbókkonᴗóǧıgorandɛ́?
　Is (s)he at home? tɛ́ŋᴗkắrᴗágná?
　Are they at home? tíŋᴗkắrᴗágrandɛ́?
　Go and see whether (s)he is at home: tékkıᴗtɛ́ŋᴗkắrᴗákkınᴗnóǧgunalᴖ.
　Let someone go and see whether (s)he is at home: tékkıᴗtɛ́ŋᴗkắrᴗágkınᴗwēǧᴗǧunalanᴖ.
homicide n. bɛ́rarᴗ (-rȧᴗ); bērídᴗ.
homonymous adj. ɛrrıkátt(ı)ᴗ.
honey n. ásalᴗ.
hoof n. súnt(ı)ᴗ.
hook n. (*fish-*) ǧákarᴗ (ǧaharᴗ), N. ǧákkarᴗ; (*to hold door, window, lid, etc.*) šɛ́ŋkɛlᴗ.
hook, fasten with a v.t. šɛŋkılɛ́.
　Fasten the open window with the hook: tắgaᴗkúzbūlgıᴗšɛŋkılɛ́ᴖ.
　Fasten the window open with the hook: tắgakᴗkussɛŋkılɛ́ᴖ.
　Open the door and fasten it with the hook: kobíttıᴗkussɛŋkılɛ́ᴖ.
hop v.i. dékk(ı).
horn n. níšš(ı)ᴗ.
horse n. kắǧᴗ.
　I shall travel on horseback: ắıᴗkắčkɛbᴗbıǧúrıᴖ.
horse-dung n. kắñᴗhóss(ı)ᴗ; kắǧlınᴗhóss(ı)ᴗ.
hot adj. ǧúgrıᴗ.
hot, become v.i. ǧúgran-.
hotel n. lokándaᴗ.
hour n. sắᴗ.
　half an hour: sắnᴗtőrt(ı)ᴗ.
house n. kắᴗ.
　Where is his (her) house? tɛ́ŋᴗkắᴗsɛ́?
　Is (s)he in his (her) house? tɛ́ŋᴗkắrᴗágná?
　Has (s)he been at your house? ɛ́nnarᴗbúgoná?
　If he is not at the office let him (i.e. the messenger) go and give it to him at his house: mắktábırᴗdắmɛŋkın, tɛ́ŋᴗkắrᴗǧútıranᴖ.
household (inmates of house) n. kắnᴗírıᴗ (kắnırıᴗ).
householder n. kắnᴗídᴗ (kắnıdᴗ).
house-top n. kắnᴗkóčč(ı)ᴗ.
how? adv. mínɛᴗ....?, mínᴗᴗ....? míŋgɛdᴗ....? (-ɛtᴗ, -ɛ́?); ısáikɛᴗ....? ('sắ-, sắ-, -áı-, -kɛ́?); ısáigɛdᴗ...? ('sắ-, sắ-, -áı-, -ɛtᴗ?, -ɛ́?).
　How are you? (a) ɛ́nᴗhắlᴗmínɛᴗbūnᴖ? (b) ɛ́nᴗhắlᴗmíŋkırírɛ́?
　How is ɛ áli today? ınnṓwwıgᴗálımínɛᴗbūn?
　See how (s)he is: tɛrᴗmínɛᴗbūŋıᴗnálᴖ.
　How did (s)he (it) get out? (a) ısáikɛᴗbélkon? (b) sáıgɛbᴗbélkon?
　X. How are you? sɛraŋágmɛn?
　Y. Thank you, I hope you are well: ắrtonᴗɛ́hᴗhắlgıᴗsɛrɛ́gırınᴖ.
　How long has (s)he been here? (a) sıntắdırtónᴗíndᴗáǧın? (b) sıntáǧırrotōnᴗíndᴗáǧın?
how much? interr. pron. míŋkótt(ı)ᴗ...? (muk-, -tırɛᴗ...?, -ti?); mıŋkóttērᴗ...? (muk-); ısáikott(ı)ᴗ...? ('s-, sắi-, -áık-, -tırɛᴗ...?, -ti?); ısáikottērᴗ...? ('s-, sắi-, -áık-).
　How much did (s)he bring? tɛrᴗmıŋkottḗgᴗéttagon?
　How much do you want? ɛrᴗmıŋkóttēdᴗdólın?
　How much does (s)he want? tɛrᴗmıŋkóttēdᴗdólın?
　How much money is there in it? dúŋgᴗısáikottērᴗtéddoᴗdábūn?
　How much money do you want? ɛrᴗdúŋgᴗısáikottēdᴗdólın?
　How many men went? (a) ógıǧᴗısáikottērᴗnókkon? (b) ógıǧᴗısáikottērᴗnókkoran?
　See how many eggs there are (count them): kumbúnčıhᴗhāsıbɛ́nalᴖ.
however conj. -mɛn- (-mɛ́n-, -mɛnᴗ; §§6093-6).
howl v.i. wíg.
　I don't like a howling dog: wélᴗwīkkáttıdᴗdólmununᴖ.
hull v.t. gáww(ı) (gắuw(ı)).
　Has (s)he hulled the beans? (a) ugúdkıᴗtɛ́ŋᴗkắččırtōŋᴗgáwwıgoná? (b) ášraŋkɛtᴗtɛ́ŋᴗkắččırtōŋᴗgáwwıgoná?
hullo! interj. hóı! (hóı!); hế!
human being n. ádɛmᴗ (ádamᴗ, ádȧmᴗ).
humble adj. mɛskínᴗ.
hump n. kúruñᴗ.
hundred card. num. ímılᴗ.
hundredweight n. guntắrᴗ.
hunger n. mínč(ı)ᴗ; orgídᴗ (órgıdᴗ); máhalᴗ.
hungry adj. mahlánᴗ.
hungry, be v.i. órıg; órıgbū-.
　I am hungry: (a) ắıgᴗmínčᴗắrınᴖ; (b) ắıgᴗórgıdᴗárınᴖ.
　Later on you will be hungry: ékkıᴗbádkɛmᴗmínčıᴗbắrınᴖ.
　(S)he is hungry: tékkıᴗtírgıᴗmínčᴗắrınᴖ.
　They are hungry: tírgıᴗmínčᴗắrırınᴖ.
hunt v.t. sɛjıdɛ́ (sējıdɛ́).
hunting n. sɛ́dᴗ.
hurry, be in a v.i. sumárk(ı).
　I am in a hurry: sumárkırıᴖ.
　I am not in a hurry: ắıᴗsumárkmununᴖ.
hurt v.t. óddıgır; (*be painful to*) ódd(ı); (*injure*) awwᵘgɛ́ (ắuwᵘgɛ́).
　My finger hurts (me): ắıgᴗánᴗsárbᴗóddınᴖ.
husband n. ógıǧᴗ.
　Where is your husband? ɛ́nnᴗógıǧᴗısắırɛ́?
　Where is her husband? ténnᴗógıǧᴗısắırɛ́?
husband v.t. waffırɛ́.
husk n. kắčč(ı)ᴗ.

hut n. (*of mud, etc.*) kå⌣; (*of straw, etc.*) kέrr(ı)⌣.
hyaena n. ɛ̆dd(ı)⌣.
Hydrocyon forskalii (*H. lineatus, H. brevis*) n. kås⌣.
Hyphaene thebaica n. hámbu⌣.

I pers. pron. âı⌣ (âı⌣, áı⌢).
ice n. télıǧ⌣.
idea n. έrıg⌣.
idle adj. (*lazy*) kússa⌣.
idleness n. (*laziness*) késɛl⌣.
if conj. use the conditional, with or without -ŏn⌣ (§§ 2998 ff., 6230 ff.).
  If (s)he (it) comes, tell me: tɛron⌣tắgın⌣ âıgı⌣wέdɛ̄n⌣.
  If I come, I shall see him (her, it, them): tågırı⌣bınállı⌢.
  If you want it (them) take it (them); if you don't want it (them) leave it (them): dólkın⌣ísa⌣; dólmɛŋkım⌣mugó⌢.
  If you go, (s)he (it) will come: έron⌣ nókkın, tέr⌣butắn⌢.
  If you do not go, (s)he (it) will not come: έr⌣nógmɛŋkın, tέr⌣butámunun⌢.
  If you look for him (her, it, them) you'll find him (her, it, them); if you don't you won't: ɛr⌣tɛbέgım⌣bélın, tɛbέmɛŋkım⌣bélmunun⌢.
  If there is fish I don't want eggs: kåre⌣ dågın⌣kúmbud⌣dólmunun⌢.
  If ɣ áli had brought it he would have got ten piastres: álon⌣έttagogıŋ⌣gírıš⌣dımíŋgı⌣ bárkon⌢.
  I should have been glad if you had killed the flies: έıoŋ⌣kúltıb⌣bέgogım⌣bımabsūd-áŋkori⌢.
ignite v.i. ǧúg.
ill, be v.i. ódd(ı); óddıbū-.
  I am ill: (*a*) âı⌣óddırı⌢; (*b*) âı⌣óddıbūrı⌢.
  Are you ill? (*a*) ɛr⌣óddıná? (*b*) ɛr⌣óddıbūná?
  (S)he (it) is ill: (*a*) tɛr⌣óddın⌢; (*b*) tɛr⌣ óddıbūn⌢.
  Is (s)he (it) ill? (*a*) tɛr⌣óddıná? (*b*) tɛr⌣ óddıbūná?
  Are they ill? (*a*) tır⌣óddırandέ? (*b*) tır⌣ óddıbūrandέ?
ill, make v.t. óddıgır.
  This makes me ill: ín⌣âıg⌣óddıgırın⌢.
  It will make you ill: έkkı⌣bóddıgırın⌢.
illness n. óddɛ⌣.
image n. tɛswíra⌣.
immediately adv. sútte⌣.
impede v.t. mír.
imperfect adj. nắgıs⌣.
implore v.t. bέdd(ı).
impregnate v.t. mɛ́ŋgır (mέwgır).
imprison v.t. kób.
improve v.i. séran-.
improve v.t. sɛrέgır.
in prep. -r⌣ after a vowel; -ır⌣ after a consonant, but -ro⌣ after -r (except of personal pronouns), -lo⌣ after -l, -do⌣ after -n and personal pronouns. See §§ 4291 ff.
  The bird is in the tree: kåuırtɛ⌣ǧówwır⌣ bún⌢.
  There is a fly in the milk: íččır⌣kúltı⌣ dábūn⌣.
  Leave it in the room: ódår⌣mugó⌢.
  in the market: súgır⌣.
  in the valley: hórro⌣.
  in the sun: masíllo⌣.
  in the coffee: búndo⌣.
  Bring some water in this: έssıg⌣íŋgɛd⌣ έtta⌣, lit.... *by means of this.*
in, come (get, go) v.i. tó.
  I can't get in: âı⌣ɛskıtómunun⌢.
in, let v.t. (*allow to enter*) tóŋgır.
  Don't let anyone in: tókkow⌣wέt⌣tóŋgırmɛn, pl. tókkow⌣wέt⌣tóŋgırmɛwwe⌢.
in order that (in order to) conj.
  I take this in order that I may eat it: (*a*) âı⌣íŋgı⌣sókkɛr⌣âı⌣káll⌣έgı⌢; (*b*) âı⌣íŋgı⌣sókkɛr⌣âı⌣kállın⌣íllår⌢.
  I took it in order that I might eat it: (*a*) âı⌣sókkɛgor⌣âı⌣káll⌣έgı⌢; (*b*) âı⌣sókkɛgor⌣kálsıŋ⌣karámır⌢.
  I came here in order to see it: (*a*) índo⌣ tågorı⌣tέkkı⌣náll⌣έgı⌢; (*b*) índo⌣ tågorı⌣tέkkı⌣nállın⌣íllår⌢.
  We came here in order to see them: (*a*) ar⌣índo⌣tågoru⌣tírgı⌣nalídd⌣έgı⌢; (*b*) ar⌣índo⌣tågoru⌣tírgı⌣nalíddun⌣ íllår⌢.
incomplete adj. nắgıs⌣.
increase n. zıáda⌣.
increase v.i. dıgrían- (dígrian-, -rıan-, -ran-); (*in size*) dúlan-.
increase v.t. dıgrígır, zīdέ; (*enlarge*) dúlgır.
incumbent, be v.i. kúǧ.
indolence n. késɛl⌣.
indolent adj. kússa⌣.
indoors adv. årɛr⌣.
industrious adj. ǧɛllıgåukátt(ı)⌣.
inexperienced adj. gaším⌣.
infant n. bıtántod⌣ (bıt-, but-).
inferior adj. bárɛd⌣.
infernal adj. ǧɛhɛnnέmd(ı)⌣.
infertile land n. bέrǧo⌣.
inform v.t. (*the speaker*) wέdɛn; (*other than the speaker*) wέtır.
information n. hábar⌣ (-bår⌣).
inhabitant n. bέlɛdn⌣íd⌣ (bɛlέdnıd⌣).
inherit v.t. nέu (nέw, néu); wɛrsέ.
inheritance n. (*act of inheriting*) nɛwíd⌣; (*what is inherited*) nέwar⌣ (-wår⌣).
inire (Latin) v.t. dέñ.
initial adj. ogólnd(ı)⌣ (ogónd(ı)⌣).
injure v.t. awwᵘgέ (åuw-).
ink n. híbır⌣ (hébır⌣).
inmate n. kån⌣íd⌣ (kånıd⌣).
inn n. lokánda⌣.
inner adj. årέnd(ı)⌣; tûnd(ı)⌣.
inoffensive adj. mɛskín⌣.
inquire v.t. ídd(ı); síkk(ı) (occ. ısík-).
inquiry n. íddar⌣ (-dår⌣); ıddíd⌣; síkkar⌣ (-kår⌣); sıkkíd⌣.
insane adj. dáhal⌣; dahálkol⌣ (dahalkól⌣); ǧómbūl⌣.
insanity n. dáhal⌣; kummɛg(ı)ríd⌣.
inscribe v.t. båǧ.
inscription n. båǧíd⌣ (båǧíd⌣, -ǧıd⌣).
  Are there any stones with inscriptions on them? kúlunčı⌣båǧbūlı⌣dårandέ?
  Where is the inscription? båǧıs⌣såirέ?
  This is an inscription, that isn't: ím⌣ båǧídun, ím⌣båǧídmunun⌢.
insect n. (*small destructive*) kósɛ⌣.
insert v.t. úndur.
inside adj. årέnd(ı)⌣; tûnd(ı)⌣.
inside adv. årɛr⌣; årɛnčır⌣; tûr⌣.
  Go inside! (*a*) tó!, pl. tówé! (*b*) årɛr⌣nók!, pl. årɛr⌣nógwέ!
  Stay inside! årɛr⌣tέp!, pl. årɛr⌣tέbwέ!
inside n. årɛ⌣; tû⌣.
inside prep. —n⌣tûr⌣ (—n-tūr⌣).
  Stay inside the house: kåırtūr⌣tέp⌢.
  Put it inside the house: kån⌣tûr⌣úndur⌢, pl.... ⌣undúrwέ⌢.
  Put them inside the house: kån⌣tûr⌣ úndurır⌢, pl.... ⌣undurívwwέ⌢.
insipid adj. bássarı⌣.
inspect v.t. ǧûñč(ı); fɛttıšέ.
inspector n. mufέttıš⌣.
instead of prep. —n⌣agárro⌣.
  Go instead of him: ténn⌣agárro⌣nók⌢.
instruct v.t. (*teach*) kúrkır.
instructor n. kúrkırıl⌣.
insufficient adj. någıs⌣.
intelligence n. (*understanding*) έrıg⌣.
intelligent adj. ɛrıkkátt(ı)⌣; ɛríkkol⌣; åǧıl⌣.
intelligible adj. wådah⌣.
intensity n. šídda⌣ (-då⌣).
interest n. (*on money due*) fåız⌣ (fáız⌣).
interior adj. årέnd(ı)⌣; tûnd(ı)⌣.
interior n. årɛ⌣; tû⌣.
internal adj. årέnd(ı)⌣; tûnd(ı)⌣.
interstice n. bárrɛ⌣.
intestine n. dúgus⌣ (dúŋus⌣).
into prep. -r⌣ after a vowel; -ır⌣ after a consonant, but -ro⌣ after -r (except of personal pronouns), -lo⌣ after -l, -do⌣ after -n and personal pronouns. See §§ 4291 ff.
  The child fell into the river: bıtån⌣úrur⌣ dıgırtógon⌢.
  Has (s)he (it) fallen into the well? gówwır⌣ dıgırtógoná?
  Put it into the box: sandúgır⌣úndur⌢.
  Put them into the box: sandúgır⌣úndurır⌢.
  Don't put pepper into the salt: úmbudır⌣ tókkon⌣fılfílg⌣uskúrmɛn⌢.
  There is some in our village: åm⌣mårro⌣ dån⌢.
  Don't put salt into the pepper: fılfíllo⌣ tókkon⌣umbúdk⌣uskúrmɛn⌢.
  Pour it into the small cup: fıŋǧándo⌣bók⌢.
intoxicate v.t. såmgır.
intoxicated, be v.i. såmbū-.
intoxicated, become v.i. såm.
intoxication n. såmar⌣ (-mår⌣); såmfd⌣.
intrigue n. fítnɛ⌣.
inundation n. (*and time of the*) dɛmírɛ⌣ (-rå⌣, -ra⌣); mısór⌣.
invert v.t. óbır; wídégır (wıdέg-, wᵘdέg-).
investigate v.t. ǧûñč(ı); fɛttıšέ.
invoke v.t. bέdd(ı).
iron n. šårt(ı)⌣; (*for smoothing linen*) mákwa⌣ (mák-).
irrigate v.t. dέǧ.
irritate v.t. (*anger*) sínnɛgır; (*annoy*) mǻgır.
irritated (angered), get v.i. sínnɛ; zålέ.
irritation n. (*anger*) sínnɛrar⌣ (-rår⌣); sınnɛríd⌣; zål⌣.
island n. årt(ı)⌣.
issue v.i. bél.
it pers. pron. tέr⌣ (tɛr⌣).
  It (the weather) is hot: gú⌣ugrín⌣.
  When it (the time or place) gets dark: gå⌣urúmmaŋkın⌣.
itch n. (*skin-disease*) kagrúss(ı)⌣.
itch v.i. kål.

its abs. poss. pron. ténd(ɪ)⌣.
its poss. pron. ténn⌣v., tén⌣c.
  its tail: ténn⌣ɛu⌣.
  its nose: tén⌣sóriñ⌣.
  its eye: tém⌣míss(ɪ)⌣.
  its meat: téŋ⌣kúsu⌣.
ivory n. fĩl-nέl⌣ (fĩlnɛl⌣); nέl⌣.

jacket n. ğak(k)έta⌣.
jar n. (*small, medium*) súlɛ⌣; (*medium*) kắdd(ɪ)⌣; (*large*) gắlo⌣; (*in water-wheel*) bế̌šɛ⌣.
jaw n. (*lower*) hánag⌣.
jerboa n. burúkk(ɪ)⌣.
jest v.i. káčč(ɪ).
Jew n. juhúdı⌣ (ğu-).
job n. ğέllı⌣.
  Is (s)he leaving his (her) job? tén⌣ğéllırtōm⌣bélbūná?
jog(gle) v.t. kɛrkɛrkídd(ɪ).
  Don't jog(gle) it: tókkoŋ⌣kɛrkɛrkíddımɛn⌣.
joint n. budúrt(ɪ)⌣.
  elbow-joint: kugúndım⌣budúrt(ɪ)⌣.
  finger-joint: ín⌣sárbɛm⌣budúrt(ɪ)⌣.
  knee-joint: kúrtım⌣budúrt(ɪ)⌣.
joke v.i. káčč(ɪ).
  I was joking: āı⌣akkáččıgori⌣.
journey n. sáfar⌣.
joy n. gúrrɛbūrar⌣ (-rắr⌣).
judge n. gắdı⌣.
judge v.t. hokmέ (huk-).
judgment n. hókum⌣ (húkum⌣, hókom⌣).
jug n. †ğắg ⌣(ğέg⌣); †ğắkk(ɪ)⌣ (ğέkk(ɪ)⌣).
  handle of jug: ğắgn⌣í⌣; ğắkkın⌣í⌣.
jump v.i. wár.
jump in v.i. wartó.
  (S)he jumped into the train: gatírro⌣wartógon⌣.
jump out v.i. warbέl.
  (S)he jumped out of the train: gatírrotōw⌣warbέlkon⌣.
just adj. (*equitable*) haggắnı⌣.
just adv. (*merely*) súdır⌣; (*only*) bέs⌣; (*now*) ékkɛnɛ⌣, íssā⌣, ıssắg⌣ (-gı⌣); (*immediate future*) use verb-complex in -dól-.
  X. What do they do? míŋg⌣āuran⌣?
  Y. They just sit (i.e. *are doing nothing*): súdır⌣agran⌣.
  Just bring it: étta⌣bés⌣.
  (S)he (it) has just gone in: ékkɛnɛ⌣tōróskó⌣.
  (S)he (it) has just come: ıssáb⌣bıdắgó⌣.
  (S)he's (it's) just coming: tāredólın⌣.
  I was just going to come: tāredólkori⌣.
  I was just going to build a house: āı⌣kắwēg⌣goñedólkori⌣.
  The moon is just going to rise: unáttı⌣bɛlɛdólın⌣.
  They mended it just before Jackson Pasha came: ğéksum⌣bā́šā⌣tāredólsuw⌣wɛkídkı⌣gɛndıgírkoran⌣.
  I want just a little: marıssoddέd⌣dólli⌣.
  Just take this away: íŋ⌣oğótta⌣.
justice n. hág⌣; hágg(ɪ)⌣.

keep
  (S)he (it) keeps quiet (*silent*): kıttotέbın⌣.
  Does (s)he keep the fast? dέrtık⌣kắgná?
keep away v.i. bắı (bắj, bắi).

keep back (**off**) v.t. (*restrain*) mír.
  Keep the dog off the sheep: wέlg⌣ɛgɛdırtōm⌣mír⌣.
keep on (*continue*) v.t. āg-complex (§§ 3831 ff.).
  The dog keeps on barking: wέl⌣agúkkın⌣.
  (S)he (it) keeps on drinking: ānnín⌣.
  The boy keeps on whistling: tód⌣ısísk⌣āğğómın⌣ (tód⌣usúsk⌣).
  I keep on telling him not to, but he keeps on doing it: āı⌣tékkı⌣tókkon⌣āumɛn⌣ɛg⌣āwwέrı⌣tér⌣agáwın⌣ (§ 6239).
Kénzi n. kunúz⌣; mottókk(ɪ)⌣ (mut-).
  Is (s)he a Kénzi? tér⌣kunúz¹ré?
Kénzi Nubian n. (*dialect*) kunuzínd(ɪ)⌣; mottokkınčínd(ɪ)⌣ (mut-).
  Do you know Kénzi? ɛr⌣kunūzíndıg⌣uñúrná?
kerosene n. ğắz⌣.
kettle n. bɛrrắd⌣ (bắr-, bar-).
key n. kúšar⌣ (-šár⌣, -šɛr⌣).
  Look for the key: kušárkı⌣tɛbé⌣.
Khalífa, the n. halífa⌣ (xa-, -fắ⌣, -fɛ⌣).
Khartoum n. hartúm⌣.
  (S)he (it) is in Khartoum: hartúmır⌣.
  the climate of Khartoum: hartúm⌣háwa⌣.
kick v.t. wádıñ.
  Mind!, it'll kick: bálko!, buwádıñın⌣.
  Did it kick you? ékkı⌣wadíñkoná?
kid n. bɛrtın-tód⌣.
kidney n. ğígılt(ɪ)⌣.
  (S)he has kidney-disease: tén⌣ğígıltı⌣tékk⌣óddın⌣.
kill v.t. bέ.
  Don't kill him (her, it): tókkom⌣bέmɛn⌣.
  Kill the flies: kúltıb⌣bérıč⌣.
kind n. ğíns(ɪ)⌣; ğínıs⌣.
  I like this kind: ín⌣ğínsıd⌣dólli⌣.
  I don't like this kind: ín⌣ğínsıd⌣dólmunun⌣.
  Bring one of this kind: ínın⌣ğínsırtōw⌣wēg⌣étta⌣ (ín⌣ğínsı- § 5122).
kindle v.t. árkır; úll(ɪ); wɛllέ.
kindness n. fádıl⌣; hέr⌣.
king n. ór⌣.
kiss v.t. dόg.
kitchen n. dέuŋ⌣kắ⌣ (dέuŋ⌣); mátbah⌣ (mát-, -báh⌣, -bax⌣, -báx⌣).
Kitchener n. kıštɛnέr⌣.
kitten n. sām-tód⌣.
knead v.t. (*mix by kneading*) ğắg; (*disintegrate by kneading*) ğúrum.
knee n. kúrt(ɪ)⌣.
kneel v.i. híkk(ɪ); húŋ(ɪ).
knife n. kánd(ɪ)⌣.
  blade of knife: kándın⌣ágıl⌣.
  handle of knife: kándın⌣ắd⌣.
  point of knife: kándın⌣kóčč(ɪ)⌣.
  sheath of knife: kándıŋ⌣kád⌣.
  Bring a knife: kándıg⌣étta⌣.
  Bring knives: kándınčıg⌣éttarır⌣.
knock v.t. kókk(ɪ); ğóm.
  Knock before you open the door: kắk⌣kúsmɛŋgon⌣ğóm⌣.
  Knock before you enter: ɛr⌣ólgon⌣tómɛŋgoŋ⌣kobídkı⌣kókki⌣.
  To (e.g.) *a messenger: Knock off:* dɛstúrk⌣áu⌣, pl. dɛstúrk⌣áuwɛ⌣.
knoll n. kútt(ɪ)⌣.
knot n. murtıgắd⌣ (-tᵘg-).
know v.t. úñur.
  I know: uñúddi⌣.

  I don't know: (*a*) āı⌣uñúrmunun⌣; (*b*) kondó⌣.
  X. Where is the cat? sab⌣ısέ?
  Y. I don't know: kondó⌣.
  I don't know you: āı⌣ékk⌣uñúrmunun⌣.
  Who knows? nĩ⌣úñurın?
  Do you know? ɛr⌣uñúrná?
  Does (s)he (it) know? tér⌣uñúrná?
  If (s)he doesn't know, let him (her) ask: téron⌣uñúrmɛŋkın, síkkan⌣.
  Let me know when the train comes in sight: bābúr⌣wándın⌣tá, āıgı⌣habárkı⌣dén⌣.
Koran n. gorán⌣ (gur-).

labium (*pudendi muliebris*) n. fássa⌣; kumáttɛn⌣ğámb(ɪ)⌣ (⌣ğέm-).
labour n. ğέllı⌣.
labour v.i. ğέllıgāu (-āw, -āū; § 1879); šuglέ (šoglέ, šogolέ).
labourer n. ğέllık⌣kόl⌣.
lacerate v.t. awwırέ (áuwı-).
ladder n. síllım⌣.
lady n. sítt(ɪ)⌣.
lamb n. ɛgɛn-tód⌣.
lame, be v.i. kohílbū- (koílbū-); tókkıbū-.
lame, go v.i. kóhıl (kóıl ́̆); tόkk(ɪ).
lamp n. lámba⌣ (-bá⌣).
  handle of lamp: lámban⌣í⌣.
  Bring my lamp: ál⌣lámbag⌣étta⌣.
lance n. šá⌣.
land n. (*ground*) árıd⌣; (*country*) bέlɛd⌣.
  infertile land: bέrğo⌣.
  high land: kútt(ɪ)⌣.
  newly-formed alluvial land: gurúnt(ɪ)⌣.
land v.i. bárran-.
landlord n. (*of house*) kắb⌣bā́ıtırıl⌣; (*of land, ground*) árın⌣tírt(ɪ)⌣.
land-tax n. árın⌣túlba⌣; árın⌣harắğ⌣.
language n. bā́ññıd⌣.
lantern n. fānús⌣.
  handle of lantern: fānúsn⌣í⌣.
  Get a lantern and bring it: fānús-sēg⌣ındétta⌣.
  Take a lantern and go: fānús-sēg⌣ındɛnnók⌣.
  Why don't you light the lantern? ɛr⌣mέn⌣fānúsk⌣úllımɛnın?
  Why didn't you light the lantern? ɛr⌣mέn⌣fānúsk⌣ullıgómɛnın?
  If I don't come back before sunset, bring a lantern: āıom⌣másıl⌣tómɛnın⌣támɛŋkırı⌣fānúsk⌣étta⌣.
large adj. dúl⌣; bárığ⌣.
  Bring a box of large matches: kıbríd⌣bárığn⌣ílbɛ-wēg⌣étta⌣.
  Give me a large box of matches: kıbrídn⌣ílbɛ⌣baríğ-gēd⌣dέn⌣.
  It's as large as a house: kắ⌣kóttın⌣.
larva n. wígıd⌣; (*of lepidoptera*) súruf⌣.
larynx n. gόz⌣ (gόs⌣).
last
  last year (*a*) n. nĩ⌣; (*b*) adv. níg⌣, -gi⌣.
late, be v.i. āhhɛrέ (āxxɛ-, -hắrέ, -hırέ); āhhɛrbū-.
  He's (she's, it's) ten minutes late: dagíga⌣dımíŋg⌣ahhɛrέbūn⌣.
  Why are you late? ɛr⌣mέn⌣ahhɛrέbūn?
  Why were you late? ɛr⌣mέn⌣ahhɛrέgon?
late, make v.t. āhhɛrέgır.
  Don't make him (her, it) late: tókkon⌣ahhɛrέgırmɛn⌣.

later (on) adv. bådɪr‿; bådk(ɪ)‿ (båtk(ɪ)‿, bått(ɪ)‿; -ki⌒, -ti⌒).
Lates niloticus n. mɪssɪgélɪñ‿; sāmús‿.
latrine n. úññíŋ-kā‿.
   Where is the latrine? úññíŋ-kā‿sɛ́?
latter adj. abǻŋd(ɪ)‿.
lattice n. šɪbbǻg‿.
laugh v.i. úsu.
   Don't laugh: tókkon‿úsumɛn⌒, pl. tókkon‿úsumɛwwɛ⌒.
   Why do you laugh at them? ɛr‿mén‿tíŋ‿kóččɪr‿úsun?
laundry n. mákwa‿ (mák-).
laundry-man n. kádeš‿šúkkɪl‿; šúkkɪl‿.
law n. hág‿, hágg(ɪ)‿; (*regulation*) gānún‿.
lawful adj. haggǻnɪ‿.
lawsuit n. gadíjɛ‿ (-jā‿, -ja‿).
lay v.t. úskur; (*egg*) múg.
   Lay the table-cloth: súfran‿fúṭag‿awíddi⌒
lay by v.t. (*save*) waffɪrɛ́.
lay on v.t. kúǧur.
laziness n. késɛl‿.
lazy adj. kússa‿; (*addicted to sleeping*) nērkátt(ɪ)‿, nalukátt(ɪ)‿.
lazy, get v.i. kússan-.
   Don't get lazy: tókkon‿kússammɛn⌒.
lead n. (*metal*) rasǻs‿.
lead v.t.
   He is leading the horse: káčkɪ‿tolléddan⌒.
leaf n. (*of plant*) úlug‿; (*of book*) táraga‿.
   Tell him (her) to take away the dead leaves: úluk‿sowwétkɪ‿sókkɛran⌒.
leak n.
   The boat has a leak: kúb‿úbbɪbūn⌒.
leak v.i. (*of vessel*) bógɪr; (*of vessel or its contents*) bóg.
   This bucket leaks: ín‿ǧérdel‿ābbógɪrɪn⌒.
   The water-skin leaks: gɪrbǻd‿bógɪn⌒.
   The water-skin is leaking: gɪrbǻd‿ābbógɪn⌒.
   Is the jug leaking? ǧákk‿ābbógná?
   The water leaks: éssɪ‿bógɪn⌒.
   The water is leaking: éssɪ‿ābbógɪn⌒.
   The water leaks from the water-skin: éssɪ‿gɪrbǻdɪrtōm‿bógɪn⌒.
leap v.i. wár.
learn v.t. kǘr.
learned man n. fagír‿.
leather n. áǧɪŋ‿kárǧel‿ (‿káǧǧel‿); áǧɪŋ‿kárǧɪbūl‿ (‿káǧǧɪbūl‿).
leave n. (*permission*) ízn‿; (*of absence*) ɪǧāza‿; (*to go off duty*) dɛstúr‿.
   You are not to go without (obtaining) leave: ízɪŋ‿ǻrmɛŋgon‿tókkon‿nógmɛn⌒.
   He has gone on leave: (a) ɪǧāzar‿nókkõ⌒; (b) ɪǧāz‿ǻŋkó⌒.
leave v.t. múg; wɛlēsɛ́ (wɛlēsé).
   Leave him (her, it) (alone, behind): mugó⌒, pl. mugówwɛ⌒.
   Leave him (her, it) alone: wɛlēsɛ́, pl. wɛlēsɛ́wɛ⌒.
   Don't leave him (her, it): tókkom‿múgmɛn⌒, pl. tókkom‿múgmɛwwɛ⌒.
   Leave this here: íŋg‿índo‿bá⌒.
   Leave the dog here: wɛ́lg‿índo‿bán⌒.
   Leave ʒáli where he is: álɪt‿tɛ́r‿ǻgindo‿mugó⌒.
   Leave him (her) where (s)he is: tɛr‿ǻgindo‿mugó⌒.
   Leave them (animate objects) where they are: tír‿ǻgrando‿múgosɪr⌒.

Leave the box where it is: sandúkkɪ‿tɛr‿búndo‿mugó⌒.
Leave it where it is: tɛr‿búndo‿mugó⌒.
Leave them (inanimate objects) where they are: (a) tɪr‿búrando‿múgosɪr⌒; (b) tɪr‿búrando‿mugó⌒.
Leave it shut: kóbban⌒.
Leave them shut: kóbbūwan⌒.
leave out v.t. (*omit*) wákk(ɪ).
   X. *The cook is making cakes:* tabbǻh‿ākkǻhkɪg-áwɪn⌒.
   Y. *Tell him to leave out the sugar:* sukkárkɪ‿wákkan⌒.
   Is he leaving it out? āwwákkɪná?
left n. (*hand*) maíñ‿.
   Go to the left: maíñgɛn‿nók⌒.
   It's on your left: ém‿maíñgɛb‿bún⌒.
   X. *Where is it?* tɛr‿sɛ́?
   Y. *On your left:* ém‿maíñgɛ́⌒.
   Stretch out your left arm: ém‿maíŋgɪ‿wárɪs⌒.
left, be v.p. (*remain over or behind*) fadlɛ́; tɛ́b.
   What's (there) left? míndo‿fadlēróskon?
   What was (there) left? míndo‿fadlégon?
   Is any of it left? (a) téddotōn‿fadlégol‿dǻná? (b) téddotōf‿fadlégollāná?
   Why was it left behind? tɛr‿méf‿fadlégon?
   There are four piastres left: gírɪš‿kémɪs‿fadlébūn⌒.
   Ten days have passed, five are left: nɛhǻr‿dímɪn‿nogóskon, díč‿tébɪn⌒.
leg n. óss(ɪ)‿.
legal adj. haggǻnɪ‿.
leisure n. súdn‿ǻgar‿; súdnagar‿.
lend v.t. (*to the speaker*) asíkkɪdɛn⌒; (*to other than the speaker*) asíkkɪtɪr.
   Don't lend it: tókkon‿asíkkɪtímmɛn⌒.
length n. nósogɪd‿.
   What is its length? tén‿nósogɪd‿mɪŋkóttērré?
lentil n. ádɛs‿.
leopard n. nímɪr‿.
less prep. ílla‿; (*obj. case*) -wakk(ɪ)‿.
   I paid the money less one dollar: dúŋgɪr‿rɪjǻl‿léwwakkɪ‿dɛfégori⌒.
lessen v.i. kíññan-; nāgɪsɛ́ (nāgsɛ́, nāksɛ́).
lessen v.t. kíññagɪr; nāgɪsɛ́gɪr (nāgsɛ́-, nāksɛ́-).
lessened adj. nágɪs‿.
lest
   Shut the door, lest the flies enter: kǻk‿kóp, kúltɪ‿tómɛnɪnn‿íllár⌒.
let v.t. (*allow*) múg.
   (*allow*) use causatives (§§ 3663 ff.).
   (*jussive*) complex in -an (§§ 3890 ff.).
   (*grant on hire* to the speaker) bǻidɛn; aǧǧɪrɛ́dɛn.
   (*grant on hire* to other than the speaker) bǻitɪr; aǧǧɪrɛ́tɪr.
   Don't let it fall: tókkon‿dɪgɪrɪ́ŋgɪrmɛn⌒, pl. tókkon‿dɪgɪrɪ́ŋgɪrmɛwwɛ́⌒.
   Don't let him (her) open it: tókkoŋ‿kúsɪŋɪrmɛn⌒.
   Don't let him (her) leave it open: tókkoŋ‿kusmugɪŋgɪ́rmɛn⌒.
   Don't let the lady lift anything heavy: tókkon‿síttɪd‿šɛ́jɪ‿dúllo-wɛ̄s‿sókkɛŋgɪrmɛn⌒.
   Don't let them take anything away: tókkon‿šɛ́jɪ-wɛ̄s‿sokkɛraŋgɪ́rmmɛn⌒.

Let him (her) burn all this: ím‿mǻlleǧ‿ǧúguran⌒.
Let Mr Dean see this: místǻr‿díŋg‿íŋgɪ‿nálan⌒.
Will (s)he let it (for hire)? baǧǧɪrɛ́tɪrná?
let be v.t. múg; wɛlēsɛ (wɛlēsé).
let in v.t. (*allow to enter*) tóŋgɪr.
   Don't let him (her, it) in: tókkon‿tóŋgɪrmɛn⌒.
   Don't let them in: tókkon‿tóraŋgɪrmɛn⌒.
   Don't let anyone in: tókkow‿wɛ́t‿tóŋgɪrmɛn⌒, pl. tókkow‿wɛ́t‿tóŋgɪrmɛwwɛ⌒.
let off v.t. (*not punish*) múg.
   Let him (her) off: mugó⌒.
   He let off the gun: búndúkkeǧ‿ǧómkon⌒.
let out v.t. bɛlkídd(ɪ); bɛlíŋgɪr.
   Let him (her, it) out: bɛlkɪddi⌒.
letter n. (*written message*) ǧawǻb‿.
liar n. mursǻǧ‿.
lick v.t. gǻñ.
lid n. tagídd(ɪ)‿; gúta‿ (gáta‿, gúta‿).
lie n. (*falsehood*) múrs(ɪ)‿.
   Don't tell lies: (a) tókkom‿múrsɪb‿bǻññɪmɛn⌒; (b) tókkom‿múrsɪw‿wɛ́mɛn⌒.
lie (down) v.i. túrb(ɪ) (túbb(ɪ)).
   Lie down: túrbi⌒, pl. túrbɪwɛ⌒.
   I shall go and lie down: aī‿bɪǧutúbbɪri⌒.
   I am just going to lie down: aī‿turbɛdólli⌒.
life n. áñɪd‿.
lift v.t. sókkɛ; índ(ɪ).
   Can you lift this? ɛr‿íŋg‿ɛskɪsókkɛná?
   Don't let the lady lift the cupboard: tókkon‿síttɪd‿dōlǻpkɪ‿sókkɛŋgɪrmɛn⌒.
light adj. (*not heavy*) šóro‿.
light n. (*illumination*) áro‿; (*lamp, etc.*) íg‿.
   Bring it here and do it in the light: índ‿árōr‿ɪndettǻu⌒.
   Light a (the) light: íkk‿úlli⌒.
   Put the light out: ígkɪ‿bé⌒.
   Whose house is that light in? mán‿íg‿níŋ‿kǻr‿bún⌒.
light v.t. (*kindle*) úll(ɪ); árkɪr; wɛllɛ́.
   Light a (the) fire: (a) íkk‿úlli⌒; (b) íkk‿árki⌒.
   Light the lantern: fānúsk‿úlli⌒.
   Light the lamp: lámbag‿árkɪr⌒.
   Don't light it: (a) tókkon‿úllimɛn⌒; (b) tókkon‿ārkírmɛn⌒.
lightning n. fɪletfɪlád‿ (fɪlat-); bérɪg‿.
like adj. -kɪrɪ‿ (-kírɪ‿; §§ 2539-40).
   What's it like? mɪŋkɪríré?
   It's like (resembles) this: íŋkírɪn⌒.
   I want one like mine: ándɪkɪrɪ-wēd‿dólli⌒.
   Leave it like that: (a, as a general rule) íŋkɛ‿múk⌒; (b, on this occasion) íŋkɛ‿mugó⌒.
   Don't leave it like that: (a) tókkon‿íŋkɛ‿múgmɛn⌒; (b) tókkon‿íŋkɛ‿mugósmɛn⌒ (‿mugómmɛn⌒).
   It was (disposed) like that: íŋkɛ‿búgon⌒.
   It was like (resembled) that: íŋkɪr‿ɛgó⌒.
like prep.[1] -náhad‿; -nahádk(ɪ)‿ (-hátk(ɪ)‿, -hátt(ɪ)‿; -hákk(ɪ)‿); -nahádkɛd‿ (-hátkɛd‿, -hákkɛd‿).
   He runs like a hare: (a) údlañ-náhab‿bódɪn⌒; (b) údláñ-nahákkɪ‿bódɪn⌒; (c) údláñ-nahákkɛb‿bódɪn⌒.

---

[1] Prep. in *FPOD* s.v.; adv. *MEG*, § 269 note.

like v.t. dól.
  Do you like it? ɛrˌtékkıˌdólná?
  Don't you like it? ɛrˌtékkıˌdólmen?
  Do they like it? tékkıˌdóllandé?
  Don't they like it? tékkıˌdólmendan?
  I like this very much: âiˌíŋgıˌdıgrīgır-dólli⌒.
  I don't like that camel (yonder): âiˌmáŋˌkámgıˌdólmununˌ⌒.
  As you like: ɛŋˌkɛ́fké⌒.
like, be v.t. gálıgˌ.
  What's it like? míŋ-gálıgın?
  It's like milk: íččıgˌgálıgın⌒.
liking n. (*fondness*) dólarˌ (-làrˌ); dolfdˌ; dólt(ı)ˌ; (كيف) kɛ́fˌ.
lime n. (*fruit*) lēmúnˌ; (*calcium oxide*) ğírˌ.
limp v.i. kóhıl (kóılˌ); tókk(ı).
  Why is (s)he (it) limping? tɛrˌméŋˌkóılın?
line n. (*fishing-*) úlˌ.
lintel n. dfuˌ (dfwˌ).
lion n. kóˌ; ésɛdˌ.
lip n. šúnd(ı)ˌ.
listen v.i., **listen to** v.t. ğíğır.
  Listen to me: ándıgˌgíğırˌ⌒.
  Listen to what I say: ámˌbaññídkıˌgíğırˌ⌒.
litter n. kášš(ı); kawíšˌ; (*sweepings*) tubínd(ı)ˌ.
little adj. (*small*) kíññaˌ.
  I want the little one, not the big one: kíññadˌdólli, dúlgımununˌ⌒.
little, a indef. pron. kínnɛrˌ; márısˌ; marísēˌ; tőddɛrˌ.
  X. *Do you want coffee?* gáhwadˌdólná?
  Y. *I want a little:* (a) kınnɛ́dˌdólliˌ⌒; (b) marıssɛ́dˌdólliˌ⌒.
  There's very little of it: marıssodunˌ⌒.
  I want a very little: marıssoddɛ́dˌdólliˌ⌒.
  Give me a very little: marıssókkırdɛ̄nˌ⌒.
  Give him (her, it) a very little: marıssókkırtırˌ⌒.
  They want a little water: ɛ́ssıˌtoddɛ́dˌdóllanˌ⌒.
  I want a little salt: úmbudˌtoddɛ́dˌdólliˌ⌒.
  I want a little boiling water: ɛ́ssıˌwäzbūlˌtoddɛ́dˌdólliˌ⌒.
  Tell him (her) to make a little: toddɛ́gˌáwanˌ⌒.
live v.i. (*be alive*) áñ; (*reside*) ág, tɛ́g.
  Do you live in the Sudan? sūdándˌágrandɛ́?
  X. *Where does (s)he live?* sáırˌ́ágın?
  Y. *In Máhas:* mássınˌdàrˌ́ágın⌒.
  Did (s)he live here? índˌ́ágkoná?
liver n. kıbdádˌ.
lizard n. ğɛŋɛníssɛˌ.
  (*Varanus niloticus*) ášk(ı) (N. ášš(ı)).
load n. dégarˌ (-gàrˌ); dɛgídˌ; kúğurarˌ (-ràrˌ); kuğurídˌ.
load v.t. (*place on and place burden on*) dég; (*superimpose*) kúğur.
  Load (pl.) the baggage sc. on to the animal(s): (a) afɛ́škıˌdégwɛˌ⌒; (b) afɛ́škıˌkúğurwɛˌ⌒.
  Load the camel: kámgıˌdɛ́kˌ⌒.
loaf n. kálˌ; (*small flat circular*) kábıdˌ.
  Is there another loaf? kálˌɛ́ččɛ́l-lɛ̄rˌdánà?
loathe v.t. síkk(ı).

lock n. dúgalˌ (-gàlˌ, -gɛlˌ); kānúnˌ; kēlúnˌ; (*padlock*) gífılˌ (gúfulˌ), táblaˌ.
  The key wouldn't go into the lock: kúšarˌdugállo ˌtōráŋgıˌmóŋkon⌒.
  Lock it: kušárkɛkˌkópˌ⌒.
  Is it locked? kušárkɛkˌkóbbūná?
locust n. báŋgaˌ.
lofty adj. álıˌ.
long adj. nósōˌ.
  This is too long: ínˌnosón⌒.
  This is not long enough: ínˌnosómununˌ⌒.
  I want a long one: nóso-wɛ̄dˌdólliˌ⌒.
  How many feet is it long? ténˌnósogıdˌgédɛmˌmukóttɛrré?
long v.i. hɛnné (hınnɛ́) constr. with -rˌ (q.v.).
loofah n. lífˌ.
look v.i. gúñč(ı).
look at v.t. nál.
  I'll look at it: âiˌbınálliˌ⌒.
  Look at this: íŋgıˌnalé⌒, pl. ....ˌnaléddɛ⌒.
  Look at them: tírgıˌnálırˌ⌒, pl. ....ˌnalíwwɛˌ⌒.
look for v.t. tɛbé.
  Look for him (her, it): tɛbé⌒, pl. tɛbɛ́wɛˌ⌒.
  Let ɛáli look for him (her, it): (a) álıtˌtékkıˌtɛbɛ́ranˌ⌒; (b §6291) álıtˌtɛbɛ́ranˌ⌒.
  Let them look for him (her, it): tɛbɛ́wanˌ⌒.
  Have you looked for him (her, it)? tɛbɛ́goná?
  X. *Did you look for him (her, it) in the market?* ɛrˌsúğırˌtɛbēnálkoná?
  Y. *I looked for him (her, it) and couldn't find him (her, it):* tɛbēmısírkoriˌ⌒.
look like it v.t. gálıg (§§5701-2).
  He is a man, though he looks like a woman: (a) ógıǧˌɛŋgonˌɛ́ŋgıˌgálıgınˌ⌒; (b) ógıǧˌɛŋgonˌɛŋgıgılunˌ⌒; (c) ógıǧˌɛŋgonˌɛŋkírınˌ⌒.
look out v.i. gúñč(ı).
  Look out! (= Take care!): bálko!, pl. bálkowɛ!
look out for v.t. gúñč(ı).
  Look out for us as we come back: árgıˌgúñčˌárˌwıdɛruˌtáˌ⌒.
  Tell him (her) to look out for them and when (s)he sees them to come here: tírgıˌgúñčırıran, nalíkkınˌíndoˌtàranˌ⌒.
  Look out for a cow that has milk: tíˌíččıkól-lɛnˌnálˌ⌒.
look well at v.t. sɛrēgırgúñč(ı).
looking-glass n. koñáll(ı)ˌ.
look-out
  Keep a good look-out: sɛrēgırgúñč(ı)ˌ⌒.
loom n. duhǎnˌ (N. dukǎnˌ).
loom-maker n. duhānfjɛˌ; duhǎŋgoñˌ (N. dukǎŋ-).
loose(n) v.t. kús.
loot v.t. ɛr.
lose v.t. dábır.
  I have lost it: dabírkoriˌ⌒.
  Have you lost it? dabírkoná?
  Don't lose it: tókkonˌdábırmenˌ⌒.
  (S)he has lost his (her) keys: téŋˌkúšarıdˌdabıróskóˌ⌒.
lose one's way v.i. tuššé (tıššɛ́).
loser n. mɛglúbˌ (mág-).
loser, be a v.i. hasrɛ́bū-.
  If (s)he sells it at that price (s)he is not a loser: tɛrˌínˌtɛmɛ́ŋgɛǧˌğántıkkın, hasrēbúmununˌ⌒.

lost, be v.i. dábbū-.
lost, get v.i. dáb.
lot
  Is that the lot? (Is that all?) gédırˌté?
loud
  This talk is too loud: ímˌbáññıdˌluzǔmˌdógorˌdálunˌ⌒.
loud, speak v.i. ğál; dúlgırbaññ(ı).
  Speak loud: dúlgırbaññiˌ⌒.
  Don't speak loud: tókkonˌdūlgırbáññımenˌ⌒.
  Don't speak so loud: tókkonˌíŋkɛˌdúlgırbaññımenˌ⌒.
louse n. íss(ı)ˌ.
love n. dólarˌ (-làrˌ); dolfdˌ; dólt(ı)ˌ.
love v.t. dól.
low v.i. wíg.
lower adj. togónd(ı)ˌ.
  It's the lower one: togóndınˌ⌒.
lower v.t. kúttɛgır; šugúdd(ı).
  Lower the flag: bɛ̄rákkıˌšugúddiˌ⌒.
luggage n. áfɛšˌ.
lunch n. gádaˌ.
  Eat your lunch: ɛŋˌgádakˌkalós⌒.
lung n. ufúff(ı)ˌ; fašfášˌ.
lupine n. aŋgállɛˌ.
lute n. kísırˌ.
luxuriant growth (of plant) n. kóšɛˌ.

mavmūr (مأمور) n. māmúrˌ.
mad adj. dáhal; dahálkōlˌ.
  Are you mad? ɛrˌdahálˌkóná? (§4672).
mad, be v.i. ğómbū-; kúmmɛbū-; dahálkŏ-.
  (S)he is mad: dahálkóˌ⌒.
magician n. gúlˌ; dógırˌ.
Máhas (دار المحس) n. mássín-daˌ.
Máhasi n. (*native of Máhas*) máss(ı)ˌ; (*dialect of Máhas*) massınčínd(ı)ˌ.
  Is (s)he a Máhasi? tɛrˌmássıré?
  Do you know Máhasi? ɛrˌmassınčíndıgˌuñúrná?
Mahdi, the n. méhedıˌ.
Mahomet n. mohámmedˌ.
maid(en) n. búruˌ.
maize n. makádaˌ.
make v.t. áu (áw, áu); (*fashion out of wood or metal*) kǎı (kǎı).
  Does (s)he make it? (a) tɛrˌ́ágauná? (b) tɛrˌ́ákkǎıná?
  (S)he is making a box: sandúg-gēgˌágawınˌ⌒.
  Let him (her) make the coffee: gáhwagˌáuan⌒.
  Where was the boat made? kúbˌsáırˌkǎıkattıgon?
  Have you made the bed? fɛríškˌawíddıgoná?
  Has (s)he made a rope? (a) ırı-wɛ̄gˌfrkoná? (b) ırı-wɛ̄gˌ́áukoná?
  What are they made of? míndotōnˌ́áukattıran?
  X. *Who make the mats?* nígüˌníbdıgˌáwığran?
  Y. *The women:* ɛ́nčiˌ⌒.
  X. *What are mats made of?* níbdıˌmíndotōnˌawíčkattıran?
  Y. *Of palm-leaves:* háurtɛrtōnˌ⌒.
  Has (s)he made the bread? kálgˌundóskoná?

male n. ónd(ı)‿.
man n. (*homo*) ádεm‿ (ádam‿, ádám‿); (*vir*) ógığ‿.
 I want a man: ogíğ-ğεd‿dólli‿.
 I want two men: ógığ‿ówwıd‿dólli‿.
 Have our men gone? án‿ğamánčı‿nogóskorandέ?
 A man may be addressed as wámbεs! (*O my brother!*).
 An old man may be addressed as wambέnna! (*O my uncle!*); wáŋgi! (*O my uncle!*).
manager n. mudír‿.
mange n. kagrúss(ı)‿.
manure n. mǎro‿.
many adj. dígrĭ (dıgrí‿).
mare n. káñ-kárr(ı)‿.
mark n. (*sign*) ír‿, alǎma‿; (*explanatory*) ıbǎr‿.
market n. súg‿.
 Has (s)he gone to (the) market? súg‿áŋkoná?
 I am going (i.e. shall go) to the market: âı‿bı-súg-andi‿.
 Is this from the market? (*a*) ín‿súgırtöndέ? (*b*) ín‿súŋdıré?
marriage n. έrkanε‿; édar‿ (édar‿); εdíd‿.
marry v.t. έd.
 Are you married? εr‿εdεdágná?
 Is (s)he married? tέr‿εdεdágná?
Mars n. (*the planet*) wíssı‿gέlε.
marvel v.i. (*marvel at* v.t.) ağabέ.
mason wasp n. fıríčč(ı)‿.
massacre v.t. bérığ.
mast n. sǎrı‿ (sǎrrı‿, sǎrrε‿); éndε‿; kúbn‿éndε‿.
master n. (*owner*) tírt(ı)‿; (*teacher*) kǔrkırıl‿.
 Who is his (her, its) master? tέn‿tírtı‿ ní‿tέ?
masticate v.t. (*food*) ğókk(ı); (*tobacco*) súkk(ı).
mat n. níbıd‿.
match n. (*for fire*) kıbríd‿.
 Have you got matches? kıbríd‿έnnarέ?
matter n. (*affair*) hǎğa‿ (-ğǎ‿, -ğε‿), ğέllı‿; (*pus*) únčε‿.
 What is the matter with you? εr‿míndέ?
 What is the matter with your leg? έnn‿óssı‿míndέ?
 It doesn't matter (It's all the same): mállε‿ wεrun‿; (*Don't trouble about it*) málέš‿.
matting, rough n. sıláttε‿.
mattress n. mέrtaba‿.
means
 Is he a man of means? hǎğakŏná?
measles n. miñmíñ‿.
measure n. (*vessel*) kέla‿; (*amount*) asídd(ı)‿.
measure v.t. ǎs; abbırέ.
 Did you measure the cloth? (*a*) εr‿kádεg‿ áskoná? (*b*) εr‿kádεg‿abbırέgoná?
measuring-rod n. šǎ‿.
meat n. kúsu‿.
medicine n. dáw(w)a‿ (dów-).
 Have you taken your medicine? (*a*) én‿ dówwag‿góllıgoná? (*b, drunk it*) én‿ dówwan‿nígoná? (*c, eaten it*) én‿ dówwak‿kálkoná? (*d, moved it*) én‿ dówwas‿sókkεgoná?
 Don't forget my medicine: án‿dówwat‿ tókkon‿íwmεn‿.

meet v.t. ábd(ı); gābılέ.
 I will meet you at the well: âı‿έkkı‿ gówwır‿bábdıri‿.
 I will meet you (pl.) at the well: âı‿írgı‿ gówwır‿babdıríddi‿.
melon n. (*sweet*) gāwún‿ (gāûún‿); (*water-*) tímε‿.
melt v.i. (*pass towards liquid state*) ğagādε (ğagādέ, ῭), tεlέwε; (*dissolve*) ğǔdε.
 It is melting: ğagādélun‿.
melt v.t. (*render liquid*) ğagádεgır (ğagādégır), tεlέwεgır; (*dissolve*) ğǔdε.
 Melt this on the fire: ıŋg‿íŋ‿kóččır‿ tεlέwεgır‿.
mend v.t. gέndıgır.
 My boots want mending: án‿ğázmǎ‿ gεndıgıddáŋgı‿dólın‿.
mended, be v.p. gέndıkattı-.
 Has it been mended? gεndıkattóskoná?
menses n. gέu‿ (gέᵘ, gέw‿, gέú‿); έŋ‿gέu‿ (‿gέᵘ, ‿gέw‿, ‿gέú‿); έŋ‿gέu‿, ‿gέu‿, ‿gέw‿, ‿gέú‿); hέd‿.
mention
 Don't mention it: (*minimising a contretemps*) málέš‿.
merchandise n. budáε‿.
merchant n. tǎğır‿, hawǎğε‿ (-ğǎ‿, -ğa‿); (*travelling*) tεššǎš‿.
mercy n. ráhma‿.
mercy, have v.i. rahmέ.
 He had mercy on him (her): téddo‿ rahmέgon‿.
 He had no mercy on him (her): téddo‿ rahmέgómunun‿.
merely adv. súdır‿.
messenger n. mıráslı‿ (mur-, -lı‿).
 Bring me a messenger: wέg‿έtta‿ıšíndi‿.
metal n. šǎrt(ı)‿.
mew v.i. wíg.
midday n. dúhur‿ (s.v. *noon*); ugrέsn‿ tǒrt(ı)‿.
 at midday: duhúrro‿.
middle adj. sεllέnd(ı)‿; (*intervening*) barrέnd(ı)‿.
 Take away the middle (intervening) one: tím‿barrέndıs‿sókkε‿.
middle n. sέllε‿.
 in the middle: sέllεr‿.
 It's in the middle: tεr‿sέllεr‿.
 It's in the middle of them: tεr‿tím‿bárrεr‿.
midnight n. ugǔntǒrt(ı)‿.
 at midnight: uguntǒrtır‿.
midrib of date-palm branch n. kárro‿.
midwife n. úskar‿.
milch adj. íččıkŏl‿.
 milch-goat: bέrt‿íččıkŏl‿.
 I want to buy a milch-cow: tí‿íččıkŏl-lεğ‿ ğandáŋgı‿dólli‿.
milk n. íčč(ı)‿.
 cow's milk: tín‿íčč(ı)‿.
 Is this milk cow's? ín‿íččı‿tíndıré?
 goat's milk: bértın‿íčč(ı)‿.
 I don't want goat's milk: âı‿bértın‿íččıd‿ dólmunun‿.
 curdled milk: mέrεl‿.
milk v.t. ğǔrr(ı).
milkman n. íččıg‿έttal‿.
mill n. tāhúna‿; (*hand-mill*) rahâıε‿ (-âıǎ‿, -âıa‿).
millet n. (*great*) márε‿; (*bulrush*) έndε‿.

mind n. (*attention*) bǎl‿.
 I gave him (her) a piece of my mind: âı‿ tέkkonon‿ğáwwıgori‿.
mind v.t. (*heed*) bǎlko.
 Mind! (Take care!) bǎlko!, pl. bǎlkowε!
 Mind (beware of) the hole (pit): kúlgı‿ bǎlko‿.
 Tell him (her) to mind: bǎlkoran‿.
 Tell him (her) to mind the wire: sílkıb‿ bǎlkoran‿.
 Mind the dog! wέlloton‿έnn-āb‿bǎlko!
 I told you to mind the dog: âı‿έkkı‿wέlloton‿έnn-āb‿bǎlkor‿εğóri‿.
 When you put it in, mind this: úndurın‿ tǎd‿íŋgı‿bǎlko‿.
 Mind you don't fall: bǎlko‿έr‿dígırmεnınn‿íllǎr‿.
 Let him (her) mind (s)he doesn't fall: tέkkı‿bǎlkoran‿tεr‿dígırmεnınn‿ íllǎr‿.
 Never mind! (*indifference*) wεlεsέ!, mugó! (*politeness*) mālέš!
 X. I can't find the key: kušárk‿εlkómunun‿, lit. *I didn't find...* (§ 5475).
 Y. Never mind! mālέš!
 X. I'm in your seat: âı‿έŋ‿kúrsır‿.
 Y. Never mind! mālέš!
mine abs. poss. pron. ánd(ı)‿.
 It's mine: ándín‿.
 Is it mine? ándırέ?
 It's not mine: ándmunun‿.
 Isn't it mine? ándmεn?
 They're mine: ándınčín‿.
 Are they mine? ándınčırέ?
 They're not mine: andínčımunan‿.
 Aren't they mine? andínčımεndan?
 Is this (that) mine? (*a*) ín‿ándırέ? (*b*) ín‿ ándı‿tέ? (*Is this the one that is mine?*).
 Are these (those) mine? íŋgu‿ándınčırέ?
mingle v.i. sǎu (sǎw, sǎú); tındımíndan.
mingle v.t. sǎwır (sǎwᵘr, sǎu(ı)r, sǎuᵘr); tındımíndıgır.
minute adj. nǒro‿.
minute n. dagíga‿.
 Wait five minutes: dagíga‿díčıkı‿tέp‿.
mirror n. koñáll(ı)‿.
miscarry v.i. bókk(ı).
miserly adj. sǒwwεd‿ (sǒwwod‿).
miss v.t. súd; mísır.
 I missed the crocodile: (*a*) εlúmgı‿sútkori‿; (*b*) έlumır‿sútkori‿; (*c*) έlumırtŏn‿ sútkori‿.
 Don't miss the train: gatírkı‿tókkom‿ mısírmεn‿.
 Did (s)he miss the steamer? bābǔrkı‿ mısírkoná?
 If you miss (=don't meet) him (her, it), come back: εrom‿mısírkıw‿wıdέ‿.
miss out v.t. wákk(ı).
mist n. níčč(ı)‿.
misty, be v.i. dúgbū- (dúggū-).
mix v.i. sǎu (sǎw, sǎú); tındımíndan-.
mix (up) v.t. sǎwır (sǎwᵘr, sǎu(ı)r, sǎuᵘr); tındımíndıgır; halbıtέ (xal-).
 Mix these: ıŋgus‿sǎuır‿.
 Don't mix these: íŋgut‿tókkon‿sǎuırmεn‿.
 Don't mix up the baggage: tókkon‿afέškı‿ tındımíndıgírmεn‿.
mixed (up) adj. tındımínd(ı)‿.
 This is all mixed up: ím‿mállε‿tındımíndín‿.

Mohammed — nephew

Mohammed n. mohámmɛd‿.
moist adj. ğáwwur‿ (ğáuwur‿).
moisten v.t. tábbɛ.
Mollugo hirta n. kóddɛ‿kárr(ı)‿.
Monday n. búš‿.
  on Monday: búšk(ı)‿ (-ki⌒).
  (S)he (it) will come on Monday: búškı‿ bıtăn⌒.
money n. dúng(ı)‿.
mongoose n. tussába‿.
monitor (*Varanus niloticus*) n. ášk(ı)‿ (N. ášš(ı)‿).
monkey n. abaláñ‿; gírıd‿.
month n. ún‿; šáhar‿.
  at the end of the month: únn‿abăgır‿.
  from now till the end of the month: ékkɛ-nɛrtōn‿únn‿abăm‿bókkon‿ (‿abăm‿mónkon‿).
moon n. unátt(ı)‿; ún‿.
  new moon: (a) unátt‿ɛ́r‿; (b) unáttı‿ ğɛdíd‿; (c) ún‿ɛ́r‿; (d) ún‿ğɛdíd‿.
  full moon: dımındokémısn‿unátt(ı)‿; arbātášarn‿unátt(ı)‿.
  when the moon rises: unáttı‿bélkın‿ (-kī⌒).
more adj. and adv. zıáda‿; (in comparison) —n‿dógōr‿; (*still, yet, further*) élgon‿ (ólg-); (*again*) ténnɛ‿.
  There is one day more: jōm‿mḗr‿ólgon‿ dăn⌒.
  Fetch some more: (a) ténn‿étta⌒; (b) tɛn-nég‿étta⌒.
  Fetch one more: ténnɛ‿wég‿étta⌒.
  Bring some more plates: (a) ténnɛ‿sáhanıg‿étta⌒; (b) sáhanıt‿ténnɛ‿étta⌒.
  Bring some more milk: (a) ténn‿íččıg‿étta⌒; (b) íččıt‿ténnɛ‿étta⌒.
  Bring some more knives: (a) ténnɛ‿kándınčıg‿étta⌒; (b) kándınčıt‿ténnɛ‿étta⌒.
  We want some more bread: (a) ar‿ténnɛ‿kálgı‿dóllu⌒; (b) ar‿kálgı‿ténnɛ‿dóllu⌒.
  Did any more children die? ténnɛ‿tónı‿ dígorandé?
  Are there more like this? ténn‿íŋkırı‿dăna?
  I don't want any more: āı‿ténnɛ‿dól-munun⌒.
  We don't want any more: ar‿ténnɛ‿dól-munun⌒.
Mormyrus caschive L. (and *M. kannume*) n. tōdágıl‿.
morning n. fáğır‿ (féğır‿).
  It's already morning: gú‿bɛjjóskon⌒.
morsel n. hítta‿ (hétta‿).
mortar (**vessel for pounding**) n. fúndug‿.
Moslem adj. mıslím(ı)‿; mıslımínd(ı)‿.
Moslem n. míslım‿.
mosque n. ğáma‿; (*small*) mısíd‿.
moth n. fírrıl‿ (fírrıl‿); (*tinea*) íttɛ‿.
mother n. -ḗn‿, always with a form of the poss. pers. pron. (§2626) prefixed:
  my mother: índ(ı)‿, obj. índıg‿.
  your mother: ınḗn‿.
  his (her, its) mother: tınḗn‿.
  our mother: antınḗn‿.
  your (pl.) mother: ıntınḗn‿.
  their mother: tıntınḗn‿.
mother-in-law n. -ogo‿, with a form of the poss. pers. pron. (§2622) prefixed:
  my mother-in-law: ánnogo‿.
  your mother-in-law: ínnogo‿.
  his (her) mother-in-law: tínnogo‿.
  our mother-in-law: antínnogo‿.
  your (pl.) mother-in-law: ıntínnogo‿.
  their mother-in-law: tıntínnogo‿.
motive n. sébɛb‿ (súbáb‿).
motor-car n. turumbíl‿.
mound n. kútt(ı)‿.
mount v.i. dárr(ı).
mountain n. ğébɛl‿.
mourner n. oñkátt(ı)‿.
mourning n. wɛğăd‿ (wáğ-).
mouse n. ğígır‿.
moustache n. šénɛb‿.
mouth n. ágıl‿.
move v.i. (*oscillate, etc.*) kérkɛr; (*go*) nóg.
  The tent-pegs are not firmly fixed, they keep on moving: hémaŋ‿kóğırı‿sɛptɛ́munan, ákkɛrkérran⌒.
move v.t. (*transport*) ɛğğú, bír.
  Tell porters to move the baggage: attălıg‿afɛ́škı‿bírwan⌒.
move (go, come) ahead v.i. ógolan-.
move along v.i. ğú; dá-.
move (go, come) on (ahead) v.i. ógolan-.
mow v.t. ğór.
much adj. dígrí‿ (dıgrí‿).
much adv. dıgríg‿ (-ígi⌒); dıgrígırg(ı)‿ (-rgi⌒).
  very much adv. désɛn‿ (-sḗ⌒, -sɛ́⌒).
  I dislike him (her, it, them) very much: désɛm‿móndi⌒.
mucus
  mucus of eye (a) míssıŋ‿kál‿; (b) míssıŋ‿kanísɛ‿; (c) míssın‿nébɛd‿ (‿né-mɛd‿).
mud n. síbɛ‿.
muddle v.t. tındımíndıgır; halbıtɛ́ (xal-).
muddled adj. tındımínd(ı)‿.
mug n. kúz‿ (kús‿).
Muhámmad n. mohámmɛd‿.
mule n. bágala‿.
murder n. bɛ́rar‿ (-ràr‿); bɛrɛ́d‿.
muscle n. ásab‿.
muscular adj. (*strong*) kógor‿.
mustard-tree n. ar̆ağ‿.
mutton n. kús‿ɛgénd(ı)‿; ɛgɛ́n‿kúsu‿.
  Tell him (her) to buy mutton: (a) kús‿ ɛgɛ́ndığ‿ğánan⌒; (b) ɛgɛ́n‿kúsuğ‿ğánan⌒.
my poss. pron. ánn‿v., án‿c.
  my salt: ánn‿úmbud‿.
  my money: án‿dúng(ı)‿.
  my house: áŋ‿ká‿.
  my hat: ám‿burnɛ́ta‿.
  my stick: áw‿wíččir‿.
  my hand: ánni‿.

nail n. (*unguis*) súnt(ı)‿; (*clavus*) musmắr‿, ókk(ı)‿.
naked adj. wírığ‿; wıríğbūl‿ (-íğğūl‿).
  Don't come when I am naked: (a) āı‿ wırığ‿tépkırı‿tókkon‿tămɛn⌒; (b) āı‿ wırığğúgırı‿tókkon‿tămɛn⌒.
  When I am naked I don't want anyone here: āı‿wırič‿tɛ́pkır‿índo‿wɛ̄d‿dól-munun⌒.
name n. érr(ı)‿.
  What's your name? ékkı‿níg‿erán?
  What's his (her) name? tékkı‿níg‿erán?
  What's its name? tékkı‿míng‿erán?
  What's the name of this? íŋgı‿míng‿ erán?
  Has (s)he the same name as you? énn‿ ɛrrıkáttıré?
name v.t. ‿é-.
namesake n. ɛrrıkátt(ı)‿.
  It's his (her) namesake: ténn‿ɛrrıkátti-taran⌒.
nape of neck n. gáfa‿.
napkin n. fúta‿; mındíl‿ (mɛn-).
narrate v.t. íg.
narrow adj. tákkar‿.
native n. bɛlɛdnırínd(ı)‿.
native n. bélɛdn‿íd‿ (bɛlɛ́dnıd‿).
natron n. ğádd(ı)‿.
navel n. sḗn‿.
near adj. ɛgétt(ı)‿; ɛgɛttínd(ı)‿.
  It's (too) near: ɛgéttın⌒.
  It's not near (enough): ɛgéttımunun⌒.
near adv. ɛgéttır‿.
  Put it near: ɛgettıgırúskur⌒, pl. ɛgettıgıruskúrwɛ⌒.
  Don't put it (so) near: tókkon‿ɛgettıgıruskúrmɛn⌒, pl. tókkon‿ɛgettıgıruskúrmɛwwɛ⌒.
  Come nearer: (a) ɛgéttır‿tá⌒, pl. ɛgéttır‿tăwɛ⌒; (b) ɛgettantá⌒, pl. ɛgettantăwɛ⌒.
near prep. —n‿ɛgéttır‿; —n‿ábtır‿ (-n‿áttır‿).
  near this: ínın‿ɛgéttır‿.
  Come near me: ánn‿ɛgéttır‿ta⌒, pl. ánn‿ ɛgéttır‿tăwɛ⌒.
  Don't put it near this: tókkon‿ínın‿ ɛgettıgıruskúrmɛn⌒, pl. ...-uskúrmɛwwɛ⌒.
nearer adj. ɛgɛttínd(ı)‿.
nearly
  They nearly died of thirst: essınɛ́rkɛd‿ dīɛdólkoran⌒.
neat adj. (*without admixture*) sáda‿.
necessary adj. lázım‿; darúrı‿.
necessity n. luzúm‿.
neck n. gúmur‿; éjjɛ‿.
  neck of bottle: gázázŋ‿gól‿.
necklace n. mútrag‿.
need n. luzúm‿.
  There is no need of this: ínıl‿luzúm‿ dámunun⌒.
need v.t. (*want*) dól.
  They are not needed: tíl‿luzúm‿dámunun⌒.
needle n. ıntíllɛ‿.
needless adj. luzúmkıññ(ı)‿.
  Your (pl.) talk is needlessly loud: ím‿ báññıd‿luzúm‿dógor‿dúlun⌒.
negro n. ógıǧ‿urúmmɛ‿.
  I saw a negro: ógıǧ‿urúmmé-wēn‿ nálkori⌒.
neigh v.i. híŋŋk(ı).
neighbour n. kānárrɛ‿.
neither...nor wála‿...wála‿.
  It is neither hot nor cold: wála‿ğúgrímu-nū‿wál‿orófélmunū⌒.
  X. Do you want a donkey or a horse? hánud‿dólná‿wálla‿kắčči?
  Y. I want neither a donkey nor a horse: wála‿hánuw‿wála‿kắčči‿.
nephew n. (*brother's son*) -bɛstŏd‿; (*sister's son*) -ssŏd‿, -ɛssın‿tŏd‿.
Always with a form of the poss. pers. pron. (§§2625, 2629, 2631) prefixed:
  my nephew (brother's son): ámbɛstŏd‿.
  your nephew (brother's son): ímbɛstŏd‿.
  his (her) nephew (brother's son): tímbɛstŏd‿.

our nephew (brother's son): antímbɛstŏd‿.
your (pl.) nephew (brother's son): ıntímbɛstŏd‿.
their nephew (brother's son): tıntímbɛstŏd‿.
my nephew (sister's son): ássŏd‿ and ánnɛssın‿tŏd‿.
your nephew (sister's son): íssŏd‿ and ínnɛssın‿tŏd‿.
his (her) nephew (sister's son): tíssŏd‿ and tínnɛssın‿tŏd‿.
our nephew (sister's son): ántıssŏd‿ and antínnɛssın‿tŏd‿.
your (pl.) nephew (sister's son): íntıssŏd‿ and ıntínnɛssın‿tŏd‿.
their nephew (sister's son): tíntıssŏd‿ and tıntínnɛssın‿tŏd‿.
nest n. kɛ́tta‿.
net n. (*large*) túkmɛ‿ (túhᵘmɛ‿), šábákà‿ (šɛ́bəkɛ‿); (*small*) turráha‿, ábɛ‿, gɛrίf‿, šɛnίf‿.
net v.t. áb.
never adv. ábadan‿ (ɛbɛdɛn‿); abadáŋ(ı)‿ (ɛbɛdɛ́ŋ(ı)‿).
With negative verb:
I have never heard it: abadáŋgı‿gıǧır-kómunun⌢.
I never drink it: âı‿tɛ́kk‿ännímunun⌢.
new adj. ɛ́r‿; ǧɛdίd‿.
Bring a new one: ɛr-rɛ́g‿ɛ́tta⌢.
It's not new, it's old: tɛr‿ɛ́rmunun, kúrusun⌢.
news n. hábar‿ (-bár‿); wɛ́rɛ‿.
good news: bıšıråd‿ (-šɛr-).
newspaper n. ǧurnǎl‿.
next
on Saturday next: sámtɛ‿tǎllo‿.
(S)he (it) is coming next Monday: búš‿ tálgu‿bıtan⌢.
Next Tuesday I shall go to Khartoum: būsnóŋ‿ǧúbúlgı‿hartúmır‿bınógrı⌢.
niece n. (*brother's daughter*) -bɛstŏd‿; (*sister's daughter*) -ssŏd‿, -ɛssın‿ tŏd‿.
Always with a form of the poss. pers. pron. (§§ 2625, 2629, 2631) prefixed:
my niece (brother's daughter): ámbɛstŏd‿ (etc., s.v. **nephew**).
my niece (sister's daughter): ássŏd‿ and ánnɛssın‿tŏd‿ (etc., s.v. **nephew**).
night n. úgū‿.
at night: ugū́g‿.
midnight: ugū́ntŏ́rt(ı)‿.
last night: wīl-ugū́g‿.
X. to Y. Good-night! hɛ́rro‿túbbi!
Y. Good-night! ékkon‿hɛ́rro‿túbbi!
X. to Y. and Z. Good-night! hɛ́rro‿túbbıwɛ!
X. answering Y. and Z. Good-night! ír̃gon‿hɛ́rro‿túbbıwɛ!
(S)he (it) comes every night: (a) úgu‿ mállɛg‿ättán‿; (b) úgu‿máll ɛt‿tán‿.
(S)he (it) stays all night: (a) úgu‿mállɛg‿ ágın‿; (b) úgu‿máll ɛt‿tégın‿.
It's almost night: ugánɛdólın⌢.
night-dress n. ugúŋ‿kádɛ‿.
Nile n. úru‿.
high Nile: (a) dɛmίrɛ‿ (-rá‿, -ra‿); (b) mısŏ́r‿.
nimble adj. šŏ́ro‿; (*swift*) bŏdkátt(ı)‿.
nine card. num. ískŏd‿.
nineteen card. num. dımındískŏd‿.
ninety card. num. dımınískŏd‿; tısáίn‿.

ninth ord. num. ıskŏdínt(ı)‿ (⌢‿‿).
nipple n. ɛ́rt(ı)‿.
nit n. íssıŋ‿kúmbu‿.
no sentence-word wǎran‿ (-rǎ⌢, -rá⌢).
— or use the negative conjugation:
X. Are you tired? ɛr‿mǎgoná?
Y. No: māgómunun⌢.
nobleman n. (*descendant of the Prophet*) šarίf‿ (šár-, šɛr-).
noblewoman n. (*descendant of the Prophet*) šarίfa‿ (šár-, šɛr-).
nobody
Nobody saw him (her, it): wɛ́r‿nalkómunun⌢.
noise n. (*of movement*) hárag‿, háraka‿; (*of voice*) híz‿, híss(ı)‿.
Does it make a noise (in moving)? harákkı‿ kŏ́ná?
I couldn't hear your voice because of the noise of the wind: túruŋ‿harágŋ‿íllɛr‿ âı‿ɛ́n‿hísk̇ı‿gıǧırkómunun⌢.
Don't make so much noise: tókkon‿hárag‿ dıgrίg‿áumɛn‿.
Don't (pl.) make so much noise: tókkon‿ hárag‿dıgrίg‿áumɛnwwɛ́‿.
I don't like noise: (a, *of movement*) âı‿ harákkı‿dólmunun⌢; (b, *voices*) âı‿ híssıg‿gıǧırráŋgı‿dólmunun⌢.
noon n. dúhur‿.
before noon: dúhurn‿ŏwwɛ́llo‿.
at noon: duhúrro‿.
after noon: dúhurm‿bádır‿.
noose n. bíǧıd‿.
nor conj. wála‿ (wálla‿).
north n. kánnɛ‿.
northwards adv. kannɛ́r‿.
nose n. sŏríŋ‿.
bridge of the nose: soríŋn‿ɛ́ndɛ‿.
nose, blow one's v.i. fúčɛ.
nose-ring n. gísma‿.
not adv. (*denying*) -munun⌢, -munan⌢ (§§ 3077, 4252); (*prohibiting*) -mɛn⌢; (*inquiring*) see negative interrogative conjugation (§ 3117; § 4256).
(S)he (it) is not this (one): ímmunun⌢.
(S)he (it) is not that (yonder): mámmunun⌢.
It is not these: ıŋgúmunan⌢.
It is not those (yonder): máŋgúmunan⌢.
Mine have come, but yours have not: ándınčı‿tágoran, ɛndınčı‿tágomunan⌢.
Put it like this, not like that: (a) íŋk‿úskur, tókkon‿íŋk‿úskurmɛn⌢; (b) íŋk‿úskur, tókkon‿íŋkémɛn⌢.
Give him (her, it) this, not that (near): íŋgı‿tír, íŋgımunun⌢.
Take this away, not that: íŋgı‿sókkɛ, íŋgımugó⌢ lit. *take this, leave that*.
X. Shall I put it here? índ‿uskúddıá?
Y. No, not there: wǎran‿, índómunun⌢.
X. Will you have a bath? bıbówwıná?
Y. Not now: ékkɛnɛmunun⌢.
Bring one, not two: wɛ́g‿ɛ́tta, ŏ́wwımunun⌢, lit. ...*it is not two*.
X. Are you going to ride? bıkučč égná?
Y. Not today: ınnówwımunun⌢, lit. *It is not today*.
Haven't you found him (her, it, them)? élkomɛn?
not at all adv. ábadan‿ (ɛbɛdɛn‿); abadáŋ(ı)‿ (ɛbɛdɛ́ŋ(ı)‿).
notable n. (*of village or district*) ómda‿.

note-book n. dáftar‿ (dáftar‿, défter‿).
nothing s.v. súd‿.
It's better than nothing: sún‿dógor‿ génun‿.
X. Is there anything? dálláná?
Y. There is nothing: dállámunun⌢.
X. What are they doing? míŋ‿ágáuran?
Y. Nothing: âuran‿dámunun⌢.
X. What did they bring? míŋ‿éttágoran?
Y. Nothing: éttāgoran‿dámunun⌢.
notice v.t. (*pay attention to*) bálko; (*perceive*) hıssɛ́.
I didn't notice: âı‿bālkogómunun⌢.
notion n. ɛ́rıg‿.
now adv. ékkɛnɛ‿ (-ɛgı‿); íŋkɛnɛ‿ (-ɛgı‿); íssá‿; ısság‿ (-gı⌢).
Nubian adj. nobínd(ı)‿.
Nubian n. (*person*) bɛ́rbɛrı‿ (bárbarı‿), nŏ́b‿ (q.v.); (*language*) núba‿, nobínd(ı)‿, rutána‿ (-ná‿), ánd(ı)‿ (s.v. ár‿ *we*), índ(ı)‿ (s.v. ír‿).
What is it called in Nubian? índıgɛm‿ míŋ‿ɛrán?, lit. *in yours (your (pl.) language) what do they call it?*
I know a little Nubian: âı‿núba‿marıssɛ́g‿uñúddi⌢.
Dóngola Nubian (language): (a) duŋguland(ı)‿; (b) duŋgulāwınčínd(ı)‿ (-lāun-).
Talk Nubian:
A native or a foreigner may say: (a) núbab‿ bánni⌢; (b) núbagɛb‿bánñi⌢; (c) nobíndıb‿bánñi⌢; (d) nobíndıgɛb‿ bánñi⌢; (e) rutánab‿bánñi⌢; (f) rutánnagɛb‿bánñi⌢.
A native may say: (g) ándıb‿bánñi⌢; (h) ándıgɛb‿bánñi⌢.
A foreigner may say to a native: (i) índıb‿ bánñi⌢; (j) índıgɛb‿bánñi⌢.
Talk Dongola Nubian: (a) duŋgulándıb‿ bánñi⌢; (b) duŋgulándıgɛb‿bánñi⌢; (c) duŋgulāwınčíndıb‿bánñi⌢; (d) duŋgulāwınčíndıgɛb‿bánñi⌢ (e, f, g, h = g, h, i, j, above).
numb v.t. bɛ́.
The cold has numbed my feet: ŏd‿ánn‿ óssıb‿bɛ̄rɛdágın⌢.
numbed, be v.i. díbū-.
My hands are numbed: ánni‿díbūn⌢.
My feet are numbed: ánn‿óssı‿díbūn⌢.
My feet are numbed with cold: ánn‿óssı‿ ŏ́tkɛd‿díbūn⌢.
number n. ír‿.

O...! interj. particle wŏ‿c....! (wŏc., wᵒv., w‿v.; § 2450).
oar n. wāwídd(ı)‿.
oath n. ǧɛ́d(ı)‿ (ǧɛ́tt(ı)‿); ǧɛ́dar‿ (-dàr‿, -dɛr‿); ǧɛdίd‿.
obese adj. túkŏl‿.
object n. (*thing*) háǧa‿ (-ǧá‿, -ǧɛ‿); šɛ́j(ı)‿ (šɛ́jj(ı)‿).
oblique adj. kɛ́rɛñ‿.
observe v.t. nál.
(S)he is observing the fast: dértıg‿ákkágın⌢.
obtain v.t. él; dúr.
obvious adj. wádah‿.
occasion n. márra‿ (-rá‿); ǧır- (§ 2762); wékıd‿ (wák-).
occupation n. ǧɛ́lli‿.

occur v.i. haslé.
 It occurred in this way: íŋkɛ‿haslégon⌒.
o'clock
 at 1 o'clock: så‿wɛ́rro‿.
odour n. írıs‿.
of
 Give me a very little of it: téddotōm‿marıssoddɛ̆d‿dēn⌒.
 What was it made of? míndotōn‿åukattıgon?
 (S)he (it) died of thirst: ɛssınɛ́rkɛd‿dígon⌒.
off
 Off with you! dáp!, pl. dábwɛ!
 Take off your shoes: ɛ́m‿mɛrkúbkı‿dúkki⌒.
 Take a little off here and a little off there too: íŋgɛkkoŋ‿kınnɛ́g‿íŋgɛkkoŋ‿kınnɛ́s‿sókkɛ⌒.
 Is (s)he well off? hågakōná‿?
 Are they well off? hågakōrandɛ́?
offence n. (*crime*) ğınájɛ‿ (-já‿, -ja‿); zémb(ı)‿.
office n. (*bureau*) máktáb‿ (mέktɛb‿).
officer n. zábıd‿; (*district, mavmúr*) māmúr‿.
official adj. máktámd(ı)‿ (mɛk-, -tɛ́m-).
 I am going to put on official dress: (a) máktám‿kádɛd‿dɛgɛdólli⌒; (b) kádɛ‿máktámdıd‿dɛgɛdólli⌒.
official n. ɛfɛ́ndı‿.
often adv. márra‿dıgríg‿.
 (S)he (it) often goes: dıgrīgırānnógın⌒.
oil n. (*vegetable*) zɛ̄d‿, dés‿; (*mineral*) ğáz‿.
 sesame oil: símsım‿zɛ̄d‿; símsım‿dés‿.
oil-cloth n. mušɛ́mma‿.
oil-press n. assåra‿.
old adj. (*stale*) kúrus‿, gɛdím‿; (*aged*) dúl‿, dúru‿ (n.).
 old man: ógiñ‿dúru‿.
 old woman: ɛ́n‿dúru‿.
 This man is old: ín‿ógığ‿dúrun⌒.
 That cow is old: ín‿tí‿dúrun⌒.
 How old is (s)he (it)? (a) ténn‿úgu‿mıŋkóttɛ̄rrɛ́? (b) ténn‿úmur‿mukóttɛ̄rrɛ́?
 This palm is old: ím‿bénti‿duranóskon⌒.
Omdurmán n. búga‿; umdurmán‿.
omit v.t. wákk(ı).
on adv.
 Come on! támɛn?, pl. támɛndu?
on prep. —ŋ‿kóččır‿; —n‿dógŏr‿; -r‿ after a vowel; -ır‿ after a consonant, but -ro‿ after -r (except of personal pronouns), -lo‿ after -l, -do‿ after -n and personal pronouns. See §§ 4291 ff.
 on this (that): ínıŋ‿kóččır‿.
 Put it on that (yonder): mánıŋ‿kóččır‿úskur⌒.
 It's on the bedstead: áŋgarɛŋ‿kóččır‿bún⌒.
 The pillow is to be on the bedstead: måháddag‿áŋgarɛr‿kúğban⌒.
 X. Where is it? tɛ́r‿ısåırɛ́?
 Y. On the shelf: ráffır⌒.
 Is the food on the table? kál‿súfrar‿bǔná?
 The money is on the table: dúŋgı‿tarabēzar‿bún⌒.
 Put the book on the table: kıtåpkı‿tarabēzar‿úskur⌒.
 The man sits on the mat: (a) ógığ‿níbıdır‿ágın⌒; (b) ógığ‿níbıdır‿tégın⌒.
 It lay on the road: dárím-tūr‿bǔgon⌒.
 Have you put the water on the fire? ɛr‿ɛ́ssıg‿ígır‿uskúrkoná?
 It's on the wound: tɛr‿kŏrro⌒.
 It's on the line: tɛr‿úllo⌒.
 It's on the plate: tɛr‿sahándo⌒.
 Go on the donkey: hánugɛn‿nók⌒.
 Bring it on a donkey: hánugɛd‿dɛ́tta⌒.
 Put it on the horse: kåğır‿úskur⌒.
 Put it on the horses: kåğlır‿úskur⌒ (kåğır…).
 on Saturday: sámtɛg‿ (-gı‿).
 (S)he (it) came on Saturday: sámtɛt‿tågon⌒.
 On seeing this (s)he (it) came out: íŋgı‿nalobbɛ́lkon⌒.
on account of prep. —n‿íllår‿ (-lar‿, -lɛr‿).
on (ahead), get (go, come) v.i. ógolan-.
on one, carry (have) v.t. kåg.
 I've no money on me: (a) åı‿dúŋgı-wɛ̄k‿kågmunun⌒; (b) åı‿dúŋgık‿kågmunun⌒.
 Have you some money on you? (a) ɛr‿dúŋgı-wɛ̄k‿kågná?, (b) ɛr‿dúŋgık‿kågná?
on, put v.t. (*wear*) dɛ́g; (*superimpose*) kúğur.
 Put the food on the table: kálgı‿súfrar‿úskur⌒.
on top of prep. —ŋ‿kóččır‿; —n‿dógŏr‿.
once num. adv. gırrɛ̆g‿.
 at once: (*immediately*) súttɛ‿; (*on the same occasion*) márra‿wɛ́gɛd‿.
 Go at once! súttɛ‿nogó!, pl. súttɛ‿nogówwɛ!
 Don't carry a lot of stuff all at once: take half: áfɛš‿dıgrít‿tókkom‿márra‿wɛ́gɛs‿sókkɛmɛn: tórtıs‿sókkɛ⌒.
one card. num. wɛ̄r‿.
 It's all one (the same, indifferent): mállɛ‿wɛ̄run⌒.
 Bring the lower one: togóndıg‿ɛ́tta⌒.
 Is there an open one? kúzbúl-lɛ̄r‿dåna?
 X. Where is the snake? kåg‿sɛ́?
 Y. The one I killed? åı‿bɛsió?
 Pull them out one by one: wɛrwɛ́gɛd‿dúkki⌒.
one-eyed adj. góška‿ (-ko‿).
onion n. bíllɛ‿.
only adv. (*merely*) súdır‿; (*just*) bés‿; (*solely*) kól‿.
 Bring two only: ówwıg‿ɛ́tta‿bés⌒.
 I want eggs only, nothing else: kúmbu‿kólgı‿dólli, šɛ́jı‿ɛččɛ́lgı‿dólmunun⌒.
 Tell him to bring the horse only: káčkı‿tɛkkólg‿ɛ́ttaran⌒.
 Give me this at breakfast only: íŋg‿åıgı‿futūr-kóllo‿dɛ́n⌒.
open v.t. kús.
 They have opened it (them): kusóskoran⌒.
 Show it to me before you open it: kúsmɛŋgon‿åıg‿amínti⌒.
 Open the door for me: åıgı‿kåk‿kúzdɛn⌒.
open, leave v.t. kusmúg.
 Leave it open: kusmúk⌒.
 Don't leave it open: tókkoŋ‿kusmúgmɛn⌒.
 Don't leave my door open: tókkon‿åŋ‿kobítkı‿kusmúgmɛn⌒.
opening n. (*aperture*) ágıl‿, úbbɛd‿.
 I want an opening in the fence: zɛ́rbɛr‿agíl-lɛ̄d‿dólli⌒.
opening, instrument for n. kúšar‿.
opinion n. ɛ́rıg‿.
opposite prep. ‿gɛ́bɛl‿ (following the genitive); ‿gɛbéllo‿ (following the genitive).
 It's opposite the door: (a) båm‿gɛ́bɛlun⌒; (b) båm‿gɛbéllo⌒.
 His (her) house is opposite the police-station: (a) téŋ‿kå‿mɛ́rkɛzŋ‿gɛ́bɛlun⌒; (b) téŋ‿kå‿mɛ́rkɛzŋ‿gɛbéllo⌒.
oppressive adj. dúllo‿.
opulence n. ırğɛ́nkanɛ‿ (-ɛ́ŋk-).
opulent adj. ırğɛ́n‿.
or conj. wálla‿.
 X. Has ɣáli come or ɣoθmán? álı‿tågoná‿wáll‿ɛsmán?
 Y. Neither ɣáli nor ɣoθmán has come: wál‿álı‿wáll‿ɛsmán‿tågomunan⌒.
 Is this today's or tomorrow's? ín‿ınnow-wındrɛ́‿wáll‿asándrɛ́?
 Bring two or three knives: kánd‿ówwı‿tóskıg‿ɛ́tta⌒.
 Don't fold it or you'll break it: tókkon‿árbırmɛn, bıtómbın⌒.
order n. (*command*) ámur‿; (*disposition*) tartíb‿ (tår-, tɛr-).
 Has an order been issued? ámur‿bɛlóskoná?
 The Government has issued orders: hukúm‿awāmírk‿ōsóskon⌒.
 This is in good order: íŋ‿gɛ́nun⌒.
order v.t. (*bid*) kallıfɛ́r‿ (kɛl-).
Orion's belt n. tóska‿.
oscillate v.i. kɛ́rkɛr.
Osmān (ɣoθmān) n. ɛsmán‿.
ostrich n. naám‿.
other adj. (*different*) ɛ́ččɛl‿; (*not at hand*) mán‿; (*of two*) őwwínt(ı)‿ (ǒuwín-, ‿‿‿).
 I want this one; if you want a light, take that other one: åı‿íŋgı‿dólli; ɛr‿ígkı‿dólkım‿máŋgı‿sókkɛ‿.
 X. Did they go? nókkorandɛ́?
 Y. Some went, others didn't: wɛ́rı‿nókkoran, wɛ́rı‿nókkomunan⌒.
 Do it every other day: jóm‿mɛ́w-wakkıg‿ówwıntír‿åu⌒.
ought
 You ought to do this: ín‿ɛ́ddo‿kúğın⌒.
 You ought to have done this: ín‿ɛ́ddo‿kúčkon⌒.
 You ought to have gone: (a) nógran‿ɛ́ddo‿kúčkon⌒; (b) nogíd‿ɛ́ddo‿kúčkon⌒.
 The sheikh ought to do it: samíllo‿kúğın⌒.
 The sheikh ought to have done it: samíllo‿kúčkon⌒.
 The sheikh ought to have come: (a) tåran‿samíllo‿kúčkon⌒; (b) tårīd‿samíllo‿kúčkon⌒.
 It's a good thing if (s)he sends it: (s)he ought to: išıntíkkın‿sɛ́rēn: téddo‿kúğın⌒.
our poss. pron. ánn‿v., án‿c.
 our salt: ánn‿úmbud‿.
 our money: án‿dúŋg(ı)‿.
 our house: áŋ‿kå‿.
 our country: ám‿bɛ́lɛd‿.
ours abs. poss. pron. ánd(ı)‿.
 It's ours: andín⌒.
 Is it ours? andırɛ́?
 It's not ours: ándımunun⌒.
 Isn't it ours? ándımɛn?
 They're ours: ándınčin⌒.

Are they ours? ándınčıré?
They're not ours: andínčımunan⌢.
Aren't they ours? andínčımendan?
Is this (that) ours? (a) ín⌣ándıré? (b) ín⌣ándı⌣té? (*Is this the one that is ours?*).
Are these (those) ours? íngu⌣ándınčıré?
out adv.
  We are now on our way out: (a) ar⌣ékkenɛ⌣bélbūru⌢; (b) ar⌣ékkenɛ⌣bóččambūru⌢.
  Don't let him (her, it) out: tókkom⌣bélıŋgırmen⌢.
  Don't let them out: tókkom⌣béllaŋgırmen⌢.
out, bring (take) v.t. ós.
  Bring (pl.) the bedstead out of the house: áŋgarɛk⌣kårtŏn⌣óswɛ⌢.
out, come (get) v.i. bél.
  I can't get out: āı⌣ɛskıbélmunun⌢.
out, go v.i. (*issue*) bél, bóččan-; (*be extinguished*) dí.
  I am going out now: ékkenɛ⌣bıbélli⌢.
  I'm just going (coming) out: āı⌣bɛlɛdólli⌢.
  I'm going out: āı⌣bóččandi⌢.
  The fire has gone out: íg⌣díoskon⌢.
out, let (send) v.t. bɛlkídd(ı); bɛlíŋgır.
out of prep. -rtŏn⌣ after a vowel; -ırtŏn⌣ after a consonant, but -dotŏn⌣ after -n, -lotŏn⌣ after -l, -rotŏn⌣ after -r.
  It feeds out of my hand: ánn⌣írtŏn⌣kálın⌢.
  Do they make it out of palm-leaves? haúrtertŏn⌣áurandé?
  out of the market: sůgırtŏn⌣.
  out of the coffee: búndotŏn⌣.
  out of the desert: ǧɛbéllotŏn⌣.
  out of the town: bɛndérrotŏn⌣.
out, put v.t. (*cause to issue*) ós; (*extinguish*) bɛ́.
  Put (pl.) the chairs out: kursínčıg⌣óswɛ⌢.
  Put the light out: íkkı⌣bé⌢.
out, take v.t. ós; (*extract*) kůl, dúkk(ı).
  Take the things out of the pockets: šɛjínčıǧ⌣ǧɛbırtŏn⌣ós⌢.
  Take a bottle out of the box: gɛzáz-zēs⌣sandůgırtŏŋ⌣kůl⌢.
  Did he take your tooth out? én⌣nélgı⌣dúkkıgoná?
outer (outside) adj. boččínd(ı)⌣.
outside adv. bóčči⌣; bóččıgɛd⌣; bárrår⌣.
  Take this dog outside: íw⌣wélgı⌣bóččır⌣ós⌢.
  (S)he sits outside: bóččıgɛd⌣ágın⌢.
  Wait outside: bóččıgɛt⌣ték⌢, pl. bóččıgɛt⌣tēgwé⌢.
  X. Where is the table? tarabéza⌣sé?
  Y. It's outside: bárrår⌣bůn⌢.
  Z. It's outside: bóččır⌣bůn⌢.
outside n. bóčč(ı)⌣.
outside (of) prep. —m⌣bóččır⌣.
oval adj. kúmbukırı⌣.
oven n. fúrun⌣.
over adv.
  When dinner is over let him (her) bring coffee: áša⌣halásaŋkıŋ⌣gáhwag⌣éttaran⌢.
over prep. —n⌣dógŏr⌣.
overcast, become v.i. dúg.
  The sky is overcast: séma⌣dúgbůn⌢.
overseer n. (*of irrigable estate*) sámɛd⌣.

overtake v.t. důr.
owe
  I owe you two pounds: ɛr⌣áddo⌣gín⌣ówwık⌣kón⌢.
  I owe him (her) two pounds: tɛr⌣áddo⌣gín⌣ówwık⌣kón⌢.
  I owe you (pl.) two pounds: ır⌣áddo⌣gín⌣ówwık⌣kóru⌢.
  I owe them two pounds: tır⌣áddo⌣gín⌣ówwık⌣kóran⌢.
  You owe me two pounds: āı⌣éddo⌣gín⌣ówwık⌣kóri⌢.
  (S)he owes me two pounds: āı⌣téddo⌣gín⌣ówwık⌣kóri⌢.
  You (pl.) owe me two pounds: āı⌣íddo⌣gín⌣ówwık⌣kóri⌢.
  They owe me two pounds: āı⌣tíddo⌣gín⌣ówwık⌣kóri⌢.
  How much do we owe you? ɛr⌣áddo⌣mukóttēk⌣kón?
  How much do you owe him (her)? tɛr⌣éddo⌣mıŋkóttēk⌣kón?
  What does (s)he owe you? ɛr⌣téddo⌣míŋgo⌣kón?
owl n. bůma⌣.
own adj. use genitive of reflexive pronoun (§ 2689).
  (S)he's his (her) own enemy: tɛr⌣ténnān⌣ádun⌢.
own v.t. kó.
owner n. tírt(ı)⌣.
ownerless adj. tırtıkómɛnıl⌣.

pace n.
  They went at a good pace: šıddagɛd-dágoran⌢.
packet n. tárıd⌣.
pad n. (*in water-wheel*) alláǧa⌣.
paddle v.t. wåu (wåw, wåu).
padlock n. gífıl⌣; tábla⌣.
page n. (*of book*) táraga⌣.
pail n. ǧérdɛl⌣.
pain n. óddɛ⌣.
  I have a pain in my back: āıg⌣án-ǧɛr⌣óddın⌢.
pain, be in v.i. óddıbü-; wéǧambü-.
paint n. bůja⌣.
paint v.t. bůjaǧ⌣ǧóm.
  Paint the small boat: kumtóttı⌣bůjaǧ⌣ǧóm⌢.
painting n. (*picture*) tɛswíra⌣.
palate n. hánag⌣.
pale adj. arogíttɛl⌣.
palm n. (*date-*) bént(ı)⌣; (*dōm-*) hámbu⌣; (*of hand*) ín-tu⌣.
palm-leaf n. hắu(ı)rtɛ⌣.
  palm-leaf fibre: awíččɛ⌣.
palm-trunk n. úmbu⌣.
pamper v.t. gåškır.
pan n. (*vessel*) dåd(ı)⌣ (dåddd(ı)⌣); (*depression in ground*) hód⌣.
pantry n. fís⌣.
paper n. wárag⌣ (wárag⌣).
  Have you got (the) paper? wárag⌣énnaré?
parcel n. tárıd⌣.
pardon v.t. āfé.
  I beg your pardon: mālɛ́š⌢.
parlour n. sála⌣.
particularly adv. hususan (xu-).
partner n. šɛríg⌣.
pasha n. båša⌣ (-šå⌣).

pass v.i. (*elapse*) nóg.
  Four days have passed and three are left: nɛhår⌣kémıs⌣nogóskon, tóskı⌣tébın⌢.
pass v.t. gašɛ́; (*hand*) ɛttå (éttå; § 3855), ɛbbıdå (§ 3851).
  Pass the house: kåg⌣gašé⌢, pl. kåg⌣gašɛ́wɛ⌢.
  Have we passed it? gašɛ́goruá?
  Pass the salt: umbúdk⌣étta⌢.
pass across v.t. múkk(ı).
pass along v.i. ǧů; då-.
Passer rufidorsalis n. zɛrzůr⌣.
pasture v.i. kål.
  The goats pasture: úrtı⌣kálın⌢.
pasture (tend at) v.t. fu (fᵘ, fw).
  The boy pastures the goats and sheep: bıtån⌣urtínčıǧ⌣íwırırın⌢.
pat v.t. tóbbɛ.
path n. dárıb⌣ (dár-, dér-, -rub); síkkɛ⌣.
patience n. sabrɛ́rar⌣ (-rår⌣); sabrɛrɛ́íd⌣.
patience, have v.i. ǧóbbɛ; sabrɛ́.
pay n. úǧrɛ⌣ (-rå⌣, -ra⌣), kıråı⌣; (*salary*) mahíja⌣ (-jå⌣, -ja⌣).
  What pay do you want? mahíja⌣mukóttēd⌣dólın⌢?
pay v.t. dɛfɛ́; (*to the speaker*) dɛfɛ́dɛn; (*to other than speaker*) dɛfɛ́tır.
  when I paid: āı⌣dɛfɛ́sı⌣wɛkídk(ı)⌣.
  I shall pay: āı⌣bıdɛfɛ́rı⌢.
  Pay me the money: āıgı⌣důŋgıd⌣dɛfɛ́dɛn⌢.
  Pay them the money: tírgı⌣důŋgıd⌣dɛfɛ́tırır⌢.
  I shall pay three pounds a month: āı⌣šahárro⌣gínɛ⌣tóskıb⌣buskúddi⌢.
  What monthly rent is (s)he paying? šahárro⌣úǧra⌣mukóttēg⌣ågúskurın? (šahárk⌣úǧra⌣...).
  I pay five piastres a day: ugrɛ́sır⌣gírıš⌣díčkı⌣dɛfɛ́rın⌢ (ugrɛ́skı⌣gírıš⌣...).
  Have you paid your debts? (a) ɛr⌣én⌣dɛ́nık⌣kópkoná? (b) ɛr⌣én⌣dɛ́nık⌣kobırríkkoná?
  Has (s)he paid his (her) debt? tɛr⌣tén⌣dɛ́ŋgı⌣kópkoná?
pea n. órrɛ⌣ (*chick-pea*).
peace n. salám⌣; géndar⌣ (-dår⌣); gɛndɛ́íd⌣.
peace of mind n. fadabål⌣.
peacemaker n. ɛǧǧwåd⌣.
peacemaking n. bɛ́war⌣ (-wår⌣); bɛwɛ́íd⌣.
peasant n. (*agricultural*) tórbar⌣.
pebble n. kórod⌣.
pedlar n. tɛššåš⌣; súlu⌣.
peel n. kåčč(ı)⌣.
peg n. kóǧır⌣.
pelican n. kårɛkal⌣.
pen n. gálam⌣.
penalty n. ǧíza⌣.
pencil n. galamrasås⌣.
penholder n. gálamn⌣åd⌣.
penis n. kúff(ı)⌣.
Pennisetum cenchroides n. kınıssɛkól⌣.
Pennisetum typhoideum n. éndɛ⌣.
people n. (*persons*) ádɛmı⌣ (ádåmı⌣).
  They counted the people: ádɛmıǧ⌣ırnálkoran⌢.
  Have our people come? (a) án⌣gamánčı⌣tågorandé? (b) án⌣ǧamánčı⌣bıdågorandé?
pepper n. fílfıl⌣.

per prep. (*for each*) -r⌣ (q.v.), or use objective case.
 I shall pay two pounds per mensem: (a) âɪ⌣ šahárro⌣ǧín⌣ówwɪb⌣bɪdɛfɛ́ri⌢; (b) âɪ⌣ šahárkɪ⌣ǧín⌣ówwɪb⌣bɪdɛfɛ́ri⌢.
 How much is it per mensem? (a) šahárro⌣ mukóttɪrɛ́? (b) šahárkɪ⌣mukóttɪrɛ́?
 They pay four piastres per diem: ugrɛ́sɪr⌣ gírɪš⌣kɛmɪsk⌣āddɛfɛ́ran⌢; (ugrɛ́skɪ⌣ gírɪš⌣kɛmɪsk⌣āddɛfɛ́ran⌢).
perceive v.t. (*feel*) hɪssɛ́.
perfect adj. kấmɪl⌣; tamắm⌣ (tàm-, tɛm-).
perforate v.t. úbbuǧ.
perform v.t. áu (áw, áû).
performance n. áwar⌣ (áwàr⌣); ắwíd⌣.
perfumed adj. númmɛl⌣ (´´).
perhaps adv. ɛddór⌣; ɛ́mkɪn⌣.
 Perhaps you won't find him (her, it, them): ɛddór⌣ɛr⌣bɪmísɪrɪn⌢.
 Perhaps there is some: ɛddór⌣dán⌢.
permission n. ízn⌣.
 Don't go without permission: ízŋg⌣ắrmɛŋ- gon⌣tókkon⌣nógmɛn⌢.
permit v.t. múg; use causative (§§ 3663 ff.).
person n. ádɛm⌣ (ádam⌣, ádàm⌣); néfɪs⌣.
 The work requires two persons: ǧɛ́llɪ⌣ néfɪs⌣ówwɪd⌣dólɪn⌢.
 It needs four persons: néfɪs⌣kɛmískɪ⌣ dólɪn⌢.
perspiration n. tɪllátt(ɪ)⌣.
perspire v.i. tíllɛ.
 I am perspiring: âɪ⌣tíllɛbúri⌢.
pestle n. mudág⌣ (múdag⌣).
pet v.t. gáškɪr.
petition n. ardahál⌣.
petition-writer n. ardahálgɪ⌣bǎǧɪl⌣.
petroleum n. ǧáz⌣.
 Put petroleum into this: índo⌣ǧázk⌣ úndur⌢.
petticoat n. tɛnnúra⌣.
Phaseolus mungo n. ašráŋkɛ⌣.
Phaseolus vulgaris n. úgud⌣.
Phoenix dactylifera n. bɛ́nt(ɪ)⌣.
piastre n. gírɪš⌣.
pick to pieces v.t. bíll(ɪ).
pick up v.t. (*lift*) índ(ɪ), sókkɛ; (*gather*) bítt(ɪ).
 Pick up that empty tin (over there) and throw it away: mán⌣ílbɛ⌣sútkɪ⌣sok- karíkkɛ⌢.
 Pick up all this rubbish and take it out: íŋ⌣kášši⌣mállɛb⌣bɪttós⌢.
pickaxe n. šákúš⌣.
picture n. tɛswíra⌣.
piece n. (*small*) hítta⌣ (hétta⌣).
 They will work by the piece, not for a daily wage: híttagɛb⌣bɪšuglɛ́ran, jōmɪ̀jagɛ́m- munun⌢.
piece-work, be on v.i. gāwɪlɛ́rɛdǎg.
pierce v.t. šɛ́g; úbbuǧ.
pig n. hallúf⌣.
pigeon n. kúru⌣; gókka⌣.
pile n. šúna⌣; kóm⌣.
pilgrim n. háǧ⌣.
pilgrimage n. háǧǧ(ɪ)⌣ (háǧɪ⌣, háǧ⌣); héǧǧ(ɪ)⌣ (héǧɪ⌣, héǧ⌣); híǧǧ(ɪ)⌣ (híǧɪ⌣, híǧ⌣).
pill n. dáwan⌣hábba⌣.
pillar n. ɛ́ndɛ⌣; (*of spindle*) núbrom⌣bɛ́r⌣, núbron⌣šúš⌣.
pillow n. mǎhádda⌣ (mah-); (*wooden support*) wɪsáda⌣ (wᵘs-).

pin n. (*small European*) dabbús⌣; (*larger wooden or metal*) nɪččínd(ɪ)⌣.
pincers n. (*large*) kammǎša⌣; (*small*) báskala⌣.
pinch v.t. sunúkk(ɪ).
pipe n. (*tube*) māsúra⌣; (*tobacco-*) kodós⌣, †bíba⌣; (*musical*) zummára⌣.
 X. Does he smoke a pipe? tɛr⌣kodóskɪ⌣níná?
 Y. No, cigarettes: wǎran, sɪǧáran⌣nín⌢.
pit n. kúl⌣.
pity n. ráhma⌣.
pity, have v.i. rahmɛ́.
 I pity him (her): âɪ⌣téddo⌣rahmɛ́ri⌢.
place n. (*position*) ágar⌣, mǎháll(ɪ)⌣ (mah-, mɛhéll(ɪ)); (*region*) ášāɪ⌣.
 Put it in its place: (a) ténn⌣agárr⌣úskur⌢; (b) tém⌣mǎhállɪr⌣úskur⌢.
 Leave it in its place: tém⌣agárro⌣mugó⌢.
 Is it in its place? tér⌣tém⌣mǎhállɪró? (-ɪré?).
place v.t. úskur.
place on v.t. kúǧur.
plain adj. (*clear*) wădah⌣; (*without admixture*) sáda⌣.
plait v.t. áwɪǧ; šír.
plant n. dɛ́ssɛ⌣; (*young*) šétɪl⌣ (šétul⌣), šégɛ⌣.
plant v.t. (*sow*) tɛ́r; (*plant out*) šég.
 Have you planted the seeds? tɛ́rɪt⌣tɛ́rkoná?
 Have you planted the seedlings? šétlɪš⌣ šékkoná?
plantain n. móz⌣.
plate n. sáhan⌣.
platform n. (*in water-wheel, under cattle-track*) ǧíbɪd⌣; (*in water-wheel, under vertical axle*) téw(ɪ)rɛ⌣.
play v.i. kácč(ɪ).
 He plays the drum: nuggáraǧ⌣ǧómɪn⌢.
 He plays on a pipe: zummáraǧ⌣ǧómɪn⌢.
please, (if you) ɛ́m⌣fadíllotōn⌣.
 Please come in (etc. تفضّل*)*: faddɪlé!, pl. faddɪlɛ́wé!
please v.t. bastɛ́gɪr.
pleased adj. mabsúd⌣.
 I am pleased: âɪ⌣mabsúd⌣ɛ́ri⌢.
 I am not pleased: âɪ⌣mabsúdmunun⌢.
 (S)he (it) is not pleased: tɛr⌣mabsúd- munun⌢.
 Are you pleased? ɛr⌣mabsúd¹ré?
 Aren't you pleased? ɛr⌣mabsúdmɛn?
pleased, be v.i. bastɛ́; gúrrɛ.
 I am pleased with you: (a) âɪ⌣éddotōm⌣ bastɛ́gori⌢; (b) âɪ⌣éddotōm⌣mabsúd⌣ éri⌢.
 I am not pleased with you: (a) âɪ⌣éddotōm⌣ bastɛ́gómunun⌢; (b) âɪ⌣éddotōm⌣ mabsúdmunun⌢.
plentiful adj. dígrí⌣ (dɪgrí⌣).
pliant adj. ǧagádɛl⌣ (¯´´, ¯´´).
pliant, be v.i. ǧagádɛ (ǧagádé, ¯´´).
plot n. (*of irrigable ground*) bá⌣, hód⌣; (*conspiracy*) fítnɛ⌣.
plumage n. dílt(ɪ)⌣.
plunder v.t. ɛ́r.
pocket n. ǧɛ́b⌣.
pod n. káčč(ɪ)⌣.
Poecilocerus hieroglyphicus n. hábɪn⌣ báŋga⌣ (hábɪm⌣).
point n. (*sharp end*) kóčč(ɪ)⌣; (*dot*) núgta⌣ (núkta⌣).
 point of knife: kándɪŋ⌣kóčč(ɪ)⌣.
 point of sword: síwɪn⌣kóčč(ɪ)⌣.

poison n. sɛ́m⌣; símm(ɪ)⌣.
poisonous, be v.i. sɛ́mko.
pole n. bɛ́r⌣; (*drawn round by cattle working water-wheel*) túhum⌣ (túgum⌣).
policeman n. áskar⌣; bōlís⌣.
police-station n. mɛ́rkɛz⌣ (mǎr-, -kàz⌣); zabtíjɛ⌣ (zapt-, -jà⌣, -ja⌣).
polish v.t. ǧígid.
pollen n. ɛ́rɛ⌣.
polo n. kúra⌣.
polo-stick n. kúrageǧ⌣ǧómran⌣.
Polypterus sp. n. ɛ́ssɪŋ⌣kǎg⌣; ɛ́ssɪn-tūŋ⌣ kǎg⌣.
pond n. mɛ́rɛ⌣.
pony n. kǎg⌣.
pool n. (*long*) básɛ⌣; (*more or less circular*) mɛ́rɛ⌣.
poor adj. fógɪr⌣; mɛskín⌣.
porcupine n. kɪnɪssɛkól⌣; abšóg⌣.
Port Sudan n. bursūdán⌣.
porter n. (*carrier*) attál⌣.
portfolio n. šǎntá⌣ (šán-, -ta⌣).
portmanteau n. šǎntá⌣ (šán-, -ta⌣).
position n. ágar⌣; árɪg⌣.
possess v.t. kó.
possibly adv. ɛddór⌣; ɛ́mkɪn⌣.
post n. (*upright*) múgdo⌣ (búgdo⌣); (*postal service*) bústa⌣.
 Take this to the post: íŋgɪ⌣bústar⌣óǧi⌢.
 There is a letter for the post: ǧawáb⌣bēr⌣ bústan⌣íllár⌣dán⌢.
 There are some letters for the post: ǧawábɪ⌣ bústan⌣íllɛr⌣dáran⌢.
 (S)he (it) won't catch the post: bústab⌣ bɪdúrmunun⌢.
 (S)he (it) is to (must) catch the post: bústad⌣ dúran⌢.
posterior adj. abáŋd(ɪ)⌣.
posterior n. (*buttocks*) abág⌣.
postmaster n. bústan⌣wakíl⌣ (-taw⌣wak-, ⌣wǎk-, ⌣wɛk-).
post-office n. bústam⌣máktab⌣.
pot n. ɪbríg⌣; bɛrrád⌣ (bàr-, bar-); (*earthenware*) súlɛ⌣.
potato n. batátɪs⌣.
potter n. búgdo⌣.
 I want the potter: búgdod⌣dólli⌢.
pound n. (*of money*) ǧíné⌣; (*weight*) rátul⌣.
pound v.t. šókk(ɪ); túkk(ɪ).
pour (out, away) v.t. bóg.
 Pour it out (away): bók⌢, pl. bógwɛ⌢.
 Don't pour it out (away): tókkom⌣ bógmɛn⌢, pl. tókkom⌣bógmɛwwɛ⌢.
 Pour this away: íŋgɪ⌣bók⌢.
 It is pouring (with rain): abbógɪn⌢.
powerful adj. (*physically*) kógor⌣.
powerless adj. ǎǧɪz⌣.
praise v.t. hamdɛ́.
 I praise God: ártɪh⌣hamdɛ́ri⌢.
 Praise be to God! (a) hámdɪlɪllá! (b) hám- dɪlla!
pray v.i. sɪgídd(ɪ), sallɛ́; v.t. (*beg*) bɛ́dd(ɪ).
prayer n. sɪgíddar⌣ (-dǎr⌣); sɪgɪddíd⌣; béddar⌣ (-dǎr⌣); bɛddíd⌣.
pregnant adj. mɛ́u⌣ (mɛ́w⌣).
 Is she pregnant? tɛr⌣mɛ́wré?
prepare v.t. haddɪrɛ́; haddɪrɛ́gɪr.
prepuce n. kúffɪn⌣úrn⌣ǎǧɪn⌣.
present n. (*gift*) hadíjɛ⌣ (-já⌣, -ja⌣).
present v.t. (*submit*) gɛddɪmɛ́ (-dumɛ́).
present, be v.i. (*of persons*) ǎg; (*of persons or things*) dá-, dábŭ-.

Was a witness present? šăhíd-dɛr‿ăkkoná?
Who was present? ní‿dăbugõ?
present, at adv. ékkɛnɛ‿; ékkɛnɛg‿ (-ɛgi⌒).
 That's enough for the present: ín‿ɛkkɛnɛn‿ íllár‿kɛfɛ́n⌒.
press v.t. ğákk(ı); úrr(ı).
press against v.t. káll(ı).
pressing (urgent), be v.i. sumárk(ı).
prevent v.t. mír.
previous adj. ogólnd(ı)‿ (ogónd(ı)‿); ŏwwélnd(ı)‿; gɛdím‿; zamánd(ı)‿ (zám-, zɛm-, -mānínd(ı)‿).
previously adv. ogóllo‿; ŏwwéllo‿; gabúllo‿; zamáŋg(ı)‿ (zám-, zɛm-).
price n. témɛn‿.
 What is the price? tén‿témɛm‿mukóttɛ̄rré?
 X. *What price did you buy at?* mukottɛ́gɛğ‿ğáŋkon? (s.v. ğán).
 Y. *At three dollars:* rıjál‿tóskıgé⌒.
prick v.t. šég.
prickle n. kınɪ́ssɛ‿.
prison n. sı́ğın‿.
 (S)*he is in prison:* sığındó⌒.
 Put him (her) into prison: sığínd‿úndur⌒.
prisoner n. (*confined*) kóbbūl‿; (*bound*) mŏ́rbūl‿.
privy n. uññíŋ-kă‿.
prize n. mukáfa‿.
probably adv. ɛddór‿.
 X. *Where is (s)he?* tér‿sɛ́?
 Y. *Probably at his (her) house:* ɛddór‿ tén‿kár‿ăgın⌒.
proceed v.i. ğú, dá-; (*go*) nóg.
produce v.t. wăndıgır.
profit n. (*gain*) máksăb‿ (méksɛb‿); (*advantage*) fáıda‿ (fáıda‿), faıdád‿.
profitable adj. faıdakŏ́l‿ (faıdakōl‿).
prohibit v.t. hağğırɛ́.
 It is prohibited: hağğırɛ́būn⌒.
promise
 They promised to send a man: ogíğ-ğēb‿ bıšıntídd‿ɛ́goran⌒.
prop n. éndɛ‿.
prop (up) v.t. sɛndɛ́.
properly adv. use sɛrē-complexes.
 Open it properly: sɛrēgırkús⌒.
 Is it properly shut? (a) sɛraŋkóbbūná? (b) sɛrēgırkóbbūná?
properly, do v.t. sɛrēgıráu (-áw, -áu).
prophet n. nébı‿.
 the Prophet: énnébı‿.
 the Prophet Muḥámmad: ɛnnɛ́m‿mohámmɛd‿.
propinquity n. ɛgétt(ı)‿.
propound v.t. íğ.
prosper v.i. hɛ́ran-; hɛ́rambŭ-.
prosperity n. hɛ́r‿.
prostitute n. dɛññára‿.
proud adj. (*in good and bad sense*) ādúlkōl‿; (*in bad sense*) nɛfɪsdúlkōl‿.
proud, be v.i. (*in good and bad sense*) ādūlkó-; (*in bad sense*) nɛfɪsdúlko.
pubes n. (*of male*) kúffın‿dílt(ı)‿, sorón‿ dílt(ı)‿; (*of female*) kumáttɛn‿dílt(ı)‿.
puff v.t. úffɛ.
pull v.t. tóllɛ.
 Pull the strap tight and fasten it: sɛ́rkı‿ tollɛdígır⌒.
 Pull yourself together: ɛn‿hɛ́lg‿áŋgır⌒.
pull down v.t. (*demolish*) wíll(ı); bŏ́rkığ.
pull out v.t. ós; dúkk(ı).

pull up v.t. dogŏgırtóllɛ.
punctual
 X. *Is the train punctual?* gátır‿tɛ́m‿ mawaídırɛ́?
 Y. *No, it's late:* wăran, ahhɛrébūn⌒.
puncture v.t. šég.
punish v.t. ğăzɛ́.
punishment n. ğíza‿.
pupil n. kŭ́rıl‿, hīrán‿; (*of eye*) míssıŋ‿ gédɛ‿.
puppy n. wɛln-tŏ́d‿ (wélntōd‿, wɛltōd‿, wɛntōd‿, ᷉‿).
pure adj. (*without admixture*) sáda‿ (q.v.).
purge v.t. (*cause to defecate*) ússıŋgır (᷉‿).
purr v.i. ñúrr(ı); fórrɛ.
purse n. kís‿.
purslane n. ğabárkal‿ (-bákkal‿).
pus n. únčɛ‿.
push v.t. káll(ı).
put v.t. úskur.
 Put it here: índ‿úskur, pl. índ‿uskúrwɛ⌒.
 Don't put it here: tókkon‿índ‿uskúrmɛn⌒, pl. ...‿uskúrmɛwwɛ⌒.
 Put it (over) there: mánd‿úskur⌒.
 Don't put it (over) there: tókkom‿mánd‿ uskúrmɛn⌒.
 Put this like this (so, like that): íŋg‿íŋk‿ úskur⌒.
 Put it so (like this, like that): tékk‿úskur⌒ (=tékké‿úskur⌒).
 Where did (have) you put it? ɛr‿sáır‿ uskúrkó?
put back v.t. (*return*) wídɛgır (wídɛgır, wᵘd-); (*put behind*) abágkır (-ákkır).
put by v.t. (*save*) waffırɛ́.
put in(to) v.t. úndur.
 Put him (her, it) in: úndur⌒, pl. undúrwɛ⌒.
 Put this in: íŋg‿úndur⌒, pl. íŋg‿undúrwɛ⌒.
 Put these in: íŋgug‿úndurır⌒, pl. íŋgug‿ undurívvɛ⌒.
 Put it into the portmanteau: šántăr‿ úndur⌒.
 What are they putting in? míŋg‿ăgundúddan?
put on v.t. (*superimpose*) kúğur; (*wear*) dég.
 Put the kettle on (sc. *the fire*): barrádkı‿ kúğur⌒.
 Put the baggage on (*the animal's back*): (a) afɛ́škı‿kúğur⌒; (b) afɛ́škı‿dék⌒.
 Put the baggage on the donkey: afɛ́škı‿ hánuŋ‿kóččır‿kúğur⌒.
 Has he put the water on? (a, *the kettle on the fire*): ɛ́ssık‿kuğúrkoná? (b, *the tank or skin on the camel*): ɛ́ssıd‿dékkoná?
 Put your turban on: ɛ́nn‿ímmad‿dék⌒.
 Let him put on his turban: ténn‿ímmad‿ dégan⌒.
 Put your clothes on: ɛŋ‿kádɛd‿dék⌒.
 Put this cloth on: íŋ‿kádɛd‿dék⌒.
 I am going to put this on (wear it): áı‿íŋgı‿ bıdégri⌒.
 Tell him (her) to put the eggs on the fire (i.e. *to cook them*): kúmbunčıg‿íğır‿kúğuran⌒.
put out v.t. (*extinguish*) bɛ́; (*cause to issue*) ós.
 Put the light out: íğkı‿bé⌒.
 Let ʒθmán go and put the light out: ɛsmáŋg‿íkkı‿ğubɛ́ran⌒.
 Put the dog out: wélg‿ós⌒.
 Put your tongue out: ɛn‿nétkı‿kúl⌒.

put up with v.t. (*tolerate*) sabrɛ́.
 We shall not put up with it: ar‿bısabrɛ́munun⌒.
pyjamas n. uğúŋ‿kádɛ‿.
pyramid n. háram‿.

quantity n. kótt(ı)‿; gédır‿.
quarrel n. támugıd‿; (*noisy*) ğáwwɛ‿ (ğáuwɛ‿).
quarrel v.i. támug, šăkılɛ́, šɛklɛ́; (*noisily*) ğáww(ı) (ğáuw(ı), -wᵘ).
 Don't quarrel with him (her): (a) tókkon‿ tékkonon‿támugmɛn⌒; (b) tókkon‿ tékkonon‿šăkılɛ́mɛn⌒.
quarter n. (¼) kɛ́msırɛ‿; rúbu‿.
question n. íddar‿ (-dăr‿); ıddíd‿; síkkar‿ (-kăr‿); sıkkíd‿.
 Don't ask questions: tókkon‿síkkımɛn⌒.
quick
 Be quick! súttɛ!, pl. súttɛwé!
quickly adv. súttɛ‿.
 Go quickly! súttɛ‿nók!, pl. súttɛ‿nógwé!
quiet
 Keep quiet! kıttottɛ́p!, pl. -tɛ́bwé!
 Tell him (her) to keep quiet: kıttottɛ́ban⌒.
 Tell them to keep quiet: kıttottɛ́bwan⌒.
quiet (silent), be v.i. kíttɛ.
 Be quiet! kíttɛ!, pl. kíttɛwé! (*more forcibly*) kíttɛmɛn?, pl. kíttɛmɛndu?
 I said 'be quiet!' kíttɛr‿ɛgóri⌒.
 I said 'be (pl.) quiet!' kíttɛw‿ɛgóri⌒.
quiet v.t. rɛjjıhɛ́.
quinine n. kína‿.
quite adv. hălıs‿ (xă-).
quiver v.i. kɛ́rkɛr.

race n. (*tribe*) ğíns(ı)‿ (ğínıs‿).
racquet n. kúragɛğ‿ğómran‿.
rag n. bílañ‿.
rage n. sínnɛrar‿ (-răr‿); sınnɛríd‿; zălɛ́‿.
 (S)*he is in a rage:* (a) sínnɛbūn⌒; (b) zălɛ́būn⌒.
rail n. (*of railway*) gadíb‿.
rain n. áru‿.
 Is it going to rain? (*now*) bōgɛdolna? (*now or later*) áru‿butáná?
 X. *Will it rain today?* ınnŏ́wwıg‿áru‿ bušúgurná? (lit. *Will rain descend today?*).
 Y. *No, it won't:* wăran, butámun⌒ (lit. *No, it will not come*).
 If it threatens to rain, take this away: bōgɛdólkın‿íŋgı‿sókkɛ⌒.
rainbow n. amrós‿ (amºrós‿, armós‿); káğıb‿bɛ́l‿.
raise v.t. dogŏ́gır; (*lift*) sókkɛ, índ(ı).
rake (*toothless, for levelling*) n. élbıl‿; wăsu‿.
ram n. dóñır‿.
ramble v.i. wíd; dáğı.
rapid n. (*cataract*) šɛllál‿.
rapidly adv. súttɛ‿.
 They walk very rapidly: (a) bagăšɛ‿ bagăšɛ‿nógran⌒; (b) tălıñ-tálıñ‿nógran⌒.
rash n. bélt(ı)‿.
rat n. ğígır‿.
rate
 It is moving at a good rate (pace): šıd-dagéddan⌒.

rather
 Tell him (her) to make the tea rather strong: šáıgıⵡkınnɛ́dⵡdúllogıranⵒ.
rattle n. kášáṵ.
rattle v.i. káraṵ; kórou; kúrub.
raven n. gurábⵡ.
raven-vulture n. gógⵡ.
ravine n. hórⵡ.
raw adj. déss(ı)ⵡ.
 The meat is raw: kúsuⵡdéssınⵒ.
 Bring a raw egg: kúmbuⵡdéssı-wēgⵡéttaⵒ.
razor n. gáññırⵡ.
reach v.t. dúr.
read v.t. gɛrjɛ́ (gɛrɛ́).
 Can you read? ɛrⵡuñurgɛrjɛ́ná?
 Let him (her) read this: tékkⵡíŋgıⵡgɛrjɛ́ranⵒ.
ready adj. hádırⵡ.
 When I am ready I shall come: áıⵡhādırándımⵡbádırⵡbıtárıⵒ.
 When they are ready let them come: tırⵡhādırándanⵡtátⵡtáwanⵒ.
 Get lunch ready: gádahⵡhaddırɛ́gırⵒ.
 When dinner is ready bring it: ášaⵡhādıráŋkınⵡɛ́ttaⵒ.
really
 It really is sugar, though it looks like flour: súkkarⵡɛ́ŋgonⵡnórtıgⵡgálıgınⵒ (ⵡnórtıgálıgınⵒ, ⵡnórtıgálıgılunⵒ).
reap v.t. mútt(ı); ğór.
rear n. (hinder part) ğɛrⵡ; (latrine) úññíŋkaⵡ.
rear v.t. dóñ.
reason n. (intelligence) ɛ́rıgⵡ; (cause) sébɛbⵡ (sábábⵡ).
 The dog is barking for no reason: wélⵡluzúmkıññıgır-āgúkkınⵒ.
reasonable adj. (sensible) ɛrıkátt(ı)ⵡ.
rebellion n. fítnɛⵡ.
recede v.i. wárran-.
receipt (written acknowledgment of) n. wésılⵡ (wás-, wās-).
receive v.t. (take over) ıstɛlɛmɛ́.
 Did you receive the money? dúŋgıgⵡıstɛlɛmɛ́goná?
 I have received the money: dúŋgıgⵡıstɛlɛmɛ̄rɛdágrıⵒ.
receptacle n. (small) ílbɛⵡ.
reception-room n. sálaⵡ.
recite v.t. gɛrjɛ́ (gɛrɛ́).
reckon v.t. hāsıbɛ́.
reckoning n. hısábⵡ.
recognize v.t. úñur.
 When I saw him (her, it) I recognized him (her, it): áıⵡtékkıⵡnálsıⵡwɛkíttıⵡuñuróskorıⵒ.
reconcile v.t. bɛ́u (bɛ́w, bɛ́u).
reconciler n. ɛğğwád̄ⵡ.
recover v.i. (from illness) kómban-; wajjɛ́.
red adj. gɛ́lɛⵡ.
reduce v.t. (make small) kíññagır.
 They will probably reduce his (her) punishment: ɛddórⵡténⵡğızabⵡbıšórogıddanⵒ.
reed n. góuⵡ (gówⵡ); gówwɛⵡ; dísⵡ.
refuse n. kášš(ı)ⵡ; kawíšⵡ.
refuse v.i. món; kɛččnɛ́.
region n. ášáıⵡ.
register n. dáftárⵡ (dáftarⵡ, déftɛrⵡ).
register v.t. (at post-office) sōkɛrɛ́.
regret n. zálⵡ.

regret v.t. nɛdmɛ́.
regulation n. gānúnⵡ.
rejoice v.i. bastɛ́; gúrrɛ.
relate v.t. íg.
relax v.i. ğagádɛ (ğagádɛ, ˊˊˊ).
relax v.t. ğagádɛgır (ğagádɛgır, ˊˊˊ).
relaxed adj. (soft) ğagádɛlⵡ (ğagádɛlⵡ, ˊˊˊ).
release v.t. kús.
 Release the dog: wélgıⵡkúsⵒ.
remain v.i. (wait) íñır (ıñír), ɛrğɛ́ (ɛrɛğɛ́, ɛrɛğğɛ́, ɛrığɛ́); (wait, remain over) tɛ́b, fadlɛ́; (remain sitting) ág, tɛ́g.
 Four days have gone and seven remain: nɛhárⵡkɛ́mısⵡnogóskon, kólotⵡtɛ́bınⵒ.
remain behind v.i. fadlɛ́.
remark n. wɛ́rɛⵡ.
remember v.t. ğílle.
 I don't remember: áıⵡğíllɛmunūnⵒ.
 Don't you remember? ɛrⵡğíllɛmɛn?
 Do you remember where (s)he put it? tɛrⵡısáırⵡuskúrsıŋⵡɛrⵡğíllɛná?
remind v.t. ğíllɛgır.
 Remind me: áıgıⵡğíllɛgırⵒ.
 Remind me of this: áıgⵡíŋgıⵡğíllɛgır.
 Remind me to give it to him (her): áıgıⵡğíllɛgırⵡáıⵡtékkıⵡtíddiⵒ (§6239).
 Remind me that I (now) gave it to him (her): áıⵡtékkıⵡtíddigⵡáıgıⵡğíllɛgırⵒ.
remote adj. wárr(ı)ⵡ.
remove v.t. sókkɛ; ārɛnnóg; ındɛnnóg; ɛğğú; índ(ı).
 Has (s)he removed it (them)? sokkɛ́dkona?
 (S)he is removing it (them): āgɛğğúnⵒ.
renovate v.t. ɛ́rkır.
rent n. úğrɛⵡ (-rāⵡ, -raⵡ).
 What is the rent of it? ténnⵡúğrɛⵡ mıŋkóttırɛ́?
 What is the rent of this house? íŋⵡkánⵡ úğrɛⵡmukóttērrɛ́?
repair v.t. géndıgır.
repent v.t. nɛdmɛ́.
reply n. rádd(ı)ⵡ (réd-).
reply v.i. rāddɛ́ (rɛd-).
reply to v.t. wıdɛgır (wıdɛg-, wᵘdɛg-); wıdɛŋgır (wᵘd-, wídɛŋgır); (to speaker) wıdɛgrɛ́m (wᵘdɛ́-); (to other than the speaker) wıdɛ́grırtır (wᵘdɛ́-).
report n. (what is said) wɛ́rɛⵡ, hábarⵡ; (sound of explosion) hízⵡ, híss(ı)ⵡ.
 Where is this report from? ínⵡhábarⵡ ısáırtōndɛ́?
 Did you hear the report of a gun? (a) búndunⵡhískıⵡgığírkoná? (b) búndunⵡhíssıgⵡgığírkoná?
 Didn't you hear the report of a gun? (a) búndunⵡhískıⵡgığırkomɛn? (b) búndunⵡhíssıgⵡgığírkomɛn?
repose n. túrbar (-bárⵡ); turbídⵡ; ráhaⵡ.
repose v.i. túrb(ı) (túbb(ı)).
representative n. wakílⵡ (wák-, wɛk-).
require v.t. (demand) talabɛ́ (tálábɛ́); (want) dól.
requital n. ğızaⵡ.
requite v.t. ğazɛ́.
rescue v.t. hallısɛ́.
resemble v.t. gálıgⵡ.
 She resembles her mother: (a) tıŋɛ́ŋgıⵡgálıgınⵒ; (b) tıŋɛ́ŋ-gálıgınⵒ.
resembling adj. use adj. in -kırıⵡ (-kírıⵡ §1701; §§2539-42).

 I saw a wild beast resembling a dog: wáhašⵡ wēnⵡnálkorıⵒ (...-kır-ɛ̄nⵡnál-§984).
reside v.i. ág; tɛ́g.
resident n. sákınⵡ.
rest n. túrbar (-bárⵡ); turbídⵡ; ráhaⵡ.
rest v.i. túrb(ı) (túbb(ı)).
rest v.t. rɛjjıhɛ́.
restrain v.t. mír.
retire v.i. (go or come backwards) abágan-; (go backwards) abágannóg.
retribution n. ğızaⵡ.
return v.i. (come back) wıdɛtá (wᵘd-), wıdɛbıdá (wᵘd-); (go back) wıdɛnóg (wᵘd-).
reverse v.t. wídɛgır (wıdégır, wᵘd-).
revile v.t. díd.
revolve v.i. gırídɛ.
reward n. kıráıⵡ; mukáfaⵡ.
rhinoceros n. †ánasaⵡ; †hartídⵡ.
rice n. rúzz(ı)ⵡ.
rich adj. ırğɛ́nⵡ; dúŋgıkōlⵡ.
Ricinus communis n. ábkoñⵡ (ápk-).
ride v.t. ɛ́gır; kuččɛ́g.
 I ride a horse: káğkⵡɛgírrıⵒ.
 I shall ride the horse: káčkıⵡbıkuččɛ́gˡrıⵒ.
 Ride! ɛgrɛ́!, pl. ɛgrɛdwɛ́!
 Ride the donkey! hánugⵡɛgrɛ́!
 I rode the donkey: hánukⵡkuččɛ́kkorıⵒ.
 Which horse did he ride? tɛrⵡkáğⵡısáıkⵡ kuččɛ́kko?
 What am I to ride? míŋⵡɛgírrı?
 I am going for a ride: káğkɛbⵡbuğúrıⵒ.
rifle n. búndugⵡ.
right adj. (correct) tamámⵡ (tám-, tɛm-); (just) haggánıⵡ.
 This is right (correct): ínⵡtámámunⵒ.
 This is not right (is incorrect): ínⵡtámám-munūnⵒ.
 X. Stay here: índoⵡtépⵒ.
 Y. All right! sɛ́rɛ́n!
 Is (s)he (it) all right? sɛ́rɛ̄rɛ́?, pl. sɛrɛ́rırɛ́?
 X. How is (s)he? tɛrⵡmínɛⵡbún?
 Y. All right: sɛrantɛ́bınⵒ ((S)he keeps well).
right n. (hand) ínⵡ; (lawful) hágⵡ, hágg(ı)ⵡ.
 Go to the right: íŋgɛnⵡnókⵒ.
 It's on your right: ɛ́nnⵡíŋgɛbⵡbúnⵒ.
 X. Where is it? tɛ́rⵡɛ́?
 Y. On your right: ɛ́nnⵡíŋgɛⵒ.
right angles, at kjátt(ı)ⵡ.
right, set v.t. géndıgır.
rigid, become v.i. déŋgɛ.
rim n. gédɛⵡ; (formed by rope, of wheel raising water) ğómboⵡáttınⵡsɛ́nⵡ.
rind n. káčč(ı)ⵡ.
ring n. kúlalⵡ; (signet-) hátımⵡ.
ring (the bell) v.i. ğaráskıⵡğóm.
 Come when I ring: ğaráskıⵡğómkırıⵡtáⵒ.
rinse v.t. úru; ɛ́lɛw (ⵡɛ́lɛuⵡ); (by shaking) šúgum.
 I want to rinse my mouth: ánnⵡagílgⵡ ururáŋgⵡdóllıⵒ.
 Rinse the cup: fıŋgáŋgⵡɛlɛwosⵒ.
 Rinse the bottle: gɛzázkıⵡšúgumⵒ.
ripe adj. kárğɛlⵡ (kážğɛlⵡ).
 It is not ripe: (a) kağğıbúmunūnⵒ; (b) déssínⵒ.
ripen v.i. kárğ(ı) (kážğ(ı)).
rise v.i. ımbɛ́l (ímbɛl); dárr(ı); (of dough) kós; (of heavenly bodies) bɛ́l; (of river) dūlan-.
 before the moon rises: unáttⵡɛ́lgomⵡbélmɛnınⵒ.

when the moon has risen: unátti⌣bélim⌣ bádir⌣.
river n. úru⌣.
Take all this and throw it into the river: ím⌣málles⌣sokkedururárki⌢.
road n. dárib⌣ (dár-, dér-. -rub⌣); síkke⌣.
roam v.i. wíd; dắǧi.
roar v.i. írr(ı).
roast v.t. níb; gélegır.
(S)he is to roast the meat: kúsun⌣níban⌢.
robber n. mágas⌣ (mágas⌣).
roll into a ball (balls) v.t. géger.
roll up v.t. *(envelop)* kátt(ı).
roof n. kắn⌣dógo⌣ (kăndógo⌣); kăŋ⌣ kóčč(ı)⌣; ságif⌣ (ségif⌣).
room n. *(apartment)* óda⌣ (óda⌣); *(space)* ágar⌣; *(intervening space)* bárre⌣.
There's no room for it: ténn⌣íllar⌣ágar⌣ dắmunun⌢.
Make room for this: ínın⌣íllar⌣agárk⌣ áû⌢.
There's no room (intervening space) between: bárre⌣dắmunun⌢.
root n. úrse⌣.
rope n. ír⌣; *(thick)* tárif⌣ (tár-, tér-), álas⌣; *(attaching yoke to pole in water-wheel)* ólos⌣.
The rope is not long (enough): ír⌣nosó-munun⌢.
Can you make rope? (a) ér⌣uñur-ırıg-áuná? *(b)* ér⌣uñur-ırıg-írná?
Does (s)he know how to make rope? tér⌣ uñurırıgírná?
rose n. wírid⌣.
round adj. gırídebūl⌣; sıláde⌣.
This is round, that isn't: íŋ⌣gırídebūn, íŋ⌣gırídebắmunun⌢.
rouse v.t. ágıs; áŋgıs.
row v.t. wắu (wắw, wắû); tólle.
royal adj. órnd(ı)⌣; orwínd(ı)⌣.
rub v.t. ǧígıd.
rub out v.t. kómıs.
rubbish n. kắšš(ı)⌣; kawíš⌣.
Take this rubbish out: íŋ⌣kắššıs⌣sokkós⌢.
place where rubbish is thrown: gumáma⌣.
rug n. sıǧǧắǧa⌣.
ruin v.t. harbé.
rule n. *(government)* hókum⌣ (húkum⌣, hókom⌣); *(law, regulation)* gănún⌣.
rule v.t. hokmé (huk-).
ruler n. *(governor)* hákum⌣.
run v.i. bót.
Run! bót!, pl. bódwe!
Run! (towards the speaker): bótta!, pl. bóttáwe!
run away v.i. bód.
(S)he (it) has run away: bōdóskon⌢.
rung n. *(in water-wheel)* áglo⌣.
runnel n. málť(ı)⌣.
rust n. ságar⌣ (-gár⌣).
rust v.i. saggıré.
rust v.t. saggıréɡır.
rustic adj. belednırínd(ı)⌣.
rustic n. béledn⌣íd⌣ (belédnıd⌣).
rusty, be v.i. saggıréḃū-.
sack n. sekíbe⌣ (sák-, sak-, -bă⌣, -ba⌣); šắwál⌣ (šaw-, šɔw-); gárar⌣; *(leathern)* búsug⌣.
sad, be v.i. weǧakattı (wǎg̀-, -ahat-).
Why are you sad? er⌣méw⌣wéǧakattın?
Why is (s)he sad? ter⌣méw⌣wéǧakattın?
saddle n. déɡır⌣.

saddle v.t. dég.
Saddle the pony: kǎčkı⌣dék⌢.
Tell him to saddle the pony: káčkı⌣dégan⌢.
Saddle the donkey: hánud⌣dék⌢.
saddle-bag n. húruǧ⌣.
saddled, be (ready) v.i. déɡbū-.
Is the horse saddled? kǎǧ⌣déɡbūná?
Saïd (Saɛíd) n. saíd⌣.
sail n. *(cloth)* kúm⌣káde⌣.
Lower the sail: kúm⌣kádek⌣kúttéɡır⌢, pl. ....kúttéɡırwe⌢.
sailing-boat n. *(large)* gajásk(ı)⌣ (gıjá-, gıá-); *(small)* kúb⌣.
sake
(S)he does it for the sake of money: dúŋgíŋ-karam⌣ắwın⌢.
salary n. mahíje⌣ (-ja⌣, -ja⌣); úǧre⌣ (-ra⌣, -ra⌣).
saliva n. ǧúrud⌣.
salt n. úmbud⌣.
salute v.t. sɛllımé (-lumé).
Salvadora persica n. aráǧ⌣.
same adj. wér⌣.
This is the same: íw⌣wérun⌢.
It's all the same (It doesn't matter): málle⌣ wérun⌢.
sand (sand-bank, sand-dune) n. síu⌣ (síʷ⌣, síw⌣).
sandal n. nál⌣ (naál⌣); tarhád⌣ (-rxád⌣).
sand-devil (column of sand) n. kašwáre⌣; kắǧbar⌣.
sand-grouse n. bugbúga⌣.
sand-storm n. gutár⌣.
satchel n. súgar⌣.
sate v.t. bérkır.
sated, be v.i. bérbū-.
sated, become v.i. bér.
satiate v.t. bérkır.
satisfactory adj. gén⌣; sére⌣.
satisfied adj. *(pleased)* mabsúd⌣.
Saturday n. sámte⌣.
on Saturday: sámteg⌣, -gi⌢.
(S)he (it) will come on Saturday: sámteb⌣ bıtán⌢.
saucepan n. *(European)* kasaróna⌣ (kaza-, kozor-); *(native earthenware)* súle⌣.
save v.t. *(rescue)* hallısé; *(husband)* waffıré.
Save him (her, it): tékkı⌣hallısé⌢.
Save your money: en⌣dúŋɡıw⌣waffıré⌢.
Are you saving your money? er⌣én⌣ dúŋɡıɡ⌣ăwwaffıréná?
sawdust n. bérn⌣kắšš(ı)⌣.
say v.t. ⌣é-; wé; án; ⌣ewé; ⌣awwé (⌣á-wé, ⌣a-wé).
What do you say? (a) er⌣míŋɡ⌣én? *(b)* er⌣ míne⌣wén?
What did you say? er⌣míne⌣wéɡon?
What does (s)he say? ter⌣míŋɡ⌣én?
(S)he said 'No': wắran⌣egri⌢.
I say 'Go': (a) áı⌣nóǧ⌣éri⌢; *(b)* áı⌣nóǧ⌣ ewéri⌢; *(c)* áı⌣nóǧ⌣awwéri⌢.
Say it again: ténne⌣wé⌢.
I said so: áı⌣íŋke⌣wéɡori⌢.
You said so: er⌣íŋke⌣wéɡon⌢.
(S)he said so: ter⌣íŋke⌣wéɡon⌢.
Don't say so: tókkon⌣íŋke⌣wémen⌢.
(S)he said (s)he would send (some)one: web⌣bišínd⌣eɡón⌢.
saying n. *(what is said)* wére⌣.
scab n. *(cicatrice)* kájjo⌣.
scabbard n. síwín⌣kă⌣.
scales n. *(for weighing)* mīzán⌣.

scanty adj. márıs⌣.
scare v.t. halé; sándıgır.
scatter v.t. gúll(ı).
school n. mádrása⌣ (médresa⌣, mídrasa⌣); *(primary)* kuttáb⌣, mısíd⌣, hálwa⌣ (xál-).
schoolmaster n. kúrkırıl⌣.
scissors n. kısór⌣.
scold v.t. díd.
(S)he scolds him (her): tér⌣tékkonon⌣ ǧáwwın⌢.
scolding n. dítt(ı)⌣.
scorch v.t. kúddeɡır.
scorched, be v.i. kúdde; kúddebū-.
scorpion n. ıččín⌣.
scrap n. kắšš(ı)⌣.
scrape v.t. kód.
scratch v.t. bắr; bárǧ; kód.
scream v.i. wíg.
screen n. dára⌣.
scrotum n. sórod⌣.
scrutinize v.t. ǧúñč(ı); fɛttıšé.
sea n. umbúdn⌣úru.
seal n. *(signet and its impression)* hítım⌣; *(signet-ring)* hắtım⌣.
seal v.t. *(affix one's seal to)* hıtmé.
Did you see that it was sealed? hıtméḃūlg⌣ nálkoná?
search v.i., *search for* v.t. tɛbé.
seat n. kúrsı⌣.
Give him (her) a seat: aɡíddi⌢.
second ord. num. ŏwwínt(ı)⌣ (ŏuwí-, ŏwwınt(ı)⌣, ŏuwí-).
sedge n. gŏu⌣ (gŏw⌣); gŏwwe⌣; dís⌣.
sediment n. tífıl⌣.
sedition n. fítne⌣.
see v.t. nál.
I see (him, her, it): áı⌣nálli⌢.
I don't see (him, her, it): áı⌣nálmunun⌢.
X. Is there any milk? ıččı⌣dáná?
Y. I'll see: nálli⌢.
X. Has the mail come? bústa⌣tắgoná?
Y. I'll go and see: nallɛnóɡri⌢.
Did you go to see? er⌣nallɛnókkoná?
Go and see at what time they open the post-office: bústam⌣mắktábkı⌣sắ⌣mukót-térro⌣kusíŋɡı⌣noǧǧunál⌢ (kúsın⌢ *he opens*).
Is (s)he (it) to be seen? nálkattıná?
Has (s)he (it) been seen? nalkáttıɡoná?
See where (s)he put the money: dúŋɡıɡ⌣ ısáı⌣uskursíŋɡı⌣nál⌢.
I don't want to see him (her, it): áı⌣nal-láŋɡı⌣dólmunun⌢.
See (to it) that I drink this: áıɡ⌣íŋɡı⌣ nían⌢, lit. *Say to me 'Drink this'*.
Did you see him (her) home? téŋ⌣kám⌣ bókkon⌣óǧıɡoná?
See (= count) how many donkeys there are: hánuɡ⌣írnal⌢.
seed n. tér⌣; bıtán⌣ (bıt-, but-).
The seed is sprouting: tér⌣abbérın⌢.
The (various) seeds are sprouting: térınč⌣ ăbbérran⌢.
seedling n. šétıl⌣ (-tul⌣).
seek v.t. *(search for)* tɛbé; *(try to obtain)* wérs(ı).
seem
There seems to be some: dáŋkırın⌢.
There seems to be none: dắmunuŋkírın⌢.
seize v.t. ár.
select v.t. bár.

self n. -néfıs‿ (-náf-, -náf-, §§2688-9); -å‿ (-ā‿, §§2688-9); -nɛwért(ı)‿ (§2691).
Let him (her) bring it himself (herself): tén-nɛfískɛd‿éttaran⌒.
Do it yourself: ɛn-nɛfísked‿åu‿.
(S)he has killed himself (herself): (a) tén-nɛfískı‿bēróskon⌒; (b) ténn-āb‿bēróskon⌒; (c) tén-nɛwértıb‿bēróskon⌒.
Did it open by itself? (a) tɛkkól‿kúskoná? (b) kól‿kúskoná?
Give me coffee by itself; I don't want milk or sugar: gáhwa‿sådad‿dén; wál‿íččıw‿wála‿sukkárkı‿dólmunun⌒.
Did you see him (her, it) yourself? ɛm‿míssıgɛn‿nálkoná?
Tell him (her) to bring each by itself: (a) baŋgı-báŋg‿éttaran⌒; (b) ɛččɛn-éččɛn‿éttaran⌒.
Put them each by itself: (a) baŋgı-báŋg‿úskurır⌒; (b) ɛččɛn-éččɛn‿úskurır⌒.
self-respecting adj. ādúlkōl‿.
sell v.t. ğán (q.v.); ɛğğuğán; (to the speaker) ğándɛn; (to other than the speaker) ğántır.
I sold the horse: káččı‿ğäntíkkori⌒.
Sell it in the market: súgır‿ɛğğuğán⌒.
I sell, I don't buy: āı‿ğántıddi, āı‿ğanár-munun⌒.
sell off v.t. ğandábır.
semaphore n. †sɛmafór‿.
semen n. téri‿.
send v.t. íšın (ıšín); éu (éw, ēu).
Has (s)he sent? ıšíŋkoná?
Send him (her) with this: íŋgɛd‿íšın⌒.
Send him (her) with the letter: ğawåbkɛd‿íšın⌒.
If (s)he sends it, let me know: tɛron‿ıšíŋkın‿åıg‿wēdēn‿.
X. *Whom did (s)he send?* níg‿ıšíŋkon?
Y. *(S)he has sent Áḥmad:* ahmɛ́tk‿ıšınɛdáğın⌒.
X. *Who (has) sent you?* n‿ékk‿ıšınɛdáğın?
Y. *The sheikh:* sámıl⌒.
Who (has) sent you (pl.)? n‿írg‿ıšınɛdáğırırın?
I want to send someone: wɛg‿ıšındáŋgı‿dólli⌒.
Send me someone: wɛt‿tåran⌒ (lit. *Tell someone to come*).
I sent him (her, it) three hours ago: āı‿tékk‿ıšınɛdāgrídduton‿så‿tóskı-taran⌒.
I am (just) going to send someone: wɛg‿ıšınɛdólli⌒.
Send this to the doctor tomorrow: íŋg‿asálgı‿hakím-nār‿íšın⌒.
I sent a telegram: tɛlɛgráfkı‿ğómkori⌒.
I sent him (her) a telegram to let him (her) know: (a) āı‿tékkı‿tɛlɛgráfkɛw‿wétıkkori⌒; (b) āı‿tékkı‿tɛlɛgráfwétıkkori⌒.
send (as a gift) v.t. (to the speaker) ıšíndɛn; (to other than the speaker) ıšíntır.
Send me one (for myself): wɛg‿åıg‿ıšín-dɛn⌒.
I will send you one: ékkı‿wéb‿bıšíntıddi⌒.
Send him (her) this: íŋgı‿tékk‿ıšíntır⌒.
Send this to the sheikh: íŋgı‿samílg‿ıšíntır⌒.
send away v.t. túr.
send for v.t. ıšınétta (ıšınétta).
Send for some ice: tɛlíčk‿ıšınétta⌒.

send out v.t. bɛlkídd(ı); bɛlíŋgır (ᵈ⁻⁻); bélkır.
senna n. (*Cassia acutifolia*) sɛnɛmékkɛ‿ (-nám-, -ká‿), sénɛ‿ (sénå‿); (*Cassia obovata*) abúrrɛ‿.
Sennār n. sınnår‿.
sense n. (*intelligence*) érıg‿.
(S)he has no sense: ɛrıkkómunun⌒.
sensible adj. (*intelligent*) ɛrıkkátt(ı)‿; érık-kōl‿.
sentence n. (*judicial*) hókum‿ (húkum‿, hókom‿); (*punishment*) ğíza‿.
sentence of imprisonment: síğın‿hókum‿.
sentence of death: díar‿hókum‿.
sentence v.t. hokmé (huk-).
The judge sentenced them to imprisonment: gádı‿tírgı‿sığíŋgɛh‿hokmérıkkon⌒.
separately adv. (*each apart from other*) baŋı-báŋ(ı)‿; ɛččɛn-éččɛn‿.
Stand (pl.) separately: (a) baŋı-báŋı‿tēbwe‿; (b) ɛččɛn-éččɛn‿tēbwe‿.
Bring each separately: (a) baŋı-báŋ‿éttarır⌒; (b) ɛččɛn-éččɛn‿éttarır⌒.
serpent n. kåg‿.
servant n. haddám‿.
serve v.i. and t. hadmé.
sesame n. símsım‿.
sesame oil: símsım‿zéd‿; símsım‿dés‿.
set v.i. kídd(ı); (*of the sun*) tó.
Has the moon set? unáttı‿kiddóskoná?
When the sun has set: másıl‿tóm‿bådır⌒.
set v.t. úskur.
set on v.t. (*superimpose*) kúğur.
settle v.i. åg; tég.
seven card. num. kólod‿.
seventeen card. num. dımındokólod‿.
seventh ord. num. kolodínt(ı)‿ (kolo-dınt(ı)‿).
seventy card. num. dımıŋkólod‿; sabaín‿.
severe adj. dúllo‿.
sew v.t. níğ.
Can you sew? (a) ɛskıníğná? (b) uñurníğná?
Let ɣáli sew this (up, on) tomorrow: álıg‿íŋg‿asálgı‿níğan⌒.
shade n. óll(ı)‿.
Put it in the shade: óllır‿úskur⌒.
shadow n. óll(ı)‿.
shaft n. (*vertical passage*) kódɛ‿.
shake v.i. šúlug; (*vibrate, etc.*) kérkɛr.
Don't let your hand shake (tremble): tókkon‿énn‿ík‿kɛrkɛrıŋgírmɛn⌒.
shake v.t. wálag; šúgum; šúlug; šulugíŋgır (óšoŋ); kɛrkɛrkídd(ı); hızzé; (*shake out*) šónd(ı).
Shake the bottle: gɛzázkı‿šúgum⌒.
Don't shake the box: sandúkkı‿tókkon‿šuluguŋgírmɛn⌒.
Don't shake the table: tókkon‿tarabēzah‿hızzémɛn⌒.
Shake the cloth: kádɛš‿šóndi⌒.
Have they shaken (out) the rugs? sığğá-gančıš‿šóndıgorandé?
Tell him (her) to shake the blanket: battāníjɛš‿šóndan⌒.
shape v.t. kåi (káj, kåi).
share n. bágıd‿.
share v.t. šɛrké.
sharp adj. (*keen-edged*) káh(ı)lí‿.
Bring a sharp knife: kándı‿káhlí-wɛg‿étta⌒.
The knife's blade is sharp: kándın‿ágıl‿káhlín⌒.

We shall start at three sharp: så‿tóskı‿tamámır‿bımbéllu‿.
sharpen v.t. ágıs; áŋgıs; kahlígır.
Sharpen this: íŋg‿ágıs⌒.
Sharpen the blade of the knife: kándın‿agílg‿áŋgıs⌒.
shave v.i. (= *shave oneself*) and v.t. gáññ(ı).
I am shaving: (a) an-nafísk‿āggáññıri⌒; (b) āggáññıri⌒.
I want to shave: āı‿gañńıráŋgı‿dólli⌒.
shaving(s) n. (*of wood*) hášam‿gábad‿; hášam‿káčč(ı)‿.
she pers. pron. tér‿ (tɛr‿).
Is it she? tér‿té?
she- kárr(ı)‿.
she-ass: hánu‿kárr(ı)‿.
she-camel: kam-kárr(ı)‿.
she-cat: sām-kárr(ı)‿.
shears n. kısór‿.
sheath n. (*case*) ká‿ (-kā‿); (*investing tissue*) kačč(ı)‿.
sheath of sword: síwín-kā‿.
sheath of knife: kandín-kā‿.
shed n. kérr(ı)‿.
sheep n. égɛd‿.
sheikh n. sámıl‿; šéh‿ (šéx‿).
shelf n. ráff(ı)‿; ráf‿.
Put it on the shelf: ráffır‿úskur⌒.
It's on the shelf: ráffır‿bún⌒.
shell n. (*husk*) kāčč(ı)‿.
shell v.t. (*hull*) gáww(ı) (gáuw(ı)).
Have you shelled the peas? órrɛg‿ğáw-wıgoná?
shine v.i. bılínč(ı); fılínč(ı) (fılítt(ı), fılát-t(ı)); tulúnč(ı).
ship n. kúb‿.
shirt n. arrǻg(ı)‿; kómán‿.
shoe n. markúb‿ (mår-, mɛr-); (*European*) ğázma‿ (ğáz-, ğéz-, -må‿).
When I get home put the irons into the shoes: kår‿ğúrı‿tåğ‿ğézmar‿šårtıg‿úndur⌒.
shoemaker n. súlu‿; ğázman‿níğı‿.
shoot n. (*young plant*) šétıl‿ (-tul‿).
shoot v.t. bundúkkɛğ‿ğóm.
I (have) shot it: bundúkkɛğ‿ğómkori⌒.
I am going gazelle-shooting: āı‿gɛ́lgı‿bērenógbūri⌒, lit. *I am going to kill gazelle.*
shooting n. (*hunting*) séd‿.
I am going shooting: āı‿sɛdır‿bığúri⌒.
shop n. dukkán‿.
shopkeeper n. hawǻgɛ‿ (-ğá‿, -ğa‿).
shore n. bárr(ı)‿; går‿; når‿; år‿.
short adj. úrtına‿ (-tuna‿); (*in measure or amount*) någıs‿.
This is too short: ín‿úrtunán⌒.
The rope is too short: ír‿úrtunán⌒.
shorten v.t. urtnágır (-tun-).
Shorten this: íŋg‿urtnágır⌒.
Shorten the rope: írıg‿urtnágır⌒.
shorts n. sagírt(ı)‿.
shoulder n. ósmar‿.
joint of shoulder: kɛffám‿budúrt(ı)‿.
shout n. kőråg‿.
shout v.i. (*talk in loud tones*) ğál; (*to call*) úwɛ.
shouting n. (*noisy talk*) ğálɛ‿.
Tell them to stop shouting: ğálɛm‿mugówwan⌒.
show v.t. amínt(ı).
(*exhibit*) wándıgır.
Show it (them) to me: åıg‿amínti⌒.

shrivel — smoke

Show it to the headman: samílg⌣amínti⌢.
Don't show it: tókkon⌣amíntımɛn⌢, pl. tókkon⌣amíntımɛwwɛ⌢.
Tell this (her) servant to show it to him (her): tɛ́n⌣haddámgı⌣tékk⌣amíntan⌢.
Go along with him (her) and show him (her) the house: tékkonon⌣nogǧukãga-mínti⌢.
shrivel v.i. ǧógor.
shrub n. ǧóww(ı)⌣; šídár⌣.
shut v.t. kób.
It is not shut (non clausum est): kobbú-munun⌢.
Shut up! (a) kíttɛ!, pl. kíttɛwɛ! (b) ɛnn⌣agílgı⌣kóp!, pl. ínn⌣áglık⌣kóbwɛ! (c) ɛr⌣kíttɛmɛn?, pl. ır⌣kíttɛmɛndu?
shut, leave v.t. kobmúg.
Leave it shut: kobmúk⌢.
Don't leave it shut: tókkoŋ⌣kobmúgmɛn⌢.
Leave them shut: kobmúgırır⌢.
Don't leave them shut: tókkoŋ⌣kob-mugırímmɛn⌢.
shuttle n. kúb⌣.
shy adj. káukáu⌣.
sick, be v.i. (*be ill*) óddıbū-; (*vomit*) ba-rísk(ı).
I'm going to be sick: barıskɛdólli⌢.
Are you going to be sick? ɛr⌣barıskɛdólná?
sickle n. túrub⌣.
handle of sickle: túrubn⌣ád⌣.
sickness n. óddɛ⌣.
side n. (*of body or other object*) bɛ́rı⌣, ǧɛ́mb(ı)⌣ (ǧám-), sábha⌣ (sápha⌣); (*place, position*) šíg⌣, árıg⌣.
Lie on your side: ɛ́m⌣bɛ́rıgɛt⌣túbbi⌢.
I have a pain in my side: án⌣ǧámb⌣ óddını⌢.
That is your side: keep to it: ín⌣ɛ́n⌣ šígun: téddo⌣tɛ́p⌢.
Keep on (keep to) your side: ɛ́n⌣šíkkɛt⌣ tɛ́p⌢.
Walk by my side: ánn⌣áttır⌣nók⌢.
Stay by his (her, its) side: tɛ́nn⌣áttır⌣ tɛ́p⌢.
Put it by the side of the chair: kúrsın⌣ áttır⌣úskur⌢.
Put them side by side: wɛrwɛ́n⌣áttır⌣ úskur⌢.
The road is on the other side of the house: dárıb⌣kártōm⌣máŋgé⌢.
The house is on the other side of the road: kã⌣dárıbırtōm⌣máŋgé⌢.
side-piece of yoke n. golmódd(ı)⌣.
sigh v.i. nɛ̄wɛdúkk(ı)⌣; nɛwɛ́rtıd⌣dúkk(ı)⌣.
sight n. nálar⌣ (-lár⌣); nalíd⌣.
sight, come in v.i. wănd(ı)⌣.
X. Hasn't (s)he (it) come in sight? wănd ıgomɛn⌢?
Y. (S)he (it) has: wăndóskó⌢.
Tell me when the steamer comes in sight: bãbúr⌣wăndıgın⌣āıgı⌣wɛ́dɛn⌢.
When they come in sight let him (her) tell me: wăndıran⌣tãd⌣āıgı⌣wɛ́dɛnan⌢.
sign n. (*mark*) ír⌣; alámа⌣; ıbár⌣.
sign v.t. (*put one's signature to*) mɛdɛ́.
I have signed the receipt: wasílgı⌣mɛdɛ́-gori⌢.
X. Is the letter signed? ǧawáb⌣mɛdɛ́búná?
Y. No, sealed: wăran, hıtmɛ́bún⌢.
signal n. (*railway*) †sɛmafór⌣.
When the signal goes down, tell me: sɛma-fór⌣šugúrkın⌣āıgı⌣wɛ́dɛn⌢.

signature n. ímdɛ⌣.
signet n. hítım⌣; hắtım⌣.
silence
Silence! kíttɛ!, pl. kíttɛwɛ́!
silent, be v.i. kíttɛ.
silver n. dúŋ(ı)⌣.
silversmith n. dúŋgın⌣tábıd⌣.
similar adj. -kırı⌣ (-kírı⌣; §§2539-40).
I want one similar to this: ıŋkırı-wɛ̄d⌣ dólli⌢.
simple adj. (*unsophisticated*) gaším⌣.
Simulium griseicolle n. nımíntɛ⌣ (-íttɛ⌣).
sin n. zɛ́mb(ı)⌣.
since conj. -ndotōn⌣ (-ddotōn⌣; §4354).
It is ten days since I saw him (her, it, them): āı⌣nalsíddotōn⌣náhár⌣dımín-taran⌢.
How many days is it since you saw him (her, it)? ɛr⌣tékkı⌣nalsúndotōn⌣jōm⌣mıŋ-kóttɛ̄r⌣té?
I haven't seen him (her, it, them) since the doctor was here: hakím⌣índ⌣āgsún-dotōn⌣nalkómunun⌢.
since prep. -rtōn⌣ after a vowel; -ırtōn⌣ after a consonant, but -rotōn⌣ after -r, -lotōn⌣ after -l, -dotōn⌣ after -n.
since Saturday: sámtɛrtōn⌣.
I haven't seen him (her, it) since Monday: (a) āı⌣tékkı⌣búšırtōn⌣nalkómunun⌢; (b) āı⌣tékkı⌣búš⌣nɛhárrotōn⌣nalkó-munun⌢.
since the great rain: áru⌣dúllotōn⌣.
since a month ago: úndotōn⌣.
sinew n. ásab⌣; kóı⌣ (kóī⌣).
sing v.t. ó.
singing n. ó⌣.
I dislike his (her) singing: tɛ́nn⌣óını⌣ móndi⌢.
sink v.i. kídd(ı)⌣; kúñ; šúgur.
The boat will sink: kúb⌣bıkíddın⌢.
The boat's just going to sink: kúb⌣kıddɛ-dólın⌢.
Sirius n. tóskan⌣abáŋ⌣wíss(ı)⌣.
sister n. -ɛss(ı)⌣, pl. -ɛssınč(ı)⌣, always with a form of the poss. pers. pron. (§2625) prefixed:
my sister: ánnɛss(ı)⌣.
your sister: ínnɛss(ı)⌣.
his (her, its) sister: tínnɛss(ı)⌣.
our sister: antínnɛss(ı)⌣.
your (pl.) sister: ıntínnɛss(ı)⌣.
their sister: tínntınnɛss(ı)⌣.
sister-in-law n. (*in general*) -ogo⌣ (= *mother-in-law* q.v.).
(*wife's sister*) ɛ́n⌣tínnɛss(ı)⌣ (s.v. -ɛss(ı)⌣).
(*husband's sister*) ógıñ⌣tínnɛss(ı)⌣ (s.v. -ɛss(ı)⌣).
(*brother's wife*) -bɛsn⌣ɛ́n⌣ (s.v. -bɛs⌣).
sit v.i. tɛ́g.
Sit down: tɛ́gos⌢, pl. tɛ́goswɛ⌢.
Sit (down) over there: mándo⌣tɛ́k⌢, pl. ...⌣tɛ́gwɛ⌢.
Go and sit down: ǧutɛ́gó⌢, pl. ǧutɛ́-gówwɛ⌢.
If (s)he comes let him (her) sit there: tékkı⌣tăgın⌣téddo⌣tɛ́gan⌢.
Tell him (her) to let me sit on a chair: tékk⌣āıgı⌣kúrsır⌣agíddan⌢.
six card. num. górıǧ⌣.
sixteen card. num. dımındogórıǧ⌣.
sixth ord. num. gorǧínt(ı)⌣ (´⌣-´).
sixty card. num. dımıngórıǧ⌣; sıttín⌣.

size n. kótt(ı)⌣.
skewer n. nıččínd(ı)⌣.
skilful adj. fála⌣.
skill n. sína⌣.
skin n. áǧın⌣; (*of fruit*) kắčč(ı)⌣; (*to hold water,* قربة) gírba⌣, gırbắd⌣; (*to hold grain,* جراب) dábja⌣; (*small, to hold milk*) bɛ́ñ⌣.
sky n. nálu⌣.
slack adj. (*lazy*) kússa⌣.
slackness n. (*laziness*) késɛl⌣.
slant downwards v.i. dɛrɛ́ñɛ; túlɛ.
slanting adj. kɛ́rɛñ⌣.
slaughter v.t. góǧ; (*massacre*) bɛ́rıǧ.
slave n. (*male*) núgud⌣; (*female*) nógo⌣.
sleep n. nálu⌣.
(S)he (it) has gone to sleep (fallen asleep): nɛrósko⌢.
sleep v.i. nɛ́r.
sleepy
I am sleepy: nalunɛ́r⌣āıg⌣ắrın⌢.
You are sleepy: nalunɛ́r⌣ékk⌣ắrın⌢.
(S)he (it) is sleepy: nalunɛ́r⌣tékk⌣ắrın⌢.
slipper n. markúb⌣ (mắr-, mɛr-).
(*European*) kắn-ǧazma⌣ (-ǧáz-, -ǧɛz-, -mắ-).
Give me my slippers: áŋ⌣kắn-ǧazmád⌣ dɛ́n⌢.
slit adj. gắgbúl⌣ (gággul⌣).
slit n. gắgar⌣ (-gắr⌣); gagíd⌣.
slit v.i. gắg; mɛ́r.
Take care! It's going to slit: bắlko! mɛrɛdólın⌢.
slit v.t. gắg.
slope v.i. dɛrɛ́ñɛ; túlɛ.
slow
Your watch is slow: ɛ́n⌣sắ⌣ahhɛrɛ́bún⌢.
slowly adv. nórɛn⌣ (-rɛ̄⌣, nórɛ́⌣).
Speak slowly: nórɛm⌣báññi⌢.
The steamer was moving slowly: bãbúr⌣ ǧobbɛnógbúgon⌢.
slowly! interj. nórɛn! (-rɛ̄!, nórɛ́!), pl. nórɛwwɛ! (´⌣-´).
small adj. kíñña⌣.
It is (too) small: tɛr⌣kíññán⌢.
Cut this into very small pieces: íŋgı⌣ nörogırmɛ́r⌢.
smell n. írıs⌣.
There is a smell: ırís-sɛ̄r⌣dán⌢.
I have not noticed its smell: āı⌣gıǧır⌣ kómunun⌢.
smell v.i. ırísko.
(S)he (it) smells: ırískı⌣kón⌢, pl. ...⌣kó-ran⌢.
(S)he (it) does not smell: ırískı⌣kómunun⌢, pl. ...⌣kómunan⌢.
This meat smells: íñ⌣kúsu⌣írís-sɛ̄k⌣kón⌢.
smell v.t. (*sniff*) súndɛ (súnnɛ); (*perceive odour of*) gíǧır.
Smell this: íŋgı⌣súndɛ⌢ (...⌣súnnɛ⌢).
smell bad v.i. síɛ (síé).
smith n. tábıd⌣.
smoke n. túlla⌣.
Can the smoke be seen? túlla⌣nálkattıná?
smoke v.t. (*tobacco*) ní.
I smoke: āı⌣tumbákkı⌣nfri⌢.
I am smoking: āı⌣tumbákk⌣ánníri⌢.
I don't smoke: āı⌣tumbákkı⌣nímunun⌢.
X. Does he smoke cigarettes? sıǧaran⌣níná?
Y. No, a pipe: wăraŋ⌣kodóskı⌣nín⌢.

snake — spring

This dish (food) is smoked: ín‿ǧákud‿ túllag‿kó⌒.
snake n. kåg‿.
snap v.i. mér.
snare n. bíɡıd‿.
sneeze v.i. átıñ; átıš.
sniff v.t. súndɛ (súnnɛ).
snore v.i. kórrɛ; fórrɛ.
snort v.i. fórrɛ.
snuff n. nušúɡ‿; tɛnšíɡa‿.
so adv. íŋkɛ‿ (íŋké⌒, íŋkɛɡ‿, -gi⌒); tékkɛ‿ (tékké⌒, tékkɛɡ‿, -gi‿); máŋkɛ‿ (máŋké⌒, máŋkɛɡ‿, -gi⌒); íŋɡɛd‿ (-ɛt⌒, íŋɡé⌒); tékkɛd‿ (-ɛt⌒, tékké⌒); máŋɡɛd‿ (-ɛt⌒, máŋɡé⌒).
(S)he said so: tɛr‿íŋkɛ‿wéɡon⌒.
so much indef. dem. pron. ıŋkóttɛr‿.
Why have you brought so much? ɛr‿mén‿ ıŋkottéɡ‿éttaɡon?
soak v.i. néñ.
soak v.t. néñɡır.
so-and-so indef. pron. fulán‿.
soap n. sābún‿.
social intercourse n. wénɛs‿.
sock n. šur(r)áb‿.
socket n. úbbur‿.
sock-suspender(s) n. †šurábkɛs‿sóllıɡıd- dan‿.
sodomite n. lúti‿ (lóti‿).
soft adj. (*pliant*) ǧaɡádɛl‿ (~~~, ~~~).
soften v.i. ǧaɡádɛ (ǧaɡádé, ~~~).
soften v.t. ǧaɡádɛɡır (ǧaɡádéɡır, ~~~).
soil n. árıd‿.
soil v.t. értıɡır; wassahé.
soldier n. áskar‿.
sole n. (*of foot*) óssín-tu‿; (*of shoe, etc.*) nāl‿ (naāl‿).
solid adj. (*hard*) déŋɡɛl‿; kóɡor‿.
solitary wasp n. fıríčč(ı)‿.
some indef. pron. and adj. -wēr‿; indef. pron. kóččɛr‿.
Tell him (her) to make some good coffee: gáhwa‿sɛré-wēɡ‿áuan⌒.
We want some more: (a) ténnɛ‿dóllu⌒; (b) tɛnnéd‿dóllu⌒.
X. Do they say so? íŋkɛ‿wérandé?
Y. Some do, some don't: wérı‿wéran, wérı‿wémunan⌒.
X. Did you see the houses? kårın‿nálkoná?
Y. I saw some, others I didn't: (a) kóččɛn‿ nálkori, kóččɛn‿nalkómunun⌒; (b) wérın‿nálkori, wérın‿nalkómunun⌒.
I want some water: éssıd‿dólli⌒.
somebody, someone indef. pron. wér‿.
Somebody has touched this: wér‿íŋɡı‿ ǧábɛɡon⌒.
Tell someone to take a lantern and go with him (her): wéf‿fānúskɛt‿tékkonon‿ nóɡan⌒.
I hear someone (α, *talking*) (a) ádɛm‿hískı‿ ɡıǧírri⌒; (b) ádɛm‿híssıɡ‿ɡıǧírri⌒; (β, *moving*) ádɛm‿harákkı‿ɡıǧírri⌒.
something indef. pron. hǎǧa‿ (-ǧa‿, -ǧɛ‿).
I hear something (α, *a voice*) (a) hískı‿ ɡıǧírri⌒; (b) híssıɡ‿ɡıǧírri⌒; (β, *a movement*) harákkı‿ɡıǧírri⌒.
sometimes adv. koččɛráŋkın‿.
It is sometimes seen: koččɛráŋkın‿nál- kattın⌒.
Sometimes (s)he (it) comes, sometimes (s)he (it) doesn't: koččɛráŋkın‿tán, koččɛráŋ- kın‿tåmunun⌒.

somewhat adv. kınnéɡ‿ (-gi⌒).
I am somewhat better: kınnés‿sɛráŋkori⌒.
son n. tód‿.
Is this your son? ín‿ɛn‿tódˈré?
song n. ố‿.
soon adv. ɛɡéttır‿; (*from now*) kínnēr‿ áŋkın‿.
Will you do it soon? ɛr‿ɛɡettıɡırbáuná?
Will they do it soon? ɛɡettıɡırbáurandé?
I shall soon go: kínnēr‿áŋkım‿bınóɡri⌒.
Bring the bath-water as soon as it is ready: hammåmn‿éssıh‿hådıranıŋɡonon‿ étta⌒.
sooner adv. õwwéllo‿; oɡóllo‿.
sooner than prep. —n‿õwwéllo‿; —n‿ oɡóllo‿.
soot n. íɡn‿úrum‿.
sorcerer n. ɡúl‿ (ɡúln‿ónd(ı)‿); dóɡır‿ (dóɡırn‿ónd(ı)‿).
sorceress n. ɡúl‿ (ɡúl‿kárr(ı)‿); dóɡır‿ (dóɡır‿kárr(ı)‿).
sore n. (*wound*) kốr‿; (*tumour*) amǧulúd‿; (*small tumour*) tússa‿.
Sorgum vulgare n. márɛ‿, *S.* máro‿.
sorghum cut while still green: mɛrmétt(ı)‿.
sorghum-stalk n. háɡɛ‿.
sorrow n. zǎl‿.
sorry, become v.i. zālé.
sort n. ǧíns(ı)‿ (ǧínıs‿).
Of what sort? mínım‿ǧínsırtōn?
I want this sort: ín‿ǧínsıd‿dólli⌒.
I don't want this sort: ín‿ǧínsıd‿dól- munun‿.
Bring some of this sort: (a) ín‿ǧínsırtōn‿ étta⌒; (b) ínın‿ǧínsırtōn‿étta⌒.
sort v.t. bár.
soul n. nɛwért(ı)‿; néfıs‿ (nåf-, náf-).
sound adj. ɡén‿; sérɛ‿.
sound n. híz‿; híss(ı)‿; (*of movement*) hárag‿, háraka‿.
Do you hear the sound of a horse (neighing, etc.)? (a) káñ‿hískı‿ɡıǧírná? (b) káñ‿ híssıɡ‿ɡıǧírná?
Don't you hear the sound of a horse (trotting, etc.)? káñ‿harákkı‿ɡıǧírmɛn?
Don't you hear the sound of persons? (α, *talking, etc.*) (a) ádɛmın‿hískı‿ɡıǧírmɛn? (b) ádɛmın‿híssıɡ‿ɡıǧírmɛn? (β, *walking, etc.*) ádɛmın‿harákkı‿ɡıǧírmɛn?
I hear the sound of the train: ɡátın‿ harákkı‿ɡıǧírri⌒.
sound condition, be in a v.i. ɡéndıbū-.
This is not in a sound condition: íŋ‿ ɡɛndıbúmunun⌒.
soup n. máraɡ‿ (máraɡ‿); mar(r)aɡád‿ (màr(r)àɡ-); šúrba‿ (-bà‿, -bɛ‿).
I want some soup: marákkı‿dólli⌒.
I don't want any soup: šúrbád‿dól- munun⌒.
X. I want my soup in a cup, I want it boiling: ám‿marákkı‿fıŋɡándo‿dólli, wázbūlɡoŋɡı‿dólli⌒.
Y. When? At dinner? sıntá? ášaró?
sour adj. nádd(ı)‿; (*of milk*) mérɛl‿.
sour milk: mérɛl‿.
south n. óŋɡo‿.
southwards adv. óŋɡōr‿.
sow v.t. tér‿; (*scattering*) ɡúll(ı)‿.
sown ground: téra‿.
space n. áɡar‿.
span n. (*9 inches*) bánd(ı)‿; (*7 inches*) šíbır‿.

spare time n. súdn‿áɡar (súdnaɡar‿).
sparkle v.i. bılínč(ı); fılítt(ı) (fılátt(ı), fılínč(ı)); tulúnč(ı).
sparrow n. zɛrzúr‿.
speak v.i. báññ(ı).
Don't speak like that: tókkon‿íŋkırıb‿ báññımɛn⌒.
spear n. šǎ‿.
specially adv. husúsan‿ (xu-).
species n. ǧíns(ı)‿ (ǧínıs‿).
speech n. báññıd‿.
spider n. kórob‿; (*large, running*) abu- šébɛd‿.
spin v.t. wéd.
spindle n. núbro‿.
notch of spindle: núbron‿dírr(ı)‿.
pillar of spindle: (a) núbrom‿bér‿; (b) núbron‿šúš‿.
top (notched end) of spindle: núbroŋ‿ɡól‿.
whorl of spindle: núbroŋ‿ɡédɛ‿.
spirit n. (*soul*) nɛwért(ı)‿, néfıs‿ (nǎf-, náf-); (*evil*) ǧǎn‿, šētán‿.
spit v.t. túff(ı).
spite of, in
They will do it in spite of him (her): téŋ‿ ɡásubır‿báuran‿.
splash v.t. físs(ı); míssɛ.
Don't splash: tókkom‿físsımɛn⌒, pl. tók- kom‿físsımɛwwɛ⌒.
Don't splash me: tókkon‿áıɡı‿físsımɛn⌒.
The water splashes me: åıɡ‿éssı‿míssɛn⌒.
split adj. ɡáɡbūl‿ (ɡáɡɡūl‿).
(S)he gave me a split stick: wíččīr‿ ɡáɡɡūlɡı‿déŋkon‿.
split n. ɡáɡar‿ (-ɡår‿); ɡaɡíd‿.
This has a split in it: íŋ‿ɡáɡbūn⌒.
split v.i. ɡáɡ.
My pipe has split: áŋ‿kodós‿ɡaɡós- kon⌒.
split v.t. ɡáɡ.
Don't split it: tókkoŋ‿ɡáɡmɛn⌒.
Split this one: íŋɡı‿ɡák⌒, pl. íŋɡı‿ɡáɡwɛ⌒.
Split the wood: bérkı‿ɡák⌒.
Are they splitting the wood? bérk‿ āɡɡáɡrandé?
I have split my pipe: áŋ‿kodóskı‿ɡaɡós- kori⌒.
split up v.t. ɡásıɡ.
Split up all this wood: ím‿bér‿mállɛɡ‿ ɡásıč⌒.
spoil v.t. (*ruin*) harbé; (*pamper*) ɡáškır.
Don't spoil the cloth: kádɛt‿tókkon‿ harbémɛn⌒.
This is (i.e. has been) spoilt: (a) ín‿harbé- kattıɡon⌒; (b) ín‿harábkattıɡon⌒ (hárabk-).
spoke n. (*of wheel raising water, thick*) duŋɡútt(ı)‿; (*of wheel raising water, thin*) tarántarɛ‿; (*of cog-wheel*) túnd(ı)‿.
spoon n. målåɡa‿ (-laɡa‿).
handle of spoon: målåɡan‿í‿.
Bring a spoon: målåɡa‿étta⌒.
Bring (some) spoons: målåɡɛnčıɡ‿éttarır⌒.
spoor n. (*footprint*) átar‿; óss(ı)‿.
sport v.i. káčč(ı).
spot n. (*dot*) núɡta‿ (núkta‿); (*place*) áɡar‿.
spout n. áɡıl‿.
spread v.t. awídd(ı).
spring n. (*of water*) míss(ı)‿.
spring v.i. wár.

sprinkle v.t. mísse.
  Sprinkle it with water: éssıgem⌣mísseᴖ.
  Sprinkle it with pepper: fılfílgem⌣mísseᴖ.
sprout v.i. bér.
squander v.t. dábır; gúll(ı).
squat v.i. ág; tég.
squeal v.i. wíg.
squeeze v.t. ğákk(ı); ğúrr(ı); ğógor; úrr(ı).
  (S)he squeezed my hand: ánn-ĭğ⌣ğogórkonᴖ.
stable n. (*of mud, brick, etc.*) káñ-kă⌣; (*of straw*) káñ⌣kérr(ı)⌣.
stack n. šúna⌣; kóm⌣.
stagger v.i. sursúkk(ı).
stair(s) n. síllım⌣.
stale adj. kúrus⌣; gedím⌣.
stalk n. (*of sorghum*) hágɛ⌣.
stamp n. (*postage-*) tába⌣.
stand v.i. tέb.
  Stand here: índo⌣tépᴖ, pl. índo⌣tébweᴖ.
stand v.t. (*endure*) sabrɛ́.
  I can't stand it: âı⌣ɛskısabrḗmununᴖ.
  I couldn't stand it: âı⌣sabrḗmâgoriᴖ.
star n. wíss(ı)⌣; (*badge*) dabbúra⌣.
start v.i. ımbél (ímbɛl).
start v.t. (*begin*) bɛtɛ́ (bɛdɛ́).
startle v.t. halɛ́.
starve v.i. mínčıgɛd⌣dí.
  I'm afraid (s)he (it) will starve: mínčıgɛb⌣bıdíŋgı⌣sándırıᴖ.
starve v.t. kálkıññıgır.
state n. (*condition*) hál⌣.
statement n. wɛ́rɛ⌣.
station n. máhátta⌣ (mah-, moh-, muh-, -tá⌣).
station-master n. máháttan⌣názır⌣;wakíl⌣ (wák-, wɛk-).
stay n. (*supporting-rope*) ɛlwíl⌣.
stay v.i. íñır (íñír), ɛrğɛ́ (ɛrɛğɛ́, ɛrɛğğɛ́, ɛrığɛ́), tέb; (*stay sitting*) ág, tég.
  Stay over there: mándo⌣tépᴖ, pl. ...⌣tébweᴖ.
  You needn't stay: go away: ɛr⌣tébıl⌣luzúm⌣dámunun: nogóᴖ.
stay behind v.i. fadlɛ́.
  Why did you stay behind? ɛr⌣méf⌣fadlɛ́gó?
  Why didn't you stay behind? ɛr⌣méf⌣fadlɛ́gómɛnın?
  Why did (s)he (it) stay behind? tɛr⌣méf⌣fadlɛ́gó?
  Why didn't (s)he (it) stay behind? tɛr⌣méf⌣fadlɛ́gómɛnın?
steal v.t. mág.
  You have stolen it: ɛr⌣mâgétkonᴖ (-kõᴖ, -kóᴖ).
steam-engine n. bâbúr⌣.
steamer n. bâbúr⌣.
steep
  steep declivity: ábol⌣.
steep v.t. nέñgır.
steersman n. réɪs⌣ (réɪs⌣).
step(s) n. (*stair*) síllım; (*stride*) bagašánd(ı)⌣.
  Mind the step: sıllímgı⌣bálko⌣.
  They walk in step: wɛrwέgonoŋ⌣gɛndınógran⌣.
step over v.t. bağášɛ.
sterile adj. mírá⌣.
stew n. ğákud⌣ (ğáhud⌣).
  I want a stew of beans: ğákud⌣fúndıd⌣dólliᴖ.

stick n. wíččır⌣ (-čír⌣).
  I have forgotten my stick (and left it) in the house: áw⌣wıččírkı⌣kár⌣íwkoriᴖ.
  Bring your stick: ɛw⌣wıččírk⌣éttaᴖ.
stick into v.t. (*implant in*) šέg.
sticky adj. ğóndo⌣.
still adv. έlgon⌣; ólgon⌣.
  Stand still, don't move: (don't shake, etc.) kɪttottɛ́pᴖ tókkoŋ⌣kɛrkέrmɛn⌣; (*don't take a step*) kɪttottɛ́pᴖ tókkon⌣nógmɛnᴖ.
sting v.t. ğóm.
stingy adj. sówwɛd⌣ (sówwod⌣).
stink v.i. síɛ (siέ).
stinking adj. síɛl⌣ (siέl⌣).
stir v.t. káše.
  Stir the tea before you pour it out: ɛr⌣ólgom⌣bógmɛŋgon⌣šáıgı⌣kášeᴖ.
  Stir the fire: íkk⌣áñgırᴖ.
stocking n. šur(r)áb⌣.
stomach n. tú⌣ (-tu⌣, -tᵘ⌣v.).
  I have a stomach-ache: án-tu⌣âıg⌣óddınᴖ.
stone n. kúlu⌣; (*small*) kóród⌣; (*for grinding, nether*) ğú⌣; (*for grinding, upper*) ğún-tód⌣.
stool n. bámbar⌣; kúrsı⌣.
stool, go to v.i. úss(ı).
  Have you been to stool today? ɛr⌣ınnówwıg⌣ussóskoná?
stoop v.i. dɛréñɛ; túlɛ.
stop v.i. (*remain*) íñır (íñír); (*remain, cease, check one's own motion*) tέb.
  I shall stop here three days: índo⌣jóm⌣tóskıb⌣bıñírrıᴖ.
  Stop here: índo⌣tέpᴖ, pl. índo⌣tébweᴖ.
  X. *Did the steamer stop here?* bābúr⌣índo⌣tέpkoná?
  Y. *No, it didn't stop*: wáran, tέpkómununᴖ.
  Let the donkey stop: hánut⌣tébanᴖ.
  When the rain stops we shall start: áru⌣tέbkım⌣bımbéllu⌣.
stop v.t. (*restrain*) mír; (*check the motion of*) ɛ́bır.
  Stop him (her, it): ɛ́bırᴖ, pl. ɛbírweᴖ.
  Stop them: ɛbırırᴖ, pl. ɛbıríwweᴖ.
  Why have they stopped the steamer? mínın⌣íllɛr⌣bābúrk⌣ɛbírkoran?
  Tell them to stop talking: bañnítt⌣mugówwanᴖ.
  I stopped him (her) and told him (her) not to do it: mírkori, tókkon⌣áumɛn⌣ɛgiᴖ.
store n. (*store-room*) máhzan⌣ (máxz-).
  There is some in the store: mahzándo⌣dánᴖ.
  There isn't any in the store: mahzándo⌣dámununᴖ.
  Put it into the store: mahzánd⌣úndurᴖ.
  I looked for it (some) in the store but couldn't find it: mahzándo⌣tēbēmɪsírkoriᴖ.
stork n. arraháu⌣ (árraháu⌣); raháu⌣ (ráháu⌣).
story n. báññid⌣; ígid⌣.
  Tell me this story: ím⌣baññídk⌣áıgı⌣wɛ́dɛnᴖ.
  How can you tell me this story? ím⌣baññídkı⌣mínɛ⌣bıwɛ́dɛnın?
stout adj. dúro⌣; kómbo⌣.
straight adj. kjátt(ı)⌣.
  This stick is not straight: íw⌣wíččır⌣kjáttımununᴖ.
stranger n. (*guest*) ıškárt(ı)⌣.

strangle v.t. gıdbɛ́.
strap n. sέr⌣.
stray v.i. tuššɛ́ (tɪššɛ́).
straw n. hasénn⌣kášš(ı)⌣ (-έn⌣k-, -έŋ⌣k-); (*broken*) sílt(ı)⌣.
street n. síkkɛ⌣; dárub⌣.
strength n. šídda⌣ (-dá⌣).
stretch (out) v.t. wárɪs.
  Stretch out your hand: έnn⌣íw⌣wárɪsᴖ.
stride n. bagašánd(ı)⌣.
strike v.t. ğóm.
  Who struck you? n⌣ékkı⌣ğómkon?
  (S)he struck him (her, it) dead: ğom-bégonᴖ.
string n. úl⌣; dubára⌣; (*of guitar*) sílıg⌣, sílk(ı)⌣, kóı⌣ (kóı⌣).
stroll v.i. gırídɛ; murrɛ́; wíd.
  We're going for a stroll: ar⌣wīd'rɛnógbúru⌣.
strong adj. kógor⌣; déŋgɛl⌣; kómbo⌣; (*of drink*) dúllo⌣.
  This donkey is not strong: ín⌣hánu⌣kogórmununᴖ.
  This wood is not strong: ím⌣bέr⌣dɛŋgέlmununᴖ.
  The wind is (too) strong: túrug⌣dıgrínᴖ.
  This wind is very strong: ín⌣túrug⌣désɛn⌣dúllonᴖ.
  Is the beer strong? mérsɛ⌣dúlloré?
  strong tea: šáı⌣dúllo⌣.
  Make the tea strong: šáıd⌣dúllogırᴖ.
  Don't make the tea strong: šáıt⌣tókkon⌣dúllogırmɛnᴖ.
struggle v.i. támug.
stubble n. hásɛd⌣.
student n. kúrıl⌣; hírán⌣.
stuff n. (*things, baggage*) áfɛš⌣.
stuffy adj. háwakıññ(ı)⌣.
stumble v.i. dátt(ı); sursúkk(ı).
stupid adj. ɛrıkkómɛnıl⌣; ɛrıkkattıbúmɛnıl⌣; kússa⌣.
subject n. (*matter*) háğa⌣ (-ğá⌣, -ğɛ⌣).
submit v.t. (*present*) gɛddımɛ́ (-dumɛ́).
subsequently adv. bádır⌣ (etc. s.v. *afterwards*).
suck v.t. ğúkk(ı).
Sudan n. sūdán⌣ (sōdán⌣, sŏgdán⌣).
Sudanese adj. sūdánd(ı)⌣ (sōd-, sŏgd-).
suddenly adv. márra⌣wέgɛd⌣.
suffice v.i. kɛfɛ́.
sufficient adj. (*that suffices*) kɛfέl⌣; (*that sufficed*) kɛfɛ́rɛl⌣.
suffocate v.t. gíd; (*to death*) gıdbɛ́.
sugar n. súkkar⌣.
  There is too much sugar in this: índo⌣súkkar⌣dıgrínᴖ.
sum n. (*calculation*) hısáb⌣.
summer n. bágōn⌣ (˘´).
summit n. kóčč(ı)⌣.
summon v.t. úwɛ.
sun n. másıl⌣.
  at sunrise: másıl⌣bélkın⌣.
  at sunset: másıl⌣tógın⌣.
  I shall not go in the sun: âı⌣masíllo⌣bınógmununᴖ.
  Don't put it in the sun: tókkom⌣masíll⌣uskúrmɛnᴖ.
  Don't leave it in the sun: tókkom⌣masíllo⌣múgmɛnᴖ.
  Don't stay in the sun: tókkom⌣masíllo⌣tέbmɛᴖ.
  Let it stay in the sun: masíllo⌣tέbanᴖ.

Sunday n. kɪrǎgɛ◡ (-áhɛ◡).
  on Sunday: kɪrǎgɛg◡ (-ɛgi⌒).
  (S)he (it) will come on Sunday: kɪrǎgɛb◡ bɪtǎn⌒.
sunset n. mígrɪb◡; šárɛ◡.
  at sunset: (a) mígrɪbɪr◡; (b) šárɛg◡ (-ɛgi⌒).
superintendent n. názɪr◡.
support n. (*post, etc.*) éndɛ◡.
support v.t. sɛndɛ́.
suppose (that) v.t. andá-; ɛdá-.
suppurate v.i. úncan-.
  The wound has suppurated: kór◡ūnčáŋkon⌒.
surprise v.t. ağabɛ́gɪr.
surprised, be v.i. höwwɪlɛ́; ağabɛ́.
  I am surprised at you: (a) âi◡éddotōn◡howwɪlɛ́ri⌒; (b) âi◡ɛkkɪ◡howwɪlɛ́ri⌒.
  I am not surprised at this: âi◡íŋgɪ◡howwɪlɛ́munun⌒.
surrender v.t. sɛllɪmɛ́ (-lumɛ́).
surround v.t. góbɪr.
suspend v.t. sóllɪgɪr.
swallow n. (*bird*) gɛrɛdún◡; ɪŋgɛlɛdúna◡.
swallow v.t. góll(ɪ).
  Swallow the medicine without chewing it: dáwat◡tókkon◡ğókkɪmɛŋŋoŋ◡gólli⌒.
swathe v.t. kátt(ɪ).
swear v.i. and t. ğéd.
  Has (s)he sworn on the Book? kɪtápkɪ◡ğɛtkoná?
swear at v.t. čubbɛ́; tubbɛ́.
  Did (s)he swear at you? ɛkkɪ◡čubbɛ́goná?
sweat n. tɪllátt(ɪ)◡.
sweat v.i. tíllɛ.
sweep v.t. túb.
  Sweep (out) the room: ódat◡túp⌒.
sweepings n. tubínd(ɪ)◡.
sweet adj. íŋg(ɪ)ri◡.
  It is sweet: íŋgrín⌒.
  Is it sweet? íŋgrīrɛ́?
sweet-scented adj. númmɛl◡ (″).
sweet-scented, be v.i. númmɛ (″).
swell v.i. nɛ́jj(ɪ).
  His (her) hand is swollen: tɛ́nn-i◡nɛ́jjɪbūn⌒.
swell v.t. nɛ́jjɪgɪr.
swift-footed adj. bōdkátt(ɪ)◡.
swim v.i. bóww(ɪ).
  Can you swim? ɛr◡uñurbówwɪná?
  Can (s)he (it) swim? tɛr◡uñurbówwɪná?, pl. uñurbówwɪrandɛ́?
switch n. kuríčče◡ (-rúč-).
swollen, be v.i. nɛ́jjɪbū-.
sword n. síwɪd◡.
  blade of sword: sɪwídn◡ágɪl◡.
  hilt of sword: (a) sɪwídn◡ǎd◡; (b) sɪwídn◡í◡.
  point of sword: síwɪn◡kóčč(ɪ)◡.
  scabbard of sword: síwín◡kǎ◡.
sycamore (*fig-tree*) n. ğɪmbɛ́z◡.
symptom n. alǎma◡.
syphilis n. hábbu◡.
  (S)he has contracted syphilis: hábbu◡tédd◡ɪmbɛlóskon⌒.

table n. tarabɛ́za◡ (-zǎ◡).
  (*for meals*) súfra◡.
table-cloth n. súfran◡fúta◡.
tail n. ɛ́u◡ (ɛ́w◡, ɛ́u◡).
tailor n. níğɪl◡; káden◡níğɪl◡; kadénčɪn◡níğɪl◡.

take v.t. (*lift*) índ(ɪ), sókkɛ; (*seize*) ǎr; (*carry*) óğɪ.
  Take it: ísa⌒, pl. ísawɛ⌒.
  Take this: íŋg◡ísa⌒.
  Take that (near): íŋg◡ísa⌒.
  Take that (yonder): máŋg◡ísa⌒.
  Have you taken the paper (away)? warákk◡ɛr◡sókkɛgoná?
  Have you taken the paper (to its destination)? warákk◡ɛr◡óğɪgoná?
  I want this light; if you want one take that over there: âi◡íŋ◡ígkɪ◡dólli; ɛr◡wɛ́d◡dólkɪm◡máŋgɪ◡sókkɛ⌒.
  Let him (her) take (carry) it to the market: súgɪr◡óğan⌒.
  I'll take (carry) it with me this afternoon: dúhurm◡bádɪr◡âɪgonom◡bóğ'rɪ⌒.
  Take the valise to him (her): šántag◡óğɪtɪr⌒.
  Take it and go: ɪndɛnnók⌒.
  Let him (her) take a lantern and go: fānús-sēg◡ɪndɛnnógan⌒.
  Take the boat to him (her): kúbk◡óğɪtɪr, pl. ...◡óğɪtɪrwwɛ⌒.
  Take the boat to them: kúbk◡óğɪtɪrɪr⌒, pl. ...◡óğɪtɪrɪwwɛ⌒.
  Take the boats to him (them): kúblɪg◡óğɪtɪrɪr⌒, pl. ...◡óğɪtɪríwwɛ⌒.
  If you put it there the cat will take it: ɛron◡tédd◡uskúrkɪn◡sáb◡bárkɪn⌒.
  Take your medicine: (*a, swallow it*) én◡dáwag◡gólli⌒; (*b, drink it*) én◡dáwan◡ní⌒; (*c, eat it*) én◡dáwak◡kál⌒; (*d, remove it*) én◡dáwas◡sókkɛ⌒.
take away v.t. sókkɛ, índ(ɪ); (*carry off*) ārɛnnóg, ɪndɛnnóg; (*drive off*) šūgɛnnóg.
  Take the glass (tumbler) away: kubâiɛs◡sókkɛ⌒.
  Come and take this away: íŋgɪ◡tasókkɛ⌒, pl. íŋgɪ◡tasókkɛwɛ⌒.
  Let him (her) take it away: sókkɛran⌒.
  Have you taken the (a) plate away from here? saháŋg◡índotōn◡sókkɛgoná?
  Has (s)he taken it (them) away? sokkédkoná? (sokkéttoná?).
  Let ɣáli take my gun away: álɪg◡ám◡bundúkkɪ◡sókkɛran⌒.
  (S)he has taken it away: ārɛnnókkon⌒.
take charge of v.t. ɪstɛlɛmɛ́.
take down v.t. (*take to pieces*) wíll(ɪ).
take off v.t. (*apparel*) dúkk(ɪ).
  Take your clothes off: ɛ́n◡káded◡dúkki⌒.
  Let him (her) take his (her) shoes off: (a) ɛ́m◡mɛrkúbkɪ◡bóttɪran⌒; (b) ɛ́m◡mɛrkúbkɪ◡dúkkan⌒.
take out v.t. ós; (*extract*) kúl, dúkk(ɪ).
  Take out a chair from the house: kúrsɪwɛ̄k◡kártōn◡ós⌒.
  Take this thorn out of my hand (i.e. extract it): íŋ◡kɪníssɛg◡ánn◡írtōn◡dúkki⌒. (...◡írtōn◡ós⌒).
take over v.t. (*receive*) ɪstɛlɛmɛ́.
  Did you take over the letter? ɛr◡ğawápk◡ɪstɛlɛmɛ́goná?
take up v.t. sókkɛ; índ(ɪ).
tale n. ígɪd◡; báññɪd◡.
talk n. báññɪd◡; (*chat*) wénɛs◡.
  I don't want talk: baññídk◡âi◡dólmunū⌒.
  I don't want a lot of talk: âi◡baññɪd◡dɪgríd◡dólmunun⌒.
  I don't want any more talk: (a) âi◡ténnɛ◡baññídkɪ◡dólmunun⌒; (b) âi◡baññídkɪ◡ténnɛ◡dólmunun⌒.
talk v.i. báññ(ɪ); (*chat*) wénnɪskatt(ɪ).
  I am talking to the cat: sápkonon◡ábbáññɪri⌒.
  Who is it keeps on talking? (a) n◡ábbáññɪn? (b) nír◡ábbáññɪn?
  Don't let anyone talk: tókkow◡wɛ́b◡báññɪŋgɪrmɛn⌒.
  What's the use (good) of talking? báññɪd◡míndo◡nɛfɛ́n?
  They talk a great deal: dɪgrīgɪrbáññɪran⌒.
tall adj. nósŏ◡.
  The man is tall: ógɪğ◡nosón⌒.
talon n. súnt(ɪ)◡.
tamarind n. aradɛ́b◡.
tamarisk n. šírɛ◡.
tan v.t. kárğɪgɪr (káğğɪ-).
tangle n. kúrt(ɪ).
tap v.t. tóbbɛ.
task n. ğɛ́ll(ɪ)◡.
tassel n. gordád◡.
taste v.t. táncɛ.
  Have you tasted it? ɛr◡táncɛgoná?
  Tell the cook to taste it: tabbáhkɪ◡táncɛran⌒.
tasteless adj. bássarɪ◡.
tax n. túlba◡; harǎğ◡ (xa-).
tea n. šâi◡.
  The tea is (too) strong: šâi◡dúllon⌒.
  The tea is (too) weak: šâi◡šŏron⌒.
  Tea is finished: clear it away: šâi◡halásun: sókkɛ⌒.
teach v.t. kúrkɪr.
teacher n. kúrkɪrɪ◡.
tea-cup n. šâiŋ◡kubâia◡; šâin◡fɪnğán◡; kubâia◡šâind(ɪ)◡; fɪnğán◡šâind(ɪ)◡.
tea-pot n. bɛrrád◡ (bár-, bar-); bɛrrád◡šâind(ɪ)◡.
  handle of tea-pot: bɛrrádn◡í◡.
tear n. (*hole torn*) úbbɛd◡; (*-drop*) óñmɪssɛ◡, umbúššɛ◡.
tear v.i. órr(ɪ); mér.
  Mind! It's tearing: bálko! ágórrɪn⌒.
tear v.t. (*from the edge*) órr(ɪ); (*tear a hole in*) úbbur.
  Don't tear it: tókkon◡órrɪmɛn⌒.
  Don't tear a hole in it: tókkon◡úbburmɛn⌒.
  It tore my clothes: áŋ◡kádɛg◡órrɪgon⌒.
  It is torn (has a hole in it): úbbubūn⌒.
tear up v.t. órɪğ.
  Don't let him (her) tear it up: tókkon◡orɪğɪŋgɪrmɛn⌒.
tease v.t. (*irritate*) sínnɛgɪr; (*worry*) mágɪr; (*tease out*) bíll(ɪ), túŋ(ɪ).
  Don't tease the monkey: (a) gɪrídkɪ◡tókkon◡sínnɛgɪrmɛn⌒; (b) gɪrídkɪ◡tókkon◡mágɪrmɛn⌒.
  X. What are they doing? míŋg◡ağáuran?
  Y. They are teasing out cotton: bɛnnákk◡ábbíllɪran⌒.
teat n. ért(ɪ)◡.
telegram n. tɛlɛgráf◡; sílɪg◡; sílk(ɪ)◡.
  I shall send a telegram: tɛlɛgráfkɪ◡bɪğómri⌒.
  I want to send him (her) with a telegram: tɛkkɪ◡tɛlɛgráfked◡ɪsɪndáŋgɪ◡dólli⌒.
  I told him (her) by telegram: tɛkkɪ◡tɛlɛgráfwɛ́tɪkkori⌒.
  (S)he let me know by telegram: âɪgɪ◡tɛlɛgráfwɛ́dɛŋkon⌒.

I shall inquire by telegram: tɛlɛgráfkɛb⌣bɪsíkkɪrɪ◠.
The news has come from Khartoum by telegram: hartûmɪrtōn⌣sílkɪgɛd⌣hábar⌣tágon◠.
telegraph n. tɛlɛgráf⌣; sílɪg⌣; sílk(ɪ)⌣.
Take this to the telegraph (office): íŋgɪ⌣tɛlɛgráfɪr⌣ógi◠.
Let him (her) take this to the telegraph (office): íŋgɪ⌣tɛlɛgráfɪr⌣ógan◠.
telephone n. tɛlɛfón⌣.
Where is the telephone? tɛlɛfón⌣ɪsáirɛ́?
tell v.t. ⌣ɛ́-; ⌣án (-an); (to the speaker) wɛ́dɛn; (to other than the speaker) wɛ́tɪr; (narrate) íg.
Did you tell him (her) to come? ɛr⌣tɛ́kkɪ⌣tắr⌣ɛgoná?
I told him (her) to come here: âi⌣tɛ́kk⌣índo⌣tằr⌣ɛgóri◠.
Tell him (her) to bring it: éttaran◠.
Tell me this later on: íŋg⌣áɪgɪ⌣bádkɛw⌣wɛ́dɛn◠.
When (s)he (it) comes, tell me: tɛr⌣tắgɪn⌣âɪgɪ⌣wɛ́dɛn◠.
I have told him (her): wɛtíkkori◠.
Who told you? n⌣ékkɪ⌣wɛtíkkŏ?
Have you told him (her)? ɛr⌣wɛtíkkoná?
Did you tell him (her)? Will (s)he come? ɛr⌣wɛtíkkoná? bɪtắná?
I tell him (her) to go: âi⌣tɛ́kkɪ⌣nóg⌣awwɛ́ri◠.
I tell you not to do it: âi⌣ékkɪ⌣tókkon⌣âumɛn⌣awwɛ́ri◠.
I keep on telling you not to do it: âi⌣ékkɪ⌣tókkon⌣âumɛn⌣ég⌣àwwɛ́ri◠.
I told him (her) to look over there in the tent: mándo⌣xɛ̄már⌣nál⌣ɛgori◠.
I told him (her) not to go: mírkori, tókkon⌣nógmɛn⌣égi◠.
Tell ɛ́ali I want to send him with a telegram: áliw⌣wɛ́tɪr⌣ékkɪ⌣tɛlɛgráfkɛd⌣išindáŋgɪ⌣dólli◠.
Tell him (her) to tell ɛ ali: (a) tɛ́kk⌣áliw⌣wɛ́tiran◠; (b §6291) áliw⌣wɛ́tiran◠.
Tell ɛ ali to tell him: (a) álit⌣tɛ́kkɪ⌣wɛ́tiran◠; (b §6291) áliw⌣wɛ́tiran◠.
Tell ɛ ali to remind me: álig⌣âigɪ⌣ğíllɛgiran◠.
Tell Muḥammad to tell me when Sálim comes: sắlum⌣tắn⌣tắm⌣mohammɛ́tt⌣âigɪ⌣wɛ́dɛnanó◠.
temple n. (*building*) bírbɛ⌣; (*of head*) tíbɪl⌣.
ten card. num. dímɪn⌣.
tenant n. (*of house*) káb⌣bájɪl⌣.
tender adj. (*soft*) ǧagádɛl⌣ (⌣́, ⌣́).
We want tender meat: ar⌣kúsu⌣ǧagādɛ́lgɪ⌣dóllu⌣.
tendon n. kóɪ⌣ (kôi).
tennis n. kúra⌣.
tent n. hɛ́ma⌣ (xɛ́-, -mɑ⌣).
tenth ord. num. dɪm(ı)nínt(ı)⌣ (dím(ı)nɪnt(ı)⌣).
tent-peg n. hɛ́maŋ⌣kóǧɪr⌣.
termite n. nórɛ⌣.
terrify v.t. sɪgíŋgɪr.
This terrified him (her, it): ín⌣tɛ́kkɪ⌣sɪgíŋgɪrkon◠.
test v.t. ǧɛrrɪbɛ́ (-rubɛ́).
Test whether it can be opened: tɛ́kkɪ⌣ǧɛrrɪbɛ́, tɛrōn⌣kúskattɪgɪn◠.
testicle n. sorón⌣kúmbu⌣ (óŋ⌣k-).

testify v.t. kárǧ(ı) (káǧǧ(ı)).
tether v.t. dígɪr; mór.
Tether the pony: káčči⌣dígɪr◠.
Tether the donkey: hánud⌣dígɪr◠.
Have you had the horse tethered? ɛr⌣káčči⌣mōrkíddɪgoná?
Tetrodon fahaka n. kɛkkɛbɛrrúd⌣.
thank v.t. šɛkkɪrɛ́; šɛkrɛ́.
Thank you! ɛn⌣hɛ́ron⌣dɪgránɪl! (§6266); éddo⌣bārɪkɛ́r⌣ɛn! (§6265).
Thank you (pl.)! íddo⌣bārɪkɛ́r⌣ɛn!
Thank you very much! éddo⌣dɪgrīgɪrbārɪkɛ́r⌣ɛn!
Thank you (pl.) very much! íddo⌣dɪgrīgɪrbārɪkɛ́r⌣ɛn!
Go and thank him (her): kattɛrhērakanǧuwɛ́tɪr◠.
that conj. (*quod*).
I know that (s)he is coming: tɛ́r⌣ǧúbūŋg⌣uñúddi◠.
Are you going to swear that you didn't see? ɛr⌣bɪǧédná⌣ɛr⌣nalménsɪŋgi?
that conj. (*ut*).
Come nearer to me that I may hear what you say: ánn⌣ɛgɛttantá, âi⌣ém⌣bɑññídkɪ⌣gɪǧɪrr⌣égi?
Bring him (her, it) here that I may see him (her, it): índ⌣étt⌣âi⌣nállíŋ-karam◠.
Bring a light that I may see: ígk⌣étt⌣âi⌣nálli◠.
that dem. pron. (*near*) ín⌣ (ɪn⌣); (*yonder*) mán⌣.
Is that ɛ ali (at hand) ín⌣áli⌣té? (*over there*) mán⌣áli⌣té?
that man: mán⌣óǧɪǧ⌣.
those men: mán⌣óǧǧi⌣.
I don't want that: âi⌣máŋgɪ⌣dólmunun◠.
I don't want that goat: âi⌣mám⌣bɛ́rtɪd⌣dólmunun◠.
I don't want those: âi⌣máŋgud⌣dólmunun◠.
I don't want those goats: âi⌣mám⌣bɛ́rtɪnčɪd⌣dólmunun◠.
That of Argo is like that of El-Ordi: argónd⌣urdíndɪkɪrɪn◠.
that rel. pron.—use the participle (§§2956–60); see Noun-clause (§§6111–57); see Adjective-clause (§§6158–72).
Where has the man gone that came yesterday? óǧɪǧ⌣wílgɪ⌣tắrɛl⌣sáikɛ⌣nókkŏ?
Bring the cheese that's in the tin: ǧíbn⌣élbár⌣dắbūlg⌣étta◠.
Call the man that's in that tent: óǧɪǧ⌣mán⌣hɛ́man⌣tűr⌣ắgɪlg⌣úwɛ◠.
Let the first that comes take this to the post: ówwɛlɛn⌣tắlg⌣íŋgɪ⌣bústar⌣ógan◠.
I shall give ten piastres to the one that brings the cat: sắbk⌣ɛttắlgɪ⌣gírɪs⌣dimíŋgɪ⌣bɪtíddi◠.
You have brought the (a) lamp that has no oil: ɛr⌣lámba⌣ǧăz⌣kōmɛnílg⌣éttagon◠.
I don't like a dog that barks: wɛ́l⌣úkkílg⌣âi⌣dólmunun◠.
The man that I saw was an Arab: óǧɪǧ⌣âi⌣náls⌣áràb⌣ɛgó◠.
Where is the knife that you found yesterday? kánd⌣ɛ́r⌣wflg⌣ɛ́lsun¹sáir⌣bún?
X. *Where is the snake?* kág⌣sɛ́?
Y. *That they killed?* bɛ́sanó?
X. *Where are the men?* óǧǧi⌣sɛ́?
Y. *That killed the snake?* kákkɪ⌣bɛ́rɛlió?

I don't like a dog that whines: âi⌣wɛ́l⌣wɪkkáttɪd⌣dólmunun◠.
that yonder dem. pron. mắman⌣.
the definite article §§4689ff.
Bring the meat: kúsug⌣étta◠.
Bring some meat: kúsug⌣étta◠.
X. *Where is the meat?* kúsu⌣sɛ́?
Y. *A dog has taken it:* wɛ́l-lɛ̄r⌣sokkɛ́tkó◠.
The dog has taken it: wɛ́l⌣sokkɛ́tkó◠.
They are men: tɪr⌣óǧǧɪn◠.
They are the men: (a) tɪr⌣óǧǧi-taran◠; (b) tɪr⌣óǧǧi-tànnan◠.
They are women: tɪr⌣ɛ́nči◠.
They are the women: (a) tɪr⌣ɛ́nči-taran◠; (b) tɪr⌣ɛ́nči-tànnan◠.
their poss. pron. tínn⌣v., tín⌣c.
their guests: tínn⌣iškari⌣.
their money: tín⌣dúŋg(ɪ)⌣.
their horses: tíŋ⌣kắǧi⌣.
their country: tím⌣bɛ́lɛd⌣.
theirs abs. poss. pron. tínd(ɪ)⌣.
It's theirs: tíndín◠.
Is it theirs? tíndɪrɛ́?
It's not theirs: tíndɪmunun◠.
Isn't it theirs? tíndɪmɛn?
They're theirs: tíndɪnčín◠.
Are they theirs? tíndɪnčɪrɛ́?
They're not theirs: tɪndɪnčɪmunan◠.
Aren't they theirs? tɪndɪnčɪmɛndan?
Is this (that) theirs? (a) ɪn⌣tíndɪrɛ́? (b) ín⌣tíndɪ⌣té? (*Is this the one that is theirs?*).
Are these (those) theirs? íŋgu⌣tíndɪnčɪrɛ́?
then adv. mán⌣wɛkídk(ɪ)⌣; see §6202.
thence adv. (*from near*) téddotōn⌣ (s.v. tɛr⌣); (*from far*) mándotōn⌣.
there adv. (*near*) índo⌣, téddo⌣; (*yonder*) mándo⌣.
Who's there? (a, to an unseen person close at hand) ɛ́r⌣nɪ́⌣té? (b, = *Who is in that place?*) nírɛ⌣mánd⌣ắgɪn?
Put it here, not there (pointing): índ⌣úskur, tókkon⌣índ⌣úskurmɛn◠.
There (yonder) implied in mán⌣:
Who's that sitting over there? ní-tɛ⌣mán⌣ắgɪl?
Call Idrís from there (i.e. from where you are): (a) tékkɛd⌣ɪdrísk⌣úwɛ◠; (b) ɪdrísk⌣úwɛ⌣tékkɛ◠.
If (s)he is there, take it to him (her): tɛrōn⌣åkkɪn⌣óǧɪtɪr◠.
If (s)he is not there, bring it back: tɛrōn⌣dắmɛŋkɪn⌣wᵘdɛgɪrétta◠.
thereby adv. íŋgɛd⌣ (etc. s.v. ín⌣); tékkɛd⌣ (etc. s.v. tɛr⌣); máŋgɛd⌣ (etc. s.v. mán⌣).
they pers. pron. tír⌣ (tɪr⌣).
X. *Let them sit down:* tɛ́gwan◠.
Y. *I'll tell them:* bɪwɛtríddi◠.
thick adj. dúro⌣; bárɪǧ⌣.
This is too thick: ɪn⌣durón◠.
This cloth is too thick: ɪŋ⌣kádɛ⌣durón◠.
Bring my thick stick: áw⌣wíččɪr⌣duróg⌣étta◠.
I want a thick one: dúro-wɛ̄d⌣dólli◠.
I want a thick cloth: kádɛ⌣dúro-wɛ̄d⌣dólli◠.
I want a thick rope: írɪ⌣baríǧ-ǧɛd⌣dólli◠.
The rope is not thick enough: írɪ⌣baríǧmunun◠.
thief n. mágas⌣ (mágɑs⌣).
thievish adj. māgkátt(ɪ)⌣ (māakát-).
thigh n. bókk(ɪ)⌣.

thin adj. (*a, deficient in one dimension*) kawwáñ‿; (*b, deficient in two dimensions*) ɛ́sɛ̃‿.
 This paper is too thin: íw‿wárág‿kawwáñun⌒.
 This stick is too thin: íw‿wíččir‿ɛsɛ̃n⌒.
 I want a thin one: (a) kawwáñ-wɛ̃d‿dólli⌒; (b) ɛsɛ̃-wɛ̃d‿dólli⌒.
 Bring those (yonder) thin ones: (a) máŋ‿kawwáñig‿ɛ́tta⌒; (b) máń‿ɛsɛ́rig‿ɛ́tta⌒.
thing n. šɛ́j(ɪ)‿ (šéjj(ɪ)‿); hága‿ (-gá‿, -gɛ‿).
 Take these things away: ín‿šéjinčis‿sókkɛrɪr⌒, pl. …‿sokkɛríwwɛ⌒.
thingamy n. hɪnãi‿.
think v.t. gílle; (*that*) andá-, ɛdá-.
 Who do you think that is (yonder)? ɛr‿máŋɪ‿ní-taran‿ándan?
 What do you think that is (yonder)? ɛr‿máŋɪ‿mínun‿ándan?
 I thought this was blood: (a) íŋ‿gɛ́un‿andágori⌒; (b) íŋ‿gɛ́un‿ɛdágori⌒.
 Do you think that there is any water? ɛr‿ɛ́ssɪ‿dán‿ɛdáná?
 I think there is some over there: go and see: ɛddɛ́r‿mándo‿dǎn: gúnal‿.
 I think it's inside a house: ãɪ‿tékkɪ‿kán-tu-wɛ́rro‿bũn‿ɛdári⌒.
 I thought it was inside a house: ãɪ‿tékkɪ‿kán-tu-wɛ́rro‿búgon‿ɛdágori⌒.
third n. (⅓) tílid‿.
third ord. num. toskínt(ɪ)‿ (́‿).
thirst n. ɛssɪnɛ́r‿; ɛ́ssɪn‿orgíd‿ (‿órgɪd‿).
 (S)he (it) is nearly dead of thirst: ɛssɪnɛ́r-kɛd‿dĩɛdólɪn⌒.
 I am thirsty: ɛssɪnɛ́r‿ãɪg‿árɪn⌒.
 Are you thirsty? ɛssɪnɛ́r‿ɛ́kk‿árná?
 (S)he (it) is thirsty: ɛssɪnɛ́r‿tékk‿árɪn⌒.
thirteen card. num. dɪmɪndotósk(ɪ)‿.
thirtieth ord. num. talatĩnínt(ɪ)‿ (́‿ ́‿).
thirty card. num. dɪmɪntósk(ɪ)‿; talatĩ́n‿.
this dem. pron. ín‿.
 this house: íŋ‿ká‿.
 these houses: íŋ‿kárɪ‿.
 I want this: íŋ‿kándɪd‿dólli⌒.
 I want this knife: íŋgud‿dólli⌒.
 I want these: íŋgud‿dólli⌒.
 I want these knives: íŋ‿kándɪnčid‿dólli⌒.
thither adv. (*near*) téddo‿; (*far*) mándo‿.
thong n. sɛ́r‿.
thorn n. kɪníssɛ‿.
thoroughly
 They were thoroughly delighted: gurrɛrɪ̃daŋ-gúrrɛgoran⌒.
thou pers. pron. ɛr‿ (ɛr‿).
though
 Though I keep on telling you not to do it you keep on doing it: ãɪ‿ɛ́kkɪ‿tókkon‿ãumɛn‿ɛ́kk‿agáwɪn⌒.
 She's a woman, though she looks like a man: ɛ́n‿ɛ́ŋgon‿ogíčkɪ‿gálɪgɪn⌒.
thought n. ɛ́rig‿.
thousand card. num. ɛ́lif‿.
thread n. úl‿.
three card. num. tósk(ɪ)‿.
thresh v.t. (*by causing cattle to tread out*) núr.
threshing-floor n. (*place where cattle tread out corn, etc.*) tága‿.
throat n. gúmur‿; ɛ́jjɛ‿.
throttle v.t. gíd; (*to death*) gɪdbɛ́.

through
 (S)he (it) broke in through the fence: zɛ́rbɛt‿tombɛttógon⌒.
throw v.t. árk(ɪ); aríkk(ɪ).
 Throw it (away): árki⌒, pl. árkɪwɛ⌒.
 Throw him (her, it) out: bóččɪr‿árki⌒.
 Don't throw it (away): tókkon‿aríkkɪmɛn⌒, pl. tókkon‿aríkkɪmɛwwɛ⌒.
 Throw a stone at it: téddo‿kúlu-wɛ̃g‿árki⌒.
throw about v.t. (*scatter*) gúll(ɪ).
 (S)he is throwing his (her) money about: tɛn‿dúŋgɪg‿aggúllɪn⌒.
through prep. —n‿túg‿ɛd‿.
 It passes through the pipe: mãsúran‿tũgɛn‿nógin⌒.
thumb n. múdul‿.
thump v.t. túkk(ɪ); šókk(ɪ).
thunder n. udúdɛ‿.
Thursday n. hamís‿.
 on Thursday: hamísk(ɪ), -ki⌒.
 (S)he (it) will come on Thursday: hamískɪ‿bɪtán⌒.
thus adv. íŋkɛ‿ (íŋké⌒, íŋkɛg‿, -gi⌒); tékkɛ‿ (tékké⌒, tékkɛg‿, -gi⌒); íŋgɛd‿ (-ɛt⌒, íŋgé⌒); tékkɛd‿ (-ɛt⌒, tékké⌒).
tick n. (*acarid*) bágg(ɪ)‿.
tickle v.t. (*the speaker*) kɪlkílg‿áudɛ̃n; (*other than the speaker*) kɪlkílg‿áutɪr.
 (S)he (it) tickled me: ãɪk‿kɪlkílg‿áudɛ̃ŋkon⌒.
 Does (s)he (it) tickle you? ɛkkɪ‿kɪlkílg‿áutɪrná?
tickling n. kílkɪl‿.
tie v.t. dígɪr; mɔ́r.
 Tie him (her, it, up): dígɪr⌒, pl. dɪgírwɛ⌒.
 Tie this (up): íŋgɪ‿dígɪr⌒.
 The camel is tied up: kám‿mɔ́rbũn⌒.
tight
 These shoes hurt me, they are too tight: ín‿gázm‿ãɪg‿óddɪgɪrɪn, tákkarun⌒.
Tilapia nilotica n. bórra‿.
till conj. ‿bókkon‿ (-kõ⌒, -kó⌒); ‿móŋkon‿ (-kõ⌒, -kó⌒); ‿kóttɪg‿ following negative subjunctive.
 Wait till (s)he (it) comes: tɛr‿tãm‿bókkon‿tɛ́p⌒.
 Wait here till (s)he (it) comes: (a) tɛr‿tãm‿bókkon‿índo‿tɛ́k⌒; (b) tɛr‿nãman‿tãm‿bókkon‿índo‿tɛ́k⌒.
till prep. —m‿bókkon‿ (-kõ⌒, -kó⌒); —m‿móŋkon‿ (-kõ⌒, -kó⌒).
 from today till Sunday: ɪnnówwɪrtõŋ‿kɪrágɛm‿bókkon‿.
 Leave it till tomorrow: asálm‿bókkom‿mugó⌒.
tillage n. tɛ́rar‿ (-rár‿); tɛrɪ́d‿.
timber n. bɛ́r‿; hášab‿ (xá-).
time n. wékid‿ (wák‿), (*hour*) sá‿; (*occasion*) márra‿ (-rá‿), gɪr‿ § 2762).
 What's the time? (a) sá‿mɪŋkóttɪré? (sá‿muk-); (b) sá‿mɪŋkóttɛ̃rré? (sá‿muk-).
 X. *At what time did they come?* sá‿mɪŋkóttɛ̃rro‿tágoran?
 Y. *At 10.30:* sá‿dɪmɪntórtɪr⌒.
 how many times? márra‿mɪŋkottɛ́g‿…?
 How many times did (s)he (it) come? márra‿mɪŋkottɛ́t‿tágon?
 three times: gɪrtóskɪg‿.
 four times: gɪrkémɪsk(ɪ)‿.

 I've said it five times: gɪrdíčk‿ɛgóri⌒.
 They've done it 100 times: gɪrɪmílg‿áukoran⌒.
 Is the train on time? gátɪr‿tɛ́m‿mawaídɪré?
 It has been here for a long time: zãmán‿dotõn‿índo‿bũn⌒.
 ancient times: wãĩ‿ (wãĩ‿).
 in ancient times: wãĩg‿, -gi⌒.
 when I have time (=leisure): ãĩ‿súdɪr‿ákkɪrɪ‿.
 Let him (her) off (don't punish him (her)) this time: ɪnnówwɪm‿mugó⌒.
timid adj. káukãu‿.
tin n. (*small receptacle of*) ílbɛ‿ (él-, -bá‿, -ba‿).
tinea n. íttɛ‿.
tin-opener n. kúšar‿ɛlbénd(ɪ)‿; kúšar‿ɛlbɛnčínd(ɪ)‿.
tip n. (*extremity*) kɛ́l‿; (*gratuity*) mukáfa‿.
tire v.t. galabɛ́; mágɪr.
 (S)he (it) tires me: ãɪg‿mágɪrɪn⌒.
tired, be v.i. mábũ-.
 I am tired: ãɪ‿mábũrɪ⌒.
 Are you tired? ɛr‿mábũná?
tired, get v.i. mã-.
 (S)he (it) will get tired: bɪmãn⌒.
to conj.
 They wait here to go in: (a) índ‿ágran‿tɔ́r‿ɛ́gi‿; (b) índ‿ágran‿tɔ́rann‿íllar⌒.
to prep. -r‿ after a vowel; -ɪr‿ after a consonant, but -ro after -r (except of personal pronouns), -lo after -l, -do after -n and personal pronouns. See §§ 4291 ff. -abd(ɪ)‿ (-add(ɪ)‿ suffixed to objective); -năr‿ (not with place-names), with ‿án go, not rendered; (*as far as*) —m‿bókkon‿ (-kõ⌒, -kó⌒); —m‿móŋkon‿ (-kõ⌒, -kó⌒); (*belonging to*) use the genitive.
 (S)he (it) has gone to the house: (a) kár‿nókkó⌒; (b) kágaddɪ‿nókkó⌒; (c) kánăr‿nókkó⌒; (d) káŋkó⌒.
 Let ɣáli go to the post: álɪb‿bústar‿nógan⌒.
 Take him (her, it) to the office: (a) máktabɪr‿óǧi⌒, pl. …‿óǧɪwɛ:⌒; (b) máktabnãr‿óǧi⌒.
 They are on their way (going) to the office: mɛktɛ́bkaddɪ‿nógbũran⌒.
 They are on their way (coming) to the office: mɛktɛ́bkaddɪ‿gúbũran⌒.
 to the valley: hɔ́rro‿.
 to the mountain: ǧɛbéllo‿.
 (S)he has gone to Aswãn: suwándo‿nókkon⌒.
 On Monday we shall go to Khartoum: (a) búškɪ‿hartúmɪr‿bɪnógru⌒; (b) búškɪ‿hartúm‿bándu‿.
 Go to the lady: síttɪnãr‿nók⌒.
 Tell him (her) to come to me: ánnar‿tãran⌒.
 (S)he (it) has gone to the market: súg‿áŋkon⌒.
 From Gebeit to Sinkat is one hour: gɛbɛdɪr‿tõn‿sɪŋkán‿bókkon‿sá‿wɛ́run⌒.
 Whom is this letter to? ín‿ǧawáb‿nínkaram?
 This is the answer to the letter: ín‿ǧawám‿ráddɪn⌒.

toad n. góglatt(ɪ)‿.

toast n. —making toast is not a Nubian practice.
toast (toasted bread): (a) fu⌣níbbūl⌣ (kál⌣ níbbūl⌣); (b) fu⌣tógbūl⌣ (kál⌣tóg-būl⌣); (c) fw⌣íkkes⌣sówwıbūl⌣ (kál⌣ ík-).
Tell him (her) to make a little toast: fu⌣ toddɛ́n⌣níban⌢.
tobacco n. tumbâg⌣; duhhân⌣ (duxxán⌣).
Where is the tin of tobacco? tumbágn⌣ ílbɛ⌣sɛ́?
today adv. ınnów(w)ıg⌣, -gi⌢ (N. ın(n)óŋ-gıg⌣, -gi⌢).
today n. ınnów(w)ı⌣ (N. ın(n)óŋg(ı)⌣).
I want some like today's: ınnowwíndı-kırıd⌣dólli⌢.
toe n. óssın⌣sárbɛ⌣.
toe-nail n. óssın⌣súnt(ı)⌣.
together, bring v.t. ğámmɛgır.
together, come v.i. *(assemble)* ğámmɛ; *(come one with another)* ğammɛtå.
together, go v.i. *(assemble)* ğámmɛ; *(go one with another)* ğammɛnóg.
token n. alǎma⌣.
tolerate v.t. sabrɛ́.
tomb n. gábur⌣; túrbɛ⌣ (-bá⌣, -ba⌣).
tomorrow adv. asálg(ı)⌣, -gi⌢.
Come tomorrow: asálgı⌣tǎrɛ⌢, pl. ...⌣tǎwɛ⌢.
(S)he (it) will come tomorrow evening: asál⌣šárɛb⌣bıtǎn⌢.
the day after tomorrow: asál⌣wa-hákk(ı)⌣.
tomorrow n. ásal⌣.
Tomorrow is Friday: ásal⌣móšonó-taran⌢.
tomorrow's water: asáln⌣ɛ́ss(ı)⌣.
tongs n. kammǎša⌣.
tongue n. néd⌣.
Put out your tongue: ɛ́n⌣nétkı⌣kúl⌢.
tonight adv. ínn⌣ugúg⌣, -gi⌢.
too adv. *(also)* -on⌣ suffixed to objective (§§ 4398-4400); *(excessively, needlessly)* luzúm⌣dógŏr⌣, not rendered unless emphatic.
Hang this up too: íŋgoŋgı⌣sóllıgır⌢.
Take this away, and these too: íŋgı⌣ sókkɛ, íŋgugoŋgı⌢.
Tell him (her) to come too: tékkoŋgı⌣ tǎran⌢.
Tell ʇoθmǎn to come too: ɛsmǎŋgoŋgı⌣ tǎran⌢.
(S)he is to go, and you too: tékkı⌣nógan, ékkon⌢ (sc. ⌣nók⌢).
I want a big one, but this is too big: dūl-lɛ̄d⌣dólli, lákın⌣íl⌣luzúm⌣dógor⌣ dúlun⌢.
This is too big and that too small: ín⌣ dúlun, íŋ⌣kíññan⌢.
There is too much of his (her) talk: tém⌣ báññid⌣désɛn⌣dıgrín⌢.
tooth n. nél⌣.
I want to clean my teeth: án⌣nélgı⌣ gɛndıgıddáŋgı⌣dólli⌢.
toothache n. nélnı⌣óddɛ⌣.
Have you got toothache? ɛn⌣nél⌣óddıná?
top n. *(highest part)* kóčč(ı)⌣; *(upper part)* dógŏ⌣; *at the top:* kóččır⌣, dógor⌣.
Cut the top of the tin: ílbɛn⌣kóččım⌣ mɛ́r⌢.
tortoise n. *(terrestrial turtle)* dárıg⌣.
totter v.i. dátt(ı); sursúkk(ı).

touch v.t. ğábɛ.
Don't touch (him, her, it): tókkon⌣ ğábɛmɛn⌢, pl. ...⌣ğábɛmɛwwɛ⌢.
Don't let anyone touch him (her, it): tókkow⌣wɛ̌ğ⌣ğábɛŋgırmɛn⌢.
Don't (pl.) let anybody touch this: tókkon⌣ íŋgı⌣wɛ̌ğ⌣ğábɛŋgırmɛwwɛ́⌢.
tough adj. déŋgɛl⌣; kógor⌣.
This fish is tough: íŋ⌣kǎrɛ⌣déŋgélun⌢.
The wood is tough: bɛ́r⌣kógorun⌢.
tow v.t. óčč(ı); ošóšk(ı); tólle.
towards prep. -nǎr⌣, -abd(ı)⌣ (-add(ı)⌣) suffixed to objective.
I am going towards him (her, it): áı⌣ték-kaddı⌣nógbūri⌢.
Go towards him (her, it): tékkaddı⌣nók⌢.
towel n. fúta⌣.
town n. bándǎr⌣ (béndɛr⌣, bándar⌣); bélɛd⌣.
track n. *(footprint)* átar⌣, óss(ı)⌣; *(path of cattle working water-wheel)* mofs⌣.
trade n. tığára⌣.
train n. *(railway)* gátır⌣.
when the train comes: gátır⌣tǎn⌣tǎd⌣.
Ask what time the train is coming: gátır⌣ sǎ⌣mukóttɛ́rro⌣bıtǎŋg⌣íddi⌢.
Ask whether the train is on time: gátıron⌣ tém⌣mawafdır⌣égın⌣síkkı⌢.
Will (s)he (it) come by this train? íŋ⌣ gatírro⌣bıtáná?, pl. ...⌣bıtarandɛ́?
transparent, be v.i. kúddɛ; kúddɛbū-.
transport v.t. ɛğğú; bír.
Tell porters to transport the baggage from the steamer to the train: attǎlıb⌣ bābūrroton⌣aféški⌣gatírr⌣ɛğğúwan⌢.
Are they transporting the baggage? aféšk⌣ ábbıfrandɛ́?
trap n. bígıd⌣.
travel v.i. *(journey)* safarɛ́; *(move along)* ğú, dǎ-; *(go)* nóg.
tray n. tábag⌣; áda⌣.
treachery n. fítnɛ⌣.
treadle n. *(of loom)* kórıs⌣.
tree n. ğów(ı)⌣ *(does not include date-palm, dōm-palm)*; šídǎr⌣ (-dar⌣, -dɛr⌣, šítǎr⌣).
tremble v.i. kérkɛr.
tribe n. ğíns(ı)⌣ (ğínıs⌣).
What is your tribe? (a) ɛ́n⌣ğínsı⌣mınɛ́llɛ́? (b) ɛ́n⌣ğínsı⌣mín¹rɛ́?
Of what tribe is this man? ín⌣ógığ⌣mínın⌣ ğínsırɛ́?
tribunal n. mahkáma⌣ (mȧh-, -kǎ-, -mȧ⌣).
trick v.t. goššɛ́.
Trigonella faenugraecum n. kárum⌣.
tripod n. kararɛ́b⌣.
trouble v.i.
Don't trouble about it! mǎlɛ́s!
trouble v.t. *(vex)* mǎgır.
troubled, be v.i. *(be anxious)* hɛmmɛ́.
I am troubled: áı⌣hɛmmɛ́rı⌢.
trough n. *(for watering animals)* hód⌣; *(in water-wheel, larger)* sáblo⌣; *(in water-wheel, smaller)* ğaráttarɛ⌣.
true adj. alɛ́⌣.
X. Is this true? ín⌣alɛ́rɛ́?
Y. Yes: alɛ́n⌢.
Is his (her) story true? tém⌣báññıd⌣ alɛ́rɛ́?
trunk n. *(portmanteau)* šánta⌣ (šán-, -ta⌣); *(of tree)* bɛ́r⌣; *(of date-palm; dōm-palm)* úmbu⌣.

trust v.t. saddıgɛ́; āmınɛ́.
truth n. alɛ́⌣; hág⌣; hágg(ı)⌣.
Tell me the truth: alɛ́w⌣wɛ̄dɛ̄n⌢.
Tell the truth: (a) hákkı⌣báññi⌢; (b) hág-gıb⌣báññı⌢.
truthful adj. haggǎnı⌣.
try v.t. ğɛrrıbɛ́ (-rubɛ́); *(judicially)* hokmɛ́ (huk-).
Try to open it: kusğɛrrıbɛ́⌢.
Did you try to go down? ɛr⌣šugurğɛr-rıbɛ́goná?
try to obtain v.t. wɛ́rs(ı).
tube n. mǎsúra⌣.
Tuesday n. būšnóñ⌣ (bıš-).
on Tuesday: būšnóñg(ı)⌣, -gi⌢.
(S)he (it) will come on Tuesday: būš-nóñgı⌣bıtǎn⌢.
tuft n. kǔğ⌣.
tumble down v.i. dígır; *(collapse)* bór.
The child tumbled down: bıtǎn⌣dıgírkon⌢.
The house tumbled down: kǎ⌣bórkon⌢.
tumbler n. kub(b)áia⌣ (-báıa⌣, -báıɛ⌣).
tumour n. amğulúd⌣, bɛ́lt(ı)⌣; *(small)* tússa⌣.
turban n. kásır⌣; ímma⌣ (-mȧ⌣).
Don't come without a turban: tókkoŋ⌣ kásır⌣mǎsır⌣tǎmɛn⌢.
turn n. *(successive occasion)* dór⌣.
Now it's your turn: ékkɛn⌣ɛ́n⌣dórun⌢.
It was his (her) turn: tén⌣dór⌣ɛgó⌢.
turn *(in any direction)* v.i. wídɛ (wıdɛ́, wᵘdɛ́).
The milk has turned sour: íččı⌣nádd⌣ anóskó⌢.
turn *(in any direction)* v.t. wídɛgır (wıdɛ́g-, wᵘdɛ́g-).
Pick it up and turn it over: sokkɛw⌣ᵘdɛ́gır⌢.
turn out v.i. *(prove to be)* ⌣án (-an).
turn round v.i. *(revolve)* gırídɛ.
turn round v.t. *(cause to revolve)* gırídɛgır; dowwırɛ́ (-wᵘrɛ́).
Turn it round and show me the back of it: dowwırɛ́, tén⌣ğɛ́rk⌣amínti⌢.
Turn the bedstead round: áŋgárɛw⌣ wᵘdɛgıruskur⌣, pl. -úskurwɛ⌢.
turtle n. *(freshwater)* amandákkɛ⌣; *(terrestrial and freshwater)* dárıg⌣.
tweezers n. báskal⌣.
twelfth ord. num. dımındówwínt(ı)⌣ (-dówwın-).
twelve card. num. dımındóww(ı)⌣.
twentieth ord. num. arínt(ı)⌣ (árın-).
twenty card. num. árı⌣.
twice num. adv. gırówwıg⌣.
twig n. áss(ı)⌣; áur⌣ (áuʳr⌣, áuɪr⌣, áwır⌣).
twilight n. šárɛ⌣.
twin n. bárs(ı)⌣.
twist n. ıbírt(ı)⌣.
twist v.t. íwıs, ıbırtıgúndur; *(form by twisting)* agáu.
Don't let the pony twist its rope: tókkoŋ⌣ káčči⌣ténn⌣írıg⌣ıbırtıgunduríŋgır-mɛn⌢.
twisted, be v.i. ıbırtıdábū-; íwızbū-.
The line is twisted: úl⌣ıbırtıdábun⌢.
The strap is twisted, put it right: sɛ́r⌣ íwızbūn, gɛ́ndıgır⌢.
twitter v.i. wíg.
two card. num. őw(ı)⌣ (őuw(ı)⌣, -wᵘ⌣, ówᵘ⌣).
tyrannical adj. dúllo⌣.

udder n. έrt(ɪ)⌣.
ugly adj. mɪšíndɪl⌣.
ulcer n. (*from tumour*) amğulúd⌣; (*from wound*) kór⌣.
umpire n. εğğwǎd⌣.
unable, be v.i. έsk(ɪ) or εskɪ-complex in the negative.
I shall be unable to eat this: āɪ⌣íŋgɪ⌣ bεskɪkálmunun⌢.
unable, become v.i. má-.
I have been unable to eat this: íŋgɪ⌣kalεmǎróskori⌢.
Was (s)he unable to finish it? hallɪsērεmǎgoná?
uncle n. (*paternal*) -bέnna⌣, -bánna⌣ (-bábna⌣); (*maternal*) -g(ɪ)⌣.
Always with a form of the poss. pers. pron. (§§ 2629–30) prefixed:
my paternal uncle: ambέnna⌣ (-bánna⌣, -bábna⌣).
your paternal uncle: ɪmbέnna⌣ (-bánna⌣, -bábna⌣).
his (her) paternal uncle: tɪmbέnna⌣ (-bánna⌣, -bábna⌣).
our paternal uncle: antɪmbέnna⌣ (-bánna⌣, -bábna⌣).
your (pl.) paternal uncle: ɪntɪmbέnna⌣ (bánna⌣, -bábna⌣).
their paternal uncle: tɪntɪmbέnna⌣ (-bánna⌣, -bábna⌣).
my maternal uncle: áŋg(ɪ)⌣.
your maternal uncle: íŋg(ɪ)⌣.
his (her) maternal uncle: tíŋg(ɪ)⌣.
our maternal uncle: antíŋg(ɪ)⌣.
your (pl.) maternal uncle: ɪntíŋg(ɪ)⌣.
their maternal uncle: tɪntíŋg(ɪ)⌣.
unclouded, be v.i. kúddε; kúddεbŭ-.
uncooked adj. déss(ɪ)⌣.
uncultivated adj. (*of land*) bŭr⌣.
under prep. —n⌣tógor⌣.
Put it under the chair: kúrsɪn⌣tógor⌣ úndur⌢.
underneath adv. tógor⌣.
underneath prep. —n⌣tógor⌣.
Mind what is underneath you: έn⌣togób⌣ bálko⌢.
understand v.t. fεhmέ; ár; úñur.
Do you understand? εr⌣fεhmέgoná?, lit. *Did you understand?*
Does (s)he understand? tεr⌣fεhmέgoná?
Don't you understand? εr⌣fεhmέgómεnɪn?
Doesn't (s)he understand? tεr⌣fεhmέgómεnɪn?
I couldn't understand him (her): āɪ⌣tέkkɪ⌣ fεhmεrεmǎgori⌢.
I don't understand what you say: āɪ⌣έm⌣ baññídk⌣uñúrmunŭ⌢.
understanding n. (*intelligence*) έrɪg⌣.
undo v.t. kús; (*unwind*) bέu (bέw, bέu).
undress
Undress yourself: έŋ⌣kádεd⌣dúkki⌢.
unfasten v.t. kús.
unfortunate adj. ákrεs⌣.
unintelligent adj. εrɪkkómεnɪl⌣; εrɪkkattɪbúmεnɪl⌣.
unjust adj. dúllo⌣.
unless conj. —use the negative conditional (§§ 3103 ff):
I don't remember it unless I see it: āɪ⌣ nálmεŋkɪrɪ⌣ğíllεmunun⌢.
Don't come unless I call you: āɪ⌣έkkɪ⌣ úwεmεŋkɪrɪ⌣tókkon⌣tǎmεn⌢.

unless (s)he calls you: tεr⌣έkk⌣úwεmεŋkɪn⌣.
unless we call you: ar⌣έkk⌣úwεmεŋkɪru⌣.
unless they call you: tɪr⌣έkk⌣úwεmεŋkan⌣.
unload v.t. (*animal*) bókk(ɪ); kúttεgɪr.
Have they unloaded the camel? kámgɪ⌣ bokkεdǎgrandέ?
Have they unloaded the donkey? hánuk⌣ kuttεgírkorandέ?
unlucky adj. ákrεs⌣.
unnecessary adj. luzúmkɪññ(ɪ)⌣.
unpardonable
This is (that was) unpardonable: ín⌣ āfēkáttɪmunun⌢.
unprofitable adj. fǎɪdakɪññ(ɪ)⌣.
unravel v.t. bέu (bέw, bέu).
unripe adj. déss(ɪ)⌣.
unripe dates: (*a*) gállo⌣; (*b*) díffε⌣.
unsaddle v.t. kúttεgɪr.
Unsaddle the pony: káčkɪ⌣kúttεgɪr⌢.
Tell him (her) to unsaddle the donkey: hánuk⌣kúttεgɪran⌢.
unsophisticated adj. gaším⌣.
untether v.t. kús.
Untether the pony: káččɪ⌣kús⌢.
Untether the donkey: hánuk⌣kús⌢.
untie kús.
until conj. ⌣bókkon⌣ (-kõ⌢, -kó⌢); ⌣móŋkon⌣ (-kõ⌢, -kó⌢); ⌣kóttɪg⌣ following negative subjunctive.
Wait until I call: āɪ⌣úwεrɪ⌣bókkon⌣ tέp⌢.
Wait (pl.) here until (s)he comes: tεr⌣ náman⌣tǎm⌣móŋkon⌣índo⌣tέgwε⌢.
Don't go until I tell you to: āɪ⌣έkkɪ⌣ wέtɪmmεndɪ⌣kóttɪt⌣tókkon⌣nógmεn⌢.
until prep. —m⌣bókkon⌣ (-kõ⌢, -kó⌢); —m⌣móŋkon⌣ (-kõ⌢, -kó⌢).
Wait until tomorrow: asálm⌣bókkon⌣ ğóbbε⌢.
untwist (come untwisted) v.i. fírt(ɪ).
untwist v.t. bέu (bέw, bέu).
unwilling, be v.i. móñ.
(S)he (it) is unwilling: móñɪn⌢.
unwind v.t. bέu (bέw, bέu).
up adv. dógor⌣.
up, come v.i. dárr(ɪ); εgέčε; (*rise*) ɪmbέl (ímbεl).
up, get v.i. ɪmbέl (ímbεl).
Don't get up, sit down: tókkon⌣ímbεlmεn, tέgó⌢.
up, go v.i. dárr(ɪ); εgέčε.
up, put (move upward) v.t. dogógɪr.
up to prep. —m⌣bókkon⌣ (-kõ⌢, -kó⌢); —m⌣móŋkon⌣ (-kõ⌢, -kó⌢).
(S)he (it) hasn't come up to now: ɪssám⌣ bókkon⌣tǎgomunun⌢.
upon prep. —ŋ⌣kóččɪr⌣ (phrases s.v. *on*); —n⌣dógor⌣.
upper adj. dogónd(ɪ)⌣.
Bring the upper one: dogóndɪg⌣έtta⌢.
uproot v.t. dúkk(ɪ).
upset v.i. ób.
The boat will upset: kúb⌣bóbɪn⌢.
upside-down, be v.i. óbbŭ-.
It is upside-down: óbbŭn⌢.
They are upside-down: óbbŭran⌢.
upside-down, turn v.i. ób.
upside-down, turn v.t. óbɪr.
urgent, be v.i. sumárk(ɪ).
This letter is urgent, that isn't: ín⌣ğawáb⌣ sumárkɪn, ín⌣sumarkɪmunun⌢.

urinate v.i. έkk(ɪ).
urine n. έkkεdn⌣έss(ɪ); έkkεd⌣.
use n. (*utility*) nεfέrar⌣ (-rár⌣), nεfεríd⌣; (*advantage*) fǎɪda⌣ (fǎɪda⌣), fǎɪdád⌣.
What's the use of this? ím⌣míndo⌣nεfέn?
It's (of) no use: nεfέmunun⌢.
It's no use (good) talking: báññɪd⌣nεfέmunun⌢.
use v.i.
I used to go: āɪ⌣annókkori⌢.
It used to howl at midnight: úgun⌣tórtɪr⌣ āwwígkon⌢.
useful adj. (*profitable*) fǎɪdakól⌣ (fǎɪdakól⌣).
useful, be v.i. nεfέ.
useless adj. (*unprofitable*) fǎɪdakɪññ(ɪ)⌣.
uterus n. kumáttέn-tu⌣.
utter v.t.
(S)he (it) uttered a loud cry: (*a*) kōrákk⌣ áukon⌢ (-ább⌣); (*b*) kōrákkɪ⌣ğómkon⌢ (-ábkɪ⌣).

vacant adj. súd⌣; fǎdɪ⌣.
vagina n. kumáttε⌣.
vain, be (conceited) v.i. nεfɪsdúlko.
valise n. šántɪ⌣ (šán-, -ta⌣).
handle of valise: šántɪn⌣ɪ́⌣.
valley n. hór⌣.
vanish v.i. dáb.
Varanus niloticus n. ášk(ɪ)⌣ (N. áss̆(ɪ)⌣).
vegetable n. (*green*) déssε⌣.
vegetables n. (*green*) hodár⌣ (xo-).
vehemence n. šídda⌣ (-dá⌣).
vehicle n. arabíjε⌣ (-jɪ⌣, -ja⌣).
vein n. kól⌣ (kóɪ⌣).
veldt n. hála⌣.
Venus n. (*evening star*) šárε-wɪss(ɪ)⌣.
very adv. désεn⌣ (-sē⌢, -sé⌢); dɪgríg⌣, -gɪ⌢; dɪgrígɪr⌣ (dɪgrígɪrg(ɪ)⌣, -gɪ⌢, dɪgrígɪr-); hálɪs⌣ (xá-).
It's very hot today: ɪnnówwɪ⌣désεn⌣ ğúgrɪn⌢.
I like it very much: désεn⌣dólli⌢.
I want a very cold one: dɪgrígɪr⌣orófέllεd⌣dólli⌢.
Bring the very small one: kíñña⌣xálɪsk⌣ étta⌢.
vex v.t. (*anger*) sínnεgɪr, zǎlέgɪr; (*harass*) mǎgɪr.
Don't vex me: tókkon⌣āɪgɪ⌣sínnεgɪrmεn⌢.
vexation n. sínnεrar⌣ (-rár⌣); sɪnnεríd⌣; zǎl⌣.
vexed, get v.i. sínnε; zǎlέ.
vibrate v.i. kέrkεr.
vibrate v.t. kεrkεrkídd(ɪ).
vicinity n. fέtt(ɪ)⌣.
in the vicinity: εgéttɪr⌣.
victor n. mεnsúr⌣ (mǎn-).
village n. mǎr⌣; híllε⌣ (-dɪ⌣, -la⌣); bέlεd⌣.
Where is your village? έm⌣mǎr⌣ɪsáɪ⌣ téddέ? lit. *Which is...?*
Do you know his (her) village? tén⌣híllag⌣ uñúrná?
violence n. gásub⌣ (-sɪb⌣); šídda⌣ (-dá⌣).
vinegar n. hál⌣ (xál⌣).
virtue n. sεrέkanε⌣.
viscous adj. ğóndo⌣.
visible, be v.i. wǎndɪbŭ-; nálkattɪ-.
Is (s)he (it) visible? wǎndɪná?
Are they visible? wǎndɪrandέ?

visible, become v.i. wånd(ı).
voice n. híz⌣; híss(ı)⌣.
  I don't like his (her, its) voice: (a) tén⌣ hísk⌣móndı⌣; (b) téh⌣híssım⌣móndi⌣.
volume n. (*book*) kıtåb⌣; (*bulk*) kótt(ı)⌣.
vomit v.t. barísk(ı).
voyage n. såfar⌣.
vulture n. fatískal⌣; šıbšıbílle⌣ (-la⌣).
vulva n. kumátte⌣.

w.c. n. úññíŋ-kå⌣.
wag v.t. wéleg.
wage n. kırå̂ı⌣.
wage, daily n. jōmíje⌣ (-jà⌣, -ja⌣).
wager v.t. díg (constr. with -ed).
wages n. mahíje⌣ (-jà⌣, -ja⌣); úğre⌣ (-rà⌣, -ra⌣).
  How much were your wages there? ém⌣ mahíja⌣mándo⌣mıŋkóttēr⌣egő?
  What are his (her) wages? tém⌣mahíja⌣ mıŋkóttērré?
  His (her) wages are five pounds a month: (a) ténn⌣úğre⌣šahárro⌣ğíne⌣díğun⌣; (b) ténn⌣úğre⌣šahárkı⌣ğıne⌣díč-taran⌣.
wail v.i. óñ.
waist-band n. (*suspending drawers*) díkke⌣.
waist-cloth, woman's n. ğåbbed⌣.
waist-fringe (رمط) n. béjje⌣.
wait v.i. íñır (ıñír), erğé (ereğé, ereğğé, erığé); (*have patience*) ğóbbe, sabré; (*remain, sitting*) åg, tég; (*remain, standing*) tê̂b.
  Wait: (a) erğé⌣, pl. erğéwe⌣; (b) ğóbbe⌣, pl. ğóbbewe⌣; (c) sabré⌣, pl. sabréwe⌣; (d) têk⌣, pl. têgwe⌣; (e) têp⌣, pl. têbwe⌣.
  Wait outside: bóččır⌣têk⌣, pl. bóččır⌣têgwe⌣.
  Don't wait: tókkon⌣têbmen⌣, pl. tókkon⌣têbmewe⌣.
  Wait a little: kınnéğ⌣ğóbbe⌣, pl. ...ğóbbewe⌣.
  Wait till we come: ar⌣tåru⌣móŋkon⌣ têp⌣.
  Wait till you see him (her, it): ğóbb⌣er⌣ nålım⌣bókkó⌣.
  Tell him (her) to wait: têban⌣.
  Did you tell him (her) to wait? er⌣tékkı⌣ têbåŋkoná?
  When (s)he comes let him (her) wait: tåğın⌣ têban⌣.
  When they come let them wait: tåğan⌣ têbwan⌣.
  Is a messenger waiting? murásli-wēr⌣ ågná?
wait for v.t. íñır (ıñír); erğé (ereğé, ereğğé, erığé).
  I shall wait for him (her, it): (a) åı⌣tékkı⌣ bıñírrı⌣; (b) åı⌣tékkı⌣berğérı⌣.
  (S)he will wait for me: (a) ter⌣åıgı⌣bíñı-rın⌣; (b) ter⌣åıgı⌣berğérın⌣.
  Don't wait for him (her, it): tókkon⌣têkk⌣ erğémen⌣.
  Whom are you waiting for? (a) er⌣níg⌣ åğíñırın? (b) er⌣níg⌣ågerğéñ? (c) er⌣níg⌣iñıredågın?
waiter n. sufråğı⌣.
wake (up) v.i. bíčč(ı).

wake (up) v.t. ågıs; åŋgıs; bíččıgır.
  Wake me before sunrise: måsıl⌣élgom⌣ belmenın⌣åıg⌣ågıs⌣.
  Wake me at five o'clock: så⌣díğır⌣åıg⌣ ågıs⌣.
  Don't wake me: (a) tókkon⌣åıg⌣bíččıgır-men⌣; (b) tókkon⌣åıg⌣ågısmen⌣ (...åŋgısmen⌣).
  If I go to sleep, wake me up again: åı⌣ nérkırı, åıg⌣ténn⌣åŋgıs⌣.
walk v.i. nóg.
walk about v.i. gıríde⌣; murré.
walking n. nógar⌣ (-går⌣); nogíd⌣.
wall n. kåt(¹)re⌣; sóbe⌣.
wander v.i. wíd; dåğı.
want n. (*desire*) dólar⌣ (-làr⌣); dolíd⌣.
want v.t. dól; wérs(ı).
  What do you want? (a) er⌣míŋgı⌣dólın? (b) er⌣míŋgı⌣wérsın?
  What does (s)he (it) want? (a) ter⌣míŋgı⌣ dólın? (b) ter⌣míŋgı⌣wérsın?
  Don't you want your money? én⌣dúŋgıd⌣ dólmen?, pl. ín⌣dúŋgıd⌣dólmendu?
  X. *Do you want this?* íŋgı⌣dólná?
  Y. *When I want it I'll say so:* åı⌣dólkırı⌣ bıwérı⌣.
  X. *I don't want any sugar:* åı⌣sukkárkı⌣ dólmunun⌣.
  Y. *All right, I won't put any in:* sérem⌣ bundúrmunun⌣.
wanting adj. (*deficient*) nåğıs⌣.
war n. tåmugıd⌣.
warm adj. kahårt(ı)⌣.
warm v.t. tóg; kahårtıgır.
warm, get v.i. kahårtan-.
warm oneself v. kåkke⌣.
warp n. (*in weaving*) ård(ı)⌣ (q.v.).
wash v.t. éu (éw, éu); šúkk(ı) (N. šúk(ı)).
  Wash your hands: énn-íg⌣éu⌣.
  Wash this: íŋgı⌣šúkki⌣.
  Don't wash it: tókkoš⌣šúkkımen⌣.
  Wash these: íŋguš⌣šúkkırır⌣.
  Don't wash these: tókkon⌣íŋguš⌣šúk-kırímmen⌣.
  Wash it in hot water: éssı⌣ğugríges⌣ šúkki⌣.
  This is going to (will) be washed: ím⌣ bišúkkıkattın⌣.
wash out v.t. (*rinse*, q.v.) úru; élew (éléu).
  Wash out your mouth: énn⌣agílg⌣úru⌣.
  Wash out the basin: tíštıg⌣eléwos⌣.
wash-basin n. (*small*) såhan⌣; (*large*) tíšt(ı)⌣.
washerman n. kådeš⌣šúkkıl⌣; šúkkıl⌣.
wasp n. (*mason, solitary*) fıríčč(ı)⌣.
waste n. (*refuse*) kåšš(ı)⌣.
waste v.t. dåbır; gúll⌣.
watch n. (*timepiece*) så⌣.
  It has stopped: têbın⌣.
  Put it right (Set it correctly): géndıgır⌣.
  It is slow: ahherébun⌣.
  Wind it up: ğåŋgi⌣.
  It is going: nógbun⌣.
  When we come back remind me to set my watch at the station: ar⌣tåru⌣wåkítk⌣ åıgı⌣ğíllegır⌣án⌣såm⌣muháttår⌣géndı-gıddın⌣íllår⌣.
watch v.i. and t. gúñč(ı); nål.
watch for v.t. gúñč(ı).
water n. éss(ı)⌣.
  cold water: éss⌣orófel⌣.

  Give me some cold water: éss⌣orófélgı⌣dén⌣.
  hot water: éssı⌣ğúğrí⌣.
  Bring (some) hot water: éssı⌣ğúğríg⌣ étta⌣.
water v.t. (*give drink to*) ıgídd(ı); (*irrigate*) dég.
  Water the pony: kåčč⌣ıgíddi⌣.
  Have you watered the pony? er⌣kåčč⌣ ıgíddıgoná?
  Water the camels: kåmlıg⌣ıgíddırır⌣.
  Has the camel been watered? kåm⌣ıgíd-dıbúná?
  Water the plants: désserd⌣dékon⌣, pl. ...dégwe⌣.
  Has (s)he watered the plants? ter⌣désserd⌣ dékkoná?
water-bottle n. (*earthenware*) gúlla⌣.
water-closet n. úññíŋ-kå⌣.
watercourse n. hór⌣.
watering-place (*way to water, place where river is accessible*) n. múšra⌣.
water-jar n. (*for carrying*) súle⌣; (*large, for storing*) gålo⌣.
water-melon n. tíme⌣.
waterproof n. mušémma⌣.
waterside n. år⌣; bárr(ı)⌣; går⌣.
water-skin n. gırbåd⌣; gírba⌣.
water-wheel n. (*irrigator*) kóle⌣; dólåb⌣.
wattle n. (*of cock*) dalål⌣ (dål-).
wave n. årre⌣.
wave v.t. wéleg.
  (S)he waves his (her) hand: ténn⌣íw⌣ wélegın⌣.
wax n. šéma⌣.
way n. (*path*) dårıb⌣ (dår-, dér-, -rub⌣); (*direction*) årıg⌣; (*method*) use -ed (-eт⌣, -é⌣) following objective.
  This is our way: ín⌣ån⌣darúb-taran⌣.
  Did (s)he (it) go this way? ín⌣arí́kken⌣ nókkoná?
  Do it this way, not that: íŋk⌣åu, tókkon⌣ íŋkémen⌣.
  Enter that way (by that entrance), not this: tókkon⌣ıŋget⌣tómen⌣, måŋget⌣to⌣.
  Go out (by) this way: íŋgeb⌣bél⌣.
  Go out (by) that (yonder) way: måŋgeb⌣ bél⌣.
  Which way did (s)he (it) go? (a) såıgen⌣ nókkon? (b) såıke⌣nókken?
  (S)he (it) is on his (her, its) way (going): ter⌣nógbun⌣; (*coming*): ter⌣ğåbun⌣.
  I am on my way out: åı⌣bélbúrı⌣.
we pers. pron. år⌣ (ar⌣).
weak adj. ğågad⌣; kússa⌣; åğız⌣.
  (S)he (it) is in a weak state: (a) ter⌣ ğagadåmbun⌣; (b) ter⌣åğızébun⌣.
  weak tea: šåı⌣šóro⌣.
wealth n. ırğénkane⌣ (-éŋk-).
wealthy adj. ırğéŋ⌣.
wear v.t. dég.
  I shall wear this: íŋgı⌣bıdégrı⌣.
weary v.t. galabé; måğır.
weary, be v.i. måbū-.
weary, grow v.i. må-.
weather n. håwa⌣.
weave v.t. góñ.
weaver n. kådeg⌣góñıl⌣; góñıl⌣; duhå-níje⌣; (N.) dukåŋgoñ⌣.
Wednesday n. árbaha⌣.
  on Wednesday: arbåhag⌣, -gi⌣.
  (S)he (it) will come on Wednesday: árba-hab⌣bıtån⌣.

week — where

week n. ğúma⌣; dór⌣.
  twice a week: ğúmar⌣márr⌣ówwɪg⌣.
  at the end of the week: ğúman⌣abáğɪr⌣.
  on next Wednesday week: árbaha⌣tálɴ⌣ dórro⌣.
  (S)he (it) will come next Wednesday week: árbaha⌣tálɴ⌣dórkɪ⌣bɪtån⌢.
weep v.i. (*aloud*) óñ.
weevil n. kóse⌣.
weft n. tůnd(ɪ)⌣.
weigh v.i.
  What does it weigh? tɛw⌣wázɪm⌣mukóttɛ̄rrɛ́?
  This weighs 2 lb.: ínɪw⌣wázɪn⌣rátul⌣ ówwɪn⌢.
weigh v.t. waznɛ́.
  Have you weighed it? ɛr⌣waznɛ́goná?
  Have they weighed it? waznɛ́gorandɛ́?
  I want to get weighed: waznɛ̄kattɪráŋgɪ⌣ dólli⌢.
weighing-machine n. mīzán⌣.
weight n. wázɪn⌣.
  What is the weight of this (that)? ínɪw⌣ wázɪm⌣mukóttɛ̄rrɛ́?
welfare n. hɛ́r⌣.
well adv. use sɛrēğɪr-complex.
  Shut it well: sɛrēğɪrkóp⌢.
  X. I'll stay here: âɪ⌣índo⌣bɪtɛ́b¹rɪ⌢.
  Y. Very well! sɛ́rɛn!
  as well (in addition): -on⌣ suffixed to objective (§§ 4398-4400).
  Take the cat as well: sábkoŋgɪ⌣sókkɛ⌢.
  Take the dog as well: wɛ́lgoŋgɪ⌣sókkɛ⌢.
well n. gɔ́ww(ɪ)⌣; (*under water-wheel*) gawátt(ɪ)⌣; (*supplying water-wheel away from river*) mítar⌣.
well pred. adj. (*in good health*) kómbo⌣, gɛ́ɴ⌣.
  Are you well? ɛr⌣kómborɛ́?
  Aren't you well? ɛr⌣kómbomɛn? (*usual inquiry*).
  Does (s)he keep well? tɛr⌣sɛrantɛ́bná?
well, be v.i. sɛranåğ; ǧárke (ǧɛ́r-).
  X. Are you well? ɛr⌣sɛranåğmɛn?, pl. ɪr⌣sɛranåğmɛndu?
  Y. ál̩rɪl̩⌣hamdɛ́ri⌢ I praise God, i.e. yes, thank you.
  Are you well? ɛr⌣ǧɛ́rkená?
  Is (s)he well? tɛr⌣ǧɛ́rkená?
well, get v.i. kómban-; wajjɛ́.
well off adj. (*pecuniarily*) dúŋgɪkɔl⌣; (*in general*) sɛ́rɛ⌣.
well-to-do adj. håğakɔl⌣ (-ǧak-, -ǧɛk-).
west n. tín⌣; tɪŋgår⌣; gárɪb⌣.
westwards adv. gárɪbɪr⌣.
wet adj. ğåuwur⌣.
  I am wet: âɪ⌣ğåuwur⌣ɛ́ri⌢.
wet v.t. tábbɛ.
what...? interr. pron. mínde⌣...?
  míndo⌣...? (*of an indefinite number*) ɪsåɪ⌣...? (¹s-, såɪ⌣, -åɪ⌣, -åi?); (=*how much*...?) mɪŋkótt(ɪ)⌣...? (mukó-, -ti?), mɪŋkóttɛr⌣...? (mukó-).
  What is it? mɪnɛ́llɛ́?
  What's this? ím⌣mɪnɛ́llɛ́?
  What's that (near)? ím⌣mɪnɛ́llɛ́?
  What's that (yonder)? mám⌣mɪnɛ́llɛ́?
  What are they? mɪnɛ́lɪrɛ́?
  What are these (those near)? íŋgu⌣mɪnɛ́lɪrɛ́?
  What are those (yonder)? máŋgu⌣mɪnɛ́lɪrɛ́?

  What is there? (Qu'y a-t-il?, Was giebts?) (a) mínde⌣dåɴ? (b) míndo⌣dåɴ?
  What has happened? (a) mínde⌣haslɛ́gon? (b) míndo⌣haslɛ́gon?
  What do you want? míŋgɪ⌣dólɪn?
  What do you clean this with? míŋgɛd⌣ íŋgɪ⌣ğɛ́ndɪgrɪn?
  What is it made of (from)? míndotɔ̄n⌣ åukattɪn?
  What is their village? tím⌣bɛ́lɛd⌣ɪsåɪ⌣tɛ́?
  What is the rent? úğrɛ⌣mukóttɛ̄rrɛ́?
  What is its price? tɛ́n⌣tɛ́mɛm⌣mɪŋkóttɛ̄rrɛ́?
  What has become of him (her, it)? s⌣åŋkó? (lit. Where has (s)he (it) gone?).
  What is his (her) father? (a) tɪmbåb⌣ mín¹rɛ́? (b) tɪmbåb⌣tɛ́n⌣ǧɛ́lli⌣mɪnɛ́llɛ́?
  What kind is it? tɛ́n⌣ǧínsɪ⌣mɪnɛ́llɛ́?
  X. What colour is it? tɛ́l⌣lɔ́n⌣mín¹rɛ́?
  Y. Red: gɛ́lɛn⌣.
  X. I am going to the market: âɪ⌣sůğ⌣ándi⌢.
  Y. What ever for? míndɛ́?
  What ever has (s)he gone for? míndɛ́⌣tɛr⌣ mɛ́ɴ⌣nókkó?
  What? (=What do you say?) mínɛ⌣wɛ́ɴ?
what rel. pron. (=*that that, those that*) see § 6122.
  Give him (her) what (s)he wants: tɛ́kkɪ⌣ tɛr⌣dolíŋgɪ⌣tír⌢.
  (S)he (it) vomited what (s)he (it) had eaten: tɛr⌣kalsúŋgɪ⌣barískɪgon⌢.
what's-its-name n. hɪnåi⌣.
wheat n. íllɛ⌣.
wheel
  wheel raising water: átt(ɪ)⌣; *cog-wheel*: árgadɛ⌣; *water-wheel*: kólɛ⌣.
when...? adv. ɪsantåd⌣...? (¹s-, san-, -sɪn-, sɪn-; -tåt?, -tå?; ɪntå?); ɪsantåğ⌣...? (¹s-, san-, -sɪn-, sɪn-; -tåk?); ɪsan- tåğk(ɪ)⌣...? (¹s-, san-, -sɪn-, sɪn-; ɪntåğ-; -tåkk(ɪ)⌣...?; -ki?).
  When do you see him (her, it)? (a) ɛr⌣ santåɴ⌣nálɪn? (b) ɛr⌣sɪntåɴ⌣nálɪn? (c) ɛr⌣santåkkɪ⌣nálɪn? (d) ɛr⌣sɪntåkkɪ⌣ nálɪn?
  When did (s)he (it) go? (a) tɛr⌣sɪbtåɴ⌣ nókkon? (b) tɛr⌣santåkkɪ⌣nókkon?
  When will (s)he (it) come? (a) tɛr⌣santåb⌣ bɪtåɴ? (b) tɛr⌣sɪntåkkɪ⌣bɪtåɴ?
  When does (s)he open his (her) shop? tɛ́n⌣ dukkåŋgɪ⌣sɪntåk⌣kúsɪn?
when conj. -do⌣ suffixed to genitive of subjunctive (§§ 4350, 6207); ⌣tåd⌣ (⌣tåt⌢, ⌣tå?); ⌣tåkk(ɪ)⌣ (-ki⌢); ⌣tåk- kɛd⌣ (-ɛt⌢, -ɛ⌢); ⌣wɛkídk(ɪ)⌣ (-ítk(ɪ)⌣, -ítt(ɪ)⌣, -ki⌢, -ti⌢); (*referring to past*) -al⌣ suffixed to objective of subjunctive present (§ 4337); (=*if*) use the conditional with or without -ɔ̃n⌣; (=*as soon as*) -onon⌣ (-onó⌢, -onó⌢, -ono⌣) suffixed to subjunctive objective (§ 4348); (=*as long as*) ⌣kóttɪg⌣, -gɪ⌢ (§ 4318).
  when they go: ⌣nógrándo⌣.
  Come when I call: âɪ⌣ůwɛrɪ⌣tåt⌣tå⌢.
  When I come (back) I shall drink tea: âɪ⌣ tårɪ⌣tåǧ⌣ǧåɪgɪ⌣bunfri⌢.
  When you see him (her) tell him (her) to come here: tɛ́kkɪ⌣nálɪn⌣tåd⌣índo⌣ tåran⌢.
  When (s)he comes, ask him (her): tɛr⌣ tåɴ⌣tå, síkki⌢.

  When the door is open, enter: båb⌣kúzbūn⌣ tåt⌣tó⌢.
  When the eggs are boiled bring them: kúmbuw⌣wåzbūn⌣tåd⌣ɛ́tta⌢.
  When you bring it, put it over there: ɛ́ttån⌣ tåkkɛm⌣månd⌣úskur⌢.
  When I heard him (her) I recognised him (her): âɪ⌣tɛ́kkɪ⌣ğíğɪssɪ⌣wɛkítt⌣uñúr- kori⌢.
  When I heard them I recognised them: âɪ⌣tírgɪ⌣ğɪğɪ́rɪssɪ⌣wɛkítt⌣uñurɪ́kkori⌢.
  When (s)he came out of the office, ɛ́ali showed it to him (her): måktåbírtɔ̄m⌣ bɛ́lsun⌣wåkítki, álɪ⌣tɛ́kk⌣amíntɪ- gon⌢.
  When I saw him (her, it) I knew him (her, it): âɪ⌣tɛ́kkɪ⌣nállɪgal⌣uñuróskori⌢.
  When (s)he (it) saw me (s)he (it) knew me: tɛr⌣åɪgɪ⌣nálɪŋgal⌣uñuróskon⌢.
  When they saw me they knew me: tɪr⌣ åɪgɪ⌣nálwaŋgal⌣uñuróskoran⌢.
  When they see us they hide: (a) árgon⌣ nálkam⌣bókkɪran⌢; (b) árgɪ⌣nálkam⌣ bókkɪran⌢.
  When (s)he (it) goes, tell me: tɛr⌣nókkɪn⌣ åɪgɪ⌣wɛ́dɛn⌢.
  When it gets dark, open the window(s): åšåɪ⌣urummåŋkɪn⌣tågak⌣kús⌢.
  Bring it when the rain stops: áru⌣tɛ́bkɪn⌣ ɛ́tta⌢.
  When you bring the hot water, tell me: ɛr⌣ ɛ́ssɪ⌣ǧugríǧ⌣ɛttåğɪn⌣åɪgɪ⌣wɛ́dɛn⌢.
  Tell me when the signal goes down: sɛmafór⌣ šugúrkɪn⌣habårkɪ⌣dɛ́n⌢.
  When they are ready bring them: håd̩ɪran- daŋgonon⌣ɛ́tta⌢.
  When (s)he (it) saw this (s)he (it) went in: íŋgɪ⌣nalottógon⌢.
  See when (ascertain at what time) (s)he shuts his (her) shop: tɛ́n⌣dukkåŋgɪ⌣sɪntåk⌣ kobíŋgɪ⌣nál⌢.
  I was on my way to him (her) when I heard that (s)he had gone on a journey: âɪ⌣tɛ́nnår⌣ğúbugori, tɛr⌣safarɛ́būŋgɪ⌣ gɪğírkori⌢ (§ 6239).
where...? adv. ɪsåɪr⌣...? (¹s-, såɪr⌣...?, -åɪr⌣); ɪs⌣v.? (¹s⌣v.?, s⌣v.?, ⌣sɛ⌣c.? § 4418).
  Where is (s)he (it)? tɛr⌣sɛ́?
  Where is (s)he (it)? (a, stressing *Where*) tɛr⌣ɪsåɪrɛ́? (b, stressing *is*) såɪr⌣bůɴ?
  Where is my handkerchief? ám⌣mɪndíl⌣ sɛ́?
  Where is the man? ógɪğ⌣sɛ́?
  Where are the camels? (a) kámlɪ⌣sɛ́? (b) kámlɪ⌣såɪrɛ́?
  Where are you? ɛr⌣såɪrɛ́?
  Where are you going (to)? (a) ɛr⌣ånɪn?, pl. ɪr⌣åndu? (b) ɛr⌣åmbūn?, pl. ɪr⌣åmbūru?
  Where has (s)he (it) gone? tɛr⌣ɪs⌣åŋkɔ̄? pl. tɪr⌣ɪs⌣åŋkorå?
  Where have you been (to)? ɛr⌣ɪs⌣åŋkon?, pl. ɪr⌣ɪs⌣åŋkoru?
where conj. -do⌣ suffixed to genitive of subjunctive (§§ 4350, 6207) use noun- clause (§ 6125).
  Stay where you were: (*sitting*) ɛr⌣ågsíndo⌣ tɛ́k⌢; (*standing*) ɛr⌣tɛ́bsíndo⌣tɛ́p⌢.
  Stay (pl.) where you were: (*sitting*) ír⌣ ågsúddo⌣tɛ́gwɛ⌢; (*standing*) ír⌣tɛ́b- súddo⌣tɛ́bwɛ⌢.

whet — with

Let him (her) remain where (s)he is: (sitting) tér‿ágíndo‿tégaŋɔ; *(standing)* tér‿tébíndo‿tébanɔ.
Let them remain where they are: (sitting) tír‿ágrándo‿tégwanɔ; *(standing)* tír‿tébrándo‿tébwanɔ.
Do you know where (s)he (it) is? (a) tér‿ısáır‿éŋg‿ér‿uñúrná? (b) ér‿uñúrná‿tér‿ısáır‿éŋgi?
Do you know where they are? (a) tír‿ısáır‿eráŋg‿ér‿uñúrná? (b) ér‿uñúrná‿tír‿ısáır‿eráŋgi?
(S)he knows where I am: (a) tér‿âı‿ısáır‿érıg‿úñurınɔ; (b) tér‿úñurın‿âı‿ısáır‿érıgiɔ.
Does (s)he know where I am? tér‿âı‿ısáır‿érıg‿uñúrná?
Do they know where I am? tír‿âı‿ısáır‿érıg‿uñúddandé?
whet v.t. ágıs; áŋgıs.
whether subord. conj.
See whether the door is shut: kobídkı‿teroŋ‿kóbbūgın‿nálɔ.
See whether (s)he is at home: tékkı‿téŋ‿kår‿åkkın‿nálɔ.
I don't know whether (s)he (it) will come tomorrow: âı‿asálgı‿butágın‿uñúrmununɔ.
Go and ask the sheikh whether he wants you or not: samílg‿ékkı‿dólkın‿wálla‿dólmeŋkın‿noğğusíkkiɔ.
which...? interr. pron. ısáı‿...? (ı's-, sáı‿, -áı‿, -áı?).
Which is it? sáı‿té?
Which is the worse (worst)? ısáı-te‿mílli?
Which could not be seen? ısáı-te‿nalkómenıl?
which rel. pron. s.v. *that* rel. pron.
while conj. ‿kóttıg‿ (-gi‿); ‿bókkon‿ (-kõ‿, -kó‿); ‿móŋkon‿ (-kõ‿, -kó‿).
Put the irons in while the shoes are damp: ğézmančı‿ğáwwur‿éraŋ‿kóttıš‿šártınčıg‿úndurɔ.
Tell him (her) to be (let it be) quiet while I work: âı‿náman‿šuglér‿bókkoŋ‿kítteranɔ.
whine v.i. wíg.
whinny v.i. híŋıŋk(ı).
whip n. kórı‿.
whisker n. såma‿ (-mɛ‿).
whistle n. *(instrument)* suffára‿.
whistle v.i. *(with lips)* ısíski‿ğóm, usúski‿ğóm; *(with instrument)* saffıré, suffåraǧ‿ğóm.
Don't let the boys whistle here: tódk‿índo‿tókkon‿ısíski‿ğomıŋgírmenɔ.
The steamer has whistled: bābūr‿saffırē-róskonɔ.
whistling n. *(with lips)* ısís‿, usús‿; *(with instrument)* saffırérar‿ (-rår‿), saffırēríd‿.
white adj. árõ‿.
white of egg n. bɛjád‿; kúmbum‿bɛjád‿.
whither...? adv. ısáır...? (etc. s.v. *where...?*).
who...? interr. pron. ní‿...? (n‿v. §1125, ní?); nírɛ‿...?
Who are you? ér‿ní‿té?
X. (hearing someone that he cannot identify, e.g. in the dark) Who is it? ér‿ní‿té? (lit. *Who are you?*).

Y. It is I: âı-taranɔ.
X. Who (pl.) are you? ír‿nígu‿té?
Y. The sheikh has sent us: sámıl‿árg‿ıšınɛdıråğırırınɔ.
Who is (s)he (it)? (a) tér‿ní‿té? (b) tér‿nehéddé?
Who's there (here, present)? n‿åǧın?
Who's that (over there)? mán‿ní‿té?
Who's that walking over there? ní-tɛ‿mán‿nóǧıl?
Who are they? (a) tír‿nígu‿téddé? (b) tír‿nígu‿té?
Who are these? íŋgu‿nígu‿té?
Who are those over there? māmáŋgu‿nígu‿téddé?
Who came (has come)? (a) ní‿tágon? (b) nírɛ‿tágon?
Who has not come? ısåı-tɛ‿tāgómenıl?
Who has not seen it? ısåı-tɛ‿nalkómenıl?
Who did (has done) this? íŋgı‿n‿åukon?
Who gave it to you? n‿ékkı‿tíkkó?
Who struck you? n‿ékkı‿ǧómkó?
Whom did you see? ɛr‿nín‿nálkon?
Whose is it? ní‿níndıré?
Whose is this? ín‿níndıré?
Whose is that horse? mán‿kåǧ‿níndıré?
who rel. pron. s.v. *that* rel. pron.
whole adj. *(complete)* kåmıl‿; tamåm‿ (tåm-, tɛm-).
whole of, the málle‿.
Has (s)he brought the whole of it? málleg‿éttāgoná?
Today (s)he slept the whole day: ınnówwın‿ugrés‿mállen‿nérkonɔ.
Did you take away the whole ten of them? ɛr‿tɛr‿dımıŋgárkı‿sókkɛgoná?
whorl n. *(of spindle)* gédɛ‿.
why...? adv. ‿mén‿...? (-mén- §5605, §§4423, 5962-3); mínın‿íllar‿...? (-lår‿, -lɛr‿).
Why is this hot? ím‿mén‿ǧúgrıré?
Why does (s)he (it) come? tér‿mén‿tån?
Why do they come? tír‿mén‿tåran?
Why did (s)he (it) come? tér‿mén‿tågon?
Why did they come? tír‿mén‿tågoran?
Why hasn't Sålım come? sålum‿tér‿mén‿tågomenın?
Why don't you come? ɛr‿mén‿tåmenın?, pl. ír‿mén‿tåmendu?
Why didn't you come? ɛr‿mén‿tågomenın?, pl. ír‿mén‿tågomendu?
Why on earth don't you bring it? mínd‿ɛr‿mén‿ɛttåmenın?
Why on earth didn't you bring it? mínd‿ɛr‿mén‿ɛttågómenın?
Why on earth is there no water? mínd‿éssı‿tɛr‿mén‿dåmenın?
wicked adj. ús‿.
wide adj. káwwa‿; bóğõ‿.
widow n. åzɛb‿; ázɛba‿.
width n. káwwagıd‿; bóğogıd‿; boğókanɛ‿.
What is its width? téŋ‿káwwagıd‿mukóttɛrré?
wife n. ɛ̄n‿, pl. ɛ̄nč(ı)‿; *(politely)* åıla‿.
my wife: ánnɛ̄n‿.
your wife: ɛ́nnɛ̄n‿.
his wife: ténnɛ̄n‿.
their wives: tínn‿ɛ̄nč(ı)‿.

will v.
They won't (are unwilling) to come near us: ánnar‿tāráŋgı‿móndanɔ.
The dog wouldn't go out: wɛl‿bɛlláŋgı‿móŋkóɔ.
Won't the key go into the lock? kúšar‿dugállo‿tōráŋgı‿mónná? (...‿móninná?).
willing, be v.i. ɛrdɛ́.
wind n. túrug‿; háwa‿.
cool wind: wɛlwétt(ı)‿.
hot poisonous wind: sumúm‿.
I like the wind: âı‿turúkkı‿dólliɔ.
I don't like this wind: âı‿ín‿turúkkı‿dólmunūɔ.
I dislike this wind: ín‿turúkkı‿móndiɔ.
If there is wind, shut it; if there is no wind, open it: túrugōn‿dåǧī, kóp; túrugōn‿dåmeŋkī, kús‿.
wind v.t. *(wrap)* kátt(ı).
window n. tåga‿ (-gå‿); šıbbåg‿.
Open the window: tågak‿kúsɔ.
Open the windows: tågančık‿kúsırırɔ.
Shut the window: tågak‿kópɔ.
Shut the windows: tågančık‿kóbırırɔ.
wine n. nɛbíd‿.
wing n. åur‿ (åu'r‿, åuır‿, áwır‿).
winged adj. fírrıl‿.
wink v.i. urútte.
winner n. mɛnsūr‿ (mån-).
winnow v.t. síll(ı).
winter n. ådır‿; šítɛ‿.
in (the) winter: adírk(ı)‿, -kiɔ; adírro‿; šítɛg‿, -gi‿; šítɛr‿.
wipe v.t. ǧígıd.
Wipe your eyes: ém‿míssır‿ǧígıtɔ.
wipe out v.t. kúmıs.
wire n. sílıg‿; sílk(ı)‿.
wise adj. årıkátt(ı)‿; åǧıl‿.
wish n. dólar‿ (-lår‿); dolíd‿; dólt(ı)‿.
wish v.t. dól.
wish for v.t. wérs(ı).
witch n. gúl‿ (gúl‿kárr(ı)‿); dóǧır‿ (dóǧır‿kárr(ı)‿).
with prep. *(accompanying)* -onon‿ (-onõ‿, -onó‿), -onó‿) suffixed to objective; *(by means of)* -ɛd‿ (-ɛt‿, -ɛ‿) suffixed to objective; *(having)* -kōl‿.
Come with me: âıgonón‿ta‿, pl. âıgonon‿tåwɛɔ.
Go with him (her, it): tékkonon‿nókɔ.
(S)he (it) is to come with you: ékkonon‿tåranɔ.
When (s)he goes, send someone with him (her); let him take the lantern and his stick with him: tɛr‿nókkın, wɛt‿tékkonon‿íšın; fånúskon‿téw‿wıččír‿koŋ‿ındennóganɔ.
Cut it with a knife: kándıgɛm‿mérɔ.
Kill it with the stick: wıččírkɛb‿béɔ.
What shall I pick this up with? íŋgı‿mínges‿sókkɛri?
X. Send someone with this: íŋgew‿wég‿íšınɔ.
Y. I'll go with it: âı‿bındennógri‿.
X. Very well, go with it: sérɛ́n, ındennókɔ.
I want to send him (her) with a letter: tékkı‿ǧawåpkɛd‿ıšındáŋgı‿dólliɔ.
I am pleased with him (her, it): (a) âı‿téddotōm‿bastégoriɔ; (b) âı‿téddotōm‿mabsúd‿ériɔ.

within — yours

Did you see a man with a donkey? ɛr⌣ógıǧ⌣hánukól-lēn⌣nálkoná?
What did you do with the key? ɛr⌣kušárkı⌣mín⌣áukon?
within adv. árɛr⌣; árɛnčır⌣.
without prep. —r⌣más(ır)⌣ (s.v. -r⌣); —n⌣más(ır)⌣ (-m⌣má-); -kıññı(ı)⌣; -kıññır⌣; -kómɛnıl⌣.
 A knife without a handle is useless:
 (a) kánd⌣ádır⌣más⌣nɛfémunun⌢;
 (b) kánd⌣ádır⌣másır⌣nɛfémunun⌢;
 (c) kánd⌣ádn⌣más⌣nɛfémunun⌢;
 (d) kánd⌣ádn⌣másır⌣nɛfémunun⌢;
 (e) kánd⌣ádkıññı⌣nɛfémunun⌢;
 (f) kánd⌣ádkıññır⌣nɛfémunun⌢;
 (g) kánd⌣ádkı⌣kómɛnıl⌣nɛfémunun⌢;
 (h) kánd⌣ádkómɛnıl⌣nɛfémunun⌢.
 What will you do without money? ɛr⌣dúŋgım⌣más⌣mínɛ⌣báwın?
 Bring tea without milk: (a) šáig⌣íččım⌣másır⌣étta⌢; (b) šáig⌣íččıkıññır⌣étta⌢.
 X. *Bring tea without milk or sugar:* šáig⌣íččım⌣másır⌣súkkarm⌣másır⌣étta⌢.
 Y. *Tea by itself?* šáı⌣sádagá?
 X. *Yes, by itself:* éjjo, sádagi⌢.
 Do it without talk: báññıdır⌣más⌣áu⌣.
 Do (pl.) it without talk: báññıdır⌣más⌣áuwɛ⌢.
 (S)he is (left) without money: dúŋgıkıññır⌣ágın⌢.
 Don't go without (first) locking the door: ɛr⌣ólgon⌣nógmɛŋgon⌣kobíttı⌣kušárkɛk⌣kóp⌢.
 (S)he has gone without (obtaining) permission: íznǧ⌣ármɛŋgon⌣nogóskō⌢.
 a cow without milk: tí⌣íččı⌣kómɛnıl⌣.
witness n. šáhıd⌣; (attestor) kárǧıl⌣ (káǧǧıl⌣), kárǧɛl⌣ (káǧǧɛl⌣; §3024).
 Was this before witnesses? ín⌣šáhıdın⌣ogóll⌣égoná?
witness, bear v.i. kárǧ(ı) (káǧǧ(ı)).
wizard n. ǧúl⌣ (ǧúln⌣ónd(ı)⌣); dóǧır⌣ (dóǧırn⌣ónd(ı)⌣).
woman n. én⌣, pl. énč(ı)⌣.
 A woman (if it is necessary to address her) may be addressed as: wánnɛssi! (*O my sister!*).
 An old woman may be addressed as: wambánɛssi! (*O my aunt!*), or wíndıkɛgıt! (*O my aunt!*).
womb n. kumáttén-tu⌣.
wonder v.i. aǧabé.
wonder at v.t. aǧabé.
wood n. (timber) bér⌣, hášab⌣ (xá-); (forest) gába⌣.
wooden adj. bérnd(ı)⌣.
 a wooden leg: óssı⌣bérnd(ı)⌣.
woof n. túnd(ı)⌣.
wool n. ábug⌣.
 sheep's wool: ɛgédn⌣ábug⌣.
 camel's wool: kámn⌣ábug⌣.
word n. báññıd⌣.
 Say this word (these words) to me: ím⌣báññıdk⌣áıgı⌣wédɛn⌢.
work n. ǧéll⌣; (action) áwar⌣ (áwar⌣), áwíd⌣.
 Do the work properly: sɛrégır⌣ǧéllıǧ⌣áu⌣, pl....áuwɛ⌢.
 X. *Are you out of work?* ɛr⌣ǧéllık⌣kómɛn?
 Y. *I have work (I am employed):* áı⌣ǧéllık⌣kóri⌢.

Z. *I am out of work:* áı⌣ǧéllık⌣kómunun⌢.
 Tell them to stop their work: ín⌣ǧéllım⌣mugówwan⌢.
work v.i. ǧéllıgáu (-āw, -áu; §1879); šuglé (šoglé, šogolé).
 Work properly: sɛrégır⌣šuglé⌢, pl....-léwɛ⌢.
 Tell him (her) to work properly: sɛrégır⌣šugléran⌢.
 Tell them to work properly: sɛrégır⌣šugléwan⌢.
 Are they working properly? sɛrégıra⌣ššugléran dé?
worm n. wígıd⌣.
worried, be v.i. (be anxious) hɛmmé.
 I am worried about him (her, it): ténn⌣íllɛr⌣hɛmméri⌢.
 They were worried about him (her, it): ténn⌣íllɛr⌣hɛmmégoran⌢.
worry v.t. (harass) máǧır.
 Don't worry me: tókkon⌣áıgı⌣máǧırmɛn⌢.
 If (s)he worries it it will bite: tér⌣tékkı⌣máǧırkım⌣báččın⌢.
worship v.t. abdé.
worst adj. bárɛd⌣.
wound n. kór⌣.
 X. *How is your wound?* ɛŋ⌣kór⌣mínɛ⌣bún?
 Y. *It's a little better:* kınnéǧ⌣áhsɛnun⌢.
 X. *How is the wound on your hand?* énn-ıŋ⌣kór⌣mínɛ⌣bún?
 Y. *It's better:* sɛranóskó⌢.
 X. *Keep it covered; if the flies touch it it will get worse:* tágban; kúltı⌣ǧábɛgım⌣bımíllanın⌢.
wound v.t. awwıré (áuwı-).
 (S)he (it) is wounded: awwırébūn⌢.
wrap (up) v.t. kátt(ı).
 Wrap it in a cloth: káde-wɛ́rro⌣kátti⌢.
 Wrap it up in paper: wáragır⌣kátti⌢.
wretchedly
 This knife is wretchedly old: íŋ⌣kándı⌣kurústodun⌢.
wring v.t. íwıs.
write (down) v.t. báǧ.
 I have written (it): báǧóskori⌢.
 I shall (will) write (it): áı⌣bıbáǧ!ri⌢.
 I shall not write: áı⌣bıbáǧmunun⌢.
 Has (s)he written? báǧóskoná?
 See that I write this down: áıg⌣íŋgı⌣báǧan⌢, lit. *Tell me to write this.*
 Have you written to him (her)? ɛr⌣tékkı⌣ǧawábk⌣išíŋkoná?
 Have you written that to him (her)? ɛr⌣tékk⌣íŋgı⌣ǧawábkew⌣wétıkkoná?
 When I am writing I don't want talking: áı⌣báččır⌣tégrı⌣táb⌣báññídkı⌣dólmunun⌢ (⌣táb⌣bañ- < ⌣tád⌣bañ-§518).
writer n. báǧıl⌣.
writing n. báǧar⌣ (-ǧar⌣); báǧíd⌣ (báǧíd⌣, -ǧıd⌣); báčč(ı)⌣.
 X. *There there is a large stone:* mándo⌣kúlu⌣dúl-lēr⌣dán⌢.
 Y. *Is there any writing on it?* báǧídkı⌣kóná?
writing-table
 It's on my writing-table: tarabéz⌣áı⌣ābbáǧ!rıŋ⌣kóččır⌣bú⌢ lit. *It is on the I-habitually-write table.*

wrong
 The account is wrong: hısáb⌣támámmunun⌢.
yard n. (slung on mast) gárja⌣.
yawn v.i. ǧaŋgídd(ı); (with sigh or groan) nēwedúkk(ı).
year n. ǧén⌣; séna⌣ (séná).
 this year: (a) n. íŋ⌣ǧén⌣ (íŋǧɛn⌣); (b) adv. ıŋǧéŋ(ı)⌣, -gi⌢.
 next year: (a) n. ǧɛn-tál⌣; (b) adv. ǧɛn-tálg(ı)⌣, -gi⌢, ǧɛn-tállo⌣.
 last year: (a) n. nî⌣, ǧɛn-nógɛl⌣; (b) adv. nîg⌣, -gi⌢, ǧɛn-nogélg(ı)⌣, -gi⌢, ǧɛn-nogéllo⌣.
 the year before last: (a) n. nísıd⌣; (b) adv. nısíd(ı)⌣ (-sítk(ı)⌣, -sítt(ı)⌣, -ki⌢, -ti⌢).
 How many years have you been here? ɛr⌣ǧém⌣mukóttég⌣índoré?
 (S)he died about ten years ago: tɛr⌣dısíndotōn⌣ǧén⌣dımíŋkırı-tánnan⌢.
 Is it this year's? ıŋǧéndıré?
 We want this year's, not last year's: ar⌣ıŋǧéndıd⌣dóllu, níndıd⌣dólmunun⌢.
yearn v.i. hɛnné (hınné), constr. with -r⌣ (q.v.).
yell v.i. wíǧ.
 Don't yell: tókkow⌣wíǧmɛn⌢.
yellow adj. gɛlíndɛl⌣.
yes sentence-word (affirming) éjjo⌣; (answering to one's name) hói! (hói!).
 X. *It won't come out* (=*I can't get it out*): bɛlláŋgı⌣mónın⌢.
 Y. *O yes it will:* bímɛmbɛlın⌢.
 X. *Have you still got that pain?* énn⌣ódd⌣olgoné?
 Y. *Yes:* ólgónun⌢.
yesterday n. wíl⌣; adv. wílg(ı)⌣, -gi⌢.
 yesterday's bread: wíln⌣kál⌣.
 the day before yesterday: n. kámıs⌣; adv. kamísk(ı)⌣, -ki⌢.
 I saw him (her, it) the day before yesterday: kamískı⌣nálkori⌢.
yet adv. élgon⌣; ólgon⌣.
 X. *Has the man come?* ógıǧ⌣tágoná?
 Y. *Not yet:* ólgónun⌢.
yoke n. íslam⌣.
 side-piece of yoke: golmódd(ı)⌣.
yolk n. gándar⌣.
yonder adv. mándo⌣.
 Who's that walking yonder? ní-tɛ⌣mán⌣nóǧıl?
you pers. pron. ér⌣ (ɛr⌣), obj. ékk(ı)⌣, -ki⌢, pl. ír⌣ (ır⌣), obj. írg(ı)⌣, -gi⌢.
young n. (progeny) bıtán⌣ (bıt-, but-).
young person n. bób⌣.
your poss. pron. (of you sg.) énn⌣v., én⌣c.
 your turban: énn⌣ímma⌣.
 your money: én⌣dúŋg(ı)⌣.
 your house: éŋ⌣ká⌣.
 your country: ém⌣bélɛd⌣.
 your hand: énn-í⌣.
your poss. pron. (of you pl.) ínn⌣v., ín⌣c.
 your singing: ínn⌣ó⌣.
 your money: ín⌣dúŋg(ı)⌣.
 your house: íŋ⌣ká⌣.
 your country: ím⌣bélɛd⌣.
yours abs. poss. pron. (of you sg.) énd(ı)⌣; (of you pl.) índ(ı)⌣.
 It's yours: éndín⌢.

youth — *Zizyphus spina-christi*

Is it yours? ɛ́ndɪrɛ́?
It's not yours: ɛ́ndɪmunun⌒.
Isn't it yours? ɛ́ndɪmɛn?
They're yours: ɛ́ndɪnčin⌒.
Are they yours? ɛ́ndɪnčɪrɛ́?
They're not yours: ɛndínčɪmunan⌒.
Aren't they yours? ɛndínčɪmɛndan?
Is this (that) yours? (a) ín⌣ɛ́ndɪrɛ́? *(b)* ín⌣ɛ́ndɪ⌣tɛ́? *(Is this the one that is yours?)*.

Are these (those) yours? íŋgu⌣ɛ́ndɪnčɪrɛ́?
It's yours (pl.): índín⌒.
Is it yours (pl.)? índɪrɛ́?
It's not yours (pl.): índɪmunun⌒.
Isn't it yours (pl.)? índɪmɛn?
They're yours (pl.): índɪnčin⌒.
Are they yours (pl.)? índɪnčɪrɛ?
They're not yours (pl.): ɪndíčɪmunan⌒.
Aren't they yours (pl.)? ɪndínčɪmɛndan?

Is this (that) yours (pl.)? (a) ín⌣índɪrɛ́?
(b) ín⌣índɪ⌣tɛ́? *(Is this the one that is yours (pl.)?)*
Are these (those) yours (pl.)? íŋgu⌣índɪnčɪrɛ́?
youth n. *(young man)* bɔ́b⌣.

Zizyphus spina-christi n. kóɪd⌣.